International Handbook of Alcohol Dependence and Problems

International Handbook of Alcohol Dependence and Problems

Edited by

Nick Heather

Centre for Alcohol and Drug Studies, University of Northumbria at Newcastle, UK

Timothy J. Peters

Department of Clinical Biochemistry, King's College School of Medicine, London, UK

Tim Stockwell

National Drug Research Institute, Curtin University of Technology, Perth, Australia

JOHN WILEY & SONS, LTD

Chichester · New York · Weinheim · Brisbane · Singapore · Toronto

National   01243 779777
International   (+44) 1243 779777
e-mail (for orders and customer service enquiries): cs-books@wiley.co.uk
Visit our Home Page on http://www.wiley.co.uk
or http://www.wiley.com

Other Wiley Editorial Offices

John Wiley & Sons, Inc., 605 Third Avenue,
New York, NY 10158-0012, USA

WILEY-VCH GmbH, Pappelallee 3,
D-69469 Weinheim, Germany

John Wiley and Sons Australia, Ltd, 33 Park Road, Milton,
Queensland 4064, Australia

John Wiley & Sons (Asia) Pte Ltd, 2 Clementi Loop #02-01,
Jin Xing Distripark, Singapore 129809

John Wiley & Sons (Canada) Ltd, 22 Worcester Road,
Rcxdalc, Ontario M9W 1L1, Canada

Library of Congress Cataloging-in-Publication Data

International handbook of alcohol dependence and problems / edited by Nick Heather,
Timothy J. Peters, Tim Stockwell.
      p. cm.
   Includes bibliographical references and index.
   ISBN 0-471-98375-6 (cased)
   1. Alcoholism.   I. Heather, Nick.   II. Peters, Timothy J.   III. Stockwell, Tim.
RC565 .I534 2001
616.86′1—dc21

2001017671

British Library Cataloguing in Publication Data

A catalogue record for this book is available from the British Library

ISBN 0-471-98375-6

Typeset in 9^1/$_2$/11 pt Times by Best-set Typesetter Ltd., Hong Kong
Printed and bound in Great Britain by Bookcraft (Bath) Limited, Midsomer Norton
This book is printed on acid-free paper responsibly manufactured from sustainable forestry, in which at
least two trees are planted for each one used for paper production.

Contents

About the Editors

Nick Heather
After working for ten years as a clinical psychologist in the UK National Health Service, in 1979 Nick Heather developed and led the Addictive Behaviours Research Group at the University of Dundee. In 1987 he became founding Director of the National Drug and Alcohol Research Centre at the University of New South Wales, Australia. He returned to the UK at the beginning of 1994 to take up a post as Consultant Clinical Psychologist at the Newcastle City Health NHS Trust. He is Director of the Centre for Alcohol and Drug Studies in Newcastle and Professor of Alcohol and Other Drug Studies at the University of Northumbria at Newcastle. He has published many scientific articles, books, book chapters and other publications, mostly in the area of addictions and with an emphasis on the treatment of alcohol problems.

Timothy J. Peters
Timothy Peters graduated in Medicine and Biochemistry from the University of St Andrews Scotland. After further training in Scotland he moved to The Royal Postgraduate Medical School, Hammersmith Hospital, as an MRC Clinical Research Fellow in gastroenterology and thence to the Laboratory of Christian de Duve at the Rockefeller University, New York, USA. Returning to London he worked successively as Lecturer, Senior Lecturer and Reader in Cell Biology at the RPMS, Hammersmith before moving in 1979 to head the Division of Clinical Cell Biology at the MRC Clinical Research Centre, Northwick Park.

In 1988 he moved to King's College, University of London as Head of the Department of Clinical Biochemistry. His research has broadly spanned biomedical aspects of alcohol misuse, especially gastrointestinal, musculoskeletal and hepatic complications in both man and the experimental animals. More recently, his interests have encompassed evaluation of treatment protocols, quality of life of alcoholics and epidemiology of substance misuse.

Tim Stockwell
Tim Stockwell has been Director of the National Drug Research Institute, Curtin University, Western Australia (formerly the National Centre for Research into the Prevention of Drug Abuse) since June 1996 and served as Deputy Director for seven years prior to that. He studied Psychology and Philosophy at Oxford University, obtained a PhD at the Institute of Psychiatry, University of London, and is a qualified clinical psychologist. He served as Regional Editor for Australasia of the journal *Addiction* for 6 years and has published

over 140 research papers, book chapters and monographs, plus several books on prevention and treatment issues. His current interests include alcohol taxation, liquor licensing legislation and the assessment of alcohol consumption and related problems at the community, regional and national levels. He has worked as a consultant to the World Health Organization and the United Nations Drug Control Program.

List of Contributors

Jeff Allison, *Jeff Allison Training Consultancy, 3 Comiston Gardens, Edinburgh EH10 5QH, UK*

Britt K. Anderson, *Addictive Behaviors Research Center, Department of Psychology, University of Washington, Seattle, WA 98195, USA*

George E. Bigelow, *Behavioral Pharmacology Research Unit, Johns Hopkins University School of Medicine, 5510 Nathan Shock Drive, Baltimore, MD 21224-6823, USA*

Kevin Boots, *Health Department of Western Australia, Perth, Western Australia, Australia*

Clara M. Bradizza, *Research Institute on Addictions, University at Buffalo—State University of New York, 1021 Main Street, Buffalo, NY 14203, USA*

Janice M. Brown, *211 MEMH, University of Arkansas, Fayetteville, AR 72701, USA*

Russell Carvolth, *Alcohol, Tobacco and Other Drug Services, Public Health Services Branch, Queensland Health, Brisbane, Queensland, Australia*

Sally Casswell, *Alcohol and Public Health Research Unit, University of Auckland, Private Bag 92019, Auckland, New Zealand*

Jonathan Chick, *Alcohol Problems Clinic, Royal Edinburgh Hospital, 35 Morningside Park, Edinburgh EH10 5HD, UK*

R. Lorraine Collins, *Research Institute on Addictions, University at Buffalo—State University of New York, 1021 Main Street, Buffalo, NY 14203, USA*

Christopher C.H. Cook, *Kent Institute of Medicine & Health Sciences, University of Kent at Canterbury, Canterbury CT2 7PD, UK*

W. Miles Cox, *School of Psychology, University of Wales, Bangor LL57 2DG, UK*

David J. Drobes, *Center for Drug and Alcohol Problems, Medical University of South Carolina, 171 Ashley Avenue, Charleston, SC 29401, USA*

Chad Emrick, *University of Colorado Health Sciences Center, 3525 South Tamatac Drive, Suite 360, Denver, CO 80237, USA*

Elizabeth E. Epstein, *Center for Alcohol Studies, 607 Allison Road, Rutgers—The State University of New Jersey, Piscataway, NJ 0885403, USA*

Ramon Estruch, *Alcohol Research Unit, Hospital Clinic, University of Barcelona, Gran Via de les Corts, Catalanes 585, 08007 Barcelona, Spain*

Paul A.T. Gilligan, *School of Psychology, University of Wales, Bangor LL57 2DG, UK*

Dennis M. Gorman, *School of Rural Public Health, Texas A and M University System Health Science Center, 260 Centeq Building, College Station, TX 77843-1266, USA*

Kathryn Graham, *Clinical Social & Evaluation Research Dept. (London), Centre for Addiction and Mental Health, 33 Russell Street, Toronto, Ontario M5S 2S1, Canada*

Thomas K. Greenfield, *Alcohol Research Group, National Alcohol Research Center on Epidemiology of Alcohol Problems, 2000 Hearst Avenue, Suite 300, Berkeley, CA 94709-2130, USA*

Paul Gruenewald, *Prevention Research Center, 2150 Shattuck Avenue, Suite 900, Berkeley, CA 94704, USA*

Hugh H.D. Gurling, *Royal Free and University College London Medical School, Gower Street, London WC1E 6BT, UK*

Nick Heather, *Centre for Alcohol and Drug Studies (CADS), University of Northumbria at Newcastle, Plummer Court, Carliol Place, Newcastle upon Tyne NE1 6UR, UK*

Linda Hill, *Alcohol and Public Health Research Unit, University of Auckland, Private Bag 92019, Auckland, New Zealand*

Harold D. Holder, *Prevention Research Center, 2150 Shattuck Avenue, Suite 900, Berkeley, CA 94704, USA*

Nils Homann, *Department of Medicine, Salem Medical Centre, Zeppelinstrasse 11-33, D-69121 Heidelberg, Germany*

Ross Homel, *School of Criminology and Criminal Justice, Griffith University, West Approach Drive, Nathan, Brisbane, Queensland 4111, Australia*

Steven G. Hosier, *School of Psychology, University of Wales, Bangor LL57 2AS, UK*

David J. Kavanagh, *Department of Psychiatry, University of Queensland, Brisbane, Queensland 4072, Australia*

Arthur L. Klatsky, *Department of Medicine, Kaiser Permanente Medical Center, 280 MacArthur Boulevard, Oakland, CA 94611, USA*

Harald K.-H. Klingemann, *University of Applied Sciences, School of Social Work, Berne, Switzerland*

Robert G. Knight, *Department of Psychology, University of Otago, PO Box 56, Dunedin, New Zealand*

Paul Lemmens, *Department of Medical Sociology, University of Limburg, PO Box 616, 6200 MD Maastrict, The Netherlands*

Charles S. Lieber, *Alcohol Research and Treatment Center, Bronx Veterans Affairs Medical Center and Mount Sinai School of Medicine, 130 West Kingsbridge Road, Bronx, New York, NY 10469, USA*

Anne Lingford-Hughes, *Psychopharmacology Unit, University of Bristol, University Walk, Bristol BS8 1TD, UK*

David Mantle, *Neurochemistry Department, Regional Neurosciences Centre, Newcastle General Hospital, Newcastle upon Tyne NE4 6BE, UK*

G. Alan Marlatt, *Addictive Behaviors Research Center, Department of Psychology, University of Washington, Seattle, WA 98195, USA*

Nyanda McBride, *National Drug Research Institute, Curtin University of Technology, GPO Box U1987, Perth 6845, Western Australia*

Gillian McIlwain, *School of Criminology and Criminial Justice, Griffith University, West Approach Drive, Nathan, Brisbane, Queensland 4111, Australia*

A. James McKnight, *Transportation Research Associates, 8201 Corporate Drive, Suite 200, Annapolis, MD 20785, USA*

Richard Midford, *National Drug Research Institute, Curtin University of Technology, GPO Box U1987, Perth 6845, Western Australia*

David Moore, *The Australian National University, Canberra, ACT 0200, Australia*

Kim T. Mueser, *Dartmouth Medical School, Dartmouth Psychiatric Research Center, Main Building, 105 Pleasant Street, Hanover, NH 03301, USA*

David J. Nutt, *Psychopharmacology Unit, University of Bristol, University Walk, Bristol BS8 1TD, UK*

Esa Österberg, *Social Research Unit for Alcohol, Studies STAKES, National Research and Development Centre for Welfare and Health, Siltasaarenkatu 18, PO BOX 220, FIN-00531 Helsinki, Finland*

George A. Parks, *Department of Psychology, University of Washington, 2611 NE 125th Street, Suite 201, Seattle, WA 98195-4357, USA*

Juha Partanen, *Social Research Unit for Alcohol Studies, PO Box 220, FIN-00531 Helsinki, Finland*

Timothy J. Peters, *GKT School of Medicine, Department of Clinical Biochemistry, King's College Hospital School of Medicine, Bessemer Road, Camberwell, London SE5 9PJ, UK*

Victor R. Preedy, *Department of Nutrition and Dietetics, King's College London, Bessemer Road, London SE5 9PJ, UK*

Duncan Raistrick, *Leeds Addiction Unit, 19 Springfield Mount, Leeds LS2 9NG, UK*

Stephen Rollnick, *Department of General Practice, University of Wales College of Medicine, PO Box 68, Cardiff CF1 3XA, UK*

Robin Room, *Centre for Social Research on Alcohol and Drugs, Stockholm University, Sveaplan, S-106 91 Stockholm, Sweden*

Michael E. Saladin, *Medical University of South Carolina, 171 Ashley Avenue, Charleston SC 29401, USA*

Helmut K. Seitz, *Salem Medical Centre, University of Heidelberg, Zeppelinstrasse 11-33, D-69121 Heidelberg, Germany*

Jussi Simpura, *Social Research Institute for Alcohol Studies, National Research and Development Centre for Welfare and Health (Stakes), PO Box 220, FIN-00531 Helsinki, Finland*

Harvey Skinner, *Department of Public Health Sciences, Faculty of Medicine, University of Toronto, McMurrich Building, Toronto, Ontario M5S 1A8, Canada*

Tim Stockwell, *National Drug Research Institute, Curtin University of Technology, GPO BOX U1987, Perth, WA 6845, Australia*

Betsy Thom, *School of Social Science, Middlesex University, White Hart Lane, London N17 8HR, UK*

Stephen T. Tiffany, *Department of Psychological Sciences, Purdue University, 1364 Psychological Sciences Building, West Lafayette, IN 47907-1364, USA*

Andrew J. Treno, *Prevention Research Center, 2150 Shattuck Avenue, Suite 900, Berkeley, CA 94704, USA*

Robert B. Voas, *Public Services Research Institute, Pacific Institute for Research and Evaluation, Calverton, MD, USA*

Paulette West, *Centre for Addiction and Mental Health, The Gordon J. Mogenson Building, 100 Collip Circle, Suite 200, London, Ontario N6G 4X8, Canada*

John B. Whitfield, *Department of Clinical Biochemistry, Royal Prince Alfred Hospital, Missenden Road, Camperdown, Sydney NSW 2050, Australia*

Malissa Yang, *Faculty of Health Sciences, McMaster University Medical School, 1200 Main Street W, Hamilton, Ontario L8N 3Z5, Canada*

Giles N. Yeates, *University of Wales, 39 College Road, Bangor LL57 2AS, UK*

Preface

A multitude of books have been written, and continue increasingly to be written, about alcohol dependence and alcohol-related problems but none, as far as we are aware, has attempted what this *Handbook* tries to do. This is to offer a high-level, comprehensive coverage of the entire field of alcohol studies, from neurochemistry to sociology and from research on the molecular basis of dependence to large-scale studies of the primary prevention of alcohol problems. Thus, our intention has been to provide, for the first time in a single volume, a complete source of information and reference for all major aspects of alcohol studies and all contributory disciplines—in short, alcohol studies from A to Z.

No book in this field can claim to be comprehensive in a literal sense; it would be impossible to cover every single issue that has ever arisen in the long history of research and scholarship on alcohol and its deleterious effects. We can predict that some people with a professional or scientific interest in alcohol problems will find their particular preoccupations and favoured theories missing from the contents. If this does happen, it may be due partly to the way we have chosen to structure the contents by subject area under six general headings rather than, say, by the groups of people who may be affected by alcohol problems. Thus, for example, no chapters will be found on "Alcohol and Women", "Alcohol and Minority Groups" or "Alcohol and Young People", etc. Attention to problems among these groups will be found scattered throughout the chapters of the book but we chose not to structure the contents in this way.

It is also possible, of course, that the editors, being fallible human beings, have overlooked some topics that others would see as essential. But what we would claim is that the *Handbook* is comprehensive in the sense that all the leading areas of research and theory—the most influential research findings, the most pressing clinical concerns, the potentially most important practical applications—are given adequate coverage in these pages.

The *Handbook* has been called "international" mainly because of the geographical spread of the authorship, with 11 different countries around the world being represented by authors' affiliations. We have also tried to cover the international literature and explore implications for treatment and preventive practice from an international rather than any particular national perspective. However, the book is clearly not international in another sense; we have made no attempt to give an adequate account of the many variations that alcohol problems show in different cultures. A special regret is that we have not been able to give anything like a satisfactory coverage of increasing alcohol-related problems in developing nations, which would have required a different kind of book.

Contributors to the book, who include many internationally recognized experts on their chosen topics, were asked to write authoritative, science-based reviews of knowledge in their areas of special interest. However, authors were asked *not* to attempt a theoretical or research "cutting edge" of their topics, since these may be found elsewhere in more narrowly-focused works or peer-reviewed journals and, in any event, would probably need more space than even this large *Handbook* could provide. Rather, they were requested to compile a general, up-to-date summary of knowledge in their respective areas, making decisions about what is of major importance and essential to include in such a summary—in short, and to fall back on another hackneyed term, the "state of the art" for their designated topics. Although relying heavily on established research findings, all chapters attempt to draw out the implications of their contents for practice in the field.

With this remit in mind, we also requested that referencing should be selective, with an emphasis on key hypotheses and the most prominent research findings. If a reader finds that a relevant study is missing from the list of references in a chapter (perhaps, for example, to the reader's own work), this does not necessarily mean that the author or authors were unaware of it, merely that they were following the editors' instructions on referencing.

Given its comprehensive coverage, the intended readership for the *Handbook* embraces all those with an academic, research, clinical, counselling or policy-orientated interest in alcohol dependence and problems. We believe that its main advantage over other books in the field will be its ability to increase communication between scientists and practitioners from the wide range of disciplines and professions that make up the world of alcohol studies—physicians, psychiatrists, general medical practitioners, ward, practice and community nurses, occupational therapists, biochemists, psychopharmacologists, academic, clinical and forensic psychologists, sociologists, anthropologists, social workers, probation officers, counsellors of all sorts, health economists, health care commissioners, policy makers and several others. The failure of communication between combinations of these groups is often deplored and we hope that the book can assist in remedying this situation by giving readers an insight into areas of knowledge that might not otherwise come to their attention. As might be expected, we also hope that the *Handbook* will prove valuable for teaching purposes at both undergraduate and postgraduate levels.

To increase the usefulness of the book to this wide range of readers, each chapter begins with a short synopsis that aims to summarize its contents in accessible language. These serve the purpose of informing readers who may not be concerned with the detail of the topic contained in the chapter. Thus, for example, therapists and counsellors may be less interested in chapters in Part II on clinical pathology but would find useful a brief summary of the key facts and issues contained in them. Conversely, physicians treating alcohol-related diseases may not need the detailed coverage of preventive policy issues included in Part VI (although many will) but will want to know broadly what are the main initiatives and barriers to implementation that have been described in the literature. At the same time, readers who wish to pursue a particular subject area in more depth will find a list of Key Works and Suggestions for Further Reading at the conclusion of each chapter. Lastly, each Part of the book is preceded by an Editor's Introduction, with the aim of describing the wider context of the subject matter in the chapters of that Part and preparing the ground so that the reader can obtain maximum benefit from them.

Although we have tried to reduce repetition as much as possible by the careful selection of subject areas, it is inevitable in a book of this kind that there will be some degree of overlap between different chapters. We have responded to this by cross-referencing where appropriate but we also decided not to attempt to eliminate overlap completely. This is because to have done so would have risked spoiling the flow of a chapter's argument or rendering it incomplete in other ways. In any case, different authors will undoubtedly offer a somewhat different interpretation of the same material.

We have also eschewed any attempt to impose a consistent terminology on authors. Thus, some authors refer to "alcoholism" and others to "alcohol dependence", while some use "problem drinking" and others "alcohol abuse", and so on. Again, to have insisted on a standard set of terms and definitions would have been to restrict the ability of authors to convey their expert understandings in full, especially since different terms often have different theoretical connotations. We trust that, even if authors do not explicitly address the task of definition, any special implications of key terms will become clear from the context of the chapters in question. Implicit in the title of the book, however, and in the Part headings, is our acceptance of the now commonly-held view that alcohol dependence and alcohol problems, while often empirically correlated on the individual level, are conceptually independent dimensions of alcohol-related harm.

Nevertheless, we wish to stress that we have not tried in any way to impose our own views on controversial or theoretically crucial issues on the authors of this book; no "party line" will be found here. As one consequence of this, it is perfectly possible that inconsistent or even conflicting viewpoints will be discovered between one chapter and another. Apart from any other consideration, if such disagreement is found, it only reflects the real situation in the world of alcohol studies.

An undertaking of the sort represented by this *Handbook* could not have been accomplished without the efforts of a number of people in addition to the editors. We would therefore like to thank Christina Allan, Ester Lee and Susan Wilson for their hard work and invaluable assistance. We are obviously grateful to all the authors who agreed to contribute to the book, particularly since they must receive many requests to write book chapters; we thank them for choosing this book to communicate their expertise. Finally, we wish to thank our editors at John Wiley & Sons, Michael Coombs and Lesley Valerio, for their consistent support and patience throughout the preparation of the manuscript.

Nick Heather
Timothy Peters
Tim Stockwell
March 2000

Part I

Alcohol and People

Edited by Nick Heather
Centre for Alcohol and Drug Studies, University of Northumbria at Newcastle, Newcastle upon Tyne, UK

EDITOR'S INTRODUCTION

This opening section of the Handbook is intended to prepare the ground for the remainder of the book. Under the very general heading of "Alcohol and People", it consists of four chapters which do not fit neatly into any other section of the book but which are essential for a full understanding of the present state of alcohol studies. Despite their diverse contents, all these chapter take a broad view of the field and they all in varying degrees present an historical perspective on the subject matter.

Bearing in mind that the focus of the book is on alcohol dependence and problems, Chapter 1 attempts to redress the balance somewhat by describing the undoubted pleasures and benefits of drinking as well as the harm it causes. The experience of National Prohibition in the USA between 1920 and 1933 proved, if proof were needed, that people do not find credible any view of alcohol that is unequivocally hostile (Lender & Martin, 1987), and this is why Chapter 1 is necessary for scene-setting purposes. To repeat here what is one of the main points of the chapter, in addressing the many forms of damage to health and welfare that alcohol produces, the editors and authors of this book freely concede that it is also responsible for a range of tangible benefits to individuals and societies and for great pleasure and enjoyment to those who drink it.

Chapter 1 also stresses, however, that while it is reasonable to call alcohol our favourite drug, it is also the most harmful drug known to humankind. These two facts in combination immediately produce a profound ambivalence and conflict in our responses to alcohol and this is briefly explored in the chapter.

This introductory section of the book then proceeds in the traditional manner with a chapter on the history of alcohol. However, Chapter 2 by Betsy Thom is far from a traditional treatment of the topic; rather than offering a mere chronological account, Thom presents the history of our uses of alcohol and our responses to alcohol-related harms in their social, political and economic contexts.

While significant developments in the history of alcohol had taken place in previous centuries, it was perhaps in the nineteenth century that the most dramatic changes occurred. In the Western world at least, "the drink question" became one of the hottest social and political issues of the time, one that was capable of unseating governments and which permeated almost all aspects of communal life (see, e.g., Harrison, 1970). It can plausibly be argued much of the history of alcohol in the twentieth century can be seen as a "hangover" from the century before and that our current view of this particular drug can only be properly understood from this perspective (e.g. Levine, 1978). All this clearly emerges from Chapter 2. The chapter concludes with important speculation on a recent development most likely to be the dominant theme in the history of alcohol during the twenty-first century—the globalization of a commercial product and the consequences of this for our attempts to limit alcohol-related problems on a world-wide basis.

An historical perspective is also present in Chapter 3 by Robin Room. Here, however, the focus is on what have been called "governing images" of alcohol problems (Room, 1974) or, in more modern parlance, "discourses" on alcohol problems, in the sense of systems of thought that shape the way in which members of a society implicitly understand the phenomena in question. More familiar to workers in the alcohol field is the related notion of "models" of alcohol problems—the moral model, the disease model, the cognitive-behavioural model, and so forth.

These shared understandings exert a typically unacknowledged influence on what society perceives to constitute alcohol-related problems and the ways it responds to them; they not only affect popular conceptions of the nature of alcohol and its harmful consequences but also scientific theory and research in the area. It is the task of sociologists in the constructivist tradition to elucidate these discourses and draw out their social and political implications in contrast to alternative and possibly coexisting discourses. In Chapter 3, Room provides an overview of the main, competing discourses, including the addiction concept, the new public health approach and the more recent emergence of a neoliberal ideology in the alcohol field that emphasizes consumer sovereignty and individual choice. The chapter concludes with what might be termed a meta-constructivist analysis—in other words, a dissection of the nature and properties of alcohol discourse analyses themselves.

The last chapter in Part I, Chapter 4 by Elizabeth E. Epstein, concerns the various ways in which alcohol-related problems and dependence are classified. This chapter again adopts an historical perspective, especially in an informative tracing of the evolution of listings for alcohol-related problems in the two major classificatory systems for mental and behavioural disorders in use today—the Diagnostic and Statistical Manual of Mental Disorders (DSM) in the USA and the International Statistical Classification of Diseases (ICD) in Europe. The end of this historical account provides the reader with the "correct" and officially recognized current terms with which to describe the varieties of individual alcohol-related harm. However, objections to these systems and alternatives to psychiatric classification are also mentioned in Chapter 4. The heterogeneity of alcohol problems is emphasized and the most prominent typologies to be found in the literature are described. Two crucial issues that bear upon the accuracy of alcohol-related diagnoses—comorbidity of alcohol and other psychiatric disorders, and ways in which medical conditions are complicated or exacerbated by alcohol use disorders—are then discussed. Epstein concludes by describing a number of important research questions in this area and by giving her view on how progress can best be made in the classification of alcohol dependence and problems.

REFERENCES

Harrison, B. (1970). *Drink and the Victorians*. London: Faber.
Lender, M.E. & Martin, J.K. (1987). *Drinking in America.* New York: Free Press.
Levine, H.G. (1978). The discovery of addiction: changing conceptions of habitual drunkenness in American history. *Journal of Studies on Alcohol*, **39**, 143–174.
Room, R. (1974). Governing images and the prevention of alcohol problems. *Preventive Medicine*, **3**, 11–23.

Chapter 1

Pleasures and Pains of Our Favourite Drug

Nick Heather

Centre for Alcohol and Drug Studies, University of Northumbria at Newcastle, Newcastle upon Tyne, UK

Synopsis

Despite the fact that some countries prohibit its use and despite many people's preference for other psychoactive substances, alcohol can reasonably be described as the world's favourite drug. There must be good reasons for this popularity and the main purpose of this chapter, in a book devoted to alcohol dependence and problems, is to concede clearly that alcohol has many benefits and affords great pleasure to those who drink it.

While the pains of alcohol are numerous and diverse, the pleasures include possible benefits to health, improvements to psychological and cognitive functioning, and various social and economic benefits. Research and theory relating to these benefits are briefly described. However, the simultaneous existence of both pleasures and pains means that individual and societal responses to alcohol are very likely to be ambivalent and contradictory, and examples of this are provided. There is inevitable conflict between the interests of public health and the interests of the drinks industry but it is concluded that there is no alternative to finding ways in which these competing interests can be reconciled on a political level.

Despite its popularity and the benefits it brings to our lives, it should not be forgotten that alcohol is also our most dangerous drug and is responsible for more harm throughout the world than any other psychoactive substance, including illicit drugs and nicotine.

Despite its previous use in the literature (Royal College of Psychiatrists, 1986), it may seem presumptuous to describe ethyl alcohol as "our favourite drug". It is common knowledge that some Moslem countries of the world find alcohol to be an extremely disruptive and dangerous substance, and prohibit and penalize its use. And it is not so long ago that similar attitudes to alcohol prevailed, officially at least, in the USA and other Western countries. At the same time, the vast illegal and international trade in other psychoactive substances suggests that, for many people on the planet, alcohol is clearly not their favourite drug. It would be difficult or impossible to compare directly the total amounts of

International Handbook of Alcohol Dependence and Problems. Edited by N. Heather, T.J. Peters and T. Stockwell.
© 2001 John Wiley & Sons Ltd.

various mood-altering substances consumed each day by the world's population but it is incontrovertible that there is a range of highly popular, convenient and, for their users, credible alternatives to assist the aim of, in Rimbaud's phrase, "the derangement of the senses" (Rimbaud, 1973, p. 200).

Nevertheless, as in their different ways both Chapters 2 and 20 of this *Handbook* make clear, recent changes in world trade have meant that a preference for alcohol can now be truly said to be a global phenomenon. If in no other way, alcohol is our favourite drug in the sense that, due to Western cultural and commercial influence on the rest of the world, it is in most societies the officially approved and "legitimate" method of artificially changing our moods and perceptions, a need that human beings seem always to have had and that may be an inherent aspect of human nature (Siegel, 1989). What can also be asserted with some confidence is that, despite the recent pandemic in problems due to usually illicit drugs like heroin, cocaine and amphetamines, and despite the moral panic these problems have created, the total harm caused by alcohol world-wide far exceeds that due to these other psychoactive substances (Murray & Lopez, 1996). Thus it is not mere ethnocentrism to claim, in an international book of this kind, that alcohol is our favourite and our most frequently misused drug.

There must be good reasons for this popularity. In other words, the long history and present status of alcohol in human behaviour and affairs must presuppose some highly pleasurable and beneficial effects. Why otherwise would we be so keen to consume it? A common reaction to books devoted to describing and analysing the dependence-producing properties and problems associated with alcohol is the assumption that those who have edited or contributed to them must be "anti-alcohol", "killjoys" or, to use the evocative Australian term, "wowsers". A common counter-reaction to this is the attempt by authors of these works to distance themselves from such sentiments of blanket disapproval, and this book will be no exception. Thus, as a prelude to all the remaining chapters focused on alcohol dependence and problems, the aims of this opening chapter are to state clearly that drinking alcohol can be, and often is, a highly pleasurable and beneficial activity, and to describe briefly research, theory and comment on the forms these pleasures and benefits take.

THE PAINS OF ALCOHOL

We begin, however, with the negative consequences of alcohol consumption, although there will be no need to dwell long on this topic here. If for the moment we regard alcohol dependence as but one of the problems caused by alcohol, alongside other types of physiological, psychological and social problems, then the pains that go with drinking alcohol are simply the subject matter of the remainder of this volume. We may merely note that these problems include harm to physical health, psychological well-being, interpersonal relationships and wider social functioning, together with criminal, legal, occupational, financial and economic varieties of harm. To this might perhaps be added spiritual problems (Miller, 1998). Harm accrues to individual drinkers, their families, their friends and people living in their neighbourhoods and to the wider society. These negative consequences are covered, in their different forms, in all six Parts of this *Handbook*.

THE PLEASURES AND BENEFITS OF ALCOHOL

In the scientific and scholarly literature on alcohol, little has been written until recently on the positive consequences of drinking. This situation has changed somewhat following the establishment in 1995 of the International Center for Alcohol Policies (ICAP) in the USA, an organization funded by the international drinks industry. Among other publications, ICAP has produced a book called *Alcohol and Pleasure: A Health Perspective* (Peele & Grant, 1999), which aims to promote the "simple, undeniable truth" that drinkers expect alcohol to satisfy them and provide a sources of personal pleasure, a truth that "somehow has been obscured by the vast literature on health and social problems associated with alcohol abuse" (Grant, 1999, p. xi). As might perhaps be expected, ICAP's activity in this respect has not been regarded by all commentators as wholly benign or disinterested. For example, McCreanor, Caswell & Hill (2000) describe the Permission for Pleasure conference in 1998, upon which the Peele & Grant book was based, as "an openly ideological move" (p. 183). McCreanor et al. see ICAP's activities in general as a strategy by the drinks industry to shape the way in which alcohol and alcohol research are perceived by policy makers and others to the benefit of industry profits, particularly in developing nations, and to the detriment of public health (see also Jernigan & Mosher, 2000).

Health Benefits

The notion that moderate alcohol consumption is good in various ways for health is possibly as old as the history of alcohol itself (see Chapter 2, this volume) and is embedded in folk wisdom on the subject (Klatsky, 1999). Traditionally, medical practitioners have recommended alcohol for pain and stress relief and for a variety of minor ailments. Within the last two decades, however, the alleged health benefits of alcohol have become the focus of intense scientific enquiry and some controversy following the putative discovery of a cardio-protective effect, i.e. the finding that moderate drinkers (principally middle-aged men) appear to have a lower risk from coronary heart disease than both heavy drinkers and non-drinkers, a topic on which literally hundreds of scientific papers have been written.

This topic is dealt with in Chapter 11 of this *Handbook* and little comment is needed here. Suffice it to say that, while most authorities in this area of epidemiological research, including Klatsky (see Chapter 11, this volume), now accept that the cardio-protective effect is a genuine finding and that a plausible biological mechanism exists to explain it, some commentators remain unconvinced (e.g. Fillmore, 2000). This is because some well-designed studies have failed to observe the effect and because there are said to be persistent methodological problems in this area of research, particularly with respect to the assurance that differences in alcohol consumption between moderate and non-drinking groups are not confounded with other variables relevant to risks for heart disease.

Claims have also been made for the protective effects of moderate drinking with respect to several other medical conditions, including ischaemic stroke, non-insulin-dependent diabetes, osteoporosis, rheumatoid arthritis and the common cold (see Pittman, 1996). It must be stressed, though, that, especially by comparison with research on alcohol and coronary heart disease, research in these areas is still in its infancy and firm conclusions are not yet possible. This research is also beset by formidable methodological problems, particularly the task of separating out differences in drinking behaviour from other lifestyle factors that may affect the risks in question, the heterogeneity of non-drinking control groups and the accurate measurement of alcohol consumption itself (Pittman, 1996). It also worth remarking that the evidence in favour of beneficial effects here is correlational, not causal, in nature.

Psychological Benefits

The claim that alcohol improves the drinker's mood in the short term is hardly contentious, since this is perhaps the main reason why most people drink. There is, indeed, a large amount of experimental evidence that the acute effects of alcohol include increased enjoyment, euphoria, happiness and the general expression of positive moods (see Baum-Baicker, 1985). Again as might be predicted, these feelings are experienced more strongly in group situations than when drinking alone (Pliner & Cappell, 1974). Lowe & Taylor (1997) reported that drinking increased the degree to which students found a film comedy funny, while Lowe & Taylor (1993) found that weekly alcohol consumption among students was positively correlated with frequency of laughter in daily life, although obviously this might not be a causative link.

Abundant research has also clearly shown that such positive effects are prominent among what people expect from drinking. Brown and colleagues (1980) classified alcohol expectancies into six types: (a) global, positive transformation of experience; (b) enhanced social and physical pleasure; (c) enhanced sexual performance and experience; (d) increased power and aggression; (e) increased social assertiveness; and (f) relaxation and reduced tension. Lighter drinkers tended to show more global expectancies, while heavier drinkers tended to show stronger expectancies of sexual and aggressive behaviour. Later research in this area has demonstrated that both strong positive and weak negative expectancies are associated with the development of drinking problems (see Jones & McMahon, 1998).

A prominent explanation of the reinforcing effects of alcohol is the *tension-reduction hypothesis*, i.e. the hypothesis that alcohol consumption is a learned instrumental response reinforced by its tension-reducing consequences (see Chapter 15). Although this hypothesis has not fared well as a general explanation of alcohol dependence (Cappell & Greeley, 1987), there is no question that alcohol is an anxiolytic drug and that its acute effects include a reduction in anxiety and the physiological response to stress. More relevant for present purposes is evidence on whether regular moderate drinking serves to help cope with stress in the longer term, the so-called *stress-buffering hypothesis* (Neff & Husaini, 1982). This evidence has been reviewed by Baum-Baicker (1987) and Brodsky & Peele (1999). Conclusions are that alcohol may be effective as a short-term calming measure but moderate drinkers are less inclined to use alcohol as a coping device than heavy and problem drinkers, and that the habitual use of alcohol to cope with stress and other negative states can be a precursor of alcohol dependence.

A variant of the tension-reducing hypothesis has been proposed by Hull (1981). This is the idea that an important effect of alcohol is to reduce, not tension and stress *per se*, but self-awareness, thereby leading to an escape from worries and low self-esteem. A great deal of evidence of various kinds has been adduced to support this hypothesis (see Hull et al., 1983; Hull & Bond, 1986) but its present status is uncertain. A related notion is that alcohol serves to increase a personal sense of power and achievement, especially in men, while at the same time lowering accumulated tension and anxiety (McLelland et al., 1972) but the evidence to support this hypothesis, as a general account of alcohol's effects, is thin. In any event, while these hypothetical effects following moderate consumption might be considered beneficial, the dangers of repeated or heavy alcohol use for these purposes are obvious.

There is also some evidence that moderate drinking is associated with reduced risk for depression and other psychiatric symptomatology. Neff & Husaini (1982) found that stressful life events were more strongly related to depressive symptoms in abstainers and heavy drinkers than in moderate drinkers, and a similar finding has been reported more recently by Lipton (1994). Neither of these studies controlled for the possibility that some of the abstainers may have been former problem drinkers or had abstained because of pre-existing health problems.

Lastly, there is quite good evidence to suggest that moderate drinking may be of benefit in the elderly (see Baum-Baicker, 1987). For example, Mishara & Kastenbaum (1980), reviewing research on this topic up to that time, concluded that the provision of daily beer or wine to patients in geriatric units and nursing homes increased social interaction and decreased the need for sleeping tablets, among other advantages. There is also a suggestion, no more than that at present, that moderate wine consumption can serve as a protective factor against dementia and Alzheimer's disease (Orgogozo et al., 1997).

Benefits for Intellectual Functioning

The possibility that alcohol can improve intellectual functioning may seem surprising, given its obviously deleterious impact on thinking and judgement. Nevertheless, there is good evidence that moderate drinkers show higher levels of intellectual abilities than non-drinkers (see Brodsky & Peele, 1999). For example, in an examination of drinking patterns and cognitive test scores among roughly 4000 pairs of twins who served in World War II, Christian et al. (1995) reported that the highest reasoning abilities were found among those who drank between eight and 16 drinks per week, while the lowest occurred in those who consumed less than one drink or more than 16 drinks a week. This does not prove, of course, that moderate drinking exerts a directly beneficial effect on intellectual functioning, but such a possibility cannot presently be ruled out (see Baum-Baicker, 1985).

A related possibility is that alcohol enhances creativity, especially given the remarkable incidence of serious drinking problems among writers of genius (see e.g. Goodwin, 1970, 1971). With regard to more moderate drinking, the evidence on this hypothesis is mixed (Brodsky & Peele, 1999).

Social Benefits

It is a truism that alcohol plays a highly useful role in everyday social life—marking births, deaths, marriages and celebrations, inspiring song and verse, cementing mutual agreements, and generally oiling the wheels of social intercourse that might otherwise be stiff and awkward. It is no less obvious that alcohol is the principal means by which many groups of friends, particularly those of similar age and gender, seek to maximize the enjoyment of each other's company and "have fun". Copious anthropological evidence confirms that this use of alcohol to enhance sociability and bonding is common throughout history and throughout the world (see e.g. Heath, 1995).

Although the link between drinking and behavioural disinhibition is complex (Room & Collins, 1981) and is undoubtedly influenced by culturally-learned expectancies about alcohol's effects on behaviour (MacAndrew & Edgerton, 1969), it is the ability of the drug to help people "lose their inhibitions" in social gatherings that is most often credited for these useful properties. So entrenched are these beliefs about alcohol that people become observably more sociable when they merely think they have consumed alcohol but actually have not (Darkes & Goldman, 1993). These positive expectancies of drinking come especially to the fore in the transition from "work" to "play".

Although adolescent and youthful drinking is rightly regarded as a matter for concern, one study has shown that college students in the USA who reported a moderate frequency of drinking binges showed better psychological and social adjustment than either those who reported a high frequency or no binges at all (Nezlek, Pilkington & Bilbro, 1994), a finding incidentally that is highly similar to one for marijuana use among high school students (Shedler & Block, 1990). Clearly, when a particular form of drug use is normative behaviour, well-adjusted individuals will tend to engage in it.

Economic Benefits

In this list of the benefits of drinking, it must not be forgotten that the manufacture, distribution and sales of alcohol provide employment for many people in our society. In the UK, for example, the total number of people employed in alcohol and tobacco production in 1997 was 53,000 (Brewers & Licensed Retailers Association, 1998), of whom 10,000 at most were employed in the tobacco industry. Numbers of people employed in public houses, hotels and restaurants are huge; in 1997, the figure for pubs and bars was 376,000, while the total figure including hotels and restaurants was 1,048,000 (Brewers & Licensed Retailers Association, 1998), although many of these were part-time workers.

Again using the UK as an example, British citizens spent over £28,000 million on alcohol in 1996, generating in excess of £10,000 million in government revenue that year (Raistrick, Hodgson & Ritson, 1999). The pre-tax profits of the six leading alcohol companies in 1995 were more than £3200 million and £190 million was spent on promoting alcohol in 1996 (Alcohol Concern, 1997). Big business indeed!

Against this, of course, must be set the economic cost to society of alcohol-related problems. The latest study in the UK (Godfrey & Hardman, 1994) estimated a total cost of over £2461 million in 1992 but even this figure was reckoned to be conservative because it did not include crime other than drink–drive or drunkenness offences, or lost productivity due to hangover and impaired performance at work. There are also several areas of cost that it is extremely difficult to quantify, such as the cost of alcohol-related injuries to the health service. Studies in countries other than the UK suggest that the total costs of excessive drinking lie between 2% and 5% of gross national product (GNP) each year (Godfrey, 1997). Using the lowest figure in this range, the costs of excessive drinking in England alone amount to nearly £11,000 million per annum (Alcohol Concern, 1999), slightly more, it will be noted, that the estimated revenue to the UK government.

ALCOHOL AND SOCIETY: AMBIVALENCE AND CONTRADICTION

Given the simultaneous existence of the pleasures and pains that have been documented in this chapter, it is small wonder that society's view of alcohol has been characterized by sociologists as profoundly ambivalent (see Room, 1976). This ambivalence was more clearly and sharply drawn in earlier historical times; in the nineteenth century in the USA and in many European countries, for example, the Temperance Movement flourished in a situation where there seemed to be only two conflicting, behavioural imperatives—teetotalism or habitual drunkenness. The twentieth century saw the emergence of a third possibility— moderate drinking—for the first time on a widespread scale. Even today, however, cultures and subcultures that have high rates of alcohol abstention tend to show higher rates of excessive and problem drinking among those who do imbibe, the extreme examples of this being drinking among some indigenous peoples such as the Australian Aborigines (Kahn et al., 1990). An interesting question concerns the extent to which, on a psychological level, all of us carry within us some representation of these conflicting societal responses to alcohol. The contradiction here is that, while the drinks industry tries to persuade us that it is only interested in promoting sensible and responsible drinking, alcohol is an essentially intoxicating drug. We drink it for its intoxicating effects, even those of us who seek only a warm glow from a few glasses or wine or a stiff gin and tonic. More to the point, many members of society, mainly but not only the younger members, deliberately and self-consciously use alcohol to pursue intoxication, i.e. to get drunk, and they too would claim to derive pleasure from this activity. Thus the benefits of moderate drinking listed above occur in spite of, not because of, the basic nature of the substance. It also follows that, notwithstanding its harmful consequences, an honest appraisal of the pleasures of drinking must include the pleasures of intoxication.

The drinks industry must be aware of these ambivalent and conflicting responses. Even a cursory examination of alcohol advertising, especially that aimed at younger people, shows that its ability to intoxicate, and the glamour and excitement with which intoxication is associated, is the product's main selling point (see Chapter 42, this volume). As Lemmens (Chapter 20 this volume) points out, a small percentage of the population is responsible for a greatly disproportionate amount of the total alcohol consumed; in the figures Lemmens quotes, 10% of the population of The Netherlands drinks between 30% and 60% of the total amount. Owing to the way in which alcohol consumption is invariably distributed in a population, the same disproportion applies to any country's drinking. Thus, if all those excessive drinkers currently drinking above medically recommended levels were magically transformed into moderate drinkers, the drinks industry's profits would disappear at a stroke.

This last observation might be seen as indicating an irreconcilable contradiction between the interests of the drinks industry and the interests of public health. The reality is, however, that the drinks industry, like the poor of Victorian times, will always be with us. In a world in which alcohol is made available mainly by private enterprise, in which the voting public mostly demands a reasonably free access to alcohol, but also in which excessive drinking poses grave risks to health and safety, there is no alternative to finding ways in which the interests of industry profits and of public health and welfare can be reconciled politically.

Alcohol, then, is our favourite and our most dangerous drug. Smoking, via nicotine addiction, kills more people each year than drinking but its victims are mostly middle-aged and over. A calculation that includes death, disability and suffering throughout the life-span, and which embraces harm to the drinker's family, neighbourhood and the wider society, shows alcohol to be top of the world league table of harmful substances and on a par with malaria and tuberculosis (Jernigan et al., in press). All societies in human history have felt the need to exert some form of control over this powerfully intoxicating, addictive and potentially poisonous drug. Drinking alcohol is, of course, a matter of individual responsibility and choice but, at the same time, it should also be a matter of collective responsibility for limiting the harms that arise from it. Any society that forgets or ignores this fact does so at its peril.

ACKNOWLEDGEMENTS

I am grateful to Christine Godfrey and Dave Place for their advice on particular points in this chapter. I am also very grateful to Tim Stockwell for helpful comments on an earlier draft of the chapter.

KEY WORKS AND SUGGESTIONS FOR FURTHER READING

Peele, S. & Grant, M. (Eds) (1999). *Alcohol and Pleasure: A Health Perspective.* Washington, DC: International Center on Alcohol Policies.

A book produced by the alcohol industry-funded International Center on Alcohol Policies, extolling the pleasures and benefits of drinking.

Baum-Baicker, C. (1987).   The psychological benefits of moderate alcohol consumption: a review of the literature. *Drug & Alcohol Dependence*, **15**, 305–322.

Although somewhat out-of-date now, this is a comprehensive and useful review of the literature in this area at that time.

McCreanor, T., Caswell, S. & Hill, L. (2000).   ICAP and the perils of partnership (Editorial). *Addiction*, **95**, 179–185.

A challenging editorial on the dangers of public health advocates and researchers "getting into bed" with the drinks industry. See also the commentaries on the editorial from various points of view in the same issue of *Addiction.*

Pittman, D. (1996).   What do we know about beneficial consequences of moderate alcohol consumption on social and physical well-being? A critical review of the recent literature. *Contemporary Drug Problems*, **23**, 389–406.

A short but useful review of this topic.

Murray, C.M. & Lopez, A. (1996).   *The Global Burden of Disease: A Comprehensive Assessment of Mortality and Disability from Diseases, Injuries, and Risk Factors in 1990 and Projected to 2020.* Geneva: World Health Organization.

This contains evidence that alcohol is more harmful world-wide than other psychoactive substances.

REFERENCES

Alcohol Concern (1997).   Spending on alcohol. *Acquire: Alcohol Concern's Quarterly Information and Research Bulletin*, **19**, 8.

Alcohol Concern (1999).   *Proposals for a National Alcohol Strategy for England.* London: Alcohol Concern.

Baum-Baicker, C. (1987).   The psychological benefits of moderate alcohol consumption: a review of the literature. *Drug & Alcohol Dependence*, **15**, 305–322.

Brewers & Licensed Retailers Association (1998).   *Statistical Handbook 1998.* London: Brewing Publications Ltd.

Brodsky, A. & Peele, S. (1999).   Psychosocial benefits of moderate alcohol consumption: alcohol's role in a broader conception of health and well-being. In S. Peele & M. Grant (Eds), *Alcohol and Pleasure: A Health Perspective* (pp. 187–207). Washington DC: International Center on Alcohol Policies.

Brown, S.A., Goldman, M.S., Inn, A. & Anderson, L.R. (1980).   Expectations of reinforcement from alcohol: their domain and relation to drinking patterns. *Journal of Consulting & Clinical Psychology*, **48**, 419–426.

Cappell, H. & Greeley, J. (1987).   Alcohol and tension reduction: an update on research and theory. In H.T. Blane & K.E. Leonard (Eds), *Psychological Theories of Drinking and Alcoholism* (pp. 15–54). New York: Guilford.

Christian, J.C., Reed, T., Carmelli, D., Page, W.F., Norton, J.A. & Breitner, J.C.S. (1995).   Self-reported alcohol intake and cognition among aging twins. *Journal of Studies on Alcohol*, **56**, 414–416.

Darkes, J. & Goldman, M.S. (1993).   Expectancy challenge and drinking reduction: experimental evidence for a mediational process. *Journal of Consulting & Clinical Psychology*, **61**, 344–353.

Fillmore, K.M. (2000).   Is alcohol *really* good for the heart? (Editorial). *Addiction*, **95**, 173–174.

Godfrey, C. (1997).   Nature and extent of the problem. In J. Chick, C. Godfrey, B. Hore, J. Marshall & T. Peters (Eds), *Alcohol Dependence: A Clinical Problem* (pp. 1–11). London: Mosby-Wolfe Medical Communications.

Godfrey, C. & Hardman, G. (1994).   *Changing the Social Costs of Alcohol.* Final Report to the Alcohol Education & Research Council. Centre for Health Economics: University of York, UK.

Goodwin, D.W. (1970). The alcoholism of F. Scott Fitzgerald. *Journal of the American Medical Association*, **212**, 86–90.

Goodwin, D.W. (1971). The alcoholism of Eugene O'Neill. *Journal of the American Medical Association*, **216**, 99–104.

Grant, M. (1999). Preface. In S. Peele & M. Grant (Eds), *Alcohol and Pleasure: A Health Perspective* (pp. xi–xiv). Washington DC: International Center for Alcohol Policies.

Heath, D.B. (1995). Some generalisations about alcohol and culture. In D.B. Heath (Ed.), *International Handbook on Alcohol and Culture* (pp. 348–361). Westport CT: Greenwood.

Hull (1981). A self-awareness model of the causes and effects of alcohol consumption. *Journal of Abnormal Psychology*, **90**, 586–600.

Hull J.G. & Bond, C.F. (1986). Social and behavioural consequences of alcohol consumption and expectancy: a meta-analysis. *Psychological Bulletin*, **99**, 347–360.

Hull, J.G., Levenson, R.W., Young R.D. & Sher, K.J. (1983). Self-awareness—reducing effects of alcohol consumption. *Journal of Personality & Social Psychology*, **44**, 461–473.

Jernigan, D.H. & Mosher, J.F. (2000). Permission for profits. Commentary on McCreanor et al., "ICAP and the perils of partnership". *Addiction*, **95**, 190–191.

Jernigan, D., Monteiro, M., Room, R. & Saxena, S. (in press). Towards a global alcohol policy: alcohol, public health and the role of WHO. *Bulletin of the World Health Organization* **78**, 491–499.

Jones, B. & McMahon, J. (1998). Alcohol motivations as outcome expectancies. In W.R. Miller & N. Heather (Eds), *Treating Addictive Behaviours* (pp. 75–92). New York: Plenum.

Kahn, M.W., Hunter, E., Heather, N. & Tebbutt, J. (1990). Australian Aborigines and alcohol: a review. *Drug & Alcohol Review*, **10**, 351–366.

Klatsky, A.L. (1999). Is drinking healthy? In S. Peele & M. Grant (Eds), *Alcohol and Pleasure: A Health Perspective* (pp. 141–156). Washington DC: International Center for Alcohol Policies.

Lipton, R.I. (1994). The effect of moderate alcohol use on the relationship between stress and depression. *American Journal of Pubic Health*, **84**, 1913–1917.

Lowe, G. & Taylor, S.B. (1993). Relationship between laughter and weekly alcohol consumption. *Psychological Reports*, **72**, 1210.

Lowe, G. & Taylor, S.B. (1997). Effects of alcohol on responsive laughter and amusement. *Psychological Reports*, **80**, 1149–1150.

MacAndrew, C. & Edgerton, R.B. (1969). *Drunken Comportment: A Social Explanation*. Chicago, IL: Aldine.

McCreanor, T., Caswell, S. & Hill, L. (2000). ICAP and the perils of partnership. (Editorial). *Addiction*, **95**, 179–185.

McLelland, D.C., David, W.N. Kalin, R. & Wanner, E. (1972). *The Drinking Man*. New York: The Free Press.

Miller, W.R. (1998). Researching the spiritual dimensions of alcohol and other drug problems. *Addiction*, **93**, 979–990.

Mishara, B.L. & Kastenbaum, R. (1980). *Alcohol and Old Age*. New York: Grune & Stratton.

Murray, C.M. & Lopez, A. (1996). *The Global Burden of Disease: A Comprehensive Assessment of Mortality and Disability from Diseases, Injuries, and Risk Factors in 1990 and Projected to 2020*. Geneva: World Health Organization.

Neff, J.A. & Husaini, B.A. (1982). Life events, drinking patterns and depressive symptomatology: the stress-buffering role of alcohol consumption. *Journal of Studies on Alcohol*, **43**, 301–318.

Nezlek, J.B., Pilkington, C.J. & Bilbro, K.G. (1994). Moderation in excess: binge drinking and social interaction among college students. *Journal of Studies on Alcohol*, **55**, 342–351.

Orgogozo, J.-M., Dartigues, J.-F., Lafont, S. et al. (1997). Wine consumption and dementia in the elderly: a prospective community study in the Bordeaux area. *Revue Neurologique*, **153**, 185–192.

Peele, S. & Grant, M. (Eds) (1999). *Alcohol and Pleasure: A Health Perspective*. Washington DC: International Center for Alcohol Policies.

Pittman, D. (1996). What do we know about beneficial consequences of moderate alcohol consumption on social and physical well-being? A critical review of the recent literature. *Contemporary Drug Problems*, **23**, 389–406.

Pliner, P. & Cappell, H. (1974). Modification of affective consequences of alcohol: a comparison of solitary and social drinking. *Journal of Abnormal Psychology*, **83**, 418–425.

Raistrick, D., Hodgson, R. & Ritson B. (Eds) (1999). *Tackling Alcohol Together: the Evidence Base for UK Alcohol Policy.* London: Free Association Books.

Rimbaud, A. (1973). *Poesies, Une Saison en Enfer, Illuminations.* Paris: Gallimard.

Room, R. (1976). Ambivalence as a sociological explanation: the case of cultural explanations of alcobol problems. *American Sociological Review* **41**, 1047–1065.

Room, R. & Collins, G. (1981). *Alcohol and Disinhibition: Nature and Meaning of the Link.* Research Monograph No. 12, National Institute on Alcohol Abuse & Alcoholism. Washington DC: US Department of Health & Human Services.

Royal College of Psychiatrists (1986). *Alcohol: Our Favourite Drug.* London: Tavistock.

Shedler, J. & Block, J. (1990). Adolescent drug use and psychological health: a longitudinal inquiry. *American Psychologist*, **45**, 612–630.

Siegel, R.K. (1989). *Intoxication: Life in Pursuit of Artificial Paradise.* New York: E.P. Dutton.

Chapter 2

A Social and Political History of Alcohol

Betsy Thom
School of Social Science, Middlesex University, Enfield, UK

Synopsis

The concern in this chapter is to trace major historical trends in the use of alcohol and in responses to problem drinking and alcohol-related harms. But how is problem drinking defined? What counts as alcohol-related harm? And why have responses to alcohol use and problem use differed radically from one historical time to another and from place to place? The argument presented in subsequent sections is that our perceptions of appropriate or inappropriate uses of alcohol and our policies for dealing with the unwanted consequences of alcohol use are embedded within social, political and economic contexts. As these evolve and change, so too, perceptions of the benefits and costs of alcohol consumption are modified or radically changed.

The chapter begins by illustrating the widespread importance of alcohol as a commodity in the economies and in the everyday lives of people from the earliest times. As well as the benefits, the harmful effects of alcohol were observed and recorded and sanctions were imposed to prevent or control the unwanted consequences of inappropriate use—usually associated with drunkenness. But, on the whole, the dominant response to drunkenness before the nineteenth century was "generalized disapproval" of the drinker's behaviour. Legislative controls were confined to curbing behaviour that posed a threat to social order, and to regulating alcohol manufacturing and distribution processes. Treatment, as a response to harmful drinking, did not exist prior to the nineteenth century. By then, rapidly changing political and social circumstances and the emergence of a medical definition of habitual drunkenness as a "disease" contributed to changing conceptions of alcohol and resulted in a re-assessment of the benefits and harms associated with its use. Temperance societies were prominent among the new interest and pressure groups, which emerged in the nineteenth century. The forces influencing the rise of the temperance movement in America and Europe and the adoption, in some societies, of a prohibition response to alcohol are briefly reviewed. Major changes have taken place also in the twentieth century. The chapter sketches the shift from a treatment response to alcoholism to a prevention and public health approach intended to address a much wider range of alcohol-

International Handbook of Alcohol Dependence and Problems. Edited by N. Heather, T.J. Peters and T. Stockwell.

related harms and to extend appropriate forms of intervention to a much larger target group of "problem drinkers". Concurrent trends, away from a philosophy of specialist care towards community-based responses, and concurrent professional develop- ments, especially in clinical psychology, social work and counselling, resulted in an expansion in the alcohol field and the injection of new perspectives and approaches to the management of alcohol. The chapter ends with a brief look to the future, arguing that the "globalization" of products, of perspectives on alcohol use and of policy and practice responses demands a different kind of historical analysis which includes, but reaches beyond, the influence of the political and social contexts of individual countries to an examination of the influence of "global markets" and "global networks" on the history of alcohol.

ALCOHOL USE

Alcohol Use in Early Societies

The origins of alcohol use pre-date recorded history and, although it is believed that ethanol was known to neolithic man, we do not know what kind of liquor was first used. In China, archaeological evidence dates the origin of alcohol from fermented grain to some 6000–7000 years ago (Yucun & Zuxin, 1998). Some historical accounts suggest that honey, the basis of mead, was the natural source of the first drinkable ethanol (Sournia, 1990) and that the grapevine was the most likely plant deliberately cultivated to produce alcohol (Keller, 1979). But early civilizations produced alcohol from a variety of different sub- stances—whatever was locally available (Charrington, 1925).

Factors such as taste, the availability of suitable ingredients, the stage of techno- logical development in a society and ease of production most certainly played a part in the spread and popularity of different kinds of alcohol. So too did war, economic needs and trade opportunities. In ancient Rome, for instance, wine was a scarce, costly commodity, reflected in laws which controlled its use, one of which forbade the sprink- ling of wine on funeral pyres. By the beginning of the second century BC, viticulture played an important economic role in the home market and wine rapidly became a valuable trade commodity and the major source of wealth in Italy (Jellinek, 1976). Certainly, the spread of wine-making throughout Europe followed in the wake of Roman conquests. Wine was brought to England by the Romans, but when they left, subsequent invaders—the Angles, Saxons, Jutes and Vikings—favoured ale and cider and the wine trade dwindled. In a later period, monastic orders often controlled the production and marketing of wine in the villages around their monasteries. They led the way both in developing new wines and in forging new trade routes (Robinson, 1988; Ferguson, 1975).

Outside Europe, age-old forms of brewing and producing alcoholic drinks persisted throughout the centuries and can still be found in some countries today. In many countries, however, traditional practices were changed dramatically during the colonization of major parts of the world by Europeans. The introduction of alcohol, an excellent "consumable" trading commodity, to people who hitherto had not known it, and of distilled spirits to soci- eties accustomed to milder forms of alcohol, often disrupted traditional patterns of alcohol production and consumption and resulted in harmful drinking practices which were, nevertheless, advantageous to the colonists (Sournia, 1990; Hall, 1986; see accounts from different countries in Grant, 1998, & in Molamu and MacDonald, 1996, for a contempo- rary example from Botswana).

The Discovery of Distilled Liquor

Part of the problem may have been the differences in strength between traditional brews and the alcohol brought in by colonists. In places such as North America, only the milder forms were available until distilled beverages and distillation techniques were introduced with colonization. Earliest forms of alcohol, which relied on a natural fermentation process, could not have been stronger than 14% alcohol; at that level natural yeast, an essential ingredient in the process, dies. Stronger beverages did not appear until the twelfth century when, with the discovery of distillation processes, an alcohol content of up to 93% could be achieved. In Europe, the first distilled drinks appeared around the mid-fifteenth century and by the end of the sixteenth century were found throughout the West (Sournia, 1990; Tannahill, 1988). By the end of the seventeenth century, American colonists had at their disposal a considerable range of fermented and distilled beverages, including whisky introduced by Irish and Scottish settlers and rum—consumed in large quantities by the colonists and used as a commodity in the slave trade between America, Africa and the plantation owners of the West Indies—as well as cider, apple brandy and a highly potent liquor known as applejack (Tannahill, 1988).

Alcohol Use, Privilege and Social Status

While the great forces of international trade, war and politics helped to shape the history of alcohol production and use across the centuries, what people drank also depended on the social organization and internal economies of the societies in which they lived. In India, kings could afford the grape wine first imported from Rome and later from Kapisi, north of Kabul; poorer people had to make do with rice ale or one of the brews made from sugarcane juice, honey, the sap of palmyra and talipot palms and other local produce (Tannahill, 1988). In countries such as England and Germany, wine remained the drink of the aristocracy and the wealthy classes for many centuries while most people drank ale, mead or whatever was cheapest and most easily produced (Vogt, 1984). Economic and social factors underpinned the "gin epidemic" in eighteenth century England, when consumption rose from 500,000 gallons in 1700 to over 5 million in 1735. The rise followed government action to help farmers find a market for excess grain and to destroy the trade in smuggled French brandy. By cancelling the tax on distilling, abolishing the control of manufacturing standards and permitting gin to be sold without a licence, the floodgates were opened to the production of cheap gin, which quickly resulted in the excesses and public health problems illustrated in Hogarth's famous depiction of "Gin Lane".

How alcohol was manufactured, distributed and used was also related to authority and power divisions within societies. Ritualistic uses of alcohol in early societies or as part of religious ceremonies often symbolized and reinforced existing power and authority relationships within families, kin groups and households, as well as within the wider community. In many societies, access to alcohol use, or rights to production and distribution of alcohol, were controlled by the ruling or land-owning classes, generally, it has been argued, to the benefit of those in power or to preserve the social order. Vogt (1984), for instance, points out how, apart from keeping prices low, demand for alcohol was deliberately raised in Germany during the first half of the nineteenth century by forcing workers into the "trucking system". For rural workers, this meant that they were obliged to accept supplies of alcohol in lieu of wages. In the case of industrial workers, factory owners commissioned saloons as centres for hiring and paying workers, thereby inducing workers to drink as much as possible. The profits went to the factory owners who had commissioned the saloons and to the entrepreneurs who ran them (Vogt, 1984). Similar illustrations of the manipulation of systems of production and distribution by the ruling classes to preserve power in the face of changing social circumstances come from other countries (e.g. feudal Poland, discussed in Levine, 1987).

In some societies, of course, access to alcohol was denied to certain groups—often women, servants or slaves—because it was thought that alcohol use would incite disruptive or rebellious behaviour (Heath, 1990). There were also formal and informal sanctions governing which groups could participate in the processes of manufacturing and distributing alcohol (see country sections in Grant, 1998). Plant (1997) discusses this in relation to women's roles within the changing economic and social structures of different societies. She notes, for instance, that brewing was traditionally a woman's task in many countries but that this changed in a variety of ways with changing social circumstances, developments in manufacturing technologies and changing relationships between the genders.

The Emergence of Legislative Controls

The emergence of legislative controls also indicates the importance of alcohol to the economies and social orders of ancient and medieval societies. In most cases, controls took the form of taxes, laws to suppress smuggling, and legislation to control trade with other countries and to regulate manufacturing and distribution processes. Legislative controls emerged in different societies at different times but were everywhere linked to economics, politics and social order rather than to individual and public health concerns. That came to the fore much later. For example, controlling the quality of the liquor traded to other countries or sold internally became an early cause for concern in many societies. The adulteration of beverages by unscrupulous dealers was commonplace from earliest times. The Sumerian code of Hammurabi (1750 BC) roundly condemned the selling of ale that was under-strength and over-priced (Tannahill, 1988). In thirteenth century Britain, the adulteration of ale—an important item in the national diet—became a political issue which led to the inclusion of a statement in the Magna Carta on standard measures for ale and wine and later, in 1266, in the "Assize of Bread and Ale", to laws controlling the price and quality of ale. Transgressions of the law were to be punished by the pillory or the tumbrel and, later, by corporal punishment (Ferguson, 1975; Wilson, 1940).

The Importance of Alcohol in Daily Life

While alcohol played a prominent role in the wider affairs of state, it was also an important element in the daily lives of the population. There is ample documented evidence of its integration in the religious, social, economic and political life of almost every civilization up to the present day (e.g. Grant, 1998). When distilled alcohol was discovered, it was a precious commodity, regarded as a medicine and called *aqua vitae* (the water of life), giving us the names *eau de vie*, aquavit, vodka and whisky (from *uisge beatha*, abbreviated to *uisge*). The benefits attributed to alcohol as a food, a safe drink (when water was often unclean), a medicine and an anaesthetic (when little else was available for the relief of sickness and pain) were widespread. According to some historical sources, the use of alcohol for medicinal purposes increased dramatically after the discovery of distillation. Used sparingly at first because of its price and scarcity, as availability increased it became "the universal remedy for all diseases and ailments, a miraculous drug which cured disease and prolonged life" (Charrington, 1925, p. 126). In the nineteenth century, alcohol was prescribed medically and it formed the base of many commercial and home remedies

(Olsen, 1994). But the rise of temperance in the nineteenth century, along with changing social and political forces in Europe and America, resulted in challenges to beliefs about the medicinal and nutritional value of alcohol. By the twentieth century, perceptions of alcohol and its use laid greater emphasis on the ill-effects rather than on the benefits of the substance.

ALCOHOL AND HARM

Knowledge of Harm

Despite the popularity of alcoholic beverages, people have always known that alcohol can be harmful as well as beneficial. Alcohol, the "good creature of God" to American colonists (sermon by Increase Mather, 1673) was also "the demon drink", "mother's ruin" (gin), and "a great and growing evil" in other times and places. Hippocrates, the Greek physician, described symptoms such as nausea, insomnia, palpitations and delirium which, centuries later, became a familiar part of the clinical picture of "alcoholism". Aristotle posed the question: "Why cannot the drunken have sexual intercourse?". Alexander the Great committed excesses of violence while under the influence of drink and later historians have speculated about the extent to which his drinking bouts contributed to his death (Jellinek, 1976; Keller, 1979; Sournia, 1990). The history of drinking in Georgian England reveals that eighteenth century physicians attributed a long list of disabilities and diseases to hard drinking, including flatulence, dropsy, gout, cirrhosis and madness. They were aware of the private tragedies as well as the public nuisances and costs of excessive consumption (Porter, 1985; Gutzke, 1984). Historical accounts of alcohol use in India, South America, China and Africa provide further illustrations that the possible ill-effects of alcohol were recognized (Grant, 1998).

Responses to Alcohol-related Harm

Philosophers, physicians, writers and preachers have been prolific in proposing ways of managing alcohol-related problems. The Greek philosopher, Plato, suggested that wine be forbidden to those under 18 years of age, that it could be used in moderation by individuals between 18 and 30, and that it need not be restricted to those over 40 (Sournia, 1990). Preachers in colonial America threatened habitual drunkards with eternal suffering (Levine, 1978) and a wide variety of punishments were meted out, including, at various times, a period in the stocks, whipping and fines (Williams & Brake, 1980). By and large, however, what is most notable about responses to intoxication or excessive use of alcohol prior to the nineteenth century is that concerns revolved around moral attitudes and social behaviours regarded as licentious, sinful or criminal that were associated with excessive drinking. Even then, the dominant social response was "generalized disapproval" (Porter, 1990).

So why, throughout most historic periods, were the personal and physical problems of alcohol and the links between private and public behaviours largely ignored for policy purposes? As noted above, economic and political factors underpinned early legislation, along with concerns to control alcohol-related harm to the community or the state. This was true at local as well as national levels. In England, licensing administration grew out of concern with public houses as unruly hotbeds of political dissent, and in 1495 an act was passed by which alehouses could be suppressed on the agreement of two justices of the peace. It was re-enacted in 1503, stating:

Forasmuch as intolerable hurts and troubles to the Commonwealth of this Realm doth daily grow and increase through such abuses and disorders as are had and used in common alehouses and other houses called "tippling houses" . . . (Wilson, 1940, p. 95).

That these sentiments were not confined to medieval times is illustrated by the testimony of a witness to the Select Committee in 1833 on the harm resulting from the Beerhouse Act (1830), by which any householder could sell beer, free from licensing or control by the justices. Among the many excesses and problems created by the speedy proliferation of outlets, not least was that: "The Act has increased the opportunities of meeting of the lower classes to discuss politics and what they call their own grievances, and thus done more harm than good". Pamphlets circulated in the beerhouses incited disruption in the cause of workers' rights with rallying cries such as, "Down with the Tithes! down with the taxes! down with the places (placeholders)! and down with the pensions!" (Wilson, 1940, p. 102).

Similar reasons motivated concerns and legislation on drunkenness. Drunkenness itself became a civil offence in England in 1552 and in 1606 an act was passed for "repressing the odious and loathsome sin of drunkenness" but, it appears, it was rarely enforced (Robinson, 1988, p. 130; Williams & Brake, 1980). Indeed, Porter (1985) makes the point that heavy drinking was prized as a manly and sociable custom in Georgian England (see Levine, 1978, for similar attitudes towards drunkenness in colonial America).

Changing Constructions of "Harm": an Example from Medieval England

Warner (1997), in her examination of alcohol-associated harm in England from late medieval to early modern times, notes that how harm is construed has been very different from place to place and from time to time. Categories of harm that existed in medieval times would no longer feature in current lists or may have changed their meaning. Drunken behaviours that were perceived as subversive of the social and moral order in medieval times included playing the fool, refusal to defer to social superiors—the local minister and the church among others—and conspicuous consumption of certain kinds of food and drink by the lower classes. Charges for disorderly conduct recorded between 1560 and 1640 included wives brawling with husbands and neighbours, parents who allowed children to run around the church during services, parishioners who sat in pews reserved for their social superiors, and other similar offences which, today, might simply attract disapproval or informal sanctions, even if linked with drunkenness. Loss of income due to drinking was recognized then, as now, as a harm but stemmed from a different perception of the nature of the problem. The concern was not with individual or family troubles but with ensuring that husbands and fathers supervised and provided for their dependants and did not place the burden on the community, the parish or the local aristocracy.

On the other hand, current lists of alcohol-related harm include items that do not appear in the medieval literature. The fact that effects of alcohol on productivity and on the workplace were *not* defined as a problem in medieval times is consistent with the widespread belief that alcohol enhanced productivity. Harm, in other words, is not a constant; it is socially constructed in the process of social interaction and social change.

How do such changes come about? Warner contends that the definition of harm depends in large part on who is in a position to represent and influence public opinion and policy.

In medieval England, the nation's political and religious elites defined harm in ways that reflected their interests in preserving the moral and social order. In the early nineteenth century, medical and psychiatric definitions of harm emerged at a time when these professions were expanding and extending their influence to encompass new client groups through the treatment of lunacy and other "deviant" behaviours.

Harm and Legislative Control

Legislation to prevent or reduce alcohol-related harm depends on how harm is defined and on the extent to which beliefs about the substance compete with or are tempered by other social and economic concerns. Summarizing the situation in Europe, Sournia (1990) concludes that, by the beginning of the eighteenth century, Western societies (or particular individuals in those societies) were beginning to express concern at levels of drunkenness. The rise in concern did not occur simultaneously in every country and did not manifest itself everywhere in the same way; but it was based on social anxieties directed especially towards drunkenness in the lower classes and the threat to social order.

In England, such anxieties were reflected in an increasing spate of legislation to control consumption, often by attempting to shift consumers from one type of beverage to another type regarded as less harmful. Earlier measures to control consumption had included the introduction of excise in 1643—imposed at that time on the makers and retailers of ale, beer, cider and perry—and the promotion of new substitute commodities, such as coffee, chocolate and tea, which, partly due to the price of these new beverages, failed to make a significant impact on the nation's drinking habits (Williams & Brake, 1980). Beer continued to be the favoured drink, with a population of around 5,000,000 consuming 12,400,000 barrels in 1688. But in 1689, Cromwell's government stopped imports of spirits from abroad and opened up the home market to the distillery trade. The result, according to Williams & Brake (1980), was a massive increase in consumption of spirits and a deterioration in behaviour and public health. In particular, the "gin epidemic" and its association with poverty, crime and disorder in the early eighteenth century prompted the famous Gin Act of 1736, intended to raise the price of spirits and reduce availability. The attempt failed, leading instead to a flourishing illicit trade and an increase in beer drinking. Later legislation was more effective in stemming the rise in consumption but it remained high and so did the attendant harm. Later, the 1830 Beerhouse Act was another failed attempt to wean consumers away from spirits; in fact, over the following 10 years, consumption of spirits increased by 32% (Williams & Brake, 1980; see Armyr et al., 1982, for examples from other countries, ranging from those that have developed highly restrictive policies and systems to those characterized by more liberal "free market" approaches).

Throughout the ages, historical continuities in responses to alcohol control can be observed—for instance, the use of legislation to reduce perceived threats to authority or the social order. But change is also a major theme in examining perceptions of harm and the emergence and evolution of responses to harm. In particular, historians have focused on changes occurring in the nineteenth century, which, it is often argued, sowed the seeds of contemporary views and policies on alcohol. Porter (1990) poses the crucial questions asked by many other historians of this period. Why and when did the traditional attitudes towards chronic drunkenness—"generalized disapproval"—begin to harden, leading to widespread temperance, abstinence and teetotal movements? How was habitual drunkenness transformed, within the mental outlooks of official society, into a deeply disturbing social problem? (Porter, 1990, pp. xi–xii).

CHANGING PERCEPTIONS AND RESPONSES TO ALCOHOL AND ALCOHOL-RELATED PROBLEMS

There is no one explanation for the changes that occurred throughout the Western world in perceptions of alcohol and alcohol-related harm around the beginning of the nineteenth century. The bare facts of consumption and harm, even given the levels of apparently harmful drinking habits and an increase in spirits drinking in America, were not enough to explain the dramatic rise in concern about alcohol and the widespread drive to provide a solution to the "alcohol problem". Equally, increased knowledge and scientific exploration of alcohol use and the effects of alcohol contributed to changing conceptualizations of its role in medicine, nutrition and social interaction but are not alone sufficient to explain its fall from grace as the century proceeded.

The Disease Concept of Alcoholism and the Emergence of a Treatment Response

Considerable emphasis has been placed on the "discovery" of the disease concept of alcoholism and the progressive understanding of the disease that developed over the century throughout Europe and America. According to Levine (1978), it was Benjamin Rush, an American physician, who provided the first clearly developed, modern conception of alcohol addiction. This included the idea of gradual and progressive addiction, bouts of drunkenness characterized by an inability to refrain from alcohol (loss of control), the description of the condition as a "disease" and total abstinence as the cure. Around the same time, in the UK, Thomas Trotter described habitual drunkenness as a "disease of the mind" to be managed by "the discerning physician".

Treatment and rehabilitation, as an organized response to habitual drunkenness or alcoholism, did not exist prior to the nineteenth century. Conceptualization of the problem as a disease meant that treatment was now an appropriate form of response and, over the course of the century, in Europe and America, a variety of treatments were offered by private doctors, voluntary and philanthropic societies; and, in the shape of inebriate asylums or reformatories, as a state response to the problem (McLaughlan, 1991; Baumhol & Room, 1987). The organization of self-help groups can also be traced to the nineteenth century. The Washingtonians group of reformed drinkers started in the 1840s in Baltimore. They espoused an approach to prevention and recovery which was a forerunner of beliefs and methods popularized again a century later by Alcoholics Anonymous. The disease concept, loss of control and the need for abstinence were central; meetings focused around the reciting of personal testimonies and "confessions". By the 1850s the Washingtonians had lost their appeal, although not before they had sown the seeds for other self-help temperance societies which flourished in the USA and in Britain throughout the remainder of the century.

Interpretations of the role of medical practitioners such as Rush and Trotter in "discovering" the concept of habitual drunkenness as a "disease" have differed. But there is agreement that both played an important role in synthesizing many of the ideas of the day within a meaningful framework appealing to policy makers, professionals and to an increasing range of philanthropical and lay groups (Levine, 1978; Porter, 1985; Olsen, 1994). Equally important is the argument that the new "medical and psychiatric discourses" emerging at the start of the nineteenth century came to the fore in an era of rapidly changing social conditions, new philosophical and political perspectives and the emergence of new power elites (MacLeod, 1967; Levine, 1978; Berridge, 1989).

The Temperance Movements

While psychiatric and medical understanding was important in formulating the new ideas, wider dissemination of these ideas to the general public and the mobilization of pressure for policy change owed much to the temperance movements. The birth of the temperance move ient in 1808 has been traced to Saratoga in the State of New York, although the foundatio of the American Society for the Promotion of Temperance in Boston in 1826 marks the start of more organized activity. In Europe, temperance messages spread unevenly to different countries over the first half of the century—sometimes meeting with strong opposition (Street et al., 1862; Bretherton, 1991). During this period, the movement was marked by tensions between protagonists of different views on alcohol and its association with individual and social harm. Rush's work had a profound influence over temperance ideology, although most historians agree that early temperance societies were not prohibitionist. To begin with, temperance meant moderation, not abstinence, although certain liquors were considered "worse" than others. Rush himself did not include wine and beer in his abstinence repertoire. In America, total abstinence from distilled spirits was advocated; but different interpretations of the problem and the solution were a feature of the movement everywhere (Street et al., 1862).

Powerful elites and pressure groups were often divided in their allegiances. Doctors and the clergy, for instance, did not all subscribe to abstinence ideals. Olsen (1994), in an examination of reactions to the temperance movement in the Church of England, distinguishes three periods: 1830–1855, when Anglican clergymen, in keeping with medical opinion, rejected teetotalism in favour of moderation; 1855–1873, a period when, in general, doctors were discouraging the use of alcohol as a medicine and a minority of clergymen attempted, unsuccessfully, to convert the Anglican church to the prohibitionist view; and 1873–1914, when the Church of England Temperance Society promoted teetotalism for the majority but affirmed the legitimacy of moderate drinking among the British medical and social elite.

While recruitment of powerful groups was an important facet of temperance strategy, its success also drew on its grass roots appeal and its relevance to the concerns and ambitions of ordinary working and middle class people in the eighteenth and early nineteenth centuries. In its heyday, the social significance of the movement went beyond its contribution to managing the alcohol problem. Through participation in temperance associations, working-class people, tradespeople and women found routes to improve their education and skills, helping them to move up the social ladder and to participate in public and political life (e.g. see Tyrrell, 1991, for a discussion of the influence of the Women's Christian Temperance Union). For young people, the Bands of Hope provided education and training through involvement in organizing activities and opened the way to future careers. Taking the pledge was not only a badge of abstinence, it was opting in to a lifestyle reflecting contemporary values of hard work, God-fearing respectability and the chance to better oneself. In some places, different phases in the development of the movement were also clearly linked to class struggles of the time. Bretherton (1991), in his history of the Irish temperance movement, describes the early movement as led by "Protestants of position and property"—Irish landlords, members of the nobility and gentry, large employers such as factory owners, canal and railway proprietors, and the wealthy "old middle class" (doctors, lawyers, bankers and clergymen). Advocacy of moderation that allowed wine and beer (the drinks of the upper classes) denied the lower orders their whiskey and other spirits. While the motives of these elite groups for promoting temperance varied, Bretherton's account indicates the familiar concern of the leadership with preserving positions of privilege and *status quo* through using mechanisms, such as the temperance movement, to manage changing social conditions and to modify social relationships by

encouraging behaviour changes in the lower classes. By contrast, most of the teetotal converts in the next phase of the movement came from humbler backgrounds. They were young
professional men, artisans, tradesmen, journeymen and apprentices who reacted against
the hierarchical order of their society and rejected the kind of temperance movement
associated with elite leadership. Teetotalism was a radical response linked to the ideals of
social reformism and the particular political circumstances of Irish history.

Prohibition

Early resistance to temperance messages was not confined to Europe. In America also,
Levine (1978) notes resistance to temperance messages, especially among elite groups, in
the early years of the century, with growing numbers of converts adopting the total abstinence approach from the mid-1830s. For a brief period, just before the Civil War, around
one-third of Americans lived under legal prohibition. The issue was revived towards the
end of the century with the establishment of groups such as the Woman's Christian Temperance Union and the Anti-Saloon League, and with the support of powerful allies such
as John D. Rockefeller and the middle and business classes. Two decades of campaigning
ended in January 1920 with the introduction of prohibition (Levine, 1985; Musto, 1997).
In contrast to America, in Canada, Britain and Europe the policy trend went towards
developing sophisticated regulatory systems for alcohol control and treatment, rather than
towards state-led prohibition (MacLeod, 1967; Levine, 1985).

   Prohibition in America was unsuccessful, not because it failed to lower consumption but
because it proved impossible to implement and police, because it was disliked by the public
and because, by the 1930s, former supporters such as Rockefeller were advocating repeal.
Levine (1985) argues that prohibition had triumphed in the first place because it had persuaded many middle-class Americans that banning alcohol would significantly reduce
major social problems. In fact, the rise in lawlessness and unrest around alcohol production and distribution and the general disrespect for the law that was seen as an offshoot of
prohibition led to fears of anarchy, communism and the violation of property laws. Increasing unrest during the Great Depression of the 1930s fed beliefs that repeal would reduce
the threat to social order, and the support of the business elite and the upper classes was
lost; prohibition was over by April 1933.

   Prohibition, as a response to alcohol control, was not confined to the USA. The influence of temperance thinking was a dominant force on late nineteenth and early twentieth
century legislation in the Nordic countries. The result was total prohibition for a time in
some countries (Finland, 1919–1932) or in some regions (municipalities in Norway around
1914). In Sweden, despite strong political influence around the beginning of the century,
temperance pressure for total prohibition was rejected; but strict controls were enforced
through the Gothenburg system, whereby municipalities set up special non-profit companies to control distribution and sale of aquavit—later extended to all spirits and wine.
This was followed by a rationing system whereby alcohol rations were allocated to Swedish
citizens according to age, sex, occupation and family circumstances. At variance with principles of justice under the social welfare system of post-war Sweden, the rationing system
was abandoned in 1955 and replaced, following a rapid rise in spirits consumption, by a
system of controls based on price. Prohibition is still exercised in some Islamic countries
and it emerged as late as 1978 in the Pacific Islands as a new way of tackling public
drunkenness and violence (Marshall & Marshall, 1990).

   It is notable that the history of alcohol in the nineteenth and early twentieth century,
just as in earlier periods, was linked to major political and economic forces and to the
interests of powerful individuals and groups able to influence beliefs, attitudes and

responses to alcohol use. What is most interesting, historically, are the changes over the centuries in the methods adopted to exercise control. As the twentieth century progressed and prohibition sentiment declined in most Western countries, alcohol control through legislation has "smoothly, quietly and effectively organized and managed not only the production, distribution and sale of alcoholic beverages, but also much of the social life associated with drinking" (Levine, 1985).

ALCOHOL IN THE TWENTIETH CENTURY

In England, by the beginning of the twentieth century, attention had strayed from the disease concept of alcoholism towards social harms, such as loss of productivity, accidents and crime, poverty and racial degeneration. All these problems were seen to be associated with excessive alcohol consumption and temperance campaigns to address the harms were aimed at public and political target groups and at the education of children and women in particular. Pressures to adopt preventive measures were supported by new groups, such as the mental hygiene movement, concerned with issues of "degeneracy" and hereditary disease, which included inebriety (Berridge, 1989). A spate of legislation to control manufacturing, distribution and consumption of alcohol, along with major changes in social and economic circumstances, resulted in a fall in consumption and related problems and a wane in policy attention to alcohol issues in general.

Similarly, in America, by the time Prohibition was repealed, the nineteenth century model of alcohol as an inherently addictive substance was lost. It did not re-appear until the 1930s in America and the late 1940s in England, by which time the social and political climate was ready to foster a new conceptualization of alcoholism as a disease. By this time, too, the temperance movement was inextricably linked in the public imagination with an approach to alcoholism seen as moralistic and unscientific, and the movement declined rapidly over the second half of the twentieth century. Paradoxically, as one historian of Scottish temperance has pointed out, by the late twentieth century legislation and attitudes towards alcohol consumption and drinking practices were to travel full circle back towards encouraging moderation—or "sensible drinking" in the new terminology (King, 1979). But by this time, the "ownership" of the new ideology and of responses to alcohol-related problems had shifted to the State and to a vast bureaucracy of professional and voluntary services. In the sections that follow, three major trends occurring over the latter half of the twentieth century are outlined: trends in beliefs about alcohol and the nature of harmful drinking, changes in the kinds of interventions seen as appropriate to address the problems and changes in forms of control to prevent or minimize harm. These trends were confined, at first, to "developed" countries. In more recent decades, perceptions of alcohol and alcohol-related harm and ideas about effective intervention have spread, largely from "developed" to "developing" parts of the world. The final section speculates on the implications of "globalization" for the future history of alcohol policy and practice.

Beliefs: from the Disease of Alcoholism to Problem Drinking and Intoxication

The re-emergence and evolution of the disease concept of alcoholism has been examined in depth elsewhere (Heather & Robertson, 1997). It came to the fore in an era which valued "science" as the rationale for policy action and which had witnessed the emergence of alcohol research in both Britain and America (Berridge, 1989). Dissemination and spread of the concept to Europe owed much to the work of E.M. Jellinek and the Yale Centre for

_.....ies, which conducted research, issued the _Quarterly Journal of Studies on Alcohol_ and started a series of summer schools in the early 1940s. Jellinek's writing and his work with the World Health Organization during the 1950s were influential in gaining medical and lay support for the new vision and in uniting groups with diverse interests around the issue of alcohol (Page, 1988).

But while the rhetoric of "science" underpinned the discourse of those who promoted the disease concept as "new", more practical reasons facilitated its eventual, widespread acceptance. Its propagandist role in mobilizing professional and public support for addressing the problem of alcoholism was particularly valuable in the early years. One concern was to change professional and public images of the habitual drunk or alcoholic from "a hopeless case", a "morally weak person", to an unfortunate individual afflicted by a disease which, like other diseases, was amenable to cure through medical and psychiatric care and appropriate lay support. This humanitarian argument also had the advantage of carving out an area of activity for medical specialism, voluntary intervention and lay organization, all of which were to expand enormously in the coming decades. What was most important, however, was that the disease concept now suited the social and political climate of post-war Europe and America. The emphasis on personal freedom and consumerism militated against any response that appeared to deny the majority of people the right to drink. The disease concept diverted attention from the majority who were not afflicted towards the minority who could be managed by treatment and rehabilitation responses. So it is not surprising that official action concentrated largely on treatment rather than prevention (Baggott, 1990; Thom, 1999). But this emphasis was short-lived. Belief in the disease concept of alcoholism has continued to exercise a strong influence in many countries up to the present time. It is especially visible in abstinence models of treatment and in the philosophy of Alcoholics Anonymous, which has spread to most parts of the world (for historical accounts, see Cook, 1988; Kurtz, 1979). But the disease concept has also undergone many modifications and changes (Heather & Robertson, 1997) and in some countries—notably the UK and Australia—has declined in importance.

Although the shift away from the disease concept occurred in different countries at different times, the 1970s is generally seen as the watershed, when an accumulation of theoretical and practical forces tipped the balance towards prevention approaches and a much broader perspective on the nature of the alcohol problem. The focus of concern now became alcohol misuse and problem drinking (rather than alcoholism) and the extent of alcohol-related harm in communities and populations as a whole (rather than in the individual and the family). The term "preventive paradox" summed up the belief that a greater level of harm accrued from drinking by the majority of the population than from the minority of "alcoholics" or excessive drinkers. The "new public health approach" proposed that both change in individual lifestyles and public health measures were required to minimize the harms related to the use of alcohol (Faculty of Public Health Medicine, 1991). By the 1990s, then, addressing harmful drinking habits became the focus of policy, prevention and intervention measures in Australia, the USA and most European countries.

Intervention: from Specialist Treatment to Community-based Interventions

Changing beliefs about the problem were accompanied by changes in ways of tackling alcohol-related harms. The disease concept had influenced a treatment approach based on a belief in the need for specialist care delivered by psychiatrists or other specially trained professionals, located in alcoholism treatment units and supported by rehabilitation hostels, services and self-help groups. This approach was dominant in England from the late 1950s till around the mid-1970s and in some countries, Germany for example, has continued to be the primary response to the provision of care for people with drinking problems. But with the emergence of the "new public health" perspective, the specialist approach became too narrow to respond effectively to the wide range of problems and groups of people identified as appropriate targets for intervention. In Europe, America and Australia by the 1980s, responses to alcohol-related problems included education and public awareness campaigns (e.g. against drink–driving), community-based approaches to detoxification and treatment delivery, efforts to encourage early intervention and to provide brief interventions and a broad range of counselling and voluntary services. Concurrent trends in professional development meant that new groups of professionals, such as clinical psychologists, social workers and counsellors, were beginning to carve out a niche in the alcohol field. They brought with them theoretical perspectives and intervention options suited to the needs of increasingly large and diverse groups of people seen as "problem drinkers" or as affected by problem drinking (Institute of Medicine, 1990; Plant, 1997; Thom, 1999). The precise nature and extent of service and treatment developments in different countries have varied according to the economic and political forces that determine priorities for resource allocation as well as the influence of different interest and pressure groups and public support for different policies.

Control: Reducing Harmful Consumption and Minimizing the Harms

With the exception of attempts to introduce prohibition, and the illegal status of alcohol in some countries, formal and informal alcohol controls have generally aimed to prevent or reduce alcohol-related harms. By the 1990s, a major shift had taken place away from a treatment response towards prevention and control approaches, a shift that challenged previous administrative and service boundaries between health, social welfare and criminal justice responses.

Even within the latter part of the twentieth century, ideas about what counts as "harmful", about how harm is measured and about what kind of controls might be effective have changed. Major social trends—such as the proliferation of research, the rise of epidemiological approaches to understanding social problems, or changes in health and welfare systems within countries—have contributed to shifts in perceptions of the uses of alcohol. The introduction of "units" measures in the 1980s is one example of how attempts to achieve a systematic, agreed measure of harm increased the size of the alcohol problem. By making problem alcohol use more easily quantifiable and therefore more visible, the size of the problem and the need for extending intervention and control to larger numbers of people was "demonstrated" (Wiener, 1990; Thom, 1999). Recent research on the possible benefits of moderate consumption of alcohol re-opens debate on the definition and nature of harm. As in the past, powerful lobbies (such as the British Medical Association or the alcohol industry) have played a part in influencing policy action and new interest groups and networks have emerged. In the latter half of the twentieth century, the role of the mass media has influenced perceptions of alcohol and drinking patterns (through industry marketing and health lobby campaigning). Media campaigns have been the primary vehicle attempting to alter perceptions of problem use and for mobilizing public support for (or against) various forms of control.

Bunton (1990) suggests that what we now have in many countries is a dispersed form of control which permeates a large number of institutions and networks of social interaction. Notions of "control" have spread beyond state and local government to include control exercised by workplaces, educational establishments, criminal justice systems and helping services. Regulation has extended beyond concern with the quantity of alcohol consumed to more widespread intervention in drinking practices and drinking settings. Whether we accept or reject Bunton's critique of the new public health approach as "control", it highlights again the importance of locating current approaches to alcohol within specific historical and social contexts. Most importantly, future analyses of the history of alcohol will have to look more closely at the impact of "globalization" on the policies and practices of individual countries.

Alcohol Use and Harm in a "Global Market"

From earlier discussion, it is clear that alcohol has always been a trading commodity between countries, that countries have learned from one another, not only about new technology or systems for the production and distribution of the product but also about systems to control use and problem use and about how to treat the unwanted physical and social consequences of excessive use. Equally, this chapter has sought to illustrate the importance of political and social contexts for the emergence of particular types of responses to alcohol use and for changing responses over the centuries. By the end of the twentieth century, interchange between countries (or different parts of the world) had taken on new dimensions. Social and political trends, such as speedier communications, increasing physical and social mobility, the rise of multi-national companies, greater international collaboration and increased professional exchange, created a "global market" for alcohol and a global network of individuals involved in the provision of responses to alcohol use and alcohol-related harm. The proliferation of research and research structures (e.g. research institutions or units) encouraged the development of shared knowledge and shared perspectives on alcohol issues, including issues of control and treatment (Babor, 1993). Definitions of harm and of effective responses are now likely to be influenced as much by policies directed from outside one's own country as by policies and practices rooted in internal cultures and social contexts.

To some extent, responses to alcohol have converged across countries and cultures, witnessed, for instance, by the widespread enthusiasm for "brief interventions", the strong international support for control of alcohol use through taxation, the importance of the self-help movement world-wide and the growing emphasis on harm-reduction measures. Since the 1950s, international effort through the work of the World Health Organization has aimed to stimulate member states to adopt common approaches to tackling alcohol-related harm (Thom, 1999)

At the same time the diversities remain, even within groups of countries sharing similar political, social and economic situations. Grant (1998) casts doubt on the validity of using the state as the unit of analysis, given the cultural diversity found in most countries but particularly in places where states have been created out of successive phenomena of colonization and decolonization. Patterns of alcohol consumption, even in politically and socially stable countries, have been changing rapidly over the past 50 years (e.g. see McDonald, 1994, for an analysis of changing patterns of drinking in the west of France.)

At a global level, differences are particularly visible in the divide between countries that are "developed", "developing" and "transitional" (i.e. countries currently or recently undergoing major political and socioeconomic change). By and large, developed countries have traded not only their beverage products to less developed countries but also their ideas about appropriate systems and approaches for treatment and control and their methods for researching and analysing alcohol-associated harm. We still know very little about the mechanisms by which policies, treatment or control approaches are transferred between countries or about the extent to which the growth of "global markets"—in products, ideas and responses—has changed the political and social contexts which give rise to particular responses to alcohol. The impact of globalization on responses to alcohol use and problem use in the twentieth century is an area where historical research is lacking. Future analyses of the history of alcohol will need to ask questions that include, but reach beyond, the political and social boundaries of individual countries.

KEY WORKS AND SUGGESTIONS FOR FURTHER READING

Baggott, R. (1990). *Alcohol, Politics and Social Policy.* Aldershot: Avebury.

This book examines the emergence and evolution of alcohol as a social and political problem in Britain from the late 1950s to the 1980s. In particular, it attempts to explain the shift in government policy in the 1970s from a treatment to a prevention response.

Barrows, S. & Room, R. (Eds) (1991). *Drinking Behaviour and Belief in Modern History.* Berkeley, CA: University of California Press.

Contributions to this volume provide an analysis of the social history of everyday drinking practices in Europe and America. Main themes covered in the chapters include: drinking cultures and sub-cultures; societal responses to drinking; temperance movements and social history; mutual help, medicalization and inebriety.

Edwards, G. (Ed.) (1991). *Addictions: Personal Influences and Social Movements.* New Brunswick, NJ: Transaction.

Based on interviews with 27 people, this book offers an insight into the interaction between individuals, networks and institutions in the formation and development of responses to substance use and problem use over the post-war period.

Grant, M. (Ed.) (1998). *Alcohol and Emerging Markets: Patterns, Problems and Responses.* London: Brunner-Mazel.

Chapters covering Africa, Asia, China, India, South America and Central and Eastern Europe locate current drinking practices and responses to problem drinking within the historical and cultural traditions of different societies. Issues specific to developing countries and "emerging markets" are identified and illustrate the importance of social and political contexts in defining and measuring alcohol-related harm.

Plant, M. (1997). *Women and Alcohol: Contemporary and Historical Perspectives.* London: Free Association Books.

Chapter 2 provides an overview of alcohol throughout the ages. It concentrates, in particular, on illustrating the role of social and moral contexts on women's use of alcohol at different historical periods.

REFERENCES

Armyr, G., Elmer, A. & Herz, U. (1982). *Alcohol in the World of the 80s: Habits, Attitudes, Preventive Policies and Voluntary Efforts.* Stockholm: Sober Forlags AB.

Babor, T.F. (1993). Beyond the invisible college: a science policy analysis of alcohol and drug research. In G. Edwards, J. Strang & J.H. Jaffe (Eds), *Drugs, Alcohol and Tobacco: Making the Science and Policy Connections* (pp. 48–69). Oxford: Oxford Medical Publications.

Baggott, R. (1990). *Alcohol Politics and Social Policy.* Aldershot: Avebury.

Baumhol, J. & Room, R. (1987).   Inebriety doctors and the state: alcohol treatment institutions since
    1940. In M. Galanter (Ed.), *Recent Developments in Alcoholism* (Vol. 5). New York: Plenum.

Berridge, V. (1989).   History and addiction control: the case of alcohol. In D. Robinson, A. Maynard
    & R. Chester (Eds), *Controlling Legal Addictions* (pp. 24–42). Basingstoke: Macmillan.

Bretherton, G. (1991).   Against the flowing tide: whiskey and temperance in the making of modern
    Ireland. In S. Barrows & R. Room (Eds), *Drinking Behaviour and Belief in Modern History*
    (pp. 147–164). Berkeley, CA: University of California Press.

Bunton, R. (1990).   Regulating our favourite drug. In P. Abbott & G. Payne (Eds), *New Directions
    in the Sociology of Health.* London: Falmer.

Charrington, E.H. (Editor-in-chief) (1925).   *Standard Encyclopaedia of the Alcohol Problem*, Vol. 1.
    Westerville OH: Aarau-Buckingham.

Cook, C.C.H. (1988).   The Minnesota model in the management of drug and alcohol dependency:
    miracle, method or myth? Part 11. Evidence and conclusions. *British Journal of Addiction*, **83**,
    735–748.

Faculty of Public Health Medicine/Royal College of Physicians (1991).   *Alcohol and the Public
    Health.* Basingstoke: Macmillan.

Ferguson, S. (1975).   *Drink.* London: Batsford.

Grant, M. (Ed.) (1998).   *Alcohol and Emerging Markets: Patterns, Problems and Responses.* London:
    Brunner-Mazel.

Gutzke, D. (1984).   The cry of the children: the Edwardian medical campaign against maternal drink-
    ing. *British Journal of Addiction*, **79**, 71–84.

Hall, R.L. (1986).   Alcohol treatment in American Indian populations: an indigenous treatment
    modality compared with traditional approaches. In T.F. Babor (Ed.), *Alcohol and Culture: Com-
    parative Perspectives from Europe and America* (pp. 168–178). New York: New York Academy of
    Sciences.

Harrison, B. (1971).   *Drink and the Victorians.* London: Faber.

Heath, D.B. (1990).   Anthropological and socio-cultural perspectives on alcohol as a reinforcer.
    In W.M. Cox (Ed.), *Why People Drink* (pp. 263–290). New York: Jardner.

Heather, N. & Robertson, I. (1997).   *Problem Drinking*, 3rd edn. Oxford: Oxford Medical
    Publications.

Institute of Medicine (1990).   *Broadening the Base of Treatment for Alcohol Problems.* Washington
    DC: National Academy Press.

Jellinek, E.M. (1976).   Drinkers and alcoholics in Ancient Rome. *Journal of Studies on Alcohol*, **37**,
    1721–1743.

Keller, M. (1979).   A historical overview of alcohol and alcoholism. *Cancer Research*, **39**, 2822–2829.

King, E. (1979).   *Scotland Sober and Free: The Temperance Movement 1829–1979.* Glasgow: Glasgow
    Museums and Art Galleries.

Kurtz, E. (1979).   *Not God: A History of Alcoholics Anonymous.* Center City, MN: Hazelden.

Levine, H. (1987).   Alcohol monopoly to protect the non-commercial sector of eighteenth century
    Poland. In M. Douglas (Ed.), *Constructive Drinking Perspectives on Drink from Anthropology*
    (pp. 250–269). Cambridge: Cambridge University Press.

Levine, H.G. (1978).   The discovery of addiction: changing conceptions of habitual drunkenness in
    America. *Journal of Studies on Alcohol*, **39**, 143–174.

Levine, H.G. (1985).   The birth of American alcohol control: prohibition, the power elite, and the
    problem of lawlessness. *Contemporary Drug Problems*, **12**, 63–115.

MacLeod, R.M. (1967).   The edge of hope: social policy and chronic alcoholism. *Journal of the History
    of Medicine and Allied Sciences*, **12**, 215–245.

Marshall, M. & Marshall, L.B. (1990).   *Silent Voices Speak: Women and Prohibition in Truk.* Belmont,
    CA: Wadsworth.

McDonald, M. (1994).   Drinking and social identity in the west of France. In M. McDonald (Ed.),
    Gender, Drink and Drugs (pp. 99–124). Oxford: Berg.

McLaughlin, P. (1991).   Inebriate reformatories in Scotland: an institutional history. In S. Barrows &
    R. Room (Eds), *Drinking Behaviour and Belief in Modern History* (pp. 287–314). Berkeley, CA:
    University of California Press.

Molamu, L. & MacDonald, D. (1996).   Alcohol abuse among the Basarwa of the Kgalagadi and
    Ghanzi Districts in Botswana. *Drugs: Education, Prevention and Policy*, **3**, 145–152.

Musto, D.F. (1997). Alcohol control in historical perspective. In M. Plant, E. Single & T. Stockwell (Eds), *Alcohol—Minimising the Harm: What Works?* (pp. 10–25). London: Free Association Books.

Olsen, G.W. (1994). Physician heal thyself: drink, temperance and the medical question in the Victorian and Edwardian Church of England, 1830–1914. *Addiction*, **89**, 1167–1176.

Page, P.B. (1988). The origins of alcohol studies: E.M. Jellinek and the documentation of the alcohol research literature. *British Journal of Addiction*, **83**, 1095–1103.

Plant, M. (1997). *Women and Alcohol: Contemporary and Historical Perspectives.* London: Free Association Books.

Porter, R. (1985). The drinking man's disease: the "pre-history" of alcoholism in Georgian Britain. *British Journal of Addiction*, **80**, 385–396.

Porter, R. (1990). Introduction. In J.-C. Sournia (Ed.), *A History of Alcoholism.* Cambridge MS: Blackwell.

Robinson, J. (1988). *On the Demon Drink.* London: Beazley.

Sournia J.-C. (1990). *A History of Alcoholism.* Cambridge, MA: Blackwell.

Street, J.C., Lees, F.R. & Burns, D. (Eds) (1862). *Proceedings of the International Temperance Prohibition Convention* (held in London, 2–4 September 1862). London: Job Cauldwell.

Tannahill, R. (1988). *Food in History*, 2nd edn. London: Penguin.

Thom, B. (1999). *Dealing with Drink: Alcohol and Social Policy—from Treatment to Management.* London: Free Association Books.

Tyrrell, I. (1991). Women and temperance in international perspective: the world's WCTU, 1880s–1920s. In S. Barrows & R. Room (Eds), *Drinking Behaviour and Belief in Modern History* (pp. 217–240). Berkeley, CA: University of California Press.

Vogt, I. (1984). Defining alcohol problems as a repressive mechanism: its formative phase in Imperial Germany and its strength today. *International Journal of the Addictions*, **19**, 551–569.

Warner, J. (1997). Shifting categories of the social harms associated with alcohol: examples from late medieval and early modern England. *American Journal of Public Health*, **87**, 1788–1797.

Wiener, C. (1981). *The Politics of Alcoholism: Building an Arena around a Social Problem.* New Brunswick, NJ: Transaction.

Williams, G.P. & Brake, G.T. (1980). *Drink in Great Britain 1900–1979.* London: Edsall.

Wilson, G.B. (1940). *Alcohol and the Nation: A Contribution to the Study of the Liquor Problem in the UK.* London: Nicholson & Watson.

Yucun, S. & Zuxin, W. (1988). China. In M. Grant (Ed.), *Alcohol and Emerging Markets: Patterns, Problems and Responses* (pp. 123–143). London: Brunner-Mazel.

Chapter 3

Governing Images in Public Discourse about Problematic Drinking

Robin Room

*Centre for Social Research on Alcohol and Drugs, Stockholm
University, Sveaplan, Sweden*

Synopsis

*This chapter reviews studies of governing images or "discursive formations" of problematic
drinking. Analyses in the late 1960s first systematically contrasted different "models of alcoholism" and conceptualizations of the "deviant drinker". These initiated a sociological tradition of "constructivist" analysis of the "medicalization of deviance", primarily focused on
the rise of the disease concept of alcoholism in the modern era. Starting in the late 1970s, historical analyses argued that the initiation of "addiction" concepts came much earlier, and were
popularized as part of nineteenth century temperance movement thinking. Recent analyses
in the cultural studies tradition have placed the alcohol discourse in a broader frame of discourse in English-speaking societies about "diseases of the will".*

    *Meanwhile, research on discursive formations has expanded to take into account
ideologies of alcohol control, including the "new public health approach", and a loosely
linked "alcohol problems" approach. Particularly in Nordic countries, attention has
been given to the competing discourses of neoliberalism and of the welfare state, which have
been the dominant discourses in the debate over Nordic alcohol control measures.*

    *In their timing and location, the appearance of analyses of a particular governing image
are themselves a signal and symptom that this conceptualization is coming under critical
scrutiny. More attention is needed in future work on discursive formations to who uses a discourse and how it is received; to the boundaries of application of a discourse, and to breaks
and imperfections in its application; and to the relation between governing images and the
images, attitudes and arguments at the level of everyday communications.*

The potential problems from drinking of alcoholic beverages have been the subject of
public discourse for all of recorded history. An ancient Egyptian text, for instance, offers
the injunction:

International Handbook of Alcohol Dependence and Problems. Edited by N. Heather, T.J. Peters and
T. Stockwell.
© 2001 John Wiley & Sons Ltd.

> Make not thyself helpless in drinking in the beer shop. For will not the words of thy report repeated slip out from thy mouth without thou knowing that thou has uttered them? Falling down, thy limbs will be broken, and no-one will give thee a hand to help thee up. As for thy companions in the swilling of beer, they will get up and say, "Outside with this drunkard" (Budge, 1972).

The text illustrates that there are at least two levels of understanding operating in any communication. In the first place, the text is an argument about drinking and its potential adverse consequences that is intended to inform or persuade. We can thus analyse the text in terms of its subject matter and message.

In the second place, the text includes within it a whole way of thinking about alcohol. We notice that the message assumes a concept of a "drunkard" as a moralized social category, carrying a negative stigma. The text is thus giving us a scrap of evidence about a way of thinking about drinking assumed by the writer to be both understood and shared by the readers.

Nowadays, the term "discourse" is used for both these aspects of communication. The meaning that concerns us here is the second, referring to a system of thinking about a particular topic, and relating back to Foucault's (1972) concept of a "discursive formation". Thus Sutton (1998), for instance, distinguishes between several major formulations of the nature of alcohol problems in Swedish history. In this sense, "a discourse may be understood as a bounded body of knowledge and associated practices, a particular identifiable way of giving meaning to reality via words or images" (Lupton, 1999, p. 15). Earlier analyses in the field had used other terms roughly in place of this sense of "discourse", talking for instance in terms of "models of alcoholism" (Siegler, Osmond & Newell, 1968; Bruun, 1971), of "conceptions" (Levine, 1978) or of "governing images" (Room, 1974, 1978; Moore & Gerstein, 1981).

The reader is thus referred elsewhere for material on discourse at the level of elements of meaning and their relationship, often discussed in the alcohol literature in terms of "representations" (e.g. Paakanen & Sulkunen, 1987), "images" (e.g. Sulkunen, 1998), or "portrayals" (e.g. Grube, 1993), and for reviews of the substantial literatures on the content of communications about alcohol and their persuasive value (Casswell, 1995; Martin & Mail, 1995; Baillie, 1996) and on representations of alcohol in fiction and other literary works (Forseth, 1999).

MORAL VS. MEDICAL MODELS

That drinking or alcohol problems can be conceptualized and discussed in very different terms has been self-evident in societies such as the USA, where the conceptualizations have been openly contested during the last two centuries. In such circumstances, it has not required scholarship to perceive that alcoholic beverages could be defined alternatively as "the good creature of God" or the "demon rum" (Levine, 1983b), and that problematic drinkers could be defined alternatively as "drunkards" or as "alcoholics".

Systematic efforts to describe and contrast different discourses or conceptualizations of problematic drinking may be dated from Gusfield's paper (1967) on "moral passage" and Siegler, Osmond & Newell's paper (1968) on "models of alcoholism" (see also Bruun, 1971). Siegler et al. laid out a number of alternative conceptualizations of the problematic drinker, and sought to systematically fill in the blanks for each model in terms of its definition of the drinker and the implications for the drinker's social handling. While "moral" and "medical" models are distinguished in the classification, the authors further distinguish within these general rubrics between different "moral" and different "medical" models. The ideas that there are multiple medical models, and that medical and moral models were not necessarily mutually exclusive, have received some further attention (Room, 1974, 1978) but are still overlooked in much analysis.

While Siegler et al. had not focused on the historical succession of conceptualizations, this issue was at the heart of Gusfield's (1967) analysis, which traced the succession of three different dominant conceptions of the "deviant drinker" in the USA in the preceding century and a half. In the first period of temperance ferment, orientated to "moral suasion", the dominant image, Gusfield proposed, was the "repentant drinker". In the latter part of the nineteenth century, as the temperance movement moved towards legislating sobriety, the image shifted to the "enemy drinker". In the 1940s, after the collapse of the temperance cause and the repeal of Prohibition, the image shifted again to the "sick drinker". Gusfield emphasizes the symbolic functions of laws and official acts expressing such conceptions, whereby the "worth of one set of norms" over others is publicly affirmed. He also stresses the role of social "movements to redefine behavior" in catalysing the "transition of the behavior from one moral status to another".

The shift towards the "disease concept of alcoholism" in the 1930s and after has drawn considerable further attention by sociologists. Building on a perspective which Gusfield's (1967) analysis pioneered, Schneider (1978) and Conrad & Schneider (1980) adopted a self-conscious framing as "historical social constructionists" (now often termed "constructivists"), emphasizing the social processes by which concepts are created and take on social authority. Conrad & Schneider fit the alcoholism story into an analysis of the "medicalization of deviance" as a general historical shift. On the other hand, focusing specifically on alcohol, Roizen (1991) analysed the repeated efforts to find a discourse about alcohol problems which the American public could accept in the 1930s and 1940s, after the debacle of Prohibition. While these analyses have focused primarily on the role of ideological entrepreneurs, and their interaction with and effects on public discourse, other analyses have shown how the shift in discourse had effects, too, on the mainstream of scientific and biomedical knowledge (Herd, 1992; Katcher, 1993).

THE RISE OF THE ADDICTION CONCEPT

In his landmark paper on "the discovery of addiction", Levine (1978) shifted the focus of attention to the early nineteenth century, more than a century earlier than the period which was the focus of discussions of the rise of the modern "disease concept of alcoholism" (see also Chapter 2, this volume). Paralleling analyses by Foucault (1975) and Rothman (1971) of the shift in perspective and discourse that brought into being the nineteenth century mental asylum, Levine argued that the addiction concept was first developed for alcohol and that it arose in connection with early temperance thinking, in a social context of a heightened concern for self-control in Jacksonian America.

Porter (1985) and Warner (1994) have since argued that the inception of the addiction concept must be pushed back from Levine's dating, with Porter finding an addiction concept in eighteenth century British medical writers and Warner in seventeenth and eighteenth century sermons. It is unclear, however, how widely such concepts were accepted then. Acknowledging Porter's and Warner's evidence, it can still be argued that Levine's dating of the rise of addiction concepts is right, in terms of broad-based popular discourse about drinking (Ferentzy, 2000). Supportive evidence can be found in McCormick's (1969) pioneering study of conceptions of problematic drinking in English literature. "When we look at fiction about 1830, when the industrial revolution was in full swing", McCormick concluded, "we find that the same drinking may be described as existed 80 years before but that a new and more desperate kind of solitary, tragic and inexplicable drinking has come into existence beside it".

These discussions of the advent of the addiction concept in the nineteenth century have been primarily limited to material from Britain and the USA. Although it is clear that addiction concepts also became rooted in other European societies in the course of the nineteenth century (e.g. Baumohl & Room, 1987), relatively little historical work has appeared, in English at least, focusing on the shift in discourse associated with the advent of the addiction concept (but see Mitchell, 1986; Sournia, 1990).

There has, however, been some research and analysis on the applicability of alcoholism or addiction concepts in a broader frame cross-culturally. The present author argued that alcoholism could be regarded as a "culture-bound syndrome" (Room, 1985), given the ethnographic evidence that interpretations of problematic drinking in terms of loss of control were culturally specific, depending among other things on a cultural expectation of personal self-control. As Lemert (1951) had earlier noted, the theme of lack of self-control at the heart of American attitudes to the alcoholic "is one of the most vivid and isolating distinctions which can be made in a culture which attributes morality, success, and respectability to the power of a disciplined will" (p. 356). In a given society, Lemert proposed:

> In order for chronic alcohol addiction or compulsive drinking to develop, there must be strong disapproval of the consequences of drinking or of drinking itself beyond a certain point of intoxication, so that the culture induces guilt and depression over drinking and extreme drunkenness *per se*" (Lemert, 1951, pp. 348–9).

Along the same line, qualitative research on a World Health Organization project has raised further questions about the cross-cultural applicability of current diagnostic concepts of dependence (Room et al., 1996; Schmidt & Room, 1999), although other studies, using quantitative factor-analytic methods, have argued for the cross-cultural applicability of the alcohol dependence syndrome (e.g. Hall et al., 1993).

Recently, the burgeoning field of cultural studies has begun to take an interest in the issue of self-control and the will as a focal conceptualization and concern in English-speaking cultures. The discourse around alcohol is brought into analyses like Sedgewick's (1992) essay on "epidemics of the will" and Keane's (1998) work, in the context of a broader discussion of the cultural position of concepts of willpower and addiction. Peele (1995) offers a more partisan critique of addiction concepts as fueling the growth of an addiction treatment industry in the USA. Valverde's (1998) recent volume on *Diseases of the Will* returns problematic drinking to a central place in the discussion, analysing it as an object both of self-control and of state control.

THE IMPACT OF THE TEMPERANCE MOVEMENT: REACTIONS AND CONTINUITIES

The historical analyses we have been discussing can be seen as driven by the central feature in the landscape of discourse on problematic drinking in English-speaking societies in the last two centuries: the rise of the temperance movement and its aftermath (including the movement's political decline). In this context, the main object of research attention has been the governing image of addiction, as a way of problematizing and understanding some or all drinking. While the "medicalization of deviance" tradition has emphasized the transition between different governing images in the twentieth century, analyses like Levine's have emphasized the transition to temperance from conceptions of earlier times, and have focused on the continuities in conceptions and discourse between the temperance era and more recent decades (see also Chapter 2, this volume.)

Temperance movement thinking about alcohol extended well beyond the domain of addiction concepts (e.g. Levine, 1983b). And temperance movements of the nineteenth and early twentieth centuries were heavily intertwined with the major "progressive" movements of the day—abolition of slavery, women's rights, socialism and, in many places, nationalism and nation-building. The extensive historical literature on these movements, and on those who opposed them, often considers or touches on the ways of thinking and discourse of those involved, but is beyond the scope of this essay. For relevant historical studies, the reader is referred to bibliographic essays by Verhey (1991) and in the pages of the *Social History of Alcohol Review*.

"ALCOHOL PROBLEMS" AND ALCOHOL CONTROL

Research on frames for problematic drinking and for social responses to it has expanded in recent years to take into account ideologies of state control of the alcohol market. As Levine (1983a) notes, the idea of state alcohol control developed explicitly as an alternative to prohibition and thus was bitterly opposed by the mainstream of the temperance movement. The idea, which often included the idea of the state monopolizing all or part of the industry, remained an elite rather than popular discourse nearly everywhere until and unless it was actually put into practice. As government monopolies were implemented, in Sweden incrementally after 1850 (Frånberg, 1987), in Russia around 1900 (McKee, 1997), in Canada in the 1920s (Smart & Ogborne, 1996) and in 18 States in the USA in 1934 (Room, 1987), they often set the frame for continuing debates in these societies about government vs. individual responsibilities for controlling problematic drinking. Thus, this framing of discourse about alcohol has figured prominently in current analyses based on Swedish (Sutton, 1998) and Canadian (Valverde, 1998) experience.

Analyses have begun to appear of a relatively recent formulation of the argument for state intervention in the alcohol market, variously called the "total consumption approach" or the "new public health approach". This framing is at centre stage in Sutton's (1998) analysis of Swedish alcohol discourses; only in the Nordic countries, and particularly in Sweden, could this framing be considered to have entered popular discourse rather than remaining an elite discussion (Sulkunen et al., 2000). The discourse also plays a part in the story in the growing field of studies of the formation of government alcohol policies, both in the Nordic countries (e.g. Holder et al., 1998) and elsewhere (e.g. Baggott, 1990).

Loosely linked with the "new public health approach" has been a conceptualization of the focus of discussion in terms of "alcohol-related problems" or "drinking problems" (see also Chapter 2, this volume.) Whereas the classic alcoholism concept had tended to regard all specific health and social problems as symptoms of a unitary alcoholism, the "alcohol problems" approach disaggregated the field into a wide diversity of health, casualty, inter-actional and social problems related to alcohol consumption or drinking comportment. Although some formulations in the "alcohol problems" tradition subsume alcoholism or alcohol dependence as one more among the problems (e.g. Edwards et al., 1977), the approach tended to be counterposed to an approach in terms of "alcoholism" (Room, 1984). For instance, one early formulation argued, after listing "the most important kinds of damage caused by alcohol", "alcoholism is excluded from the classification because the damage caused by alcoholics already appears in the above classes" (Bruun, 1973). This tradition, too, has received some constructivist scrutiny (Levine, 1984).

The Dialectic of Control: Consumer Sovereignty and External Governance

In an era in which the tide has flowed strongly in favour of privatization and the doctrine of consumer sovereignty, a framing of alcohol issues in terms of "alcohol control" or "alcohol policy"—relatively recent terms in the alcohol literature (Room, 1999)—is now seen by many as an assertion of state power at the expense of individual autonomy. As Tigerstedt (1999) points out, there is some irony in this, as the framing, with its emphasis on patterns and problems at the level of the population as a whole, was originally put forward as a justification for dismantling individual-level social controls on drinking in Nordic countries.

A number of recent studies in Nordic and neighbouring countries have paid detailed attention to the competing discourses concerning drinking and conceptualizations of drinking and alcohol problems, often in the context of general discourses about social problems (e.g. Simpura & Tigerstedt, 1992; Lagerspetz, 1994; Hanhinen & Törrönen, 1998). Contrasting the framing of newspaper discussions by public health advocates and by advocates of looser Swedish alcohol controls, Olsson (1990) noted that the public health discourse tended to use statistical and impersonal arguments, while opposing arguments were pitched at the personal and anecdotal level. Those opposed to the current controls offered an alternative "dream of a better order", in which:

> ... the central role of alcohol still remains, but ... it is less dramatic and ... the negative consequences of alcohol are believed to be minimized. The continental drinking culture is the theme of this dream, nourished by the shame felt about what is felt to be the dominating drinking culture ... the Scandinavian way of drinking, which is characterized by heavy drinking, drunkenness, and violence (Olsson, 1990).

In a participant-observation study of the ways of thinking and speaking of middle-class regular drinkers in Helsinki, Sulkunen (1992) found, among their generally relaxed views on moral questions, one strand of "militantism": an "antipathy of external control and patronizing over individuals, particularly over drinking in public" (p. 114). "Their rally against the moral barrier [between alcohol and everyday life] finds an easy target in the public alcohol control system" (p. 117). Likewise, focus groups with local influentials in a Finnish community study (Holmila, 1997) found a strong contingent of "neoliberals", who saw decisions about drinking as a matter for individual decision and autonomy, in contrast to those whose thinking ran in older liberal terms, with authority resting with the family, or the supporters of welfare state thinking, who assigned the state a substantial role in preventing problems from drinking.

SOME CONCLUSIONS AND SUGGESTIONS

A Constructivist Perspective on Constructivist Analyses

The timing and orientation of the studies we have been considering suggests that analyses of the discourse of a particular conceptualization in the alcohol field are themselves a signal and symptom of the fact that this conceptualization is under critical scrutiny and often under attack. Already in the late 1960s and early 1970s, the disease concept of alcoholism was under critical scrutiny by sociologists (Room, 1983). By treating it as just one more "model" to be ranged alongside others, analyses such as those by Siegler et al. (1968) and Bruun (1971) were implicitly putting in question the model's claim to be the "new scientific approach" which transcended all others. Likewise, Levine's (1978) analysis in terms of a continuity between temperance thinking and the alcoholism concept undercut arguments by the alcoholism movement that their conceptualization was a "new scientific" replacement for temperance models.

In a similar fashion, the new cultural studies of "epidemics of the will" (Sedgewick, 1992) and historical analyses of the idea of "diseases of the will" (Valverde, 1998) come in the wake of a new North American efflorescence of concerns about self-control, expressed among other ways in a fanning-out into other preoccupations, from its origin in Alcoholics Anonymous, of 12-step ideology (Room, 1992; Rice, 1996). Along with the new cultural studies have come more polemical critiques of these trends (e.g. Kaminer, 1992; Rapping, 1996).

Even more obviously, analyses of the discourse of alcohol control and of the "public health approach" have primarily emanated from societies (Canada and the Nordic countries) and a time when alcohol controls have been being weakened or dismantled (Holder et al., 1998; Her et al., 1999), and public discourse about a "total consumption model" has been losing ground (Sutton, 1998). These changes also provide a context for the recent Nordic studies of the competing neoliberal discourse in terms of individual consumer autonomy.

The dating and shape of the current literature suggests a slightly facetious conclusion: when an eager young scholar comes to you offering a label for the conceptual framing you have been struggling toward or working within, and proposing to study it as a discourse, then you know you are history.

That the analyses are to some extent creatures of their own time and place does not, of course, in any way invalidate them. The work we have been considering includes solid research and some brilliant thinking, and makes contributions which will last beyond its own historical moment. But the record so far does leave a question—Is there some way in which such work can be stimulated in other times and places, where there is no alternative conceptualization to lean on, and before scholars are growing uneasy with the old dispensation?

Who Uses a Discourse, and how Is It Received?

In recent decades, a revolution in historiography has broadened the attention of historians from the narrow focus of diplomatic and intellectual history to the broader spheres of social and cultural history. Imperfectly, and as yet only partially, a version of this expansion of attention is under way in analyses of public discourse on alcohol. Studies still appear which are primarily grounded on policy documents and medical, professional or research literatures, but the questions of who shares a discourse in common and of how communications within a particular discourse are received by various audiences are coming more to the fore. The use of focus groups and participant observation methods, as in the recent Nordic studies, open up the possibility of understanding how discursive formations are actually put to use in everyday reasoning and conversation, of studying who adheres to a discourse and interpersonal variations in its expression, and of testing how those holding to one discourse respond when challenged from another.

Quantitative methods such as sample surveys may also play a part in helping us understand the cultural complexes which we have been calling governing images or discursive formations. In the context of such surveys, approaches such as offering respondents vignettes to think their way through, and recording and analysing their open-ended responses, offer the promise of capturing the reasoning and associations that tie the discursive formation together.

The Reach of a Governing Image, and Its Imperfect Hegemony

A governing image or discursive formation gathers together a broad field in terms of a single frame of understanding, often summarized in a few shorthand phrases. It is thus always an imperfect fit to the reality it seeks to cover (Room, 1978); adherents will tend to downplay the discrepancies, while opponents, if any, will tend to focus on them. The conceptual terrain which a governing image seeks to cover may expand or contract over time. Thus, for instance, the extent to which drinking–driving is to be understood in terms of alcoholism has varied in the last 30 years in North America. For another example, alcoholism concepts are surprisingly absent from North American public discourse about the role of intoxication in sexual and other violent crimes (Room, 1996). More attention to the boundaries of application of governing images will give us a better understanding of their core of meaning and their social significance.

In fact, it is quite common for people, even when quite committed to a particular discursive frame, to shift into and out of it in different contexts. Someone strongly committed to talking about and understanding the world in terms of scientific rationality may nevertheless read and half believe the newspaper's horoscope column. It even seems possible and fairly common to work within supposedly antagonistic conceptual frames for the same material. Thus, Kaskutas (1992) reports that 29% of the members of Women for Sobriety also concurrently attend Alcoholics Anonymous, and Connors & Dermen (1996) report 35% concurrently attending AA for members of Secular Organizations for Sobriety (SOS)—although both WFS and SOS were founded around critiques of some of AA's central ideas. In the words of an AA slogan, it is not unusual, with respect to discursive formations, for people to "take what you can can use and leave the rest".

In the context of linguistic studies, attention is now given to these "breaks" and discontinuities in the framing and logic of speech as especially informative about the structure of thinking and discourse (e.g. Arminen, 1998). Analyses like this at the level of conceptualizations and discursive formations would give us a much better understanding of the collective thinking and social processes surrounding governing images of problematic drinking.

Discursive Formations and the Analysis of Everyday Discourse

At the level of empirical work, the boundary between studying a governing image or discursive formation and studying discourse in its other meaning—the imagery, associations and structure of argument of speech or other communications—is often unclear. We have excluded from consideration here the wide range of survey and experimental studies of attitudes and expectancies about drinking, and survey studies of reasons for drinking and of attitudes towards public policies on alcohol and on community responses to alcohol problems. For purposes of studying discursive formations, off-the-cuff responses to the precoded questions in such studies tend to offer only fragments of the picture. Along with content analysis of texts and other prepared communications, however, they do provide the material for analyses of images, attitudes and arguments in everyday life. We need some clear thinking about analyses of the relation between the two levels, that of discursive formations and that of everyday discussion, as a prelude to actual analyses of the interrelations.

The Dynamics of Competition between Discourses

The alcohol experience suggests that old discourses rarely die; they go out of fashion or they go underground as being "politically incorrect", but there are still elements of them extant in the culture in which they once flourished. Although Gusfield's (1967) early formulation was in terms of shifting designations of the deviant drinker over time, his later work fully recognizes that American social thought on problematic drinking is a matter of continually "contested meanings" (Gusfield, 1996). While the focus of the sociological constructivist tradition has often been on the ideological entrepreneurs who push forward a new conceptualization, attention is needed to the responses of various audiences to the ideological contests.

In this regard, new attention is needed to the various "moral models" of problematic drinking. Long after the demise of the North American temperance movement, it is clear that "moral models" of drinking are alive and well, and indeed riding in triumph in the context of criminal law (e.g. Keiter, 1997). New moral-accountability discourses can be found also in such contexts as cognitive-behavioural psychology and economic theories of "rational addiction" (Elster & Skog, 1999). As Valverde (1998) suggests, after documenting discontinuities between the Canadian medical-social and criminal-justice discourses, "uncovering historical connections would be helpful in breaking through vicious circles and avoiding unknowing, forgetful repetitions" (p. 203).

More sustained attention is also needed to the relation between discourses of normalized drinking—drinking as a pleasure and a social activity—and the discourses of problematic drinking that have been our focus here. For that matter, the somewhat more hidden discourses in praise of intoxication need also to be taken into account. The theme of needing to understand the "pathological" in the context of the "normal" is an old one in alcohol studies; as Gusfield (1996) found in making the point, Selden Bacon, the founder of modern alcohol sociology, had made it forcefully and repeatedly over a period of 30 years and more.

KEY WORKS AND SUGGESTIONS FOR FURTHER READING

Bruun, K. (1971). Finland: the non-medical approach. In L.G. Kiloh & D.S. Bell (Eds), *29th International Congress on Alcoholism and Drug Dependence, Sydney, Australia, February 1970* (pp. 545–559). Australia: Butterworths.

This deceptively-titled essay summarizes and comments on work by Siegler and Osmond on models of alcoholism and of drug addiction, and describes and interprets the changing definitions of alcohol problems in Finnish history.

Elster, J. & Skog, O.-J. (Eds) (1999). *Getting Hooked: Rationality and Addiction*. Cambridge: Cambridge University Press.

A collection of excellent essays by various authors revolving around consideration of the economists' concept of "rational addiction" and, more generally, of the relation of concepts of rationality and addiction.

Gusfield, J.R. (1996). *Contested Meanings: The Construction of Alcohol Problems*. Madison, WI: University of Wisconsin Press.

A collection of essays by a founder of sociological constructivism, including his landmark 1967 article on "moral passage" and other work on the changing nature of the stigma of drunkenness, studies of drinking in the history of leisure, and on social worlds of drinking and driving.

Holmila, M. (Ed.) (1997). *Community Prevention of Alcohol Problems*. London: Macmillan.

This report of a project in which researchers and community agencies worked together to reduce alcohol problems in a Finnish community includes a good example of the new analyses of competing ideologies of alcohol control in Sulkunen's chapter on the images of alcohol policy among the local elites.

Levine, H.G. (1978). The discovery of addiction: changing conceptions of habitual drunkenness in American history. *Journal of Studies on Alcohol*, **39**, 143–174.

The first application to alcohol issues of Foucault's ideas of the "shift of gaze" in the wake of the Enlightenment, this remains an article important enough that historians are still arguing over its contentions.

Valverde, M. (1998). *Diseases of the Will: Alcohol and the Dilemmas of Freedom*. Cambridge: Cambridge University Press.

A wide-ranging and historically-informed interpretation of the development of concepts of alcohol addiction which draws into its frame consideration of Alcoholics Anonymous, of government alcohol control systems, and of intoxication as a defence in criminal law.

REFERENCES

Arminen, I. (1998).   Sharing experiences: doing therapy with the help of mutual references in the meetings of Alcoholics Anonymous. *Sociological Quarterly*, **39**, 491–515.

Baggott, R. (1990).   *Alcohol, Politics, and Social Policy*. Aldershot: Avebury.

Baillie, R.K. (1996).   Determining the effects of media portrayals of alcohol: going beyond short term influence. *Alcohol and Alcoholism*, **31**, 235–242.

Baumohl, J. & Room, R. (1987).   Inebriety, doctors, and the state: alcoholism treatment institutions before 1940. In M. Galanter (Ed.), *Recent Developments in Alcoholism* (Vol. 5) (pp. 135–174). New York: Plenum.

Bruun, K. (1971).   Finland: the non-medical approach. In L.G. Kiloh & D.S. Bell (Eds), *29th International Congress on Alcoholism and Drug Dependence, Sydney, Australia, February 1970* (pp. 545–559). Australia: Butterworths.

Bruun, K. (1973).   Alkoholihaitat mahdollisimman vähäisiksi (The minimization of alcohol damage), *Alkoholipolitiikka*, 35:185–191; abstracted in *Drinking and Drug Practices Surveyor*, **8**(15), 47.

Budge, E.A.W. (1972).   *The Dwellers on the Nile*. New York: Blom, B. (originally published 1926).

Casswell, S. (1995).   Public discourse on alcohol: implications for public policy. In H.D. Holder & G. Edwards (Eds), *Alcohol and Public Policy: Evidence and Issues*. Oxford: Oxford University Press.

Connors, G.J. & Dermen, K.H. (1996).   Characteristics of participants in Secular Organizations for Sobriety (SOS). *American Journal of Drug and Alcohol Abuse*, **22**, 281–296.

Conrad, P. & Schneider, J.W. (1980).   *Deviance and Medicalization: From Badness to Sickness*, 1st edn. St. Louis, MO: Mosby.

Edwards, G., Gross, M.M., Keller, M., Moser, J. & Room, R. (Eds) (1977).   *Alcohol-Related Disabilities*. WHO Offset Publication No. 32. Geneva: World Health Organization.

Elster, J. & Skog, O.-J. (Eds) (1999).   *Getting Hooked: Rationality and Addiction*. Cambridge: Cambridge University Press.

Ferentzy, P. (2000).   *The Addiction Concept: How the Language of Sin Was Replaced by That of Disease*. Ph. D. Dissertation. Toronto, Ontario: York University.

Forseth, R. (1999).   Addiction studies: a review of the literature. *Dionysos: Journal of Literature and Addiction*, **9**(2), 29–36.

Foucault, M. (1972). Orders of discourse. *Social Science Information*, **2**(19), 7–30.

Foucault, M. (1975). *The Birth of the Clinic: An Archaeology of Medical Perception*. New York: Vintage.

Frånberg, P. (1987). "The Swedish snaps—a history of booze, Bratt, and bureaucracy"—a summary. *Contemporary Drug Problems* **14**, 557–611.

Grube, J.W. (1993). Alcohol portrayals and alcohol advertising on television: content and effects on children and adolescents. *Alcohol Health and Research World*, **17**, 61–66.

Gusfield, J. (1967). Moral passage: the symbolic process in public designations of deviance. *Social Problems*, **15**, 175–188.

Gusfield, J.R. (1996). *Contested Meanings: The Construction of Alcohol Problems*. Madison, WI: University of Wisconsin Press.

Hall, W., Saunders, J.B., Babor, T.F., Aasland, O.G., Amundsen, A., Hodgson, R. & Grant, M. (1993). Structure and correlates of alcohol dependence: the WHO Collaborative Project on the Early Detection of Persons with Harmful Alcohol Consumption—III. *Addiction*, **88**, 1627–1636.

Hanhinen, S. & Törrönen, J. (Eds) (1998). *Journalists, Administrators and Business People on Social Problems: A Study around the Baltic Sea*. NAD Report No. 35. Helsinki: Nordic Council for Alcohol and Drug Research.

Her, M., Giesbrecht, N., Room, R. & Rehm, J. (1999). Privatizing alcohol sales and alcohol consumption: evidence and implications. *Addiction*, **94**, 1125–1139.

Herd, D. (1992). Ideology, history and changing models of cirrhosis epidemiology. *British Journal of Addiction*, **87**, 179–192.

Holder, H.D., Kühlhorn, E., Nordlund, S., Österberg, E., Romelsjö, A. & Ugland, T. (1998). *European Integration and Nordic Alcohol Policies*. Aldershot: Ashgate.

Holmila, M. (Ed.) (1997). *Community Prevention of Alcohol Problems*. London: Macmillan.

Kaminer, W. (1992). *I'm Dysfunctional, You're Dysfunctional: The Recovery Movement and Other Self-Help Fashions*. Reading, MA: Addison-Wesley.

Kaskutas, L.A. (1992). An Analysis of "Women for Sobriety". Dr. P.H. Dissertation, School of Public Health, University of California, Berkeley.

Katcher, B.S. (1993). The post-Repeal eclipse in knowledge about the harmful effects of alcohol. *Addiction*, **88**, 729–744.

Keane, H. (1998). What's Wrong with Addiction? PhD Dissertation, Australian National University.

Keiter, M. (1997). Just say no excuse: the rise and fall of the intoxication defense. *Journal of Criminal Law and Criminology*, **87**, 482–520.

Lagerspetz, M. (Ed.) (1994). *Social Problems in Newspapers: Studies around the Baltic Sea*, NAD Publication No. 28. Helsinki: Nordic Council for Alcohol and Drug Research.

Lemert, E. (1951). *Social Pathology: A Systematic Approach to the Theory of Sociopathic Behavior*. New York: McGraw-Hill.

Lupton, D. (1999). *Risk*. London and New York: Routledge.

Levine, H.G. (1978). The discovery of addiction: changing conceptions of habitual drunkenness in American history. *Journal of Studies on Alcohol*, **39**, 143–174.

Levine, H.G. (1983a). The Committee of Fifty and the origins of alcohol control. *Journal of Drug Issues*, **13**, 95–116.

Levine, H.G. (1983b). The good creature of God and demon rum: colonial American and nineteenth century ideas about alcohol, crime and accidents. In R. Room & G. Collins (Eds), *Alcohol and Disinhibition: Nature and Meaning of the Link* (pp. 111–171). NIAAA Research Monograph No. 12. Rockville, MD: National Institute on Alcohol Abuse and Alcoholism, DHHS Publication No. (ADM) 83–1246.

Levine, H.G. (1984). What is an alcohol-related problem? (Or, what are people talking about when they refer to alcohol problems?) *Journal of Drug Issues*, **14**, 45–60.

Martin, S.E. & Mail, P. (Eds) (1995). *Effects of the Mass Media on the Use and Abuse of Alcohol*, NIAAA Research Monograph No. 28. Bethesda, MD: National Institute on Alcohol Abuse and Alcoholism.

McCormick, M. (1969). First representations of the gamma alcoholic in the English novel. *Quarterly Journal of Studies on Alcohol*, **30**, 957–980.

McKee, W.A. (1997). Taming the Green Serpent: Alcoholism, Autocracy, and Russian Society, 1881–1914, PhD Thesis, University of California, Berkeley.

Mitchell, A. (1986).   The unsung villain: alcoholism and the emergence of public welfare in France, 1870–1914. *Contemporary Drug Problems*, **13**, 447–471.

Moore, M. & Gerstein, D. (Eds) (1981).   *Alcohol and Public Policy: Beyond the Shadow of Prohibition*. Washington: National Academy Press.

Olsson, B. (1990).   Alkoholpolitik och alkoholens fenomenologi: uppfattningar som artikulerats i pressen (Alcohol policy and the phenomenology of alcohol: conceptions articulated in the press). *Alkoholpolitik*, **7**, 184–195.

Peele, S. (1995).   *The Diseasing of America: Addiction Treatment out of Control—How We Allowed Recovery Zealots and the Treatment Industry to Convince Us We Are Out of Control*, 2nd edn. Lexington, MA: Lexington Books.

Porter, R. (1985).   The drinking man's disease: the "pre-history" of alcoholism in Georgian Britain. *British Journal of Addiction*, **80**, 385–396.

Rapping, E. (1996).   *The Culture of Recovery: Making Sense of the Self-help Movement in Women's Lives*. Boston, MA: Beacon.

Rice, J.S. (1996).   *A Disease of One's Own: Psychotherapy, Addiction, and the Emergence of Co-dependency*. New Brunswick, NJ: Transaction.

Roizen, R. (1991).   The American Discovery of Alcoholism, 1933–1939, PhD Dissertation, University of California, Berkeley.

Room, R. (1974).   Governing images and the prevention of alcohol problems. *Preventive Medicine*, **3**, 11–23.

Room, R. (1978).   Governing Images of Alcohol and Drug Problems: The Structure, Sources and Sequels of Conceptualizations of Intractable Problems, PhD Dissertation, University of California, Berkeley.

Room, R. (1983).   Sociological aspects of the disease concept of alcoholism. In R.G. Smart et al. (Eds), *Research Advances in Alcohol and Drug Problems*, Vol. 7 (pp. 47–91). London: Plenum, 1983.

Room, R. (1984).   Alcohol control and public health. *Annual Review of Public Health*, **5**, 293–317.

Room, R. (1985).   Dependence and society. *British Journal of Addiction*, **80**, 133–139.

Room, R. (1987).   Alcohol monopolies in the US: challenges and opportunities. *Journal of Public Health Policy*, **8**, 509–530.

Room, R. (1992).   "Healing ourselves and our planet": the emergence and nature of a generalized twelve-step consciousness. *Contemporary Drug Problems*, **19**, 717–740.

Room, R. (1996).   Drinking, violence, gender, and causal attribution: a Canadian case study in science, law and policy. *Contemporary Drug Problems*, **23**, 649–686.

Room, R. (1999).   The idea of alcohol policy. *Nordic Studies on Alcohol and Drugs*, **16** (English Supplement), 7–20.

Room, R., Janca, A., Bennett, L.A., Schmidt, L. & Sartorius, N. et al. (1996).   WHO cross-cultural applicability research on diagnosis and assessment of substance use disorders: an overview of methods and selected results. *Addiction*, **91**, 199–230.

Rothman, D.J. (1971). *The Discovery of the Asylum: Social Order and Disorder in the New Republic*. Boston: Little, Brown.

Schmidt, L. & Room, R. (1999).   Cross-cultural applicability in international classifications and research on alcohol dependence. *Journal of Studies on Alcohol*, **60**, 448–462.

Schneider, J.W. (1978).   Deviant drinking as disease: alcoholism as a social accomplishment. *Social Problems*, **25**, 361–372.

Sedgewick, E.K. (1992).   Epidemics of the will. In J. Crary & S. Kwinter (Eds), (pp. 582–595). *Incorporations*. New York: Zone.

Siegler, M., Osmond, H. & Newell, S. (1968).   Models of alcoholism. *Quarterly Journal of Studies on Alcohol*, **29**, 571–591.

Simpura, J. & Tigerstedt, C. (Eds) (1992).   *Social Problems around the Baltic Sea: Report from the Baltica Study*, NAD Publication No. 21. Helsinki: Nordic Council for Alcohol and Drug Research.

Smart, R. & Ogborne, A. (1996).   *Northern Spirits*, 2nd edn. Toronto: Addiction Research Foundation.

Sournia, J.C. (1990).   *A History of Alcoholism*. Oxford: Basil Blackwell.

Sulkunen, P. (1992).   *The European New Middle Class: Individuality and Tribalism in Mass Society*. Aldershot: Avebury.

Sulkunen, P. (1998).   Images and realities of alcohol. *Addiction*, **93**, 1305–1312.

Sulkunen, P. & Paakkanen, P. (Eds) (1987). *Cultural Studies on Drinking and Drinking Problems: Report on a Conference*, Reports from the Social Research Institute of Alcohol Studies No. 176. Helsinki: SRIAS.

Sulkenen, P., Sutton, C., Tigestedt, C. & Warpenius, K. (Eds.) (2000). *Broken Spirits: Power and Ideas in Nordic Alcohol Control*. NAD Publication No. 39. Helsinki: Nordic Council for Alcohol and Drug Research.

Sutton, C. (1998). Swedish Alcohol Discourse: Constructions of a Social Problem, PhD Dissertation, Uppsala, 1998 (Studia Sociologica Upsaliensia 45, published by Uppsala University Library).

Tigerstedt, C. (1999). Alcohol policy, public health and Kettil Bruun. *Contemporary Drug Problems,* **26**, 209–235.

Valverde, M. (1998). *Diseases of the Will: Alcohol and the Dilemmas of Freedom*. Cambridge: Cambridge University Press.

Verhey, J. (1991). Sources for the social history of alcohol. In S. Barrows & R. Room (Eds), *Drinking: Behavior and Belief in Modern History*. Berkeley, CA: University of California Press.

Warner, J. (1994). "Resolv'd to drink no more": addiction as a preindustrial concept. *Journal of Studies on Alcohol*, **55**, 685–691.

Chapter 4

Classification of Alcohol-Related Problems and Dependence

Elizabeth E. Epstein
Center of Alcohol Studies, State University of New Jersey,
Piscataway, NJ, USA

Synopsis

Modern conceptions of alcohol use disorders are based on categorical, rule-governed systems of diagnosis found in the Diagnostic and Statistical Manual of Mental Disorders (DSM-IV; American Psychiatric Association, 1994) in the USA and the International Statistical Classification of Diseases (ICD; World Health Organization, 1992) in Europe. Both diagnostic systems have evolved over two centuries, and have been heavily influenced by the advent of modern psychiatric classification, the disease model of alcoholism, and research-based approaches to establish reliability in psychiatric classification.

Current formulations reflect the dual notions of the alcohol dependence syndrome and the alcohol problems (abuse or harmful use) perspectives. This chapter summarizes historical and prevailing formulations of alcohol use disorders and dependence, tracing the influences on and development of the DSM-I through IV and the ICD-8 through 10 diagnostic categories. Alternative methods to classification based on problems associated with drinking, and drinking severity, are presented. Current research on alcohol typologies is discussed as another way to organize the heterogeneity seen in alcoholic populations. Comorbidity of psychiatric and medical disorders is reviewed briefly in terms of differential diagnosis. Finally, future directions in classification of alcohol use disorders and dependence are discussed.

This chapter is designed to familiarize the reader with the history, evolution and current formulations of major diagnostic or classification approaches to alcohol use disorders and dependence.

What is an "alcoholic?" Someone who drinks too often? Too much? Someone who has lost his/her home and family due to alcohol? Someone who inherited a disease that somehow

International Handbook of Alcohol Dependence and Problems. Edited by N. Heather, T.J. Peters and T. Stockwell.
© 2001 John Wiley & Sons Ltd.

compels him/her to consume alcohol? Interestingly, current diagnostic formulations include none of the criteria typically used for popular stereotypes. In common usage, the terms "alcoholism" and "alcoholic" are mentioned freely and often with certainty. In contrast, scientific and treatment communities have grappled with the subtleties of defining and classifying alcohol use disorders for over 200 years.

This chapter will summarize historical and current formulations of scientists' and professionals' attempts to answer this question: how do we best define and classify alcohol use disorders, as well as the population of "alcoholics?" We begin with a discussion of a broader issue under which the classification of alcohol use disorders is subsumed, namely, the notion of categorical diagnoses of psychiatric disorders. Then, a brief review of historical antecedents leading to the development of successively more sophisticated and research-based definitions of alcohol problems will be presented. Current classifications of alcohol use disorders follow the USA-based DSM-IV and the European ICD-10; these will be compared and described in more detail, as will some alternative approaches to classifications based on range of severity. Heterogeneity among persons with alcohol use problems will then be discussed, in terms of prevailing typologies that have been developed in attempts to further classify the population with alcohol use disorders. A discussion of medical and psychological issues complicating diagnosis of alcohol disorders will follow. Finally, a brief review of empirical support for current diagnostic systems will focus on recent research which highlights promising innovations and future directions in the classification of alcohol problems and dependence.

CLASSIFICATION OF PSYCHIATRIC DISORDERS

Modern psychiatry, dating back to Kraepelin's classification system for mental illness at the end of the nineteenth century, is embedded in the medical model, according to which discrete diagnostic entities have common etiologies, symptom profiles and course. Diagnostic classification has several advantages. Scientists need etiological clarity to develop medications and other treatments, and standardization of diagnosis in order to calibrate research within and across laboratories. Clinicians appreciate the prognostic value of orderly symptom profiles in order to select the appropriate treatment and to gauge recovery. Health care payment systems require diagnoses to determine reimbursement allowances.

Since the 1970s, diagnostic classification has become increasingly rule-governed, as reflected in the development of successive Diagnostic and Statistical Manuals (American Psychiatric Association, 1952, 1968, 1980, 1987, 1994), the most recent three versions of which require that the patient meet particular subsets of detailed criteria in order to "meet the threshold" of a categorical diagnosis. This approach has been useful to establish reliability and ease of use of diagnostic categories; however, the classical categorical approach to diagnosis in medicine does not always capture the heterogeneity found among mental and behavioral disorders. Alternatively, dimensional approaches quantify aspects of mental disorders such that each patient is rated on a continuum of severity for each dimension. Dimensional systems avoid imposing dichotomous assignment to type; however, choice of relevant dimensions for a particular disorder can be controversial. In the alcohol field, controversy has surrounded the notion of alcoholism as a discrete disorder that people either "have or don't have". Current formulations are categorical-based systems of diagnosis and typology, but, as discussed below, researchers are investigating other, dimensional models based on drinking behavior and severity.

HISTORY OF CLASSIFICATION SCHEMES FOR ALCOHOL PROBLEMS AND ALCOHOL DEPENDENCE

Modern conceptions of alcohol use disorders are rooted in a history traceable to the early nineteenth century, when "alienists"—medical specialists in mental and addictive disorders—began to recognize such disorders as a public health problem in several different countries (Lender, 1979; Babor, 1996). Various classification systems were published by medical writers in the USA and Europe. Bruhl-Cramer (1819) introduced the concept of "dipsomania," or drink seeking (see Grant & Dawson, 1999). In 1849, the term "alcoholic" was coined by Magnus Huss in Sweden to describe people who suffered negative consequences of alcohol use (Miller & Hester, 1995). As Babor (1996) notes, 39 classifications of alcoholics were developed around the world between 1850 and 1941 (see also Babor & Lauerman, 1986). For instance, Carpenter (1850) described "oinomania" (wine mania) as a disease with types based on frequency of drinking, course and desire for alcohol. By the 1870s, the Association for the Study of Inebriety was formed by American alienists and similar societies emerged in Britain and France, as well as scientific books and journals devoted to the study of inebriety. Attempts to understand the elusive nature of excessive drinking and to capture that understanding in a useful classification system continued. For instance, Kerr (1893) described four types of inebriates based on frequency and comorbid psychopathology, and also on social versus unsocial drinking. Crothers (1911) described a complicated classification system of three types replete with subcategories, as well as a classification for etiology. This system clearly reflected the notion of inebriety as a disease and also linked inebriety to several different forms of comorbid psychopathology. Several other alienists in France and England published classification systems for dipsomania in the late nineteenth and early twentieth centuries (see Babor, 1996, for a detailed review), all of which rooted excessive alcohol use and alcohol-related problems in a disease model and as a psychiatric disorder associated with other psychiatric problems. Interestingly, although dipsomania was generally seen as a disease, alienists identified much heterogeneity among inebriates and early attempts to classify alcohol use disorders focused on differentiating among types of alcoholics.

In America, from the late nineteenth century to 1933, that is, throughout the Temperance and Prohibition movements, alcohol was seen as a dangerous substance (Hester & Miller, 1995) to be avoided by everyone. When alcohol was again legalized in 1933, the disease model became even more firmly entrenched; Alcoholics Anonymous, began in 1935, adopted and further promulgated the American disease model of alcoholism. In this view, alcohol could be used safely in moderation by most Americans, but not, however, by those afflicted with the disease of alcoholism (Hester & Miller, 1995). Individuals who had the disease deserved treatment, not punishment, according to this model. The disease model of alcoholism provided a unitary conception, focusing on physiological addiction and dependence to the exclusion of negative social and psychological consequences of excessive alcohol use (Grant & Dawson, 1999).

In 1941, Bowman & Jellinek published an elaborate classification scheme for the disease, based on pattern of drinking frequency, etiology, comorbid disorders and ability to abstain (see Babor, 1996, for a detailed description). Almost 20 years later, Jellinek (1960) published *The Disease Concept of Alcoholism*, which elaborated on his earlier work and postulated five species of alcoholism: alpha, beta, gamma, delta, and epsilon. Gamma and delta included physiological addiction and thus were considered the two main types of the disease. Jellinek's classification became the most popular alcohol typology for the next 20 years; however, little empirical research was done to substantiate the theory (Bowman & Jellinek, 1941).

MODERN DIAGNOSTIC CLASSIFICATION

Current nosology for alcohol use disorders and dependence relies on the Diagnostic and Statistical Manual of Mental Disorders (DSM; American Psychiatric Association, 1952, 1968, 1980, 1987, 1994) and the International Statistical Classification of Diseases, Injuries, and Causes of Death (ICD; World Health Organization, 1967, 1978, 1989, 1992), both of which have chronicled many changes over the past 45 years or so. This section will review the development of the modern DSM and ICD classifications for alcoholism summarized in Tables 4.1–4.4.

DSM

In the DSM-I (American Psychiatric Association, 1952), the term "alcoholism" was used but was considered a subcategory of Sociopathic Personality Disturbance, and little clinical detail was provided. DSM-II (American Psychiatric Association, 1968) reflected the influence of Jellinek's (1960) typology described above, such that alcoholism became a separate disorder. However, it was still subsumed in the "Personality Disorders and Certain Other Non-psychotic Mental Disorders" section under "Alcoholism." Due to a push for international classification at the time, the DSM-II diagnosis had the same definition as the ICD-8 (Sellman, 1994; World Health Organization, 1967). "Alcoholism" was broken down into three subtypes, the first two of which are listed here in Table 4.1 and correspond to subsequent descriptions of Alcohol Abuse; the third is listed in Table 4.2 as a precursor of current Alcohol Dependence (see Tables 4.1 and 4.2).

In 1972, the Feighner criteria (Feighner et al., 1972) were published for 15 psychiatric disorders, including alcoholism. This system was designed primarily to establish reliability of diagnoses for research purposes and was the precursor to further development in the DSM and ICD of objective, criterion- and rule-based operationalization of constructs related to alcoholism.

A comprehensive medical approach to diagnosis of alcoholism was put forth by the Criteria Committee of the National Council on Alcoholism (NCA; Criteria Committee, National Council on Alcoholism, 1972). This consisted of 86 criteria focusing on physiological, clinical, behavioral, psychological and attitudinal symptoms (Babor, 1992b). This diagnostic system, although sophisticated in its recognition of the complexities of alcohol use problems, was not widely adopted in clinical practice due to weak decision rules and lack of established validity and reliability (Babor, 1992b; Jacobson, 1980).

An additional influence on subsequent development of the classification systems in America and Europe was the Alcohol Dependence Syndrome (ADS), coined by Edwards & Gross (1976). The ADS was carefully defined by seven "essential elements" and was thought to be one component of "alcohol-related problems" (Room, 1998). The seven elements included: (1) a narrowing of the drinking repertoire; (2) subjective awareness of a compulsion to drink; (3) salience of drink-seeking behavior; (4) increased tolerance to alcohol; (5) repeated withdrawal symptoms; (6) relief or avoidance of withdrawal symptoms by further drinking, and (7) reinstatement after abstinence. Several elements of the ADS are evident in subsequent editions of the DSM and ICD classifications of alcohol dependence.

In DSM-III (1980) the term "alcoholism" was replaced with two categories, "Alcohol Abuse" and "Alcohol Dependence," each with its own set of criteria (see Tables 4.1 and 4.2), thus disaggregating the unitary disease concept of alcoholism into

Table 4.1   DSM-II, DSM-III, and DSM-III-R criteria for Alcohol Abuse

DSM-II (APA, 1968)
303.   *Alcoholism:* Alcohol intake is great enough to damage their physical health, or their personal or social functioning, or when it has become a prerequisite to normal functioning. If the alcoholism is due to another mental disorder, both diagnoses should be made.
303.0   *Episodic excessive drinking:* If alcoholism is present and the individual becomes intoxicated as frequently as four times a year, the condition should be classified here. Intoxication is defined as a state in which the individual's coordination or speech is definitely impaired or his behaviour is clearly altered.
303.1   *Habitual excessive drinking:* persons who are alcoholic and who either become intoxicated more than 12 times a year or are recognizably under the influence of alcohol more than once a week, even though not intoxicated.

DSM-III (APA, 1980)
(A)   Pattern of pathological alcohol use: need for daily use of alcohol for adequate functioning: inability to cut down or stop drinking; repeated efforts to control or reduce excess drinking by "going on the wagon" or restricting drinking to certain times of the day; binges; occasional consumption of a fifth of spirits (or equivalent in wine or beer); amnesic periods for events occurring while intoxicated (blackouts); continuation of drinking despite a serious physical disorder that the individual knows is exacerbated by alcohol use; drinking of non-beverage alcohol.
(B)   Impairment in social or occupational functioning due to alcohol use: e.g. violence while intoxicated, absence from work, loss of job, legal difficulties, arguments or difficulties with family or friends because of excessive alcohol use.
(C)   Duration of disturbance of at least one month.

DSM-III-R (APA, 1987)
(A)   A maladaptive pattern of psychoactive substance use indicated by at least one of the following:
   (1)   continued use despite knowledge of having a persistent or recurrent social, occupational, psychological, or physical problem that is caused or exacerbated by use of the psychoactive substance.
   (2)   recurrent use in situations in which use is physically hazardous
(B)   Some symptoms of the disturbance have persisted for at least one month, or have occurred repeatedly over a longer period of time.
(C)   Never met the criteria for Psychoactive Substance Dependence for this substance.

two separate disorders with varying clinical histories and prognoses (Cottler et al., 1995). Alcohol abuse and dependence were subsumed under a new "Substance Use Disorders" section, rather than the Personality Disorders section. Alcohol Dependence essentially represented a more severe form of alcohol abuse that required physiological dependence marked by either tolerance or withdrawal. DSM-III was highly successful in that it became a standard diagnostic tool in several countries. Babor (1995) attributes the success to the following factors: its use of the Kraepelinian approach to classification, its rich clinical detail, its attention to reliability issues and its usefulness in epidemiological research.

In 1987 the DSM-III-R (American Psychiatric Association, 1987) was published; this edition kept Substance Use Disorders as a separate section and formalized decision rules used to establish diagnoses. Alcohol Abuse was further distinguished from Alcohol

Table 4.2   DSM II, DSM-III, and DSM-III-R criteria for Alcohol Dependence

DSM-II (American Psychiatric Association, 1968)
  303.   *Alcoholism:* Alcohol intake is great enough to damage their physical health, or their personal or social functioning, or when it has become a prerequisite to normal functioning. If the alcoholism is due to another mental disorder, both diagnoses should be made.
  303.2   *Alcohol addiction:* when there is direct or strong presumptive evidence that the patient is dependent on alcohol. If available, the best direct evidence of such dependence is the appearance of withdrawal symptoms. The inability of the patient to go one day without drinking is presumptive evidence. When heavy drinking continues for three months or more it is reasonable to presume addiction to alcohol has been established.

DSM-III
  (A) Either a pattern of pathological alcohol use or impairment in social or occupational functioning due to alcohol use:
       Pattern of pathological alcohol use: need for daily use of alcohol for adequate functioning: inability to cut down or stop drinking; repeated efforts to control or reduce excess drinking by "going on the wagon" or restricting drinking to certain times of the day; binges; occasional consumption of a fifth of spirits (or equivalent in wine or beer); amnesic periods for events occurring while intoxicated (blackouts); continuation of drinking despite a serious physical disorder that the individual knows is exacerbated by alcohol use; drinking of non-beverage alcohol.
       Impairment in social or occupational functioning due to alcohol use: e.g. violence while intoxicated, absence from work, loss of job, legal difficulties, arguments or difficulties with family or friends because of excessive alcohol use.
  (B) Either tolerance or withdrawal:
       Tolerance: need for markedly increased amounts of alcohol to achieve the desired effect, or markedly diminished effect with regular use of the same amount.
       Withdrawal: development of Alcohol Withdrawal (e.g. morning "shakes" and malaise relieved by drinking) after cessation of or reduction in drinking.

DSM-III-R
  (A) At least three of the following:
       (1)   substance often taken in larger amounts or over a longer period than the person intended
       (2)   persistent desire or one or more unsuccessful efforts to cut down or control substance use
       (3)   a great deal of time spent in activities necessary to get the substance, taking the substance, or recovering from its effects
       (4)   frequent intoxication or withdrawal symptoms when expected to fulfill major role obligations at work, school, or home, or when substance use is physically hazardous
       (5)   important social, occupational, or recreational activities given up or reduced because of substance use
       (6)   continued substance use despite knowledge of having a persistent or recurrent social, psychological, or physical problem that is caused or exacerbated by the use of the substance
       (7)   marked tolerance: need for markedly increased amounts of the substance (at least 50%) in order to achieve intoxication or desired effect, or markedly diminished effect with continued use of the same amount
       (8)   characteristic withdrawal symptoms
       (9)   substance often taken to relieve or avoid withdrawal symptoms
  (B) Some symptoms of the disturbance have persisted for at least one month, or have occurred repeatedly over a longer period of time.

Dependence. Physiological dependence (tolerance or withdrawal) was taken away as a necessary component of Alcohol Dependence and simply listed along with seven other criteria, of which any three earned a patient the diagnosis of Alcohol Dependence (see Table 4.2). The revisions aligned the DSM Substance Use Disorders sections more closely with the dependence syndrome concept (Babor, 1995).

ICD

The International Classification of Diseases (ICD) was compiled by the World Health Organization (WHO) in order to create a common, worldwide diagnostic system (Room, 1998). The ICD-8 (World Health Organization, 1967), as noted above, used a classification for alcoholism that was identical that used for DSM-II (see Tables 4.3 and 4.4) and placed it in the section called "Neuroses, Personality Disorders, and Other Non-psychotic Mental Disorders". "Episodic" and "Habitual" excessive drinking were less severe forms, and "Alcohol Addiction" was defined more akin to today's Alcohol Dependence, as far as physiological dependence is concerned. In 1974, the terms were carefully defined, "Episodic Excessive Drinking" as "occurring as frequently as four time a year or more . . . (lasting) . . . for several days or weeks and may be associated with physical or mental stress or precipitated by cyclical mood changes," and "Habitual Excessive Drinking" as "regular consumption of excessive quantities of alcohol to the detriment of a person's health or social functioning" (WHO, 1974, p. 47; see also Babor, 1992b).

For ICD-9 (WHO, 1978), the term alcoholism was replaced with "Alcohol Dependence Syndrome," defined as drug dependence was in ICD-8 (Babor, 1992b) (see Table 4.4), including the concepts of withdrawal and tolerance, and subjective compulsion to use alcohol. A new category was created, called "Non-dependent Abuse of Drugs," under which alcohol was listed along with nine other Substances. In ICD-9 (WHO, 1978), then, it was assumed that Substance Abuse Dependence subsumes both alcohol and other drugs, and

Table 4.3 ICD 8 (WHO, 1967), and ICD 9 (WHO, 1978) criteria for Alcoholism and Alcohol Abuse

ICD-8 (WHO, 1967)

303. *Alcoholism:* Alcohol intake is great enough to damage their physical health, or their personal or social functioning, or when it has become a prerequisite to normal functioning. If the alcoholism is due to another mental disorder, both diagnoses should be made.

303.0 *Episodic excessive drinking:* If alcoholism is present and the individual becomes intoxicated as frequently as four times a year, the condition should be classified here. Intoxication is defined as a state in which the individual's coordination or speech is definitely impaired or his behaviour is clearly altered.

303.1 *Habitual excessive drinking:* persons who are alcoholic and who either become intoxicated more than 12 times a year or are recognizably under the influence of alcohol more than once a week, even though not intoxicated.

ICD-9 (WHO, 1978)

305. *Non-dependent abuse of drugs:* includes cases where a person, for whom no other diagnosis is possible, has come under medical care because of the maladaptive effect of a drug on which he is not dependent and that he has taken on his own initiative to the detriment of his health or social functioning.

305.0 *Alcohol abuse:* Drunkenness, excessive drinking of alcohol, "hangover," inebriety.

Table 4.4   ICD 8 (WHO, 1967), and ICD 9 (WHO, 1978) criteria for Alcohol Dependence Syndrome

ICD-8 (WHO, 1967)

  303. *Alcoholism:* Alcohol intake is great enough to damage their physical health, or their personal or social functioning, or when it has become a prerequisite to normal functioning. If the alcoholism is due to another mental disorder, both diagnoses should be made.

  303.2 *Alcohol addiction:* when there is direct or strong presumptive evidence that the patient is dependent on alcohol. If available, the best direct evidence of such dependence is the appearance of withdrawal symptoms. The inability of the patient to go one day without drinking is presumptive evidence. When heavy drinking continues for three months or more it is reasonable to presume addiction to alcohol has been established.

ICD-9 (WHO, 1978)
Alcohol Dependence Syndrome: A state, psychic and also physical, resulting from taking alcohol, characterized by behavioural and other responses that always include a compulsion to take alcohol on a continuous or periodic basis in order to experience its psychic effects, and sometimes to avoid the discomfort of its absence; tolerance may or may not be present.

also that Substance Use Without Physiological Dependence is deleterious enough to be classified separately (Babor, 1992b).

CURRENT DEFINITIONS AND DIAGNOSIS

DSM-IV

DSM-IV (American Psychiatric Association, 1994) was published after the DSM-IV Substance Use Disorders Work Group's effort to review relevant literatures, consult with 50 expert advisors, analyze existing data-sets, and do field trials in order to base the revision on empirical data and consensus among researchers and clinicians from psychiatry, psychology and the addictions field (National Institute on Alcohol Abuse and Alcoholism, 1995; Cottler et al., 1995; Schuckit, 1994). It is currently the accepted diagnostic tool used in the USA. The Substance Use Disorders section is similar to that of DSM-III-R, with several refinements (see Table 4.3).

The Alcohol Dependence diagnosis was similar to that in DSM-III-R, except that one of the DSM-III-R criteria was moved to the Alcohol Abuse criterion list and one (relief drinking) was dropped entirely. DSM-IV added specifiers for course and for physiological dependence. Thus, using DSM-IV, one can be diagnosed as Alcohol Dependent without having physiological dependence (tolerance or withdrawal) (see Table 4.5).

The Alcohol Abuse diagnosis is more detailed and better operationalized, and the threshold is lower, that is, only one of four symptoms must be positive in order to get a diagnosis, so it is "easier" to be labeled as such. The same exclusion criterion as was in DSM-III-R, that a patient who had ever been diagnosed with Alcohol Dependence could not be diagnosed with Alcohol Abuse, was retained in the DSM-IV, thus keeping Alcohol Abuse a residual category diagnosable only after assessing for Alcohol Dependence (Babor, 1992a). The separation of Alcohol Abuse (see Table 4.6) implies that it is not simply an early stage dependence syndrome, but rather a disorder in its own right, based on a pattern of pathological use and social or occupational impairment (Babor, 1992a).

Table 4.5 DSM-IV and ICD-10 criteria for Substance Abuse and Harmful Use

DSM-IV criteria for Substance Abuse	ICD-10 criteria for Harmful Use
A. A maladaptive pattern of substance use leading to Clinically significant impairment or distress, as Manifested by one (or more) or the following, occurring Within a 12-month period:	A pattern of psychoactive substance use that is causing damage to health. The damage may be physical (as in cases of hepatitis from the self-administration of injected drugs) or mental (e.g. episodes of depressive disorder secondary to heavy consumption of alcohol).
(1) Recurrent substance use resulting in a failure to fulfill major role obligations at work, school, or home (e.g. repeated absences or poor work performance related to substance use; substance-related absences, suspensions, or expulsions from school; neglect of children or household)	
(2) Recurrent substance use in situations in which it is physically hazardous (e.g. driving an automobile or operating a machine when impaired by substance use)	
(3) Recurrent substance-related legal problems (e.g. arrests for substance-related disorderly conduct)	
(4) Continued substance use despite having persistent or recurrent social or interpersonal problems caused or exacerbated by the effects of the substance (e.g. arguments with spouse about consequences of intoxication, physical fights)	"the fact that a pattern of use or a particular substance is disapproved of by another person or by the culture, or may have led to socially negative consequences such as arrest or marital arguments is not in itself evidence of harmful use"
B. The symptoms have never met the criteria for Substance Dependence for this class of substance	Harmful use should not be diagnosed if dependence syndrome, a psychotic disorder, or another specific form of drug- or alcohol-related disorder is present

ICD-10

ICD-10 (WHO, 1989) was heavily influenced by the Alcohol Dependence Syndrome (Edwards & Gross, 1976) and also by the concept of "disabilities caused by substance use" (Edwards, Gross, Keller & Moser, 1976; Edwards, Arif & Hodgson, 1981). The dependence syndrome focuses on subjective compulsion to drink, physiological dependence (tolerance and withdrawal) and rapid reinstatement of symptoms after a period of abstinence. In Table 4.5, the DSM-IV and ICD-10 diagnoses of Alcohol Dependence are compared. Both represent the more severe form of alcohol use problems and require at least three symptoms of seven (for the DSM) or six (for the ICD) clustering in a 12 month period to meet the diagnostic threshold. For both, physiological dependence (tolerance and withdrawal) is a possible but not a necessary component of the clinical picture, as are loss of control, drinking in lieu of other once-important activities and continuing to drink despite knowledge of

Table 4.6 Comparison of Edwards and Gross' Alcohol Dependence Syndrome, DSM-1V and ICD-10 criteria for alcohol dependence

Alcohol Dependence Syndrome	DSM-IV (APA, 1994)	ICD-10 (WHO, 1992)
	A. A maladaptive pattern of substance use, leading to clinically significant impairment or distress as manifested by three or more of the following occurring at any time in the same 12-month period:	A. Three or more of the following have been experienced exhibited at some time during the previous year:
(3) Increased tolerance to alcohol	(1) Tolerance, as defined by either of the following: (a) Need for markedly increased amounts of a substance to achieve intoxication or desired effect (b) Markedly diminished effect with continued use of the same amount of the substance	(d) Evidence of tolerance, such that increased dosages are required in order to achieve effects originally produced by lower dosages.
(4) Repeated withdrawal symptoms (5) Relief or avoidance of withdrawal by further drinking	(2) Withdrawal, as manifested by either of the following: (a) characteristic withdrawal syndrome for the substance, or (b) the same (or a closely related) substance is taken to relieve or avoid related) withdrawal symptoms.	(c) A physiological withdrawal state when substance use has ceased or been reduced as evidenced by: characteristic substance withdrawal syndrome, or use of the same (or a closely related) substance with the intention of relieving or avoiding withdrawal symptoms.
	(3) The substance is often taken in larger amounts or over a longer period than was intended	(b) Difficulties in controlling substance-taking behaviour terms of its onset, termination, or levels of use
	(4) There is a persistent desire or unsuccessful efforts to cut down or control substance use	
(2) Salience of drink-seeking behaviour	(5) A great deal of time is spent in activities necessary to obtain the substance, use the substance, or recover its effects.	

(1) Narrowing of the drinking repertoire

(6) Important social, occupational, or recreational activities are given up or reduced because of substance use.

(7) The substance use is continued despite knowledge of having a persistent or recurrent physical or psychological problem that is likely to have been caused or exacerbated by the substance.

Specifiers:
- With physiological dependence (1) or (2)
- Without physiological dependence

Course specifiers:
- Early Full Remission
- Early Partial Remission
- Sustained Full Remission
- Sustained Partial Remission
- On Agonist Therapy
- In a Controlled Environment

(e) Progressive neglect of alternative pleasures or interests because of substance use, increased amount of time necessary to obtain or take the substance or to recover from its effects.

(f) persisting with substance use despite clear evidence of overtly harmful consequences, such as harm to the liver through excessive drinking, depressive mood statesconsequent to heavy substance use, or drug-related impairment of cognitive functioning. Efforts should be made to determine that the user was actually, or could be expected to be, aware of the nature and extent of the harm.

(7) Rapid reinstatement of of symptoms after a period abstinence

(6) Subjective awareness of compulsion to drink

(a) a strong desire or sense of compulsion to take the substance its harmful effects. The DSM-IV and ICD-10 depart from one another in listing different aspects of the Alcohol Dependence Syndrome, which heavily influences both diagnostic systems. The DSM-IV lists a variant of "salience of drink seeking behavior" (Edwards & Gross, 1976), while the ICD-10 includes the concept of subjective compulsion to drink. In addition, the DSM-IV includes the inability to stop or cut down as a possible symptom, and neither the DSM nor the ICD include Edwards & Gross's (1976) seventh symptoms of the alcohol dependence syndrome, "rapid reinstatement of symptoms after a period of abstinence."

As seen in Tables 4.3 and 4.6, the term "abuse" in the ICD-9 was replaced in the ICD-10 with "harmful use," meant to identify a pattern of use that has already caused either mental or physical damage. This is quite different from the DSM-IV conception of abuse, which can be diagnosed based only on, for instance, perceived damage by family members of the alcohol abuser (Babor, 1992b). The purpose for the change in ICD-10 was to facilitate accurate reporting of health problems related to alcohol use (Babor, 1992b; Edwards et al., 1981).

Current diagnostic criteria for both the DSM and the ICD are based on years of evolution of the concept of excessive use, associated negative consequences and physical dependence (see Babor, 1992b). Both rely heavily on Edwards & Gross's (1976) Alcohol Dependence Syndrome, which itself evolved over 200 years of notions regarding the nature of excessive use and consequences of alcohol, dating back to Benjamin Rush (1785) and Samuel Woodward (1838). One thing is certain—classification of alcohol use disorders and dependence, although historically based on a medical model, is certainly not as clear-cut as other medical syndromes that have more straightforward etiologies, predictable course and similar features across patients. Alcohol use disorders and dependence are also not as clearly classified as many other psychiatric disorders. Classic symptoms of schizophrenia, for instance, involve hallucinations and delusions that are not under the patient's control. In order to become dependent on alcohol, however, an individual must seek and consume alcohol on a regular basis. The idea that one's volitional behavior can be classified as a disease is difficult to reconcile. End points of the process, such as tolerance and withdrawal symptoms related to physiological dependence on alcohol, are easier to understand as a disease state. As Babor (1995) states, "diagnostic classification in DSM-IV is dictated more by blind adherence to the description by the patient of the behavior than by a basic understanding of the underlying determinants of that behavior" (p. 78).

Confusion regarding classification of alcohol use disorders is thus apparent in the long history of scientists' and clinicians' grappling with diagnoses and definitions. Several factors contribute to the difficulties in classification, including: (a) the behavioral nature of the disorder, which may lend itself to a more dimensional approach to drinking and which has resulted in a body of literature which refutes the disease concept of alcohol use disorders; (b) the obvious heterogeneity in the population of those diagnosed with alcohol use disorders, which has resulted in a large literature on alcoholic subtypes; (c) high rates of comorbid psychiatric disorders, such as depression, anxiety, post-traumatic stress disorder (PTSD) and personality disorders; and (d) medical conditions that are complicated or exacerbated by psychoactive substance use disorders, making differential diagnosis difficult. The following sections will briefly address these issues.

ALTERNATIVES TO THE PSYCHIATRIC CLASSIFICATION OF ALCOHOL PROBLEMS

The notion of the "disease concept of alcoholism" as a unitary disorder involving the alcohol dependence syndrome, and the diagnostic approach based on a medical model, has been challenged in the USA, Europe and Australia (Drummond, 1992; Drew, 1987; Fingarette, 1988; Heather & Robertson, 1997) and alternative approaches have been offered.

In 1972, Robin Room suggested five levels of analysis of dependence, thereby disaggregating the unitary concept of a single, medically-based disease notion. Levels included: (1) physiological; (2) psychological; (3) face-to-face interaction; (4) subcultures and social worlds; and (5) cultural (see Heather, Robertson & Davies, 1985). Edwards et al. (1977), from a WHO scientific group, distinguished between the more narrowly defined alcohol dependence syndrome (meaning addiction or disease) and alcohol-related disabilities, which more closely align with today's "Heavy Drinking," "Alcohol-related Problems" and "Alcohol Abuse." Hence, the "problems perspective", which focuses more on a continuum of drinking behavior and social and psychological problems related to alcohol use, possibly in the absence of physiological dependence. Drummond (1992) describes a bi-axial concept, attributed first to Edwards et al. (1977): alcohol-related problems are on an orthogonal axis to a dependence continuum, thus problems can occur independently of dependence and both can occur in various degrees of severity.

Heather & Robertson (1997) have argued against the notion of a disease concept and suggested an alternative set of assumptions describing "problem drinking" as: (a) a complex, learned behavior rather than a discrete entity; (b) a chosen behavior; (c) a learned behavior; and (d) not necessarily progressive. Social learning theory is applied to problem drinking and its treatment (Heather & Robertson, 1997; Hodgson & Stockwell, 1985).

Philosopher Fingarette (1988) has objected to the assumption of inevitable progression of the disease state leading to a loss of control over drinking, and to the notion of a "single causal origin and . . . a single inexorable course" (p. 99). Fingarette recommends use of "heavy drinking" to refer to a continuum of excessive consumption of alcohol, rather than a clear dichotomy between alcoholics and non-alcoholics. Heavy drinkers, according to Fingarette, choose to make drinking a "central activity" in their lives. This central activity gains momentum over time and changes the drinker's perceptions of his/her world. In order to change the drinking behavior, the heavy drinker must first accept personal responsibility and then take measures to restructure his/her way of life in order to eliminate the drinking behavior and build new ways to cope and achieve satisfaction.

In Australia, Drew (1987) advocates the "minimization of harm" and the "exercise of autonomy, self-control or self-governance" in determining policy directing treatment approaches. The disease concept, he argues, tacitly communicates the notion that drug addicts are incapable of helping themselves and that they need a medical expert to "cure" their disease.

Others (Kranzler, Babor & Lauerman, 1990) have used the WHO criteria to define a range of severity of drinking problems for non-alcoholics, based on drinking quantity and frequency. Non-hazardous drinkers consume less than 40 grams ethanol per day; hazardous drinkers consume 40–80 grams per day. The notion of levels of problem drinking lends itself to various preventative, early and brief interventions to screen for hazardous drinking and help the patient gain self-control of his/her drinking behavior instead of developing physiological dependence on alcohol (Heather, 1995; see Chapter 31, this volume).

HETEROGENEITY AMONG PERSONS WITH SUBSTANCE USE PROBLEMS

This chapter thus far has centered on efforts to classify alcoholism. Other efforts have been made to classify the *population* of alcoholics, that is, among those individuals who are diagnosed or identified as alcoholic, how do we describe the apparent heterogeneity among them? These efforts to classify alcoholics into typologies began as early as the nineteenth century; Babor & Lauerman (1986) and Babor & Dolinsky (1988) have eloquently summarized early attempts. Examples of unidimensional typologies are based on gender (Del Boca & Hesselbrock, 1996), family history (V. Hesselbrock et al., 1985), antisocial personality disorder (M. Hesselbrock et al., 1984; Liskow et al., 1991) and drinking pattern (Jellinek, 1960; Epstein et al., 1995). Age of onset has been a dimension of growing interest among researchers (Irwin, Schuckit & Smith, 1990).

Type 1/Type 2

Perhaps the most influential sub-typing schema in terms of generating research was proposed by Cloninger, Bohman & Sigvardsson (1981) as Type 1/Type 2, originally derived from archival data in Sweden on 862 male adoptees with alcohol problems, all born out of wedlock (see also Chapter 13, this volume). The original study (Cloninger et al., 1981), which is quoted widely as providing evidence for Type 1/2 alcoholism in the probands, actually classified the families, not the problem drinking probands themselves, as Type 1 or 2. Families of probands who were moderate drinkers were characterized by early onset alcohol problems and criminality among the biological fathers, and no alcohol problems among the biological mothers. These families became known as "Type 2" or male-limited. Families of probands who were mild or severe drinkers showed no alcohol problem in the biological fathers and some alcohol abuse in the birth mothers. The severity of alcohol abuse in the proband depended on the socioeconomic status of the adoptive parents. These types of families were called "Type 1" or milieu-limited. In a separate study (Bohman, Sigvardsson & Cloninger, 1981), female adoptees in Sweden were classified according to the Type 1 or 2 characteristics of their biological parents, using the familial criteria established in the Cloninger et al. (1981) study. Female adoptees of Type 1, but not Type 2, biological families showed an excess of alcohol problems. It was concluded from these studies that female alcoholism is homogeneous (all Type 1) and that alcoholism in males is heterogeneous.

Although these two studies spurred a great deal of research on Type 1/2, there are methodological and interpretive issues to be noted. First, as Hill (1994) has pointed out, the conclusions about female alcoholism were based on a sample size of five alcoholic female adoptees. Second, the Type 1/2 typology has never been independently replicated using the methodology Cloninger et al. (1981) describe. Third, it should be emphasized that these 1981 studies addressed the Type 1/2 characteristics of the biological parents of alcoholic probands. That is, the only clinical feature of the proband studied was whether he drank at a mild, moderate or severe level. Nevertheless, the subtype literature routinely references the Cloninger et al. study as providing evidence for Type 1 versus 2 proband characteristics (see e.g. Gilligan, Reich & Cloninger, 1987).

Extensive research was generated by the Type 1/2 distinction; unfortunately, however, there has been little consistency among these studies in the choice of variables used to operationalize Type 1 and Type 2. Generally, the variables resemble those used by Gilligan et al. (1987), employing the clinical descriptor method rather than the family history method. The clinical descriptors thought to describe Type 1 and Type 2 alcoholics are listed in Table 4.7. In general, little success has been reported in identifying two distinct subgroups using clinical characteristics of the alcoholics themselves. In fact, Penick et al. (1990), Glenn & Nixon (1991), Irwin, Schuckit & Smith (1990) and Epstein, McCrady & Hirsch (1997) all concluded that age of symptom onset is the only variable studied that reliably differentiates alcoholics in terms of family history, associated psychopathology and/or response to treatment. As Penick et al. (1990) point out, the relative effect of age of onset is confounded with Antisocial Personality Disorder (ASP) and family history of alcoholism; all three of these

Table 4.7 Type 1/Type 2 alcoholism using the clinical descriptor method, and Type A/B alcoholism

	Type 1 Criteria (Loss of control; benders; guilt; medical problems)	Type 2 Criteria (DWIs; fights; treatment for drinking; unable to abstain; drinking-related arrest)
A. Indicators of vulnerability and risk		
1. Familial alcoholism	Low	High
2. Childhood disorder	Low	High
3. Bipolar character dimensions	Low	High
4. Onset of problem drinking	Late	Early
B. Severity of dependence		
5. Ounces of alcohol consumed per day	Low	High
6. Relief drinking	Low	High
7. Dependence syndrome	Low	High
8. Benzodiazepine use	Low	High
9. Polydrug use	Low	High
C. Chronicity and consequences of drinking		
10. Medical conditions	Low	High
11. Physical consequences	Low	High
12. Social consequences	low	High
13. Life-time severity	Low	High
14. Years heavy drinking	More	Fewer
D. Psychopathology		
15. Depressive symptom count	Low	High
16. Anxiety	Low	High
17. Antisocial Personality	Low	High

variables co-vary and the specific contribution of each has not been studied thus far. Criteria used to establish Type 2 alcoholism in both probands and first-degree relatives appear to be compatible with criteria used to diagnose ASP; however, this has never been empirically established.

In summary, replicability of both the family history and clinical descriptor methods of classifying Type 1s and 2s is inconclusive, especially for female alcoholics. The Type 1/2 literature, although often misunderstood and misquoted, has made an impact in the fields of alcohol research and treatment. It has promulgated the notion of heterogeneity among alcoholics and this has been a major contribution. On the other hand, Type 1/2 is frequently referred to by practitioners as "the two types of alcoholism", as if conclusively established; this conclusion is premature and over-simplified. In addition, the idea of two dichotomous types of alcoholics has enforced the notion of categorical classification systems in attempting to describe alcoholic samples, which has yet to be established as the most accurate or efficient way to describe psychopathology.

Type A/B

The A/B typology, briefly described, is a more recent attempt to use several dimensions of description. Seventeen variables, broken down into four domains, were used originally to differentiate two groups of alcoholics (Babor et al., 1992) and are listed in Table 4.7.

Several studies have been published since 1992 to test the replicability and validity of the A/B distinction, reviewed in more detail elsewhere (Ball, 1996). Both alcohol-only and other drug-using samples have been assessed, as well as both males and females. In general, the A/B distinction has been supported and is in fact beginning to replace the Type 1/2 schema as the most popular and more often researched typology in the field. However, methodological issues must be raised here also. For instance, all studies have reported replication of the A/B distinction; however, all studies have used a statistical analysis that automatically and perhaps artificially creates two groups for every data set examined (Bux, 1999; Grove, 1991). Also, almost every study published has been authored by at least one investigator from the laboratory that originally published on the A/B typology; thus, this schema must be verified by independent research groups. Initial findings from two studies done by an independent research team indicate that more than two clusters may be the most appropriate way to classify alcoholics, if at all. Epstein et al. (1998) attempted to replicate the A/B typology with a heterogeneous sample of treatment and non-treatment seeking males and females and found five clusters, although only three of these had numbers large enough to consider. Cluster 3 had severe dependence but no psychopathology or vulnerability indicators; cluster 4 had high vulnerability indicators, high dependence severity and high psychopathology, like the classic Type B; and cluster 5 showed fairly mild dependence severity, low vulnerability indicators and low psychopathology, like the classic Type A.

Bux (1999), in a careful and comprehensive study to clarify analytic issues related to the A/B typology, found the following: (a) the original two-cluster solution did optimally divide the sample and seemed to replicate Babor et al.'s (1992) and others' findings; (b) this two-cluster solution was based on severity of alcohol use in the sample; (c) the bi-modality of severity in the sample was not conclusive and severity was better described along a continuum; (d) cluster analysis of the 17 original variables minus the severity-related variables resulted in four or five clusters based on comorbid drug use, anxiety and depression symptoms, and antisocial traits.

Given the relatively short history of the A/B typology, the amount of good research it has generated and the focus it has taken off of the older, less reliable Type 1/2 schema is a positive step. However, the A/B typology may reflect simply a continuum of severity of alcohol dependence and several typology researchers are looking again to the more theoretical schemas, which examine combinations of severity and several comorbid psychiatric conditions, such as depression and antisocial personality, to describe the heterogeneity in alcoholic populations (Bux et al., 1998; Epstein et al., 1994, 1998).

ISSUES RELATED TO DIFFERENTIAL AND ACCURATE DIAGNOSES: PSYCHIATRIC AND MEDICAL DISORDER AND CULTURAL FACTORS

Comorbidity of Substance Use Disorders and Other Psychiatric Disorders

A large body of scientific literature has amassed in a collective effort to untangle the relationships between alcohol and comorbid psychiatric disorders (see also Chapter 34, this volume). Understanding of these relationships has clear implications for clarifying etiology and processes of all disorders involved, as well as development of targeted, effective treatments of both alcohol use and other psychiatric disorders. Alcoholic individuals with other psychiatric comorbidity have a worse clinical course and outcome (Merikangas et al., 1998). Disorders most commonly associated with alcohol use problems and dependence include depression, anxiety and antisocial personality, both in community (Farrell et al., 1998; Grant & Harford, 1995; Helzer & Pryzbeck, 1988; Kessler et al., 1997; Merikangas et al., 1998; Robins, Locke & Regier, 1990) and treatment-seeking samples (Ross, Glaser & Germanson, 1988).

The relationship between alcohol use disorders and depression, for instance, remains unclear, with varied rates of comorbid depression ranging from 2% to 53% reported in the literature (Grant, Hasin & Dawson, 1996). Over the past 25 years, the research has become increasingly sophisticated, shedding light on possible reasons for the wide range in rates of comorbid depression.

The term "primary" has been somewhat problematic in the literature, since it can suggest causation, imply greater significance or simply independence, or can refer to temporal patterning in onset *vis à vis* substance use problems. In the more recent studies, the temporal patterning criterion has typically been used, that is, life-time onset of major depression must precede life-time onset of substance abuse or dependence. Similarly, "secondary depression" usually means that onset of major depression occurs after the onset of an alcohol diagnosis.

Differentiating between depression that is primary versus secondary to substance use can be difficult. Since alcohol is a central nervous system depressant, individuals who drink heavily over time often present with symptoms of depression which are identical to such symptoms in non-alcoholic, depressed samples and are often diagnosable as a major depressive episode, yet they often subside within a few days to weeks of abstinence (Raimo & Schuckit, 1998). Also, withdrawal from certain drugs can mimic features of major depressive disorder. In contrast, some patients are alcohol- or drug-dependent and also have a depressive disorder that needs to be addressed independently of the alcohol problem.

Similarly, confusion between substance abuse and ASP, and a variety of instruments used across studies to make the diagnoses, may result in varied rates of comorbid ASP reported, from 25% to 50%. There is ample evidence that alcoholics with ASP generally have a more severe course and worse treatment response than other substance abusers (Mueser, Drake & Wallach, 1998). Typology research has confirmed these findings. As Sellman (1994) notes, alcoholism began in DSM-1 (APA, 1952) as part of Sociopathic Personality Disorder and has since been classified independently of any psychiatric disorders. As typology research progresses, more evidence accumulates for a strong link between Alcohol Disorders and Comorbid Psychiatric Disorders, both Axis I and II. As Sellman (1994) asks, "Is diagnosis of alcoholism in the future a partial return to the past?" (p. 207).

Other research has focused on severe mental illness. Forty-seven percent of individuals with schizophrenia and 56% of those with bipolar disorder have lifetime diagnoses of substance abuse or dependence (Cary & Correia, 1998). A further area of investigation into comorbidity has been on PTSD, which is associated with an elevated rate of alcohol use problems (Langley, 1997).

In summary, in terms of diagnosis, comorbid psychiatric disorders in alcoholic populations complicate matters considerably, especially when anxiety, depressive and antisocial symptoms are present. Many of these symptoms mimic legal, social, psychological and withdrawal-related symptoms of alcohol dependence. Four basic models link alcohol disorders with other psychiatric disorders (*Alcohol & Health*: National Institute and Alcohol Abuse & Alcoholism, 1993): (1) the "secondary alcoholism model," whereby psychiatric disorder causes or precedes the alcohol disorder; (2) the "secondary psychiatric disorder model," whereby the alcohol disorder causes or precedes the psychiatric disorder; (c) the "common factor model," where a third factor common to both the psychiatric and the alcohol disorder causes both; and (d) the "bi-directional model," where the alcohol and psychiatric disorders have reciprocal interaction effects on one another. In the DSM-IV there is a provision to assign diagnoses such as Substance-induced Mood Disorder, when the mood symptoms are clearly the result of alcohol or drug use. However, it is difficult to assign causality conclusively, so these diagnoses should be used with care.

Medical Conditions That Are Complicated or Exacerbated by Alcohol Use Disorders

Alcohol use disorders and dependence have deleterious effects on several body systems. This type of knowledge is important for diagnosis of both alcohol and medical disorders— to diagnose Harmful Use, for instance, which requires that medical and psychological harm be done already. Also, the information can help determine severity of the alcohol disorder, perhaps be used as motivational feedback to patients who are undecided about whether to stop drinking, and help the medical practitioner diagnose and treat particular medical problems related to alcohol use.

In terms of diagnostic confusion of alcohol use disorders, the DSM-IV specifies a separate category, Mental Disorder Due to a General Medical Condition, if the symptoms are thought to be physiologically resultant from medical disorders such as diabetic acidosis, cerebellar ataxias and other neurological conditions, hypoglycemia and diabetic keto-acdiosis. Individuals may be suffering from a medical disorder but thought to be either intoxicated or going through withdrawal from alcohol.

Briefly, alcohol has been shown to adversely effect the liver, the pancreas, the cardiovascular system to increase the risk of coronary artery disease and other cardiovascular diseases such as hypertension, arrhythmias, cardiomyopathy (heart muscle disease) and stroke, the immune system, cancers of the upper airways, mouth, and liver, the endocrine system, and also to cause neurologic disorders in both the alcoholic and in the female alcoholic's fetus (see National Institute on Alcohol Abuse and Alcoholism, 1993, Stein, 1997; see Part II, this volume, for a more complete discussion of alcohol and medical complications).

FUTURE DIRECTIONS FOR CLASSIFICATION OF ALCOHOL-RELATED PROBLEMS AND ALCOHOL DEPENDENCE

The DSM-IV Substance Use Disorders Work Group and the WHO-ADAMHA Task Force on Alcohol and Drugs may have set a new standard for establishing, evaluating and revising diagnostic classifications for substance use disorders. It will undoubtedly be difficult to justify future revisions to our classification systems based on anything less than empirical evidence. The DSM-IV Work Group had its strengths and limitations (see Cottler et al., 1995; Babor, 1995; Grant, 1995; Rounsaville, 1995), as do most projects of this magnitude and complexity. Research is in progress evaluating the reliability and validity of the DSM-IV criteria (Schuckit, 1994; Carroll, Rounsaville & Kendall, 1994), as are long-term preparations for the DSM-V (Rounsaville, 1995).

For instance, Schuckit et al. (1998) have examined the meaningfulness of distinguishing between alcohol dependence with and without physiological dependence (either tolerance or withdrawal) in a sample of 3395 subjects. Eighty-seven percent of the sample had either tolerance or withdrawal. Of these, 51% had withdrawal symptoms. Subjects with physiological dependence evidenced a more severe form of Alcohol Dependence based on several clinical indicators, thus supporting the clinical efficacy of the "with/without physiological dependence" distinction in DSM-IV. Furthermore, evidence suggested that the "withdrawal" criterion was more useful than the "tolerance" criterion in predicting the most severe clinical course.

Langenbucher et al. (1997) addressed a similar question, using a sample of subjects in treatment, and unlike Schuckit et al.'s (1998) group, found that tolerance and withdrawal not only did not put patients at risk for more immediate medical problems and a higher relapse rate but actually seemed to lower the risk for drinking during the 6 month follow-up period tested. Langenbucher et al. conclude, however, that "physiological alcohol dependence fails as a course specifier, not because it lacks merit at the conceptual level, but rather because it is not well operationalized in the DSM-IV" (p. 348). Langenbucher et al. (1997) suggest instead a multistage criterion method for "coding the severity of physiological dependence, with multiple exemplars for innate and acquired tolerance, mild and severe withdrawal, use to avoid withdrawal, preference for high-proof beverages, evidence of sustained high intake, and so on" (p. 349).

Langenbucher et al. (1996) have also studied the question of criterion weighting in the DSM-IV and cite the example of the National Council on Alcoholism (1972) Criteria Committee method of using major and minor symptoms in diagnosing alcoholism. The DSM-III essentially used a weighting system, in that tolerance or withdrawal had to be endorsed in order for a person to qualify for an Alcohol Dependence diagnosis; this system was changed with DSM-III-R. The Langenbucher study pointed to an alternative, experimental system of factorially complex criteria, including tolerance, severe withdrawal, loss of control, attempts to exert control, obsessive use, salience and negative consequences.

In yet another study, Langenbucher & Chung (1995) tested whether symptom sequencing of alcohol abuse and dependence symptoms provides evidence for the two disorders as separate or as a unitary disease concept. The data supported the notion that Alcohol Abuse, defined as "hazardous use, heedless drunkenness, and social-legal consequences" (p. 353) is a discrete syndrome that is different from and is prodromal to Alcohol Dependence.

Others have tried to operationalize alternative, more dimensional approaches to psychiatric diagnoses of alcoholism (see section above on Alternatives to the Psychiatric Classification of Alcohol Problems). For example, Tarter et al. (1992) argue that evidence calls into question the notion of alcoholism as a "chronic stable" or progressive disorder, and suggest instead a taxonomy based on a continuous trait called "alcohol involvement," consisting of 10 domains: alcohol and drug use, psychiatric disorder, behavior disposition, health, social skills, social relationships, work, school, family, and recreation/leisure. These 10 domains can be assessed via a 149-item self-report inventory and yield scaled information about severity and functioning of the patient, useful for treatment planning, outcome research and capturing the heterogeneity in alcoholic populations, according to Tarter et al. (1992).

Research reviewed in this chapter is crucial to our understanding of the nature of alcohol problems and dependence, and for progress in terms of reliable and valid classification systems used in our clinics and research. Studies testing the validity of existing schemes, as well as those proposing and testing alternative systems, will allow us to base future conceptions and classifications of alcohol use disorders on thoughtful inquiry, clinical validity and empirical evidence. Systematic and scientific, hypothesis-based observation of these disorders can only further our ability to understand and treat individuals suffering from alcohol-related problems and dependence.

KEY WORKS AND SUGGESTIONS FOR FURTHER READING

Babor, T.F. (1992). Substance-related problems in the context of international classificatory systems. In M. Lader, G. Edwards & D.C. Drummond (Eds), *The Nature of Alcohol
and Drug Related Problems.* Oxford: Oxford University Press.

This article provides a concise historical overview and comparison of DSM and ICD
diagnostic systems.

Babor, T.F. (1992a). Diagnosis of alcohol abuse and dependence. In J.H. Mendelson
& N.K. Mello (Eds), *Medical Diagnosis and Treatment of Alcoholism.* New York:
McGraw-Hill.

This chapter's emphasis is on the diagnostic approach to alcohol abuse–dependence,
covering history, the concept of harmful use, the Alcohol Dependence Syndrome, subtyping and multiple assessment.

Edwards, G. & Gross, M.M. (1976). Alcohol Dependence: provisional description of a
clinical syndrome. *British Medical Journal,* **281,** 1058–1061.

The original description of the Alcohol Dependence Syndrome.

Heather, N. & Robertson, I. (1997). *Problem Drinking,* 3rd edn. Oxford: Oxford University Press.

This is the central text to learn about alternatives to categorical diagnostic approaches.

Jellinek, E.M. (1960). *The Disease Concept of Alcoholism.* New Haven, CT: Hillhouse.

The classic text describing the early classification of alcoholism.

Room, R. (1998). Alcohol and drug disorders in the international classification of
diseases: a shifting kaleidoscope. *Drug & Alcohol Review,* **17,** 305–317.

This article proves an historical overview of the development of the Alcohol Dependence Syndrome and ICD alcohol and drug diagnostic categories.

Sellman, D. (1994). Alcoholism: development of the diagnostic concept. *Australian & New
Zealand Journal of Psychiatry,* **28,** 205–211.

This article traces diagnostic concepts over the past 40 years and compares the DSM
and ICD systems.

REFERENCES

American Psychiatric Association (APA) (1952). *Diagnostic and Statistical Manual of Mental Dis-
orders,* 1st edn. Washington, DC: APA.
American Psychiatric Association (APA) (1968). *Diagnostic and Statistical Manual of Mental
Disorders,* 2nd edn. Washington, DC: APA.
American Psychiatric Association (APA) (1980). *Diagnostic and Statistical Manual of Mental Dis-
orders,* 3rd edn. Washington, DC: APA.
American Psychiatric Association (APA) (1987). *Diagnostic and Statistical Manual of Mental
Disorders,* 3rd edn (revised). Washington, DC: APA.
American Psychiatric Association (APA) (1994). *Diagnostic and Statistical Manual of Mental Dis-
orders,* 4th edn. Washington, DC: APA.
Babor, T.F. (1992a). Diagnosis of alcohol abuse and dependence. In J.H. Mendelson & N.K. Mello
(Eds), *Medical Diagnosis and Treatment of Alcoholism* (pp. 1–24). New York: McGraw-Hill, Inc.

Babor, T.F. (1992b). Substance-related problems in the context of international classificatory systems. In M. Lader, G. Edwards & D.C. Drummond (Eds), *The Nature of Alcohol and Drug Related Problems* (pp. 83–98). Oxford: Oxford University Press.

Babor, T.F. (1995). The road to DSM-IV: confessions of an erstwhile nosologist. *Drug & Alcohol Dependence*, **38**, 71–83.

Babor, T.F. (1996). The classification of alcoholics: typology theories from the nineteenth century to the present. *Alcohol Health & Research World*, **20**, 6–14.

Babor, T.F., Hofmann, M., Del Boca, F.K., Hesselbrock, V.M., Meyer, R.E., Dolinsky, Z.S. & Rounsaville, B. (1992). Types of alcoholics: 1. evidence for an empirically derived typology based on indicators of vulnerability and severity. *Archives of General Psychiatry*, **49**, 599–608.

Babor, T.F. & Dolinsky, Z.S. (1988). Alcoholic typologies: historical evolution and empirical evaluation of some common classification schemes. In R.M. Rose & J. Barrett (Eds), *Alcoholism: Origins and Outcome* (pp. 245–266). New York: Raven.

Babor, T.F. & Lauerman, R.J. (1986). Classification and forms of inebriety: historical antecedents of alcoholic typologies. In M. Galanter (Ed.), *Recent Developments in Alcoholism*, Vol. 1 (pp. 113–144). New York: Plenum.

Ball, S.A. (1996). Type A and Type B alcoholism: applicability across subpopulations and treatment settings. *Alcohol Health & Research World*, **20**, 30–35.

Bohman, M., Sigvardsson, S. & Cloninger, C.R. (1981). Maternal inheritance of alcohol abuse: cross-fostering analysis of adopted women. *Archives of General Psychiatry*, **38**, 965–969.

Bowman, K.M. & Jellinek, E.M. (1941). Alcohol addiction and its treatment. *Quarterly Journal of Studies on Alcohol*, **2**, 98–176.

Bruhl-Cramer, C. Von (1819). *Über Die Trunksucht and Eine Rationelle*. Berlin: Heilmethode Deserlben.

Bux, D.A. (1999). The Critical Evaluation of a Dichotomous Approach to Classifying Alcoholics (unpublished dissertation). Piscataway, NJ: Rutgers University.

Bux, D.A., Labouvie, E., Epstein, E.E. & McCrady, B.S. (1998). Validity and Utility of Type A/B Alcoholism. Paper presented at the Research Society on Alcoholism Annual Conference at Hilton Head SC, June.

Carpenter, W.B. (1850). *On the Use and Abuse of Alcoholic Liquors in Health and Disease*. Philadelphia: Lea & Blanchard.

Carroll, K., Rounsaville, B.J. & Kendall, J.B. (1994). Should tolerance and withdrawal be required for substance dependence disorders? *Drug & Alcohol Dependence*, **36**, 15–22.

Cary, K.B. & Correia, C.J. (1998). Severe mental illness and addictions: assessment considerations. *Addictive Behaviors*, **23**, 735–748.

Cloninger, C.R., Bohman, M. & Sigvardsson, S. (1981). Inheritance of alcohol abuse: cross fostering analysis of adopted men. *Archives of General Psychiatry*, **38**, 861–868.

Cottler, L.B., Schuckit, M.A., Helzer, J.E., Crowley, T., Woody, G., Nathan, P. & Hughes, J. (1995). The DSM-IV field trial for substance use disorders: major results. *Drug & Alcohol Dependence*, **38**, 59–69.

Crothers, T.D. (1911). *Inebriety: a Clinical Treatise on the Etiology, Symptomatology, Neurosis, Psychosis and Treatment and the Medico-legal Relations*. Cincinnati, OH: Harvey.

Del Boca, F.K. & Hesselbrock, M.N. (1996). Gender and alcoholic subtypes. *Alcohol Health & Research World*, **20**, 56–62.

Drew, L.R.H. (1987). Beyond the disease concept of addiction: towards an integration of the moral and scientific perspectives. *Australian Drug & Alcohol Review*, **6**, 45–48.

Drummond, C.D. (1992). Problems and dependence: chalk and cheese or bread and butter? In M. Lader, G. Edwards & D.C. Drummond (Eds), *The Nature of Alcohol and Drug Related Problems* (pp. 61–82). Oxford: Oxford University Press.

Edwards, G., Arif, A. & Hodgson, R. (1981). Nomenclature and classification of drug and alcohol-related problems: a WHO memorandum. *Bulletin of the World Health Organization*, **59**, 225–242.

Edwards, G. & Gross, M.M. (1976). Alcohol dependence: provisional description of a clinical syndrome. *British Medical Journal*, **281**, 1058–1061.

Edwards, G., Gross, M.M., Keller, M. & Moser, J. (1976). Alcohol-related problems in the disability perspective. *Journal of Studies on Alcohol*, **37**, 1360–1382.

Edwards, G., Gross, M.M., Keller, M., Moser, J. & Room, R. (1977). *Alcohol Related Disabilities* (WHO Offset Publ. No. 32). Geneva: World Health Organization.

Epstein, E.E., Ginsburg, B., Hesselbrock, V. & Schwarz, J.C. (1994). Alcohol and drug abusers subtyped by antisocial personality disorder and primary or secondary depressive disorder. *Annals of the New York Academy of Sciences*, **708**, 187–201.

Epstein, E.E., Kahler, C.W., McCrady, B.S., Lewis, K.D. & Lewis, S. (1995). An empirical classification of drinking patterns among alcoholics: binge, episodic, sporadic and steady. *Addictive Behaviors*, **20**, 23–41.

Epstein, E.E., Labouvie, E., McCrady, B.S., Jensen, N. & Hirsch, L. (1998). Alcoholic Subtypes: a Multisite Study of Clinical Validity. Paper presented at the Research Society on Alcoholism Annual Conference at Hilton Head SC, June.

Epstein, E.E., McCrady, B.S. & Hirsch, L.S. (1997). Marital functioning among early versus late alcoholic couples. *Alcoholism: Clinical and Experimental Research*, **21**, 547–556.

Farrell, M., Howes, S., Taylor, C., Lewis, G., Jenkins, R., Bebbington, P., Jarvis, M., Brugha, T., Gill, B. & Meltzer, H. (1998). Substance misuse and psychiatric comorbidity: an overview of the OPCS National Psychiatric Morbidity Study. *Addictive Behaviors*, **23**, 909–918.

Feighner, J., Robins, E., Guze, S., Woodruff, R., Winokur, G. & Munoz, R. (1972). Diagnostic criteria for use in psychiatric research. *Archives of General Psychiatry*, **26**, 57–63.

Fingarette, H. (1988). *Heavy Drinking: The Myth of Alcoholism as a Disease*. Berkeley, CA: University of California Press.

Gilligan, S.B., Reich, T. & Cloninger, C.R. (1987). Etiologic heterogeneity in alcoholism. *Genetic Epidemiology*, **4**, 395–414.

Glenn, S.W. & Nixon, S.J. (1991). Applications of Cloninger's subtypes in a female alcoholic sample. *Alcoholism: Clinical and Experimental Research*, **15**, 851–857.

Grant, B.F. (1995). Commentary No. 1. *Drug & Alcohol Dependence*, **38**, 71–75.

Grant, B.F. & Dawson, D.A. (1999). Alcohol and drug use, abuse and dependence: classification, prevalence and comorbidity. In B.S. McCrady & E.E. Epstein (Eds), *Addictions: A Guidebook for Professionals*. New York: Oxford University Press.

Grant, B.F. & Harford, T.C. (1995). Comorbidity between DSM-IV alcohol use disorders and major depression: results of a national survey. *Drug & Alcohol Dependence*, **39**, 197–206.

Grant, B.F., Hasin, D.S. & Dawson, D.A. (1996). The relationship between DSM-IV alcohol use disorders and DSM-IV major depression: examination of the primary-secondary distinction in a general population sample. *Journal of Affective Disorders*, **38**, 113–128.

Grove, W.M. (1991). Validity of taxometric inferences based on cluster analysis stopping rules. In W.M. Grove & D. Cicchetti (Eds), *Thinking Clearly about Psychology: Vol. 2: Personality and Psychopathology* (pp. 313–329). Minneapolis, MN: University of Minnesota Press.

Heather, N. (1995). Brief intervention strategies. In R.K. Hester & W.R. Miller (Eds), *Handbook of Alcoholism Treatment Approaches: Effective Alternatives*, 2nd edn (pp. 105–122). Boston, MA: Allyn & Bacon.

Heather, N. & Robertson, I. (1997). *Problem Drinking*, 3rd edn. Oxford: Oxford University Press.

Heather, N., Robertson, I. & Davies, P. (1985). *The Misuse of Alcohol: Crucial Issues in Dependence, Treatment and Prevention*. New York: New York University Press.

Helzer, J.E. & Pryzbeck, T.R. (1988). The co-occurrence of alcoholism with other psychiatric disorders in the general population and its impact on treatment. *Journal of Studies on Alcohol*, **49**, 219–224.

Hesselbrock, M., Hesselbrock, V., Babor, T., Stabenau, J., Meyer, R. & Weidenman, M. (1984). Antisocial behaviour, psychopathology and problem drinking: the natural history of alcoholism. In D. Goodwin, K. van Dusen & S.A. Mednick (Eds), *Longitudinal Research in Alcoholism* (pp. 197–214) Boston, MA: Kluwer-Nijhoff.

Hesselbrock, V., Hesselbrock, M., Stabenau, J. & Babor, T. (1985). Subtyping of alcoholism in male patients by family history and antisocial personality. *Journal of Studies on Alcohol*, **49**, 89–98.

Hester, R.K. & Miller W.R. (1995). *Handbook of Alcoholism Treatment Approaches: Effective Alternatives*, 2nd edn. Boston, MA: Allyn & Bacon.

Hill, S. (1994). Etiology. In J. Langenbucher, P. Nathan, B.S. McCrady & W. Frankenstein (Eds), *Annual Review of the Addictions*. Tarrytown, NY: Elzevier Science Inc.

Hodgson, R. & Stockwell, T. (1985). The theorectical and empirical basis of the alcohol dependence model: a social learning perspective. In N. Heather, I. Robertson & P. Davies (Eds), *The Misuse of Alcohol: Crucial Issues in Dependence Treatment and Prevention* (pp. 17–34). New York: New York University Press.

Huss, M. (1849). *Alcoholismus Chronicus Eller Chronisk Alkolssjukdom.* Stockholm.

Irwin, M., Schuckit, M. & Smith, T.L. (1990). Clinical importance of age at onset in Type I and Type 2 primary alcoholics. *Archives of General Psychiatry*, **47**, 320–324.

Jacobson, G.R. (1980). Detection, assessment and diagnosis of alcoholism: current techniques. In M. Galanter (Ed.), *Recent Developments in Alcoholism*, Vol. 1 (pp. 377–413). New York: Plenum.

Jellinek, E.M. (1960). *The Disease Concept of Alcoholism.* New Haven, CT: Hillhouse.

Kerr, N. (1893). *Inebriety and Narcomania.* London: H.K. Lewis.

Kessler, R., Crum, R., Warner, L., Nelson, C., Schulenberg, J. & Anthony, J. (1997). Lifetime co-occurrence of DSM-III-R alcohol abuse and dependence with other psychiatric disorders in the National Comorbidity Study. *Archives of General Psychiatry*, **54**, 313–321.

Kranzler, H.R., Babor, T.F. & Lauerman, R.J. (1990). Problems associated with average alcohol consumption and frequency of intoxication in a medical population. *Alcoholism: Clinical & Experimental Research*, **14**, 119–126.

Langenbucher, J.W., Chung, T., Morgenstern, J., Labouvie, E., Nathan, P.E. & Bavly, L. (1997). Physiological alcohol dependence as a "specifier" of risk for medical problems and relapse liability in DSM-IV. *Journal of Studies on Alcohol*, **58**, 341–350.

Langenbucher, J.W., & Chung, T. (1995). Onset and staging of DSM-IV alcohol dependence using mean age and survival-hazard methods. *Journal of Abnormal Psychology*, **104**, 346–354.

Langenbucher, J.W., Morgenstern, J., Nathan, P.E., Labouvie, E. & Miller, K.J. (1996). On criterion weighting in the DSM-IV. *Journal of Consulting & Clinical Psychology*, **64**, 343–356.

Langley, M. (1997). Posttraumatic stress disorder and addiction: What are the links? In N.S. Miller (Ed.), *The Principles and Practice of Addictions in Psychiatry* (pp. 279–296). Philadelphia, PA: W.B. Saunders.

Lender, M.E. (1979). Jellinek's typology of alcoholism: some historical antecedents. *Journal of Studies on Alcohol*, **40**, 361–375.

Liskow, B., Powell, B.J., Nickel, E. & Penick, E. (1991). Antisocial alcoholics: are there clinically significant diagnostic subtypes? *Journal of Studies on Alcohol*, **52**, 62–69.

Merikangas, K.R., Mehta, R.L., Molnar, B.E., Walters, E.E., Swendsen, J.D., Aguilar-Gaziola, S., Bijl, R., Borges, G., Caraveo-Anduaga, J.J., Dewit, D.J., Kolody, B., Vega, W.A., Wittchen, H. & Kessler, R.C. (1998). Comorbidity of substance use disorders with mood and anxiety disorders: results of the international consortium in psychiatric epidemiology. *Addictive Behaviors*, **23**, 893–907.

Miller, W.R. & Hester, R.K. (1995). Treatment for alcohol problems: toward an informed eclecticism. In R.K. Hester & W.R. Miller (Eds), *Handbook of Alcoholism Treatment Approaches: Effective Alternatives*, 2nd edn (pp. 1–11). Boston, MA: Allyn & Bacon.

Mueser, K.T., Drake, R.E. & Wallach, M.A. (1998). Dual diagnosis: a review of etiological theories. *Addictive Behaviors*, **23**, 717–734.

National Council on Alcoholism (1972). Criteria for the diagnosis of alcoholism. *Annals of Internal Medicine*, **77**, 249–258.

National Institute on Alcohol Abuse & Alcoholism (1993). *Alcohol and Health* (EEI Contract No. ADM-281-91-0003). Alexandria, VA: US Department of Health and Human Services.

National Institute on Alcohol Abuse & Alcoholism (1995). Diagnostic criteria for alcohol abuse and dependence. *Alcohol Alert*, **30**, 359.

Penick, E.C., Powell, B.J., Nickel, E.J., Read, M.R., Gabrielli, W.F. & Liskow, B.I. (1990). Examination of Cloninger's Type I and Type II alcoholism with a sample of men alcoholics in treatment. *Alcoholism: Clinical & Experimental Research*, **14**, 623–629.

Raimo, E.B. & Schuckit, M.A. (1998). Alcohol dependence and mood disorders. *Addictive Behaviors*, **23**, 933–946.

Robins, L.N., Locke, B.Z. & Regier, D.A. (1990). An overview of psychiatric disorders in America. In L.N. Robins & D.A. Regier (Eds), *Psychiatric Disorders in America: the Epidemiologic Catchment Area Study* (pp. 328–366). New York: Free Press.

Room, R. (1998). Alcohol and drug disorders in the international classification of diseases: a shifting kaleidoscope. *Drug & Alcohol Review*, **17**, 305–317.

Ross, H.E., Glaser, F.B. & Germanson, T. (1988). The prevalence of psychiatric disorders in patients with alcohol and other drug problems. *Archives of General Psychiatry*, **45**, 1023–1031.

Rounsaville, B.J. (1995). Commentary No. 3: data and diagnoses; A comment on the DSM-IV field trial for substance use disorders. *Drug & Alcohol Dependence*, **38**, 79–82.

Rush, B.N. (1785). *An Enquiry into the Effects of Spiritous Liquors on the Human Body*. Boston, MA: Thomas & Andrews.

Schuckit, M. (1994). Substance related disorders. In T. Widiger, A. Francis, H. Pincus, M. First & W. Davis (Eds), *The DSM-IV Source Book*, Vol. 1. Washington, DC: American Psychiatric Association Press.

Schuckit, M.A., Smith, T.L., Daeppen, J., Eng, M., Li, T.K., Hesselbrock, V.M., Nurnberger, J.I. & Bucholz, K.K. (1998). Clinical relevance of the distinction between alcohol dependence with and without a physiological component. *American Journal of Psychiatry*, **155**, 733–740.

Sellman, D. (1994). Alcoholism: development of the diagnostic concept. *Australian & New Zealand Journal of Psychiatry*, **28**, 205–211.

Stein, M.D. (1997). Medical disorders in addicted patients. In N.S. Miller (Ed.), *The Principles and Practice of Addictions in Psychiatry* (pp. 144–154). Philadelphia, PA: W.B. Saunders.

Tarter, R.E., Moss, H.B., Arria, A., Mezzich, A.C. & Vanyukov, M.M. (1992). The psychiatric diagnosis of alcoholism: critique and proposed reformulation. *Alcoholism: Clinical and Experimental Research*, **16**, 106–116.

Woodward, S.B. (1838). *Essays on Asylums for Inebriates*. Worcester, MS: Worcester Asylum.

World Health Organization (1967). *Manual of the International Statistical Classification of Diseases, Injuries, and Causes of Death*, 8th revision. Geneva: World Heath Organization.

World Health Organization (1978). *Manual of the International Statistical Classification of Diseases, Injuries, and Causes of Death*, 9th revision. Geneva: World Heath Organization.

World Health Organization (1989). *Manual of the International Statistical Classification of Diseases, Injuries, and Causes of Death*, 10th revision. Geneva: World Heath Organization.

World Health Organization (1992). *The ICD-10 Classification of Mental and Behavioural Disorders: Clinical Descriptions and Diagnostic Guidelines*, 10th revision. Geneva: World Heath Organization.

Part II

Clinical Pathology

Edited by Timothy J. Peters
King's College School of Medicine, London, UK

EDITOR'S INTRODUCTION

This section of the *Handbook* is concerned with the biomedical aspects of alcohol misuse. Why, the reader may ask, should a book dominated, rightly so, by the psychosocial aspects of alcoholism, particularly the treatment thereof, contain a whole section, rather than chapters or part chapters, on this topic?

It is clear that cell and molecular biology will increasingly dominate the behavioural sciences in the new millennium. Undoubtedly, molecular sociology will, as molecular psychology is already upon us, dominate the next two or three decades. All workers, even managers and administrators, in the health care field related to substance misuse will require a degree of biomedical knowledge. The chapters on the neuropharmacological basis of alcohol dependence clearly indicate the need for basic science knowledge for workers in the field. These studies clearly link to the genetic basis of alcoholism, well summarized by Cook and Gurling in Chapter 13.

Another important reason for the major emphasis on biomedical aspects of alcohol misuse relates to practical patient care. It is well recognized that alcoholic misusers, including both harmful drinkers and dependent alcoholics, frequently have associated medical disorders, with estimates of 80% being frequently reported. Similarly, the important progression from the hazardous to the harmful drinker category is generally related to the development of physical rather than psychosocial complications.

The physical or biomedical complications can affect all body systems and can imitate all pathological processes. All the pathological process and all the systems susceptible to alcohol-mediated damage are covered in the ensuing chapters. It is essential that any underlying pathologies, cirrhosis, hypertension, tuberculosis, HIV/AIDS and malignant disease, to name but a few examples of alcohol-associated disorders, are appropriately treated before embarking on the demanding journey of psychosocial rehabilitation. Failure to do so will damage any therapeutic relationship, reduce the chances of a favourable outcome, and may have important medico-legal consequences.

A further reason for being fully aware of the biomedical aspects of alcohol misuse is the role they play in therapist–patient interactions. Patients frequently perceive their alcoholism to have a biomedical rather than a psychosocial basis (Potamiano et al., 1985). This may be interpreted by behaviourists as conscious or subconscious attempts to shift the responsibility for their condition from themselves. However, if this is their concept of their condition, their medical attendants should at least initially respond to this belief.

The system-based chapters on biomedical complications pay particular emphasis to pathogenic mechanisms, including aldehyde toxicity, reactive oxygen species generation, and effects on metabolic pathways including redox and inhibition of protein synthesis. These are common themes in the aetiopathology of cellular damage in chronic alcohol misuse, although the relative importance of each varies from tissue to tissue, with dose–duration of alcohol use, the hormonal environs and often the age of the individual. Repair processes in the aftermath of abstention are encouragingly vigorous, but become more delayed as the subject ages.

Although this brief introduction has tended to highlight the differences between the biomedical and psychosocial consequences of alcohol misuse, in reality they are integral to the clinical problem, with several areas of overlap. A recently introduced approach to integrate the two aspects is the assessment of Quality of Life (QoL) in remitting and relapsing alcoholics. Although there are no alcohol-specific QoL instruments, the applications of generic instruments have emphasized the very low level of QoL for both physical and psychological domains (Foster et al., 1999). For example, applications of the Rotterdam Cancer Symptom Checklist to alcoholics after admission and detoxification indicates worse scores than patients with advanced head and neck or bladder malignancy (Foster et al., 2000).

These studies confirm the global impairment in such patients, have abstention prognostic indicators and have opened up new lines of research, as well as integrating the psychosocial and biomedical problems in these individuals (Foster et al., 1998).

REFERENCES

Foster, J.M., Marshall, E.J., Hooper, R. & Peters, T.J. (1998). Quality of life measures in alcohol-dependent subjects and changes with abstinence and continued heavy drinking. *Addiction Biology*, **3**, 321–332.

Foster, J.H., Powell, J.E., Marshall, E.J. & Peters, T.J. (1999). Quality of life in alcohol dependent subjects—a review. *Quality of Life Research*, **8**, 255–261.

Foster, J.H., Marshall, E.J., Hooper, R.L. & Peters, T.J. (2000). Measurement of quality of life in alcohol-dependent subjects by a cancer symptom checklist. *Alcohol*, **20**, 105–110.

Potamianos, G., Winter, D., Duffy, S.W., Gorman, D.M. & Peters, T.J. (1985). The perception of problem-drinkers by general hospital staff, general practitioners and alcoholic patients. *Alcohol*, **2**, 563–566.

Chapter 5

Molecular Basis and Metabolic Consequences of Ethanol Metabolism

Charles S. Lieber
Bronx Veterans' Affairs Medical Center and Mount Sinai School of Medicine, New York, USA

Synopsis

The main pathway of ethanol metabolism proceeds via cytosolic alcohol dehydrogenase (ADH) of the liver, which has multiple isoenzymes, the genetic polymorphism of which is now being unraveled in terms of its possible clinical implications. The latest ADH isozyme to be categorized is s ADH, which is prevalent in the upper GI tract and exhibits ethnic variability with lesser activity in the majority of Japanese. It was also known that hepatic catalase, located in the peroxisomes, can break down ethanol, but it is now realized that, except for unusual circumstances, this is a minor pathway. Three decades ago, a third pathway of ethanol metabolism was discovered, namely the microsomal ethanol oxidizing system (MEOS) which, contrary to the two other pathways, is highly inducible by chronic alcohol consumption, with a 4–10-fold increase of cytochrome P4502E1 (CYP2E1), associated with proliferation of the endoplasmic reticulum, both in experimental animals and in humans. This induction contributes to the metabolic tolerance against ethanol that develops in the alcoholic and spills over to other drugs which are microsomal substrates. Administration of pure ethanol with non-deficient diets, either to rats or man (under metabolic ward conditions), resulted in accelerated blood clearance, not only of ethanol but also of meprobromate, propanolol, antipyrine, tolbutamide, warfarin, diazepam and rifamycin (Lieber, 1992), which persisted for days to weeks after the cessation of alcohol, depending on the drug. During that period, drug dosage has to be increased to offset the enhanced breakdown and also because of the central nervous system tolerance to psychoactive drugs that develops in alcoholics.

There is also cross-induction of other microsomal enzymes, especially other cytochromes P450. These, as well as CYP2E1, activate scores of xenobiotics to highly toxic and carcinogenic metabolites. These include industrial solvents (bromobenzene, vinylidene chloride),

---

International Handbook of Alcohol Dependence and Problems. Edited by N. Heather, T.J. Peters and T. Stockwell.

*anesthetics (enflurane, methoxyflurene), commonly used medications (isoniazid, phenylbu-
tazone), illicit drugs (cocaine) and over-the-counter analgesics (acetaminophen, also called
paracetamol), all shown to be substrates and/or inducers of CYP2E1. Amounts of acetaminophen well within the therapeutic range (2.5–4 g/day) can cause hepatic injury and even
death in heavy drinkers.*

*The CYP2E1 induction also contributes to increased rates of superoxide and other radical
production, resulting in lipid peroxidation which correlates with the amount of CYP2E1. Furthermore, this induction of the microsomal system enhances acetaldehyde production which,
in turn, aggravates oxidative stress directly as well as indirectly: it impairs the defense mechanisms against oxidative stress by depleting glutathione (GSH) in various ways, including
binding to cysteine and/or provoking GSH leakage out of the mitochondria and of the cell.
The ultimate precursor of cysteine (one of the three amino acids of GSH) is methionine,
which must first be activated to S-adenosylmethionine (SAMe) by a synthetase which is
depressed in alcoholic liver disease. This enzymatic block can be bypassed by SAMe administration, which restores hepatic SAMe levels and attenuates parameters of ethanol-induced
liver injury. SAMe was now found to significantly reduce the mortality of patients with
cirrhosis.*

*SAMe also contributes to the methylation of phosphatidylethanolamine to phosphatidyl-
choline (PC). The activity of the methyltransferase involved is strikingly depressed by alcohol
consumption, but this can be corrected, and hepatic PC levels restored, by the administration
of a mixture of polyunsaturated PCs (polyenyl-phosphatidylcholine: PPC). Concomitantly,
PPC provides protection against the alcohol-induced rise in hepatic F_2-isoprostanes and
hydroxynonenal, products of lipid peroxidation, with prevention of CCl_4- and alcohol-
induced lipid peroxidation in rats and baboons, and attenuation of the associated liver injury,
including fibrosis, with prevention of cirrhosis.*

*Thus, elucidation of the metabolism of ethanol and its biochemical effects now provides
prospects for improved therapy, based on "cocktails" of antifibrotic and antioxidant agents
and inhibitors of CYP2E1 (when excessively induced) and correction of deficient nutrient
activation by providing SAMe and, possibly, polyunsaturated phosphatidylcholine.*

HEPATIC METABOLISM OF ETHANOL AND ITS CONSEQUENCES

Most tissues of the body contain enzymes capable of ethanol oxidation (Figure 5.1)
or non-oxidative metabolism, but significant activity occurs only in the liver and, to a
lesser extent, in the stomach. Hence, medical consequences are predominant in
these organs. Indeed, many of the metabolic and toxic effects of alcohol in the liver
have been linked to its metabolism in that tissue. Ethanol is readily absorbed from the
gastrointestinal tract. Only 2–10% of that absorbed is eliminated through the kidneys
and lungs; the rest is oxidized in the body. The relative liver specificity of the metabolism of ethanol, coupled with the high energy content of ethanol (each gram
provides 29 kJ, or 7.1 kcal) and the lack of effective feedback control of its rate
of hepatic metabolism, may result in a displacement, by ethanol, of up to 90% of the
liver's normal metabolic substrates and probably explains why ethanol disposal produces
striking metabolic imbalances in the liver. The extent to which ethanol becomes the
preferred fuel for the total body has been demonstrated in humans: it decreased total
body fat oxidation by 79% and protein oxidation by 39%, and almost completely abolished
the 249% rise in carbohydrate oxidation seen after glucose infusion (Shelmet et al., 1988).
Through each of its three pathways, ethanol produces specific metabolic and toxic

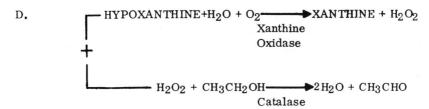

A. $$CH_3CH_2OH + NAD^+ \xrightarrow{\hspace{1cm}} CH_3CHO + NADH + H^+$$
$$\text{ADH}$$

B. $$CH_3CH_2OH + NADPH + H^+ + O_2 \xrightarrow{\hspace{1cm}} CH_3CHO + NADP^+ + 2H_2O$$
$$\text{MEOS}$$

C.
$$NADPH + H^+ + O_2 \xrightarrow{\hspace{1cm}} NADP^+ + H_2O_2$$
$$\text{NADPH Oxidase}$$

$$H_2O_2 + CH_3CH_2OH \xrightarrow{\hspace{1cm}} 2H_2O + CH_3CHO$$
$$\text{Catalase}$$

D.
$$HYPOXANTHINE + H_2O + O_2 \xrightarrow{\hspace{1cm}} XANTHINE + H_2O_2$$
$$\text{Xanthine Oxidase}$$

$$H_2O_2 + CH_3CH_2OH \xrightarrow{\hspace{1cm}} 2H_2O + CH_3CHO$$
$$\text{Catalase}$$

Figure 5.1 Ethanol oxidation by alcohol dehydrogenase (ADH) and NAD^+ (A), hepatic microsomal ethanol-oxidizing system (MEOS) and NADPH (B), a combination of NADPH oxidase and catalase (C), and xanthine oxidase and catalase (D). From Lieber (1992), with permission

disturbances and all three pathways result in the production of acetaldehyde, a highly toxic metabolite.

The Alcohol Dehydrogenase (ADH) Pathway and Associated Metabolic Disorders

ADH Isozymes

ADH is the liver's major pathway for ethanol disposition. One *raison d'être* of ADH might be to rid the body of the small amounts of alcohol produced by fermentation in the gut (Baraona et al., 1986). ADH has a broad substrate specificity, which includes dehydrogenation of steroids, oxidation of the intermediary alcohols of the shunt pathway of mevalonate metabolism and ω-oxidation of fatty acids (Bjorkhem, 1972); these processes provide the "physiologic" substrates for ADH.

Human liver ADH is a zinc metalloenzyme with several classes (Figure 5.2) of multiple molecular forms, which arise from the association of eight different types of subunits, $\alpha, \beta1, \beta2, \beta3, \gamma1, \gamma2, \pi$ and χ, into active dimeric molecules. A genetic model accounts for this multiplicity as products of five gene loci, ADH1 through ADH5 (Bosron et al., 1993). There

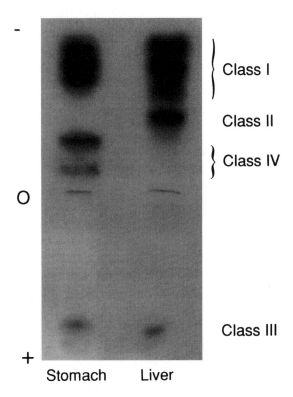

Figure 5.2 ADH isoenzymes in cytosol from liver and gastric mucosa obtained during surgery. Class II ADH is present in the liver but not in the stomach. By contrast, two bands of activity with slow cathodic mobility on starch gel electrophoresis are present in the gastric mucosa, but not in the liver. They correspond to class IV, or what has also been called μ- or σ-ADH. Data from Hernandez-Munoz et al. (1990)

are three types of subunit, α, β and γ in class I. Polymorphism occurs at two loci, ADH2 and ADH3, which encode the β and γ subunits. Class II isozymes migrate more anodically than class I isozymes and, unlike the latter, which generally have low K_m values for ethanol, class II (or π) ADH has a relatively high K_m (34 mM) and a relative insensitivity to 4-methylpyrazole inhibition. Class III (χADH) contributes to the metabolism of ethanol in the stomach (*vide infra*) but it does not participate in the oxidation of ethanol in the liver because of its very low affinity for that substrate. More recently, a new isoenzyme of ADH has been purified from human stomach, so-called σ- or μ-ADH (Class IV) and a cDNA encoding yet another new form of ADH (Class V) in liver and stomach was reported (Yasunami et al., 1991).

Metabolic Effects of Excessive ADH-mediated Hepatic NADH Generation

The oxidation of ethanol via the ADH pathway results in the production of acetaldehyde with loss of H which reduces NAD to NADH. The large amounts of reducing equivalents generated overwhelm the hepatocyte's ability to maintain redox homeostasis and a number

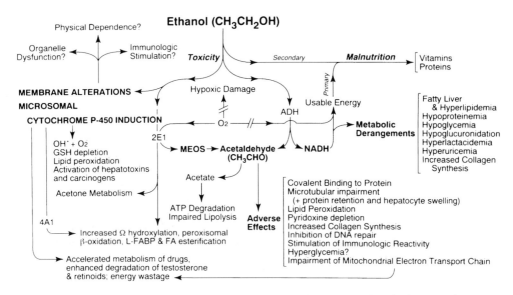

Figure 5.3 Hepatic, nutritional and metabolic abnormalities after ethanol abuse. Malnutrition, whether primary or secondary, can be differentiated from metabolic changes or direct toxicity, resulting partly from ADH mediated redox changes, or effects secondary to microsomal induction, or acetaldehyde production. From Lieber (1998), with permission

of metabolic disorders ensue (Figure 5.3) (Lieber, 1992), including hypoglycemia and hyperlactacidemia. The latter contributes to the acidosis and also reduces the capacity of the kidney to excrete uric acid, leading to secondary hyperuricemia, which is aggravated by the alcohol-induced ketosis and acetate-mediated enhanced ATP breakdown and purine generation (Faller & Fox, 1982). Hyperuricemia explains, at least in part, the common clinical observation that excessive consumption of alcoholic beverages commonly aggravates or precipitates gouty attacks. The increased NADH also promotes fatty acid synthesis and opposes lipid oxidation with, as a net result, fat accumulation (Lieber & Schmid, 1961).

The effects of ethanol were reproduced *in vitro* by an alternative NADH-generating system (sorbitol-fructose) and were blocked by a H^+ acceptor (methylene blue) (Lieber et al., 1959; Lieber & Schmid, 1961). The preventive effect of methylene blue against ethanol-induced fat accumulation was recently confirmed (Galli et al., 1999).

Hepatic Steatosis and Other Zonal Effects in the Liver

One of the earliest pathologic manifestations of alcohol abuse is the development of a fatty liver. Fatty acids of different origins can accumulate as triglycerides in the liver because of different metabolic disturbances: decreased hepatic release of lipoproteins, increased mobilization of peripheral fat, enhanced hepatic uptake of circulating lipids, enhanced hepatic lipogenesis (*vide supra*) and, most importantly, decreased fatty acid oxidation, whether as a function of the reduced citric acid cycle activity secondary to the altered redox potential (*vide supra*) or as a consequence of permanent changes in mitochondrial structure and functions (Lane & Lieber, 1966; Chedid et al., 1991; Lieber, 1992).

A characteristic feature of liver injury in the alcoholic is the predominance of steatosis and other lesions in the perivenular (also called centrilobular zone or zone 3) of the hepatic acinus. The mechanism for this zonal selectivity of the toxic effects has been postulated to involve a relative lack of oxygen (Videla & Israel, 1970). The low oxygen tensions (normally prevailing in perivenular zones) exaggerate the redox shift produced by ethanol (Jauhonen et al., 1982): ethanol increased the lactate: pyruvate ratio and decreased pyruvate more in hepatic venous blood than in total liver. In isolated rat hepatocytes, the ethanol-induced redox shift was markedly exaggerated by lowering the oxygen to a tension similar to those found in centrilobular zones. The process was also assessed in isolated perfused rat livers by varying the oxygen supply to produce the oxygen tensions prevailing *in vivo* along the sinusoid (Jauhonen et al., 1985). Hypoxia increased NADH, which in turn inhibited the activity of NAD⁺-dependent xanthine dehydrogenase, thereby favoring that of oxygen-dependent xanthine oxidase (XO) (Kato et al., 1990). It has been postulated that, due to the acetate derived from ethanol, purine metabolites accumulate and could be metabolized via XO. This process leads to the production of oxygen radicals, which may mediate toxic effects towards liver cells, including peroxidation. Physiological substrates for XO, hypoxanthine and xanthine, as well as AMP, significantly increased in the liver after ethanol, together with an enhanced urinary output of allantoin (a final product of xanthine metabolism). Allopurinol pretreatment resulted in 90% inhibition of XO activity, and also significantly decreased ethanol induced lipid peroxidation (Kato et al., 1990). Zonal distribution of some enzymes can influence the selective perivenular toxicity. Proliferation of the smooth endoplasmic reticulum after chronic ethanol consumption is maximal in the perivenular zone, with associated microsomal enzyme induction and related effects (*vide infra*). Furthermore, by means of immunohistochemical techniques, human ADH has also been demonstrated to be present mainly in hepatocytes around the terminal hepatic venule (Buhler et al., 1982). Thus, a presumably higher level of ethanol metabolism in the perivenular zone could contribute to the increased hepatotoxicity of ethanol in that area.

Pathogenic Role of ADH Polymorphism

Individual differences in the rate of ethanol metabolism may be genetically controlled. Furthermore, genetic factors influence the severity of alcohol-induced liver disease. Indeed, the frequency of an alcohol dehydrogenase 3 allele has been found to differ in patients with alcohol-related end-organ damage (including cirrhosis) and matched controls, suggesting that genetically determined differences in alcohol metabolism may explain differences in the susceptibility to alcohol-related disease (possibly through the enhanced generation of toxic metabolites) (Day et al., 1991), but this hypothesis has been questioned (Poupon et al., 1992).

Microsomal Ethanol Oxidizing System (MEOS)

Identification of the Pathway and of the Cytochromes P450 Involved

This new pathway has been the subject of extensive research, reviewed in detail elsewhere (Lieber, 1997b, 1999a). The first indication of an interaction of ethanol with the microsomal fraction of the hepatocyte was provided by the morphologic observation that alcohol consumption results in a proliferation of the smooth endoplasmic reticulum (SER) (Lane & Lieber, 1966). This increase in SER resembles that seen after the administration of a wide variety of hepatotoxins (Meldolesi, 1967), therapeutic agents (Conney, 1967) and some food additives (Lane & Lieber, 1967). Since most of the substances that induce a proliferation of the SER are metabolized, at least in part, by the cytochrome P450 enzyme system that is located on the SER, the possibility that alcohol may also be metabolized by similar enzymes was raised. Such a system was indeed demonstrated in liver microsomes *in vitro* and found to be inducible by chronic alcohol feeding *in vivo* (Lieber & DeCarli, 1968) and was named the microsomal ethanol oxidizing system (MEOS) (Lieber & DeCarli, 1968, 1970a).

That a distinct cytochrome P450 enzyme system is involved was shown by: (a) isolation of a P450-containing fraction from liver microsomes which, although devoid of any ADH or catalase activity, could still oxidize ethanol as well as higher aliphatic alcohols (e.g. butanol, which is not a substrate for catalase) (Teschke et al., 1972, 1974); and (b) recon-stitution of ethanol-oxidizing activity using NADPH-cytochrome P450 reductase, phos-pholipids, and either partially-purified or highly-purified microsomal P450 from untreated (Ohnishi & Lieber, 1977) or phenobarbital-treated (Miwa et al., 1978) rats. That chronic ethanol consumption results in the induction of a unique P450 was also shown by Ohnishi & Lieber (1977) using a liver microsomal P450 fraction isolated from ethanol-treated rats. An ethanol-inducible form of P450, purified from rabbit liver microsomes (Koop et al., 1982), catalyzed ethanol oxidation at rates much higher than other P450 isozymes. The puri-fied human protein (now called CYP2E1) was obtained in a catalytically active form, with a high turnover rate for ethanol and other specific substrates (Lasker et al., 1987). Con-trasting with hepatic ADH, which is not inducible in primates as well as most other animal species, a four-fold induction of CYP2E1 was found in biopsies of recently drinking subjects, using the Western blot technique with specific antibodies against this CYP2E1 (Tsutsumi et al., 1989), accompanied by a corresponding rise in mRNA (Takahashi et al., 1993). Other cytochromes P450 (1A2, 3A4) are also involved (Salmela et al., 1998). The induction of CYP2E1 contributes to the metabolic tolerance to ethanol that develops in chronic and heavy drinkers (Salaspuro & Lieber, 1978). In addition to this tolerance to ethanol, alcoholics tend to display tolerance to various other drugs. Indeed, it has been shown that the rate of drug clearance from the blood is enhanced in alcoholics (Kater et al., 1969a,b). Of course, this could be caused by a variety of factors other than ethanol, such as the congeners and the use of other drugs so commonly associated with alcoholism. Controlled studies showed, however, that administration of pure ethanol with non-deficient diets either to rats or man (under metabolic ward conditions) resulted in a striking increase in the rate of blood clearance of meprobamate and pentobarbital (Misra et al., 1971) and propranolol (Sotaniemi et al., 1981). The metabolic tolerance persists several days to weeks after cessation of alcohol abuse, and the duration of recovery varies depending on the drug considered (Hetu & Joly, 1985). Similarly, increases in the metabolism of antipyrine (Vessell et al., 1971), tolbutamide (Kater et al., 1969a,b; Carulli et al., 1971), warfarin (Kater et al., 1969b), propranolol (Pritchard & Schneck, 1977), diazepam (Sellman et al., 1975) and rifamycin (Grassi & Grassi, 1975) were found. Furthermore, the capacity of liver slices from animals fed ethanol to metabolize drugs such as meprobamate was increased (Misra et al., 1971), which clearly showed that ethanol consumption affects drug metabolism in the liver itself, independent of changes in drug excretion or distribution or hepatic blood flow.

Experimentally, this effect of chronic ethanol consumption is modulated, in part, by the dietary content in carbohydrates (Teschke et al., 1981), lipids (Joly & Hetu, 1975) and proteins (Mitchell et al., 1981).

It is now recognized that CYP2E1, in addition to its ethanol oxidizing activity, catalyzes fatty acid ω-1 and ω-2 hydroxylations (Laethem et al., 1993; Amet et al., 1994; Adas et al., 1998). Furthermore, acetone is both an inducer and a substrate of CYP2E1 (Koop & Casazza, 1985; Koop et al., 1989; Yang et al., 1990) (Figure 5.4). Excess ketones and fatty acid commonly accompany diabetes and morbid obesity, conditions associated with

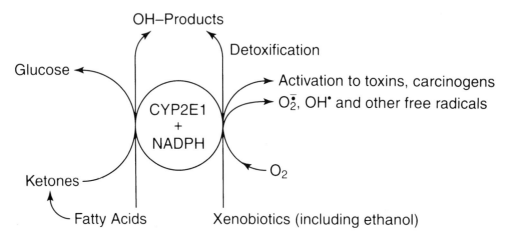

OH–Products

Detoxification

Glucose

Activation to toxins, carcinogens

CYP2E1
+
NADPH

$O_2^{\bar{}}$, OH$^\bullet$ and other free radicals

O_2

Ketones

Fatty Acids

Xenobiotics (including ethanol)

Figure 5.4 Physiologic and toxic roles of CYP2E1, the main cytochrome P450 of the microsomal ethanol oxidizing system (MEOS). Many endogenous and xenobiotic compounds are substrates for CYP2E1 and induce its activity through various mechanisms (see text), resulting in an array of beneficial as well as harmful effects. From Lieber (1999a), with permission

non-alcoholic steatohepatitis (NASH). Experimentally, obese, overfed rats also exhibit substantially higher microsomal ethanol oxidation, acetaminophen activation, and *p*-nitrophenol hydroxylation (monooxygenase activities catalyzed by CYP2E1) (Raucy et al., 1991). These diabetic rats are experimental models relevant to NASH, and indeed, the hepatopathology of NASH appears to be due, at least in part, to excess CYP2E1 induction (Weltman et al., 1998).

Clinically, a most important feature of CYP2E1 is not only ethanol oxidation, but also its extraordinary capacity to convert many xenobiotics to highly toxic metabolites (Figure 5.4), thereby explaining the increased vulnerability of the alcoholic. These agents include *industrial solvents* e.g. bromobenzene and vinylidene chloride, *anesthetic agents* e.g. enflurane (Tsutsumi et al., 1990) and methoxyflurane, commonly used *medications* (e.g. isoniazid, phenylbutazone), illicit drugs (e.g. *cocaine*) and over-the-counter *analgesics* (e.g. acetaminophen) (Sato et al., 1981), all of which are substrates for, and/or inducers of, CYP2E1. The effects of acetaminophen, ethanol, and fasting are synergistic (Whitecomb & Block, 1994), because all three deplete the level of reduced glutathione, a scavenger of toxic free radicals. Rats fed ethanol chronically have increased rates of GSH turnover (Morton & Mitchell, 1985), and ethanol produces an enhanced loss from the liver (Speisky et al., 1985). The selective loss of the compound from liver mitochondria (Hirano et al., 1992) contributes to the striking alcohol-induced oxidant stress and impairment of this organelle.

Role of CYP2E1 in Oxidative Stress and GSH Depletion

CYP2E1 generates several species of active oxygen (Figures 4.3, 4.4) which, in concert with a decrease in the level of GSH, promote injury by inactivation of enzymes and peroxidation of lipids. In patients with cirrhosis, hepatic depletion of α-tocopherol (Leo et al., 1993), a major antioxidant, potentiates this effect. GSH offers one of the mechanisms for the scavenging of toxic free radicals. Replenishment of GSH can be achieved

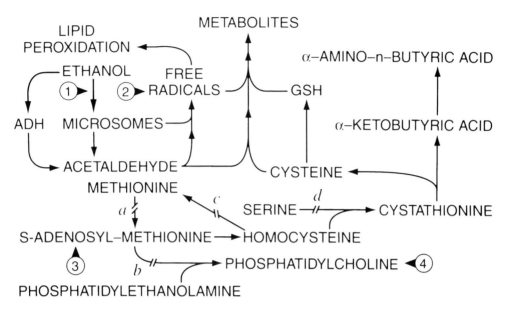

Figure 5.5 Lipid peroxidation and other consequences of alcoholic liver disease and/or increased free radical generation and acetaldehyde production by ethanol-induced microsomes, with sites of possible therapeutic interventions. Metabolic blocks caused by liver disease (a,b), folate (c), B_{12} (c) or B_6 (d) deficiencies are illustrated, with corresponding depletions in S-adenosylmethionine, phosphatidylcholine and glutathione (GSH). New therapeutic approaches include: (1) downregulation of microsomal enzyme induction, especially of CYP2E1; (2) decrease of free radicals, with antioxidants; (3) replenishment of S-adenosylmethionine; and of (4) phosphatidylcholine. From Lieber (2000), with permission

by administration of precursors of cysteine (one of the amino acids of this tripeptide) such as acetylcysteine or S-adenosyl-L-methionine (SAMe) (Lieber et al., 1990a; Lieber, 1999b) (Figure 5.5).

Methionine is not very useful to that effect. Methionine deficiency has been described and its supplementation has been considered for the treatment of liver diseases, especially the alcoholic variety, but excess methionine was shown to have some adverse effects (Finkelstein & Martin, 1986), including a decrease in hepatic ATP (Hardwick et al., 1970). Furthermore, whereas in some patients with alcoholic liver disease, circulating methionine levels are normal (Iob et al., 1967), in others elevated levels were observed (Fischer et al., 1974; Iber et al., 1957; Montanari et al., 1988). Moreover, Kinsell et al. (1947) found a delay in the clearance of plasma methionine after its systemic administration to patients with liver damage. Similarly, Horowitz et al. (1981) reported that the blood clearance of methionine after an oral load of this amino acid was slowed. Since about half the methionine is metabolized by the liver, these observations suggested impaired hepatic metabolism of this amino acid in patients with alcoholic liver disease. Indeed, for most of its functions, methionine must be activated to S-adenosylmethionine (SAMe) and, in cirrhotic livers, Duce et al. (1988) reported a decrease in the activity of SAMe synthetase, the enzyme involved, also called methionine adenosyltransferase (Figure 5.5).

Various mechanisms of inactivation of SAMe synthetase have been reviewed recently (Lu, 1998). One factor that may have contributed to the defect is relative hypoxia, with nitric oxide-mediated inactivation and transcriptional arrest (Avila et al., 1998). In addition, long-term alcohol consumption was found to be associated with enhanced methionine utilization and depletion (Finkelstein et al., 1974). As a consequence, SAMe depletion, as well as its decreased availability, could be expected and, indeed, long-term ethanol consumption under controlled conditions by non-human primates was associated with a significant depletion of hepatic SAMe (Lieber et al., 1990a). Potentially, such SAMe depletion may have a number of adverse effects. SAMe is the principal methylating agent in various transmethylation reactions which are important to nucleic acid and protein synthesis. Hirata & Axelrod (1980) and Hirata et al. (1978) also demonstrated the importance of methylation to cell membrane function with regard to membrane fluidity and the transport of metabolites and transmission of signals across membranes. Thus, depletion of SAMe, by impairing methyltransferase activity, may promote the membrane injury which has been documented in alcohol-induced liver damage (Yamada et al., 1985). Furthermore, SAMe plays a key role in the synthesis of polyamines and provides a source of cysteine for glutathione production (Figure 5.5). Thus, the deficiency in methionine activation and in SAMe production resulting from the decrease in the activity of the corresponding synthetase results in a number of adverse effects, including inadequate cysteine and GSH production, especially when aggravated by associated folate, B_6 or B_{12} deficiencies (Figure 5.5). The consequences of this enzymic defect can be alleviated by providing SAMe, the product of the reaction. SAMe is unstable, but the synthesis of a stable salt allowed for replenishment of SAMe through ingestion of this compound: blood levels of SAMe increased after oral administration in rodents (Stramentinoli et al., 1979) and in man (Bornbardieri et al., 1983). Although it has been claimed that the liver does not take up SAMe from the bloodstream (Hoffinan et al., 1980), other results indicated uptake of SAMe by isolated hepatocytes either at pharmacologic (Travers et al., 1984) or at physiologic (Pezzoli et al., 1978; Engstrom & Benevenga, 1987) extracellular levels. Results in baboons (Lieber et al., 1990a) also clearly showed hepatic uptake of exogenous SAMe *in vivo*. The effective use of SAMe for transmethylation and transsulphuration has been demonstrated *in vivo* (Giulidori & Stramentinoli, 1984).

Clinical trials also revealed that SAMe treatment is beneficial in intrahepatic cholestasis (Giudici et al., 1992) including recurrent intrahepatic cholestasis and jaundice caused by androgens or estrogens. Given either orally or parenterally, SAMe improved both the pruritus and the biochemical parameters of cholestasis, such as serum bilirubin, alkaline phosphatase and γ-glutamyl transferase. It was also used successfully in severe cholestasis of pregnancy (Frezza et al., 1984a,b) with few, if any, untoward effects. Especially noteworthy is a prospective, multicenter, double-blind, placebo-controlled trial (Frezza et al., 1984) performed in 220 inpatients with chronic liver disease (chronic active hepatitis and cirrhosis, including primary biliary cirrhosis) in whom serum markers of cholestasis and subjective symptoms significantly improved after SAMe. Oral administration of 1200 mg/day of SAMe for 6 months also resulted in a significant increase of hepatic GSH in patients with alcoholic as well as non-alcoholic liver disease (Vendemiale et al., 1989).

The most impressive therapeutic success was achieved in a recent long-term randomized, placebo-controlled, double-blind, multicenter clinical trial of SAMe in patients with alcoholic liver cirrhosis in whom SAMe improved survival or delayed liver transplantation (Mato et al., 1999). One-hundred-and-twenty-three patients with Child class A, B or C cirrhosis were studied for 2 years. The overall mortality or liver transplantation at the end of the trial was 30% in the placebo group and only 16% in the SAMe group, but the difference was not statistically significant ($p = 0.077$). However, when patients in Child class C were excluded, the overall mortality/liver transplantation was significantly greater in the placebo group (29% vs. 12%, $p = 0.025$), and differences between both groups in the 2-year survival curves were also significant. A compliance rate of greater than 75% in about 68–69% of patients was achieved, which is remarkable indeed, considering the nature of the population studied. An additional positive feature of this study is the confirmation of a virtually total lack of side effects of SAMe. Thus, despite a relatively modest number of subjects, the study of Mato et al. (1999) provides the first clinical demonstration of such a significant successful therapy of alcoholic cirrhosis in man.

Effects of Phosphatidylcholine (PC) Depletion

In the presence of liver disease, the activity of phosphatidylethanolamine methyltransferase is depressed (Duce et al., 1988), with significant pathologic effects. This enzymatic block can again be bypassed through the administration of the product of that reaction, in this case phosphatidylcholine (PC) (Lieber et al., 1994a) (Figure 5.5). This is emerging as potentially important approach to the treatment of liver disease.

Characteristic features of alcoholic liver injury include scarring or fibrosis and striking membrane alterations with associated phospholipid changes (Lieber, 1992). In an attempt to offset some of these abnormalities, polyunsaturated lecithin (extracted from soybeans) was fed to baboons given ethanol for up to 8 years (Lieber et al., 1990b). Whereas fibrosis or cirrhosis ensued in most of the baboons fed the diet with ethanol alone, no cirrhosis or septal fibrosis developed in the animals fed ethanol with the lecithin. The soybean lecithin extract used was rich in polyunsaturated phospholipids, with 55–60% phosphatidylcholine (PC). To assess whether PC was the active agent, a more purified extract was fed, comprising 94–96% PC. The feeding of this mixture rich in polyunsaturated PCs (PPC), especially dilinoleoylphosphatidylcholine (DLPC), which has a high bioavailability, exerted a remarkable protection against alcohol-induced fibrosis and cirrhosis (Lieber et al., 1994b).

Therapeutic Inhibition of CYP2E1

As reviewed above, the upregulation of CYP2E1 activity by ethanol results in increased generation of reactive radicals and toxic metabolites. Consequently, it has been suggested that CYP2E1 inhibitors may eventually provide useful tools for the prevention and treatment of the hepatotoxicity associated with heavy drinking. Indeed, experimentally, a decrease in the inducibility of CYP2E1 was found to be associated with a reduction in associated liver injury (French et al., 1997; Kim et al., 1997) but, when the liver pathology was semi-quantitated, it was only partially ameliorated by CYP2E1 inhibitors (Morimoto et al., 1993, 1995). Thus far, no corresponding human data are available, mainly because of lack of an agent suitable for chronic human use. Furthermore, the CYP2E1 inhibition was incompletely effective in reducing induction of CYP2E1 by ethanol. Whereas CYP2E1 inhibitors completely blocked lipid peroxidation, they only partially prevented other lipid abnormalities (French et al., 1997). Several inhibitors, such as chlormethiazole (Gebhardt et al., 1997), have been used and other effective inhibitors are being developed (Mathews et al., 1998) but there is still an unfulfilled need to obtain CYP2E1 inhibitors which are not only effective but also innocuous enough to be used chronically in humans. Polyenylphosphatidylcholine (PPC), a mixture of polyunsaturated phosphatidylcholine extracted from soybeans, may provide such a tool. PPC, and its main component DLPC, have an antifibrotic action (Li et al., 1992; Lieber et al., 1994a; Ma et al., 1996) and a striking capacity to oppose both CCl_4-and alcohol-induced oxidative stress (Lieber et al., 1997; Aleynik et al., 1997a,b). PPC also corrects alcohol-induced abnormalities in lipid metabolism (Navder et al., 1997a,b). Furthermore, recent results revealed a significant reduction by PPC feeding of the CYP2E1 induction by ethanol (Aleynik et al., 1998). Unlike some of the experimental CYP2E1 inhibitors referred to above, PPC is innocuous; it is currently being tested in humans.

Non-enzymatic Microsomal Ethanol Metabolism

In addition to the metabolism of ethanol to acetaldehyde via 2E1 through a typical monooxygenase mechanism, ethanol can be oxidized by liver microsomes through hydroxyl radicals (OH°), including those originating from iron-catalyzed degradation of H_2O_2 (Cederbaum, 1989). Such a non-enzymatic pathway is partially responsible for the formation of hydroxyethyl radicals (Knecht et al., 1993), an intermediate step between ethanol and its product, acetaldehyde. This mechanism may also explain the reported activity of ethanol as OH° scavenger in some experimental conditions (Cederbaum et al., 1977; Ohnishi & Lieber, 1978). Other evidence indicates that the production of such radicals might be due to an oxidizing species, possibly bound to cytochrome P450, and abstracting a proton from the alcohol α-carbon (Albano et al., 1994). This is also consistent with the inhibition of MEOS by adding iron chelators, such as 2-keto-4-thiomethylbutyric acid (Cederbaum et al., 1977). In fact, Ingelman-Sundberg & Johansson (1984) initially proposed that the microsomal ethanol oxidation does not involve a specific cytochrome P450-dependent mechanism, but rather results from OH° formed primarily in iron-catalyzed Haber-Weiss and Fenton reactions. Microsomal ethanol oxidation under *in vivo* conditions would, according to this concept, require the presence of non-heme iron. However, it was soon realized that this OH°-dependent mechanism represents only a minor contribution toward microsomal ethanol oxidation under normal conditions (Cederbaum, 1989). Its importance increased under experimental conditions promoting microsomal OH° production, such as adding ferric ethylenediaminetetraacetic acid (EDTA), and it decreased under conditions that minimize production of OH° (Cederbaum, 1989). Whereas OH° may participate in the activity of a reconstituted ethanol-oxidizing system, superoxide is not involved (Ohnishi & Lieber, 1978), although increased NADPH- and NADH-dependent production of superoxide and hydroxyl radicals by microsomes has been demonstrated after chronic ethanol treatment (Rashba-Step et al., 1993). It is not known, however, whether hydroxyethyl free radicals contribute to the damaging effects of ethanol. Hydroxyethyl radicals appear to be involved in the alkylation of hepatic proteins. *In vitro*-produced hydroxyethyl radical forms stable adducts with albumin or fibrinogen (Clot et al., 1995) and patients with alcoholic cirrhosis have increased serum levels of both IgG and IgA reacting with proteins of liver microsomes incubated with ethanol and NADPH (Clot et al., 1995), which do not cross-react with the epitopes derived from acetaldehyde-modified proteins.

The Catalase Pathway

Catalase is capable of oxidizing alcohol *in vitro* in the presence of an H_2O_2-generating system (Keilin & Hartree, 1945) and its interaction with H_2O_2 in the intact liver was demonstrated (Sies & Chance, 1970). However, its role is limited by the small amount of H_2O_2 generated (Ohnishi & Lieber, 1977) and, under physiological conditions, catalase thus appears to play no major role in ethanol oxidation.

The catalase contribution might be enhanced if significant amounts of H_2O_2 become available through β-oxidation of fatty acids in peroxisomes (Handler & Thurman, 1985). However, the peroxisomal enzymes do not oxidize short chain fatty acids such as octanoate, and peroxisomal β-oxidation was observed only in the absence of ADH activity. In its presence, the rate of ethanol metabolism is reduced by adding fatty acids (Williamson et al.,

1969) and, conversely, β-oxidation of fatty acids is inhibited by NADH produced from ethanol metabolism via ADH (Williamson et al., 1969). Similarly, generation of reducing equivalents from ethanol by ADH in the cytosol inhibits H_2O_2 generation, leading to significantly diminished rates of peroxidation of alcohols via catalase (Handler & Thurman, 1985). Various other results also indicated that peroxisomal fatty acid oxidation does not play a major role in alcohol metabolism (Inatomi et al., 1989). Furthermore, when fatty acids were used by Handler & Thurman (1985) to stimulate ethanol oxidation, this effect was very sensitive to inhibition by aminotriazole, a catalase inhibitor. Therefore, if this mechanism were to play an important role *in vivo*, one would expect a significant inhibition of ethanol metabolism after aminothiazole administration *in vivo*, when physiologic amounts of fatty acids and other substrates for H_2O_2 generation are present. A number of studies, however, have shown that aminotriazole treatment has a little, if any, effect on alcohol oxidation *in vivo* (Kato et al., 1987a,b; Takagi et al., 1986).

Despite the considerable controversy that originally surrounded this issue, it is now agreed by the principal contenders involved that catalase cannot account for microsomal ethanol oxidation (Teschke et al., 1977; Thurman & Brentzel, 1977). However, catalase could contribute to fatty acid oxidation. Indeed, long-term ethanol consumption is associated with increases in the content of a specific cytochrome (CYP4A1) that promotes microsomal ω-hydroxylation of fatty acids, which may compensate, at least in part, for the deficit in fatty acid oxidation due to the ethanol induced injury of the mitochondria (Lieber et al., 1997). Products of ω-oxidation also increase liver cytosolic fatty acid-binding protein (L-FABPc) content and peroxisomal β-oxidation (Kaikaus et al., 1990), an alternative but modest pathway for fatty acid disposition (*vide supra*).

EXTRAHEPATIC ETHANOL METABOLISM: OXIDATION OF ETHANOL IN THE STOMACH; GENDER AND ETHNIC DIFFERENCES

Extrahepatic metabolism of ethanol is low, except for the stomach, which is exposed to high ethanol concentrations that can support the activities of enzymes requiring such levels (such as ADH class IV and V). Alcohol was known to disappear from the stomach and this was considered to be part of its "absorption" from the gastrointestinal tract. It was quantitated postprandially by Cortot et al. (1986) in seven healthy subjects. They found that of the ingested alcohol, $39.4 \pm 4.1\%$ was absorbed through the stomach wall during the first postprandial hour and $73.2 \pm 4.2\%$ during the remaining time. It is now apparent that some of this absorbed ethanol is actually metabolized in the gastric wall.

It was also known that, when alcohol is taken orally, blood levels achieved are generally lower than those obtained after administration of the same dose intravenously (Julkunen et al., 1985a,b), so-called first pass metabolism (FPM). Many drugs undergo FPM, which usually reflects metabolism in the liver. However, several observations had shown that the gastric mucosa also contains enzymes with *alcohol dehydrogenase* activity. The histochemical observations of Pestallozi et al. (1983) showed that the majority of superficial mucosa cells in the stomach had significant amounts of such activity. In fact, the human gastric mucosa possesses several ADH isoenzymes (Hernandez-Munoz et al., 1990) (Figure 5.2), one of which is a class IV ADH (now called σ-ADH) and is not present in the liver. This enzyme has been purified (Stone et al., 1993), its full-length cDNA obtained and the complete amino acid sequence deduced (Farrés et al., 1994; Yokoyama et al., 1994). Furthermore, a nearly full length gene (*ADH7*) was cloned by Satre et al. (1994); the full-length gene was obtained by Yokoyama et al. (1996) and localized to

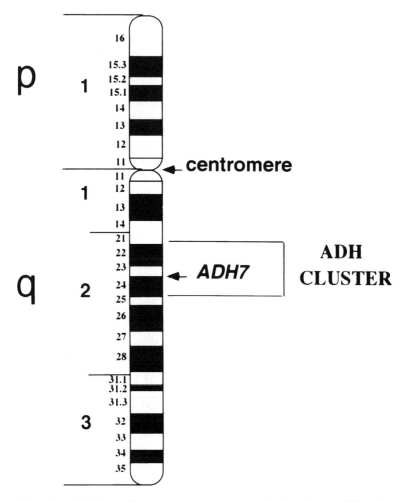

Figure 5.6 Mapping of *ADH7* on Chromosome 4. *ADH7* was found to be part of the cluster of other ADH isozymes. Data from Yokoyama et al. (1996)

chromosome 4 (Figure 5.6). The upstream structure of human *ADH7* gene and the organ distribution of its expression was also defined (Yokoyama et al., 1995). Sigma ADH was found to have a high capacity for ethanol oxidation, greater than that of the other isozymes. Its affinity for ethanol is relatively low, with a K_m of about 30 mM (Stone et al., 1993), but this is not a drawback in the stomach where ethanol is commonly present at much higher concentrations.

In vitro, gastric ADH was found to be responsible for a large part of ethanol metabolism found in cultured rat (Mirmiran-Yazdy et al., 1995) and human (Haber et al., 1996) *gastric cells*. However, the *in vivo* relative contribution of gastric and hepatic ADH to ethanol metabolism is still the subject of debate (Levitt & Levitt, 1994; Lieber et al., 1996; Smith et al., 1992; Sato & Kitamura, 1996) but studies of Lim et al. (1993) showed true gastric FPM in experiments using the same dose of alcohol given by either intragastric intubation or by intravenous, intraportal and intraduodenal infusions at a rate that mimicked

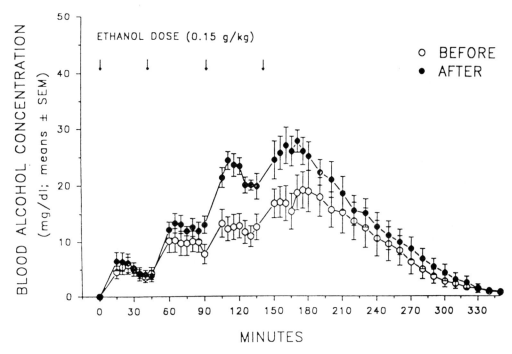

Figure 5.7 Effect of ranitidine (150 mg b.i.d. for 7 days) on blood alcohol levels after four small drinks in nine normal men. After repetitive drinking, blood alcohol levels reached clinically relevant concentrations. The decrease in FPM produced by ranitidine was associated with significant increases in blood alcohol to concentrations that are known to be accompanied by impairment of skills and judgement. From Arora et al. (1999), with permission

the loss of alcohol from the stomach. Furthermore, rats that had developed portosystemic shunts after ligation of the portal vein exhibited blood alcohol curves and FPM equivalent to those of sham-operated controls, indicating again that FPM is not dependent on first-pass flow through the liver, but reflects, at least in part, gastric metabolism (Lim et al., 1993).

The concept of ethanol metabolism in the stomach was also supported indirectly by the observation that commonly used drugs, such as *aspirin* (Roine et al., 1990), and some *H₂-blockers* (Caballeria et al., 1989), which decrease the activity of gastric ADH (Caballeria et al., 1989; Haber et al., 1996; Hernandez-Munoz et al., 1990; Mirmiran-Yazdy et al., 1995; Stone et al., 1995) and/or accelerate gastric emptying (Amir et al., 1996), also increased blood alcohol levels *in vivo*. This was particularly apparent after repeated intake of low alcohol doses, mimicking social drinking (Figure 5.7). Although questioned at first, such increases in blood levels have now been confirmed (Fraser et al., 1992; Palmer et al., 1991) for low ethanol doses. The blood level achieved by each single administration of such low doses is small, but social drinking is usually characterized by repetitive consumption of such small doses. Under those conditions, the effect of the drug is cumulative (Gupta et al., 1995), and the increase in blood alcohol becomes sufficient to reach levels known to impair cognitive and fine motor functions (Klein et al., 1967; Modell & Mountz, 1990; Moskowitz et al., 1985).

Some *ethnic* differences also support the concept of the role of gastric ADH in FPM of ethanol. Indeed, sigma-ADH is absent or markedly decreased in activity in a large percentage of Japanese subjects (Baraona et al., 1991). Their FPM is reduced correspond-ingly (Dohmen et al., 1996), in keeping with a predominant role for σ-ADH in human FPM. Thus, the FPM represents some kind of "protective barrier" against the systemic effects of ethanol, and its stimulation was invoked to explain some associated attenuation of liver damage (Battiston et al., 1994; Iimuro et al., 1996).

Gender differences have also been described: *women* have a greater vulnerability than men to the development of organ damage after chronic alcoholic abuse, in terms of both liver disease (Becker et al., 1996; Morgan & Sherlock, 1977; Parrish et al., 1993; Pequiqnot et al., 1978) and brain damage (Mann et al., 1992). It is noteworthy that in Caucasians, gastric ADH activity is lower in women than in men (Frezza et al., 1990b), at least below the age of 50 years (Seitz et al., 1993). There were associated higher blood alcohol levels, an effect more striking in alcoholic than in non-alcoholic women (Frezza et al., 1990b) because FPM is partly lost in the alcoholic (Di Padova et al., 1987), together with decreased gastric ADH activity. Furthermore, in women, the alcohol consumed is distributed in a 12% smaller water space (Frezza et al., 1990b) because of a difference in body composition (more fat and less water).

The magnitude of FPM also depends on the *concentration of the alcoholic beverages* used. Indeed, gastric ADH isozymes require a relatively high ethanol concentration for optimal activity (*vide supra*). Therefore, the concentration of alcoholic beverages affects the amount metabolized (Roine et al., 1991), with lesser FPM and higher blood levels after beer than whiskey (Roine et al., 1993) for equivalent amounts of ethanol. *Fasting* also strikingly decreases FPM (Di Padova et al., 1987), most likely because of accelerated gastric emptying, resulting in shortened exposure of ethanol to gastric ADH, and its more rapid intestinal absorption.

When alcohol is being metabolized in the stomach, it is converted to *acetaldehyde*, a toxic metabolite, and some resulting gastric injury can be expected. It is possible, of course, that alternatively, or in addition, alcohol may favor gastric injury in some other ways. For instance, the alcohol- (or acetaldehyde-)induced mucosal injury may promote implantation or persistence in the stomach of *Helicobactor pylori* (HP). An increased incidence of HP infection in the alcoholic has been observed (Pateron et al., 1990). Since both ethanol and the NH_3 generated by HP activate cysteine proteases (Nagy et al., 1996), they also could potentiate each other's gastric toxicity in a similar way and play a role in the pathogenesis of gastritis (Lieber, 1997a). Gastric NH_3 (and hence HP) can be eliminated with antibiotics (Lieber & Lefevre, 1957; Meyers & Lieber, 1976) and, with the eradication of HP, chronic gastritis usually resolves (Uppal et al., 1991).

NON-OXIDATIVE METABOLISM OF ETHANOL

Ethanol can form ethyl esters *in vivo*, and the corresponding enzyme has been purified (Mogelson & Lange, 1984). Laposata & Lange (1986) have found that, compared to controls, in short-term-intoxicated subjects, concentrations of fatty acid ethyl esters were significantly higher in pancreas, liver, heart and adipose tissue. Because in humans this non-oxidative ethanol metabolism occurs in the organs most commonly injured by alcohol abuse, and because some of these organs lack oxidative ethanol metabo-lism, Laposata & Lange (1986) postulated that fatty acid ethyl esters may have a role in the production of alcohol-induced injury. This was corroborated by more recent evidence for experimental pancreatic damage (Werner et al., 1997) but further experiments are needed to verify the possible role of this mechanism in the pathogenesis of alcohol-induced injury.

ACETALDEHYDE METABOLISM AND TOXICITY, INCLUDING GSH DEPLETION AND LIPID PEROXIDATION

Acetaldehyde, the product of ethanol oxidation, is highly toxic and rapidly metabolized to acetate, mainly by a mitochondrial low K_m *aldehyde dehydrogenase* (ALDH2), the activity of which is lacking in about 25–50% of Asians. In these individuals, even small amounts of alcohol that have almost no effect on Caucasians, can produce a rapid facial flush, frequently associated with tachycardia, headache and nausea (Wolff, 1973). This propensity for flushing is genetically determined and caused by decreased disposition secondary to the lack of ALDH2 activity (Goedde et al., 1979; Harada et al., 1979; Horowitz et al., 1981; Teng, 1981). In fact, the flushing reaction seen in susceptible Asians mimics to a lesser degree the disulfiram reaction caused by the elevation of acetaldehyde following aldehyde dehydrogenase inhibition. The latter reaction has gained widespread therapeutic use as a reinforcement for abstinence in alcoholism rehabilitation programs. Actually, the aversive cardiovascular effects of acetaldehyde may contribute to the relatively lower incidence of cirrhosis in "flushers" (Yoshihara et al., 1983). The flushing phenotype may also confer some resistance to the development of alcoholism (Harada et al., 1983). Conversely, however, Japanese alcoholics with an ALDH2 deficiency and, presumably, higher hepatic acetaldehyde levels during drinking, developed alcoholic liver disease at a lower cumulative intake of ethanol than controls (Enomoto et al., 1991).

The ALDH activity is also significantly reduced by chronic ethanol consumption (Hasumura et al., 1975). The decreased capacity of mitochondria of alcohol-fed subjects to oxidize acetaldehyde, associated with unaltered or even enhanced rates of ethanol oxidation (and therefore acetaldehyde generation because of MEOS induction: *vide supra*) results in an imbalance between production and disposition of acetaldehyde. The latter causes the elevated acetaldehyde levels observed after chronic ethanol consumption in men (Di Padova et al., 1987) and in baboons, which revealed a tremendous increase of acetaldehyde in hepatic venous blood (Lieber et al., 1989), reflecting high tissue levels.

Acetaldehyde's toxicity is due, in part, to its capacity to form *protein adducts*, resulting in antibody production, enzyme inactivation and decreased DNA repair (Lieber et al., 1989; Espina et al., 1988). It is also associated with a striking impairment of the capacity of the liver to utilize oxygen. Moreover, acetaldehyde promotes glutathione (GSH) depletion, free radical-mediated toxicity, and lipid peroxidation. Indeed, acetaldehyde was shown to be capable of causing *lipid peroxidation* in isolated perfused livers (Müller & Sies, 1983). *In vitro*, metabolism of acetaldehyde via xanthine oxidase or aldehyde oxidase may generate free radicals, but the concentration of acetaldehyde required is much too high for this mechanism to be of significance *in vivo*. However, another mechanism to promote lipid peroxidation is via GSH depletion. One of the three amino acids of this tripeptide is cysteine. Binding of acetaldehyde with cysteine and/or GSH may contribute to a depression of liver GSH (Shaw et al., 1983). Rats fed ethanol chronically have significantly increased rates of GSH turnover (Morton & Mitchell, 1985). Acute ethanol administration inhibits GSH synthesis and produces an increased loss from the liver (Speisky et al., 1985). GSH is selectively depleted in the mitochondria (Hirano et al., 1992) and may contribute to the striking alcohol-induced alterations of that organelle. GSH offers one of the mechanisms for the scavenging of toxic free radicals, as shown in Figure 5.5, which also illustrates how the ensuing enhanced GSH utilization (and thus turnover) results in a significant increase in α-amino-*n*-butyric acid (Shaw & Lieber, 1980). Although GSH depletion *per se* may not be sufficient to cause lipid peroxidation, it is generally agreed upon that it may favor the peroxidation produced by other factors. GSH has been shown to spare and potentiate vitamin E (Barclay, 1988); it is important in the protection of cells against electrophilic drug injury in general, and against reactive oxygen species in particular, especially in primates, which are more vulnerable to GSH depletion than rodents (Shaw et al., 1981).

Iron overload may play a contributory role, since chronic alcohol consumption results in increased iron uptake by hepatocytes (Zhang et al., 1993) and since iron exposure accentuates the changes of lipid peroxidation and in the glutathione status of the liver cell induced by acute ethanol intoxication (Valenzuela et al., 1983). It is also of interest that genetic factors may be involved. There is an apparent association between the occurrence of glutathione-S-transferase (GST) M1 "null" genotype and alcoholic liver disease, the "null" genotype indicating absent activity of class μ glutathione transferase (Savolainen et al., 1996). Other genetic factors have also been implicated: in addition to the ALDH2 deficiency and the CYP2E polymorphism (*vide supra*), a significant association, with alcoholic cirrhosis, of a particular restriction fragment length polymorphism (RFLP) haplotype of the COL1A2 locus of the collagen type I gene has been reported by Weiner et al. (1988) but questioned by others (Bashir et al., 1992).

EFFECTS OF ACETATE

Acetaldehyde is converted to acetate (Figure 5.3) but the role of the latter has been much less studied than that of the former, although acetate is by no means and inert product. Its various metabolic effects have been reviewed elsewhere (Israel et al., 1994). It is noteworthy that acetate was found (Liang & Lowenstein, 1978) to increase cardiac output, myocardial contractility and coronary and portal blood flow; the latter has been attributed to the adenosine formed (Carmichael et al., 1988). The effects of a rise of circulating acetate on intermediary metabolism in various tissues have not been well defined. In adipose tissue, acetate inhibits lipolysis (Nilsson & Belfrage, 1978), and it was found to be responsible, at least in part, for the decreased release of free fatty acids (FFA) and the fall of circulating FFA (Crouse et al., 1968). A fall in FFA, a major fuel for peripheral tissues, may have significant metabolic consequences. In the liver, acetate was also shown to promote steatosis (Morgan & Mendenhall, 1977).

ACKNOWLEDGEMENTS

Original studies reviewed here were supported by NIH grants AA05934, AA11115, AA11160, AA07275, the Kingsbridge Research Foundation and the Department of Veterans Affairs. Skillful typing of the manuscript by Ms D. Perez is gratefully acknowledeged.

KEY WORKS AND SUGGESTIONS FOR FURTHER READING

Ting-Kai, Li (2000).   Pharmacogenetics of responses to alcohol and genes that influence alcohol drinking. *Journal of Studies on Alcohol*, **61**, 5–12.

This review provides an excellent update on the new developments in the controversial field of the genetics of alcohol drinking.

Lieber, C.S. (2000).   Alcohol: its metabolism and interaction with nutrients. *Annual Review of Nutrition*, **20**, 395–430.

This is a comprehensive review of the progress in our understanding of the hepatic, metabolic and nutritional effects of alcohol through its interactions with other drugs, including their impact on pathogenesis and treatment.

REFERENCES

Adas, F., Betthou, F., Picart, D., Lozac'h, P., Beauge, F. & Amet, Y. (1998).   Involvement of cytochrome P450 2E1 in the (omega-1)-hydroxylation of oleic acid in human and rat liver microsomes. *Journal of Lipid Research*, **39**, 1210–1219.

Albano, E., Tomasi, A., Persson, J.O., Terelius, Y., Goria Gatti, L., Ingelman Sundberg, M. & Dianzani, M.U. (1991).   Role of ethanol-inducible cytochrome P450 (P450IIE1) in catalysing the free radical activation of aliphatic alcohols. *Biochemical Pharmacology*, **41**, 1895–1902.

Albano, E., Tomasi, A. & Ingelman-Sundberg, M. (1994).   Spin trapping of alcohol derived radicals in microsomes and reconstituted systems by electron spin resonance. *Methods in Enzymology*, **223**, 117–127.

Aleynik, M.K., Leo, M.A., Aleynik, S.I. & Lieber, C.S. (1998).   Polyenylphosphatidylcholine opposes the increase of cytochrome P4502E1 by ethanol and corrects its iron-induced decrease. *Alcoholism: Clinical and Experimental Research*, **23**, 96–100.

Aleynik, S.I., Leo, M.A., Aleynik, M.K. & Lieber. C.S. (1997a).   Polyenylphosphatidylcholine prevents carbontetrachloride induced lipid peroxidation while it attenuates liver injury and fibrosis. *Journal of Hepatology*, **27**, 554–561.

Aleynik, S.I., Leo, M.A., Takeshige, U., Aleynik, M. & Lieber, C.S. (1997b).   Dilinoleoylphosphatidylcholine (DLPC) is the active antioxidant of polyenylphosphatidylcholine (PPC). *Gastroenterology*, **112**, 1209.

Amet, Y., Berthou, F., Goasduff, T., Salaun, J.P., Le Breton, L. & Menez, J.F. (1994).   Evidence that cytochrome P450 2E1 is involved in the (ω-1)-hydroxylation of lauric acid in rat liver microsomes. *Biochemical and Biophysical Research Communications*, **203**, 1168–1174.

Amir, I., Anwar, N., Baraona, E. & Lieber, C.S. (1996).   Ranitidine increases the bioavailability of imbibed alcohol by accelerating gastric emptying. *Life Sciences*, **58**, 511–518.

Arora, S., Baraona, E. & Lieber, C.S. (2000).   Blood alcohol levels are increased in social drinkers receiving ranitidine. *American Journal of Gastroenterology*, **95**, 208–213.

Avila, M.A., Carretero, V., Rodriguez, N. & Mato, J. (1998).   Regulation by hypoxia of methionine adenosyltransferase activity and gene expression in rat hepatocytes. *Gastroenterology*, **114**, 364–371.

Baraona, E., Julkunen, R., Tannenbaum, L. & Lieber, C.S. (1986).   Role of intestinal bacterial overgrowth in ethanol production and metabolism in rats. *Gastroenterology*, **90**, 103–110.

Baraona, E., Yokoyama, A., Ishii, H., Hernandez-Munoz, R., Takagi, T., Tsuchiya, M. & Lieber, C.S. (1991).   Lack of alcohol dehydrogenase isoenzyme activities in the stomach of Japanese subjects. *Life Sciences*, **49**, 1929–1934.

Barclay, L.R. (1988).   The cooperative antioxidant role of glutathione with a lipid-soluble and a water-soluble antioxidant during peroxidation of liposomes initiated in the aqueous phase and in the lipid phase. *Journal of Biological Chemistry*, **263**, 16138–16142.

Bashir, R., Day, C.P., James, F.W., Ogilvie, D.J., Sykes, B. & Bassendine, M.F. (1992).   No evidence for involvement of type I collagen structural genes in "genetic predisposition" to alcoholic cirrhosis. *Journal of Hepatology*, **16**, 316–319.

Battiston, L., Moretti, M., Tulissi, P. et al. (1994).   Hepatic glutathione determination after ethanol administration in rat: evidence of the first-pass metabolism of ethanol. *Life Sciences*, **56**, 241–248.

Becker, U., Deis, A., Sorenson, T.I.A., Grønbaek, M., Borch Johnsen, K., Müller, C.F., Schnohr, P. & Jensen, G. (1996).   Prediction of risk of liver disease by alcohol intake, sex, and age: a prospective population study. *Hepatology*, **23**, 1025–1029.

Bjorkhem, I. (1972).   On the role of alcohol dehydrogenase in ω-oxidation of fatty acids. *European Journal of Biochemistry*, **30**, 441–451.

Bornbardieri, G., Pappalardo, G., Bernardi, L., Barra, D., Di Palma, A. & Castrini, G. (1983). Intestinal absorption of S-adenosyl-L-methionine in humans. *International Journal of Clinical Pharmacology, Therapy and Toxicology*, **21**, 186–188.

Bosron, W.F., Ehrig, T. & Li, T.-K. (1993). Genetic factors in alcohol metabolism and alcoholism. *Seminars in Liver Disease*, **13**, 126–135.

Buhler, R., Hess, M. & von Wartburg, J.-P. (1982). Immunohistochemical localization of human liver alcohol dehydrogenase in liver tissue, cultured fibroblasts and hela cells. *American Journal of Pathology*, **108**, 89–99.

Caballeria, J., Baraona, E., Rodamilans, M. & Lieber, C.S. (1989). Effects of cimetidine on gastric alcohol dehydrogenase activity and blood ethanol levels. *Gastroenterology*, **96**, 388–392.

Carmichael, F.J., Saldivia, V., Varghese, G.A., Israel, Y. & Orrego, H. (1988). Ethanol-induced increase in portal blood flow: role of acetate and A1- and A2-adenosine receptors. *Gastrointestinal and Liver Physiology*, **18**, G417–423.

Carulli, N., Manenti, I., Gallo, M. & Salvioli, G.F. (1971). Alcohol-drugs interaction in man: alcohol and tolbutamide. *European Journal of Clinical Investigation*, **1**, 421–424.

Cederbaum, A.I. (1989). Oxygen radical generation by microsomes: role of iron and implications for alcohol metabolism and toxicity. *Free Radicals in Biology and Medicine*, **7**, 559–567.

Cederbaum, A.I., Dicker, E., Rubin, E. & Cohen, G. (1977). The effect of dimethylsulfoxide and other hydroxyl radical scavengers on the oxidation of ethanol by rat liver microsomes. *Biochemical and Biophysical Research Communications*, **78**, 1254–1262.

Chedid, A., Mendenhall, C.L., Garside, P., French, S.W., Chen, T., Rabin, L. & the VA Cooperative Group. (1991). Prognostic factors in alcoholic liver disease. *American Journal of Gastroenterology*, **82**, 210–216.

Clot, P., Bellomo, G., Tabone, M., Aricò, S. & Albano, E. (1995). Detection of antibodies against proteins modified by hydroxyethyl free radicals in patients with alcoholic cirrhosis. *Gastroenterology*, **108**, 201–207.

Conney, A.H. (1967). Pharmacological implications of microsomal enzyme induction. *Pharmacology Reviews*, **19**, 317–366.

Cortot, A., Jobin, G., Ducrot, F., Aymes, C., Giraudeaux, V. & Modigliani, R. (1986). Gastric emptying and gastrointestinal absorption of alcohol ingested with a meal. *Dig. Dis. Sci.*, **31**, 343–348.

Crouse, J.R., Gerson, C.D., DeCarli, L.M. & Lieber, C.S. (1968). Role of acetate in the reduction of plasma free fatty acids produced by ethanol in man. *Journal of Lipid Research*, **9**, 509–512.

Day, C.P., Bashir, R., James, O.F., Bassendine, M.F., Crabb, D.W., Thomasson, H.R., Li, T.K. & Edenberg, H.J. (1991). Investigation of the role of polymorphisms at the alcohol and aldehyde dehydrogenase loci in genetic predisposition to alcohol-related end-organ damage. *Hepatology*, **14**, 798–801 [erratum, *Hepatology*, 1991, **15**, 750].

Di Padova, C., Worner, T.M., Julkunen, R.J.K. & Lieber, C.S. (1987). Effects of fasting and chronic alcohol consumption on the first pass metabolism of ethanol. *Gastroenterology*, **92**, 1169–1173.

Dohmen, K., Baraona, E., Ishibadsshi, H., Pozzato, G., Moretti, M., Matsunaga, C., Fujimoto, K. & Lieber, C.S. (1996). Ethnic differences in gastric sigma alcohol dehydrogenase activity and ethanol first pass metabolism. *Alcoholism: Clinical and Experimental Research*, **20**, 1569–1576.

Duce, A.M., Ortiz, P., Cabrero, C. & Mato, J.M. (1988). S-adenosyl-L-methionine synthetase and phospholipid methyltransferase are inhibited in human cirrhosis. *Hepatology*, **8**, 65–68.

Engstrom, M.A. & Benevenga, N.J. (1987). Rates of oxidation of the methionine and S-adenosyl-methionine methyl carbons in isolated rat hepatocytes. *Journal of Nutrition*, **117**, 1820–1826.

Enomoto, N., Takase, S., Takada, N. & Takada, A. (1991). Alcoholic liver disease in heterozygotes of mutant and normal aldehyde dehydrogenase-2 genes. *Hepatology*, **13**, 1071–1075.

Espina, N., Lima, V., Lieber, C.S. & Garro, A.J. (1988). *In vitro* and *in vivo* inhibitory effect of ethanol and acetaldehyde on O^6-methylguanine transferase. *Carcinogenesis*, **9**, 761–766.

Faller, J. & Fox, I.H. (1982). Evidence for increased urate production by activation of adenine nucleotide turnover. *New England Journal of Medicine*, **307**, 1598–1602.

Farrés, J., Moreno, A., Crosas, B., Peralba, J.M., Allali Hassani, A., Hjelmqvist, L., Jörnvall, H. & Parés, X. (1994). Alcohol dehydrogenase of class IV (δADH) from human stomach: cDNA sequence and structure/function relationships. *European Journal of Biochemistry*, **224**, 549–557.

Finkelstein, J.D. & Martin, J.J. (1986). Methionine metabolism in mammals. Adaptation to methionine excess. *Journal of Biological Chemistry*, **261**, 1582–1587.

Finkelstein, J.D., Cello, F.P. & Kyle, W.E. (1974). Ethanol-induced changes in methionine metabolism in rat liver. *Biochemical and Biophysical Research Communications*, **61**, 475–481.

Fischer, J.E., Yoshimura, N., Aguirre, A., James, J.H., Cummings, M.G., Abel, R.M. & Deindoerfer, F. (1974). Plasma amino acids in patients with hepatic encephalopathy. *American Journal of Surgery*, **127**, 40–47.

Fraser, A.G., Hudson, M., Sawyer, A.M., Rosalki, S.B. & Pounder, R.E. (1992). Short report: the effect of ranitidine on post-prandial absorption of a low dose of alcohol. *Aliment. Pharmacol. Ther.*, **6**, 267–271.

French, S., Morimoto, M., Reitz, R., Koop, D., Klopfenstein, B., Estes, K., Clot, P., Ingelman-Sundberg, M. & Albano, E. (1997). Lipid peroxidation, CYP2E1 and arachidonic acid metabolism in alcoholic liver disease in rats. *Journal of Nutrition*, **127**, 907S–911S.

Frezza, M., Pozzato, G., Chiesa, L., Stramentinoli, G. & Di Padova, C. (1984). Reversal of intrahepatic cholestasis of pregnancy in women after high dose S-adenosyl-L-methionine administration. *Hepatology*, **4**, 274–278.

Frezza, M., Surrenti, C., Manzillo, G., Fiaccadori, F., Bortolini, M. & Di Padova, C. (1990a). Oral S-adenosylmethionine in the symptomatic treatment of intrahepatic cholestasis: a double-blind placebo controlled study. *Gastroenterology*, **99**, 211–215.

Frezza, M., Di Padova, C., Pozzato, G. et al. (1990b). High blood alcohol levels in women. The role of decreased gastric alcohol dehydrogenase activity and first-pass metabolism. *New England Journal of Medicine*, **322**, 95–99.

Galli, A., Price, D. & Crabb, D. (1999). High-level expression of rat class I alcohol dehydrogenase is sufficient for ethanol-induced fat accumulation in transduced HeLa cells. *Hepatology*, **29**, 1164–1170.

Gebhardt, A.C., Lucas, D., Ménez, J.F. & Seitz, H.K. (1997). Chlormethiazole inhibition of cytochrome P450 2E1 as assessed by chlorzoxazone hydroxylation in humans. *Hepatology*, **26**, 957–961.

Giudici, G.A., Le Grazie, C. & Di Padova, C. (1992). The use of ademethionine (SAMe) in the treatment of cholestatic liver disorders: meta-analysis of clinical trials. In J.M. Mato, C.S. Lieber, N. Kaplowitz & A. Caballero (Eds), *Methionine Metabolism: Molecular Mechanism and Clinical Implications* (pp. 67–79). Madrid: CSIC Press.

Giulidori, P. & Stramentinoli, G. (1984). A radioenzymatic method for S-adenosyl-L-methionine determination in biological fluids. *Analytical Biochemistry*, **137**, 217–220.

Goedde, H.W., Harada, S. & Agarwal, D.P. (1979). Racial differences in alcohol sensitivity: a new hypothesis. *Human Genetics*, **51**, 331–334.

Grassi, G.G. & Grassi, C. (1975). Ethanol–antibiotic interactions at hepatic level. *Journal of Clinical Pharmacology and Biopharmacology*, **11**, 216–225.

Gupta, A.M., Baraona, E. & Lieber, C.S. (1995). Significant increase of blood alcohol by cimetidine after repetitive drinking of small alcohol doses. *Alcoholism: Clinical and Experimental Research*, **19**, 1083–1087.

Handler, J.A. & Thurman, R.G. (1985). Fatty acid-dependent ethanol metabolism. *Biochemical and Biophysical Research Communications*, **133**, 44–51.

Haber, P.S., Gentry, T., Mak, K.M., Mirmiran-Yazdy, A.A., Greenstein, R.J., Lieber, C.S. (1996). Metabolism of alcohol by human gastric cells: relation to first pass metabolism. *Gastroenterology*, **111**, 863–870.

Harada, S., Misawa, S., Agarwal, D.P. & Goedde, H.W. (1979). Studies on liver alcohol and acetaldehyde dehydrogenase variants in Japanese. *Hoppe-Seylers Z Physiol Chem*, **360**, 278.

Harada, S., Agarwal, D.P., Goedde, H.W. & Ishikawa, B. (1983). Aldehyde dehydrogenase isozyme variation and alcoholism in Japan. *Pharmacology, Biochemistry and Behaviour*, **18**, 151–153.

Hardwick, D.F., Applegarth, D.A., Cockcroft, D.M., Ross, P.M. & Cder, R.J. (1970). Pathogenesis of methionine-induced toxicity. *Metabolism*, **19**, 381–391.

Hasumura, Y., Teschke, R. & Lieber, C.S. (1975). Hepatic microsomal ethanol oxidizing system (MEOS): dissociation from reduced nicotinamide adenine dinucleotide phosphate-oxidase and possible role of form 1 of cytochrome P-450. *Journal of Pharmacology and Experimental Therapeutics*, **194**, 469–474.

Hernández-Muñoz, R., Caballeria, J., Baraona, E., Uppal, R., Greenstein, R. & Lieber, C.S. (1990). Human gastric alcohol dehydrogenase: its inhibition by H_2-receptor antagonists, and its effect on the bioavailability of ethanol. *Alcoholism: Clinical and Experimental Research*, **14**, 946–950.

Hetu, C. & Joly, J.-G. (1985). Differences in the duration of the enhancement of liver mixed-function oxidase activities in ethanol-fed rats after withdrawal. *Biochemical Pharmacology*, **34**, 1211–1216.

Hirano, T., Kaplowitz, N., Tsukamoto, H., Kamimura, S. & Fernandez-Checa, J.C. (1992). Hepatic mitochondrial glutathione depletion and progression of experimental alcoholic liver disease in rats. *Hepatology*, **6**, 1423–1427.

Hirata, F. & Axelrod, J. (1980). Phospholipid methylation and biological signal transmission. *Science*, **209**, 1082–1090.

Hirata, F., Viveros, O.H., Diliberto, E.J. Jr & Axelrod, J. (1978). Identification and properties of two methyltransferases in conversion of phosphatidylethanolamine to phosphatidylcholine. *Proceedings of the National Academy of Science of the United States of America*, **75**, 1718–1721.

Hoffinan, D.R., Marion, D.W., Cornatzer, W.E. & Duerra, J.A. (1980). S-adenosylmethionine and S-adenosylhomocysteine metabolism in isolated rat liver. *Journal of Biological Chemistry*, **255**, 10822–10827.

Horowitz, J.H., Rypins, E.B., Henderson, J.M., Heymsfield, S.B., Moffitt, S.D., Bain, R.P., Chawla, R.K., Bleier, J.C. & Rudman, D. (1981). Evidence for impairment of transsulfuration pathway in cirrhosis. *Gastroenterology*, **81**, 668–675.

Iber, F.L., Rosen, H., Stanley, M.A., Levenson, S.M. & Chalmers, T.C. (1957). The plasma amino acids in patients with liver failure. *Journal of Laboratory and Clinical Medicine*, **50**, 417–425.

Iimuro, Y., Bradford, B.U., Forman, D.T. & Thurman, R.G. (1996). Glycine prevents alcohol-induced liver injury by decreasing alcohol in the rat stomach. *Gastroenterology*, **110**, 1536–1542.

Inatomi, N., Kato, S., Ito, D. & Lieber, C.S. (1989). Role of peroxisomal fatty acid beta-oxidation in ethanol metabolism. *Biochemical and Biophysical Research Communications*, **163**, 418–423.

Ingelman-Sundberg, M. & Johansson, I. (1984). Mechanisms of hydroxyl radical formation and ethanol oxidation by ethanol-inducible and other forms of rabbit liver microsomal cytochromes P-450. *Journal of Biological Chemistry*, **259**, 6447–6458.

Iob, V., Coon, W.W. & Sloan, W. (1967). Free amino acids in liver, plasma and muscle of patients with cirrhosis of the liver. *Journal of Surgical Research*, **7**, 41–43.

Israel, Y., Orrego, H. & Carmichael, F.J. (1994). Acetate-mediated effects of ethanol, *Alcoholism: Clinical and Experimental Research*, **18**, 144.

Jauhonen, P., Baraona, E., Miyakawa, H. & Lieber, C.S. (1982). Mechanism for selective perivenular hepatotoxicity of ethanol. *Alcoholism: Clinical and Experimental Research*, **6**, 350–357.

Jauhonen, P., Baraona, E., Lieber, C.S. & Hassincn, I.E. (1985). Dependence of ethanol-induced redox shift on hepatic oxygen tensions prevailing *in vivo*. *Alcohol*, **2**, 163–167.

Joly, J.-G. & Hetu, C. (1975). Effects of chronic ethanol administration in the rat: relative dependency on dietary lipids. *Biochemical Pharmacology*, **124**, 1475–1480.

Julkunen, R.J.K., DiPadova, C. & Lieber, C.S. (1985a). First pass metabolism of ethanol: a gastrointestinal barrier against the systemic toxicity of ethanol. *Life Sciences*, **37**, 567–573.

Julkunen, R.J.K., Tannenbaum, L., Baraona, E. & Lieber, C.S. (1985b). First pass metabolism of ethanol: an important determinant of blood levels after alcohol consumption. *Alcohol*, **2**, 437–441.

Kaikaus, R.M., Chan, W.K., Lysenko, N., Ortiz, P., Montellano, D. & Bass, N.M. (1990). Induction of liver fatty acid binding protein (l-FABP) and peroxisomal fatty acid β-oxidation by peroxisome proliferators (PP) is dependent on cytochrome p-450 activity. *Hepatology*, **12**, A248.

Kater, R.M.H., Tobon, F. & Iber, F.L. (1969a). Increased rate of tolbutamide metabolism in alcoholic patients. *Journal of the American Medical Association*, **207**, 363–365.

Kater, R.M.H., Roggin, G., Tobon, F., Zieve, P. & Iber, F.L. (1969b). Increased rate of clearance of drugs from the circulation of alcoholics. *American Journal of Medical Science*, **258**, 35–39.

Kato, S., Alderman, J. & Lieber, C.S. (1987a). Respective roles of the microsomal ethanol oxidizing system (MEOS) and catalase in ethanol metabolism by deermice lacking alcohol dehydrogenase. *Archives of Biochemistry and Biophysics*, **254**, 586–591.

Kato, S., Alderman, J. & Lieber, C.S. (1987b). Ethanol metabolism in alcohol dehydrogenase deficient deermice is mediated by the microsomal ethanol oxidizing system, not by catalase. *Alcohol and Alcoholism*, **1**(Suppl), 231–234.

Kato, S., Kawase, T., Alderman, J. & Lieber, C.S. (1990). Role of xanthine oxidase in ethanol-induced lipid peroxidation in rats. *Gastroenterology*, **98**, 203–210.

Keilin, D. & Hartree, E.F. (1945). Properties of catalase: catalysis of coupled oxidation of alcohols, *Biochemical Journal*, **39**, 293–301.

Kim, N.D., Kwak, M.K. & Kim, S.G. (1997). Inhibition of cytochrome P450 2E1 expression by 2-(allylthio) pyrazine, a potential chemoprotective agent: hepatoprotective effects. *Biochemical Pharmacology*, **53**, 261–269.

Kinsell, L., Harper, H.A., Barton, H.C., Michaels, G.D. & Weiss, H.A. (1947). Rate of disappearance from plasma of intravenously administered methionine in patients with liver damage. *Science*, **106**, 589–594.

Klein, K.E., Breuker, K., Brüner, H. & Wegmann, H.M. (1967). Blutalkohol und Fluguntuchtigkeit. Versuch einer Erarbeitung von Richtwerten für die allgemeine Luftfahrt. *Int. Z. Angew. Physiol.*, **24**, 254–257.

Knecht, K.T., Thurman, R.G. & Mason, P.R. (1993). Role of superoxide and trace transition metals in the production of α-hydroxyethyl radical from ethanol by microsomes from alcohol dehydrogenase-deficient deermice. *Archives of Biochemistry and Biophysics*, **303**, 339–348.

Koop, D.R., Morgan, E.T., Tarr, G.E. & Coon, M.J. (1982). Purification and characterization of a unique isozyme of cytochrome P-450 from liver microsomes of ethanol-treated rabbits, *Journal of Biological Chemistry*, **257**, 8472–8480.

Koop, D.R. & Casazza, J.P. (1985). Identification of ethanol-inducible P-450 isozyme 3a as the acetone and acetol monooxygenase of rabbit microsomes. *Journal of Biological Chemistry*, **260**, 13607–13612.

Koop, D.R., Crump, B.L., Nordblom, G.D. & Coon, M.J. (1989). Ummunochemical evidence for induction of the alcohol oxidizing cytochrome P450 isozyme 3a (P-450IIE1) as a benzene and phenol hydroxylase. *Toxicology and Applied Pharmacology*, **98**, 278–288.

Laethem, R.M., Balaxy, M., Falck, J.R., Laethem, C.L. & Koop, D.R. (1993). Formation of 19(S)-, 19(R)-, and 18(R)-hyroxyeicosatetraenoic acids by alcohol-inducible cytochrome P450 2E1. *Journal of Biological Chemistry*, **268**, 12912–12918.

Lane, B.P. & Lieber, C.S. (1966). Ultrastructural alterations in human hepatocytes following ingestion of ethanol with adequate diets. *American Journal of Pathology*, **49**, 593–603.

Lane, B.P. & Lieber, C.S. (1967). Effects of butylated hydroxytoluene on the ultrastructure of rat hepatocytes. *Laboratory Investigation*, **16**, 341–348.

Laposata, E.A. & Lange, L.G. (1986). Presence of nonoxidative ethanol metabolism in human organs commonly damaged by ethanol abuse. *Science*, **231**, 497–499.

Lasker, J.M., Raucy, J., Kubota, S., Bloswick, B.P., Black, M. & Lieber, C.S. (1987). Purification and characterization of human liver cytochrome P-450-ALC. *Biochemical and Biophysical Research Communications*, **148**, 232–238.

Leo, M.A., Rosman, A. & Lieber, C.S. (1993). Differential depletion of carotenoids and tocopherol in liver diseases. *Hepatology*, **17**, 977–986.

Levitt, M.D. & Levitt, D.G. (1994). The critical role of the rate of ethanol absorption in the interpretation of studies purporting to demonstrate gastric metabolism of ethanol. *Journal of Pharmacology and Experimental Therapeutics*, **269**, 297–304.

Li, J., Kim, C., Leo, M.A., Mak, K.M., Rojkind, M. & Lieber, C.S. (1992). Polyunsaturated lecithin prevents acetaldehyde-mediated hepatic collagen accumulation by stimulating collagenase activity in cultured lipocytes. *Hepatology*, **15**, 373–381.

Liang, C.S. & Lowestein, J.M. (1978). Metabolic control of the circulation. *Journal of Clinical Investigation*, **62**, 1029–1038.

Lieber, C.S. (1992). *Medical and Nutritional Complications of Alcoholism: Mechanisms and Management* (pp. 579). New York: Plenum.

Lieber, C.S. (1997a). Gastric ethanol metabolism and gastritis: interactions with other drugs, *Helicobacter pylori*, and antibiotic therapy (1957–1997)—a review. *Alcoholism: Clinical and Experimental Research*, **21**, 1360–1366.

Lieber, C.S. (1997b). Cytochrome P4502E1: its physiological and pathological role. *Physiological Review*, **77**, 517–544.

Lieber, C.S. (1998). Hepatic and other medical disorders of alcoholism: from pathogenesis to treatment. *Journal of Studies on Alcohol*, **59**, 9–25.

Lieber, C.S. (1999a). Microsomal ethanol-oxidizing system (MEOS), the first 30 years (1968–1998)—a review. *Alcoholism: Clinical and Experimental Research*, **23**, 991–1007.

Lieber, C.S. (1999b). Role of S-adenosyl-L-methionine in the treatment of liver diseases. *Journal of Hepatology*, **30**, 1155–1159.

Lieber, C.S. (2000). Alcoholic liver disease: natural course, mechanisms and therapeutic strategies. In P. Johnstone (Ed.), *Liver Cirrhosis and Development*. Basel: Kluwer Academic (in press).

Lieber, C.S. & DeCarli, L.M. (1968). Ethanol oxidation by hepatic microsomes: adaptive increase after ethanol feeding. *Science*, **162**, 917–918.

Lieber, C.S. & DeCarli, L.M. (1970a). Hepatic microsomal ethanol oxidizing system: *in vitro* characteristics and adaptive properties *in vivo*. *Journal of Biological Chemistry*, **245**, 2505–2512.

Lieber, C.S. & Lefevre, A. (1957). Effect of oxytetracycline on acidity, ammonia and urea in gastric juice in normal and uremic subjects. *Complies Rendues Societe' Biologie*, (*Paris*) **151**, 1038–1042.

Lieber, C.S. & Schmid, R. (1961). The effect of ethanol on fatty acid metabolism: stimulation of hepatic fatty acid synthesis *in vitro*. *Journal of Clinical Investigation*, **40**, 394–399.

Lieber, C.S., DeCarli, L.M. & Schmid, R. (1959). Effects of ethanol on fatty acid metabolism in liver slices. *Biochemical and Biophysical Research Communications*, **1**, 302–306.

Lieber, C.S., Baraona, E., Hernandez-Munoz, R., Kubota, S., Sato, N., Kawano, S., Matsumura, T. & Inatomi, N. (1989). Impaired oxygen utilization: a new mechanism for the hepatotoxicity of ethanol in sub-human primates. *Journal of Clinical Investigation*, **83**, 1682–1690.

Lieber, C.S., Casini, A., DeCarli, L.M., Kim, C., Lowe, N., Sasaki, R. & Leo, M.A. (1990a). S-adenosyl-L-methionine attenuates alcohol-induced liver injury in the baboon. *Hepatology*, **11**, 165–172.

Lieber, C.S., DeCarli, L.M., Mak, K.M., Kim, C.-I. & Leo, M.A. (1990b). Attenuation of alcohol-induced hepatic fibrosis by polyunsaturated lecithin. *Hepatology*, **12**, 1390–1398.

Lieber, C.S., Robins, S.J. & Leo, M.A. (1994a). Hepatic phosphatidylethanolamine methyltransferase activity is decreased by ethanol and increased by phosphatidylcholine. *Alcoholism: Clinical and Experimental Research*, **18**, 592–595.

Lieber, C.S., Robins, S.J., Li, J., DeCarli, L.M., Mak, K.M., Fasulo, J.M. & Leo, M.A. (1994b). Phosphatidylcholine protects against fibrosis and cirrhosis in the baboon. *Gastroenterology*, **106**, 152–159.

Lieber, C.S., Gentry, R.T. & Baraona, E. (1996). First pass metabolism of ethanol. In J.B. Saunders & J.B. Whitfield (Eds), *The Biology of Alcohol Problems* (pp. 315–326). Elsevier Science: London.

Lieber, C.S., Leo, M.A., Aleynik, S., Aleynik, M. & DeCarli, L.M. (1997). Polyenylphosphatidylcholine decreases alcohol-induced oxidative stress in the baboon. *Alcoholism: Clinical and Experimental Research*, **21**, 375–379.

Lim, R.T. Jr, Gentry, R.T., Ito, D., Yokoyama, H., Baraona, E. & Lieber, C.S. (1993). First pass metabolism of ethanol in rats is predominantly gastric. *Alcoholism: Clinical and Experimental Research*, **17**, 1337–1344.

Lu, S.C. (1998). Methionine adenosyltransferase and liver disease: it's all about SAM. *Gastroenterology*, **114**, 403–407.

Ma, X., Zhao, J. & Lieber, C.S. (1996). Polyenylphosphatidylcholine attenuates non-alcoholic hepatic fibrosis and accelerates its regression. *Journal of Hepatology*, **24**, 604–613.

Mann, K., Batra, A., Günthner, A. & Schroth, G. (1992). Do women develop alcoholic brain damage more readily than men? *Alcoholism: Clinical and Experimental Research*, **16**, 1052–1056.

Mathews, J.M., Etheridge, A.S., Raymer, J.H., Black, S.R., Pulliam, D.W. & Bucher, J.R. (1998). Selective inhibition of cytochrome P450 2E1 *in vivo* and *in vitro* with trans-1,2-dichloroethylene. *Chem. Res. Toxicol.*, **11**, 778–785.

Mato, J.M., Cámara, J., Fernández de Paz, J., Caballería, L., Coll, S., Caballero, A. et al. (1999). S-adenosylmethionine in alcoholic liver cirrhosis: a randomized, placebo-controlled, double-blind, multicentre clinical trial. *Journal of Hepatology*, **30**, 1081–1089.

Meldolesi, J. (1967). On the significance of the hypertrophy of the smooth endoplasmic reticulum in liver cells after administration of drugs. *Biochemical Pharmacology*, **16**, 125–131.

Meyers, S. & Lieber, C.S. (1976). Reduction of gastric ammonia by ampicillin in normal and azotemic subjects. *Gastroenterology*, **70**, 244–247.

Mirmiran-Yazdy, S.A., Haber, P.S., Korsten, M.A., Mak, K.M., Gentry, R.T., Batra, S.C. & Lieber, C.S. (1995). Metabolism of ethanol in rat gastric cells and its inhibition by cimetidine. *Gastroenterology*, **108**, 737–742.

Misra, P.S., Lefevre, A., Ishii, H., Rubin, E. & Lieber, C.S. (1971). Increase of ethanol meprobamate and pentobarbital metabolism after chronic ethanol administration in man and in rats. *American Journal of Medicine*, **51**, 346–351.

Mitchell, J.R., Mack, C., Mezey, E. & Maddrey, W.C. (1981). The effects of variation in dietary protein and ethanol on hepatic microsomal drug metabolism in the rat. *Hepatology*, **1**, 336–340.

Miwa, G.T., Levin, W., Thomas, P.E. & Lu, A.Y.H. (1978). The direct oxidation of ethanol by catalase- and alcohol dehydrogenase-free reconstituted system containing cytochrome P-450, *Archives of Biochemistry and Biophysics*, **187**, 464–475.

Modell, J.G. & Mountz, J.M. (1990). Drinking and flying—the problem of alcohol use in pilots. *New England Journal of Medicine*, **323**, 455–461.

Mogelson, S. & Lange, L.G. (1984). Nonoxidative ethanol metabolism in rabbit myocardium: purification to homogeneity of fatty acyl ethyl ester synthase. *Biochemistry*, **23**, 4075–4081.

Montanari, A., Simoni, I., Vallisa, D., Trifiro, A., Colla, R., Abbiati, R., Borghi, L. & Novarini, A. (1988). Free amino acids in plasma and skeletal muscle of patients with liver cirrhosis. *Hepatology*, **8**, 1034–1039.

Morgan, D.D. & Mendelhall, C.L. (1977). The role of acetate in the pathogenesis of the acute ethanol-induced fatty liver in rats. *Gastroenterology*, **73**, 1235.

Morgan, M.Y. & Sherlock, S. (1977). Sex-related differences among 100 patients with alcoholic liver disease. *British Medical Journal*, **1**, 939–941.

Morimoto, M., Hagbjork, A.L., Nanji, A.A., Ingelman-Sundberg, M., Lindros, K.O., Fu, P.C., Albano, E. & French, S.W. (1993). Role of cytochrome P450 2E1 in alcoholic liver disease pathogenesis. *Alcohol*, **10**, 459–464.

Morimoto, M., Hagbjork, A.L., Wan, Y.J.Y., Fu, P.C., Clot, P., Albano, E., Ingelman-Sundberg, M. & French, S.W. (1995). Modulation of experimental alcohol-induced liver disease by cytochrome P450 2E1 inhibitors. *Hepatology*, **21**, 1610–1617.

Morton, S. & Mitchell, M.C. (1985). Effects of chronic ethanol feeding on glutathione turnover in the rat. *Biochemical Pharmacology*, **34**, 1559–1563.

Moskowitz, H., Burns, M.M. & Williams, A.F. (1985). Skill performance at low blood alcohol levels. *Journal of Studies on Alcohol*, **46**, 482–485.

Müller, A. & Sies, H. (1983). Inhibition of ethanol- and aldehyde-induced release of ethane from isolated perfused rat liver by pargyline and disulfiram. *Pharmacology, Biochemistry and Behaviour*, **18**, 429–432.

Nagy, L., Kusststsche, S., Hauschka, P.V. & Szabo, S. (1996). Role of cysteine proteases and protease inhibitors in gastric mucosal damage induced by ethanol or ammonia in the rat. *Journal of Clinical Investigation*, **98**, 1047–1054.

Navder, K., Baraona, E. & Lieber, C.S. (1997a). Polyenylphosphatidylcholine attenuates alcohol-induced fatty liver and hyperlipemia in rats. *Journal of Nutrition*, **127**, 1800–1806.

Navder, K., Baraona, E. & Lieber, C.S. (1997b). Polyenylphosphatidylcholine decreases alcoholic hyperlipemia without affecting the alcohol-induced rise of HDL-cholesterol. *Life Sciences*, **61**, 1907–1914.

Nilsson, N.O. & Belfrage, P. (1978). Effects of acetate acetaldehyde and ethanol on lipolysis in isolated rat adipocytes. *Journal of Lipid Research*, **19**, 737–741.

Ohnishi, K. & Lieber, C.S. (1977). Reconstitution of the microsomal ethanol-oxidizing system: qualitative and quantitative changes of cytochrome P-450 after chronic ethanol consumption, *Journal of Biological Chemistry*, **252**, 7124–7131.

Ohnishi, K. & Lieber, C.S. (1978). Respective role of superoxide and hydroxyl radical in the activity of the reconstituted microsomal ethanol-oxidizing system. *Archives of Biochemistry and Biophysics*, **191**, 798–803.

Palmer, R.H., Frank, W.O., Nambi, P., Wetherington, J.D. & Fox, M.J. (1991). Effects of various concomitant medications on gastric alcohol dehydrogenase and first-pass metabolism of ethanol. *American Journal of Gastroenterology*, **86**, 1749–1755.

Parrish, K.M., Dufour, M.C., Stinson, F.S. & Harford, T.C. (1993). Average daily alcohol consumption during adult life among decedents with and without cirrhosis: the 1986 National Mortality Followback Survey. *Journal of Studies on Alcohol*, **54**, 450–456.

Pateron, D., Fabre, M., Ink, O., Cherif, F., Hagege, H., Foissy, P., Ducreux, M., Benamouzig, R. & Buffet, C. (1990). Influence de l'alcool et de la cirrhose sur la présence de *Helicobacter pylori* dans la muqueuse gastrique. *Gastroenterology and Clinical Biology*, **14**, 555–560.

Pequignot, G., Tuyns, A.J. & Berta, J.L. (1978). Ascitic cirrhosis in relation to alcohol consumption. *International Journal of Epidemiology (London)*, **7**, 113–120.

Pestallozi, D.M., Buhler, R., von Wartburg, J.P. et al. (1983). Immunohistochemical localization of alcohol dehydrogenase in the human gastrointestinal tract. *Gastroenterology*, **85**, 1011–1016.

Pezzoli, C., Stramentinoli, G., Galli-Kienele, M. & Plaff, E. (1978). Uptake and metabolism of S-adenosyl-L-methionine by isolated rat hepatocytes. *Biochemical and Biophysical Research Communications*, **85**, 1031–1038.

Poupon, R.E., Nalpas, B., Coutelle, C., Fleury, B., Couzigou, P., Higueret, D. & the French Group for Research on Alcohol and Liver. (1992). Polymorphism of alcohol dehydrogenase, alcohol and aldehyde dehydrogenase activities: implications in alcoholic cirrhosis in white patients. *Hepatology*, **15**, 1017–1022.

Pritchard, J.F. & Schneck, D.W. (1977). Effects of ethanol and phenobarbital on the metabolism of propanolol by 9000 g rat liver supernatant. *Biochemical Pharmacology*, **26**, 2453–2454.

Raucy, J.L., Lasker, J.M., Kramer, J.C., Salazer, D.E., Lieber, C.S. & Corcoran, G.B. (1991). Induction of P450IIE1 in the obese rat. *Molecular Pharmacology*, **39**, 275–280.

Rashba-Step, J., Turro, N.J. & Cederbaum, A.I. (1993). Increased NADPH- and NADH-dependent production of superoxide and hydroxyl radical by microsomes after chronic ethanol consumption. *Archives of Biochemistry and Biophysics*, **300**, 401–408.

Roine, R.P., Gentry, R.T., Hernández-Muñoz, R., Baraona, E. & Lieber, C.S. (1990). Aspirin increases blood alcohol concentrations in human after ingestion of ethanol. *Journal of the American Medical Association*, **264**, 2406–2408.

Roine, R.P., Gentry, R.T., Lim, R.T. Jr, Baraona, E. & Lieber, C.S. (1991). Effect of concentration of ingested ethanol on blood alcohol levels. *Alcoholism: Clinical and Experimental Research*, **15**, 734–738.

Roine, R.P., Gentry, R.T., Lim, R.T. Jr, Heikkonen, E., Salaspuro, M. & Lieber, C.S. (1993). Comparison of blood alcohol concentrations after beer and whiskey: *Alcoholism: Clinical and Experimental Research*, **17**, 709–711.

Salaspuro, M.P. & Lieber, C.S. (1978). Non-uniformity of blood ethanol elimination: its exaggeration after chronic consumption. *Annals of Clinical Research*, **10**, 294–297.

Salmela, K.S., Kessova, I.G., Tsyrlov, I.B. & Lieber, C.S. (1998). Respective roles of human cytochrome P4502E1, 1A2, and 3A4 in the hepatic microsomal ethanol oxidizing system. *Alcoholism: Clinical and Experimental Research*, **22**, 2125–2132.

Sato, N. & Kitamura, T. (1996). First-pass metabolism of ethanol: an overview. *Gastroenterology*, **111**, 1143–1144.

Sato, C., Nakano, M. & Lieber, C.S. (1981). Increased hepatotoxicity of acetaminophen after chronic ethanol consumption in the rat. *Gastroenterology*, **80**, 140–148.

Satre, M.A., Zgombic-Knight, M. & Duester, G. (1994). The complete structure of human class IV alcohol dehydrogenase (retinol dehydrogenase) determined from ADH7 gene. *Journal of Biological Chemistry*, **269**, 15606–15612.

Savolainen, V.T., Pajarinen, J., Perola, M., Penttilä, A. & Karhunen, P.J. (1996). Glutathione-S-transferase GST M1 "null" genotype and the risk of alcoholic liver disease. *Alcoholism: Clinical and Experimental Research*, **20**, 1340–1345.

Seitz, H.K., Egerer, G., Simanowski, U.A., Waldherr, R., Eckey, R., Agarwal, D.P., Goedde, H.W. & von Wartburg, J.P. (1993). Human gastric alcohol dehydrogenase activity: effect of age, gender and alcoholism. *Gut*, **34**, 1433–1437.

Sellman, R., Kanto, J., Raijola, E. & Pekkarinen, A. (1975). Human and animal study on elimination from plasma and metabolism of diazepam after chronic alcohol intake. *Acta Pharmacol. Toxicol.*, **36**, 33–38.

Shaw, S. & Lieber, C.S. (1980). Increased hepatic production of alpha-amino-*n*-butyric acid after chronic alcohol consumption in rats and baboons. *Gastroenterology*, **78**, 108–113.

Shaw, S., Jayatilleke, E., Ross, W.A., Gordon. E.R. & Lieber, C.S. (1981). Ethanol induced lipid peroxidation: potentiation by long-term alcohol feeding and attenuation by methionine. *Journal of Laboratory and Clinical Medicine*, **98**, 417–425.

Shaw, S., Rubin, K.P. & Lieber, C.S. (1983). Depressed hepatic glutathione and increased diene conjugates in alcoholic liver disease: evidence of lipid peroxidation. *Dig. Dis. Sci.*, **28**, 585–589.

Shelmet, J.J., Reichard, G.A., Skutches, C.L., Hoeldtke, R.D., Owen, O.E. & Boden, G. (1988). Ethanol causes acute inhibition of carbohydrate, fat, and protein oxidation and insulin resistance. *Journal of Clinical Investigation*, **81**, 1137–1145.

Sies, H. & Chance, B. (1970). The steady state level of catalase compound I in isolated hemoglobin-free perfused rat liver. *FEBS Letters*, **11**, 172–176.

Smith, T., DeMaster, E.G., Furne, J.K., Springfield, J. & Levitt, M.D. (1992). First-pass gastric mucosal metabolism of ethanol is negligible in the rat. *Journal of Clinical Investigation*, **89**, 1801–1806.

Sotaniemi, E.A., Anttila, M., Rautio, A., Stengard, J., Saukko, P. & Jarvensivu, P. (1981). Propranolol and sotalol metabolism after a drinking party. *Clin. Pharmacol. Ther.*, **29**, 705–710.

Speisky, H., MacDonald, A., Giles, G., Orrego, H. & Israel, Y. (1985). Increased loss of decreased synthesis of hepatic glutathione after acute ethanol administration. *Biochemical Journal*, **225**, 565–572.

Stone, C.L., Thomason, H.R., Bosron, W.F. & Li, T.-K. (1993). Purification and partial amino acid sequence of a high activity human stomach alcohol dehydrogenase. *Alcoholism: Clinical and Experimental Research*, **17**, 911–918.

Stone, C.L., Hurley, T.D., Peggs, C.F., Kedishvili, N.Y., Davis, G.J., Thomasson, H.R., Li, T.K. & Bosron, W.F. (1995). Cimetidine inhibition of human gastric and liver alcohol dehydrogenase isoenzymes: identification of inhibitor complexes by kinetics and molecular modeling. *Biochemistry*, **34**, 4008–4014.

Stramentinoli, G., Gualano, M. & Galli-Kienle, G. (1979). Intestinal absorption of S-adenosyl-L-methionine. *Journal of Pharmacology and Experimental Therapeutics*, **209**, 323–326.

Takagi, T., Alderman, J., Geller, J. & Lieber, C.S. (1986). Assessment of the role of non-ADH ethanol oxidation *in vivo* and in hepatocytes from deermice. *Biochemical Pharmacology*, **35**, 3601–3606.

Takahashi, T., Lasker, J.M., Rosman, A.S. & Lieber, C.S. (1993). Induction of P450E1 in human liver by ethanol is due to a corresponding increase in encoding mRNA. *Hepatology*, **17**, 236–245.

Teng, Y.S. (1981). Human liver aldehyde dehydrogenase in Chinese and Asiatic Indians: gene deletion and its possible implications in alcohol metabolism. *Biochemical Genetics*, **19**, 107–114.

Teschke, R., Hasumura, Y., Joly, J.G., Ishii, H. & Lieber, C.S. (1972). Microsomal ethanol-oxidizing system (MEOS): purification and properties of a rat liver system free of catalase and alcohol dehydrogenase. *Biochemical and Biophysical Research Communications*, **49**, 1187–1193.

Teschke, R., Hasumura, Y. & Lieber, C.S. (1974). Hepatic microsomal alcohol oxidizing system Solubilization, isolation and characterization. *Archives of Biochemistry and Biophysics*, **163**, 404–415.

Teschke, R., Matsuzaki, S., Ohnishi, K., DeCarli, L.M. & Lieber, C.S. (1977). Microsomal ethanol oxidizing system (MEOS): current status of its characterization and its role. *Alcoholism: Clinical and Experimental Research*, **1**, 7–15.

Teschke, R., Moreno, F. & Petrides, A.S. (1981). Hepatic microsomal ethanol oxidizing system (MEOS) respective role of ethanol and carbohydrates for the enhanced activity after chronic alcohol consumption. *Biochemical Pharmacology*, **30**, 45–51.

Thurman, R.G. & Brentzel, H.J. (1977). The role of alcohol dehydrogenase in microsomal ethanol oxidation and the adaptive increase in ethanol metabolism due to chronic treatment with ethanol. *Alcoholism: Clinical and Experimental Research*, **1**, 33–38.

Travers, J., Varela, I. & Mato, J.M. (1984). Effect of exogenous S-adenosyl-L-methionine on phosphatidylcholine synthesis by isolated rat hepatocytes. *Biochemical Pharmacology*, **33**, 1562–1564.

Tsutsumi, M., Lasker, J.M., Shimizu, M., Rosman, A.S. & Lieber, C.S. (1989). The intralobular distribution of ethanol-inducible P450IIE1 in rat and human liver. *Hepatology*, **10**, 437–446.

Tsutsumi, M., Leo, M.A., Kim, C., Tsutsumi, M., Lasker, J., Lowe, N. & Lieber, C.S. (1990). Interaction of ethanol with enflurane metabolism and toxicity: role of P450IIE1. *Alcoholism: Clinical and Experimental Research*, **14**, 174–179.

Uppal, R., Lateef, S.K., Korsten, M.A., Paronetto, F. & Lieber, C.S. (1991). Chronic alcoholic gastritis: roles of ethanol and *Helicobacter pylori*. *Archives of Internal Medicine*, **151**, 760–764.

Valenzuela, A., Fernandez, V. & Videla, L.A. (1983).   Hepatic and biliary levels of glutathione and lipid peroxides following iron overload in the rat: effect of simultaneous ethanol administration. *Toxicology and Applied Pharmacology*, **70**, 87–95.

Vendemiale, G., Altomare, E., Trizio, T., Le Grazie, C., Di Padova, C., Salerno, M.T., Carrieri, V. & Albano, O. (1989).   Effect of oral S-adenosyl-L-methionine on hepatic glutathione in patients with liver disease. *Scandinavian Journal of Gastroenterology*, **24**, 407–415.

Vessell, E.S., Page, J.G. & Passananti, G.T. (1971).   Genetic environmental factors affecting ethanol metabolism in man. *Clin. Pharmacol. Ther.*, **12**, 192–201.

Videla, L. & Israel, Y. (1970).   Factors that modify the metabolism of ethanol in rat liver and adaptive changes produced by its chronic administration. *Biochemical Journal*, **118**, 275–281.

Weiner, F.R., Eskreis, D.S., Compton, K.V., Orrego, H. & Zern, M.A. (1988).   Haplotype analysis of a type I collagen gene and its association with alcoholic cirrhosis in man. *Molecular Aspects of Medicine*, **10**, 159–168.

Weltman, M.D., Farrell, G.C., Hall, P., Ingelman-Sundberg, M. & Liddle, C. (1998).   Hepatic cytochrome P450 2E1 is increased in patients with non-alcoholic steatohepatitis. *Hepatology*, **27**, 128–133.

Werner, J., Laposata, M., Fernandez-Del Castillo, C., Saghir, M., Iozzo, R.V., Lewandrowski, K.B. & Warshaw, A.L. (1997).   Pancreatic injury in rats induced by fatty acid ethyl ester, a non-oxidative metabolite of alcohol. *Gastroenterology*, **113**, 286–294.

Whitecomb, D.C. & Block, G.D. (1994).   Association of acetaminophen hepatotoxicity with fasting and ethanol use. *Journal of the American Medical Association*, **272**, 1845–1850.

Williamson, J.R., Scholz, R., Browning, E.T., Thurman, R.G. & Fukami, M.H. (1969).   Metabolic effects of ethanol in perfused rat liver. *Journal of Biological Chemistry*, **25**, 5044–5054.

Wolff, P.H. (1973).   Vasomotor sensitivity to alcohol in diverse mongoloid populations. *American Journal of Human Genetics*, **25**, 193–199.

Yamada, S., Mak, K.M. & Lieber, C.S. (1985).   Chronic ethanol consumption alters rat liver plasma membranes and potentiates release of alkaline phosphatase. *Gastroenterology*, **88**, 1799–1806.

Yang, C.S., Yoo, J.-S., Ishizaki, H. & Hong, J. (1990).   Cytochrome P450 IIE1: roles in nitrosamine metabolism and mechanisms of regulation. *Drug Metabolism Review*, **22**, 147–159.

Yasunami, M., Chen, C.-S. & Yoshida, A. (1991).   A human alcohol dehydrogenase gene (ADH6) encoding an additional class of isozyme. *Proceedings of the National Academy of Science of the United States of America*, **88**, 7610–7614.

Yokoyama, H., Baraona, E. & Lieber, C.S. (1994).   Molecular cloning of human class IV alcohol dehydrogenase. *Biochemical and Biophysical Research Communications*, **203**, 219–224.

Yokoyama, H., Baraona, E. & Lieber, C.S. (1995).   Upstream structure of human ADH7 gene and the organ distribution of its expression. *Biochemical and Biophysical Research Communications*, **216**, 216–222.

Yokoyama, H., Baraona, E. & Lieber, C.S. (1996).   Molecular cloning and chromosomal localization of ADH7 gene encoding human class IV ADH. *Genomics*, **31**, 243–245.

Yoshihara, H., Sato, N., Kamada, T. & Abe, H. (1983).   Low K_m ALDH isozyme and alcoholic liver injury. *Pharmacology, Biochemistry and Behaviour*, **18**, 425–428.

Zhang, H., Loney, L.A. & Potter, B.J. (1993).   Effect of chronic alcohol feeding on hepatic iron status and ferritin uptake by rat hepatocytes. *Alcoholism: Clinical and Experimental Research*, **17**, 394–400.

Chapter 6

Neuropharmacology of Ethanol and Alcohol Dependence

Anne Lingford-Hughes
and
David J. Nutt
*Psychopharmacology Unit, University of
Bristol, Bristol, UK*

Synopsis

Alcoholism is a heterogeneous disorder involving many different chemical or neurotransmitter systems. This chapter describes which systems are involved in mediating the central effects of alcohol. Whilst early theories of how the effects of alcohol were mediated focused on non-specific absorption into the lipid membrane of the cell, it is now recognized that alcohol disrupts specific lipid–protein interactions. The neurotransmitter receptors commonly affected are those with a transmembrane ion channel, such as the GABA-benzodiazepine and glutamatergic N-methyl-D-aspartate (NMDA) receptors. Alcohol increases function of the GABA-benzodiazepine receptor and inhibits this glutamatergic receptor. Since the GABA system is the brain's primary inhibitory system and glutamate an excitatory system, alcohol acutely reduces brain activity. In particular, ataxia, anxiolysis, sedation and amnesia are thought to be mediated through the GABA-benzodiazepine receptor. In addition, changes in this receptor are thought to underlie tolerance to alcohol. Furthermore, there is evidence to suggest that different forms of this receptor determine sensitivity to alcohol.

Dysfunction within the glutamatergic system is thought to result in alcohol intoxication, blackouts and cognitive impairment and to significantly contribute to alcohol withdrawal. The latter is due to increased glutamatergic, particularly NMDA receptor, function, which results as a compensatory mechanism to overcome the antagonism of the NMDA receptor by alcohol. Increased activity in the noradrenaline system is also thought to mediate some of the signs of alcohol withdrawal, such as autonomic instability and increased arousal. A drug whose actions include inhibiting NMDA and possibly increasing GABA-

International Handbook of Alcohol Dependence and Problems. Edited by N. Heather, T.J. Peters and T. Stockwell.
© 2001 John Wiley & Sons Ltd.

benzodiazepine receptor function, acamprosate, has been found to be efficacious in reducing the risk of relapse and maintaining abstinence in alcohol dependence.

A deficiency in serotonin or 5-hydroxytryptamine function has been proposed to be associated with vulnerability to alcoholism, particularly Type 1 alcoholism. The latter is characterized by early age of onset, male only, impulsive and antisocial personality traits. Type 2, by contrast, is associated with a later age of onset, both genders and anxiety personality traits. Whilst such an absolute dichotomy is rarely seen, there is increasing evidence to suggest that Type 1 and Type 2 alcoholism are associated, respectively, with low and high levels of serotonin, and that increased serotonergic function results in craving and increased anxiety.

The mesolimbic dopaminergic system is involved in mediating the rewarding effects of alcohol and alcohol increases dopaminergic neurotransmission within this system. Hypofunction within this system has been found to be associated with alcoholism. There are several different dopamine receptors whose role in alcoholism remains to be elucidated, but it is likely that the D3 receptors in the nucleus accumbens of the mesolimbic system will play a key role. This dopaminergic system is modulated at several sites by the opioid system. Alcohol increases the release of opiates, consequently a deficient opioid system has been proposed to be associated with alcoholism. It is unclear which receptor subtype is critically involved; however, the non-selective opiate receptor antagonist, naltrexone, is efficacious in reducing the risk of relapse in abstinent alcoholics.

Whilst various actions of alcohol can now be ascribed to specific neurotransmitters, much needs to be understood concerning their role in mediating the effects of alcohol and in alcoholism. Such increased understanding will undoubtedly inform development of improved pharmacotherapy.

Alcoholism is a heterogeneous disorder involving many different neurotransmitter systems. In this chapter the terms "alcohol" and "ethanol" are used interchangeably, since ethanol is the form commonly used in animal studies, although it is appreciated that ethanol is only one form of alcohol. Early theories of how ethanol worked assumed that it was absorbed into the lipid membrane, thus altering its fluidity in a non-specific manner. More recently, these theories have been superseded by ones emphasizing that ethanol possesses more specific actions, such as disrupting lipid–protein interactions or even the proteins or receptors themselves. It now appears that the receptor systems most commonly affected by alcohol and through which the majority of ethanol's central effects are mediated are ion channels, such as the GABA-benzodiazepine and glutamatergic N-methyl-D-aspartate (NMDA) receptors. In addition, it is now possible to begin to ascribe the various actions of alcohol to specific actions of different neurotransmitters (see Table 6.1).

Table 6.1 Possible transmitters involved in the action of ethanol

Experience	Transmitter/receptor
Euphoria/pleasure	Dopamine, opioids, 5-HT
Activation	Noradrenaline, dopamine
Anxiolysis, ataxia	GABA-benzodiazepine (increased)
Sedation/amnesia	GABA-benzodiazepine receptor (increased), NMDA receptor (decreased)
Nausea	5-HT$_3$ activation
Withdrawal	NMDA receptors (increased), GABA-benzodiazepine receptor (decreased), noradrenaline (increased)

In addition to affecting multiple neurotransmitter systems, the effects of alcohol on the brain can differ, depending on which state is being studied. For example, neuroadaptation to alcohol involves alterations in neurotransmitter function which reduce the effect of alcohol, a consequence of which is dependence associated with states such as tolerance and withdrawal. Neurotransmitter levels and function in these states will inevitably be different from others, for example, in intoxication or abstinence. In addition, the effects of alcohol may differ depending on a person's vulnerability to alcoholism. These different states and association with particular neurotransmitters will have to be taken into account when considering how pharmacotherapy may play a role in treating alcohol use and abuse. It is possible that more specific prescribing with the profile of the patient's problems in mind will improve the efficacy of drugs currently available.

GABA-BENZODIAZEPINE RECEPTOR

The GABA-benzodiazepine ($GABA_A$) receptor is regarded as a principal target for alcohol (see Figure 6.1). The GABA system provides the majority of inhibitory activity in the brain, hence its activation is associated with reduced electrical activity. It appears that the GABAergic system, together with glutamatergic system, modulates the activity of other neurotransmitters. Benzodiazepines and alcohol share many behavioural and cognitive effects, such as muscle incoordination, amnesia, sedation, anticonvulsant action and anxiolysis. Many of these effects of alcohol have been shown to be due to modulation of the GABA-benzodiazepine receptor. There is no alcohol receptor as such, but alcohol appears to alter the GABA-benzodiazepine receptor by allosteric modulation of GABA activation of the Cl^- channel, thereby potentiating GABAergic neurotransmission. The hypothesis concerning alcoholism is that a hypofunctional GABA system is associated with increased vulnerability.

There is a wealth of animal research investigating the role of the GABA-benzodiazepine receptor complex mediating the central effects of alcohol. Acutely, alcohol results in potentiation of GABA-ergic function. Physiological doses of ethanol have been shown to potentiate muscimol(GABA agonist)-stimulated Cl^- flux in a number of animal tissue preparations (see Grobin et al., 1998). However, there are regions, such as the hippocampus, in which sensitivity to ethanol is either absent or requires specific experimental conditions.

It has been increasingly recognized that the subunit profile of the GABA-benzodiazepine receptor determines sensitivity to alcohol. The GABA-benzodiazepine receptor has a heteromeric structure which is made up of five subunits, of which there are six types (α, β, γ, δ, ρ and ε), each existing in a number of different forms, e.g. isoforms $\alpha1$–$\alpha6$. Whilst this number of isoforms and subunits could potentially result in many different receptors, it is clear that certain subunit combinations are preferentially formed. The most common subtype consists of $\alpha1$, $\beta2$ and $\gamma2$. Particular subunits and isoforms have been shown to be critical for sensitivity to alcohol. For instance, a strong relationship has been found between GABA-benzodiazepine receptors with high affinity for zolpidem (a GABA agonist used as an hypnotic), sensitivity to ethanol and expression of $\alpha1$, $\beta2$ and $\gamma2$ subunits. Receptors rich in $\alpha5$ are less sensitive.

Initially, evidence suggested that the long form of the $\gamma2$ ($\gamma2L$) subunit imparted ethanol sensitivity in a frog oocyte expression system (Wafford et al., 1991); however, subsequent studies found expression of $\alpha1$, $\beta1$ and $\gamma2L$ were not necessarily sufficient. The $\gamma2L$ subunit variant contains a site for phosphorylation by protein kinase C, whose presence appears essential for ethanol to modulate GABAergic function (see below). Using a technique called quantitative trait locus mapping, which involves identifying regions on

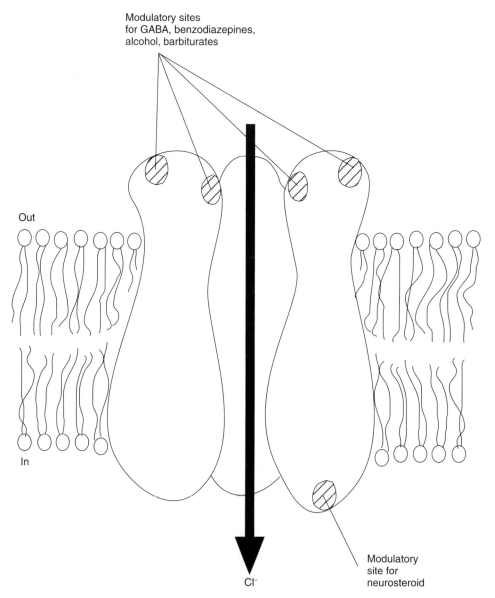

Modulatory sites
for GABA, benzodiazepines,
alcohol, barbiturates

Out

In

Cl⁻

Modulatory
site for
neurosteroid

Figure 6.1 Stylized diagram of the GABA-benzodiazepine receptor. Only three of the five subunits
are shown

chromosomes that are associated with particular characteristics of the animal studied,
regions on chromosome 1, 4 and 11 in mice have been identified as affecting genetic predisposition to acute alcohol withdrawal. In particular, a polymorphism of the $\gamma 2$ subunit
gene, Gaberg2, was found to be associated with severity of alcohol withdrawal. In another
approach, gene targeting has been used to delete part of the gene (24 base-pair exon) which
distinguishes the long ($\gamma 2$L) and short ($\gamma 2$S) form of the $\gamma 2$ subunit. Interestingly, despite

replacement of γ2L by γ2S, sensitivity to ethanol in several different behavioural paradigms was not altered, leading again to the conclusion that γ2L is not an absolute requirement for determining ethanol sensitivity.

The α6 receptor subunit is preferentially found in the cerebellum, and GABA-benzodiazepine receptors expressing this subunit bind Ro15 4513 with high affinity and are diazepam-insensitive (Luddens et al., 1990). This α6-rich GABA-benzodiazepine receptor is proposed to mediate alcohol-induced ataxia and motor incoordination. In rats bred for ethanol-induced motor impairment (alcohol-sensitive, non-tolerant rats: ANT), this behaviour is thought to be linked to expression of a mutated form of the α6 subunit. Recently mice lacking a functional α6 gene have been bred. As predicted, diazepam-insensitive Ro15 4513 binding is absent in the cerebellum of these mice. Interestingly, the hypnotic effect of ethanol was unchanged, suggesting that the α6 subunit is not necessary for ethanol-induced sedation.

Further evidence for a particular role for the α6 subunit in alcoholism is gained by studies with Ro15 4513, a partial inverse agonist at the benzodiazepine receptor, which has been shown to antagonize many but not all of the central effects of alcohol (Suzdak et al., 1986). One study showed that these effects are mediated via the benzodiazepine receptor, since they were antagonized by Ro15 1788. Although there has been debate as to whether Ro15 4513 is a specific alcohol antagonist, its ability to reverse the effects of alcohol has made it a powerful tool to investigate how the effects of alcohol are mediated.

In animals chronically exposed to alcohol, tolerance and dependence results in reduced potentiation of GABAergic neurotransmission, reduced behavioural responses and withdrawal symptomatology (see Grobin et al., 1998). Such a reduced sensitivity of GABA-ergic responses to ethanol has been shown in a number of different tissues in various animal models. However, there are regional differences and a reduction is not always apparent in every brain area studied. In addition, responsivity to other GABA-ergic neuromodulators, such as benzodiazepine agonists and barbiturates, is reduced, whilst to benzodiazepine inverse agonists enhancement is seen.

Much energy has been devoted to finding the mechanisms underlying tolerance and dependence to alcohol. Binding studies have not generally shown reductions in the level and affinity of GABA-benzodiazepine receptors, using a variety of radioligands labelling different parts of the receptor complex (see Grobin et al., 1998). The exception to this is that increased levels of Ro15 4513 binding have been reported in the cortex and cerebellum after chronic alcohol exposure; in addition, the ability of Ro15 4513 to inhibit the actions of muscimol was enhanced. In regard to tolerance and withdrawal, the role of the GABA-benzodiazepine receptor subtype(s) to which Ro15 4513 binds preferentially is unknown.

Many studies, however, have shown that chronic ethanol exposure is associated with altered expression of particular GABA-benzodiazepine receptor subunits. Receptor subunits are proteins or peptides whose structure is determined by the genetic make-up or DNA of the cell. The information stored in the DNA is transmitted to the area of the cell where the protein is synthesized by messenger RNA (mRNA). By measuring the level of mRNA, an index is obtained of which subunits of the GABA-benzodiazepine receptors are being expressed at the genetic level and synthesized by the cell. For instance, the most consistent finding is of decreased levels of the α1 sub-unit mRNA in the cerebral cortex and cerebellum (see Grobin et al., 1998). In addition, the levels of α2 and α5 receptor subunit mRNAs are reduced and α4 and α6 subunit mRNA levels increased. Finally, depending on the brain region studied, increases or no change in β1, γ1, γ2S, γ3, α4, α5 and α6 have been reported. A reduction in the expression of α1 and increase in α4 and α6 subunits could explain the increase in Ro15 4513 binding reported, since this ligand has preferential affinity for GABA-benzodiazepine receptors containing the α4 and α6 subunits.

Although changes in mRNA levels are reported, this may not necessarily be accompanied by concomitant changes in subunit peptide levels. In the rat cerebral cortex, changes in peptide levels are similar to those seen with mRNA levels. Thus, reduced levels of α1 and increased levels of α4 peptide levels have been reported (Devaud et al., 1997). However, no change in the level of γ2S peptide was seen, despite increased mRNA levels. It is expected that traditional ligand-binding studies should reflect these changes in peptide levels. However, it is possible that ligands used are not sensitive enough to detect these subtle subunit alterations.

Emphasizing the differential regional selectivity of altered subunit expression, Charlton et al. (1997) found that expression of α5 mRNA was reduced in the cerebral and cerebellar cortices and increased in the hippocampus, whilst expression of α1 mRNA was reduced in the cerebral cortex, hippocampus and ventral tegmental area. This study also illustrates the differential temporal sensitivity to ethanol. The reduction in the cerebral cortex was apparent after 1 month of ethanol exposure, whereas in the other regions a longer exposure (at least 3 months) was required to see any changes. Similarly, levels of the α4 subunit in the hippocampus were not altered after 14 days of chronic ethanol exposure, whereas increases were seen in the cerebral cortex. Reductions of the α4 subunit in the hippocampus required at least 40 days of ethanol exposure.

In addition there are different subunit profiles in a strain of mice which are either withdrawal seizure prone (WSP) or resistant (WSR). For instance, in WSP mice a reduction in levels of whole brain α1 subunit mRNA is seen after chronic ethanol exposure (Buck et al., 1997). However such a decrease is not seen in WSR mice. Interestingly the reverse is seen with the α6 subunit mRNA. A further study of ethanol-naïve mice revealed increased levels of α1, α6 and β2 subunit mRNAs in the cerebellum of WSR compared to WSP mice. No such differences were seen in the cerebral cortex. Thus, withdrawal seizure severity is associated with specific regional differences in the subunit profile of the GABA-benzodiazepine receptor.

During withdrawal from ethanol, mRNA expression for α1, α4 and γ1 subunits has been shown to revert to normal levels, whilst increased expression of β2, β3 and γ1 also occurs (Devaud et al., 1997). Despite these changes occurring in the first 8 hours of withdrawal, peptide expression is not altered with persistence of the pattern seen in ethanol dependency, such as reduced α1 and α4 peptide levels (Devaud et al., 1997). No change in γ2 peptide levels occurs in either dependence or withdrawal (Devaud et al., 1997). It has been suggested that mRNA expression reflects the rapidly changing state of CNS excitability in withdrawal, whereas peptide levels may reflect the long-term changes associated with ethanol dependence (Grobin et al., 1998). Ethanol withdrawal has also been shown to be associated with enhanced sensitivity to neurosteroids derived from progesterone and deoxycorticosterone, 3α-5α-THP and THDOC, which modulate GABA-benzodiazepine receptor activity.

It has been argued that despite evidence that GABA-ergic response is attenuated in animal studies, the inconsistent data and variable decreases reported in receptor number cast doubt on a key role for altered GABA-ergic function in withdrawal. This may account for the fact that whilst benzodiazepines are effective in controlling withdrawal symptoms for the majority of patients, it has been argued that benzodiazepines act non-specifically in reducing seizures, since GABA-ergic dysfunction is not the fundamental underlying neuropathology.

GABA-benzodiazepine receptor function can be also modulated by phosphorylation at several points during its synthesis, including control of gene expression. In addition, after the protein or peptide has been made, it can be further modified by phosphorylation, i.e. at a post-translational step. Several lines of evidence suggest that protein phosphorylation is an important factor in determining the sensitivity of the GABA-benzodiazepine receptor to alcohol. Phosphorylation by the enzyme, protein kinase C, is involved in mediating the activating effects of ethanol on GABA-benzodiazepine receptors. Mice or isolated cells expressing a mutant form of protein kinase C show reduced ethanol sensitivity. Thus ethanol tolerance and dependence may also involve altered phosphorylation of GABA-benzodiazepine receptors.

Lastly, ethanol exposure has been shown to alter the level of chaperonin proteins. These intracellular proteins are involved in moving other proteins, such as components of receptors, between organelles. Chronic ethanol exposure upregulates the level of some chaperonin proteins and hence it has been suggested that this might be another method of altering the function of GABA-benzodiazepine receptors.

There have been a number of studies investigating the role of the GABA-ergic system in ethanol reinforcement. In relation to alcoholism, reinforcement is a process by which animals or subjects will repetitively seek alcohol because it induces rewarding or pleasant feelings (positive reinforcement) or relieves an unpleasant feeling, e.g. alcohol withdrawal (negative reinforcement). Thus, the concept of reinforcement is intimately related to the repeated self-administration and use of alcohol. GABA antagonists and Ro15 4513 administered systemically reduce ethanol self-administration. GABA agonists have been shown to increase ethanol intake, although not consistently (Boyle et al., 1993). Microinjections of other GABA antagonists into the brain, particularly the central nucleus of the amygdala, also abolish reinforcement. Ro15 4513 has been shown dose-dependently to reduce alcohol self-administration. As is described below, the dopaminergic mesolimbic system is critically involved with mediating positive reinforcement. The dopamine containing cell bodies arise in the ventral tegmental area (VTA) in the brain stem and terminate in the nucleus accumbens. There are several points in this system where GABA-ergic neurons appears to play a key modulatory role. Dopaminergic neurons in the VTA are under tonic inhibition from GABA-ergic neurons. Thus, GABA antagonists increase dopamine levels in the nucleus accumbens. Recently it has been shown that picrotoxin, a GABA antagonist, applied to the VTA reduces ethanol consumption in alcohol-preferring rats.

In contrast to the wealth of evidence from animal studies, there is relatively little evidence from investigating alcohol dependence in man of a hypofunctional GABAergic system. Levels of GABA, both in the plasma and CSF, have been reported to be low in recently abstinent alcoholics and males at risk of alcoholism, although not consistently.

There have been a number of post-mortem studies measuring the level of GABA-benzodiazepine receptor in alcohol dependence, but the results are inconsistent. In the frontal cortex, an increase, decrease or no change in receptor levels has been reported (see Lewohl et al., 1996). These conflicting results may be due to the use of different radioligands, including a marker of the GABA Cl$^-$ channel, benzodiazepine agonists and antagonists. Elsewhere in the brain, a reduction in [^{3}H]-flunitrazepam (a benzodiazepine agonist) binding was reported in the hippocampus, but no such change was found in the caudate and temporal cortex. Of note, an increase in [^{3}H]-Ro15-4513 reported in rats has not been replicated in human samples. In alcohol dependence with Wernicke's encephalopathy, increased binding of [^{3}H]-muscimol (a GABA agonist) in the frontal cortex, thought to be secondary to neuronal loss, has been reported. Interestingly, no concomitant increase in benzodiazepine binding was seen; rather, a decrease in [^{3}H]-diazepam (a benzodiazepine agonist) and no change in [^{3}H]-flunitrazepam was apparent. The significance of these results is unclear.

More recently, expression of GABA-benzodiazepine receptor sub-units has been studied in post-mortem tissue from human alcoholics. Increased levels of α1 subunit mRNA expression have been found in the frontal but not the motor cortex of uncomplicated alcoholics (Lewohl, Crane & Dodd, 1997). However, interestingly, in patients with hepatic cirrhosis, increased levels of the α1 subunit mRNA were seen in the motor cortex but not in the frontal cortex. No changes were seen in α2 or α3 subunit mRNAs. Another study reported a slight increase of α1 subunit mRNA expression in the frontal cortex, with no change in α4 subunit mRNA (Mitsuyama et al., 1998). The level of β3 subunit mRNA expression was also increased. However, no changes in the α1, α4 or β2/3 subunit peptide levels were found. This study re-emphasizes that mRNA and peptide levels do not necessarily co-vary. More importantly, it appears that, since the results from human post-mortem tissue and animals are different, animal models of alcohol dependence may not adequately reflect the human condition. Animal models differ from human alcohol dependence in the pattern of alcohol consumption and, in these particular studies, in the time between the study and the last consumption of alcohol.

Recently a number of *in vivo* neuroimaging studies, using [11C]-flumazenil and positron emission tomography (PET) or [123I]-iomazenil and single photon emission tomography (SPET), have reported decreased levels of the GABA-benzodiazepine receptor in alcohol dependent subjects. The areas where decreases are consistently reported include the frontal cortex, particularly the medial frontal region (Lingford-Hughes et al., 1998; Gilman et al., 1996). In addition, reductions in the cerebellum are described but these may only occur in the presence of clinical signs of cerebellar dysfunction (Gilman et al., 1996). It is unclear whether these reductions were caused by abuse of alcohol or were pre-existing (Lingford-Hughes et al., 1998). This regional pattern of altered receptor levels strongly supports the hypothesis that only specific populations of the GABA-benzodiazepine receptor are involved in alcoholism.

There is some evidence to suggest that the GABA-benzodiazepine receptor system may be hypofunctional in alcohol dependence. Volkow et al. (1993) have used [18F]-FDG PET to measure the reduction in glucose metabolism induced by a lorazepam (a benzodiazepine agonist) challenge as an index of benzodiazepine receptor function. In the orbitofrontal cortex, thalamus and basal ganglia, lorazepam effects were attenuated in abstinent alcohol-dependent subjects compared with control subjects. In the occipital cortex and cerebellum, no such difference was seen. This likely reflects the reduction in GABA-benzodiazepine receptor levels described above. In a further study, it was shown that the relative activity of the GABA-benzodiazepine receptor did not alter during detoxification and early abstinence. It was therefore suggested that changes in GABA-ergic function were not involved in withdrawal. Lastly, Volkow et al. (1995) used the same paradigm in healthy male subjects with or without a family history of alcohol abuse. A blunted response was seen but only in the cerebellum of those subjects with such a family history. There were no differences in other regions; however, the differing cerebellar response was taken as evidence for GABA-ergic hypofunction being involved in vulnerability to alcoholism.

The intensive amount of research performed into elucidating the role of the GABA-benzodiazepine receptor in alcohol dependence has yielded a wealth of supportive evidence for this receptor complex playing a major role in mediating the central effects of alcohol and in alcohol dependence. It does appear that the GABA-ergic system is hypofunctional, although it is unclear whether this is merely as a consequence of alcohol abuse or exists as a trait characteristic. The apparent discrepancies between animal models and human alcohol dependence require further investigation. Investigation of the role of intracellular messengers in tolerance and dependence is only in its infancy.

GLUTAMATE

Glutamate dysfunction has been proposed as a unifying hypothesis of alcoholic brain injury (Tsai, Gastfriend & Coyle, 1995). Glutamate is the major excitatory neurotransmitter

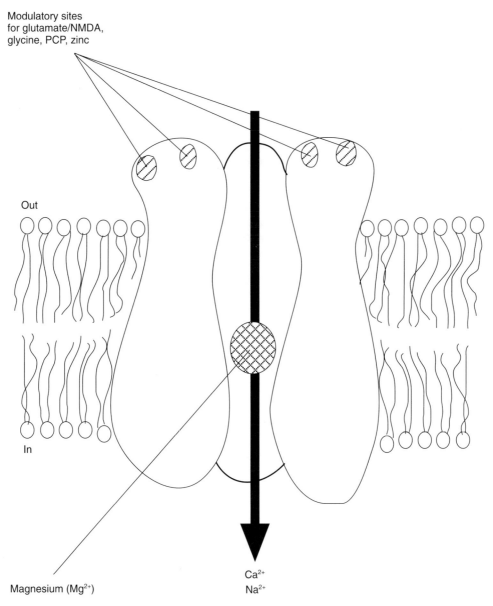

Modulatory sites
for glutamate/NMDA,
glycine, PCP, zinc

Out

In

Magnesium (Mg²⁺)

Ca²⁺
Na²⁺

Figure 6.2 Stylized diagram of the glutamate NMDA receptor. Only three of the five subunits are shown

system in the brain and alcohol is an antagonist at the N-methyl-D-aspartate (NMDA) receptor subtype (see Figure 6.2). Thus, acutely, alcohol reduces brain excitability. Like the GABA-benzodiazepine receptor, the NMDA receptor is a heteropentameric structure. Its identified subunits include NR1, NR2A-NR2D and NR3A. The NMDA receptor gates a Ca^{2+} channel which when not activated is blocked by Mg^{2+}. Located in this receptor–ionophore complex is also a binding site for glycine, which is a co-agonist to

glutamate and NMDA. There is a distinct binding site for phencyclidine (PCP) and its analogue, MK-801, which are both non-competitive antagonists, like alcohol.

There is increasing evidence that many effects of alcohol and the symptoms associated
with dependency, particularly withdrawal, appear to involve altered activity in the glutamatergic system. Alcohol intoxication, blackouts and cognitive impairment are associated
with attenuation of NMDA receptor neurotransmission. Long-term potentiation in the hippocampus, an NMDA-mediated process involved in memory, is attenuated by alcohol.
Hyperexcitability of the glutamatergic system appears to be involved in withdrawal seizures
and delirium tremens. Wernicke–Korsakoff's encephalopathy (see Chapter 8, this volume)
may result from ethanol-induced neurotoxicity through the increased number of NMDA
receptors. It is unclear whether the NMDA receptor contributes to the reinforcing effect
of alcohol.

Further evidence that alcohol acts as an NMDA antagonist is given by animal models
showing that NMDA antagonists are perceived to be like ethanol. In animal studies, NMDA
antagonists also block the acquisition of tolerance to alcohol. There appear to be regional
differences in responsivity of the glutamatergic system to alcohol. For example, ethanol
does not alter glutamate concentration in the frontal cortex but does in the hippocampus
and midbrain. There are also regional differences in the response of the NMDA receptor
to alcohol. Similarly to the situation with the GABA-benzodiazepine receptor, this is likely
due to differential subunit expression. Recently a region within two transmembrane segments (TM2, TM3) of glycine $\alpha1$ receptor subunit that confers ethanol sensitivity has been
identified.

Chronic exposure to ethanol in a number of different animal and *in vitro* models
results in NMDA supersenstivity (Hu & Ticku, 1995). This is seen as a mechanism to
overcome the antagonism of the NMDA receptor by alcohol. Some but not all studies
have found chronic ethanol exposure results in increased levels of NMDA receptors or
subunit proteins (Gulya et al., 1991; Hu & Ticku, 1995). For example, alcohol specifically
alters the NMDA channel ionophore by increasing specific subunits of the glutamate
receptor, the NMDAR1 and NMDAR2A (Snell et al., 1996). Increased levels and
activity of voltage-sensitive Ca^{2+} channels are also seen but kainate (another glutamate
receptor subtype) responses are unaltered (Gulya et al., 1991; Snell et al., 1996). As is seen
with the GABA-benzodiazepine receptor, there are regional differences. For instance, in
the hippocampus, no changes have been reported in the level of glycine or NMDA agonist
binding sites.

Lastly, as for the GABA-benzodiazepine receptor, altered phosphorylation of the receptor is thought to be important in altering sensitivity to NMDA receptors to alcohol. The
dynamic interaction between NMDA receptors and cytoskeletal-associated proteins is a
prerequisite for subcellular receptor targeting and synaptic localization (Chandler, Harris
& Crews, 1998). NMDA receptor function is regulated by this interaction and also by phosphorylation. Within these processes, there are many potential targets for ethanol to alter
NMDA receptor function (Chandler, Harris & Crews, 1998). For instance, mice deficient in
the enzyme, tyrosine kinase *Fyn*, are more sensitive to the hypnotic effect of ethanol and
do not show acute tolerance to NMDA receptor-mediated EPSPs (Chandler, Harris &
Crews, 1998). The focus on these mechanisms is likely to be intense in the future and they
may underlie tolerance and dependence.

In withdrawal, it appears that increased levels of glutamate are present in addition to
upregulation of a number of glutamate receptor subunits, NMDAR1, NMDAR2B, GluR1.
The changes seen in NMDA receptors after chronic exposure to alcohol return to normal
levels over the same time period as disappearance of withdrawal seizures (Gulya et al.,
1991). In addition to enhanced NMDA receptor function, increased voltage-sensitive Ca^{2+}
channel (VSCC)-mediated excitation is seen in hippocampal slices from mice in alcohol

withdrawal. Moreover, there is evidence to show that there are differences in NMDA and VSCC in mice bred for high and low sensitivity to ethanol withdrawal seizures.

Many animal models study the effects of chronic exposure to ethanol, which is not akin to patterns of exposure in human alcohol dependence where cycles of alcohol consumption and abstinence are the norm. The phenomenon of 'kindling' has been described, whereby the incidence and severity of seizures appears to increase with greater numbers of withdrawal cycles. This has been reproduced in animal models (Ulrichson et al., 1996). In such animals, significant decreases in [^{3}H]-α-amino-3-hydroxy-5-methyl-4-isoxazolepropionic acid (AMPA; another glutamate receptor subtype) binding in the striatum, entorhinal cortex, cerebellum and hippocampus and smaller decreases in [^{3}H]-flunitrazepam in the frontal cortex have been described (Ulrichson et al., 1996). Interestingly, in those animals who had seizures, but not in those that did not, increased [^{3}H]-MK801 (a glutamate antagonist) binding was seen within the entorhinal cortex and hippocampus. It was suggested that the reduction in [^{3}H]-AMPA binding reflected decreased glutaminergic neurotransmission which results in a protective effect to kindling.

As described, there is now increasingly strong evidence that alcohol-related changes at the NMDA receptor contribute to alcohol dependence, particularly to the symptoms associated with alcohol withdrawal. In animal models, seizures resulting from ethanol withdrawal can be blocked by NMDA antagonists (Grant et al., 1990). It is arguable that NMDA antagonists may have a role in the treatment of alcohol withdrawal, since benzodiazepines often do not afford full protection against such seizures. However, unlike the GABA-benzodiazepine receptor system, the NMDA receptor appears to play no role in tolerance, another phenomenon of dependence. Responsivity of the NMDA receptor system to alcohol does not differ, whether alcohol-naïve or after chronic exposure to alcohol.

Whilst comparable experiments have not been performed for alcohol, recent evidence suggests that glutamate may play a role in the learning of addictive behaviour (see Wicklegren, 1997). In animals given repeated doses of amphetamine or cocaine, sensitization occurs and has been shown to involve adaptations of glutamatergic neurotransmission within the nucleus accumbens. Supersensitivity of VTA dopaminergic cells to glutamate is seen after repeated amphetamine administration. In withdrawal, subsensitivity is seen and is associated with decreased expression of GluR1, GluR2 and NR1 sub-units in the nucleus accumbens. Sensitization to cocaine is associated with increased glutamatergic neurotransmission in the nucleus accumbens in rats. Glutamate appears to be crucial to acquisition of sensitization since, in those rats which did not become sensitized, no increase in glutamate was seen. Consequently, enhanced glutamate may be intimately involved with drug-seeking behaviour. It was proposed that reactivation of glutamatergic neurotransmission contributes to craving for the drug and such activation may occur with drug-related cues. However, whether this model based on studies of stimulants is generalizable to alcoholism is unclear.

Based on animal studies, studies of human alcoholism expected to find an increase in the level and function of NMDA receptors. A recent post-mortem study found no differences in binding of a glutamate agonist, antagonist or marker of the channel between alcohol-dependent subjects and controls (Freund & Anderson, 1999). The alcohol-dependent subjects had grossly normal brains and were otherwise matched with the control group. It may be that the ligands used are not sensitive enough to pick up subtle subunit changes. Other explanations include differing lengths of ethanol exposure and lack of replication of the cycles of abstinence, drinking and withdrawal.

Glutamatergic function in alcoholism has recently been investigated. Ketamine, an NMDA antagonist, has alcohol-like effects in recently abstinent alcoholics (Krystal et al., 1998). At a dose of 0.5 mg/kg, ketamine was perceived as equivalent to about nine standard drinks. Tsai et al. (1998) explored whether glutamatergic neurotransmission is increased in alcohol withdrawal by measuring CSF levels of excitatory neurotransmitters 1 week and 1 month after stopping drinking alcohol. As predicted from animal studies, increased concentrations of N-acetylaspartylglutamate and glycine were found at both time points in alcohol-dependent subjects compared to control subjects. There was very little difference between the levels at one week or one month. In addition, reductions were seen in GABA levels. It is not known, however, whether such an increase and decrease in levels are state or trait markers of alcoholism.

Manipulation of the glutamatergic system has been shown to be efficacious in maintaining abstinence from alcohol. Acamprosate (calcium acetyl-homotaurinate) has been shown to approximately double the abstinence rate, increase time to first relapse, reduce the lapse into relapse rate and has been reported to decrease craving (see Swift, 1999; Chapter 27 this volume). It also appears that the benefit of acamprosate persists after its termination. Since alcoholism is a heterogeneous disorder in which different neurotransmitters can be involved to a greater or lesser extent, it follows that acamprosate will not necessarily be uniformly efficacious. It has been shown that alcoholics who drink to overcome withdrawal or anxiety derive the greatest benefit.

The mechanism of action of acamprosate *in vivo* is unknown, but *in vitro* acamprosate is primarily an NMDA antagonist, although in hippocampal CA1 pyramidal neurons an increase in NMDA neurotransmission is seen (Lovinger & Zieglgansberger, 1996). For instance, acamprosate increases the expression of various splice variants of the NMDAR1, e.g. NMDAR1-4 in the hippocampus, but attenuates post-synaptic activity of excitatory amino acid agonists in neocortical neurons and enhances NMDA receptor-mediated synaptic neurotransmission. Acamprosate has been shown to increase glutamatergic activation in the nucleus accumbens and hippocampus in the rat. It has been proposed that in withdrawal these neurons are underactive, leading to withdrawal symptoms and craving, and that acamprosate ameliorates these processes.

Acamprosate has also been shown to block the "alcohol-deprivation" effect. This effect is the increased "work" an animal will perform to receive ethanol after a period of deprivation, or abstinence, in rats trained to lever press for alcohol. This increase only lasts for a few days. If animals are pre-treated with acamprosate or naltrexone (see below), this increase in responding is abolished (Koob, 1996). The exact neuropharmacology and regions involved in this effect remain to be elucidated but have evident similarities to patterns seen in alcoholism in man.

SEROTONIN

5-HT (hydroxytryptamine) or serotonin has been a focus of research in the search for a biochemical explanation for the genetic transmission of alcoholism and has been the subject of a number of recent reviews (LeMarquand, Pihl & Benkelfat, 1994; Sellers, Higgins & Sobel 1994). The hypothesis put forward is that serotonergic deficiency is associated with increased vulnerability to alcoholism and also to impulsivity and aggressive behaviours. Furthermore, it appears that hypofunction in the serotonergic system may be more apparent in a particular type of alcoholism. In classical adoption studies, Cloninger, Bohman & Sigvardsson (1981) described two subtypes whose characteristics are given in Table 6.2 (see also Chapters 4 and 14, this volume). There is now much evidence to suggest that a distinguishing feature of these two variants is brain 5-HT function. In addition, abnormalities of the serotonergic system are hypothesized to be present in disorders which commonly coexist with alcoholism, such as depression, anxiety, bulimia and suicidal behaviour. The primary source of serotonergic neurons in the brain is the raphe nuclei in the brainstem, from where they project widely throughout the brain. There are a number of different sero-

Table 6.2   Subtypes of alcoholism (modified from Cloninger et al., 1981)

Characteristic	Type 1	Type 2
Onset of alcoholism	>25 years	<25 years
Gender	Both	Male
Antisocial traits	No	Common
Type of drinking	Binge	Steady
Other drug use	No	Yes
Anxiety state	High	Low
Impulsivity	Low	High
Brain 5-HT function	High	Low
mCPP responses	Anxiety	"Crave"

tonin receptor subtypes, for example 5-HT_{1A}, 5-HT_{2A}, 5-HT_3. In addition, there is a transporter mechanism or reuptake site on the neuron which released serotonin, through which serotonin is removed from the synapse to terminate its activity.

Many animal studies have shown that reduced serotonergic functioning is associated with alcohol preference. Lower levels of serotonin and 5-hydroxyindoleacetic acid (5-HIAA) have been found in alcohol-preferring rats (P) compared with non-preferring rats (NP) (see McBride & Li, 1998). An increase in 5-HT_{1A} receptors is found in the cerebral cortex and a lower level of these receptors is found in the raphe nucleus reflecting a reduced number of serotonergic neurons. Reduced levels of the 5-HT_{1B} receptor are also present in many limbic regions of P rats. Further support for an association between reduced 5-HT_{1B} receptor levels and alcohol preference comes from studies of mice lacking this receptor. These mice consume approximately twice as much ethanol as their wild-type, probably because it is more rewarding (Crabbe et al., 1996). By contrast, levels of 5-HT_{2A} are reduced and 5-HT_3 receptors unchanged in P rats compared to NP rats. This receptor profile is not common to all alcohol-preferring rodents and hence cannot be taken as necessarily mediating vulnerability to alcoholism in man (see McBride & Li, 1998).

In man, supportive evidence for reduced serotonergic functioning in alcoholism has been obtained from a number of studies, although not unequivocally. Low levels of CSF 5-HIAA have been reported in some but not all studies comparing alcoholics with controls (see LeMarquand et al., 1994). A number of post-mortem studies have been performed measuring 5-HT levels, 5-HIAA and levels of reuptake sites. An initial study surprisingly reported no decrease in 5-HIAA in alcoholic subjects who committed suicide. Later studies, however, described reduced levels of 5-HT, 5-HIAA and reuptake sites in the caudate, hippocampus and hypothalamus of alcoholics.

A number of studies have used the platelet as a model for the CNS serotonergic system. Although many studies provide evidence supportive of reduced serotonergic function in alcoholism, again there are inconsistencies (see LeMarquand et al., 1994). Reduced levels of 5-HT have been reported. There is also evidence to suggest that activity of the serotonin transporter is enhanced in alcoholics, resulting in lower synaptic levels of serotonin. Since this effect persists into abstinence, this may be trait and not a state marker. Although platelet 5-HT_2 receptor function is diminished in recently detoxified alcoholics, it returns to normal within 3 weeks. Animal models of alcoholism have shown reduced 5-HT_2 receptor function in rat cortex, interestingly without reduced receptor levels. However, with prolonged abstinence, reduced 5-HT_2 receptor function is associated with reduced receptor levels. Thus, these studies suggest that chronic alcohol exposure is associated with reduced serotonergic functioning but it is not necessarily a trait marker.

As already described in relation to ethanol-preferring rodents, specific receptor subtypes may be involved with particular aspects of alcoholism. Linkage of antisocial alcoholism to the 5-HT$_{1B}$ gene has been reported in two populations (Lappalainen et al., 1998). The 5-HT$_3$ receptor is the only 5-HT receptor linked to an ion channel and there is evidence to suggest that, similarly to the NMDA and GABA-benzodiazepine receptors, it is directly modulated by ethanol (see Grant, 1995). The 5-HT$_3$ receptor plays a key role in modulating dopaminergic neurotransmission in the nucleus accumbens and hence is likely to be involved with the reinforcing effects of alcohol. This is supported by animal studies showing that selective 5-HT$_3$ antagonists decrease ethanol self-administration.

An important population of 5-HT$_2$ receptors is found on inhibitory cortical GABA interneurons where they stimulate GABA release. The reduced 5-HT function in Type 2 alcoholics means they have less cortical inhibition, which predisposes them to impulsive behaviour. The relative lack of GABA inhibition may explain their relative resistance to sedative drugs, such as alcohol and benzodiazepines (Cowley et al., 1992). Other studies in animals and man have found that 5-HT agonists are perceived as alcohol in drug discrimination paradigms, perhaps because the net effect of both is an increase in GABA function.

If a serotonergic deficit is involved in alcohol dependence, then increasing the amount of serotonin available through using reuptake inhibitors (fluoxetine, citalopram) or agonists (buspirone, mCPP) should result in reduced alcohol consumption, but this is not the case (LeMarquand et al., 1994). Similarly, 5-HT antagonists are not expected to reduce alcohol consumption. However ondansetron, a 5-HT$_3$ antagonist, has been reported to reduce alcohol consumption in man, presumably by modulating dopaminergic transmission, as described above. Serotonin reuptake inhibitors (SSRIs) have, at best, only modest efficacy in helping to control drinking in alcoholics or maintain abstinence (see also Chapter 27, this volume). It has been postulated that SSRIs only help those with comorbid depression. In one study, fluoxetine was found to actually worsen outcome for patients whose characteristics included parental family history, early onset, polydrug abuse and greater severity of dependence. This result is interesting in light of the evidence that it is this group that has serotonergic hypofunction (see below).

Neuroendocrine challenges have been used to test serotonin function in alcohol dependence. These involve giving a drug with known activity on particular neurotransmitter system or its receptor(s), which will stimulate or inhibit the release of hormones in the blood which can be measured. Therefore, from the response and changes in hormonal levels, inferences can be made about the function of the neurotransmitter system targeted by the drug. Concerning the serotonergic system, a diminished cortisol and prolactin response has been reported in response to tryptophan, a serotonin precursor, and MK-212, a 5-HT$_2$/5-HT$_{1C}$ agonist (Lee & Meltzer, 1991). There was no difference in baseline levels of cortisol or prolactin in alcoholics compared to control subjects. It appears that hypofunction in the serotonergic system may be more apparent in a particular type of alcoholism. With regard to Cloninger et al.'s (1981) typology, it appears that low levels of 5-HT, inferred from low levels of CSF 5-HIAA, are associated with the early onset, family history positive, high impulsivity Type 2 variant of alcoholism (Fils-Aime et al., 1996). There is also some evidence to suggest that serotonergic function is reduced in impulsive sons of alcoholics (Linnoila, 1989). By contrast, in the Type 1 variant, high 5-HT levels result in high levels of anxiety, which are overcome by drinking alcohol. It is unlikely that there will be such a clear dichotomy in 5-HT brain function but the evidence supporting serotonergic hypofunction in Type 2 alcoholism is increasingly robust.

In an elegant series of experiments, Linnoila's group have studied non-human primates and humans to explore the relationship between Type 2 alcoholism and serotonergic function. In non-human primates, high rates of alcohol consumption were seen under a stressful condition of social separation and were associated with low CSF 5-HIAA levels. Despite the higher levels of drinking, these monkeys were less sensitive to intoxication. There are strong parallels between these characteristics and those seen in young males at high risk of alcoholism. In addition, chronic stress early in life resulted in low brain serotonergic function, aggression, resistance to sedatives and promotion of alcohol intake (Higley & Linnoila, 1997). These studies have obvious important implications in relation to childhood experiences and later risk of alcoholism. Such studies offer the exciting prospect that neurobiology will explain important psychological observations on separation and subsequent psychopathology.

Differences in Type 1 and Type 2 alcoholism are further seen using the mixed serotonergic agonist/antagonist, m-chlorophenylpiperazine (mCPP). Several studies have reported that mCPP induces craving for alcohol and is perceived as "alcohol-like", particularly in Type 2 alcoholics. By contrast, Type 1 alcoholics respond with enhanced anxiety (George et al., 1997). As an agonist, mCPP has the greatest affinity for the $5-HT_{2C}$ subtype, where it is a partial agonist, and lower affinities for $5-HT_{1A}$, $5-HT_6$ and $5-HT_7$ receptors; mCPP also acts as an antagonist at $5-HT_{2A}$ and $5-HT_3$ receptors. The most abundant 5-HT receptor in the cortex is the $5-HT_{2C}$ subtype. In order to clarify which anatomical site(s) are involved in mCPP induced craving, a PET study measuring glucose metabolism after injection of mCPP has been performed (Hommer et al., 1997). Compared to controls, alcoholics showed a blunted response to mCPP in the head of the caudate, thalamus, orbitofrontal and prefrontal cortices and an enhanced response in the cerebellum and posterior cingulate cortex. Of note, though, craving was not induced; this is probably due to the adverse environment of the scanning procedure, which is not conducive to inducing craving. Despite the fact that the subjective state of craving was not induced, these results lend support to the hypothesis that the serotonergic system is hypofunctional in alcohol dependence.

Neuroimaging of 5-HT is in its infancy, but an *in vivo* neuroimaging SPET study using β-CIT to label the serotonergic transporter found that alcoholics had 30% less such transporters in the raphe nuclei compared to control subjects (Heinz et al., 1998). The reduction correlated with life-time alcohol consumption and with increased levels of anxiety and depression. There was no relationship with a measure of impulsivity. The reduction in transporters was thought to reflect toxic damage by alcohol. A further study in non-human primates revealed that greater β-CIT uptake correlated with low levels of 5-HIAA in the CSF, less intoxication upon initial exposure to alcohol and greater aggressiveness (Heinz et al., 1998). These *in vivo* studies support the hypothesis that serotonergic hypofunction is implicated in alcoholism, particularly Type 2.

DOPAMINE

The dopaminergic mesolimbic system, involving a projection from the ventral tegmental area (VTA) to the nucleus accumbens, has attracted much attention with regard to the positive reinforcing or pleasurable effects of alcohol. An increase in dopamine within the nucleus accumbens is hypothesized to be a prerequisite for alcohol reinforcement. It is proposed that vulnerability to alcoholism is associated with a hypofunctional mesolimbic dopaminergic system. In animal models, ethanol has been shown to increase the firing of dopaminergic neurons and to release dopamine in the striatum and particularly within the nucleus accumbens (Di Chiara & Imperato, 1985). As expected, dopamine antagonists decrease lever-pressing for alcohol in non-deprived rats. Injection of dopamine antagonists into the nucleus accumbens and dopamine agonists into the VTA reduce self-administration of ethanol (Hodge, Samson & Chappelle, 1997). It is suggested that in the VTA, dopamine agonists act via dopamine autoreceptors, resulting in decreased firing of the dopaminergic neurons to the nucleus accumbens. In alcohol withdrawal, a decrease in dopamine function is seen in the striatum. Thus from these studies it appears that dopamine does play a role in mediating the pleasurable effects of alcohol. Downregulation of these systems during repeated ethanol exposure or during abstinence may induce feelings of dysphoria or craving, which increase the likelihood of relapse.

Many studies, however, produce conflicting results and it appears that dopaminergic and non-dopaminergic pathways play a role in mediating the pleasure of drinking alcohol. The release of dopamine in the nucleus accumbens has been shown not to be critical to positive reinforcement in the rat. Denervation of the nucleus accumbens with 6-hydroxydopamine does not prevent oral self-administration of alcohol (Rassnick, Stinus & Koob, 1993). Based on studies with conventional reinforcers, such as food and water, and with other substances of abuse, it has been proposed that mesolimbic dopamine neurons do not code for generic motivational significance, but only for specific stimuli possessing a particularly high motivational impact related to their novelty, unpredictability or occurrence under a deprivation state. This was acknowledged as being at variance with the view proposed by Robinson & Berridge (1993), that mesolimbic dopamine neurons code for generic motivational salience.

Studies have shown that increased responsivity of dopaminergic neurotransmission may persist after cessation of exposure to ethanol (Nestby et al., 1997). After a period of withdrawal from ethanol, whether consumption was forced or voluntary, ethanol consumption was associated with increased dopamine release in the nucleus accumbens. Moreover, the more alcohol that was consumed, the greater the release of dopamine. Such an increase was not seen in the caudate or putamen but D_1 receptor supersensitivity was seen here. Similar changes are seen after exposure to other drugs of abuse, such as morphine and psychostimulants. These neuroadaptations could be involved in the risk of relapse, particularly if the amount of alcohol consumed is related to how pleasurable its effects are, as suggested by the above animal studies.

The neurochemistry of some alcohol-preferring rodents supports the hypothesis that dopaminergic deficits are associated with increased consumption. In alcohol-preferring (P) rats, compared with non-P rats, lower basal levels of noradrenaline and dopamine have been found, but only in the nucleus accumbens and olfactory tubercle (see McBride & Li, 1998). A similar decrease is also found in HAD rats and C57BL/6J mice, which consume high levels of ethanol. Acute alcohol exposure results in a rise in dopamine in the P rats. However, in another strain of alcohol-preferring rats (AA), no differences were found between the strains, whether ethanol-naïve or previously experienced, in the amount of dopamine released in the nucleus accumbens after acute ethanol exposure. Interestingly, a small but significant increase in dopamine was seen in those rats which self-administered alcohol compared to those that received alcohol non-contingently. Lastly, ethanol-related cues did not increase dopamine in the nucleus accumbens. Thus, in this species dopamine does not appear to be key in mediating positive reinforcement.

There has been some systematic investigation into which dopamine receptor subtypes are involved in mediating the effects of alcohol and also of positive reinforcement. There are both D_1 and D_2-like receptor subtypes within the mesolimbic system. Injections of both agonists and antagonists at the D_1, D_2 and D_3 receptor subtypes have been shown to both reduce or increase ethanol intake and preference (see McBride & Li, 1998). It is hypothesized that dopamine agonists mimic the effects of alcohol, whilst antagonists prevent the reinforcing effect of alcohol, and hence both will reduce alcohol consumption. Lower levels of D_2 receptors have been reported in the nucleus accumbens of sP but not sNP rats (see McBride & Li, 1998). Such a reduction, though, is not found in other species, including AA and HAD rats. Mice lacking the dopamine D_2 receptor show marked aversion to ethanol compared to the ethanol-consuming wild-types (Phillips et al., 1998). In addition, sensitivity to ethanol-induced locomotor impairment was also reduced in these mutant mice. It has been proposed that D_1 and D_2 receptors may mediate reinforcing effects but differentially regulate the appetitive and consummatory components of drug reinforcement (Self & Nestler, 1998). In animal models of cocaine addiction, stimulation of the D_2 but not D_1 receptors induces relapse. More recently, it has been proposed that D_3 rather than D_2 receptors are important in reducing ethanol intake. As is seen with the D_2 receptor, altered levels of the D_1 and D_3 receptors are not consistent with reductions and no changes seen, depending on the species (see McBride & Li, 1998). These studies add further support to the hypothesis that reduced function in the dopaminergic system is associated with alcohol preference, but not unequivocally, and also that particular receptor subtypes may play specific roles.

The activity of the dopaminergic system in alcoholism in man has been studied using neuroendocrine challenges. Apomorphine and bromocriptine are dopamine agonists and the resulting increase in growth hormone (GH) levels is used as an index of dopaminergic function. Apomorphine is non-specific in that it will act on D_1 and D_2 receptors, although the GH response is thought to involve only D_2 receptors. Bromocriptine is a D_2 agonist. Reduced dopaminergic responsivity has been repeatedly seen in abstinent alcoholics (Balldin, Berggren & Lindstedt, 1992). Several studies, but not all, have shown that the dopaminergic system is more sensitive in early abstinence (Annuziato et al., 1983; Heinz et al., 1996a,b). A positive correlation between withdrawal symptomatology 1 day after stopping alcohol and degree of blunted GH response to apomorphine has been reported (Heinz et al., 1996a). Interestingly, the responsivity of the dopaminergic system may predict relapse. Although all patients showed a blunted GH response, patients who subsequently relapsed showed a lower GH response than those patients who remained abstinent. This supports the view that increased dopamine is protective against relapse. These responses could not be attributed to different genotypes of either the dopamine D_1 nor dopamine D_2 (*Taq*A1 allele). These studies suggest that there are alterations in dopaminergic function within the hypothalamus/pituitary in alcohol dependence; however, it is uncertain whether such alterations are also seen within the critical mesolimbic system.

Cloninger (1978) hypothesized that high "novelty-seeking" behaviour is associated with low basal firing rates of dopaminergic neurons. Subjects with this behaviour were hypothesized to show a greater dopamine response to alcohol. This was based on an earlier study, which showed that men at high risk of developing alcoholism were more sensitive to alcohol-induced changes in prolactin levels. A subsequent study in alcoholics supported the hypothesis by showing that greater GH release in response to apomorphine was associated with "novelty seeking". A number of studies have failed, however, to support this hypothesis, since relapse, taken as a correlate of "novelty-seeking" behaviour, was not associated with increased dopaminergic sensitivity (Heinz et al., 1996b).

In regard to the treatment of alcohol dependence, it has been hypothesized that blockade of dopaminergic neurotransmission in the mesolimbic areas would reduce positive reinforcement. Consequently, drinking alcohol would be less pleasurable and it was inferred that craving would also be reduced. No specific D_1 antagonists or agonists have been used to treat alcohol dependence. Studies exploring the use of D_2 antagonists, and using bromocriptine as a dopamine agonist, have shown little efficacy, although it appears that there may be an effect in some patients. It has been reported that bromocriptine resulted in the greatest improvement in craving and anxiety in patients with the A1 allele of the dopamine D_2 receptor (Lawford et al., 1995). Thus, in these particular patients, reduced dopaminergic functioning may be present and lead to relapse, as described above. It is debatable how successful manipulation of the dopaminergic system will be in maintaining abstinence in alcohol dependence. In particular, craving is an ill-defined phenomenon which contains components other than the desire the gain pleasure from alcohol. It is possible that such pharmacological manipulation may be of more use in people who drink heavily and still derive pleasure from drinking alcohol.

There have been a number of neuroimaging studies exploring the status of the dopaminergic system in alcohol dependence. A reduction in the level of striatal D_2 receptors has been reported, but there is conflicting evidence about whether there is a change in the level of dopamine transporters, with a decrease and no change described (Volkow et al., 1996; Tiihonen et al., 1995). This latter inconsistency may, however, be due to different radiotracers used to label the dopamine transporter. Volkow et al. (1996) interpreted the reduction in striatal D_2 receptor as reflecting a loss of striatal GABA neurons. Tiihonen et al. (1995) studied the dopamine transporter with β-CIT and SPET in violent and non-violent alcoholics and found that transporter levels were significantly reduced in non-violent, but not violent, alcoholics. The significance of this finding is unclear. As yet there have been no imaging studies examining the status of the dopaminergic system in people with a high risk of developing alcoholism.

A recent study has shown that dopamine transporters are lower in alcoholics in the first few days after alcohol withdrawal and increase over the next 4 weeks to normal levels (Laine et al., 1999). This concurs with a report of reduced dopamine transporters in monkeys chronically exposed to alcohol. It was proposed that this reduction in dopamine transporters in early abstinence leads to reduced dopamine uptake and therefore to sensitization of dopamine impulses. It was suggested that this sensitization was implicated in the risk of relapse, given the role of dopamine in mediating positive reinforcement.

NORADRENALINE

The noradrenaline system has received relatively little attention in comparison to other neurotransmitter systems and is often not mentioned in reviews of the neuropharmacology of alcoholism. There is evidence to suggest that impaired noradrenergic function is associated with alcoholism and that noradrenergic hyperactivity underlies many symptoms of withdrawal (Nutt & Glue, 1986). Reduced levels of noradrenaline have been found in post-mortem examinations of chronic alcoholics in the hippocampus and cingulate cortex. It appears that acute alcohol consumption causes an increase in noradrenaline turnover, followed by a reduction. In alcohol-dependent rats, however, increased noradrenaline turnover is maintained. It has been shown that noradrenaline release in animals chronically exposed to alcohol is increased through altered Ca^{2+} mediated neuronal responses.

It is unclear whether the reduced levels in the noradrenergic system pre-date alcohol abuse. There is evidence from animal studies that noradrenergic impairment may be a trait marker. In alcohol-preferring (P) rats, noradrenaline levels in the medulla are lower and higher in the cerebral cortex compared with the non-alcohol-preferring (NP) strain prior to alcohol consumption (see McBride & Li, 1998). Other alcohol-preferring strains do not necessarily show this difference. However, no differences in cortical noradrenergic receptor numbers has been reported.

The locus coeruleus is the major noradrenergic nucleus in the brain and is involved in regulating attentional states and activity of the autonomic system. Locus coeruleus neurons show dose-dependent depression of responsiveness to sensory stimuli at low doses of ethanol (Aston-Jones, Foote & Bloom, 1982). Since this nucleus is involved in mediating attention, it is likely that this effect may contribute to alcohol-induced impairment of cognitive processes. It is not clear whether the locus coeruleus is structurally different in alcoholics. Reductions in neuronal number have been reported and disputed. It may be that more severe alcoholism is associated with neuronal loss, but this remains to be elucidated.

Increased activity within the noradrenergic system has been implicated in mediating somatic symptoms of drug withdrawal. In alcohol withdrawal, CSF and urinary levels of noradrenaline and its metabolites are elevated (see Nutt & Glue, 1986). This may be due to desensitization of inhibitory $\alpha 2$ receptors (Nutt & Glue, 1986). Levels of noradrenaline and its primary metabolite, 3-methoxy-4-hydroxyphenylethyleneglycol (MOPEG), are elevated in the urine and CSF during early withdrawal and decrease during detoxification in male patients to normal levels. Furthermore, positive correlations were found between CSF MOPEG levels and sleeping problems, restlessness, visual hallucinations, elevated muscle tension and improvement in depressive mood. An association has also been reported between the plasma level of the metabolite, 3-methoxy-4-hydroxyphenyl glycol, and the severity of withdrawal and the number of previous detoxifications.

Whilst reduced levels of β-adrenergic receptors have been described in ethanol dependent rats, in withdrawal increased levels are seen. It has been suggested that this increase probably occurs after the period of maximum withdrawal and thus is a consequence rather than a cause of withdrawal (Nutt & Glue, 1986). Notably, propanolol, a β-adrenergic antagonist, has been found to control some of the signs of alcohol withdrawal, such as tremor and hypertension. This effect was associated with reduced levels of urinary noradrenaline. Reduced levels of $\alpha 2$ receptors have also been shown in rat brain. If this reduction involved autoreceptors, then increased noradrenergic activity would result. In alcoholic patients undergoing detoxification, the response to clonidine, an $\alpha 2$-adrenergic agonist, has been found to be blunted. This suggests central $\alpha 2$-adrenergic receptors are hypofunctional and likely contribute to withdrawal symptomatology of increased arousal, insomnia and restlessness. Another study using clonidine-induced hypothermia to assess $\alpha 2$-adrenergic receptor function found subsensitivity of this receptor during early withdrawal, which had normalized 5 weeks later. This suggests that altered noradrenergic function is a state rather than a trait marker of alcoholism. Platelet $\alpha 2$-adrenoreceptors have been reported to be reduced in alcohol withdrawal, but not consistently. It appears that rapid changes in receptor levels take place in the first few days and are associated with reducing levels of plasma noradrenaline.

In opiate withdrawal, adrenergic $\alpha 2$ agonists, such as clonidine and more recently lofexidine, are used clinically to ameliorate symptoms associated with adrenergic hyperactivity, such as insomnia, agitation and elevated blood pressure. These drugs have been tested in alcohol withdrawal but are not currently widely used. Due to their ability to cause seizures, they should only be used as an adjunct to benzodiazepines.

In addition to withdrawal, noradrenaline may play a role in tolerance to alcohol. Lesion of ascending noradrenaline projections with 6-hydroxydopamine blocked the development of tolerance to the hypothermic and sedative effects of alcohol (Tabakoff & Ritzmann, 1977). This effect could be prevented by pre-treatment with a noradrenaline reuptake blocker (methylimipramine), suggesting that disruption of noradrenergic function is involved. This is important since 6-hydroxydopamine will also destroy dopaminergic projections. Such treatment had no effect on withdrawal.

OPIOID SYSTEM

There is increasing evidence to show that alcohol-induced activation of the endogenous opioid system is functionally involved in alcohol reinforcement and in mediating the pleasurable effects of alcohol. The interaction between alcohol and the opioid system has been recently reviewed (Herz, 1997; Ulm, Volpicelli & Volpicelli, 1995). The hypothesis concerning the role of the opiate system in alcohol dependence is that consumption of alcohol compensates for an opioid deficiency. Evidence from animal and human studies supports this hypothesis, since alcohol consumption results in activation of the opioid system and opioid antagonists reduce alcohol self-administration.

As described, the mesolimbic dopaminergic system is widely acknowledged as playing a central role in the rewarding effects of drugs of abuse and positive reinforcement. The opioid system is intimately involved with the mesolimbic dopaminergic system in several key areas. β-Endorphin-containing neurons from the arcuate nucleus innervate both the VTA and dopaminergic presynaptic terminals in the nucleus accumbens. In addition there are encephalinergic interneurons within the nucleus accumbens. In the nucleus accumbens, κ receptors are located on the dopaminergic terminals and their activation reduces dopamine release. The nucleus accumbens consists of a shell and a core, which are distinct in their functional connections. The shell is linked to the extended amygdala and hence to the network integrating emotional responses. The core is associated with extrapyramidal control of motor function, and μ opiate receptors are located here.

Injection of opiates into the VTA results in increased dopamine levels in the nucleus accumbens by disinhibiting dopaminergic neuronal firing (Wise, 1998). In the VTA, opiates act through μ receptors inhibiting the GABA neurons on which they are located. The GABA neurons tonically inhibit the firing of the dopaminergic neurons. Thus, activation of the μ receptor, and also the δ receptor, results in release from this tonic inhibition and dopamine levels increase in the nucleus accumbens. Through a similar mechanism, application of opioids directly into the nucleus accumbens also results in positive reinforcement.

Alcohol consumption increases activity in the opioid system. Opioid antagonists, such as naltrexone and naloxone, have been shown to reduce alcohol consumption in several animal models in a specific and dose-dependent manner. It appears that different opioid receptor subtypes may be involved. Both naltrexone and naloxone are antagonists at the μ, κ and δ receptor subtypes. To further probe which receptor subtype is involved in mediating the effects of naltrexone, a recent study in rhesus monkeys used opioid antagonists selective at the μ and κ subtypes, and also gave them in combination with naltrexone (Williams & Woods, 1998). There was no evidence to show that either the μ or the κ receptor subtype was critical in reducing alcohol consumption. It was concluded that naltrexone's efficacy lies through its interaction with another opioid receptor site, as yet uncharacterized.

δ Antagonists, such as naltrindole, have also been shown to reduce alcohol consumption (Froelich et al., 1991) but not in every study (Williams & Wood, 1998). The δ opioid receptor has been shown to be involved in the release of dopamine in the nucleus accumbens. δ Antagonists inhibit alcohol-stimulated dopamine release in this area. In neural cells expressing the δ receptor, chronic exposure to alcohol has been shown to result in increased affinity and density of the δ receptor through increased genetic expression. This persists for up to 24 hours after withdrawal before returning to normal levels.

The studies described above are performed with the opiate antagonists being given systemically. Another study has explored the anatomical sites where the opiates act to modulate reinforcement. Giving methylnaloxonium, an opioid antagonist, directly into various brain regions, it has been shown that the amygdala and nucleus accumbens are involved in reducing ethanol reinforcement (Koob et al., 1998). Thus, there is ample evidence that the opioid system is involved in mediating the positive reinforcing effects of alcohol through modulation of the mesolimbic dopaminergic system.

In addition to altering opioid release and receptor function, alcohol also modulates gene expression. Acutely, alcohol increases endorphin and encephalin gene expression in specific brain regions and increases release of opioids from the pituitary. The reverse is seen after chronic alcohol administration with decreased opioid gene expression and reduced β-endorphin release. The mechanisms involved in alcohol regulating opioid gene expression remain speculative. Proenkephalin and proopiomelanocortin (POMC; precursor of β-endorphin) gene expression are controlled by cAMP response element binding protein (CREB), a transcription factor (Hyman et al., 1994). CREB has been proposed to play an important role in learning and memory. Once phosphorylated by cAMP dependent and independent mechanisms, CREB becomes transcriptionally active and induces sensitive genes, such as POMC and proenkephalin. It has been recently shown that acute exposure to ethanol results in an increase in phosphorylated CREB and consequently increased proenkephalin and POMC expression (Hyman et al., 1994).

A difference in the response of the opioid system to alcohol has been described in rats selectively bred for high (P) and low alcohol preference (NP). Acutely, alcohol results in a greater increase of POMC mRNA in the arcuate nucleus and pituitary in P compared to NP rats (see McBride & Li, 1998). In addition, an increase in proencephalin mRNA is also seen in the nucleus accumbens of P but not NP rats. These studies suggest that the opiate system is more sensitive to the effects of alcohol in P rats. Once the blood alcohol level had returned to normal, the proenkephalin mRNA was suppressed in both strains. In AA compared to ANA rats, β-endorphin levels are higher in the anterior pituitary, lower in the amygdala and periaqueductal grey matter and equivalent in the nucleus accumbens and cerebral cortex. However, lower levels of proenkephalin and prodynorphin were found in the nucleus accumbens and VTA in AA rats. In some but not all species of alcohol-preferring rodents, different levels of μ, κ and δ opiate receptors have been reported, with both increases and decreases described compared with the non-alcohol-preferring strain (see McBride & Li, 1998). These results support the hypothesis that the opioid system plays a determining role in preference for alcohol but whether an increase or decrease in function is involved appears to be region-specific.

The ability of opioid antagonists to reduce self-administration of alcohol in animal models led to naltrexone being used in the treatment of alcohol dependence (see also Chapter 27 this volume). The first study showed that naltrexone given to recently detoxified alcohol-dependent subjects resulted in a lower relapse rate and reduced craving (Volpicelli et al., 1992). More interestingly, however, in those subjects who drank alcohol, naltrexone appeared to prevent a full relapse. It has also been shown that, even after the withdrawal of naltrexone, relapse rates remain lower and abstinence rates increase (O'Malley et al., 1996). These results were attributed to the fact that alcohol stimulates the release of opiates resulting in positive reinforcement and that, in the presence of naltrexone, this reinforcement does not occur; consequently, drinking more alcohol is not attractive. For the long-term effect after withdrawal of naltrexone, it is suggested that, once the pleasurable response to alcohol is blocked, alcohol-related cues may lose their ability to induce craving and further drinking. This is supported by evidence from animal models where opioid antagonists facilitate the extinction of the conditioned reinforcing effects of alcohol in the absence of alcohol consumption.

NEUROPEPTIDE Y

A relative newcomer to the list of neurotransmitters or neuromodulators that are involved in mediating the effects of alcohol is neuropeptide Y (NPY). This neuropeptide is an inhibitory neuromodulator thought to modulate noradrenaline. It has been shown to have anxiolytic effects, thought to be mediated via the amygdala and to increase feeding behaviour via an effect in the paraventricular nucleus. In the alcohol-preferring (P) strain of rats, NPY has been implicated as causal in their high level of alcohol consumption (Ehlers, Somes & Cloutier, 1998). Lower levels of NPY were found in the amygdala, hippocampus and frontal cortex in P compared to non-P rats. Raised NPY levels have also been described in Wistar rats in alcohol withdrawal. NPY-deficient mice, which display high levels of anxiety and greater susceptibility to seizures than wild-type mice, drank twice as much ethanol and were more resistant to its sedative effects (Thiele, 1998). Interestingly, the reverse was seen in mice bred to overexpress the NPY gene. It was suggested from all these studies that the major physiological function of NPY is to protect neural circuits. Thus, its absence is compensated for by consumption of other substances, e.g. alcohol, food.

KEY REFERENCES AND SUGGESTIONS FOR FURTHER READING

Drug and Alcohol Dependence, **51** (Special Issue) (1998).
  Concerns pharmacological aspects of drug and alcohol dependence.

Koob, G., Rocio, M., Carrera, A., Gold, L., Heyser, C., Maldonado-Irizarry et al. (1998). Substance abuse as a compulsive behaviour. *Journal of Psychopharmacology*, **12**, 39–48.

Tsai, G., Gastfriend, D. & Coyle, J. (1995). The glutamatergic basis of human alcoholism. *American Journal of Psychiatry*, **152**, 332–340.

Nutt, D. & Glue, P. (1986). Monoamines and alcohol. *British Journal of Addiction*, **81** 327–338.

Nutt, D.J. (1999). Alcohol and the brain. Pharmacological insights for psychiatrists. *British Journal of Psychiatry*, **175**, 114–119.

REFERENCES

Annuziato, L., Amoroso, S., di Renzo, G., Argenzio, F., Aurilio, C., Grella, A. & Quatrone, A. (1983). Increased GH responsiveness to dopamine receptor stimulation in alcohol addicts during the late withdrawal syndrome. *Life Sciences*, **33**, 2651–2655.
Aston-Jones, G., Foote, S. & Bloom, F. (1982). Low doses of ethanol disrupt sensory responses of brain noradrenergic neurones. *Nature*, **296**, 857–860.
Balldin, J., Berggren, U. & Lindstedt, G. (1992). Neuroendocrine evidence for reduced dopamine receptor sensitivity in alcoholism. *Alcoholism: Clinical and Experimental Research*, **16**, 71–74.
Benkelfat, C., Murphy, D., Hill, J., Nutt, D. & Linnoila, M. (1991). Ethanol-like properties of the serotonergic partial agonist *m*-chlorophenylpiperazine in chronic alcoholics. *Archives of General Psychiatry*, **48**, 383–390.
Boyle, A., Segal, R., Smith, B. & Amit, Z. (1993). Bidirectional effects of GABAergic agonists and antagonists on maintenance of voluntary ethanol intake in rats. *Pharmacology, Biochemistry and Behaviour*, **46**, 179–182.
Buck, K., Hahner, L., Sikela, J. & Harris, R. (1991). Chronic ethanol treatment alters brain levels of γ-aminobutyric acid A receptor subunit mRNAs: relationship to genetic differences in ethanol withdrawal seizure severity. *Journal of Neuroscience*, **57**, 1452–1455.
Chandler, L., Harris, R. & Crews, F. (1998). Ethanol tolerance and synaptic plasticity. *Trends in Pharmacological Sciences*, **19**, 491–495.
Charlton, M., Sweetman, P., Fitzgerald, L., Terwilliger, R., Nestler, E. & Duman, R. (1997). Chronic ethanol administration regulated the expression of GABAA receptor a1 and a5 subunits in the ventral striatum and hippocampus. *Journal of Neurochemistry*, **68**, 121–127.
Cloninger, C. (1978). Neurogenetic adaptive mechanisms in alcoholism. *Science*, **236**, 410–416.
Cloninger, R., Bohman, M. & Sigvardsson, S. (1981). Inheritance of alcohol abuse: cross-fostering analysis of adopted men. *Archives of General Psychiatry*, **38**, 861–868.
Cowley, D., Roy-Byrne, P., Godon, C., Greenblatt, D.J., Ries, R., Walker, R.D., Damson, H.H. &

Hommer, D.W. (1992). Response to diazepam in sons of alcoholics. *Alcoholism: Clinical and Experimental Research*, **16**, 1057–1063.

Crabbe, J., Phillips, T., Feller, D.J, Hen, R., Wenger, C.D., Lessov, C.N. & Schafer, G.L. et al. (1996). Elevated alcohol consumption in null mutant mice lacking 5HT1B receptors. *Nature Genetics*, **14**, 98–100.

Devaud, L., Fritschy, J., Sieghart, W. & Morrow, A. (1997). Bidirectional alterations of GABA-A receptor subunit peptide levels in rat cortex during chronic ethanol consumption and withdrawal. *Journal of Neurochemistry*, **69**, 126–130.

Di Chiara, G. & Imperato, A. (1985). Ethanol preferentially stimulates dopamine release in the nucleus accumbens of freely moving rats. *European Journal of Pharmacology*, **115**, 131–132.

Ehlers, C., Somes, C. & Cloutier, D. (1998). Are some of the effects of ethanol mediated NPY? *Psychopharmacology*, **139**, 136–144.

Fils-Aime, M., Eckardt, M., George, D., Brown, G., Mefford, I. & Linnoila, M. (1996). Early-onset alcoholics have lower cerebrospinal fluid 5-hydroxyindoleacetic acid levels than late-onset alcoholics. *Archives of General Psychiatry*, **53**, 211–216.

Freund, G. & Anderson, K. (1999). Glutamate receptors in the cingulate cortex, hippocampus, and cerebellar vermis of alcoholics. *Alcoholism: Clinical and Experimental Research*, **23**, 1–6.

Froehlich, J., Zweifel, M., Harts, J., Lumeng, L. & Li, T.-K. (1991). Importance of delta opioid receptors in maintaining high alcohol drinking. *Psychopharmacology*, **103**, 467–472.

George, D., Benkelfat, C., Nutt, D., Hill, J., Phillips, M., Wynne, D. et al. (1997). A comparison of behavioural and biochemical responses to *meta*-chloropenylpiperazine in subtypes of alcoholics. *American Journal of Psychiatry*, **154**, 81–87.

Gilman, S., Koeppe, R., Adams, K. et al. (1996). Positron emission tomographic studies of cerebral benzodiazepine-receptor binding in chronic alcoholics. *Annals of Neurology*, **40**, 163–171.

Grant, K., Valverius, P., Hudspith, M. & Tabakoff, B. (1990). Ethanol withdrawal seizures and the NMDA receptor complex. *European Journal of Pharmacology*, **176**, 289–296.

Grant, K. (1995). The role of 5-HT$_3$ receptors in drug dependence. *Drug and Alcohol Dependence*, **38**, 155–171.

Grobin, A., Matthews, D., Devaud, L. & Morrow, A. (1998). The role of GABA-A receptors in the acute and chronic effects of alcohol. *Psychopharmacology*, **139**, 2–19.

Gulya, K., Grant, K., Valverius, P., Hoffman, P. & Tabakoff, B. (1991). Brain regional specificity and time-course of changes in the NMDA receptor–ionophore complex during ethanol withdrawal. *Brain Research*, **547**, 129–134.

Heinz, A., Schmidt, K., Baum, S., Kuhn, S., Dufeu, P., Schmidt, L. & Rommelspacher, H. (1996a). Influence of dopaminergic transmission on severity of withdrawal syndrome in alcoholism. *Journal of Studies on Alcoholism*, **57**, 471–474.

Heinz, A., Dufeu, P., Kuhn, S., Dettling, M., Graf, K., Kurten, I. et al. (1996b). Psychopathological and behavioural correlates of dopaminergic sensitivity in alcohol-dependent patients. *Archives of General Psychiatry*, **53**, 1123–1128.

Heinz, A., Ragan, P., Jones, D., Hommer, D., Williams, W., Knable, M. et al. (1998). Reduced central serotonin transporters in alcoholism. *American Journal of Psychiatry*, **155**, 1544–1549.

Herz, A. (1997). Endogenous opioid systems and alcohol addiction. *Psychopharmacology*, **129**, 99–111.

Higley, J. & Linnoila, M. (1997). A nonhuman primate model of excessive alcohol intake. *Recent Developments in Alcoholism*, **13**, 191–219.

Hodge, C., Samson, H. & Chappelle, A. (1997). Alcohol self-administration: further examination of the role of dopamine receptors in the nucleus accumbens. *Alcoholism: Clinical Experimental Research*, **21**, 1083–1091.

Hommer, D., Andreasen, P., Rio, D., Williams, W., Ruttimann, U., Momenan, R. et al. (1997). Effects of *m*-chlorophenylpiperazine on regional brain glucose utilization: a positron emission tomographic comparison of alcoholic and control subjects. *Journal of Neuroscience*, **17**, 2796–2806.

Hu, X. & Ticku, M. (1995). Chronic ethanol treatment upregulates the NMDA receptor function and binding in mammalian cortical neurons. *Molecular Brain Research*, **30**, 347–356.

Hyman, S., Konradi, C., Kobieriski, L., Cole, R., Senatus, P. & Green, D. (1994). Pharmacologic regulation of striatal proenkephalin gene expression via transcription factor CREB. *Molecular Neurobiology*, **50**, 155–171.

Koob, G. (1996). The neurobiology of ethanol–opioid interactions in ethanol reinforcement. *Alcoholism: Clinical and Experimental Research*, **20**, 185A.

Koob, G., Rocio, M., Carrera, A., Gold, L., Heyser, C., Maldonado-Irizarry, C. et al. (1998). Substance abuse as a compulsive behaviour. *Jurnal of Psychopharmacology*, **12**, 39–48.

Krystal, J., Petrakis, I., Webb, E., Cooney, N., Karper, L., Namanworth, S. et al. (1998). Dose-related ethanol-like effects of the NMDA antagonist, ketamine, in recently detoxified alcoholics. *Archives of General Psychiatry*, **55**, 354–360.

Laine, T., Ahonen, A., Torniainen, P., Heikkila, J., Pyhtinen, J., Rasanen, P. et al. (1999). Dopamine transporters increase in human brain after alcohol withdrawal. *Molecular Psychiatry*, **4**, 189–191.

Lappalainen, J., Long, J., Eggert, M., Ozaki, N., Robin, R., Brown, G. et al. (1998). Linkage of anti-social alcoholism to the serotonin 5-HT$_{1B}$ receptor gene in two populations. *Archives of General Psychiatry*, **55**, 989–994.

Lawford, B., Young, R., Rowell, J., Qualichefski, J., Fletcher, B., Syndulkko, K. et al. (1995). Bromocriptine in the treatment of alcoholics with the D2 dopamine receptor A1 allele. *Nature Medicine*, **1**, 337–341.

Lee, M. & Meltzer, H. (1991). Neuroendocrine responses to serotonergic agents in alcoholics. *Biological Psychiatry*, **30**, 1017–1030.

LeMarquand, D., Pihl, R. & Benkelfat, C. (1994). Serotonin and alcohol intake, abuse, and dependence: clinical evidence. *Biological Psychiatry*, **36**, 326–337.

Lewohl, J.M., Crane, D.I. & Dodd, P.R. (1996). Alcohol, alcoholic brain damage and GABA-A receptor isoform gene expression. *Neurochemistry International*, **29**, 677–684.

Lewohl, J., Crane, D. & Dodd, P. (1997). Expression of the α1, α2, and α3 isoforms of the GABA-A receptor in human alcoholic brain. *Brain Research Report*, **751**, 102–112.

Lingford-Hughes, A., Acton, P., Gacinovic, S., Suckling, J., Busatto, G., Boddington, S. et al. (1998). Reduced levels of GABA-benzodiazepine receptor in alcohol dependency in the absence of grey matter atrophy. *British Journal of Psychiatry*, **173**, 116–122.

Linnoila, M., de Jong, J. & Virkkunen, M. (1989). Family history of alcoholism in violent and impulsive fire setters. *Archives of General Psychiatry*, **46**, 613–616.

Lovinger, D. & Zieglgansberger, W. (1996). Interactions between ethanol and drugs acting on the NMDA-type glutamate receptor. *Alcoholism: Clinical and Experimental Research*, **20**, 187A–191A.

Luddens, H., Pritchett, D., Kohler, M., Killisch, I., Keinanen, K., Money, H. et al. (1990). Cerebellar GABA-A receptor selective for a behavioural alcohol antagonist. *Nature*, **346**, 648–651.

McBride, W. & Li, T. (1998). Animal models of alcoholism: neurobiology of high alcohol-drinking behaviour in rodents. *Critical Reviews in Neurobiology*, **12**, 339–369.

Mitsuyama, H., Little, K., Sieghart, W., Devaud, L. & Morrow, A. (1998). GABA-a receptor α1, α4 and β3 subunit mRNA and protein expression in the frontal cortex of human alcoholics. *Alcoholism: Clinical and Experimental Research*, **22**, 815–822.

Nestby, P., Vanderschuren, L., De Vries, T., Hogenboom, F., Wardeh, G., Mulder, A. & Schoffelmeer, A. (1997). Ethanol, like psychostimulants and morphine, causes long-lasting hyper-reactivity of dopamine and acetylcholine neurons of rat nucleus accumbens: possible role in behavioural sensitization. *Psychopharmacology*, **133**, 69–76.

Nutt, D. & Glue, P. (1986). Monoamines and alcohol. *British Journal of Addiction*, **81**, 327–338.

O'Malley, S., Jaffe, A., Chang, G., Rode, S., Schotenfeld, R., Meyer, R. & Rounsaville, B. (1996). Six-month follow-up of naltrexone and psychotherapy for alcohol dependence. *Archives of General Psychiatry*, **53**, 217–224.

Phillips, T., Brown, K., Burkhart-Kasch, S., Wenger, C., Kelly, M., Rubinstein, M. et al. (1998). Alcohol preference and sensitivity are markedly reduced in mice lacking dopamine D2 receptors. *Nature Neuroscience*, **1**, 610–615.

Rassnick, S., Stinus, L. & Koob, G. (1993). The effects of 6-hydroxydopamine lesions of the nucleus accumbens and the mesolimbic system on oral self-administration of ethanol in the rat. *Brain Research*, **623**, 16–24.

Robinson, T. & Berridge, K. (1993). The neural basis of drug craving: an incentive–sensitization theory of addiction. *Brain Research Review*, **18**, 247–291.

Self, D. & Nestler, E. (1998). Relapse to drug seeking: neural and molecular mechanisms. *Drug and Alcohol Dependence*, **51**, 49–60.

Sellers, E., Higgins, G. & Sobell, M. (1992). 5-HT and alcohol abuse trends. *Pharmacological Science*, **13**, 69–75.

Snell, L., Nunley, K.R., Lickteig, R.L., Browning, M.D. et al. (1996). Regional and subunit specific changes in NMDA receptor mRNA and immunoreactivity in mouse brain following chronic ethanol ingestion. *Moleular Brain Research*, **40**, 71–78.

Swift, R.M. (1999). Drug therapy for alcohol dependence. *New England Journal of Medicine*, **340**, 1482–1490.

Suzdak, P., Glowa, J., Crawley, J., Schwartz, R., Skolnick, P. & Paul, S. (1986). A selective imidazobenzodiazepine antagonist of ethanol in the rat. *Science*, **234**, 1243–1247.

Tabakoff, B. & Ritzmann, R. (1977). The effects of 6-hydroxydopamine on tolerance to and dependence on alcohol. *Journal of Pharmacology and Experimental Therapeutics*, **203**, 319–332.

Thiele, T., Marsh, D., Ste Marie, L., Bernstein, I. & Palmiter, R. (1998). Ethanol consumption and resistance are inversely related to neuropeptide Y levels. *Nature*, **396**, 366–369.

Tiihonen, J., Kuikka, J., Bergstrom, K., Hakola, P., Karhu, J., Ryynanen, O. & Fohr, J. (1995). Altered striatal dopamine re-uptake site densities in habitually violent and non-violent alcoholics. *Nature Medicine*, **7**, 654–657.

Tsai, G., Gastfriend, D. & Coyle, J. (1995). The glutamatergic basis of human alcoholism. *American Journal of Psychiatry*, **152**, 332–340.

Tsai, G., Ragan, P., Chang, R., Chen, S., Linnoila, M. & Coyle, J. (1998). Increased glutamatergic neurotransmission and oxidative stress after alcohol withdrawal. *American Journal of Psychiatry*, **155**, 726–732.

Ulm, R., Volpicelli, J. & Volpicelli, L. (1995). Opiates and alcohol self-administration in animals. *Psychopharmacology*, **56**, 5–14.

Ulrichson, J., Bech, B., Ebert, B., Diemer, N., Allerup, P. & Hemmingsen, R. (1996). Glutamate and benzodiazepine receptor autoradiography in rat brain after repetition of alcohol dependence. *Psychopharmacology*, **126**, 31–41.

Volkow, N., Wang, G., Hitzemann, R., Fowler, J., Wolf, A., Pappas, N. et al. (1993). Decreased cerebral response to inhibitory neurotransmission in alcoholics. *American Journal of Psychiatry*, **150**, 417–422.

Volkow, N., Wang, G., Begleiter, H., Pappas, N., Burr, G., Piscani, K. et al. (1995). Regional brain metabolic response to lorazepam in subjects at risk for alcoholism. *Alcoholism: Clinical and Experimental Research*, **19**, 510–516.

Volkow, N., Wang, G., Fowler, J., Logan, J., Hitzemann, R., Ding, Y. et al. (1996). Decreases in dopamine receptors but not in dopamine transporters in alcoholics. *Alcoholism: Clinical and Experimental Research*, **20**, 1594–1598.

Volpicelli, J., Alterman, A., Hayashida, M. & O'Brien C. (1992). Naltrexone in the treatment of alcohol dependence. *Archives of General Psychiatry*, **49**, 876–880.

Wafford, K., Burnett, D., Leidenheimer, N., Burt, D., Wang, J., Kofuji, P. et al. (1991). Ethanol sensitivity of the GABA-A receptor expressed in *Xenopus* oocytes required eight amino acids contained in the γ 2L subunit. *Neuron*, **7**, 27–33.

Wickelgren, I. (1997). Getting the brain's attention. *Science*, **278**, 35–37.

Williams, K. & Wood, J. (1998). Oral ethanol-reinforced responding in rhesus monkeys: effects of opioid antagonists selective for the μ-, κ- or δ-receptor. *Alcoholism: Clinical and Experimental Research*, **22**, 1634–1639.

Wise, R. (1998). Drug activation of brain reward pathways. *Drug and Alcohol Dependence*, **51**, 13–22.

Chapter 7

Neurological Consequences of Alcohol Use

Robert G. Knight
*Department of Psychology, University of Otago, Dunedin,
New Zealand*

Synopsis

In this chapter, the neurological consequences of alcohol abuse and dependence are reviewed. A survey of research on the acute effects of intoxication on the brain is followed by sections focusing on the nervous system damage caused by chronic alcohol abuse.

Ingestion of alcohol has short-term effects on the central nervous system. The experimental study of intoxicated subjects has shown that alcohol impairs memory and information processing, and the more complex and novel the task, the greater the effects. The cumulative effects of prolonged alcohol use can cause long-term brain changes. At the moderate end of the spectrum of alcohol use, there has been a substantial research effort directed at determining the consequences of social drinking. The data available to date support a preliminary conclusion that a daily consumption in excess of around five standard drinks increases the risk of cognitive deficits. Furthermore, the consequences of alcohol use are not confined to the drinker. Epidemiological research has shown that prenatal exposure to alcohol is a risk factor for a variety of developmental abnormalities, including learning disorders, hyperactivity and reduced intellectual functioning.

Alcohol dependence is associated with increased tolerance to alcohol and withdrawal effects (e.g. tremor, hallucinations, seizures and delirium tremens) if alcohol is abruptly withdrawn. After detoxification, many alcoholics show signs of residual damage to the cerebellum, resulting in gait disturbances, lesions in the peripheral nervous system causing sensori-motor problems, and cortical atrophy. A range of neuroradiological, electrophysiological and neuropsychological studies have demonstrated that damage to the central nervous system is prevalent in alcoholics, and although this is reversible with abstinence, recovery is not always complete.

A small number of chronic alcoholics progress to develop Wernicke–Korsakoff syndrome. The lesions associated with this disorder are located bilaterally in the grey matter surrounding the ventricular system and the midline diencephalic structures. The damage is caused by thiamine deficiency and the neurotoxic effects of alcohol. The acute stage of this disorder,

International Handbook of Alcohol Dependence and Problems. Edited by N. Heather, T.J. Peters and T. Stockwell.

Wernicke's encephalopathy, is characterized by global confusion or apathy and pronounced ocular and gait disturbances. When this acute stage resolves, some patients are left with an irreversible and dense amnesia, usually accompanied by a considerable degree of apathy. Patients with Korsakoff's amnesia have been extensively studied because of the light they shed on the biological basis of memory and the operation of memory systems. Research on the lesions critical for producing alcoholic amnesia has implicated the circuits linking the temporal lobes with the thalamic nuclei and the mammillary bodies. Neuropsychological studies have revealed that many such patients have a circumscribed amnesia, with a well-preserved intellectual capacity. They may also perform normally on those memory tests that do not require any reference to a learning episode for remembering (indirect tests of implicit memory). Because of their extensive history of alcohol abuse, liver damage and malnutrition, however, it is common to find that amnesic alcoholics have pervasive cognitive impairments, often resulting from frontal lobe damage.

Whether or not there is continuity in the biological damage and cognitive dysfunction with the progression from social drinking to Wernicke–Korsakoff's syndrome is unclear. There is evidence that, all other things being equal, impairment is proportional to consumption in the range from moderate drinking to alcoholism. It is also likely that the extent of biological damage from alcoholism to Korsakoff's disease is continuous but that a critical lesion is necessary to produce severe amnesia.

The use of alcohol and knowledge of the consequences of drunkenness have a history that stretches back into antiquity (see Chapter 2, this volume). The specific study of the effects of alcohol on the brain and behaviour, however, began with medical accounts of memory loss in alcoholism in the mid-1800s. In the latter part of the nineteenth century, first Carl Wernicke and later Korsakoff published independent reports that recognized the severe neurological damage that resulted from chronic alcohol abuse. Since that time, there has been an increasingly intense effort to document the neurological and psychological effects caused by alcohol consumption.

In this chapter, a survey of this work is presented. The focus initially is on the effects of acute intoxication and the consequences of prenatal exposure to alcohol. Later sections focus on the neurobehavioural effects of moderate and abusive drinking, and finally on the Wernicke–Korsakoff syndrome.

ACUTE ALCOHOL INTOXICATION

Metabolism of Alcohol

The human body can metabolize a small amount of alcohol per hour, equivalent to about an ounce of whiskey, without any neurobehavioural effects. When consumption exceeds that, psychological and physical changes occur that become more pronounced as the dose increases.

Most alcohol is absorbed rapidly through the lining of the stomach and small intestine, and distributed throughout the total body water. Initial concentrations of ethanol are highest in those organs with an abundant blood supply, such as the brain, liver, lungs, and kidneys, and lowest in the muscles. The major pathway for removing alcohol involves the enzyme alcohol dehydrogenase, which oxidizes alcohol to acetaldehyde, which is in turn reduced to acetate. A secondary pathway is the microsomal ethanol oxidizing system, which becomes more significant with high concentrations of alcohol in the liver. Both these metabolic processes are located in the liver; therefore when blood alcohol levels are high, other liver functions are disturbed, indirectly affecting other functional systems, such as digestion. Sustained alcohol abuse leads to a progressive increase in the ability of the liver to metabolize alcohol, resulting in greater tolerance. Increased consumption is needed to become intoxicated, causing more disruption of normal liver function and greater likelihood of damage to the brain. Eventually, the liver sustains irreversible damage, resulting in a reduction in the efficiency of metabolizing alcohol. When this happens, tolerance may be dramatically reduced.

Acute Intoxication

Ingestion of alcohol induces effects that begin with excitement and emotional enhancement and may end in stupor, which are generally proportional to blood alcohol level (BAL). Since alcohol has a high initial concentration in the brain, neurological effects are seen almost at once. The expression of alcohol intoxication at various dosage levels, however, is mediated by a range of genetic, environmental and cultural factors, as well as by the presence or absence of other drugs that act on the central nervous system.

The behavioural and emotional effects that occur at the early stages of intoxication when the BAL is about 20–40 mg/ml, which include decreased self-consciousness and euphoria, are thought to result from alcohol's depressant effects on the reticular activating system. Changes in arousal level reduce the inhibitory control that this system exerts over the cortex. Placebo-controlled studies of the effects of intoxication on psychological performance typically use dosages in the BAL range of 50–100 mg/ml. The legal limit for driving is set in most countries within this range. At about 100 mg/ml, most drinkers appear intoxicated. Minor speech abnormalities and instability of gait will be apparent, and social judgement may be affected. The intoxicated person in the 200–300 mg/ml range will have a marked ataxic or staggering gait, poor social judgement and may feel nauseous and vomit. By the time a BAL of 300 mg/ml is reached, there is likely to be amnesia for the drinking episode.

Double-blind placebo trials with participants who have BAL readings in the 50–100 mg/ml range have consistently shown that cognition is affected by alcohol. The conclusion that intoxication affects learning and memory in both non-alcoholic and alcoholic subjects has been demonstrated in numerous studies. Such deficits cannot be explained by expectancy or placebo effects. In addition to this general finding, two interesting effects have been observed. The first is the *retrograde facilitation effect*. Lamberty et al. (1990) found that if alcohol were administered immediately after a learning session, the recall of the newly learnt information would be better than when a placebo is administered. One explanation for this facilitatory effect is that learning is made more salient by the post-session mood-enhancing properties of alcohol. The second effect is *state-dependent learning*. There are many anecdotes about occasions when alcoholics secrete bottles in places they are unable to locate when sober next day. When drunk on a later occasion, however, the memory of hiding the bottle returns. This experience exemplifies state-dependent learning; information learned in one drug-induced state is better recalled in the same state than when sober. This effect has been demonstrated in empirical studies that show that reinstatement of the drinking context facilitates retrieval of material acquired in the study session.

Few studies have investigated performance by intoxicated subjects on intelligence tests. The general conclusion is that low doses of alcohol impair performance on complex and novel tasks, but leave tests that are dependent on academic skills largely untouched.

Numerous studies have shown that psychomotor performance is affected by inebriation. Risk of accident and injury in the operation of machinery, driving or flying is increased by drinking. Generally, the more complex the task, the more likely there are to be alcohol effects. Prior practice on a task makes it more resistant to alcohol effects. There is also some evidence to suggest that it is possible to compensate for the effects of alcohol during the initial stages of the task, but that this effort cannot be sustained over time.

The experimental study of intoxicated subjects has confirmed that, as might be expected from the high concentration of alcohol in the brain, cognition is disrupted. Even at low doses equivalent to the amount consumed by the average moderate drinker, the ability to carry out complex information processing tasks will be impaired. There is some evidence that impairments may be more pronounced in the children of alcoholics, and in women, rather than men, at comparable dosage levels.

PRENATAL EXPOSURE TO ALCOHOL

Aristotle is often cited as being the first to conjecture that women who drank during pregnancy harmed their unborn children. These concerns resurfaced during the gin epidemic of 1765–1785 in England, when the price of distilled liquor was very low and drunkenness was rampant (see Chapter 2, this volume). Scientific scrutiny of the effects of exposure to alcohol on fetal development is, however, a recent phenomenon. In 1973, earlier French reports that the children of alcoholic mothers showed distinctive abnormalities of appearance and behaviour were confirmed by a group of researchers in Seattle (Jones & Smith, 1973). They documented a distinctive triad of neurobehavioural and physical characteristics that provided the basis of the foetal alcohol syndrome (FAS). The three principal abnormalities of FAS are as follows: (a) pre- and postnatal growth retardation, usually below the 10th percentile; (b) characteristic craniofacial abnormalities (including microcephaly, large low-set ears, malformed lips and deformities of the eyes, eyelids, nose and central face); (c) central nervous system dysfunction, evidenced by intellectual disability and behavioural problems.

Following the initial clinical reports, many further cases were identified. It became apparent that chronic prenatal exposure to alcohol did not always result in all the features of FAS but might lead to only one or two abnormalities. Where only part of the syndrome was manifest, the term "fetal alcohol effects" (FAE) was applied. Epidemiological studies suggest that FAS occurs in 0.29–0.48/1000 live births (Mattson & Riley, 1998). The incidence of FAE approaches 3/1000 live births. It is important to emphasize that all the abnormalities attributable to the effects of alcohol exposure *in utero* are also seen in children whose mothers abstained from alcohol during pregnancy. The diagnosis of FAS should be applied with appropriate caution. Nonetheless, the epidemiological research confirms that the affects of prenatal exposure to alcohol on development are pervasive, expensive and preventable. For example, Abel & Sokol (1991) have estimated conservatively that it costs US$74.6 million annually to care for FAS children. About 75% of this figure is made up from the costs of caring for low birth-weight children and providing institutional care for those who are intellectually disabled.

Aetiology of FAS

Considerable research has been directed at determining the process by which exposure to alcohol results in FAS. Because alcohol passes the placental barrier readily, the direct toxic effects of alcohol have been cited as the primary cause of the syndrome. Support for this view comes from studies of birds, where it is possible to demonstrate the damaging effect of alcohol on the embryo independently of the mother. The toxic effects of alcohol have also been observed in mammalian embryos cultured *in vitro*. The evidence that alcohol (or its metabolites) is toxic for the developing fetus does not preclude the possibility that maternal health is a contributing factor. Alcohol inhibits absorption of nutrients and reduced levels of glucose, vitamins, amino acids and trace elements have all been implicated in growth retardation in laboratory animals.

The mechanism whereby alcohol exerts its effects is not certain. Alcohol disrupts the placental transport of nutrients, which may lead to hypoxia and growth retardation. The nervous tissue of the developing fetus is also vulnerable to the toxic effects of alcohol (Michaelis, 1990) and this may account for the neurological deficits seen in FAS. For example, it has been proposed that the cognitive deficits in FAS may be the consequence of cell loss and abnormal migration in the first trimester. There has also been speculation about the effects of drinking at certain critical periods in fetal development. There is evidence in the animal literature that alcohol exposure at certain points in gestation is more damaging than at others, but this issue is difficult to research in humans. It has been proposed that heavy consumption throughout gestation results in the full spectrum of FAS symptoms and that binge drinking at critical times results in less pervasive FAE. The skeletal and organ abnormalities of FAS may result from damage in the first trimester, whereas brain development and growth may be affected by later exposure to alcohol. The dosage level of alcohol that results in abnormalities has been difficult to establish. It is likely that there are considerable individual differences in susceptibility to the toxic effects of alcohol and that maternal health is an important factor. A dose-related gradient of effects has been proposed (Streissguth, 1977), there being no safe level of exposure but the risk of damage to the embryo being elevated as exposure increases. Determining the effects of different dosages is problematic because of difficulties in recording and quantifying consumption accurately across the whole gestation period. It is widely accepted, however, that consumption in excess of about three drinks/day throughout the gestation period results in a measurable increase in the risk of fetal damage.

Neuropsychological Deficits

The earliest case reports noted that mental retardation was a common feature of FAS. In a comprehensive review of 79 individual cases of FAS reported in the literature, Mattson & Riley (1998) calculated an average IQ of 65.7 (SD = 20.2), range 20–120. They also located 17 group studies based on retrospective reports of maternal consumption involving 269 children with FAS. The average IQ, weighted for sample size, was 72.3 (range = 47–98). Prospective studies (e.g. Streissguth et al., 1980) have found similar reductions in IQ. The use of prospective studies has allowed the relationship between consumption levels during pregnancy and the child's IQ to be examined. These studies have revealed that level of exposure to alcohol *in utero* predicts lower intellectual functioning in childhood.

There is accumulating evidence that learning deficits, as might be expected from the results of the IQ testing, are common in alcohol-exposed infants. As with the intellectual retardation, learning and academic problems may occur in the absence of the morphological changes associated with FAS. Deficits in language skills and motor coordination have also been reported in children with FAE. In summary, there is consistent evidence that foetal exposure to alcohol results in a range of cognitive decrements that lead to learning problems in the school setting. These effects may be influenced by the poor home environment experienced by many children of alcoholics and concurrent behavioural difficulties.

Children with FAS have been usually described as displaying symptoms of hyperactivity or attentional deficit. The hyperactivity may occur in the absence of any other signs of FAS, including intellectual retardation. Similar findings are reported consistently in the animal literature, e.g. hyperactivity is an almost invariable consequence of exposing rats to alcohol prenatally. Similarly, attention deficits have been reported in both FAS and alcohol-exposed children. Even moderate maternal exposure to alcohol during pregnancy results in poorer performance on tasks measuring attention and concentration, even when there is no evidence of hyperactivity.

MODERATE ALCOHOL CONSUMPTION

The vast majority of people that use alcohol do so in moderation. Numerous studies have been conducted to determine whether drinking at socially sanctioned levels has a deleterious effect on health. One problem is determining what is meant by moderate consumption. A review of the literature revealed considerable differences in quantities regarded as constituting moderate consumption in different countries (Eckhardt et al., 1998). If a common metric is used whereby a standard drink contains 12 g of alcohol, then the definition of moderate drinking in the studies they surveyed was around 2–7 standard drinks per day. In their review of the effects of social drinking, Parsons & Nixon (1996) found that the mean number of standard drinks per occasion regarded as moderate in the studies they surveyed was 2–8. Drinking at levels of more than 10 drinks per occasion (120 g alcohol) or over 70 drinks/week is usually regarded as in excess of moderate social drinking. Intakes of 3–80 g per occasion have generally been regarded as moderate for the purposes of research. Recommended government guidelines in the UK and elsewhere set a much lower level of 2–3 drinks (24–36 g of alcohol/day) as moderate.

The effects on cognition of chronic moderate drinking have been examined in studies spanning the past two decades. Research into the neuropsychological consequences of social drinking began with Parker & Noble's (1977) study of 102 middle-aged Californians, who consumed an average quantity per occasion (QPO) of 42 ml alcohol. They administered tests of abstract problem solving, conceptual learning and free-recall memory, and examined the association between test performance and amount consumed. In doing so, they were motivated by Ryback's (1971) continuity hypothesis, which predicted that the neurological damage caused by alcohol would be proportional to the amount consumed. With the effects of age partialled out, they found significant negative correlations between QPO and the cognitive test scores. These correlations were more substantial for the subgroup of heavy social drinkers. In the discussion of their findings, Parker & Nobel suggested a number of explanations for their results.

The explanation they considered most likely was that ingestion of alcohol caused residual brain damage in proportion to the amount consumed. A variant of this proposal is that there is a threshold for consumption above which risk of neurological damage becomes probable (Parsons, 1998). Alternatively, persons with lesser intellectual or cognitive skills might be predisposed to consume more alcohol, or some third variable such as emotional distress might cause both greater consumption and/or cognitive impairment. Another possibility is that alcohol causes transient brain changes that have an effect at the time of testing that is commensurate with the amount consumed (Parker et al., 1983). Parker & Noble's initial study was followed by several others in the period up to 1985, with often mixed and inconsistent results. In an influential review, Parsons (1986) concluded that the empirical evidence to that time was not consistent with the hypothesis that alcohol played a causal role in reduced cognitive performance in social drinkers and that the other explanations could not be excluded. He detailed the many methodological shortcomings of these early studies and provided guidelines for the conduct of future investigations. Bowden (1987) drew similar conclusions and noted that the correlations between consumption levels and cognitive performance explained little of the variance and were hard to replicate.

In a later review, Parsons & Nixon (1996) revisited the issue of the effects of social drinking and reached somewhat different conclusions. They found that the methodology used had improved considerably and that the many extraneous variables that might have produced the significant correlations between cognition and drinking quantities had been controlled. For instance, no evidence had emerged that some third variable, such as stress or genetic factors, was responsible. Similarly, no support had emerged that the significant correlations were the consequence of some transient effect alcohol had on cognition. Of the 17 studies that had appeared since 1985, they found that 10 produced no evidence of any impairment in cognition for social drinkers. In the remaining seven studies, support for the alcohol-causal hypothesis was found. Parsons & Nixon (1996) computed the average consumption levels for each of the moderate drinking groups in the 17 studies. They found that those studies that reported positive findings tested social drinkers with higher weekly consumption levels (21–105 drinks/week) than those with negative findings (3–28 drinks/week). Although there was considerable overlap, they concluded that their findings provided preliminary evidence for the conclusion that cognitive impairment was induced by chronic social drinking. They found no effect of age on study outcome. The hypothesis they advanced by way of conclusion provides a fitting summary of the research to date:

> Persons drinking an average of five or six standard drinks per occasion (60–72 g of absolute alcohol) 5–7 days a week over a year or more risk the development of cognitive inefficiencies or deficits. At seven to nine drinks per day (84 g or more), cognitive deficits become likely. Drinking daily at the alcoholic level of 10 drinks (120 g) or more results in the greatest number of deficits (p. 188).

It is important to emphasize that these preliminary conclusions are based on average trends and the chronic or acute effects of alcohol depend on such factors as body weight and fat distribution, race, individual differences in metabolism rates and prior drinking experiences.

Adding to the evidence that heavy social drinkers are at some risk of brain damage are results from two electrophysiological studies. Nichols & Martin (1996) reported on the latency of event-related potentials (ERP) in male drinkers whose consumption was light (less than two drinks/day) or heavy (more than about three drinks/day). They found that the heavier drinkers had delayed latencies, a result consistent with a diminished capacity for information processing. Fox et al. (1995) similarly compared light and heavy social drinkers, and found significant differences in ERP activity during a learning and memory task. In an investigation of the relationship between consumption and brain computed topography (CT) scans, Bergman et al. (1983) found no association between alcohol consumption and CT indices of brain atrophy. However, in both this study and that of Cala (1985), average daily consumption above about 50–60 g alcohol/day was associated with evidence of tissue damage. Taken together with the neuropsychological studies, findings from neuroimaging and electrophysiological studies suggest that a chronic daily consumption above about 40 g may be associated measurable declines in brain functioning and cognitive efficiency.

CHRONIC ALCOHOLISM

Clinical Aspects

Dependence and Withdrawal

With prolonged drinking, the neurobehavioural effects of alcohol diminish as a consequence of increased tolerance. One important consequence of this process of neuroadaption is that cross-tolerance to other drugs, notably benzodiazepines and barbiturates, may occur. Related to the development of tolerance is dependence. As the brain becomes better adjusted to function in the presence of quantities of alcohol, continued exposure is needed to maintain neurobehavioural equilibrium. Consequently, if alcohol suddenly ceases to be available, a period of readjustment, or withdrawal, occurs. Even in moderate drinkers, the aftermath of intoxication may lead to symptoms similar to those experienced by the chronic alcoholic. After a heavy bout of drinking, the moderate drinker experiences a period of headache, sleeplessness, agitation and mood change. For the dependent alcoholic, however, the withdrawal effects are more severe.

The abrupt withdrawal from alcohol by dependent alcoholics may result in severe and protracted effects and should usually be attempted under some form of medical supervision (see Chapter 26, this volume). Withdrawal symptoms are unpleasant and, in the case of delirium tremens and seizures, may be life-threatening. There are four major symptoms associated with alcohol withdrawal: tremor, hallucinations, seizures and delirium tremens. The former two symptoms usually present within 3–12 hours after abstinence; any seizures that occur appear after 12–48 hours; and delirium tremens begins, in severely affected cases, 3–4 days after drinking ceases (Lishman, 1987). The intensity of the withdrawal effects is predicted by BALs before abstinence. Signs of nervous system disturbance can be observed in the development of abnormal EEG activity which becomes apparent 20–30 hours after abstinence.

Tremor, particularly in the arms and legs, is the earliest and most common sign of withdrawal, and is usually accompanied by sleep disturbance and nausea. Perceptual disturbances ranging in intensity from transitory visual flashes to prolonged auditory hallucinations are often reported in the early days of withdrawal. Abstinence or even a drastic reduction in consumption may induce seizures ("rum fits") in about 10% of hospitalized alcoholics. About 5% of patients admitted for treatment of alcohol problems develop delirium tremens. The person with delirium tremens experiences vivid hallucinations, tremor, agitation and insomnia, together with signs of autonomic hyperactivity, including tachycardia, sweating and fever. The symptoms usually progress in severity until the patient falls into a prolonged sleep. The episode typically resolves in about 3 days and has mortality rate of 5% due to cardiac complications, self-injury, infection and hyperthermia. In a small percentage of cases, as the delirium subsides, the typical features of Wernicke–Korsakoff syndrome may emerge.

Residual Neurological Effects

Once detoxification has ended, many alcoholics are left with neurological symptoms that may persist over a considerable period or, indeed, may prove to be irreversible. Wernicke–Korsakoff syndrome, which will be considered later in this chapter, is the most studied neurological condition associated with prolonged alcohol abuse. Two other residual neurological conditions are seen commonly in chronic alcoholics: cerebellar degeneration and peripheral neuropathy. In some alcoholics, damage to the anterior and superior portions of the cerebellar vermis and hemispheres results in an ataxia of the lower limbs. The affected alcoholic develops a characteristic broad-based and poorly coordinated gait that may stabilize and improve but often persists despite abstinence and enhanced diet. Peripheral neuropathy is a well-known complication of chronic alcohol dependence, resulting from damage to the peripheral nervous system. The most common features are sensory abnormalities, such as pain, numbness or burning sensations, or motor symptoms, including loss of reflexes and muscular wasting. Like the central nervous system damage, alcoholic polyneuropathy is likely to be caused by nutritional insufficiency and the neurotoxic effects of alcohol. It should also be noted that the neurological symptoms seen in alcoholics are often secondary to the alcohol abuse. As well as nutrition deficiencies, alcoholics are at greater risk for head injury, stroke and severe liver disease. Liver damage is a strong predictor of neuropsychological test performance, irrespective of length of alcohol abuse and consumption history (e.g. Tarter et al., 1988).

Neurological Research

Neuroradiological Studies of Alcoholism

The advent of CT-scanning in the 1970s allowed the investigation of brain morphology in large representative groups of alcoholics. CT-scans provide good images of the fluid-filled spaces in the brain which enlarge with atrophy of the brain, allowing damage to the brain to be quantified. Early studies consistently reported ventricular enlargement and cortical atrophy in a significant number of the alcoholics who were studied. It was apparent, however, that there was much variability in the incidence of cerebral damage across studies, which was attributable to differences in selecting participants and the scanning procedures used. In a major study, Bergman et al. (1980) evaluated the scans of 148 alcoholics undergoing detoxification. They found that some 46% of alcoholics aged 20–29, rising to 67% of patients aged 50–59, had signs of cerebral atrophy. Evidence of subcortical atrophy was seen in 15% of alcoholics aged 20–29, increasing to 37% in the 50–59 age range. In a well-controlled study, Lishman et al. (1980) also observed clear evidence of brain atrophy on a number of CT indices. They confirmed that atrophy was more pronounced in older alcoholics and that the longer the period of abstinence prior to the scan, the less pathological was the rating of atrophy on the scan. In a follow-up 1 year later, patients who were abstinent had improved, whereas those who continued drinking showed no signs of improvement. These findings were consistent with the earlier results of Carlen et al. (1978), who advocated the use of the term "reversible brain shrinkage" to describe their findings, to avoid the implication that the evidence of brain damage from CT scans was entirely due to irreversible cell loss.

Conclusions from CT studies suggest that alcoholism results in both cortical and subcortical abnormalities in many chronic drinkers. These deficits appeared to be reversible in part with prolonged abstinence but improvements were more noticeable in younger alcoholics and were far from complete. Studies of the effects of abstinence, however, are difficult to conduct because of problems in detecting and assessing abstinence. Despite the many limitations of the CT studies, they served to draw attention to the fact that brain impairments occurred in patients with a history of alcohol abuse but with no clinical signs of residual neurological impairments. Attempts to demonstrate a relationship between cognitive deficits and CT-assessed brain changes proved largely unsuccessful. Only modest correlations between scan indices and functional impairments have been reported. Several explanations for this have been advanced, but the most likely reason is that CT indices are based largely on ventricular volumes and are a relatively non-specific measure of cerebral atrophy.

The introduction of magnetic resonance imaging (MRI) in the latter part of the 1980s allowed a more precise evaluation of brain structures and the detection of small abnormalities in brain tissue. Initial uncontrolled studies with small number of chronic alcoholics tended to confirm the earlier CT studies. In a well-controlled trial, Jernigan et al. (1991) examined the relationships between cerebrospinal fluid levels, tissue damage and results on cognitive tests in a group of 28 middle-aged alcoholics. After 4–5 weeks abstinence, they found significant grey matter reductions remained which were correlated with the levels of fluid volume. They reported atrophy in the diencephalon, the striatum and regions of the cortex that included the mesial temporal lobes. Although some of the scan indices were related to the psychological test scores, the findings were not consistent.

MRI-defined abnormalities in the mammillary bodies and cerebellum have been reported in nonamnesic alcoholics. Lesions in these areas are characteristic of patients with Wernicke–Korsakoff syndrome and this evidence suggests a possible continuum of damage from chronic alcohol abuse to Korsakoff's disease. As with the CT scan data, there is evidence of improvement with long periods of abstinence; the ventricular volumes of alcoholics decrease and grey matter cortical volumes increase (Pfefferbaum et al., 1995). Sophisticated position emission tomography (PET) studies have also been conducted with alcohol-dependent patients, typically to measure regional glucose metabolism rate or cerebral blood flow. This research offers the prospect of identifying specific brain regions that are dysfunctional in the actual execution of particular processing tasks. Abnormalities in alcoholics' brains have been reported that suggest deficits in cortical processing (Volkow et al., 1992). In a review of the early literature, Eckhardt et al. (1990) concluded that the effects identified by PET scans are relatively subtle when compared with those identified by neuropathological and neuropsychological investigations. Although PET scanning has the potential to clarify the underlying brain changes that cause cognition to be impaired, this potential remains to be realized.

Neuropsychological Studies

Most reviews of the literature regarding the performance of alcoholics have reached the conclusion that such patients do have cognitive impairments (e.g. Knight & Longmore, 1994; Parsons, 1998). Evidence for this comes from an extensive literature in which neuropsychological tests assessing memory, intelligence and other functions known to be sensitive to brain impairments have been administered to alcoholics.

Intelligence

In a review of 19 studies reporting the IQ scores of alcoholics and matched controls, Knight & Longmore (1994) computed an effect size (ES) for each study. An ES gives an estimate of the difference in scores between the two groups compared in terms of the standard deviation of the control group. An ES is therefore an index expressed in standard deviation units, so that on an IQ with the usual standard deviation of 15, an ES of 1.0 equates to a 15-point difference between the two groups. The 19 studies yielded some 45 test scores and a mean ES of 0.65. The control group out-performed the alcoholic by, on average, about two-thirds of a standard deviation, or 10 IQ points. Thus, on average, 75% of the non-alcoholic controls performed better than the alcoholic patients. The latest version of the Wechsler Adult Intelligence Scale (WAIS-III) contains results from a group of 28 nonamnesic alcoholics. On this new test, the alcoholic patients performed in the average range, with their scores on speeded tests being about 10 points lower on average than their verbal IQ score. In summary, on measures of intellectual capacity that are sensitive to brain damage, typically those that use novel tasks that do not rely on academic skills, a substantial group of persons who abuse alcohol show intellectual impairments.

Memory

Groups of alcoholics constituted from those patients who do not show clinical evidence of amnesia typically show some decrements on sensitive tests of memory and learning. Controlled studies have consistently found impairments in memory that are most evident on sensitive tests of new learning and more pronounced in alcoholics over than under the age of 40. Data from the recently revised Wechsler Memory Scale (WMS-III) confirm that, on standard clinical tests of memory, non-amnesic alcoholics perform in the normal range.

Other Cognitive Processes

On a range of tests of higher cognitive functioning that are not constructed primarily to assess intelligence or memory, alcoholics have generally been found to perform relatively poorly compared with controls but seldom in the range indicative of brain impairment. For example, in studies reporting results from the Halstead Reitan Battery, an omnibus test of cognitive processes widely used in the USA to quantify brain impairments, alcoholics typically have significantly higher than average impairment scores. Only in some studies, however, do their average results place them in the range usually indicative of brain damage. Parsons (1998) reported the outcome of a large study contrasting 97 non-alcoholics with a group of 143 alcoholics on a battery of 16 tests. For each test, both accuracy and speed of completion were measured. Test scores were combined to form four factors and on each factor there was a significant difference between the two groups, although the absolute differences between the factor scores was not large (equivalent to ES values of 0.39–0.62). When efficiency scores were computed, which were the ratio of standardized accuracy scores to speed scores for each factor, they found that the alcoholics were significantly less efficient than the controls (ES values in range 0.5–0.75).

WERNICKE–KORSAKOFF SYNDROME

Clinical Aspects

In 1881, Carl Wernicke described a clinical syndrome based on his observation of three cases characterized by ophthalmoplegia, ataxia and confusion. On post-mortem examination, small haemorrhagic lesions were identified in the grey matter surrounding the third and fourth ventricles, extending into the brainstem in the region of the optic nuclei. Some 6 years later, Russian physician Sergei Korsakoff detailed a profound amnesic disorder, often accompanied by peripheral nerve disease, that persisted in patients after a period of delirium or confusion. Korsakoff observed this condition not only in chronic alcoholics but also in patients with diseases causing malabsorption of food, and speculated that the cause might be some toxin that interfered with tissue nutrition. The relationship between Wernicke's and Korsakoff's clinical syndrome was not recognized by early authors. Korsakoff attributed the mental changes in the amnesic condition to cortical damage resulting from toxicity, whereas Wernicke's encephalopathy was seen as an inflammation in the brainstem. Gradually, however, the joint occurrence of the two disorders was noted and their common neuropathological basis established. Post-mortem findings suggested that the critical lesions for the development of amnesia lay in the diencephalon and that Korsakoff patients almost invariably had brainstem lesions similar to those of patients who had Wernicke's disease. An important advance was made with the identification of thiamine deficiency as a cause of Wernicke's encephalopathy in the 1930s. Supplementing the diet of patients with Wernicke–Korsakoff's syndrome was found to lead to a more rapid reduction in the confusional state in the early stages of the disorder, although residual amnesic symptoms remained impervious to this treatment. Thus, Wernicke–Korsakoff syndrome came to be regarded as a disorder associated with alcoholism, with an acute stage that might either resolve completely or leave the patient with an irreversible and dense amnesia. The history and course of the disorder, from the earliest reports, was seen to be variable and the nature of the continuity between the psychological deficits of chronic alcoholism and later Wernicke–Korsakoff syndrome difficult to characterize.

Wernicke's Encephalopathy

The primary symptoms of this neurological condition are a global confusion or apathy, ocular abnormalities (particularly nystagmus and paralysis of the oculomotor muscles) and an unsteady or ataxic gait. The patient almost invariably displays a disturbance in consciousness, with severe disorientation, poor concentration, profound apathy and an inability to communicate coherently. Their confused condition and indifference to their surroundings make it difficult to test their cognitive functioning; nonetheless, with the clearing of consciousness, the presence of memory and intellectual disturbance may be more apparent. Victor et al. (1989) in their series of patients with Wernicke–Korsakoff syndrome, found that the most common ocular abnormalities were nystagmus, paralysis of the lateral rectus and disturbances of conjugate gaze. Patients with Wernicke's encephalopathy frequently have a broad-based, ataxic gait and may be unable to walk without support in the initial stages. Many Wernicke patients show signs of delirium tremens on initial presentation and most (82% in the Victor et al. series) have signs of peripheral nervous disease. Many patients with acute Wernicke's disease recover, except for a permanent amnesia for the confusional period. Victor et al. reported that 21% of their series showed complete or near-complete recovery.

Korsakoff's Syndrome

The most striking feature of this disorder is amnesia, which reveals itself as the patient is asked about recent life events and everyday routines. Although capable of completing intellectual challenges when the task is put before them and does not require access to recent memories, attempts to recollect recently studied information typically end in failure. Korsakoff's disease can be defined as chronic anterograde amnesia in the presence of normal or near-normal intelligence. Commonly accompanying the failure of memory is a degree of apathy and loss of initiative. Most show little inclination to respond to questions with elaborate answers and, left to themselves, will sit without discomfort in silence. Some patients are talkative or show signs of spontaneity but their conversation is often full of repetitive anecdotes or complaint. Korsakoff patients are usually orientated for place and adapt slowly to new surroundings. They typically have a degree of retrograde amnesia that may stretch back for many years, and so appear to have lost any knowledge of their recent lives. They are thus often unable to give a correct age and memories of their families may be rooted in the distant past, so that a 30-year old son is recalled as a child at school. One of the most arresting clinical characteristics is the patient's lack of insight and apparent indifference to their amnesic deficits. As Talland (1965) has noted in his studies of a series of alcoholic amnesics:

None realized the full extent of his amnesic disability; some would admit to poor memory for names or dates, others denied any memory disturbance, even in the face of the most striking evidence (p. 29).

Patients with Korsakoff's syndrome are often reported to confabulate, that is, to fabricate memories in response to questions about their personal histories. Korsakoff noted the tendency for his patients to relate events that might have happened in response to questions about the recent past, but which the clinician knew had not. This tendency is most commonly ascribed to the patient's use of events transposed or recollected from his/her earlier life to apply to present circumstances. Korsakoff patients appear to produce false memories without awareness because of their inability to recall recent happenings. Korsakoff patients do not produce detailed spontaneous confabulation of the kind seen in patients with dementing or frontal lobe disorders (Kopelman, 1987).

Neurological Research

Neuropathology

Recent post-mortem examinations have confirmed earlier findings that the most common abnormalities in Wernicke–Korsakoff's syndrome are bilaterally distributed in the grey matter surrounding the cerebral aqueduct and the third and fourth ventricles. Other consistently affected sites are the thalamus, the mammillary bodies and the cerebellum. Within the nuclei affected, regions closer to the ventricular system are more affected than those further away. The distribution of lesions is regarded as sufficiently distinctive to allow accurate post-mortem diagnosis. Of interest is the finding that this distinct pattern of neuropathology has been found in alcoholic patients who had no history of Wernicke–Korsakoff syndrome during life (Harper, 1983). This suggests that brain damage may occur more commonly than is supposed in alcoholics and emphasizes the importance of ensuring that such patients receive good nutrition.

Most interest in Korsakoff's syndrome has been in the nature of lesions critical in producing the profound amnesia; lesions in the thalamus and mammillary bodies have been most commonly regarded as responsible. Victor et al. (1989), in their post-mortem series of 82 cases, implicated lesions of the dorsomedial nucleus of the thalamus as critical in producing amnesia and concluded that atrophy of the mammillary bodies may occur without producing amnesia. This latter conclusion was based on evidence from five cases with a history of Wernicke's encephalopathy without amnesia. However, this conclusion has been challenged by reports of two post-mortem studies where lesions were observed in the mammillary bodies and the anterior thalamus but not in the medial dorsal nuclei (Mair et al., 1979; Mayes et al., 1988). At the present time, details of the neural circuits that underpin the operation of memory processes have not been resolved, rendering it difficult to provide an anatomical explanation for memory failure in Korsakoff's disease. The available evidence suggests that circuits linking the medial temporal lobe with diencephalic nuclei in the thalamus and the mammillary bodies underlie memory processing. Thus, the ongoing search for the critical lesion in Korsakoff's amnesia remains focused on lesions in diencephalic structures and the mammillothalamic tract.

Biochemical Abnormalities

In the 1940s, the role of thiamine in producing the midline brain lesions characteristic of Wernicke–Korsakoff syndrome was established in studies with pigeons. Subsequently it was found that malnourished prisoners of war who developed symptoms consistent with Wernicke's encephalopathy in conjunction with beri-beri responded favourably to thiamine. Although thiamine deficiency has been linked to both central and peripheral neural damage, there is some debate over whether this is sufficient to cause the irreversible amnesia of Korsakoff's syndrome without the neurotoxic effects of alcohol. Generally, non-alcoholic patients with Wernicke–Korsakoff syndrome have been reported to respond more rapidly and completely to thiamine treatment than alcoholic patients. Cases of amnesia that did not remit, however, have been reported where alcohol was not implicated, including several patients from Korsakoff's original series. Thiamine depletion appears to play a central part in producing the syndrome but the neurological damage may be augmented or potentiated by chronic alcohol abuse. The reason why only some alcoholics develop Wernicke–Korsakoff syndrome has been attributed to a genetic defect in the metabolism of thiamine (Blass & Gibson, 1977). Evidence for such a genetic vulnerability remains inconclusive.

Thiamine deficiency has an impact on several neurotransmitters, including acetylcholine, glutamate and γ-aminobutyric acid (GABA) (Kopelman, 1995). Most interest has centred on acetylcholine, which is affected by Alzheimer's disease. There is some evidence that the cholinergic system is damaged by thiamine deficiency and a reduction in neuron numbers in the nucleus basalis of Korsakoff patients has been reported in several studies. The nucleus basalis is a major source of innervation for the cholinergic system and damage in this region of basal forebrain is known to cause amnesia. Butters (1985) suggested that damage to this forebrain nucleus might be the critical lesion in the occurrence of severe amnesia. Recently, Cullen et al. (1997) counted cholinergic basal forebrain neurons in patients with Wernicke's disease, with or without chronic amnesia, alcoholics with no neurological symptoms and controls. They found no evidence of cell loss in alcoholics but significant and equivalent losses in Wernicke's patients, both with (21% below controls) and without (24% below controls) amnesia. These findings suggest that lesions in the basal forebrain may be an outcome of Wernicke's encephalopathy but not critical in producing amnesic symptoms.

Radiological Studies

Evidence from CT-scan studies of patients with Korsakoff's syndrome has generally produced results consistent with the findings from neuropathological investigations. Ventricular enlargement and widening of the sulci have been consistently reported, with the magnitude of the impairments on some indices being more pronounced than in matched non-amnesic alcoholics. For example, Jacobson & Lishman (1987) found greater ventricular enlargement in Korsakoff patient's than in alcoholic patients, and differences in the width of the interhemispheric fissure but no differences in Sylvian fissure widths. Reduced density in the thalamic region has been reported in Korsakoff patients in MRI and CT studies. Cortical atrophy has been found in MRI studies, together with atrophy of the mammillary bodies (Squire et al., 1990). Functional imaging studies have revealed a range of metabolic dysfunctions in Korsakoff patients. Paller et al. (1997) conducted a PET study of non-amnesic alcoholic and Korsakoff patients, and found widespread cortical reduction in glucose metabolism during a delayed recognition test in the amnesic patients. They concluded that the amnesic dysfunction of Korsakoff's syndrome is produced by damage to the thalamic and cortical circuits involved in memory processing.

Neuropsychological Functioning

The cognitive impairments of Korsakoff patients have been the focus of considerable clinical and experimental research. Most interest has centred on their profound memory failure. The first comprehensive examination of the neuropsychological functioning of persons with Korsakoff's disease was published by Talland (1965), who reported a 6-year study of alcoholic amnesic patients. He found that despite their profound amnesia, a number of skills were preserved in Korsakoff's disease. These included verbal comprehension and communication skills, knowledge of language, well-established motor skills, intellectual tests that involved the use of previously acquired knowledge, immediate memory and perception. On complex intellectual or information-processing tasks, they showed some impairments, but on any task that required learning and recall of new information, their deficits were severe. Thus, despite selecting patients for study that on clinical examination had a relatively circumscribed amnesia, Talland found that they had many signs of cognitive failure that did not require memory. He also found that Korsakoff patients, although not devoid of the capacity for new learning, nonetheless displayed a broad range of severe memory problems.

The findings are mirrored in the performance of a group of 10 patients with Korsakoff's syndrome on the WAIS-III and WMS-III. Their average Full Scale IQ score was 93, and all their mean IQ scale scores (between 92.2 and 94.5) were in the average range. On the Working Memory index of the WMS-III, their average score was also in the average range (97.8). All other memory scores were impaired, ranging from 57.8 on the General Memory index to 73.1 on the Auditory Immediate Memory index. For the purposes of comparison, 35 mildly impaired patients with Alzheimer's disease with a Full Scale IQ of about 87, had a General Memory index score of 60.4. The average memory impairment of the persons with Korsakoff's disease placed them more than two standard deviations below the mean and in the same range as the elderly demented group. Their rate of learning and retention scores placed them at below the 5th percentile of the standardization sample. In sum, patients with Korsakoff's disease have severe memory deficits that are out of proportion to any decrement in their intellect.

Amnesia in Korsakoff's Disease

The failure of memory in Korsakoff patients has attracted the ongoing interest of neuropsychologists over the past 30 years. Initial research was based on models that divided memory processing into stages of encoding/consolidation, storage and retrieval. The structure of memory was conceived as comprising three major stores: a sensory register, a short-term store (which functioned as a repository for working memory) and a long-term store containing permanent memories. Initially it was assumed that amnesia arose from a failure of consolidation, but research by Warrington & Weiskrantz (1970) demonstrated that amnesics were able to recall previous learning, provided they were given some form of retrieval cue. For example, they found that the word learning of Korsakoff patients approached normal if they were given the first three letters of the word they were to recall as a cue. This somewhat surprising result led them to propose that amnesia was primarily caused by a retrieval deficit. This implied that amnesics could register and encode new information but could not bring it to mind when instructed to do so.

Although Korsakoff patients did well on cued recall tasks, their performance seldom equalled that of control subjects. Graf et al. (1984) conducted a study in which they helped to define the nature of preserved learning in amnesics. They first primed their amnesics with a set of words (e.g. MOTEL) and then gave them the first three letters (MOT) with the instruction to give the first word that came to mind. They were careful not to hint that the procedure was a memory test. The amnesics were just as likely as controls to respond with the primed word rather than an unprimed word with the same stem (e.g. MOTOR). Their experiment gave rise to a distinction between *explicit* memory, where the person tested is directly instructed to recall information from a previous learning episode, and *implicit* memory, where no reference to the prior learning is made. The primary task that Graf et al. (1984) used is a good example of an implicit learning task; traditional free or cued recall tests are explicit memory tests. Alcoholic Korsakoff patients are thus able to demonstrate learning on implicit tasks, where learning is tested indirectly and requires no conscious recollection of the learning episode.

Preserved and Impaired Learning

On any task requiring the acquisition of perceptual or motor skills and on semantic priming tasks, Korsakoff patients show relatively preserved learning. Tasks that the Korsakoffs perform normally all involve demonstrating learning without reference to a previous learning episode. In order to execute a new motor skill, like riding a bicycle, it is not necessary to recall when the skill was acquired before performing the act of riding. In contrast, most laboratory-based memory tests require recall of the study episode. The distinction between tasks amnesic Korsakoff patients can and cannot do has been labelled in various ways. One such dichotomy is between procedural learning, which is preserved, and declarative memory, which is not. The distinction between explicit and implicit memory is more commonly used to define memory tasks that amnesics can or cannot complete. Another important distinction is between *primary* memory, which refers to the capacity to hold information in working store, and *secondary* memory, which refers to information that can be accessed but is not currently available. Primary memory is often termed "short-term memory" but the label "working memory" is more appropriate. Amnesic Korsakoff patients typically have well-preserved working memory capacity in the presence of almost total secondary memory failure.

Frontal Lobe Damage

In many cases, apathy and loss of spontaneity are the most striking features of the Korsakoff patient's disorder. These personality features are strongly suggestive of frontal lobe damage. There is evidence from several sources confirming that this is the case. CT scans have shown that Korsakoff amnesics have frontal cortical atrophy. In addition, on psychological tests that are sensitive to frontal functioning (e.g. measures of conceptual learning, temporal sequencing and tendency to perseverate), the results from Korsakoff patients lie between those of other amnesics (who tend not to show evidence of frontal damage) and patients with frontal lesions. Thus, the neuropsychological test profile of patients with Wernicke–Korsakoff syndrome is complicated by damage to cortical structures, including the frontal regions. This is not surprising, given that patients reach the stage of irreversible amnesia after a lengthy period of nutritional abuse and liver damage.

Alcoholic Dementia

As has been discussed previously, there is substantial evidence that chronic alcohol dependence leads to brain damage and cognitive deficits. When an unselected group of amnesic alcoholic patients is tested, a proportion will have signs of intellectual impairment. Because the most prominent symptom in severely brain damaged alcoholics is typically the amnesia, the term Korsakoff's syndrome has been applied to the range of severely impaired alcoholics, without regard to the specificity of the memory failure. Where there is demonstrable loss of intellectual functioning, comparable to the degree of amnesia, the diagnosis of alcoholic dementia may be more appropriate.

CONCLUDING COMMENTS

The presentation of this chapter implies that there is a series of progressive stages in the use of alcohol, ranging from moderate consumption, through alcoholism, to irreversible neurological damage. For a variety of reasons, studies of the neurological consequences of alcoholism tend to treat these three groups as distinct entities. The social drinker, who lives and functions successfully in the community, shows little if any unequivocal signs of impairment. Alcoholics are usually assessed in treatment facilities and show evidence of some neuropsychological impairment, but when abstinent are able to live independent lives in the community. Patients with Korsakoff's disease, however, are severely brain-damaged and may be dependent on continuing hospital care.

Although these groups can be separated, there is also an underlying progression from moderate social drinking to brain-damaged alcoholic. Whether this progression is continuous or not has been a matter of some debate. There is an emerging consensus, based on the findings of longitudinal studies, that there is a continuum of impairment ranging from moderate consumption to abusive drinking (Parsons, 1998). This suggests that a history of alcohol consumption results in an accumulation of damage to the brain that is expressed in neuropsychological inefficiencies. With abstinence, impairments remit, but not always and seldom completely. The relationship between chronic alcohol dependence and Wernicke–Korsakoff syndrome is not as clear. At a clinical level, there is a clear discontinuity; the recovering alcoholic may have mild to moderate brain dysfunction but the Korsakoff patient has a distinctive and profound neurological deficit. At the biological level, however, there is evidence of continuity in the brain lesions of non-amnesic and amnesic alcoholics. Research by Harper et al. (1986) has shown that many alcoholics with no clinical history of amnesia have a distribution of midline brain lesions comparable to patients with Korsakoff's disease. It is possible that the neuropsychological impairments of alcoholism and Wernicke–Korsakoff syndrome are similarly continuous. Because most research has focused on either the severely amnesic alcoholic or the alcoholic in treatment, it is conceivable that moderately to severely impaired alcoholics, who would complete the gap in the continuum, have been neglected in the literature, thereby creating an impression of discontinuity.

An alternative model proposes that Korsakoff's syndrome is the result of a traumatic episode causing a critical lesion, imposed on a history of declining cognitive efficiency. The Korsakoff patient may have recovered from previous clinical or subclinical Wernicke's episodes but, on the final occasion, a period of severe nutritional deficiency combined with an extensive history of alcoholism produces sufficient brain damage to cause amnesia. There is insufficient longitudinal research to describe with certainty the progression of brain damage in patients who are alcohol-dependent. It is indeed highly likely that there is no single path to Korsakoff's amnesia. Some severely amnesic alcoholics have an extensive history of drinking and progressive decline, and fit the continuity model best. They may also be more likely to show concurrent signs of dementia. Others may have a shorter history of alcoholism and more circumscribed brain damage, and develop Korsakoff syndrome abruptly, in a manner consistent with a traumatic model. At the present time there is no definitive explanation of how the diencephalic, cortical and basal forebrain lesions identified in chronic alcoholic patients lead to different patterns of cognitive impairment.

Finally, the obstacles to conducting research with alcoholic patients should be noted. These include problems in measuring deficits, in collecting accurate histories of alcohol consumption and in eliminating other causes of neurological deficits, including psychiatric conditions, organ damage, head injury and abuse of other substances. Alcoholism is a life-style that can lead to a range of risks of neurological damage, of which alcoholism is but one.

KEY WORKS AND SUGGESTIONS FOR FURTHER READING

Mattson, S.N. & Riley, E.P. (1998). A review of the neurobehavioural deficits in children with fetal alcohol syndrome or prenatal exposure to alcohol. *Alcoholism: Clinical and Experimental Research*, **22**, 279–294.

This reference provides a comprehensive review of research on the fetal alcohol syndrome.

Parsons, O.A. & Nixon, S.J. (1996). Cognitive functioning in sober social drinkers: a review of the research since 1986. *Journal of Studies on Alcohol*, **59**, 180–190.

The development of research on the neuropsychological consequences of moderate drinking can be followed in this survey of the research.

Lishman, W.A. (1987). *Organic Psychiatry: The Psychological Consequences of Cerebral Disorder*, 2nd edn. Oxford: Blackwell Scientific.

For a comprehensive introduction to the variety clinical disorders associated with alcohol, Lishman's well-known textbook is of value.

Knight, R.G. & Longmore, B.E. (1994). *Clinical Neuropsychology of Alcoholism*. Hillsdale, NJ: Erlbaum.

A review of the neuropsychological research on patients with cognitive damage consequent on alcoholism that elaborates on much of the material presented in this chapter.

Victor, M., Adams, R.D. & Collins, G.N. (1989). *The Wernicke–Korsakoff Syndrome*, 2nd edn. Philadelphia, PA: F.A. Dowis.

This monograph on Wernicke–Korsakoff syndrome provides an excellent account of the literature available in this area.

REFERENCES

Abel, E.L. & Sokol, R.J. (1991). A revised conservative estimate of the incidence of FAS and its economic impact. *Alcoholism: Clinical and Experimental Research*, **15**, 514–524.

Bergman, H., Borg, S., Hindmarsh, T., Idestrom, C.-M. & Mutzell, S. (1980). Computed tomography of the brain and neuropsychological assessment of male alcoholic patients and a random sample from the general male population. *Acta Psychiatrica Scandinavica*, **62**(Suppl. 286), 47–56.

Bergman, H., Axelsson, G., Idestrom, C.M., Borg, S., Hindmarsh, T., Makower, J. & Mutzell. S. (1983). Alcohol consumption, neuropsychological status and computer-tomographic findings in a random sample of men and women from the general population. *Pharmacology, Biochemistry and Behaviour*, **18**, 501–505.

Blass, J.P. & Gibson, G.E. (1977). Abnormality of a thiamine-requiring enzyme in patients with Wernicke–Korsakoff syndrome. *New England Journal of Medicine*, **297**, 1367–1370.

Bowden, S.C. (1987). Brain impairment in social drinkers? No cause for concern. *Alcoholism: Clinical and Experimental Research*, **11**, 407–409.

Butters, N. (1985). Alcoholic Korsakoff's syndrome: some unresolved issues concerning the etiology, neuropathology, and cognitive deficits. *Journal of Clinical and Experimental Neuropsychology*, **7**, 181–210.

Cala, L.A. (1985). CT demonstration of the early effects of alcohol on the brain. In M. Galanter (Ed.), *Recent Developments in Alcoholism*, vol. 3 (pp. 253–264). New York: Plenum.

Carlen, P.L., Wortzman, G., Holgate, R.C., Wilkinson, D.A. & Rankin, J.G. (1978). Reversible atrophy in recently abstinent chronic alcoholics measured by computed tomography scans. *Science*, **200**, 1076–1078.

Cullen, K.M., Halliday, G.M., Caine, D. & Kril, J.J. (1997). The nucleus basalis (Ch4) in the alcoholic Wernicke–Korsakoff syndrome: reduced cell number in both amnesic and non-amnesic patients. *Journal of Neurology, Neurosurgery & Psychiatry*, **63**, 315–320.

Eckhardt, M.J., Rohrbaugh, J.W., Rio, D.E. & Martin, P.R. (1990). Positron emission tomography as a technique for studying the chronic effects of alcohol on the human brain. *Annals of Medicine*, **22**, 341–345.

Eckhardt, M.J., Rawlings, R.R., Graubard, B.I., Faden, V., Martin, P.R. & Gottschalk, L.A. (1998). Neuropsychological performance and treatment outcome in male alcoholics. *Alcoholism: Clinical and Experimental Research*, **12**, 88–93.

Fox, A.M., Michie, P.T., Coltheart, M. & Solowiji, N. (1995). Memory functioning in social drinkers: a study of event-related potentials. *Alcohol and Alcoholism*, **30**, 303–310.

Graf, P., Squire, L.R. & Mandler, G. (1984). The information that amnesic patients do not forget. *Journal of Experimental Psychology: Learning, Memory, and Cognition*, **10**, 164–178.

Harper, C.G. (1983). The incidence of Wernicke's encephalopathy in Australia: a neuropathological study of 131 cases. *Journal of Neurology, Neurosurgery, and Psychiatry*, **46**, 593–598.

Harper, C.G., Giles, M. & Finlay-Jones, R. (1986). Clinical signs in the Wernicke–Korsakoff complex: a retrospective analysis of 131 cases diagnosed at necropsy. *Journal of Neurology, Neurosurgery, and Psychiatry*, **49**, 341–345.

Jacobson, R.R. & Lishman, W.A. (1987). Selective memory loss and global intellectual deficits in alcoholic Korsakoff's syndrome. *Psychological Medicine*, **17**, 649–655.

Jernigan, T.L., Butters, N., DiTraglia, G., Schafer, K., Smith, T., Irwin, M., Grant, I., Schuckit, M. & Cermak, L.S. (1991a). Reduced cerebral grey matter observed in alcoholics using magnetic resonance imaging. *Alcoholism: Clinical and Experimental Research*, **15**, 418–427.

Jones, K.L. & Smith, D.W. (1973). Recognition of the fetal alcohol syndrome in early infancy. *Lancet*, **ii**, 999–1001.

Knight, R.G. & Longmore, B.E. (1994). *Clinical Neuropsychology of Alcoholism*. Hillsdale, NJ: Erlbaum.

Kopelman, M.D. (1987). Two types of confabulation. *Journal of Neurology, Neurosurgery, and Psychiatry*, **50**, 1482–1487.

Kopelman, M.D. (1995). The Korsakoff syndrome. *British Journal of Psychiatry*, **166**, 154–173.

Lamberty, G.J., Beckwith, B.E. & Petros, T.V. (1990). Post-trial treatment with ethanol enhances recall of prose narratives. *Physiology and Behavior*, **48**, 653–658.

Lishman, W.A. (1987). *Organic Psychiatry: The Psychological Consequences of Cerebral Disorder*, 2nd edn. Oxford: Blackwell Scientific.

Lishman, W.A., Ron, M.A. & Acker, W. (1980). Computed tomography and psychometric assessment of alcoholic patients. In D. Richter (Ed.), *Addiction and Brain Damage* (pp. 215–227). London: Croom Helm.

Mair, W.G.P., Warrington, E.K. & Weiskrantz, L. (1979). Memory disorder in Korsakoff's psychosis: a neuropathological and neuropsychological investigation of two cases. *Brain*, **102**, 749–783.

Mattson, S.N. & Riley, E.P. (1998). A review of the neurobehavioural deficits in children with fetal alcohol syndrome or prenatal exposure to alcohol. *Alcoholism: Clinical and Experimental Research*, **22**, 279–294.

Mayes, A.R., Meudell, P., Mann, D. & Pickering, A. (1988). Location of lesions in Korsakoff's syndrome. Neuropsychological and neuropathological data on two patients. *Cortex*, **24**, 367–388.

Michaelis, E.K. (1990). Fetal alcohol exposure: cellular toxicity and molecular events involved in toxicity. *Alcoholism: Clinical and Experimental Research*, **14**, 819–826.

Nichols, J.M. & Martin, F. (1996). The effect of heavy social drinking on recall and event-related potentials. *Journal of Studies on Alcohol*, **57**, 125–135

Paller, K.A., Acharya, A., Richardson, B.C., Plaisant, O. et al. (1997). Functioning neuroimaging of cortical dysfunction in alcoholic Korsakoff's syndrome. *Journal of Cognitive Neuroscience*, **9**, 277–293.

Parker, E.S. & Noble, E. (1977). Alcohol consumption and cognitive functioning in social drinkers. *Journal of Studies on Alcohol*, **38**, 1224–1232.

Parker, D.A., Parker, E.S., Brody, J.A. & Schoenberg, R. (1983). Alcohol use and cognitive loss among employed men and women. *American Journal of Public Health*, **73**, 521–526.

Parsons, O.A. (1986). Cognitive functioning in sober social drinkers: a review and critique. *Journal of Studies on Alcohol*, **47**, 101–114.

Parsons, O.A. (1998). Neurocognitive deficits in alcoholics and social drinkers: a continuum? *Alcoholism: Clinical and Experimental Research*, **22**, 954–961.

Parsons, O.A. & Nixon, S.J. (1996). Cognitive functioning sober social drinkers: a review of the research since 1986. *Journal of Studies on Alcohol*, **59**, 180–190.

Pfefferbaum, A., Sullivan, E.V., Mathalon, D.H., Shear, P.K., Rosenbloom, M.J. & Lim, K.O. (1995). Longitudinal changes in magnetic resonance imaging brain volumes in abstinent and relapsed alcoholics. *Alcoholism: Clinical and Experimental Research*, **19**, 1177–1191.

Ryback, R. (1971). The continuum and specificity of the effects of alcohol on memory: a review. *Quarterly Journal of Studies on Alcohol*, **32**, 995–1016.

Squire, L.R., Amaral, D.G. & Press, G.A. (1990). Magnetic resonance imaging of the hippocampal formation and mammillary nuclei distinguish medical temporal lobe and diencephalic amnesia. *Journal of Neuroscience*, **10**, 3106–3117.

Streissguth, A.P. (1977). Maternal alcoholism and the outcome of pregnancy: implications for child mental health. *American Journal of Orthopsychiatry*, **47**, 422–431.

Streissguth, A.P., Barr, H.M., Martin, D.C. & Herman, C.S. (1980). Effects of maternal alcohol, nicotine and caffeine use during pregnancy on infant development at 8 months. *Alcoholism: Clinical and Experimental Research*, **4**, 152–158.

Talland, G.A. (1965). *Deranged Memory.* New York: Academic Press.

Tarter, R.E., Van Thiel, D.H., Arria, A.M., Carra, J. & Moss, H. (1988). Impact of cirrhosis on the neuropsychological test performance of alcoholics. *Alcoholism: Clinical and Experimental Research*, **12**, 619–621.

Victor, M., Adams, R.D. & Collins, G.N. (1989). *The Wernicke–Korsakoff Syndrome*, 2nd edn. Philadelphia, PA: F.A. Dowis.

Volkow, N.D., Hitzemann, R., Wang, G.J., Fowler, J.S., Burr, G., Pascani, K., Kewey, S.L. & Wolf, A.P. (1992). Decreased brain metabolism in neurologically intact healthy alcoholics. *American Journal of Psychiatry*, **149**, 1016–1022.

Warrington, E.K. & Weiskrantz, L. (1970). Amnesic syndrome: consolidation or retrieval? *Nature*, **228**, 628–630.

Chapter 8

Effect of Alcohol on the Orogastrointestinal Tract, the Pancreas and the Liver

Helmut K. Seitz
and
Nils Homann
*Salem Medical Centre, University of Heidelberg,
Heidelberg, Germany*

Synopsis

Alcohol consumption leads to significant alterations of the mucosa of the entire gastro-intestinal tract from mouth to rectum, the pancreas and the liver. While acute alcohol inges-tion may lead to disturbancies in gastrointestinal motility and secretion, such as gastric acid output and pancreatic secretion, chronic alcohol consumption leads to severe morphol-ogical and functional alterations of the gastrointestinal mucosa, pancreas and liver.

In the oropharynx and esophagus, chronic alcohol consumption, especially when com-bined with smoking, results in an increased risk of developing cancer. In the stomach, severe hemorrhagic gastritis may occur and in the large intestine, chronic alcohol consumption leads to mucosal injury associated with malabsorption and thus malnutrition and diarrhea. In the colorectum, chronic alcohol consumption is associated with an increased prevalence of ade-nomatous polyps and rectal carcinoma.

Since alcohol is metabolized to its first toxic metabolite, acetaldehyde, by mucosal alcohol dehydrogenases and also by bacterial enzymes in the oropharynx and especially in the large intestine, this acetaldehyde may make an important contribution to the mucosal cell injury. In addition to its deleterious effects on the gastrointestinal mucosa, chronic alcohol con-sumption leads to chronic pancreatitis, characterized by loss of pancreatic cells, leading to maldigestion and weight loss. The functional alterations of the pancreas are associated with severe morphological changes, such as calcification, enlargement of the pancreas head, leading to obstructive jaundice, and the occurence of pseudocysts.

Subsequently, alcohol consumption leads to alcoholic liver disease, including fatty liver, alcoholic hepatitis, alcoholic liver cirrhosis and hepatocellular cancer. The

International Handbook of Alcohol Dependence and Problems. Edited by N. Heather, T.J. Peters and T. Stockwell.
© 2001 John Wiley & Sons Ltd.

pathogenesis of alcohol liver disease includes genetic, metabolic, toxic and immunologic mechanisms.

UPPER AERODIGESTIVE TRACT

Alcohol has several important pathogenic effects on the mucosa of the upper gastro-intestinal tract. Since the mucosa of the upper aerodigestive tract is usually regarded as one epithelial lining, which is covered by the same squamous epithelium, the effects of alcohol on the mucosa of mouth, oropharynx, larynx, hypopharynx and esophagus share important similarities, although marked differences can also be observed. The effect of alcohol is most striking for the oral cavity, hypopharynx and esophagus, but deleterious effects for the larynx, where alcohol is in no direct contact, can be observed.

Oral Cavity, Pharynx and Larynx

Acute and Chronic Effects of Alcohol on the Oral Cavity, Pharynx and Larynx

Alcohol damages the salivary glands. Approximately 12% of alcoholics show an enlarged parotic gland and this association is even higher in patients with concomitant alcoholic liver cirrhosis (Bode, 1980). However, this enlargement of the salivary glands is accompanied by substantial histological changes, such as atrophy and lipomatosis and a general hyper-viscosity of the saliva (Maier et al., 1986). This leads to a decreased clearing function of the saliva in alcoholics, which itself might trigger some other clinical symptoms of chronic alcohol abuse. For example, it is well known that alcoholics suffer more frequently from stomatitis, glossitis and poor general dental hygiene than non-alcoholics (Maier, Zoller & Herrmann, 1993). An increased incidence of carious lesions and periodonditis has been observed. The reasons for these observations are unknown; direct damage of the mucosa by high ethanol concentrations, the bacterial or mucosal production of local acetaldehyde and/or a worse socioeconomic status of alcoholics in general have been suggested (Homann et al., 1997a, 1998). However, the most striking chronic effect of alcohol on these anatomic sites is the increased incidence of cancer.

Cancer of the Oropharynx and Larynx

Epidemiological Data

Alcohol, together with tobacco smoke, is the main cause of cancer of the oral cavity, pharynx and larynx (Seitz, Poschl & Simanowski, 1998). It has been estimated that up to 80–90% of these cancers can be avoided just by abstaining from these two risk factors. The relative risks associated with ethanol consumption are significantly different in distinct anatomic sites of the upper gastrointestinal tract, with the lowest values for the larynx. It is believed that these differences are due to local effects of ethanol and that the higher risk for anatomic subsites, such as tongue and hypopharynx, may be caused by a longer contact with the ingested alcohol at these sites while drinking. It is well known from epidemiological studies that there exists a strong dose-dependency between the amount of ingested ethanol and relative cancer risk and, in contrast to tobacco smoke, the attributable risks for alcohol consumption do not seem to be saturable (Brugere et al., 1986). Indeed, in a carefully designed study, a French group showed relative risks for alcohol drinking, adjusted for tobacco smoke, to be as high as 143 for the hypopharynx carcinoma in men drinking more than 160 g/day (Brugere et al., 1986).

Although alcohol and tobacco smoke are well-known, independent and strong risk factors for upper gastrointestinal tract cancer, their combined action on these epithelia is poorly understood. Studies have shown strikingly that smokers have higher cancer rates in conjunction with high exposure to alcohol than could be expected from the attributable data for each risk factor alone (Franceschi et al., 1990; Bofetta et al., 1992). Hence, in regard to upper gastrointestinal tract cancer, alcohol and tobacco act together in a more multiplicative than an additive manner and seem to have synergistic tumor-promoting effects. The reason for this is unknown; however, it is noteworthy that the attributable relative cancer risk of alcohol seems to be predominantly of more importance for the development of cancers of the oral cavity and the hypopharynx, whereas the influence of smoking is more obvious for oropharyngeal and laryngeal carcinoma (Seitz, Poschl & Simanowski, 1998; Brugere et al., 1986; Franceschi et al., 1990; Bofetta et al., 1992). Again, these differences may be explained by local effects involving direct contact while, respectively, swallowing or inhaling.

Pathomechanisms of Alcohol

The exact mechanism by which alcohol exhibits the co-carcinogenic action on the mucosa of the upper aerodigestive tract is still unknown. Ethanol could exhibit systemic co-carcinogenic effects by: (a) displacing potential cancer-protective nutrients in the diet; (b) influencing the toxification of procarcinogens via the induction of metabolizing enzymes; (c) inhibiting the detoxification of carcinogenic compounds due to inhibition of liver enzyme function; (d) increasing the oxidative exposure; (e) affecting the hormonal status; and (f) suppressing immune function (Seitz, Poschl & Simanowski, 1998). Despite these hypothetical mechanisms, the tumor-promoting effect on the mucosa of the upper gastrointestinal tract may be largely local, caused by direct contact of ethanol with the mucosa. Accelerated cell division after ethanol intake has been observed in the oral cavity (Maier et al., 1994). Accordingly, this is assumed to be one of the major effects of local ethanol-associated carcinogenesis, as it is also caused by its first metabolite, acetaldehyde, which may be the main pathogenic substance in ethanol-associated carcinogenesis (Homann et al., 1997b). Direct mucosal damage followed by compensatory regeneration may be an explanation for the hyperproliferating effects of ethanol. Other local co-carcinogenic effects may be an enhanced solubility of concomitantly inhaled or ingested carcinogens by alcohol and the intake of possible carcinogenic congeners in alcoholic beverages. For example, high concentrations of nitrosamines have been found in whisky and beer (Walker et al., 1979).

Most recently, many experimental data have indicated that acetaldehyde, the first metabolite of alcohol, plays an important role in ethanol-associated carcinogenesis (Seitz, Poschl & Simanowski, 1998). Polymorphism and/or mutation in the genes coding for enzymes responsible for acetaldehyde accumulation and detoxification are of particular interest. Such enzymes include alcohol dehydrogenases (ADH) and aldehyde dehydrogenases (ALDH). For example, a Japanese group demonstrated that individuals with heterozygous mutations in the ALDH-2 gene, leading to decreased enzyme activity and, thus, increased acetaldehyde levels, have a much higher risk of developing a malignant tumor in the oropharynx than non-mutant controls if high alcohol amounts are taken (Yokoyama et al., 1996). In addition, acetaldehyde can be produced by mucosal ADH and just recently it has been shown that, if high amounts of alcohol are consumed, individuals with predominant ADH-3 expression, leading to an enzyme expression that very rapidly converts ethanol to acetaldehyde, have a higher cancer risk at these sites than controls not expressing that gene (Harty et al., 1997). However, recent research has revealed that the main metabolic source of acetaldehyde in the oral cavity might be the microbial production of acetaldehyde by the oral microflora, leading to long-lasting and high levels of acetaldehyde in the saliva (Homann et al., 1997a; Pikkarainen et al., 1981). This would explain the epidemiological finding that alcoholics with poor dental hygiene, leading to bacterial overgrowth, have higher cancer risks than alcoholics with a normal dental status (Maier et al., 1993).

ESOPHAGUS

Esophageal Cancer

The esophagus was the first organ where a causal relation between alcohol intake and the development of a malignant tumor was decribed. At the beginning of this century, Lamu reported an increased incidence of esophageal cancer among absinth consumers in the area of Calvados, France (Lamu, 1910). Since then, numerous epidemiological studies have confirmed and extended this early description and identified chronic, heavy alcohol consumption together with tobacco smoke as the main cause for esophageal cancer (Seitz, Poschl & Simanowski, 1998; Tuyns & Masse, 1973). As for the oropharynx and the oral cavity, the relative risks associated with alcohol are dose-dependent and not saturable. In general, taking comparable data from the aerodigestive tract into account, the effect of alcohol on cancer development seems to be similar to that for the oral cavity and the hypopharynx, e.g. the influence of tobacco smoke seems to be of less importance (Seitz, Poschl & Simanowski, 1998; Tuyns & Masse, 1973). Again, alcohol and tobacco smoke act synergistically on cancer development.

The pathogenic mechanisms of ethanol-associated carcinogenesis in esophageal cancer are unknown; however, the same systemic and local effects as described for the upper aerodigestive tract have been discussed (Seitz, Poschl & Simanowski, 1998; Simanowski et al., 1993). In addition, altered metabolism of nitrosamines by alcohol may play an important role. Among other possibilities, enhanced activation of the nitrosamine may occur in the esophagus through cytochrome P4502E1 (CYP2E1) which has enhanced expresssion in the upper gastrointestinal tract of alcoholics (Seitz, Poschl & Simanowski, 1998). Such an activation is a prerequisite for an increased methylation pattern of esophageal DNA by dimethylnitrosamine as it was observed in ethanol-fed rats in contrast to control rats. Zinc deficiency, which is commonly observed in alcoholics, further enhances this activation (Seitz & Suter, 1994).

Another mechanism by which alcohol promotes esophageal cancer development is the frequently observed increased incidence of gastro-esophageal reflux disease (GERD). In patients with a long history of GERD, an increased incidence of Barretts esophagus has been described. This metaplastic conversion of the lower esophagus mucosa is a well-known precursor lesion for malignant transformation.

Other Alcohol-associated Alterations of the Esophagus

Acute alcohol ingestion has also been shown to lead to a significant gastro-esophageal reflux in healthy human volunteers. The pathomechanisms of gastro-esophageal reflux disease due to alcohol have been only partly elucidated. Alcohol lowers the pressure of the lower esophageal sphincter and its normal reaction and stimulation by pentagastrin and protein. Thus, the esophageal clearance is inhibited. Esophageal motility is also decreased by intravenous alcohol application, which also suggests systemic effects on the esophagus (Keshavarzian & Fields, 1996). In some chronic alcoholics, the disturbed motility in the distal esophagus with reduced and altered motility waves can lead to a characteristic "nut-cracker-esophagus", a clinical feature which is fully reversible after abstaining (Keshavarzian & Fields, 1996). Clinically, the occurence of esophagitis has been reported frequently; however, animal studies suggest that only alcoholic beverages with an alcohol content of 40% are able to substantially damage the esophageal mucosa (Wienbeck & Berges, 1985). Moreover, the contact time while swallowing is relatively rapid, so that acute, erosive lesions of the esophagus caused by alcohol are rare.

Another consequence of acute alcohol consumption is the Mallory–Weiss syndrome. Acute, intense vomiting due to alcohol intoxication or via hangover may lead to very high intraluminal esophageal pressure, which can cause the characteristic longitudinal mucosal lesions within the lower esophagus (Wienbeck & Berges, 1985). This is often accompanied by acute bleeding, which only rarely requires endoscopic intervention. Seldom seen, but clinically much more severe, are intramural hematoma or the Boerhaave syndrome—rupture of the esophagus caused by alcohol due to the same pathomechanism.

STOMACH

The stomach is the first organ that has long contact with alcohol. Its mucosa is damaged and altered by both acute and chronic alcohol ingestion. In contrast to other gastrointestinal sites, the stomach may contribute to overall ethanol metabolism. This so-called gastric first-pass metabolism is most likely 5–10% *in vivo* (Oneta et al., 1998). It has been subject to controversy in recent years and its contribution depends on multiple factors (Seitz & Poschl, 1997).

Gastric first-pass metabolism is mediated predominantly by class IV ADH (σ-ADH), an ADH exclusively expressed in gastrointestinal mucosa (Seitz & Oneta, 1998). In addition, other ADHs, such as class I and III, also oxidize ethanol. Gastric ADH activity is decreased by female gender, aging, medication (cimetidin, etc.), genetic factors, fasting, chronic atrophic gastritis and chronic alcoholism (Seitz & Poschl, 1997; Seitz & Oneta, 1998). In addition, rapid gastric emptying also decreases gastric first-pass metabolism (Seitz & Poschl, 1997; Pedrosa et al., 1996). Thus, many factors, varying inter-individually, modulate gastric ethanol metabolism. The absorption of ethanol from the stomach also depends on gastric emptying and can be up to 30%. Gastric emptying is stimulated when alcohol concentration is below 10% and delayed by high alcohol concentrations (Barboriak & Meade, 1970).

Acute Effects of Alcohol on Gastric Function

Alcohol stimulates gastric juice secretion, no matter whether it is taken orally, intragastrically or intravenously. Beer, wine and alcohol with an alcohol content of 1–5% are the most potent stimulators of gastric secretion, whereas strong alcoholic beverages, such as whisky and cognac, have no effect. The increase in gastric secretion by alcohol may be caused by vagal stimulation, by histamines, which are frequent congeners in alcoholic beverages, and by an increased concentration of gastrin (Seitz et al., 1995).

Alcohol itself increases mucosal permeabiltiy in different experimental animal models. This has been shown, for example, by measurement of the transmural gastric electric potential and it may be caused by direct damage by alcohol to the intracellular matrix, with local seperation of tight junctions. Thus, alcohol is a frequent cause of erosive lesions in the stomach. Erythema, hemorrhagia and infiltration of eosinophilic granulocytes can be observed 3 hours after alcohol ingestion and acute bleeding due to hemorrhagic lesions is frequently observed, especially in patients with alcoholic liver cirrhosis (Laine & Weinstein, 1988; Gottfried, Korsten & Lieber, 1978). In healthy patients, acute bleeding due to alcohol is rare. However, alcohol promotes mucosal lesions caused by other pathogens, such as acetyl salicylacid, steroids or *Helicobacter pylori*. In this context, it is notewothy that *H. pylori* expresses significant amounts of ADH and is capable of producing substantial amounts of microbially derived cytotoxic acetaldehyde (Salmela et al., 1993). However, it seems that alcoholics are no more frequently infected with *H. pylori* than non-alcoholics (Laine, Marin-Sorensen & Weinstein, 1989). Although *H. pylori* metabolizes ethanol, individuals infected with *H. pylori* reveal a reduced first-pass metabolism of ethanol due to the *H. pylori*-associated mucosal change and decrease of mucosal ADH activity (Simanowski et al., 1997).

Alcohol may cause mucosal lesions by a direct effect on the mucosa-protecting mucus. It has been shown that alcohol significantly inhibits the secretion of prostaglandin E2 (Bode et al., 1988). Moreover, an increased secretion of leukotrienes may also be involved and alcohol directly inhibits the production of the mucus, most propably via a direct inhibition of the enzyme carboanhydrase.

Chronic Effects on Gastric Function

There is disagreement about whether alcohol may be a direct cause of chronic gastritis. This possible association may become clinically relevant only for severe alcoholics with accompanying malnutrition. Alcohol may act also as an independent factor for gastric or duodenal ulcer development. However, most studies suggest that this may only be the case for heavy drinkers with an excessive consumption of more than 100 g pure alcohol per day.

SMALL INTESTINE

Alcohol is completely absorbed in the jejunum and does not reach the ileum. However, as alcohol is a water-soluble substance, it is present and distributed in the water-phase of all organs. Thus, the alcohol concentrations in the remaining gut are comparable to blood ethanol concentrations. Under certain pathological conditions, such as bacterial overgrowth or fungal infection, additional ethanol can be produced microbially from carbohydrates.

Chronic alcohol consumption leads to intestinal symptoms such as diarrhea, malabsorption, malnutrition and weight loss (Seitz & Suter, 1994). Maltnutrition and weight loss are frequently caused by the replacement of normal nutritional components by alcohol in heavy drinkers. However, alcohol has a direct impact on the absorption of many important trace elements and vitamins and on the morphology and function of the small intestine.

Effects of Alcohol on Small Intestinal Mucosa Morphology and Function

Chronic, heavy alcohol consumption leads to several alterations in the mucosa of the jejunum. A decreased surface, an invasion of mononuclear cells, a decreased height of microvilli accompanied by a reduced cell height of enterocytes, and an increased mitotic index have been described (Seitz & Simanowski, 1996). In general, an increased permeability of the small intestine as a consequence of alcohol abuse is demonstrated even in well-nourished persons. This leads to an increased transfer of various macromolecules through the intestinal membrane that are not transferred under normal circumstances. Increased permeability for hemoglobin, polyethylenglycol, peroxidase and endotoxins is described (Bjarnason, Ward & Peters, 1984; Bode & Bode, 1992). Endotoxins are metabolic toxins of the normal intestinal microflora. As bacterial overgrowth in patients with alcohol abuse has been described, it is not surprising that endotoxemia is detected in patients with acute alcohol intoxication. Endotoxins stimulate potent mediators, such as tumor necrosis factor, various leukotrienes and interleukins. These mediators may lead to disturbances in metabolism and microcirculation of the membranes and, finally, as a *circulus vitiosus*, cause mucosal damage of the small intestine. Moreover, endotoxins have been implicated in the development of alcoholic liver disease (Bode & Bode, 1992).

Alcohol consumption decreases type I motility waves in the jejunum without affecting the type III motility in the jejunum. The observed shortened transit time and the frequent symptom of diarrhea in alcoholics may be explained by these observations (Keshavarzian et al., 1986).

Effect of Alcohol on Metabolism and Transport of Various Nutritional Compounds and Drugs

The absorption and metabolism of nutritional compounds and drugs is substantially disturbed by alcohol intake, which may lead not only to the clinically frequently observed malnutrition but also can cause various health harms.

Carbohydrates, Amino Acids and Lipids

Alcohol leads, via a direct effect on cyclic AMP, to an increased secretion of water and mineral salts in the jeunum, which may further explain the observed diarrhea among alcoholics. However, this diarrhea may also be caused by osmotic mechanisms of non-absorped carbohydrates. Alcohol has been shown to worsen pre-existing lactose intolerance (Seitz et al., 1995). Chronic alcohol consumption is the major cause of secondary lactose intolerance. It decreases the expression of various carbohydrate utilizing brush-border enzymes, such as lactase, saccharidase and maltase. Moreover, the absorption of glucose and xylose is directly inhibited (Mezey, 1985).

The active transport of various important amino acids and the *in vitro* activity of membrane peptidases is also inhibited by alcohol (Seitz et al., 1995). Acute and chronic alcohol ingestion leads to an increased intestinal synthesis of triglycerids and cholesterol. The pathomechanistic role of these findings is still unclear.

Vitamins, Minerals, Trace Elements and Drugs

Since the absorptive function of the intestinal mucosa is disturbed by chronic alcohol consumption, decreased absorption of various vitamnins, minerals and trace elements occurs (Seitz & Suter, 1994). Alcoholics usually show decreased absorption of the following vitamins: folic acid, thiamine and cyanocobalamine.

Folic acid deficiency can usually only be seen in malnourished alcoholics. However, malabsorption, increased urinary or fecal secretion, block of the enterohepatic circulation, impairment of hepatic uptake or direct toxic effects of alcohol on folic acid have been reported. It is one cause for the frequently observed anemia in alcoholics (Seitz & Suter, 1994).

In the past, the prevalence of a thiamine deficiency was reported to occur in 30–80% of chronic alcoholics. Recent studies reported much lower frequencies; however, this deficiency is caused by many mechanisms. Malnutrition is thought to be the main cause, but also malabsorption and direct inhibiting interference of alcohol has been reported (Seitz & Suter, 1994). The relevent and impressive clinical feature of thiamine deficiency is acute alcoholic encephalopathy, the Wernicke–Korsakoff syndrome.

Cyanocobalamine deficiency is seen in up to 50% of alcoholics. Again, concomitant malnutrition is the main cause for this deficiency in alcoholics, but also a decreased bioavailability due to an alcohol-induced reduced intraluminal hydrolysis of the precursor FAD is described. Its clinical correlate can be megaloblastic anemia and, much more rarely, subacute combined degeneration of the spinal cord.

Zinc and selenium are trace elements which are seen in decreased serum and tissues levels in heavy drinkers (Seitz & Suter, 1994). Decreased liver concentrations are especially described. Whether disturbed absorption or decreased intake is the main cause for these findings remains unclear.

Increased iron load of the liver is commonly seen in alcoholic liver disease and it has been reported that the absorption of iron, in contrast to other minerals, is increased in alcoholics (Seitz & Suter, 1994).

The absorption of many drugs is altered by alcohol. For example, whereas the absorption of theophylline, diazepam and estradiol is increased by alcohol, the intestinal absorption of isoniacid and estrone sulphate is decreased (Mezey, 1985).

COLON

As already mentioned, the colonic ethanol concentrations equal those present in the blood. A great number of epidemiological studies, including case-control studies and prospective cohort studies, have identified the rectum as a site of enhanced alcohol-associated cancer development (Seitz et al., 1998). In addition, various prospective studies using colonoscopy to identify colorectal polyps have also emphasized the role of chronic alcohol consumption, especially in the form of beer as a risk factor for colorectal polyp development (Seitz et al., 1998). Since polyps are precursor lesions for colorectal cancer, it seems that chronic alcohol consumption is a potential risk factor to develop colorectal cancer. Taking together available epidemiological data, the risk is approximately two- to three-fold, which is low compared to upper gastrointestinal tract cancer. However, considering the high prevalence of colroectal cancer in the Western population, this observation ought to be taken into consideration. The mechanisms for the co-carcinogenic effect of alcohol on the rectum are unclear.

Various experimental studies have focused on the effect of acetaldehyde, which is produced either by fecal bacteria or mucosal ADH from ethanol (Seitz et al., 1998). It has been shown that acetaldehyde concentrations in the colorectal mucosa correlate with the number of microorganisms present in the colorectal lumen (Seitz et al., 1990). It has also been shown that acetaldehyde is associated with an increased proliferative activity in the colorectal mucosa, possibly due to primary injury of the mucosa, which is answered by compensatory hyperproliferation (Simanowski et al., 1994; Homann, Bosch & Simanowski, 1996). In addition, the proliferative compartment of the colonic crypt is extended towards the lumen. Both factors, hyperregenerativity and extension of the proliferative compartment, are known risk factors for the development of colorectal cancer, as shown in experimental animal studies as well as in humans.

The reason why predominantly rectal cancer occurs with chronic alcohol consumption is not clear. However, the fecal bacterial pattern may be of importance, since in that area aerobics are more predominant than the caecal region. Furthermore, the reason why the association is more predominant with beer than other alcoholic beverages is also unclear. It has to be pointed out that additional factors, such as folate deficiency, may further contribute to the alcohol-associated co-carcinogenesis for the rectal mucosa.

PANCREAS

Alcohol abuse is the most common cause for pancreatic injury. It leads to chronic pancreatitis, with various clinical symptoms. Although many pathomechanisms have been elucidated, the lack of an adequate animal model has left many questions unanswered. No epidemiological study could convincingly show a correlation between high alcohol intake and the incidence of pancreatic cancer.

Alcohol-induced Chronic Pancreatitis

Epidemiological Data and Clinical Course

Chronic alcohol abuse is the main cause for chronic pancreatitis. Its prevalence varies between 3% and 8% of all alcoholics (Korsten & Wilson, 1993; Korsten, Pirola & Lieber, 1992). The prevalence of autoptic changes in alcoholics characteristic for chronic pancreatitis is much higher, suggesting that symptomatic pancreatitis occurs only in a very small minority of all alcoholics (Sarles et al., 1979). Epidemiological data show that latency from the start of chronic alcohol abuse to symptomatic pancreatitis is shorter in women, suggesting that, as for alcoholic liver disease, women are more susceptible to alcohol toxicity with respect to pancreatitis (Gullo, 1991). It takes approximately 10–20 years from the beginning of alcohol abuse to the first outbreak of pancreatitis. There seems to be some tendency towards a dose–response relationship with earlier onset of alcoholic pancreatitis in patients with very high alcohol doses (>200 g/day) compared to alcoholics with lower daily alcohol intake. However, it is still unclear why only a minority of alcohol abusers develop symptomatic pancreatitis, and no marker is available to reliably detect those patients who are at high risk for development of chronic pancreatitis.

The median age at first diagnosis is about 40 years. The typical symptoms are midepigastric, heavy pain with radiation to the back. Fever, nausea and vomiting are common and the abdomen is usually tender with decreased bowel sounds. Elevation of pancreatic enzymes, such as amylase and lipase, is frequently seen in the onset; however, in long-lasting pancreatitis it might be lacking due to synthesis failure of the "burned-out" pancreas. It should be taken into account that pancreatic enzymes can also be elevated in other diseases, and that amylase especially has a much lower specifity and can be elevated over a long period of time without any clinical symptoms of pancreatitis. Diagnosis should include imaging with ultrasound and, in severe cases, computed tomography (CT), which has a much higher sensitivity for early detection of severe and progressive disease with pancreas necrosis and infection, acute hemorrhagic pancreatitis and development of pseudocysts. The assessment of severity, in addition to CT criteria, can be done by several clinical and laboratory markers. Elevated white blood cells, glucose, LDH and AST, accompanied by a decrease in calcium, hematocrit, arterial oxygen pressure and BUN, with the need of heavy transfusion, predict final prognosis and they are summarized in the clinically frequently used Ranson score or others (Agarwal & Pitchumoni, 1991; Ranson & Pasternack, 1977). Mortality in mild pancreatitis is less than 2% and it increases to a mortality of 30% in cases with infected necrosis (Gullo, Barbara & Labo, 1988).

As it is a chronic disease, relapse is seen frequently and it is more common in active drinkers compared to abstainers. Thus, life-long alcohol abstention is the best therapy. However, if complications such as calcification, duct stones or pseudocysts occur and occlude the pancreatic duct, relapse is seen frequently. Clinical signs of ongoing chronic pancreatitis are all clinical symptoms of exocrine and (usually much later) endocrine organ failure. Accordingly, malapsorption, with consequent malnutrition, diarrhea, weight loss and diabetes, can occur. Very frequently, chronic abdominal pain is the main clinical symptom, which finally leads to surgical therapy.

Pathogenesis

As for acute pancreatitis, the main pathomechanism of pancreatitis is the autodigestion of the pancreas by intraorganic activation of its own proteolytic enzymes, such as trypsin, elastase, chymotrypsin and lipase. However, how these proenzymes are activated by chronic alcohol abuse is still unclear. To date, no reliable animal experimental model exists. However, many hypothetical theories have been developed.

Malnutrition of the severe alcoholic, as well as high-fat diet and hypertriglyceridemia, have been suggested, but no well-controlled study could reveal consistent, repeated evidence for any of these conditions (Wilson et al., 1985; Johnson & Hoshing 1991). As only a minority of alcoholics develop clinical pancreatitis, genetic markers, for example different ethanol-utilizing enzymes, such as the ADH2*2 or ADH3*1 allele or genes coding for CYP2E1, have been suggested. However, the evidence has not been convinced in large cohorts (Matsumoto et al., 1996; Chao et al., 1995).

Direct toxic effects of alcohol or its first metabolite, acetaldehyde, on the pancreas in general, or on membranes of the acinar cell leading to disruption of cells, have been postulated (Nordback et al., 1991). Especially the role of acetaldehyde, mediated via free radicals, may be of importance, as free radical scavengers have been show to prevent some organ damage caused by acetaldehyde in the animal model (Schönberg, Buchler & Beger, 1992; Niederau et al., 1992). The general toxic-metabolic hypothesis of alcohol-associated pancreatitis includes various factors, such as an induced enzyme pancreas system due to alcohol, a cleavage of intercellular junctions by alcohol, disturbances in the microcirculation and direct cell damage. Sarles and colleagues postulated another hypothesis of how alcohol triggers the autodigestion of the pancreas (Sarles, 1974). In this hypothesis, ethanol is supposed to lead to precipitation of small proteins, which themselves act as small crystals that occlude small ducts, leading to an elevated intraductal pressure. Together with complexed calcium, the precipitated proteins should occur due to ethanol-induced changes in the hemostasis of solubility, with lithostatin in decreased levels as the key substance.

Another hypothesis includes an altered pancreatic juice flow and/or duodenal juice reflux via the sphincter of Oddi, both conditions which have been shown to occur after alcohol intake (Goff, 1993; Luther et al., 1995). Moreover, alcohol leads to an increased permeability of the pancreatic ducts for molecules up to a molecular size of 20 kDa, which may lead to efflux of pancreatic enzymes into the interstitial tissue space (Reber, Roberts & Way, 1979). However, this theory has not been convincingly supported by experimental studies. In general, as can be seen from the numerous hypotheses, no clear, unique pathogenic mechanism of chronic alcoholic pancreatitis exists.

LIVER

Unquestionably, chronic alcohol consumption is associated with an increased risk for the development of alcoholic liver disease, and alcohol is the major cause of liver disease in Western industrialized countries. Although no threshold level with respect to risk assessment for alcoholic liver cirrhosis exists, most epidemiological data show an increased risk of developing alcoholic cirrhosis with intake of 60 g/day in men and 20 g/day in women, consumed regularly over time (Lelbach, 1985). Strong correlation exists between the risk of cirrhosis, the product of daily consumed alcohol in grams and the time of alcohol consumption. However, only approximately 20% of alcoholics develop liver cirrhosis. The reason for this is unknown. Other factors may additionally contribute to the risk. It is well-known that woman are at higher risk of developing alcoholic liver disease at a lower alcohol intake and over a shorter time interval. Some studies show that, even when they stop drinking, 50% or more of the women develop advanced liver disease (Gavaler & Arria, 1995). Other studies point to the existence of genetic factors which predispose to alcoholic liver disease. Thus, with respect to alcoholic cirrhosis, the concordance of homozygous twins was almost 15% compared to 5% for heterozygous (Lumeng & Crabb, 1994). Polymorphism of ethanol-metabolizing enzymes and/or mutations may also contribute to the risk of alcoholic liver disease. Some studies also show that increased incidence of some HLA-antigens, such as B8, Bw40, B13, A2, DR3 and DR2, are associated with an increased risk of developing alcoholic liver disease (Lumeng & Crabb, 1994). It is interesting to note that the drinking pattern is also of importance, since periodic drinking of larger quantities of alcohol carries a lower risk compared to continuous drinking for a longer period of time. It has been shown recently that alcohol consumption in patients with hepatitis C virus infection is especially deleterious (Schiff, 1997). Finally, comedication with certain drugs, as well as vitamin A, may increase this risk (Table 8.1).

Table 8.1 Interaction between ethanol and xenobiotics at the CYP2E1 site

Drugs	Chemicals	Carcinogens	Others
5-Fluorouracil	Acetone	2-Acetylaminofluorene	Vitamin A
Acetaminophen	Aniline	2-Aminofluorene	
Barbiturates	Benzene	4-Aminobiphenyl	
Cyclophosphamide	Bromobenzene	Aflatoxin	
Enfluorane	Butanol	Amino acid Pyrrolysates	
Halothane	CCl4	Benzo(a)pyrene	
Isoniazid	Pentanol	Dimethylhydrazine	
Meprobamate	Solvents	Nitrosamines	
Methadone	Vinyl chloride		
Phenylbutazone			
Phenytoin			
Propranolol			
Rifampicin			
Tolbutamide			
Tranquilizers			
Warfarin			

Pathogenesis of Alcoholic Liver Disease

Ethanol Metabolism in the Liver

Ethanol metabolism predominantly takes place in the liver. Less than 5% of the consumed ethanol is excreted and changes through lung and kidney. Less than 8% is metabolized by gastric ADH and the rest is oxidized in the liver (Oneta et al., 1998; Lieber, 1994). Three metabolic pathways oxidize alcohol (Figure 8.1). Alcohol dehydrogenase (ADH) is localized in the cytoplasm of the hepatocyte. Four classes of ADH exist, with various kinetic properties (Table 8.2). ADH 2 and ADH 3 exhibit genetic polymorphism, and it is known that ADH 2-2 and ADH 3-1 are involved in prevalence in alcoholism and alcohol-associated organ damage (Lumeng & Crabbe, 1994). Both enzymes produce more acetaldehyde than their correspondent isoenzymes. Acetaldehyde is a very toxic compound and is involved in unpleasant general symptoms after drinking, in alcoholic liver disease and in alcohol-associated carcinogenesis. Cytochrome P4502E1 (CYP2E1)-dependent ethanol metabolism takes place in the microsomes of the hepatocyte. This pathway is inducible. Chronic alcohol consumption leads to proliferation of the smooth endoplasmatic reticulum, which is the morphologic equivalent of microsomes. The affinity of alcohol to CYP2E1 is much lower than to ADH (K_m for CYP2E1 10mM, K_m for ADH approximately 1–2mM). Thus, ethanol metabolism via CYP2E1 occurs at higher ethanol levels. Since CYP2E1 is also involved in the metabolism of various drugs and xenobiotics, including procarcinogens, an interaction between alcohol metabolism and the metabolism of these compounds occurs (Lieber, 1994) (Table 9.1). Through CYP2E1 also, carbon-centered free radicals are produced, contributing to alcoholic liver disease. One of the major compound is the hydroxyethyl radical (Albano & Clot, 1996).

Catalase does not play a major role in ethanol metabolism.

Acetaldehyde, the first metabolite of ethanol metabolism is highly toxic both to protein and DNA, and therefore a potent enzyme system for its degradation exists. The aldehyde dehydrogenases (ALDH) are four isozymes, while ALDH-2, the mitochondrial enzyme, is of major importance. It has a low K_m and metabolizes acetaldehyde rapidly. In orientals, ALDH-2 may be mutated and therefore its activity is decreased. If it is a heterozygous mutation (ALDH 2-2*1), activity is low, as shown in approximately 50% of orientals, and if alcohol is taken a flush reaction occurs. If these subjects drink alcohol, they have an increased risk of developing alcoholic liver disease, and also an increased risk of develop-

1. Ethanol + NAD$^+$ $\longrightarrow$ Acetaldehyde + NADH + H$^+$
$$\text{ADH}$$
$$\text{(cytoplasm)}$$

2. Ethanol + NADPH + H$^+$ + O$_2$ $\longrightarrow$ Acetaldehyde + NADP$^+$ + 2H$_2$O
$$\text{MEOS}$$
$$\text{(endoplasmic reticulum)}$$

3. Ethanol + H$_2$O$_2$ $\longrightarrow$ Acetaldehyde + 2H$_2$O
$$\text{catalase}$$
$$\text{(perixisomes)}$$

Figure 8.1   The three metabolic pathways of ethanol oxidation

Table 8.2 Alcohol dehydrogenases and their kinetic properties

Class	Allele	Enzyme	Gastrointestinal location	K_m (mM)
I	ADH1	$\alpha\alpha$	Most tissues,	4.2
	ADH2*1	$\beta1\beta1$	predominantly in	0.05
	ADH2*2	$\beta2\beta2$	the liver, gastrointestinal tract,	1
	ADH2*3	$\beta3\beta3$	blood vessels,	36
	ADH3*1	$\gamma1\gamma1$	pancreas, lung, skin,	1
	ADH3*2	$\gamma2\gamma2$	muscle, endocrine cells	<1
II	ADH4	$\pi\pi$	Liver	34
III	ADH5	$\chi\chi$	All tissues	n.s.
IV	ADH7	$\sigma\sigma$	Gastrointestinal mucosa	37
V	ADH6	?	Stomach	?

Values for K_m are from Lumeng & Crabb (1994).
n.s. = not saturable.

ing cancer of the upper gastrointestinal tract (Yokoyama et al., 1996; Enomoto et al., 1991). If the mutation occurs at both alleles (homozygous), no alcohol can be consumed because the flush reaction is so severe, and that individual does not drink, as shown in approximately 10% of orientals.

Effect of Alcohol on the Hepatic Intermediar Metabolism due to its Oxidation by Alcohol Dehydrogenase

The ADH reaction not only produces acetaldehyde but also produces equivalents in the form of NADH. NADH is usually oxidized in the respiratory chain to produce ATP. However, if NADH production is overwhelming, NADH-inhibits various NADH-producing reactions, including the citric acid cycle, fatty acid oxidation and gluconeogenesis (Lieber, 1994). One gramme of alcohol contains 7.1 Kcal (29.7 kJ), and if alcohol is given additionally to the daily diet, weight increase occurs. If alcohol is taken chronically in higher amounts, the microsome oxidizing system is induced, which utilizes NADPH. Calories are lost and malnutrition and weight reduction takes place (Seitz & Suter, 1994). The pathogenesis of fatty liver includes inhibition of fatty acid oxidation and an increased synthesis of triglycerides. It also includes an increased uptake of chylomicrones from the gut and an increased uptake of fatty acids from adiposed tissues. Finally, the secretion of lipoproteins from the liver is inhibited. As a result, fatty liver can be seen (Seitz & Suter, 1994).

In the presence of NADH, pyruvate is converted to lactate and lactate leads to hyperlactacidemia and to acidosis. It also decreases the pH in the kidney tubuli. Thus, uric acid is reabsorped from the tubulus and hyperuricemia occurs, leading in some predisposed individuals to acute gouty attacks. On the other hand, gluconeogenesis is blocked due to a lack in pyruvate, so that in some alcoholics with low glycogen liver storage and low glucose intake hypoglycemia may be present, which is of clinical importance (Seitz & Suter, 1994; Lieber, 1994). On the other hand, with adequate calorie intake, hyperglycemia may occur, since alcohol liberates catecholamines and stimulates glycolysis.

Porphyrin metabolism is also affected by the increased NADH : NAD ratio. Thus, ethanol can result in hepatic porphyria by inhibition of uroporphyrin-decarboxylase and an induction of δ-aminolaevulanic-acid-synthethase. Thus, ethanol enhances the genetic determined defect of uroporphyrin-decarboxylase in porphyria cutanea tarda (Doss, 1985). Finally, alcohol also interferes with hormone metabolism, leading primarily to changes in the estrogen/testosterone ratio, resulting in impotence, feminization and gynaecomastia.

Changes in Hepatic Intermediar Metabolism due to Cytochrome P4502E1 Interaction

Since CYP2E1 is involved not only in the metabolism of ethanol but also of other compounds, an interaction may occur. Chronic alcohol consumption leads to an enhanced ethanol metabolism through CYP2E1 induction, which explains the increased metabolic rate in alcoholics. Table 9.1 gives the most important drugs and xenobiotics that interfere with ethanol metabolism at the CYP2E1 site. In the presence of ethanol, these drugs are mostly not metabolized adequately and, as a result, increased levels in the serum may occur and enhance their effects. In the absence of ethanol, in an induced organism, most of the compounds are metabolized more rapidly, leading to decreased serum levels, which may be important with respect to therapeutic dosage (Lieber, 1994). Under these circumstances, the dosage of the drug has to be increased. For example, patients who chronically consume ethanol in the evening, leading to an induction of CYP2E1, may need an increased dose of medication in the morning, when alcohol is absent.

Finally, some drugs are toxified through CYP2E1 (Table 9.2). The toxic intermediates are increased due to the induction and may lead to severe liver damage (Lieber, 1994). An increased activation of toxins at the working place may explain combination injuries of the liver by these compounds and alcohol. Finally, an enhanced activation may also lead to enhancement of alcohol-associated carcinogenesis (Seitz, Pöschl & Simanowski, 1998; Seitz & Osswald, 1992).

Acetaldehyde and Its Hepatic Toxicity

Acetaldehyde binds rapidly to protein, including glutathion, resulting in decreased glutathion levels. It also binds to various enzymes, including those of the nuclear repair system of DNA alkylation. Finally, it may bind to membranes, resulting in damage of the mitochondrial membranes and also injury of the mitchondrial tubular system (Lieber, 1994). As a result, mitochondrial function decreases, including the action of ALDH activity, which is present in mitochondria. Microtubules are responsible for the secretion of macromolecules, such as albumin, transferrin and lipoproteins. These substances may be retained in the cell and then the cell not only accumulates fat but also protein and water, which leads to the typical ballooning of the hepatocyte. Acetaldehyde also leads to transformation of the stellate cells to myofibroblasts and its production of collagen, thus initiating fibrogenesis (Lieber, 1994).

Nutritional Aspects of Alcoholic Liver Disease

Chronic alcohol consumption leads to severe alterations of vitamins and trace elements status (Seitz & Suter, 1994). The effect of alcohol on vitamin A metabolism leads to a reduction of vitamin A in the liver and to the occurence of toxic metabolites, possibly involved in fibrogenesis. These metabolites are produced via CYP2E1. In addition, since retinol and alcohol both need alcohol dehydrogenase for metabolism, the levels of retinoic acid in the liver and possibly in other tissues are relatively low leading to severe alterations in cell differentiation and proliferation (Wang et al., 1998).

Folate is involved in methyl transfer. The lack of folate, together with pyridoxalphosphate, leads to reduction of methionine. In addition, the enzyme which activates methionine to S-adenosylmethionine is also decreased, resulting in a decreased S-adenosylmethionine level. This leads to a decrease in methylation of phospholipids, resulting in membrane alterations and also to a decrease in the methylation of cytosine bases in the DNA and to a reduced thymidine production. Both factors may be involved in alcohol-associated carcinogenesis. Malnutrition associated with alcoholism may decrease the immune response, thus leading to a decreased function of the immune systeme (Seitz & Suter, 1994).

Clinical Aspects of Alcoholic Liver Disease

Chronic alcohol consumption leads to (a) fatty liver, (b) alcoholic hepatitis, (c) alcoholic liver cirrhosis and (d) hepatocellular cancer.

The pathogenesis of fatty liver has already been discussed. Alcoholic fatty liver can be associated with Zieve syndrome, which is characterized by an additional hyperlipoproteinemia (type V) and hemolytic anemia with jaundice. The mechanism of the hemolysis is not clear, but is possibly due to lipid changes in the erythrocyte membrane.

Alcoholic hepatitis is diagnosed histologically by a typical morphological feature, including the appearance of polymorphic leukocytes, necrosis and fibrosis. In addition, cholestasis may occur and may determine the prognosis. The occurence of Mallory bodies, assembling condensed cytoskeletal proteins such as keratin and actin, is typical. It is believed that endotoxins from the intestine liberate cytokines in the liver, such as tumor necrosis factor and interleukins, accompanied by an increase of transforming growth factor $\beta 1$, which initiates fibrogenesis (French et al., 1993; Lieber, 1997).

Clinicially, a broad spectrum from asymptomatic forms up to fulminant hepatitis can be observed. The most frequent symptoms include weight loss, abdominal pain, nausea and vomiting, icterus, fever and leukocytosis. The complications of alcoholic hepatitis are the occurrence of ascites, hepatic encephalopathy and splenomegaly. Approximately 20% of patients with alcoholic hepatitis show additional cirrhosis. Special forms of alcoholic hepatitis include asymptomatic, anicteric alcoholic hepatitis, chronic alcoholic hepatitis, mostly with fibrosis leading to cirrhosis, and fulminant alcoholic hepatitis with a high mortality. AST is always higher than ALT, mostly not over 300 U/l. γ-Glutarytransferase and alkaline phosphatase activity are high. Orrego and co-workers have developed a combined clinical and laboratory index which correlates well with 1 year mortality (Orrego et al., 1983). General mortality in patients with alcoholic hepatitis is 15–20%. Bad prognosis is associated with the occurence of encephalopathy, poor blood coagulation, hypoalbumanemia and hepato-renal syndrome. As therapy, glucosteroids have been used, especially in patients with icterus and hepatic encephalopathy. However, only a subgroup of patients respond, namely those who have leukocytosis and an increased invasion of polynuclear leukocytes in liver biopsy (Mathurin et al., 1995). Alcohol abstinence is mandatory. However, despite alcohol abstinence, especially in women, alcoholic hepatitis advances in many cases into cirrhosis.

Alcoholic cirrhosis may develop from alcoholic hepatitis. However, fatty liver may proceed directly to alcoholic cirrhosis by an increased fibrogenesis due to an increased conversion of stellate cells into myofibroblasts capable producing various collagens. Fibrosis starts around the central vein as perivenulous sclerosis. In this location the NADH:NAD ratio is especially high, due to an increased activity of ADH, and also the production of acetaldehyde is additionally increased due to the increased action of CYP2E1. An increased NADH:NAD ratio leads to increased lactate, and lactate as well as acetaldehyde converts stellate cells to collagen-producing cells. Thus, the occurrence of perivenulous sclerosis is an early histological prognostic sign and, if alcohol is further consumed, this lesion extends to perisinusoidal fibrosis and periportal fibrosis until complete cirrhosis is reached (Lieber,

1994; French et al., 1993). Prognosis of hepatic cirrhosis due to alcohol depends on whether or not the patient continues to drink. The 5-year survival rate in continuous drinkers is half of that of abstainers. Thus, in child C cirrhosis, the 5 year survival rate is less than 30% if alcohol consumption is continued (Schenker, 1984). Complications of alcoholic cirrhosis are hepatic encephalopathy, ascites, hepato-renal syndrome, portal hypertension with esophageal variceal bleeding, and hepatocellular cancer.

Hepatocellular cancer is frequently observed in alcoholic cirrhosis and is due to cirrhosis itself, to various direct co-carcinogenic actions of alcohol as well as to concomittant infection of hepatitis C, which is more frequent in alcoholics than in non-alcoholics. The mechanisms of alcohol-associated carcinogenesis are summarized elsewhere (Seitz, Pöschl; & Simanowski, 1998).

KEY WORKS AND SUGGESTIONS FOR FURTHER READING

Agarwal, D.P., & Seitz, H.K. (Eds) (in press).   *Alcohol in Health and Diseases*. New York: Marcel Dekker.

This is the most up-to-date book on various aspects of alcohol toxicity. It contains some chapters on cancer and alcoholic liver disease written by the most distinguished scientists in the field.

Preedy, V.R. & Watson, R.R. (Eds) (1996).   *Alcohol and the Gastrointestinal Tract*. Boca Raton, FL: CRC Press.

This book entirely deals with the effect of alcohol on the gastrointestinal tract, gastrointestinal morphology and function and also on mechanisms by which alcohol is toxic.

Galanter, M. (Ed.) (1998).   *Recent Developments in Alcoholism, Vol. 14, The Consequences of Alcoholism*.

This book contains important chapters with respect to the effect of alcohol on liver, stomach and pancreas. It also contains the most up-to-date knowledge on alcohol and cancer.

Hall, P. (Ed.) (1995).   *Alcoholic liver disease: pathology and pathogenesis*, 2nd edn. London: Edward Arnold.

This book entirely discusses alcoholic liver disease from a scientific and clinical point of view. It contains chapters on alcohol metabolism, pathogenesis and differential diagnosis. It also deals with alcohol and porphyria and discusses clinical implications.

REFERENCES

Agarwal, N. & Pitchumoni, C.S. (1991).   Assessment of severity in acute pancreatitis. *American Journal of Gastroenterology*, **78**, 637.

Albano, E. & Clot, P. (1996).   Free radicals and ethanol toxicity. In V.R. Preedy & R.R. Watson (Eds), *Alcohol and the Gastrointestinal Tract* (pp. 57–68). CRC Press: Boca Raton, FL.

Barboriak, J.J. & Meade, R.C. (1970).   Effect of alcohol on gastric emptying in men. *American Journal of Clinical Nutrition*, **23**, 1151.

Bjarnason, I., Ward, K. & Peters, T.J. (1984).   The leaky gut of alcoholism: possible route of entry for toxic compounds. *Lancet*, **1**, 979.

Bode, C., Ito, T., Rollenhagen, A. et al. (1988). Effect of acute and chronic alcohol feeding on prostaglandin E2 biosynthesis in rat stomach. *Dig Dis Sci*, **33**, 814.

Bode, J.C. & Bode, C. (1992). Alcohol malnutrition and the gastrointestinal tract. In R.R. Watson & B. Watzl (Eds), *Nutrition and Alcohol* (p. 403). CRC Press: Boca Raton, FL.

Bode, J.C. (1980). Alcohol and the gastrointestinal tract. *Adv Intern Med Ped*, **45**, 1.

Bofetta, P., Mashberg, A., Winkelmann, R. et al. (1992). Carcinogenic effect of tobacco smoking and alcohol drinking on anatomic sites of the oral cavity and oropharynx. *International Journal of Cancer*, **52**, 530.

Brugere, J., Guenel, P., Leclerc, A. et al. (1986). Differential effects of tobacco and alcohol in cancer of the larynx, pharynx and mouth. *Cancer*, **57**, 391.

Chao, Y.C., Young, T.H., Chang, W.K. et al. (1995). An investigation of whether polymorphisms of cytochrome P4502E1 are genetic markers of susceptibility to alcoholic end-stage organ damage in a Chinese population. *Hepatology*, **22**, 1409.

Doss, M.O. (1985). Alcohol and porphyrin metabolism. In H.K. Seitz & B. Kommerell (Eds), *Alcohol-related Diseases in Gastroenterology* (pp. 232–252). Springer Verlag: Berlin.

Enomoto, N., Takase, S., Takada, N. & Takase, A. (1991). Alcoholic liver disease in heterozygotes of mutant and normal aldehyde dehydrogenase-2 genes. *Hepatology*, **13**, 1071.

Franceschi, S., Talamini, R., Barra, S., Baron, A.E. et al. (1990). Smoking and drinking in relation to cancers of the oral cavity, pharynx, larynx and esophagus in Northern Italy. *Cancer Research*, **50**, 6502.

French, S.W., Nash, J., Shitabata, P. et al. (1993). Pathology of alcoholic liver disease. *Seminars in Liver Disease*, **13**, 154.

Gavaler, J.S. & Arria, A.M. (1995). Increased susceptibility of alcoholic liver disease: artificial or real? In P. Hall (Ed.), *Alcoholic Liver Disease Pathology and Pathogenesis* (pp. 123–133). Edward Arnold. London.

Goff, J.S. (1993). The effect of ethanol on the pancreatic duct sphincter of Oddi. *American Journal of Gastroenterology*, **88**, 656.

Gottfried, E., Korsten, M.A. & Lieber, C.S. (1978). Alcohol-induced gastric and duodenal lesions in man. *American Journal of Gastroenterology*, **70**, 587.

Gullo, L. (1991). Chronic panreatitis in Italy. In H. Sarles, C.D. Johnson & J.F. Sauniere (Eds), *Pancreatitis: New Data and Geographical Distribution* (p. 157). Arnette: Paris.

Gullo, L., Barbara, L. & Labo, G. (1988). Effect of cessation of alcohol on the course of pancreatic dysfunction in alcoholic pancreatitis. *Gastroenterology*, **95**, 1063.

Harty, L.C., Caporaso, N.E., Hayes, R.B. et al. (1997). Alcohol dehydrogenase 3 genotype and risk of oral cavity and pharyngeal cancers. *Journal of the National Cancer Institute*, **89**, 1968.

Homann, N., Bosch, F.X. & Simanowski, U.A. (1996). Chronic alcohol consumtion has striking effects on cell proliferation and differentiation in the human rectum. *Gastroenterology*, **110**, A530 (abstract).

Homann, N., Jousimies-Somer, H., Jokelainen, K. et al. (1997a). High acetaldehyde levels in saliva after ethanol consumption: methodological aspects and pathogenetic implications. *Carcinogenesis*, **18**, 1739.

Homann, N., Kärkäinnen, P., Kovisto, T. et al. (1997b). Effects of acetaldehyde on cell regeneration and differentiation of the upper gastrointestinal tract mucosa. *Journal of the National Cancer Institute*, **89**, 1692.

Homann, N., Tillonen, J., Meurman, J. et al. (1998). Acetaldehyde in saliva: formation and pathogenic aspects. *Alcoholism: Clinical and Experimental Research*, **22** (Suppl.), A147.

Johnson, C.D. & Hoshing, S. (1991). National statistics for diet, alcohol consumption and chronic pancreatitis in England and Wales. *Gut*, **32**, 1401.

Keshavarzian, A. & Fields, J.Z. (1996). Gastrointestinal motility disorders induced by ethanol. In V.R. Preedy & R.R. Watson (Eds), *Alcohol and the Gastrointestinal Tract* (pp. 235–254). Boca Raton, FL: CRC Press.

Keshavarzian, A., Iber, F.L., Danleis, M.D. et al. (1986). Intestinal transit and lactose intolerance in chronic alcoholics. *American Journal of Clinical Nutrition*, **44**, 70.

Korsten, M.A. & Wilson, J.S. (1993). Alcohol and the pancreas: clinical aspects and mechanism of injury. *Alcohol Health Research World*, **17**, 292.

Korsten, M.A., Pirola, R.C. & Lieber, C.S. (1992). In C.S. Lieber (Ed.), *Medical and Nutritional Complications of Alcoholis* (p. 341). Plenum Medical: New York.

Laine, L. & Weinstein, W.M. (1988). Histology of alcoholic hemorrhagic "gastritis": a prospective evaluation. *Gastroenterology*, **98**, 909.

Laine, L., Marin-Sorensen, M. & Weinstein, W. (1989). *Campylobacter pylorii* in alcoholic hemorrhagic "gastritis". *Dig Dis Sci*, **34**, 677.

Lamu, L. (1910). Etudee de statistique clinique de 131 cas de cancer de l'oesophage et du cardia. *Arch Mal Appar Dig Mal Nutr*, **4**, 451.

Lelbach, W.K. (1985). Epidemiology of alcohol use and its gastrointestinal complications. In H.K. Seitz & B. Kommerell (Eds), *Alcohol-related Diseases in Gastroenterology* (pp. 1–18). Springer Verlag: Berlin.

Lieber, C.S. (1994). Alcohol and the liver: 1994 update. *Gastroenterology*, **106**, 1085.

Lieber, C.S. (1997). Alcoholic liver disease. In G. Friedman, E.D. Jacobson & R.W. McCallum (Eds), *Gastrointestinal Pharmacology and Therapeutics* (pp. 465–487). Lippincott Raven: Philadelphia, PA.

Lumeng, L. & Crabb, D.W. (1994). Genetic aspects and risk factors in alcoholism and alcoholic liver disease. *Gastroenterology*, **107**, 572.

Luther, R., Niederau, C., Niederau, M. et al. (1995). Influence of ductal pressure and infusates on activity and subcellular distribution of lysosomal enzymes in the rat pancreas. *Gastroenterology*, **109**, 573.

Maier, H., Born, I.A., Veith, S. et al. (1986). The effect of chronic alcohol consumption on salivary gland morphology and function in the rat. *Alcoholism: Clinical and Experimental Research*, **10**, 425.

Maier, H., Weidauer, H., Zöller, J. et al. (1994). Effect of chronic alcohol consumption on the morphology of the oral mucosa. *Alcoholism: Clinical and Experimental Research*, **18**, 387.

Maier, H., Zöller, J., Herrmann, A. et al. (1993). Dental status and oral hygiene in patients with head and neck cancer. *Otolaryngol. Head Neck Surg*, **108**, 655.

Mathurin, P., Rueff, S., Ramond, M.J. et al. (1995). Corticosteroid therapy in patients with severe alcoholic hepatitis. In V. Arroyo, J. Bosch & J. Rodes (Eds), *Treatments in Hepatology* (pp. 277–280). Masson: Barcelona.

Matsumoto, M., Takahashi, H., Maruyama, K. et al. (1996). Genotypes of alcohol-metabolizing enzymes and the risk for alcoholic chronic pancreatitis in Japanese alcoholics. *Alcoholism: Clinical and Experimental Research*, **20**, 289A.

Mezey, E. (1985). Effect of ethanol on intestinal morphology, metabolism and function. In H.K. Seitz & B. Kommerell (Eds), *Alcohol-related Diseases in Gastroenterology* (pp. 342–60). Springer Verlag: Berlin.

Niederau, C., Niederau, M., Borchard, F. et al. (1992). Effects of antioxidants and free radical scavengers in three different models of acute pancreatitis. *Pancreas*, **7**, 486.

Nordback, I.H., MacGowan, S., Potter, J.J. et al. (1991). The role of acetaldehyde in the pathogenesis of acute alcoholic pancreatitis. *Annals of Surgery*, **214**, 671.

Oneta, C.M., Simanowski, U.A., Martinez, M. et al. (1998). First pass metabolism of ethanol is strikingly influenced by the speed of gastric emptying. *Gut*, **43**, 612.

Orrego, H., Israel, Y., Blake, J.E. et al. (1983). Assessment of prognostic factors in alcoholic liver disease: towards a global quantitative expression of severity. *Hepatology*, **3**, 896.

Pedrosa, M.C., Russel, R.M., Saltzmann, J.R. et al. (1996). Gastric emptying and first pass metabolism of ethanol in elderly subjeccts with and without atrophic gastritis. *Scandinavian Journal of Gastroenterology*, **31**, 671.

Pikkarainen, P.H., Baraona, E., Jauhonen, P. et al. (1981). Contribution of oropharynx flora and of lung microsomes to acetaldehyde in expired air after alcohol ingestion. *Journal of Laboratory and Clinical Medicine*, **97**, 631.

Ranson, J.H.C. & Pasternack, B.S. (1977). Statistical methods for quantifying the severity of clinical acute pancreatitis. *Journal of Surgical Research*, **22**, 79.

Reber, H.A., Roberts, C. & Way, L.W. (1979). The panreatic duct mucosal barrier. *American Journal of Surgery*, **137**, 128.

Salmela, K.S., Roine, R.P., Koivisto, T. et al. (1993). Characteristic of *Helicobacter pylori* alcohol dehydrogenase. *Gastroenterology*, **105**, 325.

Sarles, H. (1974). Chronic calcifying pancreatitis–chronic alcoholic pancreatitis. *Gastroenterology*, **66**, 604.

Sarles, H., Sahhel, J., Staub, J.L. et al. (1979). Chronic pancreatitis. In *The Exocrine Pancreas*. Saunders: London, p. 402.

Schenker, S. (1984). Alcoholic liver disease: evaluation of natural history and prognostic factors. *Hepatology*, **4**, 36S.

Schiff, E.R. (1997). Hepatitis C and alcohol. *Hepatology*, **26** (suppl 1), 39S.

Schönberg, M.H., Buchler, M. & Beger, H.C. (1992). The role of oxygen radicals in experimental acute pancreatitis. *Free Radicals in Biology and Medicine*, **12**, 512.

Seitz, H.K. & Oneta, C.M. (1998). Gastrointestinal alcohol dehydrogenase. *Nutrition Review*, **56**, 35.

Seitz, H.K. & Osswald, B. (1992). Effect of ethanol on procarcinofgen activation. In R.R. Watson (Ed.), *Alcohol and Cancer* (pp. 55–72). CRC Press: Boca Raton, FL.

Seitz, H.K. & Pöschl, G. (1997). The role of gastrointestinal factors in alcohol metabolism *Alcohol and Alcoholism*, **32**.

Seitz, H.K. & Simanowski, U.A. (1996). Cell turnover in the gastrointestinal tract and the effect of ethanol. In V.R. Preedy & R.R. Watson (Eds), *Alcohol and the Gastrointestinal Tract* (pp. 273–287). CRC Press: Boca Raton, FL.

Seitz, H.K. & Suter, P.M. (1994). Ethanol toxicity and nutritional satus. In F.N. Kotsonis, M. Mackey & J. Hjelle (Eds), *Ethanol Toxicity and Nutritional Status*. New York: Raven, pp. 95–116.

Seitz, H.K., Egerer, G., Osswald, B.R. & Simanowski, U.A. (1995). Alkohol und Gastrointestinaltrakt. In H.K. Seitz, C.S. Lieber & U.A. Simanowski (Eds), *Handbuch Alkohol, Alkoholismus, Alkoholbedingte Organschäden* (pp. 293–324). J.A. Barth Verlag: Leipzig.

Seitz, H.K., Pöschl, G. & Simanowski, U.A. (1998). Alcohol and cancer. In M. Galanter (Ed.), *Recent Development in Alcoholism. Vol. 14, The Consequences of Alcoholism* (pp. 67–95). New York: Plenum.

Seitz, H.K., Simanowski, U.A., Garzon, F.T. et al. (1990). Possible role of acetaldehyde in ethanol-related rectal cocarcinogenesis in the rat. *Gastroenterology*, **98**, 406.

Simanowski, U.A., Egerer, G., Oneta, C. et al. (1997). *Helicobacter pylori* infection decreases gastric alcohol dehydrogenase activity and first-pass metabolism of ethanol in men. *Digestion*, **59**, 314.

Simanowski, U.A., Suter, P., Russell, R.M. et al. (1994). Enhancement of ethanol-induced rectal mucosal hyper-regeneration with age in F344 rats. *Gut*, **35**, 1102.

Simanowski, U.A., Suter, P., Stickel, F. et al. (1993). Esophageal epithelial hyperregeneration following chronic ethanol consumption: effect of age and salivary gland function. *Journal of the National Cancer Institute*, **85**, 2030.

Tuyns, A. & Masse, L.M.F. (1973). Mortality from cancer of the esophagus in Brittany. *International Journal of Epidemiology*, **2**, 241.

Walker, E.A., Castegnaro, M., Garren, L. et al. (1979). Intake of volatile nitrosamines from consumption of alcohols. *Journal of the National Cancer Institute*, **69**, 947.

Wang, X.D., Liu, C., Chung, J. et al. (1998). Chroni alcohol intake reduces retinoic acid concentration and enhances AP-1 (c-jun and c-fos) expression in rat liver. *Hepatology*, **28**, 744.

Wienbeck, M. & Berges, W. (1985). Esophageal and gastric lesions in the alcoholic. In H.K. Seitz & B. Kommerell (Eds), *Alcohol-related Diseases in Gastroenterology* (pp. 361–375). Springer Verlag: Berlin.

Wilson, J.S., Bernstein, L., McDonald, C. et al. (1985). Diet and drinking habits in relation to the development of alcoholic pancreatitis. *Gut*, **26**, 882.

Yokoyama, A., Muramutsu, T., Ohmori, T. et al. (1996). Multiple primary esophageal and concurrent upper aerodigestive tract cancer and the aldehyde dehydrogenase type-2 geotype of Japanese alcoholics. *Cancer*, **77**, 1986.

Chapter 9

Alcoholic Muscle, Skin and Bone Disease

Victor R. Preedy
*Department of Nutrition & Dietetics, King's College
London, London, UK*
David Mantle
*Regional Neurosciences Centre, Newcastle General Hospital,
Newcastle upon Tyne, UK*
and
Timothy J. Peters
*Department of Clinical Biochemistry, King's College Hospital,
London, UK*

Synopsis

Skeletal muscle myopathy affects up to 60% of alcohol misusers. This is characterized by atrophy of white fibres (low in mitochondria); the red fibres (with abundant mitochondria) are relatively resilient. The myopathy is accompanied by muscle weakness which occurs in about 50% of alcohol misusers. Although not life-threatening per se, pathological lesions in muscle, skin and bone will contribute to impairment of life qualities and increase morbidity. Skin abnormalities in alcohol misusers are diverse and include acne, ecchymoses, eczema, facial erythema, alcohol flushing, folliculitis, seborrhoeic dermatitis, rosacea and tinea pedis. Up to 80% of chronic alcoholics may be affected with one or more of these dermatological features. Discoid eczema is particularly associated with male alcohol misusers and is very rare in non-alcohol misusers. Bone pathologies may be present in to 50% of alcohol misusers and include osteoporosis, osteopenia and increased fracture rates due to accidents. Post-trauma healing of fractures is also impaired.

The metabolic derangements of muscle, skin and bone can occur in the absence of liver impairment, neuropathy or malnutrition. This suggests that alcohol, and/or one of its ensuing metabolites, may directly cause damage to these three tissues. This supposition has been supported by well-controlled animal studies. However, diseases of the liver, kidney and CNS and malnutrition may directly induce pathological changes in muscle, skin and bone and exacerbate the lesions that arise as a consequence of the direct effects of alcohol. Because of the

International Handbook of Alcohol Dependence and Problems. Edited by N. Heather, T.J. Peters and
T. Stockwell.

large mass of muscle, skin and bone, important changes in whole-body metabolism occur in alcoholics. However, abstinence may reverse some, but not all, of the pathological features in these tissues, whereas continued drinking either impairs patient recovery or treatment or worsens the disease.

In this review we cover three major pathologies occurring in alcohol misusers, namely lesions of skeletal muscle, skin and bone. More specific descriptions of these pathologies have been reviewed separately elsewhere, that is, skeletal muscle (Preedy et al., 1994b; Preedy et al., 1997b; Preedy et al., 1998a; Reilly et al., 1995); skin (Higgin & DuVivier, 1994a; Higgins et al., 1992) and bone (Klein, 1997; Laitinen & Valimaki, 1991; Moniz, 1994; Rico, 1990; Sampson, 1997).

EFFECT OF ALCOHOL ON SKELETAL MUSCLE

The most prevalent skeletal muscle disorder in the Western Hemisphere is probably alcohol-induced muscle disease. Paradoxically, it is one of the least studied. Difficulties in gait and mobility, impaired muscle strength, cramps and myalgia and frequent falls are distinguishing features.

Alcoholic myopathy occurs in between one- and two-thirds of all chronic alcohol misusers (Martin et al., 1985; Urbano Marquez et al., 1989). This may represent a process that affects all muscle types. Such a hypothesis was originally raised over 25 years ago in relation to acute damage by alcohol, especially in the heart and skeletal muscle (Seneviratne, 1975) and further expounded by us in relation to smooth, cardiac and skeletal muscle in laboratory animal studies (Peters and Preedy, 1991). More recent clinical studies have further strengthened this argument and have shown a relationship between alcoholic cardiomyopathy and alcohol-induced skeletal muscle disease (Fernandez Sola et al., 1994, 1997).

The diameters of fast-twitch white fibres are markedly reduced in alcoholic myopathy. The slow-twitch red fibres are generally resilient (Hanid et al., 1981; Martin et al., 1985; Trounce et al., 1987). There is no overt membrane damage, and serum creatine kinase activities are not elevated. Although there may be enhancement of lipid deposition within the muscle, there is no overt fibrosis or inflammation (Sunnasy et al., 1983; Del Villar Negro et al., 1984; Martin et al., 1985). Mitochondrial changes may occur in muscle of patients with neuropathy, but not in muscle of alcoholic patients with normal neurological indices or healthy controls (Haida et al., 1998).

Acute myopathy occurs very infrequently, i.e. in less that 5% of alcohol misusers (Douglas et al., 1966; Schneider, 1970; Ford et al., 1984; Grau et al., 1988). However, the clinical consequences of rhabdomyolysis with acute renal failure can be fatal. Unfortunately, many of the older textbooks dealing with alcoholic myopathy concentrate on the acute form of the disease, despite its rarity.

Muscle strength is decreased in chronic alcoholics with histologically proven myopathy (Martin et al., 1985; Hickish et al., 1989; Urbano Marquez et al., 1989; Pendergast et al., 1990; Sacanella et al., 1995). This forms the basis of diagnostic tests in some studies, the advantage being the non-invasive aspect and the relatively low cost of the apparatus. This is offset by the disadvantage of establishing a suitable set of control variables for each apparatus. Patients with cirrhosis have reduced muscle strength compared to healthy controls and correlate with whole body muscle mass as defined by urinary creatinine excretion (Andersen et al., 1998). However, it is important to emphasise that the myopathy can arise independently from liver disease.

Histological assessments have the disadvantage of requiring an invasive procedure, with

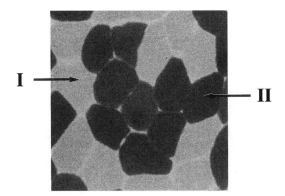

Figure 9.1   Red (I) and white (II) fibres in normal human muscle. Micrographs show a normal specimen with myosin-ATPase staining to attenuate the white fibres (also referred to as white muscle fibres)

the use of local anaesthetics. However, the histological analysis can also be used to determine whether there are any underlying skeletal muscle abnormalities and to identify whether there are other conditions such as neuropathies (Ballantyne & Hansen, 1982; Wassif et al., 1994). Attenuating the visualization of white fibres with myosin-ATPase stains facilitates the direct estimation of fibre diameters (Figure 9.1). The main feature of alcoholic myopathy is a reduction in the diameters of white fibres without overt additional pathologies (Figure 9.2). The diameters of red and white fibres can be measured with a Magiscan or other computerized imaging system, which should also be programmed to calculate the atrophy factor (Slavin et al., 1983; Martin et al., 1985). Alternatively, confirmation of myopathy may be conducted directly on photomicrographs of suitably stained preparations using appropriate standards of magnification. The atrophy factor is a measure of the relative proportion of skeletal muscle fibres with reduced diameters (Brooke & Engel, 1969).

Raised serum creatine kinase (CK) activities indicate muscle membrane damage and occur frequently in acute myopathy, whereas, in contrast, raised CK activities are not observed in chronic alcoholic myopathy. There are ethnic differences in base-line CK values (Sherwood et al., 1996). Concomitant analysis of serum aminotransaminase activities may be helpful in establishing the presence of secondary organ dysfunction (e.g. liver disease). Low levels of serum myoglobin are also found in chronic alcoholics but its relationship to alcoholic myopathy is unknown (Lundin et al., 1986).

Although chronic alcoholic myopathy has been diagnosed in terms of the proximal muscles, other muscle groups are affected (Perkoff, 1971). Urinary creatinine excretion (i.e. creatinine/height index) is reduced in myopathic subjects (Duane & Peters, 1988a). However, in practical terms, it is very often difficult to obtain an accurate collection of the urine in unreliable alcoholic patients.

There is a considerable body of evidence suggesting that in the pathogenesis of alcohol-induced liver disease, free radicals may be responsible (Cederbaum, 1991; Nordmann et al., 1992). Similar mechanisms could be responsible for the pathogenesis of muscle damage (Garcia Bunuel, 1984), although detailed studies are lacking. Nevertheless, studies in this area have been facilitated by an animal model in which anatomically distinct skeletal muscles, containing a predominance of single-fibre types, have been analysed to represent the individual muscle fibre types.

Compared to white fibre predominant muscles (i.e. the EDL, plantaris or white portions of the gastrocnemius) red fibre-rich muscles, such as the soleus or red portions of the gas-

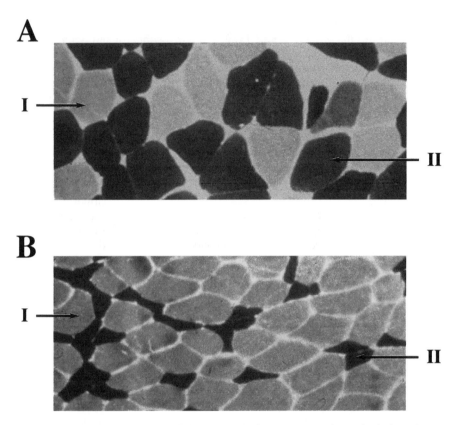

Figure 9.2 White fibre atrophy in alcoholism. Muscle from (A) control, (B) alcoholic subject. I, red fibres; II, white fibres. Note atrophy of white fibres

trocnemius, contain higher activities of cytosolic and mitochondrial superoxide dismutase, catalase, glutathione peroxidase and α-tocopherol (Higuchi et al., 1985; Asayama et al., 1986; Asayama et al., 1987; Riley et al., 1988a; Riley et al., 1988b; Laughlin et al., 1990). However, the imidazole dipeptides (anserine, homocarnosine and carnosine) are important intracellular buffering agents and antioxidants, and their concentrations are higher in white muscles compared to red fibres (Crush, 1970; Lykkeboe & Johansen, 1975; Tamaki et al., 1977; Higuchi et al., 1985; Harris et al., 1990; Mannion et al., 1992; Sewell et al., 1992; Chan & Dekker, 1994). Imidazole dipeptides have additional properties, such as regulation of phosphorylase and fructose 1,6-bisphosphatase activities (Ikeda et al., 1980; Johnson et al., 1982), perhaps suggesting a role in intermediary metabolism. In experimental myopathy, the imidazole dipeptides in both Types I and II fibre-rich muscle are not reduced (Ward et al., 1992b). The involvement of free radicals in the genesis of alcoholic myopathy has recently been reviewed (Preedy et al., 1998a).

Chronic alcoholics have a variety of nutritional disorders arising as a consequence of disadvantaged socio-economic circumstances, calorific displacement or end organ damage (e.g. gastrointestinal changes, inducing malabsorption). However, the frequencies of impaired riboflavin, pyridoxine, thiamine, vitamin B_{12}, folate and vitamin D status in patients with myopathy are not dissimilar to alcoholics, with or without myopathy (Duane

& Peters, 1988a; Hickish et al., 1989; Urbano Marquez et al., 1989). An outstanding issue, however, pertains to the observation that the serum α-tocopherol and selenium are low in myopathic alcoholics (Ward & Peters, 1992a). In contrast, in Spanish alcohol misusers, the serum and muscle levels of retinol, ascorbic acid and α-tocopherol are not significantly different to controls (Fernandez Sola et al., 1998).

Marked liver dysfunction has profound effects on skeletal muscle (Marchesini et al., 1981; Jenkins, 1984; Morrison et al., 1990; Caregaro et al., 1996; Andersen et al., 1998). However, studies have shown that there is no direct clinical relationship between alcoholic myopathy and liver impairment (Martin et al., 1985; Duane et al., 1988b). Animal studies have also supported these conclusions (Preedy et al., 1990a).

Electromyograms in alcoholic patients with white fibre atrophy are normal in general (Trounce et al., 1987). Although neuropathies frequently occur in alcoholism, their incidence (approximately 10–15%) is considerably lower than myopathies (approximately 40–65%) (Estruch et al., 1993). Neuropathies also arise as a consequence of chronic alcohol misuse and may lead to atrophy of white fibres (Chen et al., 1991). A comprehensive study of neuromorphological indices in 19 chronic alcohol misusers showed lack of necrosis, fibre grouping (indicative of re-innervation) or central nucleation in muscle biopsies (Mills et al., 1986). In 12 subjects, however, there was evidence of myopathy as defined by reductions in muscle diameter (Mills et al., 1986). Thus, one can conclude that neuropathies occur in alcoholism but their incidence is infrequent compared to myopathy and the latter can arise independently of neuropathy (Mills et al., 1986).

Chronic alcohol consumption can induce glucocorticoid excess, i.e. pseudo-Cushing's syndrome (Paton, 1976; Jeffcoate, 1993; Groote Veldman & Meinders, 1996), which may potentially be a contributing factor to the myopathy. However, this has been refuted in well-controlled endocrine studies on myopathic alcoholic misusers (Duane & Peters, 1987). Of note is the fact that alcohol-induced pseudo-Cushing's syndrome is rare (Kirkman & Nelson, 1988).

Alcoholic myopathy is characterized by a fall in the rate of muscle protein synthesis, an observation originally derived from laboratory animal studies (reviewed in Preedy & Peters, 1994a; Preedy et al., 1994c, d) and substantiated by clinical studies using stable isotopes (Pacy et al., 1991). Contributory mechanisms include reductions in total RNA (which is largely ribosomal), which has been observed in rats fed alcohol for chronic periods (Marway et al., 1990) as well as in clinical studies (Wassif et al., 1993). The fall in muscle RNA may be due to increases in substrate-specific RNase activities (Reilly et al., 1998).

EFFECTS OF ALCOHOL ON SKIN

Even the simple topical application of ethanol to skin produces deleterious changes, such as alterations in mitochondria, increased lipid accumulation in keratinocytes and loss of cells from the stratum corneum (Brown & Habowsky, 1979). In the past there have been occasional studies, e.g. a case presentation of bullous skin lesions in a patient consuming contaminated (with heavy metals) alcohol-containing beverages (Hughes et al., 1983), although systematic analyses, apart from the studies of Higgins and colleagues (see below; Higgins & DuVivier, 1994a; Higgins et al., 1994b; Hoefkens et al., 1997), are rare.

One of the earliest skin manifestations of alcohol ingestion is facial flushing due to increased blood flow and vasodilation (Mizoi et al., 1979; Iwase et al., 1995). This may in part be due to the inability to metabolise acetaldehyde in susceptible subjects (Yoshida et al., 1989; Sherman et al., 1994; Ward et al., 1994). Up to half of some populations in the Far East are deficient in the low K_m ALDH isoform, so that after acute ethanol ingestion there is raised circulating acetaldehyde with concomitant flushing (Mizoi et al., 1983).

One needs to consider the possibility of skin lesions arising indirectly in alcohol misusers. For example, pellagra-induced skin abnormalities may also arise in susceptible subjects due to niacin (i.e., nicotinamide) deficiency (Ishii et al., 1981; Vannucchi et al., 1991; Dumitrescu Lichiardopol, 1994). Features of pellagra include photosensitization of the skin and ecrolytic migratory erythema (Hendricks, 1991). Skin changes may also arise through deficiency of vitamin A (i.e. dehydrated skin) and pantothenic acid (i.e. dermatitis). Zinc deficiency, which also causes skin lesions, may arise in alcohol misusers because of poor diet or increased urinary zinc excretion or poor intestinal absorption of zinc (Prasad, 1983, 1985a, b). There may be a metabolic interaction between niacin and zinc (Vannucchi et al., 1989). The relevance of zinc deficiencies in alcoholism is underestimated, as it is also induces impaired immunological responses, which in turn may exacerbate skin lesions (Fraker et al., 1987). As a rule of thumb, half of all alcohol misusers will have either a fungal, viral or a bacterial infection of the skin in one or more regions. Vitamin E and A status is low in alcohol misusers with acral or erythrodermic psoriasis (Marrakchi et al., 1994). It is difficult to interpret this as reflecting the disease process *per se* or reflecting a dietary deficiency that precipitates the skin disorder. Clearly, reversing the nutritional deficiencies in alcohol misusers with skin disorders should be a primary strategy for the investigating clinician, together with attending to the skin lesions.

In a study of over 100 alcoholics, dermatological abnormalities were observed in over 80% of subjects (Parish & Fine, 1985). Lesions include acne, ecchymoses, rosacea, persistent facial erthema, flushing, porphyria cutanea tarda, psoriasis, psoriatic acral pustulosis, spider naevi and sweating via autonomic neuropathy (Higgins et al., 1992; Hoefkens et al., 1997; Marrakchi et al., 1994). In one study, carried out in a Finnish dermatological department, patients with psoriasis (plaque, guttate, arthropathic and pustular) were compared to 285 controls with other skin complaints (dermatitis, skin infections, acne and rosacea) (Poikolainen et al., 1990). Significantly higher alcohol intakes were obtained in the psoriatic group (43 g/day) compared to the non-psoriatic controls (21 g/day) (Poikolainen et al., 1990). The frequency of intoxication was similarly higher (i.e. mean of 62 episodes per year compared to 43; Poikolainen et al., 1990).

The relative risk of psoriasis in alcohol misusers is up to eight-fold higher than their non-alcohol misusing counterparts; 40% of patients attending dermatology clinics with psoriasis can be classified as alcohol misusers, compared to 3% of similarly attending eczema patients (Higgins et al., 1994a). However, in alcohol misusers the type of psoriasis is regional-specific, affecting predominantly the plantar and palmar regions with an element of inflammation affecting 15% of alcoholics. This contrasts with the standard prevalence of psoriasis of 2% in the general population, but discoid eczema is another particular lesion associated with male alcohol misusers and rarely occurs in non-abusing subjects (Higgins & DuVivier, 1992, 1994a).

In laboratory animals, feeding nutritionally complete ethanol containing liquid diets reduces skin weights (Preedy et al., 1988). Ethanol dosage also acutely reduces skin protein synthesis (Preedy et al., 1990b). Acute ethanol infusions have been reported to have no effect on skin blood flow, as measured by microspheres (Gulati et al., 1989). In contrast, acute alcohol-induced vasoconstriction has been reported, which may be related to the low doses of ethanol used (Tabrizchi et al., 1993). In chronic ethanol feeding, blood flow is unaffected when measured by microspheres (Preedy et al., 1997a), yet reduced when measured by non-invasive laser-Doppler methods (Preedy et al., 1992). Thus, although the flushing response in man is well recognized, laboratory animal studies have produced inconsistent results. This is probably because of the application of inappropriate methods used to measure blood flow in animals, which often requires the use of anaesthetics and other hypnotics concomitant with ethanol or invasive procedures (Preedy et al., 1992).

Acetaldehyde binds to collagen to form acetaldehyde–protein adducts (Jukkola et al., 1989). This will have the potential to form autoantibodies against skin or to alter conformational/and or functional capabilities. Free radicals may also induce conformational changes in collagen (Ryu et al., 1997).

EFFECTS OF ALCOHOL ON BONE

Post-mortem studies over 30 years ago revealed that alcohol misusers have decreased bone mass (Saville, 1965). More sophisticated studies in ambulatory subjects have confirmed these finding that chronic alcohol consumption precipitates either osteoporosis or osteopenia and it is now believed that up to 50% of all alcohol misusers have either condition (Feitelberg et al., 1987; Crilly et al., 1988; Diamond et al., 1989; Kelepouris et al., 1995). Thus, in one study of 26 heavy alcohol misusers (>150 g/day for 3 years or more) compared to 26 matched controls, bone volumes were reduced (all data as mean ± SEM: 12.7 ± 1.1% compared to 20.4 ± 1.3% $p < 0.05$; Diez et al., 1994). The incidence of fractures is also more common in chronic alcohol misusers compared to their non- or moderate-drinking counterparts (Oikarinen et al., 1992; Lauritzen et al., 1993; Kelepouris et al., 1995; Peris et al., 1995; Tuppurainen et al., 1995). Furthermore, alcohol abusers have impaired recovery from bone fractures compared to controls and develop more post-trauma complications, such as infections (Tonnesen et al., 1991; Passeri et al., 1993).

Some studies have shown little or no effect of alcohol on bone-mineral composition (Felson et al., 1995; Glynn et al., 1995; Johnell et al., 1995; Krogsgaard et al., 1995). These negative studies sometimes entail epidemiological analysis on a large population engaging in moderate or light drinking, rather than the impact of excessive alcohol, such as that seen in alcohol-dependent subjects.

Bone changes in alcoholics have been ascribed to nutritional impairments, e.g. by vitamin D-deficient diets (Feitelberg et al., 1987). A large study in over 2500 women (>45 years of age) has also shown that the risk of hip fractures is also inversely related to poor nutritional status (Huang et al., 1996). However, in strictly controlled laboratory animal studies, where both control and treated animals receive identical diets, albeit differences in alcohol, alcohol-induced bone disorders arise independently of nutritional status. Thus, bone weights decrease and urinary hydroxyproline excretion (a marker of collagen turnover) increases, compatible with clinical observations (Preedy et al., 1991a). Bone magnesium, calcium and phosphate decline, although trace elements such as zinc, iron and copper are unaltered or even increased (Preedy et al., 1991a). Ethanol induces increased loss of magnesium and calcium via the kidney.

Bone disorders or osteodystrophy occur frequently in liver disease (Diamond et al., 1990; Capra et al., 1991). In cirrhosis, serum osteocalcin (a measure of bone formation) declines, with a concomitant development of osteoporosis (Jorge Hernandez et al., 1988; Resch et al., 1990; Capra et al., 1991). In addition, serum osteocalcin levels and γ-glutamyl transferase activities (a marker of liver toxicity) correlate in acute alcohol toxicity studies (Rico et al., 1987). Overall this is suggestive of a relationship between liver dysfunction and bone disorders, but in chronic alcoholics with osteoporosis, the prevalence of liver disease is similar to that occurring in chronic alcoholics without osteoporosis (Spencer et al., 1986).

Abstinence ameliorates the changes in alcohol-induced bone mass, although at least 2 years may be required before a measurable improvement occurs (Lindholm et al., 1991; Peris et al., 1994).

The reduced bone density in alcoholism is suggestive of an imbalance between bone formation and resorption. Reduced osteoblastic function (a measure of bone formation or synthesis) has been observed in alcohol misusers (Klein et al., 1996). Bone formation rates in alcohol misusers decreases from 0.041 ± 0.004 to $0.023 \pm 0.005 \mu m^3/\mu m^2/day$ ($p < 0.01$; Diez et al., 1994). In the same study, mineral deposition rates also decreased from 0.77 ± 0.14 to $0.31 \pm 0.05 mm/day$ ($p < 0.05$). In contrast, osteoclast number (a measure of resorption or bone degradation) increased (Diez et al., 1994). Urinary hydroxyproline excretion increases in alcoholics (Crilly et al., 1988; Diamond et al., 1989). Pyridinoline and deoxypyridinoline are more specific urinary markers of bone collagen turnover (Black et al., 1988, 1989a, b; Robins et al., 1991). In rats fed alcohol for 6 weeks, urinary pyridinoline excretion declines only slightly (Preedy et al., 1991b). More significant decreases in the total, free and conjugated forms of deoxypyridinoline occur, with the decrease in the conjugated form being greater than the decline in free deoxypyridinoline (Preedy et al., 1991b). The consequences of these differential effects on conjugated and free forms is not clear (Preedy et al., 1991b).

CONCLUSION

Muscle, skin and bone account for a major proportion of whole-body mass and contribute largely to specific fields of metabolism such as glucose (muscle), lipid (skin) or mineral (bone) homeostasis. In combination, these tissues also account for no less than 50% of whole-body protein synthesis. At least half of alcoholics will have pathologies affecting one or more of these tissues. Although not life-threatening, lesions of these three tissues will contribute markedly to increased morbidity and impaired life qualities and alter whole-body metabolic control. However, muscle, skin and bone lesions occur in at least two-thirds of alcohol misusers and are thus far greater than the incidence of cirrhosis (15–25%). Some (but not all) of the lesions in muscle, skin and bone can be reversed by abstinence, in contrast to cirrhosis, which is considered irreversible. Furthermore, the relative amount of research into alcohol-induced liver disease is considerably greater than that being undertaken on alcohol-induced muscle, skin and bone disease.

KEY WORKS AND SUGGESTIONS FOR FURTHER READING

Bone

Crilly, R.G., Anderson, C., Hogan, D. & Delaquerriere Richardson, L. (1988).   Bone histomorphometry, bone mass, and related parameters in alcoholic males. *Calcified Tissue Int*, **43**, 269–276.

These studies provide compelling evidence that alcohol causes deleterious changes in bones of male alcohol misusers classified into those who were drinking or abstaining. Bone mineral density measurements and histomorphometry were combined with indices of endocrine status and urinary hydroxyproline measurements.

Preedy, V.R., Baldwin, D.R., Keating, J.W. & Salisbury, J.R. (1991).   Bone collagen, mineral and trace element composition, histomorphometry and urinary hydroxyproline excretion in chronically-treated alcohol-fed rats. *Alcohol and Alcoholism*, **26**, 39–46.

This study is a comprehensive analysis of the bone changes in tibia of rats fed alcohol for 6 weeks and illustrates the wide-ranging changes that occur. Attention is focused on collagen. There appeared to a delay before alcohol feeding reduced bone collagen. Concomitant measures included urinary hydroxyproline excretion, which was increased, analogous to the human studies by Crilly et al. (1988). Cortical bone thickness of lower tibia was reduced, which may have reflected reduced load bearing (perhaps due to muscle loss).

Skin

Higgins, E.M. & du Vivier, A.W. (1992). Alcohol and the skin. *Alcohol and Alcoholism*, **27**, 595–602.

Studies by Higgins and colleagues are arguably the most comprehensive analyses of skin changes in alcohol misusers and are recommended reading for those who wish to investigate this pathology further. In this review, the various prevalent forms of skin lesions in alcohol misusers such as psoriasis and discoid eczema, are described.

Preedy, V.R., Marway, J.S., Salisbury, J.R. & Peters, T.J. (1990). Protein synthesis in bone and skin of the rat are inhibited by ethanol: implications for whole body metabolism. *Alcoholism: Clinical and Experimental Research*, **14**, 165–186.

Usually, alcohol studies focus on a single tissue and the implications of the pathogenic changes are often considered in isolation. These studies look at protein metabolism in bone and skin in response to alcohol, with comparative reference to the changes in muscle and liver. Acute alcohol dosage reduced the synthesis rates of skin and bone proteins *in vivo*. The reduction in absolute rates of protein synthesis in bone and skin were comparable to the reductions in liver and skeletal muscle in response to acute ethanol dosage.

Muscle

Martin, F., Ward, K., Slavin, G., Levi, J. & Peters, T.J. (1985). Alcoholic skeletal myopathy, a clinical and pathological study. *Quarterly Journal of Medicine*, **55**, 233–251.

This study comprehensively investigated the diagnosis and high prevalence of alcoholic myopathy in a large group of patients. Alcoholic patients ($n = 151$) were investigated and myopathy diagnosed by quadriceps muscle biopsy. Type II muscle fibre atrophy was observed in 60% of subjects. Other measures included assessment of cirrhosis and neuropathy. However, neither liver disease nor neuropathy influenced the occurrence of myopathy, suggesting that alcohol acts directly on skeletal muscle.

Fernandez Sola, J., Villegas, E., Nicolas, J.M., Deulofeu, R., Antunez, E., Sacanella, E., Estruch, R. & Urbano Marquez, A. (1998). Serum and muscle levels of alpha-tocopherol, ascorbic acid, and retinol are normal in chronic alcoholic myopathy. *Alcoholism: Clinical and Experimental Reasearch*, **22**, 422–427.

This study examines directly some specific micronutrients in alcohol misusers. Measurements included serum and muscle levels of retinol, α-tocopherol and ascorbic acid. Forty per cent of subjects had myopathy but serum and muscle levels of the aforementioned micronutrients were similar to controls. Thus, unlike the UK study, it shows that the myopathy can develop independently of abnormal nutritional intake. In this study the authors concluded that the total life-time dose of ethanol was the only independent factor in relation to alcoholic myopathy.

Urbano Marquez, A., Estruch, R., Navarro Lopez, F., Grau, J.M., Mont, L. & Rubin E. (1989). The effects of alcoholism on skeletal and cardiac muscle. *New England Journal of Medicine*, **320**, 409–415.

This article (along with the study by Martin et al., 1985), is considered a classical investigation into the features of alcoholic myopathy with parallel studies on the heart. Assessments included skeletal muscle strength. Nearly half of subjects had skeletal muscle myopathy, as diagnosed by histological examination of biopsies. Life-time intake of alcohol correlated negatively with muscle strength.

Preedy, V.R. & Peters, T.J. (1988). The effect of chronic ethanol feeding on body and plasma composition and rates of skeletal muscle protein turnover in the rat. *Alcohol and Alcoholism*, **23**, 217–224.

This study is one of the first to show that myopathy can be induced in young and mature rats by alcohol feeding. The advantage of using young rats is that the myopathy can be induced in only 6 weeks. Chronic ethanol feeding reduced fractional rates of skeletal muscle protein synthesis and breakdown.

REFERENCES

Andersen, H., Borre, M., Jakobsen, J., Andersen, P.H. & Vilstrup, H. (1998). Decreased muscle strength in patients with alcoholic liver cirrhosis in relation to nutritional status, alcohol abstinence, liver function, and neuropathy. *Hepatology*, **27**, 1200–1206.

Asayama, K., Dettbarn, W.D. & Burr, I.M. (1986). Differential effect of denervation on free-radical scavenging enzymes in slow and fast muscle of rat. *Journal of Neurochemistry*, **46**, 604–609.

Asayama, K., Dobashi, K., Hayashibe, H., Megata, Y. & Kato, K. (1987). Lipid peroxidation and free radical scavengers in thyroid dysfunction in the rat: a possible mechanism of injury to heart and skeletal muscle in hyperthyroidism. *Endocrinology*, **121**, 2112–2118.

Ballantyne, J.P. & Hansen, S. (1982). A quantitative assessment of reinnervation in the polyneuropathies. *Muscle and Nerve*, **5**, S127–S134.

Black, D., Duncan, A. & Robins, S.P. (1988). Quantitative analysis of the pyridinium cross-links of collagen in urine using ion-paired reversed-phase high-performance liquid chromatography. *Analytical Biochemistry*, **169**, 197–203.

Black, D., Farquharson, C. & Robins, S.P. (1989a). Excretion of pyridinium cross-links of collagen in ovariectomized rats as urinary markers for increased bone resorption. *Calcified Tissue International*, **44**, 343–347.

Black, D., Marabani, M., Sturrock, R.D. & Robins, S.P. (1989b). Urinary excretion of the hydroxypyridinium cross-links of collagen in patients with rheumatoid arthritis. *Annals of Rheumatic Disease*, **48**, 641–644.

Brooke, M.H. & Engel, W.K. (1969). The histographic analysis of human muscle biopsies with regard to fiber types. 2. Diseases of the upper and lower motor neuron. *Neurology*, **19**, 378–393.

Brown, W.R. & Habowsky, J.E. (1979). Comparative ultrastructure and cytochemistry of epidermal responses to tape stripping, ethanol and vitamin A acid in hairless mice. *Journal of Investigations in Dermatology*, **73**, 203–206.

Capra, F., Casaril, M., Gabrielli, G.B., Stanzial, A., Ferrari, S., Gandini, G., Falezza, G. & Corrocher, R. (1991). Plasma osteocalcin levels in liver cirrhosis. *Italian Journal of Gastroenterology*, **23**, 124–127.

Caregaro, L., Alberino, F., Amodio, P., Merkel, C., Bolognesi, M., Angeli, P. & Gatta, A. (1996). Malnutrition in alcoholic and virus-related cirrhosis. *American Journal of Clinical Nutrition*, **63**, 602–609.

Cederbaum, A.I. (1991). Microsomal generation of reactive oxygen species and their possible role in alcohol hepatotoxicity. *Alcohol and Alcoholism* (Suppl.), **1**, 291–296.

Chan, K.M. & Decker, E.A. (1994).   Endogenous skeletal muscle antioxidants. *Critical Reviews in Food Science and Nutrition*, **34**, 403–426.

Chen, S.S., Peng, M.J. & Chen, T.J. (1991).   Study of myopathy in chronic alcoholics with neurological complication. *Kao Hsiung i Hsueh Ko Hsueh Tsa Chih*, **7**, 296–306.

Crilly, R.G., Anderson, C., Hogan, D. & Delaquerriere Richardson, L. (1988).   Bone histomorphometry, bone mass, and related parameters in alcoholic males. *Calcified Tissue International*, **43**, 269–276.

Crush, K.G. (1970).   Carnosine and related substances in animal tissues. *Comparative Biochemistry and Physiology*, **34**, 3–30.

Del Villar Negro, A., Merino Angulo, J. & Rivera Pomar, J.M. (1984).   Skeletal muscle changes in chronic alcoholic patients. A conventional, histochemical, ultrastructural and morphometric study. *Acta Neurological Scandinavica*, **70**, 185–196.

Diamond, T., Stiel, D., Lunzer, M., Wilkinson, M. & Posen, S. (1989).   Ethanol reduces bone formation and may cause osteoporosis. *American Journal of Medicine*, **86**, 282–288.

Diamond, T., Stiel, D., Lunzer, M., Wilkinson, M., Roche, J. & Posen, S. (1990).   Osteoporosis and skeletal fractures in chronic liver disease. *Gut*, **31**, 82–87.

Diez, A., Puig, J., Serrano, S., Marinoso, M.L., Bosch, J., Marrugat, J. et al. (1994).   Alcohol-induced bone disease in the absence of severe chronic liver damage. *Journal of Bone and Mineral Research*, **9**, 825–831.

Douglas, R.M., Fewings, J.D., Casley Smith, J.R. & West, R.F. (1966).   Recurrent rhabdomyolysis precipitated by alcohol: a case report with physiological and electron microscopic studies of skeletal muscle. *Australasian Annals of Medicine*, **15**, 251–261.

Duane, P. & Peters, T.J. (1987).   Glucocorticosteroid status in chronic alcoholics with and without skeletal muscle myopathy. *Clinical Science*, **73**, 601–603.

Duane, P. & Peters, T.J. (1988a).   Nutritional status in alcoholics with and without chronic skeletal muscle myopathy. *Alcohol and Alcoholism*, **23**, 271–277.

Duane, P. & Peters, T.J. (1988b).   Serum carnosinase activities in patients with alcoholic chronic skeletal muscle myopathy. *Clinical Science*, **75**, 185–190.

Dumitrescu, C. & Lichiardopol, R. (1994).   Particular features of clinical pellagra. Rom. *Journal of Internal Medicine*, **32**, 165–170.

Estruch, R., Nicolas, J.M., Villegas, E., Junque, A. & Urbano Marquez, A. (1993).   Relationship between ethanol-related diseases and nutritional status in chronically alcoholic men. *Alcohol and Alcoholism*, **28**, 543–550.

Feitelberg, S., Epstein, S., Ismail, F. & D'Amanda, C. (1987).   Deranged bone mineral metabolism in chronic alcoholism. *Metabolism*, **36**, 322–326.

Felson, D.T., Zhang, Y., Hannan, M.T., Kannel, W.B. & Kiel, D.P. (1995).   Alcohol intake and bone mineral density in elderly men and women. The Framingham Study. *Amencan Journal Epidemiology*, **142**, 485–492.

Fernandez Sola, J., Estruch, R., Grau, J.M., Pare, J.C., Rubin, E. & Urbano Marquez, A. (1994).   The relation of alcoholic myopathy to cardiomyopathy. *Annals of Internal Medicine*, **120**, 529–536.

Fernandez Sola, J., Estruch, R. & Urbano Marquez, A. (1997).   Alcohol and heart muscle disease. *Addiction Biology*, **2**, 9–17.

Fernandez Sola, J., Villegas, E., Nicolas, J.M., Deulofeu, R., Antunez, E., Sacanella, E. et al. (1998).   Serum and muscle levels of α-tocopherol, ascorbic acid, and retinol are normal in chronic alcoholic myopathy. *Alcoholism: Clinical and Experimental Research*, **22**, 422–427.

Ford, C.S., Caldwell, S.H. & Kilgo, G.R. (1984).   Acute alcoholic myopathy. *American Family Physician*, **29**, 249–252.

Fraker, P.J., Jardieu, P. & Cook, J. (1987).   Zinc deficiency and immune function. *Archises of Dermatology*, **123**, 1699–1701.

Garcia Bunuel, L. (1984).   Lipid peroxidation in alcoholic myopathy and cardiomyopathy. *Medical Hypotheses*, **13**, 217–231.

Glynn, N.W., Meilahn, E.N., Charron, M., Anderson, S.J., Kuller, L.H. & Cauley, J.A. (1995).   Determinants of bone mineral density in older men. *Journal of Bone and Mineral Research*, **10**, 1769–1777.

Grau, A., Pomes, J., Davalos, A., Gomez, E., Sola, P. & Genis, D. (1988). Computed tomography in acute alcoholic myopathy. *Journal of Computed Tomography*, **12**, 161–164.

Groote Veldman, R. & Meinders, A.E. (1996). On the mechanism of alcohol-induced pseudo-Cushing's syndrome. *Endocrinology Reviews*, **17**, 262–268.

Gulati, A., Srimal, R.C. & Bhargava, H.N. (1989). Effect of varying concentration of ethanol on systemic hemodynamics and regional circulation. *Alcohol*, **6**, 9–15.

Haida, M., Yazaki, K., Kurita, D. & Shinohara, Y. (1998). Mitochondrial dysfunction of human muscle in chronic alcoholism detected by using ^{31}P-magnetic resonance spectroscopy and near-infrared light absorption. *Alcoholism: Clinical and Experimental Research*, **22**, 108S–110S.

Hanid, A., Slavin, G., Mair, W., Sowter, C., Ward, P., Webb, J. & Levi, J. (1981). Fibre type changes in striated muscle of alcoholics. *Journal of Clinical Pathology*, **34**, 991–995.

Harris, R.C., Marlin, D.J., Dunnett, M., Snow, D.H. & Hultman, E. (1990). Muscle buffering capacity and dipeptide content in the thoroughbred horse, greyhound dog and man. *Comparative Biochemistry and Physiology*, A. **97**, 249–251.

Hendricks, W.M. (1991). Pellagra and pellagralike dermatoses: etiology, differential diagnosis, dermatopathology, and treatment. *Seminars in Dermatology*, **10**, 282–292.

Hickish, T., Colston, K.W., Bland, J.M. & Maxwell, J.D. (1989). Vitamin D deficiency and muscle strength in male alcoholics. *Clinical Science*, **77**, 171–176.

Higgins, E.M. & DuVivier, A.W. (1992). Alcohol and the skin. *Alcohol and Alcoholism*, **27**, 595–602.

Higgins, E.M. & DuVivier, A.W. (1994a). Cutaneous disease and alcohol misuse. *British Medical Bulletin*, **50**, 85–98.

Higgins, E.M., DuVivier, A.W. & Peters. T.J. (1994b). Smoking and psoriasis. *British Medical Journal*, **308**, 1572.

Higuchi, M., Cartier, L.J., Chen, M. & Holloszy, J.O. (1985). Superoxide dismutase and catalase in skeletal muscle: adaptive response to exercise. *Journal of Gerontology*, **40**, 281–286.

Hoefkens, P., Higgins, E.M., Ward, R.J. & van Eijk, H.G. (1997). Isoforms of transferrin in psoriasis patients abusing alcohol. *Alcohol and Alcoholism*, **32**, 195–199.

Huang, Z., Himes, J.H. & McGovern, P.G. (1996). Nutrition and subsequent hip fracture risk among a national cohort of white women. *American Journal of Epidemiology*, **144**, 124–134.

Hughes, G.S. Jr & Davis, L. (1983). Variegate porphyria and heavy metal poisoning from ingestion of "moonshine". *Southern Medical Journal*, **76**, 1027–1029.

Ikeda, T., Kimura, K., Hama, T. & Tamaki, N. (1980). Activation of rabbit muscle fructose 1,6-bisphosphatase by histidine and carnosine. *Journal of Biochemistry (Tokyo)*, **87**, 179–185.

Ishii, N. & Nishihara, Y. (1981). Pellagra among chronic alcoholics: clinical and pathological study of 20 necropsy cases. *Journal Neurological and Neurosurgical Psychiatry*, **44**, 209–215.

Iwase, S., Matsukawa, T., Ishihara, S., Tanaka, A., Tanabe, K., Danbara, A. et al. (1995). Effect of oral ethanol intake on muscle sympathetic nerve activity and cardiovascular functions in humans. *Journal of the Autonomic Nervous System*, **54**, 206–214.

Jeffcoate, W. (1993). Alcohol-induced pseudo-Cushing's syndrome. *Lancet*, **341**, 676–677.

Jenkins, W. (1984). Liver disorders in alcoholism. *Contempory Issues in Clinical Biochemistry*, **1**, 258–270.

Johnell, O., Gullberg, B., Kanis, J.A., Allander, E., Elffors, L., Dequeker, J. et al. (1995). Risk factors for hip fracture in European women: the MEDOS Study. Mediterranean Osteoporosis Study. *Journal of Bone and Mineral Research*, **10**, 1802–1815.

Johnson, P., Fedyna, J.S., Schindzielorz, A., Smith, C.M. & Kasvinsky, P.J. (1982). Regulation of muscle phosphorylase activity by carnosine and anserine. *Biochemical and Biophysical Research Communications*, **109**, 769–775.

Jorge Hernandez, J.A., Gonzalez Reimers, C.E., Torres Ramirez, A., Santolaria Fernandez, F., Gonzalez Garcia, C., Batista Lopez, J.N. et al. (1988). Bone changes in alcoholic liver cirrhosis. A histomorphometrical analysis of 52 cases. *Digestive Diseases and Sciences*, **33**, 1089–1095.

Jukkola, A. & Niemela, O. (1989). Covalent binding of acetaldehyde to type III collagen. *Biochemical and Biophysical Research Communications*, **159**, 163–169.

Kelepouris, N., Harper, K.D., Gannon, F., Kaplan, F.S. & Haddad, J.G. (1995). Severe osteoporosis in men. *Annals of Internal Medicine*, **123**, 452–460.

Kirkman, S. & Nelson, D.H. (1988). Alcohol-induced pseudo-Cushing's disease: a study of prevalence with review of the literature. *Metabolism*, **37**, 390–394.

Klein, R.F., Fausti, K.A. & Carlos, A.S. (1996). Ethanol inhibits human osteoblastic cell proliferation. *Alcoholism: Clinical and Experimental Research*, **20**, 572–578.

Klein, R.F. (1997). Alcohol-induced bone disease: impact of ethanol on osteoblast proliferation. *Alcoholism: Clinical and Experimental Research*, **21**, 392–399.

Krogsgaard, M.R., Frolich, A. & Lund, B. (1995). Long-term changes in bone mass after partial gastrectomy in a well-defined population and its relation to tobacco and alcohol consumption. *World Journal of Surgery*, **19**, 867–871.

Laitinen, K. & Valimaki, M. (1991). Alcohol and bone. *Calcified Tissue International*, **49** (Suppl.): S70–S73.

Laughlin, M.H., Simpson, T., Sexton, W.L., Brown, O.R., Smith, J.K. & Korthuis, R.J. (1990). Skeletal muscle oxidative capacity, antioxidant enzymes, and exercise training. *Journal of Applied Physiology*, **68**, 2337–2343.

Lauritzen, J.B., McNair, P.A. & Lund, B. (1993). Risk factors for hip fractures. A review. *Danish Medical Bulletin*, **40**, 479–485.

Lindholm, J., Steiniche, T., Rasmussen, E., Thamsborg, G., Nielsen, I.O., Brockstedt Rasmussen, H. et al. (1991). Bone disorder in men with chronic alcoholism: a reversible disease? *Journal of Clinical Endocrinology and Metabolism*, **73**, 118–124.

Lundin, L., Hallgren, R., Landelius, J., Roxin, L.E. & Venge, P. (1986). Myocardial and skeletal muscle function in habitual alcoholics and its relation to serum myoglobin. *American Journal of Cardiology*, **58**, 795–799.

Lykkeboe, G. & Johansen, K. (1975). Comparative aspects of buffering capacity in muscle. *Respiratory Physiology*, **25**, 353–361.

Mannion, A.F., Jakeman, P.M., Dunnett, M., Harris, R.C. & Willan, P.L. (1992). Carnosine and anserine concentrations in the quadriceps femoris muscle of healthy humans. *European Journal of Applied Physiology*, **64**, 47–50.

Marchesini, G., Zoli, M., Angiolini, A., Dondi, C., Bianchi, F.B. & Pisi, E. (1981). Muscle protein breakdown in liver cirrhosis and the role of altered carbohydrate metabolism. *Hepatology*, **1**, 294–299.

Marrakchi, S., Kim, I., Delaporte, E., Briand, G., Degand, P., Maibach, H.I. & Thomas, P. (1994). Vitamin A and E blood levels in erythrodermic and pustular psoriasis associated with chronic alcoholism. *Acta Dermatologia Venereologica*, **74**, 298–301.

Martin, F., Ward, K., Slavin, G., Levi, J. & Peters, T.J. (1985). Alcoholic skeletal myopathy, a clinical and pathological study. *Quarterly Journal of Medicine*, **55**, 233–251.

Marway, J.S., Preedy, V.R. & Peters, T.J. (1990). Experimental alcoholic skeletal muscle myopathy is characterized by a rapid and sustained decrease in muscle RNA content. *Alcohol and Alcoholism*, **25**, 401–406.

Mills, K.R., Ward, K., Martin, F. & Peters, T.J. (1986). Peripheral neuropathy and myopathy in chronic alcoholism. *Alcohol and Alcoholism*, **21**, 357–362.

Mizoi, Y., Ijiri, I., Tatsuno, Y., Kijima, T., Fujiwara, S., Adachi, J. & Hishida, S. (1979). Relationship between facial flushing and blood acetaldehyde levels after alcohol intake. *Pharmacology, Biochemistry and Behaviour*, **10**, 303–311.

Mizoi, Y., Tatsuno, Y., Adachi, J., Kogame, M., Fukunaga, T., Fujiwara, S. et al. (1983). Alcohol sensitivity related to polymorphism of alcohol-metabolizing enzymes in Japanese. *Pharmacology, Biochemistry and Behaviour*, **18**(Suppl. 1), 127–133.

Moniz, C. (1994). Alcohol and bone. *British Medical Bulletin*, **50**, 67–75.

Morrison, W.L., Bouchier, I.A., Gibson, J.N. & Rennie, M.J. (1990). Skeletal muscle and whole-body protein turnover in cirrhosis. *Clinical Science*, **78**, 613–619.

Nordmann, R., Ribiere, C. & Rouach, H. (1992). Implication of free radical mechanisms in ethanol-induced cellular injury. *Free Radicals in Biology and Medicine*, **12**, 219–240.

Oikarinen, K., Silvennoinen, U. & Ignatius, E. (1992). Frequency of alcohol-associated mandibular fractures in northern Finland in the 1980s. *Alcohol and Alcoholism*, **27**, 189–193.

Pacy, P.J., Preedy, V.R., Peters, T.J., Read, M. & Halliday, D. (1991). The effect of chronic alcohol ingestion on whole body and muscle protein synthesis—a stable isotope study. *Alcohol and Alcoholism*, **26**, 505–513.

Parish, L.C. & Fine, E. (1985). Alcoholism and skin disease. *International Journal of Dermatology*, **24**, 300–301.

Passeri, L.A., Ellis, E. III & Sinn, D.P. (1993). Relationship of substance abuse to complications with mandibular fractures. *Journal of Oral Maxillofacial Surgery*, **51**, 22–25.

Paton, A. (1976). Alcohol-induced cushingoid syndrome. *British Medical Journal*, **2**, 1504.

Pendergast, D.R., York, J.L. & Fisher, N.M. (1990). A survey of muscle function in detoxified alcoholics. *Alcohol*, **7**, 361–366.

Peris, P., Pares, A., Guanabens, N., del Rio, L., Pons, F., Martinez de Osaba, M.J. et al. (1994). Bone mass improves in alcoholics after 2 years of abstinence. *Journal of Bone and Mineral Research*, **9**, 1607–1612.

Peris, P., Guanabens, N., Monegal, A., Suris, X., Alvarez, L., Martinez de Osaba, M.J. et al. (1995). Aetiology and presenting symptoms in male osteoporosis. *British Journal of Rheumatology*, **34**, 936–941.

Perkoff, G.T. (1971). Alcoholic myopathy. *Annual Review of Medicine*, **22**, 125–132.

Peters, T.J. & Preedy, V.R. (1991). Chronic alcoholic myopathy: An overview. In T.N. Palmer (Ed.), *Alcoholism: A Molecular Perspective* (pp. 301–308). Plenum: New York.

Poikolainen, K., Reunala, T., Karvonen, J., Lauharanta, J. & Karkkainen, P. (1990). Alcohol intake: a risk for psoriasis in young and midle aged men? *British Medical Journal*, **300**, 780–783.

Prasad, A.S. (1983). Zinc deficiency in human subjects. *Progress in Clinical and Biological Research*, **129**, 1–33.

Prasad, A.S. (1985a). Clinical, endocrinological and biochemical effects of zinc deficiency. *Journal of Clinical Endocrinology and Metabolism*, **14**, 567–589.

Prasad, A.S. (1985b). Clinical manifestations of zinc deficiency. *Annual Reviews in Nutrition*, **5**, 341–363.

Preedy, V.R. & Peters, T.J. (1988). The effect of chronic ethanol feeding on body and plasma composition and rates of skeletal muscle protein turnover in the rat. *Alcohol and Alcoholism*, **23**, 217–224.

Preedy, V.R., Gove, C.D., Panos, M.Z., Sherwood, R., Portmann, B., Williams, R. & Peters, T.J. (1990a). Liver histology, blood biochemistry and RNA, DNA and subcellular protein composition of various skeletal muscles of rats with experimental cirrhosis: implications for alcoholic muscle disease. *Alcohol and Alcoholism*, **25**, 641–649.

Preedy, V.R., Marway, J.S., Salisbury, J.R. & Peters, T.J. (1990b). Protein synthesis in bone and skin of the rat are inhibited by ethanol: implications for whole body metabolism. *Alcoholism: Clinical Experimental Research*, **14**, 165–168.

Preedy, V.R., Baldwin, D.R., Keating, J.W. & Salisbury, J.R. (1991a). Bone collagen, mineral and trace element composition, histomorphometry and urinary hydroxyproline excretion in chronically-treated alcohol-fed rats. *Alcohol and Alcoholism*, **26**, 39–46.

Preedy, V.R., Sherwood, R.A., Akpoguma, C.I. & Black, D. (1991b). The urinary excretion of the collagen degradation markers pyridinoline and deoxypyridinoline in an experimental rat model of alcoholic bone disease. *Alcohol and Alcoholism*, **26**, 191–198.

Preedy, V.R., Cook, E.B. & Siddiq, T. (1992). Non-invasive laser-Doppler assessment of cutaneous blood-flow in alcohol studies: effects of chronic ethanol consumption on peripheral blood-flow in unanaesthetised rats. *Alcohol and Alcoholism*, **27**, 165–169.

Preedy, V.R. & Peters, T.J. (1994a). Alcohol and muscle disease. *Journal of the Royal Society of Medicine*, **87**, 188–190.

Preedy, V.R. & Peters, T.J. (1994b). Alcohol and muscle disease. *Journal of the Royal Society of Medicine*, **87**, 188–190.

Preedy, V.R., Peters, T.J., Patel, V.B. & Miell, J.P. (1994c). Chronic alcoholic myopathy: transcription and translational alterations. *FASEB Journal*, **8**, 1146–1151.

Preedy, V.R., Salisbury, J.R. & Peters, T.J. (1994d). Alcoholic muscle disease: features and mechanisms. *Journal of Pathology*, **173**, 309–315.

Preedy, V.R., Nott, D.M., Yates, J., Venkatesan, S., Jenkins, S.A. & Peters, T.J. (1997a). Hepatic haemodynamics and reticuloendothelial function in the rat in response to chronic ethanol administration. *Addiction Biology*, **2**, 445–454.

Preedy, V.R., Peters, T.J. & Why, H. (1997b). Metabolic consequences of alcohol dependency. Adverse. Drug React. *Toxicological Reviews*, **16**, 235–256.

Preedy, V.R., Reilly, M., Mantle, D. & Peters, T.J. (1998a). Free radicals and antioxidants in the pathogenesis of alcoholic myopathy. In A.E. Reznick, D.L. Packer, C.K. Sen, J.O. Holloszy & M.J. Jackson (Eds), *Free Radicals and Skeletal Muscle* (pp. 283–293). Birkhauser Verlag: Basel.

Preedy, V.R., Reilly, M.E., Mantle, D. & Peters, T.J. (1998b). Oxidative damage in liver disease. *Journal of International and Federal Clinical Biochemistry*, **10**, 16–20.

Reilly, M.E., Preedy, V.R. & Peters, T.J. (1995). Investigations into the toxic effects of alcohol on skeletal muscle. Adverse. Drug React. *Toxicological Reviews*, **14**, 117–150.

Reilly, M.E., Imren-Eryilamaz, E., Amir, A., Peters, T.J. & Preedy, V.R. (1998). Skeletal muscle ribonuclease activities in chronically ethanol-treated rats. *Alcoholism: Clinical Experimental Research*, **22**, 876–883.

Resch, H., Pietschmann, P., Krexner, E., Woloszczuk, W. & Willvonseder, R. (1990). Peripheral bone mineral content in patients with fatty liver and hepatic cirrhosis. *Scandinavian Journal of Gastroenterology*, **25**, 412–416.

Rico, H., Cabranes, J.A., Cabello, J., Gomez Castresana, F. & Hernandez, E.R. (1987). Low serum osteocalcin in acute alcohol intoxication: a direct toxic effect of alcohol on osteoblasts. *Bone and Mineral*, **2**, 221–225.

Rico, H. (1990). Alcohol and bone disease. *Alcohol and Alcoholism*, **25**, 345–352.

Riley, D.A., Bain, J.L., Ellis, S. & Haas, A.L. (1988a). Quantitation and immunocytochemical localization of ubiquitin conjugates within rat red and white skeletal muscles. *Journal of Histochemistry and Cytochemistry*, **36**, 621–632.

Riley, D.A., Ellis, S. & Bain, J.L. (1988b). Catalase-positive microperoxisomes in rat soleus and extensor digitorum longus muscle fiber types. *Journal of Histochemistry and Cytochemistry*, **36**, 633–637.

Robins, S.P., Black, D., Paterson, C.R., Reid, D.M., Duncan, A. & Seibel, M.J. (1991). Evaluation of urinary hydroxypyridinium cross-link measurements as resorption markers in metabolic bone diseases. *European Journal of Clinical Investigation*, **21**, 310–315.

Ryu, A., Naru, E., Arakane, K., Masunaga, T., Shinmoto, K., Nagano, T. et al. (1997). Cross-linking of collagen by singlet oxygen generated with UV-A. *Chemical and Pharmacological Bulletin (Tokyo)*, **45**, 1243–1247.

Sacanella, E., Fernandez Sola, J., Cofan, M., Nicolas, J.M., Estruch, R., Antunez, E. & Urbano Marquez, A. (1995). Chronic alcoholic myopathy: diagnostic clues and relationship with other ethanol-related diseases. *Quarterly Journal of Medicine*, **88**, 811–817.

Sampson, H.W. (1997). Alcohol, osteoporosis, and bone regulating hormones. *Alcoholism: Clinical and Experimental Research*, **21**, 400–403.

Saville, P.D. (1965). Changes in bone mass with age and alcoholism. *Journal of Bone and Joint Surgery*, **47**, 492–499.

Schneider, R. (1970). Acute alcoholic myopathy with myoglobinuria. *Southern Medical Journal*, **63**, 485–489.

Seneviratne, B.I. (1975). Acute cardiomyopathy with rhabdomyolysis in chronic alcoholism. *British Medical Journal*, **4**, 378–380.

Sewell, D.A., Harris, R.C., Marlin, D.J. & Dunnett, M. (1992). Estimation of the carnosine content of different fibre types in the middle gluteal muscle of the thoroughbred horse. *Journal of Physiology (London)*, **455**, 447–453.

Sherman, D.I., Ward, R.J., Yoshida, A. & Peters, T.J. (1994). Alcohol and acetaldehyde dehydrogenase gene polymorphism and alcoholism. *EXS*, **71**, 291–300.

Sherwood, R.A., Lambert, A., Newham, D.J., Wassif, W.S. & Peters, T.J. (1996). The effect of eccentric exercise on serum creatine kinase activity in different ethnic groups. *Annals of Clinical Biochemistry*, **33**, 324–329.

Slavin, G., Martin, F., Ward, P., Levi, J. & Peters, T.J. (1983). Chronic alcohol excess is associated with selective but reversible injury to type 2B muscle fibres. *Journal of Clinical Pathology*, **36**, 772–777.

Spencer, H., Rubio, N., Rubio, E., Indreika, M. & Seitam, A. (1986). Chronic alcoholism. Frequently overlooked cause of osteoporosis in men. *American Journal of Medicine*, **80**, 393–397.

Sunnasy, D., Cairns, S.R., Martin, F., Slavin, G. & Peters, T.J. (1983). Chronic alcoholic skeletal muscle myopathy: a clinical, histological and biochemical assessment of muscle lipid. *Journal of Clinical Pathology*, **36**, 778–784.

Tabrizchi, R. & Pang, C.C. (1993). Influence of intravenous infusion of ethanol on regional blood flow in conscious rats. *Journal of Pharmacy and Pharmacology*, **45**, 151–153.

Tamaki, N., Nakamura, M., Harada, M., Kimura, K. & Kawano, H. (1977).   Anserine and carnosine contents in muscular tissue of rat and rabbit. *Journal of Nutrition Science and Vitaminology (Tokyo)*, **23**, 319–329.

Tonnesen, H., Pedersen, A., Jensen, M.R., Moller, A. & Madsen, J.C. (1991).   Ankle fractures and alcoholism. The influence of alcoholism on morbidity after malleolar fractures. *Journal of Bone and Joint Surgery*, **73**, 511–513.

Trounce, I., Byrne, E., Dennett, X., Santamaria, J., Doery, J. & Peppard, R. (1987).   Chronic alcoholic proximal wasting: physiological, morphological and biochemical studies in skeletal muscle. *Australia and New Zealand Journal of Medicine*, **17**, 413–419.

Tuppurainen, M., Kroger, H., Honkanen, R., Puntila, E., Huopio, J., Saarikoski, S. & Alhava, E. (1995). Risks of perimenopausal fractures—a prospective population-based study. *Acta Obstetrica Gynecologia Scandinavica*, **74**, 624–628.

Urbano Marquez, A., Estruch, R., Navarro Lopez, F., Grau, J.M., Mont, L. & Rubin, E. (1989).   The effects of alcoholism on skeletal and cardiac muscle. *New England Journal of Medicine*, **320**, 409–415.

Vannucchi, H. & Moreno, F.S. (1989).   Interaction of niacin and zinc metabolism in patients with alcoholic pellagra. *American Journal of Clinical Nutrition*, **50**, 364–369.

Vannucchi, H., Moreno, F.S. Amarante, A.R., de Oliveira, J.E. & Marchini, J.S. (1991).   Plasma amino acid patterns in alcoholic pellagra patients. *Alcohol and Alcoholism*, **26**, 431–436.

Ward, R.J. & Peters, T.J. (1992a).   The antioxidant status of patients with either alcohol-induced liver damage or myopathy. *Alcohol and Alcoholism*, **27**, 359–365.

Ward, R.J. & Preedy, V.R. (1992b).   Imidazole dipeptides in experimental alcohol-induced myopathy. *Alcohol and Alcoholism*, **27**, 633–639.

Ward, R.J., McPherson, A.J., Chow, C., Ealing, J., Sherman, D.I., Yoshida, A. & Peters, T.J. (1994). Identification and characterization of alcohol-induced flushing in Caucasian subjects. *Alcohol and Alcoholism*, **29**, 433–438.

Wassif, W.S., Preedy, V.R., Summers, B., Duane, P., Leigh, N. & Peters, T.J. (1993).   The relationship between muscle fibre atrophy factor, plasma carnosinase activities and muscle RNA and protein composition in chronic alcoholic myopathy. *Alcohol and Alcoholism*, **28**, 325–331.

Wassif, W.S., Sherman, D., Salisbury, J.R. & Peters, T.J. (1994).   Use of dynamic tests of muscle function and histomorphometry of quadriceps muscle biopsies in the investigation of patients with chronic alcohol misuse and chronic fatigue syndrome. *Annals of Clinical Biochemistry*, **31**, 462–468.

Yoshida, A., Dave, V., Ward, R.J. & Peters, T.J. (1989).   Cytosolic aldehyde dehydrogenase (ALDH1) variants found in alcohol flushers. *Annals of Human Genetics*, **53**, 1–7.

Chapter 10

Nutrition and Infectious Disease

Ramon Estruch
Alcohol Research Unit, University of Barcelona, Barcelona, Spain

Synopsis

In early studies, the rather high incidence of malnutrition in alcoholics can be related to the patients included, consisting of indigent skid-row patients or those with severe somatic complications. Later studies have revealed that nutritional deficiencies are rare among middle-class alcoholics without significant somatic complications. However, nutritional deficiencies may be found among low-income and homeless alcoholic populations, and in those who suffer from ethanol-related complications, especially liver disease or neurological disorders.

Over time, alcoholism and malnutrition have been discussed jointly with regard to the pathogenesis, prognosis and even therapy of the ethanol-related diseases. Epidemiological, clinical and experimental studies have demonstrated that ethanol has a direct effect on most body tissues. Nevertheless, since not all heavy drinkers exhibit all types of ethanol-related complications, other factors, such as nutritional deficiencies, environmental circumstances or genetic predisposition, may enhance or prevent the effects of ethanol on cells. In fact, several studies have suggested that poor nutrition may have an additive effect, thereby contributing to the toxic effects of ethanol.

Several diseases in chronic alcoholics are due to specific nutritional deficiencies (e.g. Wernicke encepahopathy). However, since the metabolism of ethanol in the liver alters the activation and degradation of key nutrients, restoring nutritional balance and the use of specific nutrients may also be useful in the treatment of ethanol-related disease of non-nutritional cause (e.g. alcoholic hepatitis).

Another complication of alcohol abuse is altered immune regulation, leading to immunodeficiency. The consequences of this immunodeficiency include increased susceptibility to bacterial pneumonia, tuberculosis and other infectious diseases. Alcohol abuse also facilitates the spread of human immune deficiency virus and the progression of the disease in those subjects already infected. In addition, the process of liver disease due to hepatitis C virus is accelerated in patients who consume alcohol. Several mechanisms have been proposed to explain the immunodeficiency observed in chronic alcoholics. Malnutrition and liver disease

International Handbook of Alcohol Dependence and Problems. Edited by N. Heather, T.J. Peters and T. Stockwell.
© 2001 John Wiley & Sons Ltd.

have additive effects on the immune system which may contribute to the effects of ethanol on this system.

Although nutritional status and infectious disease are closely related in chronic alcoholics, this chapter has been divided into two parts. In the first part, the relationship of alcohol abuse and nutrition is discussed. Chronic alcoholism continues to be the main cause of malnutrition in Western countries. In the second part, one of the least-appreciated medical complications of alcohol abuse is reviewed-altered immune regulation due to ethanol intake leading to immunodeficiency, which explains the increased susceptibility of chronic alcoholics to acquire bacterial pneumonia, tuberculosis and other infectious diseases.

ALCOHOL AND NUTRITION

Several studies have reported a dose–response relationship between alcohol consumption and the risk of developing organic ethanol-related complications (Thakker, 1998). However, despite many alcoholics having drunk huge amounts of alcohol, ethanol-related diseases appear only in a small proportion of heavy drinkers and alcoholics. For instance, only 20–30% of severe alcohol misusers develop liver cirrhosis. Thus, besides ethanol itself, other factors, such as individual predisposition, environmental circumstances, immunologic disturbances and malnutrition, may contribute to the development of such complications. The pathogenesis of the complications arising from alcoholism and their relationship with the nutritional status of alcoholics have been widely discussed over the last 50 years. Malnutrition was formerly believed to be paramount in the development of alcohol-related diseases. Lately, reports on the dose–response relationship between alcohol intake and several ethanol-related diseases has led many researchers to attribute these diseases directly to the toxic effects of ethanol and to consider nutritional status to be less important. Currently, the situation has moved to a middle point and the predominant idea is that malnutrition increases the toxic effects of ethanol and contributes to the development of ethanol-related diseases.

Caloric Value of Ethanol

One of the key questions in the relationship between alcohol intake and nutritional status is the caloric value of ethanol. Alcoholic beverages contribute significantly to the overall calories in the diet of most Western countries. Based on epidemiologic consumption data, the estimated contribution of alcohol to the diet of the general population varies between 4.5% and 5.7% of the total calories, but the figure is higher in most persons who consume ethanol regularly, with alcohol accounting for up to 18% of total energy. In heavy drinkers ethanol may supply more than 50% of dietary energy.

Atwater & Rosa (1899) determined the metabolizable energy value of ethanol as a metabolic fuel to humans to be 6.9 kcal/g (28.8 kJ/g), similar to that of carbohydrates. However, experimental and epidemiologic studies have suggested an apparent low yield of useful energy from ethanol. Energy metabolism from ingested ethanol was assessed by metabolic studies measuring thermogenesis and oxygen consumption in healthy volunteers who received 25% of their total energy requirements as ethanol. Either added to the diet or substituted for other foods, ethanol increased 24 h energy expenditure and decreased lipid oxidation. The conclusion was that habitual consumption of ethanol favours lipid storage and weight gain, but the results suggested that the metabolizable energy from ethanol was 80%, as useful as that from carbohydrates (Rumpler et al., 1996; Suter et al., 1992). In other studies, weight loss occurred in volunteers when 35% of carbohydrate calories were replaced by ethanol and was maximal at 50%, the highest rate tested. The inefficiency of the utilization of ethanol could be explained, at least in part, by induction of the microsomal ethanol oxidizing system (MEOS) for the metabolism of ethanol, rather than the traditional oxidation of ethanol through the alcohol dehydrogenase (ADH) system. The MEOS pathway yields 10 ATP/mol of ethanol oxidized to carbon dioxide, whereas the ADH pathway yields 16 ATP per unit. Thus, the oxidation of ethanol via the MEOS pathway yields only 67% of the useful energy from the ADH path (Lieber, 1997). Other mechanisms to explain energy wasting is the uncoupling of mitochondrial NADH oxidation, perhaps promoted by catecholamine release or a hyperthyroid state.

Many epidemiological studies have observed a negative relationship between ethanol consumption and body weight. Thus, the major study performed by Colditz et al. (1991) indicated that the consumption of ethanol results in a greater energy intake but not an associated increase in body mass. However, in other surveys alcoholics were above the ideal body weight and a positive correlation was found between alcohol consumption and obesity. The variability in the results of epidemiological studies may be due to the difficulty of assessing ethanol intake in free-living subjects and to the fact that some consumers add ethanol to their usual food intake, whereas others replace carbohydrates or fats with ethanol (for review, see Rumpler et al., 1996; Suter et al., 1992).

Mechanisms of Malnutrition in Chronic Alcoholics

Dietary Deficiencies

Many early studies reported grossly deficient diets in alcoholics and suggested that poor dietary intake may be the principal cause of nutritional deficiencies encountered in these patients. Thus, studies performed in alcoholics with evidence of ethanol-related diseases, mainly liver cirrhosis, or with very poor socioeconomic background, pointed out that chronic alcoholics frequently report nutritional deficiencies, with a reduction in protein or carbohydrate intake. In contrast, more recent studies performed in alcoholics free of major complications have reported that the mean daily intake of protein, fat and carbohydrates was similar to that in a control population. Thus, although the dietary intake of chronic alcoholics is grossly imbalanced because of the caloric value of ethanol, the diets of most alcoholics seem to be adequate in terms of major nutrient intake when compared with healthy control populations. However, low real calorie intake may play an important role in the genesis of malnutrition in alcoholics from low socioeconomic levels and/or in some with ethanol-related diseases.

Increase in Nutritional Requirements

Chronic alcoholics usually exhibit an increased oxygen consumption due to an hypermetabolic state similar to hyperthyroidism, which is associated with an increased Na^+-K^+ ATPase activity and an increased consumption of ATP. On the other hand, mitochondrial damage due to the toxic effects of ethanol or its metabolites reduces the synthesis of ATP. To equilibrate these high energetic requirements, an increase in nutrient oxidation is needed, with an increase in nutrient uptake. In addition, increased requirements for certain vitamins, particularly those used for tissue repair, such as folic acid, pyridoxine and vitamin B_{12}, have been reported. Thus, low serum folic acid levels must be corrected to normal by giving extra folate doses when patients maintain ethanol intake. When the intake is insufficient, alcoholics start to lose weight and became malnourished. Finally, ethanol increases faecal loss of nitrogen, as well as urinary loss of zinc, magnesium, calcium and phosphate, which must be replaced by increased intake of these ions.

Malabsorption

Ethanol has a direct toxic effect on the gastrointestinal tract. Acute administration of ethanol induces gastric secretion and modifies the mucous barrier of the stomach, leading to the development of acute gastritis and duodenitis. In addition, acute ingestion of large amounts of alcohol inhibits intestinal absorption of D-xylose in humans and impairs absorption of amino acids, glucose and vitamins in laboratory animals.

Chronic ethanol intake causes chronic gastritis and delay in gastric emptying and induces changes in the motility, structure and function of the small intestine. Significant differences have also been observed in the bacteria flora of the jejunum of chronic alcoholics compared to non-alcoholic controls, which may produce disturbances of the small intestine. Intravenous alcohol administration inhibits pancreatic exocrine secretion, even in non-alcoholic patients. In addition, chronic alcoholics frequently show evidence of pancreatic exocrine insufficiency, i.e. a decrease in the output of bicarbonate and pancreatic enzymes after stimulation of the pancreas with secretin and pancreozymin hormones. Finally, nutritional deficiencies may, by themselves, adversely affect intestinal and pancreatic function. Thus, folate-deficient alcoholics show a significantly higher incidence of xylose and vitamin B_{12} malabsorption than folate-replete alcoholics.

Chronic alcoholics with liver cirrhosis frequently report steatorrhoea, which may persist for several weeks after ethanol withdrawal. Malabsorption in these patients is multifactorial and may be caused by pancreatic insufficiency, decreased intraluminal bile salts, altered intestinal motility, small intestinal mucosal abnormalities or enteropathy caused by some commonly used drugs such as neomycin.

Effects in the Storing and Metabolism of Nutrients

Chronic alcoholics, specially those with liver disease, have a decreased capacity to store nutrients, such as folic acid, riboflavin, nicotinamide, pantothenic acid, vitamin B_{12} and vitamin A. On the other hand, ethanol causes wide-ranging effects on the metabolism of nutrients. Ethanol inhibits albumin synthesis, impedes protein release from the liver, inhibits gluconeogenesis and impairs vitamin utilization (e.g. thiamine).

Nutritional Assessment and Classification of Malnutrition

Nutritional Assessment

Although only a minority of alcoholics have clinically manifest nutritional problems, they still represent the largest group of patients with treatable nutritional deficiencies in Western countries. Thus, complete nutritional assessment should be performed on every alcoholic patient, including a dietary recall history, anthropometric assessment and laboratory analyses (Table 10.1). Dietary recall history should be obtained by an expert physician or nurse-dietician through repeated interviews and, whenever possible, data should be verified by relatives and friends: a 3-day, 5-day, week or month diet history may be used. However, lack of patient cooperation, urgency of treatment, lack of qualified personnel and time-consuming interviews make proper evaluations in clinical practice difficult. Type, average quantity per year and frequency of ethanol intake should also be recorded, as should signs and symptoms that may be related to nutritional problems, such as under- or overwight, poor oral hygiene, glossitis, vomiting, diarrhoea, abdominal pain, oedema, enlarged liver or jaundice.

Anthropometric measures should include height, weight, circumference of the upper non-dominant arm and tricipital skin fold. Since chronic alcoholics tend to accumulate fat

Table 10.1 Nutritional parameters assessed in chronic alcoholics and controls

	Alcoholics (n = 250)	Controls (n = 100)	p
Total daily kcal	3250 ± 622	2650 ± 353	<0.001
Total daily kcal (EtOH excluded)	1620 ± 450	2650 ± 353	<0.001
Ideal body weight (%)	99.5 ± 16.3	105.4 ± 11.4	<0.001
Tricipital skin fold thickness (cm)	0.81 ± 0.47	1.17 ± 0.42	<0.001
Arm circumference (cm)	25.7 ± 3.2	28.0 ± 3.2	<0.001
Arm muscle circumference (cm)	23.2 ± 2.6	24.3 ± 2.9	<0.001
Arm muscle area (cm^2)	43.6 ± 10.0	47.9 ± 9.7	<0.001
Arm fat area (cm^2)	8.7 ± 4.2	12.9 ± 4.4	<0.001
Lean body mass (kg)	48.9 ± 5.4	53.1 ± 4.8	<0.001
Total protein (g/l)	71.0 ± 6.6	70.0 ± 7.2	NS
Albumin (g/l)	41.6 ± 6.8	43.7 ± 5.8	0.049
Transferrin (mg/dl)	235 ± 54	250 ± 40	0.011
Prealbumin (mg/dl)	27.4 ± 12.1	31.2 ± 6.2	0.002
Retinol-binding protein (mg/dl)	4.56 ± 2.24	5.98 ± 2.11	<0.001
Haemoglobin (g/l)	144 ± 17	145 ± 15	NS
Lymphocytes (×10^6/l)	1887 ± 664	2300 ± 430	<0.001
Vitamin B$_{12}$ (pg/ml)	871 ± 793	616 ± 614	NS
Serum folate (ng/ml)	6.66 ± 3.34	9.53 ± 5.14	0.001
Red-cell folate (ng/ml)	420 ± 300	484 ± 163	NS
Erythrocyte-transketolase activity*	16.6 ± 6.8	15.8 ± 6.5	NS

EtOH, ethanol; *percentage difference in enzymatic activity with and without the addition of thiamine pyrophosphate (TPP effect). NS, not significant.

in the abdomen, the waist:hip ratio should also measured in these patients. Overall nutrition may be assessed in terms of the proportion of actual to ideal weight and the body mass index. The lean body mass may be calculated from the creatinine–height index or the circumference of the upper non-dominant arm and the thickness of the tricipital skin fold. The muscular area of the arm may also be calculated from these two last parameters and is an estimation of the skeletal muscle mass (protein reserve). The fatty area of the arm may be calculated from the tricipital skin fold and it is an estimation of the total body fat (energy reserve). Although arm muscle and fat areas may be better indicators of nutrition than tricipital skin fold thickness and mid-arm circumference, it may be unnecessary to use upper-arm muscle and fat areas for clinical purposes (Lieber, 1997).

The following laboratory parameters should also be measured in each case: haemoglobin, total lymphocytes, albumin, transferrin, prealbumin and retinol-binding protein. Other interesting laboratory tests are serum electrolytes, liver enzymes, bilirubin, blood urea nitrogen, creatinine, glucose, uric acid, cholesterol and triglycerides. Other authors include an evaluation of cellular immune function made from the response to multiple skin tests, but in our experience these tests are not specific (Colditz et al., 1991; Blackburn et al., 1977; Bishop et al., 1981).

On the other hand, lack of specific nutrients (vitamins and minerals) may be observed in chronic alcoholics. Specific vitamin, mineral and trace element levels may easily be measured in serum/plasma and red cells. This is extremely unsatisfactory, providing only indirect evidence of nutritional balance. The main vitamins that should be evaluated in chronic alcoholics are folate, pyridoxine, thiamine, nicotinic acid, riboflavin, pantothenic acid, biotin and vitamins A, B$_{12}$, C, D, E and K. Finally, chronic alcoholics may also present mineral deficiencies, such as in zinc, magnesium and selenium.

Classification of Malnutrition

The main types of malnutrition in Western countries are marasmus (*caloric malnutrition*) and kwashiorkor-like conditions (*protein malnutrition*). Patients are considered to have caloric malnutrition if their actual weight is less than 80% of the ideal weight or if the calculated lean body mass is more than 10% below the normal value. Patients are considered to be affected by protein malnutrition when three or more of the following parameters are diminished: total lymphocytes, haemoglobin, transferrin, albumin, prealbumin and retinol-binding protein. Diagnosis of mixed malnutrition should be made when tests show both caloric and protein malnutrition. Finally, chronic alcoholics may present a lack of specific nutrients (vitamins or minerals) (see Lieber, 1997, for review).

Prevalence and Severity of Malnutrition in Chronic Alcoholics

Caloric and Protein Malnutrition

The prevalence and severity of malnutrition in chronic alcoholics depend on the diagnostic criteria used, age, ethnic composition, socioeconomic status and underlying diseases of the subjects included in the study. Thus, most published nutritional studies have reported a high proportion of malnutrition in patients with alcoholic liver disease (Chawla et al., 1989). However, these studies have used vitamin deficiency or low measurements of serum albumin as the main indices for diagnosing malnutrition. These measurements are inappropriate to assess nutritional status in the presence of liver disease because the liver plays a major role in vitamin and protein metabolism. Therefore, measurement of serum albumin, prealbumin, retinol-binding protein, transferrin and lymphocyte counts are not reliable indicators of nutritional status in the presence of chronic liver disease. Using anthropometry, in another study with 132 patients with chronic liver disease, only 2% showed a weight index below the 80th percentile and 1% were between the 80th and 90th percentiles. However, 19% had reduced energy reserves (determined by arm fat area) and 35% had reduced protein reserves (determined by arm muscular area). Thus, a significant number of patients with chronic liver disease, irrespective of the aetiology, are malnourished (Thuluvath & Triger, 1994).

The prevalence of malnourished alcoholics also depends on the social levels of the subjects included in the study. Goldsmith et al. (1983) detected protein-calorie malnutrition in only 8% of upper-middle class alcoholics. Other studies have demonstrated that chronic alcoholics have body weights equal to or even higher than their ideal body weight.

In another study of an ethnically, socially and geographically homogeneous group of 250 chronic alcoholics (mean age, 41 ± 11 years), whose sole motivation for seeking medical attention was their desire to rid themselves of alcohol dependence, all the patients studied had stable social and employment histories and supportive relationships with members of their families, who usually accompanied them to the clinic. They were drawn from the middle socioeconomic class, with no indigents included in the study.

The dietary histories of these chronic alcoholics showed adequate nutrition. Slight but significant differences were observed in the anthropometric parameters between alcoholics and controls (Table 11.1). However, only 25 (10%) alcoholics showed evidence of energy (calorie) malnutrition, 15 (6%) of protein malnutrition and 6 (2%) of mixed malnutrition. In the univariate analysis, caloric-malnourished alcoholic patients were older, had a more prolonged history of alcoholism and a higher total lifetime dose of ethanol consumption, reported lower calorie intake (ethanol excluded) and showed a higher prevalence of peripheral neuropathy than well-nourished alcoholics (Table 10.2). However, in the multi-

Table 10.2   Risk factors for caloric malnutrition in chronic alcoholics

	Malnourished (n = 31)	Well-nourished (n = 219)	Univariate p	Multivariate p
Age (years)	47.7 ± 9.2	40.9 ± 9.7	0.007	–
Duration of intake (years)	28.2 ± 11.3	20.9 ± 9.8	0.015	–
Daily ethanol intake (g)	238 ± 92	232 ± 101	NS	–
TLDE (kg/kg)	45.4 ± 13.7	23.7 ± 13.3	0.001	0.0001
Dietary intake* (kcal/day)	1120 ± 157	1653 ± 237	0.001	0.0229

TLDE, total lifetime dose of ethanol. *Daily calorie intake (ethanol excluded).

Table 10.3   Nutritional data in chronic alcoholics with and without ethanol-related diseases

	Alcoholics with complications (n = 151)	Alcoholics without complications (n = 99)	p
Ideal body weight (%)	95.5 + 19.7	103.0 ± 14.8	<0.01
Tricipital skin fold thickness (cm)	0.81 ± 0.36	1.10 ± 0.38	<0.001
Arm circumference (cm)	24.6 ± 3.6	27.5 ± 2.8	<0.001
Arm muscle circumference (cm)	22.1 ± 3.0	24.1 ± 2.2	<0.001
Arm muscle area (cm^2)	39.7 ± 11.1	46.6 ± 8.5	<0.001
Arm fat area (cm^2)	8.5 ± 4.2	11.5 ± 4.3	<0.001
Lean body mass (kg)	48.2 ± 5.7	51.5 ± 5.5	<0.001
Total protein (g/l)	69.5 ± 7.6	70.2 ± 6.1	NS
Albumin (g/l)	38.2 ± 7.2	41.2 ± 6.8	<0.01
Transferrin (mg/dl)	215 ± 69	246 ± 52	<0.01
Prealbumin (mg/dl)	23.3 ± 13.8	30.3 ± 12.5	<0.001
Retinol-binding protein (mg/dl)	4.14 ± 2.62	5.17 ± 2.29	<0.001
Haemoglobin (g/l)	142 ± 17	143 ± 20	NS
Lymphocytes (×10^6/l)	1776 ± 643	2108 ± 720	NS
Vitamin B$_{12}$ (pg/ml)	892 ± 693	774 ± 645	NS
Serum folate (ng/ml)	5.66 ± 3.74	7.93 ± 3.64	<0.001
Red-cell folate (ng/ml)	403 ± 199	453 ± 414	NS
Erythrocyte-transketolase activity*	15.6 ± 6.1	16.1 ± 6.6	NS

*Percentage difference in enzymatic activity with and without the addition of thiamine pyrophosphate (TPP effect). NS, not significant.

variate analysis, the only two independent risk factors in the development of energy malnutrition were the total lifetime dose of ethanol and daily calorie intake. On the other hand, the independent risk factors for developing protein malnutrition were the total lifetime dose of ethanol, daily ethanol intake and the presence of cirrhosis ($p < 0.01$, all) (Nicolas et al., 1993).

Among these patients, ethanol-related diseases were ruled out and alcoholic cirrhosis was diagnosed in 20 cases (9%), skeletal myopathy in 117 (48%), dilated cardiomyopathy in 20 (9%) and peripheral neuropathy in 41 (16%). Patients with ethanol-related diseases exhibited significantly lower nutritional parameters than alcoholics without complications (Table 10.3). In fact, alcoholics without ethanol-related diseases did not show nutritional deficiencies compared to the control group. It is difficult to compare these results with other reports in which hospitalized patients, alcoholics with severe complications, older subjects or indigents have been included. However, the group of alcoholics studied may be more representative of patients that the practising physician usually encounters (Estruch et al., 1993).

In summary, malnutrition is not as frequent as previously thought in middle socioeconomic class alcoholics, but it should be suspected in alcoholics who have consumed high amounts of ethanol or present ethanol-related diseases.

Lack of Specific Nutrients

Several studies have reported deficiencies in essential nutrients, including vitamins A, B_1, B_2, B_6, C and E. Vitamin B_{12} and folate may also be deficient, but B_{12} deficiency is relatively uncommon in chronic alcoholics and levels may even be raised. The percentage of chronic alcoholics with a reduction of these vitamins varies from 6% to 80% in different studies. However, more recent studies of heavy drinkers have showed only decreased serum levels of folic acid and vitamin E. It is particularly interesting that none of the parenterally administered vitamins, which are commonly prescribed for alcoholics during detoxification (ascorbic acid, nicotinamide, pyridoxine, riboflavine and thiamine) are found to be reduced in alcoholics compared to controls (Cook et al., 1991; Glória et al., 1997).

Serum homocysteine concentrations have been shown to be a sensitive functional indicator of intracellular folate, vitamin B_{12} and vitamin B_6 status. In concordance with the reduction in levels of red blood cell folate concentrations observed in chronic alcoholics, mean serum homocysteine is twice as high in alcoholics compared to controls. In recent years, there has been a growing interest in mild elevations of plasma homocysteine because of its association with the increased risk of occlusive vascular disease (Cravo et al., 1996).

On the other hand, studies performed in subjects who consumed different amounts of alcohol reported significantly lower plasma concentrations of vitamin E, ascorbic acid and selenium in alcoholics compared to non-drinkers. These results were associated with a significant increase in serum malondialdehyde, a marker of oxidative stress. Thus, chronic alcoholics show high plasma oxidative stress, which may contribute to the development of some ethanol-related diseases (Lecomte et al., 1994).

Deficiency in trace elements has also been reported in chronic alcoholics, including magnesium, zinc and selenium. Blood lead has been found to be elevated in chronic alcoholics, particularly in those who preferentially drink wine (Ringstad et al., 1993).

Nevertheless, despite all these considerations, alcoholics still represent the largest group of patients with treatable nutritional disorders in Western countries. Management of alcohol-related nutritional deficiencies should include identification of high-risk individuals and result in improving health status and reducing morbidity and mortality. Vitamin administration, mainly parenteral thiamine, is recommended in all chronic alcoholics who have consumed large amounts of ethanol and/or show neurological manifestations (see below).

Malnutrition and Ethanol-related Diseases

Malnutrition has been implicated in the pathogenesis and prognosis of several ethanol-related diseases. Currently, nobody questions the nutritional basis of some ethanol-related diseases, such as Wernicke–Korsakoff syndrome, pellagra, nutritional amblyopia, cerebellar degeneration and some haematological abnormalities. The relationship between alcoholic dementia or alcoholic peripheral neuropathy is more controversial. With respect to alcoholic liver disease, although a direct hepatotoxic effect has been demonstrated on the liver in humans and animals (primate), nutritional deficiencies also have an important role in the development of liver cirrhosis. Finally, alcoholic myopathy and cardiomyopathy have been related to a direct toxic effect on skeletal and heart muscle fibres, respectively, without requiring an additional nutritional deficiency.

On the other hand, malnutrition has been demonstrated to be an independent risk factor for the prediction of operative mortality in alcoholic patients undergoing major surgery. Nutritional status also determines the survival in patients with alcoholic hepatitis and in patients with chronic liver disease. Short- and long-term studies have shown that nutritional supplements may improve survival in patients with chronic liver disease. Thus, malnutrition also seems to be an important prognostic factor in patients with ethanol-related disease.

Alcoholic Liver Disease

Since the earliest clinical descriptions of alcoholic cirrhosis were primarily in derelict alcoholics with severe malnutrition, it was held that liver damage was due to altered nutrition rather than alcohol *per se*. In fact, alcoholic cirrhosis was known by the term "fatty nutritional cirrhosis". Experimental studies have shown that rats fed choline–methionine-deficient diets and 15% ethanol in drinking water, developed fatty liver. In 1941, Patek & Post (1941) studied chronic alcoholics with liver cirrhosis and severe malnutrition. In these patients, fed a hypercaloric and hyperproteic diet and with concomitant administration of modest amounts of alcohol, recovery from alcohol liver injury was not impaired. This fact suggested that ethanol was not hepatotoxic *per se* when the patient was correctly fed. In another study (Summerskill et al., 1957), concomitant to the administration of 160 g of ethanol a day, some patients received a high-protein diet and others a low-protein diet. Those who were fed a high-protein diet showed a steady clinical improvement, but no significant changes in the histological parameters of liver injury. In contrast, the patients who received the low-protein diet showed neither changes nor slight deterioration in liver function tests nor histological changes. Similarly, other researchers observed that, once the nutritional status of alcoholics had become normal, the administration of ethanol in doses of up to 300 g a day did not impede the recovery of liver injury.

On the other hand, epidemiological studies have shown a close correlation between ethanol intake and mortality due to cirrhosis. In experimental studies, alcoholics and non-alcoholic volunteers developed fatty liver despite adequate dietary intake. Likewise, baboons fed with the Lieber–DeCarli diet developed the entire spectrum of alcoholic liver disease, i.e. fatty liver, alcoholic hepatitis and even cirrhosis. However, examination of these experimental models revealed that the animals were actually malnourished because they had ingested an inadequate intake of macro- and micronutrients or both in diets that were incomplete or unbalanced (Rao & Larkin, 1997).

Other observations in non-alcoholic subjects have also allowed malnutrition and liver disease to be linked. Patients who have undergone small bowel bypass for the treatment of obesity develop liver lesions that are indistinguishable from alcoholic liver injury. Fatty liver, acute "alcoholic" hepatitis and even liver cirrhosis have been observed in these patients. Furthermore, liver damage improves by either restoration of intestinal continuity or parenteral hyperalimentation (Kishi et al., 1996).

Several studies have investigated the influence of the diet and nutritional status in the development of alcoholic liver disease. In a study which included 309 hospitalized alcoholics, patients with cirrhosis reported a significantly lower intake of calories and proteins than patients without cirrhosis. In two Veterans Administration Cooperative Studies that enrolled 666 patients, an association was found between the degree of protein-calorie malnutrition and the severity of illness and mortality. In addition, since protein-calorie malnutrition in patients with alcoholic hepatitis correlated significantly with mortality, the authors concluded that malnutrition has prognostic significance in alcoholic hepatitis and suggested that nutritional therapy may have a beneficial role in the management of alcohol-induced liver damage (Mendenhall et al., 1995). Several major controlled studies have been performed on this issue and the predominant conclusions were that nutrition therapy improves nutritional status and abnormal liver tests, but does not decrease early mortality. However, since voluntary food intake is likely to be poor in patients with moderate to severe alcoholic hepatitis, it would seem essential to ensure that all these patients are adequately nourished, whenever possible, by the oral and enteral route. If difficulties are encountered in meeting requirements, then a proportion should be given parenterally. However, it is important to remember that the long-term outcome of these patients is determined largely by their ability to maintain abstinence from alcohol and that a small, carefully selected subgroup of very sick patients may benefit, at least in the short term, from treatment with corticosteroids (De la Maza et al., 1995).

In addition, in a study performed in our institution, 85 chronic alcoholics were divided into three groups (normal liver, steatosis and alcoholic hepatitis). No differences were observed between the three groups in the amount and duration of ethanol intake. However, patients with alcoholic hepatitis reported a significantly lower intake of carbohydrates and proteins (Figure 10.1) than patients with normal liver or steatosis. In addition, diets followed by patients contained vitamins, minerals and oligo-elements in amounts below the recommended requirements (Table 10.4). On the other hand, 78% and 22% of patients with normal liver exhibited data of mild or moderate malnutrition, respectively. Thus, mal-

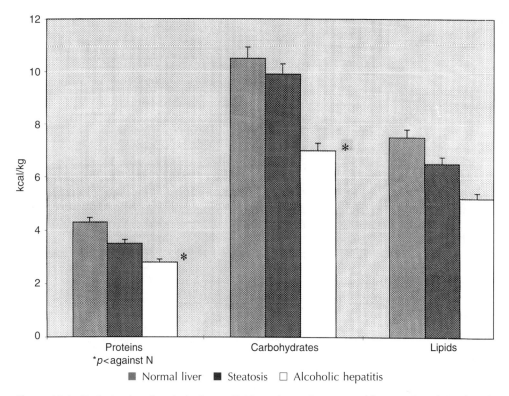

Figure 10.1 Daily intake of carbohydrates, lipids and proteins reported by a series of 85 chronic alcoholics with different types of liver disease

Table 10.4 Daily intake of vitamins in a cohort of chronic alcoholics classified according to their liver disease

Vitamins	Daily requirements	Normal ($n = 50$)	Steatosis ($n = 25$)	Alcoholic hepatitis ($n = 20$)	Cirrhosis ($n = 50$)
A	5000 U	1950 ± 205	2062 ± 397	1976 ± 354	2105 ± 1234
B_1	1.2 mg	5.9 ± 3.2	7.3 ± 4.1	4.2 ± 2.9	7.2 ± 3.8
B_2	1.2–1.6 mg	1.2 ± 0.2	1.2 ± 0.3	1.1 ± 0.2	1.2 ± 0.3
Niacin	13–16 mg	21.6 ± 5.3	22.5 ± 7.4	14.6 ± 5.3	21.4 ± 7.1
B_6	2–2.2 mg	2.4 ± 0.3	2.1 ± 0.5	1.9 ± 0.4	2.3 ± 0.4
B_{12}	3 mg	3.6 ± 0.4	2.8 ± 0.5	2.5 ± 0.4	2.4 ± 0.2
Biotin	100–200 μg	133 ± 15	119 ± 21	112 ± 19	105 ± 12
C	60 mg	89 ± 17	97 ± 18	87 ± 24	119 ± 21
D	5 μg	0.89 ± 0.15	0.89 ± 0.18	0.88 ± 0.17	0.74 ± 0.13
E	8–10 mg	2.4 ± 0.3	2.3 ± 0.5	2.0 ± 0.4	2.1 ± 0.3
Pantothenic acid	4–7 mg	2.6 ± 0.3	2.3 ± 0.4	2.2 ± 0.4	1.8 ± 0.2
Folic acid	400 μg	190 ± 16	189 ± 24	148 ± 24	105 ± 12

nutrition may precede the development of alcoholic liver disease and not be attributed to liver insufficiency. Although ethanol undoubtedly has a direct effect on the liver, there is compelling evidence that malnutrition may play a role in the pathogenesis of alcohol-induced damage.

Theoretically, there are a number of mechanisms by which nutrition may modify alcohol-induced liver damage. First, protein-calorie deficiency may enhance the toxicity of alcohol on the liver. Recent studies have suggested the importance of energy homeostasis, detoxification of oxygen-derived peroxides, membrane integrity and formation and elimination of the metabolites of ethanol, especially acetaldehyde. Nutrients, mainly some amino acids, are essential for the maintenance of these processes, especially when they are "stressed" by ethanol. Liver glutathione concentration decreases substantially in rats exposed to low-calorie diets. Glutathione availability and its transfer into the mitochondria seems to be vital to protect the cells from peroxidative injury. Furthermore, glutathione depends on the provision of precursor amino acids (cysteine). Peroxidation has been associated with the development of ethanol-induced hepatic fibrosis and, by contrast, administration of S-adenosyl-L-methionine, a source of cysteine for glutathione production, to baboons exposed to chronic ethanol, attenuates part of the ethanol-induced liver injury and decreases mitochondrial injury. Thus, glutathione may play a role in alcohol-induced peroxidative injury.

Glycine also has protective effects in some types of hepatic injury and some studies have emphasized the role of another antioxidant, vitamin E, especially in mitochondria. However, vitamin E supplementation during 1 year did not influence liver function tests, mortality or hospitalization rates of decompensated alcoholic cirrhosis, although serum levels on the vitamin significantly increased (Morgan, 1996). In addition, membrane integrity depends on the provision of phospholipids. In baboons fed alcohol for several years, supplementation with oral phospholipids (i.e. polyunsaturated lecithin) prevented the development of septal fibrosis.

Finally, malnutrition may limit repair of damage processes. Protein deprivation may impair repairing processes since it reduces liver protein stores, RNA and polyamines, and desegregate ribosomal protein in the rough endoplasmic reticulum.

Pancreas and Gastrointestinal Tract

The gastrointestinal tract is exposed to a high alcohol concentration from oral ingestion and also to alcohol absorbed in the blood stream. Indeed, the effects of ethanol include increased mucosal permeability, promotion of bacterial overgrowth, altered gut motility and impaired salt, water, vitamin and nutrient absorption. On the other hand, malnutrition itself may cause disturbances in the gastrointestinal tract. Thus, folate deficiency induces marked morphologic alterations of the mucosa, which are normalized after diet supplementation with folate. These changes hinder the treatment of nutritional deficiencies by oral or enteral nutrient preparations, which should be administered parenterally via to assure its efficacy.

Ethanol intake is the main risk factor for the development of acute and chronic pancreatitis in men. However, epidemiological studies have suggested that protein and fat consumption may also play a role in the pathogenesis of chronic pancreatitis. Ethanol intake combined with a high-protein, high-fat diet enhances the concentration of pancreatic enzymes, which may lead to protein precipitation in the pancreatic ducts, a key process in the development of chronic pancreatitis. By contrast, other studies have reported that patients with chronic pancreatitis consumed a low dietary intake of protein, carbohydrate and fat. Thus, the role of nutrition on the pathogenesis of chronic pancreatitis is a matter of controversy (Mezey et al., 1988).

Cardiovascular System

At one time, nutritional deficiency (especially thiamine deficit) was thought to play an essential role in the pathogenesis of ethanol-induced damage in the heart of chronic alcoholics, but clinical differences between alcoholic cardiomyopathy (low output failure) and wet beri-beri (high output failure), the lack of the former to improve with thiamine treatment and the lack of correlation with nutritional status, have led to the current view that large amounts of alcohol are toxic to the myocardium. Studies performed in the last decade have observed that the nutritional status of patients with definite alcoholic cardiomyopathy was excellent. In fact, none of these patients exhibited clinical or laboratory evidence of malnutrition. In addition, the estimated total lifetime amount of ethanol correlated inversely with ejection fraction ($r = -0.58$; $p < 0.001$) and directly with ventricular mass ($r = 0.59$; $p < 0.001$) (Urbano-Márquez et al., 1989). According to these results, poor nutrition appeared to play no part in the development of alcoholic cardiomyopathy. However, an additive effect of malnutrition contributing to the effects of ethanol may not be ruled out.

Haematological System

Haematological abnormalities, mainly anaemia and/or thrombocytopenia, have been reported in 13–62% of the chronic alcoholics admitted to a General Hospital. The aetiology of these disorders includes nutritional deficiencies, alcoholic liver disease and infections and the direct effect of ethanol on the haematological system. Malnourished alcoholics commonly present megalobastic anaemia due to folic acid deficiency and less frequently to vitamin B_{12} deficit. Folic acid deficiency is usually seen in wine, brandy or whisky drinkers, and less frequently in beer drinkers because of the high folate content of this beverage. Chronic alcoholics may also show sideroblastic changes on bone-marrow examination. These changes have been attributed to a defect in the synthesis of the group haem secondary to pyridoxine deficiency. In fact, sideroblastic changes have been reproduced in healthy volunteers who received high doses of ethanol together with a diet deficient in pyridoxine and folic acid. Finally, chronic alcoholics may present severe haemolysis secondary to hypophosphataemia, due to poor intake or urinary loss of phosphates.

Chronic alcoholics often exhibit an alteration in the number of platelets (thrombocytopenia and thrombocytosis), as well as in their function. These abnormalities may be due to a direct effect of ethanol and/or a severe folate deficiency (Lindenbaum, 1987).

Central and Peripheral Nervous System

Neurologic disorders in chronic alcoholic patients have been related to a combination of three factors: (a) the neurotoxic effects of ethanol and/or its metabolites; (b) nutritional factors (malnutrition and vitamin deficiencies); and (c) individual susceptibility, probably related to genetic predisposition. The combination of these factors explains why not everyone who consumes ethanol to an excess has neurologic complications. The neurotoxic effects of ethanol have been related to a direct toxic action of this toxin or its oxidative metabolites on the nervous system, although neurological damage has also been related to effects of the non-oxidative metabolites of ethanol (fatty-acid ethyl esters), changes in neuronal calcium channels, the effects of excitatory amino acids on N-methyl-D-aspartate (NMDA) receptors or an excessive accumulation of hydroxyl radicals. Malnutrition and vitamin deficiency may enhance the effects of ethanol on the nervous system and/or determine the development of specific nutritional disorders (e.g. Wernicke's encephalopathy) in alcoholic patients. Finally, genetic factors may also determine the susceptibility of certain alcoholics to neurologic disorders. The main neurological complications seen in chronic alcoholics and related to malnutrition and/or vitamin deficiencies are Wernicke–Korsakoff syndrome, pellagra and nutritional amblyopia. Other diseases, such as cerebellar degeneration and peripheral and autonomic neuropathies, have previously been attributed to nutritional deficiencies, but there is increasing evidence that they are due to the toxic effects of ethanol (Charness, 1993; Neiman, 1998; Nicolas et al., 1997).

Wernicke–Korsakoff Syndrome

This syndrome is characterized by an acute phase (Wernicke's encephalopathy) and a chronic phase (Korsakoff syndrome). Wernicke's encephalopathy is a common neurological disease due to a deficiency of thiamine, which is seen, although not exclusively, in chronic alcoholics. These patients suddenly present focal neurological symptoms (nystagmus, oculomotor palsies), ataxia and deterioration of consciousness. The characteristic pathological lesions occur symmetrically in the structures surrounding the aqueduct as well as in the third and fourth ventricles. The diagnosis of the disease is based on a rapid reversibility of the symptoms after thiamine administration supported by the demonstration of thiamine deficiency or the presence of characteristic lesions in pathological studies. In acute cases, MRI demonstrates an increased T_2 signal surrounding the paraventricular regions of the thalamus and hypothalamus (diencephalon) and the periaqueductal region of the midbrain (mesencephalon), consistent with the location of the pathological lesions. In subacute and chronic cases, atrophy of mammilary bodies can be identified by imaging. A high proportion of alcoholic patients recovering from Wernicke's encephalopathy maintain a selective deficit of anterograde and retrograde memory, together with an intact sensorium, known as Korsakoff's amnaestic syndrome (Estruch et al., 1998).

Thiamine is an essential co-factor for several enzymes of the nervous system, such as transketolase, α-ketoglutarate dehydrogenase, pyruvate dehydrogenase, and branched-chain α-keto acid dehydrogenase. A deficiency in thiamine produces a diffuse decrease in the use of glucose by the cerebrum. The reduction of pyruvate dehydrogenase activity determines a shift from aerobic metabolism to rapid glycolysis, a sequence similar to the events observed in hypoxic-ischaemic injury. It has been proposed that glutamic acid, an excitatory amino acid neurotransmitter, may play a role in the pathogenesis of this disorder (Reuler et al., 1985).

Pellagra

This disorder is characterized by the triad of dementia, diarrhoea and dermatitis, and has been attributed to a nicotinic acid deficiency. Neurological symptoms reported by these patients include mental retardation, recent memory loss and melancholia to psychiatric disturbance weeks or months before the development of other manifestations. Typical dermatitis is commonly absent because of the lack of sun exposure in most alcoholics.

Nutritional Amblyopia

This disease is also known as alcohol-tobacco amblyopia and is diagnosed primarily in chronic alcoholics. It involves retrobulbar neuritis affecting maculo-papillary fibres and has been related to a deficiency in thiamine, vitamin B_{12} and riboflavin.

Cerebellar Degeneration

Almost half of alcoholics show degeneration of Purkinje cells in the cerebellar cortex and especially in the midline cerebellar structures (anterior and superior vermis). However, the clinical and neurological signs are not always in agreement. Asymptomatic alcoholics showing cerebellar atrophic findings on CT scans or MRIs have been described. It is unclear whether these patients have a subclinical cerebellar syndrome or will develop symptoms. Only a small proportion of chronic alcoholics complain of ataxia, which affects mainly gait and less frequently the limbs and trunk.

The similarity of the cerebellar lesions with those observed in Wernicke encephalopathy may suggest that the former could be related to thiamine deficiency. However, there is some evidence to suggest that they may be due to the toxic effects of ethanol. Thus, a long-term intake of alcohol is needed to cause cerebellar damage. On the other hand, a study which includes a morphometric analysis of MRI scans reported that malnourished alcoholics showed a significantly greater cerebellar shrinkage compared to well-nourished alcoholics. In addition, in multivariate analysis, ethanol intake and nutritional status were independent risk factors related to the degree of cerebellar shrinkage. Thus, alcoholic cerebellar degeneration seems to be related to both ethanol intake and malnutrition (Johnson-Greene et al., 1997).

Peripheral and Autonomic Neuropathy

Alcoholic neuropathy is a gradually progressive disorder due to the involvement of sensory, motor and autonomic nerves. The clinical symptoms are typically symmetrical and affect mainly the lower limbs. Autonomic disturbances include orthostatic hypotension, diarrhoea, impotence and sweating disorders. Although these symptoms are less common, their presence has been associated with increased mortality.

Alcoholic neuropathy has also been attributed to associated malnutrition or a specific lack of thiamine. However, studies performed in experimental animals and in chronic alcoholics have suggested that this peripheral neuropathy may be secondary to the toxic effects of ethanol or its metabolites. In fact, the only risk factor for the development of peripheral neuropathy in chronic alcoholics was the total lifetime amount of alcohol. Patients with peripheral neuropathy exhibited significantly lower anthropometric parameters than their counterparts, but the former had also drunk significantly higher doses of ethanol than the latter. Thus, ethanol seems to have a profound direct effect on the peripheral nervous system, but further studies are require to delimit the exact role of malnutrition in the development of alcoholic peripheral neuropathy (Monforte et al., 1995).

ALCOHOL AND INFECTIOUS DISEASES

Because alcohol can exert potent suppressive effects on the immune system, the susceptibility of alcohol misusers to a wide spectrum of infections is significant and poses an important public health problem. Among these, pulmonary infections have the strongest and best-documented association with alcohol abuse (see Cook, 1998 for review).

Diseases Related to Immune Deficiency

Alcohol abuse has been associated with an increase in infectious diseases caused by pathogens and opportunistic microorganisms. The frequency and severity of infections are so pronounced among alcoholics that a conviction has long existed among physicians that alcohol itself directly inhibits the body's specific immune mechanisms. The evidence varies from clinical observations that alcoholics have increased susceptibility to infection to laboratory studies showing depressed *in vitro* function of immune effector cells in the presence of ethanol. However, the frequent presence of data of malnutrition, liver disease or other concomitant processes in chronic alcoholic with infectious diseases makes it difficult to attribute susceptibility to infection to ethanol intake only. On the other hand, the results of *in vitro* studies, in which it is easy to control these confounding factors, may not be extrapolated to a clinical setting (Fernández-Sola et al., 1995; MacGregor, 1986).

Pneumonia

The connection between alcohol abuse and pneumonia has been recognized for centuries, considering that alcohol is perhaps the most potent predisposing factor to lobar pneumonia. Alcoholism induces an increased susceptibility to more severe pneumococcal pneumonia, with a higher incidence of subsequent bacteriaemia and fatality rates reaching >50% in some studies. In addition, numerous investigators have reported evidence that alcoholics are at increased risk of pneumonia caused by other microorganisms, such as *Klebsiella pneumoniae* and *Haemophilus influenzae*, and that they are prone to aspiration lung abscesses. More recent well-designed case-control studies have confirmed that high alcohol intake is the main risk factor for developing community-acquired pneumonia in middle-aged people. Response therapy is often suboptimal in these patients, who have increased mortality rates even with appropriate antibiotic therapy and modern intensive care facilities. Thus, alcoholism also confers a worse prognosis in patients with community-acquired pneumonia, who should be treated with broad-spectrum antibiotics for a longer period of time. Another striking consistent characteristic of pneumonia in alcoholics is the high rate of recurrence. In a study of 158 patients admitted to Johns Hopkins Hospital with recurrent pneumonia, the most common predisposing condition was alcoholism, present in 40% of the patients. Thus, from a clinical point of view, there is no doubt that alcohol abusers are more susceptible to bacterial pneumonia than normal subjects, regardless of the presence of malnutrition or alcoholic liver disease (Fernández-Sola et al., 1995).

Tuberculosis

Chronic alcoholic patients also show an increase in the incidence and severity of pulmonary tuberculosis. Cohorts of alcoholics followed for many years have been found to have a prevalence of tuberculosis of 15–200 times the control populations. The presence of human immunodeficiency virus (HIV) disease in some alcoholic patients has also increased the prevalence of tuberculosis in this population. However, even when this fact is taken into account, the increased morbidity and mortality due to tuberculosis in alcohol abusers persists. Since compliance with treatment is low in a high proportion of alcoholics, implementation of institutional intervention programmes may be needed. The rise of drug-resistant strains of *Mycobacterium tuberculosis* in immunocompromised individuals, including alcoholics, is of increasing national and world-wide concern (MacGregor & Louria, 1997).

Human Immune Deficiency Virus (HIV) Infection

The interactions between alcohol abuse and HIV infection are well recognized, because there is a high prevalence of alcoholism in the HIV-positive population, and alcohol ingestion increases the risk-taking behaviour for acquisition of HIV. The subsequent question that has arisen is what role, if any, alcohol plays in either the spread of HIV or in the progression of symptoms in those already infected. It has been suggested that excessive alcohol consumption potentially influences the progression of HIV disease. Some experimental evidence has suggested that ethanol may act as a co-factor in HIV disease. Ethanol selectively impairs the *in vitro* antigenic proliferative response to HIV env–gag peptide and natural killer activity by lymphocytes from acquired immunodeficiency syndrome (AIDS) patients; this situation therefore impairs the ability to set up a host response against HIV-infected cells. In another *in vitro* study, HIV replication has been shown to increase when ethanol is added to HIV-infected cells. On the hand, alcohol-induced liver disease increases the expression of proinflammatory cytokines, which have also been implicated as promoters of HIV replication. Thus, all these experimental data suggest that alcohol consumption may alter the host defence system in a way that might adversely influence HIV disease progression. In respect to human studies, a heavy alcohol abuser was identified as one who rapidly progresses to AIDS shortly after seroconversion. Other human studies have shown an improvement in CD4$^+$ cell counts after alcohol withdrawal in HIV alcoholic patients However, the results of clinical studies have been less conclusive. It has also been reported in a group of HIV-positive intravenous drug abusers, followed for up to 5 years, that abnormalities of T cell subsets were significantly greater in heavy alcohol users than in non-users or light users. However, since the results of other clinical studies have been inconclusive regarding the acceleration of HIV disease in drinkers, the interaction between alcohol and HIV disease remains an attractive issue for research (Bagby et al., 1998).

Viral Hepatitis

Several studies have evaluated the presence of antibodies against hepatitis B virus (HBV) and hepatitis C virus (HCV) in chronic alcoholics. Careful studies have concluded that after correction for the most important non-alcohol-related risk factors for HBV and HCV (intravenous drug abuse and homosexual and bisexual behaviours), there was no increased incidence of HBV in pure alcoholics but an increased incidence of 10% for HCV was still present in alcoholics. This may indicate increased susceptibility to HCV in alcoholics. On the other hand, it is important to remember that hepatitis-positive alcoholics have two diseases (alcoholism and viral hepatitis) that may have additive or synergistic effects on the development of liver disease, and both conditions may affect the immune system to produce immunodeficiency (Imperial, 1999).

Other Infections

Alcohol abusers are also more susceptible than normal patients to septicaemia from pneumonia or other sources of infection (urinary tract infections, bacterial peritonitis and biliary infections), as well as to several less common infections, such as lung abscess, empyema, spontaneous bacterial peritonitis, diphtheria, cellulitis and meningitis due to Gram-negative organisms, e.g. *Listeria monocytogenes* (MacGregor & Louria, 1997).

Mechanisms of Immunodeficiency in Chronic Alcoholism

Factors that contribute to the high incidence of infection among alcoholics include dulled mental function, breakdown of local protective barriers, aspiration, environmental exposure, liver disease and malnutrition, as well as the toxic direct effect of ethanol on the immune system. Both malnutrition and liver cirrhosis are known to adversely affect the body's immune response and it is often difficult to ascribe a specific infection to the direct effect of ethanol on immune system. Currently, malnutrition is a common form of acquired immunodeficiency. Malnourished patients generally show a depression in phagocytic function and a reduction in total lymphocytes, circulating T lymphocytes and relative CD8 lymphocytes. In addition, deficiencies in riboflavin, thiamine, pantothenic acid, folic acid and vitamin C are associated with increased susceptibility to infection. Finally, zinc deficiency may produce an impairment in cell-mediated immunity and increase susceptibility to infection. Liver disease, mainly cirrhosis, is another cause of immunodeficiency in chronic alcoholics. However, since the prevalence of liver disease is so high in chronic alcoholic patients, it is really difficult to differentiate between the effects of liver disease and those of ethanol itself on the immune system. The main abnormalities of the immune system observed in chronic alcoholics with and without liver disease are the following:

Serum Immunoglobulin Elevations and Tissue Deposits

Chronic alcoholics frequently have greatly increased serum immunoglobulins. Typically, IgA is elevated in alcoholics with and without liver disease, IgG is increased in patients with alcoholic liver disease and IgM in those with active liver disease, such as alcoholic hepatitis. In addition, tissue deposits of IgA are often observed in these patients, especially in skin, liver and kidney. However, despite the elevated immunoglobulin levels, chronic alcoholics are immunodeficient, since this increase is due to an abnormal regulation of the synthesis of antibodies.

Reduced Cell-mediated Immunity

Lymphocytes obtained from alcoholics show a reduction in their growth response to stimulation by several different agents (mitogens). This fact explains the reduced response of alcoholics to tuberculin and fungal skin tests (delayed hypersensitivity).

Reduced Lymphocyte Numbers, Alteration of Subsets and Persistent Activation

Alcoholics with liver disease typically have lymphopenia, depending on the stage and severity of disease. Alcoholics without liver disease have normal numbers of lymphocytes in peripheral blood. In addition, alterations in the percentage of various lymphocyte types (subsets) are frequently observed in chronic alcoholics. Thus, these patients show a normal or elevated ratio of CD4$^+$:CD8$^+$ T cells, together with an increase in the percentage of cells displaying the histocompatibility molecule MCH-II, and other changes in adhesion molecules that fit under the heading of "persistent activation" of T cells. B cells (antibody-producing lymphocytes) in alcoholics without liver disease tend to be normal or slightly reduced, but they are often significantly reduced in alcoholics with liver disease. Abnormal interactions between T and B cells may also explain inappropriate immunoglobulin production and other defects of immune regulation in alcoholics. Natural killer cells also display reduced functional activity in alcoholics.

Increased Numbers and Activation of Monocytes and Neutrophils

Neutrophils, one of the first line of defence against bacteria, are often increased in alcoholic hepatitis, both in peripheral blood and in damaged liver. Other abnormalities of neutrophils in the presence of alcohol have been described, including reduced emigration into sites of inflammation and decreased bacterial killing. Alterations of monocytes and macrophages have been described in chronic alcoholics.

Other Abnormalities

Finally, alcohol have been shown to affect production of the regulatory molecules called cytokines. Alcoholics with liver disease present serum increase levels of cytokines, interleukins (IL-1, IL-6 and IL-8) and tumor necrosis factor alpha (TNFα) (Cook, 1998).

KEY WORKS AND SUGGESTIONS FOR FURTHER READING

Lieber, C.S. (1997).   Ethanol metabolism, cirrhosis and alcoholism. *Clinica Chimica Acta*, **257**, 59–84.

> One of the latest reviews on the metabolism of ethanol and its relation to nutritional deficiencies observed in chronic alcoholism.

Estruch, R., Nicolas, J.M., Villegas, E., Yungué, A. & Urbano-Marquez, A. (1993).   Relationship between ethanol-related diseases and nutriitonal status in chronicaly alcoholic men. *Alcohol and Alcoholism*, **28**, 543–550.

> One of the largest and most complete studies on nutritional status of chronic alcoholic patients. This and other recent studies demonstrated that alcoholics from the middle class do not show evidence of malnutrition, and alcohol-related diseases in these alcoholics appear to be due to an accumulative toxic effect of ethanol.

MacGregor, R.R. (1986).   Alcohol and immune defence. *Journal of the American Medical Association*, **256**, 1474–1479.

> A classical review of the relationship between alcohol and immune defence. Although published in 1986, it will be useful as an introduction to the issue.

Cook, R.T. (1998).   Alcohol abuse, alcoholism and damage to the immune system—a review. *Alcoholism: Clinical and Experimental Research*, **22**, 1927–1942.

> An interesting and extensive review of the effects of alcohol abuse on the immune system leading to immunodeficiency and autoimmunity.

REFERENCES

Atwater, W.O. & Rosa, E.B. (1899). *Description of New Respiratory Calorimeter and Experiments on the Conservation of Energy in the Human Body.* Washington, DC: US Government Printing Office.

Bagby, G.J., Stoltz, D.A., Zhang, P., Bohm, R.P. & Nelson, S. (1998). Simian immunodeficiency virus, infection, alcohol and host defense. *Alcoholism: Clinical and Experimental Research*, **22**, 193S–195S.

Bishop, C.W., Bowen, P.E. & Ritchey, S.J. (1981). Norms for nutritional assessment of American adult by upper anthropometry. *American Journal of Clinical Nutrition*, **34**, 2530–2539.

Blackburn, G.L., Bistrain, B.R., Maini, B.S., Schlamm, B.A. & Smith, M.F. (1981). Nutritional and metabolic assessment of the hospitalised patient. *Journal of Parenteral Nutrition*, **1**, 11–22.

Charness, M.E. (1993). Brain lesions in alcoholics. *Alcoholism: Clinical and Experimental Research*, **17**, 2–11.

Chawla, R.K., Wolf, S.C., Kutner, M.H. & Bonkovsky, H.L. (1989). Choline may be an essential nutrient in malnourished patients with cirrhosis. *Gastroenterology*, **97**, 1514–1520.

Colditz, G.A., Giovannucci, E., Rimm, E.B. et al. (1991). Alcohol intake in relation to diet and obesity in women and men. *American Journal of Clinical Nutrition*, **54**, 49–55.

Cook, C.C.H., Walden, R.J., Graham, B.R., Gillham, C., Davies, S. & Prichard, B.N.C. (1991). Trace element and vitamin deficiency in alcoholic and control subjects. *Alcohol and Alcoholism*, **26**, 541–548.

Cook, R.T. (1998). Alcohol abuse, alcoholism, and damage to the immune system—A review. *Alcoholism: Clinical and Experimental Research*, **22**, 1927–1942.

Cravo, M.L., Glória, L.M., Selhub, J.S. et al. (1996). Hyperhomocysteinemia in chronic alcoholism: correlation with folate, vitamin B_{12} and vitamin B_6 status. *American Journal of Clinical Nutrition*, **63**, 220–224.

De la Maza, M.P., Petermann, M., Bunout, D. & Hirsch, S. (1995). Effects of long-term vitamin E supplementation in alcoholic cirrhotics. *Journal of the American College of Nutrition*, **14**, 192–196.

Estruch, R., Bono, G., Laine, P. et al. (1998). Brain imaging in alcoholism. *European Journal of Neurology*, **5**, 119–135.

Estruch, R., Nicolas, J.M., Villegas, E., Junqué, A. & Urbano-Márquez, A. (1993). Relationship between ethanol-related diseases and nutritional status in chronically alcoholic men. *Alcohol and Alcoholism*, **28**, 543–550.

Fernández-Sola, J., Junque, A., Estruch, R., Monforte, R., Torres, A. & Urbano-Márquez, A. (1995). High alcohol intake as a risk and prognostic factor for community-acquired pneumonia. *Archives of Internal Medicine*, **155**, 1649–1654.

Glória, L., Cravo, M., Camilo, M.E. et al. (1997). Nutritional deficiencies in chronic alcoholics: relation to dietary intake and alcohol consumption. *American Journal of Gastroenterology*, **92**, 485–489.

Goldsmith, R.H., Iber, F.L. & Miller, P.A. (1983). Nutritional status of alcoholics of different socio-economic class. *Journal of the American College of Nutrition*, **2**, 215–220.

Imperial, J.C. (1999). Natural history of chronic hepatitis B and C. *Journal of Gastroenterology and Hepatology*, (Australia), **14**, 1S–5S.

Johnson-Greene, D., Adams, K.M., Gilman, S. et al. (1997). Impaired upper limb coordination in alcoholic cerebellar degeneration. *Archives of Neurology*, **54**, 436–439.

Kishi, M., Maeyama, S., Koike, J., Asida, Y., Yoshida, H. & Uchikoshi, T. (1996). Correlation between intrasinusoidal neutrophilic infiltration and ceroid-lipofuscinosis in alcoholic liver fibrosis with and without fatty change: clinicopathological comparison with nutritional fatty liver. *Alcoholism: Clinical and Experimental Research*, **20**, 366A–370A.

Lecomte, E., Herberth, B., Pirollet, P. et al. (1994). Effect of alcohol consumption on blood oxidant nutrients and oxidative stress indicators. *American Journal of Clinical Nutrition*, **60**, 255–261.

Lieber, C.S. (1997). Ethanol metabolism, cirrhosis and alcoholism. *Clinica Chimica Acta*, **257**, 59–84.

Lindenbaum, J. (1987). Haematologic complications of alcohol abuse. *Seminars Liver Dis* **7**, 169–178.

MacGregor, R.R. & Louria, D.B. (1997). Alcohol and infection. *Current Clinical Topics in Infectious Disease*, **17**, 291–315.

MacGregor, R.R. (1986). Alcohol and immune defense. *Journal of the American Medical Association*, **256**, 1474–1479.

Mendenhall, C., Roselle, G.A., Gratside, P., Mortiz, T. & The Veterans Administration Cooperative Study Group, 119 and 275. (1995). Relationship of protein calorie malnutrition to alcoholic liver disease: a re-examination of data from two veterans administration cooperative studies. *Alcoholism: Clinical and Experimental Research*, **19**, 635–641.

Mezey, E., Kolman, C.J., Diehl, A.M., Mitchell, M.C. & Herlong, H.F. (1988). Alcohol and dietary intake in the development of chronic pancreatitis and liver disease in alcoholism. *American Journal of Clinical Nutrition*, **48**, 148–151.

Monforte, R., Estruch, R., Valls-Solé, J., Nicolas, J.M., Villalta, J. & Urbano-Márquez, A. (1995). Autonomic and peripheral neuropathies in patients with chronic alcoholism. A dose-related toxic effect of alcohol. *Archives of Neurology*, **52**, 45–51.

Morgan, M.Y. (1996). The treatment of alcoholic hepatitis. *Alcohol and Alcoholism*, **31**, 117–134.

Neiman, J. (1998). Alcohol as a risk factor for brain damage: neurological aspects. *Alcoholism: Clinical Experiment Research*, **22**, 346S–351S.

Nicolas, J.M., Estruch, R., Antúnez, E., Sacanella, E. & Urbano-Márquez, A. (1993). Nutritional status in chronically alcoholic men from the middle socioeconomic class and its relation to ethanol intake. *Alcohol and Alcoholism*, **28**, 551–558.

Nicolas, J.M., Estruch, R., Salamero, M., et al. (1997). Brain impairment in well-nourished chronic alcoholics is related to ethanol intake. *Annals of Neurology*, **41**, 590–598.

Patek, A.J. & Post, J. (1941). Treatment of cirrhosis of the liver by a nutritious diet and supplements rich in vitamin B-complex. *Journal of Clinical Investigation*, **20**, 481–505.

Rao, G.A. & Larkin, E.C. (1997). Nutritional factors required for alcoholic liver disease in rats. *Journal of Nutrition*, **127**, 896S–898S.

Reuler, J.B., Girard, D.E. & Cooney, T.G. (1985). Wernicke encephalopathy. *New England Journal of Medicine*, **312**, 1035–1039.

Ringstad, J., Knutsen, S.F., Nilssen, O.R. & Thomassen, Y. (1993). A comparative study of serum selenium and vitamin E levels in a population of male risk drinkers and abstainers. a population-based matched-pair study. *Biological Trace Element Research*, **36**, 65–71.

Rumpler, W.V., Rhodes, D.G., Baer, D.J., Conway, J.M. & Seale, J.L. (1996). Energy value of moderate alcohol consumption by humans. *American Journal of Clinical Nutrition*, **64**, 108–114.

Summerskill, W.H.J., Wolfe, S.J. & Davidson, C.S. (1957). Response to alcohol in chronic alcoholics with liver disease. *Lancet*, **1**, 335–340.

Suter, P.M., Schutz, Y. & Jequier, E. (1992). The effect of ethanol on fat storage in healthy subjects. *New England Journal of Medicine*, **326**, 983–987.

Thakker, K.D. (1998). An overview of health risks and benefits of alcohol consumption. *Alcoholism: Clinical and Experimental Research*, **22**, 285S–298S.

Thuluvath, P.J. & Triger, D.R. (1994). Evaluation of nutritional status by using anthropometry in adults with alcoholic and non-alcoholic liver disease. *American Journal of Clinical Nutrition*, **60**, 269–273.

Urbano-Márquez, A., Estruch, R., Navarro-López, F., Grau, J,M., Mont, L.L. & Rubin, E. (1989). Effects of alcoholism on skeletal and cardiac muscle. *New England Journal of Medicine*, **320**, 409–415.

Chapter 11

Cardiovascular System

Arthur L. Klatsky
Kaiser Permanente Medical Center, Oakland, CA, USA

Synopsis

Disparities in the relationships between alcohol consumption and various cardiovascular conditions are now evident, with complex interrelationships between conditions. Thus, it is best to consider separately the relationships of alcohol to several disorders, as follows:

1. *The evidence continues to mount that susceptible persons may suffer heart muscle damage from chronic use of large amounts of alcohol, leading to* alcoholic cardio-myopathy.
2. *Strong, consistent epidemiologic data support a relationship of heavier drinking to higher blood pressure* (hypertension*). Clinical experiments confirm a hypertensive effect of alcohol, which appears and regresses within several days, but a mechanism has not yet been established.*
3. *Heavier, and possibly lighter drinking is related to higher risk of* hemorrhagic stroke *(due to ruptured blood vessels), but lighter drinking is associated with lower risk of* ischemic stroke *(due to blocked blood vessels).*
4. *Heavier drinking, especially binge drinking, is associated with certain* heart rhythm disturbances.
5. *An inverse relationship of alcohol use to* coronary heart disease *is consistently supported by many population studies. Interpretation of these data as a protective effect of alcohol against coronary disease is strengthened by plausible mechanisms, including increased high-density-lipoprotein (HDL) cholesterol in alcohol drinkers, and anti-clotting actions of alcohol. Because coronary disease is so common, causing about 60% of all cardiovascular deaths and about 25% of all deaths, lighter alcohol drinking has an impact upon total mortality statistics, such that lighter drinkers are at slightly lower risk than abstainers of death within a given time period.*

International comparisons suggest that wine may be more protective against coronary disease than liquor or beer. Reports of protective substances, other than alcohol, in wine (especially red) support the hypothesis of possible extra benefit from wine. However, prospective population studies show no consensus; apparent protection has been found for beer, wine or liquor, and it has been suggested that favorable traits or drinking patterns of wine drinkers

International Handbook of Alcohol Dependence and Problems. Edited by N. Heather, T.J. Peters and T. Stockwell.

might explain the international study findings. Furthermore, observational and experimental data are inconclusive, at best, with respect to benefits from antioxidant supplements. Whatever the facts, it is worth noting that prominent lay media dissemination has probably led to widespread public acceptance of specific benefits of red wine.

As with most aspects of alcohol and health effects, the evidence does not suggest evenly graded relationships of alcohol with any cardiovascular condition. Thus, the amount of alcohol taken is a crucial consideration. Advice to concerned persons needs to take into account individual risk/benefit factors in drinkers or potential drinkers. For drinkers, there are no compelling health-related data which preclude personal preference as the best guide to choice of beverage.

This chapter will deal primarily with alcohol and the various cardiovascular conditions, with relevant discussion of lipid and metabolic factors pertinent to these relationships.

Evident disparities in relationships between drinking alcoholic beverages and various cardiovascular (CV) conditions (Klatsky, 1995b, 1998) make it desirable to consider several disorders separately. Because of past misunderstandings about alcohol–CV relationships, it is relevant to include historical review in this presentation. The following will be covered:

1. Although perceived 150 years ago, understanding of alcoholic cardiomyopathy (heart muscle disease) was later clouded by recognition of beriberi (vitamin B_1 deficiency) and of combined toxicity from alcohol with arsenic or cobalt.
2. A report of a link between heavy drinking and hypertension (HTN) in World War I French soldiers was apparently ignored for >50 years. Epidemiologic studies and experiments have now firmly established this association, but a mechanism remains elusive.
3. The "holiday heart syndrome", an increased risk of certain rhythm disturbances in binge drinkers, has been widely known to clinicians for 25 years. Data remain sparse about the total role of heavier drinking in cardiac rhythm disturbances.
4. Failure of earlier studies to distinguish types of stroke impeded understanding; it now seems probable that alcohol drinking increases risk of stroke due to ruptured blood vessels but lowers risk of stroke due to blocked blood vessels.
5. In 1786, William Heberden reported angina pectoris relief by alcohol, and pathologists observed that alcoholics had little atherosclerosis in the early 1900s. Recent population studies and plausible mechanisms suggest that alcohol protects against coronary heart disease (CHD). International comparisons dating back to 1819 suggest that wine may be more protective than liquor or beer, but this issue remains unresolved.

DEFINITIONS OF MODERATE AND HEAVY DRINKING

Any definition of moderate drinking is arbitrary. The operational definition here used is based upon the level of drinking in epidemiologic studies above which net harm is usually seen. Thus, less than three drinks per day is called "lighter" or "moderate" drinking, and three or more drinks per day "heavy" drinking. Sex, age and individual factors lower the upper limit for some persons and raise it for others. In data based upon surveys, systematic "underestimation" (lying) probably tends to lower the *apparent* threshold for harmful alcohol effects, because some heavy drinkers allege lighter drinking.

Fortunately, the amount of alcohol in a standard-sized drink of wine, liquor or beer is approximately the same. Since people think in terms of "drinks", not milliliters or grams of alcohol, it seems to this author best to describe alcohol relations in terms of drinks per day or per week. When talking with patients, health professionals should always remember the importance of defining the size of drinks.

ALCOHOLIC CARDIOMYOPATHY

Definition of Cardiomyopathy

The word "cardiomyopathy" (CM) is used by some to mean heart muscle disease, regardless of the cause. Others use it to refer to heart muscle disease only of unknown cause ("idiopathic"). Many, including this author, use the term to mean heart muscle disease independent of the valves, coronary arteries, pericardium and congenital malformations. Some cases have known causes; many do not. A common type of CM is characterized by an enlarged heart with weakened contraction, which is called "dilated CM". Sustained heavy alcohol drinking is believed to be one of the causes of dilated CM (Kasper et al., 1994). The clinical picture of dilated CM ranges from abnormalities detectable only by testing ("subclinical"), to severe illness with heart failure and high mortality rate.

Alcohol's Role in Dilated Cardiomyopathy

A number of famous nineteenth century physicians commented about an apparent relationship between chronic intake of large amounts of alcohol and heart disease (Klatsky, 1998). A German pathologist (Böllinger, 1884) described cardiac dilatation and hypertrophy among Bavarian beer drinkers, who averaged 432 l/year; this became known as the "Münchener bierherz".

In 1900, an epidemic of heart disease due to arsenic-contaminated beer occurred in Manchester, UK. Before this event, Graham Steell, a great British cardiologist, had recognized alcoholism as one of the causes of muscle failure of the heart but, following the arsenic-beer episode, Steell (1906) wrote: "in the production of the combined affection of the peripheral nerves and the heart met with in beer drinkers, arsenic has been shown to play a conspicuous part". In his textbook, *The Study of the Pulse*, William MacKenzie (1902) described cases of heart failure attributed to alcohol and first used the term "alcoholic heart disease". Early in the twentieth century, there was general doubt that alcohol had a direct role in producing heart muscle disease, although some (Vaquez, 1921) took a strong view in favor of such a relationship. After the detailed descriptions of cardiovascular beri-beri (Aalsmeer & Wenckebach, 1929; Keefer, 1930), the concept of "beri-beri heart disease" dominated thinking about the effects of alcohol upon the heart for several decades.

In recent decades increasing interest has been evident in possible direct toxicity of alcohol upon the myocardial cells and the existence of alcoholic CM has now become solidly established (Moushmoush & Abi-Mansour, 1991; Richardson et al., 1998). Many series of cases in various types of practice have been reported. Varying proportions of chronic heavy alcohol users have been reported to have evidence of the condition, probably dependent mostly upon the drinking habits of the study population. The absence of diagnostic tests has been a major impediment to epidemiologic study, since the entity has been indistinguishable from other forms of dilated CM. Most cases of dilated CM remain of unknown cause, with a post-viral autoimmune process and genetic factors the leading causal hypotheses. The proportion of heavy drinkers who develop cardiomyopathy is not known, but is smaller than the proportion who develop liver cirrhosis. Also not known is the proportion that improves with abstinence, but data showing that such regression occurs have been present for decades (Demakis et al., 1974). The most convincing evidence that alcohol can cause cardiomyopathy consists of extensive data, in animals and humans, of non-specific functional and structural abnormalities related to alcohol (Moushmoush & Abi-Mansour, 1991; Urbano-Marquez et al., 1989; Richardson et al., 1998). These data include autopsy studies, cardiac biopsies and non-invasive measures of heart function, such as nucleide and echocardiographic studies. Subclinical abnormalities of function and structure may precede evident illness for years.

A landmark study (Urbano-Marquez et al., 1989) showed a clear relation in alcoholics of life-time alcohol consumption to structural and functional myocardial and skeletal muscle abnormalities. The large amounts of alcohol needed—equivalent to 120 g alcohol/day for 20 years—make the term "cirrhosis of the heart" appropriate.

A possible non-oxidative metabolic pathway for alcohol has been reported (Lapasota & Lange, 1986) in the heart, muscle, pancreas and brain, related to fatty acid metabolism. Increased enzymatic activity in myocardial cells has also been reported (Richardson et al., 1998) but it is not clear whether the reported enzymatic activity reflects causative processes or an adaptive reaction. The histologic findings include evidence of inflammation, fatty deposits, focal or diffuse scarring and submicroscopic abnormalities. Some (Richardson et al., 1998) believe that heart muscle thickening, scarring and cell nuclear disruption are greater in alcoholic than in other forms of dilated CM, but this has not been generally considered sufficiently characteristic for specific diagnosis.

Diagnosis and Clinical Picture

The diagnosis depends upon the combination of a compatible alcohol drinking history and the presence of heart muscle disease without other evident cause. When clinical evidence appears, early manifestations are non-specific electrocardiographic findings and, possibly, rhythm disturbances. Evans (1959) described electrocardiographic variations, which he considered characteristic, but these have not been widely reported. The late picture includes (congestive) heart failure, chronic rhythm disturbances, conduction abnormalities, systemic emboli and death (Burch et al., 1966; Regan, 1984). The onset may be insidious, but sometimes seems subacute.

Possible Co-factors with Alcohol in Cardiomyopathy

Because the diagnosis of alcoholic CM is based on excluding other causes of CM and other types of heart disease, the quantitative role of alcohol as a contributing factor remains unknown. It seems plausible that amounts of drinking substantially less than needed to produce CM might act in concert with other conditions or co-factors to cause heart muscle dysfunction. In this connection, it seems appropriate to consider further the arsenic and cobalt beer-drinker episodes and thiamine (co-carboxylase or vitamin B_1) deficiency—or beri-beri heart disease. *Arsenic-beer drinkers' disease* refers to a 1900 epidemic (6000+ cases with 70+ deaths) in Manchester, UK, which proved to be due to contamination of beer by arsenic with prominent cardiovascular manifestations, especially heart failure. It was determined that the affected beer had 2–4 parts per million of arsenic, not—in itself—an amount likely to cause serious toxicity, and that some persons seemed to have a "peculiar idiosyncrasy" (Reynolds, 1901). An appointed committee report (Royal Commission, 1903) suggested that "alcohol predisposed people to arsenic poisoning" but, apparently, no one suggested the converse. *Cobalt-beer drinkers' disease*, recognized 65 years after the arsenic-beer episode, was similar in some respects. In the mid-1960s reports appeared of heart failure epidemics among beer drinkers in Omaha and Minneapolis, USA, Quebec, Canada, and Leuven, Belgium, generally with abrupt onset in chronic heavy beer drinkers. The explanation proved to be the addition of small amounts of cobalt chloride by certain breweries to improve the foaming qualities of beer. This etiology was tracked down largely by Quebec investigators (Morin & Daniel, 1967), and the condition became justly known as "Quebec beer-drinkers cardiomyopathy". Removal of the cobalt additive ended the epidemic in all locations. Even in Quebec, where cobalt doses were greatest, 121 contaminated beer provided only about 8 mg cobalt, less than 20% of the dose sometimes used as a blood stimulant. Such cobalt use had not been implicated as a cause of heart disease. Most exposed persons did not develop the condition. Thus, it was established that both cobalt and substantial amounts of alcohol seemed needed to produce this condition. Despite much speculation, biochemical mechanisms were not established. One observer (Alexander, 1969) summed up the arsenic and cobalt episodes thus: "This is the second known metal-induced cardiotoxic syndrome produced by contaminated beer".

The arsenic and cobalt episodes raise the possibility of other co-factors in alcoholic cardiomyopathy, such as cardiotropic viruses, drugs, selenium, copper and iron. Deficiencies of zinc, magnesium, protein and various vitamins have also been suggested as co-factors, but deficiency of thiamine is probably the only one with solid proof of cardiac malfunction.

Cardiovascular beri-beri dominated thinking about alcohol and cardiovascular disease for many years. The classical description (Aalsmeer & Wenckebach, 1929) described heart failure in Javanese polished-rice eaters, with high cardiac output due to wide open peripheral small blood vessels. It became assumed that heart failure in heavy alcohol drinkers in the West was due to associated nutritional deficiency states. Although some heart failure cases in North American and European alcoholics fitted this clinical pattern, most did not, as they had a cardiac output, were well-nourished and responded poorly to thiamine. Some felt that these facts were due to the chronicity of the condition, which ultimately might become irreversible. However, Blacket & Palmer (1960) stated the following: "It (beri-beri) responds completely to thiamine, but merges imperceptibly into another disease, called alcoholic CM, which doesn't respond to thiamine". Modern physiologic techniques have confirmed that, in beri-beri, there is generalized dilatation of peripheral arterioles, not heart muscle disease, and a few cases of complete recovery with thiamine within 1–2 weeks have been documented. Thus, it is evident that many cases earlier called "cardiovascular beri-beri" would now be called "alcoholic heart disease". Does chronic thiamine deficiency play a role in some cases of alcoholic CM? This currently unpopular thesis has not been proved or disproved.

In view of the history just cited, it seems noteworthy that there has been little work so far about possible co-factors or predisposing traits for alcoholic cardiomyopathy.

HYPERTENSION (HTN)

Background

Although an association between heavy drinking and HTN was reported in 1915 in middle-aged French servicemen (Lian, 1915), it was more than 50 years before further attention was paid to this subject. Since the mid-1970s, dozens of cross-sectional and prospective epidemiologic studies have solidly established an empiric alcohol–HTN link, and clinical experiments have confirmed this (MacMahon, 1987; Keil et al., 1993; Klatsky, 1995a). So far, a mechanism has not been demonstrated. The evidence is sufficient so that clinicians should consider heavy alcohol drinking to be a probable HTN risk factor.

Epidemiologic Studies

Almost all of approximately 50 cross-sectional studies show higher mean blood pressures and/or higher HTN prevalence with increasing alcohol drinking. This observation has been made in North American, European, Australian and Japanese populations and seems independent from adiposity, salt intake, education, cigarette smoking and several other potential indirect explanations. Most studies do *not* show any increase in blood pressure at light–moderate alcohol drinking, and several show the lowest pressures in lighter female drinkers. Data (Klatsky et al., 1977) from the first Kaiser Permanente study (Figure 11.1) show these relationships in the two sexes in each of three racial groups. A later Kaiser Permanente study (Klatsky et al., 1986a) confirmed these relationships. The data from this later study suggested that ex-drinkers had similar blood pressures to those of non-drinkers and that elevated blood pressures regressed within a week upon abstinence from alcohol. In both studies, HTN prevalence was approximately doubled among the heaviest (≥6 drinks daily) drinkers, compared to abstainers or light drinkers.

Data from prospective studies show higher risk of HTN development among heavier alcohol drinkers, as detailed in reviews (Keil et al., 1993; Klatsky, 1995a). Several of these were well-controlled for multiple nutritional factors.

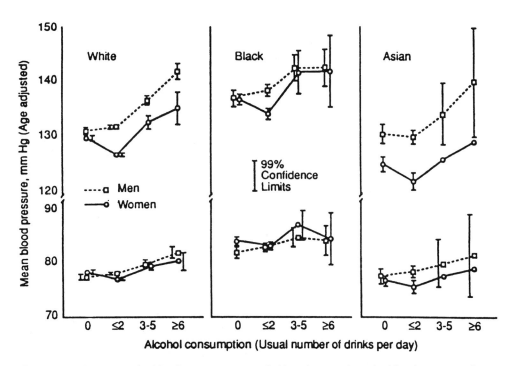

Figure 11.1 Mean systolic blood pressures (upper half) and mean diastolic blood pressures (lower half) for White, Black or Asian men and women with known drinking habits. Small circles represent data based on fewer than 30 persons. From Klatsky et al. (1977), with permission.

Intervention Studies

A landmark study (Potter & Beevers, 1984) showed in hospitalized hypertensive men that 3–4 days of intake of 4 pints of beer raised blood pressure and that 3–4 days of abstinence resulted in lower pressures. A 12 week cross-over design trial (Puddey et al., 1985) showed similar results in ambulatory normotensives and the observation was later confirmed in hypertensives (Puddey et al., 1987). Other studies show that heavier alcohol intake interferes with drug treatment of HTN, and that moderation or avoidance of alcohol supplements betters other non-pharmacologic interventions for blood pressure lowering, such as weight reduction, exercise or sodium restriction (Keil et al., 1993; Klatsky, 1995a).

Possible Mechanisms

The alcohol–HTN relationship is a subacute one, developing in days to weeks. Acute human and animal experiments show no consistent increase in blood pressure after alcohol administration (MacMahon, 1987; Keil et al., 1993; Klatsky, 1995a). Ambulatory monitoring has shown a depressor effect of a substantial dinner-time alcohol dose, lasting up to 8 hours, with a pressor effect the next morning (Kawano et al., 1992).

Much work has failed to uncover a biological mechanism, including no consistent relationships to various potential neuroendocrine mechanisms. Experiments suggest independence from acetaldehyde-induced flushing, common in Asians (Kawano et al., 1992). All suggested physiologic mechanisms and remain speculative. One hypothesis is the existence of a heightened responsiveness of the sympathetic nervous system (Coca et al., 1992; Randin et al., 1995). An overactive sympathetic nervous system exists during the alcohol withdrawal state, but this is not the likely explanation for the alcohol–HTN relationship at the drinking levels seen in the studies.

Sequelae of Alcohol-associated HTN

Complex interactions of alcohol, various cardiovascular conditions and risk factors make the study of this important subject difficult. Since CHD and strokes of all types are major cardiovascular sequelae of HTN, the lower risk of CHD and ischemic stroke among drinkers confound study of this aspect. A counter-balancing role of HTN has been observed in two alcohol–CHD studies (Criqui, 1987; Langer et al., 1992). An attempt to study whether alcohol-associated HTN had the same prognosis as HTN not so associated led to the conclusion that alcohol's harmful and beneficial effects so dominated the outcome that the basic question could not be answered (Klatsky, 1995a).

Interpretive Problems and Conclusions

A satisfactory long-term clinical trial of alcohol, HTN and HTN sequelae is unlikely to be performed. Thus, the closest practical alternatives are prospective observational studies and short–intermediate-term clinical trials. The intrinsic problems in studies of alcohol and health effects are well-known (Klatsky, 1995a). Under-reporting of heavier alcohol intake is one of these, but is incorrectly cited as a factor in the alcohol–HTN relationship, since the major effect of such under-reporting would produce an apparent, but spurious, relationship of HTN to *lighter* drinking. The threshold for the relationship could be higher than suggested by the epidemiologic data.

Because many traits are related to alcohol drinking or to HTN, it is difficult to rule out all indirect explanations. Psychological or social stress is especially difficult to exclude. The intervention studies provide good evidence against most indirect explanations.

Except for the failure, so far, to demonstrate a biologic mechanism, other criteria for causality are satisfactorily fulfilled. It is the author's opinion that the relationship between heavier drinking and higher risk of HTN is causal and that alcohol-related HTN is the commonest reversible form of HTN. Alcoholic beverage type (wine, liquor or beer) seems to be a minor factor. Estimates of the proportion of HTN due to heavy drinking vary with the population involved; the contribution of alcohol depends substantially upon the drinking habits of the group under study. Among the lowest estimates are 5% (Friedman et al., 1993) or 7% (MacMahon, 1987) of hypertension, considering both sexes together. This translates into 1–2 million people with alcohol-associated HTN in the USA, using 20–40 million hypertensives as the denominator. It is probable that alcohol restriction plays a major role in HTN management and prevention (Joint National Committee on Detection Evaluation and Treatment of High Blood Pressure, 1993).

CARDIAC ARRHYTHMIAS

An association of heavier alcohol consumption with atrial arrhythmias has been suspected for decades, with typical occurrence after a large meal accompanied by much alcohol. The concept of the "holiday heart phenomenon" has become widely known. The basis of this term was the observation (Ettinger et al., 1978) that supraventricular arrhythmias in alcoholics without overt cardiomyopathy were most likely to occur on Mondays or between Christmas and New Year's Day. Various atrial arrhythmias have been reported to be associated with spree drinking, with atrial fibrillation the commonest manifestation. The arrhythmia typically resolves with abstinence, with or without other specific treatment. A Kaiser Permanente study (Cohen et al., 1988) compared atrial arrhythmias in 1322 persons reporting 6+ drinks/day to arrhythmias in 2644 light drinkers. The relative risk in the heavier drinkers was at least doubled (Table 11.4).

Increased ventricular ectopic activity has been documented after ingestion of substantial amounts of alcohol, although epidemiologic studies have not shown a higher risk of sudden death in drinkers (Siscovick et al., 1986).

Speculation about mechanisms for the relationship between heavier drinking and arrhythmias has included myocardial damage, electrolyte/metabolic effects, vagal reflexes, effects upon conduction/refractory times and possible roles for catecholamines or acetaldehyde. A recent report from Finland (Maki et al., 1998) studied these in men with recurrent alcohol-associated AF. In controlled analyses of a number of tests and measurements, there was some evidence for exaggerated sympathetic nervous system reaction in these persons.

CEREBROVASCULAR DISEASE

Earlier studies of relationships of alcohol drinking to stroke were made difficult by imprecise diagnosis of stroke type before modern imaging techniques improved diagnostic accuracy. Risk factors differ somewhat for the two major stroke types; these are hemorrhagic stroke, due to ruptured blood vessels on the brain surface (subarachnoid hemorrhage) and in the brain substance, and ischemic (occlusive) stroke, due to blockage of blood vessels by clot formation in the brain blood vessels, blood clot emboli to the brain from the heart or elsewhere, or blockage of blood vessels outside the brain (most notably the carotid arteries). All studies of alcohol and stroke are greatly complicated by the disparate relationships of both stroke and alcohol to other cardiovascular conditions. Age and HTN are major risk factors for all stroke types, and most cardiovascular conditions have differing relations to various types of stroke. When we add in the disparities in alcohol–CV relationships and the lighter/heavier/binge drinking differences, we end up with almost Byzantine complexity in alcohol–stroke relationships.

As indicated in a comprehensive review (Van Gign et al., 1993), several reports suggest that alcohol use, especially heavier drinking, is associated with higher risk of stroke. Some studies examined only drinking sprees; some others did not differentiate between hemorrhagic and ischemic strokes. The importance of these deficiencies is highlighted by several recent studies suggesting that regular lighter drinkers may be at higher risk of hemorrhagic stroke types, but at lower risk of several types of ischemic stroke (Van Gign et al., 1993). For example, The Nurse's Health Study (Stampfer et al., 1988) showed drinkers to be at higher risk of subarachnoid hemorrhage but lower risk of occlusive stroke. Another example is a Kaiser Permanente study which looked at the relations between reported alcohol use and the incidence of hospitalization for several types of cerebrovascular disease (Klatsky et al., 1989). Daily consumption of 3+ drinks, but not lighter drinking, was related to higher hospitalization rates for hemorrhagic stroke; higher blood pressure appeared to be a partial mediator of this relationship. Alcohol use was associated with lower hospitalization rates for ischemic stroke, an inverse relationship present in both sexes, Whites and Blacks, and for extracranial and intracerebral occlusive lesions. A much larger Kaiser Permanente study is now under way.

CORONARY ARTERY DISEASE (CHD)

Background

Although incidence is decreasing in developed countries, CHD remains the leading cause of death in men and women. Since it causes a majority of all cardiovascular deaths, CHD dominates statistics for cardiovascular mortality and has substantial impact upon total mortality. Population studies have uncovered several, probably causal, CHD risk factors, including cigarette smoking, HTN, diabetes mellitus, high low-density lipoprotein (LDL) cholesterol, and low high-density lipoprotein (HDL) cholesterol. Sometimes, the LDL is called the "bad" cholesterol and HDL the "good" cholesterol. Atherosclerotic narrowing of major epicardial vessels is the usual basis, with clot formation in narrowed vessels playing a critical role in major events, such as acute myocardial infarction ("heart attack") or sudden death. Angina pectoris is a common symptom of CHD. Since Heberden's description of angina relief by alcohol (Heberden, 1786), many have assumed that alcohol is a coronary vasodilator, but exercise tests (Orlando et al., 1976) suggest that alcohol's effect is purely subjective. Thus, it is probably dangerous for CHD patients to drink before exercise.

In the early 1900s, reports appeared showing that heavy alcohol drinkers had little atherosclerotic disease, but this was explained this as an artifact due to premature deaths of many heavy drinkers (Klatsky, 1994). Early studies of alcoholics and problem drinkers suggested a high CHD rate, but these studies did not allow for the role of traits associated with alcoholism, such as cigarette smoking (Klatsky, 1994). Studies of heavy drinkers can tell nothing about the role of light–moderate drinking.

Epidemiologic Studies

Epidemiologic studies consistently show reduced risk of acute myocardial infarction and CHD death in light–moderate drinkers (Maclure, 1993; Renaud et al., 1993; Klatsky, 1994;

Rehm et al., 1997). While angina pectoris is a common CHD symptom, it is subjective and difficult to quantify and thus has been relatively little studied epidemiologically in relation to alcohol. Studies showing more CHD events in alcohol abstainers than in drinkers include international comparisons of CHD mortality in relation to mean alcohol consumption, time-trend analyses of CHD over many years in relation to drinking, case-control studies, prospective population studies, and studies of coronary arteriograms in relation to drinking (Renaud et al., 1993; Klatsky, 1994). The reasons for the increased CHD risk of heavier vs. lighter drinkers may include the effects of spree drinking, alcohol-associated HTN or arrhythmias, misdiagnosis of other conditions (e.g. dilated cardiomyopathy as CAD), or a truly different effect of heavier drinking upon CHD.

Some population studies did not separate life-long abstainers from ex-drinkers, or did not adequately control for baseline CHD risk. This led to the "sick quitter" hypothesis, which stated that the non-drinking referent groups in these studies were at higher risk for reasons other than abstinence (Shaper et al., 1988). This hypothesis is refuted by prospective studies that separate ex-drinkers from life-long abstainers and that also control well for baseline CHD (Maclure, 1993; Renaud et al., 1993; Klatsky, 1994). A few examples will suffice:

1. Data from Kaiser Permanente studies are summarized in Tables 11.1–11.3. Analysis of alcohol habits in relation to CHD hospitalizations (Klatsky et al., 1986a) showed (Table 11.1) that ex-drinkers and infrequent (<1/month) drinkers were at risk similar to that of life-long abstainers. A lower CHD risk was present among all other drinkers, independent of a number of potential indirect explanations, baseline CHD risk at examination (Table 11.2) and beverage choice. In a study of total CV mortality (Klatsky et al., 1990a), ex-drinkers had higher age-adjusted CHD and overall CV mortality risk than life-long abstainers, but the difference disappeared when adjusted for other traits. Among drinkers there were U-shaped mortality curves, independent of baseline risk, relating amounts of alcohol to CV and CAD deaths, with a nadir at 1–2 and 3–5 drinks/day. The study demonstrated the expected disparities between alcohol and various CV conditions (Table 11.3).

Table 11.1 Relative risk of coronary artery disease hospitalization* according to alcohol use

Alcohol use	RR**	95% CI	p Value
Non-drinkers			
Abstainer	1.0[†]	–	–
Ex-drinker	1.0	(0.7, 1.4)	0.9
Drinkers			
<1/month	0.9	(0.7, 1.2)	0.6
<1/day, >1/month	0.7	(0.5, 0.8)	<0.001
1–2/days	0.6	(0.5, 0.7)	<0.0001
3–5/days	0.5	(0.4, 0.8)	<0.001
6–8/days	0.5	(0.3, 1.1)	0.1
≥9/days	0.5	(0.2, 1.5)	0.2

*First for any CAD diagnosis ($n = 756$).
**Computed from coefficients estimated by Cox proportional hazards model; co-variates include sex, age, race, smoking, education, coffee.
RR, relative risk; CI, confidence interval.
[†]Referent.
Adapted from Katsky et al. (1986b).

Table 11.2 Relative risk of coronary artery disease hospitalization according to alcohol use among persons free of coronary risk/symptoms or recent major illness*

Alcohol use	RR**	95% CI	p value
Non-drinkers			
Abstainer	1.0[†]	–	–
Ex-drinker	0.9	(0.6, 1.6)	0.8
Drinkers			
<1/month	0.9	(0.6, 1.3)	0.8
<1/day, >1/month	0.6	(0.4, 0.9)	<0.01
1–2/days	0.5	(0.3, 0.7)	<0.0001
3–5/days	0.5	(0.3, 0.8)	<0.01
6–8/days	0.7	(0.2, 1.8)	0.4
≥9/day	0.5	(0.1, 3.8)	0.5

*First for any CAD diagnosis ($n = 336$) among persons with no CHD risk/symptoms (12 items) or other major illness in the past year.
**Computed from coefficients estimated by Cox proportional hazards model; co-variates include sex, age, race, smoking, education, coffee.
RR, relative risk; CI, confidence interval.
[†]Referent.
Adapted from Katsky et al. (1986b).

Table 11.3 Relative risk* of death of various cardiovascular conditions and cirrhosis by alcohol use

Condition (n deaths)	RR for each drinking category vs. lifelong abstainers					
	Ex-drinkers	<1/month	>1/day; <1/month	1–2/day	3–5/day	6+/day
All CAD (600)	1.0	0.9	0.8[a]	0.7[b]	0.7[b]	0.8
AMI (284)	1.0	0.7	0.8	0.6[b]	0.5[b]	0.6
Other CAD (316)	0.9	1.0	0.7	0.8	0.7	1.0
Stroke (138)	1.0	0.8	0.8	0.8	0.7	1.4
Hemorrhagic (41)	1.4	1.5	1.6	1.8	1.3	4.7
Ischemic (34)	0.9	0.5	0.5	0.3	0.4	–[d]
Non-specific (63)	1.1	0.7	0.9	1.0	1.0	1.2
Hypertension (64)	2.8	2.4	1.9	1.3	2.2	2.1
Cardiomyopathy (24)	3.4	8.5[a]	4.0	5.6	2.4	8.0
Syndromes (82)**	0.6	0.6	0.5	0.4[a]	0.6	1.0
Arterial (41) ***	–[d]	1.1	1.6	0.4[a]	1.7	–[d]
Cirrhosis (42)	10.8[c]	1.4	1.0	4.3	8.1[b]	22.0[c]

*Computed from coefficients estimated by Cox proportional hazards model; co-variates include sex, age, race, smoking, education, coffee; reference group is lifelong abstainers.
**Includes "symptomatic heart disease" ($n = 32$); disorders of heart rhythm ($n = 22$); and ill-defined heart disease ($n = 28$).
***Includes arteriosclerosis ($n = 15$); aneurysms ($n = 23$); peripheral vascular disease ($n = 2$); and arterial embolism and thrombosis ($n = 1$).
[a]$p < 0.05$; [b]$p < 0.01$; [c]$p < 0.001$; [d]insufficient cases for estimate.
RR, relative risk; CAD, coronary artery disease; AMI, acute myocardial infarction.
Adapted from Katsky et al. (1990a).

Table 11.4 Relative risk* of supraventricular arrhythmia in persons with high vs. low daily alcohol intake

Rhythm	Persons with arrhythmia				RR (6+/<1)	p Value
	6+ Drinks day (n = 1332)		<1 Drink day (n = 2664)			
	(No.)	(%)	(No.)	(%)		
Atrial fibrillation	15	1.1	13	0.5	2.3	0.02
Atrial flutter	8	0.6	6	0.2	3.0	0.05
SVT	5	0.4	2	0.1	5.0	0.03
APBs	43	3.3	32	1.3	3.0	<0.01
Fibrillation, flutter or SVT	21	1.6	19	0.7	2.3	<0.01

*Relative risks and p values estimated using McNemar's method for matched pairs.
RR, relative risk; SVT, supraventricular tachycardia; APBs, atrial premature beats.
Adapted from Cohen et al. (1988).

2. A large prospective study among women free of CHD at examination (Stampfer et al., 1988) showed a progressive lower risk of CHD events with increasing alcohol use, independent of prior reduction in alcohol intake and nutrient intake. Further analysis of these data in women (Fuchs et al., 1995), demonstrated that net beneficial effects of moderate alcohol use in women was limited by adverse effects, except in persons clearly at above-average CHD risk, primarily those above 50 years of age.
3. The 12 year prospective American Cancer Society Study (Boffetta & Garfinkel, 1990) of 276,802 men showed a U-shaped curve for CHD mortality, with a RR of 0.8 (vs. abstainers) at 1–2 drinks/day.
4. In the Health Professional Followup Study of 51,529 men (Rimm et al., 1991) well controlled for dietary habits, newly diagnosed CHD was inversely related to increasing alcohol intake.
5. A study in both sexes, the Auckland Heart Study (Jackson et al., 1991), designed to study the hypothesis that persons at high CHD risk are likely to become non-drinkers, showed that moderate drinkers had lower CHD risk than both life-long abstainers and ex-drinkers.

Possible Mechanisms for CAD Protection by Alcohol

Via Blood Lipid Factors

The most studied mechanism, and the most plausible for overall protection by alcohol against atherosclerotic disease, is a link via blood lipid factors. These play a central role in development of this condition (Criqui & Golomb, 1998), with a positive relationship between CHD and higher levels of LDL cholesterol, the so-called "bad cholesterol", and an inverse relationship between higher levels of HDL cholesterol, the so-called "good cholesterol". Triglycerides may play an independent role and some feel that the ratio between total cholesterol and HDL cholesterol, which indirectly incorporates data about LDL, HDL and triglycerides, may be the best single CHD risk indicator (Criqui & Golomb, 1998). A subset of heavier drinkers have a substantial increase in triglyceride levels, but this is infrequently seen with lighter/moderate drinking. Alcohol may be associated with lower LDL levels (Hein et al., 1996), but it is unclear that this is independent of other dietary factors. The case for a lipid link for alcohol's protection against CHD currently rests primarily upon HDL effects.

HDL levels are inversely related to CHD risk (Renaud et al., 1993; Criqui & Golomb, 1998), possibly acting by abetting removal of lipid deposits in large blood vessels. HDL binds with cholesterol in the tissues and may aid in preventing tissue oxidation of LDL cholesterol; it then carries it back to the liver for elimination or reprocessing. The net effect is reduction of cholesterol build-up in the walls of large blood vessels, such as the coronary arteries. In the absence of severe liver impairment, alcohol ingestion raises HDL levels (Rimm et al., 1991; Renaud et al., 1993; Gaziano et al., 1993; Criqui & Golomb, 1998). The biochemical pathways for the HDL effect of alcohol are incompletely understood. Also pertinent are data that show elevation by alcohol of apolipoproteins A_1 and A_2, associated with HDL particle formation (Camargo et al., 1985; Moore et al., 1988).

The hypothesis that the apparent protective effect of alcohol against CHD is mediated by higher HDL cholesterol levels in drinkers has been examined quantitatively in three separate studies (Criqui, 1987; Suh et al., 1992; Gaziano et al., 1993). All three analyses yielded similar findings, suggesting that higher HDL levels in drinkers mediated about half of the lower CHD risk. One of these studies (Gaziano et al., 1993) suggested that both major HDL subfractions, HDL2 and HDL3, are involved. HDL3 may be more strongly related to lighter alcohol intake, but is probably related as strongly as HDL2 to lower CHD risk.

Via Antithrombotic Mechanisms

There are data that support an inhibitory effect of alcohol upon various aspects of clotting (Klatsky, 1994; Renaud et al., 1993; Hendriks & van der Gang, 1998), including decreased platelet stickiness and lower fibrinogen levels. Perhaps the evidence about anti-clotting effects of alcohol is best for fibrinogen lowering (Hendriks & van der Gang, 1998). Antithrombotic actions of alcohol could partially account for the lower CHD risk at very light drinking levels (e.g. several drinks per week) seen in several of the epidemiologic studies.

Via Glucose Metabolism

Although alcohol drinking, especially heavier intake, has been associated with higher blood glucose levels (Gerard et al., 1977), lighter drinking has also been associated with possible beneficial changes in insulin and glucose metabolism (Mayer et al., 1993; Facchini et al., 1994; Kiechl et al., 1996; Lazarus et al., 1997). Since glucose intolerance and decreased insulin sensitivity are major CHD risk factors, these effects could hypothetically play a role in protection by alcohol against CHD.

Via Stress Reduction

Hypothetical considerations about possible benefit from anti-anxiety or stress-reducing effects of alcohol have no good supporting data.

Role of Beverage Choice (Wine, Liquor, Beer)

In 1819, Dr Samuel Black, a perceptive Irish physician with a great interest in angina pectoris, wrote probably the first commentary pertinent to the "French Paradox". Noting apparent angina disparity between Ireland and France, he attributed the low prevalence in the latter to "the French habits and modes of living, coinciding with the benignity of their climate and the peculiar character of their moral affections" (Black, 1819). It was to be 160 years before data were presented from the first international comparison study to suggest less CHD in wine-drinking countries than in beer- or liquor-drinking countries (St. Leger et al., 1979), and there are confirmatory international comparison studies (Renaud & de Lorgeril, 1992; Criqui & Ringel, 1994). The "French paradox" concept has arisen from these data; it refers to the fact that France tends to be an outlier on graphs of mean dietary fat intake vs. CHD mortality, unless adjusted for wine alcohol intake (Renaud & de Lorgeril, 1992; Criqui & Ringel, 1994). Reports of non-alcohol antioxidant phenolic compounds or antithrombotic substances in wine, especially red wine, have appeared (Renaud et al., 1993; Klatsky, 1994; Rimm et al., 1996). Inhibition of oxidative modification of LDL cholesterol is probably antiatherogenic, although prospective clinical trials of antioxidant supplements, vitamin E possibly excepted, are not yet conclusive (Virtamo et al., 1998).

A Kaiser Permanente cohort study of 221 persons who died of CHD (Klatsky & Armstrong, 1993) and who took 80–90% of their beverage alcohol as the preferred beverage, showed that, compared to non-drinkers, CAD risk was significantly lower among preferrers of each beverage type. When the CHD risk of the beverage preferrer groups was compared to each other, there was a gradient of apparently increasing protection from liquor to beer to wine. There were substantial differences in traits between the preference groups (Klatsky et al., 1990b). The wine drinkers had the most favorable CHD risk profiles, leading to the hypothesis that favorable uncontrolled traits (e.g. dietary habits, physical exercise, use of antioxidant supplements) of wine preferrers might explain the findings.

An analysis of the role of beverage choice among 3931 persons hospitalized for coronary disease used a proxy variable for reported frequency of drinking each beverage type, enabling use of all available beverage choice data (Klatsky et al., 1997). Adjusted analyses, not controlled for total alcohol intake, showed inverse relationships to CHD risk for each beverage type, weakest for liquor use. In sex-specific data this inverse relation was significant for beer use in men and for wine use in women. When controlled for total alcohol intake, only beer use in men remained significantly related. There were no significant differences in risk between drinkers of red, white, both red and white, and other types of wine. It was concluded that all beverage types protect against CHD, with additional protection by specific beverages likely to be minor.

Although antioxidant and other substances in wine are an attractive hypothetical explanation for CHD protection, the prospective population studies provide no consensus that wine has additional benefits, and various studies show benefit for wine, beer, liquor or all three major beverage types (Klatsky, 1994; Klatsky et al., 1997; Renaud et al., 1993; Hein et al., 1996; Rimm et al., 1996). The traits of the beverage users differ, with wine drinkers having the most favorable CHD risk profile (Klatsky et al., 1990b), and drinking pattern differences among the beverage types could also play a role. The wine/liquor/beer issue is unresolved at this time (Rimm et al., 1996; Klatsky et al., 1997; Keil et al., 1997), but it seems likely that ethyl alcohol is the major factor with respect to lower CHD risk. There seem to be no compelling health-related data which preclude personal preference as the best guide to choice of beverage.

A Causal Relation?

It remains theoretically possible that life-long abstainers could differ from drinkers in psychological traits, dietary habits, physical exercise habits, or some other way which could be related to CAD risk, but there is no good evidence for such a trait. The various studies indi-

Table 11.5 Relationships of alcohol drinking to cardiovascular conditions

Condition	Amount of alcohol drinking		Comment
	Small	Large	
Dilated cardiomyopathy	No relationship	Probably causal	?Unknown co-factors
Beri-beri	No relationship	No relationship	Thiamine deficiency
Arsenic/cobalt-beer disease	No relationship	Synergistic	Examples of co-factors
Hypertension	Little or no relationship	Probably causal	Mechanism unknown
Coronary disease	Protective	?Protective	Via HDL, antithrombotic effects; beverage type minor factor
Arrhythmia	?None	Probably causal	?Susceptibility factors
Hemorrhagic stroke	?Increased risk	Increased risk	Via higher BP, antithrombotic actions
Ischemic stroke	Protective	?Protective	Complex interactions with other conditions

cate that such a correlate would need to be present in persons of both sexes, various countries and multiple racial groups. While it remains possible that other factors play a role, a causal, protective effect of alcohol is a simpler and more plausible explanation.

Thus, some data suggest that heavier drinking increases the risk of hemorrhagic cerebrovascular events, but that alcohol use may lessen the risk of occlusive lesions. In stroke risk the antithrombotic (or anticlotting) actions of alcohol may be important, increasing risk of hemorrhagic strokes and decreasing risk of ischemic strokes. At this time there is no consensus about the relations of alcohol drinking to the various types of cerebrovascular disease and agreement only that more study of this important are is needed (Marmot & Brunner, 1991).

CONCLUSION

This survey documents the evidence for disparity in the relations of alcohol and CV disorders. Table 11.5 summarizes the relations, with emphasis on the disparity between the overall favorable relations of lighter drinking and the overall unfavorable relations of heavier drinking. Advice to the general public or concerned persons about the health effects of alcohol drinking needs to be individualized according to the persons' specific medical history and risks (Friedman & Klatsky, 1993; Pearson & Terry, 1994). A few rules seem sensible: (a) the overall health risk of a heavier drinker is likely to be reduced by reduction or abstinence; (b) because of the unknown risk of progression to heavier drinking, abstainers cannot be indiscriminately advised to drink for CV health benefit; (c) the majority of persons who are light/moderate drinkers need no change in drinking habits, except in special circumstances.

ACKNOWLEDGEMENT

Some of the material here reported was supported by research performed with a grant from the Alcoholic Beverage Medical Research Foundation, Baltimore, MD, USA.

KEY WORKS AND SUGGESTIONS FOR FURTHER READING

Fuchs, C.S., Stampfer, M.J., Colditz, G.A., Giovannucci, E.L., Manson, J.E., Kawachi, I. et al. (1995).   Alcohol consumption and mortality among women. *New England Journal of Medicine*, **332**, 1245–1250.

A prospective study in a large population of women, which shows the risk/benefit factors in population subsets.

Klatsky, A.L. (1995).   Blood pressure and alcohol intake. In J.H. Laragh & B.M. Brenner (Eds), *Hypertension: Pathophysiology, Diagnosis and Management*, 2nd edn. New York: Raven, pp. 2649–2667.

A comprehensive review of all aspects of the alcohol–hypertension relationship.

Renaud, S., Criqui, M.H., Farchi, G. & Veenstra, J. (1993).   Alcohol drinking and coronary heart disease. In P.M. Verschuren (Ed.), *Health Issues Related to Alcohol Consumption*. Washington, DC: ILSI Press, pp. 81–124.

A comprehensive review of the alcohol coronary disease topic.

Rimm, E., Klatsky, A.L., Grobbee, D. & Stampfer, M.J. (1996).   Review of moderate alcohol consumption and reduced risk of coronary heart disease: is the effect due to beer, wine, or spirits? *British Medical Journal*, **312**, 731–736.

An analysis of studies pertinent to the beverage choice issue and discussion of the problems inherent in such studies.

Urbano-Marquez, A., Estrich, R., Navarro-Lopez, F., Grau, J.M. & Rubin, E. (1989).   The effects of alcoholism on skeletal and cardiac muscle. *New England Journal of Medicine*, **320**(7), 409–415.

A key article and elegant study about alcoholic cardiomyopathy.

Van Gign, J., Stampfer, M.J., Wolfe, C. & Algra, A. (1993).   The association between alcohol consumption and stroke. In P.M. Verschuren (Ed.), *Health Issues Related to Alcohol Consumption*. Washington, DC: ILSI Press, pp. 43–80.

A comprehensive review of the alcohol–stroke topic.

REFERENCES

Aalsmeer, W.C. & Wenckebach, K.F. (1929).   Herz und Kreislauf be der Beri-Beri Krankheit. *Wein. Arch. Inn. Med.*, **16**, 193–272.

Alexander, C.S. (1969).   Cobalt and the heart. *Annals of Internal Medicine*, **70**, 411–413.

Black, S. (1819).   *Clinical and Pathological Reports*. [A. Wilkinson (Ed.)]. Newry, pp. 1–47.

Blacket, R.B. & Palmer, A.J. (1960).   Haemodynamic studies in high output beri beri. *British Heart Journal*, **22**, 483–501.

Boffetta, P. & Garfinkel, L. (1990).   Alcohol drinking and mortality among men enrolled in an American Cancer society prospective study. *Epidemiology*, **1**, 342–348.

Böllinger, O. (1884).   Ueber die Haussigkeit under Ursachen der idiopathischen Herzhypertrophie in Menchen. *Disch. Med. Wochenschr.*, **10**, 180.

Burch, G.E., Phillips, J.H.Jr & Ferrans, V.J. (1966).   Alcoholic cardiomyopathy. *American Journal of Medical Science*, **252**, 123/89–138/104.

Camargo, C.A.J., Williams, P.T., Vranizan, K.M., Albers, J.J. & Wood, P.D. (1985).   The effect of moderate alcohol intake on serum apolipoproteins A-I and A-II. A controlled study. *Journal of the American Medical Association*, **253**, 2854–2857.

Coca, A., De la Sierra, A., Sanchez, M., Picado, M.J., Lluch, M.M. & Urbano-Marquez, A. (1992). Chronic alcohol intake induces reversible disturbances on cellular Na^+ metabolism in humans: its relationship with changes in blood pressure. *Alcoholism: Clinical and Experimental Research*, **16**, 714–720.

Cohen, E.J., Klatsky, A.L. & Armstrong, M.A. (1988). Alcohol use and supraventricular arrhythmia. *American Journal of Cardiology*, **62**, 971–973.

Criqui, M.H. (1987). Alcohol and hypertension: new insights from population studies. *European Heart Journal*, **8**(Suppl. B), 19–26.

Criqui, M.H. & Ringel, B.L. (1994). Does diet or alcohol explain the French paradox? *Lancet*, **344**, 1719–1723.

Criqui, M.H. & Golomb, B.A. (1998). Epidemiologic aspects of lipid abnormalities. *American Journal of Medicine*, **105**, 48S–57S.

Demakis, J.G., Proskey, A., Rahimtoola, S.H., Jamil, M., Sutton, G.C., Rosen, K.M. et al. (1974). The natural course of alcoholic cardiomyopathy. *Annals of Internal Medicine*, **80**, 293–297.

Ettinger, P.O., Wu, C.F., De La Cruz, C.Jr, Weisse, A.B., Ahmed, S.S. & Regan, T.J. (1978). Arrhythmias and the holiday heart: alcohol-associated cardiac rhythm disorders. *American Heart Journal*, **95**, 555–562.

Evans, W. (1959). The electrocardiogram of alcoholic cardiomyopathy. *British Heart Journal*, **21**, 445–456.

Facchini, F., Chen, Y.D. & Reaven, G.M. (1994). Light-to-moderate alcohol intake is associated with enhanced insulin sensitivity. *Diabetes Care*, **17**, 115–119.

Friedman, G.D. & Klatsky, A.L. (1993). Is alcohol good for your health? *New England Journal of Medicine*, **329**, 1882–1883.

Fuchs, C.S., Stampfer, M.J., Colditz, G.A., Giovannucci, E.L., Manson, J.E., Kawachi, I. et al. (1995). Alcohol consumption and mortality among women. *New England Journal of Medicine*, **332**, 1245–1250.

Gaziano, J.M., Buring, J.E., Breslow, J.L., Goldhaber, S.Z., Rosner, B., VanDenburgh, M. et al. (1993). Moderate alcohol intake, increased levels of high density lipoprotein and its subfractions, and decreased risk of myocardial infarction. *New England Journal of Medicine*, **329**, 1829–1834.

Gerard, M.J., Klatsky, A.L., Friedman, G.D., Siegelaub, A.B. & Feldman, R. (1977). Serum glucose levels and alcohol consumption habits in a large population. *Diabetes*, **26**, 780–785.

Heberden, W. (1786). Some account of a disorder of the breast. *Medical Transactions of the Royal College of Physicians, London*, **2**, 59–67.

Hein, H.O., Suadicani, P. & Gyntelberg, F. (1996). Alcohol consumption, serum low density lipoprotein cholesterol concentration, and risk of ischaemic heart disease: six year follow-up in the Copenhagen male study. *British Medical Journal*, **312**, 736–741.

Hendriks, F.J. & van der Gang, M.S. (1998). Alcohol, anticoagulation and fibrinolysis. In D.J. Chadwick & J.A. Goode (Eds), *Alcohol and Cardiovascular Diseases* (pp. 111–124). Chichester: Wiley.

Jackson, R., Scragg, R. & Beaglehole, R. (1991). Alcohol consumption and risk of coronary heart disease. *British Medical Journal*, **303**, 211–216.

Joint National Committee on Detection Evaluation and Treatment of High Blood Pressure. The fifth report of the Joint National Committee (1993). *Archives of Internal Medicine*, **153**, 158–183.

Kasper, E.K., Willem, W.R.P., Hutchins, G.M., Deckers, J.W., Hare, J.M. & Baughman, K.L. (1994). The causes of dilated cardiomyopathy: clinicopathologic review of 673 consecutive patients. *Journal of the American College of Cardiology*, **23**, 586–590.

Kawano, Y., Abe, H., Kojima, S., Ashida, T., Yoshida, K., Imanishi, M. et al. (1992). Acute depressor effect of alcohol in patients with essential hypertension. *Hypertension*, **20**, 219–226.

Keefer, C.S. (1930). The beri-beri heart. *Archives of Internal Medicine*, **45**, 1–22.

Keil, U., Swales, J.D. & Grobbee, D.E. (1993). Alcohol intake and its relation to hypertension. In P.M. Verschuren (Ed.), *Health Issues Related to Alcohol Consumption* (pp. 17–42). Washington, DC: ILSI Press.

Keil, U., Chambless, L.E., Doring, A., Filipiak, B. & Stieber, J. (1997). The relation of alcohol intake to coronary heart disease and all-cause mortality in a beer-drinking population. *Epidemiology*, **8**, 150–156.

Kiechl, S., Willeit, J., Poewe, W., Egger, G., Oberhollenzer, F., Muggeo, M. & Bonora, E. (1996).   Insulin sensitivity and regular alcohol consumption: large, prospective, cross sectional population study. *British Medical Journal*, **313**, 1040–1044.

Klatsky, A.L., Friedman, G.D., Siegelaub, A.B. & Gerard, M.J. (1997).   Alcohol consumption and blood pressure. *New England Journal of Medicine*, **296**, 1194–2000.

Klatsky, A.L., Friedman, G.D. & Armstrong, M.A. (1986a).   The relationship between alcoholic beverage use and other traits to blood pressure: a new Kaiser Permanente study. *Circulation*, **73**, 628–636.

Klatsky, A.L., Armstrong, M.A. & Friedman, G.D. (1986b).   Relations of alcoholic beverage use to subsequent coronary artery disease hospitalizations. *American Journal of Cardiology*, **58**, 710–714.

Klatsky, A.L., Armstrong, M.A. & Friedman, G.D. (1989).   Alcohol use and subsequent cerebrovascular disease hospitalizations. *Stroke*, **20**, 741–746.

Klatsky, A.L., Armstrong, M.A. & Friedman, G.D. (1990a).   Risk of cardiovascular mortality in alcohol drinkers, ex-drinkers and non-drinkers. *American Journal of Cardiology*, **66**, 1237–1242.

Klatsky, A.L., Armstrong, M.A. & Kipp, H. (1990b).   Correlates of alcoholic beverage preference: Traits of persons who choose wine, liquor or beer. *British Journal of the Addictions*, **85**, 1279–1289.

Klatsky, A.L. & Armstrong, M.A. (1993).   Alcoholic beverage choice and risk of coronary artery disease mortality: do red wine drinkers fare best? *American Journal of Cardiology*, **71**, 467–469.

Klatsky, A.L. (1994).   Epidemiology of coronary heart disease—influence of alcohol. *Alcoholism: Clinical and Experimental Research*, **18**, 88–96.

Klatsky, A.L. (1995a).   Blood pressure and alcohol intake. In J.H. Laragh & B.M. Brenner (Eds), *Hypertension: Pathophysiology, Diagnosis, and Management* (pp. 2649–2667). 2nd edn. New York: Raven.

Klatsky, A.L. (1995b).   Cardiovascular effects of alcohol. *Scientific American Science and Medicine*, **2**, 28–37.

Klatsky, A.L., Armstrong, M.A. & Friedman, G.D. (1997).   Red wine, white wine, liquor, beer, and risk for coronary artery disease hospitalization. *American Journal of Cardiology*, **80**, 416–420.

Klatsky, A.L. (1998).   Alcohol and cardiovascular diseases: a historical overview. In D.J. Chadwick & J.A. Goode (Eds), *Novartis Foundation Symposium 1998*, **216**, 2–12; Discussion 12–18, 152–158.

Langer, R.D., Criqui, M.H. & Reed, D.M. (1992).   Lipoproteins and blood pressure as biologic pathways for the effect of moderate alcohol consumption on coronary heart disease. *Circulation*, **85**, 910–915.

Lapasota, E.A. & Lange, L.G. (1986).   Presence of nonoxidative ethanol metabolism in human organs commonly damaged by ethanol abuse. *Science*, **231**, 497–499.

Lazarus, R., Sparrow, D. & Weiss, S.T. (1997).   Alcohol intake and insulin levels. The normative aging study. *American Journal of Epidemiology*, **145**, 909–916.

Lian, C. (1915).   L'alcoholisme cause d'hypertension artrielle. *Bulletin of the Academy of Medicine (Paris)*, **74**, 525–528.

MacKenzie, J. (1902).   The study of the pulse. In *The Study of the Pulse* (p. 237). Edinburgh: Y.J. Pentland.

Maclure, M. (1993).   Demonstration of deductive meta-analysis: ethanol intake and risk of myocardial infarction. *Epidemiology Review*, **15**, 328–351.

MacMahon, S. (1987).   Alcohol consumption and hypertension. *Hypertension*, **9**, 111–121.

Maki, T., Toivonen, L., Koskinen, P., Naveri, H., Harkonen, M. & Leinonen, H. (1998).   Effect of ethanol drinking, hangover, and exercise on adrenergic activity and heart rate variability in patients with a history of alcohol-induced atrial fibrillation. *American Journal of Cardiology*, **82**, 317–322.

Marmot, M. & Brunner, E. (1991).   Alcohol and cardiovascular disease: the status of the U-shaped curve. *British Medical Journal*, **303**, 365–368.

Mayer, E.J., Newman, B., Quesenberry, C.P.Jr, Friedman, G.D. & Selby, J.V. (1993).   Alcohol consumption and insulin concentrations. Role of insulin in associations of alcohol intake with high-density lipoprotein cholesterol and triglycerides. *Circulation*, **88**, 2190–2197.

Moore, R.D., Smith, C.R., Kwiterovich, P.O. et al. (1988).   Effect of low-dose alcohol use vs. abstraction on apolipoproteins A–I and B. *American Journal of Medicine*, **84**, 884–896.

Morin, Y. & Daniel, P. (1967).   Quebec beer-drinkers' cardiomyopathy: etiologic considerations. *Canadian Medical Association Journal*, **97**, 926–928.

Moushmoush, B. & Abi-Mansour, P. (1991). Alcohol and the heart. *Archives of Internal Medicine*, **151**, 36–42.

Orlando, J.F., Aronow, W.S. & Cassidy, J. (1976). Effect of ethanol on angina pectoris. *Annals of Internal Medicine*, **842**, 652–655.

Pearson, T.A. & Terry, P. (1994). What to advise patients about drinking alcohol. *Journal of the American Medical Association*, **272**, 957–958.

Potter, J.F. & Beevers, D.G. (1984). Pressor effect of alcohol in hypertension. *Lancet*, **1**, 119–122.

Puddey, I.B., Beilin, I.J., Vandongen, R., Rouse, I.L. & Rogers, P. (1985). Evidence of a direct effect of alcohol consumption on blood presure in normotensive men: a randomized controlled trial. *Hypertension*, **7**, 707–713.

Puddey, I.B., Beilin, L.J. & Vandongen, R. (1987). Regular alcohol use raises blood pressure in treated hypertensives. *Lancet*, **1**, 647–651.

Randin, D., Vollenweider, P., Tappy, L., Jequier, E., Nicod, P. & Scherrer, U. (1995). Suppression of alcohol-induced hypertension by dexamethasone. *New England Journal of Medicine*, **332**, 1733–1737.

Regan, T.J. (1984). Alcoholic cardiomyopathy. *Progress in Cardiovascular Disease*, **27**, 141–152.

Rehm, J.T., Bondy, S.J., Sempos, C.T. & Vuong, C.V. (1997). Alcohol consumption and coronary heart disease morbidity and mortality. *American Journal of Epidemiology*, **146**, 495–501.

Renaud, S. & de Lorgeril, M. (1992). Wine, alcohol, platelets, and the French paradox of coronary heart disease. *Lancet*, **339**, 1523–1526.

Renaud, S., Criqui, M.H., Farchi, G. & Veenstra, J. (1993). Alcohol drinking and coronary heart disease. In P.M. Verschuren (Ed.), *Health Issues Related to Alcohol Consumption* (pp. 81–124). Washington, DC: ILSI Press.

Reynolds, E.S. (1901). An account of the epidemic outbreak of arsenical poisoning occurring in beer drinkers in the north of England and the Midland Counties in 1900. *Lancet*, **1**, 166–170.

Richardson, P.J., Patel, V.B. & Preedy, V.R. (1998). Alcohol and the myocardium. In D.J. Chadwick & J.A. Goode (Eds), *Alcohol and cardiovascular diseases* (Novartis Foundation Symposium No. 216) (pp. 2–18).

Rimm, E.B., Giovannucci, E.L., Willett, W.C., Colditz, G.A., Ascherio, A., Rosner, B. & Stampfer, M.J. (1991). Prospective study of alcohol consumption and risk of coronary heart disease in men. *Lancet*, **388**, 464–468.

Rimm, E., Klatsky, A.L., Grobbee, D. & Stampfer, M.J. (1996). Review of moderate alcohol consumption and reduced risk of coronary heart disease: is the effect due to beer, wine or spirits? *British Medical Journal*, **312**, 731–736.

Royal Commission Appointed to Inquire into Arsenical Poisoning from the Consumption of Beer and other Articles of Food or Drink (1903). *Final Report*, Part I. London: Wyman and Sons.

St. Leger, A.S., Cochrane, A.L. & Moore, F. (1979). Factors associated with cardiac mortality in developed countries with particular reference to consumption of wine. *Lancet*, **1**, 1017–1020.

Shaper, A.G., Wannamethee, G. & Walker, M. (1988). Alcohol and mortality in British men: explaining the U-shaped curve. *Lancet*, **2**, 1267–1273.

Siscovick, D.S., Weiss, N.S. & Fox, N. (1986). Moderate alcohol consumption and primary cardiac arrest. *American Journal of Epidemiology*, **123**, 499–503.

Stampfer, M.J., Colditz, G.A., Willett, W.C., Speizer, F.E. & Hennekens, C.H. (1988). Prospective study of moderate alcohol consumption and the risk of coronary disease and stroke in women. *New England Journal of Medicine*, **319**, 267–273.

Steell, G. (1906). *Textbook on Diseases of the Heart* (p. 79). Philadelphia, PA: Blakiston.

Suh, I., Shaten, J., Cutler, J.A. & Kuller, L. (1992). Alcohol use and mortality from coronary heart disease: the role of high-density lipoprotein cholesterol. *Annals of Internal Medicine*, **116**, 881–887.

Urbano-Marquez, A., Estrich, R., Navarro-Lopez, F., Grau, J.M., L., M. & Rubin, E. (1989). The effects of alcoholism on skeletal and cardiac muscle. *New England Journal of Medicine*, **320**, 409–415.

Van Gign, J., Stampfer, M.J., Wolfe, C. & Algra, A. (1993). The association between alcohol consumption and stroke. In P.M. Verschuren (Ed.), *Health Issues Related to Alcohol Consumption* (pp. 43–80). Washington, DC: ILSI Press.

Vaquez, H. (1921). Quebec beer drinkers' cardiomyopathy. In *Maladies du Coeur*. Paris: Baillière, p. 308.

Virtamo, J., Rapola, J.M., Ripatti, S., Heinonen, O.P., Taylor, P.R., Albanes, D. & Huttunen, J.K. (1998). Effect of vitamin E and β-carotene on the incidence of primary non-fatal myocardial infarction and fatal coronary disease. *Archives of Internal Medicine*, **158**, 668–675.

GLOSSARY

Angina pectoris   A common symptom of inadequate heart muscle oxygen supply, usually caused by coronary artery blockage, often characterized by poorly defined central anterior chest discomfort, which may radiate to the neck, shoulders and arms.

Arrhythmia   Irregularity of the heart beat, with various types ranging in importance from inconsequential to life-threatening.

Atherosclerosis   A condition characterized by thickening, internal irregularity, and stiffening of the large arteries (e.g. aorta, coronary arteries to the heart muscle, carotid and vertebral arteries to the head, and femoral arteries to the legs). It is due substantially to deposition of fatty substances just beneath the inside lining (endothelium) of the blood vessels, producing lesions known as *plaques*.

Cardiomyopathy   Heart muscle disease independent of disorders of the valves, coronary arteries, pericardium and congenital malformations. Some cases have known causes; many do not. Very heavy alcohol drinking, sustained over many years, is one cause.

Case-control study   The study of an attribute of a condition by comparison of the frequency of an attribute or trait in a group of persons with the condition (cases) to the frequency of the attribute in a group without the condition (controls). The validity of the results is strongly dependent on the similarity of the case and control groups, excepting the trait under study.

Coronary heart disease   A heart disease due to *atherosclerosis* of the coronary arteries, which obstructs the heart's blood supply and is exacerbated by a tendency for blood clot formation in the affected arteries. It can produce *angina pectoris*, *myocardial infarction* ("heart attack") and sudden death.

Dilated cardiomyopathy   A type of cardiomyopathy characterized by an enlarged heart with weakened contraction; sustained heavy alcohol drinking can cause this.

Epidemiology   The study of disease and health in large populations, with primary concern about groups of persons rather than individuals.

Heart failure   Often called *congestive heart failure*, this is a constellation of symptoms, physical findings, and measurements due to inadequate heart pumping function. Common symptoms are breathlessness, easy fatigability and accumulation of excess body fluid.

Hemorrhagic stroke   An acute brain injury due to a ruptured blood vessel in the brain or on its surface. The brain injury results from deprived blood supply and tissue swelling or damage from accumulating blood. A large proportion of hemorrhagic strokes result in death or serious disability, but complete recovery is also possible.

Hypertension   High blood pressure, often defined as 140/90 mmHg or higher on several measurements.

Ischemic stroke   An acute brain injury due to a blocked blood vessel supplying the brain. The brain injury results primarily from deprived blood supply. The blood vessels may be blocked by clots forming in diseased brain arteries or by clots traveling in the circulation from elsewhere (the heart or large arteries between the heart and brain). Most strokes (~85%) are ischemic; they range in severity from minor attacks with complete recovery to severe ones with major disability or death.

Myocardial infarction Commonly called "heart attack", a manifestation of *coronary heart disease* in which deficiency of oxygen supply leads to death of part of the heart muscle and sometimes sudden death of the person affected. The acute condition is followed by scar formation, which causes continued impairment of heart muscle function.

Prospective population study The study of the relationship of a trait to the development of a condition in a population after the trait has been measured or determined, e.g. the risk of coronary heart disease may be studied in relation to sex, ethnicity or alcohol drinking, with resultant comparison of risk in relation to a large number of known traits. Statistical models enable control for indirect explanations of results.

Chapter 12

Diagnostic and Monitoring Investigations

John B. Whitfield
Royal Prince Alfred Hospital, Sydney, New South Wales, Australia

Synopsis

A number of biochemical or structural changes induced by chronic excessive alcohol intake have been used as biological markers of alcohol dependence or recent consumption. Such markers have been applied to diverse groups, including the general population or high-risk subgroups, patients presenting for treatment without known alcohol-related problems, and patients with known alcohol dependence who have a treatment goal of abstinence or controlled drinking.

The place of biological markers in relation to questionnaires and history-taking, and the points of difference between markers of alcohol use and other diagnostic tests, should be appreciated. Alcohol intake in the population is a continuum and, although risk of such adverse consequences as dependence or physical disease is increased by high levels of consumption, the population cannot be divided into "healthy" and "diseased" groups. Therefore, laboratory tests indicate the probability of current or future problems, rather than providing a diagnosis.

Of the currently available laboratory tests, carbohydrate-deficient transferrin (CDT) offers the best combination of specificity and sensitivity for clinical purposes. Measurement of 5-hydroxytryptophol also has high sensitivity and specificity, but values return to normal within a few hours of completion of ethanol metabolism and it is therefore mainly of research use. g-Glutamyl transferase (GGT) lacks specificity, being abnormal in liver disease from any cause and also in patients taking enzyme-inducing drugs and in some people with obesity. However, GGT is the only marker of alcohol intake that has been shown in prospective studies to predict mortality and health-care or social security utilization. Erythrocyte mean cell volume (MCV) lacks both sensitivity and specificity, but may still be useful in alerting the doctor to alcohol abuse if a routine haematological profile returns an abnormal MCV with no obvious explanation.

Since the diagnosis will usually be evident in patients with severe alcohol dependence and massive current alcohol intake, the main uses of laboratory tests are to detect lesser degrees of hazardous or harmful use and to monitor abstinence in patients receiving treatment. Sen-

International Handbook of Alcohol Dependence and Problems. Edited by N. Heather, T.J. Peters and T. Stockwell.
© 2001 John Wiley & Sons Ltd.

sitivity in detecting hazardous alcohol intake is low, but people with abnormal GGT values might benefit more from intervention. Monitoring abstinence with whichever test was abnormal at presentation or another time of known excessive drinking (usually CDT or GGT) is better than applying the same test to all patients. Detection of the medical complications of alcoholism relies on conventional liver (or other organ) function tests.

Progress is likely to come through further development of markers of risk, and their use in conjunction with questionnaires for the detection of hazardous or harmful alcohol use. Genetic markers of alcohol dependence risk may be discovered within the next 5 years, and their clinical use will raise important practical and ethical issues. Non-genetic markers, of the risk of death or disease among hazardous drinkers, are a more immediate prospect.

This chapter aims to provide a summary of the more useful biological markers of alcohol intake or alcohol-related disease, with information on the sensitivity and specificity of the tests in various situations related to alcohol problems. Where possible, information is given on the biochemical and pathological events leading to test abnormality, and on the prognostic significance of abnormalities. Briefer accounts are given of tests that are less effective or not yet widely available, and of the prospects for tests for genetic susceptibility to alcohol dependence or alcohol-related disease.

This chapter is aimed at clinicians, laboratory scientists and students, and is intended to provide:

1. An improved understanding of the role and limitations of laboratory tests in the assessment and management of people with alcohol-related conditions.
2. A resource for subsequent checking of key facts and for access to the original work on which these facts are based.

LABORATORY INVESTIGATIONS ON THE ASSESSMENT AND MANAGEMENT OF ALCOHOL-RELATED CONDITIONS

There is a substantial literature, dating back many years, on the pathological and biochemical changes that occur in people affected by alcohol dependence or alcohol-related disease. This knowledge can be applied to evaluation of individual patients, with a view to obtaining information which will help in their management. Nevertheless, there is little point in doing investigations for clinical purposes unless there is a clinical question to be answered and some action that may be influenced by the result.

The questions that may occur are, in principle, similar to those that occur in the management of any other physical or mental illness:

- Can a provisional diagnosis be confirmed or ruled out?
- Has the patient's condition improved or deteriorated with the passage of time or in response to treatment?
- Is the person at above-average risk for development of disease or for development of a complication of their existing disease or condition?

In addition, there is a question that needs to be answered in a research or clinical trial setting. This is basically the same as the second question above; have patients (on average) got better or worse after some intervention? Objective evidence of change or improvement is important in all trials, but it is particularly relevant when the main endpoint is behaviour change as reported by the patient or client.

The questions outlined above may occur at a number of points in the course of the disease or condition, for example:

- Before alcohol dependence or hazardous alcohol use commences.
- During periods of excessive alcohol consumption, with or without dependence.
- During treatment, whether the goal is abstinence or controlled drinking.
- After medical consequences of excessive drinking have developed.

DEFINITIONS AND CLASSIFICATIONS

A distinction should be made between a test that indicates current disease, and a test that evaluates the risk of a disease developing in the future. Most clinical laboratory tests are of the former type, in that they are normal before the disease develops and, generally, they revert to normal after the disease resolves. They reflect the current state of the patient and, in the context of markers of alcohol consumption, they have become known as *state markers*.

Other tests, of which cholesterol is probably the most widely known example, give a measure of the probability of some adverse event occurring in future. Variation in these *risk factors* may be due to multiple factors, such as genetic make-up or diet, but although the level of the risk factor and therefore of the risk may vary with time, they are not tied closely to the current state of the patient. In the extreme case of risk associated with a particular allele at a genetic locus, the genotype, and therefore the risk, are set at conception and remain constant (apart from age-related expression of the trait) throughout life. In the context of alcohol dependence, tests that measure risk have become known as *trait markers*; but at present there are few thoroughly validated trait markers for risk of alcohol dependence.

It is therefore possible to classify biological markers related to alcohol in two dimensions; the state/trait difference, and the major stages or events in the natural history of the condition. State and trait markers are potentially applicable to hazardous alcohol consumption, alcohol dependence or organ damage. Markers could exist in each of these six categories, but at present there are no examples of state markers for dependence. (Although dependence in a currently drinking person may be easily detectable, it might be useful to determine whether neurochemical changes associated with dependence are still present and the symptoms of dependence would reappear after any exposure to alcohol.)

For a state marker, it is important to understand the concepts of test *sensitivity* and *specificity* and the relevance of the prevalence of the condition in the population tested. Sensitivity is the proportion of people with the condition who will be detected by the test, while specificity is the proportion of people who do not have the disease who have normal or negative results. These two proportions are interdependent, because one can always improve the sensitivity at the cost of poorer specificity, or vice versa, by changing the cut-off point that defines a normal or abnormal result. For this reason, estimates of test performance should always quote both sensitivity and specificity, and comparisons are easiest if specificity is set at 95% for all the tests being compared or evaluated.

The prevalence of a condition among the population tested, together with the sensitivity and specificity, will determine the proportion of *false positives* and *false negatives* produced by testing.

The sensitivity and specificity should not vary not vary with the prevalence of the condition sought, but they will be affected by the nature of the control and affected groups used in the test evaluations. A control group comprising hospital or laboratory staff will often lead to higher specificity than can be expected during the application of the test to a mixed group of patients, while a severely affected patient group will produce a higher sensitivity estimate than the mixture of more and less severe cases usually seen in practice. Therefore evaluations of test performance should be assessed with the control and study groups' characteristics in mind.

For a qualitative risk factor marker, the concept of relative risk is more appropriate than sensitivity. One genotype (say the homozygote of the commonest allele) is chosen as the reference point and the increase or decrease in risk of having or developing the condition for each of the other possible genotypes is calculated. For quantitative risk factors, the difference between people in the highest and lowest quintiles, or the difference in risk between the 25th and 75th centiles, is sometimes quoted.

SPECIAL CONSIDERATIONS RELEVANT TO ALCOHOL

Several considerations apply to markers of alcohol consumption or dependence which are absent from the more common applications of laboratory tests:

- In contrast to diseases which are either present or absent, alcohol consumption is common in most countries, and the frequency distribution of alcohol intake is continuous. Many people drink at levels that are either harmless or beneficial; it is only the minority who drink at hazardous levels who may benefit from testing. Furthermore, although there are expert guidelines on what constitutes safe or hazardous drinking, it is very likely that the threshold for alcohol-related harm differs between individuals. What is safe for one person may be harmful for another. This adds to the difficulty of defining who is in the "abnormal" group and who is in the "normal" one.
- Even for dependence, which can be dichotomized, these are quantitative aspects. Some people will have multiple symptoms and frequent relapses, whereas for others alcohol dependence may only be present for a short time and cause comparatively minor problems. Studies based on subjects recruited from clinical sources are likely to show greater differences between the subjects and unaffected controls than studies based on community recruitment. As mentioned above, this will affect statistics such as test sensitivity.
- Because there is no entirely reliable method or "gold standard" for the measurement of alcohol consumption, it is hard to evaluate the absolute sensitivity or specificity of a test. Unreliable measures of the independent variable (alcohol intake) will decrease the correlation with marker results and diminish the separation between two contrasted groups. Only the relative performance of different tests can be compared.
- Ethanol metabolism is rapid compared to that of many other drugs, and essentially complete. The products of this metabolism are carbon dioxide and water, and are indistinguishable from the products of metabolism of foodstuffs or body energy stores. Therefore, it is necessary to use markers of the consequences of alcohol use, which are inherently less reliable than detection of drug metabolites—but which may, paradoxically, be more informative.

For all these reasons, the use of biochemical tests for estimation of alcohol intake has limitations, which should be understood and acknowledged. Besides, alcohol intake is irrelevant apart from its association with risk of problems and alcohol-induced disease; wherever possible, we should concentrate on detecting or predicting the harm that excessive alcohol use can cause. Because validation of markers of long-term harm requires long-term studies, such an approach has been rare.

Conversely, some people benefit from their alcohol intake. On a population basis, there will be some level of intake at which the chance of an average person benefiting from alcohol is exceeded by the chance of sustaining damage. Some individuals will presumably differ quite widely from this average safe limit, and it might be possible to use biochemical tests to assess both benefit and harm and the balance between them. However, this does not appear to have been done.

It is reasonable to ask whether screening with laboratory tests is a useful activity. Perhaps interviewing techniques, or simple questionnaires, offer a cheaper substitute. Detection of dependence and problems arising from alcohol are more directly approached in this way. However, there are an increasing number of long-term prospective studies to show that testing can have predictive value, and that intervention based on results of laboratory tests can be beneficial. The optimum strategy may be to use a short verbal or written checklist first, followed by laboratory investigations in those found to be at high risk. Nevertheless, it must be appreciated that the group at risk from their drinking is wider than just the group meeting diagnostic criteria for dependence.

BIOCHEMICAL CONSEQUENCES OF ALCOHOL USE

In this section, we consider analytes whose mean values change in 'alcoholics' and which have been proposed as markers of alcohol intake. It is not necessary to consider the large number of tests where mean values can be shown to be affected by alcohol; for a diagnostic test it is necessary to have a minimum overlap between the frequency distributions for the affected and unaffected groups.

Potentially there are three groups of interest, which unfortunately have no absolute boundaries; control subjects or safe drinkers, hazardous drinkers, and dependent drinkers. It is necessary to distinguish between studies that have contrasted actively drinking alcoholics and control subjects, and those that have contrasted subjects believed to be taking safe quantities of alcohol and subjects taking hazardous amounts. For each test we will consider:

- Reference ranges and any factors affecting them.
- Test performance, including any sex and age effects on marker effectiveness.
- Information relevant to test interpretation.
- Prognostic value.

These topics have previously been reviewed by Goldberg & Kapur (1994), Conigrave et al. (1995), Sharpe et al. (1996) and, in part, by Stibler (1991).

γ-Glutamyl Transferase (GGT)

GGT is an enzyme with poorly understood physiological functions, but which seems to be associated with amino acid transport at cell membranes, and with glutathione uptake. It is easily measured in serum or plasma using chromogenic substrates, and inexpensive methods are available for automated photometric analysers and for some near-patient testing systems.

Reference Range

Most laboratories and textbooks quote a reference range up to 55 u/l at 37°C for men and 40 u/l for women. Our own unpublished data show that the 95th centiles of the GGT frequency distribution for people reporting consumption of up to 70 g alcohol in the past week are 66 for men and 44 for women. Because of the effects of alcohol and of obesity on GGT, the reference range depends on the degree to which people with these characteristics are excluded.

Test Performance

The specificity of GGT as an alcohol intake marker is diminished by its abnormal values in many kinds of liver disease (including the increasingly common chronic hepatitis of viral origin), its induction by microsomal enzyme-inducing drugs (Rosalki et al., 1971), and increases in mean value associated with obesity (van Barneveld et al., 1989) and non-insulin-dependent diabetes (Barbieux et al., 1990). In the general population, lack of specificity is less of a problem than in a hospital environment.

Sensitivity, like specificity and the reference range, depends on the definition of the group studied. For dependent or alcoholic patients, sensitivity is in the range 60–90% (Conigrave et al., 1995). For people drinking hazardous amounts of alcohol but not known to be dependent, sensitivity values of 20–50% have been found. Interpretation of these values is made more difficult by the wide range of specificities reported (55–100%).

Test Interpretation

The limited sensitivity of GGT for detecting hazardous drinking has the corollary that some hazardous and heavy drinkers have an elevated GGT, while others do not, as can be seen in Figure 12.1 (adapted from Whitfield et al., 1978). The range of GGT results seen in the sampled population becomes greater as alcohol intake increases. Because the physiological function of GGT is uncertain, we cannot define the underlying difference between a heavy drinker with a normal GGT and one with an elevated GGT, but we can look for other differences between these groups and for differences in prognosis.

First, subjects with raised GGT are more likely to show abnormalities in the liver function tests, aspartate aminotransferase (AST) and alanine aminotransferase (ALT) (Whitfield et al., 1981; Whitfield and Martin, 1985a). This is consistent with each test responding to alcohol-induced liver damage, and indeed, it has been shown that alcoholics with raised GGT are more likely to have evidence of liver steatosis, fibrosis or cirrhosis on liver biopsy (Wu, Slavin and Levy, 1976; Kryszewski et al., 1977; Frezza et al., 1989). For reasons that are not yet understood, subjects with excessive alcohol consumption and raised GGT are also likely to have increased serum triglycerides and urate (Whitfield et al., 1981), and increased blood pressure (Henningsen et al., 1980). Second, several groups have shown that subjects with raised GGT have an increased incidence of mortality or morbidity in prospective studies.

Prognostic Value

A number of independent studies have shown that an increased GGT is a predictor of increased mortality, morbidity or use of health and social security resources. Some studies have taken into account variations in alcohol use, obesity, or other risk factors and shown that the effect of GGT is independent of these. Some studies have classified causes of death or types of illness, e.g. into "alcohol-related deaths", cardiovascular deaths and deaths from cancer. The overall picture is that GGT is a significant risk factor, but it is not so clear that it only predicts "alcohol-related" death.

The earliest studies were performed in Malmö, Sweden, from 1974 onwards (Kristenson et al., 1980; Peterson et al., 1980; Kristenson et al., 1983; Trell, Kristenson & Petersson, 1985; Hood et al., 1990). Men aged in the 40s were screened for a number of health-related

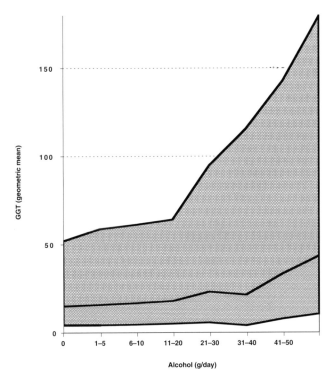

Figure 12.1 Geometric mean and 95% confidence intervals for GGT by self-reported average daily alcohol intake in men. Note that the variance of the GGT distribution increases progressively above 20 g alcohol/day. Data from Whitfield et al. (1978)

variables, and those with a GGT result in the top decile were investigated further and, if appropriate, enrolled in an intervention trial that aimed to reduce drinking. Participants were followed-up after the screening process and a strong association between high GGT and mortality was established (see Figure 12.2). High GGT was also a good predictor of alcohol-related admissions to hospital, orthopaedic hospitalization, and other events that would be expected to occur more frequently in heavy drinkers. It was also, unexpectedly, a predictor of coronary heart disease.

Investigation of men admitted to hospital in Helsinki, Finland, following injury (Antti-Poikka & Karaharju, 1988) revealed that high GGT among heavy drinkers was a predictor of increased complications and longer hospital stay.

A study conducted in Sydney, Australia (Conigrave et al., 1993), also assessed GGT results as a predictor of mortality and healthcare utilization. Again, significant results were obtained and it could be shown that this was not solely due to GGT acting as a marker of alcohol intake; a high GGT adds information to that obtained from an estimate of alcohol consumption.

At least three other studies, in Germany, Japan and England, have investigated the relationship between cardiovascular risk and GGT. The Japanese study (Miura et al., 1994) showed a high GGT to be a predictor of the development of hypertension; the English study (Wannamethee et al., 1995) found an increased risk of ischaemic heart disease and deaths from all causes; and the German study (Brenner et al., 1997; Arndt et al., 1998) showed increased all-cause mortality and retirement from work due to disability in men with high GGT.

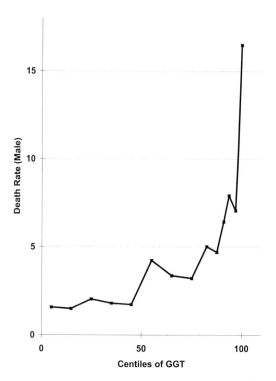

Figure 12.2   Deaths from all causes except cancer during 5–11 years follow-up of middle-aged men in Sweden, by centiles of GGT at screening. (Modified from Hood et al., 1990)

The exact relationships between elevated GGT, alcohol intake, coronary heart disease, alcoholic liver disease and all-cause mortality are uncertain. Nevertheless, it is clear that an alcohol-dependent person or a hazardous drinker with a high GGT has a worse prognosis than one with a normal GGT value. One must also conclude that drinkers with high GGT are not among the people who improve their cardiovascular risk through their alcohol use.

Erythrocyte Mean Cell Volume (MCV)

The size of erythrocytes is affected by genetic factors (Whitfield and Martin, 1985b) and also by a number of anaemias caused by deficiency of iron, folate and vitamin B_{12}. Alcoholism may cause both anaemia and macrocytosis, but the recognition that the mean cell volume was increased in a high proportion of people consuming large amounts of alcohol came after technical advances made it possible to measure MCV with much greater precision. The cause of this alcohol-related macrocytosis is unknown; folate deficiency or altered folate metabolism may play a role, but folate supplementation will not necessarily normalize MCV if drinking continues.

Reference Range

Ranges for MCV by automated haematology analysers vary, with values quoted as 83–98 fl (Rodger et al., 1987) or 82–95 fl (Davidson and Hamilton, 1978). Papers evaluating

MCV as a marker of excessive alcohol intake have generally set an upper limit of normal of 94 or 95 fl and have found that specificity at this cut-off point is around 90% (Bell et al., 1994; Wickramasinghe et al., 1994; Yersin et al., 1995).

Test Performance

The specificity of MCV for alcohol is affected by the population studied, and in particular by the presence of patients with megaloblastic anaemias. The review by Conigrave et al. (1995) found a range of sensitivities of 40–50% for "alcoholics" (alcohol-dependent subjects in treatment) and 20–30% for subjects with hazardous alcohol consumption. Results should be interpreted with knowledge of the subjects' smoking status, which also increases MCV (Whitehead et al., 1995), but also with the knowledge that smoking and alcohol dependence are strongly associated.

Test Interpretation

The lack of knowledge about the cause of increased MCV in people with excessive alcohol consumption makes it difficult to assess its significance. Although there is experimental evidence that folate absorption and metabolism can be changed by alcohol (Blocker & Thenen, 1987), and some alcoholics will have low folate intake and definite folate deficiency, effects of alcohol on erythrocyte size through other mechanisms are thought to exist.

Prognostic Value

There is no information on relationships between MCV values and prognosis.

Glycoproteins

Chronic excessive alcohol consumption brings about a number of changes to plasma glycoproteins, particularly transferrin. For reasons which are not entirely clear, the terminal residues on the carbohydrate side-chains of transferrin are more often absent and, because the usual terminal carbohydrate residue is sialic acid, this leads to a change in charge and isoelectric point of the protein.

Animal experiments have provided evidence that both post-translational modification of transferrin is incomplete and normal hepatic uptake of asialoglycoproteins is impaired after chronic alcohol administration (Xin et al., 1995). Taken together, these hepatic changes increase the circulating concentration of carbohydrate-deficient transferrin (CDT).

Isotransferrins (varying in sialic acid content) can be separated by isoelectric focusing or by ion-exchange chromatography, and their concentration can be measured by immunoblotting and densitometry or by immunoassay. These are standard laboratory techniques but comparatively time-consuming and therefore expensive. Commercially available methods are also expensive.

Reference Range

The reference ranges depend on the method used and on the reference base for the result (by volume of serum, or as a proportion of total transferrin). Values are higher in women than men, and higher in younger (presumably premenopausal) women than in women aged over 50 (Whitfield et al., 1998). There have also been reports of higher values in pregnant than in non-pregnant women (Godsell et al., 1995; Stauber et al., 1996). Some of this variation may be due to variation in serum total transferrin.

By the commonest method, based on anion exchange and transferrin immunoassay, the reference ranges are up to 20 u/l for men and 30 u/l for women. Older methods based on anion exchange gave reference ranges up to 80 or 100 mg/l because more of the trisialo-transferrin was included in the "carbohydrate-deficient" fraction. With methods that express results as a percentage of total transferrin, the reference ranges also vary according to the mixture of isotransferrins included; up to 2.5% for the %CDT RIA and up to 6% for the %CDT TIA, for both men and women.

Test Performance

Specificity for alcohol is better than older tests such as GGT or MCV, but CDT is abnormal in patients with some non-alcoholic forms of liver disease (Bell et al., 1993) and in a group of rare carbohydrate-deficient glycoprotein disorders (Stibler et al., 1998) and galactosaemia (Stibler et al., 1997). CDT, as measured by column anion-exchange methods, can be affected by uncommon variants of the transferrin protein, which vary in isoelectric point (Stibler et al., 1988).

The reported sensitivity of CDT in currently drinking alcohol-dependent subjects is 65–95%, and for hazardous alcohol intake 25–60% (Conigrave et al., 1995).

Test Interpretation

The reasons for variation in the sensitivity of CDT for alcohol abuse have recently become clearer. Initial reports were that subjects with insulin resistance or hypertension (Fagerberg et al., 1994a, b) were likely to show false negatives (poorer sensitivity). These results were confirmed in further studies (Whitfield et al., 1998) and effects of smoking, past alcohol dependence, obesity and dyslipidaemia and were also found, at least among subjects with hazardous alcohol use. Non-smokers showed substantially lower sensitivity of CDT for hazardous alcohol consumption, while obesity/high triglyceride/low HDL were also associated with lower sensitivity.

Prognostic Value

There is no information on the value of CDT in predicting morbidity or mortality in alcoholics or hazardous drinkers. In view of the reports of association between dyslipidaemia, hypertension and insulin resistance and a diminished CDT response to alcohol, it is likely that a raised CDT has no adverse implications, except as an indicator of excessive alcohol intake.

Acetaldehyde–Protein Adducts and Antibodies

Ethanol is metabolized to acetaldehyde by alcohol dehydrogenase, followed by conversion to acetate by aldehyde dehydrogenase. Acetaldehyde concentrations in the blood during ethanol metabolism are normally very low (in the micromolar range or below). Acetaldehyde can react with free amino groups in proteins to produce acetaldehyde–protein adducts, by a mechanism analogous to the formation of glycoproteins by glucose (Braun et al., 1997).

Measurement of such adducts as markers of alcohol intake is based on the premise that the more alcohol is ingested, the greater the time during which acetaldehyde is present and the greater the degree to which reactions between acetaldehyde and proteins will occur. The reaction is believed to occur in two steps, the second of which is irreversible, so that the proteins retain their modified form for their lifetime in the circulation. In principle, any protein may become modified but most studies have focused on haemoglobin because of its high concentration in the blood.

These reactions were first demonstrated *in vitro* using unrealistically high concentrations of acetaldehyde, but there is now substantial evidence for the production of such adducts *in vivo* during alcohol metabolism, and for their persistence in the circulation after ethanol elimination is complete.

Because the chemical modification of the proteins changes their antigenic properties, antibodies to them are formed, and so the presence of either the modified protein or of the antibody may be used as a marker of high alcohol intake. Measurement of the modified protein has been by enzyme immunoassay, with antibodies directed against the acetaldehyde-modified epitopes on proteins (Worrall et al., 1998) or by ion exchange separation of modified haemoglobins (Sillanaukee et al., 1991; Chen et al., 1995). Measurements of the antibodies may distinguish between different classes of immunoglobulins (Viitala et al., 1997).

Reference Range

Ranges, and units of measurement, vary with the method used.

Test Performance

There appears to be no information on specificity, although industrial exposure or smoking might lead to formation of acetaldehyde–protein adducts. Sensitivity has been assessed in a small number of studies using differing analytical approaches (Sillanaukee et al., 1991, 1992; Lin et al., 1993; Worrall et al., 1996; Hazelett et al., 1998; Hurme et al., 1998), with results varying between 20% and 80%.

Test Interpretation

Since this test has not been widely used, there is little information on factors that might modify the results or their interpretation. The assumption is that this test would give an index of "ethanolic control" in the same way that glycated proteins give an index of glycaemic control in diabetics; a time-integrated measure of blood ethanol (in fact, blood acetaldehyde) concentrations. However, since acetaldehyde modification of proteins may have a role in the pathogenesis of alcohol-related organ damage, some interpretation as a risk factor may become possible.

Prognostic Value

There is no direct evidence that measurement of adducts or antibodies to them has value in the prediction of alcoholic liver disease or other consequences of alcohol use. However, they do appear to have significance in the pathogenesis of liver disease, because experimental animals treated with ethanol and immunized with acetaldehyde-modified proteins show more liver damage than animals treated with ethanol alone (Yokoyama et al., 1995). Moreover, alcoholic patients with ALDH deficiency, who will be more likely to form acetaldehyde–protein adducts, have a higher risk of alcoholic liver disease (Enomoto et al., 1991). There has been one report that pregnant women with increased acetaldehyde–haemoglobin adducts were more likely to give birth to babies affected by

fetal alcohol syndrome (Niemela, Halmesmaki & Ylikorkala, 1991), and another that antibodies to acetaldehyde-modified cardiac cytosolic proteins are detectable in alcoholic heart
disease (Harcombe et al., 1995). Further prognostic studies of acetaldehyde adducts or
antibodies to them are warranted.

Serotonin Metabolites

The actions of both alcohol dehydrogenase and aldehyde dehydrogenase lead to conversion of NAD to NADH in hepatocytes, and a consequent change in the equilibrium
between any pair of compounds interconverted by an NAD-dependent dehydrogenase
enzyme. Serotonin (5-hydroxytryptamine, 5-HT) is normally metabolized via an aldehyde
intermediate to the carboxylic acid, 5-hydroxyindoleacetic acid (5-HIAA), with traces
of 5-hydroxytryptophol (5-HTOL). The change in NADH:NAD ratio during ethanol
metabolism leads to a relative increase in formation and excretion of 5-HTOL and an
increase in the urine 5-HTOL:5-HIAA ratio (Voltaire et al., 1992). Being based on the
effects of ethanol metabolism, this is a comparatively short-term marker, but abnormalities in the urine ratio persist for some hours after ethanol elimination is complete. The test
has mainly been applied to intensive surveillance of patients in outpatient treatment
programmes in Sweden, and to validation of other biological markers in patients under
treatment.

Measurement of the 5-HTOL:5-HIAA ratio is performed using gas chromatography–
mass spectrometry, which is now fairly widely available but still expensive for a routine test.

Reference Range

Values of 4–20 pmol 5-HTOL/nmol 5-HIAA were reported by Voltaire et al. (1992).

Test Performance

Because this test depends on a metabolic consequence of alcohol use, it would be expected
that all occasions of alcohol consumption would increase the 5-HTOL:5-HIAA ratio
within any individual subject. Sensitivity of 90% for men and 60% for women was reported
by Helander et al. (1996a) for as little as 7 g alcohol. When the ratio is used, foods containing 5-hydroxyindoles do not interfere and polymorphisms in alcohol and aldehyde
dehydrogenases have no effect. However, ALDH inhibitors increase the ratio.

Test Interpretation

Results must be interpreted in the light of information on the time since drinking may have
taken place; if testing is infrequent, then it will be difficult to assess the significance of
normal results.

Prognostic Value

There is no information on relationships between 5-HTOL values and prognosis.

Alcohols and Alcohol Metabolites

Blood, plasma and urine ethanol concentrations rise after consumption of alcoholic beverages, and both the concentration and the time for which detectable amounts persist is

proportional to the ethanol intake. Ethanol is easily measured in blood or breath but, because most people consume alcohol from time to time, a positive result is of little value unless the subject denies taking alcohol. Presence of alcohol in the morning, or during a medical consultation, might be thought unusual and worthy of further investigation but there appears to be no data on this.

Tolerance to ethanol develops in people who habitually consume large amounts, and this takes two forms; metabolic tolerance (in which ethanol is metabolized more quickly than normal, possibly because of induction of hepatic microsomal systems) and neurological tolerance (in which symptoms or signs of intoxication are less than would normally occur at the blood ethanol concentration present). Neurological tolerance allows very high blood ethanol concentrations to occur while the patient remains conscious and this is a classical clinical indication of alcohol dependence.

Because of metabolic tolerance, ethanol metabolism is faster and concentrations of ethanol metabolites (particularly acetate) during ethanol metabolism are higher in alcoholics than in normal subjects (Olsen et al., 1989; Roine et al., 1988; Girela et al., 1994). Each of these has been proposed as a marker of excessive alcohol intake, but they suffer from the disadvantage of requiring alcohol to be administered or else performing the test while the subject is intoxicated. The main role for such tests would be after emergency admission to hospital. Although the principle has been validated, and Girela et al. (1994) reported sensitivity of acetate to be comparable to that of GGT or MCV, there are few studies on the practicality or effectiveness of such testing.

Methanol is present in small amounts in alcoholic beverages and may also be produced by gut flora. It is normally metabolized by alcohol dehydrogenase and, because ethanol is the preferred substrate for this enzyme, methanol metabolism is reduced after ethanol consumption. This has led to proposals for the measurement of methanol as a marker of alcohol intake but available data have not made the case for this (Roine et al., 1989; Buchholtz, 1993; Haffner et al., 1993; Helander et al., 1996a). In principle, methanol should only be detectable while ethanol is also present and for a short time afterwards.

Because ethanol distributes to all body fluids and tissues, measurement of ethanol in sweat has been exploited through the "patch test". An absorbent patch is attached to the skin of a subject and the ethanol content of the collected sweat is measured after 24 or 48 hours (Phillips and McAloon, 1980; Phillips, 1984; Phillips et al., 1995). Adhesive type, which reveals evidence of removal and re-application, helps to avoid the more obvious forms of deceit. A similar device based on a sensor which measures transdermal ethanol diffusion has also been developed (Swift et al., 1992). This approach may be the closest to a "gold standard" that is available. An accurate method of measuring alcohol intake in free-living subjects over a significant period of time would be valuable because it could be used to calibrate other methods of estimation, such as laboratory tests, but it would be difficult to recruit and retain sufficient heavy-drinking volunteers for such studies.

Fatty acid ethyl esters are formed enzymatically in the presence of ethanol. A small number of investigations have been conducted, mainly using tissue samples in experimental animals or post-mortem samples from humans. Such esters have been detected in human blood for up to 24 hours after consumption of ethanol (Doyle et al., 1994, 1996). Another minor metabolite of ethanol, ethyl glucuronide, has recently been found to persist for a few hours after ethanol elimination is complete (Schmitt et al., 1997; Wurst et al., 1999) and may be useful in a similar way to the measurement of 5-hydroxytryptophol.

Test Performance

There are few reports of evaluations of sensitivity and specificity of tests for ethanol or its metabolites, or other alcohols. Consequently, no summary of test performance can be given.

Test Interpretation

Results of test in this class will need to be interpreted in relation to the time of ethanol consumption, because false negatives will occur when, or soon after, ethanol elimination is complete.

Prognostic Value

There are no formal evaluations of prognostic value for any of this group of tests. Fatty acid ethyl esters are believed to be toxic and might play a role in organ damage (Laposata, 1998), but whether they have an important role in alcohol-related disease is still uncertain.

PRECURSORS OF HARMFUL ALCOHOL USE

There has long been a clinical impression that alcoholism runs in families. Adoption and twin studies have now shown that genetic factors account for most, if not all, of this family resemblance. The effect is reasonably strong; a large study of families in the USA (Dawson et al., 1992) estimated that life-time alcoholism risk was increased by 167% by having both first- and second-degree relatives with alcoholism, and in Australia, Heath et al. (1997) found that having an identical twin who was affected increased alcoholism risk around four-fold.

As a consequence of this evidence for genetic factors in alcoholism, many investigators have embarked upon the search for "genes for alcoholism" (more accurately, alleles for alcoholism). The main lesson learned so far is the need to reserve judgement until a number of independent reports have come to the same conclusions.

Genetic variation in the two major enzymes of ethanol metabolism, alcohol dehydrogenase (ADH) and aldehyde dehydrogenase (ALDH), has been shown to affect alcohol dependence risk. There is also some evidence that *ADH* variation affects the risk of alcoholic liver disease among patients who are alcohol dependent. However, the polymorphism of *ALDH2* occurs only in Asians and the polymorphism in *ADH2* that affects alcohol use is present in only a small proportion (less than 10%) of Caucasian subjects. Although these enzyme variants are of considerable theoretical interest, showing some connection between alcohol metabolism and alcohol dependence, they do not have predictive or diagnostic value in the ethnic groups most prone to alcohol dependence.

Because of the role of dopamine in neurotransmission and its postulated role in reward and dependence mechanisms, genetic variants of dopamine receptors, such as DRD2 and DRD4, have been investigated for associations with alcohol dependence. This has been a particularly controversial and contradictory area of research but it can reasonably be said that these genetic markers have no role in the diagnosis or management of alcohol problems.

Two enzymes have been claimed to be markers of genetic susceptibility to alcohol dependence. The most widely studied one, monoamine oxidase, now seems to be a state marker of smoking and its apparent role as a trait marker for alcohol dependence is due to the strong association between smoking and alcohol (Anthenelli et al., 1998). The other, adenyl cyclase, has been less widely studied but appears to be a trait marker for alcohol dependence when measured after several days' abstinence, and may also have associations with depression (Menninger et al., 1998).

A comprehensive strategy for detecting genes affecting alcoholism risk requires a large number of subjects, related to each other in some way so that linkage analysis can be used, and results from around 300 genetic markers on each subject. So far, this approach has yielded suggestive, but not conclusive, results, which need replication and further refinement (Foroud et al., 1998; Long et al., 1998; Reich et al., 1998). Diagnostic applications appear some years away and may require a profile of gene typings to build up an assessment of risk. This would be impractical at present but is likely to become technically feasible within such a time-frame. Genetic markers may be found that indicate subtypes of alcoholism, or likely co-morbidity from other psychiatric problems, or possibly susceptibility to specific types of alcohol-induced organ damage.

CHANGES EXPECTED DURING ABSTINENCE AND AFTER RELAPSE

By definition, state markers should return to normal when the abnormal condition has resolved. Some markers may remain elevated if liver damage is irreversible, and use of markers for characterization of patients as abstinent or relapsing is limited by the sensitivity of the tests since some patients will never show abnormal results.

The practicality of using tests as relapse markers will also depend on the half-life of their return to normal. As 5-hydroxytryptophol only remains abnormal for a few hours after drinking, most attention has been paid to GGT and CDT. MCV is very slow to return to normal, and there is no information on acetaldehyde-modified proteins in this role.

Over the past 20 years, at least 13 papers have explored the use of GGT and/or CDT as markers of abstinence or relapse. Earlier studies demonstrated a decline with abstinence, while more recent ones have concentrated more on identification of individual bouts of drinking. The topic has been reviewed by Borg (1996).

Initial papers reported that GGT decreased with abstinence in alcoholics, with a half-life of around 25 days. Some of these papers (Shaw et al., 1979; Montiero & Masur, 1986) found no decrease in MCV in the same patients. More recent papers have compared GGT and CDT directly; CDT decreases more quickly than GGT, with a half-life around 15 days. Nearly all these papers found CDT to be better (e.g. Helander et al., 1996b; Schmidt et al., 1997), but several recommended use of either as appropriate because not all patients had raised CDT. It became clear that even patients with normal CDT or GGT could show decreases with abstinence, and an individual reference range could be more useful than a universal one (Weill et al., 1988; Borg et al., 1995). The more recent papers have identified individual occasions of relapse by use of 5-HTOL and evaluated other markers by reference to this (Borg et al., 1995).

Ultimately, the use of test results in managing the treatment of alcohol-dependent patients will need to be justified by controlled trials measuring outcomes with and without test results.

EVALUATION OF ALCOHOL-RELATED DISEASE

The use of laboratory tests to detect and evaluate organ damage resulting from alcohol abuse is no different in principle from their use for other diseases. In many cases the tests are not specific for alcohol-related damage. The organs most often affected are the liver, heart, pancreas and brain and there are some important but rare vitamin deficiencies that can be investigated.

Liver Function Tests, and Markers of Fibrosis and Cirrhosis

Mild degrees of liver abnormality, such as fatty liver, produce no changes in serum markers beyond the increases in GGT and aminotransferases that may be present in any heavy drinker. Alcoholic hepatitis will produce substantial increases in AST and ALT and, of course, bilirubin.

Cirrhosis or fibrosis are generally biochemically silent until very advanced stages are reached, but a number of markers of fibrosis have been advocated and evaluated. These are based on collagen metabolism and do show statistical associations with the presence or progress of fibrosis, but may not be reliable in the evaluation of individual patients. Fibrosis markers were reviewed by Plebani & Burlina (1991), and since that time more than a dozen reports have investigated single or multiple markers for fibrosis or cirrhosis in general, or alcoholic cirrhosis in particular. Tsutsumi et al. (1996) compared six assays in patients with alcoholic and non-alcoholic liver disease and found that five of them reflected the histologically assessed degree of fibrosis, with the triple-helix domain of Type IV collagen showing the most significant results in alcoholics. Values for this marker were higher in alcoholics, for any degree of fibrosis, than in non-alcoholic liver disease, and decreased to normal over eight weeks of abstinence from alcohol. This suggests that it is a marker of collagen turnover and active fibrosis rather than a marker of accumulated damage.

Hepatocellular carcinoma (HCC) is a serious complication of cirrhosis and might be detectable through measurement of α-fetoprotein (AFP) in serum. However, there are a number of obstacles to such screening programmes (see Khakoo et al., 1996). First, the increased risk is associated with cirrhosis and not alcohol *per se*, so defining the high-risk group encounters the difficulty of deciding which drinkers have cirrhosis. Second, treatable (small) tumours do not always produce elevated serum AFP values, particularly when the reference range is adjusted to allow for increased AFP in liver disease. Third, evidence so far suggests that ultrasound screening is more sensitive and specific than AFP screening, although combinations could be useful.

Other Complications of Alcohol Abuse

Thiamine deficiency may be detectable by measurement of erythrocyte transketolase activity (ETKA) in the absence and presence of added thiamine pyrophosphate. This requires a blood sample before any supplementation of the patient with thiamine is undertaken. The previous view, that alcoholics who become thiamine-deficient have a genetically abnormal form of transketolase, has not been confirmed.

Pancreatitis may arise from alcohol abuse. If the diagnostic question is whether pancreatitis is present, then amylase and lipase are used. If the question is whether the pancreatitis is alcoholic in origin, then CDT is reported to be the best test, with GGT abnormal regardless of aetiology. Some authors have suggested that amylase is less elevated in alcoholic than non-alcoholic pancreatitis and therefore that the lipase:amylase ratio might be relevant, but this is not generally felt to be useful.

Muscle damage may occur in alcoholics, and measurement of creatine kinase may be useful. For other complications, such as cardiomyopathy or brain damage, laboratory tests have little to offer at present.

LABORATORY TESTS IN CLINICAL TRIALS

A number of treatments have been proposed or instituted for alcohol dependence. Whether these are based on psychological or pharmacological sciences, resource allocation considerations require that they should be evaluated and compared; and ethical considerations require that the most effective treatment should be offered. Such evaluations need to define desired outcomes, which may be abstinence, controlled drinking or reduction in harmful effects of alcohol. If self-report of alcohol use is taken as a measure of treatment effectiveness, then optimism and bias may lead to incorrect conclusions but biological markers should be more objective.

As discussed earlier, application of biological markers to individual patients has limitations because of poor sensitivity or specificity. However, when the object is to compare two or more groups of people, then the individual differences in marker response to alcohol intake will become less important and differences between treatment groups will be readily detected. This approach has been applied to a number of trials of pharmacotherapy for alcohol dependence, of treatment based on counselling or combinations of each (Kristenson et al., 1983; Persson and Magnusson, 1989; Martinez Ruiz et al., 1995; Anton, Moak and Latham, 1996; O'Connor et al., 1997; Wilde and Wagstaffe, 1997).

CONCLUSIONS: WHAT INVESTIGATIONS, WHEN, AND IS THERE EVIDENCE OF EFFECTIVENESS?

A summary of the usefulness of biological markers in various clinical situations is attempted in Table 12.1. In each case, except for genetic markers of susceptibility, biological markers can presently provide useful information to be considered alongside clinical and interview data. The more expensive tests cannot be justified for universal application, but may play a role in particularly critical situations where alcohol use is denied and where public safety may be at risk if the patient successfully deceives his/her doctor. Continuing research using the more expensive tests is justified because a major clinical benefit from any of them would increase utilization and lead to development of cheaper methods.

Future research on biological markers may be most productive where it focuses on risk. The course of alcohol dependence and the development of complications is variable and some of the tests discussed (particularly GGT) have been shown to have predictive value. Other markers may also have this useful property, particularly acetaldehyde-modified proteins and fatty acid ethyl esters, and these, too, should be investigated in prospective studies.

Variation in risk of alcohol dependence may soon be assessable through use of genetic markers. This will undoubtedly raise ethical issues, but the same issues are already confronting clinical geneticists dealing with many diseases, and will become significant for many psychiatric conditions apart from alcohol dependence. A great deal of work will be required in order to understand the pathophysiology of the tests and the disease and to delineate the genotype–phenotype relationships with multiple genetic markers. As with state markers, the best test of whether genetic markers have clinical utility will be the effect on outcomes for the patients.

KEY WORKS AND SUGGESTIONS FOR FURTHER READING

Borg, S., Helander, A., Voltaire Carlsson, A. & Hogstrom Brandt, A.M. (1995). Detection of relapses in alcohol-dependent patients using carbohydrate-deficient transferrin: improvement with individualized reference levels during long-term monitoring. *Alcoholism: Clinical and Experimental Research*, **19**, 961–963.

This paper investigated one of the major uses for biological markers of alcohol intake, in the detection of continuing alcohol consumption in patients under treatment.

Table 12.1 Summary of the role of biological makers in various clinical situations

Phase	Question	Tests	Status
Prior to alcohol use or development of problems	Is this person at high risk for alcohol-related problems?	Genetic markers of susceptibility	None yet confirmed, except ALDH2 and ADH2 (only relevant in some populations). Others tentative and unlikely to become useful for several years
Drinking but no definite alcohol-related diagnosis	Is this person currently drinking excessive amounts of alcohol?	State markers: CDT and GGT	Well-documented test characteristics, less than 100% sensitivity. GGT may have predictive value. CDT has better specificity and possibly sensitivity, but is expensive
During treatment for alcohol dependence	Has the patient ceased drinking, or controlled his/her drinking to safe levels?	State markers: CDT and 5-HTOL	Both responsive to reduction in alcohol use and to its resumption; 5-HTOL short-term and CDT medium-term; both expensive tests
Alcohol dependence with continuing excessive drinking	Is there evidence of organ damage due to alcohol?	Organ damage markers	GGT and other LFTs; possibly amylase, CK, thiamine, depending on organ affected

Relapses were monitored by a combination of self-report (three times a week) and urine 5-HTOL (daily). The use of individual rather than collective reference ranges for CDT approximately doubled the number of relapses detected, and around 80% of these were verified by self-report or 5-HTOL.

Brenner, H., Rothebacher, D., Arndt, V., Schuberth, S., Fraisse, E. & Fliedner, T.M. (1997). Distribution, determinants and prognostic value of γ-glutamyl transferase for all-cause mortality in a cohort of construction workers from southern Germany. *Preventive Medicine*, **26**, 305–310.

This study covers sources of variation in, and predictive value of, GGT measurement in a large cohort of men from the working population. As expected, alcohol consumption, body mass index and hypertension had the greatest effect on serum GGT. However, GGT had predictive value which was independent of these variables, suggesting that it could be used to identify individuals or groups who are at highest risk.

Kristenson, H., Ohlin, H., Hulten-Nosslin, M.B., Trell, E. & Hood, B. (1983). Identification and intervention of heavy drinking in middle-aged men: results and follow-up of 24–60 months of long-term study with randomized controls. *Alcoholism: Clinical and Experimental Research*, **7**, 203–209.

This is one of a series of valuable papers from the Malmö group, who investigated the importance of alcohol and the role of biological markers in an integrated public health screening project. Although it addresses the broad issues of early intervention, subjects were randomized to intervention or control groups after screening based on GGT results. Discussion of changes in GGT during treatment was used as a means of reinforcing reduced alcohol consumption in the intervention group.

Stibler, H. (1991). Carbohydrate-deficient transferrin in serum: a new marker of potentially harmful alcohol consumption reviewed. *Clinical Chemistry*, **37**, 2029–2037.

The author played a major role in the development of carbohydrate-deficient transferrin as a marker of alcohol intake. In this review she summarized the methods used and the characteristics and value of this test. Sensitivity and specificity data from 21 studies are tabulated and the causes of false positives are discussed. Although the paper was published some time ago, when the available data were mainly from severely affected currently drinking alcohol-dependent subjects, it still provides a good starting point.

REFERENCES

Anthenelli, R.M., Tipp, J., Li, T.-K., Magnes, L., Schuckit, M.A., Rice, J., Daw, W. & Nurnberger, J.I. (1998). Platelet monoamine oxidase activity in subgroups of alcoholics and controls: results from the Collaborative Study on the Genetics of Alcoholism. *Alcoholism: Clinical and Experimental Research*, **22**, 598–604.

Anton, R.F., Moak, D.H. & Latham, P. (1996). Carbohydrate-deficient transferrin as an indicator of drinking status during a treatment outcome study. *Alcoholism: Clinical and Experimental Research*, **20**(5), 841–846.

Antti-Poika, I. & Karaharju, E. (1988). Heavy drinking and accidents—a prospective study among men of working age. *Injury*, **19**, 198–200.

Arndt, Y., Brenner, H., Rothenbacher, D., Zschenderlein, B., Fraisse, E. & Fliedner, T.M. (1998). Elevated liver enzyme activity in construction workers: prevalence and impact on early retirement and all-cause mortality. *International Archives of Occupational and Environmental Health*, **71**(6), 405–412.

Barbieux, J.P., Bacq, Y., Schellenberg, F., Weill, J., Constans, T. & Lamisse, F. (1990). Increase of serum γ-glutamyl transferase activity in diabetic patients is not linked to diabetes itself. *Pathologie Biologie (Paris)*, **38**, 93–98.

Bell, H., Tallaksen, C., Sjaheim, T., Weberg, R., Raknerud, N., Orjasaeter, H., Try, K. & Haug, E. (1993). Serum carbohydrate-deficient transferrin as a marker of alcohol consumption in patients with chronic liver diseases. *Alcoholism: Clinical and Experimental Research*, **17**, 246–252.

Bell, H., Tallaksen, C.M., Try, K. & Haug, E. (1994). Carbohydrate-deficient transferrin and other markers of high alcohol consumption: a study of 502 patients admitted consecutively to a medical department. *Alcoholism: Clinical and Experimental Research*, **18**, 1103–1108.

Blocker, D.E. & Thenen, S.W. (1987). Intestinal absorption, liver uptake, and excretion of ³H-folic acid in folic acid-deficient, alcohol-consuming nonhuman primates. *American Journal of Clinical Nutrition*, **46**, 503–510.

Borg, S. (1996). Treatment of alcohol dependence: experiences of using biological markers in monitoring and prevention of relapse. *Alcohol and Alcoholism*, **31**, 621–624.

Borg, S., Helander, A., Voltaire Carlsson, A. & Hogstrom Brandt, A.M. (1995). Detection of relapses in alcohol-dependent patients using carbohydrate-deficient transferrin: Improvement with individualized reference levels during long-term monitoring. *Alcoholism: Clinical and Experimental Research*, **19**, 961–963.

Braun, K.P., Pavlovich, J.G., Jones, D.R. & Peterson, C.M. (1997). Stable acetaldehyde adducts: structural characterization of acetaldehyde adducts of human hemoglobin N-terminal beta-globin chain peptides. *Alcoholism: Clinical and Experimental Research*, **21**, 40–43.

Brenner, H., Rothenbacher, D., Arndt, V., Schuberth, S., Fraisse, E. & Fliedner, T.M. (1997). Distribution, determinants and prognostic value of γ-glutamyl transferase for all-cause mortality in a cohort of construction workers from southern Germany. *Preventive Medicine*, **26**, 305–310.

Buchholtz, U. (1993). Blood methanol as a marker of alcoholism. A diagnostic component within the scope of expert assessment of driving competence in alcoholic intoxication. *Blutalkohol*, **30**, 43–51.

Chen, H.M., Scott, B.K., Braun, K.P. & Peterson, C.M. (1995). Validated fluoimetric HPLC analysis of acetaldehyde in hemoglobin fractions separated by cation exchange chromatography: three new peaks associated with acetaldehyde. *Alcoholism: Clinical and Experimental Research*, **19**, 939–944.

Conigrave, K.M., Saunders, J.B., Reznik, R.B. & Whitfield, J.B. (1993). Prediction of alcohol-related harm by laboratory test results. *Clinical Chemistry*, **39**, 2266–2270.

Conigrave, K.M., Saunders, J.B. & Whitfield, J.B. (1995). Diagnostic tests for alcohol consumption. *Alcohol and Alcoholism*, **30**, 13–26.

Davidson, R.J. & Hamilton, P.J. (1978). High mean red cell volume: its incidence and significance in routine haematology. *Journal of Clinical Pathology*, **31**, 493–498.

Dawson, D.A., Harford, T.C. & Grant, B.F. (1992). Family history as a predictor of alcohol dependence. *Alcoholism: Clinical and Experimental Research*, **16**, 572–575.

Doyle, K.M., Bird, D.A., Al-Salihi, S., Hallaq, Y., Cluette-Brown, J.E., Goss, K.A. & Laposata, M. (1994). Fatty acid ethyl esters are present in human serum after ethanol ingestion. *Journal of Lipid Research*, **35**, 428–437.

Doyle, K.M., Cluette-Brown, J.E., Dube, D.M., Bernhardt, T.G., Morse, C.R. & Laposata, M. (1996). Fatty acid ethyl esters in the blood as markers for ethanol intake. *Journal of the American Medical Association*, **276**, 1152–1156.

Enomoto, N., Takase, S., Takada, N. & Takada, A. (1991). Alcoholic liver disease in heterozygotes of mutant and normal aldehyde dehydrogenase-2 genes. *Hepatology*, **13**, 1071–1075.

Fagerberg, B., Agewall, S., Urbanavicius, V., Atlvall, S., Lundberg, P.-A. & Lindstedt, G. (1994a). Carbohydrate-deficient transferrin is associated with insulin sensitivity in hypertensive men. *Journal of Clinical Endocrinology and Metabolism*, **79**, 712–715.

Fagerberg, B., Agewall, S., Berglund, A., Wysocki, M., Lundberg, P.-A. & Lindstedt, G. (1994b). Is carbohydrate-deficient transferrin in serum useful for detecting excessive alcohol consumption in hypertensive patients? *Clinical Chemistry*, **40**, 2057–2063.

Foroud, T., Bucholz, K.K., Edenberg, H.J., Goate, A., Neuman, R.J., Porjesz, B. et al. (1998). Linkage of an alcoholism-related severity phenotype to chromosome 16. *Alcoholism: Clinical and Experimental Research*, **22**, 2035–2042.

Frezza, M., Pozzato, G., Chiesa, L., Terpin, M., Barbone, F. & Di Padova, C. (1989). Abnormal serum gamma-glutamyltranspeptidase in alcoholics. Clues to its explanation. *Netherlands Journal of Medicine*, **34**, 22–28.

Girela, E., Villanueva, E., Hernandez-Cueto, C. & Luna, J.D. (1994). Comparison of the CAGE questionnaire versus some biochemical markers in the diagnosis of alcoholism. *Alcohol and Alcoholism*, **29**, 337–343.

Godsell, P.A., Whitfield, J.B., Conigrave, K.M., Hanratty, S.J. & Saunders, J.B. (1995). Carbohydrate deficient transferrin levels in hazardous alcohol consumption. *Alcohol and Alcoholism*, **30**, 61–66.

Goldberg, D.M. & Kapur, B.M. (1994). Enzymes and circulating proteins as markers of alcohol abuse. *Clinica Chimica Acta*, **226**, 191–209.

Haffner, H.T., Batra, A., Wehner, H.D., Besserer, K. & Mann, K. (1993). Methanol level and methanol elimination in alcoholic patients. *Blutalkohol*, **30**, 52–62.

Harcombe, A.A., Ramsay, L., Kenna, J.G., Koskinas, J., Why, H.J., Richardson, P.J. et al. (1995). Circulating antibodies to cardiac protein-acetaldehyde adducts in alcoholic heart muscle disease. *Clinical Science*, **88**, 263–268.

Hazelett, S.E., Liebelt, R.A., Brown, W.J., Androulakakis, V., Jarjoura, D. & Truitt, E.B. (1998). Evaluation of acetaldehyde-modified hemoglobin and other markers of chronic heavy alcohol use: effects of gender and hemoglobin concentration. *Alcoholism: Clinical and Experimental Research*, **22**, 1813–1819.

Heath, A.C., Bucholz, K.K., Madden, P.A.F., Dinwiddie, S.H., Slutske, W.S., Statham, D.J. et al. (1997). Genetic and environmental contributions to DSM-IIIR alcohol dependence risk in a national twin sample: consistency of findings in women and men. *Psychological Medicine*, 27, 1381–1396.

Helander, A., Beck, O. & Jones, A.W. (1996a). Laboratory testing for recent alcohol consumption: comparison of ethanol, methanol and 5-hydroxytryptophol. *Clinical Chemistry*, 42, 618–624.

Helander, A., Carlsson, A.V. & Borg, S. (1996b). Longitudinal comparison of carbohydrate-deficient transferrin and gamma-glutamyl transferase: complementary markers of excessive alcohol consumption. *Alcohol and Alcoholism*, 31, 101–107.

Henningsen, N.C., Ohlsson, O., Mattiasson, I., Trell, E., Kristensson, H. & Hood, B. (1980). Hypertension, levels of serum gamma glutamyl transpeptidase and degree of blood pressure control in middle-aged males. *Acta Medica Scandanavica*, 207, 245–251.

Hood, B., Kjellstrom, T., Ruter, G. & Kristenson, H. (1990). Serum cholesterol, serum triglyceride, alcohol, myocardial infarction and death (2): necessary to pay attention to serum GT in assessment of risks of myocardial infarction and death. *Lakartidningen*, 87, 3295–3298.

Hurme, L., Seppa, K., Rajaniemi, H. & Sillanaukee, P. (1998). Chromatographically identified alcohol-induced haemoglobin adducts as markers of alcohol abuse among women. *European Journal of Clinical Investigation*, 28, 87–94.

Khakoo, S.I., Grellier, L.F., Soni, P.N., Bhattacharya, S. & Dusheiko, G.M. (1996). Etiology, screening, and treatment of hepatocellular carcinoma. *Medical Clinics of North America*, 80, 1121–1145.

Kristenson, H., Ohlin, H., Hulten-Nosslin, M.B., Trell, E. & Hood, B. (1983). Identification and intervention of heavy drinking in middle-aged men: results and follow-up of 24–60 months of long-term study with randomized controls. *Alcoholism: Clinical and Experimental Research*, 7, 203–209.

Kristenson, H., Trell, E., Fex, G. & Hood, B. (1980). Serum γ-glutamyltransferase: statistical distribution in a middle-aged male population and evaluation of alcohol habits in individuals with elevated levels. *Preventive Medicine*, 9, 108–119.

Kryszewski, A., Bardzik, I., Kilkowska, K., Vogel-Pienkowska, M. & Schminda, R. (1977). Gamma glutamyl transpeptidase activity in serum and liver in chronic alcoholism. *Acta Medica Polonica*, 18, 199–211.

Laposata, M. (1998). Fatty acid ethyl esters: ethanol metabolites which mediate ethanol-induced organ damage and serve as markers of ethanol intake. *Progress in Lipid Research*, 37, 307–316.

Lin, R.C., Shahidi, S., Kelly, T.J., Lumeng, C. & Lumeng, L. (1993). Measurment of hemoglobin-acetaldehyde adduct in alcoholic patients. *Alcoholism: Clinical and Experimental Research*, 17, 669–674.

Long, J.C., Knowler, W.C., Hanson, R.L., Robin, R.W., Urbanek, M., Moore, E., Bennett, P.H. & Goldman, D. (1998). Evidence for genetic linkage to alcohol dependence on chromosomes 4 and 11 from an autosome-wide scan in an American Indian population. *American Journal of Medical Genetics*, 81, 216–221.

Martinez Ruiz, M., Llobell Segui, G., Peralba Vano, J.L. & Toral Revuelta, J.R. (1995). Evaluation of the efficacy of naltrexone in alcoholism by the determination of serum carbohydrate-deficient transferrin. *Anales de Medicina Interna*, 12, 589–592.

Menninger, J.A., Baron, A.E. & Tabakoff, B. (1998). Effects of abstinence and family history for alcoholism on platelet adenylyl cyclase activity. *Alcoholism: Clinical and Experimental Research*, 22, 1955–1961.

Miura, K., Nakagawa, H., Nakamura, H., Tabata, M., Nagase, H., Yoshida, M. & Kawano, S. (1994). Serum gamma-glutamyl transferase level in predicting hypertension among male drinkers. *Journal of Human Hypertension*, 8(6), 445–449.

Montiero, M.G. & Masur, J. (1986). Monitoring alcoholism treatment: the appropriateness of choice between gamma GT or MCV evaluation after a short time of abstinence. *Alcohol*, 3, 223–226.

Niemela, O., Halmesmaki, E. & Ylikorkala, O. (1991). Hemoglobin-acetaldehyde adducts are elevated in women carrying alcohol-damaged fetuses. *Alcoholism: Clinical and Experimental Research*, 15, 1007–1010.

O'Connor, P.G., Farren, C.K., Rounsaville, B.J. & O'Malley, S.S. (1997). A preliminary investigation of the management of alcohol dependence with naltrexone by primary care providers. *American Journal of Medicine*, 103, 477–482.

Olsen, H., Sakshaug, J., Duckert, F., Stromme, J.H. & Morland, J. (1989). Ethanol elimination rates determined by breath analysis as a marker of recent excessive ethanol consumption. *Scandinavian Journal of Laboratory and Clinical Investigation*, **49**, 359–365.

Persson, J. & Magnusson, P.-H. (1980). Early intervention in patients with excessive consumption of alcohol: a controlled study. *Alcohol*, **6**, 403–408.

Peterson, B., Kristenson, H., Sternby, N.H., Trell, E., Fex, G. & Hood, B. (1980). Alcohol consumption and premature death in middle-aged men. *British Medical Journal*, **280**, 1403–1406.

Phillips, M. (1984). Sweat-patch testing detects inaccurate self-reports of alcohol consumption. *Alcoholism: Clinical and Experimental Research*, **8**, 51–53.

Phillips, M., Greenberg, J. & Andrzejewski, J. (1995). Evaluation of the Alcopatch, a transdermal dosimeter for monitoring alcohol consumption. *Alcoholism: Clinical and Experimental Research*, **19**, 1547–1549.

Phillips, M. & McAloon, M.H. (1980). A sweat-patch test for alcohol consumption: evaluation in continuous and episodic drinkers. *Alcoholism: Clinical and Experimental Research*, **4**, 391–395.

Plebani, M. & Burlina, A. (1991). Biochemical markers of hepatic fibrosis. *Clinical Biochemistry*, **24**, 219–239.

Reich, T., Edenberg, H.J., Goate, A., Williams, J.T., Rice, J.P., Van Eerdewegh, P. et al. (1998). Genome-wide search for genes affecting the risk for alcohol dependence. *American Journal of Medical Genetics*, **81**, 207–215.

Rodger, R.S., Fletcher, K., Fail, B.J., Rahman, H., Sviland, L. & Hamilton, P.J. (1987). Factors influencing haematological measurements in healthy adults. *Journal of Chronic Diseases*, **40**, 943–947.

Roine, R.P., Korri, U.M., Ylikahri, R., Penttila, A., Pikkarainen, J. & Salaspuro, M. (1988). Increased serum acetate as a marker of problem drinking among drunken drivers. *Alcohol and Alcoholism*, **23**, 123–126.

Roine, R.P., Eriksson, C.J., Ylikahri, R., Penttila, A. & Salaspuro, M. (1989). Methanol as a marker of alcohol abuse. *Alcoholism: Clinical and Experimental Research*, **13**, 172–175.

Rosalki, S.B., Tarlow, D. & Rau, D. (1971). Plasma gamma-glutamyl transpeptidase elevation in patients receiving enzyme-inducing drugs. *Lancet*, **2**, 376–377.

Schmitt, G., Droenner, P., Skopp, G. & Aderjan, R. (1997). Ethyl glucuronide concentration in serum of human volunteers, teetotalers, and suspected drinking drivers. *Journal of Forensic Sciences*, **42**, 1099–1102.

Schmidt, L.G., Schmidt, K., Dufeu, P., Ohse, A., Rommelspacher, H. & Muller, C. (1997). Superiority of carbohydrate-deficient transferrin to gamma-glutamyltransferase in detecting relapse in alcoholism. *American Journal of Psychiatry*, **154**, 75–80.

Sharp, P.C., McBride, R. & Archbold, G.P. (1996). Biochemical markers of alcohol abuse. *Quarterly Journal of Medicine*, **89**, 137–144.

Shaw, S., Worner, T.M., Borysow, M.F., Schmitz, R.E. & Lieber, C.S. (1979). Detection of alcoholism relapse: comparative diagnostic value of MCV, GGTP and AANB. *Alcoholism: Clinical and Experimental Research*, **3**, 297–301.

Sillanaukee, P., Seppa, K. & Koivula, T. (1991). Effect of acetaldehyde on hemoglobin: HbA1ach as a potential marker of heavy drinking. *Alcohol*, **8**, 377–381.

Sillanaukee, P., Seppa, K., Koivula, T., Israel, Y. & Niemela, O. (1992). Acetaldehyde-modified hemoglobin as a marker of alcohol consumption: comparison of two new methods. *Journal of Laboratory and Clinical Medicine*, **120**, 42–47.

Stauber, R.E., Jauk, B., Fickert, P. & Hausler, M. (1996). Increased carbohydrate-deficient transferrin during pregnancy: relation to sex hormones. *Alcohol and Alcoholism*, **3**, 389–392.

Stibler, H., Borg, S. & Beckman, G. (1988). Transferrin phenotype and level of carbohydrate-deficient transferrin in healthy individuals. *Alcoholism: Clinical and Experimental Research*, **12**, 450–453.

Stibler, H. (1991). Carbohydrate-deficient transferrin in serum: a new marker of potentially harmful alcohol consumption reviewed. *Clinical Chemistry*, **37**, 2029–2037.

Stibler, H., von Dobeln, U., Kristiansson, B. & Guthenberg, C. (1997). Carbohydrate-deficient transferrin in galactosaemia. *Acta Paediatrica*, **86**, 1377–1378.

Stibler, H., Holzbach, U. & Kristiansson, B. (1998). Isoforms and levels of transferrin, antithrombin, alpha(1)-antitrypsin and thyroxine-binding globulin in 48 patients with carbohydrate-deficient glycoprotein syndrome type I. *Scandinavian Journal of Laboratory and Clinical Investigation*, **58**, 55–61.

Swift, R.M., Martin, C.S., Swette, L., LaConti, A. & Kackley, N. (1992). Studies on a wearable, electronic, transdermal alcohol sensor. *Alcoholism: Clinical and Experimental Research*, **16**, 721–725.

Trell, E., Kristenson, H. & Petersson, B. (1985). A risk factor approach to the alcohol-related diseases. *Alcohol and Alcoholism*, **20**, 333–345.

Tsutsumi, M., Takase, S., Urashima, S., Ueshima, Y., Kawahara, H. & Takada, A. (1996). Serum markers for hepatic fibrosis in alcoholic liver disease: which is the best marker, type III procollagen, type IV collagen, laminin, tissue inhibitor of metalloproteinase, or prolyl hydroxylase? *Alcoholism: Clinical and Experimental Research*, **20**, 1512–1517.

Van Barneveld, T., Seidell, J.C., Traag, N. & Hautvast, J.G.A.J. (1989). Fat distribution and gamma-glutamyl transferase in relation to serum lipids and blood pressure in 38-year old Dutch males. *European Journal of Clinical Nutrition*, **43**, 809–818.

Viitala, K., Israel, Y., Blake, J.E. & Niemela, O. (1997). Serum IgA, IgG, and IgM antibodies directed against acetaldehyde-derived epitopes:relationship to liver disease severity and alcohol consumption. *Hepatology*, **25**, 1418–1424.

Voltaire, A., Beck, O. & Borg, S. (1992). Urinary 5-hydroxytryptophol: a possible marker of recent alcohol consumption. *Alcoholism: Clinical and Experimental Research*, **16**, 281–285.

Wannamethee, G., Ebrahim, S. & Shaper, A.G. (1995). Gamma-glutamyltransferase: determinants and association with mortality from ischaemic heart disease and all causes. *American Journal of Epidemiology*, **142**, 699–708.

Weill, J., Schellenberg, F., Le Goff, A.M. & Benard, J.Y. (1988). The decrease of low serum gamma glutamyl transferase during short-term abstinence. *Alcohol*, **5**, 1–3.

Whitehead, T.P., Robinson, D., Allaway, S.L. & Hale, A.C. (1995). The effects of cigarette smoking and alcohol consumption on blood haemoglobin, erythrocytes and leucocytes: a dose related study on male subjects. *Clinical and Laboratory Haematology*, **17**, 131–138.

Whitfield, J.B., Hensley, W.J., Bryden, D. & Gallagher, H. (1978). Effects of age and sex on biochemical responses to drinking habits. *Medical Journal of Australia*, **ii**, 629–632.

Whitfield, J.B., Allen, J.K., Hensley, W.J. & Adena, M.A. (1981). The effect of drinking on correlations between biochemical variables. *Annals of Clinical Biochemistry*, **18**, 143–145.

Whitfield, J.B. & Martin, N.G. (1985a). Individual differences in plasma ALT, AST and GGT: contributions of genetic and environmental factors, including alcohol consumption. *Enzyme*, **33**, 61–69.

Whitfield, J.B. & Martin, N.G. (1985b). Genetic and environmental influences on the size and number of cells in the blood. *Genetic Epidemiology*, **2**, 133–144.

Whitfield, J.B., Fletcher, L.M., Murphy, T.L., Powell, L.W., Halliday, J., Heath, A.C. & Martin, N.G. (1998). Smoking, obesity and hypertension alter the dose-response curve and test sensitivity of carbohydrate-deficient transferrin as a marker of alcohol intake. *Clinical Chemistry*, **44**, 2480–2489.

Wickramasinghe, S.N., Corridan, B., Hasan, R. & Marjot, D.H. (1994). Correlations between acetaldehyde-modified haemoglobin, carbohydrate-deficient transferrin (CDT) and haematological abnormalities in chronic alcoholism. *Alcohol and Alcoholism*, **29**, 415–423.

Wilde, M.I. & Wagstaffe, A.J. (1997). Acamprosate. A review of its pharmacology and clinical potential in the management of alcohol dependence after detoxification. *Drugs*, **53**, 1038–1053.

Worrall, S., de Jersey, J., Wilce, P.A., Seppa, K., Hurme, L. & Sillanaukee, P. (1996). Relationship between alcohol intake and immunoglobulin A immunoreactivity with acetaldehyde-modified bovine serum albumin. *Alcoholism: Clinical and Experimental Research*, **20**, 836–840.

Worrall, S., de Jersey, J., Wilce, P.A., Seppa, K., Hurme, L. & Sillanaukee, P. (1998). Comparison of carbohydrate-deficient transferrin, immunoglobulin A antibodies reactive with acetaldehyde-modified protein and acetaldehyde-modified albumin with conventional markers of alcohol consumption. *Alcoholism: Clinical and Experimental Research*, **22**, 1921–1926.

Wu, A., Slavin, G. & Levi, A.J. (1976). Elevated serum gamma glutamyl transferase (transpeptidase) and histological liver damage in alcoholism. *American Journal of Gastroenterology*, **65**, 318–323.

Wurst, F.M., Kempter, C., Seidl, S. & Alt, A. (1999). Ethyl glucuronide—a marker of alcohol consumption and a relapse marker with clinical and forensic implications. *Alcohol and Alcoholism*, **34**, 71–77.

Xin, Y., Lasker, J.M. & Lieber, C.S. (1995). Serum carbohydrate-deficient transferrin: mechanism of increase after chronic alcohol intake. *Hepatology*, **22**, 1462–1468.

Yersin, B., Nicolet, J.F., Dercrey, H., Burnier, M., van Melle, G. & Pecoud, A. (1995).   Screening for excessive alcohol drinking. Comparative value of carbohydrate-deficient transferrin, gamma-glutamyltransferase, and mean corpuscular volume. *Archives of Internal Medicine*, **155**, 1907–1911.

Yokoyama, H., Nagata, S., Moriya, S., Kato, S., Ito, T., Kamegeya, K. & Ishii, H. (1995).   Hepatic fibrosis produced in guinea pigs by chronic ethanol administration and immunisation with acetaldehyde adducts. *Hepatology*, **21**, 1438–1442.

Part III

Antecedents of Drinking, Alcohol Problems and Dependence

Edited by Nick Heather
Centre for Alcohol and Drug Studies, University of Northumbria at Newcastle, Newcastle upon Tyne, UK

EDITOR'S INTRODUCTION

Part III of this book is about the antecedents of drinking, alcohol problems and alcohol dependence—in plainer language, about the causes of these things. Scientists tend to avoid speaking of "cause" because philosophers tell us it is not an empirical concept, i.e. causes cannot be observed or inferred via the senses. All that can be said with any certainty is that one event precedes another with sufficient regularity in similar circumstances to be described as an antecedent of it. Be that as it may, for the purposes of this book, the reader can assume that we are concerned here with what would be called in ordinary language the causes of the alcohol consumption and alcohol use disorders.

Scientific accounts of what causes people to drink problematically have varied considerably and have been subject to intellectual fashions that determine more general perspectives on human behaviour. These general influences, complete with their particular implications for what can be done about alcohol-related problems, have competed with each other in transient fashion in time and place over the last 200 years. In some periods or schools of thought, it was assumed that the roots of "habitual drunkenness" or "alcoholism" lay in heredity and found expression in biological differences between those who are adversely affected by drinking and those who are not; the task of scientific research was to identify and hopefully find ways, usually pharmacological, of correcting these biological abnormalities. At other times, it was assumed that it was the individual's psychological make-up, resulting in the psychoanalytic view from early learning experiences, that accounted for the origins of problem drinking; according to this view, the main kinds of psychopathology associated with problematic drinking could be identified by scientific enquiry and cured by some form of psychotherapy or other psychological intervention. At yet other times, it was sociocultural factors that were chiefly blamed for high rates of drinking problems; the attention of research turned to describing social norms and other features of the drinker's surrounding culture that encouraged heavy drinking and to how these precipitating factors could be altered.

Over the last 20 years or so, however, a broad consensus has emerged among theorists and researchers that all three kinds of factors—biological, psychological and sociocultural—need to be taken into account to reach a satisfactory explanation of the origins of alcohol dependence and problems. This perspective is known, naturally enough, as the "biopsychosocial" model of alcohol problems. It must immediately be conceded that such a model can easily become an excuse for intellectual laziness—the bland assertion that all three kinds of causation must in some way apply—but this need not be the case. Even within a comprehensive theory of this sort, there is still plenty of room for disagreement about the relative contributions of the three types of antecedent and for the delineation of their precise roles at different points in the theory of causation. What can be claimed is that no adequate account of the causes of alcohol dependence and problems can afford to leave out the contribution of any one of these three general influences.

We have spoken so far of the causes of alcohol dependence and problems but, clearly, the circumstances giving rise to dependence need not be the same, and indeed will almost certainly be different, from those underlying various kinds of alcohol-related problems. This is especially true of problems arising from acute alcohol intoxication, such as accidents and violence; these problems can occur in the absence of dependence or with only low levels of dependence (Thorley, 1985) and different kinds of explanation from those applying to dependence will be needed. The same is true of problems due to regular excessive consumption, such as liver cirrhosis and other organic diseases; these too can occur in individuals who are not highly alcohol-dependent (Wodak et al., 1983). Furthermore, it is only relatively recently that serious scientific attention has been paid to explaining why some people drink at all and others do not; previously, this must have been regarded as self-evident. While it is obvious that those who do not drink cannot show any form of self-induced alcohol-related harm, an explanation of why people begin drinking will be only a starting point in theories of alcohol dependence and problems. It is probably fair to say that the chapters in Part III focus on theories of alcohol dependence and chronic problems, with some attention to explanations of drinking itself. The causes of acute, intoxication-related problems are more relevant to the subject matter in Parts IV and VI.

The development of a fully integrated biopsychosocial model of alcohol problems is a major scientific undertaking and a task for the future. It is certainly not attempted here. What Part III does offer, however, is a series of accounts of the major components that will eventually comprise this model. Thus, the latest evidence on the genetic predisposition to alcohol dependence and problems is given in Chapter 13. This, combined with information on the neuropharmacological basis of dependence in Chapter 6, provides coverage of the biological substrate of alcohol dependence. The "psychological" component of theory is represented by chapters on the two major forms of learning—classical conditioning in Chapter 14 and operant/instrumental learning in Chapter 15. Sociocultural factors are included in Chapter 16, although this chapter focuses on social and cognitive learning processes at the individual level, rather than the broader sociological variables relevant to the prevention of alcohol problems that are mentioned in Parts IV and VI. Then, cutting across these components of a full theory, the origins of alcohol dependence and problems are considered from a developmental perspective in Chapter 17. Similarly, in Chapter 18 various causative factors are combined in a description of differences between those who show or are at risk of alcohol problems and those who do not.

Important research on the genetic basis of dependence and problems, mainly using twin and adoption studies, has been carried out since the end of World War II and the results of these earlier studies are summarized in Chapter 13 by Cook & Gurling. More recently, however, rapid advances in research methods and knowledge in the field of molecular biology have transformed this area of study and introduced, as in many other areas of disease and disability, a most exciting period in research on predisposing genetic factors. These latest developments are described in some detail in Chapter 13. Of particular note is the funding of a very large, multicentre study in the USA, the Collaborative Study on the Genetics of Alcoholism (COGA), aimed at searching for associations with alcohol dependence across the entire human genome (see Begleiter et al., 1995). The results of the study to date are described by Cook & Gurling.

The idea that alcohol dependence can be explained by some form of classical conditioning is attractive in its simplicity and plausibility, and was first mooted in a seminal paper by Abraham Wikler as early as 1948. Part of its attraction is that it has obvious implications for how the condition could be treated by using principles from the same body of conditioning theory. Unfortunately, as Chapter 14 by Drobes and his colleagues points out, research designed to validate and explore the implications of this idea has run into considerable difficulties, and the conditioning theory of drug dependence, while not quite in disarray, is certainly in a state of flux. Nevertheless, interesting theories of drug dependence based wholly or partly on the concept of the classically conditioned response have been developed, a prime example being the incentive-sensitization model of Robinson & Berridge (1993). This, however, in common with several other theories in this area, does not escape criticism in Chapter 14. One of the authors of the chapter (Tiffany, 1990) has proposed an influential alternative to existing conditioning theories, using the concepts of automatic and non-automatic cognitive processing, which attempts to integrate conflicting findings in the literature and this too is described in the chapter. The chapter concludes with a discussion of the implications of conditioning theory for the assessment and treatment of alcohol dependence and thus provides a link with Part V.

As George Bigelow complains in Chapter 15, compared with the attention given to classical conditioning in research and applications in the alcohol problems field, the potential of concepts from instrumental learning theory, based on the pioneering work of B.F. Skinner (e.g. Skinner, 1953), has been relatively neglected. In simplified terms, classical conditioning applies to involuntary, mainly emotional responses to alcohol and drinking, whereas operant conditioning (or instrumental learning) applies to intentional actions. It is therefore obvious that a satisfactory explanation of persistent harmful drinking must include contributions from both forms of learning and the relevance of key principles from the science of instrumental learning is made clear in Chapter 15. Bigelow also devotes a major part of his chapter to describing the therapeutic applications of operant principles and research findings, again forming links with the subject matter of Part V.

It is now commonplace to claim that a revolution occurred during the latter part of the twentieth century in the science of psychology—usually know as "the cognitive revolution". With regard to learning theory, Albert Bandura (1969) and other scientists advocated a conception of the learning process in which its specifically human aspects were incorporated. This new theory recognized that much human learning was acquired by observation and modelling (i.e. imitation) of other people. So too, the role of cognitions—expectancies, causal attributions and beliefs related to the self or to others—was introduced. This did not mean that more basic forms of learning represented by classical and operant conditioning were now seen as irrelevant; rather, these more primitive conditioning processes were seen as finding expression in behaviour via the human capacity for thought and language. This new account of human learning was called *social learning theory* (Bandura, 1977) and its application to the causation of alcohol dependence and problems is the subject matter of Chapter 16 by Collins & Bradizza. The authors also draw out the implications of research and theory in this area for the treatment of alcohol problems.

A great deal of theory and research has been devoted to factors contributing to the development of alcohol problems in childhood and adolescence. Chapter 17 by Dennis Gorman summarizes this large body of work, concentrating in particular on three major developmental models—the Social Development Model (Hawkins et al., 1992), Problem Behavior Theory (Jessor & Jessor, 1977) and the alcohol-specific integrative model of Wagenaar & Perry (1994). Common ground and differences between these models are described. The chapter concludes by discussing the implications of the evidence reviewed for the prevention of alcohol problems, this time making connections with Part VI of the book.

Finally in this section, Chapter 18 by Miles Cox and his colleagues is devoted to the topic of individual differences. More specifically, the chapter addresses the issues of individual differences as antecedents of alcohol problems, the personality characteristics of problem drinkers, and the subtypes of problem drinkers that have been described in the literature. Strictly speaking, the last two of these topics are not concerned with the antecedents of alcohol problems *per se* but with the personality and other correlates of alcohol use disorders. They have been included here, however, for the sake of convenience. Among other conclusions, Chapter 18 rectifies a common misconception by making clear that there is no such thing as a single "alcoholic personality".

REFERENCES

Bandura, A. (1969). *Principles of Behavior Modification.* New York: Holt, Rinehart and Winston.

Bandura, A. (1977). *Social Learning Theory.* Englewood Cliffs, NJ: Prentice-Hall.

Begleiter, H., Reich, T., Hesselbrock, V., Porjesz, B., Li, T-K, Schukit, M.A., Edenberg, H.J. & Rice, J.P. (1995). The Collaborative Study on the Genetics of Alcoholism. *Alcohol Health & Research World,* **19**, 228–236.

Hawkins, J.D., Catalano, R.R. & Miller, J.Y. (1992).   Risk and protective factors for alcohol and other drug problems in adolescence and early adulthood: implications for substance abuse prevention. *Psychological Bulletin*, **112**, 64–105.

Jessor, R. & Jessor, S.L. (1977).   *Problem Behavior and Psychosocial Development: A Longitudinal Study of Youth.* New York: Academic Press.

Robinson, T.E. & Berridge, K.C. (1993).   The neural basis of drug craving: an incentive-sensitization theory of addiction. *Brain Research Reviews*, **18**, 247–291.

Skinner, B.F. (1953).   *Science and Human Behaviour.* New York: Macmillan.

Thorley, A. (1985).   The limitations of the alcohol dependence syndrome in multi-disciplinary service development. In N. Heather, I. Robertson & P. Davies (Eds), *The Misuse of Alcohol: Crucial issues in Dependence, Treatment and Prevention.* London: Croom Helm.

Tiffany, S.T. (1990).   A cognitive model of drug urges and drug-use behaviour: role of automatic and nonautomatic processes. *Psychological Review*, **97**, 147–168.

Wagenaar, A.C. & Perry, C.L. (1994).   Community strategies for the reduction of youth drinking: theory and application. *Journal of Research on Adolescence*, **4**, 319–345.

Wikler, A. (1948).   Recent progress in research on the neurophysiological basis of morphine addiction. *American Journal of Psychiatry*, **105**, 329–338.

Wodak, A.D., Saunders, J.B., Ewusi-Mensah, I., Davis, M. & Williams, R. (1983).   Severity of alcohol dependence in patients with alcoholic liver disease. *British Medical Journal*, **287**, 1420–1422.

Chapter 13

Genetic Predisposition to Alcohol Dependence and Problems

Christopher C.H. Cook
Kent Institute of Medicine and Health Sciences, University of Kent,
Canterbury, UK
and
Hugh H.D. Gurling
Molecular Psychiatry Laboratory, Royal Free and University College
London Medical School, London, UK

Synopsis

The familiality of alcohol dependence and problems has long been recognized. Over the last half-century considerable evidence has accumulated, from twin and adoption studies, to suggest that this has a partly genetic basis. Genetic marker studies are required in order to identify the genetic loci responsible for conferring a predisposition to alcohol dependence and problems, and the attainable power of these studies has increased rapidly with recent advances in molecular biology.

The best-established and confirmed genetic effect of this sort, to date, is the alcohol flushing syndrome, due to a point mutation in the ALDH2 locus on chromosome 12q. This mutation, which occurs with high frequency in parts of the Far East but not in Caucasian populations, confers a protection against alcohol-related problems by virtue of an aversive effect experienced following alcohol consumption. This effect tends to considerably limit alcohol consumption by affected individuals.

Although results to date have been somewhat conflicting, there is also some evidence to support the role of the D2 dopamine receptor gene in conferring a genetic predisposition to alcohol dependence and problems in some Caucasian populations. A large collaborative US study, which is currently attempting to replicate its own initial findings, promises the possibility of identifying a range of other predisposing, and possibly also protective, genetic loci which increase, or reduce, the risk of developing alcohol dependence or problems.

International Handbook of Alcohol Dependence and Problems. Edited by N. Heather, T.J. Peters and T. Stockwell.
© 2001 John Wiley & Sons Ltd.

The observation that alcohol dependence and other alcohol-related problems run in families, and thus the idea that they may be the result of heredity, dates back to antiquity (Bynum, 1984). For example, in 1884 George Harley stated:

> . . . the drunkard does not transmit to his offspring the craving for alcohol, but the abnormal organic bodily tissue which gives rise to the craving (quoted in Berridge, 1990).

This understanding sits remarkably well with contemporary ideas regarding the genetic transmission of alcohol-related problems. However, psychological explanations of the familiality of these problems also have a long history:

> No doubt tastes and dispositions are frequently acquired in infancy and childhood, which are afterwards regarded as innate. I should on a general principle be more inclined to believe that the child of intemperate parents would be tainted by example than by hereditary predispositions. But making all due allowances, there may be instances where such a disposition is inherited (Sweetser, 1829, quoted in Bynum, 1984).

The role of genetic factors in the aetiology of alcohol-related problems was almost totally dismissed in the 1930s and 1940s, but regained acceptance in the 1950s and has remained popular since.

Given a population distribution of liability to the development of problems and dependence, increased levels of consumption appear to increase the probability that an individual will develop drinking problems, including dependence (Bruun et al., 1975). *Level of consumption* of alcohol, *complications* secondary to consumption and *physical dependence* thus represent three interacting conceptual levels at which aetiological factors, including genetic predisposition, appear to operate (Cook & Gurling, 1990). This chapter will focus predominantly on alcohol-related problems, including both dependence and other complications of consumption.

A now considerable body of research has addressed the question of whether a predisposition to alcohol dependence and problems may be inherited. Family studies have consistently shown that alcohol dependence and problems occur more frequently among the relatives of those affected than among the relatives of those not affected (Cotton, 1979), but this alone does not distinguish between genetic and environmental influences in aetiology. When compared and contrasted, twin and adoption studies offer the opportunity for a better separation of genetic and environmental effects. Genetic marker studies—using either association or linkage methods—offer the possibility of identifying specific genetic loci that may confer a predisposition to alcohol-related problems.

TWIN STUDIES OF ALCOHOL-RELATED PROBLEMS

Twin studies of alcohol dependence and problems, based upon clinically ascertained samples, are summarized in Table 13.1. Of these six independent studies, five show greater monozygotic (MZ) than dizygotic (DZ) concordance, suggesting a significant genetic effect. One other study (in which concordance rates were not quoted) showed no evidence of a genetic effect (Allgulander et al., 1991). Of three acceptably sized studies based upon population samples, two have shown evidence for a genetic effect (Kendler et al., 1992; Prescott et al., 1994) and one has shown little or no such evidence (Partanen et al., 1966). However, several of the studies are subject to methodological criticisms (Cook & Gurling, 1990). There is also some question as to whether the classical twin method used in these studies is appropriate for studying alcohol dependence and other alcohol-related problems.

Table 13.1 Twin studies of alcohol dependence and problems

Author	Twin pairs (n)	Sex	Criticisms	Criteria	Concordance MZ (%)	Concordance DZ (%)	MZ/DZ
Kaij, 1960	174	M	Antisocial subject bias	Official records	25.4	15.8	1.6
				All records	53.5	28.3	1.9
				Chronic alcoholism	71.4	32.3	2.2
Hrubec & Omenn, 1981	7962	M	No interviews Low ascertainment (?DZ > MZ)	V-A records: alcoholism,	26.3	11.9	2.2
				alcoholic psychosis,	21.1	6.9	3.5
				cirrhosis	14.6	5.4	2.7
Kendler, 1985	81	M	As for Hrubec & Omenn, 1981 (represents a subset of their sample)	V-A records (probands identified with both alcoholism and schizophrenia): results here are for ICD-8 alcoholism only	64.7	8.5	7.6
Gurling et al., 1981, 1989	79	M + F	?Validity of twin method in alcoholism	ICD-9 Alcoholism	23.0	36.0	0.6
				RDC Alcoholism	30.0	36.0	0.8
Koskenvuo et al., 1984	244	M	No interviews ?Migration DZ > MZ Low ascertainment	Hospital admission Death certification ICD-8 Alcoholism	23.1	10.8	2.1
Pickens et al., 1991	169	M + F	?Validity of twin method in alcoholism	DSM-III Alcohol: Male Abuse	74.0	57.8	1.3
				Dependence	59.0	36.2	1.6
				Female Abuse	26.7	27.3	1.0
				Dependence	25.0	5.0	5.0
Caldwell & Gottesman, 1991	154	M + F	?Validity of twin method in alcoholism	DSM-III Alcohol: Male Abuse	68	46	1.5
				Dependence	40	13	3.1
				Female Abuse	47	42	1.1
				Dependence	29	25	1.2

V-A, Veterans Administration.
ICD, International Classification of Diseases; ICD-8, 8th Revision (World Health Organization, 1965); ICD-9, 9th Revision (World Health Organization, 1978).
DSM-III, Diagnostic and Statistical Manual of Mental Disorders, 3rd edn (American Psychiatric Association, 1980).
DSM-IIIR, Diagnostic and Statistical Manual of Mental Disorders, 3rd edn (Revised) (American Psychiatric Association, 1987).
RDC, Research Diagnostic Criteria (Spitzer et al., 1978).

The twin method assumes that any excess in concordance for MZ over DZ twins can be attributed to heredity and not to unequal family environments in MZ and DZ families. However, MZ twins are more likely to live together in adult life than DZ twins and this proximity could increase their concordance for drinking behaviour. Unequal family environments may also reduce concordance by a within-pair "competition" effect, whereby heavy drinking effects reduced consumption in the co-twin. The possibility of a competition effect has been suggested by the results of twin studies of normal drinking (e.g. Clifford et al., 1984).

One of the early samples of twins has recently been followed up after 16 years (Reed et al., 1996). Unsurprisingly, the number of twins with a lifetime diagnosis of alcoholism was increased. Monozygotic concordance rates remained higher than dizygotic concordance rates for ICD alcoholism, alcoholic psychosis and cirrhosis. Statistical analysis suggested, however, that the genetic predisposition to end-organ damage was largely shared with the predisposition to alcoholism and was not independent from the latter.

Observations of twins have thus confirmed a genetic effect in alcohol dependence and problems in some, but not all, studies published to date. This suggests that twin studies should be viewed in the light of adoption and half-sib studies in order to further disentangle genetic and environmental effects.

ADOPTION STUDIES OF ALCOHOL-RELATED PROBLEMS

Adoption studies have been widely employed in psychiatric research as a means of separating genetic and environmental influences, since adoptees receive their genes from one set of parents and their family upbringing from another. Four different groups of researchers have used the adoption strategy to study alcohol dependence and problems (see Table 13.2). Roe's (1944) study is the only one to have shown no evidence of a genetic effect and there is some doubt as to the diagnosis of "alcoholism" in the fathers of her subjects. The methodology of the other studies has also been criticized on various grounds, but they continue to provide strong evidence in favour of a genetic influence upon the aetiology of alcohol dependence and other alcohol-related problems.

The Iowa studies (Cadoret & Gath, 1978; Cadoret et al., 1987) are of interest by virtue of having shown a genetic effect in females as well as males and an environmental

Table 13.2 Adoption studies of alcohol dependence and problems

Authors	Influence of adoptive family demonstrated	Increased incidence of alcoholism among adoptees with alcoholic biological parents
Roe, 1944		Male and female—no
Cadoret & Gath, 1978		Male and female—yes
Cadoret et al., 1985	Males—yes	Males—yes
Cadoret et al., 1987	Females—no	Females—yes
Goodwin et al., 1973 & Goodwin et al., 1974	Males—no	Males—yes
Goodwin et al., 1977	Females—no	Females—no
Bohman, 1978		Males—yes
		Females—no

effect in males but no environmental effect in females. However, the Copenhagen Study (Goodwin et al., 1973, 1977) is probably the best to date on methodological grounds. It showed a four-fold increase in the incidence of "alcoholism" amongst male adoptees adopted away from their alcoholic parent(s) soon after birth. An effect of alcoholism in the adoptive family was not demonstrated (except in terms of the increased incidence of depression amongst female adoptees). Goodwin et al.'s criteria for "alcoholism" may have been too lenient and over-inclusive but nevertheless they produce a curious anomaly. If the cut-off point for abnormality is widened to include an even broader group of "problem drinkers", then there is no significant difference between index and control adoptees. This finding contradicts the evidence of several twin studies, and of Cloninger's analysis of Bohman's adoption study (Cloninger et al., 1981), that not only alcoholism but also milder alcohol misuse is under some degree of genetic influence. It also runs counter to the evidence that heavy drinking and alcoholism are closely related.

Bohman (1978) also demonstrated a genetic effect in males but no such genetic effect in females. Since alcohol misuse was uncommon among women at the time this study was carried out, it may have been that the sample was too small to show any significant effect. Adoptees who lived with their biological mother for more than 6 months had 1.5 times more risk of later alcohol abuse than others but this did not account for the differences between the biological children of alcoholics and controls. Cloninger et al. (1981) re-examined and enlarged Bohman's data on male adoptees. They identified two types of alcoholism (see Tables 4.7 and 6.2, this volume). Taken together, the findings of Bohman and Cloninger are quite remarkable but it remains to be seen whether their classification of alcoholism will stand the test of time. It has certainly not received universal support and many subjects appear not to fit clearly into either category (Schuckit & Irwin, 1989). However, Cloninger and colleagues have recently replicated the Stockholm adoption study and have produced confirmatory evidence in support of Type 1 and Type 2 alcoholism as clinically distinct forms of alcoholism (Sigvardsson et al., 1996).

Half-siblings of offspring of alcoholics also offer opportunities for separating possible genetic and environmental effects on drinking behaviour. Schuckit et al. (1972) found that it seemed to matter little whether the half-siblings were raised by an alcoholic parental figure or not, since the same proportion of both groups became alcoholic. The only consistent predictor of alcoholism in half-siblings was the presence of an alcoholic biological parent.

GENETIC MARKER STUDIES

Genetic marker studies offer the potential to determine not only whether alcohol-related problems are genetically determined, and to what extent, but also to provide information on what it is that is inherited. In other words, they offer the potential to identify the genetic location (locus) or the gene(s) responsible for conferring a predisposition to alcohol-related problems.

A good genetic marker should be of known chromosomal location, preferably highly polymorphic (i.e. with many different variations), of known mode of inheritance (dominant/recessive, etc.) and of readily determinable type (i.e. it is easily possible to identify which variant any given individual has inherited). A genetic marker may be an observable characteristic of an organism, a protein, a gene or a DNA sequence. Good genetic markers were in short supply prior to recent advances in DNA technology. Now, restriction fragment length polymorphisms (RFLPs) and other DNA markers, such as microsatellite repeat polymorphisms, provide readily available markers with all the above characteristics, which are available for study across the entire human genome.

Genetic markers may be used to study differences between populations or groups by use of statistical tests of association between marker variants and different alcohol-related problems. Alternatively, genetic markers may be used to study the transmission of alcohol-related problems within families. Here, evidence of genetic transmission is obtained by searching for genetic "linkage" within a family or an affected sibling pair between particular genetic markers and the disorder or trait under study. Where there is perfect genetic linkage, individuals who inherit the particular marker will always also inherit the index disorder (e.g. alcohol dependence).

Genetic Association Studies of Alcohol Dependence and Problems

Genetic, or "allelic", association studies attempt to demonstrate a statistical association between a genetic marker and a disorder (or trait), relative to a suitable control group, within a given population. Demonstration of such an association may be indicative of a direct causal effect between a genetic variation and the disorder, or it may be evidence of linkage disequilibrium between a locus predisposing to the disorder and a nearby marker on the same chromosome. (Linkage disequilibrium exists where the two genetic loci are situated very close together on the same chromosome, so that a particular allele at one locus tends always to be found with a particular allele at the other).

Genetic association studies have methodological weaknesses because hidden population stratifications in control and disease populations may be present. For example, selection of heavy drinkers may inadvertently lead to selection of a particular ethnic or racial group that displays a higher frequency of the marker type than does the control population. On the other hand, strong *a priori* evidence for the involvement of a protein and its specific gene in a disease may justify the use of this approach.

Prior to recent developments in molecular biology, a large number of genetic markers were studied in an attempt to find an association with alcohol dependence, or other alcohol-related problems, at the population level.

Blood Groups

Thirteen or more studies of alcohol dependence and problems have been conducted in which blood groups have been used as genetic markers. The 12 different blood groups employed in total are situated on only eight of the 23 human chromosome pairs. Given that these markers are also generally not highly polymorphic, they are greatly lacking in power to detect genetic effects.

Blood group A was associated with alcoholism in at least two studies (Nordmo, 1959; Kojic et al., 1977) but numerous attempts to replicate these findings failed to find any association with the ABO system. Hill (S.Y.) et al. (1975) found that the ss phenotype of the MNSs system was significantly less common in alcoholics as compared with their non-alcoholic first-degree relatives and suggested that this phenotype may be protective against alcoholism. The prevalence of the ss phenotype in alcoholics did not differ greatly from that reported for the general population, although an unrelated control group was not included in the study. Hill et al. were not at that stage able to show linkage between this locus and alcoholism in the sibling pairs included in their sample (see below), and Winokur et al. (1976) and Hill (E.M.) et al. (1988) were unable to replicate their association result in studies of similar design. No significant allelic association of this locus with alcoholism was found by Hill (S.Y.) et al. (1988) in a later paper where they used general population data as a control.

Two other association studies of the MNSs blood group system and alcoholism have been published. Kojic et al. (1977) found a significantly greater incidence of the SS group in alcoholics, as compared with controls. No association between alcoholism and MNSs blood groups was found by Tanna et al. (1988). One further study found that the SS group was significantly reduced amongst heavy drinkers (Gleiberman et al., 1981).

Other Blood Protein Markers

Six or more association studies of alcoholism have utilized polymorphic serum proteins as genetic markers. The 24 different proteins employed in these studies are located on only 15 different chromosomes. As with the blood group association studies, this limited distribution of a small number of only slightly polymorphic markers provides limited power to detect genetic effects. All of these studies compared affected subjects with unaffected relatives as controls, except for the one by Kojic et al. (1977). Only complement component 3 (C3; Hill, S.Y. et al., 1975) and haptoglobin (HP; Kojic et al., 1977) have yielded positive results in association studies of alcoholism and these results have not been replicated.

HLA Antigens

Numerous studies have employed HLA antigens as genetic markers to study alcohol-related liver disease, but the results have been inconsistent (Eddleston & Davis, 1982; Arria et al., 1991). It is doubtful that any conclusions can be drawn at present concerning the importance of these immune susceptibility genes as potential loci for genetic predispositions to alcohol-related problems.

Alcohol-metabolizing Enzymes

Perhaps the most studied, and certainly the best established, example of a single gene effect that alters drinking behaviour and the incidence of alcohol dependence and problems is the flushing reaction to alcohol, which is conferred by the "Oriental" or inactive form of ALDH2 (ALDH2-2). A large number of papers have now studied the various associations between ALDH2 status, flushing (e.g. Shibuya, 1993), quantity of alcohol consumption and alcohol dependence and problems. Subjects with the inactive form of ALDH2 drink less than controls (Higuchi et al., 1992), presumably because of the aversive effects of the flushing reaction that they experience when they do drink. Many studies have shown an association with alcoholic liver disease. For example, in one study of Oriental subjects, the frequency of the ALDH2-2 gene was 0.35 in controls but only 0.07 in patients with alcoholic liver disease (Shibuya & Yoshida, 1988). In various studies, the frequency of the ALDH2-2 gene was reduced in patients diagnosed according to DSM-IIIR (e.g. Maezawa et al., 1995) or ICD10 (Shen et al., 1997) criteria for alcohol dependence. No association has been found with brain atrophy (Maezawa et al., 1996) and conflicting results have been obtained in studies of alcoholic pancreatitis (Day et al., 1991; Chao et al., 1997). The ALDH2-2 allele is apparently not found in Caucasians (Agarwal & Goedde, 1991) and thus this particular single dominant gene effect cannot be implicated in models of predisposition to alcohol dependence and other alcohol-related problems in European populations.

There has also been some research, albeit less consistent, in support of an effect of polymorphisms at the alcohol dehydrogenase (ADH) loci on genetic predisposition to alcohol-related problems. There is evidence from several studies that ADH*1 and ADH3*2 may be associated with alcohol dependence or alcoholic liver disease in oriental populations (e.g. Chao et al., 1997). However, this apparently does not apply in Caucasian groups

(Gilder et al., 1993). Whitfield (1997) has suggested that ADH2*2 reduces the risk of alcohol dependence but increases the risk of alcoholic liver disease in alcoholics. Some associations have also been found with alcoholic pancreatitis (e.g. Chao et al., 1997) and alcoholic brain atrophy (Maezawa et al., 1996).

The ethanol inducible form of the enzyme cytochrome p450 has also been the subject of various studies. However, the majority have shown no association with either alcohol consumption or a range of alcohol-related problems (e.g. Chao et al., 1997).

D_2 Dopamine Receptor Gene Locus (DRD2)

In 1990, a study employing DNA markers demonstrated a highly significant association between the A1 allele of the D_2 dopamine receptor gene locus and severe alcoholism (Blum et al., 1990). These workers found that the A1 allele was present in 69% of 35 post-mortem brain samples from alcoholics, diagnosed according to DSM-IIIR criteria after death, as compared with only 20% of 35 similar specimens from controls. Subsequently, there have been numerous attempts at replication, some successful and others not.

A number of reviewers have combined results from the various studies in order to demonstrate either that there is an overall significant association between the A1 allele of this marker and alcoholism (e.g. Noble, 1993) or else to demonstrate that there is not (e.g. Gelernter et al., 1993)! Since new studies have continued to appear in the literature at a rapid rate, each review has considered a different combination of studies and most are not currently up to date. At the time of writing this chapter, we were able to identify 26 studies, which we combined (excluding Neiswanger et al., 1993, for which the relevant data were not available) by similar means to those used by Gelernter et al. (1993) and Noble (1993). The overall association, combining results from all the studies in this way, remains significant. If the original study by Blum et al. (1990) is excluded, as recommended by Gelernter et al. (1993), then the overall result still remains significant. If the meta-analysis is limited to studies of Caucasian subjects, then the overall result is much more highly significant.

Much of the controversy surrounding this research has concerned the allele frequencies in the control populations rather than in the subjects, and allele frequencies evidently do vary considerably from one racial group to another (Barr & Kidd, 1993). It is also interesting to note that some of the earlier negative studies failed to take steps to screen their controls to exclude those with drinking problems.

Several studies (e.g. Blum et al., 1991) found that the association with the A1 allele depended upon the severity of alcoholism. Lack of agreement on the precise criteria for use of the term "severe" has introduced further problems into this debate, and others have not found "severity" to have any significant impact on their findings (e.g. Cook B.L. et al., 1992).

In one study, a significant association has been shown in unaffected subjects between the A1 allele of the TaqI RFLP and having a family history of alcoholism in siblings (Neiswanger et al., 1993). Remarkably few association studies of alcoholism and the DRD2 locus have employed genetic markers other than the TaqI A RFLP. Of three studies employing the TaqI B RFLP, one has shown an association with alcoholism (Blum et al., 1993) and two have not (Lu et al., 1993, 1996). These studies were all conducted in populations that had also been studied with the TaqI A RFLP, the results being consonant in each case. Neiswanger et al. (1993) and Lu et al. (1996) have employed microsatellite repeat polymorphisms at the DRD2 locus. Again, results were consonant with those obtained with the TaqI A RFLP, the former group finding positive results with both markers and the latter group finding negative results with both markers. A [311]Cys variant of the DRD2 receptor has been shown to be associated with DSM-IIIR alcohol dependence (Higuchi et al., 1994) in one study but not with ICD-10 alcohol dependence in another (Finckh et al., 1996).

Methodological and statistical questions aside, this research gave rise to some scepticism because there were no particularly strong *a priori* reasons for suspecting that the DRD2 locus might have a role to play in conferring a predisposition to alcoholism. However, examination of the literature before and since does yield evidence for the involvement of this locus. In animal studies, dopamine receptor agonists and antagonists have been shown to influence alcohol consumption (e.g. Dyr et al., 1993). Other research has suggested that abstinent alcoholics show reduced dopamine receptor sensitivity (e.g. Wiesbeck et al., 1995), although not all studies have found evidence for this (Heinz et al., 1996) and receptor binding studies in rats have also shown mixed results (e.g. Stefanini et al., 1992). Blum's own group have published a paper showing that the binding affinity (K_d) of DRD2 receptors is reduced in alcoholics and that the number of binding sites (B_{max}) is reduced in subjects with the A1 allele (Noble et al., 1991). Healthy subjects with the A1 allele also show different regional brain glucose metabolism on PET scanning (Noble et al., 1997) and poorer performance on visuospatial tasks (Berman & Noble, 1995). Perhaps the most interesting possibility, however, is the proposed role of dopamine in the tridimensional theory of personality elaborated by Cloninger (1987) and the role of dopamine in reward pathways in the brain.

In his tridimensional model, Cloninger associates dopaminergic activity with "novelty-seeking" personality traits based upon animal studies. He quotes research that has shown that low doses of ethanol stimulate ventral tegmental dopaminergic neurones, thus providing a pharmacological reinforcement of alcohol-seeking behaviour (see also a more recent review by Harris et al., 1992). Indeed, it has been proposed elsewhere that dopamine plays a key role in reward pathways for a range of different drugs of abuse and that it may be involved in a common neurochemical basis for alcohol and drug addictions (e.g. Miller & Gold, 1993).

Rolfs et al. (1993) have demonstrated single point mutations in non-coding regions of the DRD2 gene in alcohol-dependent patients. The functional significance of these mutations remains to be evaluated. However, Gejman (1993) was unable to find any structural mutation in the coding regions of the DRD2 gene, even though he had chosen as subjects 113 alcoholics from a series in which an association of the A1 allele and alcoholism had already been demonstrated. Gejman did not study some parts of the gene (the "enhancer" or "promoter" regions) and so it remains possible that a mutation could be found there. Alternatively, it is possible that the DRD2 locus is not the susceptibility locus itself and that the findings of the association studies implicating DRD2 are due to another neighbouring, tightly-linked gene in which a mutation predisposes to alcoholism.

As remarked above, it is well known that population "stratification" effects can produce spuriously significant results in association studies. However, it is also possible that a genuine, aetiologically significant association may only be observed in certain racial groups. The Oriental "flushing" syndrome is a good example of this (see above). So far, significant results have been found in Black, Caucasian and Oriental populations (e.g. Blum et al., 1990; Arinami et al., 1993) but not in an American Indian population (Goldman et al., 1993). Negative results have also been found in Caucasian and Oriental populations (e.g. Gelernter et al., 1991; Chen et al., 1996). Combining the results of studies, as described above, there is a highly significant association between the A1 allele and alcoholism in combined Caucasian and Black subject groups. (These studies include mainly Caucasian subjects. Based on published sources, less than 6% of the total alcoholic and control subjects appear to have been Black). Combined data for the Oriental groups alone reveals no overall significant association.

Potentially, the greatest significance of involvement of the DRD2 locus in conferring a predisposition to alcohol misuse could be in terms of the implications for prevention and treatment. Treatment with tiapride (a dopamine receptor-blocking agent) has been claimed to improve abstinence rates following detoxification and also to exert a beneficial effect upon associated neurotic symptoms (Shaw et al., 1987; see also Chapter 27, this volume). In a double-blind study, bromocriptine (a DRD2 agonist) was found to produce the greatest improvements in craving and anxiety in alcoholics with the A1 allele (Lawford et al., 1995; see also Chapter 6, this volume). However, others have not found an association between clinical outcome and DRD2 genotype following detoxification and 6 months of non-pharmacological treatment (Heinz et al., 1996).

Research is beginning to emerge suggesting that if the DRD2 locus does have a role in the aetiology of alcohol dependence and/or other alcohol-related problems, it may not be completely specific to alcohol alone. Smith et al. (1992) have found an increased incidence of the A1 allele amongst heavy polysubstance abusers relative to controls. (However, see also the negative findings of Berrettini & Persico, 1996, who studied substance abuse in African-Americans). Comings et al. (1991a, 1996) found that the A1 allele frequency was elevated not only in alcoholism but also in Gilles de la Tourette's syndrome, autism, attention deficit hyperactivity disorder and post-traumatic stress disorder, and this group have also found some evidence that DRD2 genotype may be associated with impaired ability to deal with conflict (Comings et al., 1995).

Other Dopamine Receptor and Transporter Gene Loci

Research on the DRD2 locus has generated interest in other possible influences of dopaminergic systems in the genetic predisposition to alcohol-related problems. These studies have employed genetic markers at other dopamine receptor loci (DRD1, DRD3 & DRD4) and at the dopamine transporter locus (DAT). Although most of these studies have produced negative results, the work of Muramatsu and colleagues (Muramatsu & Higuchi, 1995; Muramatsu et al., 1996) is of interest by virtue of its consideration of a two or three gene model, where DRD4 and/or DAT loci may influence risk in those with the ALDH2*2 genotype. (Of course, if this occurred in Caucasian populations, we might consider this to be a single gene model, since virtually everyone is of ALDH2*2 genotype!). Other studies have found an association between DRD1 alleles and Tourette's syndrome, smoking and pathological gambling (Comings et al., 1997) and an association between DRD4 alleles and opioid dependence, smoking or other drug misuse (George et al., 1993; Kotler et al., 1997).

Other DNA Markers

Other published DNA marker studies of alcohol dependence and problems are largely negative (e.g. Chan et al., 1994; Isoe et al., 1996; Geijer et al., 1997). A few positive findings deserve further study (e.g. Harada et al., 1996; Hsu et al., 1996).

The Genetic Association Method and Alcohol-related Problems

The inconsistent findings of several allelic association studies in this field raise important questions as to the usefulness of the method and the correct interpretation of the results. In particular, it is important to distinguish between use of the allelic association method to study a particular locus for which there were strong *a priori* reasons to implicate it in conferring a predisposition to alcohol dependence or problems, and use of the same method to study a large number of loci for which there were no *a priori* reasons for such interest. This points to the potential importance of studies such as those on Oriental alcohol intolerance, where such prior hypotheses existed, as compared with the uncertain significance of the findings of many of the early studies on blood groups. However, such "screening" studies do pave the way for subsequent research and offer the opportunity for replication of their findings. Thus, initial scepticism concerning the association between DRD2 and alcoholism may have been well founded but it is now difficult to dismiss completely a result that has been replicated in so many different laboratories. This locus has demonstrated more consistent and reproducible results than any other genetic marker so far used in association studies of alcohol dependence or other alcohol-related problems in Caucasian populations.

As discussed earlier, it is extremely likely that genetic heterogeneity exists for genetic susceptibility to alcohol dependence and problems, such that distinct genetic effects may contribute to the predisposition to specific problems, in specific families and in specific populations. A replication in a different population is thus more convincing than a failure to replicate. In the latter case, doubt will remain as to whether the results could have been confirmed had the study been repeated in a genetically more similar group. Such concerns are obvious where racial and genetic differences are great, as in Caucasian and Oriental studies of alcohol intolerance. However, variations in the prevalence of blood groups also exist at the level of populations drawn from the same county (e.g. Mourant et al., 1976).

A further problem, which has attracted particular attention in the case of the recent studies of the DRD2 locus, concerns the choice of a suitable control group. This includes both the need to find a truly comparable population and also the need to ensure that alcohol-related problems are excluded from control subjects. Control subjects who are included in a study need to be assessed every bit as rigorously as affected subjects. They also need to be drawn from the same population, so that differences are not introduced due to genetic differences between populations. Comparisons should be made with other psychiatric disorders in order to examine the specificity of the findings. It has proved only partly possible to address these issues in respect of the recent research into the DRD2 locus, and they remain largely unaddressed in earlier research, such as the studies of blood groups.

GENETIC LINKAGE STUDIES OF ALCOHOL DEPENDENCE AND PROBLEMS

Linkage analysis attempts to demonstrate, within families, the co-segregation of an allele of a marker locus with the allele of a gene determining the disorder, disease or trait. Linkage studies offer a more powerful approach to identifying single gene effects than do association studies. In particular, they are capable of detecting the presence and effects of genes at a much greater genetic distance along chromosomes than the genetic association method. At the simplest level, linkage may be detected merely by observing co-segregation between a marker allele and a disease within a family. However, such an inspection of the data offers no indication of the probability that such co-segregation could have occurred by chance and it does not readily accommodate the difficulties introduced by complex modes of inheritance, recombination between loci, incomplete penetrance, and occurrence of phenocopies, etc. Various statistical methods have therefore been introduced in order to quantify these probabilities and to allow incorporation of such complexities into the analysis (Ott, 1991).

Two main variations of the linkage method are routinely used. The lod score method of analysis employs an odds ratio for the odds in favour of linkage between the disorder and marker loci and the odds in favour of non-linkage, given the observed segregation of marker alleles and disease phenotype within the pedigree. The lod score is actually a $\log_{10}$ of this ratio. The lod score method requires specification of the mode of inheritance of the disease gene, which is often not known in diseases of complex inheritance. Problems of incomplete penetrance can be overcome by study of only the affected members of the pedigree but a frequent incidence of phenocopies still reduces the power of the analysis.

The sib-pair method offers some superficial advantages over the lod score method of analysis because it does not require the mode of inheritance to be specified and it does not raise the issue of whether to exclude families where there is evidence of bilineal inheritance. It is also relatively robust to the effects of low penetrance. However, it is statistically less powerful than the lod score method. The sib-pair method of analysis examines sharing of alleles between siblings in a pedigree. Where it is possible to determine that two sibs share an allele from the same parent, they are said to be "identical by descent". Where they share a particular allele but with no evidence that it was inherited from the same parent, they are said to be "identical by state". Observations on the frequency with which pairs of affected sibs are identical by descent allow a calculation that tests for evidence of linkage (Ott, 1991, pp. 78–79). Where information on identity by descent is unavailable, identity by state may be used but this further reduces the power of the analysis.

Application of linkage analysis to mouse or other animal populations follows the same basic principles as that for human studies. However, much more carefully designed and statistically powerful experiments can be carried out by virtue of the possibilities for experimental breeding and prior selection of mouse strains that may or may not exhibit target characteristics.

Animal Linkage Studies of Alcohol Response

Studies of tolerance, withdrawal effects, dependence and many other facets of alcohol consumption have been studied in specially bred ("recombinant inbred") strains of mice (Crabbe et al., 1994). The mouse linkage approach has great power to identify genetic loci that increase or decrease response to alcohol-related variables. The overall results of such studies are beyond the scope of this review. However, because the whole human genome has been mapped by homology to the whole mouse genome, some of the mouse genetic studies can be used to identify or confirm genetic loci that are of importance in conferring a predisposition to heavy drinking or alcohol-related problems in humans. For example, Crabbe et al. (1994) drew attention to several components of alcohol and drug response as well as taste sensitivity that map near the mouse dopamine D2 gene locus. Thus, the mouse work points to a possible role for this locus in the human in a variety of aspects of drug and alcohol misuse.

A recent example of recombinant inbred strain methodology is demonstrated in the study by Belknap et al. (1997), which employed a second generation intercross of two mouse strains which were then selected according to high or low ethanol preference over four generations. The resultant high and low alcohol preference strains were found to have a locus on chromosome 3, near or at the mouse ADH1 gene that is homologous to human chromosome 4q. Buck et al. (1997) used a similar strategy to map three loci associated with increased risk for alcohol withdrawal in mice. They calculated that genes at these loci accounted for 68% of the genetic variability in withdrawal severity. Candidate genes at these loci encode a γ-aminobutyric acid (GABA)-A receptor, glutamic acid decarboxylase, and a locus influencing seizure phenotype. Crabbe (1998) also studied mice for withdrawal severity and identified loci that influenced this trait on eight chromosomes. The locus on chromosome 1 had previously been identified but the others were novel. Such studies in humans would be difficult, although not impossible. Carr et al. (1998) identified a locus on mouse chromosome 4 that showed significant evidence of linkage with the Neuropeptide Y gene, which encodes an endogenous anxiolytic protein. All of these alcohol response loci identified in the mouse may indicate roles for the homologous loci in the human. Thus the mouse data can be used to shorten the length of time that research would have taken using genetic linkage analysis in human populations.

Linkage Studies of Alcohol Dependence and Problems in Humans

Until recently, remarkably few linkage studies of alcohol dependence and problems had been carried out. Research interest and activity in this promising field is now increasing.

Blood Groups

Early interest in the possibility of linkage between the MNSs locus and alcoholism was not subsequently replicated (Hill et al., 1993). The MNSs locus on chromosome 4q is situated in a region that also contains a gene encoding tryptophan oxygenase, a potential candidate gene for predisposition to alcohol dependence (Comings et al., 1991b). Tryptophan oxygenase provides an alternative path to tryptophan hydroxylase in the metabolism of tryptophan and thus may indirectly influence levels of serotonin. Serotonin deficiency has been proposed as providing a possible biochemical predisposition to alcohol dependence (Kent et al., 1985; see also Chapter 6, this volume).

Tanna et al. (1988) studied 30 polymorphic genetic markers, including eight blood groups, in a group of 41 families. The lod score and sib-pair linkage analyses revealed no significant evidence of linkage for any of the blood groups studied. A significant exclusion of linkage was obtained for six loci (including MNSs).

Hill (E.M.) et al. (1988) studied 29 genetic markers, including nine blood groups, in a series of 34 nuclear families ascertained for the *NIMH Collaborative Depression Study*. Sib pair analyses yielded no significant evidence of linkage. Both this study and four other published studies failed to find any notable evidence of linkage between blood groups and DSD (Wilson et al., 1991).

Esterase D

Tanna et al. (1988) and Hill (E.M.) et al. (1988), using a sib-pair method, found inconsistent evidence for linkage between alcoholism and esterase D. However, it is possible that esterase D is linked to depression rather than alcoholism (Wilson et al., 1991).

A more recent study (Wesner et al., 1991) has utilized a RFLP marker to study linkage with the esterase D locus in 15 of the 26 families studied in the original paper by Tanna et al. (1988). Tight linkage to alcoholism was excluded for both alcoholism alone and also for a combination of unipolar depression and alcoholism. This study does deal a severe blow to any hopes that the esterase D locus, or a linked locus, may be confirmed as a true alcohol susceptibility locus. However, this region of chromosome 13q14.1 has not yet been completely excluded.

Other Protein Markers

Polymorphic protein markers other than ESD and blood groups have not yielded significant positive results when applied to linkage studies of alcohol dependence and other alcohol-related problems (Wilson et al., 1991).

Tanna et al. (1976) found evidence for linkage of DSD with HP and C3 using a sib-pair method. In a re-analysis of the data using the lod score method, Tanna et al. (1979) found only weak (non-significant) evidence for linkage with HP and no evidence for linkage with C3. Evidence in support of the linkage of DSD with ORM was first published by Hill (E.M.) et al. (1988). The result was statistically significant if individuals with other psychiatric diagnoses were considered to be unaffected but not if they were excluded from the analysis. Linkage of DSD with C3 or HP was not supported.

Wilson et al. (1989) found weak (non-significant) evidence of linkage between DSD and ORM using a sib-pair analysis. Linkage with the same locus was demonstrated also where the affection status was broadened to include any psychiatric illness. Re-analysis of these data (Wilson et al., 1991) found significant results for both DSD and "any psychiatric illness". Weitkamp et al. (1980) found no evidence for linkage with any of 19 protein markers.

D_2 Dopamine Receptor Gene Locus (DRD2)

There have been six linkage studies of the DRD2 locus and alcoholism. Bolos et al. (1990) studied two Caucasian families with a total of eight affected (RDC Alcoholism) and six "unaffected" members. In each family one parent was affected and the alcoholism was described as "early onset" (age 12–22 years). Highly negative results were reported for a dominant model of transmission with high penetrance. However, other models do not appear to have been excluded. Furthermore, the families described in this paper actually contain more cases of drug abuse (total = 10) than alcoholism (total = 8) and also display a range of other psychiatric disorders. This raises interesting questions as to what kind of predisposition might be inherited and how the phenotype should be defined in genetic studies of these families.

Parsian et al. (1991) studied 21 families using the TaqI DRD2 RFLP and found no evidence of linkage using a sib-pair method. However, nine families were not informative and some of the remaining families contained only one case of "alcoholism".

Neiswanger et al. (1995) studied 20 "high-density families segregating for alcoholism only", which showed no evidence of linkage between the DRD2 locus and alcoholism using either sib-pair or lod score analyses. The markers studied were the TaqI A RFLP and a microsatellite repeat sequence polymorphism. However, subjects taken from the same families and compared with subjects from control families in which alcoholism was not segregating demonstrated a significant association between alcoholism and the A1 allele of the TaqI RFLP. Thus, evidence for association was found in the absence of evidence for linkage.

Cook and colleagues (Cook et al., 1996) used the sib-pair and lod score linkage methods in families multiply affected by alcoholism, using both the TaqI "A" RFLP and a microsatellite repeat polymorphism at the DRD2 locus. The identity by descent analysis provided significant evidence of an effect of the DRD2 locus on the liability to develop heavy drinking and RDC alcoholism in the first sample of families studied. However, this result was explicable by the segregation of alleles in a single large sibship and it was not replicated in a second sample of families. Although the results did not support linkage between the DRD2 locus and alcoholism in most of the families studied, it remains possible that this locus influences the predisposition to alcoholism in some families.

More recently, a large-scale collaborative study of the genetics of alcoholism ("COGA") has employed linkage analysis to screen the entire human genome. DNA from 105 families with at least three first-degree relatives affected by alcoholism was analysed using microsatellite markers. Analysis did not provide evidence of linkage or allelic association of the DRD2 gene with alcoholism (Edenberg et al., 1998). However a re-analysis of the

COGA D2 linkage data, using model free methods of analysis that had greater statistical power, produced significant evidence of linkage (Curtis et al., 1999). Another large sib-pair linkage study of alcoholism in a South-Western American Indian population found no role for the DRD2 locus in alcoholism (Goldman et al., 1997).

Caution must be exercised in comparing the results of linkage analyses provided by these six linkage studies. The mode of transmission of susceptibility genes for alcohol dependence and other alcohol-related problems is unknown and the application of different methods of linkage analysis may yet tease out evidence for involvement of the D2 gene under specific models. In general, the sib-pair method of analysis is a less powerful form of analysis than the lod method (especially where there is genetic heterogeneity) and it is the sib-pair method that has been used in most of the studies so far. All that can be concluded overall is that the lod score and sib-pair linkage analyses do not so far find significant evidence of linkage with alcohol dependence or other alcohol-related problems at the DRD2 locus. At the same time, some weak positive lod scores have been found, indicating that any claim of exclusion of the locus by linkage analysis is premature.

Other DNA Markers

Devor et al. (1993) have published evidence suggestive of linkage between "alcoholism" and D9S67, a genetic marker on chromosome 9q. This marker is adjacent to both the ABO blood group locus and also the dopamine β-hydroxylase gene. Wesner et al. (1990) found no evidence for linkage of c-Harvey-ras-1 (H-ras) or insulin (INS) DNA markers on chromosome 11p, with either alcoholism or DSD, but neither could the possibility of such linkage be excluded. The family sample included relatively few alcoholics.

The large USA-based collaborative study ("COGA"), which has employed linkage analysis to screen the entire human genome, found evidence for a locus affecting alcohol dependence on chromosome 4, near the ADH gene cluster, which appeared to provide a protective factor (Reich et al., 1998). Linkage results were also highly suggestive that chromosomes 1 and 7 had a role in the genetic susceptibility to alcohol dependence and less significant evidence was found on chromosome 2.

The COGA investigators are now analysing results from a second genome scan in a similarly ascertained replication sample with 157 families and 1313 informative members. For linkages confirmed by the replication, investigators will use multiple genetic markers to narrow the region of interest on each chromosome. An extension of the original COGA study has examined electrical event-related potentials (ERPs) in the brain produced in response to sensory stimuli. The P3 or P300 ERP component usually peaks between 300 and 500 ms after a stimulus, and people with low P3 amplitude are believed to have difficulty in distinguishing significant from insignificant stimuli (Begleiter et al., 1998). Previous studies have repeatedly found that the P3/P300 evoked potential is abnormal in alcoholics, even if they are abstinent. Such a result may indicate that low P3 amplitudes occur before the onset of heavy drinking and could be inherited. The whole-genome scan used to detect linkage with alcoholism provided significant evidence for linkage on chromosomes 2 and 6. Suggestive evidence for linkage was found on chromosomes 5 and 13. It is not yet clear which genes at these loci affect P3 amplitude. However, genes encoding ionotropic glutamate receptors and two subunits of the acetylcholine receptor are nearby.

In the NIAAA study of US American Indians by Long et al. (1998) significant evidence for linkage with alcohol dependence was found with the marker D11S1984, which is on chromosome 11p near the locus for the DRD4 dopamine receptor. Evidence for linkage was also found with the marker D4S3242, which is situated near the locus for the γ-aminobutyric acid receptor subunit A. In accordance with the COGA scan in predominantly Caucasian families, Goldman and colleagues (Goldman et al., 1997; Long et al., 1998) identified a second region on chromosome 4, near the ADH gene cluster, which showed linkage to alcoholism resistance in this population.

Another recent linkage study of alcoholism by Nielsen et al. (1998) has also supported linkage on chromosome 11p. Nielsen et al. investigated the role of tryptophan hydroxylase (TPH) in predisposing individuals to suicidality, alcoholism and the development of personality traits in a large Finnish cohort. They showed that a variation in the TPH gene was linked with suicidality and alcoholism. The field of linkage analysis of alcoholism is moving ahead quickly and efforts to clone and sequence the various susceptibility and modifying genes are soon likely to be successful. The whole project has been enormously helped by the systematic cloning and sequencing of the human genome and by the information provided by animal studies.

GENETIC PREDISPOSITION TO ALCOHOL DEPENDENCE AND PROBLEMS

Given that there is evidence in favour of a genetic effect, how may a genetic predisposition to alcohol dependence and problems be mediated? Genetic effects may influence levels of alcohol consumption, incidence of alcohol-related problems and onset of physical dependence. We have reviewed elsewhere some of the mechanisms by which such influences may be mediated (Cook & Gurling, 1990). However, as discussed above, the exact genetic loci responsible, and thus the specific genetic effects, have yet to be identified in respect of the great bulk of cases of alcohol dependence and problems, at least in Caucasian populations.

Modern reviewers tend to see alcohol dependence and problems as having a multifactorial aetiology (Cook, 1994). However, such problems are also heterogeneous and for different individuals may be the result of varying and interacting aetiological factors. Unfortunately, much genetic research has tended to ignore psychosocial issues, and psychosocial studies have in turn tended to neglect biological variables (Fillmore, 1988). It is therefore important to view genetic research on alcohol dependence and problems in the broader context of studies of environmental and psychological effects upon aetiology.

KEY WORKS AND SUGGESTIONS FOR FURTHER READING

Crabbe, J.C., Belknap, J.K. & Buck, K.J. (1994).   Genetic animal models of alcohol and drug abuse. *Science*, **264**, 1715–1723.

A review of use of animal genetic models.

Reich, T., Edenberg, H.J., Goate, A. et al. (1998).   A genome-wide search for genes affecting the risk for alcohol dependence. *American Journal of Medical Genetics*, **81**, 207–215.

Paper describing the major US collaborative study on the genetics of alcohol misuse. The biggest genetic research project in this field ever!

Cook, C.C.H. & Gurling, H.M.D. (1990).   The genetic aspects of alcoholism and substance abuse: a review. In G. Edwards & M. Lader (Eds), *The Nature of Drug Dependence* (pp. 75–111). Oxford: Oxford University Press.

A previous review by the present authors in which the possible "mechanisms" by which a genetic predisposition might affect drinking/problems/dependence are explored in more detail than in the present chapter.

McGuffin, P. et al. (1994). *Seminars in Psychiatric Genetics*. London: Gaskell.

A book reviewing psychiatric genetics for psychiatrists (and others), with accessible introductions for the beginner, covering basic genetics, molecular biology, linkage and association methods, etc. Also includes a chapter on alcoholism.

REFERENCES

Agarwal, D.P. & Goedde, H.W. (1991). The role of alcohol metabolising enzymes in alcohol sensitivity, alcohol drinking habits, and incidence of alcoholism in Orientals. In T.N. Palmer (Ed.), *The Molecular Pathology of Alcoholism* (pp. 211–237). Oxford: Oxford University Press.

Allgulander, C., Nowak, J. & Rice, J.P. (1991). Psychopathology and treatment of 30,344 twins in Sweden. II. Heritability estimates of psychiatric diagnosis and treatment in 12,884 twin pairs. *Acta Psychiatrica Scandinavica*, **83**, 12–15.

American Psychiatric Association (1980). *Diagnostic and Statistical Manual of Mental Disorders*, 3rd Edn (DSM-III). Washington, DC: APA.

American Psychiatric Association (1987). *Diagnostic and Statistical Manual of Mental Disorders*, 3rd edn (Revised) (DSM-IIIR). Washington, DC: APA.

Arinami, T., Itokawa, M., Komiyama, T., Mitsushio, H., Mori, H., Mifune, H. et al. (1993). Association between severity of alcoholism and the A1 allele of the dopamine D2 receptor gene TaqI A RFLP in Japanese. *Biological Psychiatry*, **33**, 108–114.

Arria, A.M., Tarter, R.E. & Van Thiel, D.H. (1991). Vulnerability to alcoholic liver disease. *Recent Developments in Alcoholism*, **9**, 185–204.

Barr, C.L. & Kidd, K.K. (1993). Population frequencies of the A1 allele at the dopamine D2 receptor locus. *Biological Psychiatry*, **34**, 204–209.

Begleiter, H., Porjesz, B., Reich, T., Edenberg, H.J., Goate, A., Blangero, J. et al. (1998). Quantitative trait loci analysis of human event-related brain potentials: P3 voltage-evoked potentials. *Electroencephalography acid Clinical Neurophysiology*, **108**, 244–250.

Belknap, J.K., Richards, S.P., O'Toole, L.A., Helms, M.L. & Phillips, T.J. (1997). Short-term selective breeding as a tool for QTL mapping: ethanol preference drinking in mice. *Behavioral Genetics*, **27**, 55–66.

Berman, S.M. & Noble, E.P. (1995). Reduced visuospatial performance in children with the D2 dopamine receptor A1 allele. *Behavioral Genetics*, **25**, 45–58.

Berrettini, W.H. & Persico, A.M. (1996). Dopamine D2 receptor gene polymorphisms and vulnerability to substance abuse in African-Americans. *Biological Psychiatry*, **40**, 144–147.

Berridge, V. (1990). Dependence: historical concepts and constructs. In G. Edwards & M. Lader (Eds), *The Nature of Drug Dependence* (pp. 1–18). Oxford: Oxford University Press.

Blum, K., Noble, E.P., Sheridan, P.J., Montgomery, A., Ritchie, T., Jagadeeswaran, P. et al. (1990). Allelic association of human dopamine D2 receptor gene in alcoholism. *Journal of the American Medical Association*, **263**, 2055–2060.

Blum, K., Noble, E.P., Sheridan, P.J., Finley, O., Montgomery, A., Ritchie, T. et al. (1991). Association of the A1 allele of the D2 dopamine receptor gene with severe alcoholism. *Alcohol*, **8**, 409–416.

Blum, K., Noble, E.P., Sheridan, P.J., Montgomery, A., Ritchie, T., Ozkaragoz, T. et al. (1993). Genetic predisposition in alcoholism: association of the D2 dopamine receptor TaqI B1 RFLP with severe alcoholics. *Alcohol*, **10**, 59–67.

Bohman, M. (1978). Some genetic aspects of alcoholism and criminality. *Archives of General Psychiatry*, **35**, 269–276.

Bolos, A.M., Dean, M., Lucas-Derse, S., Ramsburg, M., Brown, G.L. & Goldman, D. (1990). Population and pedigree studies reveal a lack of association between the dopamine D2 receptor gene and alcoholism. *Journal of the American Medical Association*, **264**, 3156–3160.

Bruun, K., Edwards, G., Lumio, M., Makela, K., Pan, L., Popham, R.E. et al. (1975). *Alcohol Control Policies in Public Health Perspective*, Vol. 25. Forssa: The Finnish Foundation for Alcohol Studies.

Buck, K.J., Metten, P., Belknap, J.K. & Crabbe, J.C. (1997). Quantitative trait loci involved in genetic predisposition to acute alcohol withdrawal in mice. *Journal of Neuroscience*, **17**, 3946–3955.

Bynum, W.F. (1984). Alcoholism and degeneration in 19th century European medicine and psychiatry. *British Journal of Addiction*, **79**, 59–70.

Cadoret, R.J. & Gath, A. (1978).   Inheritance of alcoholism in adoptees. *British Journal of Psychiatry*, **132**, 252–258.

Cadoret, R.J., O'Gorman, T.W., Troughton, E. & Heywood, E. (1985).   Alcoholism and antisocial personality. Interrelationships, genetic and environmental factors. *Archives of General Psychiatry*, **42**, 161–167.

Cadoret, R.J., Troughton, E. & O'Gorman, T.W. (1987).   Genetic and environmental factors in alcohol abuse and antisocial personality. *Journal of Studies on Alcohol*, **48**, 1–8.

Carr, L.G., Foroud, T., Bice, P., Gobbett, T., Ivashina, J., Edenberg, H. et al. (1998).   Quantitative trait locus for alcohol consumption in selectively bred rat lines. *Alcoholism: Clinical and Experimental Research*, **22**, 884–887.

Chan, R.J., McBride, A.W., Thomasson, H.R., Ykenney, A. & Crabb, D.W. (1994).   Allele frequencies of the preproenkephalin A (PENK) gene CA repeat in Asians, African-Americans, and Caucasians: lack of evidence for different allele frequencies in alcoholics. *Alcoholism: Clinical and Experimental Research*, **18**, 533–535.

Chao, Y.-C., Young, T.-H., Tang, H.-S. & Hsu, C.-T. (1997).   Alcoholism and alcoholic organ damage and genetic polymorphisms of alcohol metabolizing enzymes in Chinese patients. *Hepatology*, **25**, 112–117.

Chen, C.-H., Chien, S.-H. & Hwu, H.-G. (1996).   Lack of association between TaqI A1 allele of dopamine D2 receptor gene and alchol-use disorders in Atayal natives of Taiwan. *American Journal of Medical Genetics*, **67**, 488–490.

Clifford, C.A., Fulker, D.W. & Murray, R.M. (1984).   Genetic and environmental influences on drinking patterns in normal twins. In N. Krasner, J.S. Madden & R.J. Walker (Eds), *Alcohol-related Problems* (pp. 115–126). New York: Wiley.

Cloninger, C.R. (1987).   Neurogenetic adaptive mechanisms in alcoholism. *Science*, **236**, 410–416.

Cloninger, C.R., Bohman, M. & Sigvardsson, S. (1981).   Inheritance of alcohol abuse: cross-fostering analysis of adopted men. *Archives of General Psychiatry*, **38**, 861–868.

Comings, D.E., Comings, B.G., Muhleman, D., Dietz, G., Shahbahrami, B., Tast, D. et al. (1991a).   The dopamine D2 receptor locus as a modifying gene in neuropsychiatric disorders. *Journal of the American Medical Association*, **266**, 1793–1800.

Comings, D.E., Muhleman, D., Dietz, G.W. & Donlan, T. (1991b).   Human tryptophan oxygenase localized to 4q31: possible implications for alcoholism and other behavioural disorders. *Genomics*, **9**, 301–308.

Comings, D.E., MacMurray, J., Johnson, P., Dietz, G. & Muhleman, D. (1995).   Dopamine D2 receptor gene (DRD2) haplotypes and the defense style questionnaire in substance abuse, Tourette syndrome, and controls. *Biological Psychiatry*, **37**, 798–805.

Comings, D.E., Muhleman, D. & Gysin, R. (1996).   Dopamine D2 receptor (DRD2) gene and susceptibility to posttraumatic stress disorder: a study and replication. *Biological Psychiatry*, **40**, 368–372.

Comings, D.E., Gade, R., Wu, S., Chiu, C., Dietz, G., Muhleman, D. et al. (1997).   Studies of the potential role of the dopamine D1 receptor gene in addictive disorders. *Molecular Psychiatry*, **2**, 44–56.

Cook, B.L., Wang, Z.W., Crowe, R.R., Hauser, R. & Freimer, M. (1992).   Alcoholism and the D2 receptor gene. *Alcoholism: Clinical and Experimental Research*, **16**, 806–809.

Cook, C.C.H. (1994).   Aetiology of alcohol misuse. In J. Chick & R. Cantwell (Eds), *Seminars in Psychiatry: Alcohol and Drug Misuse* (pp. 94–125). London: Royal College of Psychiatrists.

Cook, C.C.H. & Gurling, H.M.D. (1990).   The genetic aspects of alcoholism and substance abuse: a review. In G. Edwards & M. Lader (Eds), *The Nature of Drug Dependence* (pp. 75–111). Oxford: Oxford University Press.

Cook, C.C.H., Palsson, G., Turner, A., Holmes, D., Brett, P., Curtis, D. et al. (1996).   A genetic linkage study of the D2 dopamine receptor locus in heavy drinking and alcoholism. *British Journal of Psychiatry*, **169**, 243–248.

Cotton, N.S. (1979).   The familial incidence of alcoholism. *Journal of Studies on Alcohol*, **40**, 89–116.

Crabbe, J.C. (1998).   Provisional mapping of quantitative trait loci for chronic ethanol withdrawal severity in BXD recombinant inbred mice. *Journal of Pharmacology and Experimental Therapeutics*, **286**, 263–271.

Crabbe, J.C., Belknap, J.K. & Buck, K.J. (1994).   Genetic animal models of alcohol and drug abuse. *Science*, **264**, 1715–1723.

Curtis, D., Jing, H.Z. & Sham, P.C. (1999).   Comparison of GENEHUNTER and MFLINK for analysis of COGA linkage data. *Genetic Epidemiology*, **17**, Suppl. 1, S115–120.

Day, C.P., Bashir, R., James, O.F., Bassendine, M.F., Crabb, D.W., Thomasson, H.R. et al. (1991).   Investigation of the role of polymorphisms at the alcohol and aldehyde dehydrogenase loci in genetic predisposition to alcohol-related end-organ damage. *Hepatology*, **14**, 798–801.

Devor, E.J., Dill-Devor, R.M., Tanna, V.L. & Winokur, G. (1993).   New evidence of genetic linkage of alcoholism in chromosome 9q34. *Alcoholism: Clinical and Experimental Research*, **17**, 452 (Abstract).

Dyr, W., McBride, W.J., Lumeng, L., Li, T.K. & Murphy, J.M. (1993).   Effects of D1 and D2 dopamine receptor agents on ethanol consumption in the high-alcohol-drinking (HAD) line of rats. *Alcohol*, **10**, 207–212.

Eddleston, A.L.W.F. & Davis, M. (1982).   Histocompatibility antigens in alcoholic liver disease. *British Medical Bulletin*, **38**, 13–16.

Edenberg, H.J., Foroud, T., Koller, D.L., Goate, A., Rice, J., Van Eerdewegh, P. et al. (1998).   A family-based analysis of the association of the dopamine D2 receptor (DRD2) with alcoholism. *Alcoholism: Clinical and Experimental Research*, **22**, 505–512.

Fillmore, K.M. (1988).   *Alcohol Use Across the Life Course: A Critical Review of 70 Years of International Longitudinal Research.* Toronto: Addiction Research Foundation.

Finckh, U., von Widdern, O., Giraldo-Velasquez, M., Podschus, J., Dufeu, P., Sander, T. et al. (1996).   No association of the structural dopamine D2 receptor (DRD2) variant 311Cys with alcoholism. *Alcoholism: Clinical and Experimental Research*, **20**, 528–532.

Geijer, T., Jönsson, E., Neiman, J., Persson, M.-L., Brené, S., Gyllander, A. et al. (1997).   Tyrosine hydroxlase and dopamine D4 receptor allelic distribution in Scandinavian chronic alcoholics. *Alcoholism: Clinical and Experimental Research*, **21**, 35–39.

Gejman, P.V. (1993).   No structural mutation in the dopamine D2 receptor gene in alcoholism or schizophrenia. *Psychiatric Genetics*, **3**, 130–131.

Gelernter, J., O'Malley, S., Risch, N., Kranzler, H.R., Krystal, J., Merikangas, K. et al. (1991).   No association between an allele at the D2 dopamine receptor gene (DRD2) and alcoholism. *Journal of the American Medical Association*, **266**, 1801–1807.

Gelernter, J., Goldman, D., Risch, N. (1993).   The A1 allele at the D2 dopamine receptor gene and alcoholism. A reappraisal. *Journal of the American Medical Association*, **269**, 1673–1677.

George, S.R., Cheng, R., Nguycn, T., Israel, Y. & O'Dowd, B.F. (1993).   Polymorphisms of the D4 dopamine receptor alleles in chronic alcoholism. *Biochemical and Biophysical Research Communications*, **196**, 107–114.

Gilder, F.J., Hodgkinson, S. & Murray, R.M. (1993).   ADH and ALDH genotype profiles in Caucasians with alcohol-related problems and controls. *Addiction*, **88**, 383–388.

Gleiberman, L., Gershowitz, H., Harburg, E. & Kuusinen, S. (1981).   Blood groups and alcohol use. *Journal of Studies on Alcohol*, **42**, 557–563.

Goldman, D., Brown, G.L., Albaugh, B., Robin, R., Goodson, S., Trunzo, M. et al. (1993).   DRD2 dopamine receptor genotype, linkage disequilibrium, and alcoholism in American Indians and other populations. *Alcoholism: Clinical and Experimental Research*, **17**, 199–204.

Goldman, D., Urbanek, M., Guenther, D., Robin, R. & Long, J.C. (1997).   Linkage and association of a functional DRD2 variant (Ser311Cys) and DRD2 markers to alcoholism; substance abuse and schizophrenia in south-western American Indians. *American Journal of Medical Genetics*, **74**, 386–394.

Goodwin, D.W., Hermansen, L., Guze, S.B. & Winokur, G. (1973).   Alcohol problems in adoptees raised apart from alcoholic biological parents. *Archives of General Psychiatry*, **28**, 238–243.

Goodwin, D.W., Schulsinger, F., Moller, N., Hermansen, L., Winokur, G. & Guze, S.B. (1974). Drinking problems in adopted and non-adopted sons of alcoholics. *Archives of General Psychiatry*, **31**, 164–169.

Goodwin, D.W., Schulsinger, F., Knop, J., Mednick, S.A. & Guze, S.B. (1977).   Alcoholism and depression in adopted-out daughters of alcoholics. *Archives of General Psychiatry*, **34**, 751–755.

Harada, S., Okubo, T., Tsutsumi, M., Takase, S. & Muramatsu, T. (1996).   Investigation of genetic risk factors associated with alcoholism. *Alcoholism: Clinical and Experimental Research*, **20**, 293A–296A.

Harris, R.A., Brodie, M.S. & Dunwiddie, T.V. (1992). Possible substrates of ethanol reinforcement: GABA and dopamine. *Annals of the New York Academy of Science*, **654**, 61–69.

Heinz, A., Sander, T., Harms, H., Finckh, U., Kuhn, S., Dufeu, P. et al. (1996). Lack of allelic association of dopamine D1 and D2 (TaqIA) receptor gene polymorphisms with reduced dopaminergic sensitivity in alcoholism. *Alcoholism: Clinical and Experimental Research*, **20**, 1109–1113.

Higuchi, S., Muramatsu, T., Shigemori, K., Saito, M., Kono, H., Dufour, M.C. & Harford, T.C. (1992). The relationship between low K_m aldehyde dehydrogenase phenotype and drinking behavior in Japanese. *Journal of Studies on Alcohol*, **53**, 170–175.

Higuchi, S., Muramatsu, T., Murayama, M. & Hayashida, M. (1994). Association of structural polymorphism of the dopamine D2 receptor gene and alcoholism. *Biochemical and Biophysical Research Communications*, **204**, 1199–1205.

Hill, E.M., Wilson, A.F., Elston, R.C. & Winokur, G. (1988). Evidence for possible linkage between genetic markers and affective disorders. *Biological Psychiatry*, **24**, 903–917.

Hill, S.Y., Goodwin, D.W., Cadoret, R., Osterland, C.K. & Doner, S.M. (1975). Association and linkage between alcoholism and eleven serological markers. *Journal of Studies on Alcohol*, **36**, 981–992.

Hill, S.Y., Aston, C. & Rabin, B. (1988). Suggestive evidence of genetic linkage between alcoholism and the MNS blood group. *Alcoholism: Clinical and Experimental Research*, **12**, 811–814.

Hill, S.Y., Neiswanger, K. & Kaplan, B. (1993). Exclusion of linkage between alcoholism and the MNS blood group region on chromosome 4q in multiplex families. *Psychiatric Genetics*, **3**, 170.

Hsu, Y.-P.P., Loh, E.W., Chen, W.J., Chen, C.-C., Yu, J.-M. & Cheng, A.T.A. (1996). Association of monoamine oxidase A alleles with alcoholism among male chinese in Taiwan. *American Journal of Psychiatry*, **153**, 1209–1211.

Isoe, K., Urakami, K., Ji, Y., Adachi, Y. & Nakashima, K. (1996). Presenilin-1 polymorphism in patients with Alzheimer's disease, vascular dementia and alcohol-associated dementia in Japanese population. *Acta Neurologia Scandinavica*, **94**, 326–328.

Kendler, K.S., Heath, A.C., Neale, M.C., Kessler, R.C. & Eaves, L.J. (1992). A population-based twin study of alcoholism in women. *Journal of the American Medical Association*, **268**, 1877–1882.

Kent, T.A., Campbell, J.L., Pazdernik, T.L., Hunter, R., Gunn, W.H. & Goodwin, D.W. (1985). Blood platelet uptake of serotonin in men alcoholics. *Journal of Studies on Alcohol*, **46**, 357–359.

Kojic, T.O., Stojanovic, A., Dojcinova, A. & Jakulic, S. (1977). Possible genetic predisposition for alcohol addiction. *Advances in Experimental Medicine and Biology*, **85A**, 7–24.

Kotler, M., Cohen, H., Segman, R., Gritsenko, I., Nemanov, L., Lerer, B. et al. (1997). Excess dopamine D4 receptor (D4DR) exon III seven repeat allele in opioid-dependent subjects. *Molecular Psychiatry*, **2**, 251–254.

Lawford, B.R., Young, R.McD., Rowell, J.A., Qualichefski, J., Fletcher, B.H., Syndulko, K.L. et al. (1995). Bromocriptine in the treatment of alcoholics with the D2 dopamine receptor A1 allele. *Nature Medicine*, **1**, 337–341.

Long, J.C., Knowler, W.C., Hanson, R.L., Robin, R.W., Urbanek, M., Moore, E. et al. (1998). Evidence for genetic linkage to alcohol dependence on chromosomes 4 and 11 from an autosomewide scan in an American Indian population. *American Journal of Medical Genetics*, **81**, 216–221.

Lu, R.-B., Chang, R.-M., Ko, H.-C., Castiglione, C.M., Schoolfield, G., Kidd, J.R. & Kidd, K.K. (1993). No association between alcoholism and the A1 at DRD2 gene in Han Chinese. *Psychiatric Genetics*, **3**, 172.

Lu, R.-B., Ko, H.-C., Chang, F.-M., Castiglione, C.M., Schoolfield, G., Pakstis, A.J. et al. (1996). No association between alcoholism and multiple polymorphisms at the dopamine D2 receptor gene (DRD2) in three distinct Taiwanese populations. *Biological Psychiatry*, **39**, 419–429.

Maezawa, Y., Yamauchi, M., Toda, G., Suzuki, H. & Sakurai, S. (1995). Alcohol-metabolizing enzyme polymorphisms and alcoholism in Japan. *Alcoholism: Clinical and Experimental Research*, **19**, 951–954.

Maezawa, Y., Yamauchi, M., Searashi, Y., Takeda, K., Mizuhara, Y., Kimura, T. et al. (1996). Association of restriction fragment-length polymorphisms in the alcohol dehydrogenase 2 gene with alcoholic brain atrophy. *Alcoholism: Clinical and Experimental Research*, **20**, 29A–32A.

Miller, N.S. & Gold, M.S. (1993). A hypothesis for a common neurochemical basis for alcohol and drug disorders. *Psychiatric Clinics of North America*, **16**, 105–117.

Mourant, A.E., Kopec, A.C. & Domaniewska-Sobczak, K. (1976). *The Distribution of the Human Blood Groups and Other Polymorphisms.* Oxford: Oxford University Press.

Muramatsu, T. & Higuchi, S. (1995). Dopamine transporter gene polymorphism and alcoholism. *Biochemical and Biophysical Research Communications,* **211**, 28–32.

Muramatsu, T., Higuchi, S., Murayama, M., Matsushita, S. & Hayashida, M. (1996). Association between alcoholism and the dopamine D4 receptor gene. *Journal of Medical Genetics,* **33**, 113–115.

Neiswanger, K., Hill, S.Y. & Kaplan, B.B. (1993). Association between alcoholism and the TaqI A RFLP of the dopamine receptor gene in the absence of linkage. *Psychiatric Genetics,* **3**, 130.

Neiswanger, K., Hill, S.Y. & Kaplan, B.B. (1995). Association and linkage studies of the TaqI A1 allele at the dopamine D2 receptor gene in samples of female and male alcoholics. *American Journal of Medical Genetics,* **60**, 267–271.

Nielsen, D.A., Virkkunen, M., Lappalainen, J., Eggert, M., Brown, G.L., Long, J.C. et al. (1998). A tryptophan hydroxylase gene marker for suicidality and alcoholism. *Archives of General Psychiatry,* **55**, 593–602.

Noble, E.P. (1993). The D2 dopamine receptor gene: a review of association studies in alcoholism. *Behavioral Genetics,* **23**, 119–129.

Noble, E.P., Blum, K., Ritchie, T., Montgomery, A. & Sheridan, P.J. (1991). Allelic association of the D2 dopamine receptor gene with receptor-binding characteristics in alcoholism. *Archives of General Psychiatry,* **48**, 648–654.

Noble, E.P., Gottschalk, L.A., Fallon, J.H., Ritchie, T.L. & Wu, J.C. (1997). D2 dopamine receptor polymorphism and brain regional glucose metabolism. *American Journal of Medical Genetics,* **74**, 162–166.

Nordmo, S.H. (1959). Blood Groups in schizophrenia, alcoholism, and mental deficiency. *American Journal of Psychiatry,* **116**, 460–461.

Ott, J. (1991). *Analysis of Human Genetic Linkage,* revised edn. Baltimore, MD: Johns Hopkins University Press.

Parsian, A., Todd, R.D., Devor, E.J., O'Malley, K.L., Suarez, B.K., Reich, T. & Cloninger, C.R. (1991). Alcoholism and alleles of the human D2 dopamine receptor locus. *Archives of General Psychiatry,* **48**, 655–663.

Partanen, J., Bruun, K. & Markkanen, T. (1966). *Inheritance of Drinking Behaviour.* Helsinki: Finnish Foundation for Alcohol Studies.

Prescott, C.A., Hewitt, J.K., Truett, K.R., Heath, A.C., Neale, M.C. & Eaves, L.J. (1994). Genetic and environmental influences on lifetime alcohol-related problems in a volunteer sample of older twins. *Journal of Studies on Alcohol,* **55**, 184–202.

Reed, T., Page, W.F., Viken, R.J. & Christian, J.C. (1996). Genetic predisposition to organ-specific endpoints of alcoholism. *Alcoholism: Clinical and Experimental Research,* **20**, 1528–1533.

Reich, T., Edenberg, H.J., Goate, A., Williams, J.T., Rice, J.P., Van Eerdewegh, P. et al. (1998). A genome-wide search for genes affecting the risk for alcohol dependence. *American Journal of Medical Genetics,* **81**, 207–215.

Roe, A. (1944). The adult adjustment of children of alcoholic parents raised in foster-homes. *Quarterly Journal of Studies on Alcohol,* **5**, 378–393.

Rolfs, A., Finckh, U., Pautzke, A., Hegerl, U., Schmidt, L.G. & Rommelspacher, H. (1993). Characterization of the dopamine 2 receptor gene (D2DR) as possible predisposing gene for alcoholism. Proceedings of the 3rd World Congress on Psychiatric Genetics, New Orleans.

Schuckit, M.A. & Irwin, M. (1989). An analysis of the clinical relevance of type 1 and type 2 alcoholics. *British Journal of Addiction,* **84**, 869–876.

Schuckit, M.A., Goodwin, D.W. & Winokur, G. (1972). A study of alcoholism in half siblings. *American Journal of Psychiatry,* **128**, 1132–1136.

Shaw, G.K., Majumdar, S.K., Waller, S., MacGarvie, J. & Dunn, G. (1987). Tiapride in the long-term management of alcoholics of anxious or depressive temperament. *British Journal of Psychiatry,* **150**, 164–168.

Shen, Y.-C., Fan, J.-H., Edenberg, H.J., Li, T.-K., Cui, Y.-H., Wang, Y.-F. et al. (1997). Polymorphism of ADH and ALDH genes among four ethnic groups in China and effects upon the risk for alcoholism. *Alcoholism: Clinical and Experimental Research,* **21**, 1272–1276.

Shibuya, A. (1993).   Genotypes of alcohol dehydrogenase and aldehyde dehydrogenase and their significance for alcohol sensitivity. *Nippon Rinsho*, **51**, 394–399.

Shibuya, A. & Yoshida, A. (1988).   Genotypes of alcohol metabolising enzymes in Japanese with alcohol liver diseases: a strong association of the usual caucasian type aldehyde dehydrogenase gene (ALDH1/2) with the disease. *American Journal of Human Genetics*, **43**, 744–748.

Sigvardsson, S., Bohman, M. & Cloninger, C.R. (1996).   Replication of the Stockholm adoption study of alcoholism. *Archives of General Psychiatry*, **53**, 681–687.

Smith, S.S., Ohara, B.F., Persico, A.M., Gorelick, D.A., Newlin, D.B., Vlahov, D. et al. (1992).   Genetic vulnerability to drug abuse. *Archives of General Psychiatry*, **49**, 723–727.

Spitzer, R.L., Endicott, J. & Robins, E. (1978).   Research diagnostic criteria. *Archives of General Psychiatry*, **35**, 773–782.

Stefanini, E., Frau, M., Garau, M.G., Garau, B., Fadda, F. & Gessa, G.L. (1992).   Alcohol-preferring rats have fewer dopamine D2 receptors in the limbic system. *Alcohol and Alcoholism*, **27**, 127–130.

Tanna, V.L., Winokur, G., Elston, R.C. & Go, R.C.P. (1976).   A linkage study of depression spectrum disease: the use of the sib pair method. *Neuropsychobiology*, **2**, 52–62.

Tanna, V.L., Go, R.C.P., Winokur, G. & Elston, R.C. (1979).   Possible linkage between alpha hapto-globin (hp) and depression spectrum disease. *Neuropsychobiology*, **2**, 102–113.

Tanna, V.L., Wilson, A.F., Winokur, G. & Elston, R.C. (1988).   Possible linkage between alcoholism and esterase-D. *Journal of Studies on Alcohol*, **49**, 472–476.

Weitkamp, L.R., Pardue, L.H. & Huntzinger, R.S. (1980).   Genetic marker studies in a family with unipolar depression. *Archives of General Psychiatry*, **37**, 1187–1192.

Wesner, R.B., Tanna, V.L., Palmer, P.J., Goedken, R.J., Crowe, R.R. & Winokur, G. (1990).   Linkage of c-Harvey-ras-1 and INS DNA markers to unipolar depression and alcoholism is ruled out in 18 families. *European Archives of Psychiatry and Neurological Science*, **239**, 356–360.

Wesner, R.B., Tanna, V.L., Palmer, P.J., Thompson, R.J., Crowe, R.R. & Winokur, G. (1991).   Close linkage of esterase-D to unipolar depression and alcoholism is ruled out in eight pedigrees. *Journal of Studies on Alcohol*, **52**, 609–612.

Whitfield, J.B. (1997).   Meta-analysis of the effects of alcohol dehydrogenase genotype on alcohol dependence and alcoholic liver disease. *Alcohol and Alcoholism*, **32**, 613–619.

Wiesbeck, G.A., Mauerer, C., Thome, J., Jakob, F. & Boening, J. (1995).   Alcohol dependence, family history, and D2 dopamine receptor function as neuroendocrinologically assessed with apomorphine. *Drug Alcohol Dependence*, **40**, 49–53.

Wilson, A.F., Tanna, V.L., Winokur, G., Elston, R.C. & Hill, E.M. (1989).   Linkage analysis of depression spectrum disease. *Biological Psychiatry*, **26**, 163–175.

Wilson, A.F., Elston, R.C., Mallot, D.B., Tran, L.D. & Winokur, G. (1991).   The current status of genetic linkage studies of alcoholism and unipolar depression. *Psychiatric Genetics*, **2**, 107–124.

Winokur, G., Tanna, V., Elston, R. & Go, R. (1976).   Lack of association of genetic traits with alcoholism and the C3, Ss and ABO systems. *Journal of Studies on Alcohol*, **37**, 1313–1315.

World Health Organization (1965).   *International Classification of Diseases, 8th Revision (ICD-8).* Geneva, WHO.

World Health Organization (1978).   *International Classification of Diseases, 9th Revision (ICD-9).* Geneva: WHO.

GLOSSARY

Allele   "Alleles" are the different variants of a gene that may be inherited. Every normal individual possesses two copies of every gene, which may thus be identical or different alleles.

Concordance   In genetic twin studies, members of a twin pair may be alike (concordant) or unlike (discordant) for a particular trait or disorder. Concordance rates may be calculated as a proportion of the total number of twins studied (the probandwise rate) or as a proportion of the total number of twin pairs (the pairwise rate). Modern studies have preferred to use the former statistic.

Co-segregation   See *segregation*.

Genome   The complete genetic material of an individual or species.

Linkage   Genetic linkage refers to the *co-segregation* of two genetic loci, or of a genetic locus and a trait or disorder, within a family pedigree. Usually, in scientific research, linkage is sought between a genetic marker, of known inheritance, and a trait or disorder of unknown inheritance. Detection of linkage provides evidence that the genetic marker locus must be situated close to (or at) the genetic locus determining the disorder or trait.

Microsatellite marker   This is a more variable, and thus more powerful, genetic marker detected using the "polymerase chain reaction" (PCR). Variation occurs as a result of repetition of DNA base pairs, with different alleles displaying a different number of repeats of the base pair sequence.

Penetrance   This refers to the situation where a gene is inherited but its effects are not expressed.

Phenocopy   A "phenocopy" is a case of a disorder that occurs due to completely non-genetic causes, but which is indistinguishable from cases that occur due to genetic causes.

Polymorphism   A DNA polymorphism is a genetic sequence that occurs in different forms, or variants, in different individuals. The more variants there are, the more "polymorphic" a gene or marker is said to be. For research purposes, a highly polymorphic marker provides greater power to detect *linkage* with a genetic disorder or trait.

Recombination   Genetic loci that are adjacent to each other on a given chromosome will be in *linkage* with each other. The *alleles* at each locus on each chromosome of the pair will therefore tend to *segregate* together, and thus the same combination of *alleles* will tend to be found together in the offspring as in the parents. Of course, one chromosome, and thus one combination of *alleles*, will be inherited from each parent, and by the same token one chromosome (with its particular combination of *alleles*) will not be inherited. However, *alleles* may still become separated due to breaking and reconnection of chromosomes during the processes of cell division (meiosis) which leads to formation of ova or sperm. Thus, the combination of *alleles* in the offspring may be different to that found in the parents. This process is known as recombination. The greater the genetic distance between two loci on the same chromosome, the greater the likelihood of recombination occurring between them.

Restriction fragment length polymorphism (RFLP)   RFLPs are *polymorphisms* that are detected by use of restriction enzymes. These enzymes cut the DNA chain at specific genetic sequences, thus producing DNA strands of varying length. These strands, or fragments, may be separated by electrophoresis and identified using a radioactive "label". Mutations that add or remove a sequence that is cleaved by a particular restriction enzyme will result in fragments of varying length after digestion of the DNA with the enzyme, and may thus identified in the laboratory.

Segregation   During the process of cell division (meiosis) that leads to the formation of gametes (ova or sperm), each gamete receives randomly only one chromosome from each of the parental chromosome pairs. Thus, for each genetic locus, the offspring receives randomly one or other of the *alleles* from each parent. This process is referred to as segregation. *Alleles* on different chromosomes will segregate completely independently of each other. *Alleles* on the same chromosome, to a degree depending upon the genetic distance between them, are more likely to remain together or "co-segregate".

Chapter 14

Classical Conditioning Mechanisms in Alcohol Dependence

David J. Drobes
and
Michael E. Saladin
Medical University of South Carolina, Charleston, SC, USA
and
Stephen T. Tiffany
Department of Psychological Sciences, Purdue University,
West Lafayette, IN, USA

Synopsis

Cue reactivity studies demonstrate that alcohol-dependent individuals respond to alcohol-related cues with enhanced subjective and physiological reactions, and these reactions are deemed to be functionally related to the motivation to drink. According to classical conditioning conceptualizations of cue reactivity findings, enhanced reactions to alcohol cues among alcoholics occur due to the formation of an association between environmental cues and alcohol consumption over a history of drinking. Several prominent applications of classical conditioning theory are reviewed in this chapter, including withdrawal-based, appetitively-based, incentive-motivation and classical-operant interaction theories.

In general, these theories have not been well supported by the empirical literature and a number of conceptual problems in applying these theories to cue reactivity findings are discussed. We briefly describe Tiffany's cognitive model as an alternative theoretical framework, in which automatic and non-automatic cognitive processes are invoked to explain the disparate findings across the cue reactivity literature. The chapter concludes with an overview of clinical applications of classical conditioning theory within the treatment of alcohol dependence and we discuss some directions that may benefit both clinical and theoretical development in this area.

International Handbook of Alcohol Dependence and Problems. Edited by N. Heather, T.J. Peters and T. Stockwell.
© 2001 John Wiley & Sons Ltd.

Jerry is alcohol-dependent and he has not had a drink in 3 weeks. He is beginning to feel confident that he has overcome his drinking problem and he has started to repair some of the damage he has done to his life through his destructive drinking life-style. His desire to drink has been gradually weakening. On the way home from a particularly stressful and difficult day at work, Jerry looks up and sees the neon sign for Joe's Bar, one of his favourite haunts where he used to spend many hours with his drinking buddies. His mouth begins to water and he remembers how a drink after a hard day's work helped him to calm down and enjoy himself. He notices that he feels excitement in his stomach. He decides to stop and get a pack of cigarettes at the drug store next to the bar. As Jerry pays for the cigarettes, he looks at his watch and realises that happy hour is just getting under way next door at Joe's. He knows that several of his friends are probably in there, and he starts to think that the best way to forget about the worries of the day is to go and get a drink. He does.

Individuals who study and treat alcohol dependence often assume that reactions to environmental stimuli that have been associated with previous drinking episodes can play an important role in ongoing alcohol consumption and relapse to drinking. The typical scenario described above highlights the potential involvement of alcohol-related cues in an episode of relapse drinking. Numerous investigations have attempted to systematically evaluate the impact of alcohol cues by presenting them to alcohol-dependent individuals in a controlled laboratory setting. In these studies, alcohol-dependent individuals confronted with relevant cues generally report increased cravings for alcohol and they often display distinct patterns of physiological reactions, such as increased heart rate and salivation. In some cases, they show evidence of increased alcohol seeking and consumption. Responsivity to alcohol-related cues has been termed cue reactivity *(Drummond et al., 1995).*

Cue reactivity phenomena are often interpreted by appealing to classical conditioning mechanisms. Simply put, alcohol-dependent individuals have an extensive history of drinking in the presence of certain alcohol-related cues, such as the sight or smell of the alcoholic beverage itself, or the environmental context in which drinking typically occurs. It is assumed that these stimuli, through repeated pairings with the alcohol unconditioned stimulus (US), become conditioned stimuli (CSs) that are capable of eliciting conditioned responses (CRs). From this perspective, responses to alcohol-relevant cues presented in a cue reactivity study are thought to represent CRs.

If stimuli that have been associated with previous alcohol consumption can acquire the ability to control conditioned responses that influence alcohol consumption, then it is both theoretically and clinically important to elucidate the functional role of classical conditioning mechanisms in alcohol-related disorders. Identification of these mechanisms will promote theory development, drive empirical evaluation and refinement of these theories, and ultimately enhance our ability to develop treatments that will directly address the impact of conditioned cues on alcohol-related disorders.

This chapter will review findings and theories pertaining to classical conditioning mechanisms in alcohol dependence. Despite potentially important differences between "classical" and "Pavlovian" conditioning, these terms are often used interchangeably by cue reactivity researchers. For the purposes of the present chapter, we will integrate studies that may actually be better specified as relating to either Pavlovian or classical conditioning. Our coverage of the relevant literature will be selective and will be designed to provide the reader with an overview of contemporary work and theorizing in this area. When necessary, pertinent findings from other drugs of abuse will be included, as many of the theories that will be reviewed were originally developed from studies of opiates, nicotine and cocaine. In response to identified shortcomings of the most widely recognized theories, we will consider the potential benefit of an alternative framework from which to interpret alcohol cue reactivity findings. Finally, this chapter will conclude with a brief consideration of clinical applications of classical condi-

tioning approaches and consider some potential directions for further research that we hope will facilitate theoretical and clinical progress.

BASIC ALCOHOL CUE REACTIVITY EFFECTS

In most alcohol cue reactivity studies, alcohol-dependent or social drinkers are presented with *in vivo* presentations of stimuli that are closely associated with past drinking, such as the sight, smell and/or taste of a preferred alcoholic beverage (e.g. Monti et al., 1987). A few researchers have utilized alcohol-relevant videos or pictures (e.g. Stormark et al., 1993) and recent studies have incorporated imagery procedures for the induction of alcohol craving (e.g. Weinstein et al., 1998). Across these studies, there is typically some measurement of self-reported urges or craving to drink alcohol in response to the cue presentations and a number of studies have included various psychophysiological measures. This is an important feature of this work, as most of the theories described below make specific predictions regarding the physiological responses that should accompany craving reports.

Carter & Tiffany (1999) recently provided an empirical evaluation of alcohol cue reactivity effects by conducting a meta-analysis of cue reactivity effects across a range of addictive substances. Consistent with the assumption that alcohol-dependent individuals will report increased urges and cravings for alcohol in response to alcohol cues, this meta-analysis revealed a reliable positive effect size (i.e. the number of standard deviation units for the difference, in this case, between responding to the alcohol cue and a comparison neutral cue) for alcohol craving. It is important to note that the effect size for self-reported alcohol craving was in the medium range (Cohen, 1988), whereas the corresponding effect sizes in studies of opiate, cocaine and nicotine cue reactivity were substantially larger. For psychophysiological measures, the meta-analysis indicated significant increases in heart rate and sweat gland activity in response to alcohol cues and a non-significant decrease in skin temperature. The effect sizes for heart rate and sweat gland activity were both in the small to medium range and there was substantial variability in the effect sizes reported across the studies included in this analysis. One relevant physiological measure that was not included in this meta-analysis is salivation. Previous reviewers have suggested that salivation is reliably increased in the presence of alcohol cues (e.g. Rohsenow et al., 1990). A recent meta-analytic review of this measure in alcohol studies (Tiffany, Carter & Singleton, 1999) indicates that presentations of alcohol cues induce significant increases in salivation with an effect size in the average range.

OPPORTUNISTIC VS. CONDITIONING STUDIES

Behaviour elicited by alcohol-related cues in the vast majority of human cue reactivity studies is often *assumed* to be a function of previous alcohol–cue pairings (see Glautier & Tiffany, 1995). Thus, human cue reactivity research is generally opportunistic in nature and the occurrence of classical conditioning can only be inferred. In contrast, direct evidence of conditioning is very rare and comes from laboratory studies in which neutral cues are explicitly paired with the administration of alcohol. In one such study, McCaul, Turkkan & Stitzer (1989) paired situational and drink cues with either alcohol or placebo in separate groups of non-treatment-seeking alcohol-dependent subjects. Following four daily sessions of conditioning, all subjects were presented with the CS paired with a placebo drink. Interestingly, the alcohol group exhibited decreased heart rate and skin conductance, as well as greater desire to drink scores, during the test session. These results were interpreted as evidence of a conditioned response to the alcohol-paired cues for these subjects. Similar studies have yielded further evidence of alcohol conditioning effects in social drinkers (e.g. Newlin, 1985; 1986). While several studies have permitted a direct examination of the development of conditioned responses to alcohol cues in humans, most of these studies are somewhat limited in that they are usually conducted with social drinkers as subjects. Clearly, psychological and neurobiological mechanisms involved in alcohol–cue learning and its expression may differ considerably between social drinkers and those with an extensive history of alcohol consumption.

In contrast to the limited number of studies involving explicit drug conditioning in humans, a substantial body of animal research has examined mechanisms of associative learning in drug administration studies. These animal studies have augmented findings from the human literature by directly examining various features of classical conditioning, such as the role of drug-paired cues on the development of tolerance (e.g. Siegel, 1979; Tiffany, Drobes & Cepeda-Benito, 1992). One limitation of this literature is that it is difficult to represent the numerous possible alcohol–cue conditioning schedules that can occur in humans. For instance, a relatively common pattern among alcohol-dependent individuals is binge drinking, which may involve substantial alcohol consumption on the weekend interspersed with relatively mild or no mid-week drinking. The animal drug conditioning studies have not yet addressed this pattern, even though it is clear that the relative spacing of conditioning trials may substantially influence the development and retention of conditioned responses in general (Frey & Misfeldt, 1967; Prokasky & Ebel, 1964). Furthermore, it is important to note that, while there are numerous demonstrations of conditioning effects as a result of alcohol–cue pairings, there are no published data demonstrating that the conditioned behaviour controlled by alcohol-related cues has a measurable impact on the instrumental behaviours emitted to procure and consume alcohol. The animal literature is replete with illustrations of the mediation of instrumental behaviour by classical conditioning (e.g. Overmier & Lawry, 1979) but this literature does little to inform us about the direct effects of cue reactivity on alcohol procurement and ingestion in the natural environment. Additional research is needed to demonstrate that the processes reflected in cue reactions have some impact on alcohol-related behaviour.

CLASSICAL CONDITIONING THEORIES

Conditioned Withdrawal Models

The first model to apply principles of classical conditioning to the study of drug addiction was that of Wikler (1948). Originally developed to account for opiate withdrawal-like reactions observed in situations where drug withdrawal had previously taken place, this model was later applied to conditioned alcohol withdrawal (e.g. Ludwig & Wikler, 1974). According to the model, repeated pairings between situational cues and withdrawal states eventually imbue the cues with the ability to elicit withdrawal-like CRs when they are encountered in the natural environment. A more recent model (Poulos, Hinson & Siegel, 1981) posits that withdrawal-like effects are elicited by the presence of cues associated with previous alcohol consumption, rather than alcohol withdrawal. This theory is built on the hypothesis that stimuli reliably paired with alcohol administration come to elicit CRs that are opposite in direction to, or compensatory for, the direct or unconditioned effects of alcohol. The functional significance of these compensatory responses is to maintain a homeostatic balance in the drinker. This conditioning leads to tolerance when alcohol is consumed and to withdrawal-like responses when alcohol is not consumed in the presence of alcohol cues. In both the conditioned withdrawal and compensatory response models, the

CR is thought to elicit craving and an aversive emotional state that is sufficient to motivate drug-seeking behaviour and increase the probability of relapse.

Several animal studies have claimed support for the withdrawal-based models by demonstrating conditioned tolerance to the temperature reducing effects of alcohol. For example, Mansfield & Cunningham (1980) repeatedly injected rats with ethanol or saline in the presence of distinctive environmental cues. Testing for both groups of animals occurred in the distinctive context following administration of saline. Rats that had received the prior alcohol–cue pairings evidenced relatively greater temperature increases than the saline control animals. As this is opposite in direction to the direct effect of alcohol on temperature, these findings are consistent with the development of a conditioned compensatory response to alcohol cues. Alternatively, the observed temperature increases can be interpreted as a non-specific conditioned arousal that is unrelated to the direction of the unconditioned effects of alcohol (Cunningham & Schwarz, 1989).

Despite obvious similarities, there are important differences in the two withdrawal-based theories described above. The clearest difference is in the nature of the cues that should come to attain properties of a CS, withdrawal-paired or drug-paired. Realistically, this may not be an important difference, as it may often be the case that cues available during alcohol consumption cannot be differentiated from those present during alcohol withdrawal. There are also differences in the extent to which the empirical literature has supported these two theories. While there is considerable evidence that alcohol tolerance involves classical conditioning (see review by Tiffany & Baker, 1986), there is little experimental support for the occurrence of conditioned withdrawal effects. Another advantage of the compensatory model is that it expressly allows conditioning to proceed throughout an individual's drinking history. In contrast, the withdrawal model requires that sufficient experience with the alcohol US must occur to permit the development of withdrawal URs before any conditioning can occur. This is problematic for two reasons. First, direct conditioning studies have demonstrated basic conditioning effects in social drinkers who have no withdrawal history (e.g. Newlin, 1986). Second, the theory implies that prior to the onset of withdrawal, individuals are experiencing unreinforced exposures to stimuli that will subsequently be involved in the conditioning of withdrawal CRs. However, a vast body of basic learning research has shown that prior exposure to putative CSs results in profound retardation of conditioning during subsequent CS–US pairings involving those CSs, a phenomenon widely known as latent inhibition (Lubow & Moore, 1959). Thus, it is difficult to argue that withdrawal conditioning is a viable phenomenon, given the potential development of considerable latent inhibition to putative CSs prior to withdrawal conditioning.

Both of the conditioned withdrawal models that have been described are conceptually attractive, and each has played an important role in terms of bringing conditioning theory into the mainstream of addiction research. However, there are several grounds upon which these theories have been seriously undermined as viable accounts of alcohol dependence. First, although classical conditioning does appear to play a role in many instances of drug tolerance, there is little support for the assumption that these conditioned tolerance effects are necessarily subserved by conditioned compensatory responses. Second, conditioned withdrawal-based theories predict that patterns of physiology that accompany presentations of drug-paired cues should resemble the physiology of withdrawal. However, most of the available evidence suggests that the direction of autonomic responses elicited by drug-paired cues are not always drug-opposite or withdrawal-like (Carter & Tiffany, 1999). Furthermore, there is little evidence from experimental studies to support the notion that alcohol cue-elicited physiological responses are strongly associated with various indices of drinking behaviour, and alcohol-dependent individuals who have relapsed rarely cite withdrawal-like reactions as proximal to their relapse (e.g. Marlatt & Gordon, 1980). Finally, the withdrawal-based models all presume that drug-paired CSs are experienced as aversive. This being the case, alcohol-dependent individuals should readily learn to avoid or escape the aversive environments associated with previous drinking. To the contrary, clinical lore and experimental evidence suggests that these cues are not avoided; in fact, animals can readily develop preferences for environments paired with a variety of drugs, including alcohol (e.g. Cunningham et al., 1992).

In sum, there are reasons to question whether the conditioned withdrawal effects posited by either Wikler's (1948) or Siegel's (1975) models of drug conditioning provide the motivational substrate of alcohol dependence. Nevertheless, there are aspects of these models, in particular the proposal that tolerance can come under the associative control of environmental stimuli, that may be of profound importance in the development of alcohol dependence. Tolerance, in general, could promote excessive alcohol consumption in two ways. First, to the extent that an individual develops tolerance to some positive effects of alcohol, he/she would have to escalate levels of consumption to maintain the same level of effect. Second, certain of the aversive effects of alcohol, for example, dizziness and nausea, may curb the intake of excessive quantities of alcohol. Tolerance to these effects would permit consumption of increasingly greater quantities of alcohol (Tiffany & Baker, 1986).

Patterns of alcohol consumption over the early phases of alcohol exposure may work against the development of substantial tolerance to either the positive or aversive effects of alcohol. That is, for many drinkers, the early stages of alcohol consumption may be characterized by somewhat intermittent, spaced exposures to alcohol. This pattern of drug exposure would not allow for the accumulation of much pharmacological (i.e. non-associative) tolerance across exposures to the drug (Baker & Tiffany, 1985). However, associative tolerance processes could easily bridge long intervals between alcohol exposures. The potential contributions of classically conditioned tolerance to an escalation of alcohol consumption over the early phases of alcohol dependence have received virtually no attention in the research literature.

Conditioned Appetitive Models

Conditioned appetitive models are based on the assumption that alcohol produces positively reinforcing effects which are experienced as subjective pleasure or euphoria, and that these effects provide strong motivation for repeated episodes of drinking. Thus, reactions to alcohol-paired cues may involve memory for positively reinforcing alcohol effects, anticipation of alcohol-induced euphoria or expectancies of alcohol-related positive outcomes. The most influential model of this type is the conditioned incentive model proposed by Stewart, de Wit & Eikelboom (1984). A major feature of this model is that stimuli associated with previous drug ingestion become positive incentive stimuli that propel further drug use. Several models of this type postulate that cues paired with alcohol administration will develop the capacity to elicit CRs that are characterized by the same constellation of appetitive, autonomic and affective reactions elicited by alcohol itself (e.g. Wise, 1988). According to some models, a priming dose of alcohol or positive affect alone should serve as cues for activating an appetitive motivational state (e.g. Baker, Morse & Sherman, 1987).

Appetitively-based conditioning models can be contrasted with withdrawal-based models on several grounds. First, drug conditioning effects are attributed to the appetitive features of drugs, rather than drug withdrawal. Second, most appetitive models adopt a single process theory of drug learning, in that conditioned incentive stimuli elicit a motivational state that directly primes drug-taking behaviour. In contrast, the conditioned withdrawal models rely on a two-factor approach, in which classical conditioning elicits a withdrawal-like response and relief from withdrawal via drug-seeking behaviour is seen primarily as an instrumental conditioning process. Third, while withdrawal-based models predict responses to drug-paired CSs that are opposite in direction from direct drug effects, most appetitively-orientated models predict drug cue reactivity responses that resemble direct drug effects.

While attributing a primary role to positive emotional states, several appetitively-orientated models suggest that negative emotional states may serve to enhance the incentive value of the drug, thereby augmenting craving and increasing the probability of substance use. Some models suggest that both withdrawal- and appetitively-based conditioning mechanisms can contribute to the experience of alcohol cravings. For instance, the dual affect model (Baker et al., 1987) suggests that different types of CSs can elicit distinct patterns of alcohol cue reactions. According to this model, CSs associated with the ingestion of alcohol or with positive affect should elicit CRs that resemble direct alcohol effects, while CSs associated with alcohol withdrawal or negative affect should elicit CRs that are opposite from alcohol's direct effects.

Considerable animal data has tended to support the conditioned appetitive model of alcohol and drug use behaviour. Among these are studies showing that animals will readily self-administer alcohol (e.g. Shelton & Macenski, 1998). These studies illustrate that alcohol can serve as a powerful positive reinforcer, even in the absence of withdrawal. Furthermore, animals will show a preference for environments paired with alcohol administration (e.g. Kelly, Bandy & Middaugh, 1997), which suggests that drug-paired contexts become secondary reinforcers that motivate approach behaviour. From the human cue reactivity literature, patterns of autonomic activity upon presentations of alcohol-paired stimuli are generally consistent with the activating or stimulating drug effects rather than the physiology of withdrawal *per se* (Carter & Tiffany, 1999). These findings appear to support the appetitively-orientated characterization of drug conditioning better than the withdrawal-based models.

As with the withdrawal-based accounts, there are several problems with the appetitively-based models as they have been articulated. While the pattern of autonomic responses elicited by drug-paired cues in cue reactivity studies have generally been consistent with an appetitive motivational model, it is not feasible to unequivocally attribute these patterns to activation of an appetitive motivational system (Tiffany, 1995). First, there have been vastly different autonomic profiles observed across different cue reactivity paradigms and laboratories and it is unlikely that a unique autonomic profile of appetitive motivational or positive-affect states will ever be identified. Indeed, it has not been established that autonomic physiology can clearly differentiate positive from negative affect states (Levenson, 1992). Second, autonomic drug–cue reactivity patterns observed in many studies are compatible with several plausible alternate explanations. For instance, the finding that alcohol cues can increase heart rate (Carter & Tiffany, 1999) might reflect the activation of an appetitive motivational state, but it may also reflect preparation for physical activity, cognitive effort associated with urge processing, defensive responding, negative affect provoked by frustration over not being able to consume alcohol at the present time, or even conditioning of the initial direct stimulatory effects of alcohol. These possibilities illustrate how difficult it is to unambiguously attribute an autonomic response profile during an alcohol cue reactivity experiment to a specific motivational process (see also Cacioppo & Tassinary, 1990).

Another problem with the appetitive account of alcohol conditioning is the pattern of findings across response systems in studies of human cue reactivity. If cue reactivity responses reflect the activation of an appetitive motivational state, then there should be strong relationships between various indices of this state, such as physiology, self-reported craving, mood and drug use. As mentioned above, the literature provides little evidence of meaningful relationships between cue-induced physiological responses and self-reported craving or mood, as well as a pervasive lack of association between physiological drug cue responding and drug-use behaviour (Tiffany, 1990). Furthermore, the prediction that presentations of drug-paired cues to addicts should elicit a positive affect state has received little support. Studies have shown that expectancy of alcohol consumption is associated with no overall impact on mood (Hull & Bond, 1986) and various types of cue reactivity studies have found that presentations of drug-relevant stimuli generally enhance negative mood and/or decrease positive mood (e.g. Drobes & Tiffany, 1997).

Incentive-sensitization Model

Robinson & Berridge (1993) introduced a biopsychological theory that attempts to account for the interplay between neurobiological changes and associative learning mechanisms in the development of addictive behaviour. According to this theory, specific neural systems become sensitized over the course of repeated and intermittent drug use, such that the drug effects are augmented over time. In particular, the mesotelencephalic dopaminergic pathways involved in drug pleasure and addiction are thought to become sensitized in the addicted individual. Classical conditioning is thought to play a crucial role in mediating this neural sensitization, in that the expression of sensitized drug effects is controlled by the presence of drug-related cues. The model differentiates drug "liking", which is associated with pleasurable drug effects, from drug "wanting", which is akin to an unconscious motivational process involving the attribution of excessive incentive salience and attractiveness towards drug use. As drug wanting is fundamentally an unconscious process, other cognitive events are necessary to translate drug wanting into subjective awareness, or craving (Berridge & Robinson, 1995).

The incentive-sensitization model goes further than the previously described theories in that it incorporates a specific role for associative learning mechanisms in mediating the neurophysiological changes that occur in an addicted individual. As the motivational process underlying compulsive drinking behaviour in alcohol-dependent individuals is thought to be unconscious, the theory is consistent with the frequent observation, both clinically and in alcohol cue reactivity research studies, that alcohol craving and drinking behaviour are not highly correlated (see Tiffany, 1990). This model can also account for the increase in craving and "loss of control" drinking that alcohol-dependent individuals often experience when they begin drinking, since the cue constellation associated with drinking will be better matched by the taste and flavour associated with consumption of an alcoholic beverage (i.e. ingestion of a small quantity of alcohol may be a subthreshold US but may serve as an extremely powerful CS). Kim, Siegel and Patenall (1999) have provided a recent demonstration of this phenomenon using morphine in rats. Withdrawal-based models, on the other hand, would predict a temporary decrease in craving after the first drink due to the immediate pleasurable or withdrawal-suppressing effects of drinking.

Most of the research pertinent to the incentive-sensitization model comes from animal studies of opiates, cocaine and other psychostimulants (e.g. Robinson & Berridge, 1993). There is some recent evidence that dopamine release undergoes sensitization with repeated alcohol administrations in rats (e.g. Nestby et al., 1997) and that conditioned cues repeatedly paired with alcohol can enhance behavioural sensitization effects of alcohol (Cunningham & Noble, 1992). However, central tenets of this model have not yet been translated into testable hypotheses for human alcohol dependence.

An important limitation of the incentive-motivational model is the assertion that "wanting a drug" or craving operates, primarily, at an unconscious level and is only occasionally evident in conscious awareness. This position certainly finesses, to some extent, the bothersome findings that craving reports and drug-use behaviour are often uncoupled

(Tiffany, 1990). However, it provides no guidance regarding the cognitive processes responsible for translating unconscious wanting into conscious craving, neither does it permit any predictions about when craving and drug use might and might not be coupled (Tiffany & Carter, 1998). Equally troublesome is the theory's proposal that unconscious craving is only sometimes available to conscious experience. This portrayal of craving is contrary to a considerable number of research and clinical findings suggesting that addicts are exquisitely aware of their craving and perfectly willing to express it. For example, cue reactivity research reveals that reports of craving are easily and replicably triggered by presentations of drug-paired cues and these reports are extremely robust (e.g. Carter & Tiffany, 1999).

Interactions between Classical and Instrumental Conditioning

Two-process Theory

Stasiewitz & Maisto (1993) recently extended Mowrer's (1947) two-factor theory of avoidance by asserting that negative emotion is a major aetiological factor in the development and maintenance of addictive behaviour. This model posits that aversive conditioned emotional responses (CERs) develop to neutral stimuli that have been paired with aversive life events. The basic process giving rise to CERs is synonymous with classical aversive conditioning described in the original formulation of two-factor theory. A second associative process, known as conditioned avoidance response (CAR), occurs when the individual engages in behaviour that eliminates or reduces the amount of negative emotion experienced as a result of CERs. Consistent with Mowrer's original formulation, this model assumes that the avoidance of negative emotion serves to reinforce the CAR. In the case of addiction, substance use is a CAR that is reinforced, and hence maintained, by reduction or elimination of a CER. While this modified version of two-factor theory is open to many of the critiques levelled against its predecessor (e.g. Mineka, 1979), it does have the virtue of accounting for the high level of comorbidity between affective and anxiety-based disorders and addictive disorders (e.g. Swendsen et al., 1998).

Cue and Manipulandum Theory

Tomie (1993) has derived a theory of human drug taking from his analysis of animal discrimination learning studies. In a typical experiment of this type, food-deprived pigeons might receive food reinforcement for pecking a response key with a green light but they are not reinforced for pecking when the response key is red. Tomie argues that excessive and compulsive responding can result from a close physical arrangement between the reinforcement cue and the response device, or manipulandum. This particular physical arrangement is referred to as cue and manipulandum (CAM). In the example, when the pigeon responds by pecking the green light, then CAM is arranged because the reinforcement cue and the response manipulandum are in the same location. Tomie proposes that CAM behaviour occurs at a higher rate or with a higher probability than that observed under non-CAM conditions (e.g. when the reinforcement cue is physically separate from the response manipulandum). In addition, he suggests that CAM behaviour is compulsive in that it occurs reliably even when it results in the delay or loss of opportunity for food reinforcement. With its emphasis on the properties of the stimulus that signal reinforcement, this theory is closely aligned with other two-process accounts of the influence of classical conditioning factors on response–consequence learning.

Tomie (1995) suggests that the compulsive nature of CAM-derived behaviour corresponds closely with several prominent features of alcohol dependence, such as drinking that occurs despite clear knowledge that it creates physical and emotional problems. Further-more, Tomie asserts that the alcohol cue reactivity literature supports his notion of CAM because the glassware associated with drinking elicits physiological arousal and self-reported alcohol craving. Alcohol glassware would meet the definition of CAM in that it is both a cue for reinforcement and a manipulandum essential to alcohol consumption. A problematic aspect of this theory is the assertion that CAM behaviour is a function of the correlation between the cue and the reinforcing effects of alcohol. Since glassware is often used in the consumption of other non-alcohol beverages, the correlation between the glass-ware and alcohol's reinforcing effects might be expected to be quite low. At the very least, these conditions would be less than optimal for the development of CAM. In fact, one might expect CAM behaviour to be controlled most by the sight and smell of a drinker's pre-ferred beverage, because these cues are most physically proximal to the manipulandum used in the consumption of alcohol (i.e. any glassware) and are most highly correlated with the effects of alcohol. This alternative interpretation highlights Tomie's narrow emphasis on the roll of "manipulandum" cues in the development and maintenance of alcohol misuse behaviour. The model may be more readily applied to forms of addictive behaviour where there is a great deal of ritualized use of specific drug-taking paraphernalia (e.g. cocaine and heroin). At best, this model may apply to a limited portion of alcohol-conditioned cues, and the theory awaits empirical evaluation in the alcohol research arena.

General Evaluation of Theories

The classical conditioning theories that have been reviewed here all suffer from short-comings that raise the possibility that other types of models may better account for cue reactivity phenomena. To summarize, cue responses are generally not opposite from direct drug effects, which seriously undermines the conditioned withdrawal theories (Carter & Tiffany, 1999). Although cue reactivity responses are generally consistent with the direct or stimulatory effects of alcohol, research on alcohol cue reactivity is not consistent with the general assumption that there should be a high degree of concordance between verbal reports of craving, alcohol-related behaviours and physiological reactivity. This is especially problematic for traditional models of cue reactivity that assume self-reported urges or cravings to be a direct function of physiological, classically conditioned responses to drug cues. In general, cue reactivity studies cannot directly support the assumption that alcohol cue reactions necessarily represent classically conditioned responses. In most cue reactiv-ity experiments, the subject is involved in a wide variety of tasks, which may include per-ceptual processing, motor activity, problem solving and a diverse array of cognitive processes. These activities, both physical and mental, invoke physiological reactions that may override any conditioned responses to alcohol cues that are presented. This is not to say that classical conditioning is not important, but it may be only one of several factors that influence physiological reactions, or self-reported craving, displayed in the presence of alcohol cues. Many of the models discussed are either silent or vague on the role of emotion as a potential cue for drinking. In other cases, the scope of the model is too limited to include predictions regarding the impact of critical individual difference and situational variables on affective consequences of a CR. For instance, factors that might influence the affective nature of a response to a cue that has previously been associated with drinking may include the individual's drinking history and current drinking status, including the current motivation to either drink or to avoid drinking. In addition, the length of alcohol deprivation, degree of withdrawal, or whether or not the cue implies an explicit opportu-nity for drinking, as opposed to a cue that may invoke a frustrative non-reward response, may also contribute importantly to alcohol cue reactions.

AN ALTERNATIVE INTERPRETATION OF CUE REACTIVITY

Alcohol-dependent individuals clearly exhibit differential patterns of reactivity to alcohol-relevant cues and studies have demonstrated the development of alcohol-related cue effects in the laboratory. As discussed above, the common assumption that cue reactivity patterns represent the operation of classical conditioning has met with substantive challenges, both conceptually and empirically (see Tiffany, 1990). Given these discrepant findings, it is questionable to assume that alcohol cue reactions necessarily represent classically conditioned responses. Therefore, it is important to consider alternative interpretations of cue reactivity findings.

Tiffany (1990) has proposed a theory in which cognitive processing plays a primary role in the control of addictive behavior in general and cue reactivity patterns in particular. According to this model, repeated practice of cognitive and behavioral tasks related to drug use results in the development of automatized drug-use action plans that are quickly and easily retrieved from memory. These automatic processes are enacted whenever the proper eliciting stimulus conditions are present, which are presumed to involve those cues that have been most reliably paired with previous drug consumption. The drug-use action plans are thought to be cognitively effortless, fast and efficient, stereotyped, stimulus-bound and difficult to inhibit. In contrast, non-automatic cognitive processes are activated in parallel with drug-use action plans whenever these automatized schema are impeded. This can occur when there is an intent to thwart the automatized sequence in an attempt to maintain abstinence or when there are situational obstacles to the completion of the automatized sequence. For example, an alcohol-dependent individual who is attempting to remain sober may be suddenly confronted with a situation that has been closely associated with drinking in the past (as in the scenario described at the outset of this chapter), or an alcohol-dependent individual who is not attempting abstinence cannot find a liquor store that is open. In both types of situations, non-automatic processing is necessary to resolve a problem. This processing would be characterized as slow, flexible, cognitively effortful and limited by available cognitive resources. Furthermore, non-automatic processes should give rise to urge responding, which can be manifest across verbal report, physiology and overt behavior.

A critical feature of Tiffany's (1990) theory is that physiological responses within an urge-eliciting situation should reflect cognitive and metabolic demands of the situation (e.g. problem solving, motor activity involved with obtaining or avoiding drug use) rather than being primarily mediated through classical conditioning. Importantly, there is a central role afforded to negative affect in this model, in that non-automatic processes involved in urge responding are presumed to give rise to negative mood states, such as irritability and frustration. In turn, negative emotional states may increase the risk of relapse because they may activate other non-automatic processing, which competes with the non-automatic cognitive resources necessary for the task of maintaining abstinence.

There are several distinct advantages to the proposals contained in Tiffany's (1990) model. First and foremost, the model builds on a simple associative analysis by positing a central role for higher-order cognitive processes in addiction, while differentiating processes that link alcohol cues and drinking behaviour from those associated with craving. This is entirely consistent with the frequent failure of cue reactivity studies to demonstrate meaningful relationships between craving report and drinking behaviour. Furthermore, the proposal that physiological responding during cue reactivity studies is not inherently due to classically conditioned withdrawal or appetitive effects, but rather is multiply determined and may reflect a variety of situational demands, is consistent with the diverse patterns of physiology seen across studies and laboratories. From this perspective, it is unlikely that a particular urge physiology could ever be detected. Furthermore, it suggests that conceptualizations of cue reactivity phenomena that are based exclusively on classical conditioning mechanisms may be insufficient and that researchers may have to begin incorporating concepts from the broader perspective of cognitive psychophysiology in order to adequately interpret physiological findings from these studies.

CLINICAL APPLICATIONS

There are several areas in which classical conditioning concepts have been applied to the treatment of alcohol dependence. We will briefly discuss two particularly relevant and novel applications that stem directly from this general theoretical approach and that clearly have potential to improve alcohol treatment if integrated into the mainstream (the reader is referred to chapters in Part V of this volume for more extended discussions of treatment and treatment effectiveness).

Cue Reactivity and Treatment Outcome

Several recent cue reactivity studies have demonstrated a predictive relationship between laboratory responding to alcohol stimuli and drinking outcomes. For instance, Rohsenow et al. (1994) found that salivary reactivity to alcohol cues in treatment-seeking alcohol-dependent individuals within 1 week of achieving abstinence was positively related to drinking frequency during a 3-month follow-up period. Similarly, Drummond & Glautier (1994) reported that autonomic activity during the final session of a 10-session cue exposure treatment protocol (see below) predicted heavy drinking during a 6-month follow-up period. Although not employing psychophysiological measures, Cooney et al. (1997) determined that self-reported urge to drink alcohol during a trial that combined negative mood imagery with traditional alcohol cue exposure predicted time to relapse after inpatient treatment. Taken together, findings from these studies offer clear evidence that cue reactivity is an important feature of alcohol dependence, as it bears a relationship with relapse risk. This being the case, it is suggested that the use of cue reactivity procedures be expanded within clinical assessment protocols, as this may improve allocation of treatment resources to those most at risk. Further research will be needed to determine the optimal and most efficient cue reactivity paradigms for use in clinical settings, as well as parameters such as the time to conduct these assessments (e.g. before, during or after an active treatment period). In addition, future research should determine if those who display particular patterns of cue reactivity are able to benefit maximally by being matched to particular modes of treatment that specifically address associative mechanisms in their alcohol addiction.

Cue Exposure

Despite the lack of consensus concerning the precise mechanisms of cue reactivity, the natural extension of this work into the clinical arena—namely, cue exposure treatment—has not awaited theoretical unanimity in this area. From the perspective of behaviour therapy, the premise is that if conditioned responses to alcohol cues bear a functional relationship with the motivation to drink, then non-reinforced exposures to the alcohol-related CS should eventually result in extinction of the CR, thereby decreasing drinking behaviour. This is analogous to the application of exposure-based treatment of anxiety disorders, which are now considered the treatment of choice for a range of disorders involving autonomic fear reactions to various interoceptive and exteroceptive stimuli.

Several laboratory studies have demonstrated that initial reactivity to an alcohol cue will diminish with prolonged or repeated exposures to the stimulus within a single session (e.g. Staiger & White, 1991). More recently, controlled treatment studies have reported that multiple sessions of cue exposure treatment decreased both the frequency and intensity of future drinking (e.g. Drummond & Glautier, 1994). Considering that the application of this treatment methodology within the alcohol area is still in its infancy, these results are promising. It is likely that ongoing and future research will refine cue exposure treatment and consequently improve outcomes. In particular, research in this area may benefit from: (a) incorporating exposure to a broader range of personally-relevant alcohol cues, such as affective material and personalized guided imagery; (b) determining which patients are most likely to benefit from exposure treatment; and (c) establishing how best to combine this technique with other treatment components.

It is important to acknowledge that cue exposure may deter future drinking by mechanisms other than that of simple extinction. For instance, a recent case report (Heather, Tebbutt & Greeley, 1993) demonstrated that cue exposure subsequent to ingestion of two priming drinks was associated with decreased drinking over a 1 year follow-up period, an enhanced sense of control over drinking and a diminished desire to drink during a laboratory consumption assessment.

Using a similar approach, Sitharthan et al. (1997) trained patients to stop drinking after two to three priming drinks. Patients who received this modified cue exposure treatment reported fewer drinking episodes and consumed less per occasion over a 6 month follow-up period relative to a standard cognitive-behavioural therapy comparison group (see also Heather et al., in press). It is important to note that both of these studies involved a goal of moderated drinking, rather than abstinence. Given that CS–US pairings were explicitly continued in these studies, it seems unlikely that the improved outcomes were purely the result of extinction of classically conditioned responses. Rohsenow, Monti & Abrams (1995) have suggested that cue exposure may be beneficial to alcohol-dependent individuals by breaking behavioural chains leading to drinking, by disconfirming expectations about the effects of exposure to drinking cues or by strengthening efficacy expectations about one's ability to cope without drinking when confronted with such cues. These authors suggest that cue exposure may be most efficacious if patients are able to rehearse behavioural and cognitive coping skills while under simulated alcohol cue conditions (cf. Monti et al., 1993a). From a controlled drinking perspective, the primary conditions for skill rehearsal may be under the influence of priming alcohol doses.

SUMMARY AND CONCLUSIONS

We began by reviewing empirical findings suggesting that alcohol-dependent individuals exhibit enhanced verbal and physiological reactivity to alcohol-relevant cues, and that these reactions appear to result from previous pairings of these cues with alcohol ingestion. We then examined a number of classical conditioning theories that have been developed to account for these cue reactivity phenomena. Despite wide support for the existence of alcohol cue reactivity, particular theoretical conceptualizations based on theories of classical conditioning have not been well supported by the available empirical research and there are important conceptual inconsistencies in applying these theories. We briefly reviewed an alternative theoretical framework (Tiffany, 1990) in which the cognitive concepts of automatic and non-automatic information processing are invoked to explain diverse patterns of cue reactivity. Notably, Tiffany's model posits that cue reactivity effects can be multiply determined, with a primary emphasis on the behavioural and cognitive demands of the eliciting situation. Since the causal path of cue reactivity is multiply determined, the model can account for the lack of a uniform psychophysiology of alcohol craving and for the lack of meaningful relationships between verbal, physiological and behavioural craving indices. Finally, we discussed some current and potential clinical applications of alcohol cue reactivity findings.

Reactions to motivationally-relevant cues have been an important topic within the general study of normal and abnormal psychological processes. For instance, there is a growing literature using the startle reflex to index emotional reactions elicited by various sorts of perceptual stimuli (e.g. Lang, 1995). Perhaps methods of this sort might serve to better inform cue reactivity investigators about the role of emotion in alcohol cue reactivity and craving. This is particularly important in light of recent studies demonstrating a link between emotion, cue reactivity and treatment outcome (Cooney et al., 1997). In addition, research methodologies that have received a great deal of attention in the study of general learning processes (e.g. occasion setting; Holland, 1985) should be utilized more vigorously in studies of alcohol cue reactivity. Finally, there are numerous potential applications of more recent theoretical and empirical developments in the area of classical conditioning (e.g. AESOP theory; Wagner and Brandon, 1989) and classical–instrumental interactions (see Allan, 1998) that may advance our understanding of alcohol cue reactivity phenomena.

KEY WORKS AND SUGGESTIONS FOR FURTHER READING

Carter, B.L. & Tiffany, S.T. (1999).   Meta-analysis of cue-reactivity in addiction research. *Addiction*, **94**, 327–340.

This article presents the first empirical analysis of the magnitude and direction of effects across cue reactivity studies, including analyses of both self-report and physiological dependence measures. It begins with a thoughtful overview of important methodological and theoretical issues in drug cue reactivity research.

Drummond, D.C., Tiffany, S.T., Glautier, S. & Remington, B. (Eds) (1995).   *Addictive Behaviour: Cue Exposure Theory and Practice*. New York: Wiley.

This book consists of a cohesive set of chapters written by a renowned group of cue exposure experts critically examining theoretical, methodological and applied aspects of cue exposure research.

Glautier, S. & Drummond, D.C. (1994).   Alcohol dependence and cue reactivity. *Journal of Studies on Alcohol*, **55**, 224–229.

This empirical study provides an example of how cue reactivity findings obtained within a treatment-based cue exposure protocol can be informative regarding individual differences in alcohol dependence and dependence severity.

Niaura, R.S., Rohsenow, D.J., Binkoff, J.A., Monti, P.M., Pedraza, M. & Abrams, D.B. (1988). Relevance of cue reactivity to understanding alcohol and smoking relapse. *Journal of Abnormal Psychology*, **97**, 133–152.

This article provides an early review of the alcohol and smoking cue reactivity literature, along with a discussion of the relevance of this area of research for understanding and preventing relapse.

REFERENCES

Allan, R.W. (1998). Operant–respondent interactions. In W. O'Donohue (Ed.), *Learning and Behaviour Therapy* (pp. 146–168). Needham Heights, MA: Allyn & Bacon.

Baker, T.B., Morse, E. & Sherman, J.E. (1987). The motivation to use drugs: a psychobiological analysis of urges. *Nebraska Symposium on Motivation*, **34**, 257–323.

Baker, T.B. & Tiffany, S.T. (1985). Morphine tolerance as habituation. *Psychological Review*, **92**, 78–108.

Berridge, K.C. & Robinson, T.E. (1995). The mind of an addicted brain: neural sensitization of wanting versus liking. *Current Directions in Psychological Science*, **4**, 71–76.

Cacioppo, J.T. & Tassinary, L.G. (1990). Inferring psychological significance from physiological signals. *American Psychologist*, **45**, 16–28.

Carter, B.L. & Tiffany, S.T. (1999). Meta-analysis of cue-reactivity in addiction research. *Addiction*, **94**, 327–340.

Cohen, J. (1988). *Statistical Power Analysis for the Behavioural Sciences*, 2nd edn. Hillsdale, NJ: Erlbaum.

Cooney, N.L., Litt, M.D., Morse, P.A., Bauer, L.O. & Gaupp, L. (1997). Alcohol cue reactivity, negative-mood reactivity, and relapse in treated alcoholic men. *Journal of Abnormal Psychology*, **106**, 243–250.

Cunningham, C.L., Niehus, D.R., Malott, D.H. & Prather, L.K. (1992). Genetic differences in the rewarding and activating effects of morphine and ethanol. *Psychopharmacology*, **107**, 385–393.

Cunningham, C.L. & Noble, D. (1992). Conditioned activation induced by ethanol: role in sensitization and conditioned place preference. *Pharmacology, Biochemistry & Behaviour*, **43**, 307–313.

Cunningham, C.L. & Schwarz, K.S. (1989). Pavlovian-conditioned changes in body temperature induced by alcohol and morphine. *Drug Development Research*, **16**, 295–303.

Drobes, D.J. & Tiffany, S.T. (1997). Induction of smoking urge through imaginal and *in vivo* procedures: physiological and self-report manifestations. *Journal of Abnormal Psychology*, **106**, 15–25.

Drummond, D.C. & Glautier, S. (1994). A controlled trial of cue exposure treatment in alcohol dependence. *Journal of Consulting and Clinical Psychology*, **62**, 809–817.

Drummond, D.C., Tiffany, S.T., Glautier, S. & Remington, B. (1995). Cue exposure in understanding and treating addictive behaviours. In D.C. Drummond, S.T. Tiffany, S. Glautier & B. Remington (Eds), *Addictive Behaviour: Cue Exposure Theory and Practice* (pp. 1–17). New York: Wiley.

Frey, P.W. & Misfeldt, T.S. (1967). Rabbit eyelid conditioning as a function of the intertrial interval. *Psychonomic Science*, **9**, 137–138.

Glautier, S. & Tiffany, S.T. (1995). Methodological issues in cue reactivity research. In D.C. Drummond, S.T. Tiffany, S. Glautier & B. Remington (Eds), *Addictive Behaviour: Cue Exposure Theory and Practice* (pp. 75–97). New York: Wiley.

Heather, N., Brodie, J., Wale, S., Wilkinson, G., Luce, A., Webb, E. & McCarthy, S (2000). A randomized controlled trial of moderation-oriented cue exposure. *Journal of Studies on Alcohol*, **61**, 560–570.

Heather, N., Tebbutt, J. & Greeley, J. (1993). Alcohol cue exposure directed at a goal of moderate drinking. *Journal of Behaviour Therapy and Experimental Psychiatry*, **24**, 187–195.

Holland, P.C. (1985). The nature of conditioned inhibition in serial and simultaneous feature negative discriminations. In R.R. Miller & N.E. Spear (Eds), *Information Processing in Animals: Conditioned Inhibition* (pp. 267–297). Hillsdale, NJ: Erlbaum.

Hull, J.G. & Bond, C.F. Jr (1986). Social and behavioural consequences of alcohol consumption: a meta-analysis. *Psychological Bulletin*, **99**, 347–360.

Kelly, B.M., Bandy, A.E. & Middaugh, L.D. (1997). A study examining intravenous ethanol-conditioned place preference in C57BL/6J mice. *Alcoholism: Clinical and Experimental Research*, **21**, 1661–1666.

Kim, S.A., Siegel, S. & Patenall, V.R.A. (1999). Drug-onset cues as signals: intra-administration associations and tolerance. *Journal of Experimental Psychology; Animal Behavior Processes*, **25**, 491–504.

Lang, P.J. (1995). The emotion probe: studies of motivation and attention. *American Psychologist*, **50**, 372–385.

Levenson, R.W. (1992). Autonomic nervous system differences among emotions. *Psychological Science*, **3**, 23–27.

Lubow, R.E. & Moore, A.V. (1959). Latent inhibition: the effect of non-reinforced pre-exposure of the CS. *Journal of Comparative and Physiological Psychology*, **52**, 415–419.

Ludwig, A.M. & Wikler, A. (1974). "Craving" and relapse to drink. *Quarterly Journal of Studies on Alcohol*, **35**, 108–130.

Mansfield, J.G. & Cunningham, C.L. (1980). Conditioning and extinction of tolerance to the hypothermic effect of ethanol in rats. *Journal of Comparative and Physiological Psychology*, **94**, 962–969.

Marlatt, G.A. & Gordon, J.R. (1980). Determinants of relapse: implications for the maintenance of behaviour change. In P.O. Davidson & S.M. Davidson (Eds), *Behavioural Medicine: Changing Health Lifestyles* (pp. 410–452). New York: Brunner/Mazel.

McCaul, M.E., Turkkan, J.S. & Stitzer, M.L. (1989). Conditioned opponent responses: effects of placebo challenge in alcoholic subjects. *Alcoholism: Clinical and Experimental Research*, **13**, 631–635.

Mineka, S. (1979). The role of fear in theories of avoidance learning, flooding, and extinction. *Psychological Bulletin*, **86**, 985–1010.

Monti, P.M., Binkoff, J.A., Abrams, D.B., Zwick, W.R., Nirenberg, T.D. & Liepman, M.R. (1987). Reactivity of alcoholics and nonalcoholics to drinking cues. *Journal of Abnormal Psychology*, **96**, 122–126.

Monti, P.M., Rohsenow, D.J., Rubonis, A.V., Niaura, R.S., Sirota, A.D., Colby, S.M. & Abrams, D.B. (1993a). Alcohol cue reactivity: effects of detoxification and extended exposure. *Journal of Studies on Alcohol*, **54**, 235–245.

Mowrer, O.H. (1947). On the dual nature of learning—a re-interpretation of "conditioning" and "problem-solving". *Harvard Educational Review*, **17**, 102–148.

Nestby, P., Vanderschuren, L.J.M.J., De Vries, T.J., Hogenboom, F., Wardeh, G., Mulder, A.H. & Schoffelmeer, A.N.M. (1997). Ethanol, like psychostimulants and morphine, causes long-lasting hyperreactivity of dopamine and acetylcholine neurons of rat nucleus accumbens: possible role in behavioural sensitization. *Psychopharmacology*, **133**, 69–76.

Newlin, D.B. (1985). The antagonistic placebo response to alcohol cues. *Alcoholism: Clinical and Experimental Research*, **9**, 411–416.

Newlin, D.B. (1986). Conditioned compensatory response to alcohol placebo in humans. *Psychopharmacology*, **88**, 247–251.

Overmier, J.B. & Lawry, J.A. (1979). Pavlovian conditioning and the mediation of behaviour. In G.H. Bower (Ed.), *The Psychology of Learning and Motivation*, Vol. 13. New York: Academic Press.

Poulos, C.X., Hinson, R.E. & Siegel, S. (1981). The role of Pavlovian processes in drug tolerance and dependence: implications for treatment. *Addictive Behaviours*, **6**, 205–211.

Prokasy, W.F. & Ebel, H.C. (1964). GSR conditioning and sensitization as a function of intertrial interval. *Journal of Experimental Psychology*, **67**, 113–119.

Robinson, T.E. & Berridge, K.C. (1993). The neural basis of drug craving: an incentive-sensitization theory of addiction. *Brain Research Reviews*, **18**, 247–291.

Rohsenow, D.J., Niaura, R.S., Childress, A.R., Abrams, D.B. & Monti, P.M. (1990). Cue reactivity in addictive behaviours: theoretical and treatment implications. *The International Journal of the Addictions*, **25**, 957–993.

Rohsenow, D.J., Monti, P.M., Rubonis, A.V., Sirota, A.D., Niaura, R.S., Colby, S.M., Wunschel, S.M. & Abrams, D.B. (1994). Cue reactivity as a predictor of drinking among male alcoholics. *Journal of Consulting and Clinical Psychology*, **62**, 620–626.

Rohsenow, D.J., Monti, P.M. & Abrams, D.B. (1995). Cue exposure treatment in alcohol dependence. In D.C. Drummond, S.T. Tiffany, S. Glautier & B. Remington (Eds), *Addictive Behaviour: Cue Exposure Theory and Practice* (pp. 169–196). New York: Wiley.

Shelton, K.L. & Macenski, M.J. (1998). Discriminative stimulus effects of self-administered ethanol. *Behavioural Pharmacology*, **9**, 329–336.

Siegel, S. (1975). Evidence from rats that morphine tolerance is a learned response. *Journal of Comparative and Physiological Psychology*, **89**, 498–506.

Siegel, S. (1979). The role of conditioning in drug tolerance and addiction. In J.D. Keehn (Ed.), *Psychopathology in Animals: Research Applications* (pp. 143–168). New York: Academic Press.

Sitharthan, T., Sitharthan, G., Hough, M.J. & Kavanagh, D.J. (1997). Cue exposure in moderation drinking: a comparison with cognitive-behaviour therapy. *Journal of Consulting and Clinical Psychology*, **65**, 878–882.

Staiger, P.K. & White, J.M. (1991). Cue Reactivity in alcohol abusers: stimulus specificity and extinction of the responses. *Addictive Behaviours*, **16**, 211–221.

Stasiewicz, P.R. & Maisto, S.A. (1993). Two-factor avoidance theory: the role of negative affect in the maintenance of substance use and substance use disorder. *Behaviour Therapy*, **24**, 337–356.

Stewart, J., de Wit, H. & Eikelboom, R. (1984). Role of unconditioned and conditioned drug effects in the self-administration of opiates and stimulants. *Psychological Review*, **91**, 251–268.

Stormark, K.M., Laberg, J.C., Bjerland, T. & Hugdahl, K. (1993). Habituation of electrodermal reactivity to visual alcohol stimuli in alcoholics. *Addictive Behaviours*, **18**, 437–443.

Swendsen, J.D., Merikangas, K.R., Canino, G.J., Kessler, R.C., Rubio-Stipec, M. & Angst, J. (1998). The comorbidity of alcoholism with anxiety and depressive disorders in four geographic communities. *Comprehensive Psychiatry*, **39**, 176–184.

Tiffany, S.T. (1990). A cognitive model of drug urges and drug-use behaviour: role of automatic and nonautomatic processes. *Psychological Review*, **97**, 147–168.

Tiffany, S.T. (1995). Potential functions of classical conditioning in drug addiction. In D.C. Drummond, S.T. Tiffany, S. Glautier & B. Remington (Eds), *Addictive Behaviour: Cue Exposure Theory and Practice* (pp. 47–71). New York: Wiley.

Tiffany, S.T. & Baker, T.B. (1986). Tolerance to alcohol: psychological models and their application to alcoholism. *Society of Behavioural Medicine*, **8**, 7–12.

Tiffany, S.T. & Carter, B.L. (1998). Is craving the source of compulsive drug use? *Journal of Psychopharmacology*, **12**, 23–30.

Tiffany, S.T., Carter, B.L. & Singleton, E.G. (in press). Challenges in the manipulation, assessment and interpretation of craving relevant variables. *Addiction*.

Tiffany, S.T., Drobes, D.J. & Cepeda-Benito, A. (1992). Contribution of associative and nonassociative processes to the development of morphine tolerance. *Psychopharmacology*, **109**, 185–190.

Tomie, A. (1993). Locating reward cue at response manipulandum (CAM) induces symptoms of drug abuse. *Neuroscience & Biobehavioral Reviews*, **20**, 505–536.

Tomie, A. (1995). CAM: an animal learning model of excessive and compulsive implement-assisted drug-taking in humans. *Clinical Psychology Review*, **15**, 145–167.

Wagner, A.R. & Brandon, S.E. (1989). Evolution of a structured connectionist model of Pavlovian conditioning (ÆSOP). In S.B. Klein & R.R. Mower (Eds), *Contemporary Learning Theories: Pavlovian Conditioning and the Status of Traditional Learning Theory* (pp. 149–190). Hillsdale, NJ: Erlbaum.

Weinstein, A., Lingford-Hughes, A., Martinez-Raga, J. & Marshall, J. (1998). What makes alcohol-dependent individuals early in abstinence crave for alcohol: exposure to the drink, images of drinking, or remembrance of drinks past? *Alcoholism: Clinical and Experimental Research*, **22**, 1376–1381.

Wikler, A. (1948). Recent progress in research on the neurophysiological basis of morphine addiction. *American Journal of Psychiatry*, **105**, 329–338.

Wise, R.A. (1988). The neurobiology of craving: implications for the understanding and treatment of addiction. *Journal of Abnormal Psychology*, **97**, 118–132.

Chapter 15

An Operant Behavioral Perspective on Alcohol Abuse and Dependence

George E. Bigelow
Behavioral Pharmacology Research Unit, Johns Hopkins University School of Medicine, Baltimore, MD, USA

Synopsis

The central principle of operant behavioral psychology is that behavior is controlled by its consequences. This and other principles of operant behavior are described as they relate to the development and perseverance of problem drinking—of excessive alcohol self-administration despite adverse consequences. Animal laboratory research on alcohol self-administration supports the view that alcohol and other drugs of abuse produce biologically rewarding effects through normal neuropharmacological mechanisms present in most individuals. Animal laboratory operant alcohol self-administration procedures have been developed and provide valuable models of the behavioral disorders of alcohol abuse and dependence. These self-administration procedures are widely accepted and widely used in laboratory studies of genetic, neurobiological and pharmacological influences on alcohol self-administration. Progressive ratio and behavioral choice procedures are described as examples of operant procedures that have proven especially useful.

Human laboratory studies of alcohol self-administration with problem drinkers and with social drinkers are summarized. The principle is emphasized that alcohol self-administration can be modified by appropriate arrangement of contingencies of reinforcement related to drinking and to alternative non-drinking behaviors. Several controlled therapeutic clinical trial examples of operant behavioral or contingency management behavior therapies are reviewed. These examples illustrate the successful use of operant behavioral reinforcement principles and methods to improve outcomes in treatment of alcohol abuse and dependence.

Operant or instrumental learning is that portion of learning related to action—to typically overt, apparently volitional behaviors—as opposed to cognitions or associations, which are

International Handbook of Alcohol Dependence and Problems. Edited by N. Heather, T.J. Peters and T. Stockwell.

more passive. It refers to behavior that operates on or manipulates the environment, to behavior that has an instrumental function. The behaviors of getting and consuming alcohol are operant or instrumental behaviors. Consequently, the science of operant or instrumental behavior is important to understanding and studying the behavioral disorders of alcohol abuse and dependence.

The central principle of the science of operant behavior is that operant behavior is controlled by its consequences. In casual-usage terminology, this is the view that behavior is controlled by reward and punishment, but the reader is cautioned—lest usage and thinking become too casual—that these terms have specific technical definitions. This chapter summarizes research and practice in the application of operant behavior methods and principles to the conceptualization and study of alcohol self-administration behavior and to the treatment of alcohol problems. The emphasis is on human research.

It should be noted here at the outset that, despite an extensive scientific base documenting the relevance and applicability of operant behavioral science principles and procedures to understanding and treating alcohol abuse and dependence, the operant perspective has not developed a strong leadership position in the alcohol field. This is in interesting contrast to the drug abuse field, i.e. the study and treatment of abuse and dependence on illegal drugs, drugs other than alcohol. There, the operant perspective plays quite a dominant role. The contrast between the two fields can be seen by examining the programs of the annual scientific meetings of leading research societies in the alcohol and drug abuse fields—in the USA, for example, these are the Research Society on Alcoholism (RSA) and the College on Problems of Drug Dependence (CPDD), respectively. CPDD meetings tend to have a heavy representation of operant behavior research and treatment presentations, whereas RSA meetings have relatively little representation from this scientific perspective. This difference between the two societies and the two fields in their scientific emphasis does not reflect differences in the applicability of operant behavioral science to alcohol-use vs. drug-use disorders. Rather, the difference reflects primarily the differing scientific theories or paradigms dominant in the two fields. The operant behavior conceptualization and approach has developed and prospered largely unopposed in the drug abuse field over the past three to four decades. In contrast, the alcohol field has remained dominated, at least in the USA, by the previously-established disease-model conceptualization of alcohol abuse and dependence. In a Kuhnian (Kuhn, 1962) sense, this is a case of a new conceptualization and approach—a new paradigm, in Kuhn's terminology—having failed to displace a previously entrenched alternative paradigm in the alcohol field. Some of the reasons for this failure, and some of the reasons why the alcohol and drug abuse fields have differed in their receptivity to the operant approach, have been discussed elsewhere (Bigelow & Silverman, 1999).

PRINCIPLES OF OPERANT BEHAVIOR

The central principle of the science of operant behavior is that behavior is controlled by its consequences. Secondary principles also of great importance for understanding how alcohol reinforcement can gain such powerful control over behavior are that: (a) immediate consequences are much more powerful than delayed consequences; (b) certain (or frequent, or probable) consequences are much more powerful than uncertain (or less frequent, or less probable) consequences; (c) variation and progressive escalation of the response requirement can engender remarkably persistent behavior; and (d) a given behavior is affected not only by its own contingencies and consequences but by the contingencies and consequences prevailing on alternative behavioral options.

Superficial examination of the lives of many alcohol abusers often does not suggest that alcohol drinking is a behavior developed and maintained by its reinforcing consequences. Instead, one is typically struck by the apparent self-destructiveness of the behavior— repeated excessive drinking that continues despite multiple adverse consequences. In severe cases there is progressive deterioration, with progressive loss of friends, family, job, health and self-respect. It is through the operation of the above-mentioned secondary principles of operant behavior that one is able to interpret how abusive drinking patterns can develop through biologically normal contingencies of reinforcement. In contrast to the variable and uncertain rewards available in other domains of his/her life, the problem drinker faces the availability of rapid and certain effects from alcohol consumption. Gradual tolerance development progressively increases the amount of drinking required to achieve the same effect. Impairments or disruptions consequent to drinking can further reduce the availability of rewards in non-drinking domains of life functioning, and a spiraling behavioral deterioration can ensue in which non-drinking-related behavioral repertoires are progressively displaced by drinking-related behaviors.

BEHAVIORAL PHARMACOLOGICAL VIEW OF ALCOHOL ABUSE AND DEPENDENCE

The apparent self-destructiveness of alcohol abuse and dependence is one of the features that leads to their being viewed as pathologies. The persistence of alcohol use despite adverse consequences can appear illogical and abnormal. One speculation or interpretation, based on this appearance of abnormality, is that alcohol abuse is a compulsion, with the drinker being out of control and driven by neurobiological defects to drink independently of drinking's consequences. In contrast, the behavioral pharmacological interpretation is that alcohol abuse is learned operant behavior that is reinforced and controlled by its consequences. Rather than being out of control, alcohol abuse is seen as being too powerfully controlled by the immediate reinforcing effects of alcohol, and inadequately controlled by other, less immediate, less certain, and less powerful reinforcers and contingencies. Reinforcement of behavior by alcohol or other drugs of abuse is seen as biologically normal, with the substance use disorder resulting from abnormalities or inadequacies in the environmental contingencies of reinforcement rather than from defects within the individual.

An extensive scientific literature supports this view of the biological normality of alcohol reinforcement. Major elements of that evidence include: widespread vulnerability to alcohol reinforcement under certain conditions; development of animal models of alcohol abuse that rely on operant behavioral self-administration procedures; and cross-species commonalities between animals and humans regarding drug and alcohol reinforcement, the temporal patterns of their self-administration, and the effects on self-administration of manipulated independent variables (Griffiths, Bigelow & Henningfield, 1980). This operant view of alcohol reinforcement as biologically normal does not contend that reinforced operant learning is the only process relevant to the complex disorder of alcohol abuse. It recognizes that vulnerability to alcohol reinforcement can be modulated by a broad range of biological, environmental and behavioral variables (e.g. genetics, access, social or cultural context, personality, etc.).

The biological normality of alcohol reward or reinforcement is supported by basic neuroscientific research that identifies the sites and neuropharmacological mechanisms of alcohol reward in the normal brain (Koob et al., 1998). But the operant view that alcohol self-administration is a behavior controlled by its consequences does not rely solely on this mechanism of direct neuropharmacological reward. Other consequences of alcohol consumption may also contribute to its reinforcing effects. Alcohol may produce behavioral changes in the drinker that increase exposure to other sources of reward (e.g. changes in social behavior), and alcohol consumption may alter the way others in the environment behave in response to the drinker. These types of non-pharmacological consequence are likely an important component of the overall array of reinforcement contingencies that can, under appropriate conditions (or perhaps we should say inappropriate conditions), contribute to the development and maintenance of abusive and inappropriate patterns of alcohol self-administration.

Excessive self-administration of drugs or alcohol—i.e. substance abuse or dependence—is often thought of as compulsive substance use. From the operant reinforcement perspective, excessive alcohol self-administration is more appropriately thought of as a disorder of attraction rather than a disorder of compulsion. Elsewhere (Bigelow, Brooner & Silverman, 1998), we have discussed this attraction-vs.-compulsion distinction with respect to drug abuse; the distinction is equally relevant to alcohol abuse. The "attraction" conceptualization recognizes the biologically reinforcing effects of alcohol, and tends to focus the search for causes of alcohol self-administration on those reinforcing effects and on other potentially reinforcing consequences or events that *follow* self-administration. In contrast, the "compulsion" conceptualization tends to direct attention—from the operant perspective, to misdirect attention—to events that *precede* alcohol self-administration and to carry connotations of irresistibility and uncontrollability. The operant reinforcement conceptualization focuses attention on the controllability or malleability of alcohol self-administration through contingencies of reinforcement and learning. It directs attention to the rewarding and/or positive reinforcing effects of alcohol as prime determinants of alcohol self-administration, abuse and dependence, and it is compatible with the reinforcement-based behavior therapy principle that the most effective way to reduce and eliminate an undesirable behavior is to provide a competing attraction, i.e. positive reinforcement of alternative behavior.

BEHAVIORAL LABORATORY RESEARCH IN ANIMALS

Perhaps the most direct and compelling support for the operant behavior conceptualization of alcohol abuse comes from laboratory research showing that alcohol functions as a reinforcer that maintains alcohol/drug seeking and self-administration in animal subjects. In their review comparing animal and human drug self-administration, Griffiths, Bigelow & Henningfield (1980) noted that the same substances abused by humans are generally self-administered by animals in laboratory behavioral models, and that a broad range of variables that affect self-administration affect animals and humans similarly. Of all psychiatric/behavioral disorders, substance abuse is perhaps the class of disorders most adequately represented by experimental animal models. Laboratory alcohol self-administration models have great face validity, and the extensive research documenting factors that influence self-administration and the consistency of these influences between animal models and human observations builds a strong case for their functional validity as well.

Alcohol is self-administered by the intravenous route (Woods, Ikomi & Winger, 1971) and several different techniques have been developed for establishing self-administration by the oral route (Meisch, 1975; Samson, 1986). In their review of the role of stress in drug and alcohol self-administration, Piazza & Le Moal (1998) note that acquisition of alcohol self-administration, like that of many other abused substances, is facilitated by a variety of stress-inducing manipulations.

Operant alcohol self-administration procedures have become well-accepted and widely adopted. They are widely used in research related to the behavioral genetics, neuropharmacology and pharmacological treatment of alcohol abuse and dependence. Operant methods serve in these research areas primarily as assessment or measurement tools for quantifying the impact of genetic or pharmacological influences on alcohol self-administration (e.g. Heyser et al., 1999). Less attention is devoted to studying the environmental and operant learning factors involved in the acquisition, maintenance and modification of alcohol self-administration; this is an area deserving of more research attention.

Despite the value of operant self-administration procedures, Hughes & Bickel (1997) have noted that they do not fully and adequately represent many of the clinical phenomena of substance use disorders that make substance use problematic. They have suggested operant paradigms that might be developed and studied to operationalize and to focus research on such clinical diagnostic features of substance use as: using more than intended; giving up other activities in order to use; using despite harm; failing to stop or cut down; spending excessive time obtaining, using and recovering from use.

Two animal laboratory operant methods deserve special mention here because they have significantly advanced the sensitivity of operant procedures for assessing and understanding important influences on alcohol self-administration behavior. These are progressive ratio procedures and operant choice procedures.

Operant drug/alcohol self-administration procedures are often used to assess reinforcing efficacy, or to assess whether some pretreatment procedure affects the reinforcing efficacy of the self-administered drug or alcohol. For example, these methods have supported the conclusion that opioid antagonists, such as naloxone and naltrexone decrease the reinforcing efficacy of alcohol (Hyytia & Sinclair, 1993; Stromberg, Volpicelli & O'Brien, 1998). However, sometimes self-administration data can be difficult to interpret. Self-administration rates are often an inverted-U-shaped function of dose. Consequently, when an experimental manipulation changes self-administration rate it can be difficult to know whether this is analogous to an increase or a decrease in reinforcer magnitude. Progressive ratio and choice procedures solve this interpretation problem by providing an index of reinforcing efficacy that is independent of the rate of self-administration.

Progressive Ratio Procedures

In progressive ratio procedures (Hodos, 1961), the number of responses required for reinforcer delivery (the ratio) progressively increases and the largest ratio successfully completed for reinforcement is called the breaking point. The ratio might increase across successive reinforcements or successive trials within a single session, or it might increase across successive sessions. The breaking point is used as an index of reinforcing efficacy. By appropriate arrangement of temporal procedures, it is possible to eliminate or minimize the chance that performance is distorted by the pharmacological effects or behavior-impairing effects of prior drug/alcohol intake. In their review of progressive ratio self-administration research, Stafford, LeSage & Glowa (1998) note there has been a substantial increase since 1988 in the annual number of published self-administration studies using progressive ratio procedures.

Choice Procedures

Operant choice procedures, in which two or more potential reinforcers are concurrently available, provide another tool for assessing reinforcing efficacy independently of rate of self-administration. When two alternatives are available under comparable schedules of reinforcement, the relative amount of responding for each alternative can serve as an index of reinforcing efficacy. An important outgrowth of this area of research has been the demonstration that the relative reinforcing efficacy of drug or alcohol self-administration is significantly influenced by the availability, and schedule of availability, of alternative reinforcers (Carroll, Rodefer & Rawleigh, 1995; Carroll, 1996). Operant analysis and interpretation of these behavioral choice studies has recently blended with behavioral economic analyses of alcohol self-administration (Rodefer & Carroll, 1996; Rodefer et al., 1996).

BEHAVIORAL LABORATORY RESEARCH IN HUMANS

For approximately two decades, in the 1960s and 1970s, several laboratories conducted residential human laboratory research focusing on behavioral study of alcohol self-administration by volunteers who were alcohol-dependent or alcohol abusers and who were given supervised experimental access to substantial quantities of beverage alcohol on a chronic daily basis. Prior laboratory research on chronic alcohol exposure in humans had used experimenter-scheduled dosing regimens (Mendelson, 1964), rather than volitional self-administration regimens. The elevation of alcohol consumption from the status of an independent variable to that of a dependent variable represented a significant advance in the application of behavioral science to the study of alcohol use disorders; for the first time it was possible to observe and study these disorders directly in the laboratory.

Early studies of human alcohol self-administration were largely descriptive, but later studies turned to systematic experimental manipulation to assess factors that might influence alcohol self-administration behavior. The progressive methodological development of human alcohol self-administration studies has been described by Bigelow, Griffiths & Liebson (1975) as being from initial descriptive observational studies of relatively unrestricted drinking, to subsequent studies that manipulated independent experimental variables in an effort to assess effects on drinking, and still later to studies that included experimental manipulations but also placed various restrictions on drinking in an effort to enhance sensitivity to the experimental manipulations.

Descriptive Observational Studies of Drinking

Descriptive observational studies revealed several things:

1. The problem drinker volunteers engaged in orderly operant behavioral performances to gain access to beverage alcohol (Mello & Mendelson, 1965).
2. They appeared to regulate their drinking and not to be out of control, i.e. they did not drink themselves to stuporousness/anesthetization; they did not drink all available alcohol as soon as it was available and, anecdotally, their drinking appeared to be influenced by social factors within the study setting.
3. The temporal pattern of operant alcohol self-administration was widely varying and erratically cyclic across days, rather than steady and sustained (Mello & Mendelson, 1971)—the same type of erratic temporal pattern seen in animals, given similar relatively unrestricted access to alcohol for self-administration (Woods, Ikomi & Winger, 1971).
4. Drinking appeared not to be substantially driven or controlled by physical dependence or the alcohol withdrawal syndrome; a feature of the erratically varying temporal pattern was that participants would occasionally abstain from alcohol voluntarily and spontaneously, despite its ready availability and despite the occurrence of withdrawal signs and symptoms, and would re-initiate episodes of drinking even when withdrawal signs and symptoms were absent (Griffiths, Bigelow & Henningfield, 1980).

5. Drinking appeared not to be driven by anxiety or anxiety reduction; on the contrary, anxiety tended to increase, not decrease, over the course of drinking periods (McNamee, Mello & Mendelson, 1968; Mendelson & Mello, 1966).

Role of Antecedent or Setting Conditions

Studies that varied the antecedent or setting conditions of drinking generally observed little or no systematic effect on alcohol self-administration. Varying whether subjects lived (and drank) in isolation or in social circumstances had no systematic effect (Nathan & O'Brien, 1971; Nathan et al., 1970a,b; Goldman et al., 1973). Varying whether subjects were exposed to procedures intended to induce stress or anxiety had no effect (Allman, 1973; Allman, Taylor & Nathan, 1972); however, this failure may be due to the weakness of this stress manipulation (being informed of the inadequacy of one's operant task performance to earn a financial bonus) since in other studies social stress has increased alcohol self-administration in alcoholics (Miller et al., 1974) and in heavy social drinkers (Marlatt, Kosturn & Lang, 1975).

Influence of Schedule of Availability

Studies that varied the operant behavioral contingencies related to alcohol availability—either the schedule of reinforcement for alcohol delivery, the availability or schedule of alternative reinforcers, or the scheduled consequences of drinking vs. abstinence—generally observed substantial and orderly effects on alcohol self-administration. When the amount of operant behavior required to obtain doses of alcohol was varied, higher response requirements resulted in reduced alcohol self-administration (Mello, McNamee & Mendelson, 1968; Liebson et al., 1971; Bigelow & Liebson, 1972). When money was offered as an alternative to drinking in a choice procedure, larger-magnitude alternative reinforcement was more effective than lower-magnitude in achieving abstinence; and efficacy of the alternative reinforcer was reduced when delays of reinforcement were introduced between the choice occasion and the reinforcer delivery (Cohen et al., 1971b).

Influence of Behavioral Consequences

Among the most impressive human laboratory demonstrations of the power and efficacy of operant contingency management procedures to influence alcohol drinking among seriously problematic drinkers is a series of studies by Cohen, Liebson and colleagues (Cohen et al., 1971a; Cohen, Liebson & Faillace, 1971, 1972, 1973). These were the first studies to focus on the central operant behavioral principle that behavior is controlled by its consequences and to evaluate the effects on drinking of systematically varying the consequences of choosing to drink. In the Cohen et al. (1971a) study, volunteer chronic alcoholics in a residential laboratory were given access to 24 ounces (720 ml) of 95-proof beverage alcohol daily, 5 days/week for 5 weeks (no alcohol on weekends). A within-subject experimental design was used in which excessive drinking had scheduled consequences during weeks 1, 3 and 5 (the contingent weeks), but not during weeks 2 or 4 (the non-contingent, or control, weeks). During contingent weeks, subjects lived in an "enriched" environment so long as they did not drink excessively; however, as soon as they drank excessively (defined as more than five one-ounce drinks) they were restricted to an "impoverished" environment. During the non-contingent control weeks drinking had no scheduled consequences and subjects were restricted to the impoverished environment independently of their drinking behavior. The enriched environment provided access to a variety of privileges, including social contacts, use of a recreation room, access to preferred regular hospital meals, opportunity to work in the hospital laundry for pay, and permission to receive visitors. In the impoverished environment, subjects were restricted to their bedrooms, their opportunities for activities and socialization were severely restricted, and they received a pureed diet. During the contingency, excessive drinking also resulted in loss of alcohol access on the following day, so consecutive days of excessive drinking were not possible. The contingency had a dramatic effect on drinking; excessive drinking was rare during the contingency but commonplace during the non-contingent periods. Other studies in the series extended these findings about the efficacy of contingent consequences for controlling drinking by showing that it was not exposure to the impoverished environment that caused excessive drinking, but the absence of contingencies, and by showing that the contingency could be effective even when prolonged continuous periods of excessive drinking were possible.

Subsequent studies have shown that drinking can be controlled by consequences of much smaller magnitude than were used in the Cohen et al. studies. In a residential laboratory study, Bigelow, Liebson & Griffiths (1974) demonstrated that the drinking of chronic problem drinkers could be suppressed by about half by scheduling a brief period of isolation immediately contingent upon receipt of each drink. This "time out" isolation contingency resulted in immediate, though brief, loss of availability of a broad range of potential reinforcers—physical activities, sensory stimulation, social stimulation and interaction. Griffiths, Bigelow & Liebson (1974, 1977) showed that contingent time out from social interactions alone was also effective in reducing drinking by chronic problem drinkers, although apparently less so than the contingent isolation procedure.

Influences of Other Parameters

One of the features noted during these contingent time out studies and related studies with problem drinkers is that the ability of alcohol to serve as a reinforcer is a graded function of many different parameters. These include characteristics of the alcohol itself, of its schedule of availability, of the consequences of alcohol selection, of the available alternatives, and of the schedules of availability of those alternatives. Variations in any of these factors, and probably others, can influence the occurrence of alcohol seeking and alcohol self-administration behavior. Over the range tested, larger alcohol doses appear to be more effective reinforcers than smaller doses (Griffiths, Bigelow & Liebson, 1976); higher beverage alcohol concentrations appear to be more effective reinforcers than lower concentrations (Bigelow, Griffiths & Liebson, 1977); drinks that can be closely spaced appear to be more effective reinforcers than drinks that must be more widely spaced in time (Bigelow, Griffiths & Liebson, 1975; Griffiths, Bigelow & Liebson, 1976). Sometimes, variables that influence drinking behavior may demonstrate their influence only under limited sets of conditions, e.g. only when doses or availability are limited, or only when other behavioral options are restricted (Bigelow, Griffiths & Liebson, 1975; Griffiths, Bigelow & Liebson, 1977).

Influence of Alternative Behavioral Options

The operant behavioral principle that the occurrence of a particular behavior is influenced by the availability of and contingencies affecting other behavioral options is often insufficiently appreciated in discussions and considerations of the operant behavioral perspective. Alcohol self-administration behavior can be more completely studied and understood when it is viewed as operant choice behavior in the context of a potentially vast smorgasbord of concurrent schedules of reinforcement leading to different consequent events. Selection and pursuit of the alcohol self-administration option is governed not just by the contingencies related to alcohol, but also by the contingencies related to the other options and their consequences. Extensive animal laboratory operant behavior research has focused on study of concurrent schedules of reinforcement and their interactions. Vuchinich & Tucker (1983, 1988, 1996) have extended to human alcohol self-administration this analysis of how concurrent behavioral options can influence a specific target behavior, such as drinking. In a series of naturalistic studies they have documented that drinking is an inverse function of the availability of non-drinking rewards (Tucker, Vuchinich & Gladsjo, 1994; Tucker, Vuchinich & Pukish, 1995; Vuchinich & Tucker, 1996). More recently, this operant choice perspective on drinking has blended with the behavioral economic perspective (Vuchinich & Simpson, 1998). Both perspectives recognize that delayed rewards are less effective as determinants of behavior than are immediate rewards. Individuals are seen as facing choices in their natural circumstances between smaller rewards delivered sooner and larger rewards delivered later (e.g. the immediate small rewards of drinking vs. the delayed larger rewards of more successful and rewarding life-style functioning. Experimentally, this has been modeled as choices between different amounts of money to be received immediately vs. after various delays. Using this model, Vuchinich & Simpson (1998) have reported that delays reduce reward value more in problem drinkers than in normal social drinkers. This differential delay-discounting may be one factor that contributes to problem drinkers' coming under excessive control of the immediate small rewards of drinking.

Effects on Other Behaviors and Reinforcers

Alcohol's behavioral pharmacological actions are not limited to serving as a reinforcer of drinking behavior. Alcohol also has other direct effects on behavior that may influence the reinforcing effects of drinking. Administration of alcohol produces increases in both social interactions and verbal behavior in both problem drinkers and normals (Griffiths, Bigelow & Liebson, 1974; Stitzer et al., 1981a,b; Higgins & Stitzer, 1988). These consequent increased social behaviors and social interactions may contribute to reinforcing alcohol self-administration, although they are certainly not essential elements.

Alcohol consumption may also alter the reinforcing efficacy of potential reinforcers. Griffiths, Bigelow & Liebson (1975) evaluated the effect of alcohol administration on the choices of problem drinkers between money and opportunities to socialize. Results showed that alcohol consumption increased the relative preference for socializing over money. It is not clear whether this was due to a decrease in the efficacy of money as a reinforcer or to an increase in the efficacy of socializing as a reinforcer, or perhaps to both. But one can imagine how this type of alcohol-induced change in relative reinforcing efficacy of these alternatives might contribute to shaping a preference for drinking and a discounting of the importance of its economic and personal consequences.

Operant Studies in Non-problem Drinkers

In the 1980s and 1990s human laboratory research concerning alcohol's reinforcing effects moved from problem/dependent alcohol abuser volunteers to non-problem social drinker volunteers. de Wit & Chutuape (1993) reported that alcohol preloads increased alcohol self-administration, in a money vs. alcohol choice procedure, in social drinkers just as it is reported to do in problem drinkers. Doty & de Wit (1995) reported that the positive subjective effects of alcohol were greater when it was administered in a social setting vs. in isolation, and also that subjects were more likely to self-administer alcohol in the social setting. de Wit, Svenson & York (1999) reported that naltrexone decreased alcohol self-administration in social drinkers, but that its effects were non-specific in that it also decreased self-administration of the placebo control beverage. Roehrs et al. (1999) compared social drinkers with vs. without insomnia in an alcohol/placebo choice procedure and concluded that insomnia contributed to alcohol's reinforcing effects.

CONTINGENCY MANAGEMENT TREATMENT RESEARCH

Clinical trials of behavioral treatments explicitly based on contingency management procedures have provided strong evidence in support of the operant behavioral perspective on alcohol abuse. Detailed review of several of these clinical trials is useful for illustrating the efficacy of the approach.

Contingency Management Treatment of Chronic Public Drunkenness Offenders

Miller (1975) reported a randomized trial that focused on chronic public drunkenness offenders. At the time of the study, public drunkenness was commonly treated as a criminal offense, so arrest records could be used as one objective index of public drunkenness frequency. Participants were individuals with eight or more public drunkenness arrests in the preceding 12 months, at least 5 year histories of abusive drinking, unstable housing and unstable employment—a so-called "skid row" population.

The study assessed whether a positive reinforcement approach of providing desirable goods and services contingent upon sobriety would be more successful than the usual-care procedure, which typically provided resources non-contingently to these needy skid-row residents. Twenty subjects were enrolled and randomized equally among the two treatment conditions. For participants in the positive reinforcement treatment, the investigator made arrangements with agencies serving the skid row community to provide their goods and services only contingent upon sobriety, and to discontinue those goods and services for 5 days contingent upon any instance of observed intoxication or elevated breath alcohol concentration (greater than 10mg/100ml blood alcohol concentration); breath alcohol recordings were obtained on a random schedule in the community. Goods and services included in the contingency included housing and meals at a relatively desirable service agency, employment, clothing donations, and Veterans Administration canteen booklets exchangeable for cigarettes, meals, or clothing. For patients in the usual-care treatment condition the same goods and services were available non-contingently. Outcomes of the two groups were compared for the 2 months before and the 2 months after study initiation.

The primary outcome measures were public drunkenness arrests and hours employed per week. The two groups were similar on these indices before treatment. Both measures showed a clinically and statistically significant superiority of the contingency management treatment during the randomized differential treatment; both measures showed significant improvement in the contingency management group and no significant change in the usual-care group. Mean public drunkenness arrests fell from 1.7 to 0.3 with contingency management treatment, but were unchanged with usual-care treatment—means of 1.4 and 1.3. Mean hours employed per week increased nearly four-fold, from 3.2 to 12, with contingency management treatment, but were not significantly changed with usual-care treatment—means of 4.4 and 3.2. In addition to these primary outcomes, breath alcohol samples that were collected from half the contingency management group both before and during the intervention showed a large and significant reduction in mean blood alcohol level from 50 mg% to 0.002 mg%.

Miller (1975) concluded that behavioral treatment strategies based on the principles of contingency management could have substantial beneficial impact on the drinking behavior, drunkenness arrests and employment of skid row alcoholics. He noted that the common usual-care procedures for allocating service resources might actually be counter-therapeutic, in that they might result in delivery of more services to alcoholics when they are intoxicated than when they are sober, and that such an unintended contingency might actually help to maintain inappropriate and abusive drinking patterns. From a cost–benefit perspective, an attractive feature of this particular contingency management therapy was that improved outcomes were not dependent on the provision of more or different services, but simply on appropriate arrangement of the contingencies under which existing services were dispensed. Thus, this study demonstrated both the efficacy of contingency management treatment of problem drinking and also that improved outcomes might be achieved by incorporating appropriate contingencies into existing community services and agencies.

Contingency Management Treatment of Alcohol Abuse in Methadone Patients

Another example of the efficacy of introducing behavioral contingencies into settings where reinforcing goods and services are otherwise routinely dispensed non-contingently is provided by clinical research on the treatment of alcohol abuse among methadone maintenance patients. Methadone is an orally effective and long-acting opioid substitution medication that, when administered daily in adequate doses, is a very effective treatment for heroin dependence (Strain et al., 1999). Concurrent alcohol abuse has been one of the leading reasons for failure of patients enrolled in methadone maintenance treatment. Liebson, Tommasello & Bigelow (1978) evaluated the efficacy of a contingency management intervention for promoting successful treatment of alcohol abuse among methadone patients. The therapeutic target was to promote the routine ingestion of disulfiram (Antabuse®). Disulfiram inhibits ethanol's metabolism and causes accumulation of the partial metabolic product acetaldehyde; acetaldehyde poisoning is aversive and serves to deter ethanol consumption. In form, disulfiram treatment is pharmaceutical, but in function its effectiveness is via the mechanism of behavioral avoidance (i.e. abstinence from ethanol avoids the aversive ethanol–disulfiram reaction). As typically used in medical practice (patients receive a prescription, with instructions to purchase the medication and to use it daily) disulfiram has shown little or no clinical effectiveness, despite its unquestioned pharmacological efficacy (Swift, 1999; Garbutt et al., 1999); patients apparently avoid the disulfiram more readily than the ethanol. Methadone, in contrast, is a positively-reinforcing medication that maintains good patient adherence. Liebson and colleagues used the reinforcing efficacy of methadone to arrange a behavioral contingency that would reinforce disulfiram ingestion.

Patients were 25 volunteer alcohol-abusing methadone patients who were about to be, or had recently been, discharged from their methadone maintenance treatment programs because of their alcohol abuse. All patients were initially treated for alcohol withdrawal as needed, which typically involved brief hospitalization, and all were treated for 14 days with supervised disulfiram (administered daily under observation immediately before methadone administration). Two (8%) dropped out during this initial detoxification and disulfiram induction. The remaining 23 patients were randomly assigned to either of two procedures; both procedures involved continued methadone maintenance, and both involved disulfiram, to which all consented. All patients were counseled to stop drinking and about the effects of disulfiram, instructed to take disulfiram daily as an aid to abstinence, and warned that resumption of drinking could result in their termination from methadone treatment. Patients in the control condition were given a supply of disulfiram weekly and instructed to use it. Patients in the contingency management condition were required to continue taking their disulfiram under nursing supervision as a precondition to receiving their daily methadone dose—i.e. methadone treatment was used to reinforce disulfiram ingestion. The interventions were of 6-months duration, except that patients in the control condition who relapsed to drinking were then transferred to the contingency management condition for ethical and compassionate reasons. Outcomes were assessed in terms of relapse rate, amount of drinking, criminal behavior, and illicit drug use.

Treatment outcomes for the two groups differed dramatically. In the contingency management treatment, 11 of 13 patients (85%) completed 6 months without a serious drinking relapse; in the control condition only 1 of 10 (10%) did so. The percentage of days drinking (confirmed by breath alcohol test) was 10 times greater in the control treatment than in the contingency management treatment—21% vs. 2%. The arrest rate was eight times higher with the control treatment than with contingency management—0.8 vs. 0.1 per 100 patient-days. With the control treatment, 57% of arrests were drinking-related; no drinking-related arrests occurred with the contingency management treatment. Urinalysis testing for illicit drug abuse showed no evidence of increased use (i.e. no symptom substitution); in fact, the trend, though non-significant, was toward reduced illicit drug use.

This study's demonstration of disulfiram's efficacy in reducing drinking when its ingestion was assured is a powerful demonstration that alcoholic drinking behavior can be controlled by its consequences. The study also illustrates again the success of incorporating into therapeutic contingency management relationships the dispensing of goods or services that would otherwise be dispensed non-contingently, without beneficial utilization of their reinforcing potential.

Community Reinforcement Treatment of Alcohol Abuse and Dependence

Another important illustration of the effectiveness of contingency management therapies for alcohol problems is provided by the Community Reinforcement Approach, originally developed by Hunt & Azrin (1973). The two previous illustrations focused on creating therapeutic contingencies involving a small number of specific reinforcers already routinely dispensed within patients' life setting. The Community Reinforcement Approach attempts to achieve a much more comprehensive transformation of the contingencies within patients' lives. The Community Reinforcement Approach is based on the same operant behavior/contingent reinforcement conceptualization of how behavior is influenced and controlled. But instead of only establishing contingencies with existing potential reinforcers, it also intervenes to introduce into patients' lives a broad range of activities expected to be effective reinforcers for most individuals—employment, social relationships, recreation, etc.—and then to establish therapeutic contingent reinforcement relationships involving these activities.

Hunt & Azrin (1973) reported the results of a random-assignment clinical trial comparing the outcomes of alcohol abuse/dependence patients treated with the Community

Reinforcement Approach to the outcomes of similar, matched patients treated with a usual-care approach that emphasized alcohol education and the 12-step self-help/peer-support program of Alcoholics Anonymous. Both treatment groups received the usual-care treatment, but the community reinforcement group also received treatment that focused on establishing vocational, family and social-recreational reinforcers in the lives of patients and arranging that drinking would result in a rapid loss of (time-out from) these reinforcers. Community reinforcement patients received assistance with employment, with marital and family interactions, and with arranging non-alcohol-related social/recreational activities. Contingent relationships were arranged such that access to these activities was contingent on abstinence from alcohol, and such that instances of drinking would result in relatively immediate and certain exclusion or time-out from these reinforcers. Participants were alcohol-dependent; their drinking had resulted in physical dependence and they had been admitted to a State hospital for treatment. Treatment outcomes were assessed over a 6-month post-hospitalization period; outcomes were quantified as percentages of days drinking, unemployed, absent from home or institutionalized.

Outcomes of the two treatment groups differed significantly on all four of the outcome indices throughout the 6-month follow-up comparison period; the community reinforcement treatment had, by far, the better outcome. Each of the adverse-outcome indices was 4–13 times more frequent in usual-care patients than in community reinforcement patients—drinking, 79% vs. 14% of days; unemployed, 62% vs. 5% of days; absent from home, 66% vs. 16% of days; and institutionalized, 27% vs. 2% of days. These are impressive results, and they offer strong support for the value of the operant behavior conceptualization of alcohol use disorders and for the contingency management approach to treatment of alcohol abuse and dependence.

Community reinforcement treatment has subsequently been extended to homeless alcohol-dependent persons and to a larger sample of participants, thus documenting the replicability and generalizability of the effectiveness of this approach (Smith, Meyers & Delaney, 1998). The 106 participants were randomized to community reinforcement treatment vs. standard care. Standard care consisted of housing and meals, 12-step counseling, a jobs program, and case management. Community reinforcement treatment consisted of housing and meals, behavioral counseling and skills training, a jobs club, a non-drinking social club; it included randomly-scheduled breathalyzer tests to detect alcohol use and it provided abstinence-contingent incentives. Outcomes from the two treatment conditions were compared over a 12-month assessment period. Both groups showed substantial improvements from pretreatment, the community reinforcement outcomes were significantly superior to those of standard treatment, especially on outcome indices directly related to drinking behavior. These data further strengthen the case for the clinical utility and effectiveness of operant incentive-based behavior therapy for alcohol dependence by extending its demonstrated efficacy to the very difficult population of homeless alcohol abusers.

CONCLUSIONS AND COMMENTS

The current status of the operant behavior perspective in the alcohol abuse/dependence field is quite mixed. Within the basic science arena, the appropriateness and utility of operant behavioral approaches are well-accepted, and operant approaches are widely used. Operant alcohol self-administration procedures are seen as appropriate models of alcohol abuse/dependence and extensively used as tools for assessing the influence on alcohol self-administration of a broad range of biological factors—genetics, neurological interventions, neuropharmacological manipulations, pharmacological/pharmaceutical interventions, and behavioral/environmental manipulations. Extensive animal and human laboratory research has shown clearly that operant principles and methods are relevant to understanding and to changing alcohol self-administration behavior.

However, in the treatment and treatment research arenas there is relatively little attention paid to operant behavioral approaches, such as contingency management, as therapeutic approaches to alcohol problems. The overwhelming therapeutic emphasis continues to be on verbal therapies. Nearly all of the encouraging and successful clinical trials in alcoholism treatment described earlier represent work conducted 20–30 years ago. At present, there is relatively little contingency management work in the alcoholism field; this is in contrast to the drug abuse treatment field, where operant contingency management approaches are quite prominent (cf. Higgins & Silverman, 1999). Recent major clinical trials of psychosocial treatments for alcoholism—evaluating what are regarded as the accepted, state-of-the-art effective treatments—have focused only on comparing variations of verbal therapies (Project MATCH Research Group, 1997), with no involvement of contingency management procedures.

Regardless of the reasons for the current situation, it is certainly hoped that both laboratory research and therapeutic research derived from the operant perspective will flourish and bloom again in the future. The perspective has much to offer, not the least of which is its rigorous empiricism, which ensures that data will prevail.

KEY WORKS AND SUGGESTIONS FOR FURTHER READING

Griffiths, R.R., Bigelow, G.E., Henningfield, J.E. (1980). Similarities in animal and human drug-taking behavior. In N.K. Mello (Ed.), *Advances in Substance Abuse: Behavioral and Biological Research*. (pp. 1–90). Greenwich, CT: JAI.

Reviews, from an operant behavioral perspective, the functional commonalities across substances and across species of influences on drug/alcohol self-administration behavior. These cross-species commonalities make a strong case for the biological normality of drug/alcohol reinforcement.

Higgins, S.T., Silverman, K. (Eds) (1999). *Motivating Behavior Change Among Illicit-Drug Abusers*. Washington, DC: American Psychological Association.

Provides a comprehensive review of operant behavioral treatments for substance abuse as these have been developed and applied to treatment of abuse and dependence on illicit drugs.

Meyers, R.J., Smith, J.E. (1995). *Clinical Guide to Alcohol Treatment: The Community Reinforcement Approach*. New York: Guilford.

Provides a practical clinical guide to the implementation of operant-behavior-based community reinforcement treatment of alcohol abuse and dependence.

REFERENCES

Allman, L. (1973). Group drinking during stress: effects on alcohol intake and group process. *International Journal of Addition*, **8**, 475–488.

Allman, L.R., Taylor, H.A. & Nathan, P.E. (1972). Group drinking during stress: effects on drinking behavior, affect and psychopathology. *American Journal of Psychiatry*, **129**, 669–678.

Bigelow, G.E., Brooner, R.K. & Silverman, K. (1998). Competing motivations: drug reinforcement vs. non-drug reinforcement. *Journal of Psychopharmacology*, **12**, 8–14.

Bigelow, G.E., Griffiths, R.R. & Liebson, I.A. (1975). Experimental models for the modification of human drug self-administration: methodological developments in the study of ethanol self-administration by alcoholics. *Federation Proceedings*, **34**, 1785–1792.

Bigelow, G.E., Griffiths, R.R. & Liebson, I.A. (1977). Pharmacological influences upon ethanol self-administration. In M.M. Gross (Ed.), *Alcohol Intoxication and Withdrawal*, Vol. IIIB (pp. 523–538). New York: Plenum.

Bigelow, G.E. & Liebson, I.A. (1972). Cost factors controlling alcoholic drinking. *Psychological Record*, **22**, 305–314.

Bigelow, G.E., Liebson, I.A. & Griffiths, R.R. (1974). Alcoholic drinking: suppression by a brief time-out procedure. *Behaviour Research and Therapy*, **12**, 107–115.

Bigelow, G.E. & Silverman, K. (1999). Theoretical and empirical foundations of contingency management treatments for drug abuse. In S.T. Higgins & K. Silverman (Eds), *Motivating Behavior Change Among Illicit-Drug Abusers* (pp. 15–31). Washington, DC: American Psychological Association.

Carroll, M.E. (1996). Reducing drug abuse by enriching the environment with alternative non-drug reinforcers. In L. Green & J.H. Kagel (Eds), *Advances in Behavioral Economics* (pp. 37–68). Norwood, NJ: Ablex Publishing.

Carroll, M.E., Rodefer, J.S. & Rawleigh, J.M. (1995). Concurrent self-administration of ethanol and an alternative non-drug reinforcer in monkeys: effects of income (session length) on demand for drug. *Psychopharmacology*, **120**, 1–9.

Cohen, M., Liebson, I.A. & Faillace, L.A. (1971). The role of reinforcement contingencies in chronic alcoholism: an experimental analysis of one case. *Behaviour Research and Therapy*, **9**, 375–379.

Cohen, M., Liebson, I.A. & Faillace, L.A. (1972). A technique for establishing controlled drinking in chronic alcoholics. *Diseases of the Nervous System*, **33**, 46–49.

Cohen, M., Liebson, I. & Faillace, L. (1973). Controlled drinking by chronic alcoholics over extended periods of free access. *Psychological Reports*, **32**, 1107–1110.

Cohen, M., Liebson, I.A., Faillace, L.A. & Allen, R.P. (1971a). Moderate drinking by chronic alcoholics: a schedule-dependent phenomenon. *Journal of Nervous and Mental Disorders*, **153**, 434 444.

Cohen, M., Liebson, I.A., Faillace, L.A. & Speers, W. (1971b). Alcoholism: controlled drinking and incentives for abstinence. *Psychological Reports*, **28**, 575–580.

de Wit, H. & Chutuape, M.A. (1993). Increased ethanol choice in social drinkers following ethanol preload. *Behavioral Pharmacology*, **4**, 29–36.

de Wit, H., Svenson, J. & York, A. (1999). Non-specific effect of naltrexone on ethanol consumption in social drinkers. *Psychopharmacology*, **146**, 33–41.

Doty, P. & de Wit, H. (1995). Effect of setting on the reinforcing and subjective effects of ethanol in social drinkers. *Psychopharmacology*, **118**, 19–27.

Garbutt, J.C., West, S.L., Carey, T.S., Lohr, K.N. & Crews, F.T. (1999). Pharmacological treatment of alcohol dependence: a review of the evidence. *Journal of The American Medical Association*, **281**, 1318–1325.

Goldman, M., Taylor, H., Carruth, M. & Nathan, P. (1973). Effects of group decision-making on group drinking by alcoholics. *Quarterly Journal of Studies on Alcoholism*, **34**, 807–822.

Griffiths, R.R., Bigelow, G.E. & Henningfield, J.E. (1980). Similarities in animal and human drug-taking behavior. In N.K. Mello (Ed.), *Advances in Substance Abuse: Behavioral and Biological Research* (pp. 1–90). Greenwich, CT: JAI.

Griffiths, R.R., Bigelow, G.E. & Liebson, I.A. (1974). Suppression of ethanol self-administration in alcoholics by contingent time-out from social interactions in alcoholics. *Behaviour Research and Therapy*, **12**, 327–334.

Griffiths, R.R., Bigelow, G.E. & Liebson, I.A. (1975). Effect of ethanol self-administration on choice behavior: money vs. socializing. *Phamacology. Biochemistry and Behavior*, **3**, 443–446.

Griffiths, R.R., Bigelow, G.E. & Liebson, I.A. (1976). Human sedative self-administration: effects of inter ingestion interval and dose. *Journal of Pharmacology and Experimental Therapeutics*, **197**, 488–494.

Griffiths, R.R., Bigelow, G.E. & Liebson, I.A. (1977). Comparison of social time-out and activity time-out procedures in suppressing ethanol self-administration in alcoholics. *Behaviour Research and Therapy*, **15**, 329–336.

Heyser, C.J., Roberts, A.J., Schulteis, G. & Koob, G.F. (1999). Central administration of an opiate antagonist decreases oral ethanol self-administration in rats. *Alcoholism: Clinical and Experimental Research*, **23**, 1468–1476.

Higgins, S.T. & Silverman, K. (Eds) (1999). *Motivating Behavior Change Among Illicit-Drug Abusers*. Washington, DC: American Psychological Association.

Higgins, S.T. & Stitzer, M.L. (1988). Effects of alcohol on speaking in isolated humans. *Psychopharmacology*, **95**, 189–194.

Hodos, W. (1961). Progressive ratio as a measure of reward strength. *Science*, **134**, 943–944.

Hughes, J.R. & Bickel, W.K. (1997). Modeling drug dependence behaviors for animal and human studies. *Pharmacology Biochemistry and Behaviour*, **57**, 413–417.

Hunt, G.M. & Azrin, N.H. (1973). A community reinforcement approach to alcoholism. *Behaviour Research and Therapy*, **11**, 91–104.

Hyytia, P. & Sinclair, J.D. (1993). Responding for oral ethanol after naloxone treatment by alcohol-preferring AA rats. *Alcoholism: Clinical and Experimental Research*, **17**, 631–636.

Koob, G.F., Roberts, A.J., Schulteis, G., Parsons, L.H., Heyser, C.J., Hyytia, P., Merlo-Pich, E. & Weiss, F. (1998). Neurocircuitry of targets of ethanol reward and dependence. *Alcoholism: Clinical and Experimental Research*, **22**, 3–9.

Kuhn, T.S. (1962). *The Structure of Scientific Revolutions*. Chicago, IL: University of Chicago Press.

Liebson, I.A., Cohen, M., Faillace, L.A. & Ward, R.F. (1971). The token economy as a research method in alcoholism. *Psychiatry Quarterly*, **45**, 574–581.

Liebson, I.A., Tommasello, A. & Bigelow, G.E. (1978). A behavioral treatment of alcoholic methadone patients. *Annals of Internal Medicine*, **89**, 342–344.

Litten, R.Z. & Allen, J.P. (1998). Advances in development of medications for alcoholism treatment. *Psychopharmacology*, **139**, 20–33.

Marlatt, G.A., Kosturn, C.F. & Lang, A.R. (1975). Provocation to anger and opportunity for retaliation as determinants of alcohol consumption in social drinkers. *Journal of Abnormal Psychology*, **84**, 652–659.

McNamee, H.B., Mello, N.K. & Mendelson, J.H. (1968). Experimental analysis of drinking patterns of alcoholics: concurrent psychiatric observations. *American Journal of Psychiatry*, **124**, 1063–1069.

Meisch, R.A. (1975). The function of schedule-induced polydipsia in establishing ethanol as a positive reinforcer. *Pharmacological Reviews*, **27**, 465–473.

Mello, N.K., McNamee, H.B. & Mendelson, J.H. (1968). Drinking patterns of chronic alcoholics: gambling and motivation for alcohol. In J.O. Cole (Ed.), *Clinical Research in Alcoholism* (pp. 83–118). Psychiatric Research Report No 24. Washington, DC: American Psychiatric Association.

Mello, N.K. & Mendelson, J.H. (1965). Operant analysis of drinking patterns of chronic alcoholics. *Nature*, **206**, 43–46.

Mello, N.K. & Mendelson, J.H. (1971). Drinking patterns during work contingent and non-contingent alcohol acquisition. In N. Mello & J. Mendelson, (Eds), *Recent Advances in Studies of Alcoholism* (pp. 647–686). Washington, DC: Government Printing Office.

Mendelson, J.H. (Ed.) (1964). Experimentally induced chronic intoxication and withdrawal in alcoholics. *Quarterly Journal of Studies on Alcoholism*, **2**(Suppl.).

Mendelson, J.H. & Mello, N.K. (1966). Experimental analysis of drinking behavior of chronic alcoholics. *Annals of the New York Academy of Science*, **133**, 828–845.

Miller, P.M. (1975). A behavioral intervention program for chronic public drunkenness offenders. *Archives of General Psychiatry*, **32**, 915–918.

Miller, P.M., Hersen, M., Eisler, R.M. & Hilsman, G. (1974). Effects of social stress on operant drinking of alcoholics and social drinkers. *Behaviour Research and Therapy*, **12**, 67–72.

Nathan, P. & O'Brien, J. (1971). An experimental analysis of the behavior of alcoholics and non-alcoholics during prolonged experimental drinking: a necessary precursor of behavior therapy. *Behavioural Therapy*, **2**, 455–476.

Nathan, P., Titler, N., Lowenstein, L., Solomon, P. & Rossi, A. (1970a). Behavioral analysis of chronic alcoholism. *Archives of General Psychiatry*, **22**, 419–430.

Nathan, P., Zare, N., Ferneau, E. & Lowenstein, L. (1970b). Effects of congener differences in alcoholic beverages on the behavior of alcoholics. *Quarterly Journal of Studies on Alcoholism*, **5**(Suppl.), 87–100.

Piazza, P.V. & Le Moal, M. (1998). The role of stress in drug self-administration. *Trends in Pharmacological Sciences*, **19**, 67–74.

Project MATCH Research Group (1997). Matching alcoholism treatments to client heterogeneity: Project MATCH posttreatment drinking outcomes. *Journal of Studies on Alcohol*, **58**, 7–29.

Rodefer, J.S. & Carroll, M.E. (1996). Progressive ratio and behavioral economic evaluation of the reinforcing efficacy of orally delivered phencyclidine and ethanol in monkeys: effects of feeding conditions. *Psychopharmacology*, **128**, 265–273.

Rodefer, J.S., DeRoche, K.K., Lynch, W.A. & Carroll, M.E. (1996). A behavioral economic analysis of the effects of food deprivation and satiation on self-administration of phencyclidine and ethanol. *Experimental and Clinical Psychopharmacology*, **4**, 61–67.

Roehrs, T., Papineau, K., Rosenthal, L. & Roth, T. (1999). Ethanol as a hypnotic in insomniacs: self-administration and effects on sleep and mood. *Neuropsychopharmacology*, **20**(3), 279–286.

Samson, H.H. (1986). Initiation of ethanol reinforcement using a sucrose-substitution procedure in food- and water-sated rats. *Alcoholism: Clinical and Experimental Research*, **10**, 436–442.

Smith, J.E., Meyers, R.J. & Delaney, H.D. (1998). The community reinforcement approach with homeless alcohol-dependent individuals. *Journal of Consulting and Clinical Psychology*, **66**, 541–548.

Stafford, D., LeSage, M.G. & Glowa, J.R. (1998). Progressive-ratio schedules of drug delivery in the analysis of drug self-administration: a review. *Psychopharmacology*, **139**, 169–184.

Stitzer, M.L., Griffiths, R.R., Bigelow, G.E. & Liebson, I.A. (1981a). Social stimulus factors in drug effects in human subjects. In T. Thompson & C.E. Johanson (Eds), *Behavioral Pharmacology of Human Drug Dependence* (pp. 130–154). NIDA Research Monograph 37, DHHS Publication No. (ADM) 81–1137. Washington, DC: US Government Printing Office.

Stitzer, M.L., Griffiths, R.R., Bigelow, G.E. & Liebson, I.A. (1981b). Human social conversation: effects of ethanol, secobarbital and chlorpromazine. *Pharmacology, Biochemistry and Behaviour*, **14**, 353–360.

Strain, E.C., Bigelow, G.E., Liebson, I.A. & Stitzer, M.L. (1999). Moderate- vs. high-dose methadone in the treatment of opioid dependence: a randomized trial. *Journal of the American Medical Association*, **281**, 1000–1005.

Stromberg, M.F., Volpicelli, J.R. & O'Brien, C.P. (1998). Effects of naltrexone administered repeatedly across 30 or 60 days on ethanol consumption using a limited access procedure in the rat. *Alcoholism: Clinical and Experimental Research*, **22**, 2186–2191.

Swift, R.M. (1999). Drug therapy for alcohol dependence. *New England Journal of Medicine*, **340**, 1482–1490.

Tucker, J.A., Vuchinich, R.E. & Gladsjo, J.A. (1994). Environmental events surrounding natural recovery from alcohol-related problems. *Journal of Studies on Alcohol*, **55**, 401–411.

Tucker, J.A., Vuchinich, R.E. & Pukish, M.A. (1995). Molar environmental events surrounding recovery from alcohol problems in treated and untreated problem drinkers. *Experimental and Clinical Psychopharmacology*, **3**, 195–204.

Vuchinich, R.E. & Simpson, C.A. (1998). Hyperbolic temporal discounting in social drinkers and problem drinkers. *Experimental Clinical Psychopharmacology*, **6**, 292–305.

Vuchinich, R.E. & Tucker, J.A. (1983). Behavioral theories of choice as a framework for studying drinking behavior. *Journal of Abnormal Psychology*, **92**, 408–416.

Vuchinich, R.E. & Tucker, J.A. (1988). Contributions from behavioral theories of choice to an analysis of alcohol abuse. *Journal of Abnormal Psychology*, **97**, 181–195.

Vuchinich, R.E. & Tucker, J.A. (1996). Alcoholic relapse, life events and behavioral theories of choice. *Experimental and Clinical Psychopharmacology*, **4**, 19–28.

Woods, J.H., Ikomi, F.I. & Winger, G. (1971). The reinforcing properties of ethanol. In M.K. Roach, W.M. McIsaac & P.J. Creaven (Eds), *Biological Aspects of Alcoholism* (pp. 371–388). Austin, TX: University of Texas Press.

Chapter 16

Social and Cognitive Learning Processes

R. Lorraine Collins
and
Clara M. Bradizza
Research Institute on Addictions, University at Buffalo,
State University of New York, USA

Synopsis

In this chapter we examine the contributions made by research on social and cognitive learning models of antecedents to alcohol use, alcohol problems, and dependence. Social learning theory is the basis of many of the approaches we will describe, so we begin by outlining principles relevant to alcohol use and dependence. They include alcohol as a positive reinforcer that maintains or increases drinking, and alcohol as a punisher that produces negative consequences that can lessen drinking. Social learning principles also suggest that vicarious learning (learning through observing the behavior of others) provides models of alcohol-related behavior. Models include family members, media portrayals, and peers. Research on direct social influences indicate that individuals drink more when exposed to a sociable "in person" model who drinks heavily and drink less when exposed to a light drinking model. This research has implications for treatment in that light drinkers may serve as models for moderation training.

Social influence processes also are apparent in the development of drinking behavior in adolescents. Parents seem to have more influence over the initiation of alcohol use, while peers seem to influence the adolescent's later frequency and pattern of drinking. When drinking becomes a problem, social influence processes that support abstinence from alcohol have proven to be effective treatment strategies. A broad-based community reinforcement approach, which focuses on functioning in a variety of areas, also has been successful for some individuals in treatment and for concerned others in their social networks.

Cognitive learning antecedents of alcohol use and dependence encompass a wide variety of topics. We review the literatures on expectancies (i.e. beliefs about the effects of alcohol), reasons for drinking, confidence in one's ability to handle alcohol (i.e. self-efficacy), urges to drink, loss of control and impaired control over drinking, as well as drinking restraint (i.e.

International Handbook of Alcohol Dependence and Problems. Edited by N. Heather, T.J. Peters and T. Stockwell.

the preoccupation with setting limits on alcohol consumption). Each of these constructs may be involved in the development of drinking and/or treatment of alcohol problems and dependence.

Expectancies represent the individual's indirect learning experiences with alcohol, while reasons for drinking represent the outcomes they hope to attain from a particular drinking episode. In either case, positive expectancies and reasons for drinking motivate alcohol use in adolescents and adults. Experimental research also suggests that beliefs about alcohol effects are expressed in socially-mediated behavior, such that individuals who believe they have consumed alcohol will behave in a manner consistent with the belief, regardless of whether or not they actually have consumed alcohol. Attempts to decrease positive expectancies or increase negative expectancies have shown short-term success in reducing alcohol intake.

A lack of confidence in one's ability to handle alcohol (i.e. low self-efficacy) can perpetuate maladaptive drinking and contribute to the development of alcohol dependence. Generally, those lower in self-efficacy manifest more severe problems with alcohol. Self-efficacy tends to increase during treatment and higher levels of self-efficacy are related to the maintenance of abstinence following treatment. Even so, relapse is a common occurrence. Constructs related to excessive drinking and/or relapse are the urge to drink, impairment in the individual's sense of control over drinking, and being overly preoccupied with limiting drinking. By examining these cognitive constructs, we hope to better understand alcohol use, alcohol problems and alcohol dependence.

SOCIAL LEARNING CONSTRUCTS AS ANTECEDENTS TO ALCOHOL USE AND DEPENDENCE

In his seminal book outlining social learning theory, Bandura (1969) described the use of alcohol and similar substances as socially mediated activities. Substance use was said to develop via mechanisms such as the positively reinforcing pharmacological properties of the substance, punishment and vicarious learning. Each of these will be described in turn.

The Role of Positive Reinforcement

Alcohol is a powerful positive reinforcer because its immediate pharmacological effects (e.g. disinhibition) are experienced as positive and its delayed effects (e.g. depression of the central nervous system) are negative. The individual drinks alcohol to experience or maintain rewards related to its use. Along with disinhibition, alcohol helps to relieve aversive stimulation (e.g. stress, boredom, frustration). These positive effects can lead to alcohol consumption becoming a primary response, as is the case for dependent drinkers. Once alcohol use is established as the response of choice, the drinker may continue use not only to experience benefits, but also to forestall aversive reactions associated with withdrawal, thereby establishing a secondary mechanism for maintaining use. This notion is consistent with psychological theories that link excessive substance use to attempts to forestall withdrawal (Shipley, 1987).

The positive reinforcement of alcohol's pharmacological properties is enhanced by the fact that drinking often occurs in a social context, thereby linking alcohol use to social reinforcement. Cultural norms and related social contingencies for drinking vary with demographic characteristics (e.g. gender, age) as well as variables such as location (urban vs. rural), religion, and socioeconomic status (including education and occupation). These norms are transmitted through socializing agents (e.g. family, peers, media) who use substances and serve as models of its use.

The Role of Punishment

In learning theory, the nature and effects of punishment are complex. Simply put, the experience of negative consequences (i.e. punishment) following a behavior tends to reduce the occurrence of that behavior. Punishment suppresses a behavior, but does not remove it from the individual's repertoire, so the behavior may return once the punishment is removed. Given the biphasic properties of alcohol, the experience of even short-term negative consequences (e.g. nausea) is delayed and usually does not outweigh the positive cognitive and social benefits of drinking. In the case of alcohol dependence, the experience of the more significant negative consequences (e.g. loss of family, poor health) may be delayed for many years. Typically, punishment alone is not an effective strategy for changing drinking behavior. Therefore, interventions based on social learning principles focus on providing alternatives to drinking (e.g. other ways of coping) rather than using punishment to change drinking behavior.

Vicarious Learning and Modeling

New behaviors and reinforcement contingencies can be learned vicariously (i.e. by observation) or by actually engaging in the behavior. Through vicarious learning, models teach new behaviors, strengthen or weaken the performance of previously learned behaviors or enhance the value of a particular stimulus or behavior. Thus, observing that a behavior is followed by positive reinforcement (or a lack of negative consequences) leads to that behavior being learned/exhibited. Observing that a behavior is followed by punishment or other negative consequence leads to inhibition of that behavior, even if the behavior remains part of the observer's repertoire. Exposure to persons who achieve positive outcomes as a function of substance use (e.g. become more sociable, report less stress) is likely to enhance the observer's substance use. Models also can provide guidance on how to use the substance, the situations in which substance use is appropriate (e.g. drink wine with meals) and the likely outcomes of use.

Bandura's general description of social learning principles in substance use and misuse has served as the basis for other models. For example, Wills & Shiffman's (1985) ideas concerning the role of stress and coping on substance use are consistent with Bandura's ideas concerning substance use as helping to relieve aversive stimulation. Similarly, cognitive-behavioral approaches such as Marlatt & Gordon's (1980, 1985) relapse prevention model suggest that relapse following abstinence is a function of many of the components described in social learning theory. They include the individual's lack of effective responses for coping with aversive stimulation, a low sense of confidence for maintaining abstinence, and beliefs about the reinforcement available from the substance (see Chapter 29, this volume). These and other social and cognitive learning antecedents of alcohol use, alcohol problems and dependence will be discussed in the remainder of this chapter.

MODELING OF ALCOHOL CONSUMPTION

One of the key components of Bandura's (1969) social learning explanation of the development of drinking behavior was the role of vicarious learning, including social influence processes linked to modeling. Modeling of alcohol use by others in the environment was said to provide information on what to drink, how to drink and what consequences to expect. More recently, Bandura (1997) has declared social modeling to be "a powerful shaper and regulator of alcohol consumption" (p. 358). Potential models for alcohol use include family members, media portrayals of drinking, peers, and other persons in the immediate drinking environment. Issues related to the social influence of peer and family drinking practices are mentioned in the "Social Reinforcement" section of this chapter. The literature on media portrayals (particularly advertising) of alcohol consumption will be presented in Chapter 42. In this chapter, we will focus on research that examines the experimental manipulation of the modeling of alcohol consumption, with emphasis on the social influence of "in-person" models.

The basic modeling research paradigm was developed by Caudill & Marlatt (1975). To test the impact of "in-person" models on alcohol intake, they exposed moderate to heavy drinking males to research confederates who modeled either "heavy drinking" or "light drinking". A control group drank with no model present. Individuals exposed to heavy drinking models consumed more alcohol than those in the other two conditions. These results were replicated in subsequent studies of social drinkers, which varied aspects of the modeling situation (setting, type of alcohol), the characteristics of the participants (e.g. age, drinking history) and the characteristics of the model (e.g. gender, nature of the interaction). Modeling effects have also been identified in dependent drinkers (Caudill & Lipscomb, 1980).

A qualitative review of the early research on the modeling of alcohol consumption (Collins & Marlatt, 1981) concluded that there existed "a powerful effect wherein an individual's consumption of alcohol will vary to match that of a drinking partner" (p. 235). A recent meta-analytic review of modeling research reached a similar conclusion based on empirical criteria (Quigley & Collins, 1999). Modeling effects were found for the total amount consumed as well as for aspects of the topography of drinking, including sip rate/frequency and sip volume. Quigley & Collins concluded that "modeling can produce a strong effect on the consumption of alcohol" (p. 95) and outlined several moderators of this effect. Three moderators that are of particular relevance to alcohol problems and dependence are gender, drinking history and the nature of the interaction between the model and the participant.

The results for gender generally suggest that participants will match the drinking behavior of a model of the same gender, particularly among males. The results for dyads that included men and women were mixed; generally, men model men more readily than they model women, while women will model men or women. The findings concerning gender of the model are consistent with research on the development of excessive drinking. For example, some studies have suggested that women who drink to match or provide companionship to their heavy-drinking spouses may develop drinking problems of their own (Wilsnack & Wilsnack, 1990). However, given the possible convergence of men's and women's drinking (Mercer & Khavari, 1990), gender may play a less important role in the future.

The results for drinking history indicate that moderate to heavy social drinkers are responsive to models who drink heavily and will drink to match their level of intake. Thus, drinkers who spend time with heavy drinkers are at risk for maintaining heavy-drinking patterns. Dependent drinkers who return to their drinking buddies following treatment are at increased risk for relapse. Acknowledging the latter observation, Marlatt's (1996) taxonomy of the precipitants of relapse includes a category of "indirect social pressure", which refers to substance use in response to "the observation of another person or group that is using the substance or serves as a model of substance use for the user." (p. S45). Research using Marlatt's relapse taxonomy has identified direct (e.g. being offered a drink) and indirect social pressure as being involved in 12–24% of alcohol relapses, dependent on the clinical sample and the phase of treatment during which data were collected (Lowman, Allen & Stout, 1996). These data support the role of modeling in the initiation, reinforcement and maintenance of maladaptive drinking.

The nature of the interaction between the model and the subject illustrates an intriguing effect of social influence on alcohol intake. Subjects exposed to a "cold", unsociable model will drink more than those exposed to a "warm" sociable model. It is likely that an unsociable model is experienced as aversive and so individuals either drink to cope with the negative situation or leave it. These findings are consistent with the identification of aversive social interactions as high risk situations for excessive drinking and relapse (Lowman et al., 1996; Marlatt & Gordon 1980; 1985). They also highlight the importance of helping dependent drinkers to identify aversive social situations as contributing to relapse, and providing them with the skills to cope with such situations by using strategies other than drinking. These and other findings from modeling research can be incorporated into treatments for alcohol problems.

Implications of Modeling Research for the Treatment of Alcohol Dependence

Light drinkers will not drink to match the drinking level of a heavy-drinking model, suggesting that light drinkers may have a "ceiling" on the amount they consume. However, moderate to heavy social drinkers will try to match the drinking behavior of light-drinking models, and thereby consume less alcohol. In some cases, alcohol intake in response to a light-drinking model is even less than the alcohol intake seen when there is no model present, suggesting a broad range of malleability in the drinking behavior of moderate to heavy social drinkers. For dependent drinkers, this malleability can be utilized in moderation training programs to reduce alcohol intake. In such programs, relationships with and exposure to persons who are light drinkers could provide dependent drinkers with positive models for appropriate drinking behaviors, partners with whom to practice such behaviors, and social contexts within which to experience reinforcement for drinking less. Findings concerning the sociability of the model suggest that a warm relationship will enhance the model's ability to influence the drinker.

SOCIAL REINFORCEMENT AS ANTECEDENTS TO ALCOHOL DEPENDENCE

Social reinforcement describes a process by which social factors are used to influence drinking and related behaviors of individuals. These social influences are thought to play an important role in the development of drinking (normally occurring in adolescence) and also in the modification of drinking and associated dysfunctional behaviors in problem drinkers.

Development of Drinking Behaviors in Adolescents

Adolescents begin drinking in the context of a social environment that consists of both distal and proximal elements (White, Bates & Johnson, 1991). Distal environments include the larger culture in which an adolescent lives. In general, broad cultural influences function to determine the range of acceptable behaviors, that is, which behaviors will generally be reinforced. Proximal environments include more immediate influences, such as peer groups and family. These social influences shape adolescent drinking by providing rewards and punishments through overt instruction, modeling and setting behavioral expectations.

Kandel & Andrews (1987) have proposed a model to explain the processes by which social factors influence or alter alcohol use in adolescents. These processes can be viewed as having a direct, indirect or contingent effect. Direct effects occur when social events have immediate consequences for the adolescent. For example, a parent warns an adolescent that he/she will suffer negative consequences if he/she is found to be using alcohol. Indirect effects occur when an individual influences the development of an adolescent's attitudes, expectancies or behaviors other than the behavior of interest. These indirect influences can then be used to alter the behavior of interest. For example, a peer might positively influence the attitude of the adolescent towards risk-taking, which in turn may result in initiation of drinking by the adolescent. The third route is a contingent effect in which one source of social influence modifies the adolescent's susceptibility to another person's influence. For example, a close parent–child relationship may allow parents to influence the behavior of their child, such that they are able to encourage their child to select a non-drinking peer group.

A number of studies have examined parental and peer influences on the initiation and maintenance of alcohol use during adolescence. Studies examining parental influence have found that parents have the strongest influence over the initiation of adolescent alcohol use (Barnes & Welte, 1986; Kandel & Andrews, 1987; White et al., 1991). The quality of the parent–child bond and the child-rearing practices of parents are strongly related to offspring drinking behavior, as are parental attitudes towards drinking. Pendergrast & Schaefer (1974) found that adolescents who had a positive relationship with their parents were less likely to start drinking and drank less than adolescents who reported poor parent–child relationships. Barnes & Welte (1986) found that adolescents who perceived their parents as having a neutral or mildly approving attitude towards drinking were significantly more likely to drink, as compared with those adolescents who perceived parental disapproval of drinking.

Once drinking has begun, peers are most influential in determining the frequency of adolescent alcohol use (Kandel & Andrews, 1987; White et al., 1991). This peer influence is thought to operate through two mechanisms. The first is assortive pairing, in which adolescents with similar attitudes towards alcohol use are drawn to associate together. The second involves social influence within the peer group, whereby adolescents develop similar attitudes and behaviors through a process of mutual influence. Having friends who drink regularly or get drunk frequently is a strong predictor of drinking in adolescents (Barnes & Welte, 1986).

Overall, it appears that parents have a significant degree of influence over the initiation of adolescent alcohol use; however, once drinking has begun, peers more strongly influence the pattern of alcohol use. Similar social influence factors also assist treatment providers and family members in modifying the drinking-related behaviors of alcohol-dependent individuals.

Social Reinforcement and the Treatment of Alcohol Dependence

Behavioral principles, such as positive and negative reinforcement, can be used in social situations to modify the drinking behavior of treatment-seeking alcoholics. Mallams et al. (1982) assessed the effects of a resocialization program aimed at decreasing alcohol use among alcoholics in treatment and reducing the negative consequences resulting from alcohol use. Patients in the experimental group were strongly encouraged to attend a non-alcoholic social club aimed at promoting abstinence and appropriate social behavior. As compared with a control group, this group drank significantly less alcohol during the 3-month experimental period and demonstrated greater improvement on a measure of negative consequences of alcohol consumption. Alterman et al. (1974) assessed the impact of a social intervention that subtly reinforced either abstinence or continued alcohol use on subsequent drinking behavior of inpatient alcoholics. They found that the group receiving social reinforcement for abstinence drank significantly less than a control group that had not received any instructional set. No differences were found between the control group and the group receiving the social reinforcement for continued drinking. The results of these studies suggest that social reinforcement can be used effectively to decrease drinking in alcoholics undergoing treatment.

The Community Reinforcement Approach

The Community Reinforcement Approach (Hunt & Azrin, 1973; Smith & Meyers, 1995) is a treatment program that utilizes behavioral principles to modify alcohol-related problems. It is based on the idea that problems with alcohol are reflected in functioning in many areas of the individual's life. Thus, the approach involves broad-based interventions that attempt to improve the individual's social, familial, vocational and recreational functioning by replacing maladaptive behaviors (e.g. excessive drinking) with more adaptive ones. This approach requires that the alcohol-dependent individual willingly and actively participates in treatment. For those who resist treatment, principles of social reinforcement can be taught to families and concerned others (CO). These principles can be used by the CO to shape the behavior of the alcohol-dependent individual. Strategies include positive reinforcement and/or the termination of negative consequences during periods of abstinence (Meyers, Dominguez & Smith, 1996; Sisson & Azrin, 1986). Punishment for intoxication and extinction or ignoring of undesirable behaviors are also used to influence drinking behavior. Meyers et al. developed a structured treatment program for individuals concerned with a partner or family member's drinking. This program, known as CRAFT (Community Reinforcement and Family Training), instructs family members and COs in the use of social reinforcement to decrease drinking and other destructive behaviors exhibited by the dependent drinker. Components of this program include: providing COs with basic information about substance abuse, training them in the principles of reinforcement, instructing them in handling abusive situations, and helping the COs to motivate the drinker to enter treatment. Although a large body of research supports the use of behavioral principles in treating alcohol-use disorders, more research is needed to examine the efficacy of programs such as CRAFT.

COGNITIVE LEARNING CONSTRUCTS AS ANTECEDENTS TO ALCOHOL USE AND DEPENDENCE

Alcohol Expectancies: Beliefs about the Effects of Alcohol

Much of the research on alcohol expectancies derives from the work of MacAndrew & Edgerton (1969), who argued that intoxicated behaviors were primarily determined by cultural beliefs or expectations about the effects of alcohol and not its pharmacological effects.

Alcohol expectancies have typically been defined as cognitive representations of an individual's past direct and indirect learning experiences with alcohol (Connors & Maisto, 1988a). More recently, there has been an emphasis on viewing outcome expectancies in the context of long-term memory processes using associative memory models, such that memory functioning mediates the effects of previous alcohol use on later alcohol use (Rather & Goldman, 1994; Stacy, 1997).

Expectancy Set: Laboratory Research and the Balanced Placebo Design

The impact of expecting to consume alcohol on social and non-social behaviors has been investigated in controlled laboratory studies using the balanced placebo design. This experimental methodology allows the investigator to manipulate separately the actual beverage content and the expected beverage content in a 2 × 2 factorial design. In this way, the separate and combined effects of expecting to drink alcohol and the pharmacological effects of alcohol can be examined (Marlatt & Rohsenow, 1980; Rohsenow & Marlatt, 1981). In the context of the balanced placebo design, "expectancy set" is defined as the subject being led to expect that he/she will receive either an alcoholic or a non-alcoholic beverage.

Hull & Bond's (1986) now classic meta-analytic review of the impact of expectancy set within the balanced placebo design found consistent differences between social vs. non-social behaviors. Social behaviors that can be viewed as somewhat more aberrant, such as sexual arousal and alcohol consumption, are strongly influenced by expecting to drink alcohol. Individuals who believe they have consumed alcohol (regardless of whether or not they actually have) are more likely to demonstrate increased motivation to consume more alcohol and greater sexual arousal in response to erotica, as compared with individuals who expected to receive non-alcoholic beverages.

In contrast to the expectancy effects found for social behaviors, the pharmacological properties of alcohol had a significant effect on non-social behaviors such as memory functioning, mood, internal bodily sensations and motor performance. Alcohol consumption was found to disrupt memory and information processing and to enhance self-reported mood by increasing positive mood and decreasing negative mood. Physical sensations such as feelings of warmth, anesthesia, subjective impairment and gastrointestinal functioning all increase following alcohol consumption. In addition, alcohol impairs an individual's ability to perform motor tasks.

Measurement of Alcohol Outcome Expectancies

Researchers have developed a number of questionnaires to assess beliefs about the effects of alcohol, often referred to as outcome expectancies. One of the most frequently used questionnaires, the Alcohol Expectancy Questionnaire (AEQ; Brown et al., 1980) consists of 90 items that assess positive beliefs. They contribute to six factors: global positive transformation, enhanced sexual functioning, social and physical pleasure, increased social assertiveness, tension reduction, and increased power and aggression. The AEQ and its variants have been used in studies with adults and adolescents as well as with clinical and community samples. Research indicates that alcoholics consistently score higher than social drinkers on all scales of the AEQ, except the Increased Power and Aggression scale (Brown, Goldman & Christiansen, 1985; Connors et al., 1986).

The Alcohol Effects Scale (Southwick et al., 1981) has been used primarily with social drinkers. Its innovations include stipulation of the alcohol dose (moderate vs. heavy) and assessment of beliefs concerning negative effects (cognitive/physical impairment) of alcohol. The Alcohol Beliefs Scale (Connors & Maisto, 1988b) assesses dose-related expectancies and the usefulness of alcohol for different purposes. The expectancy portion of the scale can be divided into four factors: control issues, sensations, capability issues and social issues. The usefulness section consists of three factors describing alcohol as useful for feeling better, feeling in charge, and relieving emotional distress. More recently, scales devoted to assessing negative expectancies and/or beliefs about positive and negative effects have been developed (Jones & McMahon, 1998). The Negative Alcohol Expectancy Questionnaire consists of 60 items that describe negative consequences of drinking. The three temporally-linked subscales represent consequences that occur in the same day as drinking, the day after drinking, and the long-term consequences related to months and years of heavy drinking. The proliferation and refinements in expectancy measures is indicative of strong interest in this construct. Even so, expectancy research has been criticized on theoretical and methodological grounds, so more research on this topic is likely (Goldman et al., 1991; Leigh, 1989).

Alcohol Expectancies and Drinking during Adolescence

Studies involving adolescents have examined the relationship between alcohol expectancies and the onset of alcohol use. Research findings indicate that alcohol expectancies are present in children well before they begin to drink, suggesting that observational learning from the broader culture, parents and other adult models contribute to the early acquisition of beliefs about the effects of alcohol. Generally, the self-reported strength of alcohol expectancies is positively related to drinking, such that stronger expectancies are associated with higher reported levels of alcohol use. Several studies have found that alcohol use and problem drinking in adolescents can be predicted both cross-sectionally and longitudinally from expectancies (e.g. Christiansen et al., 1989).

Altering Outcome Expectancies to Prevent Alcohol Problems and Treat Alcohol Dependence

The decision to drink is at least partly based on the expectation that alcohol will serve certain functions. Most prevention and cognitive-behavioral treatment programs for adolescents devote a portion of their curriculum to restructuring expectancies. Connors & Maisto (1988a) have proposed several strategies aimed at altering positive expectancies as means of changing alcohol use. They include self-monitoring to determine the congruence of expectancies and the actual consequences of drinking, educational interventions that present ways in which expectancies mediate environmental events and alcohol use, and cognitive restructuring to modify specific thoughts and beliefs that mediate the relationship between emotional responses and alcohol misuse.

Jones & McMahon (1998) have suggested that expectancy-based interventions should target reductions in positive expectancies (to reduce drinking) while enhancing negative expectancies (to increase regulation of drinking). The former would help to prevent alcohol problems and the latter would enhance outcomes for alcohol treatment. Among clinical samples, there is indirect evidence that lower levels of positive expectancies are related to better treatment outcomes (e.g. Connors, Tarbox & Faillace, 1993). Direct evidence of this relationship was provided by Darkes & Goldman (1993, 1998) when they tested whether changing expectancies would influence alcohol use. They assigned moderate to heavy drinking male college students to one of three conditions: an "expectancy challenge" condition, specifically designed to decrease positive expectancies; a "traditional" information program similar to college prevention programs; and an "assessment-only" control condition. The expectancy challenge consisted of two sessions in which students consumed either an alcohol or placebo beverage in a group situation and then were asked to identify which beverage each individual (themselves included) had consumed. The third session involved a didactic presentation emphasizing the role of expectancies in producing behavioral effects that might be attributed to the pharmacological properties of alcohol. The expectancy challenge condition was the only one effective in reducing social/sexual expectancies for alcohol. More importantly, subjects in this condition reduced their alcohol intake significantly more than the other two groups, with this effect being stronger for heavier drinkers. These results suggests that expectancy challenge may be an effective secondary prevention strategy.

Although there are no studies using expectancy challenge in alcohol treatment, Marlatt (1985) has described case examples of using a "programmed relapse" to disconfirm positive expectancies held by problem drinkers. Beliefs concerning a specific effect of alcohol (e.g. relaxation) are challenged in the context of consuming a placebo beverage that the individual believes contains alcohol. Alternatively, Jones & McMahon (1998) have described a program of research focused on enhancing negative expectancies to increase motivation for treatment. They found that higher levels of negative expectancies were related to better treatment outcomes, including maintenance of abstinence and more time to the first drink. Positive expectancies did not predict these treatment outcomes. Thus, positive and negative expectancies seem to play important and complementary roles in the development and treatment of problem drinking.

Reasons for Drinking

Cox & Klinger (1988) have proposed a motivational model of alcohol use in which the decision to drink is affected by the immediate environmental context and current positive and negative incentives for drinking vs. participating in alternative activities. Their model suggests that motives provide the final common pathway to alcohol use and misuse. They propose four classes of motives: enhancement, conformity, social and coping. Enhancement motives involve drinking to heighten positive mood and are likely to be internally generated. Conformity motives are externally generated and involve drinking to avoid social rejection. Social motives involve drinking to obtain positive social rewards, are externally generated and are considered to be specific to social contexts. Coping motives involve drinking to reduce negative emotions, which are more likely to be controlled by internal rather than social factors.

Social and coping motives have received the most attention in the literature. Drinking for social motives is generally considered to be a normative, non-pathological and socially appropriate, while drinking for coping reasons is considered pathological and inappropriate. There is evidence that at least partially supports this view. A number of studies have found that coping reasons for drinking are significant predictors of heavy or excessive drinking patterns among adult and adolescent samples drawn from treatment and from the community (e.g. Cooper et al., 1995; Windle & Windle, 1996). In contrast, only two studies with adolescent samples found that social or enhancement reasons were more strongly related to heavy or problematic alcohol use (Cronin, 1997; Ratliff & Burkhart, 1984). Cooper et al. (1995) have suggested that individuals who drink to cope are less able to exercise control over their consumption, as compared with individuals who drink for enhancement reasons. They may become more psychologically dependent on alcohol to cope with negative emotions and, as a result, are more likely to drink in situations that lead to problems (e.g. on the job, before driving) and to continue to drink despite the occurrence of these problems. This explanation is consistent with studies that have identified negative affect as a high-risk situation for relapse (Cannon et al., 1992; Marlatt & Gordon, 1985). The role of drinking motives in relapse among alcohol-dependent samples warrants further attention.

Relationship between Expectancies and Reasons for Drinking

Although alcohol expectancies and reasons for drinking are theoretically related constructs, they differ in important ways. Expectancies were defined earlier as cognitive representations of an individual's past direct and indirect learning experiences with alcohol. In contrast, reasons for drinking are an individual's specific motivations for using alcohol, that is, the outcomes they hope to attain by drinking. When alcohol expectancies and their corresponding motives are assessed together, they are found to be moderately positively correlated. There is evidence to suggest that the formation of expectancies precedes drinking motives among social drinkers. The presence of an expectancy is almost always necessary before a motive will be endorsed; however, the reverse is not usually true (Leigh, 1990). In addition, there is evidence that drinking motives more directly predict alcohol use. When the relationship between expectancies, motives and alcohol consumption is examined, drinking motives account for a greater proportion of the variance in predicting drinking outcomes, as compared with expectancies (Cronin, 1997). These findings suggest that motives are more proximal or direct determinants of alcohol use than are expectancies.

SELF-EFFICACY, ALCOHOL USE, AND ALCOHOL DEPENDENCE

Bandura (1977) described self-efficacy as the individual's confidence in his/her ability to handle a stressful situation. The individual's strength of self-efficacy in specific situations determines the likelihood that he/she will perform adaptive behaviors in those situations. Self-efficacy theory suggests mechanisms for the development of alcohol use and dependence. For the beginning drinker, low efficacy expectations for resisting social pressure to try alcohol can lead to the initiation of alcohol use. For the social drinker, the failure of initial attempts to control specific episodes of excessive drinking could undermine the individual's confidence in his/her ability to "handle" alcohol, thus perpetuating maladaptive drinking and contributing to the development of alcohol dependence. For the problem drinker, low self-efficacy for handling a range of high-risk situations can lead to relapse following treatment. Thus, the individual's sense of efficacy is important in all phases of drinking.

   Much of the research on self-efficacy and alcohol use has focused on high-risk situations related to the cessation of drinking and relapse following treatment (Annis & Davis, 1988; Marlatt & Gordon, 1980, 1985). Marlatt & Gordon (1980) suggested that decreased self-efficacy for coping with high-risk situations combined with positive expectations of the effects of the substance could precipitate relapse. Annis and colleagues developed a therapeutic approach and related measures based on the notion that procedures that enhance self-efficacy will lead to better treatment outcomes (Annis, 1990; Annis & Davis, 1988). This is based on the idea that the strength of the individual's expectations of personal efficacy will determine the nature, course, and duration of efforts to cope with adverse situations. In the case of the dependent drinker who has completed treatment, drinking is an adverse situation fraught with risk. In Annis's program, a hierarchy of personally-relevant high-risk situations is developed. Individuals are gradually exposed, via performance-based homework assignments, to situations that are progressively riskier. Consistent with Bandura's tenets, the aim is to expose the individual to situations that enhance efficacy by being challenging but not requiring extraordinary effort. The individual must not only successfully cope with the situation, but also should attribute the success of coping to his/her own efforts, rather than to external sources. With repeated experiences of mastery, the individual comes to see him/herself as able to cope with drinking. This enhanced sense of self-efficacy is then available when the individual is faced with the next high-risk situation for drinking.

Measurement of Self-efficacy for Drinking

Two assessment instruments, the Situational Confidence Questionnaire and the Inventory of Drinking Situations, are central to Annis' individualized approach to conceptualizing and implementing self-efficacy-based treatment. The Situational Confidence Questionnaire (SCQ; Annis & Davis, 1988) is designed to assess the individual's confidence in his/her ability to cope with alcohol-related situations. Individuals imagine situations (e.g. "If I had an argument with a friend") and rate their confidence in their ability to resist the urge to drink in that situation. The SCQ has been validated for monitoring changes in self-efficacy during treatment. A more generic Drug Taking Confidence Questionnaire for assessing self-efficacy in individuals who use alcohol, cocaine, heroin, cannabis and other drugs also has been developed and validated (Sklar, Annis & Turner, 1997).

The Inventory of Drinking Situations (IDS) consists of items drawn from the eight categories of high-risk drinking situations (e.g. negative emotions, urges/temptations) outlined by Marlatt & Gordon (1980, 1985). Responses to the IDS are used to develop a profile, which serves as the basis for the hierarchy of high-risk situations that is used in treatment. An Inventory of Drug Taking Situations has also been developed (Sobell, Toneatto & Sobell, 1994). Other self-efficacy measures have addressed some of the limitations of the measures developed by Annis and colleagues. The Alcohol Abstinence Self-Efficacy Scale (AASS) measures efficacy for maintaining abstinence (DiClemente et al., 1994). Individuals rate their confidence that they will not drink in situations representing each of four factors (e.g. negative affect, withdrawal and urges) that exemplify precipitants of relapse. The AASS's focus on abstinence contrasts with the SCQ's focus on avoiding heavy drinking.

Self-efficacy and Treatment of Alcohol Dependence

Self-efficacy tends to increase during treatment for alcohol dependence. Level of self-efficacy tends to be related to treatment outcomes, such as length of stay in treatment, abstinence and relapse. Generally, those lower in self-efficacy are likely to manifest more severe symptoms of alcohol dependence and to relapse during follow-ups (Burling et al., 1989; Rychtarik et al., 1992). However, the nature of the relationship between self-efficacy and treatment outcomes are complex. For example, Burling et al. (1989) found that low self-efficacy at intake led to longer stays in inpatient treatment, which produced better conditions at discharge. Patients who showed the largest gains in self-efficacy while in treatment were better able to maintain abstinence following treatment. Rychtarik et al. (1992) found that self-efficacy at the start (rather than at the end) of treatment was the best predictor of relapse following treatment. This finding is consistent with Burling et al.'s report that high self-efficacy at the end of treatment was not predictive of relapse during follow-up. Most recently, self-efficacy for maintaining abstinence from alcohol was found to be one of the strongest predictors of long-term (3 year) outcomes. The study involved a sample of 952 alcoholics participating in different forms of outpatient treatment (Project MATCH Research Group, 1998). Even with these promising results, some have suggested that because alcohol dependence and relapse are multiply determined, concepts such as self-efficacy and related measures such as the SCQ cannot fully capture the nature of the high-risk situations drinkers face, their motivation during treatment, and their ability to maintain treatment gains (Langenbucher et al., 1996). Whatever the case, self-efficacy has contributed to our understanding of the development and treatment of alcohol dependence. Future research will refine that understanding and related methodological and psychometric issues.

URGES TO DRINK

Traditionally, terms such as "urge", "craving" and "desire" have been used interchangeably in research and clinical settings, resulting in a lack of precise meanings and difficulties in interpreting the outcome of studies on substance abuse. Kozlowski & Wilkinson (1987) suggested differentiating the meaning of the term "cravings" as a strong desire and reserving the terms "urges" and "desires" to refer to milder forms of longing for a substance. Despite researchers' efforts to clarify the meanings of these terms, there is some evidence to suggest that individuals who misuse substances do not differentiate among the terms in the same way as researchers (Shiffman, 1987). We will use the more generic term "urges" to refer to the entire range of desire for alcohol.

Measurement of Urges to Drink

Urges have most often been assessed in research studies by one or two items. This has allowed for rapid assessment of urges (as a proxy for alcohol use), most commonly in alcohol cue reactivity studies (e.g. Cooney et al., 1984). However, Tiffany (1992) has criticized the use of these scales, stating that their reliability is often unknown and that so few items may not adequately identify the range of terms that alcoholics use to describe their own urge experiences. In an effort to improve the measurement of urges, several questionnaires have been developed and evaluated.

Among those scales that have proven psychometrically sound are the Alcohol Use Questionnaire (AUQ; Bohn, Krahn & Staehler, 1995) and the Desires for Alcohol Questionnaire (DAQ). The AUQ is a brief, unidimensional scale that consists of eight items that assess the desire to drink, positive expectancies and the inability to avoid drinking. It was developed using an alcohol-dependent sample. The DAQ consists of 36 items that yield three factors: strong intentions and desires to use alcohol; negative and positive reinforcement; and mild desires and intentions to use alcohol. It discriminates between excessive and social drinkers (Love, James & Willner, 1998). Despite some promising initial research, more work is needed on the development and refinement of measures, particularly with alcohol-dependent samples.

Urges and the Prediction of Drinking Behavior

Social learning theory suggests that urges should predict drinking behavior in social and problem drinkers. The few studies that have examined the relationship between urges and alcohol use suggest that urges may be better predictors of drinking in alcohol-dependent samples than among social drinkers. Johnson & Fromme (1994) found no significant relationship between college drinkers' craving and both latency to first sip and total time spent drinking a placebo. In contrast, several studies that have examined urges and post-treatment alcohol use in alcoholics have noted significant relationships. For example, Monti et al. (1990) found that greater urges to drink following alcohol-relevant role plays were positively correlated with number of drinks per drinking day and negatively correlated with number of days abstinent during the 6-month follow-up. Similarly, alcoholics' urges to drink during alcohol-relevant and general social situation role plays were positively related to frequency of heavy drinking days at 6–24-month follow-ups (Kadden et al., 1992).

Despite some promising research on the relationship between urges and drinking, the role of urges in the maintenance of problem drinking remains unclear. One new approach that may shed light on both theoretical and practical issues in this area are neuroimaging studies that examine the relationship of subjective aspects of craving to brain activation (Maas et al., 1998).

Drinking Urges and Models of Relapse

Drinking urges are often described as a motivational component in the relapse process. In the most prominent social-learning model of relapse, Marlatt & Gordon (1980, 1985) proposed that high-risk situations can lead to a resumption of alcohol use in abstinent individuals if they lack the resources to cope effectively with the situations. Although most high-risk situations in this model involve emotional or social triggers, urges and cravings also can function as triggers for alcohol use. Not all models view urges as necessary to explain relapse. Tiffany's (1990) cognitive model proposes that urges to use a substance and relapse are parallel processes that can operate with little mutual influence. He suggests that for addicted individuals, substance use is a well-practiced behavior that can occur "automatically" without much conscious thought, whereas urges are "controlled" processes that require effortful cognitive processing and are more available to conscious awareness. Tiffany's model implies that urges may not be necessary for relapse and that a return to alcohol use can occur in the absence of any urges.

LOSS OF CONTROL DRINKING

The disease model of alcoholism has had an enduring influence on the conceptualization and treatment of alcohol dependence. The model, which was fully articulated by Jellinek (1960), suggested that for certain types of dependent drinkers, characterized as "gamma alcoholics", any exposure to alcohol would lead to an inability to control subsequent alcohol intake. The notion of "loss of control" within a drinking episode served as the basis for recommending abstinence as the only responsible treatment goal for persons with alcohol dependence. Challenges to this notion began with an experiment by Merry (1966), who tested the effects of consuming one dose of alcohol on alcoholics in treatment. His sample of nine alcoholics did not show differences in either craving or physical dependence after they consumed either alcohol or water disguised as an orange-flavored "vitamin mixture". Merry interpreted his results as suggesting that psychological and environmental factors may be more important than alcohol in initiating "loss of control" drinking. Subsequent research has used more elaborate designs to test the effects of alcohol's pharmacological properties vs. cognitive/psychological factors in craving and loss of control among alcoholics. These studies showed that exposure to the pharmacological properties of alcohol in a single dose did not produce loss of control. However, cognitive factors, such as being told that one was consuming alcohol, led to greater alcohol intake regardless of whether the individual drank an alcoholic or a placebo beverage. This research challenged notions about one drink of alcohol serving as an automatic trigger for loss of control drinking. It also contributed to the birth of a new area of experimental research, in which the cognitive/expectancy effects of alcohol were contrasted with pharmacological effects of alcohol in the balanced placebo design, described earlier.

Challenges to the meaningfulness of disease model notions concerning "loss of control" do not mean that alcohol-dependent individuals do not have problems regulating their alcohol intake. Descriptions of "types" of alcoholics and diagnostic criteria for alcohol dependence often incorporate constructs related to loss of control and the inability to abstain from drinking (Penick et al., 1999). Kahler, Epstein & McCrady (1995) found overlap in the conceptualization and measurement of "loss of control" and "inability to abstain" from drinking. Their research provided support for "a single dimension of impaired control" (p. 1035), impaired control being defined as "difficulties in controlling when and how much to drink." (p. 1035). More recent theorizing and research has focused on impaired control as contributing to the development of alcohol dependence and/or relapse following treatment.

Measurement of Impaired Control

Heather (1995) defined impaired control as "a breakdown of an intention to limit or refrain from drinking." (p. 1046) and described it as occurring relatively early in the development of alcohol dependence. He and his colleagues developed and tested a measure of impaired control in which control is conceptualized as a continuous variable. The Impaired Control Scale (ICS; Heather et al., 1993) consists of three parts designed to assess intentions/attempts to control drinking, frequency of episodes of impaired control during the past 6 months, and belief in ability to exert control over drinking. Results suggest that the scale is reliable and valid. Aspects of impaired control have been related to alcohol dependence, alcohol problems and treatment outcomes, such that individuals with higher ICS scores were less successful in abstinence-orientated treatment (Heather, Booth & Luce, 1998).

DRINKING RESTRAINT AS ANTECEDENT TO ALCOHOL DEPENDENCE

Drinking restraint has been defined as one's preoccupation with controlling alcohol intake. Results from studies of social drinkers have suggested that drinking restraint serves as a risk factor for excessive drinking and have supported the link between drinking restraint, binge drinking and alcohol problems (Bensley, 1991; Collins, 1993). Collins and colleagues proposed that some individuals become preoccupied with controlling their alcohol consumption and therefore set limits on their intake. They modified Marlatt & Gordon's (1980, 1985) abstinence violation effect to suggest that restrained drinkers experienced a limit violation effect (LVE; Collins & Lapp, 1991). In the LVE, the failure to control/regulate consumption leads to negative affective states (e.g. depression, guilt) that may include negative, self-blaming attributions (e.g. "I am a bad person because I can't control my drinking"). The individual then continues to drink to repair these negative states, thereby drinking to excess and further exacerbating his/her concern about the need to regulate alcohol intake.

Over time, a cycle that includes limit setting, failures to regulate intake, and negative affective and attributional reactions results in episodes of excessive drinking that contribute to the development of problem drinking.

Measurement of Drinking Restraint

A psychometrically sound measure of the components of drinking restraint, the Temptation and Restraint Inventory (TRI), was developed using different samples of social drinkers (Collins & Lapp, 1992) and confirmed with a sample of inpatient alcoholics (Connors et al., 1998). The TRI represents drinking restraint as encompassing five factors: Govern (perceived difficulty controlling alcohol intake); Restrict (attempts to change/cut down on drinking); Emotion (drinking related to negative affect); Concern about Drinking (plans to reduce drinking, worry about controlling drinking); and Cognitive Preoccupation (thoughts about drinking). These five factors form two higher-order factors that conform to the bifactorial nature of the restraint construct: Cognitive and Emotional Preoccupation (the temptation to drink) and Cognitive and Behavioral Control (control/restriction of alcohol intake).

A second measure of restrained drinking, the Drinking Restraint Scale (DRS; Curry, Southwick & Steele, 1987) was developed on a sample of college students and has not been tested with clinical samples. The seven items are summed to provide a single measure of drinking restraint, which has been found to be related to heavier drinking, more cyclical and extreme patterns of drinking, and external responsiveness to alcohol-related cues

Drinking Restraint and Treatment of Alcohol Dependence

Treatment strategies derived from models of drinking restraint have not been developed and tested with clinical samples. However, Collins' model suggests that successful treatment for problem drinkers could include a focus on moderation goals, particularly for those who are experiencing problems with alcohol but who do not meet diagnostic criteria for dependence. Generally, such treatment should focus on helping restrained drinkers to maintain a balance between the two competing inclinations of being tempted to drink and regulating alcohol intake.

To date, two moderation training programs have included restraint as a predictor of treatment outcome. Walitzer & Connors (1994) used a multi-component behavioral intervention to help 133 heavy-drinking women lessen their alcohol intake. Results indicated that (pre- to post-treatment) changes on four of the five TRI subscales accounted for post-treatment changes in the participants' alcohol use (e.g. days drunk, quantity and frequency). Specifically, increases in negative affect (Emotion), perceived difficulty (Govern), and drinking-related thoughts (Cognitive Preoccupation) predicted heavier drinking. Increases in behavioral attempts to reduce drinking (Restrict) were associated with lower levels of alcohol use. Changes in restraint did not predict alcohol use at a 6 month follow-up. A more recent study involved 37 heavy drinkers randomly assigned to either an 8 week outpatient behavioral drinking moderation program or a waiting-list control (Collins et al., 1998). Results indicated that during the program, participants in the moderation training program showed significantly greater reductions in the average number of drinks consumed per week and in the average number of drinks consumed during each drinking episode. Drinking restraint was not a significant predictor of excessive drinking during the program, but this may be due to the small sample.

Research on drinking restraint is in its relative infancy and more work, particularly related to treatment, needs to be done. The same can be said for many of the approaches described in this chapter. Alcohol use and dependence are complex phenomena that encompass a wide variety of components. Social and cognitive learning processes offer useful frameworks for conceptualizing the nature of the alcohol dependence, measuring key components and developing strategies for prevention and treatment. However, more research is needed to evaluate the contributions that these processes make to our understanding of alcohol use and related issues.

KEY WORKS AND SUGGESTIONS FOR FURTHER READING

Bandura, A. (1997). *Self-efficacy: The Exercise of Control*. New York: W.H. Freeman.

Bandura's most recent book reviews research and theorizing on self-efficacy, including research on alcohol abuse.

Goldman, M.S., Del Boca, F.K. & Darkes, J. (1999). Alcohol expectancy theory. In K.E. Leonard & H.T. Blane (Eds), *Psychological Theories of Drinking and Alcoholism*, 2nd edn. New York: Guilford.

Provides an overview of research on alcohol expectancies, with emphasis on the role of memory networks in expectancies and drinking behavior.

Maisto, S.A., Carey, K.B. & Bradizza, C.M. (1999). Social learning theory. In K.E. Leonard & H.T. Blane (Eds), *Psychological Theories of Drinking and Alcoholism*, 2nd edn. New York: Guilford.

An overview of social learning theory, including current research, as it relates to alcohol use and alcohol dependence. Includes some discussion of alcohol expectancies.

Marlatt, G.A. & Gordon, J.R. (Eds) (1985). *Relapse Prevention*. New York: Guilford.

Although published in the mid-1980s, this is still the best source of information about Marlatt and Gordon's cognitive-behavioral model of relapse. This model has contributed to many areas of research on alcohol use, including self-efficacy and drinking restraint.

Tiffany, S.T. (1997). New perspectives on the measurement, manipulation and meaning of drug craving. *Human Psychopharmacology*, **12**, S103–S113.

A review of the current state-of-the-art in research on craving.

REFERENCES

Alterman, A.I., Gottheil, E., Skoloda, T.E. & Grasberger, J.C. (1974). Social modification of drinking by alcoholics. *Quarterly Journal of Studies on Alcohol*, **35**, 917–924.

Annis, H.M. (1990). Relapse to substance abuse: empirical findings within a cognitive-social learning approach. *Journal of Psychoactive Drugs*, **22**, 117–124.

Annis, H.M. & Davis, C.S. (1988). Assessment of expectancies. In D.M. Donovan & G.A. Marlatt (Eds), *Assessment of Addictive Behaviors* (pp. 84–111). New York: Guilford.

Bandura, A. (1969). *Principles of Behavior Modification*. New York: Holt, Rinehart & Winston.

Bandura, A. (1977). Self-efficacy: toward a unifying theory of behavior change. *Psychological Review*, **84**, 191–215.

Bandura, A. (1997). *Self-efficacy: The Exercise of Control*. New York: W.H. Freeman.

Barnes, G.M. & Welte, J.W. (1986). Patterns and predictors of alcohol use among 7–12th-grade students in New York State. *Journal of Studies on Alcohol*, **47**, 53–62.

Bensley, L.S. (1991).   Construct validity evidence for the interpretation for drinking restraint as a response conflict. *Addictive Behaviors*, **16**, 139–150.

Bohn, M.J., Krahn, D.D. & Staehler, B.A. (1995).   Development and initial validation of a measure of drinking urges in abstinent alcoholics. *Alcoholism: Clinical and Experimental Research*, **19**, 600–606.

Brown, S.A., Goldman, M.S. & Christiansen, B.A. (1985).   Do alcohol expectancies mediate drinking patterns of adults? *Journal of Consulting and Clinical Psychology*, **53**, 512–519.

Brown, S.A., Goldman, M.S., Inn, A. & Anderson, L.R. (1980).   Expectations of reinforcement from alcohol: their domain and relation to drinking patterns. *Journal of Consulting and Clinical Psychology*, **48**, 419–426.

Burling, T.A., Reilly, P.M., Moltzen, J.O. & Ziff, D.C. (1989).   Self-efficacy and relapse among inpatient drug and alcohol abusers: a predictor of outcome. *Journal of Studies on Alcohol*, **50**, 354–360.

Cannon, D.S., Rubin, A., Keefe, C.K., Black, J.L., Leeka, J.K. & Phillips, L.A. (1992).   Affective correlates of alcohol and cocaine use. *Addictive Behaviors*, **17**, 517–524.

Caudill, B.D. & Lipscomb, T.R. (1980).   Modeling influences on alcoholics' rates of alcohol consumption. *Journal of Applied Behavior Analysis*, **13**, 355–365.

Caudill, B.D. & Marlatt, G.A. (1975).   Modeling influences in social drinking: an experimental analogue. *Journal of Consulting and Clinical Psychology*, **43**, 405–415.

Christiansen, B.A., Smith, G.T., Roehling, P.V. & Goldman, M.S. (1989).   Using alcohol expectancies to predict adolescent drinking behavior after one year. *Journal of Consulting and Clinical Psychology*, **57**, 93–99.

Collins, R.L. (1993).   Drinking restraint and risk for alcohol abuse. *Experimental and Clinical Psychopharmacology*, **1**, 44–54.

Collins, R.L. & Lapp, W.M. (1991).   Restraint and attributions: evidence of the abstinence violation effect in alcohol consumption. *Cognitive Therapy and Research*, **15**, 69–84.

Collins, R.L. & Lapp, W.M. (1992).   The temptation and restraint inventory for measuring drinking restraint. *British Journal of Addiction*, **87**, 625–633.

Collins, R.L. & Marlatt, G.A. (1981).   Social modeling as a determinant of drinking behavior: implications for prevention and treatment. *Addictive Behaviors*, **6**, 233–239.

Collins, R.L., Morsheimer, E.T., Shiffman, S., Paty, J.A., Gnys, M. & Papandonatos, G.D. (1998).   Ecological momentary assessment in a behavioral drinking moderation training program. *Experimental and Clinical Psychopharmacology*, **6**, 306–315.

Connors, G.J., Collins, R.L., Dermen, K.H. & Koutsky, J.R. (1998).   Substance use restraint: an extension of the construct to a clinical population. *Cognitive Therapy and Research*, **22**, 75–87.

Connors, G.J. & Maisto, S.A. (1988a).   The alcohol expectancy construct: overview and clinical applications. *Cognitive Therapy and Research*, **12**, 487–504.

Connors, G.J. & Maisto, S.A. (1988b).   The Alcohol Beliefs Scale. In M. Hersen & A.S. Bellack (Eds), *Dictionary of Behavioral Assessment Techniques* (pp. 24–26). New York: Pergamon.

Connors, G.J., O'Farrell, T.J., Cutter, H.S.G. & Thompson, D.L. (1986).   Alcohol expectancies among alcoholics, problem drinkers, and nonproblem drinkers. *Alcoholism: Clinical and Experimental Research*, **10**, 667–671.

Connors, G.J., Tarbox, A.R. & Faillace, L.A. (1993).   Changes in alcohol expectancies and drinking behavior among treated problem drinkers. *Journal of Studies on Alcohol*, **53**, 676–683.

Cooney, N.L., Baker, L.H., Pomerleau, O.F. & Josephy, B. (1984).   Salivation to drinking cues in alcohol abusers: toward the validation of a physiological measure of craving. *Addictive Behaviors*, **9**, 91–94.

Cooper, M.L., Frone, M.R., Russell, M. & Mudar, P. (1995).   Drinking to regulate positive and negative emotions: a motivational model of alcohol use. *Journal of Personality and Social Psychology*, **69**, 990–1005.

Cox, W.M. & Klinger, E. (1988).   A motivational model of alcohol use. *Journal of Abnormal Psychology*, **97**, 168–180.

Cronin, C. (1997).   Reasons for drinking versus outcome expectancies in the prediction of college student drinking. *Substance Use & Misuse*, **32**, 1287–1311.

Curry, S., Southwick, L. & Steele, C. (1987).   Restrained drinking: risk factor for problems with alcohol? *Addictive Behaviors*, **12**, 73–77.

Darkes, J. & Goldman, M.S. (1993). Expectancy challenge and drinking reduction: experimental evidence for a meditational process. *Journal of Consulting and Clinical Psychology*, **61**, 344–353.

Darkes, J. & Goldman, M.S. (1998). Expectancy challenge and drinking reduction: process and structure in the alcohol expectancy network. *Experimental and Clinical Psychopharmacology*, **6**, 64–76.

DiClemente, C.C., Carbonari, J.P., Montgomery, R.P.G. & Hughes, S.O. (1994). The alcohol abstinence self-efficacy scale. *Journal of Studies on Alcohol*, **55**, 141–148.

Goldman, M.S., Brown, S.A., Christiansen, B.A. & Smith, G.T. (1991). Alcoholism and memory: broadening the scope of alcohol-expectancy research. *Psychological Bulletin*, **110**, 137–146.

Heather, N. (1995). Impaired control: a concept of fundamental significance. [Commentary on Kahler et al.'s article "Loss of control and inability to abstain: the measurement of and the relationship between two constructs in male alcoholics"]. *Addiction*, **90**, 1046–1047.

Heather, N., Booth, P. & Luce, A. (1998). Impaired control scale: cross-validation and relationships with treatment outcome. *Addiction*, **93**, 765–775.

Heather, N., Tebbutt, J.S., Mattick, R.P. & Zamir, R. (1993). Development of a scale for measuring impaired control over alcohol consumption: a preliminary report. *Journal of Studies on Alcohol*, **54**, 700–709.

Hull, J.G. & Bond, C.F. (1986). Social and behavioral consequences of alcohol consumption and expectancy: a meta-analysis. *Psychological Bulletin*, **99**(3), 347–360.

Hunt, G.M. & Azrin, N.H. (1973). A community-reinforcement approach to alcoholism. *Behavior Research and Therapy*, **11**, 91–104.

Jellinek, E.M. (1960). *The Disease Concept of Alcoholism*. New Brunswick, NJ: Hillhouse.

Johnson, C.N. & Fromme, K. (1994). An experimental test of affect, subjective craving, and alcohol outcome expectancies as motivators of young adult drinking. *Addictive Behaviors*, **19**, 631–641.

Jones, B.T. & McMahon, J. (1998). Alcohol motivations as outcome expectancies. In W.R. Miller & N. Heather (Eds), *Treating Addictive Behaviors*, 2nd edn. (pp. 75–91). New York: Plenum.

Kadden, R.M., Litt, M.D., Cooney, N.L. & Busher, D.A. (1992). Relationship between role-play measures of coping skills and alcoholism treatment outcome. *Addictive Behaviors*, **17**, 425–437.

Kahler, C.W., Epstein, E.E. & McCrady, B.S. (1995). Loss of control and inability to abstain: the measurement of and the relationship between two constructs in male alcoholics. *Addiction*, **90**, 1025–1036.

Kandel, D.B. & Andrews, K. (1987). Processes of adolescent socialization by parents and peers. *International Journal of the Addictions*, **22**, 319–342.

Kozlowski, L.T. & Wilkinson, D.A. (1987). Use and misuse of the concept of craving by alcohol, tobacco, and drug researchers. *British Journal on Addiction*, **82**, 31–36.

Langenbucher, J., Sulesund, D., Chung, T. & Morganstern, J. (1996). Illness severity and self-efficacy as course predictors on DSM-IV alcohol dependence in a multisite clinical sample. *Addictive Behaviors*, **21**, 543–553.

Leigh, B.C. (1989). In search of the seven dwarves: issues of measurement and meaning in alcohol expectancy research. *Psychological Bulletin*, **105**, 361–373.

Leigh, B.C. (1990). Alcohol expectancies and reasons for drinking: comments from a study of sexuality. *Psychology of Addictive Behavior*, **4**, 91–96.

Love, A., James, D. & Willner, P. (1998). A comparison of two alcohol craving questionnaires. *Addiction*, **93**, 1091–1102.

Lowman, C., Allen, J., Stout, R.L. & The Relapse Research Group (1996). Replication and extension of Marlatt's taxonomy of relapse precipitants: overview of procedures and results. *Addiction*, **91**, S51–S71.

Maas, L.C., Lukas, S.E., Kaufman, M.J., Weiss, R.D., Daniels, S.L., Rogers, V.W., Kukes, T.J. & Renshaw, P.F. (1998). Functional magnetic resonance imaging of human brain activation during cue-induced cocaine craving. *American Journal of Psychiatry*, **155**, 124–126.

MacAndrew, C. & Edgerton, R.B. (1969). Drunkenness as time out: an alternative solution on the problem of drunken changes-for-the-worse. In C. MacAndrew & R.B. Edgerton (Eds), *Drunken Comportment*, (pp. 83–99). New York: Aldine.

Mallams, J.H., Godley, M.D., Hall, G.M. & Meyers, R.J. (1982). A social-systems approach to resocializing alcoholics in the community. *Journal of Studies on Alcohol*, **43**, 1115–1123.

Marlatt, G.A. (1985). Cognitive assessment and intervention procedures for relapse prevention. In G.A. Marlatt & J.R. Gordon (Eds), *Relapse Prevention* (pp. 201–279). New York: Guilford.

Marlatt, G.A. (1996). Taxonomy of high-risk situations for alcohol relapse: evolution and develop-
  ment of a cognitive-behavioral model. *Addiction*, **91**, S37–S49.
Marlatt, G.A. & Gordon, J.R. (1980). Determinants of relapse: implications for the maintenance of
  behavior change. In P.O. Davidson & S.M. Davidson (Eds), *Behavioral Medicine: Changing Health
  Lifestyles* (pp. 410–452). New York: Brunner/Mazel.
Marlatt, G.A. & Gordon, J.R. (Eds) (1985). *Relapse Prevention*. New York: Guilford.
Marlatt, G.A. & Rohsenow, D.J. (1980). Cognitive processes in alcohol use: expectancy and the
  balanced-placebo design. In N.K. Mello (Ed.), *Advances in Substance Abuse: Behavioral and
  Biological Research* (pp. 159–199). Greenwich, CT: JAI.
Mercer, P.W. & Khavari, K.A. (1990). Are women drinking more like men? An empirical examina-
  tion of the convergence hypothesis. *Alcoholism: Clinical and Experimental Research*, **14**, 461–466.
Merry, J. (1966). The "loss of control" myth. *Lancet*, **1**, 1257–1258.
Meyers, R.J., Dominguez, T.P. & Smith, J.E. (1996). Community reinforcement training with con-
  cerned others. In V.B. VanHasse & M. Hersen (Eds), *Sourcebook of Psychological Treatment
  Manuals for Adult Disorders* (pp. 257–294). New York: Plenum.
Monti, P.M., Abrams, D.B., Binkoff, J.A., Zwick, W.R., Liepman, M.R., Nirenberg, T.D. & Rohsenow,
  D.J. (1990). Communication skills training, communication skills training with family and cogni-
  tive behavioral mood management training for alcoholics. *Journal of Studies on Alcohol*, **51**,
  263–270.
Penick, E.C., Nickel, E.J., Powell, B.J., Liskow, B.I., Campbell, J., Dale, T.M., Hassanein, R.E. & Noble,
  E. (1999). The comparative validity of eleven alcoholism typologies. *Journal of Studies on
  Alcohol*, **60**, 188–202.
Prendergast, T.J. & Schaefer, E.S. (1974). Correlates of drinking and drunkenness among high school
  students. *Quarterly Journal of Studies on Alcohol*, **35**, 232–242.
Project Match Research Group (1998). Matching alcoholism treatment to client heterogeneity:
  Project MATCH three-year drinking outcomes. *Alcoholism: Clinical and Experimental Research*,
  22, 1300–1311.
Quigley, B.M. & Collins, R.L. (1999). The modeling of alcohol consumption: a meta-analytic review.
  Journal of Studies on Alcohol, **60**, 90–98.
Rather, B.C. & Goldman, M.S. (1994). Drinking-related differences in the memory organization of
  alcohol expectancies. *Experimental and Clinical Psychopharmacology*, **2**, 167–183.
Ratliff, K.G. & Burkhart, B.R. (1984). Sex differences in motivations for and effects of drinking
  among college students. *Journal of Studies on Alcohol*, **45**, 26–32.
Rohsenow, D.J. & Marlatt, G.A. (1981). The balanced placebo design: methodological considera-
  tions. *Addictive Behaviors*, **6**, 107–122.
Rychtarik, R.G., Prue, D.M., Rapp, S.R. & King, A.C. (1992). Self-efficacy, aftercare, and relapse in
  a treatment program for alcoholics. *Journal of Studies on Alcohol*, **53**, 435–440.
Shiffman, S. (1987). Craving: don't let us throw the baby out with the bath water. [Commentary on
  Kozlowski & Wilkinson's article "Use and misuse of the concept of craving by alcohol, tobacco,
  and drug researchers"]. *British Journal of Addiction*, **82**, 37–38.
Shipley, T.E. Jr. (1987). Opponent process theory. In H.T. Blane & K.E. Leonard (Eds), *Psychological Theories of Drinking and Alcoholism* (pp. 346–387). New York: Guilford.
Sisson, R.W. & Azrin, N.H. (1986). Family-member involvement to initiate and promote
  treatment of problem drinkers. *Journal of Behavioral Therapy and Experimental Psychiatry*, **17**,
  15–21.
Sklar, S.M., Annis, H.M. & Turner, N.E. (1997). Development and validation of the drug-taking
  confidence questionnaire: a measure of coping self-efficacy. *Addictive Behaviors*, **22**, 655–670.
Smith, J.E. & Meyers, R.J. (1995). The community reinforcement approach. In R.K. Hester & W.R.
  Miller (Eds), *Handbook of Alcoholism Treatment Approaches: Effective Alternatives* (pp. 251–266).
  Boston, MA: Allyn and Bacon.
Sobell, L.C., Toneatto, T. & Sobell, M.B. (1994). Behavioral assessment and treatment planning for
  alcohol, tobacco, and other drug problems: current status with an emphasis on clinical applications.
  Behavior Therapy, **25**, 533–580.
Southwick, L., Steele, C., Marlatt, A. & Lindell, M. (1981). Alcohol-related expectancies: defined by
  phase of intoxication and drinking experience. *Journal of Consulting and Clinical Psychology*, **49**,
  713–721.

Stacy, A.W. (1997).   Memory activation and expectancy as prospective predictors of alcohol and marijuana use. *Journal of Abnormal Psychology*, **106**, 61–73.

Tiffany, S.T. (1990).   A cognitive model of drug urges and drug-use behavior: role of automatic and nonautomatic processes. *Psychological Review*, **97**, 147–168.

Tiffany, S.T. (1992).   A critique of contemporary urge and craving research: methodological, psychometric, and theoretical issues. *Advances in Behaviour Research and Therapy*, **14**, 123–139.

Walitzer, K.S. & Connors, G.J. (1994).   Drinking restraint and mediation of changes in heavy drinking. Research Society on Alcoholism, Maui, Hawaii, June.

White, H.R., Bates, M.E. & Johnson, V. (1991).   Learning to drink: familial, peer, and media influences. In D.J. Pittman & H.R. White (Eds), *Society, Culture, and Drinking Patterns Re-examined* (pp. 177–197). New Brunswick, NJ: Rutgers Center of Alcohol Studies.

Wills, T.A. & Shiffman, S. (1985).   Coping and substance use: a conceptual framework. In S. Shiffman & T.A. Wills (Eds), *Coping and Substance Use* (pp. 3–24). Orlando, FL: Academic Press.

Wilsnack, S.C. & Wilsnack, R.W. (1990).   Women and substance abuse: research directions for the 1990s. *Psychology of Addictive Behaviors*, **4**, 46–49.

Windle, M. & Windle, R.C. (1996).   Coping strategies, drinking motives, and stressful life events among middle adolescents: associations with emotional and behavioral problems and with academic functioning. *Journal of Abnormal Psychology*, **105**, 551–560.

Chapter 17

Developmental Processes

Dennis M. Gorman
School of Rural Public Health, Texas A&M University System Health Science Center, College Station, TX, USA

Synopsis

This chapter reviews theories and empirical data pertaining to developmental processes associated with alcohol dependence and alcohol-related problems. Developmental theories are primarily concerned with identifying variables in childhood and adolescence that predict later alcohol abuse/dependence, specifically those involving relationships with family members and peers. These are discussed in detail, along with the intervening mechanisms that link factors such as poor family management practices and peer group affiliation to later problems related to alcohol use.

Following this, three specific models that attempt to link these developmental processes to alcohol abuse/dependence are described, along with research evidence pertaining to each theory. Two of these theories are broad-based, in that they attempt to explain alcohol problems as part of a whole range of other types of anti-social and health-compromising behaviors, including drug use, early sexual activity, violence, smoking, poor diet and mental health problems. These theories are the Social Development Model (developed by Hawkins & Catalano) and Problem Behavior Theory (first described by Richard and Shirley Jessor). An alcohol-specific integrative model developed by Wagenaar & Perry is also described in detail.

Two key issues related to the analysis of developmental processes arise from this review of integrative theories; the first involves the distinction between alcohol abuse/dependence as a "time-limited" vs. "life-course-persistent" form of behavior, and the second involves the nature of the relationship between alcohol abuse/dependence and other types of problem behaviors. Each issue is discussed in detail and the relevant empirical evidence reviewed. The chapter concludes with a discussion of the implications of the evidence pertaining to developmental processes for alcohol prevention interventions.

DEVELOPMENTAL PROCESSES, RISK AND RESILIENCY

Developmental explanations of problem behaviors, including problems related to alcohol abuse and dependency, focus primarily on occurrences during childhood and adolescence

International Handbook of Alcohol Dependence and Problems. Edited by N. Heather, T.J. Peters and T. Stockwell.
© 2001 John Wiley & Sons Ltd.

(Compas, Hinden & Gerhardt, 1995; Moffit, 1993). There are sound reasons for this focus. First, most people initiate these behaviors during adolescence. In the case of alcohol use, three out of four 17 year-olds in the USA and 90% of those in the UK have initiated this behavior (Johnston, O'Malley & Bachman, 1998; Goddard, 1991). Second, the occurrence of most problem behaviors, including heavy drinking, peaks during late adolescence and early adulthood (Chen & Kandel, 1995). For example, results from the annual household survey conducted in the USA show that both "heavy" and "binge" drinking peak among 18–25 year-olds (US Department of Health and Human Services, 1998). In a recent survey conducted in England and Wales, the proportion exceeding "sensible limits" of alcohol consumption was greatest among this same age group, as was the proportion reporting at least one heavy drinking session during the previous week (Goddard, 1991). Third, a sizable proportion of those who are going to have a persistent problem over the course of their life manifest the initial signs of this problem, or related antecedents, during adolescence and childhood (Tarter, 1988; Zucker, 1994). Finally, most of those who exhibit the problem during adolescence desist by their late 20s to early 30s—that is, they "mature out" (Chen & Kandel, 1995; Labouvie, 1996). The latter two points are among the most well-established facts of development research—problem behaviors exhibit marked temporal stability for a minority of individuals but show marked instability over time for the majority (Moffitt, 1993)—issues we shall return to later.

Another key feature of development models is that they explain problem behaviors in terms of *risk factors* (Compas et al., 1995). Risk refers to a statistical probability that a specific outcome will occur at some later date (Zucker, 1996). The list of 17 risk factors proposed by Hawkins, Catalano & Miller (1992a) is fairly typical of such inventories and has been one of the most influential in the field of alcohol and drug prevention research. The 17 factors fall within three broad domains: those describing characteristics of the *environment* (e.g. laws, norms, availability, neighborhood disorganization and poverty), those describing characteristics of *individuals* (e.g. physiological differences, attitudes towards drugs, educational achievement, and more general dispositions such as non-conformity and alienation), and those describing *interpersonal relations* (e.g. relations with family members and peers). Developmental theories are primarily concerned with risk variables from the latter domain, although, as we will see, they frequently involve hypotheses linking these factors and alcohol abuse/dependence in terms of mediating traits or dispositions of individuals.

While there are certainly limitations to the way in which risk factor models have been used in the area of drug and alcohol prevention, their potential benefits in terms of targeting appropriate intervention activities at those most in need cannot be overlooked (Gorman, 1996a). Some researchers, however, argue that the risk factor approach has inherent limitations and that as an alternative we should focus on *protective factors*. This view has been most fully articulated by Brown & Horowitz (1993), who argue that the two concepts (risk and protection) have developed through independent areas of research and represent distinct "paradigms".

Most developmental theorists, however, consider risk and protection to be complementary concepts. Indeed, the very terms "protection" and "resiliency" carry with them the assumption of adversity or risk of adversity—the variables one is concerned with are, presumably, protecting individuals from some other adverse influence or set of influences. A cohesive, harmonious family, in order to be protective, must be buffering the effects of negative influences (such as ease of availability and permissive norms or, alternatively, biological susceptibility) in a way that a non-cohesive, conflict-ridden family does not. Seminal writing on resiliency and protective factors reflects this view. For example, Werner (1986) was concerned with identifying protective factors that differentiated offspring of alcoholics who did not develop serious coping problems from those who did. In this study, children of alcoholics were described as "one of the most prevalent high-risk groups in this country" (Werner, 1986, p. 34). Similarly, Rutter (1985) examined protective factors in the context of the negative influences, such as parental psychiatric disorder, stressful life events and social adversity. He described resiliency research as a phase in the broader area of stress research, and stated that "protective factors may have no detectable effect in the absence of any subsequent stressor: their role is to modify the response to later adversity rather than to foster normal development in any direct sense" (Rutter, 1985, p. 600).

Thus, while the study of risk factors in developmental research is not without problems, it remains central to any comprehensive attempt to explain the developmental pathways leading to specific problem behaviors (Compas et al., 1995). Greater clarity is needed in distinguishing variables that increase the likelihood that a certain type of behavior will occur from those that decrease the likelihood, as well as in identifying the different domains from which these influences emanate. However, this should not negate the use of risk factor models in understanding the development of alcohol abuse and dependence.

DEVELOPMENTAL PROCESSES THAT INFLUENCE ALCOHOL ABUSE/DEPENDENCE

Before beginning this review, it should be noted that developmental theories are primarily concerned with identifying variables and relationships in childhood and adolescence that predict later problem behavior (in this case, alcohol abuse/dependence) of either a time-limited form (i.e. restricted to adolescence and early-adulthood) or of a type that is life-course-persistent. However, as Holder (1994) observes, many alcohol-related problems, especially those that befall young drinkers (e.g. drunk–driving and altercations while drinking) do not result from the actions of individuals who meet the diagnostic criteria of alcohol abuse or dependence. Thus, the types of risk factors identified herein may be of little use in explaining the occurrence of such problems; rather, issues of access and availability may be far more important (see Chapters 35 and 36, this volume).

Family Processes

There exists a large body of empirical research that has established family influences as important co-variates of alcohol abuse and dependence (Jacob & Leonard, 1994). There are two principal social (as compared to biological) explanations of the relationship between family risk factors and alcohol abuse. According to *social learning theory*, processes such as conditioning, modeling, imitation and observational learning are the key factors linking an individual's drinking behavior with the behavior of family members (see Chapters 14, 16 and 18, this volume). In contrast, much of the developmental literature stresses interactions within the family as the principal way in which parents influence the drinking-related behaviors of their children. The quality of the interaction between the child and his/her parents and the quality of the home environment have been shown to influence adolescents' drinking behavior, independent of parents' personal use of alcohol. The aspects of family life that act as risk factors include low levels of attachment and bonding to family members, ambiguous or paradoxical communication styles, excessive discipline (either too lax or too punitive), conflict, absence of parental love and support, low parental control and inadequate monitoring, and poor management techniques (Hawkins et al., 1992a).

Although less attention has been paid to protective mechanisms, certain aspects of "family culture", including maintenance of rituals and goal-setting by parents, have been shown to afford protection in families in which alcohol dependence is an issue (Bennett & Wolin, 1990). In addition, as Reifman and colleagues observe, much of the research on family influence on alcohol use has focused on initiation rather than heavier use (Reifman et al., 1998). In their recent longitudinal study, however, they found that parental monitoring of children's behavior at age 13–16 years was predictive of both "regular drinking" and "heavy episodic drinking" 2 years later.

Peer Relationships

Virtually all studies that include drinking among peers as a variable find it to be one of the most, if not the most, powerful predictors of adolescent alcohol use, although the strength of the effects vary by ethnicity, age and gender (Jacob & Leonard, 1994; Kandel, 1996). Research on the influence of peer groups on alcohol and other drug use has been criticized for its reliance on cross-sectional designs, its use of measures based solely on adolescents' descriptions of friends' behavior rather than on their actual behavior, failure to consider parental influences on children's selection of peers, and failure to consider genetic contributions to parental effects (Kandel, 1996). For example, Aseltine (1995) found that while friends' behavior was the strongest predictor of a youth's own behavior, the estimate of influence was greatly overestimated in analyses that relied only on respondents' perceptions of friends' behavior.

The association between an adolescent's drinking behavior and that of his/her peers is generally assumed to be the result of peer socialization. However, although research has established that peers influence one another's alcohol use, it is as likely that adolescents select friends whose behavior is similar to their own as it is that the behavior is learned from the peer group. Indeed, current research suggests that association with alcohol-using peers is just as much a consequence of an individual's drinking behavior as it is a cause of it (Jacob & Leonard, 1994; Kandel, 1996). Adolescents select friends who are like themselves in terms of shared behaviors and attitudes; they then mutually influence one another's behavior through their continued associations. In the case of drinking, these shared attitudes and behaviors need not be alcohol-specific but may relate to more general tendencies, such as aggressiveness and antisocial behavior (Jacob & Leonard, 1994).

The latter point is especially noteworthy as it relates to early peer rejection, which has been shown to be a strong predictor of later persistent problem behavior (Hawkins et al., 1992a, 1995; Jacob & Leonard, 1994; Moffitt, 1993). Young children who are aggressive and antisocial are much more likely to be rejected by peers than those who are not. These antisocial, rejected children tend to band together and engage in problem behaviors at a relatively early age. During adolescence, when engaging in antisocial behavior is more or less normative, these early starters become role models for heavy drinking, drug use and other problem behaviors (Moffitt, 1993). Most of the late-starters will desist in these behaviors once they reach their mid-20s, whereas early starters are more likely to have life-course-persistent problems (see discussion of "limiteds" and "persistents", below).

In an attempt to estimate the bias resulting from the types of methodological and theoretical limitations described above, Kandel (1996) concluded that assessment of peer effects on alcohol use and other problem behaviors, relative to parent effects, was overestimated in published empirical studies by at least a factor of five. Thus, the influence of parents on behavior has generally been underestimated in the alcohol and drug prevention literature which so heavily emphasizes the role of peers. However, the more general developmental literature has consistently shown parenting and other family factors to be of primary importance. For example, Brown et al. (1993) found that parenting practices such as monitoring and joint decision-making were associated with both membership in specific types of adolescent peer groups (e.g. drug-using peers vs. academically-orientated peers) and with specific types of adolescent behaviors (e.g. drug use and academic achievement) among individuals as old as 15–19 years. Indeed, many developmental theories consider disruptions in family management practices (e.g. inadequate monitoring and inconsistent discipline) to be the key influences that initiate adolescent involvement in problem behaviors such as alcohol and drug use, initiating a process that affects social and emotional development, bonding to prosocial others, friendship networks and academic achievement (see description of the Social Development Model, below).

Intervening Mechanisms

Behavioral Traits

Developmental theories typically explain the link between socialization experiences within the family and peer group and alcohol abuse/dependence in terms of their effects on *behavioral traits*, principally those describing a tendency towards sadness and low self-worth, and those describing an inability to exhibit self-control and behave in a conventional manner. The former is generally referred to as *negative affect* and describes a proneness to experience depressed mood, high levels of stress, poor self-concept and difficulties in coping. Such feelings and emotions have been shown to be important in shaping behavior, including alcohol and drug using behaviors (Labouvie et al., 1990). In addition, the development of such feelings and emotions has been shown to be fundamentally influenced by socialization experiences within the family (Harris, Brown & Bifulco, 1990).

As for *self-control*, this has been described primarily in terms of *emotionality* and *conventionality*. Emotionality describes, at a psychological level, a susceptibility to becoming easily and intensely distressed and, at a physiological level, excessive autonomic liability (Tarter, 1988). These are considered behavioral traits that, while genetically endowed, are fundamentally modified and shaped by the physical and social environment, thereby influencing the development of personality and predisposing individuals toward engaging in certain behaviors and refraining from others. Both emotionality and high activity level in childhood and adolescence, and related characteristics such as risk-taking and impulsivity, have been linked to later alcohol abuse/dependence. Tarter (1988) also states that children who are highly emotional and impulsive have more difficulty exerting self-control and are at greater risk for engaging in non-conventional behaviors.

Conventionality–unconventionality has been defined as a generalized dimension of individual differences ". . . underlying and summarizing an orientation toward, commitment to, and involvement in the prevailing values, standards of behavior, and established institutions of the larger . . . society" (Donovan, Jessor & Costa, 1991, p. 52). Conventional youth are intolerant of deviance, have high educational attainment, are more likely to be religious, and are more likely to engage in behaviors that are socially approved, normatively expected and institutionalized as appropriate for adolescents. Thus, conventional youth are more likely to bond to prosocial others and prosocial agencies. Unconventional youth display the opposite motivational structure and pattern of behaviors, and are therefore more prone to associating with antisocial others and engaging in deviant behaviors, including alcohol abuse.

These two very general paths to alcohol abuse are not mutually exclusive. Indeed, research shows that there are important interactions between behavioral traits. For example, Labouvie et al. (1990) found two developmental pathways to adolescent substance abuse, one involving negative affect and emotionality, and one involving positive affect and emotionality.

Stressful Life Events

Stressful life events have been linked to both the development of alcohol dependence and the development of behavioral traits such as emotionality and negative affect (Gorman & Brown, 1992). Individuals raised by alcohol-dependent parents and/or in families characterized by conflict and poor management practices are likely to experience more stressful and disruptive life events, such as frequent relocations, parental separations and economic hardships, than individuals raised in conflict-free families (Hoffman & Su, 1998). Furthermore, parenting practices fundamentally influence peer group affiliation in adolescence and youth who associate with antisocial peers are also more likely to experience negative life events, such as accidents and illness among those friends, than are youths who associate with non-using, prosocial peers (Hoffman & Su, 1998). Thus, parental and peer influences can exert influence on alcohol use behavior, not only through the types of socialization and developmental mechanisms described above, but also through the differential levels of stress to which they expose individuals.

Age of Onset

A number of studies have shown that lower age of initiation of alcohol use is predictive of later alcohol dependence and related problems (Grant & Dawson, 1997; Hawkins et al., 1997; Pedersen & Skrondal, 1998). Moreover, some of these studies showed that the effects of parental and peer influences, such as alcohol use, norms and family management practices, are mediated through age of initiation (Hawkins et al., 1997; Pedersen & Skrondal, 1998). This suggests that age of onset is itself an important risk factor in the developmental process, leading to fundamental changes in behavior repertoire, self-identity and relations with others (Pedersen & Skrondal, 1998). Unfortunately, most studies of alcohol initiation have methodological limitations, notably asking subjects to retrospectively recall age of onset (e.g. Grant & Dawson, 1997). In addition, longitudinal studies have typically followed subjects only into their late teens (up to 19 years in Pedersen & Skrondal's study and 17–18 years in Hawkins et al.'s study), a time at which alcohol use peaks.

In two studies designed to assess these limitations, Labouvie and colleagues found that age of initiation of alcohol use was an extremely weak predictor of alcohol use, alcohol-related consequences or dependence at age 30 (Labouvie & White, 1998; Labouvie, Bates & Pandina, 1997). Individuals' use histories were better predicted by developmental trajectories that combined age of onset and use intensity (Labouvie & White, 1998). By age 30, two groups of individuals were identifiable: one comprised individuals who were earlier initiators and above-average users during adolescence but average users in early adulthood, and one comprised individuals who were early initiators and whose higher than average adolescent use had persisted into adulthood. This is in line with the distinction between adolescence-limited and life-course-persistence problem behaviors found in the more general developmental literature (Moffit, 1993; see below for details).

INTEGRATIVE DEVELOPMENTAL MODELS

The above might give the impression that key developmental processes within the family and peer group and the mechanisms that link these to alcohol abuse and dependence are treated in isolation in the research literature. In fact, many developmental theories are *integrative*, in that they endeavor to include a wide array of variables in their explanatory frameworks. The theories differ in terms of the *breadth* of behaviors they purport to explain (i.e. just alcohol abuse, or alcohol abuse and other drug-using behavior, or alcohol abuse, drug use and other problem behaviors), and in terms of the *range* of explanatory variables included in the theoretical model (i.e. some include variables from beyond the domain of socialization processes). In recent years, the trend has been in the direction of greater explanatory breadth, that is, attempting to explain the occurrence of a wide range of behaviors in terms of a common developmental process.

A comprehensive review of integrative theories is beyond the scope of this chapter (see the Key Works and Suggestions section for detailed accounts of a wide range of integrative theories). Here we examine two of the most influential theories and the empirical work accumulated in support of these: the Social Development Model (Catalano et al., 1996) and Problem Behavior Theory (Jessor & Jessor, 1977). In addition, we shall discuss the integrative model developed by Wagenaar & Perry (1994). This is focused specifically on alcohol but has greater range than the Social Development Model and Problem Behavior Theory in terms of the explanatory variables included.

Social Development Model

The Social Development Model is a hybrid theory combining elements of three other theories—social control, social learning and differential association (Catalano et al., 1996). The model stresses the importance of children developing strong bonds to the principal institutions of socialization within society, namely family, peers, community and school. Children, it is argued, learn patterns of behavior from these socializing agents; these patterns can either be *prosocial* or *antisocial*, depending on the values, attitudes and behavior of those with whom an individual bonds. More specifically, socialization has four dimensions, according to the theory: perceived opportunities for involvement with others; degree of interaction and involvement; skills to actively participate; and perceived reinforcement from participation.

According to the model, the risk factors for alcohol use and other problem behaviors occur sequentially. For example, family risk factors precede both school-based and peer-related factors. Those who establish bonds with prosocial family members in childhood are less likely to be rejected by their peers and display early attitudinal and behavioral problems, and therefore will be more committed to school and more likely to succeed academically. This, in turn, will reduce the chances of them associating with deviant peers, and hence their engaging in alcohol and drug use and other problem behaviors. In contrast, strong attachment to a heavy-drinking family member will facilitate movement down an antisocial path, involving attachment to antisocial peers and commitment to deviant activities. However, movement down this path is by no means inevitable, as it is the *preponderance of influences* that determines outcome. If an individual from a heavy-drinking family develops attachments to prosocial peers and others, and has sufficient opportunities to engage in prosocial activities that he/she perceives to be rewarding, then these bonds and experiences will offset the antisocial family influences and promote prosocial behavior, including responsible and appropriate use of alcohol.

Tests of the Social Development Model have primarily come from the Seattle Social Development Project, which is a theoretically-driven intervention program based on the model. In a study using structural equation techniques with data collected from 590 subjects, Catalano et al. (1996) concluded that constructs derived from the model (e.g. attachment and commitment to prosocial others and skills for interaction) measured at ages 9–10 and 13–14 provided an "acceptable fit" to predict alcohol and drug use at 7–18 years.

In addition to this longitudinal study, data from the project have also been used to test the effects of a combined parent and school-based intervention on constructs derived from the model and on problem behaviors such as alcohol use. The school-based intervention had two components—one targeted at teachers and one targeted at students (Hawkins et al., 1992b). The former involved training teachers in the use of proactive classroom management, interactive teaching and cooperative learning techniques. It was hypothesized that use of these techniques would increase the opportunities for students to become involved in classroom activities, which in turn would strengthen their bond to school. This increased bonding would reduce academic failure, early conduct disorder and peer rejection, thereby reducing risk of alcohol and drug use. The child skills training component also attempted to reduce early conduct disorder and peer rejection, as well as involvement with antisocial others, through instruction in communication, decision-making, negotiation and conflict resolution skills. It was hypothesized that an increase in such skills would lead to improvements in social adjustment, involvement in conventional activities and groups, and bonding to school, and hence reduce the aforementioned risk factors. Finally, the parenting program had two components, each built on a different curriculum and designed to enhance children's bonds to family and school. Specifically, the curricula were designed to teach parents how to monitor children's behavior, teach expectations for appropriate behavior, provide positive reinforcement of desired behavior, improve parent–child communication, create a positive learning environment in the home, and develop shared family activities and appropriate family roles.

The intervention study compared 200 students who had received at least one semester of the intervention with a comparison group of 700 students (Hawkins et al., 1992b). Those in the intervention group reported significantly more use of proactive family management practices by their parents, greater family communication, greater family involvement, greater bonding to family, greater attachment to school and greater commitment to school, and perceived school as more rewarding, as compared to comparison group subjects. Thus, the program was effective in influencing many of the processes posited in the Social Development Model to be of etiologic importance in the development of alcohol abuse and other problem behaviors. However, while statistically significant, the effect sizes for family variables were all small (e.g. scores of 3.54 vs. 3.41 on a six-point scale of family management). Intervention group subjects also reported significantly less delinquency and lower rates of alcohol initiation than comparison subjects (21% vs. 27%).

A follow-up of a small subsample of high-risk, low-income subjects (44 in the intervention group, 62 comparisons) 1 year later produced what the researchers termed "somewhat mixed" results (O'Donnell et al., 1995a). Of 35 outcome variables assessed, there were just seven statistically significant differences between female intervention and comparison subjects, and six statistically significant differences between the two groups of male subjects. None of the differences pertained to alcohol use.

Problem Behavior Theory

Like the Social Development Model, Problem Behavior Theory attempts to explain a broad range of deviant or antisocial behaviors in addition to alcohol abuse. The central tenet of the theory is that problem behavior is learned behavior and, as such, functional, purposeful and instrumental toward the attainment of goals (Jessor & Jessor, 1977).

Fundamental to the conceptual structure of the theory is the idea of three systems—personality, perceived environment and behavior. Within each system is a set of explanatory variables, some of which are *instigators* to engage in problem behaviors and some of which are *controls* against engaging in such behaviors. For example, within the personality system, alienation and low self-esteem are considered instigators, while greater religiosity and high academic achievement are considered controls. Within the perceived environment system, greater peer approval of problem behavior and greater friends-than-parents influence on behavior are instigators of problems, while the opposite of these variables act as controls. The output from the entire system of instigators and controls is termed *proneness*, considered synonymous with risk.

Also like Social Development Theory, Problem Behavior Theory considers drinking behavior to cluster with other behaviors that depart from societal norms, such as drug use, delinquency, sexual activity and risky behaviors. According to the theory, all of these behaviors serve the same function for adolescents, namely repudiating norms of conventionality, affirming independence from parents and a sense of maturity, coping with stress, having fun and signaling commonality with peers. Given this clustering, proneness to one type of behavior (e.g. alcohol abuse) is increased through involvement in other problem behaviors. Absence of these behaviors, and the presence of conventional behaviors such as church attendance, decreases the probability of engaging in alcohol abuse.

In an effort to expand the explanatory range of the theory, Perry & Jessor (1985) proposed that the tripartite model was appropriate in explaining the development of health-compromising behaviors, such as insufficient exercise and sleep, poor diet and non-use of seat belts, in addition to deviant behaviors. Problem drinking and drunk–driving were said to fall within both the problem behavior and health-compromising behavior domains. More recently, Jessor (1993) further broadened the list of health-compromising behaviors to include limited work skills, school failure, social isolation and amotivation.

Over the past two decades, Jessor and his colleagues have conducted a number of empirical tests, using both cross-sectional and longitudinal datasets, of the central tenets of Problem Behavior Theory as they pertain to problem drinking. These studies, along with those of other types of drug-using behaviors, are reviewed by Donovan (1996) and, for the most part, support the main tenets of the theory concerning the generality of problem behaviors and the predictive power of variables within the three systems. Other research groups have also conducted empirical tests of the theory and found the three systems to be predictive of adolescent alcohol abuse and problem drinking, and these behaviors to cluster with other types of problem behaviors into a single underlying construct (Farrell, Danish & Howard, 1992; Schlegel et al., 1987). Others, however, report that problem behaviors cluster into at least two underlying factors, that associations between these behaviors are unstable over time, and that predictors vary from one point in time to another. This is discussed in more detail below.

An Alcohol-specific Integrative Model

Wagenaar and Perry have developed an integrative model which is narrow in the sense that it attempts to explain only adolescent alcohol use, but broad in terms of the range of explanatory variables included in the theoretical model (Wagenaar & Perry, 1993). The model is very eclectic, drawing as it does on problem behavior theory, social learning theory, strain theory, cognitive and operant conditioning theories, and sociological perspectives such as symbolic interactionism, social control theory and anomie theory. However, it is in the inclusion of variables pertaining to norms (e.g. the legitimacy conferred by adult usage), economics (e.g. utility and cost) and availability (e.g. access and physical availability) that the model is most specific to alcohol use. Influencing drinking behavior is only possible, it is argued, if these environmental antecedents, as well as personal and interpersonal antecedents, are changed.

Project Northland was designed in accordance with this theoretical model and intended to reduce the incidence and prevalence of alcohol use among a cohort of 11 year-olds from 14 communities in Minnesota (Perry et al., 1996). In line with the theory, adolescent alcohol use was considered to result from interactions between environmental, interpersonal and personality variables, and an attempt was made to reduce both the *supply* of alcohol in the community and home and the *demand* for alcohol among adolescents. The intervention, delivered over a 3-year period, comprised a parenting program, a school-based skills-training program and a community program. The parenting program was orientated around activity books which students worked on at home. The activities focused on facts and myths about adolescent alcohol use, consequences of use, advertising, peer pressure, adult role models and establishing family guidelines about alcohol. A family fun night was also held at school. The school component comprised two curricula, delivered over consecutive years. Each was peer-led and comprised eight sessions; in addition to learning interpersonal resistance skills, activities were included (e.g. a theater production and the introduction of students to the organizations in their communities with influence over alcohol policy), designed to encourage bonding with prosocial others and development of community participation skills. The community component was intended to empower citizens to develop their own alcohol prevention capacity and encourage broad-based participation, and was built around task forces comprising representatives from various community organizations. The primary goal of these groups was to develop strategies to reduce the access of adolescents to alcohol. Community organizers were responsible for the formation of the task force in each community.

The intervention was evaluated in a randomized controlled trial of over 2000 adolescents. Subjects were followed-up at 6, 18 and 30 months. For the purposes of assessing the effects of the intervention, a tendency-to-use-alcohol scale was created, combining survey items about intentions to use alcohol and actual alcohol use. Analyses were conducted separately for baseline users of alcohol and non-users, and the effects of the program were very different for the two groups. By final follow-up, there was a statistically significant difference on the tendency-to-use scale between the baseline non-user group and comparisons. In addition, significantly fewer of the intervention group non-users than comparisons reported using alcohol at least once during the past week (5% vs. 10%) and using alcohol at least once during the past month (15% vs. 21%) (Perry et al., 1996). In contrast, there were no statistically significant differences between the baseline user intervention and comparison conditions on any measure of alcohol use at any of the three follow-up points. There were also significant differences between the baseline non-user intervention and comparison groups on measures of self-efficacy and peer influence at final follow-up, but no differences between the two baseline user conditions on these scales. Thus, the intervention effects were confined to a subsample of the target population, namely those who had not initiated alcohol use at baseline.

TYPOLOGIES AND PATHS

The above review of three major integrative theories raises two issues that are of fundamental importance in any understanding of developmental processes and alcohol abuse: first, to what extent is alcohol abuse related to other behavioral and health problems and to what extent do these have a common developmental path; second, to what extent is alcohol abuse a life-course-persistent problem rather than a time-limited problem?

"Generalists" vs. "Specialists"

According to both Problem Behavior Theory and the Social Development Model, alcohol abuse clusters with other types of problem behaviors, such as drug use and delinquency, and these behaviors result from a common developmental process. Individuals differ in terms of their proneness to display these behaviors, according to the former theory, while it is a preponderance of influences that determines whether an individual follows an anti-social or prosocial path in the latter theory.

In contrast to this "generalist" perspective, other researchers have argued that problem behaviors, such as alcohol and drug abuse, sexual activity and delinquency, cluster into at least two underlying factors, that the associations between these behaviors are unstable over time, and that the predictors of them differ by gender and from one point in time to another (Grube & Morgan, 1990; White & Labouvie, 1994). Indeed, data from the Social Development Project itself support the view that the underlying structure of problem behaviors is multidimensional, with delinquent behavior and drug/alcohol use represent-ing two distinct dimensions and somewhat different variables derived from the model being predictive of each (Gillmore et al., 1991; O'Donnell, Hawkins & Abbott, 1995b).

This issue is further complicated when health-related behaviors (both physical and psy-chological), in addition to problem behaviors, are considered. White (1992), for example, reported that mental health problems did not cluster with problem behaviors (including alcohol use) for males and did so only modestly for females. Brack, Brack & Orr (1994) identified three clusters in their analysis of more than 30 variables pertaining to alcohol and drug use, mental and physical health, delinquency, sexual activity and self-destructive behaviors. Alcohol use clustered with variables that the authors described as indicative of "rebellion from adult norms", namely other drug-using behaviors, problems at school, sexual intercourse, running away and getting arrested. It did not cluster with coping and affective variables, such as self-esteem, nervousness and sadness. In a study assessing 25 problem- and health-related behaviors, Basen-Engquist, Edmundson & Parcel (1996) found that drinking and other health-related behaviors considered deviant by adults but com-monly engaged in by adolescents (e.g. smoking and sexual intercourse) formed a distinct cluster, separate from more violent and self-destructive behaviors such as fighting, cocaine use and suicidal actions.

Even among "high-risk" youth, different clusters of problem behaviors can be identi-fied. Lavery et al. (1993), for example, found that health-related risk factors formed a dif-ferent pattern to drug-related and deviant activities among youth at a mental health clinic, while Spatz Widom & White (1997) found a substantial proportion of "specialists" (i.e. indi-viduals engaged in just one problem behavior) in a sample of court-substantiated cases of child abuse and neglect.

The question of whether alcohol abuse as a behavior clusters with other types of problem and/or health-related behaviors has a profound impact on the development of prevention interventions. To take but one example, if adolescent drinking is primarily a health-related behavior it will require quite different types of interventions than if it is primarily a deviant behavior. A related issue concerns the extent to which problem drinking is a life-course-persistent behavior for some individuals and an adolescence-limited behavior for others, and whether these two types of behavior have distinct developmental trajectories.

"Persistents" vs. "Limiteds"

Both cross-sectional and longitudinal studies show that, among general population samples, frequency of heavy alcohol use peaks during the late teens and early 20s and declines there-after (Chen & Kandel, 1995; US Department of Health and Human Services, 1998). Thus, for most individuals, alcohol abuse is limited in duration to late adolescence and early adulthood, while for others it persists into later years. In an attempt to understand this phenomenon, some longitudinal studies have sought to identify clusters among adolescent drinking behaviors, on the assumption that less extreme forms of use (e.g. late initiators who drink primarily for social reasons) have a different developmental trajectory from more extreme forms (e.g. those exhibiting early-onset or those associated with other types of antisocial behaviors).

In one such study conducted as part of an evaluation of a prevention program known as Project SMART, Weber et al. (1989) identified two pathways into alcohol use, one followed by "normally socialized adolescents" and one followed by problem behavior-prone adolescents. Although both groups increased their alcohol use over a 1 year period, the latter displayed a more rapid onset, greater use and more episodes of drunkenness than the former. As part of another longitudinal evaluation of a prevention program (Project ALERT), Ellickson & Hays (1991) assessed drinking patterns of 12 year-olds who had initiated alcohol use and those who had not over a 12-month period. Among the latter group, both frequency of use and heavy drinking over the subsequent year were best predicted by peer and family influences, while the same behaviors among alcohol initiates were best explained by behavioral variables (e.g. deviance) and expectancies and attitudes in addition to social influences. Finally, Labouvie, Pandina & Johnson (1991) identified four trajectories in drinking patterns between the ages of 12 and 18 years: a "normative" trajectory of slow and steady increase in use, very low use, very high use, and very rapid increase in use. Those who showed rapid initiation and subsequent heavy use also reported problems at school, disciplinary problems, low attachment to parents, more stressful life events, lower self-esteem and fewer sources of personal satisfaction when compared to those exhibiting the normative trajectory. In a later follow-up of this sample into their late 20s and early 30s, the authors distinguished between a pattern of adolescent-limited alcohol and drug use and a pattern that persists into adulthood (Labouvie & White, 1998). The former was predicted by "social" risk factors (e.g. peer use) encountered by normally socialized youth and the latter by social and "personal" risk factors (e.g. impulsivity and lack of control) displayed by "problem-prone" youth. In all three of these studies, a "normative" increase in alcohol use among adolescents predicted by normal socialization processes was distinguished from a more extreme type of drinking behavior in which personality and behavioral variables played a part in its development.

Studies that have followed subjects into their 20s and early 30s have lent further support to the idea that some forms of alcohol problems are limited to adolescence, while others follow a more pernicious and persistent course. In addition, these studies have endeavored to identify the types of life events and experiences that distinguish those who mature out from those that do not. In a study of drunkenness between ages 18 and 24, Schulenburg et al. (1996) were able to classify the drinking pattern of close to 90% of subjects into distinct trajectories. Half of the subjects reported little or no drunkenness over the 6 year period. Of the remainder, about 16% exhibited chronically high levels of drunkenness throughout the four waves of the study or increased their episodes of drunkenness over the 6 years. However, another group, comprising about one-fifth of the sample, appeared to mature out of their excessive drinking by the time they reached age 24; some had reached their peak as early as 18 while other did most of their bingeing in their early 20s. Marital status was the best predictor of the divergent trajectories, with chronic cases and those increasing their episodes of drunkenness being more likely to have remained single than those exhibiting other trajectories.

These findings are consistent with previous research that shows that marriage is associated with a reduction in alcohol consumption. Chilcoat & Breslau (1996) assessed the effects of marriage and parenthood on alcohol abuse and dependence in a sample of nearly 1000 21–30 year-olds over a period of 3.5 years. Transition into these roles was associated with a lower incidence of alcohol dependence/abuse, defined according to DSM-III-R, as well as a lower incidence of positive symptoms in the absence of meeting the criteria for full caseness. Risk of disorder was also greater among those who divorced compared to those who remained married, although in this case the data indicated a reciprocal relationship: alcohol abuse/dependence was more common among those who divorced but the incidence of divorce was increased for those with the disorder at baseline. Similarly, Labouvie (1996) found marriage to be associated with maturing out of alcohol and drug use among young adults (aged 28–31 years) but, in line with results of Chilcoat & Breslau and the research on adolescent peer group selection discussed above, found a reciprocal relationship between the two events. That is, individuals were inclined to select spouses and/or friends on the basis of shared behavioral norms regarding alcohol and other drug use, and these spouses and/or friends influenced subsequent drinking and drug use.

CONCLUSIONS AND IMPLICATIONS

The research on "generalists" and "specialists", along with the research pertaining to "limiteds" and "persistents", suggests that there are a number of subtypes of alcohol dependence, based on duration and co-occurrence with other types of problems. Eight possible subtypes are shown in Table 17.1. Some of these have been described in the research literature in detail, especially those that involve behavioral problems (e.g. Tarter, 1988). Forty years ago, Jellinek (1960) described five distinct "species" of alcoholism, including one involving primarily psychological problems, one involving physical problems and one alcohol-specific and progressive in nature. More recently, Zucker (1994) identified four subtypes (broadly corresponding to cells 2, 5, 6 and 7 of Table 17.1) and variations in family-based risk factors relevant to each.

This type of approach to understanding developmental processes is quite different from that proposed by integrative theorists, who maintain that different types of behaviors have a common developmental path. However, as Compas et al. (1995) observe, while these broad integrative models have undoubtedly helped explicate the developmental processes underlying behaviors such as alcohol abuse, there is also a danger that in attempting to describe so much behavior they succeed in explaining too little.

The main implication for prevention is that we are likely to need to develop specific types of interventions for specific subgroups of individuals, that is, we need to move from *universal* interventions to *targeted* interventions (Gorman, 1996a). The trend in prevention "science" has, however, been in the opposite direction, with the expansion of programs designed initially to address one problem (e.g. smoking) into an array of other problem areas. This trend is driven conceptually by the broad integrative approach: people are considered to engage in different behaviors (e.g. alcohol use, drug use, sex, and violence) for essentially the same reasons (e.g. deficient life skills) (see e.g. Botvin, Schinke & Orlandi, 1995). The research reviewed here suggests otherwise. Indeed, it seems to indicate that people engage in the same behavior (drinking alcohol) for different reasons.

Table 17.1 Possible subtypes according to duration and presence or absence of accompanying problems

	Alcohol specialist	Generalist—problem behaviors	Generalist—psychological problems	Generalist—health compromising behaviors
Limited	1	2	3	4
Persistent	5	6	7	8

If there are distinct subgroups of alcohol users and abusers with distinct developmental paths, one would not expect interventions based on a universal approach to have much success in reducing alcohol use, and indeed they do not (Gorman, 1995, 1996b). Not surprisingly, both Project SMART and Project ALERT which, as noted above, found subtypes of drinkers within their target populations, were unable to influence drinking behavior using a universal social skills training curriculum (see Gorman, 1995). Similarly, Perry et al.'s (1996) social influence-based program had no effect on early initiates of alcohol, while Hawkins and colleagues' Social Development Project had very minimal effects on subjects identified as "high risk" (O'Donnell et al., 1995b). These subgroups probably have distinct developmental antecedents to their problems that are not appropriately addressed through the use of standardized, universal interventions.

Before concluding, it is necessary to address one final issue that relates to the distinction between risk and protective factors raised in the introduction. Brown & Horowitz (1993) argue that a risk factor approach leads inevitably to the development of abstinence-orientated interventions that accentuate individual deficits and pathology, while a protective model leads to the development of harm-reduction interventions that promote general well-being. Basically there are two issues being raised here: one pertaining to the *goal* of programs—abstinence vs. harm reduction—and one pertaining to the *focus* of programs—individual deficits vs. individual and environmental strengths. With regard to the latter, there is no reason why the use of a risk factor model to develop an intervention program should lead to an exclusive emphasis on individual weaknesses. For example, one might identify as "at-risk" youth living in a community with a high concentration of alcohol outlets and ease of access to alcohol. In response to this, one might choose to employ an intervention which draws attention to individual-level deficiencies, such as inadequate life skills (e.g. Botvin et al., 1995). Alternatively, one might choose to raise awareness of, and facilitate action on, issues pertaining to alcohol availability through organizing people in the community (e.g. Holder et al., 1997; see also Chapter 39 this volume). Programmatic options are in no way inexorably tied to either a risk or protective model. The same is true of the program goals; indeed, examples of harm reduction interventions targeted at high risk drinkers can already be found in the research literature (e.g. Barber, Bradshaw & Walsh, 1989).

KEY WORKS AND SUGGESTIONS FOR FURTHER READING

Glantz, M. & Pickens, R. (1992). *Vulnerability to Drug Abuse.* Washington, DC: American Psychological Society.

White, H.R. (1996). Empirical Validity of Theories of Drug Abuse. *Journal of Drug Issues* (Special Issue), **26**(2).

Zucker, R.A., Boyd, G. & Howard, J. (1994). *The Development of Alcohol Problems: Exploring the Biopsychosocial Matrix of Risk.* NIAA Research Monograph No. 26. Rockville, MD: US Department of Health and Human Services.

These three edited editions contain detailed accounts of most of the key integrative theories in the area of alcohol and drug studies.

Compas, B.E., Hinden, B.R. & Gerhardt, C.A. (1995). Adolescent development: pathways and processes of risk and resilience. *Annual Review of Psychology*, **46**, 265–293.

Moffit, T.E. (1993). Adolescence-limited and life-course-persistent antisocial behavior: a developmental taxonomy. *Psychological Bulletin*, **100**, 674–701.

These two papers discuss most of the key issues relevant to the analysis of developmental processes that affect alcohol and drug use and other types of problem behaviors.

Gerstein, D.R. & Green, L.W. (1993). *Preventing Drug Abuse: What Do We Know?* Washington, DC: National Academy Press.

This book is the most thorough and objective review of programs that attempt to influence the developmental processes underlying alcohol and drug problems.

REFERENCES

Aseltine, R.H. Jr (1995). A reconsideration of parental and peer influences on adolescent deviance. *Journal of Health and Social Behavior*, **36**, 103–121.

Barber, J.G., Bradshaw, R. & Walsh, C. (1989). Reducing alcohol consumption through television advertising. *Journal of Consulting and Clinical Psychology*, **57**, 613–618.

Basen-Engquist, K., Edmundson, E.W. & Parcel, G.S. (1996). Structure of health risk behavior among high school students. *Journal of Consulting and Clinical Psychology*, **64**, 764–775.

Bennett, L.A. & Wolin, S.J. (1990). Family culture and alcoholism transmission. In R.L. Collins, K.E. Leonard & J.S. Searles (Eds), *Alcohol and the Family: Research and Clinical Perspectives* (pp. 194–219). New York: Guilford.

Botvin, G.J., Schinke, S. & Orlandi, M.A. (1995). School-based health promotion: substance abuse and sexual behavior. *Applied and Preventive Psychology*, **4**, 167–184.

Brack, C.J., Brack, G. & Orr, D.P. (1994). Dimensions underlying problem behaviors, emotions, and related psychological factors in early and middle adolescents. *Journal of Early Adolescents*, **14**, 345–370.

Brown, B.B., Mounts, N., Lamborn, S.D. & Steinberg, L. (1993). Parenting practices and peer group affiliation. *Child Development*, **64**, 467–482.

Brown, J.H. & Horowitz, J.E. (1993). Deviance and deviants: why adolescent substance use prevention programs do not work. *Evaluation Review*, **17**, 529–555.

Catalano, R.F., Kosterman, R., Hawkins, J.D., Newcomb, M.D. & Abbott, R.D. (1996). Modeling the etiology of adolescent substance use: a test of the social development model. *Journal of Drug Issues*, **26**, 429–455.

Chen, K. & Kandel, D.B. (1995). The natural history of drug use from adolescence to the mid-thirties in a general population sample. *American Journal of Public Health*, **85**, 41–47.

Chilcoat, H.D. & Breslau, N. (1996). Alcohol disorders in young adulthood: effects of transitions into adult roles. *Journal of Health and Social Behavior*, **37**, 339–349.

Compas, B.E., Hinden, B.R. & Gerhardt, C.A. (1995). Adolescent development: pathways and processes of risk and resilience. *Annual Review of Psychology*, **46**, 265–293.

Donovan, J.E. (1996). Problem-behavior theory and the explanation of adolescent marijuana use. *Journal of Drug Issues*, **26**, 379–404.

Donovan, J.E., Jessor, R. & Costa, F.M. (1991). Adolescent health behavior and conventionality-unconventionality: an extension of problem-behavior theory. *Health Psychology*, **10**, 52–61.

Ellickson, P.L. & Hays, R.D. (1991). Antecedents of drinking among young adolescents with different alcohol use histories. *Journal of Studies on Alcohol*, **52**, 398–408.

Farrell, A.D., Danish, S.J. & Howard, C.W. (1992). Relationship between drug use and other problem behaviors in urban adolescents. *Journal of Consulting and Clinical Psychology*, **60**, 705–712.

Gillmore, M.R., Hawkins, J.D., Catalano, R.F., Day, L.E., Moore, M. & Abbott, R. (1991). Structure of problem behaviors in preadolescence. *Journal of Consulting and Clinical Psychology*, **59**, 499–506.

Goddard, E. (1991). *Drinking in England and Wales in the Late 1980s*. London: HMSO.

Gorman, D.M. (1995). Are school-based resistance skills training programs effective in preventing alcohol misuse? *Journal of Alcohol and Drug Education*, **41**, 74–98.

Gorman, D.M. (1996a). Etiological theories and the primary prevention of drug use. *Journal of Drug Issues*, **26**, 505–520.

Gorman, D.M. (1996b).   Do school-based social skills training programs prevent alcohol use among young people? *Addiction Research*, **4**, 191–210.

Gorman, D.M. & Brown, G.W. (1992).   Recent developments in life-event research and their relevance for the study of addictions. *British Journal of Addiction*, **87**, 837–849.

Grant, B.F. & Dawson, D.A. (1997).   Age of onset of alcohol use and its association with DSM-IV alcohol abuse and dependence: results from the National Longitudinal Alcohol Epidemiologic Survey. *Journal of Substance Abuse*, **9**, 103–110.

Grube, J.W. & Morgan, M. (1990).   The structure of problem behaviors among Irish adolescents. *British Journal of Addiction*, **85**, 667–675.

Harris, T.O., Brown, G.W. & Bifulco, A.T. (1990).   Depression and situational helplessness/mastery in a sample selected to study childhood parental loss. *Journal of Affective Disorders*, **20**, 27–41.

Hawkins, J.D., Catalano, R.R. & Miller, J.Y. (1992a).   Risk and protective factors for alcohol and other drug problems in adolescence and early adulthood: implications for substance abuse prevention. *Psychological Bulletin*, **112**, 64–105.

Hawkins, J.D., Catalano, R.F., Morrison, D.M., O'Donnell, J., Abbott, R.D. & Day, L.E. (1992b).   The Seattle Social Development Project: effects of the first four years on protective factors and problem behaviors. In J. McCord & R.E. Tremblay (Eds), *Preventing Antisocial Behavior: Interventions from Birth through Adolescence* (pp. 139–161). New York: Guilford.

Hawkins, J.D., Graham, J.W., Maguin, E., Abbott, R., Hill, K.G. & Catalano, R.F. (1997).   Exploring the effects of age of alcohol use initiation and psychosocial risk factors on subsequent alcohol misuse. *Journal of Studies on Alcohol*, **58**, 280–290.

Hoffman, J.P. & Su, S. (1998).   Parental substance use disorder, mediating variables and adolescent drug use: a non-recursive model. *Addiction*, **93**, 1351–1364.

Holder, H.D. (1994).   Alcohol availability and accessibility as part of the puzzle: thoughts on alcohol problems and young people. In R.A. Zucker, G. Boyd & J. Howard (Eds), *The Development of Alcohol Problems: Exploring the Biopsychosocial Matrix of Risk* (pp. 249–254). NIAA Research Monograph No. 26. Rockville, MD: US Department of Health and Human Services.

Holder, H.D., Saltz, R.F., Grube, J.W., Voas, R.B., Gruenewald, P.J. & Treno, A.J. (1997).   A community prevention trial to reduce alcohol-involved accidental injury and death: overview. *Addiction*, **92**(Suppl. 2), S155–S171.

Jacob, T. & Leonard, K. (1994).   Family and peer influences in the development of adolescent alcohol abuse. In R.A. Zucker, G. Boyd & J. Howard (Eds), *The Development of Alcohol Problems: Exploring the Biopsychosocial Matrix of Risk* (pp. 123–155). NIAA Research Monograph No. 26. Rockville, MD: US Department of Health and Human Services.

Jellinek, E.M. (1960).   *The Disease Concept of Alcoholism.* New Brunswick, NJ: Hillhouse.

Jessor, R. (1993).   Successful adolescent development among youth in high-risk settings. *American Psychologist*, **48**, 117–126.

Jessor, R. & Jessor, S.L. (1977).   *Problem Behavior and Psychosocial Development: A Longitudinal Study of Youth.* New York: Academic Press.

Johnston, L.D., O'Malley, P.M. & Bachman, J.G. (1998).   *National Survey Results on Drug Use from the Monitoring the Future Study, 1975–1997: Vol. I—Secondary School Students.* Rockville, MD: US Department of Health and Human Services.

Kandel, D.B. (1996).   The parental and peer contexts of adolescent deviance: an algebra of interpersonal influences. *Journal of Drug Issues*, **26**, 289–315.

Labouvie, E.W. (1996).   Maturing out of substance use: selection and self-correction. *Journal of Drug Issues*, **26**, 457–476.

Labouvie, E.W. & White, H.R. (1998).   Drug sequences, age of onset, and use trajectories: antecedents and adult use outcomes. Paper presented at the Conference on Stages and Pathways of Drug Involvement: Examining the Gateway Hypothesis, Los Angeles, CA, 28 June.

Labouvie, E.W., Bates, M. & Pandina, R.J. (1997).   Age of first use: its reliability and predictive utility. *Journal of Studies on Alcohol*, **58**, 638–643.

Labouvie, E.W., Pandina, R.J. & Johnson, V. (1991).   Developmental trajectories of substance use in adolescence: differences and predictors. *International Journal of Behavioral Development*, **14**, 305–328.

Labouvie, E.W., Pandina, R.J., White, H.R. & Johnson, V. (1990).   Risk factors of adolescent drug use: an affect-based interpretation. *Journal of Substance Abuse*, **2**, 265–285.

Lavery, B., Siegal, A.W., Cousins, J.H. & Rubovits, D.S. (1993). Adolescent risk-taking: an analysis of problem behaviors in problem children. *Journal of Experimental Child Psychology*, **55**, 277–294.

Moffit, T.E. (1993). Adolescence-limited and life-course-persistent antisocial behavior: a developmental taxonomy. *Psychological Bulletin*, **100**, 674–701.

O'Donnell, J., Hawkins, J.D., Catalano, R.F., Abbott, R.D. & Day, L.E. (1995a). Preventing school failure, drug use, and delinquency among low-income children: long-term intervention in elementary schools. *American Journal of Orthopsychiatry*, **65**, 87–100.

O'Donnell, Hawkins, J.D. & Abbott, R.D. (1995b). Predicting serious delinquency and substance use among aggressive boys. *Journal of Consulting and Clinical Psychology*, **63**, 529–537.

Pedersen, W. & Skrondal, A. (1998). Alcohol consumption debut: predictors and consequences. *Journal of Studies on Alcohol*, **59**, 32–42.

Perry, C.L. & Jessor, R. (1985). The concept of health promotion and the prevention of adolescent drug use. *Health Education Quarterly*, **12**, 169–184.

Perry, C.L., Williams, C.L., Veblen-Mortenson, S., Toomey, T.L., Komro, K.A., Anstine, P.S., McGovern, P.G., Finnegan, J.R., Forster, J.L., Wagenaar, A.C. & Wolfson, M. (1996). Project Northland: outcomes of a community-wide alcohol use prevention program during early adolescence. *American Journal of Public Health*, **86**, 956–965.

Riefman, A., Barnes, G.M., Dintcheff, B.A., Farrell, M.P. & Uhteg, L. (1998). Parental and peer influences on the onset of heavier drinking among adolescents. *Journal of Studies on Alcohol*, **59**, 311–317.

Rutter, M. (1985). Resilience in the face of adversity: protective factors and resistance to psychiatric disorder. *British Journal of Psychiatry*, **147**, 598–611.

Schlegel, R.P., d'Avernas, J.R., Zanna, M., DiTecco, D. & Manske, S.R. (1987). Predicting alcohol use in young adult males: a comparison of the Fishbein–Ajzen model and Jessor's Problem Behavior Theory. *Drugs and Society*, **1**, 7–24.

Schulenberg, J., O'Malley, P.M., Bachman, J.G., Wadsworth, K.N. & Johnston, L.D. (1996). Getting drunk and growing up: trajectories of frequent binge drinking during the transition to young adulthood. *Journal of Studies on Alcohol*, **57**, 289–304.

Spatz Widom, C. & White, H.R. (1997). Problem behaviors in abused and neglected children grown up: prevalence and co-occurrence of substance abuse, crime, and violence. *Criminal Behavior and Mental Health*, **7**, 287–310.

Tarter, R.E. (1988). Are there inherited behavioral traits that predispose to substance abuse? *Journal of Consulting and Clinical Psychology*, **56**, 189–196.

US Department of Health and Human Services (1998). *Preliminary Results from the 1997 National Household Survey on Drug Abuse*. Rockville, MD: US Department of Health and Human Services.

Wagenaar, A.C. & Perry, C.L. (1994). Community strategies for the reduction of youth drinking: theory and application. *Journal of Research on Adolescence*, **4**, 319–345.

Weber, M.D., Graham, J.W., Hansen, W.B., Flay, B.R. & Anderson, C.A. (1989). Evidence for two path of alcohol use onset in adolescents. *Addictive Behaviors*, **14**, 399–408.

Werner, E.E. (1986). Resilient offspring of alcoholics: a longitudinal study from birth to age 18. *Journal of Studies on Alcohol*, **47**, 34–40.

White, H.R. (1992). Early problem behavior and later drug problems. *Journal of Research in Crime and Delinquency*, **29**, 412–429.

White, H.R. & Labouvie, E.W. (1994). Generality versus specificity of problem behavior: psychological and functional differences. *Journal of Drug Issues*, **24**, 55–74.

Zucker, R.A. (1994). Pathways to alcohol problems and alcoholism: a developmental account of the evidence for multiple alcoholisms and for contextual contributions to risk. In R.A. Zucker, H. Boyd & J. Howard (Eds), *The Development of Alcohol Problems: Exploring the Biopsychosocial Matrix of Risk* (pp. 255–289). NIAA Research Monograph No. 26. Rockville, MD: US Department of Health and Human Services.

Chapter 18

Individual Differences

W. Miles Cox
Giles N. Yeates
Paul A.T. Gilligan
and
Steven G. Hosier
School of Psychology, University of Wales, Bangor, UK

Synopsis

In this chapter we review the literature on characteristics of people who abuse alcohol and those who are likely to do so in the future. Specifically, we discuss: (a) individual differences as antecedents of alcohol abuse; (b) personality characteristics of alcohol abusers, along with the comorbidity of alcohol abuse and other psychological disorders; and (c) subtypes of alcohol abusers.

Researchers have used several methods to determine if alcohol abusers have distinguishing personality characteristics that predate their problems with alcohol. First, current alcohol abusers have been asked to recall what they were like before they began to abuse alcohol. In some cases, information has been available to verify the accuracy of the self-reports. Second, a limited number of studies have measured participants' personality characteristics across time to the point when some of them began to develop problems with alcohol. In these cases, it has been possible to determine if those individuals who would later develop alcohol problems were recognizably different from those who would not. In a similar vein, other studies have compared persons who were at high risk for developing problems with alcohol (identified, for example, on the basis of their family history) with those not at risk. Finally, studies of adolescents who drink excessively have been valuable for identifying variables that influence the transition from non-problematic to problematic drinking. A common theme that emerges from these different methodologies is that a large subset of the people who develop problems tend to be antisocial, aggressive and impulsive early in life. They also often come from dysfunctional families and are influenced negatively by their peers. The manner in which they react to alcohol makes drinking especially rewarding for these people.

To determine the personality characteristics of people who are currently abusing alcohol, two methods have been used. One is the in-depth study of individual clinical cases. The other is to compare average personality test scores of a group of alcoholics with those of a group

---

International Handbook of Alcohol Dependence and Problems. Edited by N. Heather, T.J. Peters and T. Stockwell.

of non-alcoholics. With these two methods, two broad personality dimensions have been found to distinguish alcoholics from non-alcoholics. The first dimension is called behavioural disinhibition, which manifests itself as impulsivity, unconventionality and emotional overactivity. The second dimension is negative emotionality, which reflects subjective discomfort and distress. The first dimension seems to be an antecedent of alcohol abuse; the second one is more a consequence of the abuse.

The research has also made it clear that there is not one alcoholic personality. Instead, subtypes of alcoholics have been identified, of which two have been replicated across various studies. One type is distinguished by later onset, slower course of development, less psychological impairment, fewer complications and better prognosis than the other type, which is more genetically determined and characterized by early onset, more rapid course of development, more severe symptoms, greater psychological problems and poorer prognosis. Classifying alcoholics into subtypes has potential practical benefits, such as being able to match each subtype with the kind of treatment that is most effective.

Personality psychology has been defined as:

> ... the scientific study of the whole person. Personality psychologists ... seek to understand both the universal and the unique in persons ... both the most important species-typical characteristics ... and the most important individual differences (McAdams, 1994, p. 4).

In this chapter, our concern is with the uniqueness of persons who abuse alcohol and those who are likely to do so in the future. We discuss personality characteristics of current and future abusers of alcohol that distinguish these persons from non-abusers. We consider: (a) individual differences as antecedents of alcohol abuse; (b) personality characteristics of alcohol abusers, and the comorbidity of alcohol abuse and other psychological disorders; and (c) subtypes of alcohol abusers.

ANTECEDENTS OF ALCOHOL ABUSE

The idea that an idiosyncratic combination of personality characteristics predisposes an individual to develop alcohol dependence is an old one, being rooted in the early psychoanalytic explorations of alcohol dependence. Key investigators in this field (e.g. Knight, 1937) considered alcohol dependence to develop from a characteristic maladaptive personality pattern, and that successful treatment of people with alcohol dependence required a fundamental change in their personality. The view that people with alcohol dependence have a personality "defect" was shared by Alcoholics Anonymous, whose treatment consisted of specifying the faulty personality structure and then remediating it.

The notion that a specific personality structure was the basis for alcohol dependence reached its extreme in the 1940s, when the concept of an "alcoholic personality" was proposed. It was suggested that a unique constellation of personality characteristics differentiated people with alcohol dependence from other individuals before the onset of alcohol dependence. However, further attempts to identify this personality structure proved unsuccessful and researchers began to acknowledge the heterogeneity in the personality characteristics of people with alcohol dependence.

The recent conceptualization of alcohol dependence as a biopsychosocial phenomenon has enabled researchers to identify a variety of variables in addition to personality (e.g. genetic, biological, neuropsychological, learning, cognitive, familial) that differentiate people who develop alcohol dependence from those who do not. The development of sensitive and objective ways to measure these variables has also enabled different patterns of alcohol dependence to be identified that vary in terms of onset, course and outcome. Finally, modern statistical analytic techniques have allowed complex relationships among the biopsychosocial variables to be identified that help explain the heterogeneity of alcohol problems.

Methods of Study

Research on individual differences in the antecedents of alcohol dependence has involved five kinds of studies: retrospective, archival longitudinal, prospective longitudinal, high-risk, and adolescent drinking. Retrospective studies have relied on recollections of people with alcohol dependence regarding salient factors in their development (e.g. personality, family disturbances) that predated the onset of their alcohol problems. Such recollections are, of course, generally considered highly subjective and are susceptible to memory distortions and interpretative biases. Therefore, this form of evidence requires additional support from other sources. Chaplin & Orlofsky (1991), however, were able to validate the early memories of people with alcohol dependence about their prealcoholic personality characteristics against objective measures of the same variables, suggesting that the retrospective method can be used effectively to identify variables for further study. Other researchers have simply used whatever information happened to have been recorded from one point in time to another before the onset of participants' alcohol dependence. This method of study, known as archival longitudinal, is restricted to data that often are not entirely objective and otherwise not optimal for answering the questions under study. Hence, the results of such studies are not widely generalizable.

By contrast, prospective longitudinal studies have offered a wealth of information about the role of individual differences in the development of alcohol dependence. These studies have followed participants for as few as 3 and as many as 30 years in order to differentiate those individuals who ultimately develop alcohol dependence from those who do not. Such studies are both time consuming and expensive to run, but their payoff can be invaluable. For example, the identification of a multitude of factors that place people "at risk" for developing problems with alcohol has been accomplished largely through prospective longitudinal research. Finally, the study of adolescents who are heavy users of alcohol and/or show signs of early dependence has been vital for assessing variables that influence the transition from non-problematic to problematic drinking. The findings of studies using these various methodologies are reviewed in the following section and their commonalities discussed.

Research Findings

Retrospective and Archival Longitudinal Studies

Several personality characteristics that were apparent in persons prior to the onset of their alcohol dependence have been revealed through retrospective and archival longitudinal studies. Males with alcohol dependence have often recalled themselves as having been impulsive, hyperactive, masculine and antisocial (Tarter et al., 1977), although there are some exceptions (Chaplin & Orlofsky, 1991). Ohannessian, Stabenau & Hesselbrock (1995) found that alcohol and other substance abusers recalled more symptoms of conduct disorder from their childhood and exhibited more antisocial behaviour during adulthood than did non-abusers. Andreasson et al. (1992) found that adults' recall of social, behavioural and psychological risk indicators for future alcohol use was associated with greater actual use of alcohol during adulthood. Similar conclusions have been drawn from studies using archival data, which include objective personality measures, such as the Minnesota Multiphasic Personality Inventory (MMPI), suggesting that pre-alcoholics are impulsive, rebellious, independent, non-conforming and undercontrolled. However, gender differences in pre-alcoholic personalities have been found in archive longitudinal studies. Jones (1968, 1971) found that pre-alcoholic males were extraverted, rebellious and masculine, whereas female pre-alcoholics were pessimistic, withdrawn and self-defeating, and were less independent and less self-satisfied than their male counterparts. Similarly, male pre-alcoholics have shown a higher incidence of sociopathy than female pre-alcoholics, who have displayed a higher incidence of affective disorders (see Benson & Wilsnack, 1983).

Recollections of alcohol-dependent people about their childhood behaviour and temperament also reveal some distinguishing characteristics. Andreasson et al. (1992) found early deviant behaviour to be a stronger predictor of heavy alcohol consumption than were other social risk indicators. Ohannessian, Stabenau & Hesselbrock (1995) investigated how alcohol-dependent people's and other substance abusers' problem behaviours earlier in life (gained from participants' recollections of different points in their lives) and their current behaviour problems were associated with their substance abuse in adulthood. They found that both degree of childhood conduct disorder and degree of adult antisocial behaviour predicted the degree of adult substance-use involvement (ranging from alcohol abuse only, to drug abuse only, to abuse of both alcohol and other drugs). However, adult antisocial behaviour was the stronger of the two behavioural predictors of adult substance-use involvement.

As Benson & Wilsnack (1983) discussed, people with alcohol dependence have recalled a greater incidence of aversive life experiences than have control participants. However, there are notable gender differences. Female who are alcohol-dependent, more than males, have reported high rates of disruption early in life (e.g. parental absence) and more specific life stressors (such as abortion, birth of a child, health problems, menopause, divorce, children leaving home, death in the family) which were associated with the onset of their heavy drinking. It also appears that parental alcohol dependence is a common factor in the pre-alcoholic's life; it has been described as a moderate-to-severe risk factor for children's later substance use (Chassin, Rogosch & Barrera, 1991). In short, it is evident that pre-alcoholics' lives (as evidenced by recollections and archival data) were often characterized by behavioural, intrapersonal and familial factors that were not conducive to healthy development. These antecedents have been validated by similar findings from prospective longitudinal studies, which have differentiated individuals who later develop dependence on alcohol from those who do not.

Prospective Longitudinal Studies

Longitudinal studies published in the 1970s and 1980s found converging evidence that participants who developed problems with alcohol were distinguished by the following personality characteristics: independence, aggression, rejection of societal values, antisocial behaviour, impulsivity and hyperactivity (Zucker, 1979). More recently, the original findings have been supported (Zucker, 1987) and additional variables have been identified. Kwapil (1996) found that individuals who were initially non-conforming and prone to psychosis exceeded control groups in the rate with which they had developed substance-abuse disorders at a 10 year follow-up. Masse & Tremblay (1997) observed that young children in kindergarten who were rated high on novelty seeking and low on harm avoidance were later more likely than their peers to develop problems with alcohol. Finally, Bates & Pandina's (1991) longitudinal study of the role of personality in the development of alcohol dependence found that individuals who exhibited a stable personality pattern did not encounter any future difficulties with alcohol. These investigators concluded that subsequent heavy use of alcohol is associated, not with a specific personality structure but with a significant change in personality structure during adolescence.

Several studies have called attention to the role of combined intra- and interpersonal variables as influential in the development of alcohol dependence. Ellickson & Hays (1991), evaluating variables that predicted adolescent drinking 3 and 12 months later, noted the combined influence of cognitive (alcohol expectancies) and social (parental and peer influences) factors. Jessor et al. (1995) concluded that early problem behaviour as a risk for later alcohol problems was mediated by various psychosocial factors, including personality, perceived environment and behaviour systems. Similarly, Bates & Labouvie (1995) identified a specific constellation of personality and environmental characteristics (high impulsivity, disinhibition, membership in deviant peer groups, low parental control) that influenced a high-risk course to future alcohol problems.

The discovery of intrapersonal and psychosocial variables that differentiate prealcoholics from control participants has been mirrored by concurrent identification of psychobiological variables. Hill et al. (1995) found that a particular pattern of electrical activity in the brain of some participants predicted high levels of substance use 4 years later. Schuckit et al. (1996) have identified low reactivity to alcohol as an antecedent of alcohol dependence at 8 and 10 year follow-ups, together with a successful replication using a more heterogeneous sample (Schuckit & Smith, 1996).

In conclusion, the longitudinal evidence corroborates the results of retrospective and archival longitudinal studies in identifying a collection of individual differences that are precursors of later alcohol problems. Collectively, the data have been used to specify which individuals are at high risk for later developing problems with alcohol. These are individuals who have a family history of alcohol dependence (either parental or multigenerational) and who exhibit personality characteristics similar to those of many people with alcohol dependence. Studies that have compared high- and low-risk individuals identified on the basis of these variables are discussed below.

High-risk Studies

A number of researchers have contended that children of alcoholics (COAs) can be distinguished from children of non-alcoholics (nonCOAs) on the basis of their personality characteristics. Jacobs (1991) reviewed evidence to suggest that COAs have a characteristic view of themselves that is acquired from dysfunctional family processes and includes an exaggerated perception of responsibility and self-hatred. Tomori (1994) found that COAs scored higher on aggression and anxiety and lower on self-image variables than did controls. Such a differentiation of COAs from nonCOAs has been supported by a variety of other studies, including that of Hill & Muka (1996). On the other hand, some studies (e.g. Howard et al., 1996) have failed to detect differences between COAs and nonCOAs. The lack of consistency in findings might be partly explained by the fact that other studies (e.g. Finn et al., 1997) have found subtypes of COAs which are differentiated by different clusters of personality characteristics. That is, the heterogeneity of COA characteristics may account for differences in samples from one study to another. It should also be noted that particular personality characteristics, regardless of genetic linkage, have been found to place individuals at risk for alcohol problems. Examples include: alexithymia (a person's inability to identify his/her own emotions); temperamental difficulties; and high novelty seeking, low harm avoidance and low reward dependence. Additionally, the relative contribution of personality characteristics and other factors (e.g. familial dysfunction) that place COAs at risk for developing alcohol problems needs to be closely examined.

Additional factors that differentiate high- and low-risk individuals include gender roles, neuropsychological variables, perceived consequences of drinking, electrical activity of the brain, behavioural disinhibition, and physiological and subjective reactions to alcohol. As in the longitudinal studies discussed above, several studies of high- and low-risk individuals have assessed the combined role of various variables (Knop et al., 1993), and analysed the direction of causality among the variables (i.e. which variables affect other variables and which variables are affected by other variables). Studies using path analysis have evaluated mediational effects of these variables (Woldt & Bradley, 1996). The current view that a variety of variables combines to determine particular individuals' risk status is further supported by studies of adolescents who are problem drinkers. Characteristics that distinguish these individuals from adolescents who drink moderately or not at all are discussed in the following section.

Adolescent Studies

Antisocial behaviour has often been observed among adolescent problem drinkers. Sigurdsson & Gudjonsson (1996), for instance, noted even higher levels of antisocial behaviour and dishonesty among adolescent alcohol and drug users than other juvenile offenders. Nevertheless, the heterogeneity of adolescent problem drinkers is striking. Donat, Hume & Hiner (1992), for example, identified five subtypes of adolescent substance abusers, and Colder & Chassin (1997) identified multiple, interrelated dimensions of adolescent temperament. Mezzich et al. (1993) found that one personality subtype of adolescents was characterized by negative affect and another by behavioural dyscontrol and hypophoria. In addition to personality antecedents, Pogge, Stokes & Harvey (1992) observed attentional deficits in alcohol-dependent adolescent inpatients. Simon et al. (1994) observed a cultural difference in personality, such that high sensation seeking was a predictor of substance use among Latino adolescents but low-to-moderate sensation seeking predicted use among White adolescents.

Finally, a number of studies have examined multiple variables in addition to personality characteristics that are associated with adolescent problem drinking (see Chapter 17, this volume). The set of predictors includes: easy access to alcohol; parental alcohol use and abuse; deviant peer influences; positive alcohol expectancies; antisocial, aggressive and impulsive personality traits; high emotional intensity; early intoxication; childhood and adolescent deviant behaviour; male gender; a family history of depression; sexual and physical abuse; and parental control. It is apparent that this list of variables is similar to those identified with other methods of study for identifying antecedents to adolescent problem drinking.

Conclusions

The methodologies described above are diverse, yet obvious commonalties exist in the collection of findings. First, there is a set of intrapersonal and psychosocial antecedents of alcohol dependence. The variables include: level of brain-wave activity; physiological and subjective reactivity to alcohol; family history of alcohol dependence; antisocial, aggressive and impulsive personality characteristics; a maladaptive self-concept; childhood conduct disorder; familial dysfunction; and deviant peer influences. Additional differentiating variables include age, gender and sociocultural membership. Hence, the antecedent research has thus far identified a set of variables that is clearly implicated in the development of alcohol dependence. Further investigation is needed to understand more clearly the relationships among these variables, especially inasmuch as the heterogeneity of alcohol dependence (in terms of onset, course and outcome) appears explicable only when such relationships are taken into account. There will be many opportunities for practical application of this knowledge, such as with prevention strategies. For example, individuals at high risk for developing problems with alcohol can be identified and interventions undertaken to influence a developmental path that is free of alcohol abuse.

PERSONALITY CHARACTERISTICS OF ALCOHOL ABUSERS

This section discusses those personality characteristics that have been found to distinguish individuals who already abuse alcohol from those who do not. As we will see, some of these personality characteristics appear to have been antecedents of the alcohol-related problems and contributed to their development. Other characteristics seem to be a consequence of the abuse of alcohol.

Epistemology

With the advent of professional psychotherapy for individuals suffering from alcohol abuse, clinicians sought to understand the nature of alcohol dependence by applying an idiographic epistemology, using clinical case studies. Measurement took the form of narrative accounts of individual experiences or projective testing with a focus on identifying intrapsychic needs that were satisfied by drinking alcohol. However, as structured group treatments for alcohol dependence developed, access to small groups of alcoholic patients facilitated a shift towards a nomothetic epistemology. That is, an attempt was now made to identify the aetiology of alcohol dependence by comparing alcoholic patients with non-alcoholic control groups. In addition, publication of the Diagnostic and Statistical Manual of Mental Disorders (DSM) and its successive revisions served as a catalyst for accelerated research to compare the personality characteristics of alcoholics and non-alcoholics. Specifically, the DSM facilitated communication of research findings and their replication and offered a framework within which disparate psychological perspectives on the nature of alcohol dependence could contribute to a common understanding of its aetiology (see also Chapter 4, this volume).

Research Findings

As we have seen, there is no evidence to suggest that there is a single personality profile that reflects an "alcoholic personality". Nevertheless, research findings indicate that alcoholics and non-alcoholic samples respond differently to a variety of unidimensional and multidimensional measures of personality.

The MacAndrew Alcoholism scale (MAC) resulted from one early attempt to develop a psychometric device for distinguishing alcoholics from non-alcoholics. The MAC scale isolated 49 items from the MMPI that were answered differently by alcoholic male outpatients and non-alcoholic male psychiatric outpatients. The ability of the MAC scale to discriminate between alcohol abusers and non-abusers is well documented (Miller & Streiner, 1990). Additionally, the MAC-R, from the re-standardized MMPI-2, appears to have the same factor structure as the original MAC scale (Weed, Butcher & Ben Porath, 1995). As Graham (1990) summarized, individuals who score high on the MAC-R scale have often had early behavioural problems, are socially extraverted, self-confident and assertive, and enjoy competition and taking risks. However, care must be taken when drawing inferences from a single psychometric test score. As Sawrie et al. (1996) described, two identical scores from the MAC scale do not necessarily reflect the same personality characteristics.

Despite such possible divergence, comparisons of alcoholic and non-alcoholic samples have consistently indicated two overarching personality dimensions that distinguish the two groups. The first dimension is behavioural disinhibition, which is associated with impulsivity, unconventionality and emotional overactivity. The second dimension is negative emotionality, which reflects subjective discomfort and distress.

Behavioural Disinhibition

Behavioural disinhibition is observed both among alcoholics and pre-alcoholics (McGue et al., 1997) and differentiates the offspring of people with alcohol dependence from those of non-alcoholics (Sher, 1991). Behaviourally disinhibited alcoholics are characterized by impulsivity, an inability to learn from mistakes and difficulties in forming close relationships (Schuckit et al., 1994). Such characteristics, particularly when associated with early-onset alcohol dependence, appear to have a strong genetic component (McGue et al., 1997), although they are also mediated by environmental influences (Tarter et al., 1994).

The behavioural disinhibition of alcohol-dependent people has also been described as reflecting high novelty seeking and low harm avoidance (Galen, Hendersen & Whitman, 1997). Some recent research has focused on how the association between these characteristics and alcohol abuse manifests itself in society. Cherpitel (1993), for instance, reported that individuals admitted to hospital with injuries were more likely to report being moderate-to-heavy drinkers than were individuals admitted without injuries. Brotman et al. (1995) reported that three-quarters of adults admitted to hospital suffering with alcohol-related injuries regularly failed to use seat belts. Donovan (1993) found that risky driving practices were associated with problem drinking. There is also evidence for an association between alcohol abuse and high-risk sexual behaviours. For example, Stinson et al. (1992), reviewing data from the 1988 *National Health Interview Survey* in the USA, found that individuals meeting the criteria for alcohol dependence were at much higher risk of exposure to HIV and developing AIDS than were non-alcohol-dependent individuals. Finally, it should be noted that, in its most extreme form, the behavioural disinhibition of alcohol-dependent people manifests itself as antisocial personality disorder (APD). In fact, the comorbidity of alcohol dependence and APD has often been observed (Sher & Trull, 1994; see also Chapter 32, this volume).

Negative Emotionality

People with alcohol dependence who enter treatment have consistently shown high levels of negative emotionality. In fact, there is a high prevalence of comorbid anxiety and mood disorders (particularly bipolar manic-depressive disorder) among alcohol-dependent individuals (Raimo & Schuckit, 1998). Much of the evidence suggests that negative emotionality is a consequence, rather than a precursor, of the abuse of alcohol (e.g. McGue et al., 1997). There are, however, exceptions to this general conclusion (e.g. Sieber, 1981). It seems reasonable to attribute alcohol-dependent people's negative emotionality to the negative life events that they have experienced as a result of their excessive drinking. In fact, it has been demonstrated that in their recent past (e.g. the previous year) people with alcohol dependence have experienced a greater number of stressful life events than have "normal" controls (Thankachan & Kodandaram, 1992). Moreover, among some people with alcohol dependence, traumatic life events appear to have precipitated the abuse of alcohol (McFarlane, 1998).

The extent of alcohol-dependent people's excessive drinking has been found to co-vary with their level of depression (Roy et al., 1991) and anxiety (Dryman, Anthony & DePaulo, 1989). Moreover, people with alcohol dependence are more likely to drink when they experience negative emotions and abstinent alcohol-dependent people are more likely to relapse at these times (Marlatt & Gordon, 1985). Finally, experimental studies have indicated that alcohol-dependent people's negative mood states serve as a potential cue for them to consume alcohol. Litt et al. (1990), for example, found that people with alcohol dependence showed an increased desire to drink following an experimental negative mood induction, irrespective of the presence or absence of exteroceptive cues.

Typologies of Alcoholics

Dissatisfaction with the conceptualization of alcohol dependence as a single entity has existed for more than a century, with attempts to identify subtypes of people with alcohol dependence recorded as long ago as 1850 (see Chapter 4, this volume). However, typologies of alcohol-dependent people that had been proposed prior to Prohibition in the USA were replaced by more objective taxonomies after this period. These were initially unidimensional models that explored single discriminating variables; nevertheless, they formed the basis for subsequent multi-dimensional classifications of alcohol-dependent people into subtypes.

Several attempts to divide people with alcohol dependence into subgroups occurring during the late nineteenth and early twentieth centuries included a prominent typology by Knight (1937). Developed from psychoanalytic case studies of people with alcohol dependence, Knight's typology differentiated alcohol-dependent people who had inherited a susceptibility to developing alcohol dependence ("essential alcoholics") from those who developed alcohol dependence as a reaction to a major life stressor ("reactive alcoholics"). Jellinek's (1960) distinction between delta and gamma alcoholics was also influential in its time. These two types were differentiated by their pattern of alcohol use, antecedents of their problem drinking and detrimental consequences of their drinking. Although these early typologies were not developed through empirical research, they bear striking similarities to recent dichotomies that were developed empirically. Therefore, as Cook et al. (1994) pointed out, the foundation laid by the early typologies should be acknowledged.

Advances in objective measurement of individual differences made it possible to develop empirically valid subtypes of alcohol-dependent people that have been distinguished in terms of their personality characteristics, pattern of alcohol use, psychiatric comorbidity and optimal treatment. The instruments that have been used are numerous and varied. This situation partly accounts for the fact that diverse typologies have been identified that differ in terms of the dimensions of personality along which they vary.

The MMPI is the personality test that has been most commonly used with people with alcohol dependence and on several occasions it has been used to develop alcoholic typologies. Using this instrument in combination with other measures, Morey, Roberts & Penk (1987) identified three subtypes (early-stage problem drinkers and affiliative and schizoid alcoholics), whereas Graham & Strenger (1988) found six subtypes, which were differentiated on the basis of personality, psychopathology, drinking history and treatment variables. Allen, Fertig & Mattson (1994) criticized use of the MMPI to develop personality-based typologies because the MMPI emphasizes disordered behaviour, the concepts that it measures are complex and it tends to view people from an intrapersonal rather than an interpersonal perspective. Instead, Allen et al. used the Personality Research Form (PRF), which yielded five subtypes: hostile–dependent; cooperative–non-reflective; socially uninvolved; impulsive–unsociable; and hostile–overcontrolled. Several studies have used the Millon Clinical Multiaxial Inventory (MCMI) and each study found five subtypes of drinkers. By contrast, Mayer & Scott (1988) and Matano, Locke & Schwartz (1994) found four and three subtypes, respectively, with the MCMI. In all of the studies using the MCMI, the subtypes were differentiated by their degree of elevation on MCMI scales measuring personality style, personality disorder and emotional symptomatology. In summary, the aforementioned lack of consistency in subtypes identified across different studies has caused confusion in the overall conceptualization of alcoholic personality subtypes. Hence, it would appear that standard measures and methodologies will be required to facilitate comparison across different studies.

Another common basis for subgrouping people with alcohol dependence has been the presence (and type) or absence of comorbid psychopathology (see Chapter 4, this volume). Kendall & Clarkin (1992), in fact, consider the study of comorbidity to be the key challenge to current mental health research in general. People with alcohol dependence have been found to display various psychopathologies, including antisocial personality disorder (Penick et al., 1994), borderline personality disorder (Morgenstern et al., 1997), paranoid personality disorder (Morgenstern et al., 1997), depression (see Poikolainen, 1994), mania (Penick et al., 1994), attention deficit disorder (Vaeth, Horton & Ahadpour, 1992), and anxiety disorders (see Schuckit & Hesselbrock, 1994). A prominent distinction (to be discussed later) that has been put forward by MacAndrew (1983) and Schuckit (1985) is that of primary vs. secondary alcohol dependence. Primary alcohol dependence refers to alcohol dependence that precedes (and perhaps contributes to) other psychiatric disorders, whereas secondary alcohol dependence is viewed as a symptom of a pre-existing disorder (commonly antisocial personality disorder). Cook et al. (1994) observed that primary alcohol dependence is more severe and has stronger familial aetiology than does secondary alcohol dependence.

A practical implication of alcoholic typologies is to use them to match patients with their optimal treatment modality. Kadden et al. (1989), for example, differentiated people with alcohol dependence in terms of their degree of antisocial tendency, disordered behaviour and impaired brain functioning. These researchers used either training in cognitive-behavioural coping skills (for patients highest on these scales) or interactional group therapy (for patients who were lowest). Patients so matched showed significantly better recovery than control patients who were not matched. Another variable that is clearly needed in applied research is patients' level of motivation. DiClemente & Hughes (1990) and Carney & Kivlahan (1995) delineated four and five motivational types of drinkers, respectively, and Isenhart (1994) identifed three motivational types. It will now be important to determine which motivational type responds best to which kind of intervention.

Evaluating the comparative validity of different alcoholic typologies, Yates & Meller (1993) concluded that the most valid typologies (in decreasing order) were those defined on the basis of presence or absence of antisocial personality disorder, presence or absence of other drug abuse or dependence, age of onset, primary vs. secondary alcohol dependence, and presence or absence of parental alcohol dependence. Comparing the relative merits of using typologies for scientific vs. clinical purposes, Brown et al. (1994) concluded that typologies that are used in scientific investigations may have limited clinical usefulness because of their highly specific inclusion criteria, whereas typologies that are useful in clinical practice may lack the rigorous assumptions of homogeneity that are required for scientific inquiry. It is widely acknowledged that progress in typological conceptualization and application has occurred mainly through recently developed typologies that vary along multiple dimensions. The most notable of these typologies are Cloninger's (1983) neurobiological learning model, Morey & Skinner's (1986) hybrid model, Zucker's (1987) developmental model and Babor et al.'s (1992) vulnerability–severity classification.

Combining genetic and psychosocial variables in a cross-fostering analysis, Cloninger, Bohman & Sigvardsson (1981) differentiated people with alcohol dependence into two types, milieu-limited (Type I) and male-limited (Type II) (see also Chapters 4, 6 and 13, this volume). Compared to Type II, Type I alcohol-dependent people are characterized by later onset, are relatively more psychologically (than physically) dependent on alcohol and are more strongly influenced by environmental factors. Type II alcohol-dependent people are strongly genetically influenced and are characterized by frequent alcohol-seeking behaviours and an early onset of problem drinking. More common in men than women, this form of alcohol dependence is often associated with criminality. The distinction between these two types of people with alcohol dependence is based on hypothesized differences in three personality dimensions (harm avoidance, reward dependence and novelty seeking) that are assessed with the Tridimensional Personality Questionnaire (TPQ). This dichotomy has been systematically supported by other studies using biological and psychological measures, such as the TPQ (e.g. Yoshino et al., 1994), the MacAndrew Alcoholism scale (Svanum & Ehrmann, 1992), serotonin levels (Virkkunen & Linnoila, 1993), and levels of platelet monoamine oxidase (Hallman, von Knorring & Oreland, 1996). It has also been supported by two successful replications (Cloninger, Sigvardsson & Bohman, 1988, 1996). Nevertheless, other studies have challenged Cloninger' dichotomy (e.g. Rubio et al., 1998) and the validity of the TPQ (e.g. Cannon et al., 1993). It appears that the mixed support for the model can be attributed to inconsistencies in the variables that have been studied. Biological measures seem to support the model (see above) but personality and familial variables have been used both to support (Cloninger et al., 1996) and challenge (Hill, 1992) the dichotomy. Further, an attempted replication in a Spanish sample was unsuccessful (Rubio et al., 1998). Several investigators have suggested that Cloninger' distinction is indistinguishable from the primary vs. secondary distinction. Noting the prominence of antisocial personality disorder and early onset in Type II alcohol dependence, these researchers suggest that this disorder is actually primary antisocial personality disorder with secondary alcohol dependence.

Using multivariate cluster analysis, Morey & Skinner (1986) developed the Hybrid Model, which differentiated three types of drinkers on the basis of demographics, personality characteristics (measured with the PRF), intellectual functioning, psychopathology, social interaction and alcohol-use variables from the Alcohol Use Inventory (AUI). One type, early-stage drinkers, reported a later onset of drinking, lower quantity of alcohol consumed and fewer detrimental consequences of their drinking. Additional characteristics that differentiate this type from the other two are stronger needs for achievement, greater abstract-thinking ability, and lower levels of aggressiveness and impulsivity. A second type, the affiliative alcoholic, showed more continuous drinking than the first type and tended to drink socially but with more interpersonal problems. Finally, the schizoid alcoholic displayed the most problematic pattern of drinking and generally drank alone and in binges. This type had greater anxiety and guilt than the other types, and reported higher levels of aggression and impulsivity and lower levels of affiliation.

Zucker's developmental model (1987), based on longitudinal evidence, suggests four "alcoholisms": antisocial, developmentally cumulative, developmentally limited and negative-affect alcohol dependence. Antisocial alcohol dependence is characterized by an early onset of alcohol abuse and antisocial behaviour. Developmentally cumulative alcohol dependence evolves from normal drinking to an extreme level of consumption that is characteristic of alcohol dependence. Developmentally limited alcohol dependence is distinguished by frequent heavy drinking early in life, which is followed by a period of abstention when the person adopts a career and a family role. Finally, negative affect alcohol dependence occurs primarily in women who have used alcohol to regulate their mood and enhance social interaction. Zucker maintains that non-drinking-related variables interact significantly with drinking variables to influence the development of each type of alcohol dependence. He also emphasizes the importance of viewing patients' alcohol problems within the context of their total life history when designing and implementing treatment.

Finally, Babor et al. (1992) proposed a Type A/Type B dichotomy of people with alcohol dependence. The former type is characterized by less premorbid risk, later onset, less severe dependence, fewer resultant problems, a less chronic course and less comorbid psychopathology. In contrast, Type B alcohol-dependent people have greater antecedent risk factors, earlier onset, more severe dependence, more severe outcomes, a more chronic course and greater chronic psychopathology. The latter type, of course, has a poorer prognosis. This model, derived from complex statistical techniques, has been supported in replications by Brown et al. (1994) and Litt et al. (1992). The latter study both reproduced the original clusters and successfully matched the two types with their optimal treatments (coping skills training for Type A alcohol-dependent people, interactional therapy for Type B alcohol-dependent people). This application supports the clinical efficacy and construct validity of Babor's typology.

It is evident that there are notable differences among the four multi-dimensional typologies discussed here in terms of the number of subtypes identified and the variables used to differentiate them. Research is still needed to reduce such differences and develop a standardized classification system for alcohol dependence that can be used for both clinical and research purposes. Despite the differences, Babor (1994) has suggested that most typology theories refer to two basic types of alcohol dependence. One type is similar to Knight's reactive, Jellinek's delta, Cloninger's Type I, Morey & Skinner's affiliative and Babor's Type A alcoholic. It is distinguished by later onset, slower course, less psychological impairment, fewer complications and better prognosis. Conversely, the other type is more genetically determined and characterized by early onset, more rapid course, more severe symptoms, greater psychological problems and poorer prognosis. This type resembles Knight's essential, Jellinek's gamma, Cloninger's Type II, Morey & Skinner's schizoid, Zucker's antisocial and Babor's Type B alcoholic.

The criticisms of Cloninger's model, described above, seem also applicable to the other typologies discussed here, namely, those of Morey & Skinner, Zucker, and Babor. That is, because each of these models uses the presence or absence of antisocial personality and early vs. late onset as differentiating factors, the older primary vs. secondary distinction still seems relevant. Future research needs to establish whether this basic dichotomy (perhaps with embellishments and/or subdivisions) will still be useful. Refinements that are likely to be required include the addition of variables related to gender and other life roles (as Zucker has suggested).

CONCLUSIONS

From this chapter's review of the literature, it is apparent that a wealth of research has been conducted to investigate individual differences related to the abuse of alcohol. Nevertheless, several overarching themes emerge from the research findings. From both the studies of individual differences that antedate alcohol abuse and those that co-vary with the abuse, we saw two broad constellations of personality characteristics. One of these we called behavioural disinhibition, a dimension of personality that manifests itself as impulsivity, non-conformity, reward-seeking and antisocial tendencies. For people who are behaviourally disinhibited, alcohol abuse seems often to be a part of their life-style. We called the other dimension negative emotionality, which includes various kinds of negative affect, particularly anxiety and depression. Alcohol abusers who are marked by negative emotionality seem to have adopted overindulgence in alcohol as their way of coping with their negative feelings.

Observing these two broad constellations of personality provided the logical next step of identifying various typologies of alcohol-dependent people. A variety of types of alcohol-dependent people have been defined but the particulars of each type seem largely to depend on the instruments that were used to identify them. Notwithstanding this variety, two types of alcohol-dependent people have been observed repeatedly. We saw that people belonging to one of these types have been called primary alcohol-dependent people; they are the antisocial alcohol-dependent people whose difficulties appear to be partly under genetic control. Their problems with alcohol begin to manifest themselves early in life and eventually become chronic and severe. People belonging to the other type have been called secondary alcohol-dependent people. Compared to primary alcohol-dependent people, their problems with alcohol are more likely to appear later in life; the excessive drinking occurs in reaction to the negative affect that the person experiences and the onset of the negative affect can sometimes be traced to specific negative life events. For the most part, secondary alcohol-dependent people's drinking problems are less severe and more likely to remit than are those of primary alcohol-dependent people.

It is clear that individual differences play a critical role in the development and maintenance of problems with alcohol. However, it is equally apparent that a unique constellation of personality characteristics (the "alcoholic personality") cannot be viewed as the exclusive cause for alcohol abuse. Instead, alcohol problems result from a complex interplay of biological, psychological, environmental and sociocultural determinants (e.g. Cox & Klinger, 1988). For this reason, it is perhaps most accurate to view personality as a modulator of the impact of the other kinds of variables. For example, people who are exposed to heavy-drinking environments would be at increased risk to drink heavily themselves because of the social reinforcement they would derive from doing so. However, whether or not this potential motivator of excessive drinking is translated into actual drinking behaviour could well be modulated by whether or not the person's personality characteristics also promote excessive drinking. Ultimately, research on individual differences related to alcohol abuse would have its greatest practical benefit by enabling us to lessen the impact of modulating influences that promote excessive drinking.

KEY WORKS AND SUGGESTIONS FOR FURTHER READING

Babor, T.F., Hesselbrock, V.M., Meyer R.E. & Shoemaker, W. (Eds) (1994). *Types of Alcoholics: Evidence from Clinical, Experimental and Genetic Research.* New York: New York Academy of Sciences.

This useful book is a complete coverage of the empirical and theoretical aspects of types of alcoholics, and with helpful suggestions for clinical applications.

Cox, W.M. (Ed.) (1983). *Identifying and Measuring Alcoholic Personality Characteristics.* San Francisco, CA: Jossey-Bass.

This book concisely depicts the personality characteristics that distinguish both alcoholics and "pre-alcoholics" from those of other people.

Cox, W.M. (1985). Personality correlates of substance abuse. In M. Galizio & S.A. Maisto (Eds), *Determinants of Substance Abuse: Biological, Psychological and Environmental Factors* (pp. 209–246). New York: Plenum.

In this chapter, the personality correlates of both alcohol abuse and other kinds of substance abuse are covered in detail.

Cox, W.M. (1987). Personality theory and research. In H.T. Blane & K.E. Leonard (Eds), *Psychological Theories of Drinking and Alcoholism* (pp. 55–89). New York: Guilford.

Personality theories of excessive drinking and alcoholism are considered, along with research findings related to these theories.

Cox, W.M. (Ed.) (1990). *Why People Drink: Parameters of Alcohol as a Reinforcer.* New York: Amereon.

This edited book considers the biological, psychological and sociocultural reasons why people drink alcohol. It then attempts to integrate the various viewpoints in a motivational model of alcohol use.

Rivers, P.C. (Ed.) (1987). *Alcohol and Addictive Behaviour: Nebraska Symposium on Motivation, 1986.* Lincoln, NE: University of Nebraska Press.

Leading alcohol researchers present their theoretical and empirical perspectives on what causes addiction to alcohol.

REFERENCES

Allen, J.P., Fertig, J.B. & Mattson, M.E. (1994). Personality-based subtypes of chemically dependent patients. In T.F. Babor, V. Hesselbrock, R.E. Meyer & W. Shoemaker (Eds), *Types of Alcoholics: Evidence from Clinical, Experimental, and Genetic Research*, Vol. 708 (pp. 7–22). New York: Annals of the New York Academy of Sciences.

Andreasson, S., Allebeck, P., Brandt, L. & Romelsjo, A. (1992). Antecedents and covariates of high alcohol consumption in young men. *Alcoholism: Clinical and Experimental Research*, **16**, 708–713.

Babor, T.F. (1994). *De gustibus non est disputandum*: lumpers, splitters and the disconfirmation dilemma. *Addiction*, **89**, 1059–1061.

Babor, T.F., Hofmann, M., DelBoca, F.K., Hesselbrock, V.M., Meyer, R.E., Dolinsky, Z.S. & Rounsaville, B. (1992). Types of alcoholics: I. Evidence for an empirically derived typology based on indicators of vulnerability and severity. *Archives of General Psychiatry*, **49**, 599–608.

Bates, M.E. & Labouvie, E.W. (1995). Personality-environment constellations and alcohol use: a process-oriented study of intraindividual change during adolescence. *Psychology of Addictive Behaviors*, **9**, 23–35.

Bates, M.E. & Pandina, R.J. (1991). Personality stability and adolescent substance use behaviors. *Alcoholism: Clinical and Experimental Research*, **15**, 471–477.

Benson, C.S. & Wilsnack, S.C. (1983). Gender differences in alcoholic personality characteristics and life experiences. In W.M. Cox (Ed.), *Identifying and Measuring Alcoholic Personality Characteristics*. San Francisco, CA: Jossey-Bass.

Brotman, S., Indeck, M.C., Leonard, D. & Huber, J. (1995). Study of the relationship between lifestyle characteristic self-reported drinking patterns and trauma. *American Surgeon*, **61**, 975–979.

Brown, J., Babor, T.F., Litt, M.D. & Kranzler, H.R. (1994). The Type A/Type B distinction: subtyping alcoholics according to indicators of vulnerability and severity. In T.F. Babor, V. Hesselbrock, R.E. Meyer & W. Shoemaker (Eds), *Types of Alcoholics: Evidence from Clinical, Experimental, and Genetic Research*, Vol. 708 (pp. 23–33). New York: Annals of the New York Academy of Sciences.

Cannon, D.S., Clark, L.A., Leeka, J.K. & Keefe, C.K. (1993). A reanalysis of the Tridimensional Personality Questionnaire (TPQ) and its relation to Cloninger's Type 2 alcoholism. *Psychological Assessment*, **5**, 62–66.

Carney, M.M. & Kivlahan, D.R. (1995). Motivational subtypes among veterans seeking substance abuse treatment: Profiles based on stages of change. *Psychology of Addictive Behaviors*, **9**, 135–142.

Chaplin, M.P. & Orlofsky, J.L. (1991). Personality characteristics of male alcoholics as revealed through their early recollections. *Individual Psychology: Journal of Adlerian Theory, Research and Practice*, **47**, 356–371.

Chassin, L., Rogosch, F. & Barrera, M. (1991). Substance use and symptomatology among adolescent children of alcoholics. *Journal of Abnormal Psychology*, **100**, 449–463.

Cherpitel, C.J. (1993). Alcohol, injury, and risk-taking behavior: data from a national sample. *Alcoholism: Clinical and Experimental Research*, **17**, 762–766.

Cloninger, C.R. (1983). Genetic and environmental factors in the development of alcoholism. *Journal of Psychiatric Treatment and Evaluation*, **5**, 487–496.

Cloninger, C.R., Bohman, M. & Sigvardsson, S. (1981). Inheritance of alcohol abuse: cross-fostering analysis of adopted men. *Archives of General Psychiatry*, **38**, 861–868.

Cloninger, C.R., Sigvardsson, S. & Bohman, M. (1988). Childhood personality predicts alcohol abuse in young adults. *Alcoholism: Clinical and Experimental Research*, **12**, 494–505.

Cloninger, C.R., Sigvardsson, S. & Bohman, M. (1996). Type I and type II alcoholism: an update. *Alcohol Health and Research World*, **20**, 18–23.

Colder, C.R. & Chassin, L. (1997). Affectivity and impulsivity: temperament risk for adolescent alcohol involvement. *Psychology of Addictive Behaviors*, **11**, 83–97.

Cook, B.L., Winokur, G., Fowler, R.C. & Liskow, B.I. (1994). Classification of alcoholism with reference to comorbidity. *Comprehensive Psychiatry*, **35**, 165–170.

Cox, W.M. & Klinger, E. (1988). A motivational model of alcohol use. *Journal of Abnormal Psychology*, **97**, 168–180.

DiClemente, C.C. & Hughes, S.O. (1990). Stages of change profiles in outpatient alcoholism treatment. *Journal of Substance Abuse*, **2**, 217–235.

Donat, D.C., Hume, A. & Hiner, G.L. (1992). Personality subtypes of adolescent substance abusers: a cluster analysis of Millon Adolescent Personality Inventory (MAPI) personality scales. *Medical Psychotherapy: An International Journal*, **5**, 95–102.

Donovan, J.E. (1993). Young adult drinking-driving: Behavioral and psychosocial correlates. *Journal of Studies on Alcohol*, **54**, 600–613.

Dryman, A., Anthony, J.C. & DePaulo, J.R. (1989). Relationship between psychiatric distress and alcohol use: findings from the Eastern Baltimore Mental Health Survey. *Acta Psychiatrica Scandinavica*, **80**, 310–314.

Ellickson, P.L. & Hays, R.D. (1991). Antecedents of drinking among young adolescents with different alcohol use histories. *Journal of Studies on Alcohol*, **52**, 398–408.

Finn, P.R., Sharkansky, E.J., Viken, R., West, T.L., Sandy, J. & Bufferd, G.M. (1997). Heterogeneity in the families of sons of alcoholics: the impact of familial vulnerability type on offspring characteristics. *Journal of Abnormal Psychology*, **106**, 26–36.

Galen, L.W., Hendersen, M.J. & Whitman, R.D. (1997). The utility of novelty seeking, harm avoidance, and expectancy in the prediction of drinking. *Addictive Behaviors*, **22**, 93–106.

Graham, J.R. (1990). *MMPI-2: Assessing Personality and Psychopathology*. New York: Oxford University Press.

Graham, J.R. & Strenger, V.E. (1988). MMPI characteristics of alcoholics: a review. *Journal of Consulting and Clinical Psychology*, **56**, 197–205.

Hallman, J., von Knorring, L. & Oreland, L. (1996). Personality disorders according to DSM-III-R and thrombocyte monoamine oxidase activity in Type 1 and Type 2 alcoholics. *Journal of Studies on Alcohol*, **57**, 155–161.

Hill, S.Y. (1992). Absence of paternal sociopathy in the etiology of severe alcoholism: is there a Type III alcoholism? *Journal of Studies on Alcohol*, **53**, 161–169.

Hill, S.Y. & Muka, D. (1996). Childhood psychopathology in children from families of alcoholic female probands. *Journal of the American Academy of Child and Adolescent Psychiatry*, **35**, 725–733.

Hill, S.Y., Steinhauer, S., Lowers, L. & Locke, J. (1995). Eight-year longitudinal follow-up of P300 and clinical outcome in children from high-risk for alcoholism families. *Biological Psychiatry*, **37**, 823–827.

Howard, M.O., Cowley, D.S., Roy-Byrne, P.P. & Hopfenbeck, J.R. (1996). Tridimensional personality traits in sons of alcoholic and nonalcoholic fathers. *Alcoholism: Clinical and Experimental Research*, **20**, 445–448.

Isenhart, C.E. (1994). Motivational subtypes in an inpatient sample of substance abusers. *Addictive Behaviors*, **19**, 463–475.

Jacobs, P.S. (1991). Characteristics of the self in children of alcoholics: a review. *Alcoholism Treatment Quarterly*, **8**, 67–74.

Jellinek, E.M. (1960). *The Disease Concept of Alcoholism*. New Haven, CT: Hillhouse.

Jessor, R., Van Den Bos, J., Vanderryn, J., Costa, F.M. & Turbin, M.S. (1995). Protective factors in adolescent problem behavior: moderator effects and developmental change. *Developmental Psychology*, **31**, 923–933.

Jones, M.C. (1968). Personality correlates and antecedents of drinking patterns in adult males. *Journal of Consulting and Clinical Psychology*, **32**, 2–12.

Jones, M.C. (1971). Personality antecedents and correlates of drinking patterns in women. *Journal of Consulting and Clinical Psychology*, **36**, 61–69.

Kadden, R.M., Cooney, N.L., Getter, H. & Litt, M.D. (1989). Matching alcoholics to coping skills or interactional therapies: posttreatment results. *Journal of Consulting and Clinical Psychology*, **57**, 698–704.

Kendall, P.C. & Clarkin, J.F. (1992). Introduction to special section: comorbidity and treatment implications. *Journal of Consulting and Clinical Psychology*, **60**, 833–834.

Knight, R.P. (1937). The psychodynamics of chronic alcoholism. *Journal of Nervous and Mental Disease*, **86**, 538–548.

Knop, J., Goodwin, D.W., Jensen, P., Penick, E., Pollock, V., Gabrielli, W., Teasdale, T.W. & Mednick, S.A. (1993). A 30-year follow-up study of the sons of alcoholic men. *Acta Psychiatrica Scandinavica*, **87**(Suppl. 370), 48–53.

Kwapil, T.R. (1996). A longitudinal study of drug and alcohol use by psychosis-prone and impulsive-nonconforming individuals. *Journal of Abnormal Psychology*, **105**, 114–123.

Litt, M.D., Babor, T.F., DelBoca, F.K., Kadden, R.M. & Cooney, N.L. (1992). Types of alcoholics: II. Application of an empirically derived typology to treatment matching. *Archives of General Psychiatry*, **49**, 609–614.

Litt, M.D., Cooney, N.L., Kadden, R.M. & Gaupp, L. (1990). Reactivity to alcohol cues and induced moods in alcoholics. *Addictive Behaviors*, **15**, 137–146.

MacAndrew, C. (1983). Alcoholic personality or personalities: scale and profile data from the MMPI. In W.M. Cox (Ed.), *Identifying and Measuring Alcoholic Personality Characteristics*. San Francisco, CA: Jossey-Bass.

Marlatt, G.A. & Gordon, J.R. (1985). *Relapse Prevention: Maintenance Strategies in the Treatment of Addictive Behaviors*. New York: Guilford.

Masse, L.C. & Tremblay, R.E. (1997). Behavior of boys in kindergarten and the onset of substance use during adolescence. *Archives of General Psychiatry*, **54**, 62–68.

Matano, R.A., Locke, K.D. & Schwartz, K. (1994). MCMI personality subtypes for male and female alcoholics. *Journal of Personality Assessment*, **63**, 250–264.

Mayer, G.S. & Scott, K.J. (1988). An exploration of heterogeneity in an inpatient male alcoholic population. *Journal of Personality Disorders*, **2**, 243–255.

McAdams, D.P. (1994). *The Person: An Introduction to Personality Psychology*, 2nd edn. San Diego, CA: Harcourt Brace Jovanovich.

McFarlane, A.C. (1998). Epidemiological evidence about the relationship between PTSD and alcohol abuse: the nature of the association. *Addictive Behaviors*, **23**, 813–825.

McGue, M., Slutske, W., Taylor, J. & Iacono, W.G. (1997). Personality and substance use disorders: I. Effects of gender and alcoholism subtype. *Alcoholism: Clinical and Experimental Research*, **21**, 513–520.

Mezzich, A.C., Tarter, R., Kirisci, L., Clark, D., Buckstein, O. & Martin, C. (1993). Subtypes of early age onset alcoholism. *Alcoholism: Clinical and Experimental Research*, **17**, 767–770.

Miller, H.R. & Streiner, D.L. (1990). Using the Millon Clinical Multiaxial Inventory's Scale B and the MacAndrew Alcoholism Scale to identify alcoholics with concurrent psychiatric diagnoses. *Journal of Personality Assessment*, **54**, 736–746.

Morey, L.C., Roberts, W.R. & Penk, W. (1987). MMPI alcoholic subtypes: replicability and validity of the 2–8–7–4 subtype. *Journal of Abnormal Psychology*, **96**, 164–166.

Morey, L.C. & Skinner, H.A. (1986). Empirically derived classifications of alcohol-related problems. In M. Galanter (Ed.), *Recent Developments in Alcoholism* (pp. 145–168). New York: Plenum.

Morgenstern, J., Langenbucher, J., Labouvie, E. & Miller, K.J. (1997). The comorbidity of alcoholism and personality disorders in a clinical population: prevalence and relation to alcohol typology variables. *Journal of Abnormal Psychology*, **106**, 74–84.

Ohannessian, C.M., Stabenau, J.R. & Hesselbrock, V.M. (1995). Childhood and adulthood temperament and problem behaviors and adulthood substance use. *Addictive Behaviors*, **20**, 77–86.

Penick, E.C., Powell, B.J., Nickel, E.J., Read, M.R., Gabrielli, W.F. & Liskow, B.I. (1990). Examination of Cloninger's Type I and Type II alcoholism with a sample of men alcoholics in treatment. *Alcoholism: Clinical and Experimental Research*, **14**, 623–629.

Pogge, D.L., Stokes, J. & Harvey, P.D. (1992). Psychometric vs. attentional correlates of early onset alcohol and substance abuse. *Journal of Abnormal Child Psychology*, **20**, 151–162.

Poikolainen, K. (1994). Depression in alcoholism: a review. *Psychiatria Fennica*, **25**, 75–87.

Raimo, E.B. & Schuckit, M.A. (1998). Alcohol dependence and mood disorders. *Addictive Behaviors*, **23**, 933–946.

Roy, A., DeJong, J., Lamparski, D., George, T. & Linnoila, M. (1991). Depression among alcoholics: relationship to clinical and cerebrospinal fluid variables. *Archives of General Psychiatry*, **48**, 428–432.

Rubio, G., Leon, G., Ferre, F., Pascual, J. & Santo Domingo, J. (1998). Clinical significance of Cloninger's classification in a sample of alcoholic Spanish men. *Addiction*, **93**, 93–101.

Sawrie, S.M., Kabat, M.H., Dietz, C.B., Greene, R.L., Arredondo, R. & Mann, A.W. (1996). Internal structure of the MMPI-2 Addiction Potential Scale in alcoholic and psychiatric inpatients. *Journal of Personality Assessment*, **66**, 177–193.

Schuckit, M.A. (1985). The clinical implications of primary diagnostic groups among alcoholics. *Archives of General Psychiatry*, **42**, 1043–1049.

Schuckit, M.A. & Hesselbrock, V. (1994). Alcohol dependence and anxiety disorders: what is the relationship? *American Journal of Psychiatry*, **151**, 1723–1734.

Schuckit, M.A., Klein, J., Twitchell, G. & Smith, T.L. (1994). Personality test scores as predictors of alcoholism almost a decade later. *American Journal of Psychiatry*, **151**, 1038–1042.

Schuckit, M.A. & Smith, T.L. (1996). An 8-year followup of 450 sons of alcoholic and control subjects. *Archives of General Psychiatry*, **53**, 202–210.

Schuckit, M.A., Tsuang, J.W., Anthenelli, R.M., Tipp, J.E. & Nurnberger, J.I. (1996). Alcohol challenges in young men from alcoholic pedigrees and control families: a report from the COGA project. *Journal of Studies on Alcohol*, **57**, 368–377.

Sher, K.J. (1991). *Children of Alcoholics: A Critical Appraisal of Theory and Research*. Chicago, IL: University of Chicago Press.

Sher, K.J. & Trull, T.J. (1994). Personality and disinhibitory psychopathology: alcoholism and antisocial personality disorder. *Journal of Abnormal Psychology*, **103**, 92–102.

Sieber, M.F. (1981). Personality scores and licit and illicit substance use. *Personality and Individual Differences*, **2**, 235–241.

Sigurdsson, J.F. & Gudjonsson, G.H. (1996). Psychological characteristics of juvenile alcohol and drug users. *Journal of Adolescence*, **19**, 121–126.

Simon, T.R., Stacy, A.W., Sussman, S. & Dent, C.W. (1994). Sensation seeking and drug use among high risk Latino and Anglo adolescents. *Personality and Individual Differences*, **17**, 665–672.

Stinson, F.S., DeBakey, S.F., Grant, B.F. & Dawson, D.A. (1992). Association of alcohol problems with risk for AIDS in the 1988 National Health Interview Survey. *Alcohol Health and Research World*, **16**, 245–252.

Svanum, S. & Ehrmann, L.C. (1992). Alcoholic subtypes and the MacAndrew Alcoholism Scale. *Journal of Personality Assessment*, **58**, 411–422.

Tarter, R., Kirisci, L., Hegedus, A., Mezzich, A. & Vanyukov, M.M. (1994). Heterogeneity of adolescent alcoholism. *Annals of the New York Academy of Sciences*, **708**, 172–180.

Tarter, R.E., McBride, H., Buonpane, N. & Schneider, D.U. (1977). Differentiation of alcoholics: childhood history of minimal brain dysfunction, family history, and drinking pattern. *Archives of General Psychiatry*, **34**, 761–768.

Thankachan, M.V. & Kodandaram, P. (1992). A study of life events and personality among alcohol dependent individuals. *Journal of Personality and Clinical Studies*, **8**, 27–34.

Tomori, M. (1994). Personality characteristics of adolescents with alcoholic parents. *Adolescence*, **29**, 949–959.

Vaeth, J.M., Horton, A.M. & Ahadpour, M. (1992). Attention deficit disorder, alcoholism, and drug abuse: MMPI correlates. *International Journal of Neuroscience*, **63**, 115–124.

Virkkunen, M. & Linnoila, M. (1993). Brain serotonin, Type II alcoholism and impulsive violence. *Journal of Studies on Alcohol*, **11**, 163–169.

Weed, N.C., Butcher, J.N. & Ben Porath, Y.S. (1995). MMPI-2 measures of substance abuse. In J.N. Butcher & C.D. Speilberger (Eds), *Advances in Personality Assessment*, Vol. 10. (pp. 121–146). Hillsdale, NJ: Erlbaum.

Woldt, B.D. & Bradley, J.R. (1996). Precursors, mediators and problem drinking: path analytical models for men and women. *Journal of Drug Education*, **26**, 1–12.

Yates, W.R. & Meller, W.H. (1993). Comparative validity of five alcoholism typologies. *American Journal on Addictions*, **2**, 99–108.

Yoshino, A., Kato, M., Takeuchi, M., Ono, Y. & Kitamura, T. (1994). Examination of the tridimensional personality hypothesis of alcoholism using empirically mutlivariate typology. *Alcoholism: Clinical and Experimental Research*, **18**, 1121–1124.

Zucker, R.A. (1979). Developmental aspects of drinking through the young adult years. In H.T. Blane & M.E. Chafetz (Eds), *Youth, Alcohol, and Social Policy* (pp. 91–146). New York: Plenum.

Zucker, R.A. (1987). The four alcoholisms: a developmental account of the etiologic process. In P.C. Rivers (Ed.), *Alcohol and Addictive Behavior: Nebraska Symposium on Motivation*, 1986 (pp. 27–83). Lincoln: University of Nebraska Press.

Part IV

Drinking Patterns and Types of Alcohol Problem

Edited by Tim Stockwell
*National Drug Research Institute, Curtin University of Technology,
Perth, WA, Australia*

EDITOR'S INTRODUCTION

The idea that drinking alcohol sometimes causes social, medical or other harms is now so well-established as to be trivial. Indeed, this understanding is probably as old as the manufacture and consumption of alcoholic beverages. Looking down the millennia, it is clear that alcohol has been, and continues to be, the most widely used mood-altering substance in the history of mankind. Nearly all pre-industrial cultures have created some form of alcoholic beverage from available fruit and other crops (see Chapter 2, this volume). As outlined in the opening chapter of Part IV, the more efficient production of alcohol with the advent of industrial production, followed by the recent globalization of commerce, has resulted in ever greater varieties of alcoholic beverages being made more readily accessible to drinkers from almost all countries and cultures. Pre-industrial patterns of occasional ritual social drinking while the beverage was still fit to drink have given way to more varied, context-specific, individualized and frequent patterns of drinking—and a plethora of consequences, both positive and negative. The international alcohol market is now dominated by a shrinking number of very large multinational companies who, while maintaining their core markets in developed countries, have also been active in creating new markets in developing and transitional countries, e.g. post-communist European societies (Jernigan, 1997). There is more alcohol being consumed now than ever before.

A major concern of this section is to describe how all of this alcohol use is patterned over place, time and circumstance and how different patterns relate to different consequences. The term "drinking pattern" is now used widely in the alcohol field but is rarely defined. A series of international conferences has been held in the 1990s around the unifying theme of drinking patterns and their consequences under the auspices of the Kettil Bruun Society for Social and Epidemiological Studies on Alcohol. A book with the title *Drinking Patterns* has been published by the alcohol industry-funded International Center for Alcohol Policy (Grant & Litvak, 1998). The term is used in both a narrow and a broad sense: narrowly, to refer to the pattern of variation in the amounts of ethyl alcohol consumed by a drinker on different occasions, or by a population of drinkers over the years; broadly, to refer to the different contexts in which drinking takes place.

The recent interest and focus on drinking patterns has its origin in a number of debates (for review, see Stockwell et al., 1997; Roche, 1998). Inevitably, it is the discipline of epidemiology that has provided the key data on the relationship between alcohol consumption and disease. As many commentators have noted (including Greenfield in Chapter 21), the ways in which alcohol use has been measured by epidemiologists has usually obscured the contribution of drinking patterns (in the narrow sense). Instead, epidemiology has mostly focused on rather crude measures of the estimated volumes consumed by individuals over periods of at least 1 month's duration. Partly this is because such studies are also investigating the contribution of many other risk factors to morbidity and mortality and include only two or three questions about alcohol use. This means that the importance of a highly variable or "binge" pattern of drinking vs. a pattern of consistent daily drinking cannot be determined in many studies. This oversight is beginning to be corrected with growing evidence that heavy consumption days increase the risk of serious illness as well as accident and injury (Rehm et al., 1996).

The drinking pattern paradigm can also be understood as a reaction to decades of alcohol research concerned almost exclusively with the longer-term consequences of regular excessive alcohol consumption, such as dependence and liver cirrhosis. While serious, these conditions affect a relatively small proportion of the drinking population. The Prevention Paradox is discussed in two of the following chapters (Lemmens, Chapter 20; Greenfield, Chapter 21). As applied to alcohol-related problems, this so-called paradox refers to the finding that it is the great number of low- to medium-volume drinkers who contribute the majority of cases of alcohol-related harm, especially when these are of the "acute" variety, i.e. associated with an episode of intoxication. More systematic analysis of underlying drinking patterns uncovers the somewhat prosaic explanation that many low-volume drinkers are actually occasional "binge" drinkers (e.g. Stockwell et al., 1996). Although it is widely understood that drinking alcohol contributes greatly to preventable death and injury on the roads, it is less widely known that intoxication contributes 40–50% of all alcohol-related deaths in some countries and about two-thirds of potential life years lost (Chikritzhs et al., 1999; Single et al., 1998).

A third major debate that has contributed to the renewed interest in drinking patterns has mostly been played out between public health advocates, the alcohol industry and their respective sympathisers. For decades the battle lines have been clearly drawn around the importance of per capita alcohol consumption as a predictor of the level of alcohol-related harm in a population. As will be discussed in Part VI on Prevention, later in this volume, a total population approach to alcohol problems is extremely threatening to the well-being of this major industry, as it encourages the adoption of policies such as increased taxes in order to reduce consumption and hence harm (and profits). As explained by Lemmens (Chapter 20), a drinking patterns approach points to factors other than the total volume of alcohol being consumed by a population as contributors to the levels of harm, e.g. extent of drinking to intoxication, beverage preferences, diet and drink–driving counter-measures. While this approach may deflect attention from a policy goal of reducing total consumption, it also focuses attention on the need for more precise measurement of drinking behaviour and its consequences. This, in turn, may lead to the adoption of policies which happen to reduce total volume of consumption as a consequence of successfully targeting high-risk drinking occasions and contexts (Stockwell et al., 1997).

As discussed in earlier sections of this book, the 1990s have seen the accumulation of evidence that low-volume drinking is associated with a reduced risk of death from heart disease, especially if episodes of high intake are avoided. There have been some studies that have failed to find a protective effect of moderate drinking (e.g. Fillmore et al., 1998). However, this particular debate, with its implication that different drinking patterns can be associated with either increased or decreased risks of premature mortality has also driven alcohol researchers to focus more carefully on "patterns", at least in the narrow sense of this term.

The new imperative to explore drinking patterns and contexts with greater rigour is a demanding one that invites numerous disciplines and perspectives into the wider discussion. This is well-illustrated by the analyses offered on the issue of alcohol and violence in Part IV, from anthropology on the one hand (Moore, Chapter 23) and social psychology and behavioural pharmacology on the other (Graham & West, Chapter 22). It is not the intention of this volume to try and close off debate with a fixed party line on such matters, but rather to allow experts in their field of study to outline the research evidence and its interpretation. The work cited by Moore emphasizes the enormous cultural diversity regarding whether violent behaviour follows drinking—it usually does not—and suggests that the causes of violent behaviour are always interpersonal and culturally embedded. Graham reviews an extensive range of epidemiological, social and pharmacological studies, which identifies the undeniable association of alcohol with the occurrence of violence as well as theoretical explanations as to how intoxication can be a contributory cause in situations where human conflict and frustration are already present. Moore also challenges accepted clinical conceptions of "alcoholism", "alcohol dependence" and "alcohol problems" by pointing to the functionality and social meanings of even ultimately self-destructive behaviour. He overviews ethnographic studies from around the world that indicate that not only do patterns of alcohol use vary a great deal, but so also do local understandings of what constitutes an "alcohol problem". Somehow, modern alcohol studies must accommodate these different perspectives and be mindful of the impact of both the biological and sociocultural contexts in which drinking behaviours are acted out.

It is hoped that Part IV will leave the reader with a sense of the importance of studying the patterns and settings within which alcohol is drunk, as well as the overall amounts consumed, to arrive at an understanding of the causes of alcohol-related problems.

REFERENCES

Chikritzhs, T., Jonas, H., Heale, P., Dietze, P., Hanlin, K. & Stockwell, T. (1999). *Alcohol-caused Deaths and Hospitalizations in Australia, 1990–1997*. National Alcohol Indicators, Bulletin No. 1. Perth, Western Australia: National Drug Research Institute, Curtin University of Technology.

Grant, M. & Litvak, J. (Eds) (1998). *Drinking Patterns and Their Consequences*. Washington, DC: Taylor & Francis.

Jernigan, D. (1997). *Thirsting for Markets: the Global Impact of Corporate Alcohol*. San Rafael, CA: Marin Institute for the Prevention of Alcohol and Other Drug Problems.

Fillmore, K.M., Golding, J.M., Graves, K.L., Kniep, S., Leino, E.V., Romelsjo, A., Shoemaker, C., Ager, C.R., Allebeck, P. & Ferrer, H.P. (1998). Alcohol consumption and mortality. I. Characteristics of drinking groups. *Addiction*, **93**, 183–203.

Roche, A. (1998). The shifting sands of alcohol research and prevention. *Australian & New Zealand Journal of Public Health*, **21**, 621–625.

Rehm, J., Ashley, M.J., Room, R., Single, E., Bondy, S., Ferrence, R. & Giesbrecht, N. (1996). On the emerging paradigm of drinking patterns and their social and health consequences. *Addiction*, **91**, 1615–1621.

Single, E., Robson, L., Xie, X. & Rehm, J. (1998). The economic costs of alcohol, tobacco and illicit drugs in Canada, 1992. *Addiction*, **93**, 991–1006.

Stockwell, T., Single, E., Rehm, J. & Hawks, D. (1997). Sharpening the focus of alcohol research and policy, from aggregate consumption to harm and risk reduction. *Addiction Research*, **5**, 1–9.

Chapter 19

International Trends in Alcohol Production and Consumption

Juha Partanen
and
Jussi Simpura
Social Research Unit for Alcohol Studies, Helsinki, Finland

Synopsis

Industrialization resulted in a definite break in the history of alcohol and drinking. While throughout most of history alcohol had been produced and consumed locally at the level of household or small community, in the nineteenth century industrial production transformed it into a market commodity in industrializing countries and a major item in colonial trade. At the same time, industrialization brought in its wake changes that affected the social position of alcohol. In the early nineteenth century the level of consumption was high in most countries of Europe and North America. It started to decline towards the end of the century, and this continued throughout the period between the two World Wars. This trend was reversed after World War II, and increasing levels of alcohol consumption were recorded from the late 1940s to the middle 1970s. During the last quarter of this century, consumption has leveled off and even declined in a number of countries. These "long waves of alcohol consumption" have been most pronounced in Northern and Central Europe and in North America.

Today there are major differences in alcohol consumption between the macro-regions of the world. In affluent Western societies, consumption levels are relatively stable and different countries have tended to become more alike in their drink preferences. In the developing world the gaps between macro-regions have widened. In Eastern and South-Eastern Asia alcohol consumption has grown fast since the 1960s. In Latin America, and especially in Africa, consumption increased until the mid-1970s, and has since then been decreasing. These differences correspond roughly to the different economic development of these regions. What is common to all developing countries, however, is the dual character of alcohol markets, reflecting deep income inequalities between the elite and the poor majority. In the ex-

---

International Handbook of Alcohol Dependence and Problems. Edited by N. Heather, T.J. Peters and T. Stockwell.
© 2001 John Wiley & Sons Ltd.

socialist transitional societies of Eastern Europe, especially in Russia, the unstable economic and political situation has led to dramatic and largely uncontrolled changes in the production, trade and consumption of alcohol.

Faced with stagnant or declining demand in their most important markets in affluent industrialized countries, the producers and traders of alcohol, especially of spirits and wines, have had to develop new strategies in order to keep up profitability and remain in business. As a consequence, the production and distribution of alcoholic beverages has become concentrated in fewer and bigger enterprises, the assortment of beverage types and brands has been expanded, typically accompanied by vigorous marketing efforts, and new markets have been sought, especially from the developing world and the transitional societies of Eastern Europe. The field is dominated by a relatively small number of big transnational companies, often in alliance with each other. The most significant change in the global market for industrially produced alcohol within the last 20 or 30 years is the increasing popularity of beer.

Societies differ greatly in the role drinking plays in their social life and culture, and these differences can be described from different perspectives, at different levels of generality. Ethnographic fieldwork over the past half-century, guided by the view that alcohol use is always part of a larger cultural configuration, has produced an impressive array of in-depth accounts of drinking behavior from various quarters of the world, and its accumulated results provide a mosaic-like picture of the immense variety of the uses of alcohol. This evidence definitely dismantles the view that alcohol produces uniform, consistent and predictable changes in human behavior. More recent ethnographic research has highlighted ongoing changes that are brought about by closer links to larger society and commodification of alcohol.

In polymorphous contemporary societies, population surveys, together with statistical data, have become essential tools to monitor changes and make comparisons in drinking patterns and their harmful consequences. The interpretation of such data requires that one has to look at the social transformations and formative influences created by the ongoing economic globalization. Three aspects of social change in particular, viz. urbanization, relationships between genders and the position of young people, appear to give rise to new or altered patterns of alcohol use everywhere in the world. The power of traditions and customs has weakened; drinking has become a more individualistic affair; differences between men and women have become smaller; and special youth cultures, distinct from the adult world, have emerged. Such considerations suggest that drinking will remain a significant part of social life in the future.

REMARKS ON THE HISTORY OF ALCOHOL AND DRINKING

For most of their history of several thousand years, alcoholic beverages have mostly been produced locally at the level of household or small community, using local raw materials and methods that have been handed down from generation to generation. Such beverages are nearly always fermented, contain at most a few per cent of ethanol and are often regarded as an important part of nutrition. Limited means of storage and transport have meant that what was produced had to be consumed soon, and alcohol seldom travelled far from its point of production. As a rule such beverages were not sold on the market. They were consumed within the household, given away as a sign of generosity and hospitality, or shared at communal festivals and within local circles of exchange, to celebrate the completion of harvest or a joint work project.

The production of alcohol presupposes, however, the existence of some agricultural surplus above the minimum necessary for survival. For this reason, as well as because of their intoxicating power, alcoholic beverages have in many societies been regarded as special commodities. Their consumption has been restricted to privileged population groups, to particular occasions and to religious ceremonies. And whenever possible, they have been traded as items of luxury. Already in antiquity vessels of wine traveled widely along the Mediterranean coasts and beyond.

The technique of distillation, invented in China and introduced to Europe by the Arabs in the twelfth century, has since the sixteenth century given rise to various distilled beverages. Their use has been a significant part of alcohol consumption, especially in the countries where grapes cannot be cultivated. Distillation provided a means to transform part of the harvest into a commodity that could be easily stored and transported without spoiling.

Distilled beverages became a major item in colonial trade (Pan, 1975). Rum flowed from the Caribbean area to North America, and cheaper varieties of industrial alcohol, so-called "trade spirits", were exported from Europe to its African and Asian colonies. The motives were not solely commercial. Alcohol also played a significant part in the subjugation of colonial work force and it provided income for colonial administration. At the later stage of colonialization these interests somewhat conflicted with concerns about productivity and maintenance of public order. Efforts to curb alcohol trade and its consumption among indigenous populations were not successful, however.

Industrialization brought in its wake changes that have profoundly transformed human life, and it has affected the social position of alcohol as well. In the early nineteenth century the consumption level was high in most countries of Europe and North America. It started to decline towards the end of the century, and this continued throughout the period between the two World Wars. This trend was reversed after World War II, and increasing consumption was recorded from the late 1940s to the middle 1970s in nearly all countries, providing reasonably accurate statistics. This period has been called "The Golden Age" in the history of mankind, an unexpected and uniquely fast economic growth accompanied with wide-reaching processes of social and cultural change (Hobsbawm, 1995). The last quarter of this century is characterized by recurring economic and political crises in various parts of the world and insecurity about the future. Alcohol consumption has leveled off and even declined in a number of countries since the late 1970s or early 1980s.

These "long waves of alcohol consumption", as they have been called (Sulkunen, 1976), have been most pronounced in Northern and Central Europe, North America, Australia and New Zealand. In the countries where wine has traditionally been used as a daily nutrient, they have taken place somewhat later and been smaller. In France, for example, consumption remained at a relatively high level until steady decline started in the mid-1950s, mainly because of the diminishing popularity of wine. In Japan, alcohol consumption increased throughout the post-war period until the 1990s. Presumably there have been historical changes in alcohol intake in other parts of the world as well, but available statistical sources do not tell much about trends or magnitudes of change.

Three general remarks can be made about the character of these historical macro-level changes in alcohol consumption. It is significant, first, that the trends and reversals of trends have been recorded roughly within the same period in countries at different stages of economic development and representing a wide variety of alcohol cultures.

Second, it does not seem that the changes in alcohol consumption can be attributed primarily to the efforts of the Temperance Movement or the government controls on the availability of alcohol which it instigated. From its beginnings in the early nineteenth century USA, the ideal of temperance gave rise to an international and highly visible social reform movement, especially in English-speaking and Nordic countries. Its achievements culminated in prohibition of alcohol in some countries during and after World War I, and since that period its influence has been on the wane. But the decline of alcohol consumption started well before the Temperance Movement gained political influence, and the changes in alcohol consumption took place also in countries where the Temperance Movement was not a significant political or social actor. It seems appropriate to consider the long waves of alcohol consumption and the ups and downs of the Temperance Movement as parallel historical processes, both generated by the industrial revolution, but each displaying its own socioeconomic and political dynamics. On the one hand, the role of the Temperance Movement has always depended on ideological and political conjuncture; on the other hand, fiscal, agricultural and industrial considerations have always weighed heavily on the availability of alcohol.

Thirdly, it is worth observing that these long-term changes in alcohol consumption bear no simple or uniform relationship to changes in affluence, amount of leisure time, social misery, industrialization or urbanization, which are often invoked when trying to explain differences in alcohol use between societies and population groups. Such factors are of significance, but their effects vary, depending on the historical and societal context of alcohol use. Poverty appears to be the most consistent limiting factor on alcohol use, but more affluence does not invariably lead to more drinking. Religion is an important factor, and major religions have adopted quite different stands to alcohol, ranging from the prohibitionism of Islam and fundamentalist Protestantism to the lenient attitudes of Catholic Christianity.

THE GLOBAL PANORAMA OF ALCOHOL AND DRINKING

To get an overview on the social position of alcohol in the present-day world it is necessary to consider the different socioeconomic contexts of alcohol production and consumption. The basic division is that between the industrialized, affluent societies and the developing societies. Inequality is a fundamental fact in today's world, and its dominant component is inequality between countries. Economic globalization has widened the gap between the rich and poor countries.

The *developed world*, which in the main consists of Western Europe and North America, is characterized by stable or decreasing alcohol consumption levels. A major exception is Japan, where per capita alcohol intake has increased up to the 1990s. According to published figures for the year 1995 (e.g. Hurst et al., 1997, p. 528) the annual per capita consumption in 100% alcohol varies roughly from 41 (Norway) to 121 (Luxembourg, France), and although part of the consumption is not registered, these figures are probably not very widely off the mark. In the post-war period, the differences in average consumption levels among countries have narrowed and countries have tended to become more alike in their drink preferences (Sulkunen, 1976; Mäkelä et al., 1981). Cultural differences persist, but increasing internationalization of life-styles has smoothed them out by adding new patterns of drinking upon the more traditional ways of using alcohol.

In economic terms, the production and distribution of alcohol typically has a 1–2% share of gross domestic product (GDP). It is thus not a major factor in national economies, even though agricultural and industrial interests, as well as those linked to catering and tourism, keep alcohol issues on the political agenda. There is an increasing awareness about the deleterious effects of alcohol use on health but, in the name of free enterprise and unrestricted trade, governmental controls on the availability of alcohol have weakened rather than become more efficient. The pressure from the European Union, for example, has made the Nordic countries start dismantling their relatively strict traditional systems of regulation (Holder et al., 1998).

In a long-term historical perspective it seems that, although alcohol is quite freely available and its use is quite extensive in the developed world, it is seldom the case that drinking for its own sake becomes the focus of social life in the same way as in pre-modern societies. Affluent consumption-orientated society provides a large number of alternatives for people to spend their time and money, and the dysfunctions of drunkenness put strict limits on the occasions in which it is possible to indulge in serious drinking. Alcohol does not belong to offices or factories, and its role in traffic arouses growing concern. Heavy and problematic drinking occurs, often linked to social exclusion but also among the well-to-do, and a minority of alcohol users become addicted to it, but in welfare societies there are specialized treatment services to deal with addictions.

As regards *developing societies*, one of the consequences of economic globalization is that the notion of "the Third World" has lost its analytical value; first, because the collapse of the Soviet Union brought down the global frontier line between capitalism and socialism, which formed the main axis of politics in the post-war era, and second, because of the highly divergent economic development in the countries that were called "the Third World" a generation ago. Singapore's GNP per capita is one of the highest in the world, South Korea is now a member in the OECD group of wealthy nations, all the larger South American countries belong to the upper middle income group of the World Bank classification. This means that one has to deal with a highly heterogeneous assembly of societies, geographically as well as economically and culturally. For an overview it seems advisable to look at three macro-regions separately, without forgetting their inter-country and intra-country differences.

Eastern and South-Eastern Asia have been characterized by consistently high rates of economic growth and rapid social transformations. Financial crises have lately blurred the picture and there are doubts whether their growth can continue. Nevertheless, most experts seem to think that the recent difficulties are temporary and that South-east Asia, together with China, is on its way of becoming one of the major power houses in the global economy.

South American countries have tried to repeat the Asian success story, but the record is mixed. After the rapid economic growth until the mid-1970s, based on exports of primary commodities and import-substitution industrialization, came the "lost decade" of the 1980s, with its debt crises that forced them to adopt austere economic policies imposed by international financial institutions.

Sub-Saharan Africa presents the saddest stories of development. After a rapid growth in the 1960s and a moderate increase in the 1970s, the industrial structure of many countries collapsed in the 1980s and even the agricultural production has been lagging behind the 3% annual population growth rate, leaving the survival dependent on international aid and foreign borrowing in most African countries. Famines, epidemics, violence, civil wars, massacres, mass exodus, social and political chaos are visible signs of Africa's present plight.

The available data on alcohol and drinking in the developing world is typically of narrow scope, not fully reliable, or not representative for whole countries, and not suitable for aggregation or comparison. For an overview of alcohol consumption per capita, geographically the most comprehensive source is the data bank of the United Nations Food and Agriculture Organization (FAO). It consists of time series on the production, trade and consumption of foodstuffs, including alcoholic beverages, starting from the year 1961. The figures are mainly based on the data produced by individual countries, and the quality of these varies. In most Islamic countries, for example, alcohol does not officially exist, and the statistics show zero consumption, although undoubtedly there is some. In many other countries a major part of alcoholic beverages remain unregistered, because they are produced in the informal sector of the economy, which is covered only in part or not included at all. Available figures of per capita consumption in the developing world are therefore not very reliable. Information on time trends, however, may be less dependent on the quality of data, assuming that errors remain more or less similar from one year to the next.

In the Appendix the changes in per capita consumption from 1970–1972 to 1994–1996, reported by WHO (2000), are presented for a number of countries.

The FAO data suggest that, broadly speaking, the changes in alcohol consumption in the three macro-regions correspond to their economic development. In major Asian countries, registered alcohol consumption has increased very fast and the rate of increase has remained nearly constant throughout the period 1961–1996. In Latin America and Africa the consumption increased until the middle 1970s, and has since then been decreasing slightly in Latin America and somewhat more in Africa. Individual countries exhibit more variation and some diverge from these general patterns of change.

Even though the available figures do not warrant a discussion on the level of consumption in developing societies, it nonetheless seems pertinent to note that the registered liters per capita are, with a few exceptions such as the Republic of Korea, quite low and certainly considerably less than in most industrialized countries. This is partly due with the large share of unregistered consumption in many developing countries. It is also the case that in many cultures women drink very little in comparison with their sisters in Europe or North America. But perhaps the main reason is widespread poverty. According to World Development Indicators (1997, p. 31), 29% of the population in the developing world live on less than 1 US$/day, and their numbers have been increasing. Lack of buying power sets strict limits to consumption—for them drinking is just not affordable. Low averages, even if they are not spurious, because of deficiencies of data, may nevertheless conceal heavy drinking in some localities and in some groups of population. They should not be taken as an indication of *absence* of heavy and problematic use of alcohol.

Despite all the geographic, economic and sociocultural differences among the developing societies there is, however, a structural aspect that is common to nearly all of them—the social reality of the developing world is deeply divided, far more deeply than in affluent industrial societies. In every developing country, unless it is in total disarray, there is the small elite that governs the country and is connected to the global economy. And, depending on how far industrialization has proceeded, there is also the middle class. Their lifestyle is characterized by *bricolage*; it is a combination, in variable proportions and ways, of Western consumption patterns and traditional status symbols. The majority of the population, on the other hand, are poor people working in cities and living in slums and shantytowns, with their congestion, squalor and lack of basic amenities, or trying to eke out their livelihood in the country. Large parts of the developing world are still predominantly rural. In China, the proportion of rural population is 70%, in India 73%, in Sub-Saharan Africa 69%, whereas Latin America with its 26% is far more urbanized (World Development Indicators, 1997, pp. 114–116). Yet urbanization continues relentlessly, and it also brings changes in the countryside, which becomes dependent on the city and its industries, and the earnings of the migrants.

The class structure cuts across the production, trade and consumption of alcohol in the whole developing world. The production and the markets of alcoholic beverages have a dual character in all macro-regions . On the one hand, there are the Western-type alcoholic beverages that are imported for the elite, and produced locally, in cheaper versions, for the middle-class. On the other hand, there are the traditional fermented or brewed products and their distillates, most often illegally manufactured: East African *pombe* and *chang'aa* and West African palm wine; *pulque* and *chicha* in Latin America; *samsu*, *toddy* and *arrack* in South Asia. The bulk of the alcohol that is consumed in some developing countries actually comes from the informal sector. In some African countries its proportion has been estimated up to 90% and its production and trade provide livelihoods, especially for many women who have to take care of the needs of their families (Maula, 1997). The production and trade of alcohol is a major component in the informal economies of developing societies.

The *ex-socialist transitional societies of Eastern Europe* provide a multi-faceted picture of changes in production, trade, consumption and patterns of use. The countries differ from each other, so that the most widely reported Russian experience cannot be generalized to cover the whole region.

In the production of alcoholic beverages, the transition since the mid-1980s, starting with the Gorbachev anti-alcohol campaign in 1985 in Russia, initially led to an increase of home-produced *samogon* and to a dramatic decline of wine production in the ex-Soviet wine-growing regions. The same goes for wine growing in ex-Yugoslavia, although production is now increasing again. Domestic production of alcoholic beverages by distilleries and breweries has recovered more quickly than wine-growing. In some parts of the region, most notably in the Czech republic, breweries and distilleries have become interlinked with major international companies.

Changes in trade have been even more dramatic than changes in production. Largely uncontrolled foreign trade with alcoholic beverages has flourished, and new legal and illegal forms of retailing have mushroomed. The Eastern European transition has opened new markets and in some countries led to "wild market practices" (Simpura, 1997; Swiatkiewicz, 1997). As a consequence, per capita alcohol consumption has increased in many countries in the region until the mid-1990s. Lacking reliable information, it is almost impossible to say how large the increase has been in different countries. Again, the Russian experience leaves in shadow even more striking changes in some smaller countries. For instance, the estimates of per capita alcohol consumption for Latvia have systematically exceeded those for Russia. The fluctuations of Polish consumption figures have been remarkable, although consumption has not reached the levels of Latvia or Russia. In many countries, drink preferences have shifted, reflecting shortages in supply.

TRENDS IN THE INDUSTRIAL PRODUCTION OF ALCOHOL

As noted above, for the last 20 years the producers and traders of alcohol, especially of spirits and wines, have had to face stagnant or declining demand in their most important markets in affluent industrialized countries. This has meant that they have had to develop new strategies in order to keep up profitability and remain in business. As a consequence, the production and distribution of alcoholic beverages has concentrated in fewer and bigger enterprises, the assortment of beverage types and brands has been expanded, typically accompanied by vigorous marketing efforts, and new markets have been sought, especially from the developing world and the transitional societies of Eastern Europe.

Starting from small family firms supplying local demand, the dominant trend in the alcohol beverage industry has been the development towards bigger production units, larger enterprises and widening spheres of marketing. Apart from some beverage types, such as champagne at the very high end of the product range and real ale for connoisseurs, in the alcohol business large-scale industrial production offers significant economies of scale. Of equal if not even more importance are the costs of marketing. One brand of vodka, whisky or lager beer is not essentially different from the next one produced for mass consumption. The brand, and the special identity it gives to the product, is what really matters. And brands are created by marketing and advertising, the costs of which are best borne by the largest producers. They create an effective barrier for potential new entrants into business.

By far the largest part of all alcohol in the world is still consumed in the same country where it is produced. Alcohol is an insignificant category in global trade flows, and most of its trade takes place between developed countries. This state of affairs should not, however, obscure the fact that nowadays the leading forces in the global alcohol business are transnational alcohol companies. Together they form a complex and dynamic network of shifting alliances, and in many cases they are subsidiaries of larger business or financial corporations. The development has been most dynamic in brewing, but this is often combined with distillation and wine production as well.

The major transnational breweries have pursued, according to Jernigan (1997), more or less similar strategies for growth. Starting with a dominant position, or at least a major share in the domestic market, and using this as a springboard for international expansion, they first export their brands in order to make them available and visible in other markets. They can then license a local brewery to distribute their international brands, positioned at the high end of the product range, alongside its own brands. They can also resort to contract brewing, in which a licensed local brewery takes care of production as well. They negotiate agreements about cross-licensing and division of markets between one another. Eventually this leads to more long-term alliances, joint ventures, part ownerships and mergers of companies.

Brewing is indeed becoming concentrated into fewer hands. In 1980, according to the study of Cavanaugh & Clairmonte (1985), the share of the top 30 brewers was below 50%. In 1995 20 companies brewed more than half of the world's industrially produced beer, and the share of the top 10 was 35% (Jernigan, 1997, p. 12). Of distilled spirits, more than half are brands hardly known outside their local markets, but in more cosmopolitan contexts the consumption is heavily concentrated on widely advertised international brands, such as Bacardi or Johnny Walker. The wine industry appears to be far more dispersed across the various viticultural countries. Their number has been on the increase, and it also includes some developing countries, although Italy and France still are by far the two largest producers (Bulletin de l'OIV, 1998, p. 110).

As a result of the increasing concentration of the brewing industry, the world has become divided into "spheres of influence" between the leading beer producers (Jernigan, 1997, p. 18). Mainland South-east Asia is dominated by Carlsberg (Denmark) and Heineken (The Netherlands), allied with Guinness (Ireland), which also has a strong position in Africa, together with South African Breweries. The three US breweries among the world's top 10 have not been able to penetrate these markets, but they have established alliances with Latin American breweries. China and Eastern Europe are still open for competition for a number of different companies.

The strategies pursued by the leading alcohol producers are based on and lead to the strengthening of the images of the key brands. Another strategy is the widening of the beverage spectrum. This has been towards less alcoholic drinks, even leading to an overlap with non-alcoholic beverages, in order to keep up with changing tastes and to win new customers, especially among women and young people. Sweet and flavored drinks containing alcohol, "alcopops", entered the market in the mid-1990s. They have been targeted at youthful consumers by the taste of the beverage and appropriate design for product names, packaging and advertising. The wine segment is struggling with recurring problems of overproduction (Bulletin de l'OIV, 1998), which have not been solved by the Common Wine Policy of the European Union (Spahni, 1988). There has been a shift away from cheap table wines to quality wines aimed for middle-class consumers, as well as efforts to extend markets beyond the core of wine-producing countries.

Considered as a whole, the biggest change in the global market for industrially produced alcohol within the last 20–30 years has been the increasing popularity of beer. It has become the dominant type of alcoholic beverage in nearly all industrialized countries, especially among young consumers even in wine-drinking regions. It is a coveted symbol of modernity and affluence among the less well-to-do populations of developing societies. This is the message conveyed by the transnational companies, resorting at times to approaches that would be considered unethical in countries where advertising is more strictly controlled. The lack of purchasing power and the influence of Islam appear to be the only factors limiting further growth of beer consumption in the developing world.

LOOKING AT THE VARIETIES OF DRINKING

There are but few known societies where alcohol has not been used at all, and in those societies some other psychoactive substance has replaced alcohol, like *kawa* in Oceania, or psychedelic mushrooms or cacti in Central America and among some North American Indians. But societies differ greatly in the role drinking plays in their social life and culture, and there are various approaches in trying to describe these differences, at different levels of generality.

At the most concrete level, ethnographic fieldwork over the past half-century has produced an impressive array of in-depth accounts of drinking behavior from various quarters of the world, and its accumulated results provide a mosaic-like picture of the immense variety of the uses of alcohol (Marshall, 1979). This work is guided by the view that alcohol use is always part of a larger cultural configuration. It seeks to relate drinking to other aspects of social life and it illuminates the ways in which traditions and norms regulate the use of alcohol. As MacAndrew & Edgerton (1969) showed in their influential book, ethographic evidence definitely dismantles the view that alcohol produces uniform, consistent and predictable changes in human behavior, apart from basic sensomotoric functions.

Across all this diversity, one can nevertheless identify certain common factors. At the most general and abstract level, it seems that societies differ along two separate dimensions in their attitudes towards alcohol. There is, first, the degree to which society is engaged with alcohol, that is, to what extent social life is permeated by its use. This is indicated by the frequency of drinking, its ritualization, its ceremonial uses and its linkages to food and eating. Second, societies vary in the degree to which they seek intoxication and tolerate its eventually harmful consequences.

It is even possible to discern certain basic commonalities, "anthropological constants", aspects that are present in the use of alcohol in all times and at all places. Alcohol is a psychoactive drug, but unlike all other drugs it also belongs to the realm of food. This links alcohol to conviviality, makes it a part of the primordial social act of sharing the drink and the experience. Drinking induces sociability, it is one of the strong bonding instruments in social life at the level of direct contact and primary group. The former aspect makes alcohol a risky substance: alcohol intoxicates, the sociability it produces is fragile (Douglas, 1987; Partanen, 1991). Anthropologists have been searching for cultures of problem-free, "integrated" drinking, with no lasting success. In all functioning societies, drinking is framed with social controls of one kind or another, but societies differ in their capability of preventing problems or dealing with them.

While earlier anthropology focused on relatively isolated societies as static entities, "frozen in time" as it were, considering culture as a template for behavior, more recent research is paying attention to historical change. The sad experiences with alcohol of the peoples whose lives were thoroughly dislocated by colonialism and neocolonialism, such as American Indians, Inuits, Australian Aborigines, New Zealand Maoris and the peoples of Siberia, are well known. Works like Colson & Scudder (1988), Marshall & Marshall (1990), and Kunitz & Levy (1994) highlight in detail the contemporary changes that are brought about by closer links of the community to larger society, commodification of alcohol, and deterioration of local economy. They tell about people's struggles to control one's life and maintain one's identity in a fast-changing world.

In polymorphous contemporary societies, population surveys, together with statistical data, have become essential tools to monitor changes and make comparisons in drinking patterns and their harmful consequences. They are routinely carried out in many developed countries and increasingly also in the developing world. Such information, however, in order to have meaning beyond administrative monitoring or mechanical comparisons, needs interpretation. One has to look at the formative influences created by the ongoing economic globalization.

CONTEMPORARY SOCIAL TRANSFORMATIONS

More specifically, three aspects of social change, viz. urbanization, relationships between genders and the position of young people, are affecting patterns of alcohol use everywhere in the world. To single out these three aspects of social transformation should not, however, make one to forget that there are other processes of change, especially in developing countries. Industrialization is likely to create industrial working classes demanding workers' rights and labour unions, as well as educated professionals, eager to consume and longing for a more liberal atmosphere. In addition, inequalities feed resentments, which give rise to ethno-religious nationalisms. We are living in an highly unstable and inflammable world.

One of the truly dramatic changes in the latter part of this century has been the shrinkage of peasantry and rural labor that has resulted from increasing productivity in agriculture and created a push away from the country. The other side of the coin is the rapid urbanization that has created megacities and urban agglomerations, especially in the developing world, places like Mexico City, Sao Paulo, New Delhi and Shanghai, where the highrise downtown areas are surrounded by slums and shanty-towns, with their concentrated poverty and uncontrolled sprawl.

For migrants this is a new world, where traditional networks of mutual obligation and custom come under heavy strain. Unemployment is endemic, especially in the poorest countries, and migrants are forced to live by their wits, trying to earn a livelihood as petty traders, or to find some other means to fit into the networks of the informal economy. The migrant has to construct an identity and a way of life combining the old and the new. In city-life drinking places, like African *shebeens* or Mexican *pulquerias*, provide a "home from home", a place to get together with others from one's village or region. Thus, the traditions of communal drinking assume new forms and functions, and home production or a cottage industry provide urbanized and commodified versions of traditional drinks. In the old life, one could have a drink-laden celebration or fiesta perhaps a few times a year; now, one can have a fiesta whenever one can afford it.

Traditionally, drinking has been a highly gendered social practice. The difference between men's and women's drinking varies, reflecting their social positions and gender roles in general; yet substantial alcohol use has always been principally a male affair, sometimes a male prerogative. "Heroic drinking" at a male drinking session provides a kind of *Urgestalt* of alcohol use.

So far, full equality between men and women has not been attained in any society, but during the past 30 years some progress has been made in most of the developed world. Survey results indicate that the differences in male and female drinking patterns have likewise decreased nearly everywhere. Women's share of alcohol-related problems appears to be on the increase as well.

In developing societies, the waves of Western feminism have at best reached educated urban middle-class women. Traditional male attitudes, be they Confucian or macho, are still very much in evidence. Yet there are structural factors that are essentially changing women's position and that have made visible their vital role in economic and social development. In newly industrialized countries, employers in export industries often prefer female to male labor, regarding it as cheaper and more docile. Elsewhere, especially in Sub-Saharan Africa, the exodus of men to cities after work has in practice made rural women heads of families, leaving them to take care of family and subsistence farming. In the long run, the strengthening of women's economic and social position will undoubtedly increase mankind's capacity to cope with its problems. In the short run, it creates tensions between men and women, strain on family life and emotional insecurity, aggravating men's feelings of worthlessness. Many men are puzzled by the fact that "women do not fear their husbands as before", but they can find some consolation in male drinking groups where men meet in order to socialize and escape from their daily reality, money troubles and reproachful wives. This tends to strengthen the traditional pattern, in which men do most of the drinking, while women suffer most of the consequences.

In the developed world, birth rates are low, but for a visitor in a developing country the sheer number of children and young people all around is striking. The emergence of youth as a distinct social category is a global phenomenon. This has mainly resulted from the expansion and lengthening of formal education, creating an enormous gap between generations. Political radicalism, almost always leftist, has been one of its visible signs. It has flared up not just in Paris and American campuses, but also in Mexico City, Korea, Tianmen Square, Nairobi, Djakarta.

Another highly visible aspect of the emergence of youth is that it has created a global market for the entertainment industry and popular music, sometimes condemned as "cultural nerve gas", destroying traditional culture in the developing world. Its inspirations and its performers may nowadays come from anywhere in the world, but more often than not they are recycled by US companies and distributed all over the world. It provides the stuff from which youth cultures around the world are built up. These reflect the needs and aspirations of all those young people who have no established place in the social order and who are facing an uncertain future. Traditional rites of passage have become mere relics, and youth cultures have replaced them, as it were, as a means to distance oneself from one's family. For young people, drinking, and nowadays increasingly also drugs, serve as a way to manifest one's independence and to distinguish oneselves from the adult world.

The emergence of such new contexts for alcohol use does not in itself tell anything about the quantitative trends in alcohol consumption. There are too many other factors at play, especially the economic circumstances. But it tells something about the change in the styles of drinking and in the meanings attached to it, and, accordingly, in the consequences of drinking. Despite the huge economic and cultural diversity in the world, there appear to be some aspects that are common to highly different contexts of alcohol use. There has been a definite shift from communal to more individualistic patterns of alcohol use. Traditions and established customs tell less than in the past where, when and how to drink; the choices are left to individuals. There is more room for hedonism in the lives of the well-to-do as well as among those who have lost control of their lives and lack a clear perspective of the future. Life has to be lived here and now. This attitude is manifested in elitist and middle-class pleasure-seeking in affluent consumption-orientated societies, but also in the violent "cultures of urgency" among the street children in Latin American cities or in the ghettos and inner cities of the affluent world. Such considerations suggest that social as well as problematic drinking will remain a significant part of social life in the future.

Note

In addition to the listed references, materials for this chapter have been drawn from the unpublished working papers of the ongoing research project, "Alcohol Policies in Developing Societies". The project was started in 1996 by the initiative of the World Health Organization, and is led by Robin Room. The final report and a separate volume of country studies will be published in 2001.

KEY WORKS AND SUGGESTIONS FOR FURTHER READING

Colson, E. & Scudder, T. (1988). *For Prayer and Profit: the Ritual, Economic, and Social Significance of Beer in Gwembe District, Zambia, 1950–1982*. Stanford, CA: Stanford University Press.

An ethnographic study of the changes in the economic and sociocultural significance of alcohol among the Gwembe in Zambia from the 1950s to the 1980s.

Edwards, G. et al. (1994). *Alcohol Policy and the Public Good*. Oxford: Oxford University Press.

A comprehensive account of the significance of alcohol in the developed world, from the public health point of view.

Jernigan, D. (1997). *Thirsting for Markets—the Global Impact of Corporate Alcohol*. San Rafael, CA: The Marin Institute for the Prevention of Alcohol and Other Drug Problems.

A study of alcohol trade and marketing practices in Estonia, Malesia and Zimbabwe.

Mäkelä, K. et al. (1981). *Alcohol, Society and the State. A Comparative Study of Alcohol Control*. Toronto: Addiction Research Foundation.

A study of the economic and social role of alcohol and drinking in California, Finland, Ireland. The Netherlands, Ontario, Poland and Switzerland in the period 1950–1975.

Room, R. et al. (2001). *Alcohol in a Changing World: Drinking Patterns and Problems in Developing Societies*. Cambridge: Cambridge University Press.

An up-to-date account of the economic and social role of alcohol and drinking in the developing world.

REFERENCES

Bulletin de l'OIV, Vol. 71 (1998).   Paris: Office International de la Vigne et du Vin.

Cavanagh, J. & Clairmonte, F. (1985). *Alcoholic Beverages: Dimensions of Corporate Power*. New York: St. Martin's Press.

Colson, E. & Scudder, T. (1988). *For Prayer and Profit: The Ritual, Economic, and Social Significance of Beer in Gwembe District, Zambia, 1950–1982*. Stanford, CA: Stanford University Press.

Douglas, M. (Ed.) (1987). *Constructive Drinking*. Cambridge: Cambridge University Press.

Hobsbawm, E. (1995). *Age of Extremes. The Short Twentieth Century, 1914–1991*. London: Abacus.

Holder, H., Kühlhorn, E., Nordlund, S., Österberg, E., Romelsjö, A. & Ugland, T. (1998). *European Integration and Nordic Alcohol Policies*. Aldershot: Ashgate.

Hurst, W., Gregory, E. & Gussman, T. (1997). *Alcoholic Beverage Taxation and Control Policies*, 9th edn. Ottawa: Brewers' Association of Canada.

Jernigan, D. (1997). *Thirsting for Markets—the Global Impact of Corporate Alcohol.* San Rafael, CA: The Marin Institute for the Prevention of Alcohol and Other Drug Problems.

Kunitz, S.J. & Levy, J.E. (1994). *Drinking Careers: A Twenty-five-year Study of Three Navajo Populations.* New Haven, CT: Yale University Press.

MacAndrew, C. & Edgerton, R.B. (1969). *Drunken Comportment: A Social Explanation.* Chicago, IL: Aldine.

Marshall, M. (Ed.) (1979). *Beliefs, Behaviors, and Alcoholic Beverages: A Cross-cultural Survey.* Ann Arbor, MI: University of Michigan Press.

Marshall, M. & Marshall, L.B. (1990). *Silent Voices Speak: Women and Prohibition in Truk.* Belmont, CA: Wadsworth.

Mäkelä, K., Room, R., Single, E., Sulkunen, P. & Walsh, B. (1981). *Alcohol, Society, and the State. A Comparative Study of Alcohol Control.* Toronto: Addiction Research Foundation.

Maula, J. (1997). *Small-scale Poduction of Food and Traditional Alcoholic Beverages in Benin and Tanzania. Implications for the Promotion of Female Entrepreneurship.* Helsinki: Finnish Foundation for Alcohol Studies.

Pan, L. (1975). *Alcohol in Colonial Africa.* Helsinki: Finnish Foundation for Alcohol Studies, Vol. 22.

Partanen, J. (1991). *Sociability and Intoxication. Alcohol and Drinking in Kenya, Africa, and the Modern World.* Helsinki: Finnish Foundation for Alcohol Studies.

Sulkunen, P. (1976). Drinking patterns and the level of alcohol consumption: an international overview. In R.J. Gibbins et al. (Eds), *Research Advances in Alcohol and Drug Problems* (pp. 223–281), Vol. 3. New York: Wiley.

Simpura, J. (1997). Alcohol and European transformation. *Addiction,* **92**(Suppl. 1), S33–42.

Spahni, P. (1988). *The Common Wine Policy and Price Stabilization.* Aldershot: Avebury.

Swiatkiewicz, G. (1997). Regulating unregulated markets. *Addiction,* **92**(Suppl. 1), S67–72.

World Development Indicators (1997). Washington, DC: World Bank.

World Health Organization (WHO) (2000). *The Global Alcohol Report.* Geneva: WHO.

APPENDIX

Estimates of Trends in Per Capita Consumption, 1970–1996

Quantitative estimates of average annual consumption of alcohol for different countries are available from a number of sources. All of these have their limitations, although the most complete and reliable are thought to be those provided by an international body called the Food and Agricultural Organization. This reports alcohol statistics for approximately 200 countries, although they are reliant on the adequacy of reporting by each country. At the very least, this source underestimates informal sources of production, which are highly significant in many countries. When calculating per capita consumption, this is normally conducted for the estimated resident population of the country in question with no allowances made for different age profiles or for flows of tourists both into and out of the country. A selection of estimates reported for a recent WHO (2000) publication is reproduced in Table 19.1.

A more detailed temporal display at a global economic regional level is displayed in Figure 19.1 also reproduced from WHO (2000). It is evident that while total global alcohol consumption has remained fairly stable over the 27 years examined, underlying trends are in opposite directions for the developed (downwards) and the developing (upwards) countries. Those countries identified as being "in transition" also evidence a marked decline in per capita consumption since the early 1980s. However, this marked decline is most readily explained by the rise of black-market economies in post-communist societies, resulting in large quantities of unrecorded consumption, i.e. the downward trend in official statistics is likely to be apparent, not real.

Table 19.1 Trends in recorded per capita consumption of pure alcohol, (litres) per adult 15 years of age and over, 1970–1996

Country	1970–1972	1994–1996	Change (%)
China	1.03	5.17	401.94
Thailand	1.93	8.37	333.68
Nigeria	0.23	0.68	195.65
The Philippines	2.44	6.94	184.43
Republic of Korea	5.23	14.4	175.33
India	0.45	0.93	106.67
Mauritius	2.01	4.07	102.49
Liberia	2.97	5.9	98.65
Malaysia	0.45	0.89	97.78
Brazil	3.18	5.55	74.53
Egypt	0.31	0.54	74.19
Lebanon	3.45	5.72	65.80
Turkey	0.86	1.42	65.12
South Africa	5.07	7.69	51.68
Colombia	4.32	6.47	49.77
Cuba	2.67	3.85	44.19
Costa Rica	4.15	5.97	43.86
Mexico	3.67	5.11	39.24
Greece	7.88	10.62	34.77
Finland	6.19	8.27	33.60
Venezuela	7.06	9.28	31.44
Ireland	9.11	11.82	29.75
Japan	6.1	7.88	29.18
Denmark	9.42	12.08	28.24
Bolivia	2.64	3.38	28.03
UK	7.35	9.25	25.85
Romania	8.25	10.14	22.91
Barbados	7.47	9.07	21.42
Zimbabwe	2.57	2.95	14.79
The Netherlands	8.53	9.75	14.30
Luxembourg	13.19	14.66	11.14
Uruguay	7.41	8.2	10.66
Bulgaria	9.13	9.8	7.34
Trinidad and Tobago	4.55	4.8	5.49
Honduras	2.32	2.41	3.88
Ecuador	1.81	1.86	2.76
Poland	8.04	8.16	1.49
Cameroon	1.65	1.65	0.00
Ghana	0.46	0.46	0.00
Hungary	13.11	13.09	−0.15
Mongolia	2.05	2.03	−0.98
Ethiopia	0.96	0.95	−1.04
Norway	4.94	4.84	−2.02
Belize	5.9	5.76	−2.37
Czech Republic	14.63	14.28	−2.39
Iceland	4.94	4.75	−3.85
Jamaica	4.19	3.98	−5.01
Singapore	2.1	1.98	−5.71
Belgium	11.92	11.07	−7.13

Table 19.1 (*continued*)

Country	1970–1972	1994–1996	Change (%)
Papua New Guinea	1.15	1.06	−7.83
USA	9.92	8.98	−9.48
Slovakia	13.75	12.37	−10.04
Kenya	1.78	1.6	−10.11
Netherlands Antilles	9.74	8.48	−12.94
Sweden	7.33	6.36	−13.23
Germany	13.81	11.88	−13.98
Australia	11.44	9.68	−15.38
Canada	9.16	7.62	−16.81
Haiti	6.93	5.72	−17.46
Switzerland	14.13	11.46	−18.90
Portugal	16.77	13.37	−19.60
Austria	14.97	11.91	−20.27
Democratic People's Republic of Korea	3.89	3.07	−21.08
New Zealand	11.58	9.11	−21.33
Fiji	2.57	1.81	−29.57
Bahamas	17.42	12.15	−30.25
Spain	16.42	11.4	−30.57
Israel	2.48	1.72	−30.65
France	21.37	14.02	−34.39
Congo	2.94	1.78	−39.46
Peru	7.12	4.3	−39.61
Chile	13.01	7.46	−42.66
Nicaragua	4.71	2.62	−44.37
Argentina	17.52	9.73	−44.46
Italy	18.08	9.72	−46.24
New Caledonia	20.75	10.19	−50.89
Yugoslavia	23.28	11.26	−51.63
Angola	4.17	1.78	−57.31
Algeria	0.68	0.27	−60.29
United Arab Emirates	10.61	3.79	−64.28
Zambia	1.82	0.65	−64.29

Primary Sources: FAO Statistical Databases, 1998; United Nations Statistical Office, 1997. From WHO (2000), with permission. Only a selection of countries for whom data were provided has been included.

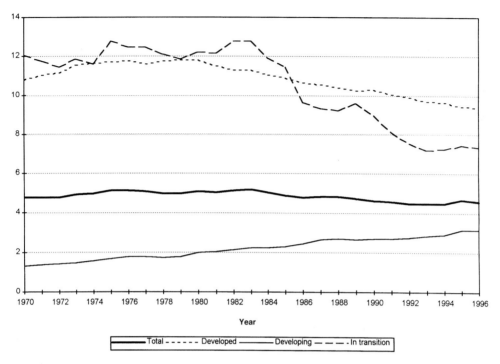

Figure 19.1 Recorded adult (15+) per capita consumption 1970–1996 by economic region (in litres of pure alcohol). Primary Sources: FAO Statistical Databases, 1998; United Nations Statistical Office, 1997. From WHO (2000), with permission. Based on all countries reviewed in that document

Chapter 20

Relationship of Alcohol Consumption and Alcohol Problems at the Population Level

Paul Lemmens

Department of Medical Sociology, University of Maastrict, Maastrict, The Netherlands

Synopsis

Individual alcohol consumption is the result of a complex combination of personal, external, and social or environmental factors. Taking the variability in individual drinking into account, it is remarkable that per capita consumption in societies is relatively stable under normal circumstances. Research has shown that not only is per capita consumption relatively stable, but so also is the way consumption is distributed among drinkers. Empirical consumption distributions are unimodal and usually skewed, with a mean higher than the median, which again is higher than the mode. This implies that the heaviest drinkers take account of a disproportionally large part of the total consumption in a population. Empirically, the top 10% have been found to consume 30–60% of the total consumption. There is both a logical necessity and empirical proof of a positive relationship between the mean and the proportion of heavy drinkers in a society. This relationship has been put forward as relatively invariant, implying that the higher the mean, the higher the incidence of alcohol-related harm. This invariance has been used as an argument for alcohol prevention measures to be directed at all drinkers and all drinking situations, in practice consisting of restrictions in availability (e.g. price and outlet density).

In this chapter, it has been argued that, although undoubtedly one can speak of a certain regularity in the way alcohol consumption is distributed in a population, what is seen at the aggregate level should be regarded with caution. A stable distribution does not imply stable consumption patterns of individuals. Chronicity of heavy drinking has been found to vary across (sub)populations and over time. Similarly, a particular consumption level can be

International Handbook of Alcohol Dependence and Problems. Edited by N. Heather, T.J. Peters and T. Stockwell.
© 2001 John Wiley & Sons Ltd.

attained in different ways. Drinking patterns, as well as the drinking contexts, seem to be important determinants of how consumption relates to harm. Acceptability of drinking that leads to intoxication varies by culture, and seems quite unrelated to per capita consumption. Cultural homogeneity as determined by shared norms seem to be important in how well alcohol is integrated in society. Regularity of distributions has in part been explained by a social interaction mechanism, implying a collective shift in drinking of the entire population. There are, however, many exceptions to the rule of concerted change. The proportion of non-drinkers in a population, an indicator of social integration of drinking, has been found not to be related to per capita consumption, nor to average consumption per drinker in the population. In the literature, many instances have been found where changes in overall drinking were not reflected in all segments of society. Part of the uncertainty surrounding this issue lies in measurement difficulties. Distributions are based on survey estimates of annual consumption, in which assessment is limited in validity and reliability. Because of the skewness, estimates of distributional shape are particularly affected by measurement error in the tail end, i.e. the consumption of the relatively few excessive drinkers.

The notion of a fixed distribution, brought to the fore in the late 1960s, and the discussion thereafter, have changed the focus of a public health policy towards alcohol, including all drinkers as possible targets of prevention, and not only alcoholics. Strategies for dealing with widespread risk factors for disease may entail measures aimed at a reduction of exposure to that risk factor. Two main issues have emerged here: whether to aim specifically at heavy drinkers, or to aim for general measures affecting all drinkers in more or less the same way. The issue emerged as the preventive paradox, due to the observation that, for some alcohol-related outcomes, the bulk of the problems occur among light and moderate drinkers. Such a situation would be yet another argument in favour of a prevention effort aimed at reduction in all drinkers.

Recently, some authors have proposed the idea that the paradox vanishes if frequency of intoxication, rather than average consumption, is taken into the equation. Others have suggested that research often fails to take into account the severity and frequency of the outcome measures. It may then seem appropriate that future research would look more carefully into these assessment issues, both of consumption and of outcomes. As the effects of consumption seem to be modified by drinking pattern, chronicity of drinking, drinking contexts, cultural values and patterns of social interaction, the research field should direct its attention to these issues for more refined assessments of the association between aggregate levels of consumption and harm.

The issue of individual risk factors is discussed in the next chapter, and one may ask why it might be of interest to consider aspects of alcohol consumption at the aggregate, population level? When discussing alcohol problems, one should logically look first at what is available at the individual level. Population level assessments of risk, generally referred to in epidemiological textbooks as ecological designs, do not yield results that can be interpreted at the individual level.

The main scientific interest in drinking and the effects of drinking at the population level is not the assessment of risk, but lies in the observation of a large variation in the way individual risks translate and combine into prevalence and incidence of alcohol problems at the population level. Consider, for example, the connection between drinking and liver cirrhosis. At the individual level, heavy alcohol consumption of longer duration is a fairly well-established risk factor for cirrhosis of the liver, i.e. an exponential, strongly convex dose–response curve, with a sharply increasing risk at higher levels of drinking. However, this risk does not imply that a high per capita consumption in a population automatically leads to high cirrhosis rates. An illustration is given in Figure 20.1, showing the empirical

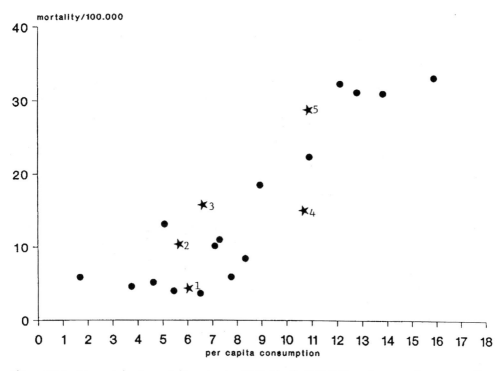

Figure 20.1 Liver cirrhosis mortality rates in 1974 (deaths/100,000) and per capita consumption (average over 1970–1972 in litres 100% alcohol) in 21 Western countries. 1 = Netherlands, 2 = Sweden, 3 = USA, 4 = Switzerland, 5 = West Germany. From Hoogendoorn (1978), with permission

association between age-adjusted liver cirrhosis mortality rates and per capita alcohol consumption in different Western countries in a particular year.

Obviously, similar average consumption rates in the figure lead to outcomes that can differ by a factor of 2. Similarly, equal rates of cirrhosis do not imply similar population consumption levels. Although the correlation between average consumption and cirrhosis mortality over all countries is positive, there is ample variation. What is observed here between countries has also been observed within countries over time. It would seem too simplistic, therefore, to assume that whenever per capita consumption goes up, so too would the rate of alcohol-related misery, and to the same degree. As an aside, it should be noted that different diagnostic practices in different countries in different times may be a source of error in the observed association.

Apparently, many factors co-determine how a particular risk affects the rate of alcohol-related problems in a population. One obvious factor is the way in which total consumption is distributed across the entire population, i.e. the population distribution. Other factors affecting the incidence rate are, among conceivable others: drinking pattern (e.g. concentrated or spaced in time); the general diet and hygienic conditions; temporal dynamics of the effects of (heavy) drinking (e.g. the time-lag of negative effect); differences in the number of treatment facilities for alcoholism and dependence; and differences in treatment facilities and care for patients with liver cirrhosis. Of these factors, the shape of the distribution of alcohol consumption has raised particular scientific interest, and has caused considerable controversy.

DISTRIBUTION OF CONSUMPTION

Formally, population incidence of a particular outcome that is causally related to alcohol consumption can be regarded as the product of two variates, the risk function for that outcome and the population distribution (Kleinbaum et al., 1982). It has been shown analytically that only in the case of a linearly increasing risk (viz. a linear alcohol dose–response curve) is the incidence in the population independent of the distribution of alcohol consumption (Skog, 1991a), implying that every sip of alcohol in a population adds to the increased incidence, regardless of the type of drinker. In all other instances (i.e. non-linear risks), the resulting incidence is dependent to a varying degree on the shape of the distribution of consumption. Since most risk curves for alcohol-related outcomes are non-linear (Holder & Edwards, 1995), the shape of the distribution is an important parameter to consider.

Generally, the population distribution of alcohol consumption, as assessed by survey methods, is positively skewed, with a mean higher than the median and much higher than the mode, as shown in Figure 20.2. The more (positively) skewed a distribution, the larger the proportion of the total consumption will be consumed by the heaviest drinkers. For example, on the basis of survey data it was estimated that the top 10% of both male and female drinkers consumed slightly more than one-third of all alcohol available in The Netherlands in 1985 (Lemmens, 1991). The degree of skewness, and hence this relationship of proportions, has been found to vary across populations (Skog, 1991b), and is dependent upon the type of data collection method used (Lemmens, 1991). For example, Greenfield & Rogers (1999) reported that, for two general populations surveys in the USA utilizing a summary measure of consumption, the heaviest, top 10% drinkers account for more than half of all consumption. Skewness could be regarded as an indicator of social integration

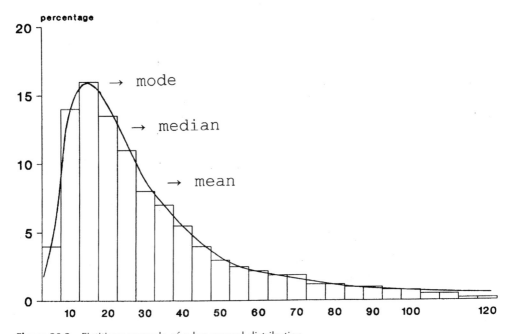

Figure 20.2 Fictitious example of a log-normal distribution

of drinking, together with its variance (i.e. the sum of inter-individual differences). In practice, this means that populations with equal means may and will differ as regards the proportion of heavy drinkers, and thus in the level of social integration of alcohol.

The way in which total consumption is distributed over the population has led to considerable controversy in the alcohol research field. The central issue is the relative invariance of the distribution of consumption. What was meant by "relative invariance" is, however, not an easy concept to explain, and has been a cause of confusion. In the following sections, a brief summary of the discussion on the distribution issue is presented.

LEDERMANN'S DISTRIBUTION MODEL

In 1956, the French demographer, Ledermann, published results of studies on excess mortality and overall consumption in different French regions. He hypothesized a strong link between overall consumption in a population and excessive use. In his view, no sharp distinction between normal drinking levels and excessive, alcoholic levels could be made (unimodal distribution, with only one peak, as in Figure 20.2). Differences between drinkers were regarded as being gradual (no separate populations of alcoholics and social drinkers). He suggested a mathematical model for the relationship between average consumption in a population and the proportion of excessive use, exceeding a particular daily average. Figure 20.3 shows the hypothetical relationship according to the Ledermann formula.

Since the model has only one parameter, i.e. average consumption, Ledermann's model implied that a public health policy aimed at prevention of alcohol-related diseases had but one option: "... the suppression of alcohol in all the forms in which it is consumed" (Ledermann, 1964). Within an emerging public health ideology, this was interpreted as that

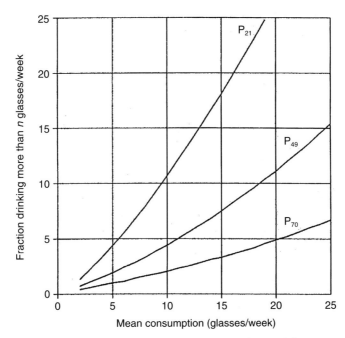

Figure 20.3 Relationship between average consumption (per drinker) and the proportion of the drinking population consuming more than 21, 49 and 70 glasses/week, according to the Ledermann formula

an effective preventive policy should target all drinkers, not only heavy drinkers or alcoholics. Only those general measures that succeeded in bringing down total consumption in a population would be effective in reducing alcohol-related harm. The adoption of Ledermann's basic idea meant a shift in focus of a alcohol health policy from the alcoholic derelict to a hitherto-considered "normal" drinker, and could be seen as a return to a call for general measures suggested at the turn of the century, when Western society was "plagued" by a drunken urban proletariat (Katcher, 1993).

In the research literature, many studies have criticized the Ledermann model on both theoretical and empirical grounds (Skog, 1985). The variation in the relationship was large, and unimodality of the distribution has been challenged (Miller & Agnew, 1974; Duffy, 1997), mainly on the grounds of insufficient sample sizes of the empirical survey data. Criticisms also related to the fact that conclusions about longitudinal change were based on cross-sectional studies. The idea of a mathematically fixed relationship, as proposed by Ledermann, had to be relaxed. The claim of a close association between average consumption and the proportion of heavy drinkers was, however, maintained (Bruun et al., 1975), concretely implying that "a lowering of the total consumption of alcohol is likely to be accompanied by a reduction of heavy users" (ibid, p. 90).

COLLECTIVITY OF DRINKING CULTURES

Skog has formulated an influential theory to account for the apparent regularities in the population distribution, and for the connection between total consumption and the proportion of excessive users and incidence of harm in a population (Skog, 1985). His collectivity of drinking cultures rests on two postulates: (a) social influences are major determinants of a person's drinking behaviour; and (b) factors influencing drinking combine multiplicatively, resulting in a change of drinking proportionate to the initial drinking level. Through a complicated set of deductions, the theory suggests a diffusion of drinking habits (resulting in an increase or decrease of total consumption) in the population with a synchronized effect in a way that ". . . people move in concert up and down the consumption scale" (ibid, p. 97). In the model, people's drinking is seen as interrelated through various social networks, in such a way that any (independent) change in individual consumption will have an equi-directional impact on the consumption of all others.

With this notion of interdependency of all actors (or, at least, all drinkers) in society, Skog has presented his theory as a theoretical underpinning, and a further argument in favour of a prevention policy aimed at the general population. Such a policy is often considered to consist of general measures aimed at limiting and controlling supply, consisting of maintaining a high price of alcoholic beverages and restricted availability. Essentially, however, the notion of a large interdependence does not preclude measures aimed at reducing demand. What it does imply is that measures effectively reducing consumption of any drinker in the population will have an effect, to a varying degree, on all drinkers, and hence, on the incidence of excessive use, and, through that, on the rate of alcohol-related problems (Skog, 1991b).

PROBLEMS OF CAUSALITY: "WETNESS"

The importance of the general consumption level in a country as an indicator of the level of harm has remained giving rise to confusion. It is often regarded as an independent, causal factor. The tautological nature of such an argument is obvious: as the number of excessive drinkers in a population increases, logically, so does the mean of that population.

The problem arises when the mean value in a population is viewed as an independent factor affecting people's drinking. Skog, among others, has maintained the argument that "wetness" of a person's environment is a key factor in the formation of a person's drinking career. "Wetness" is the degree to which alcohol has penetrated into a particular environment, and is expressed as the aggregate sum of all drinking, and thus is conceptually closely linked to or indicated by the population mean. In Skog's view, a typical or "potential heavy drinker" in a "wet" culture will drink more than an otherwise similar person in a "dry" culture (Skog, 1991b, p. 580). In this view, mean consumption has a generic effect, and it becomes important to keep a society dry in order to prevent those being susceptible to heavy drinking to become heavy drinkers. Critics may ask what constitutes a "potential heavy drinker", especially if one holds the view, as Skog does, that drinking is primarily a social affair rather than a result of individual, constitutional factors (personality, physiology). Depicted caricaturally, heavy drinking results in a wet environment or culture which, in turn, causes people to drink heavily.

There is no easy way out of these conceptual problems. At a social level, it is often difficult to disentangle cause and effect, since all factors are part of a reciprocal, reactive process. If one looks at historical examples, this becomes all the more evident. As in many Western countries at the end of the nineteenth century, consumption in Holland dropped dramatically from 10 litres per capita to 21 in 1938. This process was characterized by changes in legislation, marked by the first drink law in 1880. Drunkenness then became a criminal offence, and sales were regulated by a restrictive permit system. As De Lint (1981) has noted, however, it is debatable whether these drink laws, which were intended to restrict outlet density, were ever effective, since in no single jurisdiction was the maximum legal density of outlets ever reached. Outlet density has been governed by economic (open market) rather than legal restraints. A similar effect is visible regarding criminal acts. In the first year after implementation of the Act outlawing public drunkenness, the number of recorded criminal offences was highest (ca. 33,000), but this number started dropping steadily and remained doing so until the present day (to less than 5% of the initial level), even though after World War II alcohol consumption has risen to levels equal to those during the first enactment. Before the war, one could have concluded that the measures had had the desired effect. The post-war evidence showed that the legal restraints did not prevent consumption from going up. This ineffectiveness of an upper limit on outlet density was the reason for its abolition in the Dutch Drink Act of 1967.

In sum, although the Dutch legal reform and change in per capita consumption were contingent, it is questionable whether the association was of a truly causal nature. Perhaps both phenomena were the result of a broader change in society, affecting drinking morals and attitudes, rather than an independent factor causing consumption to go down. This problem, termed in economics as endogeneity of change, clearly poses a challenge to all researchers of public policy formation. The example of the Dutch situation is, nevertheless, a clear indication that social values and norms, with or without a legal base, are important determinants of consumption in the population, and of what kind and number of problems this consumption may cause.

HOMOGENEITY OF THE POPULATION

The extent to which norms and values concerning drinking in a society are shared by all members of the population determines its homogeneity regarding drinking behaviour. The more homogeneous a population, the more likely it is that factors affecting drinking will have similar effects on the drinkers. In this section, changes in overall consumption in relation to social integration of drinking will be discussed. It is often expected that a low per capita consumption is associated with a marginal social role of alcohol in society. However, this may not be generally the case.

When looking at different populations, often demarcated by national boundaries or permanent characteristics such as age and gender, one can observe large differences in the proportion of non-drinkers. There is no consistent relationship between this proportion and the level of consumption in that (sub)population. In the USA, even a slightly negative association was found between proportion of abstainers and per-drinker consumption (Hilton, 1988). Nordic countries are characterized by a low average consumption level but a high proportion of regular drinkers of alcohol, and one could speak of a high level of integration of alcohol in society. Integration of alcohol in daily life, as expressed in the proportion of drinkers, thus appears not to be associated with per capita consumption.

Since it is hypothesized by those who emphasize the large impact of social interaction that changes in drinking are general and unidirectional, it could be expected that no large social segment of the population would deviate from this rule. However, for the UK, Tuck (1980) found that the increase in total consumption from 1974 to 1979 was caused by an increase in the number of drinkers at moderate frequencies, but not in the number of daily (heavier) drinkers. Based on similar evidence covering the years following (1979–1989), Duffy (1991) concluded that the changes in average consumption were due to changes in the frequency pattern of lower frequency drinkers, and thus not consistently along the entire consumption scale, as would be predicted by the social interaction model. There are also many examples to be found of cohorts, age groups or population segments that run counter to the trend. For example, Lemmens (1995) reported a counter-trend development, especially for younger men, among whom an increase in mean had not led to an increase in the proportion of heavy drinking. Lemmens concluded that changes in mean or per capita consumption in a large population may not always accurately reflect changes in segments or subpopulations. Fillmore et al. (1994) concluded from their database of 25 longitudinal studies that "aggregate level changes do not carry equal weight among all groups in society". They found that a large change in overall consumption in society was particularly associated with an increased frequency of drinking among women. These examples show that, although per capita consumption is an important indicator of heavy drinking in a society, one cannot rely on it as a sole indicator.

Skog (1991c) has given many examples of the "relative stability" or regularity of consumption distributions across populations. Lemmens et al. (1990) have presented several examples of regularity of distributions in samples over time when alcohol consumption increased. In the latter case, the regularity observed was captured by a linear shift function, meaning that the posterior distribution could be predicted by a linear function of log-transformed data. This finding supports the idea of Skog and Ledermann of a relative aggregate stability in the way total consumption is distributed. The latter examples of change, however, still concerned small differences in average consumption, in natural situations without major policy interventions.

Ledermann (1964) proposed the idea that, if alcohol consumption distributions show a strong regularity, it would imply a generalistic control-of-supply approach to prevention, necessarily denying individuals a freedom of choice. It has, however, been suggested that major interventions affecting people's "liberty of choice" may actually affect the way alcohol is distributed. An example of such redistribution is given by Norström (1987). His data concern a situation in which the "connection between reasonable and unreasonable consumption" (Ledermann, 1964, p. 8) was broken. He found that after abrupt abolition of the Swedish alcohol rationing system, average consumption in Sweden did not change, but the prevalence of heavy drinking did (and so did the incidence of liver cirrhosis). Light and moderate drinkers decreased consumption, while heavy drinkers drank more after the reform. Apparently, the much higher prices of alcohol did affect light and moderate drinkers but had little effect on heavy drinkers, who found availability of alcohol to be less restricted than before the reform, even though the nominal price was higher. When looking at the differential change, the apparent impact of social interaction on the behaviour of drinkers was negligible relative to the effect of price. The distribution of consumption became more skewed, and one might speculate whether the abolition meant a return to a more "natural" situation. The differential price effect in the example should not be taken as general proof that heavy drinkers are not sensitive to price, however scarce individual-level research is on price and income elasticities among different types of drinkers (Edwards et al., 1994, pp. 118–9).

Summarizing the discussion so far, it is generally acknowledged that the population distribution is skewed and, thus, that the bulk of the alcohol is consumed by a limited number of drinkers. Although mean consumption and prevalence of excessive are related, an exact shape of the distribution cannot be predicted solely from the mean. Certain regularities in distribution can be observed over time, and trends in overall consumption often reflect similar changes in several segments of society. However, societies differ in many respects, and exceptions to the general rule are quite frequent. It is beyond doubt that people affect each other in their drinking, but social interaction as a theoretical foundation for the way alcohol is distributed in a population is still disputable. When comparing overall consumption across societies, one should keep in mind that it is neither an indication of social integration of alcohol (e.g. proportion of drinkers) nor the sole indicator of prevalence of heavy drinking (tail of the distribution) and of consequent alcohol problems.

DRINKING PATTERN AND CHRONICITY OF DRINKING

Given a certain overall consumption level, distributional form (i.e. degree of concentration of consumption) is only one, albeit important, parameter affecting alcohol-related problem rates in a population. Another factor is the degree of stability of drinking in a population, or chronicity of abuse. For example, heavy drinking over a prolonged period of time seems to be necessary for liver tissue to become affected. A distribution of (annual) consumption does not contain information as to the duration of the exposure to a particular dose of alcohol. Assessment of individual consumption over longer periods of time, either retrospectively or prospectively, is, however, difficult, and measurement issues are a consistent problem in this area. From what is known, it seems that individual drinking fluctuates over time, both cyclical (e.g. diurnal, weekly and seasonal cycles), and across the life-course (causing period, age and cohort effects). This implies that the tails of otherwise similar distributions may at different times be composed of different heavy drinkers. Few general rules can be given as to the effect of the dynamics of drinking behaviour on the composition of the (compound) consumption distribution. An example of this complexity is given by Fillmore (1987), who reported the highest prevalence of heavy drinking, but also the highest remission rates, among the young in the USA. Most stable in their drinking were middle-aged drinkers. A similar conclusion was reached by Hajema et al. (1997) in a Dutch general population survey. They did not find any changes in aggregate indices of consumption between 1980 and 1989, but only half of the Dutch men and less than 25% of the women reported in both years to be drinkers of higher amounts (i.e. 6 glasses weekly or more per occasion). (Sub)populations, characterized by a similar per capita consumption, and even similar distributions, may thus be composed of individuals with quite different risk profiles.

What goes for chronicity of drinking, is also relevant when considering differences in drinking pattern. The alcohol consumption of individuals can be considered a composite variable, and its distribution a compound distribution of two variates, frequency and quantity of drinking (Alanko, 1997). A similar total annual consumption of alcohol can be reached by quite different frequencies. It is known, for example, that young people in Western societies drink in a temporally much more concentrated fashion than the older people in the population, i.e. they drink less frequently but more per occasion, especially during weekends. Such a concentrated drinking pattern leads to higher BACs, and thus to higher incidences of particularly acute effects of intoxication. Tragic examples are the high weekend traffic casualty rate among younger drivers and the much higher involvement of alcohol in injured young people. Populations have been found to differ also as regards daily drinking frequency. Until recently, European countries differed greatly in prevailing drinking patterns. Traditionally, countries bordering the Mediterranean Sea had high per capita drinking levels, with a high, mostly daily, frequency of wine drinking, usually with meals. In Italy in the 1950s, for example, drinking with meals was common (>80%), but drinking between meals or after meals was relatively rare (<30%; Lolli et al., 1958). Although Italian per capita consumption ranked as one of the highest in the world, intoxication was uncommon and rates of "alcoholism" were relatively low. In the Nordic countries, daily drinking was rare, and drinking to intoxication was a pervasive habit, with spirits as beverage of preference. Such aspects of drinking, of course, have an effect on the way overall consumption is expressed in incidences of negative and harmful effects. The larger the differences in the drinking customs of populations considered, the larger the variance in the association of total consumption and harm. In recent decades, an increasing European integration of drinking pattern can be observed, with the erosion of traditional drinking patterns (Sulkunen, 1989; Hupkens et al., 1993). This process will have an effect not only on alcohol-related problem rates but also on per capita consumption.

MEASUREMENT OF CONSUMPTION AND HARMFUL EFFECTS

When looking at the distribution of consumption, it is important to pay attention to the reference period over which consumption is assessed, and to the methods that are used to measure alcohol consumption. Due to limited memory capacities, elicited self-reports of actual intake have to be limited to 1 or 2 weeks (Mäkelä, 1971). It is known that drinking is a rather dynamic behaviour, temporally complex (Ekholm, 1968). With methods of actual consumption, using a time window of only 1 or 2 weeks, the bias due to time variability is quite large (Duffy & Alanko, 1992). In other words, the generalizability of self-reported consumption into average, annual consumption at the individual level is limited. Methods covering reference periods longer than 1 week rely on summary measures, inquiring about usual or typical frequency and quantity over weeks or months. The validity of estimates of total consumption obtained by these types of methods may be questioned too. Usual frequency and usual quantity reports are combined by the researcher into a composite, individual "average consumption", with the implicit assumption that the respondents report their average frequency and ditto quantity. There are, however, indications that people tend to report modal frequency and modal amounts (Duffy & Alanko, 1992). Since frequency and quantity have their own, expectedly non-symmetrical distribution, in order to correctly combine these two data into a composite total consumption, one should first model frequency and quantity of drinking (Alanko & Lemmens, 1996). The true implications of this bias in consumption data for conclusions in alcohol epidemiology still remain to be researched (Alanko, 1997).

Few empirical results are available studying the impact of methods used to collect data on distributional form, even at the aggregate level. Lemmens (1991) has compared distributions in the Dutch general population data from 1985, obtained by means of prospective, daily diary self-reports, with self-reports from a retrospective method recalling actual consumption in the preceding week, and a summary measure (composed of quantity and frequency measures), the latter being the measure most often used in assessing distributions. Diary data are considered to be less affected by memory errors. The comparisons of distributions for males are shown in Figure 20.4.

A deviation from linearity would signify a non-linear error, and hence, a bias in the empirical distribution due to method of assessment. The width of the confidence bands signify the error variance. It is noted that the function in Figure 20.4A, signifying the relationship between daily diary and recall of actual consumption, is approximately linear and relatively stable across the consumption scale. In Figure 20.4B the result is less smooth, but it does not show a large deviation from linearity. The author concluded that method seemed to have little effect on the shape of the distribution. However, more research is needed on the effect of empirical method on estimated shape of the distribution in other populations.

Non-response or differential under-reporting may add to the problems interpreting the distribution of consumption, and, hence, the link with negative outcomes. If heavy drinkers are more likely not to be included in the sample frame, to be absent or to refuse when being interviewed, and to under-report (as is often presumed), the empirical distribution will be less skewed. Differences in the social acceptability of (heavy) drinking, the perceived level of threat a personal inquiry into drinking may entail, and the likelihood of such response effects in a survey to occur may be associated with the level of integration of alcohol in society. Hence, this may produce either a positive or negative bias in the empirical relationship using the consumption data.

Summarizing this section, it can be concluded that problems with the measurement of alcohol consumption have not yet been solved. The way alcohol is conceptualized and measured may have an effect on the shape of the empirical distribution. In Chapter 21, Greenfield discusses the problems concerning possible information biases as to harmful effects. Although a less than perfect reliability in the measure applied will produce a bias to the null, and in effect underestimate associations between consumption and harm, information bias may also produce spurious correlations.

THE PREVENTION PARADOX

In the past decades, epidemiological research on alcohol-related problems has surged, and perspectives on prevention of these problems have changed (Katcher, 1993). The increasing body of research establishing dose-specific risks related to the consumption of alcohol has resulted in changing views on how society should deal with these negative effects. In the 1940s and 1950s, the emphasis was on the alcoholic abuser and on treatment. The public health model widened its focus to include all drinkers, normal and excessive, as potential targets of preventive interventions. In that view, the entire drinking population is at risk. The primary goal of prevention is to either decrease the number of those being exposed to the risk factor or to mitigate the negative effects of the exposure. Using a traffic metaphor, the choice would be either to make people drive less fast, or to make safer cars. The latter option will be left undiscussed here.

The former involves two principle strategic options. First, one screens for those at high risk and then devises a strategy deemed effective in eliminating the exposure to that risk factor. For example, in the case of the coronary risk factor LDL-cholesterol, one screens the population for cases over a certain limit (and maybe for other risk factors), and then prescribes medication that could effectively bring the patient within "safe limits". The second option is that one leaves out the screening altogether, and directs attention to the

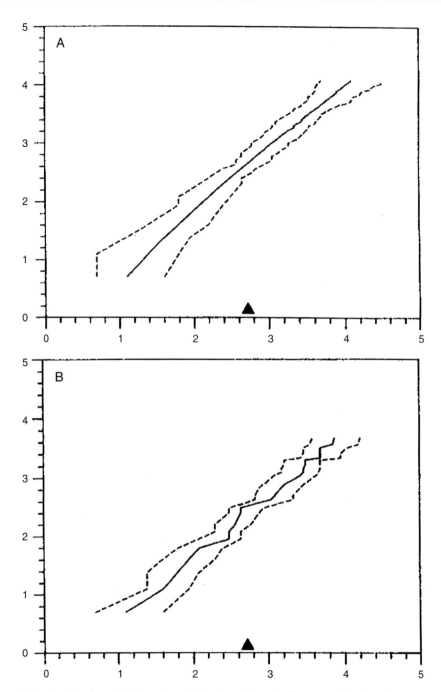

Figure 20.4 Empirical probability plots of Dutch 1985 male diary consumption data (*x* axis) and linearly transformed distributions obtained by a method measuring actual consumption (A) and a summary measure (B) from the same sample (*y* axis). All data log-transformed. Triangles denote the median

entire population that is more or less exposed to the risk factor, and hopes for a downward shift of the entire distribution. For example, one informs the public about food substances and diets that raise cholesterol blood levels, or one advertises the use of low-fat margarine as a substitute for butter.

The potential effectiveness of these approaches is dependent upon several factors. One is the incidence or dose–response relationship of the outcome in the population. The population distribution of the risk factor is the other main factor (except in the case of a linear risk curve, as noted earlier). Depending on the combination of particular risk curve and population distribution, either of these two approaches is potentially more successful.

These two approaches, and their potential effectiveness in reducing the incidence in a population, have given rise to controversy over what has become known as "the prevention paradox". The term was originally proposed by Rose (1981) in an article in the *British Medical Journal*. In the paper, Rose described a seemingly contradictory situation in which a minimal decrease in exposure to the risk factor in the entire population (e.g. cholesterol or fat intake) would be more effective in reducing incidence of the negative outcome (e.g. coronary disease) than a vast change in exposure of a select, but high-risk, group (below a safe cholesterol level). In other words, a slight shift of the entire distribution of the risk factor to the left would be more effective than a large change to the left of those considered to be at high risk.

This strategic contrast was developed for some negative social drinking problems by Kreitman (1986). He found that the bulk of the problems were caused not by excessive drinkers but by moderate drinkers, with average drinking levels below the safe limits set by the Royal College of Psychiatrists. A focus solely on heavy drinkers would, therefore, affect only a limited fraction of all problems in society. For these alcohol problems, a policy directed at all drinkers, not only heavy drinkers, would thus be indicated. A practical difficulty is to convince light drinkers to drink less in order to prevent problems for which they are at a very low risk, and thus less motivated to comply with the advice. It may be helpful to note a similar strategic dilemma in convincing all car drivers to use safety belts. Risk for most drivers is next to zero, but large-scale compliance does make a large difference in overall fatality rates. The preventive paradox has been used as an additional argument for a public health alcohol policy directed at the entire population: attempts to focus on particular heavy-drinking categories or groups may prove less effective than general availability measures which affect the behaviour of all drinkers.

The paradox has recently been challenged as an artifactual finding in a study showing that when drinking pattern is taken into account, the paradoxical situation would "disappear" (Stockwell et al., 1996). This disappearance is caused by the high(er) correlation between risk and frequency of intoxication. When intoxication is controlled for, little variance is left for the variable "average consumption". Infrequent bouts of heavy drinking of otherwise (average) light or moderate drinkers explain most of the co-variation between drinking and harm. In summary, the prevention paradox may be caused by a conceptual omission or model misspecification: by neglecting drinking pattern, one may overlook the real causal link between drinking and (certain indicators of) harm.

Concerning the other end of the paradox, the incidence of alcohol problems, it has been argued by Mäkelä (1991) that, in risk assessments, severity and frequency of occurrence of the recorded drinking problems are often ignored, treating all alcohol problems as equal. For instance, in survey assessments all hangovers are treated alike, whether they occur every other day or only once in the past year. Similar to Stockwell's argument of misspecification of the exposure measure, the paradox could then be partly the result of this crude assessment of harm, due to the collapsing of categories, obscuring the greater intensity of pain and harm among heavy drinkers. With more refined instruments, the paradox would again be less obvious. Mäkelä proposed a synthesis of the epidemiologic and clinical traditions, bridging the gap between what has been termed by Room (1977) as the "two worlds of alcohol problems". Epidemiologists and demographers tend to look at general drinking practices in relation to general health problems, but overlook the difference between a Sunday hangover and the solemn cruelty of alcoholism and dependence. Those working in the clinic often forget that the individuals they are treating form only the tail-end of the continuum, the tip of an iceberg. The confusion over the implications of the so-called prevention paradox can be regarded as a manifestation of this difference in perspective.

CONCLUDING REMARKS

The idea of a fixed distribution of alcohol consumption, as originally proposed by Leder-mann, has contributed to a widening of the focus of a public health approach to the prob-lems associated with alcohol consumption, to include not only alcoholics but all drinkers as potential cases. With Katcher (1993), one could be puzzled by the "eclipse" in knowledge in post-repeal times concerning the medical effects of excessive drinking, as he showed that several risks of heavy drinking were already known in the first part of the twentieth century. It is now undisputed that even among social, moderate drinkers the risk of experiencing harmful effects of drinking is not negligible. Per capita consumption is undoutedly an indication of how many people are exposed to high risk levels. The mean level should, however, not be taken as the sole indicator. Social interaction has been brought forward by Skog as an explanation for distributional regularity, and as such, as an additional argument for an alcohol control policy. Although it is clear that people affect each other in the way they drink, its suggested implication, that an alcohol control policy is the single effective option, is less obvious. Changing beliefs about harmfulness, or norms regarding the accept-ability of drinking alcohol, may affect the diffusion of drinking habits regardless of legal or economic restraints, as exemplified by the Dutch example. The Swedish case presented here showed that external influences on drinking may be selective, producing a redistribution. From the research literature on drinking habits, particularly the longitudinal data that has accumulated over the years, it becomes clear that the expression of the harmful effects of overall consumption is modified by several factors or blurred by measurement error. The conclusion, then, is that it may seem appropriate that future research would look more carefully into assessment issues, concerning both consumption and outcomes. As the effects of consumption seem to be modified by drinking pattern (e.g. frequency of intoxica-tion), chronicity of drinking, drinking contexts, cultural values and patterns of social interaction, the research field should direct its attention to these issues for more refined assessments of the association between aggregate levels of consumption and harm.

KEY WORKS AND SUGGESTIONS FOR FURTHER READING

Bruun, K., Edwards, G., Lumio, M. et al. (1975).   *Alcohol Control Policies in Public Health Perspective*. Helsinki: Finnish Foundation for Alcohol Studies.

The "purple book". The classic study in which the arguments for the public health model have been submitted. The adagium of the report was that "changes in the overall con-sumption of alcoholic beverages have a bearing on the health of the people in any society. Alcohol control measures can be used to limit consumption: thus, control of alcohol availability becomes a public health issue". The report was written in times of dramatic increases in overall consumption.

Edwards, G., Anderson, P., Babor, T.F. et al. (1994). *Alcohol Policy and the Public Good*. Oxford: Oxford University Press.

Intended as an update to the "purple book". The target readership is the public health official; this is a lay version of the Holder & Edwards book. Much more research on the risks of alcohol consumption was available in the early 1990s than in the early 1970s. This book was written in times of a stabilized overall consumption. The launching of the book was accompanied by a row in the British press over an attempt of the alcohol industry to discredit the book, a sign of the potential political and economic implications of a public health model.

Holder, H.D. & Edwards, G. (Eds) (1995). *Alcohol and Public Policy: Evidence and Issues*. Oxford: Oxford University Press.

Systematic reviews of trends in alcohol, and of alcohol-related medical and social risks. Evaluation studies of treatment, prevention and control measures are systematically reviewed. Includes a review of studies on price effects and economic evaluation of policies. The contributions formed the ground material for *Alcohol Policy and the Public Good*.

Skog, O.-J. (1991b). Implications of the distribution theory for drinking and alcoholism. In D.J. Pittman & H. Raskin White (Eds), *Society, Culture, and Drinking Patterns Reexamined* (pp. 576–597). New Brunswick, NJ: Alcohol Research Documentation.

Skog, O.-J. (1991c). Drinking and the distribution of alcohol consumption. In D.J. Pittman & H. Raskin White (Eds), *Society, Culture, and Drinking Patterns Reexamined* (pp. 135–156). New Brunswick, NJ: Alcohol Research Documentation.

Both chapters offer a review of the empirical and theoretical background of the single distribution model of alcohol. Description of the mechanism of social interaction and multiplicative change as explanations for the regularities in distribution.

REFERENCES

Alanko, T. (1997). *Statistical Models for Estimating the Distribution Function of Alcohol Consumption*. Helsinki: Finnish Foundation for Alcohol Studies, Monograph 44.

Alanko, T. & Lemmens, P.H. (1996). Response effects in consumption surveys: an application of the beta-binomial model to self-reported drinking frequencies. *Journal of Official Statistics*, **12**, 253–273.

Bruun, K., Edwards, G., Lumio, M. et al. (1975). *Alcohol Control Policies in Public Health Perspective*. Helsinki: Finnish Foundation for Alcohol Studies.

De Lint, J. (1981). Anti-drink propaganda and alcohol control measures: a report on the Dutch experience. In E. Single, P. Morgan & J. de Lint (Eds), *Alcohol, Society and the State*, Vol. 2. Toronto: Addiction Research Foundation.

Duffy, J.C. (1991). *Trends in Alcohol Consumption Patterns, 1978–1989*. Henley-on-Thames: NTC.

Duffy, J.C. (1997). Unimodality and the distribution of alcohol consumption. Paper presented at the 22nd Annual Alcohol Epidemiology Symposium of the Kettil Bruun Society, Edinburgh.

Duffy, J.C. & Alanko, T. (1992). Self-reported consumption measures in sample surveys: a simulation study of alcohol consumption. *Journal of Official Statistics*, **8**, 327–350.

Edwards, G., Anderson, P., Babor, T.F. et al. (1994). *Alcohol Policy and the Public Good*. Oxford: Oxford University Press.

Ekholm, A. (1968). A study of the drinking rhythm of Finnish males. Paper presented at the 25th International Congress on Alcohol and Alcoholism, September 15–20, Washington, DC.

Fillmore, K.M. (1987). Prevalence, incidence, and chronicity of drinking patterns and problems among men as a function of age: a longitudinal and cohort analysis. *British Journal of Addiction*, **82**, 77–83.

Fillmore, K.M., Golding, J.M., Leino, E.V. et al. (1994).   Societal level predictors of groups' drinking patterns: a research synthesis from the collaborative alcohol-related longitudinal project. *American Journal of Public Health*, **84**, 247–253.

Greenfield, T.K. & Rogers, J.D. (1999).   Who drinks most of the alcohol in the US? The policy implications. *Journal of Studies on Alcohol*, **60**, 78–89.

Hajema, K.J., Knibbe, R.A. & Drop, M.A. (1997).   Changes in alcohol consumption in a general population in The Netherlands: a 9 year follow-up study. *Addiction*, **92**, 49–60.

Hilton, M. (1988).   Regional diversity in United States drinking practices. *British Journal of Addiction*, **83**, 519–532.

Holder, H.D. & Edwards, G. (Eds) (1995).   *Alcohol and Public Policy: Evidence and Issues*. Oxford: Oxford University Press.

Hupkens, C.L.H., Knibbe, R.A. & Drop, M.J. (1993).   Alcohol consumption in the European Community: uniformity and diversity in drinking patterns. *Addiction*, **88**, 1391–1404.

Katcher, B.S. (1993).   The post-repeal eclipse in knowledge about the harmful effects of alcohol. *Addiction*, **88**, 729–744.

Kleinbaum, D.G., Kupper, L.L. & Morgenstern, H. (1982).   *Epidemiologic Research*. New York: Van Nostrand Reinhold.

Kreitman, N. (1986).   Alcohol consumption and the prevention paradox. *British Journal of Addiction*, **81**, 353–363.

Ledermann, S. (1956).   *Alcool, Alcoolism, Alcoolisation*. Vol. 1. Paris: Presses Universitaires de France.

Ledermann, S. (1964).   Can one reduce alcoholism without changing total alcohol consumption in a population? Paper presented at the 27th International Congress, "Alcohol and Alcoholism", Frankfurt am Main, Germany.

Lemmens, P.H. (1991).   *Measurement and Distribution of Alcohol Consumption* (dissertation) Maastricht: University of Limburg.

Lemmens, P.H. (1995).   Individual risk and population distribution of alcohol consumption. In H.D. Holder & G. Edwards (Eds), *Alcohol and Public Policy: Evidence and Issues*. Oxford: Oxford University Press.

Lemmens, P.H.H.M., Tan, E.S. & Knibbe, R.A. (1990).   Comparing distributions of alcohol consumption: empirical probability plots. *British Journal of Addiction*, **85**, 751–758.

Lolli, G., Serianni, E., Golder, G.M. & Luzzatto-Fegiz, P. (1958).   *Alcohol in Italian Culture: Food and Wine in Relation to Sobriety among Italians and Italian Americans*. New Haven, CT: Yale Center of Alcohol Studies.

Mäkelä, K. (1971).   *Measuring the Consumption of Alcohol in the 1968–1969 Alcohol Consumption Study*. Report No. 2. Helsinki: Finnish Foundation for Alcohol Studies.

Mäkelä, K. (1991).   Impact of changes in availability of alcohol on heavy and dependent drinkers. Paper presented at the International Symposium in Drug Dependence, Mexico City.

Miller, G.H. & Agnew, N. (1974).   The Ledermann model of alcohol consumption. *Quarterly Journal of Studies on Alcohol*, **35**, 877–898.

Norström, T. (1987).   The abolition of the Swedish rationing system: effects on consumption distribution and cirrhosis mortality. *British Journal of Addiction*, **82**, 633–641.

Room, R. (1977).   Measurement and distribution of drinking patterns and problems in general populations. In G. Edwards, M.M. Gross, M. Keller, J. Moser & R. Room (Eds), *Alcohol-related Disabilities* (pp. 61–87). Geneva: WHO, Publication No. 32.

Rose, G. (1981).   Strategy of prevention: lessons from cardiovascular disease. *British Medical Journal*, **282**, 1847–1851.

Skog, O.-J. (1985).   The collectivity of drinking cultures. A theory of the distribution of alcohol consumption. *British Journal of Addiction*, **80**, 83–99.

Skog, O.-J. (1991a).   Epidemiological and biostatistical aspects of alcohol use, alcoholism, and their complications. In P.C. Erickson & H. Kalant (Eds), *Windows on Science*, No. 40. Toronto: Addiction Research Foundation.

Skog, O.-J. (1991b).   Implications of the distribution theory for drinking and alcoholism. In D.J. Pittman & H. Raskin White (Eds), *Society, Culture, and Drinking Patterns Reexamined* (pp. 576–597). New Brunswick, NJ: Alcohol Research Documentation.

Skog, O.-J. (1991c). Drinking and the distribution of alcohol consumption. In D.J. Pittman & H. Raskin White (Eds), *Society, Culture, and Drinking Patterns Reexamined* (pp. 135–156). New Brunswick, NJ: Alcohol Research Documentation.

Stockwell, T., Hawks, D., Lang, E. & Rydon, P. (1996). Unravelling the preventive paradox for acute alcohol problems. *Drug and Alcohol Review*, **15**, 7–15.

Sulkunen, P. (1989). Drinking in France, 1965–1979. An analysis of household consumption data. *British Journal of Addiction*, **84**, 61–72.

Tuck, M. (1980). *Alcoholism and Social Policy*. Home Office Research Study No. 65. London: HMSO.

Chapter 21

Individual Risk of Alcohol-related Disease and Problems

Thomas K. Greenfield
National Alcohol Research Center, Alcohol Research Group,
Berkeley, CA, USA

Synopsis

This chapter addresses the distinctive role individual-level epidemiologic studies play in determining the relationship between alcohol consumption, especially drinking patterns, and alcohol-related disorders, morbidity, mortality and negative consequences of heavy consumption. Measurement and methodologic issues are reviewed. Drinking variables important for identifying patterns of consumption are summarized, including frequency, quantity, volume in a given reference period, variability, and measures of heavy drinking. Validity of self-reported alcohol intake and critical analytic issues are briefly considered. Disconfounding life-style factors, like diet, physical activity, social isolation, tobacco and other drug use, is essential in attributing risks to alcohol. How health and social consequences are measured in surveys is briefly discussed, emphasizing the importance of assessing problem severity, duration and permanence. Several approaches to identifying risks are noted, giving definitions of relative risks and attributable fractions.

Evidence on risk of alcohol-related diseases is overviewed, based on expert reviews of the role of alcohol in chronic or acute effects of alcohol consumption, with examples from key studies. The role of drinking patterns in relation to risks is emphasized where evidence is available. Conditions considered include: toxic effects; alcohol dependence and abuse; comorbidity with serious psychiatric disorders; suicide, neurological conditions and fetal development (FAS); cancer, heart and circulatory diseases; casualties, such as pedestrian accidents and motor vehicle crashes, drowning, falls and other injuries (noting emergency room studies). Wherever possible, evidence from risk function analyses and dose–response findings are included, with implications for vulnerable groups, and the degree to which morbidity or mortality of various types can be attributed to alcohol use. Public health implications, based on research on risk perception, are briefly examined at the conclusion.

International Handbook of Alcohol Dependence and Problems. Edited by N. Heather, T.J. Peters and
T. Stockwell.
© 2001 John Wiley & Sons Ltd.

Individual-level epidemiologic studies of the relationship between alcohol consumption and alcohol-related disorders, morbidity, mortality and negative consequences play a crucial role in the overall epidemiology of alcohol problems. They allow assessment of effect on outcomes of individuals' characteristics, including patterns of alcohol consumption. In addition, these studies often control demographic and other influences that may confound relationships (variables that might be responsible for the influence otherwise attributed to alcohol). Unfortunately, certain co-occurring risk factors affecting the alcohol–outcome relationship, such as smoking and some life-style factors like diet, physical activity and social support, when *functionally* associated with drinking, cannot always readily be disentangled from the alcohol effect (Andréasson, 1998). (In some populations where the association is strong, one may not find sufficient cases in which the alcohol and confounding risk behaviors do not co-occur.) Nevertheless, with increasing numbers of well-designed large studies, effects of volume and, in certain instances, patterns of drinking are becoming well established. This chapter reviews recent work bearing on alcohol consumption's effects on morbidity and mortality, frequently the cumulative result of chronic heavier drinking but often also resulting from acute consequences of heavy drinking episodes. Since the next chapter addresses drink–driving, this will not be covered here in detail. Drinking pattern goes beyond an individual's average alcohol intake, or volume. A simple (overly simple) indication of volume is the person's usual frequency of drinking, say the number of drinking days in a typical month, multiplied by the quantity usually consumed, in standard drinks, grams or ounces of pure alcohol. This estimation of volume as a product is referred to as a QF measure. Quantity and frequency of drinking are among the most basic parameters of drinking, but these "features" of a pattern are not necessarily "steady" and may vary markedly depending on circumstances and other "contextual" aspects, such as social opportunities, producing fluctuations. Despite apparently random variation, for many people a weekly cycle is discernable, peaking on weekends, especially Friday through Sunday. Individual-level survey-based studies can consider the volume and pattern of drinking of each individual, rather than a population's aggregate or per capita consumption (see Lemmens, Chapter 20). Thus, individual studies have the great advantage of being able to assess pattern, not just average consumption, which is critical for some kinds of risks (Rehm et al., 1996; Stockwell et al., 1997).

Various ways of characterizing drinking pattern have tradeoffs, each being most appropriate for particular purposes. Volume variability (V-V) was one early approach (Cahalan et al., 1969), classifying drinking not only as an average but also by the style of obtaining that volume—either by regular smaller amounts ("spacers") or by irregular, heavier and fluctuating amounts ("bingers" or "episodic heavy drinkers"). These and other typological pattern measures, defining subgroups of drinkers with distinguishable styles of drinking, abound (see Room, 1990; Greenfield, 1986). Variability is an important aspect of drinking pattern, since a volume achieved by irregular quantities generally implies a higher maximum, or peak intake on certain occasions, than the same volume resulting from steady lower amounts. Drinkers consuming variable amounts incur greater risks of problems linked to intoxication (like accidents and injuries) than those drinking the same volume in more modest amounts, never experiencing high blood alcohol concentration (BAC). So at a given volume level, those who sometimes say they drink above a specific threshold, such as five or more or eight or more drinks/day typically have higher variability *and* acute risks than those never drinking above these levels (Greenfield, 1986). Maximum amount consumed is therefore also a serviceable pattern indicator.

Continuous pattern measures are often more useful than typological ones, especially in studying dose–response or consumption–risk relationships. An individual's frequency of heavy drinking is one such measure—reported days per month or per year drinking five or more drinks/day. Another is the proportion of total consumption that involves heavy drinking (or hazardous amounts) (Rogers & Greenfield, 1999; Oddy & Stockwell, 1995).

It must be pointed out that rate of consuming a particular amount, beverages chosen (strength of drink, like low- vs. high-strength beer, beer vs. malt liquor, or table vs. fortified wines or sherry), and pour sizes all affect BAC. Other factors, including gender, concurrent eating and body water (Graham et al., 1998), also moderate BAC and so risks of acute (and possibly even chronic) consequences.

An advantage of individual-level designs (cohort, cross-sectional, longitudinal or case control studies), is that they permit estimation of dose–response relationships (Greenfield, 1998; Mäkelä & Mustonen, 1988; Midanik et al., 1996b). Studies have examined the effects on specific disorders or problems of volume and heavy quantity drinking (Caetano et al., 1997b; Cherpitel et al., 1995; Room et al., 1995).

Chemical toxicity studies have found it important to consider dose–response relation- ships for sensitive population groups. Sensitivity to a chemical or drug such as alcohol may be from metabolic differences due to genetic polymorphism, age (youth or elderly), or gender. Gender is especially relevant as regards pregnant women but also there are a range of gender differences, like weight-for-weight body water, absorption rates, etc. (Graham et al., 1998). Life-style choices like diet, physical activity or drinking with meals, can also affect uptake rate and so BAC (Victorin et al., 1998). Occupational factors related to alcohol exposure may be relevant; various ecological and life-style factors may betoken either special proclivity for exposure or degree of risk given exposure, for example, whether or not one is a driver, or engaged in hazardous jobs such as commercial fishing. Thus, indi- vidual-level epidemiological studies, particularly population surveys, may consider the rela- tionship between drinking behaviors and problematic outcomes in subgroups with special sensitivities.

Lastly, it is well established from chemical toxicity studies that peak exposures are important for toxicity (Victorin et al., 1998). Alcohol overdoses provide one clear example but a more general implication is the importance of considering drinking pattern in risk assessment (Greenfield, 1998).

MEASUREMENT AND METHODOLOGIC ISSUES AND TERMINOLOGY

Alcohol Consumption—Current Drinking

Self-reported alcohol consumption measurement, as most individual-level studies must rely on, is an extremely complex and involves estimation of a number of dimensions of drink- ing (Room, 1990), with specific choices determined by study aims, historical traditions, and needs for retaining consistent measurement in longitudinal (Caetano & Kaskutas, 1996) and cross-sectional trend analyses (Greenfield et al., 2000; Greenfield & Room, 1997; Midanik & Clark, 1994). Overall, if well developed and presented in confidential scientific surveys, self-report measures have been found reasonably valid (Babor & Del Boca, 1992; Midanik, 1982).

Among continuous parameters of drinking pattern assessed are quantity (expressed in drinks/day, g or ml pure ethanol), frequency, and volume (Rehm, 1998), variability (Gruenewald & Nephew, 1994), or a related indicator maximum amount per occasion (Greenfield, 1986). A key issue is the reference period for characterizing drinking. Typical periods have been the prior 12 months (Greenfield & Rogers, 1999), probably the most common; last 30 days (Greenfield, 1986; the standard period for current drug use adopted by NIDA, the Substance Abuse and Mental Health Services Administration, 1996); and daily drinking for the last 7 days (Eliany et al., 1990), although occasionally other periods, such as 90 days (Miller, 1996) or 14 days, are chosen. Short periods may inadequately capture variation beyond the commonly observed weekly cycle; longer periods, such as the fairly standard 12 months, can better tap episodic heavy drinking if the measure is so designed (Armor & Polich, 1982). Conversely, recall for specific drinking occasions may be more accurate for shorter periods, such as the prior 7 days, but should be supplemented by other longer-duration questions to include intermittent heavy drinkers. There is a wide consensus that usual quantity, usual frequency (QF) measures alone, without supplemental questions on frequencies of unusually heavy drinking, are less than adequate (Armor & Polich, 1982) and cannot record pattern.

In addition, if the period chosen also defines current drinking status (vs. abstention), as is often so, the choice of period, by affecting the base population of "current drinkers", will result in marked differences between study results (Greenfield & Rogers, 1999). Differences in abstinence rates (from the more standard 12-month definition) are also seen when drinkers are defined in other ways, as in the US National Health Interview Survey's (HIS) requirement that a "current drinker" (to whom detailed drinking assessment is limited) have had at least 12 drinks in the last year (Dawson & Archer, 1993; Midanik et al., 1996b). (In the NHIS, the period of assessment is determined by the recency of last drinking, as in some Scandinavian methods, e.g. Room, 1990).

It has been shown that differences are great between long-period measures assessing several levels of heavy drinking occasions, like the graduated frequencies (GF) approach developed at the Alcohol Research Group (Greenfield & Rogers, 1999; Hilton, 1989), and QF or detailed drinking recall measures (Rehm et al., 1999). Differences were most pronounced for a harmful level defined by a volume of >60 g/day pure alcohol for men (women > 40 g), where the GF measure gave a prevalence almost five times that of the weekly drinking measure. As Rehm et al. (1999) note, "Failure to account for heavy drinking is important, since rare heavy drinking occasions tend to have the most harmful immediate consequences (e.g. accidents and injuries)" (p. 220).

Alcohol Consumption—Lifetime Drinking Perspectives

Concern with adequacy of long-term recall (Simpura & Poikolainen, 1983) and life-time history measures have only recently seen a resurgence of interest. Many national alcohol surveys only assess recent drinking, although most can index having ever drunk alcoholic beverages vs. lifetime abstention. Prior drinkers who quit represent a distinctive group compared with those who have never drunk alcohol for cultural or religious reasons; abstainers generally over-represent the older, poorer and sicker (Hilton, 1986), and those not drinking for ideological reasons, who tend to have lower problem risks (Andréasson, 1998). Thus, studies try to distinguish types of abstainers.

Quite often, age of drinking onset, observed to be inversely related to risk of later alcohol dependence (Grant & Dawson, 1997), is assessed. However, this tells little about drinking history and there is a clear need for serviceable survey measures of life-time drinking (Lemmens, 1998), briefer than those used for clinical studies. Fortunately, research has suggested that simpler measures may provide useful information, comparable to more comprehensive drinking histories assessed with more elaborate "floating" formats associating changes in drinking with important recalled life events. Russell et al. (1997) found correlations in the 0.80s or high 0.70s between a detailed floating lifetime measure and a simpler decade-based version with "fixed" periods. Thus, survey applications of the simpler fixed period-based variety are feasible (Greenfield et al., 1998). The lifetime drinking perspective is crucial for mortality studies, which have seldom been based on multi-point consumption measurement (Greenfield et al., 1999). Single-point drinking assessments provide inadequate estimates of cumulative exposure.

Work is only beginning in this area with studies of the aging process (Welte & Mirand, 1994), of natural vs. treated recovery from drinking problems (Greenfield et al., 1998; Sobell et al., 1993; Watson and Sher, 1998), and the sequencing and severity of health harms associated with drinking at various life phases (Greenfield & Rogers, 1997). Prospective studies find distinct drinking "trajectories" over time. Even in longitudinal panel studies, retrospective prior lifetime measures are desirable because individuals' early adult drinking trajectories affect risks of later alcohol dependence (Muthén, 1999).

Recent studies have established reasonably unbiased recall for "remote" (meaning a few years) recall for use in retrospective data imputation for missing measurements in longitudinal studies (Grant et al., 1997). Methodological problems remain and retrospective reporting has inherent limitations. Lemmens (1998) cites three problems requiring further work: (a) how much detail can researchers expect respondents to give with reasonable reliability?; (b) how is recall of earlier periods influenced by current drinking?; and (c) how are inconsistencies in reported histories to be resolved (similar to contradictory results in longitudinal waves)?

International Perspectives in Consumption Measurement

Useful guidelines for monitoring alcohol use and problems on an international basis have been developed for the World Health Organization by an international team of researchers and an expert panel (WHO, 2000). A number of highlighted methodological concerns and solutions are relevant for both cross-national comparisons and within any one country. Measurement issues addressed include choice of reference period; quantity per drinking *day* vs. quantity per *occasion*; and the importance of estimating typical beverage strength and serving sizes (Dawson, 1998a).

Time of drinking session, whether drinking is during meals, other metabolic factors, and period over which drinks are consumed (longer for women in America) may greatly affect peak BAC and therefore the risks of acute alcohol consequences (Dawson, 1998b; Graham et al., 1998). The WHO guidelines also discuss criteria for defining drinkers and nondrinkers (considered earlier), and different ways of characterizing degrees of hazardous consumption (Rogers & Greenfield, in press; WHO, 2000). Improved assessment of drink size and drink strength, which will depend on the particular mix of products and context of consumption, is important in many countries where new alcoholic beverage products are emerging (WHO, 2000). It is particularly relevant for special populations including heavy drinkers (Kaskutas & Graves, 1999).

Measures of Health and Social Harms, Including "Alcoholism"

Much has been done in recent years to achieve a consensus on the nosology of alcoholism and alcohol abuse including the type, number and duration of symptoms required to meet diagnostic criteria (Caetano, 1997). Cross-cultural and cross-ethnic-group studies provide a mixed picture showing both some relevance of major constructs (Caetano & Clark, 1998; Caetano et al., 1997a) and the difficulty of applying identical definitions in different cultural contexts across the world (Room et al., 1996). Full consideration of these issues is beyond the scope of this review, excepting several issues regarding risk assessment. One is the importance of assessing problems on a continuum of severity, and a second involves the need for empirical study of distinct relationships between drinking patterns and specific types of problems (Muthén, 1996). Attention has been called to a disconnection between practitioners, who want yes–no "caseness" classifications, and researchers, for whom alcoholism and alcohol abuse vary in severity (Helzer, 1999). Polcin (1997), exploring clinical and epidemiological differences in perceived causes and diagnostic approaches, noted that integrating concepts of the Alcohol Dependence Syndrome construct into treatment practice would lead to greater emphasis on *degrees* of alcohol dependence, antithetical to the typical practitioner's view of dependence as a unitary phenomenon. Alcohol problems are not always chronic, progressive and irreversible, and loss of control is an impairment to varying degrees (Edwards, 1986; Polcin, 1997). The view of a continuum of severity fits findings from general population longitudinal studies that observe individuals' transitions between problem and non-problem status (Caetano & Kaskutas, 1996; Fillmore & Midanik, 1984). Regarding the multidimensional view of problems—that people may exhibit some but not all problems—there is a strong research tradition of "disaggregating" reported social alcohol-related consequences when the research aim is to estimate risks associated with drinking patterns (Mäkelä & Mustonen, 1988). Yet combined dependence and consequences scales have also been developed (Clark & Hilton, 1991) to assess number of reported problems.

The importance of measuring severity is not only for assessing dependence syndromes but applies to other consequences of acute drinking. Much research on the risk curves linking alcohol use and specific problems has relied on dichotomous (present/absent) indicators of problem occurrence, which is problematic (Midanik et al., 1996a). A recent study showed the importance for risk curves (average risk plotted against level of drinking or heavy drinking) of accounting for *frequency* of drinking–driving, not just whether or not there was an occurrence within a period (Greenfield and Rogers, 1999). The last decade of alcohol studies has seen much focus on a phenomenon called "the prevention paradox" (Kreitman, 1986; Stockwell et al., 1996b). The prevention paradox was postulated because the heaviest drinkers experience, on average, more consequences (like job-related problems and drinking–driving) than lower-drinking counterparts, but the former are few while the latter are many. Thus, the combined proportion of a problem's toll to society can stem more from lower-volume drinkers (many with problems stemming from intermittent heavy drinking) than from the heaviest drinkers (fewer in number but with more problems). Noting many illustrative findings that launched the prevention paradox concept (e.g. Kreitman, 1986) were based on dichotomous measures (did a given problem occur or not?), Greenfield & Rogers (in press) asked if the paradox would be less paradoxical if frequency rather than occurrence measures were used. For self-reported drinking–driving, using an 80/20 percentile split on volume (equivalent to dividing at just more than 2 drinks/day), 45% of the occurrence-based drinking–driving came from the lower and 55% from the upper volume group; in contrast, with the frequency-based measure, estimates of the risk burden shifted significantly upward, partitioned 32% and 68%, respectively. Conclusions were that "continuous severity measures may better model risks of acute harm from alcohol consumption than dichotomous indicators" (Greenfield & Rogers, 1999) and that the paradox was reduced but not eliminated. The study also showed the importance of drinking *pattern*: heavy beer (but not wine or spirits) drinking predicted risk of driving when intoxicated, particularly when combined with risk denial (Greenfield & Rogers, 1999).

Recent work (Muthén, 1996) highlights the importance of studying the dimensionality of widely used diagnostic criteria, such as DSM-IV (Caetano & Greenfield, in press). Muthén and associates identified an abuse factor and a distinct, albeit correlated, dependence factor in DSM-based survey items. Muthén (1992) found that the two empirical factors had distinctly different, replicable, correlates with background variables. Positive family (blood relative) history had a stronger effect on dependence than on abuse, controlling for consumption and demographics. This finding, confirming genetic studies, demonstrates the importance of measuring distinct diagnostic "elements". The measures distinguishing abuse and dependence also revealed ethnic differences: Hispanics were found at differential risk for abuse and dependence (Muthén, 1992) in contrast to Anglos. As mentioned before, ethnic and other subgroup differences in problem expression may affect the appropriateness of nosological constructs, warranting further study (Caetano et al., 1997a). A strength of the structural equation modeling approach is to place the dependent problem variables on a continuous rather than a dichotomous basis, assessing severity and using maximum information to achieve greater measurement sensitivity.

Other Useful Definitions

Several approaches to identifying risks are ecological studies (discussed in the last chapter), individual-level mortality studies, case control designs, cross-sectional and prospective cohort studies, and risk curve approaches. As mentioned earlier, individual-level studies have the potential to control for co-occurring lifestyle confounds and to establish dose–response relationships. The prospective study design is stronger than the cross-sectional, since it can add the temporal (and hence causal) link between exposure and outcome, as Svärdsudd (1998) notes. However, prospective studies with initial data collection in the days of yore could not avail themselves of advances in measurement that have subsequently occurred. Many lack sophisticated measures of drinking (and cannot establish drinking pattern), adequate controls for confounders like smoking, or multiple time points. In the reviews that lie behind this chapter, strength of design has been used in weighing evidence.

Regarding alcohol consumption levels, the relative risk (RR) for a specific morbidity or mortality condition, generally a category in the International Classification of Diseases (ICD-9 or ICD-10, for the 9th and 10th editions), is customarily defined as the risk of experiencing the indicated category within a given range of drinking (usually a volume) relative to the risk (1.0) of abstainers or these and extremely light drinkers. Because of gender differences, RR is generally specific to sex. A set of drinking ranges fairly widely used in risk attribution studies is shown in Table 21.1.

A meta-analysis by English et al. (1995) provides the most comprehensive current source of RRs for ICD-9 categories, although it must be recognized that this is at best suitable for developed countries with populations of largely European ancestry. These RRs have been termed "method unspecific" since they are not based on a specific operationalization of volume measurement (Rehm et al., 1999). Estimates of RRs have relied on principal diagnosis alone—the main cause of hospital admission or death (WHO, 2000). Tables 21.2 and 21.3 provides the RRs for the main alcohol-related conditions.

Table 21.1 Alcohol consumption ranges widely used in defining degree of risk

Gender	Volume range (g pure ethanol/day, on average)			
	Abstainer/light drinker[a]	Low risk	Hazardous	Harmful
Male	0–2.5	2.6–40	40.1–60	60.1+
Female	0–2.5	2.6–20	20.1–40	40.1+

[a] Abstainers may be distinguished from light drinkers in some studies.
Source: Rehm et al. (1999) and see World Health Organization (1994).

Table 21.2 Proportion of deaths attributed to alcohol in major reviews of the epidemiological literature from Australia, the USA and Canada. Conditions caused mainly by long-term or chronic effects of alcohol consumption

Disorder	ICD-9 codes	English et al. (1995) (Australia)	Schulz et al. (1991) (USA)	Single et al. (1998) (Canada)
Respiratory tuberculosis	011, 012	NA	0.25[1]	NA
Lip cancer	140	NA	0.50[1]	Added to next entry
Oropharyngeal cancer	141, 143, 146, 148, 149	0.21 (m), 0.08 (f)	0.50[1]	0.29 (m), 0.15 (f)
Oesophageal cancer	150	0.14 (m), 0.06 (f)	0.75[1]	0.38 (m), 0.22 (f)
Stomach cancer	151	NA	0.20[1]	NA
Colorectal cancer	153, 154	NA	0.20[1]	NA
Liver cancer	155	0.18 (m), 0.12 (f)	0.15[1]	0.29 (m), 0.16 (f)
Laryngeal cancer	161	NA	0.50[1]	0.41 (m), 0.26 (f)
Female breast cancer	174	0.03 (f)	NA	0.04 (f)
Diabetes	250	NA	0.05[1]	NA
Alcoholic psychosis	291	1.00 (m & f)	1.00[2]	1.00 (m & f)
Alcohol dependence	303	1.00 (m & f)	1.00[2]	1.00 (m & f)
Alcohol abuse	305.0	1.00 (m & f)	1.00[2]	1.00 (m & f)
Epilepsy	345	0.15 (m), 0.15 (f)	NA	0.15 (m & f)
Alcoholic polyneuropathy	357.5	1.00 (m & f)	1.00[2]	1.00 (m & f)
Hypertension	401–405	0.11 (m), 0.06 (f)	0.08[1]	0.05 (m), 0.01 (f)
Ischaemic heart disease	410–414	0.005 (m & f)	NA	NA
Alcoholic cardiomyopathy	425.5	1.00 (m & f)	1.00[2]	1.00 (m & f)
Supraventricular cardiac arrhythmias	427.0, 427.2, 427.3	0.08 (m), 0.05 (f)	NA	0.26 (m), 0.13 (f)
Heart failure	428–429	NA	NA	0.004 (m), 0.002 (f)
Stroke	430–438	0.14 (m), 0.16 (f)	0.07[1]	0.023 (m), 0.001 (f)
Oesophageal varices	456.0–456.2	0.54 (m), 0.43 (f)	NA	0.388 (m), 0.217 (f)
Pneumonia and influenza	480–487	NA	0.05[1]	Not included
Gastro-oesophageal	530.7	0.47 (m & f)	0.10[1]	0.47 (m & f)
Peptic ulcer	531–534	NA	0.10[1]	Not included
Alcoholic gastritis	535.3	1.00 (m & f)	1.00[2]	1.00 (m & f)
Alcoholic liver cirrhosis	571.0–571.3	1.00 (m & f)	1.00[2]	1.00 (m & f)
Unspecified cirrhosis*	571.5–571.9	0.54 (m), 0.43 (f)	0.50[1]	0.54 (m & f)
Cholelithiasis	574	−0.05 (m), −0.02 (f)	NA	No cases
Chronic pancreatitis	577.1	0.84 (m & f)	0.60[1]	0.84 (m & f)
Spontaneous abortion	634	0.04 (f)	NA	0.20 (m & f)
Low birthweight	656.5, 764, 765	−0.02 (m & f)	NA	No cases
Psoriasis	696.1	0.03 (m), 0.01 (f)	No cases	No cases

* Includes both specified and unspecified cases of liver cirrhosis in estimates made by English et al. and Single et al.

[1] Age range 35–85 or older.

[2] Age range 15–85 or older.

NA, not applicable; m, males; f, females.

Table 21.3 Proportion of disorders attributed to alcohol in major reviews of the epidemiological literature. Conditions caused mainly by short-term or acute effects of alcohol consumption

Disorder	ICD-9 codes	English et al. (1995) (Australia)	Schulz et al. (1991) (USA)	Single et al. (1998) (Canada)
Other ethanol poisoning	E860.1, E860.2	1.00 (m & f)[1]	1.00[1]	1.00 (m & f)
Fall injuries	E880–E888	0.34 (m & f)	0.35[1]	0.238 (m), 0.152 (f)
Fire injuries	E890–E899	0.44 (m & f)	0.45[2]	0.375 (m & f)
Accidental excessive cold	E901	NA	NA	0.25 (m & f)
Drowning	E910	0.34 (m & f)	0.38[2]	0.299 (m), 0.227 (f)
Aspiration	E911	1.00 (m & f)[1]	0.25[1]	0.25 (m & f)
Work/machine injuries	E919, E920	0.07 (m & f)	0.25[1]	0.07 (m & f)
Accidents with firearms	E922	NA	NA	0.25 (m & f)
Suicide	E950–E959	0.41 (m), 0.16 (f)	0.28[1]	0.272 (m), 0.168 (f)
Assault	E960, 65, 66, 68, 69	0.47 (m & f)	0.46[1]	0.27 (m & f)
Child abuse	E967	0.16 (m & f)	NA	0.16 (m & f)
All-cause mortality	All of above	0.07 (m), 0.04 (f)	NA	0.034 (m & f)
Acute pancreatitis	577.0	0.24 (m & f)	0.423	0.24 (m & f)
Ethanol toxicity	980.0	1.00 (m & f)[1]	1.004	1.00 (m & f)
Methanol toxicity	980.1	1.00 (m & f)[1]	NA	1.00 (m & f)
Road injuries	E810–E819	0.37 (m), 0.18 (f)	0.425	0.43 (m & f)
Other road accidents	E826, E829	NA	0.20[2]	0.20 (m & f)
Water transport accidents	E839, E838	NA	0.20[2]	0.20 (m & f)
Air/space transport accident	E840–E845	NA	0.20[2]	0.20 (m & f)
Alcohol beverage poisoning	E860.0	1.00 (m & f)	1.00[1]	1.00 (m & f)

[1] Age range 35–85 or older.
[2] Age range 15–85 or older.
NA, not applicable; m, males; f, females.

Attributable fractions (AFs) indicate, for a given ICD category, the fraction of cases or deaths that can be attributed to alcohol use/misuse (not just those resulting from dependence or heavy use). When beverage alcohol is the direct cause of the condition (alcohol-specific causation) the AF is 1.0, meaning that all instances of morbidity or mortality ascribed to this condition are causally associated with alcohol. For a variety of types of morbidity and mortality with mixed causes known from multiple studies to involve alcohol in part, the AF may be indirectly estimated by combining drinking-level prevalence data (the percentage of the drinking distribution of the population in question occupying each volume level in the above table) and the RRs by the following formula given in Rehm et al. (1999), p. 221:

$$AF = |\Sigma P_i\, RR_i^{-1}| / \Sigma P_i\, RR_i$$

where P_i = prevalence of drinking category i (0 = abstainer/light drinker; 1 = low risk, 2 = hazardous, and 3 = harmful) and RR_i = RR (risk for category relative to abstainer/light drinker with RR_0 = 1.0). Note that the application of AF presupposes a causal role of alcohol, and must depend on assessments of causality derived from comprehensive literature reviews, such as the English et al. (1995) meta-analysis (see also Single et al., 1996). For directly estimated AFs this indirect approach is unnecessary, as with conditions classified in the ICD as aetiological (alcohol-specific conditions), such as alcoholic gastritis, alcoholic psychoses or alcohol dependence with an AF of 1.0. Where RRs are not available, as for many acute conditions like accidents, other data must be used to directly estimate the AF (see English et al., 1995; Single et al., 1996).

REVIEW OF EVIDENCE ON RISK OF ALCOHOL-RELATED DISEASES, DISORDERS AND PROBLEMS

A useful distinction is to divide conditions into those related to short-term and long-term consequences of drinking, although the distinction is not always clear, as with suicide and stroke, where both chronic heavy drinking and single bouts of heavy drinking may be involved (WHO, 2000). Short-term consequences, typically associated with intoxication, may occur in those with heavy drinking sustained for years but may also occur among intermittent heavy drinkers with low volumes.

Death by Overdose—Accidental Poisoning

These events due to overdoses and the sedative–hypnotic properties of alcohol, which depress the CNS, appear to occur most often when relatively inexperienced drinkers consume very large amounts of alcohol in a short time, usually as spirits, such that a coma develops followed by death, sometimes due to anoxia from aspiration. Adequate statistics, particularly of overdoses by university students, are hard to come by. In the USA there are press reports each year, generally associated with fraternity parties, that "pressure" inexperienced drinkers to overdrink to unconsciousness and then leave them to "sleep it off". In some fatal alcohol overdoses, BALs have been found to be above 0.4.

Alcohol Dependence

Diagnosis with alcohol dependence (and abuse) is causally and definitionally related to "over-involvement" in consumption of beverage alcohol, with alcohol "dependence" requiring greater chronicity of drinking than does "abuse". In the alcohol dependence syndrome (Edwards, 1986) model, dependence generally requires sustained, regular, very heavy drinking (100–200 g or 7–15 drinks/day and up are not clinically untypical), to physiologically induce tolerance and withdrawal (Caetano et al., 1998). The topic is covered in other chapters, so here recent risk function analyses and implications are the thrust.

A recent risk function analysis included ICD-10 dependence as a dependent measure (Midanik et al., 1996b). Using the 1988 NHIS sample, with over 22,000 current US drinkers, the risks were examined of classification as dependent in the prior 12 months with respect to volume, frequency of five or more drinks/day, age and sex. Those aged 18–30 had higher levels of dependence than older groups. This reflects both heavier drinking patterns and inclusion of ICD-based problem items that may be endorsed not only by longer-term heavier drinkers but heavy episodic drinkers (ICD-10 combines elements of consequences and dependence). Younger men, especially, drink a larger proportion of their consumption than others in hazardous quantities (Rogers & Greenfield, 1999) and are high users of alcohol treatment (Weisner et al., 1995). As in other epidemiological findings (Grant & Harford, 1990), no gender difference was seen throughout most of the volume range. Only above eight drinks/day did women carry an excess risk for dependence (approximately 0.7 vs. 0.5). Differing drinking patterns, beverage choices, reporting, and factors such as rates of drinking a given number of drinks compared to men (see Graham et al., 1998) may all be implicated in this robust but surprising result, whose explanation requires more study. The study also showed how routine heavy drinking affects dependence: risks rise rapidly to 0.3 for weekly heavy drinking, then more slowly up to about 0.6 when drinking occurs on five or more drinks/day out of 4 days. Conversely, in the absence of any heavy days, the risks of dependence never exceed 0.1, even with an average of above 4.4 drinks/day, around the harmful 60 g threshold. Drinking with an even pattern (Cahalan et al., 1969), appears protective for the self-reported symptoms of dependence as well, although a caution is that severity of problems of dependence may not be well assessed by symptom counts (see section on Measures of Health and Focal Harms, above).

Consistent with the Midanik et al. (1996b) finding, using the same NHIS dataset, Dawson & Archer (1993) found relative frequency of heavy drinking (implemented as a proportion of five or more drinking occasions during the year) was predictive of DSM-III-R dependence independent of volume, which was also predictive. The risk of alcohol dependence rose from 0.03 for drinkers never drinking as five or more occasions/year to 0.5 for drinkers drinking heavily above half the time. Because analyses made body water adjustments, the findings cannot be directly compared to the Midanik et al. (1996b) results. Younger drinking onset and a positive family history of alcohol problems elevated the risks. The interactions found suggested the merit of distinguishing dependence criteria that are subject to social influences, such as disapproval of women's heavy drinking, or violating subgroup norms (Dawson & Archer, 1993). Dependence measures, including social approbation, can lead to "problem inflation" (Midanik & Greenfield, 2000), based on more stringent drinking norms in a time of "drying" cultural trends (Greenfield & Room, 1997).

Caetano et al. (1997b) re-analysed the NHIS US data with DSM-IV-based dependence as the criterion but without body water corrections (accepting self-reported consumption without biological adjustments appears to have greater relevance for informing safe drinking guidelines for men and women). Volume and heavy drinking predicted risk of dependence, but again gender was inconsequential. Drinkers with any 5+ occasions had a six-fold greater chance of being classified dependent than ones without. Starting at prevalence rates around 1–1.5% among those with no heavy days, the risk increased most rapidly up to 50 (women) and 75 (men) 5+ days, then flattened as it approached a level where most days involved heavy drinking. About 56% of all dependent individuals drank heavily *less* than once a week (37% dependent men; 70% dependent women). Thus, about half the symptomatic load of the population of dependent individuals might be prevented were interventions able to limit their heavy (5+) drinking to *less than once a week* (Caetano et al., 1997b). In general populations, alcohol abuse and dependence account for at least a quarter of psychiatric disorders, the second most common disorder after depression (Medical Research Council, 1998); DSM-III lifetime diagnoses of alcohol use disorders in various countries have been in the range 13–27%, with current prevalence of 3–7% (Berglund & Ojehagen, 1998). In the USA, the prevalence of alcohol dependence (Caetano & Greenfield, in press) and other alcohol-related consequences (Midanik & Greenfield, 2000) for both genders has remained static in recent years, despite reductions of drinking levels (Greenfield et al., 2000).

Comorbidity with Psychiatric Disorders

Alcohol dependence is more common among people with psychiatric disorders such as schizophrenia (risk 3.3 times normal), depression or affective disorders (1.9) and anxiety (1.5) than in the general population; overall, the prevalence of dependence is almost twice as high as in the general population, based on the US Epidemiological Catchment Area (ECA) samples (Regier et al., 1990). In the ECA study, excluding substance abuse disorders, 19.9% of the sample had at least one DIS-classified psychiatric disorder, vs. 36.6% for those with alcohol abuse or dependence. The same is true in reverse: according to ECA data, 13.5% were diagnosed with an alcohol use disorder, but among those with psychiatric disorders the prevalence was 22.3%. The same general conclusion may be drawn from the US National Comorbidity Survey (NCS); on a life-time basis, roughly half of those with a lifetime DSM-III-R addictive disorder have life-time mental disorders, and vice versa (Berglund & Ojehagen, 1998; Kessler et al., 1994). Drug use is higher among those with alcohol use disorders and vice versa; in the ECA study, 18% with alcohol use disorders also had a drug use disorder. The ECA study found those with antisocial personality disorder (ASPD) had 21 times the non-diagnosed population's risk of having alcohol-related disorder. Accordingly, prison samples in the USA have also shown very high rates of DIS-based lifetime alcohol (and substance) use disorders (Greenfield, 1988).

Excepting ASPD, all DIS-based psychiatric comorbidities with alcohol use disorders are more prevalent for women than men (Robins et al., 1988; Secretary of Health and Human Services, 1993). Psychiatric disorder(s) preceded dependence in about four-fifths of the cases for men and one-third for women (Berglund & Ojehagen, 1998). Some 83% of those with life-time comorbidity indicated an earlier psychiatric disorder than an addictive one (Kessler et al., 1994).

Some dose–response findings are suggestive. A 15-year follow-up of 50,000 male Swedish conscripts controlled for demographics and compared those with heavy (>250 g/week) vs. moderate (1–100 g/week) drinking. Heavy drinkers had almost twice the odds of later psychiatric admission, with no difference between moderate drinkers and abstainers. Also, initial "neurotic depression" was found to elevate risk of admission for alcoholism, implying a bidirectional association (Leifman et al., 1995).

Alcohol dependence worsens psychiatric prognoses. Based on longitudinal ECA Los Angeles data, Lipton (1994) observed that moderate drinkers had lower depression scores than abstainers, light and heavy drinkers; when stress was present, depression increased for all but the moderate group, suggesting some buffering effect of moderate consumption (Lipton, 1994). Recent reviews have concluded that patients with serious mental disorders who also abuse alcohol tend to have worse clinical outcomes; there is scant evidence of positive effects of "normal" alcohol use in those with various psychiatric disorders

(Berglund & Ojehagen, 1998; Secretary of Health and Human Services, 1993). Findings on drinking pattern appear to be absent.

Suicide

Alcohol dependence is among the main risk factors for suicide: depression and alcohol use disorders are prevalent preceding suicide (Berglund & Ojehagen, 1998). Alcoholism is common among male suicides and suicide risk greater with early onset and longer duration; it is also involved in women's suicides (Gomberg, 1989). A Finnish study of suicides found 43% with alcohol dependence or abuse, with dependence higher among males (39%) than females (18%) (Berglund & Ojehagen, 1998). It has been estimated that from one-fifth to one-third of excess mortality in alcohol-dependent persons is from suicide (Medical Research Council, 1998). Studies indicate that heavy drinking interacts with such prognostic conditions as hopelessness and significant interpersonal losses to elevate suicide risk (Berglund & Ojehagen, 1998). Among adolescents, alcohol consumption has been linked to later suicidal thoughts and attempts (Reifman & Windle, 1995). With suicide a significant part of mortality in this age group, this result takes on public health importance.

Neurological Conditions

Alcohol is consumed because of the phenomenological counterpart to central nervous system (CNS) effects; even relatively moderate consumption affects the cerebellum (Medical Research Council, 1998). Alcohol-induced brain damage has been known for a long time but today may still be "grossly underestimated" (Neiman, 1998). Neiman (1998) cites a post-mortem study indicating that only one of 22 acute Wernicke's encephalopathy cases (characteristic neuropathological lesions manifest as ocular abnormalities, ataxia, and global confusion) was diagnosed before death. Ethanol itself and its metabolites appears responsible for toxic brain damage, suggesting that patterns leading to elevated BACs (possibly including spirits consumption), are implicated; however, the effects of pattern are not well understood (Medical Research Council, 1998). Episodes of heavy drinking can trigger epileptic seizures and increase risks for hemorrhagic and ischemic stroke (Hillbom, 1998; see further below). Chronic high exposure to alcohol has modest relationships with effects on brain morphology, especially shrinkage of the third ventricle (Neiman, 1998) and may cause "slowly progressive cognitive defects" (Medical Research Council, 1998). Thus, mechanisms that may account for brain damage can involve both chronic *and* acute heavy drinking. The direct consequences of chronic heavy alcohol use are difficult to distinguish from the severe vitamin deficiency often associated with alcoholism; polyneuropathy probably involves the classic admixture of toxicity and vitamin deficiencies, although even short periods of extremely heavy drinking can result in nerve damage (e.g. radial nerve paresis) (Medical Research Council, 1998). Little is known about age- and gender-related vulnerability, but the elderly and women may have heightened susceptibility to brain damage (Neiman, 1998).

Effects on Fetal Development

FAS (considered more extensively in Chapter 7) is characterized by certain facial anomalies, including short eye openings, thin lips and elongated, flattened midface with indistinct philtrum (zone between nose and mouth), prenatal or postnatal growth retardation, and mental retardation (CNS disorders, including neurological abnormality, developmental delays, intellectual impairment and structural abnormalities); the term "alcohol related birth defects" (ARBD) has been proposed for individuals exhibiting only some attributes (US National Institute on Alcohol Abuse and Alcoholism, 1997). Diagnosis based on morphology is difficult in infants, becomes easier in mid-childhood, but again more difficult in adolescence; racial differences compound the problem of early assessment. Cognitive and behavioral deficits continue and can severely affect development, with IQ deficits, learning problems, concentration disorders and behavioral deficits found in 7-year-old children of mothers with alcohol problems (Streissguth et al., 1989). In a US sample of persons aged 12–40 with FAS, mean IQ was 68, ranging from 20 (severely retarded) to 105 (normal); 58% had scores at or below 70 (developmentally disabled, requiring special education) (US National Institute on Alcohol Abuse and Alcoholism, 1997). Attention deficit hyperactivity disorder is common among individuals with FAS.

A review of 19 worldwide studies led to an estimate of 1.9 cases per 1,000 live births, with wide variation across studies (see Allebeck & Olsen, 1998). A more recent estimate is 9.7 per 10,000 live births in the general obstetric population (Abel & Hannigan, 1995). Rates up to 4.3% of children born annually among (very) heavy drinkers, or 2,000 per year for the USA are cited (US National Institute on Alcohol Abuse and Alcoholism, 1997). The incidence of FAS among Blacks is reported to be up to seven-fold that of Whites in the USA (Schinke & Cole, 1999).

A consistent finding is that high exposure is a necessary but not sufficient cause (Allebeck & Olsen, 1998). Jacobson & Jacobson (1994) proposed that neurobehavioral effects appear to have thresholds of 1–4 drinks per day on average, although for some indicators, such as reaction times, no threshold was found. A comprehensive NIAAA review suggests that one drink per day may be the lower threshold for neurobehavioral effects, noting studies of mothers where few drank at or below this level found no neurobehavioral effects (US National Institute on Alcohol Abuse and Alcoholism, 1997). These results may be conservative, given many measurement problems in the classification of drinker volumes (Jacobson & Jacobson, 1994), with low volume levels including those who sometimes drink heavily, skewing the results (Knupfer, 1991). Improved assessment of pattern is vital, since high BAC is the critical variable (US National Institute on Alcohol Abuse and Alcoholism, 1997). Most epidemiological studies are plagued by the fact that heavy drinking is associated with poverty, nutrition deficiencies, lack of prenatal care, smoking and drug use (Allebeck & Olsen, 1998). One may conclude that FAS-like facial features are probable only with heavy drinking episodes (at least five or more drinks/day) and generally after sustained high consumption, 60+ g ethanol/day; growth retardation and low birth weight are, however, seen after 10–20 g/day (Medical Research Council, 1998).

Cancer

Organ system malignancies are covered in Chapter 8. No mutagenic effects are known for ethanol itself and no *in vitro* studies indicate malignant transformation effects (Medical Research Council, 1998). Nonetheless, alcohol consumption still may give rise to malignant tumors in humans via the metabolite acetaldehyde, which is mutagenic and carcinogenic, although the precise mechanism remains uncertain. Ethanol may promote the carcinogenic process by damaging epithelial cells, leading to cell proliferation, although many other processes have been postulated. Through ingestion, alcohol comes into direct contact with anatomical sites harboring alcohol-associated cancers (considered presently), and so may damage the mucosa, facilitating the actions of carcinogens. However, vitamin deficiencies have also been thought responsible. Alcohol's causal connection with cancer of the mouth, pharynx, larynx, and esophagus is uncontroversial (Ringborg, 1998). A study of the oral cavity and the use of mouthwashes with 25% or more alcohol found an association with cancer, supporting mechanisms other than poor nutrition. For esophageal cancer, several studies showed a higher risk with spirits than with other alcoholic beverages. In many cases, studies were limited to males and only for cancers of the pharynx has risk been demonstrated for women.

To summarize, dose–response relationships have been found for alcohol in many instances, with synergistic effects of smoking also observed. Some 25 to 50% of all cancer to the head and neck have been estimated as due to alcohol, with 75% due to alcohol and tobacco.

Regarding liver cancer, Chapter 8 should be consulted. A number studies support a "small" causal relationship between consumption and risk of developing liver cancer. Two problems are distinguishing primary tumors from metastases and the known causal relationship between Hepatitis B and liver cancer. Studies have not shown whether cirrhotic processes can induce liver cancer, and the confounding roles of aflotoxins, smoking and viral hepatitis remain to be worked out (Ringborg, 1998). Development of liver cancer requires a long period of drinking and volumes greater than 10 g/day (Medical Research Council, 1998). In the US, rates of cirrhosis and other liver diseases associated with alcohol use for African Americans are approximately 3-fold those of whites (Herd, 1989; Schinke and Cole, 1999).

There is "suggestive but not conclusive" evidence of some relationship between heavy drinking and colorectal cancer and a "weak but significant association" with breast cancer based on meta-analysis (Ringborg, 1998). There probably is no relationship with cancers of lung, stomach, pancreas, prostate, ovaries, and malignant melanoma (Medical Research Council, 1998). An AF for all cancers has been estimated at 3%, with sex differences primarily attributable to men's heavier consumption (Medical Research Council, 1998).

Heart and Circulatory Diseases

This area is summarized, being also treated in Chapter 11. The acute effects of a heavy (high BAC) episode diminish myocardial contraction, according to Waldenström (1998), with effects lasting a few hours. Tolerance develops, but in alcoholics with heart disease there is increased sensitivity to the acute effects. Even an acute intake by a subject with healthy heart can reduce output and increase the risk of arythmias (Rosenqvist, 1998). Atrial fibrillation has been noted to follow binges in people without chronic heavy drinking. Studies have found that 30–60% of all cases with arterial fibrillation, with other causes excluded, are owing to alcohol, more marked with those aged under 65, generally males, with little known about females. Important for alcohol's mortality burden, Rosenqvist (1998) cites strongly suggestive evidence that sudden deaths (in the absence of other causes), especially in drinking alcoholics, may stem from this cause, noting that: "Sudden cardiac death seems to be more common among men with chronic alcohol abuse, irrespective of the presence of coronary heart disease . . . it seems reasonable to suggest that ventricular arrhythmia is a common cause" (p. 321S).

High levels of consumption can damage heart muscle (cardiomyopathy), increasing the risk of, CHD, congestive heart failure and sudden cardiac death (Medical Research Council, 1998). An AF for alcohol abuse of 0.45 has been described for dilated cardiomyopathy (Waldenström, 1998), with alcoholic cardiomyopathies clinically indistinguishable.

Heavy drinking can cause high blood pressure and may harm brain blood vessels, leading to higher risks of stroke, brain hemorrhage and infarction (Medical Research Council, 1998), with mechanism involving the coagulation and fibrinolytic systems. Cerebral hemorrhage has a linear dose–response relationship (Hillbom, 1998). Traumatic and blood pressure-related hemorrhagic strokes associated with heavy drinking are well documented. These include rare events with high AFs, such as subarachnoid hemorrhage with rupture of the vertebral artery, due to the uncontrolled neck movements sometimes associated with intoxication; alcohol triggering aneurysmal rupture in migraine attacks (even moderate doses of, especially, red wine); lacunar infarction in young adults during intoxication; and episodes of heavy drinking (>80 g/day) in carotid atherosclerosis due to rapid heart rate and circulatory stress (even with the consensus beneficial effect of regular moderate drinking) (Hillbom, 1998). Drinking patterns generating high BACs are clearly associated in all these events, although cardiomyopathy associated with chronic use also causes cardio-embolic brain infarctions.

Coronary heart disease (CHD) has been found to have the only known potential protective effect, with the dose–response curve often J-shaped, although problems with interpretation are noted, e.g. Svärdsudd (1998) and Andréasson (1998). Svärdsudd (1998) reported that an Italian rural cohort study with an exceptionally wide range of wine intake found a shift from positive to negative effect between 78 and 108 g ethanol/day (a "fifth" bottle of wine has about 100 g). In contrast, the Nurses Health Study found no breakpoint for the positive effect up to 30 g/day (although negative effects on other organs occurred at lower levels). Compared to non-drinkers, low to moderate even intake at 1–2 drinks/day lowers CHD risk 20–30% (Medical Research Council, 1998). Increased high density lipoprotein (HDL)-cholesterol and estrogen may be a mechanism, also lowering the risk of clot formation, as summarized by Svärdsudd (1998). Recent work (Klatsky et al., 1997) and reviews find little evidence of beverage specificity (Rimm et al., 1996) and the proposed mechanisms involve ethanol.

While the J- or U-shaped curve for this morbidity and mortality (and all cause mortality) is widely found, with the lowest risks for moderate consumption, the following issues reduce the certainty in the causal interpretation (Andréasson, 1998). There are many potential confounders: measurement of pattern and even volume of drinking is often poor; age and sex differences (generally controlled); inappropriate use of abstainers as a reference group because of heterogeneity; unique life-styles (religious and ideological abstainers); earlier problem drinking or ill health ("sick abstainer" hypothesis). Although some might be induced to moderate their drinking, enthusiasm for advising moderate, low-quantity drinking is diminished given how few people drink in this pattern. One US survey found that only 2% of adults drank with a daily light pattern (Knupfer, 1987). While smoking has been generally controlled in today's studies, the same is not necessarily true of physical activity and social support. With moderate drinking the norm, very heavy plus very light drinkers and abstainers are deviant, having weaker social networks than moderate drinkers (Skög, 1995), citing evidence that social isolation has a J- or U-shaped relationship with consumption. Findings from attempts to control these variables in mortality studies, although suggestive, remain ambiguous (Greenfield et al., 1999). Thus, the cautious consensus for a preventive effect for CHD mortality is not without opponents. However, experts argue that the consistency and scope of recent findings which followed "vastly different" populations in large samples lend "strong support to the hypothesis that alcohol in moderation lowers risk of coronary disease" (Rimm, 1999, p. 6). The beneficial effect, probably similar for older men and women, is probably limited to those above 50, where risk of CHD is greatest (Medical Research Council, 1998).

Accidents, Violence and Criminal Behavior

Alcohol affects cognitive, perceptual and motor functions and reviews conclude that there is a causal role of intoxication and/or alcohol abuse in almost all types of accidents and violent behaviors (Brismar & Bergman, 1998). Strong dose–response relationships are seen for many accidents and casualties, and weaker ones for violence. Thus, alcohol contributes substantially to accident and injury mortality and morbidity. The influence of drinking pattern has been investigated in some cross-county comparisons, and different countries' consumption patterns are reflected in casualty statistics (Cherpitel et al., 1993) and emergency room (ER) data (Cherpitel, 1993). US studies observe ethnic differences, with Blacks less likely than Hispanics or Whites to report large numbers of drinks prior to injury (Cherpitel, 1998). In ER samples, self-reported consumption within 6 hours of admission is often higher for injured than uninjured patients, both elevated compared to general population levels. Intoxication is seen in 20–40% of ER admissions, with a night-time rate higher by some 80% (Medical Research Council, 1998). In general population surveys, dose–response relationships for non-fatal injuries have been observed, especially for frequency of heavy drinking (Cherpitel et al., 1995). Alcohol involvement has been shown to alter the treatment course of injured patients and may cause surgical complications (Smith et al., 1999).

Males are over-represented in the ER studies' intoxicated groups (Cherpitel, 1993). Similarly, in most countries young men are more prone to accidents and hence to the number of, years of life lost to mortality; in one study males constituted 77% of all injured drivers and 84% of those were intoxicated with alcohol (Brismar & Bergman, 1998). A study of pedestrian accidents showed that 53% of the injured had measurable BAC vs. 15% in sex–age-matched groups of uninjured from the same areas (Brismar & Bergman, 1998); consistently, younger men predominate in such statistics. Reviewing 21 studies from eight countries, Hingson & Howland (1987) found that 20–77% were alcohol-related, and those with multiple ER admissions for fall injuries were problem drinkers. Dose–response findings are strong for injuries and especially clear with traffic accidents. Summaries of US findings show this effect: BAC > 0.8% increased risk of vehicular crashes two-fold; 1.0% seven-fold; 1.5% 10-fold; and 2.0% 20-fold (Brismar & Bergman, 1998). Results show relationships between accident severity and degree of alcohol involvement and also level of intoxication. The alcohol AF is estimated at 0.3 for traffic crashes and 0.5 for drownings (Medical Research Council, 1998).

Beer is implicated in drinking–driving statistics in both roadside surveys and population surveys of self-reported problems, as described earlier (Greenfield & Rogers, 1999). Research on risk perception in relation to the alcohol is an important area of study.

Violent behavior and criminality are discussed in the next chapter, so this review is brief. Perpetrators and victims have often been drinking or intoxicated prior to the event (Brismar & Bergman, 1998; Scott et al., 1999) and criminal behaviors are associated with alcohol (and other drug) consumption and drinking problems (Greenfield & Weisner, 1995). Some findings show dose–response relationships and effects of drinking patterns. For example, in one US national study with sociodemographic variables controlled, volume and maximum amount, but especially self-reported drunkenness, predicted the breadth of criminal behaviors (Greenfield, 1998). Those who never drank heavily had virtually no risk of criminality; conversely, those with high maximum quantities (12+/day) showed increasing risks from very low volumes (episodic heavy drinkers), although high-quantity, high-volume drinkers showed the highest risk; victimization had similar but weaker relationships (Greenfield, 1998).

It appears true today, as Greenfield & Weisner (1995) commented, "while progress has been made toward establishing that there *is*, on the broadest empirical level, a relationship between alcohol and crime, the association is not well understood. Many basic questions important to understanding the origin and details of the relationship remain unanswered" (p. 361). However, important advances are being made, especially with the use of multi-level and geospatial ecological modeling (see Greenfield, 1999, for more extensive treatment). These methods allow discovery of concentrations of acute alcohol-related problems and of their relationship to both personal and environmental influences, such as policy regimes or drinking/purchase sites (Gruenewald et al., in preparation; Gruenewald et al., 1999; Parker, 1995).

There is a consensus that while many cultural and ecological factors affect the relationship, the association between intoxication and violent death is strong, especially among younger males (Medical Research Council, 1998). In one Northern Californian study of unnatural death (385 cases), persons reporting consuming six or more drinks/day had a six-fold risk of suicide and a seven-fold risk of being murdered (Klatsky & Armstrong, 1993). Men are exposed to violence mainly in public places and are as likely to be perpetrators as to be victims; women are more often the recipients of violence, often in the home. Violent behavior associated with heavy drinking in young men is linked with other risky behaviors (Brismar & Bergman, 1998), including impulsivity and risky sexual behavior (Trocki, 1993). Generalized risk-taking behavior, leading to antisocial problems, suicidal attempts, drug use and heavy drinking, has been postulated from studies of adolescence (Brismar & Bergman, 1998). For alcohol-related assaults and homicides, see also Chapter 22.

CONCLUSIONS

There are many social and health harms associated with even low levels of overall volume, generally associated with heavy drinking occasions. In the health arena, only one or two possibly beneficial effects (especially CHD reduction) associated with low quantity, regular drinking patterns have some consensus. Even so, many have pointed out that the CHD benefit, if not mainly an artifact of lifestyle and other factors, could perhaps be better achieved by "less risky" life-style changes, such as ceasing smoking, reducing fat intake and increasing regular exercise (Thakker, 1998). However, regular low-quantity drinking carries little risk and may secure pleasure and some benefit. It is relevant that we know that people, especially young people, are willing to accept much higher risks that appear self-controlled (rock climbing, speeding, substance use) than ones seen as externally imposed, beyond personal influence (airplane safety, environmental contamination). In this spirit, a recent alcohol beverage industry-sponsored conference (Permission for Pleasure, International Council on Alcohol Policy, New York, March, 1998) held that public health researchers have largely ignored the enormous benefits that lead people to drink in spite of the potential for negative consequences. Indeed, few have investigated the pleasurable effects in the same framework as the negative ones (but cf. Mäkelä & Mustonen, 1988). For public health remedies, such as safe drinking guidelines to reach target audiences, we must understand better how risk groups appreciate drinking. The acceptability of *drunkenness* to some people in certain circumstances (Greenfield & Room, 1997) must be taken up. The attractiveness of healthy living is likely to be a stronger suit for young heavy drinkers than fear induction. It is sobering to recall that in this protected era, extreme sports and adventure tourism are gaining ground: risk taking entices us, serving "to remind ourselves, at the risk of death—that we are alive!" (Richard Rodriguez, Radio Editorial on "All Things Considered", PBS, 19 May 1999.

ACKNOWLEDGEMENTS

Preparation of this chapter was supported in part by a National Alcohol Research Center Grant (AA-05595) and in part by grant "Alcohol and Mortality Ethnic and Social Influences" (R01 AA10960), both from the US National Institute on Alcohol Abuse and Alcoholism to the Alcohol Research

Group, Public Health Institute. Opinions expressed are those of the author and do not necessarily reflect those of the sponsoring institutions.

KEY WORKS AND SUGGESTIONS FOR FURTHER READING

Dawson, D.A. (Ed.) (1998). Proceedings: International Workshop on Consumption Measures and Models for Use in Policy Development and Evaluation. *Alcoholism: Clinical and Experimental Research*, **22**(2), 1S–81S.

This collection of articles was based on summaries of presentations and discussions occurring at the workshop of the same name sponsored by US NIAAA, which took place in Bethesda, MD, May 12–14 1997. Excellent state-of-the-art overview of measurement issues by methodologists and leaders in the field of alcohol measurement, including consumption measures, context measures, cultural and subgroup issues, lifetime drinking histories, measurement in longitudinal studies, modeling distribution of drinking and problems, evaluating competing models of alcohol-related harm, drinking guidelines and hazardous drinking, and pattern measurement.

Rydberg, U.S. & Allebeck, P. (Eds) (1998). Proceedings: State of the Art Conference: Risks and Protective Effects of Alcohol on the Individual. *Alcoholism: Clinical and Experimental Research*, **22**(7), 269S–373S.

This supplement, based on a conference sponsored by the Swedish Medical Council, provides a comprehensive overview of research on risks of alcohol consumption in relation to biophysical systems and syndromes, such as cancer, cardiovascular disease, cardiac arrhythmias, stroke, fetal damage, and including neurological and psychiatric conditions.

Midanik, L.T., Tam, T.W., Greenfield, T.K. & Caetano, R. (1996). Risk functions for alcohol-related problems in a 1988 US national sample. *Addiction*, **91**, 1427–1437.

Editor (1996). Six commentaries and a response: comments on Midanik et al.'s "Risk functions for alcohol-related problems in a 1988 US national sample". *Addiction*, **91**, 1439–1456.

This paper and associated comments by six well-known international researchers provides evidence of risk curves for ICD-10 dependence syndrome work problems and drunk driving, based on a large US national sample, examining both volume and rates of heavy drinking. The commentaries engage in important discussion of interpretive caveats and implications for research and policy.

English, D.R., Holman, C.D.J., Milne, E., Winter, M.J., Hulse, G.K., Codde, J., Bower, C.I., Corti, B., de Klerk, N., Lewin, G.F., Knuiman, M., Kurinezuk, J.J. & Ryan, G.A. (1995). *The quantification of drug caused morbidity and mortality in Australia, 1992*. Canberra: Commonwealth Department of Human Services and Health.

The most thorough literature review and collection of meta-anlayses regarding alcohol and health outcomes ever produced. It is regarded by many alcohol researchers internationally as a "bible". Its material and methodology are being updated but it is still the major text available on quantifying the links between alcohol consumption levels and different health outcomes.

Single, E., Ashley, M., Bondy, S., Dobbins, M., Rankin, J. & Rehm, J. (in press). *Evidence Regarding the Level of Alcohol Consumption Considered to be Low-risk for Men and*

Women. Commonwealth Department of Health and Aged Care. Canberra: Australian Government Publishing Service.

Another comprehensive international literature review which seeks to establish the links between level and pattern of alcohol consumption and various health outcomes. It updates the literature contained in English et al. and examines it from the point of view of establishing a basis for designing national guidelines for low risk alcohol consumption.

REFERENCES

Abel, E.L. & Hannigan, J.H. (1995).   Maternal risk factors in fetal alcohol syndrome: provocative and permissive influences. *Neurotoxicology and Teratology*, **17**, 445–462.

Allebeck, P. & Olsen, J. (1998).   Alcohol and fetal damage. *Alcoholism: Clinical and Experimental Research*, **22**, 329S–332S.

Andréasson, S. (1998).   Alcohol and J-shaped curves. *Alcoholism: Clinical and Experimental Research*, **22**, 359S–364S.

Armor, D.J. & Polich, J.M. (1982).   Measurement of alcohol consumption. In E.M. Pattison & E. Kaufman (Eds), *Encyclopedic Handbook of Alcoholism* (pp. 72–80). New York: Gardner.

Babor, T.F. & Del Boca, F.K. (1992).   Just the facts: enhancing measurement of alcohol consumption using self-report methods. In R.Z. Litten & J.P. Allen (Eds), *Measuring Alcohol Consumption: Psychosocial and Biochemical Methods* (pp. 3–19). Totowa, NJ: Humana.

Berglund, M. & Ojehagen, A. (1998).   The influence of alcohol drinking and alcohol use disorders on psychiatric disorders and suicidal behavior. *Alcoholism: Clinical and Experimental Research*, **22**, 333S–345S.

Brismar, B. & Bergman, B. (1998).   The significance of alcohol for violence and accidents. *Alcoholism: Clinical and Experimental Research*, **22**, 299S–306S.

Caetano, R. (1997).   The epidemiology of alcohol-related problems in the US: concepts, patterns and opportunities for research. *Drugs and Society*, **11**, 43–71.

Caetano, R. & Clark, C. (1998).   Trends in alcohol-related problems among Whites, Blacks, and Hispanics: 1984–1995. *Alcoholism: Clinical and Experimental Research*, **22**, 534–538.

Caetano, R., Clark, C. & Greenfield, T.K. (1998).   Prevalence, trends, and incidence of alcohol withdrawal symptoms: analysis of general population and clinical samples. *Alcohol, Health and Research World*, **22**, 63079.

Caetano, R. & Greenfield, T.K. (in press).   Trends in DSM-IV alcohol dependence: 1990 and 1995 US national alcohol surveys. *Alcohol, Health and Research World*.

Caetano, R. & Kaskutas, L.A. (1996).   Changes in drinking problems among Whites, Blacks and Hispanics: 1984–1992. *Substance Use and Misuse*, **31**, 1547–1571.

Caetano, R., Mora, M.E.M. & Schafer, J. (1997a).   *The Structure of DSM-IV Alcohol Dependence in a Treatment Sample of Mexican and Mexican-American Men*. Berkeley, CA: Alcohol Research Group.

Caetano, R., Tam, T., Greenfield, T.K., Cherpitel, C.J. & Midanik, L.T. (1997b).   DSM-IV alcohol dependence and drinking in the US population: a risk analysis. *Annals of Epidemiology*, **7**, 542–549.

Cahalan, D., Cisin, I.H. & Crossley, H.M. (1969).   *American Drinking Practices: A National Study of Drinking Behavior and Attitudes*, Monograph No. 6. New Brunswick, NJ: Rutgers Center of Alcohol Studies.

Cherpitel, C.J. (1993).   Alcohol and injuries: a review of international emergency room studies. *Addiction*, **88**, 923–937.

Cherpitel, C.J. (1998).   Drinking patterns and problems and drinking in the injury event: an analysis of emergency room patients by ethnicity. *Drug and Alcohol Review*, **17**, 423–431.

Cherpitel, C.J., Parés, A. & Rodés, J. (1993).   Prediction of alcohol-related casualties in the emergency room: a U.S.-Spain comparison. *Journal of Studies on Alcohol*, **54**, 308–314.

Cherpitel, C.J., Tam, T.W., Midanik, L.T., Caetano, R. & Greenfield, T.K. (1995).   Alcohol and nonfatal injury in the US general population: a risk function analysis. *Accident Analysis and Prevention*, **27**, 651–661.

Clark, W.B. & Hilton, M. (Eds) (1991). *Alcohol in America: Drinking Practices and Problems*. Albany, NY: State University of New York Press.

Dawson, D.A. (1998a). Measuring alcohol consumption: limitations and prospects for improvement. *Addiction*, **93**, 658–680; discussion, 969–977.

Dawson, D.A. (1998b). Volume of ethanol consumption: effects different approaches to measurement. *Journal of Studies on Alcohol*, **59**, 191–197.

Dawson, D.A. & Archer, L.D. (1993). Relative frequency of heavy drinking and the risk of alcohol dependence. *Addiction*, **88**, 1509–1518.

Edwards, G. (1986). The Alcohol Dependence Syndrome: a concept as stimulus to enquiry. *British Journal of Addiction*, **81**, 171–183.

Eliany, M., Giesbrecht, N., Nelson, M., Wellman, B. & Wortley, S. (1990). *National Alcohol and Other Drugs Survey (1989). Highlights report: Action on Drug Abuse*. Ottawa: Health and Welfare Canada.

English, D.R., Holman, C.D.J., Milne, E., Winter, M.J., Hulse, G.K., Codde, J., Bower, C.I., Corti, B., de Klerk, N., Lewin, G.F., Knuiman, M., Kurinezuk, J.J. & Ryan, G.A. (1995). *The Quantification of Drug Caused Morbidity and Mortality in Australia, 1992*. Canberra: Commonwealth Department of Human Services and Health.

Fillmore, K.M. & Midanik, L. (1984). The chronicity of drinking problems among men: a longitudinal study. *Journal of Studies on Alcohol*, **45**, 228–236.

Gomberg, E.S.L. (1989). Suicide risk among women with alcohol problems. *American Journal of Public Health*, **79**, 1363–1365.

Graham, K., Wilsnack, R., Dawson, D. & Vogeltanz, N. (1998). Should alcohol consumption measures be adjusted for gender differences. *Addiction*, **93**, 1137–1147.

Grant, B. & Harford, T. (1990). The relationship between ethanol intake and DSM-III alcohol dependence. *Journal of Studies on Alcohol*, **51**, 448–456.

Grant, B.F. & Dawson, D.A. (1997). Age at onset of alcohol use and its association with DSM-IV alcohol abuse and dependence: results from the National Longitudinal Alcohol Epidemiologic Survey. *Journal of Substance Abuse*, **9**, 103–110.

Grant, K.A., Arciniega, L.T., Tonigan, J.S., Miller, W.R. & Meyers, R.J. (1997). Are reconstructed self-reports of drinking reliable? *Addiction*, **92**, 601–606.

Greenfield, T.K. (1986). Quantity per occasion and consequences of drinking: a reconsideration and recommendation. *International Journal of Addictions*, **21**, 1059–1079.

Greenfield, T.K. (1988). A study of major mental disorders in California prisons: survey methodology and preliminary estimates. Presented at the Annual Meeting of the American Academy of Psychiatry and Law, San Francisco, October.

Greenfield, T.K. (1998). Evaluating competing models of alcohol-related harm. *Alcoholism: Clinical and Experimental Research*, **22**, 52s–62s.

Greenfield, T.K. (1999). Methodology and analysis in alcohol epidemiology: recent advances and opportunities. Presented at the National Institute on Alcohol Abuse and Alcoholism Extramural Scientific Advisory Board Meeting, Bethesda, MD, 5–6 May.

Greenfield, T.K., Midanik, L.T. & Rogers, J.D. (2000). A ten-year national trend study of alcohol consumption, 1984–1995: is the period of declining drinking over? *American Journal of Public Health*, **90**, 47–52.

Greenfield, T.K., Rehm, J. & Rogers, J.D. (1999). Alcohol and all-cause mortality: ethnic and social influences in a tri-ethnic US sample. Presented at the Kettil Bruun Society, Montreal, Quebec, 31 May–4 June.

Greenfield, T.K., Rogers, J. & Weisner, C. (1998). Heavy drinking in the life course of treated and untreated groups: results from a 1995 US general population survey. Presented at the Annual Alcohol Epidemiological Symposium, Kettil Bruun Society for Social and Epidemiological Research on Alcohol, Florence, Italy, 1–6 June.

Greenfield, T.K. & Rogers, J.D. (1997). Lifetime drinking and the cost of health harms: how problem severity informs the prevention paradox. Presented at the Annual Alcohol Epidemiological Symposium, Kettil Bruun Society for Social Epidemiological Research on Alcohol, Reykjavík, Iceland, 1–6 June.

Greenfield, T.K. & Rogers, J.D. (1999). Who drinks most of the alcohol in the US? the policy implications. *Journal of Studies on Alcohol*, **60**, 78–89.

Greenfield, T.K. & Rogers, J.D. (1999).   Alcoholic beverage choice, risk perception, and self-reported drunk driving: effects of measurement on risk analysis. *Addiction*, **94**, 1735–1743.

Greenfield, T.K. & Room, R. (1997).   Situational norms for drinking and drunkenness: trends in the US adult population, 1979–1990. *Addiction*, **92**, 33–47.

Greenfield, T.K. & Weisner, C. (1995).   Drinking problems and self-reported criminal behavior, arrests and convictions: 1990 US alcohol and 1989 county surveys. *Addiction*, **90**, 361–373.

Gruenewald, P., Stockwell, T., Beel, A. & Dyskin, E.V. (1999).   Beverage sales and drinking and driving: the role of on-premise drinking places. *Journal of Studies on Alcohol*, **60**, 47–53.

Gruenewald, P.J. & Nephew, T. (1994).   Drinking in California: theoretical and empirical analyses of alcohol consumption patterns. *Addiction*, **89**, 707–723.

Helzer, J.E. (1999).   Nosology National Institute on Alcohol Abuse and Alcoholism Extramural, Scientific Advisory Board Meeting, Bethesda, MD, 5–6 May.

Herd, D. (1989).   The epidemiology of drinking patterns and alcohol-related problems among US Blacks. In D. Spiegler, D. Takte, S. Aitken & C. Christian (Eds), *Alcohol Use Among US Ethnic Minorities*. Proceedings of a conference on the epidemiology of alcohol use and abuse among ethnic minority groups (pp. 3–50). Washington, DC, GPO.

Hillbom, M. (1998).   Alcohol consumption and stroke: benefits and risk. *Alcoholism: Clinical and Experimental Research*, **22**, 352S–358S.

Hilton, M.E. (1986).   Abstention in the general population of the USA. *British Journal of Addiction*, **81**, 95–112.

Hilton, M.E. (1989).   A comparison of a prospective diary and two summary recall techniques for recording alcohol consumption. *British Journal of Addiction*, **84**, 1085–1092.

Hingson, R. & Howland, J. (1987).   Alcohol as a risk factor for injury or death resulting from accidental falls: a review of the literature. *Journal of Studies on Alcohol*, **48**, 212–219.

Jacobson, J.L. & Jacobson, S.W. (1994).   Prenatal exposure and neurobehavioral development: where is the threshold? *Alcohol Health and Research World*, **18**, 30–36.

Kaskutas, L.A. & Graves, K. (1999). *An Alternative to Standard Drinks as a Measure of Alcohol Consumption*. Berkeley, CA: Alcohol Research Group.

Kessler, R.C., McGonagle, K.A., Zhao, S., Nelson, C.B., Hughes, M., Eshleman, S., Wittchen, H.-U. & Kendler, K.S. (1994).   Lifetime and 12-month prevalence of DSM-III-R psychiatric disorders in the United States. Results from the National Co-Morbidity Survey. *Archives of General Psychiatry*, **51**, 8–19.

Klatsky, A. & Armstrong, M.A. (1993).   Alcohol use, other traits, and risk of unnatural death: a prospective study. *Alcoholism: Clinical and Experimental Research*, **17**, 1156–1162.

Klatsky, A., Armstrong, M.A. & Friedman, G.D. (1997).   Red wine, white wine, liquor, beer, and risk for coronary artery disease hospitalization. *American Journal of Cardiology*, **80**, 416–420.

Knupfer, G. (1987).   Drinking for health: the daily light drinker fiction. *British Journal of Addiction*, **82**, 547–555.

Knupfer, G. (1991).   Abstaining for foetal health: the fiction that even light drinking is dangerous. *British Journal of Addiction*, **86**, 1063–1073.

Kreitman, N. (1986).   Alcohol consumption and the preventive paradox. *British Journal of Addiction*, **81**, 353–363.

Leifman, H., Kühlhom, E., Allebeck, P., Andreasson, S. & Romelsjö, A. (1995).   Antecedents and covariates to a sober lifestyle and its consequences. *Social Science and Medicine*, **41**, 113–121.

Lemmens, P.H. (1998).   Measuring lifetime drinking histories. *Alcoholism: Clinical and Experimental Research*, **22**, 29s–36s.

Lipton, R. (1994).   The effects of moderate alcohol use on the relationship between stress and depression. *American Journal of Public Health*, **84**, 1913–1917.

Mäkelä, K. & Mustonen, H. (1988).   Positive and negative experience related to drinking as a function of annual alcohol intake. *British Journal of Addiction*, **83**, 403–408.

Medical Research Council (1998).   Individual harmful and protective effects of alcohol. *Alcoholism: Clinical and Experimental Research*, **22**, 365S–373S.

Midanik, L. & Greenfield, T.K. (2000).   Trends in social consequences and dependence symptoms in the United States: the National Alcohol Surveys, 1984–1995. *American Journal of Public Health*, **90**, 53–56.

Midanik, L., Tam, T., Greenfield, T.K. & Caetano, R. (1996a).   On taking risks. *Addiction*, **91**, 1453–1456.

Midanik, L.T. (1982). The validity of self-reported alcohol consumption and alcohol problems: a literature review. *British Journal of Addiction*, **77**, 357–382.

Midanik, L.T. & Clark, W.B. (1994). The demographic distribution of US drinking patterns in 1990: descriptions and trends from 1984. *American Journal of Public Health*, **84**, 1218–1222.

Midanik, L.T., Tam, T.W., Greenfield, T.K. & Caetano, R. (1996b). Risk functions for alcohol-related problems in a 1988 US national sample. *Addiction*, **91**, 1427–1437.

Miller, W.R. (1996). *Manual for Form 90: A Structured Assessment Interview for Drinking and Related Behaviors*. Rockville, MD: National Institute on Alcohol Abuse and Alcoholism.

Muthén, B. (1999). Methodological issues in random coefficient growth modeling using a latent variable framework: applications to the development of heavy drinking, ages 18–37. In J. Rose, L. Chassin, C. Presson & J. Sherman (Eds), *Multivariate Applications in Substance Use Research*, Hillsdale, NJ: Erlbaum.

Muthén, B.O. (1992). *Covariates of Alcohol Dependence and Abuse: A Multivariate Analysis of a 1988 General Population Survey in the United States*. Los Angeles, CA: University of California at Los Angeles.

Muthén, B.O. (1996). Psychometric evaluation of diagnostic criteria: application to a two-dimensional model of alcohol abuse and dependence. *Drug and Alcohol Dependence*, **41**, 101–112.

Neiman, J. (1998). Alcohol as a risk factor for brain damage: neurologic aspects. *Alcoholism: Clinical and Experimental Research*, **22**, 346S–351S.

Oddy, W. & Stockwell, T.R. (1995). How much alcohol in Western Australia is consumed in a "hazardous" or "harmful" way? (Letter to the editor). *Australian Journal of Public Health*, **19**, 404.

Parker, R. (1995). Bringing "booze" back. In The relationship between alcohol and homicide. *Journal of Research in Crime and Delinquency*, **32**, 3–38.

Polcin, D.L. (1997). The etiology and diagnosis of alcohol dependence: differences in the professional literature. *Psychotherapy*, **34**, 297–306.

Regier, D.A., Farmer, M.E., Rae, D.S., Locke, B.Z., Keith, S.J., Judd, L.L. & Goodwin, F.K. (1990). Comorbidity of mental disorders with alcohol and other drug abuse: results from the Epidemiologic Catchment Area (ECA) study. *Journal of the American Medical Association*, **264**, 2511–2518.

Rehm, J. (1998). Measuring quantity, frequency, and volume of drinking. *Alcoholism: Clinical and Experimental Research*, **22**, 4s–14s.

Rehm, J., Ashley, M.J. & Room, R. (1996). On the emerging paradigm of drinking patterns and their social and health consequences. *Addiction*, **9**, 1615–1622.

Rehm, J., Greenfield, T.K., Walsh, G., Xie, X., Robson, L. & Single, E. (1999). Assessment methods for alcohol consumption, prevalence of high risk drinking and harm: a sensitivity analysis. *International Journal of Epidemiology*, **28**, 219–224.

Reifman, A. & Windle, M. (1995). Adolescent suicidal behavior as a function of depression, hopelessness, alcohol use, and social support: a longitudinal investigation. *American Journal of Community Psychology*, **23**, 329–354.

Rimm, E. (1999). The epidemiology of moderate alcohol consumption and the risk of chronic disease. Presented at National Institute on Alcohol Abuse and Alcoholism Extramural Scientific Advisory Board Meeting, Bethesda, MD, 5–6 May.

Rimm, E.B., Klatsky, A., Grobbee, D. & Stampfer, M.J. (1996). Review of moderate alcohol consumption and reduced risk of coronary heart disease: is the effect due to beer, wine, or spirits? *British Medical Journal*, **312**, 731–736.

Ringborg, U. (1998). Alcohol and the risk of cancer. *Alcoholism: Clinical and Experimental Research*, **22**, 323S–328S.

Robins, L.N., Helzer, J.E., Przybeck, T.R. & Regier, D.A. (1988). Alcohol disorders in the community: a report from the Epidemiologic Catchment Area. In R.M. Rose (Ed.), *Alcoholism: Origins and Outcomes* (pp. 15–29). New York: Raven.

Rogers, J.D. & Greenfield, T.K. (1999). Beer drinking accounts for most of the hazardous alcohol consumption reported in the United States. *Journal of Studies on Alcohol*, **60**, 732–739.

Room, R. (1990). Measuring alcohol consumption in the United States: methods and rationales. In L. Kozlowski, H.M. Annis, H.D. Cappell, F.B. Glaser, M.S. Goodstadt, Y. Israel, H. Kalant, E.M. Sellers & E.R. Vingilis (Eds), *Research Advances in Alcohol and Drug Problems*, Vol. 10 (pp. 39–80). New York: Plenum.

Room, R., Bondy, S. & Ferris, J. (1995). The risk of harm to oneself from drinking, Canada 1989. *Addiction*, **90**, 499–513.

Room, R., Janca, A., Bennett, L.A., Schmidt, L. & Sartorius, N. (1996). WHO cross-cultural applicability research on diagnosis and assessment of substance use disorders: an overview of methods and selected results. *Addiction*, **91**, 199–220.

Rosenqvist, M. (1998). Alcohol and cardiac arrhythmias. *Alcoholism: Clinical and Experimental Research*, **22**, 318S–322S.

Russell, M., Marshall, J.R., Trevisan, M., Freudenheim, J., Chan, A.W.K., Markovic, N., Vana, J.E. & Priore, R.L. (1997). Test–retest reliability of the Cognitive Lifetime Drinking History. *American Journal of Epidemiology*, **146**, 975–982.

Schinke, S.C. & Cole, K.C. (1999). Alcohol use among members of American ethnic-racial minority groups: a review of scientific knowledge. Presented at the National Institute on Alcohol Abuse and Alcoholism, Extramural Scientific Advisory Board Meeting, Bethesda, MD, 5–6 May.

Scott, K.D., Schafer, J.C. & Greenfield, T.K. (1999). The role of alcohol in physical assault perpetration and victimization. *Journal of Studies on Alcohol*, **60**, 528–536.

Secretary of Health and Human Services (1993). *Eighth Special Report to the US Congress on Alcohol and Health*. Rockville, MD: US Department of Health and Human Services, Public Health Services, National Institutes of Health, National Institute on Alcohol Abuse and Alcoholism.

Simpura, J. & Poikolainen, K. (1983). Accuracy of retrospective measurement of individual alcohol consumption in men: a reinterview after 18 years. *Journal of Studies on Alcohol*, **44**, 911–917.

Single, E., Easton, B., Collins, D., Harwood, H., Lapsley, H. & Maynard, A. (1996). *International Guidelines for Estimating the Costs of Substance Abuse*. Ottawa: Canadian Centre on Substance Abuse.

Skög, O.J. (1995). The J-curve, casuality, and public health. *Addiction*, **90**, 490–492.

Smith, G.S., Spicer, R.S. & Streicker, J. (1999). The epidemiology of alcohol-related injuries: current knowledge and research needs for intentional and unintentional injuries. Presented at the National Institute on Alcohol Abuse and Alcoholism Extramural Scientific Advisory Board Meeting, Bethesda, MD, 5–6 May.

Sobell, L.C., Cunningham, J.A., Sobell, M.B. & Toneatto, T. (1993). Life-span perspective on natural recovery (self-change) from alcohol problems. In J.S. Baer, G.A. Marlatt & R.J. McMahon (Eds), *Addictive Behaviors across the Life Span: Prevention, Treatment and Policy Issues* (pp. 34–66). Newbury Park, CA: Sage.

Stockwell, T., Daly, A., Phillips, M., Masters, L., Midford, R., Gahegan, M. & Philp, A. (1996a). Total versus hazardous per capita alcohol consumption as predictors of acute and chronic alcohol related harm. *Contemporary Drug Problems*, **23**, 441–464.

Stockwell, T., Hawks, D., Lang, E. & Ryon, P. (1996b). Unravelling the preventive paradox for acute alcohol problems. *Drug and Alcohol Review*, **15**, 7–15.

Stockwell, T., Single, E., Hawks, D. & Rehm, J. (1997). Sharpening the focus of alcohol policy from aggregate consumption to harm and risk reduction. *Addiction Research*, **5**, 1–9.

Streissguth, A.P., Sampson, P.D. & Baur, H.M. (1989). Neurobehavioral dose–response effects of prenatal alcohol exposure in humans in infancy to adulthood. *Anuals of the New York Academy of Sciences*, **562**, 142–158.

Substance Abuse and Mental Health Services Administration (1996). *National Household Survey on Drug Abuse: Main Findings, 1994*. Rockville, MD: SAMHSA—Office of Applied Studies.

Svardsudd, K. (1998). Moderate alcohol consumption and cardiovascular disease: is there evidence for a preventive effect? *Alcoholism: Clinical and Experimental Research*, **22**, 307S–314S.

Thakker, K.D. (1998). An overview of health risks and benefits of alcohol consumption. *Alcoholism: Clinical and Experimental Research*, **22**, 285S–298S.

Trocki, K. (1993). Predictors of risky sex and other problem behaviors in adolescents. In T. Colthurst (Ed.), *HIV and Alcohol Impairment: Reducing Risks* pp. 137–151. San Diego, CA: University of California at San Diego.

US National Institute on Alcohol Abuse and Alcoholism (1997). *Alcohol and Health*. Ninth special report to the US Congress. Rockville, MD: US Department of Health and Human Services.

Victorin, K., Haag-Gronlund, M. & Skerfving, S. (1998). Methods for health risk assessment of chemicals: are they relevant for alcohol? *Alcoholism: Clinical and Experimental Research*, **22**, 270S–276S.

Waldenström, A. (1998). Alcohol and congestive heart failure. *Alcoholism: Clinical and Experimental Research*, **22**, 315S–317S.

Watson, A.L. & Sher, K.J. (1998).   Resolution of alcohol problems without treatment: methodological issues and future directions of natural recovery research. *Clinical Psychology: Science and Practice*, **5**, 1–18.

Weisner, C., Greenfield, T. & Room, R. (1995).   Trends in the treatment of alcohol problems in the US general population, 1979–1990. *American Journal of Public Health*, **85**, 55–60.

Welte, J.W. & Mirand, A.L. (1994).   Lifetime drinking patterns of elders from a general population survey. *Drug and Alcohol Dependence*, **35**, 133–140.

World Health Organization (1994).   *Lexicon of Alcohol and Drug Terms*. Geneva: World Health Organization.

World Health Organization (2000).   *International Guide for Monitoring Alcohol Consumption and Related Harm*. Geneva: Department of Mental Health and Substance Dependence, Noncommunicable Diseases and Mental Health Cluster, World Health Organization, Publication No. WHO/MSD/00-4.

Chapter 22

Alcohol and Crime: Examining the Link

Kathryn Graham
and
Paulette West
Centre for Addiction and Mental Health, London, Ontario, Canada

Synopsis

Most studies suggest that alcohol is involved in 40–50% of violent crimes and a lesser but substantial proportion of other types of crimes. Alcohol is, by definition, involved in 100% of drinking driving violations. The available evidence suggests there are multiple contributing factors to the relationship between alcohol and crime, including the effects of alcohol, the characteristics of the person, the drinking situation and the cultural framing of both drinking and criminal behavior (as modeled in Figure 22.1). First, there is considerable evidence to suggest that alcohol intoxication plays a contributing role in aggression and other crimes, and possibly an even greater role in the escalation of violent crime. The effects of alcohol on risk taking, problem solving, emotions and power concerns tend to increase the probability that people will respond aggressively or violently in certain situations, engage in other crimes such as robbery, and choose to drive while impaired and then possibly drive aggressively or carelessly. However, it is also clear that the effects of alcohol depend not only on how much alcohol is consumed but by whom and under what circumstances (Lang, 1993). To begin with, the way that society views alcohol-related crime, both informally, through attitudes and expectations, and formally, through laws and policies, is likely to affect this relationship. Anthropological studies identified high variability in the extent that people became violent when drinking. More recently, the success of interventions to prevent drinking–driving have demonstrated the powerful cultural control over intoxicated behavior. Drinking settings also exercise considerable control over behavior through expectations, the physical and social characteristics of the settings and the intoxication level and characteristics of others in the setting. Violent crimes and drinking–driving are disproportionately associated with drinking in licensed premises in some countries. In addition, alcohol-related criminal behavior is more likely in social settings where more than one person is intoxicated. Finally, drinkers vary considerably in predispositions, attitudes

International Handbook of Alcohol Dependence and Problems. Edited by N. Heather, T.J. Peters and T. Stockwell.

and concerns that may determine whether they will engage in aggressive or criminal behavior while drinking. Alcohol-related crime tends to be most frequent among young unmarried males and has been associated with deviance, power concerns and attitudes, and expectations that aggression, drinking driving and other crimes will be more acceptable if alcohol is involved.

The possible role of alcohol in criminal behavior has intrigued researchers from many disciplines, including criminology, psychology, epidemiology, pharmacology, sociology, anthropology, law and women's studies. There is growing consensus that the pharmacological effects of alcohol play a role in the commission of violent and other crimes; however, there is also a general consensus that the relationship between alcohol and crime is affected by a complex and varying array of other factors as well (Graham et al., 1998).

One indication of the relationship between alcohol and crime is the association between level of drinking and crime rates over time within a country (Cook & Moore, 1993; Lenke, 1982; Norström, 1998). Similarly, geographic analyses show a consistent relationship of regional differences in rates of alcohol consumption with night-time road crashes and accidental and violent injuries (Midford et al., 1998). Murdoch, Pihl & Ross (1990) reviewed studies from a number of countries and concluded that being under the influence of alcohol is associated with violent crime at a greater than chance level. Although the relationship between level of alcohol use and crime could be due to social factors that influence both alcohol consumption and crime, meta-analyses of experimental studies of the effects of alcohol on aggression in controlled settings have concluded that alcohol consumption results in a measurable increase in aggressive behavior (Bushman, 1997; Bushman & Cooper, 1990; Lipsey et al., 1997). This alcohol-related increase in aggression may account, at least in part, for the relationship between alcohol and violent crime. However, the extent of involvement of alcohol in crime is highly variable (see MacAndrew & Edgerton, 1969; Murdoch et al., 1990), suggesting that a simple, direct pharmacological impact of alcohol on criminal behavior is highly unlikely. Therefore, recent research has explored both how the pharmacological effects of alcohol might make aggression more likely and how the personal, situational and cultural factors that surround drinking might affect the relationship between drinking and crime.

The chapter begins with a brief overview of statistics relating to drinking by perpetrators and victims of crime. This is followed by a description of an explanatory model linking alcohol and crime. The remainder of the chapter explores the links between alcohol and crime by examining the different aspects of drinking that might account for an increased likelihood of criminal behavior. These include: (a) the effects of alcohol; (b) the characteristics of the drinker; (c) situational factors; and (d) cultural influences. Much of the research relating alcohol and crime has focused on either aggression/violent crime or drinking and driving; therefore, this review draws primarily on this literature, although inferences regarding other alcohol-related crime such as robbery will be made where possible. Crimes defined solely by societal controls on consumption (under-age drinking, public intoxication) are excluded.

DRINKING BY PERPETRATORS AND VICTIMS OF CRIME

In one of the earliest studies of the relationship between crime and alcohol, Wolfgang (1958) examined records collected by the Police Department in Philadelphia, USA, for the period 1948–1952 to determine whether there was any relationship between alcohol and criminal homicide. According to Wolfgang, alcohol was present in the "homicide situation", meaning that the victim and/or offender and/or both were drinking, in 64% of the 588 cases he reviewed. In total, the proportion of cases in which alcohol was present was 9% for the victim only, 11% for the offender only, and 44% for both the victim and offender. Murdoch, Pihl & Ross (1990) reviewed studies measuring the involvement of alcohol in violent crime in different countries spanning the years 1951–1985. Studies varied considerably in scope and rigor, with only six of the 23 studies reviewed using comparison groups and only three using tests of statistical significance. Based on their review of these studies, Murdoch et al. concluded that alcohol consumption by the offender, victim or both was involved in over 50% of homicides and assaults overall, although this figure was highly variable across different studies.

The following sections and Table 22.1 summarize recent statistics on the proportion of perpetrators and victims who had been drinking at or near the time the crime occurred, based on interviews with offenders, court records, autopsy records, and victimization surveys done as part of large-scale, usually country-wide, studies.

Drinking by Offenders according to Interview Data and Arrest Records

A number of researchers have used survey data from the US Bureau of Justice Statistics to report on the prevalence of alcohol involvement among various populations convicted of non-violent and violent crimes (e.g. Beck et al., 1993; Harlow, 1998; Mumola & Bonzar, 1998) (see Table 22.1). According to these data, the percentage of offenders who were under the influence of alcohol at the time of the commission of a violent crime was 37–42% (42–47% for homicides). In contrast, 18–34% of non-violent offenders (excluding those convicted of driving while intoxicated and other public order offenses) had reportedly been drinking around the time the crime was committed. Statistics Canada data for 1995 (Fedorowycz, 1996) estimated that 43% of homicide offenders were drinking alcohol prior to the crime (see Table 22.1). However, for 29% of Canadian homicides, information regarding alcohol or drug use by the offender was unknown; therefore, these statistics probably underestimate the actual rate of alcohol involvement. In Australia, about one-fifth of offenders convicted of a violent crime who were surveyed as part of the National Prison Census (1988–1991) reported being under the influence of alcohol at the time of the offense (Wallace & Travis, 1994) (see Table 22.1). Most studies have found a higher rate of alcohol involvement for violent vs. non-violent crime; however, although violent crimes more often involve alcohol consumption by the perpetrator than non-violent crimes, the *amount* consumed by those who had been drinking has been found to be similar across different types of crimes (Greenfield, L.A., 1998).

Drinking by Offenders and Victims according to Victimization Surveys

Survey studies of crime victimization provide data on crimes some of which may not have been reported to police or otherwise entered into official records. Based on estimates from the 1993 Canadian General Social Survey (see Table 22.1), 24% of adult Canadians reported being victims of one or more crimes (Statistics Canada, 1994). Victims reported that 39% of assaults and sexual assaults and 22% of personal robberies were related to someone else's drinking or drug use (5% of assaults, 8% of sexual assaults and less than 1% of personal robberies related to the victim's use).

For victimizations reported as part of the US National Crime Victimization survey (Greenfield, L.A., 1998), 70% of victims were able to report on whether or not alcohol or

Table 22.1 National data sets showing the prevalence of alcohol involvement in crime

Data source	Country	n	Type of crime	Drinking by offenders (%)		
				Using at the time of offense	Alcohol only	Alcohol and drugs	Drugs only
Beck et al. (1993), Survey of inmates in state correctional facilities (Bureau of Justice Statistics)	USA (1991 data)	13,986	All offenses		18	14	17
			Violent Offenses		21	16	12
			Homicide		25	17	10
			Rape/sexual assault		22	14	5
			Robbery		15	18	19
			Assault		27	14	8
			Property Offenses		18	14	21
			Drug Offenses		8	10	26
			Public order offenses		31	9	10
			DWI		70	8	3
			Other public order		20	10	11
Mumola & Bonczar (1998), Survey of adults on probation (Bureau of Justice Statistics)	USA (1995 data)	2,030	Violent offenses		40.7	43.5	10.7
			Sexual assault		31.8	33.0	10.9
			Assault		45.5	47.5	9.3
			Property offenses		18.5	23.0	9.8
			Burglary		38.5	49.4	23.3
			Larceny/theft		16.3	20.8	9.6
			Fraud		9.7	13.3	8.2
			Drug offenses		16.3	38.4	31.7
			Possession		14.4	33.5	26.6
			Trafficking		16.2	42.2	36.6
			Public order offenses		75.1	77.0	6.4
			DWI		98.3	98.5	3.3
			Other		26.8	32.0	12.8

Data source	Country	n	Type of crime	Drinking by offenders (%)					Drinking by victims[1] (%)				
				Alcohol only	Alcohol and drugs	Drugs only	No alcohol or drugs	Unknown	Alcohol only	Alcohol and drugs	Drugs only	No alcohol or drugs	Unknown
Harlow (1998), Survey of local jail inmates (Bureau of Justice Statistics)	USA (1996 data)	6,133	Violent offenses	55.2	27.4		14.3	13.5					
			Homicide	50.3	31.0		15.9	3.4					
			Sexual assault	44.8	23.1		8.4	13.3					
			Robbery	63.2	18.8		19.5	24.9					
			Assault	54.2	33.3		13.8	7.1					
			Property offenses	55.2	17.9		16.3	21.0					
			Burglary	55.9	20.7		18.6	16.6					
			Larceny/theft	56.5	18.5		15.1	22.9					
			Fraud	52.4	7.2		15.0	30.2					
			Drug offenses	65.2	6.0		23.5	35.7					
			Possession	64.3	7.1		22.2	35.0					
			Trafficking	64.7	4.5		24.7	35.5					
			Public-order offenses	65.4	46.2		10.6	8.6					
			DWI	95.1	83.2		10.4	1.5					
			Other	47.7	24.2		10.7	12.8					
Wallace & Travis (1994), (National Prison Census)	Australia (1991 data)	5,143	Violent	19.8	80.2								
			Homicide	15.8	84.2								
			Assault	30.2	69.8								
			Sex offense	22.4	77.6								
			Robbery	23.0	77.0								
			Non-Violent	19.8	80.2								
			Breaking and entering	18.9	81.1								
			Fraud	4.9	95.1								
			Trafficking	2.2	97.8								
			Other theft	19.1	80.9								
Fedorowycz (1996), Statistics Canada	Canada (1995 data)	586	Homicide	30	13	4	24	29	25	8	5	41	21

continued overleaf

Table 22.1 (continued)

Data source	Country	n	Type of crime	Drinking by offenders (%)					
				Alcohol	Drugs and alcohol	Drugs or alcohol	Drugs	Neither	Unknown
Victimization Data									
Greenfield, L.A. (1998), National Crime Victimization Survey (Bureau of Justice Statistics	USA (1992–1995)	Approximately 50,000 households annually	Rape/sexual assault	30	7	2	4	24	34
			Robbery	10	5	1	9	59	16
			Aggravated assault	21	7	1	6	42	23
			Simple assault	21	4	1	4	35	36

Data source	Country	n	Type of crime	Drinking by offenders (%)		Drinking by victims (%)	
				Alcohol or drugs	Unknown	Alcohol or drugs	Unknown
Statistics Canada (1994), General social survey	Canada (1993)	Approximately 10,000 households (3,740 crime incidents)	Assaults	38.9	6.2	4.6	0.3
			Sexual assaults	39.4	6.0	8.4	0.0
			Robbery	21.8	7.3	0.7	0.0

[1] Based on autopsy records.

drug use by the offender was a factor (see Table 22.1). Among these victimizations, alcohol consumption by the perpetrator was considered a factor in 39% of sexual assaults, 29% of aggravated assaults, 26% of simple assaults, and 16% of robberies. Alcohol involvement was more likely among current or former spouses, boyfriends or girlfriends (40%) than among victimizations involving casual or well-known acquaintances (21%).

Wallace & Travis (1994) summarized data collected in Australia as part of the 1993 National Household Survey. Among the 3500 respondents, 13% reported being physically abused by someone affected by alcohol, 15% had property damaged by someone who had been drinking, and 7% had stolen property. For each type of victimization the percentage who indicated that they did not know whether the perpetrator had consumed alcohol was approximately 3%. A smaller percentage of respondents reported being perpetrators of the aforementioned crimes while under the influence of alcohol (4%, 3% and 1%, respectively).

Drinking by Homicide Victims According to Autopsy Records

Many studies have reported on the prevalence of drinking by crime victims, primarily homicide victims. It has been argued that drinking by the victim may precipitate an attack due to the victim's perceived vulnerability, or because the victim may be more likely to provoke an attack due to the effects of alcohol (see Wolfgang, 1958). Although few victims included in victimization surveys attributed the crimes they reported to their own substance use (Statistics Canada, 1994), autopsy reports from homicides suggest a high rate of alcohol consumption by victims, ranging from 32% in Canada in 1995 (Fedorowycz, 1996) to 46% in Los Angeles, California in 1970–1979 (Goodman et al., 1986). As might be expected given gender differences in the use of alcohol, the results generally indicate that male victims are more likely than female victims to have consumed alcohol. Fedorowycz (1996) reported that male homicide victims in Canada were twice as likely as female victims to have consumed alcohol and/or drugs. Similarly, in their study of Los Angeles homicide victims, Goodman et al. (1986) found that males were significantly more likely than females to have positive blood alcohol readings (51% vs. 26%). However, a study of New York City Medical Examiner records for 1981 (Tardiff, Gross & Messner, 1986) found approximately equal proportions of male and female victims had consumed alcohol (38% of males and 36% of females).

Alcohol use by victims also varied with the circumstances within which the homicide occurred. Goodman et al. found that when the murder followed a *physical* altercation, 68% of victims had positive BAC readings, compared to 55% when the murder was precipitated by a *verbal* argument. In their study of New York victims, Tardiff, Gross & Messner (1986) found that victims killed during disputes were more likely than fatalities arising from robbery and drug-related crime to have alcohol in their blood at the time of death. Studies of alcohol consumption by homicide victims have also found that alcohol is more likely to be present in victims aged 30–39, and in victims of homicides that occurred during warmer months, in the evenings, in bars and restaurants (Welte & Abel, 1989) and in the street rather than in the home (Tardiff et al., 1995).

Although it has been concluded that alcohol involvement in crime is higher than might be expected by chance, rates vary enormously, depending not only on the type and geographic location of the crime (Murdoch et al., 1990; Roizen, 1997) but also on the methodology for assessing alcohol involvement (see Fagan, 1993; Greenfield, T.K., 1998). The remainder of this chapter examines other kinds of research directed towards explaining the alcohol–crime relationship and identifying possible reasons for variability in this relationship.

A MODEL OF THE FACTORS CONTRIBUTING TO ALCOHOL-RELATED CRIME

The model presented in Figure 22.1 shows the general sources of influence on the alcohol–crime relationship. The outer circle represents the *cultural context* for both drinking and criminal behavior. How much people drink, how they behave when they drink, the frequency of crime, and the forms of social control over both drinking and crime, all vary across cultures. The culture sets the norms and determines generally the way people behave when drinking. Despite this cultural framing, however, there is wide variability in alcohol-related behavior *within* cultures. For example, within a culture, characteristics of different drinking settings, such as crowding, types of activities and other aspects, may affect the probability of aggressive or criminal behavior. Moreover, people tend to moderate their behavior in accordance with the norms and expectations of particular settings. Thus, the *particular social and physical context* within which alcohol is consumed also affects drinking behaviors, including behaviors such as violence, drinking–driving and other criminal acts. In addition, *even among people who consume alcohol within the same setting and culture*, there are large individual differences in violence, drinking–driving and crime generally. Thus, *characteristics of the individual*, such as attitudes and personality, are directly relevant to the relationship between alcohol and crime. Finally, the *effects of alcohol* are also likely to play a role; that is, the same person in the same setting is likely to behave differently when intoxicated compared to when sober, and the effects of intoxication may increase the probability of that person becoming aggressive or committing a crime. Crimes associated with drinking–driving are, of course, defined by the consumption of alcohol, but even for these offenses, the *effects of alcohol* may have an impact on the likelihood of the crime occurring, by affecting the person's assessment of risks or judgement about his/her driving ability. In sum, the relationship between alcohol and crime is subject to multiple influences that

Figure 22.1   Factors contributing to alcohol-related crime

operate simultaneously, although for any individual crime, certain factors may contribute more than others.

Not only do the same general processes (i.e. cultural, situational, personal characteristics and effects of alcohol) operate on aggressive behavior, drinking–driving and crime generally, but a number of studies suggest that specific factors that contribute to one type of criminal behavior may contribute to others. For example, there are a number of common predictors of both drinking–driving and alcohol-related violence. Therefore, part of the present review will include linking these and other alcohol–related crimes into a common explanatory framework. The following sections examine the alcohol-crime relationship for each part of Figure 22.1: effects of alcohol, personal characteristics, situational variables and cultural context.

The Effects of Alcohol that May Increase the Probability of Criminal Behavior

During the 1970s and 1980s, many researchers questioned whether alcohol actually played *any* active role in the relationship between alcohol and crime. In terms of aggression, while it was clear that heavy and problem drinkers have a high rate of aggression and that aggressive people are more likely to be heavy drinkers (see review by Graham, Schmidt & Gillis, 1996), it is possible that this relationship could be entirely a function of certain personal characteristics being associated *both* with heavy alcohol use and with aggression. However, recent results from epidemiological and experimental research suggest that alcohol intoxication (not just drinking pattern) plays a *contributing* role in at least some proportion of alcohol-related aggressive and criminal behavior. Specifically, at least two epidemiological studies have found that the correlation between usual drinking and crime disappears when drinking *at the time of the crime* is controlled for (Collins & Schlenger, 1988; Wiley & Weisner, 1995). Similarly, Borges, Cherpitel & Rosovsky (1998) found that drinking prior to the event was a more powerful predictor of violent vs. non-violent injury than was usual alcohol consumption. Second, the experimental literature also suggests that, even though expectation cannot be clearly separated from the pharmacological effects of alcohol, there is some basis for assuming that the effects of alcohol, as experienced by the drinker, make a contribution to the likelihood of that drinker engaging in violent behavior (Bushman, 1997; Lipsey et al., 1997) and possibly other criminal behavior.

Much theoretical and some empirical research has attempted to identify the particular *effects* of alcohol that might increase the likelihood of aggression or violent crimes. The general premise is that alcohol consumption leads to changes in the individual that make the individual more likely to behave aggressively or commit crimes. For example, one hypothesis is that alcohol leads to reduced problem-solving ability, which causes the drinker to be less able to deal with frustrating stimuli which, in turn, would make the drinker more likely to respond aggressively than he/she would when sober. Therefore, the general effect of reduced problem solving ability due to alcohol would be to increase the probability of aggression. Further, not only are the effects of alcohol likely to increase the probability of aggression, there is some research to suggest that the effects of alcohol also increase escalation or severity of aggression. In their analyses of US National Crime Victimization Survey data, Martin & Bachman (1997) found that men's encounters with strangers were significantly more likely to escalate from threat to physical attack when the assailant had been drinking, and that women were more likely to sustain injury in an assault by an intimate partner if he had been drinking. Similarly, in his community survey, Pernanen (1991) found that more severe incidents of aggression (e.g. kicking, punching) were more likely than less severe incidents to involve alcohol. Considerable research has been devoted to identifying the effects of alcohol that would affect aggressive behavior. No comparable literature exists relating specific effects of alcohol to the *propensity* to drink and drive or commit other crimes; however, as described in the following examples, many of the explanations of the effects of alcohol on aggression can be generalized to other intoxicated criminal behavior, especially behaviors involving impulsivity and risk-taking, such as driving while impaired.

Biological Mechanisms and Increased Risk Taking

A number of physiological processes have been identified as potentially involved in the alcohol–aggression relationship (see *Journal of Studies on Alcohol*, Supplement No. 11, 1993; Graham, Wells & West, 1997). One promising direction of recent research has focused on two specific brain receptor sites (5-HT and GABA) to explain why drinking might lead to aggression. Interest in GABA receptors has linked the anxiolytic effects of alcohol and the effects of some benzodiazepines with aggression (see discussion by Pihl, Peterson & Lau, 1993). Essentially, the theory that has been proposed suggests that this anxiolytic effect results in less fear of threat or consequences; therefore, the person affected by the drug will behave less cautiously than he/she would in a more sober state, especially in response to threat. A variety of empirical findings have provided at least partial support for this hypothesis. First, as with alcohol, certain benzodiazepines have been reliably linked to aggression (Bond, Lader & Da Silveira, 1997; Gantner & Taylor, 1988). In addition, animal research has provided further support for the specific role of GABA receptors, in that: (a) aggressive animals show differences from non-aggressive animals at the $GABA_A$–benzodiazepine receptor complex; (b) the effects of alcohol on aggression can be potentiated by the addition of a benzodiazepine agonist; and (c) aggression can be reduced by administration of a benzodiazepine antagonist (Miczek, Weerrts & DeBold, 1993). Third, the effects of alcohol on risk-taking have been demonstrated in relation to both aggression (Pihl & Peterson, 1993; Graham, West & Wells, 2000) and simulated driving tasks (Mongrain & Standing, 1989). Mongrain & Standing also found that subjects in their experimental study underestimated the amount of alcohol they had been given. They noted that their results suggested that the most important impairment from alcohol may be on decision making, rather than on skills *per se*.

Cognitive Effects of Alcohol

In his seminal review of the relationship between alcohol and violence, Pernanen (1976) described a number of possible causal explanations for the relationship, including a well-developed theory relating the effects of alcohol on cognitive functioning to the increased likelihood of aggression. Alcohol is known to impair cognitive functioning in a number of ways that may be relevant to aggressive and criminal behavior, including making the person less self-reflective, less able to process multiple cues, more likely to focus on salient cues, more single-minded, less able to evaluate contingencies and less able to problem-solve effectively (see Graham et al., 1997). Although complex theories have been proposed involving the role of alcohol-impaired cognitions in aggressive behavior (Gibbs, 1986; Pernanen, 1976), there have been relatively few empirical studies demonstrating that aggression is actually related to alcohol-induced cognitive impairment. In one of the few empirical studies on the role of alcohol on cognitions related to aggressive responding, Sayette, Wilson & Elias (1993) randomly assigned 40 male university students aged 21–30 to one of four experimental conditions (control, placebo, low alcohol (0.45 g/kg) and high alcohol (0.85 g/kg)) and showed them a videotape of a person behaving in a way that would provoke an angry reaction from another person. Subjects were then asked to suggest how the second person should respond and to predict how the provoker would react to this response. The video then showed the provoker as uncompromising, and subjects were asked how they would respond at this point. Results indicated that those in the high-alcohol condition were less able to generate non-aggressive solutions to the initial provocation, less likely to select non-aggressive solutions (when given a choice of solutions) and more likely to respond aggressively when the hypothetical provoker did not back down.

In sum, a large theoretical literature supported by some important empirical research suggests that the effects of alcohol on cognitive functioning may increase the likelihood of alcohol-related violence. Although there appears to be no *direct* empirical evidence regarding impaired cognitive functioning from alcohol on decision-making regarding driving while intoxicated, it seems likely that impaired problem solving due to alcohol will make people less able to (a) assess their ability to drive, (b) evaluate the potential risks of driving while intoxicated, and (c) problem solve in order to find alternative forms of transportation.

Attentional and Emotional Effects of Alcohol

In a recent study in which the relevance of different alcohol effects was assessed for incidents of naturally occurring aggression in bars frequented by young people (Graham et al., 2000), the effect of alcohol most frequently implicated as contributing to naturally occurring incidents was "being focused on the present" (i.e. increased value of present rewards and reduced subjective penalty of future consequences) (rated as contributing to 84% of incidents). This was followed by reduced anxiety or fear regarding social or physical sanctions or danger (73% of incidents), heightened emotionality or emotional lability (71%) and increased psychomotor stimulation (69%). In sum, although impaired problem solving and other strictly cognitive functions were implicated in over 60% of incidents, emotional/attentional factors played a role in a larger proportion of incidents. This is consistent with suggestions by Washburne (1956) and Pernanen (1976) that alcohol leads people to focus on the present, and the argument by Steele & Josephs (1990) that alcohol-related aggression is a result of alcohol-induced "myopia" (i.e. a short-sighted focus on the immediate situation), including reduced awareness of or access to inhibiting cues. Unplanned robbery committed by groups of individuals drinking together has also been linked to being carried away with the immediate situation and focusing on short-term situational rewards, rather than long-term negative consequences (Cordilia, 1986).

Studies of marital conflict have also suggested that alcohol affects the cognitive–emotional interaction process between couples (see review by Leonard, 1993). In particular, experimental studies of couple interactions have found that alcohol increases negative interactions and increases problem-solving attempts by the husband (Leonard & Roberts, 1998). The increased problem-solving attempts in this context might actually be a negative effect, given alcohol's deleterious effects on problem-solving *ability*.

Effects of Alcohol on Power Concerns

Issues of power and dominance have been linked to male violence generally (Archer, 1994). With regard to the role of alcohol, it has been proposed that alcohol increases the likelihood of aggression by increasing power concerns among some males (McClelland et al., 1972). Results from several recent observational studies are consistent with this hypothesis. Specifically, observational studies of young males in public drinking settings suggest that much aggression involves "macho" posturing and male honor (Oliver, 1993; Tomsen, 1997). It may also be that increased power concerns interact with impaired cognitive functioning.

For example, alcohol-impaired cognitive appraisal may lead to an inappropriate sense of mastery, control or power (Gibbs, 1986; Pernanen, 1976). Alternatively, alcohol's "ego-enhancing" effects (see Steele & Josephs, 1990) may exacerbate conflict relating to power concerns. While an increase in power concerns is implicated as one *effect of alcohol* associated with increased likelihood of aggression, there is also some evidence linking power and "macho" concerns as a *personality* trait to drinking and criminal behavior (see subsequent section on personal characteristics that moderate the relationship between alcohol and aggression).

Amount of Alcohol Consumed—the Role of Intoxication

How much people drink will partially determine the effects of alcohol. For example, experimental studies of the effects of alcohol on aggression suggest that higher doses of alcohol (BAL of 0.80 or higher) increase aggression more than lower doses (see review by Graham et al., 1996). Accordingly, a number of studies have found that aggression, drinking–driving and other alcohol-related problems are associated with a pattern of drinking involving high quantities or greater intoxication on drinking occasions. With regard to crime generally, Harrison & Gfroerer (1992) found that getting drunk monthly was significantly related to self-reported criminal behavior, even after controlling for other variables such as age, race, income, education and marital status.

A number of studies of aggression and violence have related this behavior to regularly drinking to intoxication. Midanik et al. (1996) used data from a large national health survey in the USA to derive risk curves for three types of alcohol-related problems, including drunk-driving. They found that the risk for all problems at lower and moderate levels of drinking was significantly higher for respondents who reported having consumed five or more drinks when drinking. Among those who consumed five or more drinks in a day at least once a week, the probability of drinking–driving was 0.50. The authors argue that when considering risks for alcohol-related problems, such as drinking–driving, both overall volume of drinking and quantity per occasion need to be taken into account. Results of other surveys support this point. Kantor & Straus (1987) found that husband-to-wife violence was highest among husbands who were binge drinkers, followed by those defined as "high" drinkers (three or four times a week up to daily; three or more drinks a day). Studies in the USA (Dawson, 1997) and Norway (Rossow, 1996) have found that alcohol-related violence is significantly associated with both overall volume of alcohol consumption *and* the proportion of drinking days resulting in intoxication, controlling for demographic variables.

High-quantity drinking has been clearly associated with drinking and driving. Liu et al. (1997) found that driving after having "had perhaps too much to drink" during the past month was 30 times more likely among survey respondents who consumed five or more drinks in a day at least once during the previous month. Similarly, Foss & Perrine (1993) found that drivers who had been stopped at roadside sobriety checkpoints and had a BAC above 50 mg/dl reported typically consuming a larger number of drinks at one sitting and more frequent intoxication than other drivers. Vingilis et al. (1994) studied hospital admissions to a large trauma unit in Ontario, Canada and found that crash-involved drivers who had positive BAC readings reported a lower age for first intoxication and more frequent intoxication. Lee et al. (1997) found that among teenage males and females, the risk of self-reported impaired driving rose significantly with the frequency of binge drinking.

Type of Beverage Consumed

A number of studies have found that aggression is more likely after distilled rather than brewed beverage alcohol (Boyatzis, 1974; Pihl, Smith & Farrell, 1984). In his analysis of the relationship of consumption of spirits, beer and wine with homicide and assault rates in Sweden over the period 1956–1994, Norström (1998) found that assaults were linked to consumption of beer and spirits in bars and restaurants and homicide was linked to consumption of spirits in private locations. In his review of behavioral and social consequences of different beverage types, Smart (1996) concluded that problems were more likely to be associated with consumption of spirits and beer vs. wine. Although it is well-known that people have different expectations regarding behavior following consumption of beer vs. spirits vs. wine (Hennessy & Saltz, 1990; Klein & Pittman, 1990), it is not known whether expectation alone accounts for beverage-specific associations with criminal behavior, or whether the differences can be explained by other aspects of beverage type, such as higher blood alcohol concentrations with spirits (Smart, 1996). A recent study relating consumption patterns and assault within geographic areas (Stockwell et al., 1998) concluded that relative price per alcohol content may be a more important factor than beverage type *per se*. As an alternative explanation for beverage differences in rates of drinking-driving, Gruenewald et al. (2000) concluded from their survey of over 5,000 drinkers that drinking-driving was associated with beer drinking in the US because of the particular circumstances (e.g., drinking in a bar) in which beer drinkers frequently drank.

Characteristics of People who Become Aggressive, Drive while Impaired or Engage in Other Criminal Behavior when They Drink

The relationship between alcohol and crime is highly variable, depending on a number of factors, including the characteristics of the drinker. It is well known that some people frequently become aggressive when they drink, while others never become aggressive. While socialization probably plays a role, the results of animal research suggest that an aggressive response to alcohol may also be biological. Miczek et al. (in press) found that only a subsample of mice reliably respond aggressively when given alcohol. Although research on mice found that the tendency to become aggressive under the influence of alcohol was unrelated to non-drinking aggressiveness of the mice, research on human subjects suggests that those characteristics that generally predispose a person to aggression or crime (e.g. aggressive personality, deviant attitudes) also predispose the person to alcohol-related aggression and crime, and that these characteristics may even potentiate the effects of alcohol. For example, Zhang, Wieczorek & Welte (1997) found that heavier drinking was more strongly related to assault for those who showed more deviant attitudes. In addition, certain people may be more likely to engage in alcohol-related crime because they are predisposed both to drink heavily *and* to engage in criminal behavior (Bohman, 1995). The following describes the person characteristics that have been found to be associated with alcohol-related aggressive or criminal behavior and explores some possible explanations for these associations.

Demographic Predictors

Demographic variables such as gender, age and marital status have been associated with alcohol-related crimes. In terms of gender, although some studies of violence between intimates have found women to be as aggressive as men (McLaughlin, Leonard & Senchak, 1992; Straus & Gelles, 1990; White & Koss, 1991), it is very clear that most crimes, including alcohol-related crimes of violence and drinking–driving, are committed by men (see reviews by Fagan, 1990; Macdonald & Mann, 1996). Gruenewald, Mitchell & Treno (1996) have argued that the predictive power of many demographic and other characteristics of drinking drivers disappears when drinking patterns are taken into account. However, recent analyses of survey responses suggested that the higher rate of alcohol-related consequences (measured using a composite score, including family, work and health problems) among men cannot be accounted for entirely by higher rates of alcohol consumption (Bongers et al., 1998; Kunz & Graham, 1998). Thus, although men drink more than women, this higher rate of consumption does not necessarily account for the higher rate of alcohol-related social problems among men. Consistent with this conclusion, Bushman's (1997) meta-analysis of the literature on alcohol-related aggression found a much larger effect of alcohol on aggression for men than for women. In a recent study, Giancola & Zeichner (1995) found that male aggressive behavior in an experimental setting could be predicted by aggressive personality, subjective intoxication and BAC, but none of these factors predicted the aggressive behavior of women. Moreover, they found that women generally behaved less aggressively than the men in the study. Similarly, in their analyses of a US national survey database, Robbins & Martin (1993) found that women were less likely than men to become intoxicated, and when they did were less likely to experience problems related to uncontrolled behavior, such as aggression. Pernanen (1998) reported that his study of alcohol-related violence in a Canadian city found that women were somewhat more likely than men to become angry in drinking situations, but that men were much more likely to become violent when they became angry while drinking.

Age has also been consistently related to crime generally (Beck et al., 1993; Fedorowycz, 1996; Johnson, 1996), to marital violence (Straus, Gelles & Steinmetz, 1980; Suitor, Pillemer & Straus, 1990) and alcohol-related crimes specifically (Wallace & Travis, 1994). Victimization surveys indicate that the youngest age group (24 and under) report the highest rates of violence victimization (Johnson, 1996; Rossow, 1996), with rates reported by those aged 15–24 years five times higher than those aged 45 and older (Johnson, 1996). Age is also associated with drinking–driving. Liu et al. (1997) found that drinking–driving was most frequent among persons aged 21–34 years. According to L.A. Greenfield (1998), Driving Under the Influence (DUI) arrestees are over-represented among licensed drivers aged 18–44.

Being unmarried has also been found to be associated with being involved in aggressive incidents (Pernanen, 1991). Johnson (1996) found that single people in Canada reported rates of violent victimization that were almost four times the rate for married persons.

In sum, although a wide range of people behave aggressively or drive after drinking, one demographic subgroup, namely young, single males, is disproportionately involved in alcohol-related violence and drinking–driving, and in criminal behavior generally. The importance of this population subgroup has been described not only in reviews of alcohol-related violence (Collins & Messerschmidt, 1993) and drinking–driving (Lang & Stockwell, 1991; Macdonald & Mann, 1996), but also in anthropological studies of intoxicated behavior (Marshall, 1979).

Males and Deviant Behavior

Roebuck & Murty (1996) used a general deviance model related to a "macho" world view to explain drinking–driving, especially by repeat offenders. They categorized 2786 persons convicted of DUI (i.e. that alcohol made them incapable of safe driving, as determined by the arresting officer's field test or a BAC of 0.12) in the State of Georgia, USA, into four groups in terms of recidivism and involvement in other offenses, and found that most offenders had other alcohol-related charges, other driving charges or other criminal offenses. To better understand the frame of reference for DUI among offenders, they conducted a qualitative study of a subsample of 311 white male offenders, of whom all but 22 were recidivists. Common among all three recidivist groups, but not first-time offenders, was a "macho" world view that included routine drinking and violence:

> To them manhood was based on the legitimacy of violence, domination, and independence. They also insisted on the privilege of getting completely drunk at certain time intervals and conceived of heavy drinking as a masculine trait tied in with virility, toughness, courage, and violence in settling disputes (Roebuck & Murty, 1996, p. 115).

For this group of southern White males, this macho view appeared to be related to working- or lower-class views and resentment of those seen as more privileged. Similar acceptance of alcohol-related violence was evident among young working-class male bar patrons in Sydney, Australia (Tomsen, 1997) and male drinkers in the UK (Marsh & Kibby, 1992). It should also be noted that, although Roebuck & Murty provided a sociological description of deviance relevant to alcohol-related crime, it has also been hypothesized that biological factors such as testosterone and serotonin levels may also contribute to some forms of male deviant behavior (see Archer, 1994).

General Deviance Explanations

Violence and drinking–driving, especially among adolescents and young adults, have also been explained using a *general* deviance model (i.e. not specific to males or "macho" views). In this model, the relationship between alcohol and problem behavior is explained primarily by the actions of a population subsample, for whom drinking-related deviance or criminal behavior is part of a general propensity to be less controlled by societal conventions. In support of this premise, longitudinal research indicates that childhood aggression is linked to later alcohol use by adolescents (White, 1997). Similarly, a number of studies have found that childhood hyperactivity and aggression have been linked to *both* subsequent alcohol problems and adult aggression (Klinteberg et al., 1993; Pulkkinen & Pitkänen, 1993). Based on these findings, White (1997) postulated that alcohol and aggression among adolescents is linked through common causes and described the overlap in predictors of both alcohol use/misuse and aggression. These include childhood hyperactivity, impulsivity, poor parenting, problems at school, familial criminal behavior and other characteristics associated with deviance. These predictors are similar to characteristics associated with drinking–driving (Donovan, 1993; Karlsson & Romelsjö, 1997; Roebuck & Murty, 1996). Other analyses by Osgood et al. (1988) confirmed that a general deviance explanation was able to account for interrelationships among criminal behavior, dangerous driving, heavy alcohol use and use of marijuana and other drugs among adolescents.

Both the male deviance model proposed by Roebuck & Murty (1996) and the general deviance model argued by White (1997) are common-cause models—that is, that heavy and problem drinking and criminal behavior are linked because the same factors lead to both. However, it is also possible that this link is reinforced by certain groups being more vulnerable to the effects of alcohol that increase the probability of aggression and crime. Zhang et al. (1997) used data from the Buffalo (USA) Longitudinal Survey of Young Men to test the *moderating role of alcohol use* on four predictors of aggravated assault among males aged 16–19. These predictors were: deviant attitudes, aggression and hostility, impulsivity, and problem-solving abilities. Although deviant attitudes and aggression and hostility were very strong predictors of the prevalence of assault in the predictive model prior to adding interaction terms, these two main effects became non-significant when interactive terms were added. Further analyses revealed that the relationship between deviant attitudes and prevalence of assault was significantly greater for high alcohol consumers compared to low consumers. The same significant interaction effect with alcohol consumption was found for aggression/hostility. Impulsivity showed a significant main effect (the interaction of impulsivity with alcohol consumption was not significant), but problem-solving abilities were unrelated to prevalence of assault (both as a main effect and as part of an interaction term). Alcohol consumption (as measured by an index combining frequency and quantity of alcohol use in the past year) did not contribute significantly to predicting assault, once the interaction terms were in the model. These results support the argument that alcohol is linked to violent crime through an interaction effect of alcohol with a predisposition to deviance or aggression.

Finally, analyses by Lastovicka (1988) suggested that there may be two different risk groups for drinking–driving and perhaps other alcohol-related problems and crimes. He identified a "problem behavior" group in his sample of 18–24 year-old males, which would correspond to the deviance group; however, he also identified a group of "good-timers" who scored high on partying, sensation seeking and machoism factors. The "good-timers" actually had the highest incidence of drinking–driving, higher than the deviant group. It may well be that the macho deviant group identified by Roebuck & Murty (1996) reflected their sample of recidivist drinking–drivers, while first-time drinking–drivers among young people and much of the problem behavior of young males in bars documented by Tomsen (1997) and Marsh and Kibby (1992) are more reflective of the "good-timers" risk group.

Power Concerns

As noted in a previous section, one effect of alcohol may be to increase power concerns in some individuals. However, it has also been proposed that people who have greater concern with personal power or greater feelings of powerlessness may be more likely to drink heavily (McClelland et al., 1972; Scoufis & Walker, 1982) and more likely to become aggressive when they drink. As summarized by Boyatzis (1976, p. 279):

> It appears that the arousal of power concerns in the individual, either through culture-wide concerns, his place in the social structure, or social demands for demonstrating his importance or prowess, causes the person to seek outlets which make him feel more powerful.

Boyatzis also cited a 1973 conference paper by Pelz & Schuman, which found that drinking was related to reckless driving among young men who felt hostile or alienated/powerless, but not among males who did not have these feelings. These findings are consistent with those of Roebuck & Murty that the "macho" world view that was part of deviant behavior among American southern males includes considerable resentment toward those seen as more privileged. Other studies have noted high rates of alcohol-related aggression among marginalized subpopulations who have less access than mainstream groups to societal rewards, such as prestige and material success (Graham et al., 1980; Fagan, 1990; Levinson, 1983; Pernanen, 1991), suggesting further support for the hypothesis that powerlessness and alcohol-related crime may be inter-related. Recent findings by Parker & Rehbun (1995), demonstrating that high alcohol consumption enhances the impact of poverty on homicide, and by Karlsson and Romelsjö (1997), who found a relationship between lower social class and drinking–driving, are also consistent with the hypothesis that power concerns, especially feelings of powerlessness, may moderate the relationship between alcohol and criminal behavior, with the relationship between drinking and crime more pronounced among subpopulations who are higher on power concerns, either because of lower status in society or because of subcultural values such as "machoism".

Attitudes and Expectations

Attitudes and expectations appear to be important factors in predicting whether someone will drink–drive or behave aggressively after drinking. In a study of male college students, Dermen & George (1989) found that average weekly consumption of alcohol was more strongly related to frequency of physical aggression for those who expected alcohol to increase aggression than for those who expected no effect or a decrease. Similarly, Leonard & Senchak (1993) found that heavy drinking was associated with higher premarital aggression only for those who expected alcohol to facilitate aggression. In an experimental study of alcohol and aggression, Chermack & Taylor (1995) found that the highest shocks were set by those who both had a high dose of alcohol and expected that alcohol would increase aggression.

Attitudes may play a particularly important role in violence against women by men. In her analysis of the literature linking alcohol consumption and acquaintance rape, Abbey (1991) identified a number of attitudinal variables that might be implicated in this form of male violence against women, including expectancies about the effects of alcohol on sexuality, the belief that intoxication can serve as an excuse, and the stereotype that women who consume alcohol are inviting sex. Kantor & Straus (1987) found that alcohol consumption was much more strongly associated with husband-to-wife violence among husbands who approved of violence than among those who did not approve. Findings by Leonard & Senchak (1993), however, suggest that the husband's personality may also play a role in the association between drinking, violence and attitudes. In particular, among very hostile men, drinking and violence were associated regardless of their beliefs about the effects of alcohol, while for men low on hostility, the relationship between the man's drinking and violence against the wife was greater if the man believed that drinking is an excuse for violence.

With regard to expectancies and drinking–driving, Foss & Perrine (1993) found that drivers identified at checkpoints as having blood alcohol levels higher than 50 mg/dl were more likely than other drivers to believe that driving was not affected by alcohol and that they could drink large quantities of beer and still drive safely. Similarly, Lee et al. (1997) found a positive relationship between whether teenagers reported drinking–driving and their estimates of the number of drinks required to impair their driving.

Situational Factors that May Increase the Probability of Alcohol-related Crime

Geographical analyses have been conducted to identify the association between crime and alcohol consumption, alcohol availability and specific types of alcohol outlets. Primarily studies have focused on alcohol outlet density showing relationships with drinking–driving, traffic crashes and violence (see Scribner et al., 1999). These results provide further support for the alcohol–crime link; however, they may also implicate specific situational aspects related to the social interaction occurring at alcohol outlets. For example, alcohol and crime may be linked because of certain routine activities common to drinking settings—that is, activities or situations that increase opportunities for crime, decrease control over behavior or increase the availability of potential targets (see discussions by Fagan, 1993; Miethe & Meier, 1994; as well as research on licensed premises as "hot spots" for crime by Roncek & Maier, 1991). A recent analysis conducted in Australia attempted to tease apart the separate effects of alcohol consumption *per se* vs. density of retail outlets (Stevenson, Lind & Weatherburn, 1999). Their analysis confirmed the association between alcohol consumption and assault (controlling for potential confounders across geographic areas such as poverty and the proportion of males and aboriginals in the population) but provided mixed evidence regarding the additional contribution of outlet density and type of outlet (once overall alcohol consumption was controlled for). Outlet density was associated with assault in the urban area of Sydney but not in the country area of New South Wales. Outlet type contributed to explaining assault in both geographic areas, with assaults associated with alcohol outlets at hotels, restaurants and off-licenses in Sydney but with hotel and off-licenses in country New South Wales. These results suggest some situational contribution of liquor outlets (both on and off the premises) *per se* to assault. This is consistent with other literature on licensed premises as high-risk drinking locations (see subsequent section).

Although situational factors associated with drinking may independently lead to crimes such as violence, both aggressive behavior and drinking–driving are likely to involve an interaction of the characteristics of the person, the characteristics of the situation and the effects of alcohol. One model suggests that situational factors *moderate* the relationship between alcohol and aggression (see review by Chermack & Giancola, 1997). To explore the moderating role of situational factors on the alcohol–aggression relationship, Ito, Miller & Pollock (1996) conducted a meta-analysis of 49 experimental studies of the effects of alcohol on aggression. They found that the effects of alcohol on aggressive behavior were greater in situations rated high on anxiety, inhibition conflict and frustration, while differences between sober and intoxicated aggressive behavior were less in situations where there was high provocation and self-focused attention. Similarly, a number of experimental studies have demonstrated that although alcohol consumption tends to increase aggressive behavior, this increase can be reduced or eliminated in experimental settings when the situation involves a lack of provocation (see Gustafson, 1993), third party intervention (Taylor & Gammon, 1976), provision of an explicit non-aggressive norm (Jeavons & Taylor, 1985) or monetary incentives not to aggress (Hoaken, Assad & Pihl, 1998).

Four general aspects of drinking situations have been related to aggression, drinking–driving or other crime. These include: (a) drinking situations with high social involvement; (b) the presence of other intoxicated persons; (c) the nature of social control and social influences; and (d) drinking in licensed premises, especially certain kinds of licensed premises.

Drinking Situations with High Social Involvement

The social setting *per se* may contribute to both the perceived effects of alcohol (Pliner & Cappell, 1974) and moral reasoning relevant to drinking–driving and violent or aggressive behavior. Denton & Krebs (1990) found that people scored lower on moral reasoning when tested while drinking in a natural social drinking setting, compared to scores when tested after a similar amount of alcohol in a university laboratory. This finding applied especially to those who consumed higher amounts of alcohol in the two settings. The greater effect of alcohol on moral reasoning in real social drinking situations suggests that cognitive impairment from alcohol is potentiated when the drinker is involved in social interaction. Thus, although a decrement in moral reasoning is not a necessary outcome of consuming alcohol (Graham, Turnbull & LaRocque, 1979), this decrement apparently does occur when people are drinking in natural drinking settings. Moreover, Denton & Krebs found that drinking in natural settings also leads to impaired moral *behavior* in the form of drinking–driving. Subjects were asked at the time of the interview additional questions on whether one *should* drive after drinking and whether they *would* actually drive. Despite being informed about their blood alcohol level and being cautioned not to drive, and despite consistent agreement by subjects that they *should not* drive after drinking, follow-up interviews with subjects indicated that all but one of the 26 who drove to the drinking location did drive home, including 12 who had been legally impaired at the time of testing.

The Presence of Other Intoxicated Persons

An important and often neglected variable in studies of alcohol-related violence and drinking–driving is the role of *other intoxicated* persons besides the aggressor or the drinking driver. For example, alcohol-related violent crimes often involve the victim drinking as well as the perpetrator, and the person who ends up being the "victim" is sometimes the one who actually initiated the aggressive interaction (Murdoch et al., 1990). It is simple logic that, if alcohol intoxication makes a person more emotional, more likely to take risks, less able to problem solve, less aware of contingencies and more concerned with personal power (see previous section on the effects of alcohol), it is likely to be having similar effects on other intoxicated people in the drinking situation. Therefore, the risk of violence is increased, because not just one *but two or more individuals* have impaired abilities (due to alcohol) to access non-aggressive responses to any real or perceived provocation. Finally, aggression is probably best conceptualized as a *transactional* process involving a series of behaviors by more than one person, rather than a simple interaction of situation and individual factors leading to a single aggressive behavior (Fagan, 1993; Goldstein, 1994; Luckenbill, 1977). Thus, the other people in the drinking setting play a key role in both the occurrence and the seriousness of alcohol-related aggression or crimes, and alcohol intoxication is likely to affect the way people respond *to one another* (see arrows linking people in Figure 22.1). Pernanen (1976) provided a good example of the possible interaction of the effects of alcohol on power concerns among young males in the following comment:

> The greater proportion of people displaying power concerns and resulting attitudes and behavior, the smaller will be the probability of compliance with anyone's wishes (pp. 406–407).

Consistent with the premise that aggression arises out of the effects of alcohol on more than one person in the drinking situation, an experimental study in which pairs of male subjects set shocks for one another in a competitive reaction-time task (Leonard, 1984) found that escalation of aggression was greatest when *both* members of the pair had consumed alcohol. Similarly, studies in bars have consistently found that the greater the level of intoxication of patrons, the more frequent (Graham et al., 1980; Homel & Clark, 1994) and more severe the aggression (Graves et al., 1981). Finally, Cordilia (1986) identified drinking *in groups* as a contributor to increased likelihood of criminal behavior.

The presence of other intoxicated persons also appears to play a role in drinking–driving. Vegega & Klitzner (1989) noted that young people who reported drinking–driving recognized that they themselves were impaired but drove because the others in their group were even more intoxicated! Similarly, Loxley et al. (1992) identified a group of "rescuers" (those who drove home although they had been driven to the drinking setting by someone else) and concluded that many of these individuals drove despite knowing that they had consumed too much alcohol, presumably because the person who drove them to the drinking location was unable to drive home. Thus, the level of intoxication of others in a drinking setting may have a significant impact, especially on unplanned driving after drinking.

Social Control and Social Influences

Social control and social influences in the drinking situation appear to play a large role in both aggression and drinking–driving. For example, a number of studies have found that bars with a lot of aggression tend to have permissive environments (e.g. unrestricted swearing, sexual activity, drug dealing, over-serving of alcohol), with the most violent bars characterized by an "anything goes" atmosphere (Graham et al., 1980; Homel & Clark, 1994) and a low staff to patron ratio (Homel & Clark, 1994). A recent qualitative study of the behavior of bar security staff (Wells et al., 1998) found that aggression often resulted from ineffectual social control, as well as overly aggressive behavior by the agents of social control (i.e. the bar staff). A major aspect of social control in bar settings is the level of intoxication of patrons that the bar will tolerate. Thus, drinking situations with highly intoxicated persons not only increases the risk of aggression arising from the effects of alcohol on more than one person (see previous section), but also signals to people in the situation that social controls generally are relaxed.

Social control in particular drinking situations also affects drinking–driving. Nelson et al. (1999) surveyed males aged 21–35 (oversampling heavy episodic drinking drivers) to identify factors that influence planning to avoid drinking driving. Their results indicated that having a wife or girlfriend with them on the drinking occasion greatly increased plans to avoid drinking–driving and was also associated with self-reported success at avoiding drinking–driving. Similarly, a descriptive study of youth who had driven while impaired indicated that social factors such as pressure to drive, the need to get home or to get a passenger home, and the lack of a more sober person to take the wheel, influenced their decision to drive after drinking (Vegega & Klitzner, 1989).

Drinking in Licensed Premises

At least in some cultures, licensed premises have been identified as generally high-risk drinking environments for both violence and drinking–driving (Homel, Tomsen & Thommeny, 1991; O'Donnell, 1985; Stockwell, Lang & Rydon, 1993). In a 1985 review of situations associated with drinking–driving, O'Donnell found that in 10 of 11 studies identifying drinking location prior to impaired driving, bars were the most frequently named location (bars were second most frequent in the eleventh study). Similarly, over half (57%) of DWI offenders in a study in New Mexico, USA, reported drinking in a bar prior to their arrest (Lapham et al., 1998). Drinking in bars has also been associated with impaired driving in Canada (Single & McKenzie, 1992) and alcohol-related accidents in Switzerland (Fahrenkrug & Rehm, 1995). In a study of alcohol involvement in incidents attended by the police in Sydney, Australia, Ireland & Thommeny (1993) found that 60% of alcohol-related offenses occurred in or near licensed premises.

Although bars are generally high-risk drinking locations for crime, there is also high variability among bars, suggesting that crime may be associated with certain attributes of bars, not just drinking in bars *per se*. In a study of assaults, drinking–driving charges and alcohol purchases related to a sample of bars in Perth, Australia, Stockwell, Somerford & Lang (1991) found a significant correlation between the rate of assaults and drinking–driving violations, even when the amount of alcohol purchased by the bar was controlled for; that is, a subsample of bars could be identified as high-risk for both aggression and drinking–driving (see also Stockwell, Somerford & Lang, 1992). As described in the following, a number of specific characteristics of the bar-room settings have been found to be associated with aggression and to some extent other crimes (see also reviews by Graham & Homel, 1997; Graham, Schmidt & Gillis, 1996).

Reputation and Expectations Regarding the Setting

Burns's (1980) ethnographic study, in which he accompanied a group of young men to several different bars over the course of an evening, is valuable in demonstrating that (a) bar patrons modify their behavior to suit the bar environment, and (b) patrons who are looking for trouble seek out particular environments. Thus, as might be expected, Homel & Clark (1994) found higher aggression in bars that had a reputation for violence. Lawrence & Leather (1997) studied expectations by showing subjects photos of bars and "bouncers" (door staff, security staff). They found that more aggression was expected if the bar was not well-maintained and if the bar used door security staff.

The Social Environment of the Bar

As described in the previous section, social control and the social context of drinking generally affect drinking behavior. In terms of the social environment of bars, the type of people who patronize the bar has been associated with both aggression and drinking–driving. Higher levels of aggressive behavior have been associated with bars frequented by skid row and aboriginal patrons (Graham et al., 1980; Homel & Clark, 1994) and by groups of males (Homel, Tomsen & Thommeny 1992), and with nightspots frequented by young people (Homel & Clark, 1994; Marsh & Kibby, 1992). A previous section identified young males as high risk for crime. The social context of young men drinking in *licensed premises*, in particular, has been repeatedly associated with crime (Burns, 1980; Graham, West & Wells, in press; Lang et al., 1995; Martin, Wyllie & Casswell, 1992; Tomsen, 1997). A household survey of alcohol-related harm in Australia linked young males, drinking in licensed premises, violence and drinking–driving. In this study, Stockwell et al. (1993) found that both violent incidents and drunk–driving were most common among *heavy-drinking young men who drank in licensed premises*. Other elements of the social environment associated with aggression include crowding and congestion (Graham, 1985; Homel & Clark, 1994; MacIntyre & Homel, 1997), pool playing, patrons milling about and bored patrons (see review by Graham & Homel, 1997).

Physical Environment

The physical environment may also play a role in bar-room aggression, not only in setting up expectations for behavior (Lawrence & Leather, 1997) but also by increasing levels of irritation or frustration. The following aspects of the physical environment have been associated with higher rates of aggression: irritants such as smoke and stuffiness (Graham et al., 1980) and aversive noise (Homel et al., 1992), care and maintenance of the bar (Graham et al., 1980; Homel & Clark, 1994) and poor layout, leading to crowding and bumping (MacIntyre & Homel, 1997).

Closing Time and the Wider Social Context of the Bar

Alcohol-related crime often occurs after midnight on weekend nights (Gerson & Preston, 1979; Pernanen, 1991) and appears to be associated with areas of a community where there is a high concentration of licensed premises and a large number of very intoxicated patrons leaving these bars at the same time (Homel et al., 1997; Marsh & Kibby, 1992; Tomsen, 1997).

The Effects of Cultural Framing on the Relationship between Alcohol and Crime

As shown in Figure 22.1, alcohol consumption occurs within the broad framing of cultural norms and expectations. Both crime rates and alcohol consumption patterns differ greatly across cultures. Moreover, the extent that drinking is associated with aggression or criminal behavior is also highly variable across cultures. Cross-cultural anthropological studies (Heath, 1975; MacAndrew & Edgerton, 1969) documented this variability and provided a number of insights regarding the alcohol–crime relationship. First, it is clear from these studies that there is no simple causal relationship between alcohol and crime. Not only was the relationship between alcohol and violent or criminal behavior highly variable, these studies found that there are some cultures in which aggressive or criminal behavior rarely or never occurs when people drink. Second, although aggressive and other unruly behaviors often do accompany drinking, these behaviors typically have boundaries (i.e. certain behaviors are considered so heinous that people do not engage in them, drunk or sober) and are often highly scripted or stylized. For example, drunken violence may involve only young men fighting with each other (while no violence occurs among other drinkers). In some cultures, men drink and beat their wives but are rarely violent to anyone other than their wives. Thus, while alcohol intoxication involves changes in mood and thinking often associated with aggression and crime, the culture exerts considerable control over both the form and nature of drunken behavior.

An excellent example of the powerful role of cultural framing on drinking-related crime is the dramatic decrease in acceptability of drinking–driving in many countries and the corresponding decrease in the rate of drinking–driving. A behavior that was once considered to be a fairly normative outcome of drinking has now become deviant. The evidence regarding the importance of cultural framing on drinking–driving is derived mainly from intervention studies. For example, one way that cultures indicate that drinking–driving will not be tolerated is by setting clear laws regarding drinking–driving and by active enforcement of such laws. This approach has generally been effective, especially if enforcement is sufficiently visible to increase perception that drinking drivers will be caught (see McKnight & Voas, Chapter 38). Educational efforts regarding drinking–driving are also geared to changing drinking–driving behavior by changing the cultural context. Messages such as "friends don't let friends drive drunk" specifically target the culture of drinking, by making drinking–driving a concern of the group, not just the individual. In general, educational interventions have typically not demonstrated an impact on behavior (with some possible exceptions—see Chapter 38); however, it may be that cultural attitude changes brought about by educational interventions are a necessary precondition to policy or structural changes that do produce an impact (Graham & Chandler Coutts, 2000; Room, 1998). Regardless of the mechanism, the dramatic decrease in drinking–driving in some countries provides a classic case study of the power of cultural framing to affect alcohol-related criminal behavior.

Attitudes and Expectations Regarding Alcohol and Crime

Recent research on the variability of cultural framing for drinking behavior has focused primarily on attitudes and expectations within the general population. The earlier anthropological literature suggested that two aspects of cultural understanding of alcohol-related behavior affected the probability of violence and other excesses: culturally defined "time out" and "deviance disavowal". MacAndrew & Edgerton (1969) argued that drinkers are more likely to be unrestrained in their behavior if drinking is generally seen by the culture as "time out" from usual expectations for comportment. "Deviance disavowal" involves the related but separate notion that the culture not only accepts that an individual is likely to behave in a deviant manner while drinking but that the individual may also disclaim personal responsibility for the behavior by attributing the blame to alcohol (McCaghy, 1968).

Studies of attitudes and expectations regarding violence have examined: (a) whether people expect drinking to result in aggression; (b) whether people believe that alcohol contributes to this behavior in a causal way; and (c) whether alcohol can mitigate blame for violence or other crimes committed while drinking. Regarding expectations about drinking behavior, it is apparent that people in North America and elsewhere *believe* that aggression is one effect of alcohol consumption (Leigh, 1989; Lindman & Lang, 1994; Roizen, 1983). In fact, alcohol and drug use is one of the most frequently mentioned perceived causes of crime in general population surveys (see Kidder & Cohn, 1979). At the same time, cross-cultural studies (Lindman & Lang, 1994) and research on factors that affect expectations (such as type of beverage and gender of drinker) (Crawford, 1984; Leigh, 1987) have found high variability in expectations regarding the effects of alcohol on behavior.

Although people may see alcohol use as causally related to aggression and crime, this does not necessarily mean that being intoxicated is accepted as an "excuse" for violent or criminal behavior. In fact, most studies of attitudes regarding alcohol as an excuse for aggressive or criminal behavior indicate that people do *not* consider intoxication to be an excuse (Aramburu & Leigh, 1991; Dent & Arias, 1990). On the other hand, despite general population attitudes that appear to reject alcohol as an excuse for criminal behavior, it is clear that many legal systems *do* consider intoxication to be a mitigating factor in the ability to form intent, and intoxication may be taken into consideration in sentencing (Fischer & Rehm, 1996; Mosher, 1983; Shain & Higgins, 1997). Thus, the legal response to alcohol-related crime demonstrates at least some increased tolerance for some kinds of crime if alcohol is involved.

Laws relating to drinking–driving are the exception to the general legal assumption of alcohol as a mitigating factor. In most countries, a hard line has been taken with regard to drinking–driving, and lack of ability to form intent due to intoxication is simply not a factor. Interestingly, this legal position has been extremely successful, not only in changing drinking–driving behavior but also in reinforcing attitude change. Homel, Carseldine & Kearns (1988) documented attitude change in the 5 years following the implementation of random breath testing in New South Wales. They identified increasingly negative attitudes toward drinking–driving and extremely positive views on interventions such as random breath testing. In fact, the proportion who reported that they thought random breath testing should continue went from 64% in 1982 to 97% in 1987. Loxley et al. (1992) compared attitudes of young people in New South Wales (where random breath testing had been implemented) to young people in Western Australia (where this intervention had not been implemented and which had a higher rate of alcohol-related crashes or injuries). They found that young people in New South Wales were more likely that those in Western Australia to use strategies to avoid drinking–driving (e.g. planning for a sober driver on drinking occasions), believe that others used strategies to avoid drinking–driving, and believe that friends would disapprove of drinking–driving.

In sum, it is clear that while alcohol intoxication is an important factor in violent and other crimes and probably plays a role in decisions regarding drinking–driving, and while personality characteristics are also a major factor in the commission of alcohol-related crimes, and while the situation in which drinking occurs is also an important determinant of crime; nevertheless, cultural framing in the form of attitudes, policies and laws can make a measurable difference in the level of alcohol-related criminal behavior. Drinking–driving interventions have been most successful in changing cultural framing. It appears that the impact of these interventions involves a combination of factors, including perceived risks of getting caught, perceptions of acceptability of specific crimes and, and to some extent, identification of alternatives to the behavior to be avoided (e.g. considering driving plans *prior* to the drinking occasion). No similar interventions relating to alcohol-related violent crime or crime generally have been implemented. It would be interesting to explore whether a similar reduction in alcohol-related violence could be brought about by applying the principles identified in drinking–driving interventions.

KEY WORKS AND SUGGESTIONS FOR FURTHER READING

The following provide suggestions for general reading on the topic of alcohol and crime, alcohol and aggression or violence and factors associated with drinking–driving. For papers on specific issues, see references cited in the text.

The Role of Alcohol in Crime

Statistics cited within this review were based on major national studies while smaller local or regional studies were not included. Murdoch, Phil & Ross (1990) (see References) is the best comprehensive review published to date covering a range of studies from a number of different countries. In addition, the following papers provide statistics on alcohol involvement in crime based on smaller studies from a variety of countries:

Fendrich, M., Mackesy-Amiti, M.E., Goldstein, P., Spunt, B. & Brownstein, H. (1995). Substance involvement among juvenile murderers: comparisons with older offenders based on interviews with prison inmates. *International Journal of the Addictions*, **30**, 1363–1382.

Gerson, L.W. (1978). Alcohol-related acts of violence: who was drinking and where the acts occurred. *Journal of Studies on Alcohol*, **39**, 1294–1296.

Martin, J., Nada-Raja, S., Langley, J., Feehan, M., McGee, R., Clarke, J. et al. (1998). Physical assault in New Zealand: the experience of 21 year-old men and women in a community sample. *New Zealand Medical Journal*, **111**, 158–160.

Myers, T. (1982). Alcohol and violent crime re-examined: self-reports from two subgroups of Scottish male prisoners. *British Journal of Addiction*, **77**, 399–413.

Nunes-Dinis, M.C. & Weisner, C. (1997). Gender differences in the relationship of alcohol and drug use to criminal behavior in a sample of arrestees. *American Journal of Drug and Alcohol Abuse*, **23**, 129–141.

Roslund, B. & Larson, C.A. (1979). Crimes of violence and alcohol abuse in Sweden. *International Journal of the Addictions*, **14**, 1103–1115.

Spunt, B., Brownstein, H.H., Crimmins, S.M., Langley, S. & Spanjol, K. (1998). Alcohol-related homicides committed by women. *Journal of Psychoactive Drugs*, **30**, 33–43.

Alcohol and Aggression or Violence

The following edited books, special journal issues and review papers provide a broad coverage of the literature on alcohol and aggression/violence:

Galanter, M. (Ed.) (1997). *Recent Developments in Alcoholism, Vol. 13, Alcohol and Violence*. New York: Plenum.

Martin, S.E. (Ed.) (1993). *Alcohol and Interpersonal Violence: Fostering Multidisciplinary Perspectives*, Rockville, MD: NIH.

Alcohol Health and Research World, **17**(2) (entire issue), 1993.

Contemporary Drug Problems, **24**(4) (entire issue), Winter 1997.

Journal of Studies on Alcohol, **11** (Suppl.) (entire issue), 1993.

Bushman, B.J. & Cooper, H.M. (1990). Effects of alcohol on human aggression: an integrative research review. *Psychological Bulletin*, **107**, 341–354.

Graham, K., Leonard, K.E., Room, R., Wild, T.C., Pihl, R.O., Bois, C. & Single, E. (1998). Current directions in research in understanding and preventing intoxicated aggression. *Addiction*, **93**, 659–676.

Graham, K., Schmidt, G. & Gillis, K. (1996). Circumstances when drinking leads to aggression: an overview of research findings. *Contemporary Drug Problems*, **23**, 493–557.

Pernanen, K. (1976). Alcohol and crimes of violence. In B. Kissin & H. Begleiter (Eds), *The Biology of Alcoholism* (pp. 351–444). New York: Plenum.

Pernanen, K. (1991). *Alcohol in Human Violence*. New York: Guilford.

Drinking and Driving

The following papers provide significant coverage of factors associated with drinking–driving:

Donovan, J.E. (1993). Young adult drinking–driving: behavioral and psychosocial correlates. *Journal of Studies on Alcohol*, **54**, 600–613.

Foss, R.D. & Perrine, M.W.B. (1993). Predictors of Impaired Driving. In H.D. Utzelmann, G. Berghaus & G. Kroj (Eds), *Alcohol, Drugs and Traffic Safety*, Vol. 2 (pp. 1139–1144). Cologue: Rheinland GmbH, Verlag TUV.

Macdonald, S. & Mann, R. (1996). Distinguishing causes and correlates of drinking and driving. *Contemporary Drug Problems*, **23**, 259–290.

Vingilis, E.R. & Mann, R.E. (1986). Towards an interactionist approach to drinking–driving behaviour: implications for prevention and research. *Health Education Research*, **1**, 273–288.

REFERENCES

Abbey, A. (1991). Acquaintance rape and alcohol consumption on college campuses: how are they linked? *Journal of American College Health*, **39**, 165–169.

Aramburu, B. & Leigh, B. (1991). For better or worse: attributions about drunken aggression toward male and female victims. *Violence and Victims*, **6**, 31–41.

Archer, J. (1994). Power and male violence. In J. Archer (Ed.), *Male Violence* (pp. 310–331). London: Routledge.

Beck, A., Gilliard, D., Greenfield, L., Harlow, C., Hester, T., Jankowski, L., Snell, T., Stephan, J. & Morton, D. (1993). *Survey of State Prison Inmates, 1991*. (Bureau of Justice Statistics, Special Report, March 1993, NCJ-136949). Washington, DC: US Department of Justice.

Bohman, M. (1995). Predisposition to criminality: Swedish adoption studies in retrospect. *Genetics of Criminal and Antisocial Behaviour, CIBA Foundation Symposium*, Vol. **194** (pp. 99–114). Chichester: Wiley.

Bond, A.J., Lader, M.H. & da Silveira, J.C.C. (1997). *Aggression. Individual Differences, Alcohol and Benzodiazepines*. Hove: Psychology Press.

Bongers, I.M.B., Van de Goor, L.A.M., Van Oers, J.A.M. & Garretsen, H.F.L. (1998). Gender differences in alcohol-related problems: controlling for drinking behaviour. *Addiction*, **93**, 411–421.

Borges, G., Cherpitel, C.J. & Rosovsky, H. (1998). Male drinking and violence-related injury in the emergency room. *Addiction*, **93**, 103–112.

Boyatzis, R.E. (1974). The effect of alcohol consumption on the aggressive behavior of men. *Quarterly Journal of Studies on Alcohol*, **35**, 959–972.

Boyatzis, R. (1976). Drinking as a manifestation of power concerns. In M.W. Everett, J.O. Waddell & D.B. Heath (Eds), *Cross-cultural Approaches to the Study of Alcohol: an Interdisciplinary Perspective* (pp. 265–285). Chicago: Aldine.

Burns, T.F. (1980). Getting rowdy with the boys. *Journal of Drug Issues*, **10**(2), 273–286.

Bushman, B.J. (1997). Effects of alcohol on human aggression: validity of proposed mechanisms. In M. Galanter (Ed.), *Recent Developments in Alcoholism. Vol. 13, Alcohol and Violence* (pp. 227–244). New York: Plenum.

Bushman, B.J. & Cooper, H.M. (1990). Effects of alcohol on human aggression: an integrative research review. *Psychological Bulletin*, **107**, 341–354.

Chermack, S.T. & Giancola, P.R. (1997). The relation between alcohol and aggression: an integrated biopsychosocial conceptualization. *Clinical Psychology Review*, **17**, 621–649.

Chermack, S.T. & Taylor, S.P. (1995). Alcohol and human physical aggression: pharmacological versus expectancy effects. *Journal of Studies on Alcohol*, **56**, 449–456.

Collins, J. & Messerschmidt, P. (1993). Epidemiology of alcohol-related violence. *Alcohol Health and Research World*, **17**, 93–100.

Collins, J.J. & Schlenger, W.E. (1988). Acute and chronic effects of alcohol use on violence. *Journal of Studies on Alcohol*, **49**, 516–521.

Cook, P.J. & Moore, M.J. (1993). Violence reduction through restrictions on alcohol availability. *Alcohol Health and Research World*, **17**, 151–156.

Cordilia, A.T. (1986). Robbery arising out of a group drinking context. In A. Campbell & J.J. Gibbs (Eds), *Violent Transactions—the Limits of Personality* (pp. 167–180). New York: Basil Black.

Crawford, A. (1984). Alcohol and expectancy II. Perceived sex differences in the role of alcohol as a source of aggression. *Alcohol and Alcoholism*, **19**, 71–75.

Dawson, D.A. (1997). Alcohol, drugs, fighting and suicide attempt/ideation. *Addiction Research*, **5**, 451–472.

Dent, D.Z. & Arias, I. (1990). Effects of alcohol, gender, and role of spouses on attributions and evaluations of marital violence scenarios. *Personality and Social Psychology Bulletin*, **5**, 185–193.

Denton, K. & Krebs, D. (1990). From the scene to the crime: the effect of alcohol and social context on moral judgement. *Journal of Personality and Social Psychology*, **59**, 242–248.

Dermen, K.H. & George, W.H. (1989). Alcohol expectancy and the relationship between drinking and physical aggression. *Journal of Psychology*, **123**, 153–161.

Donovan, J.E. (1993). Young adult drinking-driving: behavioral and psychosocial correlates. *Journal of Studies on Alcohol*, **54**, 600–613.

Fagan, J. (1990). Intoxication and aggression. In M. Tonry & J.Q. Wilson (Eds), *Drugs and Crime* (pp. 241–320). Chicago: University of Chicago Press.

Fagan, J. (1993). Set and setting revisited: influences of alcohol and illicit drugs on the social context of violent events. In S.E. Martin (Ed.), *Alcohol and Interpersonal Violence: Fostering Multidisciplinary Perspectives*, Vol. 24 (pp. 160–192). Rockville, MD: NIH.

Fedorowycz, O. (1996). *Homicide in Canada, 1995*. Canadian Centre for Justice Statistics, Juristat Report 16(11). Ottawa: Statistics Canada.

Fahrenkrug, H. & Rehm, J. (1995). Drinking contexts and leisure-time activities in the prephase of alcohol-related road accidents by young Swiss Residents. *SUCHT*, **41**, 169–180.

Fischer, B. & Rehm, J. (1996). Alcohol consumption and the liability of offenders in the German criminal system. *Contemporary Drug Problems*, **23**, 707–729.

Foss, R.D. & Perrine, M.W.B. (1993). Predictors of Impaired Driving. In H.D. Utzelmann, G. Berghaus & G. Kroj (Eds), *Alcohol, Drugs and Traffic Safety*, Vol. 2 (pp. 1139–1144). Cologne: Rheinland GmbH, Verlag TUV.

Gantner, A.B. & Taylor, S.P. (1988). Human physical aggression as a function of diazepam. *Personality and Social Psychology Bulletin*, **14**, 479–484.

Gerson, L. & Preston, D. (1979). Alcohol consumption and the incidence of violent crime. *Journal of Studies on Alcohol*, **40**, 307–312.

Giancola, P.R. & Zeichner, A. (1995). Alcohol-related aggression in males and females: effects of blood alcohol concentration, subjective intoxication, personality, and provocation. *Alcoholism: Clinical and Experimental Research*, **19**, 130–134.

Gibbs, J. (1986). Overview. In A. Campbell & J. Gibbs (Eds), *Violent Transactions* (pp. 107–113). New York: Basil Blackwell.

Goldstein, A.P. (1994). *The Ecology of Aggression*. New York: Plenum.

Goodman, R.A., Mercy, J.A., Loya, F., Rosenberg, M.L., Smith, J.C., Allen, N.H., Vargas, L. & Kolts, R. (1986). Alcohol use and interpersonal violence: alcohol detected in homicide victims. *American Journal of Public Health*, **76**, 144–149.

Graham, K. (1985). Determinants of heavy drinking and drinking problems: the contribution of the bar environment. In E. Single & T. Storm (Eds), *Public Drinking and Public Policy* (pp. 71–84). Toronto: Addiction Research Foundation.

Graham, K. & Chandler Coutts, M. (2000). Community action research: who does what to whom and why? Lessons learned from local prevention efforts (international experiences). *Substance Use and Misuse*, **35**, 87–109.

Graham, K. & Homel, R. (1997). Creating safer bars. In M. Plant, E. Single & T. Stockwell (Eds), *Alcohol: Minimising the Harm* (pp. 171–192). London: Free Association Press.

Graham, K., LaRocque, L., Yetman, R., Ross, T.J. & Guistra, E. (1980). Aggression and bar-room environments. *Journal of Studies on Alcohol*, **41**, 277–292.

Graham, K., Leonard, K.E., Room, R., Wild, T.C., Pihl, R.O., Bois, C. & Single, E. (1998). Current directions in research in understanding and preventing intoxicated aggression. *Addiction*, **93**, 659–676.

Graham, K., Schmidt, G. & Gillis, K. (1996). Circumstances when drinking leads to aggression: an overview of research findings. *Contemporary Drug Problems*, **23**, 493–557.

Graham, K., Turnbull, W. & LaRocque, L. (1979). Effects of alcohol on moral judgment. *Journal of Abnormal Psychology*, **88**, 442–445.

Graham, K., Wells, S. & West, P. (1997). A framework for applying explanations of alcohol-related aggression to naturally occurring aggressive behavior. *Contemporary Drug Problems*, **24**(4), 625–666.

Graham, K., West, P. & Wells, S. (2000). Evaluating theories of alcohol-related aggression using observations of young adults in bars. *Addiction*, **95**, 847–863.

Graves, T.D., Graves, N.B., Semu, V.N. & Sam, I.A. (1981). The social context of drinking and violence in New Zealand's multi-ethnic pub settings. In T.C. Harford & L.S. Gaines (Eds), *Social Drinking Contexts*, Research Monograph No 7 (pp. 103–120). Rockville, MD: NIAAA.

Greenfield, L.A. (1998). *Alcohol and Crime: An Analysis of National Data on the Prevalence of Alcohol Involvement in Crime*. Bureau of Justice Statistics. Report prepared for the Assistant Attorney General's National Symposium on Alcohol Abuse and Crime, April 1998, NCJ 168632. Washington, DC: US Department of Justice.

Greenfield, T.K. (1998). Evaluating competing models of alcohol-related harm. *Alcoholism: Clinical and Experimental Research*, **22**(2), 52S–62S.

Gruenewald, P.J., Johnson, F.W., Miller, A. & Mitchell, P.R. (2000). Drinking and driving: explaining beverage-specific risks. *Journal of Studies on Alcohol*, **61**, 515–523.

Gruenewald, P., Mitchell, P. & Treno, A.J. (1996). Drinking and driving: drinking patterns and drinking problems. *Addiction*, **91**(11), 1637–1649.

Gustafson, R. (1993). What do experimental paradigms tell us about alcohol-related aggressive responding? *Journal of Studies on Alcohol*, **11**(Suppl.), 20–29.

Harlow, C. (1998). *Profile of Jail Inmates, 1996*. Bureau of Justice Statistics, Special Report, April 1998, NCJ 164620. Washington, DC: US Department of Justice.

Harrison, L. & Gfroerer, J. (1992). The intersection of drug use and criminal behavior: results from the national household survey on drug abuse. *Crime & Delinquency*, **38**, 422–443.

Heath, D.B. (1975). A critical review of ethnographic studies of alcohol use. In R.J. Gibbins, Y. Israel, H. Kalant, R.E. Popham, W. Schmidt & R.G. Smart (Eds), *Research advances in alcohol and drug problems*, Vol. 2 (pp. 1–92). Toronto: Wiley.

Hennessy, M. & Saltz, R.F. (1990). The situational riskiness of alcoholic beverages. *Journal of Studies on Alcohol*, **51**, 422–427.

Hoaken, P.N.S., Assaad, J.M. & Pihl, R.O. (1998). Cognitive functioning and the inhibition of alcohol-induced aggression. *Journal of Studies on Alcohol*, **59**, 599–607.

Homel, R., Carseldine, D. & Kearns, I. (1988). Drink-driving countermeasures in Australia. *Alcohol, Drugs and Driving*, **4**, 113–144.

Homel, R. & Clark, J. (1994). The prediction and prevention of violence in pubs and clubs. *Crime Prevention Studies*, **3**, 1–46.

Homel, R., Hauritz, M., Wortley, R., McIlwain, G. & Carvolth, R. (1997). Preventing alcohol-related crime through community action: the Surfers' Paradise Safety Action Project. *Crime Prevention Studies*, **7**, 35–90.

Homel, R., Tomsen, S. & Thommeny, J. (1991). The problem of violence on licensed premises: the Sydney study. In T. Stockwell, E. Lang & P. Rydon (Eds), *The Licensed Drinking Environment: Current Research in Australia and New Zealand* (pp. 33–40). Melbourne: National Centre for Research into the Prevention of Drug Abuse.

Homel, R., Tomsen, S. & Thommeny, J. (1992). Public drinking and violence: not just an alcohol problem. *Journal of Drug Issues*, **22**, 679–697.

Ireland, C.S. & Thommeny, J.L. (1993). The crime cocktail: licensed premises, alcohol and street offences. *Drug and Alcohol Review*, **12**, 143–150.

Ito, T.A., Miller, N. & Pollock, V.E. (1996). Alcohol and aggression: a meta-analysis on the moderating effects of inhibitory cues, triggering events, and self-focused attention. *Psychological Bulletin*, **120**, 60–82.

Jeavons, C.M. & Taylor, S.P. (1985). The control of alcohol-related aggression: redirecting the inebriate's attention to socially appropriate conduct. *Aggressive Behavior*, **11**, 93–101.

Johnson, H. (1996). *Violent Crime in Canada.* Canadian Centre for Justice Statistics, Juristat Report, 16(6). Ottawa: Statistics Canada.

Kantor, G.K. & Straus, M.A. (1987). The "drunken bum" theory of wife beating. *Social Problems*, **34**, 213–230.

Karlsson, G. & Romelsjö, A. (1997). A longitudinal study of social, psychological and behavioural factors associated with drunken driving and public drunkenness. *Addiction*, **92**, 447–457.

Kidder, L. & Cohn, E. (1979). Public views of crime and crime prevention. In I. Frieze, D. Bar-Tal & J. Carroll (Eds), *New Approaches to Social Problems*, (pp. 237–264). San Francisco, CA: Jossey-Bass.

Klein, H. & Pittman, D.J. (1990). Perceived consequences associated with the use of beer, wine, distilled spirits, and wine coolers. *International Journal of the Addictions*, **25**, 471–493.

Klinteberg, B., Andersson, T., Magnusson, D. & Stattin, H. (1993). Hyperactive behavior in childhood as related to subsequent alcohol problems and violent offending: a longitudinal study of male subjects. *Personality and Individual Differences*, **15**, 381–388.

Kunz, J.L. & Graham, K. (1998). Drinking patterns, psychosocial characteristics and alcohol consequences. *Addiction*, **93**(7), 1079–1090.

Lang, A.R. (1993). Alcohol-related violence: psychological perspectives. In S.E. Martin (Ed.), *Alcohol and Interpersonal Violence: Fostering Multidisciplinary Perspectives*. Research Monograph No.24 (pp. 121–148). Rockville, MD: NIH.

Lang, E. & Stockwell, T. (1991). Drinking locations of drink-drivers: a comparative analysis of accident and non-accident cases. *Accident Analysis and Prevention*, **23**, 573–584.

Lang, E., Stockwell, T., Rydon, P. & Lockwood, A. (1995). Drinking settings and problems of intoxication. *Addiction Research*, **3**, 141–149.

Lapham, S.C., Skipper, B.J., Chang, I., Barton, K. & Kennedy, R. (1998). Factors related to miles driven between drinking and arrest locations among convicted drunk drivers. *Accident Analysis and Prevention*, **30**, 201–206.

Lastovicka, J.L. (1988). Speculations on the social psychology of young male drinking–driving. *Alcohol, Drugs and Driving*, **4**, 225–232.

Lawrence, C. & Leather, P. (1997). Perceiving violence: a test of attributional response and environmental context (submitted to *British Journal of Social Psychology*).

Lee, J.A., Jones-Webb, R.J., Short, B.J. & Wagenaar, A.C. (1997). Drinking location and risk of alcohol-impaired driving among high school seniors. *Addictive Behaviors*, **22**, 387–393.

Leigh, B.C. (1987). Beliefs about the effects of alcohol on self and others. *Journal of Studies on Alcohol*, **48**, 467–475.

Leigh, B.C. (1989). Attitudes and expectancies as predictors of drinking habits: a comparison of three scales. *Journal of Studies on Alcohol*, **50**, 432–440.

Lenke, L. (1982). Alcohol and crimes of violence: a causal analysis. *Contemporary Drug Problems*, **11**, 355–365.

Leonard, K.E. (1984). Alcohol consumption and escalatory aggression in intoxicated and sober dyads. *Journal of Studies on Alcohol*, **45**, 75–80.

Leonard, K.E. (1993). Drinking patterns and intoxication in marital violence: review, critique, and future directions for research. In S.E. Martin (Ed.), *Alcohol and Interpersonal Violence: Fostering Multidisciplinary Perspectives*. Research Monograph No. 24. (pp. 253–281). Rockville, MD: NIH.

Leonard, K.E. & Roberts, L.J. (1998). The effects of alcohol on the marital interactions of aggressive and nonaggressive husbands and their wives. *Journal of Abnormal Psychology*, **107**, 602–615.

Leonard, K. & Senchak, M. (1993). Alcohol and premarital aggression among newlywed couples. *Journal of Studies on Alcohol*, Supplement, **11**, 96–108.

Levinson, D. (1983). Social setting, cultural factors and alcohol-related aggression. In E. Gottheil, K.A. Druley, T.E. Skoloda & H.M. Waxman (Eds), *Alcohol, Drug Abuse, and Aggression* (pp. 41–58). Springfield, IL: Charles C. Thomas.

Lindman, R.E. & Lang, A.R. (1994). The alcohol-aggression stereotype: a cross-cultural comparison of beliefs. *International Journal of the Addictions*, **29**, 1–13.

Lipsey, M.W., Wilson, D.B., Cohen, M.A. & Derzon, J.H. (1997). Is there a causal relationship between alcohol use and violence? In M. Galanter (Ed.), *Recent Developments in Alcoholism. Vol. 13, Alcohol and Violence* (pp. 245–282). New York: Plenum.

Liu, S., Siegel, P., Brewer, R., Mokdad, A.H., Sleet, D.A. & Serdula, M. (1997). Prevalence of alcohol-impaired driving. *Journal of the American Medical Association*, **277**, 122–125.

Loxley, W., Homel, R., Berger, D. & Snortum, J. (1992). Drinkers and their driving: compliance with drinking-driving legislation in four Australian States. *Journal of Studies on Alcohol*, **53**, 420–426.

Loxley, W., Lo, S.K., Homel, R., Berger, D.E. & Snortum, J.R. (1992). Young people, alcohol, and driving in two Australian states. *International Journal of the Addictions*, **27**, 1119–1129.

Luckenbill, D.F. (1977). Criminal homicide as a situated transaction. *Social Problems*, **25**, 176–186.

MacAndrew, C. & Edgerton, R.B. (1969). *Drunken Comportment. A Social Explanation*. Chicago, IL: Aldine.

Macdonald, S. & Mann, R. (1996). Distinguishing causes and correlates of drinking and driving. *Contemporary Drug Problems*, **23**, 259–290.

MacIntyre, S. & Homel, R. (1997). Danger on the dance floor: a study of interior design, crowding and aggression in nightclubs. In R. Homel (Ed.), *Policing for Prevention: Reducing Crime, Public Intoxication and Injury*, Vol. 7 (pp. 91–113). Monsey, NY: Criminal Justice Press.

Marsh, P. & Kibby, K. (1992). *Drinking and Public Disorder*. A report of research conducted for the Portman Group by MCM Research. London: Portman.

Marshall, M. (1979). *Weekend Warriors. Alcohol in a Micronesian Culture*. Palo Alto, CA: Mayfield.

Martin, C., Wyllie, A. & Casswell, S. (1992). Types of New Zealand drinkers and their associated alcohol-related problems. *Journal of Drug Issues*, **22**, 773–796.

Martin, S.E. & Bachman, R. (1997). The relationship of alcohol to injury in assault cases. In M. Galanter (Ed.), *Recent Developments in Alcoholism*. Vol. 13, Alcohol and Violence (pp. 42–56). New York: Plenum.

McCaghy, C.H. (1968). Drinking and deviance disavowal: the case of child molesters. *Social Forces*, **16**, 43–49.

McClelland, D.C., Davis, W.N., Kalin, R. & Wanner, E. (1972). *The Drinking Man—Alcohol and Human Motivation*. Toronto: Collier-Macmillan Canada.

McLaughlin, I.G., Leonard, K.E. & Senchak, M. (1992). Prevalence and distribution of premarital aggression among couples applying for a marriage license. *Journal of Family Violence*, **7**, 309–319.

Miczek, K.A., Barros, H.M., Sakoda, L. & Weerts, E.M. (in press). Alcohol and heightened aggression in individual mice. *Alcoholism: Clinical and Experimental Research*.

Miczek, K.A., Weerts, E.M. & DeBold, J.F. (1993). Alcohol, benzodiazepine-GABA receptor complex and aggression: ethological analysis of individual differences in rodents and primates. *Journal of Studies on Alcohol*, **11**(Suppl.), 170–179.

Midanik, L.T., Tam, T.W., Greenfield, T.K. & Caetano, R. (1996). Risk functions of alcohol-related problems in a 1988 US national sample. *Addiction*, **91**, 1427–1437.

Midford, R., Masters, L., Phillips, M., Daly, A., Stockwell, T., Gahegan, M. & Philp, A. (1998). Alcohol consumption and injury in Western Australia: a spatial correlation analysis using geographic information systems. *Australian and New Zealand Journal of Public Health*, **22**, 80–85.

Miethe, T.D. & Meier, R.F. (1994). *Crime and Its Social Context*. Albany, NY: State University of New York Press.

Mongrain, S. & Standing, L. (1989). Impairment of cognition, risk-taking, and self-perception by alcohol. *Perceptual Motor Skills*, **69**, 199–200.

Mosher, J. (1983). Alcohol: both blame and excuse for criminal behavior. In R. Room & G. Collin (Eds), *Alcohol and Disinhibition: Nature and Meaning of the Link* (pp. 437–460). Rockville, MD: NIAAA.

Mumola, C.J. & Bonczar, T.P. (1998). *Substance Abuse and Treatment of Adults on Probation, 1995*. Bureau of Justice Statistics, Special Report, March 1998, NCJ 166611. Washington, DC: US Department of Justice.

Murdoch, D.D., Pihl, R.O. & Ross, D. (1990). Alcohol and crimes of violence: present issues. *International Journal of the Addictions*, **25**, 1065–1081.

Nelson, T.F., Isaac, N.E., Kennedy, B.P. & Graham, J.D. (1999). Factors associated with planned avoidance of alcohol-impaired driving in high risk men. *Journal of Studies on Alcohol*, **60**, 407–412.

Norström, T. (1998). Effects on criminal violence of different beverage types and private and public drinking. *Addiction*, **93**, 689–700.

O'Donnell, M. (1985). Research on drinking locations of alcohol-impaired drivers: implications for prevention policies. *Journal of Public Health Policy*, **6**, 510–525.

Oliver, W. (1993). *Violent Confrontations between Black Males in Bars and Bar Settings*. PhD Dissertation, State University of New York at Albany.

Osgood, W., Johnston, L.D., O'Malley, P.M. & Bachman, J.G. (1988). The generality of deviance in late adolescence and early adulthood. *American Sociological Review*, **53**, 81–93.

Parker, R. & Rehbun, L.A. (1995). *Alcohol and Homicide. A Deadly Combination of Two American Traditions*. Albany, NY: State University of New York Press.

Pernanen, K. (1976). Alcohol and crimes of violence. In B. Kissin & H. Begleiter (Eds), *The Biology of Alcoholism* (pp. 351–444). New York: Plenum.

Pernanen, K. (1991). *Alcohol in Human Violence*. New York: Guilford.

Pernanen, K. (1998). Prevention of alcohol-related violence. *Contemporary Drug Problems*, **25**, 477–509.

Pihl, R.O. & Peterson, J.B. (1993). Alcohol and aggression: three potential mechanisms of the drug effect (pp. 149–159). In S.E. Martin (Ed.), *Alcohol and Interpersonal Violence: Fostering Multidisciplinary Perspectives*. Research Monograph No. 24. Rockville, MD: NIH.

Pihl, R.O., Peterson, J.B. & Lau, M.A. (1993). A biosocial model of the alcohol-aggression relationship. *Journal of Studies on Alcohol*, **11**(Suppl.), 128–139.

Pihl, R.O., Smith, M. & Farrell, B. (1984). Alcohol and aggression in men: a comparison of brewed and distilled beverages. *Journal of Studies on Alcohol*, **45**, 278–282.

Pliner, P. & Cappell, H. (1974). Modification of affective consequences of alcohol: a comparison of social and solitary drinking. *Journal of Abnormal Psychology*, **83**, 418–425.

Pulkkinen, L. & Pitkanen, T. (1993). Continuities in aggressive behavior from childhood to adulthood. *Aggressive Behavior*, **19**, 249–263.

Robbins, C.A. & Martin, S.S. (1993). Gender, styles of deviance, and drinking problems. *Journal of Health and Social Behavior*, **34**, 302–321.

Roebuck, J.B. & Murty, K.S. (1996). *The Southern Subculture of Drinking and Driving. A Generalized Model for the Southern White Male*. New York: Garland.

Roizen, J. (1997). Epidemiological issues in alcohol-related violence. In M. Galanter (Ed.), *Recent Developments in Alcoholism*. Vol. 13, Alcohol and Violence (7–40). New York: Plenum.

Roizen, R. (1983). Loosening up: general population views of the effects of alcohol. In R. Room & G. Collins (Eds), *Drinking and Disinhibition: Nature and Meaning of the Link* (pp. 236–257). Rockville, MD: NIAAA.

Roncek, D.W. & Maier, P.A. (1991).   Bars, blocks and crimes revisited: linking the theory of routine activities to the empiricism of "hot spots". *Criminology Australia*, **29**, 725–753.

Room, R. (1998).   Seeds on stony ground: recent experience in the community prevention of alcohol problems. Paper presented at the 4th Symposium on Community Action Research and the Prevention of Alcohol and Other Drug Problems, Russell Bay of Islands, New Zealand.

Rossow, I. (1996).   Alcohol related violence: the impact of drinking pattern and drinking context. *Addiction*, 91, 1651–1661.

Sayette, M.A., Wilson, T. & Elias, M.J. (1993).   Alcohol and aggression: a social information processing analysis. *Journal of Studies on Alcohol*, **54**, 399–407.

Scoufis, P. & Walker, M. (1982).   Heavy drinking and the need for power. *Journal of Studies on Alcohol*, **43**, 1010–1019.

Scribner, R., Cohen, D., Kaplan, S. & Allen, S.H. (1999).   Alcohol availability and homicide in New Orleans: conceptual considerations for small area analysis of the effect of alcohol outlet density. *Journal of Studies on Alcohol*, **60**, 310–316.

Shain, M. & Higgins, G. (1997).   The intoxication defense and theories of criminal liability: a praxeological approach. *Contemporary Drug Problems*, **24**, 731–764.

Single, E. & McKenzie, D. (1992).   The epidemiology of impaired driving stemming from licensed premises. Paper presented at the annual meeting of the Kettil Bruun Society for Social and Epidemiological Research on Alcohol, Toronto, Canada.

Smart, R.G. (1996).   Behavioral and social consequences related to the consumption of different beverage types. *Journal of Studies on Alcohol*, **57**, 77–84.

Statistics Canada (1994).   The 1993 General Social Survey—Cycle 8 Personal Risk. *Public Use Microdata File Documentation and User's Guide*. Ottawa: Statistics Canada.

Steele, C.M. & Josephs, R.A. (1990).   Alcohol myopia: its prized and dangerous effects. *American Psychologist*, **45**, 921–933.

Stevenson, R.J., Lind, B. & Weatherburn, D. (1999).   The relationship between alcohol sales and assault in New South Wales, Australia. *Addiction*, **94**, 397–410.

Stockwell, T., Lang, E. & Rydon, P. (1993).   High risk drinking settings: the association of serving and promotional practices with harmful drinking. *Addiction*, **88**, 1519–1526.

Stockwell, T., Masters, L., Phillips, M., Daly, A., Gahagan, M., Midford, R. & Philp, A. (1998).   Consumption of different alcoholic beverages as predictors of local rates of night-time assault and acute alcohol-related morbidity. *Australian and New Zealand Journal of Public Health*, **22**, 237–242.

Stockwell, T., Somerford, P. & Lang, E. (1991).   The measurement of harmful outcomes following drinking on licensed premises. *Drug and Alcohol Review*, **10**, 99–106.

Stockwell, T., Somerford, P. & Lang, E. (1992).   The relationship between license type and alcohol-related problems attributed to licensed premises in Perth, Western Australia. *Journal of Studies on Alcohol*, **53**, 495–498.

Straus, M.A. & Gelles, R.J. (1990).   Societal change and change in family violence from 1975 to 1985 as revealed by two national surveys. In M.A. Straus & R.J. Gelles (Eds), *Physical Violence in American Families* (pp. 113–131). New Brunswick, NJ: Transaction.

Straus, M.A., Gelles, R.J. & Steinmetz, S.K. (1980).   Measuring violence with the "Conflict Tactics Scales". In *Behind Closed Doors: Violence in the American family* (pp. 253–284). New York: Anchor.

Suitor, J.J., Pillemer, K. & Straus, M.A. (1990).   Marital violence in a life course perspective. In M.A. Straus & R.J. Gelles (Eds), *Physical Violence in American Families*, (pp. 305–317). New Brunswick, NJ: Transaction.

Tardiff, K., Gross, E. & Messner, S.F. (1986).   A study of homicides in Manhattan, 1981. *American Journal of Public Health*, **76**, 139–143.

Tardiff, K., Marzuk, P.M., Leon, A.C., Hirsch, C.S., Stajic, M., Portera, L. & Hartwell, N. (1995).   A profile of homicides on the streets and in the homes of New York city. *Public Health Reports*, **110**, 13–17.

Taylor, S. & Gammon, C. (1976).   Aggressive behavior of intoxicated subjects: the effect of third-party intervention. *Journal of Studies on Alcohol*, **37**, 917–930.

Tomsen, S. (1997).   A top night out—social protest, masculinity and the culture of drinking violence. *British Journal of Criminology*, **37**, 990–1002.

Vegega, M.E. & Klitzner, M.D. (1989).   Drinking and driving among youth: a study of situational risk factors. *Health Education Quarterly*, **16**, 373–388.

Vingilis, E., Stoduto, G., Macartney-Filgate, M.S., Liban, C.B. & McLellan, B.A. (1994).   Psychosocial characteristics of alcohol-involved and non alcohol-involved seriously injured drivers. *Accident Analysis and Prevention*, **26**, 195–206.

Wallace, A. & Travis, G. (1994).   *The Incidence and Prevalence of Alcohol Use and Violence in the Australian Community*. Prepared for the National Symposium on Alcohol Misuse and Violence, Report 1. Commonwealth of Australia.

Washburne, C. (1956).   Alcohol, self, and the group. *Quarterly Journal of Studies on Alcohol*, **17**, 108–123.

Wells, S., Graham, K. & West, P. (1998).   "The good, the bad, and the ugly": responses by security staff to aggressive incidents in public drinking settings. *Journal of Drug Issues*, **28**, 817–836.

Welte, J.W. & Abel, E.L. (1989).   Homicide: drinking by the victim. *Journal of Studies on Alcohol*, **50**, 197–201.

White, H.R. (1997).   Longitudinal perspective on alcohol use and aggression during adolescence. In M. Galanter (Ed.), *Recent Developments in Alcoholism, Vol. 13, Alcohol and Violence* (pp. 81–103). New York: Plenum.

White, J.W. & Koss, M.P. (1991).   Courtship violence: incidence in a national sample of higher education students. *Violence and Victims*, **6**, 247–256.

Wiley, J.A. & Weisner, C. (1995).   Drinking in violent and nonviolent events leading to arrest: evidence from a survey of arrestees. *Journal of Criminal Justice*, **23**, 461–476.

Wolfgang, M.E. (1958).   *Patterns in Criminal Homicide*. Philadelphia, PA: University of Pennsylvania.

Zhang, L., Wieczorek, W.F. & Welte, J.W. (1997).   The nexus between alcohol and violent crime. *Alcoholism: Clinical and Experimental Research*, **21**, 1264–1271.

Chapter 23

The Anthropology of Drinking

David Moore
*Australian National University,
Canberra, ACT, Australia*

Synopsis

As the other chapters in this book demonstrate, empirical research on the psychology, epidemiology and physiology of alcohol use is vital to those working in the prevention, treatment and policy fields but it provides only part of an holistic perspective on the act of drinking alcohol. Such approaches pay little heed to the meaning of the drinking act for those doing the drinking. An anthropological focus on the meaning of the drinking act therefore differs from other types of alcohol research, and at least some of this difference is related to the methodology usually employed by anthropologists, viz. ethnography. There are many ways of defining ethnography, but its essential characteristic is long-term field research with a specified set of socially related people. The ethnographer endeavours to understand the emic (or insider) point of view regarding alcohol and to locate it within broader social, economic, political and cultural contexts.

Early anthropological studies of drinking in various cross-cultural contexts emphasized aspects of celebration. Such studies were usually conducted as afterthoughts to more conventional anthropological studies of political, legal, religious and kinship systems. Later studies attempted to formulate universal hypotheses about drinking based on ethnographic research in particular social and cultural contexts, such as the argument that drinking was primarily a means of reducing anxiety or of expressing power. Due to methodological and conceptual flaws, such studies fell from favour, to be replaced by the idea that the beliefs and practices associated with drinking were intimately linked to central aspects of culture and social organization. While alcohol, as a pharmacological agent, produced certain kinds of sensorimotor changes in the human body, the meaning given to these physiological changes varied with culture. Thus, the social and cultural context was more important in shaping "drunken comportment" than the pharmacological properties of alcohol.

More recent anthropological work, while continuing to argue that alcohol is more often associated with celebration than with problems, has attempted to incorporate a political-economy dimension into alcohol studies and has argued that drinking associated with indisputably harmful outcomes can still be seen as meaningful behaviour. Some anthropologists have taken a more interdisciplinary stance, employing quantitative methods to supplement

International Handbook of Alcohol Dependence and Problems. Edited by N. Heather, T.J. Peters and T. Stockwell.
© 2001 John Wiley & Sons Ltd.

ethnographic research, employing ethnographic or qualitative work as a precursor to the development of more culturally sensitive survey approaches, or working in multidisciplinary research teams. Another recent development is the argument that the previous conceptual distinction between substance (i.e. alcohol) and culture is invalid and that there is no culture-free position from which to view alcohol.

As a way of exploring these issues in more detail, this chapter examines ethnographic research on Australian Aboriginal drinking, and on the drinking behaviour of young people, to demonstrate both the usefulness of an anthropological perspective on alcohol use, and how it might differ from and complement studies conducted by researchers from other disciplines.

As the other chapters in this section demonstrate, much of the empirical research on alcohol use focuses on assessing levels of consumption in specified populations, investigating the relationship between consumption levels and morbidity and mortality, analysing the multiple risk factors contributing to alcohol-related problems, and exploring the relationship between alcohol use and crime, violence and drink–driving. Research of this kind is vital to those working in the prevention, treatment and policy fields but it provides only part of an holistic perspective on alcohol use. Such approaches pay little heed to the meanings of the drinking act for those who drink, meanings grounded in specific social and cultural contexts. In this chapter, I do not attempt to review the massive body of anthropological literature that deals with drinking. Heath (1975, 1976, 1986, 1987a, 1987b, 1991a) has provided several comprehensive (and overlapping) reviews of such literature. Nor do I presume much anthropological knowledge on the part of the reader. Rather, I provide a highly selective review of the various types of work done from an anthropological perspective, outlining some key studies and their central features and assessing their strengths and limitations, before moving on to a discussion of drinking amongst Australian Aborigines and amongst young people. For convenience, I use the term "anthropological" throughout this chapter but I also cover some research conducted by sociologists (e.g. Dorn, 1983; Gusfield, 1981).

In its focus on the meanings of drinking in social and cultural contexts, an anthropological perspective differs from psychological, epidemiological, medical and (some) sociological research into alcohol use, and at least part of this difference is related to the methodology usually employed by anthropologists, i.e. ethnography. The essential characteristic of ethnography is long-term field research with a specified set of socially related people. Although participant observation is the central element of ethnography (i.e. spending time participating in and observing the everyday practices of the members of the identified group), it also involves collecting sociodemographic information on the study population, conducting in-depth, relatively unstructured interviews, and attempting to relate the chosen group to the broader social, economic, political and cultural contexts in which it is located. Above all, the ethnographer endeavours to understand the emic (or insider) point of view. Put simply, how do drinkers understand their drinking? How do they define "normal" and "pathological" drinking? In what ways do their drinking practices express and constitute central aspects of their lives?

COMPARATIVE STUDIES

One of the first anthropological publications specifically focused on drinking was written by Bunzel (1940). She conducted her fieldwork in two Latin American communities— Chamula (Mexico) and Chichicastenango (Guatemala)—and used the method of "controlled comparison", i.e. taking two similar communities and attempting to show the differences in drinking practices. She showed that alcohol use was associated with child-rearing practices (as well as other social institutions and practices) and that Chichicastenango drinking was deeply embedded in social life, while Chamula drinking was destructive. This pioneering article explored a theme that was to become central to anthropological work: how does drinking express and constitute aspects of culture and social relations in a particular context? It was also representative of another theme in anthropological studies of drinking until the 1970s (and beyond): that many anthropological studies were conducted as afterthoughts—"felicitous by-products" (Heath, 1975, p. 4)—to more conventional field studies of political, legal, religious and kinship systems.

The method of controlled comparison was taken a step further by the cross-cultural (or hologeistic or holocultural) studies conducted from the 1940s through to the 1970s. These studies shared a methodology whereby the existing data for a large number of societies from around the world were used to test particular universal hypotheses. One important source of data was the Cross-Cultural Survey, later and more famously known as the Human Relations Area Files (HRAF), compiled by George Murdock and his associates at Yale University. These files contained systematic data on religion, economy, politics, social behaviour and other social and cultural aspects. The first such study employing these files was conducted by Horton (1943). On the basis of data from 56 societies, his oft-quoted conclusion was that: "*The primary function of alcoholic beverages in all societies is the reduction of anxiety*" (Horton, 1943, p. 223, original emphasis). According to Horton, this anxiety was created by subsistence problems, war or contact with more powerful and dominant societies. Another hologeistic study was conducted by Bacon, Barry & Child (1965), in which the authors argued, on the basis of HRAF data from 139 societies, that heavy drinking and drunkenness was associated with cultural contexts featuring "conflict over dependency", that is, where there was a disjunction between childhood roles encouraging a high degree of dependence and adulthood roles emphasising independence. Using thematic apperception tests, content analysis of cross-cultural data on folktales, and role-playing, McClelland et al. (1972) concluded that, for men, drinking was primarily a means of attaining, or regaining, feelings of power and strength, particularly in societies where personalized power was deemed important. Field (1962) also employed a cross-cultural approach but attempted to move away from the psychological explanation of Horton. On the basis of HRAF data on 62 societies, Field (1962, p. 58) argued that the degree of drinking was directly related to the degree of social organization in a society:

> Drunkenness . . . is determined less by the level of fear [i.e. Horton's "anxiety"] in a society than by the absence of corporate kin groups with stability, permanence, formal structure, and well-defined functions.

The hologeistic studies drew attention to the relationship between drinking and the sociocultural context and exercised a surprising influence over thinking in alcohol studies. As Heath (1991a) notes, popular "psychological" ideas about the role of drinking in reducing anxiety, in resolving conflict in families and in making men feel powerful were originally drawn from this ethnographic material. However, there were also numerous problems. The HRAF data categories were too simplistic and, as is the case with closed questionnaire responses, forced complex and sometimes inconsistent ethnographic materials into a pre-existing descriptive framework. As well, the universal hypotheses were falsified by the many ethnographic cases that did not fit, and the idea that all drinking, or even drinking in similar contexts, could be understood through recourse to monotypic explanations was fallacious.

CULTURE AND DRUNKEN COMPORTMENT

A more enduring contribution to alcohol studies made by anthropologists was the idea that the ideologies and practices associated with drinking were intimately linked to central aspects of culture and social relations (a finding previously stressed by Bunzel, 1940). Cultural beliefs were viewed as determining who could and could not drink in a society, what they could drink, with whom they could drink, how fast they could drink, in what situations they could drink, why they drank, what topics they would discuss while drinking, what they would define as "normal" and "pathological" drinking, and how they would behave at different levels of intoxication.

Because of the enormous cultural diversity in the world, drinking was similarly variable and this assertion was supported by ethnographic research in Africa, Latin America, North America, Scandinavia and the Pacific. Alcohol, in varying social and cultural contexts, was associated, *inter alia*, with religious practices, sociability, the maintenance of group boundaries, the creation of social identities and gender roles. In this particular type of anthropological work, it was accepted that alcohol, as a pharmacological agent, produced certain kinds of sensorimotor changes in the human body—e.g. changes in locomotor ability, motor coordination, visual acuity and reaction time—but that the meaning given to these physiological changes varied with culture.

This type of thinking was prevalent in anthropological circles for some years before being codified in 1965 by David Mandelbaum, then Professor of Anthropology at the University of California, Berkeley, in his widely-cited article "Alcohol and Culture". Mandelbaum (1965, p. 282) succinctly put the anthropological position thus:

> When a man [sic] lifts a cup, it is not only the kind of drink that is in it, the amount he is likely to take, and the circumstances under which he will do the drinking that are specified in advance for him, but also whether the contents of the cup will cheer or stupefy, whether they will induce affection or aggression, guilt or unalloyed pleasure. These and many other cultural definitions attach to the drink even before it touches the lips.

The authors of ethnographic studies contested the oft-stated positions that heavy drinking inevitably led to problems and to disinhibited behaviour, arguing that the social and cultural context was more important in shaping "problems" and "drunken comportment" than levels of consumption and the pharmacological properties of alcohol (e.g. Marshall, 1981). Two studies, written either side of Mandelbaum's statement, were central to these contestations: those of Heath (1958) and MacAndrew & Edgerton (1969).

Heath's (1958) work on the Camba of eastern Bolivia remains one of the most interesting and important ethnographic case studies of drinking. On their numerous festive occasions and on weekends, Camba adults drank a highly concentrated sugar cane alcoholic beverage (89% ethyl alcohol). Drinking and drunkenness were highly valued, and drinking bouts lasted several days, with drinkers frequently passing out before resuming drinking. Heath noted, however, that there were no alcohol-related problems (e.g. violence, hangovers, "alcoholism") other than minor irritation of the throat due to the strength of the liquor. The drinking group, he argued, was one of the few primary reference groups in Camba society, which was highly individualistic, fragmented and atomistic. Drinking facilitated rapport between individuals who were normally isolated and introverted. Later work (Heath, 1991b) confirmed the ongoing absence of alcohol-related problems and also that, with the formation of other communal institutions (i.e. peasant leagues), drinking parties were held less frequently and were of shorter duration.

MacAndrew & Edgerton (1969) are generally credited with the most important statement of the drunken-comportment thesis. On the basis of extensive ethnohistorical and ethnographic material from North and South America, Africa and the Pacific, they (1969, p. 165) cogently argued that drunken comportment was not merely a "function of toxically disinhibited brains operating in impulse-driven bodies" but learned behaviour. The way people conducted themselves when intoxicated was shaped by "what their society makes of and imparts to them concerning the state of drunkenness" (1969, p. 165). They also argued that in many societies around the world, alcohol served to demarcate "time-out" periods in which cultural rules that governed sober behaviour were exchanged for a different set of rules. Even apparently disinhibited behaviour, such as drunken fighting, was not random but was usually targeted at specific persons or groups. This position was supported by Marshall (1979, 1981), in his summaries of the relevant ethnographic evidence, as well as by other ethnographic studies from many parts of the world.

Several summaries of these anthropological contributions to the study of drinking exist (e.g. Marshall, 1979; Heath, 1987b) but that of Douglas (1987a, pp. 3–4) is admirably succinct:

- That the biological inheritance of different populations (Douglas employs the contentious term "races") is not a determinant of lowered ability to withstand the ill-effects of alcohol use.
- That there is no clear relationship between alcohol use and criminal or aggressive behaviour.
- That alcohol-related behaviour is culturally shaped in much the same way as any other human behaviour and does not represent some desocialized aberration.
- That drinking is a social act.
- That alcohol use is, in cross-cultural perspective, more often associated with celebration than with complication and so an anthropological perspective provides an essential corrective to the problem-focused analyses of other disciplines.

The propensity of anthropologists to draw attention to the non-problematic nature of drinking in many of the world's societies prompted Room (1984) to argue that they had systematically underestimated the problems of alcohol use. He argued that several factors shaped this "problem deflation":

- That ethnographers worked within a functionalist paradigm that emphasized societal consistency and integration over dysfunction.
- That ethnography—as a set of methods—was less able than epidemiology to uncover problems and more attuned to the pleasures of drinking.
- That ethnographers belonged to a "wet" generation of progressive, liberal, middle-class academics who were culturally antagonistic to prohibitionist and temperance culture.
- That, in their fieldwork, ethnographers were usually concerned with distancing themselves from other "outsiders"—such as missionaries and colonial administrators—who may have explicitly sought to control indigenous people.

The responses of those anthropologists invited to consider Room's comments (published with his article) ranged from agreement to outright hostility and an anthropological volume published 3 years later was provocatively entitled *Constructive Drinking: Perspectives on Drink from Anthropology* (Douglas, 1987b).

Several commentators on Room's article (e.g. Michael Agar, Dwight B. Heath) noted that his linking of problem deflation to the "culture" of ethnographers (a perfectly valid observation about the sociology of knowledge) could equally well be made about "problem amplification" amongst those focusing on alcohol "problems" (a point made by Room himself in his 1984 and 1991 publications; see also Douglas, 1987b; Heath, 1991a; McDonald, 1994). One study that has dealt with this issue, and which has perhaps not received the kind of attention it deserves, is Gusfield's (1981) *The Culture of Public*

Problems: Drinking–Driving and the Symbolic Order. This book grew out of Gusfield's involvement in a study of drink–driving in California in the 1970s. He realized that it might be profitable to bring to bear on drink–driving research an ethnographic and sociological perspective similar to that normally applied to the study of drinking. Put baldly, Gusfield's thesis was that the "problem of drinking–driving" in the USA was constructed in certain ways—as a "drama of individualism" centring on the "killer drunk"—rather than as, say, a problem in transportation (e.g. how do we prevent drunken people from crashing, or why do we build drinking establishments near busy roads?): "[e]very perspective is a way of *not* seeing as well as a way of seeing" (Gusfield, 1981, p. 187; original emphasis). The "culture" of drink–driving research emphasized alcohol as the problem and located the source of motor-vehicle accidents in the moral failings of the individual motorist, rather than in the social institutions in which the motorist was enmeshed or in the physical environment through which the motorist drove.

Gusfield's work can be seen as an early example of a constructionist trend more fully elaborated in McDonald's (1994) introduction to the edited collection, *Gender, Drink and Drugs*. She explicitly targets the earlier view of the relationship between beverage alcohol and culture—perhaps best exemplified in Marshall's (1979, p. 1) statement that:

> ... [t]he cross-cultural study of alcohol presents a classic natural experiment: a single species ..., a single drug substance ..., and a great diversity of behavioural outcomes

and seemingly adhered to by Heath, arguably the most prominent anthropologist in alcohol studies—by arguing that there is no "culture-free" substance called "alcohol" and no "culture-free" position from which to view it. The "real world" is not just "out there" but is constantly being constructed by scientific discourses that claim a position external to culture (e.g. pharmacology, medicine, biology). She is careful to qualify her comments, arguing that accepting her position does not mean denying that scientific claims are "right" but acknowledging that they, too, are cultural claims:

> [A] substance has no reality external to perceptions of it, or to the context of its use ... The substance is always the cultural values invested in it, and this applies whether the values be those of the police, the pharmacologist or the user ... (McDonald, 1994, p. 18).

McDonald's position is one also taken up recently by some anthropologists in relation to the distinction between "sex" (biology) and "gender" (culture)—that is, that *any* understandings of "biology" are also "cultured" (McDonald, 1994, p. 19; see also Errington, 1992). It is also consistent with the constructionist approach to "science" (e.g. Foucault, 1973; Knorr-Cetina, 1981).

THE POLITICAL ECONOMY OF DRINKING

In the 1980s, anthropologists, responding to more general developments in social theory, began increasingly to argue that cultural behaviour needed to be understand within broader, historically shaped political, economic and social systems (e.g. Wolf, 1982; Roseberry, 1989). This reflected the resurgence of interest in Marxist approaches to culture in the 1970s and in the analysis of an increasingly dominant and interconnected "capitalist world system". In the anthropology of drinking, this trend was first given expression by Singer (1986), although it had also been the subject of an earlier, more sociologically inclined, account by Sargent (1979). This approach (also known as "materialist") seeks to explain human social behaviour in the context of the political and economic relations in which individuals and groups operate. These historically derived relations set certain constraints on what is possible in human action. Those individuals and groups possessing power (whether political, economic, military or cultural) have greater control over their lives than those lacking such power. In Marx's famous maxim:

> [m]en [sic] make their own history, but they do not make it just as they please; they do not make it under circumstances chosen by themselves, but under circumstances directly encountered, given, and transmitted from the past (McLellan, 1977, p. 300).

However, humans are not solely determined by these relations and contemporary systems of relations are the product of historical processes and interactions between such systems and the people constituting them.

In his political-economy critique of the anthropology of drinking, Singer is particularly scathing of those studies of "traditional [indigenous] drinking" which neglect the fact that these societies have often been colonized or shaped by capitalist expansion for decades and even centuries. These accounts treat drinking as a local phenomenon somehow unrelated to, or independent of, extra-local contexts. This is particularly a problem for the hologeistic studies, in which each society for which data are entered in the HRAF is treated as a separate, bounded whole, rather than being part of a complex and increasingly interconnected capitalist world system.

The trend to political economy has been particularly noticeable in studies of the drinking of marginalized groups, particularly indigenous peoples who have been subjugated in the growth of colonialism and capitalism (e.g. Hunter, 1993; Saggers & Gray, 1998). The proponents of this type of work argue that indigenous drinking associated with indisputably harmful outcomes—as measured by the standard epidemiological and other indices of morbidity and mortality, liver cirrhosis and criminality—can still be seen as meaningful behaviour in the context of ongoing powerlessness and oppression. In this sense, the political-economy approach is not antithetical to the "drunken comportment" model, but rather calls for a broader framework for analysis than the local cultural and social context. Political-economy approaches are flawed in that they cannot account for variations at the individual level, nor for different group responses to similar political and economic contexts, such as "spontaneous remission" amongst heavy-drinking Aborigines (e.g. Brady, 1995). They also seem to reduce much cultural behaviour to mere responses to the capitalist world system. However, as Saggers & Gray (1998) argue, political economy may still provide the best way of explaining the aggregate-level differences in heath status between indigenous and non-indigenous populations.

ETHNOGRAPHY AND MULTIDISCIPLINARITY

The constructionism of Gusfield and McDonald is one position current within an anthropology that does not seek a sustained engagement with alcohol studies, neither is it so directly concerned with policy and prevention/treatment (see also Gefou-Madianou, 1992). Another distinctively anthropological type of work has taken a more multidisciplinary stance, rejecting the "Lone Ranger syndrome" (Bennett, 1988, p. 96) of the single ethnographer and acknowledging the importance of "scientific" methods, such as epidemiological surveys and other quantitative measures. These anthropologists employ quantitative methods to supplement ethnographic research (e.g. Marshall, 1990), employ ethnographic or qualitative work as a precursor to the development of more culturally sensitive survey approaches (e.g. Ames et al., 1996; Delany & Ames, 1993), work in multidisciplinary research teams (e.g. Kunitz & Levy, 1994; see also the references in Bennett, 1988) or gain additional qualifications in other disciplines. This trend to multidisciplinarity echoes earlier calls in urban anthropology (e.g. Hannerz, 1980) for ethnographers to adopt survey techniques and to use historical and other documentary data in order to gain a more comprehensive perspective on urban life.

Having outlined the main trends of analysis in anthropological research on drinking in the most general of terms, I now want to examine ethnographic research on drinking amongst Australian Aborigines and amongst young people in order to demonstrate the ways in which these general trends manifest themselves in particular studies, the usefulness of an anthropological perspective on drinking, and how an anthropological perspective might differ from and complement the research of other disciplines.

AUSTRALIAN ABORIGINAL DRINKING

The use of alcohol by Aboriginal people has been identified as a major social problem by government committees, public health workers and academic researchers. This conclusion is supported by the available statistics on the contribution of alcohol consumption to Aboriginal mortality and morbidity, to arrest and imprisonment rates (although such figures should be treated with circumspection, due to the often public nature of Aboriginal drinking and the consequently greater likelihood of arrest), and to violence against persons, violence against property, and family disruptions in Aboriginal communities. Perhaps most importantly, alcohol use has also been identified as a major social problem by Aboriginal organizations and individuals.

Perhaps because of its obvious impact on Aboriginal communities, Aboriginal drinking has been researched by those drawn from a number of disciplines, including psychiatry, psychology, medicine, sociology and anthropology (for literature reviews, see Brady, 1992; Davis, 1998; Hunter, 1993; the National Aboriginal Health Working Party, 1989; Saggers & Gray, 1998). Some of these studies, particularly those conducted in earlier periods, are ethnocentric and functionalist in outlook. Particularly problematic are those analyses built on the assumption that contemporary Aborigines are suffering from "cultural disintegration", "cultural breakdown" or "anomie" (an absence of societal norms) when compared with idealized and pristine "traditional" or "tribal" Aborigines of the past (in the following, I have italicized the relevant words and phrases).

For example, Kamien (1978, p. 149) begins his discussion of the measurement of alcohol consumption in Bourke with the following sentence: "Australian Aborigines, like all *disintegrated* societies, drink excessive amounts of alcohol, and this in turn leads to further *breakdown* of their society". Spencer (1988) refers to "transitional alcoholism", which arises when "historically earlier" social forms (read "simple" or "from an earlier evolutionary phase") undergo "complex transformation" and Aboriginal people find themselves "torn between two systems" with a consequent "*lack of normative restraints* on their behaviour". Lickiss (1971, p. 211) states that research into the role of "problem drinking" amongst Aborigines needed to be seen within the context of "culture contact or *detribalization*". Rowley (1986, p. 1) writes of "the values that enabled successive [White] generations to accept the degradation of the *Aboriginal remnants*". Even two of the most influential anthropological observers of Aborigines were moved to write that: "[i]n the southern and south-eastern areas, where European settlement expanded rapidly, it [contact with outsiders] meant the *complete destruction* of the Aboriginal way of life" (Berndt & Berndt, 1981, p. 520; see also Berndt, 1977; Larsen, 1979; Gumbert, 1984).

More recent anthropological descriptions and interpretations of urban and/or contemporary Aboriginal cultures conflict with those presented above (e.g. Sansom, 1980; Chase,

1981; Langton, 1981, 1997; Beckett, 1988; Povinelli, 1993). In these works, anthropologists stress the elements of continuity between the "culture of Aboriginal people of 'settled' Australia and of people more remote from the area of dense European settlement, implying the reproduction of some cultural forms from the pre-colonial era" (Keen, 1988, p. 2), and argue against the settler distinction between "bush" or "full-blood" and "urban" or "half-caste" Aborigines. They are also cognisant of the political-economic context in which indigenous lives are lived, a noticeable absence in earlier work on "cultural disintegration". These writers examine the ways in which Aborigines drink and attempt to describe and understand the meanings of the drinking act. Is Aboriginal drinking "pathological", "anomic" and the result of cultural disintegration, or is it rule-governed, an activity laden with meanings?

Beckett (1965), in one of the earliest studies, identified two major influences on Aboriginal drunkenness: the "work and bust" pattern of White pastoral workers, who squandered their earnings of several months in a few days of explosive drinking; and the illegality of alcohol consumption for Aborigines (prior to 1962 in New South Wales, later in some other states). Other writers have noted that, in Aboriginal representations, the right to drink is often tied to the partial relaxation of oppressive laws and to the granting of citizenship (e.g. Barber, Punt & Albers, 1988; Brady, 1992; Rowse, 1993; Sansom, 1977). For example, Brady & Palmer (1984) argue that drinking at Diamond Well is a "means whereby they [Aborigines] mythically seek to redress their powerlessness and subordinate status in a world dominated by European Australians".

The ways in which drinking in and around Alice Springs has been incorporated into contemporary Aboriginal patterns of dependence and interdependence, especially between men and women, has been examined by Collmann (1979). Spending extra cash on liquor for the community gains one credit with which to counter the long-term inconsistencies in cash resources. Men must develop access to the domestic resources of women (e.g. government pensions) through sharing liquor bought with money earned in pastoral work. Women manipulate their own resources in order to make claims on the men's intermittent, but sometimes plentiful, resources. Moreover, the purchasing of liquor is an index of personal productivity and independence.

Collmann also argues, in a later and more wide-ranging analysis (Collmann, 1988), that greater interference in the everyday lives of central Australian Aborigines by White welfare workers, considered justified by concern over living conditions and certain practices (e.g. heavy drinking and prostitution), actually helped to perpetuate these practices. In his view, the fringe-camp, the site of many such practices and a potent symbol of "degenerate" Aboriginality, emerged as a means whereby Aborigines attempted to control and limit the increased power and involvement of White welfare agencies in their affairs. Thus fringe-camp drinking is a reaction to increased White interference and decreased Aboriginal autonomy. Sackett (1988) reaches a similar conclusion on the basis of research at Wiluna in Western Australia; that moves to foster social and economic development are interpreted by Aborigines as yet another form of state intervention in their already heavily-governed lives. Through their drinking, they express their resistance to White administration and, in the Western Desert context, this reflects a cultural ideology which emphasizes personal autonomy.

On the basis of field research in central Australia, O'Connor (1984) takes issue with the concept of "alcohol dependence", directing attention to the social factors involved in heavy drinking in Aboriginal groups. He argues that Aborigines are not "dependent" on alcohol except in a group sense. When heavy-drinking Aborigines find themselves outside of their customary drinking contexts, without their usual drinking partners, they may exhibit total abstinence. Even more surprisingly, given the "disease" concept of alcoholism out of which grew the dependence approach, these same drinkers may display moderation in their drinking. O'Connor suggests the concept of "contingent drunkenness" (see also Merlan, 1998, pp. 200–201). Collectively, these anthropologists argue that Aborigines appropriate the act of drinking and remodel it to conform to Aboriginal conceptions of behaviour. In their analyses, attention is paid to the patterns, social circumstances and social outcomes of drinking, features which owe much of their character to Aboriginal cultural notions of status, social credit and communal life.

Two themes unite these anthropological studies of Aboriginal drinking. First, while drinking frequently has extremely negative consequences, it is also indisputably an act that has meaning for participants: Aboriginal drinking is expressive of a desire for equality with Whites, group membership, personal autonomy and reciprocity between family and friends. Drinking is related to the sociocultural processes through which Aborigines construct and interpret their everyday world. Second, drinking can be interpreted as an act of political resistance. It constitutes a refusal to accept the imposition of a non-indigenous socio-cultural reality through the interventionist mechanisms of the Australian state. Studies of this kind suggest that those subscribing to the "cultural disintegration" model are guilty of ethnocentric pronouncements which render their analyses crude and simplistic. To say that Aboriginal culture is "lost" legitimizes ignorance of Aboriginal conceptions of drinking and promotes the view that drinking is solely a destructive and problematic activity. It allows the transplanting of existing medical, psychiatric and social orthodoxies to the Aboriginal situation, with token gestures towards acknowledging what are seen as virtually extinct cultural differences. Mugford (1988) has described the similarly restrictive influence of what he terms the "pathology paradigm" on theorizing about motivations to use drugs. In like fashion, those who maintain that modern Aboriginal cultures are mere "remnants" of traditional modalities, continue to shape, explicitly and implicitly, representations of contemporary Aborigines.

DRINKING AMONGST YOUNG PEOPLE

Studies of the relationship between young people and alcohol use most often explore the efficacy of various youth-orientated prevention/education programmes; national or regional patterns of youthful alcohol use; youthful attitudes to, beliefs about and behaviours involving alcohol; the role of parents and/or peers in shaping these attitudes, beliefs and behaviours; and the role of various sociological factors in youth drinking patterns (e.g. ethnicity, gender, social class).

Somewhat surprisingly, while young people have been the subject of countless studies by sociologists and, to a lesser extent, anthropologists, there is yet to develop an extensive ethnographic literature on their drinking practices. In this absence, I intend to focus more closely on several accounts of young people's drinking—those of Burns (1980), Dorn (1983) and O'Nell & Mitchell (1996)—in order to illustrate the kinds of analyses produced by ethnography. All of the cited studies deal, *inter alia*, with levels or styles of drinking that would be categorized as "problematic" by most public health practitioners. However, the kinds of analyses they provide are diverse.

Burns (1980) seeks to understand drinking in the context of the creation of social identity. He focuses on the meaning of drinking for young (18–22 year-old), working-class "Townies"—residents of Charlestown, a working-class, Irish-Catholic area of Boston. Burns opens his account with an extended description of a single evening, in which a party of young "Townies" aims to "get rowdy". Over the course of the evening, the young men drink many rounds of beer in various, and diverse, drinking contexts, with Burns estimating their consumption to be approximately two ounces of absolute alcohol per hour. After drinking in local bars, the men head off to the "Combat Zone", an adult entertainment area in which they drink more beer, get "felt up" by female sex workers, get into a fight and generally "get rowdy".

Burns argues that alcohol acts as a facilitator for the management of role conflict. The young men he befriends are expected to be sociable, affable, respectful to their elders and to women in general (with sex workers being considered an exception, judging by his account) and civil and polite in everyday life. There is also an ideology about how men enact their Townie-ness. For older men, this is primarily through their being the head of a family, a good provider and a good member of the local social clubs. For younger men, who occupy a liminal status between "boy" and "man", there are various ways of enacting masculine identity, such as playing sport and "hanging around" on the street, but the primary avenue is "getting rowdy": that is, drinking heavily, becoming raucous in conversation, getting into fights, standing with one's friends in threatening situations, and defying others to prevent one from engaging in such activities. The difficulty is that "getting rowdy" places them in conflict with the norms for everyday behaviour outlined above.

Getting rowdy is thus a "time-out" behaviour in which drinking allows Townies to step outside mundane roles and social settings and to enact alternative forms of masculine self-hood. There are, however, rules governing drunken comportment in this time-out period. Round drinking means that everyone drinks the same amount and there is pressure applied to round participants to "keep up". In North American culture, alcohol is also seen as providing an excuse to behave in certain, socially sanctioned, ways. Burns shows—in relation to drunken comportment—that Townies not only drink in ways appropriate to the settings in which they find themselves; they actively seek out settings in which it is more permissible to "get rowdy". They manage the possible repercussions of "getting rowdy" for their everyday work and family identities by confining their rowdiness to the Combat Zone.

Dorn (1983) gives an account of drinking, including "getting paralytic" (i.e. very drunk), amongst a sample of young people (in their mid-teens) in a "declining" inner-London borough. He employs interviews, participant observation and documentary sources in his case study. Although, like Burns, his method is ethnography and his focus the culture of drinking, his theoretical approach is "materialist", i.e. he conceptualizes the practices of young people, including drinking, as collective class responses to prevailing economic, social and political circumstances. There are two main areas of youth employment in the borough: a shrinking small-manufacturing sector and a relatively prosperous service sector. He chooses to focus on those young people—girls and boys—involved in the transition from secondary school to the service labour market who are, for the most part, drawn from the middle strata of the working class. His main point, echoing the drunken-comportment thesis, is that "learning to drink is also learning to labour, and vice versa" (1983, p. 192); i.e. the drinking of teenagers is closely connected to their learning about the world of adult work.

The drinking of this group—done mainly in a local pub—is characterized by mixed-sex round buying in which each person, regardless of age, gender or financial considerations, takes a turn to stand a round for the rest of the group. Because of their employment in the service sector, girls are as well-off financially as boys but those who are still at secondary school or unemployed experience financial constraints. However, despite these financial disparities, Dorn states that each person takes a turn willingly and is not subject to pressure from the others present. He argues that participating in round buying is motivated by the desire to be seen as equal, independent and adult. This reflects the ideology of the labour market, which maintains that wage-earners are independent and free agents.

Round drinking during the week serves to limit consumption. Teenagers drink half-pints of beer in groups of two or three. Newcomers to the pub either buy their own drinks or some or all of those already present leave to avoid becoming part of a larger round. However, at weekends, the teenagers strive to get "paralytic" and rounds become the vehicle for heavy drinking. Those who are not working or who are working part-time avoid the mid-week drinking in order to save their money for the Friday or Saturday night episodes of heavy drinking. Getting "pissed" once-a-week is regarded as a better option than either having to rely on others for financial handouts (and thus imply dependence and "child" status) or visiting the pub more often but being forced to leave early by a lack of money. In this way, they resolve the contradiction of having little money, yet wanting to participate in round-drinking and all that it signals about independence, adulthood and equality.

In summary, Dorn concludes that round drinking amongst young people employed in the service sector is a celebration (in the sphere of consumption and leisure) of the social relations of production in which these teenagers are becoming actors. For Dorn, "getting paralytic" is a "normal" part of their culture and does not result from some "internal and personal motivation" but emerges as a response to the material and contradictory conditions created by the slow process of transition from "youth" dependence to "adult" independence in the labour market.

O'Nell & Mitchell (1996) deal with another type of youthful drinking, that amongst Native American "adolescents" in the small town of Agency on the Northern Plains Reservation. The ethnographic research was conducted by O'Nell on a part-time basis over a 3 year period. She employed in-depth, repeat interviews, group discussions with young people and adults, informal questioning, and participant observation at community events. Again, their analysis, while ethnographic, differs from those offered by Burns and Dorn, in that they argue that teenage drinking is best understood in the historical context of Northern Plains culture. Despite a history of mistreatment and mismanagement at the hands of the dominant society, certain aspects of Plains Indian culture have survived, in modified form, into the present (cf. the discussion of Aboriginal drinking). Chief amongst these is the high value placed on one's contribution to one's family.

Classic Plains Indian cultural themes run through the lives of contemporary reservation teenagers. There is a culturally valued style of sociability—acts of friendship, generosity, competition and humour—and an emphasis on family loyalty and honour, courage and modesty. Adolescence is a time of new opportunities and responsibilities with respect to family, partners, peers and the general community. One's primary allegiance remains to one's family and kin but it is also important for teenagers to establish links to other teenagers. Both boys and girls are concerned with displays of courage and strength, while women must also show modesty. Irrespective of gender, one's behaviour reflects on one's family honour. Older teenagers should also take more interest in spiritual matters and participate in conversations with adults. They must negotiate a course where they have friends and romantic interests but also preserve their kin relations and responsibilities.

In this context, teenage drinking is normal and is done at "social" occasions, such as parties, where peer friendships are established and maintained. Definitions of "pathological" drinking refer to drinking that interferes with the gender-specific "developmental tasks" (i.e. "age-relevant responsibilities which arise out of culturally-based expectations for developing selves" [1996, p. 571]) facing adolescents: that is, maintaining strong and respectful ties with peers and family members while avoiding potentially shaming incidents for the family in the outside community (e.g. going to school with a hangover). Problematic drinking, therefore, is not rooted in frequency and quantity measures but in what is deemed to be culturally abnormal.

One important finding to emerge from this study is that *both* "normal" *and* "pathological" drinking are culturally defined. Whereas the idea that the parameters of "normal" drinking are culturally defined is by now uncontroversial, they argue that alcohol-related problems—the "contours of pathology"—are still perceived as universally recognizable. However, for O'Nell & Mitchell, pathological drinking is drinking the wrong beverage, at the wrong time, in the wrong place, with the wrong people, for the wrong reasons, where what counts as "wrong" is also constituted within a cultural value system. Both "normal" and "pathological" are culturally patterned valuations rather than objectively-defined categories. In their application by non-ethnographic researchers, such categories are also political, in that certain disciplines have the authority to define particular behaviours as "problematic". There is a risk, caution the authors, of imposing Euro-American values and problem definitions onto less powerful indigenous groups (there are obvious parallels here with the Australian Aboriginal situation). Unfortunately, while there is much to admire in their study of the continuities between past and present Plains Indian cultural forms, their article is not entirely free of the conceptual imposition that they caution against. The application of the term "adolescence" to a non-Western cultural setting appears to be problematic, given its location within a mainstream developmental psychology derived from and containing Western cultural notions regarding individualized identity (see Wyn & White, 1997, pp. 51–71, for a related discussion).

These three studies emphasize different aspects of the anthropological analysis of drinking amongst young people. Burns provides an ethnography of social identity and drinking, drawing attention to the sociocultural context in which young, male, working-class Bostonians must work to become men. Dorn frames his materialist analysis in terms of the ways in which a particular set of teenagers moves into the labour market. O'Nell & Mitchell give an account of teenage drinking which stresses continuities between earlier forms of Native American culture and contemporary reservation life. These studies focus on the universal transition from pre-adult to adult status but demonstrate that this transition is differentially constructed in various sociocultural and political-economic contexts. They also caution against assuming that there is an homogeneous category of "youthful drinking" that can be defined by quantitative measures.

CONCLUDING REMARKS

There is no unitary anthropological perspective on drinking alcohol, although there are common themes which receive different emphasis. The constructionist position applies an anthropological perspective to both drinking and to those researching drinking. Political-economic approaches emphasize the intersections between broader political, economic and social relations, particularly those of capitalism and post-colonialism, and local contexts for drinking. Multidisciplinary approaches look to incorporate ethnography's unique contribution with the strengths of other disciplines involved in alcohol studies. There is, of course, nothing to prevent anthropological studies employing elements of all of these approaches. Distinctive anthropological perspectives on drinking derive from the use of ethnographic methods and from the development of more general anthropological and social theory. They can contribute much that is unique and original, as well as complementing, supplementing and, sometimes, subverting existing orthodoxies in alcohol studies. I close with the words of arguably the most prominent social scientist working in alcohol studies, Robin Room (1985, p. xvi):

> [i]f we are to understand and reduce the occurrence of problems related to alcohol, we must know more about the cultural meanings attached to its use.

ACKNOWLEDGEMENTS

I thank Tim Stockwell and Nick Heather for helpful comments on an earlier version of this chapter.

KEY WORKS AND SUGGESTIONS FOR FURTHER READING

MacAndrew, C. & Edgerton, R.B. (1969).   *Drunken Comportment: A Social Explanation*. London: Nelson.

> The authors of this book, drawing on ethnographic and ethnohistorical data, advance the thesis that "drunken comportment" is shaped by the sociocultural context in which it occurs. Although this idea was not new in anthropological circles, the book was also widely read by those beyond anthropology.

Gusfield, J.R. (1981).   *The Culture of Public Problems: Drinking–Driving and the Symbolic Order*. Chicago: University of Chicago Press.

> Gusfield provides a constructionist analysis of drinking–driving research in the United States. More specifically, he argues that the construction of the individual "killer drunk" is, in itself, a product of North American culture with its emphasis on individual-level explanations.

Room, R. (1984).   Alcohol and ethnography: a case of problem deflation? [with comments by M. Agar, J. Beckett, L.A. Bennett, S. Casswell, D.B. Heath, J. Leland, J.E. Levy, W. Madsen, M. Marshall, J. Moskalewicz, J.C. Negrete, M.B. Rodin, L. Sackett, M. Sargent, D. Strug & J.O. Waddell]. *Current Anthropology*, **25**(2), 169–191.

> Room argues that anthropologists, for a variety of reasons, have consistently under-played the problems associated with alcohol use. Anthropological responses to his argument range from agreement to angry counter-critique.

Heath, D.B. (1991).   Continuity and change in drinking patterns of the Bolivian Camba. In D.J. Pittman & H.R. White (Eds), *Society, Culture, and Drinking Patterns Re-examined* (pp. 78–108). New Brunswick, NJ: Rutgers Center of Alcohol Studies.

> A companion piece to his classic 1958 article on the Camba, in which he argued that, despite explosive drinking parties involving a highly alcoholic drink, the Camba experienced virtually no alcohol-related problems. He reports new evidence that provides further support for his original thesis regarding the link between the nature of Camba drinking and the atomistic nature of Camba society.

Kunitz, S.J. & Levy, J.E. (1994).   *Drinking Careers: A Twenty-five-year Study of Three Navajo Populations*. New Haven, CT: Yale University Press.

> *Drinking Careers* is an example of the merits of combining epidemiological and ethnographic research in order to gain a more comprehensive understanding of drinking amongst Native Americans; a continuation of their earlier and highly-regarded multi-disciplinary work [Levy, J.E. & Kunitz, S.J. (1974). *Indian Drinking: Navajo Practices and Anglo-American Theories*. New York: Wiley].

Saggers, S. & Gray, D. (1998).   *Dealing with Alcohol: Indigenous Usage in Australia, New Zealand and Canada*. Melbourne: Cambridge University Press.

> This book is a recent example of the political-economy approach which provides a comprehensive review of the available research and policy literature on alcohol use amongst indigenous peoples in Australia, New Zealand and Canada.

REFERENCES

Ames, G., Schmidt, C., Klee, L. & Saltz, R. (1996). Combining methods to identify new measures of women's drinking problems. Part 1: The ethnographic stage. *Addiction*, **91**(6), 829–844.

Bacon, M.K., Barry, H.J. & Child, I.L. (1965). A cross-cultural study of drinking, II: Relations to other features of culture. *Quarterly Journal of Studies on Alcohol*, **3**(Suppl.), 29–48.

Barber, J.G., Punt, J. & Albers, J. (1988). Alcohol and power on Palm Island. *Australian Journal of Social Issues*, **23**(2), 87–101.

Beckett, J. (1965). Aborigines, alcohol and assimilation. In M. Reay (Ed.), *Aborigines Now* (pp. 32–47). Sydney: Angus and Robertson.

Beckett, J. (Ed.) (1988). *Past and Present: The Construction of Aboriginality*. Canberra: Aboriginal Studies Press.

Bennett, L.A. (1988). Alcohol in context: anthropological perspectives. *Drugs and Society*, **2**, 89–131.

Berndt, R. (Ed.) (1977). *Aborigines and Change: Australia in the 1970s*. Canberra: Australian Institute of Aboriginal Studies.

Berndt, C.H. & Berndt, R.M. (1981). *The World of the First Australians*. Sydney: Lansdowne.

Brady, M. (1992). Ethnography and understandings of Aboriginal drinking. *Journal of Drug Issues*, **22**(3), 699–712.

Brady, M. (Ed.) (1995). *Giving Away the Grog: Aboriginal Accounts of Drinking and Not Drinking*. Canberra: Commonwealth Department of Human Services and Health.

Brady, M. & Palmer, K. (1984). *Alcohol in the Outback: Two Studies of Drinking*. Darwin: Australian National University North Australia Research Unit.

Bunzel, R. (1940). The role of alcoholism in two Central American cultures. *Psychiatry*, **3**, 361–187.

Burns, T.F. (1980). Getting rowdy with the boys. *Journal of Drug Issues*, **10**, 273–286.

Chase, A. (1981). Empty vessels and loud noises: views about Aboriginality today. *Social Alternatives*, **2**(2), 23–27.

Collmann, J. (1979). Social order and the exchange of liquor: a theory of drinking among Australian Aborigines. *Journal of Anthropological Research*, **32**(2), 208–224.

Collmann, J. (1988). *Fringe-Dwellers and Welfare: The Aboriginal Response to Bureaucracy*. St Lucia: University of Queensland Press.

Davis, J. (1998). Alcohol and Aboriginal society: is racism dead in the alcohol and drug field? In M. Hamilton, A. Kellehear & G. Rumbold (Eds), *Drug Use in Australia: A Harm Minimisation Approach* (pp. 84–97). Melbourne: Oxford University Press.

Delaney, W. & Ames, G. (1993). Integration and exchange in multidisciplinary alcohol research. *Social Science and Medicine*, **37**(1), 5–13.

Dorn, N. (1983). *Alcohol, Youth and the State*. London: Croom Helm.

Douglas, M. (1987a). A distinctive anthropological perspective. In M. Douglas (Ed.), *Constructive Drinking: Perspectives on Drink from Anthropology* (pp. 3–15). Cambridge: Cambridge University Press.

Douglas, M. (Ed.) (1987b). *Constructive Drinking: Perspectives on Drink from Anthropology*. Cambridge: Cambridge University Press.

Errington, S. (1990). Recasting sex, gender, and power. In J.M. Atkinson & S. Errington (Eds), *Power and Difference: Gender in Island Southeast Asia* (pp. 11–37). Stanford, CT: Stanford University Press.

Field, P.B. (1962). A new cross-cultural study of drunkenness. In D. Pittman & C. Snyder (Eds), *Society, Culture, and Drinking Patterns* (pp. 48–74). New York: Wiley.

Foucault, M. (1973). *The Order of Things: An Archaeology of the Human Sciences*. New York: Vintage Press.

Gefou-Madianou, D. (1992). Introduction: Alcohol commensality, identity transformations and transcendence. In D. Gefou-Madianou (Ed.), *Alcohol, Gender and Culture* (pp. 1–34). London: Routledge.

Gumbert, M. (1984). *Neither Justice Nor Reason: A Legal and Anthropological Analysis of Aboriginal Land Rights*. St Lucia: University of Queensland Press.

Gusfield, J.R. (1981). *The Culture of Public Problems: Drinking–Driving and the Symbolic Order*. Chicago: University of Chicago Press.

Hannerz, U. (1980). *Exploring the City: Inquiries Toward an Urban Anthropology*. New York: Colum-
    bia University Press.
Heath, D.B. (1958). Drinking patterns of the Bolivian Camba. *Quarterly Journal of Studies on
    Alcohol*, **19**, 491–508.
Heath, D.B. (1975). A critical review of ethnographic studies of alcohol use. In R. Gibbins, Y. Israel,
    H. Kalant, R. Popham, W. Schmidt & R. Smart (Eds), *Research Advances in Alcohol and Drug
    Problems* (pp. 1–92). New York: Wiley.
Heath, D.B. (1976). Anthropological perspectives on alcohol: an historical review. In M.W. Everett,
    J.O. Waddell & D.B. Heath (Eds), *Cross-Cultural Approaches to the Study of Alcohol: An Inter-
    disciplinary Perspective* (pp. 41–101). The Hague: Mouton.
Heath, D.B. (1986). Drinking and drunkenness in transcultural perspective: Parts I and II. *Trans-
    cultural Psychiatric Research Review*, **23**, 7–42, 103–126.
Heath, D.B. (1987a). Anthropology and alcohol studies: current issues. *Annual Review of Anthro-
    pology*, **16**, 99–120.
Heath, D.B. (1987b). A decade of development in the anthropological study of alcohol use,
    1970–1980. In M. Douglas (Ed.), *Constructive Drinking: Perspectives on Drink from Anthropology*
    (pp. 16–69). Cambridge: Cambridge University Press.
Heath, D.B. (1991a). The mutual relevance of anthropological and sociological perspec-
    tives in alcohol studies. In P.M. Roman (Ed.), *Alcohol: The Development of Sociological
    Perspectives on Use and Abuse* (pp. 125–144). New Brunswick, NJ: Rutgers Center of Alcohol
    Studies.
Heath, D.B. (1991b). Continuity and change in drinking patterns of the Bolivian Camba. In D.J.
    Pittman & H.R. White (Eds), *Society, Culture, and Drinking Patterns Re-examined* (pp. 78–108).
    New Brunswick, NJ: Rutgers Center of Alcohol Studies.
Horton, D.J. (1943). The functions of alcohol in primitive societies: a cross-cultural study. *Quarterly
    Journal of Studies on Alcohol*, **4**, 199–320.
Hunter, E. (1993). *Aboriginal Health and History: Power and Prejudice in Remote Australia*. Mel-
    bourne: Cambridge University Press.
Kamien, M. (1978). The measurement of alcohol consumption in Australian Aborigines. *Community
    Health Studies*, **2**(3), 149–151.
Keen, I. (Ed.) (1988). *Being Black: Aboriginal Cultures in "Settled" Australia*. Canberra: Aboriginal
    Studies Press.
Knorr-Cetina, K.D. (1981). *The Manufacture of Knowledge: An Essay on the Constructivist and Con-
    textual Nature of Science*. Oxford: Pergamon.
Kunitz, S.J. & Levy, J.E. (1994). *Drinking Careers: A Twenty-Five-Year Study of Three Navajo Popu-
    lations*. New Haven, CT: Yale University Press.
Langton, M. (1981). Urbanizing Aborigines: the social scientists' great deception. *Social Alternatives*,
    2(2), 16–22.
Langton, M. (1997). Rum, seduction and death: "aboriginality" and alcohol. In G. Cowlishaw &
    B. Morris (Eds), *Race Matters: Indigenous Australians and "Our" Society* (pp. 77–94). Canberra:
    Aboriginal Studies Press.
Larsen, K.S. (1979). Social crisis and Aboriginal alcohol abuse. *Australian Journal of Social Issues*,
    14(2), 143–160.
Lickiss, J.N. (1971). Alcohol and Aborigines in cross-cultural situations. *Australian Journal of Social
    Issues*, **6**(3), 210–216.
MacAndrew, C. & Edgerton, R.B. (1969). *Drunken Comportment: A Social Explanation*. London:
    Nelson.
McClelland, D.C., Davis, W.N., Kalin, R. & Wanner, E. (1972). *The Drinking Man*. New York: Free
    Press.
McDonald, M. (1994). Introduction: a social-anthropological view of gender, drink and drugs. In M.
    McDonald (Ed.), *Gender, Drink and Drugs* (pp. 1–31). Oxford: Berg.
McLellan, D. (Ed.) (1977). *Karl Marx: Selected Writings*. Oxford: Oxford University Press.
Mandelbaum, D.G. (1965). Alcohol and culture [with comments by V.S. Erlich, K.A. Hasan, D.B.
    Heath, J.J. Honigmann, E.M. Lemert & W. Madsen]. *Current Anthropology*, **6**(3), 281–293.
Marshall, M. (1979). Introduction. In M. Marshall (Ed.), *Beliefs, Behaviours, and Alcoholic
    Beverages: A Cross-Cultural Survey* (pp. 1–11). Ann Arbor, MI: University of Michigan Press.

Marshall, M. (1981). "Four hundred rabbits": an anthropological view of ethanol as a disinhibitor. In R. Room & G. Collins (Eds), *Alcohol and Disinhibition: Nature and Meaning of the Link* (pp. 186–204). NIAAA Research Monograph No. 12. Rockville, MD: US Department of Health and Human Services.

Marshall, M. (1990). Combining insights from epidemiological and ethnographic data to investigate substance use in Truk, Federated States of Micronesia. *British Journal of Addiction*, **85**, 1457–1468.

Merlan, F. (1998). *Caging the Rainbow: Place, Politics, and Aborigines in a North Australian Town.* Honolulu: University of Hawaii Press.

Mugford, S. (1988). Pathology, pleasure, profit and the state: towards an integrated theory of drug use. Paper presented to the Annual Conference of the Australian and New Zealand Society of Criminology, Sydney.

National Aboriginal Health Strategy Working Party (1989). *A National Aboriginal Health Strategy.* Canberra: AGPS.

O'Connor, R. (1984). Alcohol and contingent drunkenness in central Australia. *Australian Journal of Social Issues*, **19**(3), 173–183.

O'Nell, T.D. & Mitchell, C.M. (1996). Alcohol use among American Indian adolescents: the role of culture in pathological drinking. *Social Science and Medicine*, **42**(4), 565–578.

Povinelli, E.A. (1993). *Labor's Lot: The Power, History, and Culture of Aboriginal Action.* Chicago: University of Chicago Press.

Room, R. (1984). Alcohol and ethnography: a case of problem deflation? [with comments by M. Agar, J. Beckett, L.A. Bennett, S. Casswell, D.B. Heath, J. Leland, J.E. Levy, W. Madsen, M. Marshall, J. Moskalewicz, J.C. Negrete, M.B. Rodin, L. Sackett, M. Sargent, D. Strug & J.O. Waddell]. *Current Anthropology*, **25**(2), 169–191.

Room, R. (1985). Foreword. In L.A. Bennett & G.M. Ames (Eds), *The American Experience with Alcohol: Contrasting Cultural Perspectives* (pp. xi–xvii). New York: Plenum.

Room, R. (1991). Social science research and alcohol policy making. In P.M. Roman (Ed.), *Alcohol: The Development of Sociological Perspectives on Use and Abuse* (pp. 315–339). New Brunswick, NJ: Rutgers Center of Alcohol Studies.

Roseberry, W. (1989). *Anthropologies and Histories: Essays in Culture, History, and Political Economy.* New Brunswick, NJ: Rutgers University Press.

Rowley, C.D. (1986). *Recovery: The Politics of Aboriginal Reform.* Ringwood: Penguin.

Rowse, T. (1993). The relevance of ethnographic understanding to Aboriginal anti-grog initiatives. *Drug and Alcohol Review*, **12**(4), 393–399.

Sackett, L. (1988). Resisting arrests: drinking, development and discipline in a desert context. *Social Analysis*, **24**, 66–77.

Saggers, S. & Gray, D. (1998). *Dealing with Alcohol: Indigenous Usage in Australia, New Zealand and Canada.* Melbourne: Cambridge University Press.

Sansom, B. (1977). Aborigines and alcohol: a fringe camp example. *Australian Journal of Alcohol and Drug Dependence*, **4**(2), 58–62.

Sansom, B. (1980). *The Camp at Wallaby Cross.* Canberra: Australian Institute of Aboriginal Studies.

Sargent, M. (1979). *Drinking and Alcoholism in Australia: A Power Relations Theory.* Melbourne: Longman Cheshire.

Singer, M. (1986). Toward a political economy of alcoholism: the missing link in the anthropology of drinking. *Social Science and Medicine*, **23**(2), 113–130.

Spencer, D.J. (1988). Transitional alcoholism—the Australian Aboriginal model. *Technical Information Bulletin on Drug Abuse*, **79**, 15–23.

Wolf, E. (1982). *Europe and the People Without History.* Berkeley, CA: University of California Press.

Wyn, J. & White, R. (1997). *Rethinking Youth.* Sydney: Allen and Unwin.

Part V

Treatment and Recovery

Edited by Nick Heather
Centre for Alcohol and Drug Studies, University of Northumbria at Newcastle, Newcastle upon Tyne, UK

EDITOR'S INTRODUCTION

This is a very exciting time in the science of treatment for alcohol dependence and problems, a time of uncertainty but also of great promise. It should always be remembered that the scientific study of treatment in this field is a relatively recent phenomenon, with very few outcome studies or controlled trials appearing before the end of World War II. In the 50 or so years since then, the volume of scientific work has steadily grown from a trickle to a veritable flood and we are now confronted with a massive number of relevant publications in the scientific literature. More important than quantity, the quality of research, too, has greatly increased over this period; sample sizes, levels of methodological and statistical sophistication, and standards of scientific reporting have all shown marked improvements. We are now seeing a growing tendency towards multicentre and cross-cultural research and this can only increase the amount of secure knowledge in the field. The closing years of the twentieth century witnessed the publication of results from the largest and most expensive randomized controlled trial ever mounted, not only of treatment of alcohol problems but of any kind of psychosocial treatment for any type of disorder (Project MATCH Research Group, 1997a,b, 1998). Any evaluation of the "state of the art" of alcohol treatment research must use this study as its starting point.

Ironically, it is the results of Project MATCH that have been partly responsible for the present uncertainty in the field. There was a time during the late 1970s and early 1980s when, following the classic publications by Emrick (1975) and Edwards et al. (1977), the question was seriously asked whether treatment for alcohol problems could be said to work at all (see Chapter 31, this volume). During the 1980s, the great hope for an improvement in success rates was perceived to lie in the potential for client–treatment matching (Institute of Medicine, 1990), i.e. the simple idea, commonplace in many areas of health care, that certain types of client need certain types of treatment to show maximum benefit. It was this matching hypothesis that Project MATCH was designed to test. While four clinically useful matching effects were identified in the project (see Project MATCH Research Group, 1997a,b, 1998), the more general hypothesis, that careful matching would improve overall success rates, was not confirmed. While this result does not completely invalidate the potential usefulness of client–treatment matching, since several possible forms of matching were not investigated by Project MATCH (see Heather, 1999), it is clearly disappointing to those who believed that matching represented the best prospect for a radical improvement in the effectiveness of treatment for alcohol problems.

Another unsettling finding from Project MATCH was that, irrespective of any client–treatment matches that did or did not appear, the overall effectiveness of the three treatments studied—Cognitive-behavioural Coping Skills Therapy (CBT), Motivational Enhancement Therapy (MET) and Twelve-step Facilitation Therapy (TSF)—was about the same. This pattern did not change throughout a 3 year follow-up period (Project MATCH Research Group, 1998). This certainly does not mean that the treatments studied were ineffective; on the contrary, although the design did not include a "no treatment" control group, the absolute success and improvement rates of all three treatment modalities were impressive—higher than reported in most other studies and clearly higher than those typically found among routine treatment services. This encourages the idea that, if routine treatment were carried out to the high standards of therapist training and quality control of treatment delivery shown in Project MATCH, the effectiveness of everyday service provision could be significantly increased; in short, Project MATCH showed that treatment *can* be highly effective if delivered in the right way.

Nevertheless, the lack of statistical and clinically relevant differences between the three MATCH treatments is disappointing to those who had hoped for unambiguous answers to crucial questions regarding the possible superiority of one form of treatment over others—in other words, to the clear identification of a main "treatment of choice" for alcohol problems. From the most pessimistic point of view, the conclusion from the MATCH findings might be that it does not matter what kind of treatment one gives problem drinkers, they will show the same degree of improvement from all of them. While this is obviously to overstate the case, views of this kind are often heard and suggest that variables other than treatment type—perhaps client motivation to change, level of therapist skill or empathy, or a combination of both—are mainly responsible for variations in treatment outcome.

How can all this be reconciled with the main conclusion of Janice M. Brown's overview of the treatment effectiveness literature in Chapter 24—the conclusion that there are clear and large differences in the effectiveness of different types of treatment for alcohol problems? In fact, the difficulty is more apparent than real. In the first place, two of the MATCH treatments, CBT and MET, are among those listed by Brown as effective treatments; many of the components of CBT, such as social skills training and relapse prevention methods, are well supported by research evidence; and the effectiveness of MET is consistent with evidence that motivational interviewing receives "overwhelming support" (Chapter 24, p. 499) from the literature. Although most of the studies supporting motivational interviewing targeted the non-treatment population of heavy drinkers (see Chapter 31), the evidence at least shows that this is an effective way of persuading people to change their drinking behaviour. TSF, the other treatment modality included in Project MATCH, had not previously been examined in a controlled trial and it has not been possible, for obvious reasons, to conduct a randomized controlled trial of the effectiveness of Alcoholics Anonymous (see Chapter 34, this volume). Thus the literature prior to Project MATCH provides no evidence either way on the effectiveness of Twelve-step approaches.

There is still the difficulty that, with a few exceptions, Project MATCH gave no grounds for the encouragement of client–treatment matching and, while a number of effective treatments are listed in Chapter 24, there is little clear guidance available on which types of client should be offered each of them. However, the MATCH findings apply only to *systematic* client–treatment matching, i.e. to a formal treatment system with rules to channel clients into specific types of therapeutic approach; they have little or no bearing on the traditional clinical skill of tailoring treatment to the unique needs, goals and characteristics of a particular client in the individual case. Thus, the evidence shows that treatment providers have available to them a range of effective treatments from which to select the approach that appears, on clinical grounds, to give the client the best chances of improvement—in the words of Miller et al. (1998), a "wealth of alternatives" from which to choose.

Another valuable conclusion from Chapter 24 is that there is a range of treatments for which there is no evidence of effectiveness. This does not mean that there has been no research on these treatments but that there has been research, in some cases extensive, that has failed to provide any grounds for confidence in these treatments. From her own national perspective, Brown remarks that all these ineffective approaches are typically offered in US treatment programmes and, combined with the fact that the effective treatments are typically not used (Miller & Hester, 1986), this is one of the most outstanding examples one could find of the oft-lamented gap between research evidence and clinical practice. Although this situation might not be so bad in some other countries, there is probably no national treatment service to which it does not apply to some extent.

Yet another useful aspect of Chapter 24 is the focus on the economic aspects of treatment delivery. It cannot be repeated often enough that, even in the richest countries of the world, demand for health care provision will always exceed supply. Thus, the recent emphasis in research on the cost–benefits and cost–effectiveness of treatment for alcohol problems should not be seen as an attempt to palm off problem drinkers with second-best treatment but, on the contrary, as a rational response to the situation of ever-increasing demands for treatment in the face of limited health care resources, with the aim of ensuring that alcohol treatments retain their place in the panoply of treatment services on offer. This issue is especially relevant to an evaluation of brief intervention and is explored further in Chapter 31.

However potentially effective a treatment might be, it is essential that it is appropriate to the client's needs and circumstances, and also that there is a solid basis for deciding whether or not it has been successful and to what degree. This is the area of assessment and is the topic of Chapter 25 by Yang & Skinner. The authors include both brief intervention and specialized treatment within the remit of their chapter and make a useful practical distinction between two forms of assessment—alcohol problem identification and comprehensive assessment. It is often said that assessment, rather than being a quite separate process from treatment proper, is the first step in a competent and effective treatment programme, and this emerges clearly from Chapter 25.

In many ways, detoxification is the least controversial aspect of treatment for alcohol problems and the one where there is most agreement among practitioners and researchers alike. In Chapter 26, Duncan Raistrick describes the alcohol withdrawal syndrome in detail before stating that detoxification is usually a very straightforward procedure. However, the exceptions to this rule are sufficiently serious in their consequences that clinicians are advised to maintain vigilance throughout the detoxification procedure. The indications for and uses of a number of drug treatments and adjunctive therapies are described, while the need for accurate measurement of withdrawal severity and the outcome of detoxification is stressed. What may be found controversial is Raistrick's view that "dependence should be seen as a purely psychological phenomenon to which withdrawal makes some, quite limited contribution" (p. 524). This well-argued case deserves serious consideration.

Pharmacological agents are, of course, the main method of treatment for the alcohol withdrawal syndrome. However, Chapter 27 by Jonathan Chick is not concerned with this use of therapeutic drugs but with the effort to change harmful drinking behaviour and, in particular, with ways to prevent relapse (see also Chapter 29). Linked to the research advances described in Chapters 6 and 13 of this book, the last decade has seen major developments in this area, most notably research and implementation in practice of acamprosate, naltrexone and other opioid antagonists, and serotonin-enhancing drugs such as fluoxetine (Prozac). These drugs are described in Chapter 27, as well as more traditional agents used in the treatment of alcohol problems, such as disulfiram and other deterrent drugs. In a useful review, Chick provides information on mode of action, evidence of efficacy, characteristics of responders, interaction with other therapies, unwanted effects, use in practice and what to tell patients. An important conclusion of this chapter is that evidence favours the use of these drugs in combination with some form of psychosocial therapy and that, at best, they "are only an aid to establishing a change in lifestyle" (p. 552).

Part V then proceeds with chapters written by the same team of authors (Parks, Marlatt & Anderson) on two related treatment approaches. However, the extensive research evidence on them and their importance in the spectrum of currently available treatment modalities justifies the inclusion of separate chapters in the book. Both chapters form part of a cognitive-behavioural approach to problem drinking, but Chapter 28 deals with assessment and intervention procedures designed to facilitate an initial change in behaviour, whereas Chapter 29 is concerned with the attempt to ensure that initial gains are maintained over time. With regard to the latter, the work of G. Alan Marlatt and his colleagues in the late 1970s and early 1980s, summarized in the book by Marlatt & Gordon (1985), ushered in a revolutionary change in thinking about and treating alcohol use disorders. While others may have observed before that alcohol dependence and other addictive behaviours were essentially relapsing conditions, the implications of this simple observation had not previously been logically explored, rigorously investigated and developed into a highly practical approach to treatment. As a consequence, relapse prevention therapy came to exert a profound influence on research and practice in the addictions field throughout the world. With regard to the more general cognitive-behavioural perspective, it is fair to say that, as a body of treatment principles, methods and procedures, it is the approach to treatment of alcohol problems best supported by research evidence of any yet devised. These secure scientific foundations, together with the flexibility and usefulness of the approach, are well illustrated in Chapters 28 and 29.

The approach to treatment that could be considered in the last decade to have rivalled or even surpassed cognitive-behavioural therapy in popularity among professionals in the alcohol field is motivational interviewing, and this is the topic of Chapter 30 by Rollnick & Allison. Beginning with a classic article by W.R. Miller in 1983, the principles and methods of motivational interviewing have exerted a profound and lasting influence on therapeutic interactions with problem drinkers all over the world, an influence that was reinforced with the publication of a widely-read text by Miller and one of the authors of Chapter 30 (Miller & Rollnick, 1991). The very popularity of this approach means that it must have struck a chord in the experience of many people working to help problem drinkers. The chapter outlines the practice of motivational interviewing, and the key principles and core skill areas of the method. The relevant research evidence is briefly reviewed and the main opportunities and limitations of motivational interviewing are discussed.

The chapters in this section described so far include a number of important and relatively recent changes in the treatment of alcohol problems. Yet another of these crucial developments is what has become known as the "broadening of the base" of treatment, i.e. the move away from an almost exclusive preoccupation in the disease theory of alcoholism with the relatively few severely dependent individuals in society to a wider focus on the total range of alcohol-related harm, as represented by the many levels and varieties of harm that exist. This expansion of concern, which can best be seen as part of a public health perspective on alcohol problems, was first evident in the late 1970s (see Heather & Robertson, 1981) but was well summarized by a book by the Institute of Medicine in the USA in 1990. In practical terms, the chief component of this broadening of the base of treatment is the advent of "brief interventions" and this is the subject matter of Chapter 31 by Nick Heather. However, the chapter begins by making a clear distinction between two different classes of activity that have been called brief interventions—brief treatment and opportunistic brief intervention—and the need for this distinction, for the purposes of clarity and progress in the field, is explained. The chapter goes on to consider the origins of interest in both classes of brief interventions, the evidence bearing on their effectiveness, the range of applications associated with them and their potential benefits for the effort to reduce alcohol-related harm on a widespread scale. Both classes of intervention have important implications for the cost-effectiveness of services which are also described in the chapter.

The most recent issue to have captured the attention of treatment providers is the difficulty in providing adequate help to people who suffer from both addictive disorders and other psychiatric disturbances. This difficulty has been long recognized in the literature but it is only within the last decade or so that research and practice have given serious attention to ways it might be solved. Certainly, no book claiming to cover the current treatment of alcohol problems could be considered complete without separate attention to the area of comorbidity with psychiatric disorder. In Chapter 32, Mueser & Kavanagh begin by reviewing research on the prevalence of various types of comorbidity before describing the main principles and methods underlying treatment. The authors make a strong case for an integrated and systematic approach to the treatment of comorbidity and for the need to provide specialized approaches to particular psychiatric disorders among those with alcohol use disorders.

Despite justified optimism about the actual and potential effectiveness of treatment for alcohol problems, it is always salutary to remind ourselves that many people recover from alcohol dependence and problems, sometimes of a severe kind, without any professional help. Apart from any other consideration, it is obvious that treatment providers, theorists and researchers alike can learn a great deal from the study of such people. The two main ways in which recovery is accomplished without professional assistance are described in the remaining chapters of the section. In Chapter 33, Harald K.-H. Klingemann discusses natural recovery from alcohol problems by placing it within the context of recovery from addictive disorders in general, arguing that the nature of "self-change" demands revisions to standard conceptions of addiction itself. In reviewing research evidence in this area, Klingemann highlights the methodological problems this research faces. The chapter concludes with a discussion of the implications of the evidence on self-change for both treatment and policy regarding addictive disorders.

In the second chapter concerned with recovery without professional help, and the last in Part V, Chad Emrick describes and discusses the Fellowship of Alcoholics Anonymous (AA) and other mutual-aid groups in Chapter 34. In modern times, AA affiliates were the first to offer any kind of organized help to people suffering from alcohol dependence and problems in the 1930s and did so, moreover, in the face of professional and scientific indifference; there is no doubt that the Fellowship has saved the lives of hundreds of thousands of people since that time. It must also be recognized that there has often been a conflict of beliefs, perspectives and priorities between AA and the formal treatment and scientific community interested in alcohol problems, a conflict summarized some time ago as that between the "craftsman" and the "professional" (Kalb & Propper, 1976; Cook, 1985). More recently, however, there are signs that a form of *rapprochement* has been reached between the two sides, especially since the abatement of the so-called "controlled drinking controversy" (see Heather & Robertson, 1981; Roizen, 1987). One mark of this is the publication of a volume on research approaches to AA (McCrady & Miller, 1993). Another is that the primary purpose of Chapter 34 is "to inform health care workers and other interested readers about Alcoholics Anonymous" (p. 664). In addition to this advice and several other useful kinds of information, Emrick describes a range of mutual-aid groups from around the world that are not based on the AA Twelve Steps. The significance of these groups, and especially of the newer ones such as Rational Recovery, Secular Organizations for Sobriety and Women for Sobriety, is that they may be able to retain the considerable benefits of mutual aid without also insisting on the spiritual content of AA which, while many find it essential to their recovery, others find unacceptable.

REFERENCES

Cook, D.R. (1985). Craftsman vs. professional: analysis of the controlled drinking controversy. *Journal of Studies on Alcohol*, **46**, 433–442.

Edwards, G., Orford, J., Egert, S., Guthrie, S., Hawker, A., Hensman, C., Mitcheson, M., Oppenheimer, E. & Taylor, C. (1977). Alcoholism: a controlled study of "treatment" and "advice". *Journal of Studies on Alcohol*, **38**, 1004–1031.

Emrick, C.D. (1975). A review of psychologically oriented treatment of alcoholism: II. The relative effectiveness of different treatment approaches and the effectiveness of treatment vs. no treatment. *Quarterly Journal of Studies on Alcohol*, **36**, 88–108.

Heather, N. (1999). Some common methodological criticisms of Project MATCH: are they justified? *Addiction*, **94**, 36–39.

Heather, N. & Robertson, I. (1981). *Controlled Drinking*. London: Methuen.

Institute of Medicine (1990). *Broadening the Base of Treatment for Alcohol Problems*. Washington, DC: National Academy Press.

Kalb, M. & Propper, M.S. (1976).   The future of alcohology: craft or science? *American Journal of Psychiatry*, **133**, 641–645.

McCrady, B.S. & Miller, W.R. (Eds) (1993).   *Research on Alcoholics Anonymous: Opportunities and Alternatives.* New Brunswick, NJ: Rutgers Center of Alcohol Studies.

Marlatt, G.A. & Gordon, J.R. (1985).   *Relapse Prevention: Maintenance Strategies in the Treatment of Addictive Behaviors.* New York: Guilford.

Miller, W.R. (1983).   Motivational interviewing with problem drinkers. *Behavioural Psychotherapy*, **1**, 147–172.

Miller, W.R. & Hester, R.K. (1986).   The effectiveness of alcoholism treatment: what research reveals. In W.R. Miller & N. Heather (Eds), *Treating Addictive Behaviors: Processes of Change* (pp. 121–174). New York: Plenum.

Miller, W.R. & Rollnick, S. (1991).   *Motivational Interviewing: Preparing People to Change Addictive Behavior.* New York: Guilford.

Miller, W.R., Andrews, N.R., Wilbourne, P. & Bennett, M.E. (1998).   A wealth of alternatives: effective treatments for alcohol problems. In W.R. Miller & N. Heather (Eds), *Treating Addictive Behaviors*, 2nd edn (pp. 203–216). New York: Plenum.

Project MATCH Research Group (1997a).   Matching alcoholism treatments to client heterogeneity: Project MATCH posttreatment drinking outcomes. *Journal of Studies on Alcohol*, **58**, 7–29.

Project MATCH Research Group (1997b).   Project MATCH secondary *a priori* hypotheses. *Addiction*, **92**, 1655–1682.

Project MATCH Research Group (1998).   Matching alcoholism treatments to client heterogeneity: Project MATCH three-year drinking outcomes. *Alcoholism: Experimental & Clinical Research*, **22**, 1300–1311.

Roizen, R. (1987).   The great controlled-drinking controversy. In M. Galanter (Ed.), *Recent Developments in Alcoholism*, Vol. 5 (pp. 245–279). New York: Plenum.

Chapter 24

The Effectiveness of Treatment

Janice M. Brown
University of Arkansas, Fayetteville, AR, USA

Synopsis

Over the past decade, the treatment outcome research has consistently shown that there are effective treatment approaches. These approaches include brief interventions and motivational interviewing, social skills training, community reinforcement, behavior contracting, relapse prevention and some aversion therapies. The commonality among these treatment approaches is the focus on actively engaging the client in the processes of suppressing use and teaching alternative coping skills. Research has also indicated that some of the more typical US treatment components are not effective and typically show no improvement or worse outcomes when compared to well-articulated approaches.

Pharmacologic agents that suppress the desire to drink have shown promise in reducing alcohol consumption. Naltrexone, an opiate receptor antagonist, has demonstrated effectiveness in several well-controlled studies. Withdrawal medications, psychiatric agents, and disulfiram show more limited effectiveness in US populations.

There are a number of additional factors to consider when determining treatment effectiveness. Comorbidity of psychiatric diagnoses often complicates the picture and calls for a broader focus. Factors such as therapist characteristics and treatment setting frequently interact with treatment type. Research indicates that, in general, an empathic approach, in which one demonstrates respect and support of patients, appears to be most effective. The ongoing issue of inpatient vs. outpatient treatment remains equivocal. However, recent concerns over containment of health care costs supports a growing trend to favor outpatient approaches.

The total economic costs of substance abuse remain high. Cost–benefit analyses show that the dollars invested in treatment serve to reduce overall health and social costs. The data indicate that including substance abuse treatment in a comprehensive health care plan can have a significant impact on savings.

A growing body of literature points to the differential effectiveness of treatment approaches for alcohol problems (Finney & Monahan, 1996; Holder et al., 1991; McCaul & Furst, 1994; Miller et al., 1995). The increased emphasis on accountability in addictions treatment and the current efforts to contain health-care costs have resulted in demands for

International Handbook of Alcohol Dependence and Problems. Edited by N. Heather, T.J. Peters and T. Stockwell.
© 2001 John Wiley & Sons Ltd.

the various approaches. Treatment outcome research is used by prac-
makers to determine the impact of specific treatments, with a particu-
ffectiveness and cost-offset. Effectiveness concerns whether specific
,. family relationships, general functioning, emotional/physical health)
ha,. n the application of a particular modality. Cost-offset refers to whether
addictions u.._ ient "pays" for itself by reducing subsequent expenses (e.g. reduced accidents, improvements in work performance).

Over the past 40 years, treatments for alcohol problems have included insight psychotherapy, brief interventions and motivational approaches, psychosurgery, psychotropic
and psychedelic medications, drug agonists and antagonists, electric shock, behavior contracting, marital and family therapy, acupuncture, controlled use, self-help groups, hospitalization, social skills training, hypnosis, outpatient counseling, nausea aversion, relaxation
therapy, bibliotherapy, cognitive therapy and surgical implants. With such a diversity of
approaches, an important issue is to determine efficacy while at the same time keeping
client characteristics and cost-effectiveness at the forefront. This chapter provides a
summary of treatment approaches with documented effectiveness as well as those with
limited or no treatment efficacy. An economic evaluation of treatment approaches and
predictors of treatment outcome are also included.

TREATMENT EFFECTIVENESS

Research indicates that the majority of individuals drink less frequently and consume less
alcohol when they do drink following alcoholism treatment (McKay & Maisto, 1993; Moos,
Finney & Cronkite, 1990), although short-term outcomes (e.g. 3 months) are more favorable than those from studies with at least a year follow-up. Positive outcomes yield benefits for alcoholics and their families, as well as leading to savings to society in terms of
decreased costs for medical, social and criminal justice services. Reviews of treatment
outcome for alcohol problems have developed from early efforts to summarize findings
(Bowman & Jellnick, 1941), to reports which derived outcome statistics (Emrick, 1974), to
more recent publications examining efficacy in controlled studies with data on cost-
effectiveness (Finney & Monahan, 1996; Holder et al., 1991; Miller et al., 1995). Clearly, the
literature suggests that a variety of approaches can be effective, some more than others
because of the nature of the treatment and the intensity of the approach.

Treatment Approaches with Documented Effectiveness

There are a number of treatment protocols for which controlled research has consistently
found positive results, with more recent treatment outcome studies taking into account
methodological quality (Miller et al., 1995) and cost-effectiveness (Finney & Monahan,
1996; Holder et al., 1991). Research continues to clarify the mechanisms for successful
treatment outcome and provided here is a summary of interventions receiving strong
support.

Brief Interventions and Motivational Interviewing

Brief interventions (see also Chapter 31, this volume) vary in length from a few minutes
to one to three sessions of assessment and feedback. The goals of brief interventions include
problem recognition, commitment to change, reduced alcohol consumption and brief skills
training. In a review of 32 controlled studies using brief interventions, Bien et al. (1993)

reported that brief interventions were more effective than no treatment and often as effective as more extensive treatment. Individuals whose alcohol consumption is high, but who are not necessarily alcohol-dependent, are the primary targets for brief interventions. These approaches have several common components, including providing feedback, encouraging client responsibility for change, offering advice, providing a menu of alternatives, using an empathic approach and reinforcing the client. Brief interventions have also proved effective in reducing tobacco use and other drug use (Heather, 1998). In an atmosphere that promotes harm reduction, brief interventions offer an exciting alternative to more extensive treatment approaches.

Motivational interviewing strategies (see also Chapter 30, this volume) seek to initiate a client's intrinsic motivation to change (Miller & Rollnick, 1991). The approaches are based on the philosophy that ultimately it is the client who holds the key to successful recovery, once a commitment has been established. Understanding ambivalence as a central feature of a client's hesitance to change and using encouragement and empathy to discover what makes it worthwhile to change are central. Tapping into values and providing feedback of risk and harm appear to strengthen clients' commitment. A recent review of motivational treatment approaches offered overwhelming support for the use of these strategies in the early treatment of heavy drinkers in a variety of settings (Miller et al., 1998).

Social Skills Training

Social skills training (see also Chapter 28, this volume) is usually incorporated into a more comprehensive "broad spectrum" approach and includes a focus on communication skills, such as assertiveness, for social relations. In general, the underlying assumption has been that drinking problems arise because the individual lacks specific coping skills for sober living. These deficits can include inability to cope with interpersonal situations as well as deficits in environmental (i.e. work) situations. The competent therapist will investigate the underlying sources of an individual's vulnerability that can precipitate problem drinking. Research suggests that there are a number of domains for skills training: (a) interpersonal skills; (b) emotional coping for mood regulation; (c) coping skills for dealing with life stressors, and (d) coping with substance cues (Monti et al., 1995). The research evidence for the efficacy of social skills training in a comprehensive treatment package is strong and the core elements can be found in many other approaches. Compared with other approaches, social skills training yielded efficacy scores second only to brief interventions and motivational interviewing (Miller et al., 1998). Social skills training can be delivered individually or in group interactions and appears to be particularly appropriate for more severely dependent individuals who are more likely to experience serious psychopathology.

Community Reinforcement

The community reinforcement approach (CRA) attempts to increase clients' access to positive activities and makes involvement in these activities contingent on abstinence (Azrin et al., 1982) (see also Chapter 28). This approach combines many of the components of other behavioral approaches, including monitored disulfiram, behavior contracting, behavioral marital therapy, social skills training, motivational counseling and mood management. Some of the largest treatment effects in the literature have been associated with the community reinforcement approach (Miller et al., 1995). Compared to more traditional treatment approaches, the CRA has been shown to be more successful in helping inpatient or outpatient alcoholics remain sober and employed. Although community reinforcement is a more intense treatment approach, it is consistent with the basic philosophy of several other effective approaches. The ability to establish rewarding relationships, to focus on changing the social environment so that positive reinforcement is available, and to reduce reinforcement for drinking are emphasized with the community reinforcement and other approaches. The key appears to be helping the client to find and become involved in activities that are more rewarding than drinking.

Behavior Contracting

Behavior contracting approaches are drawn from operant conditioning principles (see Chapter 15) and are used to establish a contingent relation between specific treatment goals (e.g. attending AA meetings) and a desired reinforcer. Written behavioral contracts are a way of actively engaging the client in treatment. Drinking goals are made explicit and specific behaviors to achieve these goals are outlined. Behavioral contracts are also useful for providing alternative behaviors to drinking. When evaluated either as an individual treatment approach or as part of marital therapy, behavior contracting consistently yielded positive results (Miller et al., 1995).

Aversion Therapies

The primary goal of aversion therapies is to produce an aversive reaction to alcohol by establishing a conditioned response to cues associated with drinking (see Chapter 14). The conditioning can be accomplished by using electric shock, apneic paralysis, chemical agents or imaginal techniques. Overall, results indicate that aversion therapies are effective in the short term with respect to a reduction in alcohol consumption (Miller et al., 1995). However, there appears to be a differential effect for the various forms of aversion. Nausea aversion therapy, in which a drug is administered so that nausea and emesis occur immediately following sipping and swallowing alcoholic beverages, has demonstrated a positive outcome in a number of studies and covert sensitization, which uses imaginal techniques to induce a conditioned aversion, has also shown promising findings, while apneic paralysis and electric shock have shown less encouraging results (Holder et al., 1991; Miller et al., 1995). In general, studies that have carefully defined procedures and which have documented the occurrence of classical conditioning have shown the strongest results.

Relapse Prevention

Relapse prevention constitutes a behavioral approach with the goal of reducing the cues that precipitate relapse to alcohol (see also Chapter 29). Relapse can be triggered by stress, emotional states, craving or environmental stressors, and strategies that teach individuals how to cope with these events have demonstrated success in preventing relapse (Monti et al., 1995). Early approaches to treatment focused on initiating change, but paid little attention to strategies designed to maintain behavior change, with the result that relapse to drinking was the most common outcome of alcohol treatment. Subsequent research on the study of the determinants of relapse led to the development of interventions to increase self-efficacy and coping skills.

Evaluations of the efficacy of relapse prevention efforts have yielded mixed results (Miller et al., 1995), but evidence suggests that interventions focusing on modifying cognitions related to failure and teaching individuals to quickly recover from lapses can be successful (Weingardt & Marlatt, 1998). A number of studies have demonstrated an interaction between self-efficacy and aftercare participation. Individuals with high self-efficacy who also participated more frequently in aftercare sessions had significantly better outcomes than all other groups, but aftercare participation improved treatment outcomes for those initially low in self-efficacy (Rychtarik et al., 1992). Similar results were found in a randomized trial of aftercare participation (McKay, Maisto & O'Farrell, 1993). Additional research has indicated that relapse prevention may be more effective for certain subtypes of alcoholics, and compliance may be indicative of a type of motivation for sustaining change (Donovan, 1998). From a harm-reduction perspective, relapse prevention efforts may serve to lessen the severity of relapse and minimize the harm associated with continuing alcohol use.

Summary

Effective treatments appear to have several common strategies: suppressing use, eliciting motivation for change, and teaching alternative coping skills. Treatment approaches which actively engage the client in the treatment process appear to produce more positive outcomes. Furthermore, studies yielding positive outcomes may provide insight into both the etiology and mechanisms for resolution of alcohol problems.

Treatment Approaches with Limited Evidence of Effectiveness

There are also a number of commonly used treatment approaches that do not show any evidence of effectiveness. These approaches comprise the largest number of treatment studies and are summarized below.

Insight Psychotherapy

Psychotherapy seeks to uncover unconscious causes for a person's alcohol problems. The goal is insight and psychotherapy is frequently studied as an adjunctive component to alcohol treatment. In general, studies do not reveal consistent positive results; in fact, the trend favors patients who did not receive psychotherapy (Miller et al., 1995).

Confrontational Counseling

Confrontational interventions seek to break down defenses, particularly denial. Historically, confrontation has been considered an essential component of alcohol treatment, yet no studies have shown positive findings for approaches using confrontation (Finney & Monahan, 1996; Holder et al., 1991; Miller et al., 1995). In a controlled evaluation of therapist styles, Miller and colleagues (1993) found that confrontation yielded significantly more resistance and predicted poorer outcomes 1 year after a brief intervention. Miller & Rollnick (1991) suggested that confrontation is a *goal* rather than a procedure and that the occurrence of client resistance during a session should serve as immediate feedback for altering the therapeutic approach.

Relaxation Training

The use of relaxation training or other stress reduction techniques has intuitive appeal but there is no scientific evidence to support their use (Miller et al., 1998). The impact of these findings supports the growing doubts that individuals drink to relieve stress.

General Alcoholism Counseling

This type of counseling is usually directive and supportive but not specifically confrontational. One of the difficulties in evaluating general strategies is that they are frequently poorly defined and contrasted with additive components. However, the results of controlled evaluations indicate that alcoholism counseling is ineffective.

Education

Education is without question one of the most common components of standard alcohol treatment programs. The intent is to convey information to help the person change drinking problems. Controlled studies of the use of educational lectures and films have consistently revealed negative findings (Finney & Monahan, 1996; Miller et al., 1998). There is no research support for the notion that alcohol problems result from a lack of knowledge and thus, no impact on outcome from providing the "missing" knowledge.

Milieu Therapy

Implicit in the use of milieu therapy is the idea that recovery is aided by the *place* in which therapy occurs. The therapeutic atmosphere is itself thought to be beneficial. This idea is commonly associated with inpatient or residential programs which seek to promote an atmosphere of healing. Results of controlled research do not provide evidence to support residential/milieu therapy over less costly outpatient treatment and in fact, milieu therapy most frequently yields a less positive outcome when compared to a brief intervention (Miller et al., 1995).

Summary

It is surprising that virtually all of the ineffective treatment approaches are precisely those offered in the typical US treatment program. Historically, the treatment of alcohol problems has been regularly followed by relapse; thus, one could assume that the "standard" treatment is ineffective. One common theme among ineffective approaches is their vague and imprecise description and, as Miller et al. (1995) have pointed out, well-articulated studies serve to promote treatment effectiveness.

Pharmacologic Approaches

Pharmacological agents for the treatment of alcohol disorders (see also Chapter 27, this volume) have a long history and can be classified according to several major categories: (a) intoxication agents that reverse the effects of alcohol; (b) withdrawal agents; (c) psychiatric comorbidity agents, and (d) desire and compulsion agents. Much has been written about the effectiveness of disulfiram, and treatment outcome reviews generally agree that its effectiveness is limited. Likewise, withdrawal and psychiatric medications appear to be appropriate only for select populations of alcoholics, although this may not be applicable to countries other than the USA.

The current research interest appears to be in medications that target the desire for alcohol. A potential area for study is the opioid system, which has been implicated in alcohol's rewarding effects. Several studies have examined the effectiveness of naltrexone (ReVia), an opiate receptor antagonist, for decreasing alcohol consumption (O'Malley et al., 1992; Weinrieb & O'Brien, 1997). These studies have provided evidence of naltrexone's effectiveness in decreasing alcohol craving and drinking days. Among patients who did return to drinking, those taking naltrexone and who received coping skills training were least likely to return to heavy drinking but the cumulative rate of abstinence was highest for patients who received naltrexone and supportive therapy.

Naltrexone appears to be well-tolerated and effective in helping to stop resumption of binge drinking. There are presently more than a dozen studies examining the various aspects of using naltrexone as an adjunct to alcohol treatment. Future studies will need to determine more specific doses, the optimal duration of treatment, and whether subtypes of alcoholics would benefit from using naltrexone.

PATIENT–TREATMENT MATCHING

An emerging trend in the early 1990s was to look beyond the issues of whether alcohol treatment worked or which treatment was most effective to the possibility that matching individuals to treatment based on individual characteristics would improve treatment outcomes. The idea of matching individuals to treatment was not new to the alcohol field and a review of matching studies indicated that some treatment approaches were, in fact, more effective than others for patients with certain characteristics (Mattson et al., 1994). In order to more clearly make recommendations about patient–treatment matching, the National Institute on Alcohol Abuse and Alcoholism initiated a multisite clinical trial entitled Project MATCH (Matching Alcoholism Treatment to Client Heterogeneity). The goal was to determine whether different types of alcoholics respond selectively to particular treatment approaches. For example, cognitive-behavioral therapy was hypothesized to be more effective for patients with higher alcohol involvement, cognitive impairment and sociopathy. Twelve-step facilitation therapy was hypothesized to be useful for individuals with greater alcohol involvement and meaning seeking. Motivational enhancement therapy was hypothesized to be more effective for clients with high conceptual levels and low readiness to change (Project MATCH Research Group, 1997).

Unfortunately, the results from Project MATCH challenged the view that patient–treatment matching would yield more positive outcomes. That is, there were few differences in outcomes when patients were randomly assigned to three distinctly different treatment approaches (Project MATCH Research Group, 1997). These results should be interpreted cautiously. Clearly, support for various treatment approaches does not mean that all clients will benefit from those approaches, or that no client ever benefits from less effective approaches. The trial demonstrated that regardless of treatment, patients had a greater number of abstinent days and a significant decrease in the number of drinks on drinking days. The results are further complicated by the nature of the study. This was the largest clinical trial ever conducted and each of the treatment approaches was manualized. The careful monitoring of treatment delivery, limiting attrition and delivering an adequate amount of treatment may have served to make the modalities more similar than different with respect to therapist involvement.

PREDICTORS OF TREATMENT OUTCOME

Treatment modality is not the only criterion that influences treatment outcome. The existence of other psychopathology, the specifics of treatment setting, and therapists' effects all interact to determine treatment effectiveness. These additional variables are gaining interest in the alcohol treatment field and serve to guide treatment decisions.

Cormorbidity

It is only within the last decade that dual-diagnosis patients have received research attention (see also Chapter 32, this volume). The rates of concurrent psychiatric disorders are high and a summary of recent research findings indicated that individuals with comorbid psychiatric diagnoses have poorer alcohol treatment outcomes (McKay & Maisto, 1993). This research takes on significance with respect to matching patients to more appropriate (e.g. psychotherapy) treatments. For example, Longabaugh et al. (1994) reported that alcoholics with antisocial personality disorder (ASP) had better outcomes with a cognitive-behavioral approach when compared to a relationship enhancement approach, and a second study indicated that alcoholics with ASP showed significant improvement in several drinking measures when treated with nortriptyline (Powell et al., 1995). Relatedly, recent studies have examined the effectiveness of treatment for individuals with comorbid drug dependence and reported an increased rate of relapse to both substances (Brower et al., 1994; Brown, Seraganian & Tremblay, 1993). Two of the challenges in treating dual-diagnosed patients are the differences in the nature of their problems and variability in their degree of motivation. Clearly there is a need for longitudinal studies of dual-diagnosis patients. Such research may identify the most effective treatment, provide insight into the temporal order of symptoms in those with anxiety or depressive disorders, and help to provide a theoretical base from which to develop appropriate treatment approaches.

Therapist Effects

Therapist effects can have a significant impact on treatment outcome, yet few studies have controlled for them. The primary characteristics appear to be empathy and respect for patients (Najavits & Weiss, 1994). Given the variability in therapist's styles, the alcohol treatment field has placed more of an emphasis on manualized treatment. Manual-driven treatment controls for variability and attempts to maximize the effects of successful therapist styles. Importantly, the success of brief interventions and motivational interviewing may well be due to the focus placed on empathy and support from the therapist.

Treatment Setting and Treatment Type

Alcohol treatment services are delivered in two primary settings: inpatient and outpatient. Inpatient services typically consist of short-term residential care and are often used for acute detoxification (Brown & Baumann, 1998). Inpatient care also provides intensive, highly structured treatment. Outpatient settings provide more long-term maintenance and can be either intensive, which have been modeled after day treatment programs, or typical, which usually include weekly group therapy sessions. Because of concern over rising health care costs, more emphasis is being placed on outpatient care for all phases of treatment (McCaul & Furst, 1994). Evidence from controlled clinical efficacy studies on the advantages of inpatient vs. outpatient treatment suggests little difference in effectiveness (Institute of Medicine, 1989; Miller et al., 1995). Other treatment variables, such as modality, duration of treatment and therapist characteristics, appear to have a more direct impact on treatment outcome.

There is some evidence that comprehensive treatments are more effective than less intensive approaches (McKay & Maisto, 1993). However, these findings appear to be based on studies of more severe or dual-diagnosed alcoholics. In general, the data do not support intense inpatient treatment for all alcoholics, particularly those with uncomplicated alcohol dependence, but research is lacking on the role of these settings for individuals with additional diagnoses (McCrady & Langenbucher, 1996). With respect to treatment type, a number of approaches have been used, including 12-Step-based approaches, psychodynamic therapy and cognitive-behavioral interventions. Holder et al. (1991) concluded that brief interventions and cognitive-behavioral approaches appear to be more effective overall.

COST-EFFECTIVENESS

Costs Associated with Treatment

Whether alcohol treatment services are cost-effective is a fundamental question in this era of cost containment. The issue is one of determining which alcohol treatment modalities are the most effective for the least cost. The results of a meta-analysis of 33 treatment modalities suggested that brief interventions are the most cost-effective treatment and residential-milieu therapies are the least cost-effective (Holder et al., 1991). More recent research differs from these original findings in both cost and effectiveness determinations and points to the need to consider patient subgroups (Finney & Monahan, 1996). Nonetheless, both studies agreed that the more effective modalities consistently were in the medium-low to low cost range, and modalities with poor evidence were associated with higher costs. An important caveat to these findings is that none of the comparisons were done with individuals who were matched to treatment. It is likely that more expensive, intensive treatments may be necessary and cost-effective for more severe patients.

Cost-offset

Cost-offset has as it fundamental objective cost savings and alone may not be a realistic social policy goal. Decisions not to fund more expensive treatments in an effort to contain costs may have important implications, because if the substance abuse problem worsens, the eventual result will be much higher costs (Fox et al., 1995). Estimates of the extent of alcohol-related hospital utilization are typically based on reviews of medical records and studies indicate that alcohol-related admissions have a significant impact on the cost of inpatient care (Gordis, 1987). In general, the cost-offset literature has focused on the health care costs following treatment and a recent study demonstrated 24% lower health-related costs for treated vs. untreated alcoholics over a 14 year follow-up period (Holder & Blose, 1992). Other researchers have found that treated alcoholics' use of medical care decreased by 61% in the first year after treatment (Hoffman, De Hart & Fulkerson, 1993), absenteeism and medical claims were reduced (McDonnell Douglas Corporation, 1989) and arrests and incarcerations were decreased (Finigan, 1996).

SUMMARY

The past 40 years have brought with them a wealth of information about the treatment of alcohol problems. We have convincing evidence for the effectiveness of treatment and are at the frontier of developing new medications to reduce craving and relapse. Typically, in alcoholism treatment, lower cost treatments are at least as effective as more expensive ones and successful treatment is associated with lowered health care costs. Clearly, no one treatment will work for everyone. Perhaps encouraging professionals to adopt a comprehensive treatment program with a variety of approaches will allow more individuals to seek treatment. Allowing individuals to understand that they have options and that they can be active participants in recovery represents a more sensitive approach to treatment.

KEY WORKS AND SUGGESTIONS FOR FURTHER READING

Hester, R.K. & Miller, W.R. (1995). *Handbook of Alcoholism Treatment Approaches: Effective Alternatives*, 2nd edn. Needham Heights, MA: Allyn and Bacon.

This handbook describes a variety of alternative treatment methods for helping those with alcohol problems. The book is written for practitioners and chapters have been contributed by some of the leading researchers in the field. Each clinical chapter includes an overview of the technique, special clinical considerations and guidelines for clinical applications.

Miller, W.R. & Heather, N. (1998). *Treating Addictive Behaviors*, 2nd edn. New York: Plenum.

Written from the perspective of the transtheoretical model of change, this edited book is a compilation of works by authors who base their writing on the latest research in the addictions field. Sections focus on understanding change, preparing for and facilitating change, and sustaining change in individuals who present with addictive behaviors. The book represents a collaboration between basic and applied research.

Miller, W.R. & Rollnick, S. (1991). *Motivational Interviewing: Preparing People to Change Addictive Behavior.* New York: Guilford.

This volume is a must for clinicians working with individuals who are ambivalent about changing. This clearly written and immensely useful book outlines the steps to working with challenging clients. Motivational interviewing is detailed and practice exercises are included.

Project MATCH Research Group (1997). Matching alcoholism treatments to client heterogeneity: Project MATCH post-treatment drinking outcomes. *Journal of Studies on Alcohol*, **58**, 7–29.

This article represents an excellent overview of Project MATCH, including methodological details, research hypotheses, and directions for future research. The authors discuss the benefits of matching clients to treatment and provide a useful set of references for treatment delivery.

REFERENCES

Azrin, N.H., Sisson, R.W., Meyers, R. & Godley, M. (1982). Alcoholism treatment by disulfiram and community reinforcement therapy. *Behavior Research and Therapy*, **14**, 339–348.

Bien, T.H., Miller, W.R. & Tonigan, J.S. (1993). Brief interventions for alcohol problems: a review. *Addiction*, **88**, 315–336.

Bowman, K.M. & Jellnick, E.M. (1941). Alcohol addiction and its treatment. *Quarterly Journal of Studies on Alcohol*, **2**, 98–176.

Brower, K.J., Blow, F.C., Hill, E.M. & Mudd, S.A. (1994). Treatment outcome of alcoholics with and without cocaine disorders. *Alcoholism: Clinical and Experimental Research*, **18**, 734–739.

Brown, J.M. & Baumann, B.D. (1998). Recent advances in assessment and treatment of alcohol abuse and dependence. In L. Vandecreek, S. Knapp & T.L. Jackson (Eds), *Innovations in Clinical Practice: A Sourcebook*, Vol. 16 (pp. 81–93). Sarasota, FL: Professional Resources Press.

Brown, T.G., Seraganian, P. & Tremblay, J. (1993). Alcohol and cocaine abusers 6 months after traditional treatment: do they fare as well as problem drinkers? *Journal of Substance Abuse Treatment*, **10**, 545–552.

Donovan, D.M. (1998). Continuing care: promoting the maintenance of change. In W.R. Miller & N. Heather (Eds), *Treating Addictive Behaviors*, 2nd edn (pp. 317–336). New York: Plenum.

Emrick, C.D. (1974). A review of psychologically oriented treatment of alcoholism: I. The use and interrelationships of outcome criteria and drinking behavior following treatment. *Quarterly Journal of Studies on Alcohol*, **35**, 523–549.

Finigan, M. (1996). Societal outcomes and cost savings of drug and alcohol treatment in the state of Oregon. Prepared for the Office of Alcohol and Drug Abuse Programs, Oregon Department of Human Resource, and Governor's Council on Alcohol and Drug Abuse Programs, Salem, OR.

Finney, J.W. & Monahan, S.C. (1996). The cost-effectiveness of treatment for alcoholism: a second approximation. *Journal of Studies on Alcohol*, **57**, 229–243.

Fox, K., Merrill, J.C., Chang, H.H. & Califano, J.A. Jr (1995). Estimating the costs of substance abuse to the Medicaid hospital care program. *American Journal of Public Health*, **85**, 48–54.

Gordis, E. (1987). Accessible and affordable health care for alcoholism and related problems: strategy for cost containment. *Journal of Studies on Alcohol*, **48**, 579–585.

Heather, N. (1998). Using brief opportunities for change in medical settings. In W.R. Miller & N. Heather (Eds), *Treating Addictive Behaviors*, 2nd edn (pp. 133–147). New York: Plenum.

Hoffman, N.G., De Hart, S.S. & Fulkerson, J.A. (1993). Medical care utilization as a function of recovery status following chemical addictions treatment. *Journal of Addictive Disease*, **12**, 97–108.

Holder, H.D. & Blose, J.O. (1992). The reduction of health care costs associated with alcoholism treatment: a 14-year longitudinal study. *Journal of Studies on Alcohol*, **53**, 293–302.

Holder, H.D., Longabaugh, R., Miller, W.R. & Rubonis, A.V. (1991). The cost-effectiveness of treatment for alcoholism: a first approximation. *Journal of Studies on Alcohol*, **52**, 517–540.

Institute of Medicine (1989). *Prevention and Treatment of Alcohol Problems: Research Opportunities*. Washington, DC: Institute of Medicine.

Longabaugh, R., Rubin, A., Malloy, P. Beattie, M., Clifford, P.R. & Noel, N. (1994). Drinking outcomes of alcohol abusers diagnosed with antisocial personality disorder. *Alcoholism: Clinical and Experimental Research*, **18**, 778–785.

Mattson, M.E., Allen, J.P., Longabaugh, R., Nickless, C.J., Connors, G.J. & Kadden, R.M. (1994). A chronological review of empirical studies matching alcoholic clients to treatment. *Journal of Studies on Alcohol*, **12**(Suppl.), 16–29.

McCaul, M.E. & Furst, J. (1994). Alcoholism treatment in the United States. *Alcohol Health and Research World*, **18**, 253–260.

McCrady, B.S. & Langenbucher, J.W. (1996). Alcohol treatment and health care system reform. *Archives of General Psychiatry*, **53**, 737–746.

McDonnell Douglas Corporation & Alexander Consulting Group (1989). *Employee assistance program financial offset study, 1985–1988*. Washington DC: McDonnell Douglas Corporation.

McKay, J.R. & Maisto, S.A. (1993). An overview and critique of advances in the treatment of alcohol use disorders. *Drugs & Society*, **8**, 1–29.

McKay, J.R., Maisto, S.A. & O'Farrell, T.J. (1993). End-of-treatment self-efficacy, aftercare and drinking outcomes of alcoholic men. *Alcoholism: Clinical and Experimental Research*, **17**, 1078–1083.

Miller, W.R., Andrews, N.R., Wilbourne, P. & Bennett, M.E. (1998). A wealth of alternatives: effective treatments for alcohol problems. In W.R. Miller & N. Heather (Eds), *Treating Addictive Behaviors*, 2nd edn (pp. 203–216). New York: Plenum.

Miller, W.R., Benefield, R.G. & Tonigan, J.S. (1993). Enhancing motivation for change in problem drinking: a controlled comparison of two therapist styles. *Journal of Consulting and Clinical Psychology*, **61**, 455–461.

Miller, W.R., Brown, J.M., Simpson, T.L., Handmaker, N.S., Bien, T.H., Luckie, L.F., Montgomery, H.A., Hester, R.K. & Tonigan, J.S. (1995). What works? A methodological analysis of the alcohol treatment outcome literature. In R.K. Hester & W.R. Miller (Eds), *Handbook of Alcoholism Treatment Approaches: Effective Alternatives*, 2nd edn (pp. 12–44). Needham Heights, MA: Allyn and Bacon.

Miller, W.R. & Rollnick, S. (1991). *Motivational Interviewing: Preparing People to Change Addictive Behavior*. New York: Guilford.

Monti, P.M., Rohsenow, D.J., Colby, S.M. & Abrams, D.B. (1995). Coping and social skills training. In R.K. Hester & W.R. Miller (Eds), *Handbook of Alcoholism Treatment Approaches: Effective Alternatives*, 2nd edn (pp. 221–241). Needham Heights, MA: Allyn and Bacon.

Moos, R.H., Finney, J.W. & Cronkite, R.C. (1990). *Alcoholism Treatment: Context, Process, and Outcome.* New York: Oxford University Press.

Najavits, L.M. & Weiss, R.D. (1994). Variations in therapist effectiveness in the treatment of patients with substance use disorders: an empirical review. *Addiction,* **89**, 679–688.

O'Malley, S.S., Jaffe, A.J., Chang, G., Schottenfeld, R.S., Meyer, R.E. & Roundsaville, B. (1992). Naltrexone and coping skills therapy for alcohol dependence: a controlled study. *Archives of General Psychiatry,* **49**, 881–887.

Powell, B.J., Campbell, J.L., Landon, J.F., Liskow, B.I., Thomas, H.M., Nickel, E.J., Dale, T.M., Penick, E.C., Samuelson, S.D. & Lacoursiere, R.B. (1995). A double-blind, placebo-controlled study of nortriptyline and bromocriptine in male alcoholics subtyped by comorbid psychiatric disorders. *Alcoholism: Clinical and Experimental Research,* **19**, 462–468.

Project MATCH Research Group (1997). Matching alcoholism treatments to client heterogeneity: Project MATCH posttreatment drinking outcomes. *Journal of Studies on Alcohol,* **58**, 7–29.

Rychtarik, R.G., Prue, D.M., Rapp, S.R. & King, A.C. (1992). Self-efficacy, aftercare and relapse in a treatment program for alcoholic. *Journal of Studies on Alcohol,* **53**, 435–440.

Weingardt, K.R. & Marlatt, G.A. (1998). Sustaining change: helping those who are still using. In W.R. Miller & N. Heather (Eds), *Treating Addictive Behaviors,* 2nd edn (pp. 337–351). New York: Plenum.

Weinrieb, R.M. & O'Brien, C.P. (1997). Naltrexone in the treatment of alcoholism. *Annual Review in Medicine,* **48**, 477–487.

Chapter 25

Assessment for Brief Intervention and Treatment

Malissa Yang
McMaster University Medical School, Hamilton, Ontario, Canada
and
Harvey Skinner
*Department of Public Health Sciences, University of Toronto,
Toronto, Ontario, Canada*

Synopsis

Our understanding of alcohol problems has evolved such that they are viewed as multifactorial and existing on a continuum ranging from milder forms of problem drinking to severe alcohol dependence. Clinicians need practical tools for screening and assessment that encompass the social, behavioral and biological factors influencing a client's alcohol use and life functioning. The chapter describes a two-stage process, including alcohol problem identification (screening, case finding) followed by comprehensive assessment.

The identification stage addresses the basic questions of whether an alcohol problem is present and further action is necessary. This may take place in a range of community and primary care settings. The aim is to detect individuals with alcohol problems and either provide brief intervention (advice, counseling) or refer for further assessment and specialized treatment. There is good evidence that identifying individuals with early-stage or less severe alcohol problems and providing brief intervention is effective in reducing alcohol consumption and related problems.

The comprehensive assessment stage is essential for characterizing the specific nature and severity of the client's alcohol problems, as well as for providing a basis for intervention planning. Ongoing assessment throughout treatment and follow-up is crucial for adjusting the treatment plan and for giving feedback on goal attainment to the client (outcomes). Moreover, assessment functions well beyond that of information gathering. The process of assessment and personalized feedback are vital components in behavior change. Clinicians can provide assessment feedback in supportive ways to built readiness and motivation for change, using the principles of motivational interviewing. For example, assessment results can be used

International Handbook of Alcohol Dependence and Problems. Edited by N. Heather, T.J. Peters and
T. Stockwell.
© 2001 John Wiley & Sons Ltd.

to highlight a discrepancy between the client's drinking and a related goal (e.g. improve rela-
tionships with family).

The identification and assessment of alcohol problems is a challenge because no single
assessment method or instrument has been found to give a complete picture of the nature
and severity of problems. Therefore, convergence of information gathered across several
assessment modalities, including standardized instruments, collateral sources (e.g. family),
medical examinations and biological tests, is important for getting an accurate picture of the
client's level of alcohol consumption and related problems. The selection of assessment pro-
cedures will be guided by the specific purposes of assessment and practical constraints of the
clinical setting.

In brief, assessment is essential for assisting the client and clinician in developing a "shared"
treatment plan, fine-tuning the intervention process and monitoring progress toward goal
attainment. The basics are: (a) to think clearly through the particular need and role of assess-
ment in a given setting; (b) to incorporate a sequential, comprehensive regimen that fits the con-
straints of everyday clinical practice; and (c) to ensure that accurate and timely information is
provided for motivation enhancement, clinical decision making and outcome evaluation.

In the past 25 years, important strides have been made in understanding alcohol problems
and diverse intervention approaches have been developed. Alcohol problems are no longer
viewed as a unitary, "all-or-nothing" clinical entity (e.g. "alcoholism") for which there is a
single best treatment. Rather, alcohol problems are now broadly conceptualized as disorders that range from mild forms to very severe manifestations, with treatment considerations varying in accordance with the severity and unique characteristics of the individual's
problem and situation (Tucker, Donovan & Marlatt, 1999; Institute of Medicine, 1990;
Skinner, 1990).

Before the clinician and client begin the treatment process, a comprehensive assessment
is essential. The primary aims are two-fold: (a) to assess the severity of problems related
to drinking and degree of alcohol dependence (i.e. none, mild, moderate, severe); and (b)
to determine which intervention approach and level of treatment (e.g. brief vs. intensive)
is most appropriate for this client. A clear picture is needed of the physiological, social and
behavioral antecedents and consequences of alcohol problems. However, alcohol use and
problems must also be understood and interventions applied considering the environment
in which the individual is embedded.

Assessment is not just a discrete step occurring prior to treatment. Rather, it is a systematic, continuous process which elucidates the initial clinical impression of the individual and alcohol problem, aids in the formulation of a treatment plan, helps match the client
to an appropriate intervention, provides feedback on the course of treatment and evaluates treatment outcome. This chapter examines these purposes and stages of assessment in
alcohol problems, reviews current assessment methods and highlights issues regarding
assessment in special populations.

CHARACTERIZING THE PROBLEM AND THE INDIVIDUAL

The severity and specific manifestations of alcohol problems can differ widely between individuals. During the assessment, the clinician's goal is to gain knowledge about the particular kind of alcohol problems an individual is experiencing and to understand the evolution
of the individual's alcohol problem over time. The domains of interest include the client's
physical or medical condition, the environment in which the drinking occurs, the frequency

of drinking and amount of alcohol consumed, the drinking history, the consequences of alcohol use, and past treatment history. Individual clients will vary greatly along these domains and gathering specific information about these assessment variables allows the clinician to define and prioritize issues for intervention.

Using a variety of assessment modalities, the clinician seeks to determine the individual client's characteristics and his/her life situation, which ultimately influence treatment decisions and contribute to treatment outcome (Allen & Columbus, 1995). Although assessment allows the clinician to characterize the individual and the nature of the alcohol problem, it also yields clinical benefits. For example, giving individualized feedback based on assessment results can enhance motivation for and commitment to behavior change and can help clients formulate personal goals for improvement (Skinner et al., 1985).

SEQUENTIAL AND MULTIDIMENSIONAL ASSESSMENT

Although it is important to implement systematic procedures for alcohol assessment, the extent to which an individual client is assessed and the manner in which the assessment takes place will depend on the unique characteristics of the client and the particular community or clinical setting. The process of assessment can be considered in stages, each of which may or may not lead to the next stage. The *first stage* in alcohol assessment begins with identification (screening or case finding), where the basic question is whether an alcohol problem is present and whether further assessment is necessary (Connors, 1995). The objective is to detect individuals with alcohol problems and to set the stage for further assessment and intervention, as warranted. Increasingly, evidence indicates that identifying individuals with early-stage, less severe alcohol abuse and providing brief intervention (advice or counselling) is effective in reducing alcohol consumption and related problems (Zweben & Fleming, 1999; Heather, 1996; Bien et al., 1993).

Identification is mostly performed in primary health care settings where individuals generally present for health concerns that are not related to alcohol abuse. A number of well-studied screening instruments, such as the CAGE and AUDIT, can aid in the identification of alcohol problems among ambulatory populations (Allen et al., 1995). Clinicians should select a screening measure based on test acceptability to clients and providers, whether there are adequate resources (i.e. time, financial, personnel) and whether it is logistically possible to incorporate reliable screening procedures into routine clinical practice. Screening should have responsive procedures for feedback to clients and appropriate referrals for further evaluation.

Once a screen alerts the clinician to the presence of an alcohol problem, further assessment is needed to diagnose an alcohol disorder. The *second stage* in alcohol assessment involves using a variety of modalities, including standardized psychometric instruments or questionnaires, diagnostic interviews, medical examinations, physiological measures, or some combination thereof, to describe as fully as possible the extent and nature of the problem(s) experienced by the individual who is drinking. At this stage, the clinician should aim to learn as much as possible about the client's use of alcohol, signs and symptoms of alcohol abuse and dependence, and the consequences of alcohol use (Skinner, 1984). Although there is a tendency for clinicians, particularly those not involved specifically in treating alcohol problems, to rely solely on alcohol consumption (i.e. quantity of use) in diagnosing alcohol abuse or dependence, a comprehensive assessment should elicit information along a variety of important dimensions. An individual's level of alcohol use alone does not fully characterize his/her alcohol problems.

One crucial dimension that requires extensive assessment is the individual's drinking history. In addition to quantity and frequency of alcohol use, the clinician must obtain a clear and detailed description of variables such as drinking style (i.e. continuous vs. binge), typical drinking situations and antecedents of drinking (Sobell & Sobell, 1995). Knowledge about the duration of the individual's alcohol abuse and previous attempts to stop drinking helps the clinician to deduce which treatment methods may or may not work. A second dimension that must be explored during the assessment is the extent of the individual's dependence on alcohol, including the degree of impairment of control over drinking, physical tolerance to alcohol (i.e. a decrease in response to alcohol that occurs with continued use), withdrawal symptoms (i.e. tremor, nausea and vomiting, insomnia, delirium, anxiety, restlessness, fatigue, etc.) and compulsivity of drinking (Davidson, 1987; Skinner & Allen, 1982)

The third dimension incorporates biomedical and psychosocial problems related to the client's alcohol abuse. These may include medical conditions resulting from prolonged abuse of alcohol, problems with family members or other social relationships, legal or vocational problems, intellectual or cognitive impairment and anxiety or depression. Clinicians are also advised to explore for the presence of psychiatric conditions, which often accompany alcohol problems and can play a role in its etiology, development and treatment (Miller & Ries, 1991; Nathan, 1997).

Yet another important dimension to assess is the client's motivation and readiness to change drinking behavior, a factor which is key in deciding the next appropriate treatment step (Donovan & Rosengren, 1999; Miller & Rollnick, 1991). Finally, collecting additional information regarding use of other psychoactive substances, demographic data, family structure and circumstances, family history of alcohol use, social stability and personality ensures that an assessment is comprehensive. Convergence of detailed information along multiple dimensions will give the clinician a clear picture of the severity of the alcohol problem experienced by a given individual and guide the direction of the treatment process.

PLANNING AND GUIDING THE TREATMENT PROCESS

Using various assessment modalities (e.g. standardized assessment instruments, medical history, physiological measures, collateral sources), the clinician aims to combine the characterization of a given individual with knowledge of intervention options in order to provide appropriate and effective treatment. For example, clients exhibiting signs of more severe alcohol dependence are generally referred for intensive treatment at specialized addiction clinics. On the other hand, individuals in the early stages of alcohol problems may not manifest classic signs and symptoms and may show resistance to change. Clinicians must rely on assessment indicators, such as marital or job problems, relationship conflicts and mood disorders, to identify the presence of an alcohol problem and build motivation for treatment alternatives, such as brief counseling (Donovan & Rosengren,1999; Zweben & Fleming, 1999). Optimally, assessment and treatment should be continuous and reciprocal, so that initial assessment guides treatment goals and interventions, and subsequent assessment throughout the course of treatment provides feedback to clinician and patient as well as indicating new or ongoing problem areas to pursue. Assessment should be regarded as an ongoing activity that supports clinical decision making throughout the course of treatment.

ASSESSMENT MODALITIES

Standardized Instruments

Screening is used to identify individuals who have alcohol-related problems or who are at risk for such problems. A number of standardized instruments are available to help the clinician screen for alcohol problems. The CAGE, MAST, TWEAK, and AUDIT are commonly used for adults and are considered to be acceptably reliable and valid in a variety of situations (Connors, 1995; Crowe et al., 1997; Allen et al., 1995). Preference for screening measures will vary between individual clinicians and different settings. Decisions should be based on the kind of population being assessed, amount of time and resources available, clinical or community setting and goals of screening. Providing personal and non-confrontational feedback to clients regarding screening results can be a significant component of brief intervention.

When a screening result alerts the clinician to a potential alcohol problem, a more exhaustive assessment is in order. This gives a greater understanding of how much drinking is taking place and how drinking fits into the client's activities, resources and relationships. A myriad of psychometric instruments have been designed to aid the clinician in this endeavor. Structured diagnostic interview instruments are designed to help clinicians formally diagnose alcohol dependence and alcohol abuse according to the categorical DSM-IV (Structured Clinical Interview for DSM-IV; First et al., 1995) and ICD (Composite International Diagnostic Interview, Robins et al., 1988) systems. Before selecting and using a diagnostic measure, clinicians must be clear about what constructs are to be measured and what the purpose of measurement is. Individual cases may call for different assessment instruments or measures (Maisto & McKay, 1995).

Whether the assessment is for clinical or research purposes will influence the choice of the diagnostic instrument. The clinician, whose main priority is to develop an appropriate treatment strategy for the individual client, will be primarily interested in using an instrument that identifies the unique needs of the client and guides treatment planning. Standardized instruments, particularly those that are brief, less structured and easy to administer, can be very useful for the busy clinician (e.g. Alcohol Dependence Scale: Skinner & Horn, 1984; Drinking Inventory of Consequences: Miller, Tonigan & Longabaugh, 1995). In contrast, researchers tend to explore a wider range of variables related to alcohol problems. Lengthier and more detailed questionnaires may be more appropriate for research purposes. For example, formal diagnostic interviews require resources, including trained personnel, money to pay for a measure and time for administration, which may not be available in clinical settings, particularly busy primary care facilities.

The choice of instrument will also vary between clinical settings. Formal diagnostic interviews may be warranted in specialized alcohol treatment settings, while more concise questionnaires may be more appropriate in community or primary health centers. Several measures designed to assess multiple dimensions of alcohol problems may also be effective (e.g. Addiction Severity Index: McLellan et al., 1992; Alcohol Use Inventory: Horn et al., 1987). An important consideration is the availability of psychometric evidence for a particular measure. Validity and reliability are the two primary psychometric characteristics to consider in an assessment instrument. Other things being equal, stronger psychometric characteristics will make one measure preferable to another (Maisto & McKay, 1995).

Instruments are also available to assess various other factors, including readiness to change (Readiness to Change Questionnaire: Rollnick et al., 1992) and self-efficacy (Inventory of Drinking Situations: Annis et al., 1987), which may be of interest to the clinician. The extent to which information is gathered for these variables and the extent to which these issues require exploration will vary between individuals and should be undertaken as needed (Institute of Medicine, 1990).

Additional issues to address when choosing an alcohol assessment instrument include the assessment time-frame (i.e. period of client functioning that is of interest), administrative options (i.e. self-administered vs. structured interview), training required for administration, and scoring and fee for use. It is recommended that, in selecting a suitable instrument, clinicians who are assessing clients for treatment should seek a measure (or a combination of measures) which balances the need to obtain extensive information regarding the client's alcohol use and life functioning with the need to be efficient and parsimonious, given the wide array of possible areas that could be assessed. At present, there is no universally accepted gold standard for the assessment of alcohol problems. Treatment of alcohol problems can be enhanced by the judicious use of standardized psychometric instruments to characterize clients during the course of treatment. Clinicians should be aware of the strengths and weaknesses of alternative psychometric instruments that can assist them in the assessment process.

Whether an individual's self-report of alcohol use and related problems can be trusted is an issue of ongoing debate. The balance of the scientific literature suggests that alcohol abusers' self-reports are relatively accurate and can be used with confidence if the assessment takes place under appropriate conditions (for reviews, see Babor et al., 1990; Maisto et al., 1990; Sobell & Sobell, 1995; Skinner, 1984). In many circumstances, self-report instruments are significantly more accurate than other assessment modalities, including physical examination and laboratory findings. It should be noted that, with the exception of self-monitoring, all measures of alcohol use and alcohol-related problems rely on retrospective self-reporting, and some amount of error is to be expected. Self-reports should not be considered inherently valid or invalid. Rather, whether confidence can be placed on individuals' self-reported alcohol use and related problems will depend on the individual client, the context in which assessment takes place, the specific information that is elicited and the purposes for which assessment is undertaken. Conditions that enhance truthful self-reporting include individuals being sober and alcohol-free during assessment, assurance of confidentiality, a comfortable, non-threatening clinical environment, and clear, understandable questions.

Medical History

A medical history and examination may accompany routine screening for alcohol problems, be undertaken when a screening measure indicates that an alcohol problem potentially exists, or be incorporated into a comprehensive assessment of an individual with an identified alcohol problem (Skinner & Holt, 1987). Primary care physicians are in an optimal position to perform such examinations. Clinical signs and symptoms associated with alcoholism can range from subtle and relatively benign to more severe and dramatic. Common physical indicators to look for include skin vascularization, hand or tongue tremor, modest hypertension, stigmata of accidents or trauma, history of gastrointestinal problems, gastric or duodenal ulcers and cognitive deficits (Saunders & Conigrave, 1990; Skinner et al., 1986). A history of alcohol problems in the family raises the index of suspicion that a patient might be at increased risk. Signs of neuropsychological and cognitive impairment are also indicators of hazardous alcohol consumption.

While medical conditions such as liver cirrhosis usually confirm alcohol dependence, the absence of alcohol-related medical problems does not rule out the diagnosis. Furthermore, no distinct symptom or test result can clearly establish a diagnosis of alcohol abuse or dependence. Clinicians should keep in mind that the most readily recognized symptoms of alcohol problems generally arise only in later stages of alcohol dependence, after years of heavy drinking. A complete history must probe for earlier, more subtle signs and patterns of alcohol abuse, including job-related problems, marital discord and/or domestic violence, difficulties in sleeping, chronic relationship difficulties, financial trouble, depression and anxiety, and so on. Structured or semi-structured interviewing, with the use of standardized questions, is preferred over free-form interviewing, which can be inconsistent in collecting essential kinds of assessment information.

Biological Measures

Accurate information on alcohol consumption during the pretreatment assessment is important for diagnosis and treatment outcome evaluation. Several biological measures demonstrate strong reliability for indicating an individual's alcohol use in the past 24 hour period. The breathalyser, which measures the presence of alcohol in the breath, is an efficient method to determine whether an individual has consumed alcohol in the immediate past. Simple laboratory testing of blood, urine and sweat can also accurately indicate recent alcohol intake. These markers are direct measures of alcohol in bodily fluids and are considered to be sensitive, specific, inexpensive and easy to administer (Anton, Litten & Allen, 1995). (See also Chapter 12, this volume.)

Detection of alcohol use over longer periods through physiological testing is more challenging and relies on measuring the effects of alcohol on the body rather than directly measuring the presence of alcohol (Anton, Litten & Allen, 1995). Abnormalities in γ-glutamyltransferase (GGT), mean corpuscular volume (MCV), aspartate aminotransferase (AST) or alanine aminotransferase (ALT) are indicators of chronic alcohol consumption. These markers of heavy and sustained alcohol use are well studied, routinely used, relatively cost-efficient and widely available. However, the results must be interpreted with caution because they generally lack sufficient sensitivity and specificity (Leigh & Skinner, 1988). Furthermore, conventional biological markers are insensitive to early-stage problem drinking (Saunders & Conigrave, 1990). High-density lipoproteins, 5-hydroxytryptophol, β-hexosaminidase, carbohydrate-deficient transferrin (CDT), alcohol congeners, and blood acetaldehyde adducts (AA) are newer biological measures under investigation.

In choosing a biological test, clinicians will want to consider the window of assessment (i.e. the amount of time that a marker will remain positive following drinking), the nature of the population (i.e. ambulatory vs. alcoholics), and the sensitivity and specificity of the particular test. While physiological tests are often considered to be the most "objective" measure of alcohol abuse, no single test can definitively identify or give a comprehensive assessment for this complex condition. The only true indicator of alcohol consumption is the detection of alcohol or one of its metabolites in body fluids. No laboratory test possesses both high sensitivity and specificity for detecting alcohol use outside of the previous 24 hours.

Clinicians are also advised to consider alternative factors that may be causing abnormal laboratory results. Individuals from an ambulatory population who drink excessively but are otherwise relatively healthy will have normal test results but may still require intervention for alcohol problems. The level of "abnormal" intake will vary from person to person (e.g. male vs. female). Furthermore, not all clients with hazardous alcohol use or dependence will demonstrate abnormalities in laboratory tests. Thus, standard laboratory tests are not sufficiently sensitive to be used as the primary basis of screening and assessment. The most valuable role for a physiological test is the detection of hazardous levels of alcohol intake. Biological measures are also useful for monitoring treatment progress by corroborating self-reported alcohol use and comparing subsequent tests with baseline levels. It is recommended that laboratory tests alone should not be relied upon to identify alcohol problems and should always be used in combination with data from other assessment modalities.

Other Modalities

In light of concerns regarding the accuracy of clients' self-reports, clinicians may explore collateral sources to gather further assessment information. Such sources may include clients' spouses, family members or employers (Nathan, 1997). However, it should not be assumed that collateral observers give unbiased, accurate and detailed reports. For clients who lack social supports there may not be any suitable individuals who can consistently observe and report their behavior. Friends and co-workers may be fairly accurate in reporting frequency of drinking but can generally only provide a gross estimate of the actual quantity of alcohol consumed or of the presence of alcohol dependence symptoms (Sobell & Sobell, 1995; Skinner, 1984). Examining court documents, police and employment records may also give a clearer picture of the client's previous alcohol problems.

Self-monitoring is an assessment technique that involves having an individual record the occurrences of alcohol as well as the conditions that precede, accompany and follow drinking. The client is requested to keep a daily log of the number and types of drinks consumed and the particular situations and times when drinking occurred. This method is ideal because it does not depend on retrospective self-reporting and can increase motivation to reduce the drinking behavior. Self-monitoring procedures are especially useful for assessing alcohol consumption and problems after treatment initiation and during follow-up. Both the clinician and the client can use self-monitoring information as a relatively objective and continuous record with which to evaluate progress and setbacks.

Self-monitoring is also valuable for providing information surrounding relapse episodes. Recording urges to drink or thoughts and actions related to alcohol may aid in identifying situations or events that place the client at risk for relapse and in modifying treatment goals. Having the client play an active role in the assessment and treatment process can also enhance motivation to reduce or quit drinking. However, client compliance in keeping a consistent record may be problematic, particularly among chronic alcohol abusers who may lack motivation, organizational skills and social supports. Also, clinicians must decide the level of confidence they have that clients are reporting alcohol use and related problems honestly and accurately.

Clinicians may wish to combine different assessment tools. Composite indices of alcohol problems can be derived both within and across assessment modalities. For example, a composite of medical history and laboratory tests can substantially increase diagnostic accuracy (Skinner et al., 1986, Skinner & Holt, 1987). A battery of questionnaires, incorporating various standardized scales, may also elucidate the extent of alcohol-related problems experienced by the client. Combining a physical examination for signs and symptoms of excessive alcohol use with brief questionnaires and laboratory tests may also improve assessment. Indeed, a most valuable use of laboratory tests is to corroborate clients' self-reports of alcohol consumption during treatment and follow-up. The choice of measures or components that make up the composite index can also be modified to suit the stage of treatment.

Collecting assessment information from multiple modalities will enhance the degree of confidence that clinicians can have in clients' self-reports regarding alcohol use and in the overall characterization of the alcohol problem. Ultimately, selection of the components of a comprehensive clinical assessment will be at the discretion of the clinician. In choosing any modality for alcohol assessment, the limitations of particular tests and the unique situational needs must be kept in mind. Ultimately, confidence in the accuracy of assessments is enhanced by convergence among a variety of alternative measurement modalities.

SPECIAL POPULATIONS

Adolescents

A comprehensive assessment plays an equally important role in the identification and treatment of alcohol problems among adolescents. From a preventive perspective, the negative consequences of excessive drinking may be curtailed if problems are identified and treated in earlier, less serious stages. The diagnostic criteria for alcohol abuse and dependence have largely been developed from research with adult populations. However, withdrawal symptoms, tolerance and medical problems present differently in adolescents than in adults. Clinicians should be aware that adolescents with alcohol problems demonstrate very heterogeneous patterns of symptoms, which are mainly psychosocial rather than physical (Alexander, 1991; Martin et al., 1995). Physical examination and laboratory testing are not as helpful for identifying alcohol problems as a comprehensive interview and full appreciation of the more subtle signs in this population (Alderman, Schonberg & Cohen, 1992).

Adolescents' patterns of alcohol and other drug use can vary considerably over time according to variables over which they may not have much control, including availability of money, the opportunity to use and the influence of peers. Multiple drug use and coexisting psychiatric problems can make assessment among adolescents particularly challenging (Upfold, 1997). Routine screening for alcohol problems in primary care settings is particularly important in the adolescent population in order to prevent the development of more serious and health-threatening alcohol abuse and dependence.

It is crucial for the clinician to develop a sense of trust and rapport with the adolescent in order to gather accurate and complete assessment information and, ultimately, to achieve positive treatment outcomes. Clinicians are encouraged to develop and use innovative methods of assessment, which may be more helpful than conventional assessment tools in eliciting accurate information from adolescent clients (Leccese & Waldron, 1994). The adolescent should be assessed separately and then, if possible, the family can be assessed as a unit.

Several assessment procedures have been designed specifically for adolescents for whom detection and diagnosis may be tricky (Connors, 1995). Available assessment instruments include the Adolescent Drinking Index (ADI), the Personal Experience Inventory (PEI: Winters & Henly, 1989), the Adolescent Alcohol Expectancy Questionnaire (AEQ-A: Brown, Christianson & Goldman, 1987), the Adolescent Drug Abuse Diagnosis (ADAD: Friedman & Utada, 1989), the Personal Experience Screening Questionnaire (PESQ) and the Substance Abuse Screening Test (SAST) (Nathan, 1997; Rogers, Speraw & Ozbek, 1995). As with adults, the use of composite indices that combine assessment modalities will enhance assessment of adolescent clients. Although treatment programs have been developed for adolescents, better assessment procedures to determine the most appropriate course of treatment for individual adolescents are needed.

Populations with Coexisting Psychiatric Conditions

In both clinical and community contexts, alcohol problems are commonly accompanied by coexisting psychiatric conditions (Miller & Ries, 1991). Estimates vary on the prevalence of comorbidity. However, as many as half to two-thirds of clinical samples of patients with alcohol dependence are likely to have a lifetime diagnosis of another psychiatric disorder (Davidson & Ritson, 1993). The psychiatric syndromes that most often coexist with alcohol disorders are anxiety disorders, personality disorders and abuse of other psychoactive substances. Accurate assessment of coexisting psychiatric disorders in alcoholic clients is crucial to treatment planning and outcome (Nathan, 1997). Failure to detect other psychiatric problems can deprive clients of potentially helpful treatments. Prescription of medication must proceed with care to avoid the development of further substance dependence. (See also Chapter 32, this volume.)

Early research proposed that psychiatric clients used alcohol as a way to reduce tension, stress and anxiety. However, this "tension reduction" hypothesis has been challenged and does not appear to adequately explain the etiology or maintenance of alcohol abuse. Anxiety is a frequently found condition in patients with alcohol dependence. It appears that in most cases, anxiety is a consequence rather than a cause of heavy drinking (Allan, 1995). Generally, most depressive and anxiety symptoms recede once the alcoholic client is detoxified and has been abstinent from alcohol for a period of time (Allan, 1995; Davidson & Ritson, 1993). However, it should not be assumed that one disorder which preceded another necessarily caused the second condition. As in all clients with alcohol problems, it is recommended that clinicians take a broad and comprehensive approach to assessment and attempt to look at the alcohol use in the life context. This approach will aid in meeting the distinct assessment and treatment needs of the client.

A particular challenge in assessing and treating clients with both alcohol problems and psychiatric disorders is to determine the relative importance of each condition. Also, the intoxication and withdrawal from alcohol can produce psychiatric symptoms that characterize psychiatric disorders. Structured clinical interviews, such as the Composite International Diagnostic Interview (CIDI), the Schedules for Clinical Assessment in Neuropsychiatry (SCAN) and the Structured Clinical Interview for DSM-IV (SCID), will be most helpful in assessing cases where comorbidity is suspected (Albanese et al., 1994). Such in-depth evaluation allows the clinician to probe the severity of both the alcohol abuse and the psychiatric symptoms, their history and the context surrounding their occurrence, in order to arrive at proper diagnoses. Before a comprehensive assessment can take place, the clinician must ensure that clients are not intoxicated or experiencing alcohol withdrawal at the time of the assessment. Physiological testing may be appropriate for this determination.

Clinicians should be aware that comorbid psychiatric conditions can play a role in the etiology of alcohol dependence and make treatment more difficult. Alcohol dependence and co-occurring morbidity must both be assessed and treated, often by different means. Having an additional psychiatric disorder can alter the course of alcohol dependence in various ways, including hastening the development of dependence on alcohol, exhibition of impulsivity, aggression and risky behavior by the client, and poorer prognosis.

CONCLUSION

There is no shortage of tools to aid the clinician in the identification and assessment of alcohol problems. The key is: (a) to think clearly through the particular need and role of assessment in a given setting; (b) to incorporate a sequential, comprehensive regimen that fits the constraints of everyday clinical practice; and (c) to ensure that accurate and timely information is provided for motivation enhancement, clinical decision making and outcome evaluation. Ultimately, the purpose of assessment is to assist the client and clinician in developing a "shared" treatment plan, adjusting or fine-tuning the intervention and monitoring progress toward goal attainment.

KEY WORKS AND SUGGESTIONS FOR FURTHER READING

Allen J.P. & Columbus M. (1995). *Assessing Alcohol Problems: A Guide for Clinicians and Researchers.* National Institute on Alcohol Abuse and Alcoholism Treatment Handbook Series 4. Bethesda, MD: US Department of Health and Human Services, Public Health Service, National Institutes of Health, National Institute on Alcohol Abuse and Alcoholism.

Provides a very practical review of assessment approaches and instruments.

Institute of Medicine (1990). *Broadening the Base of Treatment for Alcohol Problems.* Washington, DC: National Academy Press.

Provides the most comprehensive yet readable discussion of key concepts and methods for identification of alcohol problems in the community (Chapter 9), assessment (Chapter 10), client–treatment matching (Chapter 11) and treatment outcome (Chapter 12).

Tucker J.A., Donovan D.M. & Marlatt G.A. (1999). *Changing Addictive Behavior: Bridging Clinical and Public Health Strategies.* New York: Guilford.

Provides an excellent overview of latest thinking regarding the integration of clinical and public health approaches to addictions. Of particular note for assessment are chapters on motivation (Chapter 5), stages of change (Chapter 6), brief interventions (Chapter 9) and stepped care (Chapter 12).

REFERENCES

Adger, H. Jr (1991). Problems of alcohol and other drug use and abuse in adolescents. *Journal of Adolescent Health,* **12**, 606–613.

Albanese, M.J., Bartel, R.L., Bruno, R.F., Morgenbesser, M.W. & Schatzberg, A.F. (1994). Comparison of measures used to determine substance abuse in an inpatient psychiatric population. *American Journal of Psychiatry,* **151**, 1077–1078.

Alderman, E.M., Schonberg, S.K. & Cohen, M.I. (1992). The pediatrician's role in the diagnosis and treatment of substance abuse. *Pediatrics in Review,* **13**, 314–318.

Alexander, B. (1991). Alcohol abuse in adolescents. *American Family Physician,* **43**, 527–532.

Allan, C.A. (1995). Alcohol problems and anxiety disorders—a critical review. *Alcohol & Alcoholism,* **30**, 145–151.

Allen, J.P., Maisto, S.A. & Connors, G.J. (1995). Self-report screening tests for alcohol problems in primary care. *Archives of Internal Medicine,* **155**, 1726–1730.

Allen, J.P., & Columbus, M. (1995). *Assessing Alcohol Problems: A Guide for Clinicians and Researchers.* National Institute on Alcohol Abuse and Alcoholism Treatment Handbook Series, 4. Bethesda, MD: US Department of Health and Human Services, Public Health Service, National Institutes of Health, National Institute on Alcohol Abuse and Alcoholism.

Annis, H.M., Graham, J.M. & Davis, C.S. (1987). *Inventory of Drinking Situations (IDS) User's Guide.* Toronto: Addiction Research Foundation.

Anton, R.F., Litten, R.Z. & Allen, J.P. (1995). Biological assessment of alcohol consumption. In J.P. Allen & M. Columbus (Eds), *Assessing Alcohol Problems: A Guide for Clinicians and Researchers* (pp. 31–39). National Institute on Alcohol Abuse and Alcoholism Treatment Handbook Series, 4. Bethesda, MD: US Department of Health and Human Services, Public Health Service, National Institutes of Health, National Instate on Alcohol Abuse and Alcoholism.

Babor, T.F., Brown, J. & Del Boca, F.K. (1990). Validity of self-reports in applied research on addictive behaviors: fact or fiction? *Addictive Behaviors,* **12**, 5–32.

Bien, T., Miller, W. & Tonigan, J. (1993). Brief interventions for alcohol problems: a review. *Addiction*, **88**, 315–336.

Brown, J. Kranzler, H.R. & Del Boca, F.K. (1992). Self-reports by alcohol and drug abuse inpatients: factors affecting reliability and validity. *British Journal of Addiction*, **87**, 1013–1024.

Brown, S.A., Christiansen, B.A. & Goldman, M.S. (1987). The Alcohol Expectancy Questionnaire: an instrument for the assessment of adolescent and adult alcohol expectancies. *Journal of Studies in Alcohol*, **48**, 483–491.

Connors, G.J. (1995). Screening for alcohol problems. In J.P. Allen & M. Columbus (Eds), *Assessing Alcohol Problems: A Guide for Clinicians and Researchers* (pp. 17–29). National Institute on Alcohol Abuse and Alcoholism Treatment Handbook Series, 4. Bethesda, MD: US Department of Health and Human Services, Public Health Service, National Institutes of Health, National Institute on Alcohol Abuse and Alcoholism.

Crowe, R.R., Kramer, J.R., Hesselbrock, V., Manos, G. & Bucholz, K.K. (1997). The utility of the Brief MAST and the CAGE in identifying alcohol problems: results from national high-risk and community samples. *Archives of Family Medicine*, **6**(5), 477–483.

Davidson, K.M. & Ritson, E.B. (1993). The relationship between alcohol dependence and depression. *Alcohol & Alcoholism*, **28**(2), 147–155.

Davidson, R. (1987). Assessment of the alcohol dependence syndrome: a review of self-report screening questionnaires. *British Journal of Clinical Psychology*, **26**, 243–255.

Donovan, D.M. (1995). Assessments to aid in the treatment planning process. In J.P. Allen & M. Columbus (Eds), *Assessing Alcohol Problems: A Guide for Clinicians and Researchers* (pp. 75–122). National Institute on Alcohol Abuse and Alcoholism Treatment Handbook Series, 4. Department of Health and Human Services, Public Health Service, National Institutes of Health, National Institute on Alcohol Abuse and Alcoholism.

Donovan, D.M. & Rosengren, D.B. (1999). Motivation for behavior change and treatment among substance abusers. In J.A. Tucker, D.M. Donovan & G.A. Marlatt (Eds), *Changing Addictive Behavior: Bridging Clinical and Public Health Strategies*. New York: Guilford.

First, M.G., Spitzer, R.L., Gibbon, M. & Williams, J.B.W. (1995). *Structured Clinical Interview for SDM-IV—Patient Version*. New York: Biometrics Department, New York State Psychiatric Institute.

Friedman, A.S. & Utada, A. (1989). A method for diagnosing and planning the treatment of adolescent drug abusers: the Adolescent Drug Abuse Diagnosis (ADAD) instrument. *Journal of Drug Education*, **19**, 285–312.

Heather, N. (1996). The public health and brief interventions for excessive alcohol consumption: the British experience. *Addictive Behaviors*, **21**, 857–863.

Horn, J.L., Wanberg, K.W. & Foster, F.M. (1987). *Guide to the Alcohol Use Inventory*. Minneapolis, MN: National Computer Systems.

Institute of Medicine (1990). *Broadening the Base of Treatment for Alcohol Problems*. Washington, DC: National Academy Press.

Kaminer, Y., Bukstein, O.G. & Tarter, R.E. (1991). The Teen Addiction Severity Index: rationale and reliability. *International Journal of Addiction*, **26**, 219–226.

Leccese, M. & Waldron, H.B. (1994). Assessing adolescent substance use: a critique of current measurement instruments. *Journal of Substance Abuse Treatment*, **11**(6), 553–563.

Leigh, G. & Skinner, H.A. (1988). Physiological assessment. In D.M. Donovan & G.A. Marlatt (Eds), *Assessment of Addictive Behaviors* (pp. 112–136). New York: Guilford.

Liftik, J. (1995). Assessment. In S. Brown (Ed.), *Treating Alcoholism* (pp. 57–93). San Francisco, CA: Jossey-Bass.

Maisto, S.A. & McKay, J.R. (1995). Diagnosis. In J.P. Allen & M. Columbus (Eds), *Assessing Alcohol Problems: A Guide for Clinicians and Researchers* (pp. 41–54). National Institute on Alcohol Abuse and Alcoholism Treatment Handbook Series, 4. Bethesda, MD: US Department of Health and Human Services, Public Health Service, National Institutes of Health, National Instate on Alcohol Abuse and Alcoholism.

Maisto, S.A., McKay, J.R. & Connor, G.J. (1990). Self-report issues in substance abuse: state of the art and future directions. *Behavioral Assessment*, **12**, 117–134.

Martin, C.S., Kaczynski, N.A., Maisto, S.A., Bukstein, O.M. & Moss, H.B. (1995). Patterns of DSM-

IV alcohol abuse and dependence symptoms in adolescent drinkers. *Journal of Studies on Alcohol*, **56**(6), 672–680.

McLellan, A.T., Kushner, H., Metzger, D., Peters, R., Smith, I., Grissom, G., Pettinati, H. & Argeriou, M. (1992). The fifth edition of the Addiction Severity Index. *Journal of Substance Abuse Treatment*, **9**, 199–213.

Miller, N.S. & Ries, R.K. (1991). Drug and alcohol dependence and psychiatric populations: the need for diagnosis, intervention, and training. *Comprehensive Psychiatry*, **32**(3), 268–276.

Miller, W. & Rollnick, S. (1991). *Motivational Interviewing: Preparing People to Change Addictive Behavior.* New York: Guilford.

Miller, W.R., Tonigan, J.S. & Longabaugh, R. (1995). *The Drinker Inventory of Consequences (DrInC): An Instrument for Assessing Adverse Consequences of Alcohol Abuse.* Test Manual. Project MATCH Monograph Series. Rockville, MD: US Department of Health and Human Services.

Nathan, P.E. (1997). Assessing substance abusers. In L.L. Murphy & J.C. Impara (Eds), *Assessment of Substance Abuse* (pp. xvii–xxix). Lincoln, NE: University of Nebraska.

Robins, L.N., Wing, A.U. & Wittchen, R. *et al.* (1988). The Composite International Diagnostic Interview. *Archives of Genered Psychiatry*, **45**, 1069–1077.

Rogers, P.D., Speraw, S.R. & Ozbek, I. (1995). The assessment of the identified substance abusing adolescent. *Pediatric Clinics of North America*, **42**(2), 351–369.

Rollnick, S., Heather, N., Gold, R. & Hall, W. (1992). Development of a short "Readiness to Change" Questionnaire" for use in brief, opportunistic interventions among excessive drinkers. *British Journal of Addiction*, **87**, 743–754.

Samet, J.H., Rollnick, S. & Barnes, H. (1996). Beyond CAGE: A brief clinical approach after detection of substance abuse. *Archives of Internal Medicine*, **156**, 2287–2293.

Saunders, J.B. & Conigrave, K.M. (1990). Early identification of alcohol problems. *Canadian Medical Association Journal*, **143**, 1060–1068.

Schorling, J.B. & Buchsbaum, D.G. (1997). Screening for alcohol and drug abuse. *Alcohol & Other Substance Abuse*, **81**, 845–865.

Skinner, H.A. (1984). Assessing alcohol use by patients in treatment. In R.C. Smart, H. Cappell, F.B. Glaser, Y. Israel, H. Kalant, W. Schmidt & E.M. Sellers (Eds), *Research Advances in Alcohol & Drug Problems*, Volume 8 (pp. 183–207). New York: Plenum.

Skinner, H.A. (1990). Spectrum of drinkers and intervention opportunities. *Canadian Medical Association Journal*, **143**, 1054–1059.

Skinner, H.A. & Allen, B.A. (1982). Alcohol dependence syndrome: measurement and validation. *Journal of Abnormal Psychology*, **91**, 199–209.

Skinner, H.A. & Horn, J.L. (1984). *Alcohol Dependence Scale: Users' Guide.* Toronto: Addiction Research Foundation.

Skinner, H.A. & Holt, S. (1987). *The Alcohol Clinical Index: Strategies for Identifying Patients with Alcohol Problems.* Toronto: Addiction Research Foundation.

Skinner, H., McIntosh, M. & Palmer, W. (1985). Lifestyle assessment: just asking makes a difference. *British Medical Journal*, **290**, 214–216.

Skinner, H.A., Holt, S., Sheu, W.J. & Israel, Y. (1986). Clinical versus laboratory detection of alcohol abuse: the Alcohol Clinical Index. *British Medical Journal*, **292**, 1703–1708.

Sobell, L.C. & Sobell, M.B. (1995). Alcohol consumption measures. In J.P. Allen & M. Columbus (Eds), *Assessing Alcohol Problems: A Guide for Clinicians and Researchers* (pp. 55–73). National Institute on Alcohol Abuse and Alcoholism Treatment Handbook Series, 4. Bethesda, MD: US Department of Health and Human Services, Public Health Service, National Institutes of Health, National Instate on Alcohol Abuse and Alcoholism.

Upfold, D.N. (1997). Assessment and outpatient counselling for adolescents and young adults. In S. Harrison & V. Carver (Eds), *Alcohol & Drug Problems: A Practical Guide for Counsellors* (pp. 319–339). Toronto: Addiction Research Foundation.

Tucker, J.A., Donovan, D.M. & Marlatt, G.A. (1999). *Changing Addictive Behavior: Bridging Clinical and Public Health Strategies.* New York: Guilford.

Winters, K.C. & Henly, G.A. (1989). *Personal Experience Inventory (PEI) Test and Manual.* Los Angeles, CA: Western Psychological Services.

Zweben, A. & Fleming, M.F. (1999).   Brief interventions for alcohol and drug problems. In J.A. Tucker, D.M. Donovan & G.A. Marlatt. *Changing Addictive Behavior: Bridging Clinical and Public Health Strategies* (pp. 251–282). New York: Guilford.

Chapter 26

Alcohol Withdrawal and Detoxification

Duncan Raistrick
Leeds Addiction Unit, Leeds, UK

Synopsis

The characteristics of alcohol withdrawal are well known. Under experimental conditions anyone can be made tolerant to the effects of alcohol and experience withdrawal symptoms on abrupt withdrawal or marked reduction of intake; in vivo it is usually after several years of regular drinking that a person begins to experience withdrawal symptoms. The severity of withdrawal can be seen to exist along a continuum ranging from the mild tremulous state through seizures and on to alcoholic delirium. It is probable that this continuum is, in reality, made up of different symptom clusters which are associated with different neurochemical systems. All of these systems are under the influence of g-aminobutyric acid (GABA) and hence the rationale for using benzodiazepines and other central nervous system depressants for the treatment of withdrawal.

Detoxification is usually a very straightforward procedure. When complications do happen they are often serious and it is, therefore, important that clinicians maintain vigilance through-out all detoxification procedures. There are a number of standardized scales to measure the severity of alcohol withdrawal and use of these scales has been shown to be helpful in the early identification of complications during detoxification and in minimizing the dose of sedative medication used to control withdrawal. There is evidence to support the use of chlor-diazepoxide as the drug of first choice for the management of alcohol withdrawal; chlor-diazepoxide is relatively safe, even in combination with alcohol, has a low addictive potential and can be uniquely identified on toxicology screening. Chlormethiazole is, however, supe-rior where there is a risk of seizures or delirium but it has a lower safety profile. Potentially dangerous medical conditions are frequently associated with the more severe withdrawal states, indicating the need for full medical work-up in these cases. The setting in which detoxi-fication should take place needs to be judged on the basis of the expected severity of with-drawal and the social support available to an individual. Home or inpatient detoxifications are costly compared to other options and can normally be offered only in circumstances where there is clinical or social need.

International Handbook of Alcohol Dependence and Problems. Edited by N. Heather, T.J. Peters and T. Stockwell.
© 2001 John Wiley & Sons Ltd.

The relationship between withdrawal symptomatology and alcohol dependence has long been controversial. There is no doubt that relief drinking is powerfully reinforced when it occurs but this is insufficient to justify the dominance of withdrawal over other drinking cues that feed into the learning processes, underpinning dependence. Dependence should be seen as a purely psychological phenomenon to which withdrawal makes some, quite limited, contribution. Tolerance and withdrawal can be subsumed under the umbrella of "neuro-adaptation" rather than using the more confusing terminology of "physical dependence".

KEY ISSUES OF UNDERSTANDING

Detoxification services are generally seen to be an important component of any alcohol treatment system. The purpose of detoxification is to minimize the severity of the withdrawal symptoms that occur when alcohol consumption is abruptly stopped or markedly reduced. Detoxification is not as straightforward or mundane a procedure as it may appear at first sight; however, it is not so much the management of withdrawal that has excited controversy but, rather, the meaning of withdrawal in understanding dependence—for example, Stockwell (1994) argues that alcohol withdrawal symptoms are of little practical importance and Tober (1992) argues that withdrawal symptoms have no place in the definition of dependence. After nearly 50 years of scientific investigation, the understanding of alcohol tolerance and withdrawal has reached a maturity, so that their final resting place in the whole spectrum of alcohol problems and problem drinking is closer to being settled.

Alcohol Withdrawal

There have been descriptions throughout history of symptoms and signs that would now be recognized as belonging to an alcohol withdrawal syndrome. The Edinburgh physician Thomas Sutton is credited with describing delirium tremens in 1813 and attributing the condition to alcohol withdrawal. Confirmation of the connection between drinking, stopping drinking and the experience of withdrawal is, however, relatively recent. In the classic study by Isbell et al. (1955), 10 ex-morphine addicts received daily dosing with alcohol for periods of up to 12 weeks. On abrupt withdrawal of alcohol, the subjects experienced significant symptoms, including tremor, sweating, vomiting, diarrhoea, hyper-reflexia, fever, raised blood pressure and insomnia; two subjects experienced convulsions and four subjects experienced hallucinations or delirium. The work of Isbell and colleagues left questions unanswered but was a sufficient basis for proceeding with further elucidation of the nature of withdrawal by the use of laboratory-style experimentation in human beings. In a selective review of this research, Gross (1977) concluded that the severity of the alcohol withdrawal syndrome would relate to alcohol intake modified by the contribution of residual effects of previous drinking and the abruptness of withdrawal. He went on to describe a factor structure of withdrawal: *Factor 1—hallucinogenic* consists of nausea, tinitus, visual disturbance, pruritis, parasthesiae, muscle pain, agitation, sleep disturbance, tactile hallucinations, and hallucinations which are auditory or visual or both: *Factor 2—affective and physiological* consists of anxiety, depression, tremor and sweats: *Factor 3—delirium* consists of clouding of the sensorium, impairment of consciousness and impairment of contact with the observer. Factors 1 and 2 were seen as existing along a continuum of severity, whereas factor 3 appeared more complex, since it increased both during drinking and on withdrawal.

In a sophisticated analysis of alcohol withdrawal symptoms, Hershon (1977) reasoned

Table 26.1 The 10 most common and the 10 most specific symptoms of alcohol withdrawal

	Most common symptoms	Most specific symptoms
1	Depression	Whole body shakes
2	Anxiety	Facial tremulousness
3	Irritability	Hand and finger shakes
4	Tiredness	Cannot face the day
5	Craving	Panicky
6	Restlessness	Guilty
7	Insomnia	Nausea
8	Confusion	Visual hallucinations
9	Sweating	Weakness
10	Weakness	Depression

Source: adapted from Hershon (1977).

that symptoms of withdrawal should (a) be absent during periods of light drinking, (b) be present during periods of heavy drinking, (c) disappear after 10 days of abstinence, (d) be present first thing in the morning, and (e) be relieved by further drinking—he applied these criteria as a series of filters to symptoms reported by 100 male drinkers in the previous month, so that he was able to separate those symptoms most specific to alcohol withdrawal from symptoms that happen to be commonly present during withdrawal (see Table 26.1). The implications of these data are that commonly occurring symptoms, perhaps the result of minor stress or the consequence of accumulated alcohol-related problems, may incorrectly be attributed to alcohol withdrawal and may lead to inaccurate assessment and inappropriate pharmacotherapy as part of a detoxification programme.

Edwards (1990) concludes that the evidence from animal and human research suggests that anyone can develop tolerance and withdrawal symptoms within a short space of time, days or weeks, provided that a sufficiently high and regular dose of alcohol is taken. Whether or when withdrawal symptoms occur is largely a function of dose and frequency scheduling, or in other words an individual's drinking pattern; typically, but not necessarily, persistent withdrawal symptoms are a feature of the later stages of a drinking career. Once withdrawal symptoms have occurred, then subsequent manifestations in terms of both frequency and severity will depend upon a complex interaction of factors, but above all blood alcohol level seems to be important. Vinson & Menezes (1991), for example, found significant but low-order correlations between blood alcohol on admission to rehabilitation services and severity of withdrawal symptoms. Alcohol affects several different neurochemical systems which probably accounts for the variable picture of alcohol withdrawal.

It appears to be the case that the more severe withdrawal states are associated with additional and multiple risk factors, although high blood alcohol levels remain an important element within the aetiology. Schuckit et al. (1995) report on a cohort of 1648 alcohol-dependent men and women where 12.8% of subjects had experienced at least one episode of alcoholic delirium or convulsions during withdrawal. The most powerful discriminating variables between those with histories of more and less severe withdrawal were the maximum number of drinks per day and the total number of withdrawal episodes; the use of non-prescribed depressant drugs and a greater number of medical problems were also significant. In a cohort of 72 "alcoholics" hospitalized for detoxification, Essardas et al. (1994) report that 46% of subjects had convulsions and 25% developed alcoholic delirium.

In contrast, Mayo-Smith & Bernard (1995) report on a cohort of 1044 subjects admitted for inpatient detoxification and given unlimited oxazepam titrated against severity of alcohol withdrawal: only 1.1% of subjects experienced seizures, with peak incidence occurring 12–48 hours after the last oxazepam dose, and without progression to alcoholic delirium. Tsuang et al. (1994) found that 9% of 532 subjects attending a day programme had a diagnosis of alcoholic hallucinosis; compared to those without a history of hallucinations, these subjects had an earlier onset of alcohol problems, consumed more alcohol per occasion and were more likely to experiment with a variety of illicit drugs.

It is not possible to say with any degree of precision what withdrawal symptomatology will be associated with what kind of drinking pattern in what kind of person. In broad brush terms, alcohol withdrawal can be seen as existing along a continuum from mild tremulousness, with or without affective change, through to seizures, hallucinations, and delirium. Whether or not this is truly a continuum or, more likely, different symptom clusters (see Hershon, 1977; Gross, 1977; Stockwell et al., 1979), reflecting withdrawal responses by different neurochemical mechanisms, is unclear. Alcoholic delirium is in some ways an exception to this general proposition. Kramp et al. (1979) compared 20 subjects with tremor and hallucinations against 20 patients with tremor, hallucinations and delirium. The main difference between subjects was that the delirium group had embarked on a drinking binge prior to the onset of symptoms and continued drinking in spite of symptoms. However, both groups required the same amount of sedation, which was carefully titrated to achieve the end-point of inducing sleep. It was therefore concluded that delirium may be qualitatively different to the simple hallucinatory state and, once triggered, have a natural history of its own. The data on the latency from abstinence or marked reduction of intake to the manifestation of different withdrawal elements are inconsistent; nonetheless there is a clear ordering of symptoms. It is plausible to think in terms of a hierarchy of neurochemical systems, each requiring greater biochemical disturbance to launch different aspects of the withdrawal syndrome. It may be that kindling and the long elimination time from high blood alcohol concentrations combine to produce this effect.

Withdrawal Symptoms and Dependence

The International Classification of Diseases (World Health Organization, 1992) defines alcohol dependence as a psychobiological state based on the provisional description of alcohol dependence by Edwards & Gross (1976). The important advance here is that dependence is seen as a unitary concept and the old distinction between psychological and physical dependence is dispensed with. Physical dependence was almost synonymous with what is now referred to as neuro-adaptation, that is, tolerance to the effects of alcohol and withdrawal symptoms, but implicit in the use of the word "dependence" was a notion that neuro-adaptation of itself was driving an individual's drinking. The centrality to dependence of withdrawal symptoms continues to excite debate.

Edwards (1990) has argued that withdrawal symptoms should be seen as a special case drinking cue which is integral to the concept of dependence. He has proposed some kind of "watershed", a threshold beyond which individuals experience withdrawal, which thereafter becomes the dominant drinking cue; this is at odds with ideas about continua of severity. While acknowledging that the scientific evidence in support of this view is weak, Edwards (p. 458) asserts that the clinical evidence is strong: "science is not science . . . until it is tested against what our . . . patients have to tell us". The veracity of this position will continue to be debated: one difficulty of the clinicians' viewpoint is that clinicians usually see a rather small segment of the drinking population and what is really needed is research that spans the whole range of drinkers. The preferred synthesis is that the mix of cues for current drinking start out as predominantly social but are then progressively replaced by pharmacological and then physiological cues. Progression is not inevitable and a mix of all three categories of drinking cue can usually be found, even in circumstances where withdrawal has come to be a preoccupation.

Hershon (1977) looked specifically at the question of which withdrawal symptoms provoked drinking and which were then relieved by drinking, or in other words whether the drinking behaviour was then reinforced. The three most commonly reported symptoms in the Hershon study—depression, anxiety and irritability—were said to have provoked drinking by 83%, 85% and 66% of subjects, respectively, and to have been 70%, 82% and 66% successful at relieving the symptoms. One interpretation of these data is that negative mood states, whether or not part of physiological withdrawal, are commonly associated with withdrawal and are likely to provoke relief drinking. This is consistent with other evidence that negative mood states are powerful triggers of drinking (see Marlatt, 1985, pp. 37–44). As dependence increases, then so drinking becomes a response triggered by ever more cues and cue complexes; for example, Rankin et al. (1982) present evidence that subjects who experience more withdrawal symptoms at one and the same time experience more drinking cues. In a strict sense, detoxification is intended to ameliorate the severity of withdrawal symptoms and thereby eliminate the negative reinforcement of relief drinking. In practice, a broad spectrum of drinking cues are diminished as the process of detoxification progresses.

Raistrick et al. (1994) have conceptualized dependence as a purely psychological phenomenon which is best understood in terms of classical and operant conditioning mechanisms. At a day-to-day clinical practice level, dependence can be thought of as an over-learned collection of thoughts and behaviours related to drinking that are the product of repeated episodes of positive and negative reinforcement: examples of positive reinforcement might be *increased sociability* or *desire for intoxication*, examples of negative reinforcement might be *avoidance of withdrawal* or *relief of depressed mood*. In short, withdrawal symptoms are seen as one among many sources of reinforcement which contribute to dependence in any individual.

The purely psychological formulation of dependence takes account of withdrawal symptoms which, however important and self-generating as drinking cues, need to be taken in the wider context. For example, Tabakoff (1990) has argued that if relief drinking were solely to do with alleviating withdrawal symptomatology, then a single "dose" of alcohol would normally be sufficient for several hours' relief. In practice, early morning drinking often becomes continuous, as if to recapture an alcohol effect: this can be seen as an example of impaired control. Giving undue emphasis to substance specific withdrawal has two further problems: first, it does not take account of the transferability of dependence from one substance to another; second, it does not allow for the measurement of dependence in people who have achieved abstinence, which will have important implications for future treatment. Raistrick et al. (1994) have developed an instrument, the Leeds Dependence Questionnaire, which balances cognitive and behavioural markers of psychological dependence. It is to be expected that this instrument will correlate highly with measures of dependence that emphasize withdrawal symptoms, provided that dependence is being measured during a heavy drinking phase, in people who experience withdrawal, and provided that dependence remains focused on one substance. In short, the psychological view of dependence is a theoretically more satisfactory account of dependence than the psychobiological model.

THE MANAGEMENT OF DETOXIFICATION

Carroll (1997) argues that it is unhelpful for psychosocial therapies and pharmacotherapies to develop separately; rather, it is the integration of therapies that will deliver the most cost-effective outcomes and should, therefore, be the basis of good practice. Broadly speaking, pharmacotherapies are targeted at a narrow-spectrum of symptoms or psychiatric disorder, in this case withdrawal, and stand in contrast to broader-spectrum psychosocial treatments. Detoxification is, however, something of an exception to the general rule of integrating therapies in that it is largely a stand-alone procedure, which can be used in or out of a therapy programme as circumstances demand but with the caveat that detoxification should always be seen as a therapy opportunity.

Timing of Detoxification

The Transtheoretical Stages of Change Model described by Prochaska & DiClemente (1984) has become a popular clinical tool in the addiction field. Notwithstanding the "transtheoretical" label, the model has much to do with motivation to change. The Model has been criticized for lacking empirical support and for attempting to define change in stages, rather than along a continuum (see Davidson, 1992). More importantly the five stages of change described in the Model have proved resistant to accurate identification, either by means of clinical assessment or by self-completion questionnaire. The Model predicts that detoxification is an intervention matched to the "action stage", albeit that there are good reasons for detoxification at other stages. Detoxification is commonly misprescribed: first, because practitioners are likely to want their problem drinkers to be at the "action stage" where people are seen to be moving out of addictive behaviour; second, problem drinkers themselves put forward the seductive argument, "If I can go away and detox, then everything will be alright"; and third, doctors find it easy to prescribe medication when they have no other appropriate response to make. The problem with careless prescribing is that a failed detoxification risks lowering a patient's self-efficacy and increasing therapist pessimism.

The key to a successful, planned detoxification is preparation. Before proceeding with detoxification, it is the job of the therapist to bring the problem drinker through to the point of readiness to change; this is not to do with transient thoughts about wanting to stop drinking or even actual changes in drinking when these have been occasioned by short-term negative consequences of drinking. The hallmark features of readiness to change are having a positive outcome expectancy or, in other words, a well-considered belief that life will be better without drinking, and self-efficacy or, in other words, a belief that a change in drinking can be achieved. Repeated failure at detoxification will make it more difficult to build self-efficacy in the future. It is a crucial part of the preparation work to identify a supportive other person, to plan activities for the detoxification period and the week immediately following, and to check that any practical arrangements, such as childcare or time off from work or travel, are planned in advance.

For opiate users, Phillips et al. (1986) found that a general neuroticism factor and the degree of expected distress during withdrawal were related to subsequent severity of symptoms. Detoxification is likely to be more problematic where individuals are frightened of what might happen to them and it follows that allaying anxiety is an important part of preparation. Green & Gossop (1988) have shown that simple information giving can be effective at reducing the severity and duration of withdrawal symptoms. Johnston et al. (1991) found that patients with a DSM-III-R diagnosis of anxiety disorder and alcohol dependence experienced significantly greater levels of anxiety throughout detoxification as compared to alcohol dependence only patients. Milby et al. (1986) identified a pathological fear of detoxification in 22–32% of patients attending different methadone maintenance programmes. This detoxification phobia was found in people with longer drug using histories: the phobias seem to have been acquired during treatment with methadone and can therefore be seen as iatrogenic. There is no direct counterpart in heavy drinkers but there is every reason to suppose that the general principle of involving patients in their detoxification will ameliorate anxieties and improve outcome. Coexisting anxiety disorder may require concurrent therapy.

While it is ideal to plan detoxification with people who have reached the stage of wanting to change their drinking, there are other occasions when detoxification is indicated. First, it may be expedient to detoxify someone experiencing withdrawal symptoms after an enforced abstinence, such as admission to hospital or imprisonment. Second, it is standard practice to detoxify prior to treatment in a residential programme. Whether it makes sense routinely to detoxify prior to outpatient therapy is less certain, unless someone's drinking is so out of control that there is no prospect of any psychosocial therapy succeeding without prior detoxification. Third, the person who has relapsed after securing a period of abstinence may require detoxification to restabilize.

The Setting for Detoxification

Alcohol treatment has been in rapid evolution over the last 20 years: the treatment population has been extended from the severe "alcoholic" to include people with a relatively mild alcohol problem and the variety of therapists has been extended to include psychologists, counsellors, nurses and doctors, among others. Detoxification programmes have also evolved to take advantage of the range of professional skills available and to respond to the changing needs of problem drinkers who have come forward for treatment. The aims of a detoxification programme are to monitor the severity of withdrawal, identify any complications of withdrawal in order to ensure safety, and to manage withdrawal with a minimum of discomfort for the patient.

Community-based detoxification can be delivered in the home, on an outpatient or day-patient basis or within a supported residential facility. Home detoxification is relatively expensive and should be reserved for people unable to travel to an outpatient unit, for example, people who have child care problems, disabled people, the elderly. In rural areas it is likely to be the case that home detoxification is more convenient and no more costly than the outpatient option. The model of home detoxification developed by Stockwell et al. (1990) involves daily visits from a psychiatric nurse trained to assess withdrawal and monitor for complications; any prescribing or medical care is provided by a consultant led team or on a shared care basis with a general practitioner. Successful home detoxification also requires supportive and sensible friends or relatives to stay with the patient during the detoxification. For people without a home or without the support of friends or relatives, a community-based facility is a safe alternative to inpatient care. For example, in a recent study of 1629 admissions to a detoxification centre staffed by care workers, only four people required transfer to psychiatric care and 17 to a general hospital (Mortimer & Edwards, 1994). The homeless tend to drink relatively modest quantities of alcohol, spread throughout the day, and usually do not experience marked withdrawal problems. The management of uncomplicated alcohol withdrawal in whatever setting may or may not include the use of medication. Whitfield et al. (1978) describe the safe detoxification of 1024 people who presented to non-drug detoxification centres with a variety of medical complications and severities of withdrawal. The success of these centres depends upon training staff to feel confident about monitoring withdrawal in order to identify those clients who are in need of medical help, and training that enables staff quickly to form a helping alliance with clients.

Consideration should always be given to home or residential detoxification for elderly people. Comparing a small group of elderly residents, mean age 69 years, with a younger group, mean age 30 years, who had been admitted for alcohol withdrawal, Brower et al.

(1994) found the elderly group experienced significantly more withdrawal symptoms for a longer duration, even though the medication regimes were similar. The elderly group were more likely to show cognitive impairment, day-time sleepiness, weakness and raised blood pressure and were therefore at greater risk.

Standard Pharmacotherapy

The rationale for the pharmacotherapy of alcohol withdrawal is based on the capacity of alcohol to enhance the inhibitory effects of the neurotransmitter γ-aminobutyric acid (GABA) and to diminish the activity of the excitatory N-methyl-D-aspartate, NMDA, receptors. Glue & Nutt (1990) have suggested that the clinical symptoms of withdrawal can be explained by overactivity of the dopaminergic (hallucinations), NMDA (seizures) and noradrenergic (sympathetic activity) systems: each of these systems is under the influence of GABA.

The incidence of withdrawal symptoms requiring pharmacotherapy will vary markedly, depending upon the population of drinkers attending a particular service. Factors that will predict severe withdrawal are (a) recent high levels of alcohol consumption; (b) previous history of severe withdrawal; (c) previous history of seizures or delirium; (d) concomitant use of psychoactive drugs; (e) poor physical health; and (f) high levels of anxiety and other psychiatric disorder. There is an evidence base to support the good practice of detoxification but the apparently forgiving nature of withdrawal management can lead clinicians into being complacent and unsafe.

For the majority of patients, withdrawal symptoms begin to emerge after some 6–8 hours and peak within the next 24 hours—only rarely do major symptoms persist beyond 5 days. The risk of seizures is small after 2 days and delirium is unlikely to emerge anew in patients who have been adequately treated. In untreated patients, status epilepticus may be the presenting problem (see Alldredge & Lowenstein, 1993). Delirium may be the presenting problem in patients who are still drinking but have markedly reduced their alcohol intake (Kramp & Hemmingsen, 1979), although the incidence is more usually seen to peak at around 4 days post-abstinence. It follows from these time scales that the general aim of pharmacotherapy is rapidly to achieve therapeutic levels of medication and to taper the dose after 48 hours.

The most effective treatments for withdrawal are all GABA-enhancing. The first-line drugs are all sedatives and, to a lesser or greater extent, have the problem that they may cause undue sedation, particularly if taken in the presence of alcohol or other central nervous system depressants. Aside from the medical treatment of alcoholic delirium, there are three basic protocols for detoxification, each of which suits different circumstances:

- *Fixed dose regimen.* In this regimen patients are assessed according to some rather crude measure of withdrawal severity and assigned to a starting point on a predetermined reduction programme. This kind of regime is clinically questionable but may be a satisfactory approach for patients with less severe withdrawal problems or as an expedience where nursing and medical resources are limited.
- *Variable dose regime.* This is probably the most widely used approach and well suited to outpatient or home detoxification. The aim is to prescribe a sufficient but minimal dose of sedative according to a clinical rating of withdrawal severity; ratings should be made using one of the standardized measurement scales that are discussed below. This approach requires the regular availability of medical, nursing and pharmacy staff.
- *Loading dose regime.* This approach is best suited to inpatient or possibly home detoxification. The principle is that a loading dose of a long-acting sedative is given

incrementally to achieve an end-point of light sleep. No further medication is given and detoxification depends on the slow elimination of the drug. This can be a cost-effective approach but skilled supervision and monitoring are required in the initial stages.

In a review of drug treatments for alcohol withdrawal, Williams & McBride (1998) evaluate 14 randomized, double-blind placebo-controlled and 22 randomized, double-blind controlled trials. They highlight serious methodological problems in most of the studies reviewed but, in overview, conclude that benzodiazepines and chlormethiazole are superior to placebo and of similar effectiveness to each other in treating withdrawal, including preventing seizures and delirium. Shaw (1995) concurs with this general conclusion but also concludes that the different pharmacokinetics of benzodiazepines may be used to advantage. A further consideration in favour of benzodiazepines is the availability of the benzodiazepine antagonist flumazenil in the event of overdose. The differences between chlordiazepoxide, diazepam, lorazepam and chlormethiazole as first-line treatments for alcohol withdrawal are marginal, and so it is sensible that clinicians select one or possibly two drugs and become totally familiar with their characteristics.

Chlordiazepoxide

Chlordiazepoxide is long-acting, half-life 5–15 hours, and has active metabolites with half-lives up to 100 hours; there is therefore a risk of an accumulation of active drug leading to unwanted sedation and confusion, especially in the elderly. Chlordiazepoxide has a low addictive potential and a high margin of safety when taken with alcohol. The metabolites of chlordiazepoxide are unique and can, therefore, be separately identified on urine toxicology screening. There is a strong argument for using chlordiazepoxide as the first-line drug in non-residential settings using fixed or variable protocols (see Duncan & Taylor, 1996). A typical reduction regime is presented in Table 26.2.

Diazepam

Diazepam is long-acting, half-life 10–30 hours, and has active metabolites with half-lives up to 100 hours. Accumulation problems are the same as for chlordiazepoxide. Diazepam is more rapidly absorbed than chlordiazepoxide, which gives it a greater addictive potential but also makes it more suitable for a loading regime. Ritson & Chick (1986) have favoured diazepam, noting its smooth action and its effect on relieving anxiety and depression.

Table 26.2 Fixed protocol for chlordiazepoxide withdrawal regimen

	Morning (mg)	Midday (mg)	Evening (mg)	Night (mg)	Total daily dose (mg)
Day 1	30	30	30	30	120
Day 2	30	20	20	30	100
Day 3	20	20	20	20	80
Day 4	20	10	10	20	60
Day 5	10	10	10	10	40
Day 6	10	10	0	10	30
Day 7	10	0	0	10	20

For moderate severity of withdrawal start at day 3, and for mild severity day 5.

Salloum et al. (1995) found that of 37 patients requiring pharmacotherapy and given a loading dose regime, 15 required a single 20 mg dose, 14 required 40–100 mg and 8 required 120–220 mg. They reported no complications related to this treatment.

Lorazepam

Lorazepam is short-acting, half-life 10–20 hours, and has no active metabolites. Lorazepam is well absorbed intramuscularly and can be seen as suited to loading regimes, particularly in patients presenting with more severe symptoms, the elderly and patients with markedly impaired liver function. The short half-life increases the addictive potential of lorazepam and also increases the potential for seizures if the drug is tapered without due caution. Hosein et al. (1978) report on the treatment of 21 patients with incipient alcoholic delirium who were successfully treated with an initial injection of lorazepam 5 mg followed by a tapering dose of oral lorazepam.

Chlormethiazole

Chlormethiazole is short acting, half-life 3–6 hours. The potency of chlormethiazole and its short half-life confer a high addictive potential. It is more likely than benzodiazepines to complicate respiratory insufficiency and to be lethal in combination with alcohol. On the other hand, chlormethiazole is consistently found to be superior to benzodiazepines in preventing seizures and delirium, suggesting that it is the drug of choice for more severe withdrawal and use on an inpatient basis only. Morgan (1995) advises that severe withdrawal symptoms are best controlled by an intravenous infusion of 0.8% chlormethiazole; this should only occur in a general medical setting where there are skilled staff to monitor fluid balance and so forth. She recommends an initial drip rate of 3.0–7.5 ml/minute to induce shallow sleep and thereafter reducing the infusion rate to 0.5–1.0 ml/minute with regular checks to ensure that the patient can be roused.

If hallucinations are a feature of withdrawal, then haloperidol is the treatment of choice and regimens should reflect standard psychiatric practice. Shaw (1995) has estimated that regularly drinking more than 24 units of alcohol on heavy days increases the risk of severe withdrawal, which includes hallucinations in 7.3–32%. Anticipation of severe withdrawal should provoke a full medical work-up, to include examination for Wernicke's encephalopathy, hepatic failure, subdural haematoma, checks for hypoglycaemia, electrolyte balance (including magnesium) and toxicology screen. Where an individual has neglected his/her diet or is scoring in the high risk area of a standard rating scale, then there is strong evidence in favour of giving multivitamin supplements, which should contain at least thiamine 300 mg daily and magnesium supplements. There is an argument for giving vitamin supplements on a routine basis, given that the potential benefits are so great and the cost so small (Cook & Thompson, 1997).

Williams & McBride (1998) concluded that carbamazepine may be an alternative first-line drug to benzodiazepines. Carbamazepine has the advantage of being effective in severe alcohol withdrawal, including alcoholic delirium. It does not interact with alcohol, it is not contraindicated for patients with liver damage and it is thought to prevent the kindling process, which has been implicated in the genesis of seizures and delirium. Carbamazepine is somewhat more expensive than benzodiazepines and there is a risk of serious haematological side effects.

Given the complexity of alcohol effects on neurotransmitter systems, a logical approach to alcohol withdrawal is to use ethanol itself as a pharmacological agent. This is usually not practical because of the problems of dispensing pharmaceutical ethanol and the problem of blood alcohol being a major cue for loss of control over further drinking. However, one setting in which ethanol substitution can be convenient is the intensive care unit. Wilkens et al. (1998) successfully treated 11 postoperative patients for alcohol withdrawal by means of ethanol infusion. They found ethanol elimination rates of 18–50 mg/100 ml/hour, which is rather higher than the widely assumed elimination rate of 15 mg/100 ml/hour.

Adjunctive Therapies

Much of the alcohol withdrawal syndrome is due to adrenergic overactivity. It follows that in cases where either benzodiazepines are deemed unsuitable or where autonomic over-activity is marked, then both α-2-adrenergic agonists, such as lofexidine, and β-adrenergic blockers, such as atenolol, may be beneficial. These drugs can be used either alone or in combination with benzodiazepines (see Brewer, 1995). Neither of these groups of drugs have any effect on preventing seizures or delirium, nor are they expected to have an impact on mood or sleep disturbance. Among other drugs that have found a rationale in the treatment of alcohol withdrawal, Williams & McBride (1998) found insufficient evidence to recommend the use of lithium, bromocryptine or γ-hydroxybutyric acid.

The use of non-pharmaceutical, non-specific "feel-good" therapies has become increasingly popular. These treatments, which include acupuncture, aromatherapy, massage and homeopathy, can be used either on a stand-alone basis for patients with mild withdrawal symptoms or as an adjunctive to pharmacotherapy. Auricular acupuncture has particular appeal, in that it is easy to organize in a variety of settings, it can be done on an individual or group basis, it is inexpensive and there is limited evidence supporting efficacy beyond a generalized "feel-good effect" (Bullock et al., 1989).

Aftercare

In an ideal situation, detoxification will be part of a therapy programme and so aftercare will be planned in advance. The need for post-detoxification treatment will vary enormously from one person to another, depending upon their social circumstances, their psychological well-being and previous levels of dependence. Whatever the long-term drinking goal, a period of total abstinence is usually desirable post-detoxification. Whether or not the detoxification service should offer disulfiram as an aid to abstinence or anti-craving drugs, at least in the period between finishing detoxification and the follow-up key worker appointment, is a policy issue for clinical teams.

If there was any suggestion of mental illness in the pre-detoxification assessment, then the service should also make a full psychiatric assessment post-detoxification. As many as 80% of problem drinkers entering treatment experience psychological symptoms, often as a mixed picture of dysphoria, anxiety, depression, panic and insomnia; in severe cases, ideas of self-harm and hopelessness may be cause for concern. Usually these symptoms fall short of a psychiatric disorder and melt away after a period of abstinence. For example, Driessen et al. (1996) found that for inpatients, who are expected to have high rates of comorbidity, the prevalence of psychiatric disorders 2 weeks post-detoxification was 3% schizophrenia, 13% affective disorder, 22% phobic disorders and 2% generalized anxiety. Brown & Irwin (1991) demonstrated a week-on-week fall in anxiety scores post-detoxification, which continued through to 3 months follow-up. Psychiatric disorder can complicate the management of detoxification; however, Araujo et al. (1996) found no differential effect on drop-out rates between those with and those without disorder. It follows that any treatment for psychiatric disorder should be delayed, preferably for as long as 4 weeks post-detoxification (see Raimo & Schuckit, 1998).

MEASURING WITHDRAWAL AND AUDIT OF DETOXIFICATION

It is usual to use a rating scale to measure the severity of alcohol withdrawal for the dual purpose of determining the dose of medication prescribed to attenuate withdrawal symptomatology and to identify any complications of detoxification. The commonly used scales are all derived from a 20-item scale developed by Gross et al. (1971), who themselves went on to develop a shortened *Selected Severity Assessment Scale* (Gross et al., 1973, pp. 365–376). The original instrument developed by Gross and colleagues had good inter-rater reliability, except on the item "quality of contact". "Visual disturbances" were differentiated from "visual illusions" or "visual hallucinations": "visual disturbances" were thought to be toxic in origin and consist of phenomena such as flashes of light or moving coloured spots. In addition to the 20 items, the scale is supplemented by charting temperature, pulse and number of seizures should any occur.

Shaw et al. (1981) developed a reliable and validated 15 item scale, the Clinical Institute Withdrawal Assessment for Alcohol (CIWA-A), which was designed for hourly administration. Sullivan et al. (1989) have revised this scale and produced the CIWA-Ar, which has only 10 items. Competent nurses can complete an evaluation in less than 2 minutes. The scale excludes seizures on the grounds that these are rare events which can be noted in the clinical assessment. Equally, pulse and blood pressure, which were not found to correlate with severity of withdrawal, are recorded as indicators of the whole clinical picture. The authors recommend that pharmacological treatment is not indicated for scores less than 10 and clinical judgement should determine the use of pharmacotherapy for scores between 10 and 20.

Metcalfe et al. (1995) also developed a 10 item modification of the CIWA-A but reached rather different clinical judgements to the previous authors. In contrast to the CIWA-Ar, they retained the seizures, "quality of contact" and "thought disturbance" items from the parent instrument. In this case, seizures were included on the grounds that they are relatively common (5–15% of problem drinkers referred for detoxification) and for the reason that around one-third of cases of alcoholic delirium are preceded by one or more seizures. "Quality of contact" and "thought disturbance" items were judged to provide early warning of more severe withdrawal. Thus, the Windsor Clinic Alcohol Withdrawal Assessment Scale (WCAWAS) was designed to be clinically more relevant than CIWA-Ar and the items chosen were seen to be objective. Of the 142 patients in their validation study, 8% developed complicated withdrawals: five developed visual hallucinations, one alcoholic delirium and five had grand mal seizures.

Wetterling et al. (1997) have also devised a scale which also seeks to improve upon the CIWA-Ar. As with the CIWA-Ar, the Alcohol Withdrawal Syndrome Scale (AWSS) was derived from a statistical analysis of CIWA-A; seizures were eliminated on the grounds of rarity and irrelevance as a clinical predictor. In their validation study of 256 subjects referred for detoxification, 10.5% developed alcoholic delirium. The authors recommend that scores of five or less be considered mild withdrawal, requiring no medication, and scores 10 or greater be considered severe withdrawal and high risk for complications. The three shorter rating scales, CIWA-Ar, WCAWAS and AWSS, can each be seen as a suitable instrument for monitoring the clinical progress of detoxification. In choosing a particular scale, clinicians will apply their own preferences and intuition; a key issue is whether or not to include withdrawal seizures. The scoring system for different scales is presented in Table 26.3.

Measuring the effectiveness of treatment at minimizing the severity of withdrawal and at preventing complications is one valid indicator of outcome. Equally, detoxification has the clear aim of achieving an alcohol-free state and so, logically, outcome could be assessed

Table 26.3 Scoring systems for different alcohol withdrawal scales

	DCCRS Gross et al. (1971)	CIWA-A Shaw et al. (1981)	CIWA-Ar Sullivan et al. (1989)	WCAWAS Metcalfe et al. (1995)	AWSS Wetterling et al. (1997)
Pulse rate					0–3
Blood pressure					0–3
Temperature					0–3
Respiration rate					0–3
Sweating	0–7	0–7	0–7		0–3
Anxiety	0–7	0–7	0–7	0–4	0–2
Tremor	0–7	0–7	0–7	0–8	0–3
Depression	0–7				
Agitation	0–7	0–7	0–7	0–8	0–4
Snout reflex	0–2				
Hallucinations	0–4	0–3			0–4
Tactile		0–6	0–7		
Auditory		0–6	0–7	0–8	
Visual		0–6	0–7	0–10	
Nausea and vomiting	0–7	0–7	0–7	0–6	
Pruritus	0–7				
Muscle pain	0–7				
Sleep disturbance	0–7				
Nightmares	0–7				
Tinitus	0–7				
Headache		0–7	0–7		
Eating disturbed	0–7				
Thought disturbance		0–3		0–6	
Orientation	0–4	0–4	0–4	0–10	0–3
Impaired consciousness	0–7				
Quality of contact	0–7	0–7		0–6	0–3
Impaired gait	0–7				
Visual disturbance	0–7				
Flushing of the face		0–2			
Insight	0–7				
Seizures		0 or 7		0 or 10	
Max. Score	129	86	67	76	34

on this basis. However, these limited goals lack conviction as outcome measures, and another solution is to tailor outcomes to include more of a feel for the local clinicians' views of success. For example, it may be useful to report the percentage of patients prescribed disulfiram or anti-craving drugs, the percentage of patients attending their therapist post-detoxification or the percentage that continue to take prescribed medication. As well as following the clinical course of detoxification, there is also a need to audit the process of detoxification. First, audit should show evidence of preparation—has the patient been given adequate information? Has a supportive other person been involved? Has a plan of daily activities been worked out? Second, there should be monitoring of the clinical ratings of withdrawal against prescribing practice and complications of withdrawal. Third, there should be some measure of engagement in ongoing therapy where this is appropriate.

There are two things that are important to remember about detoxification. First, improved case management has reduced the mortality rate for the most severe withdrawal state, alcoholic delirium, from in excess of 15% 20 years ago to under 5% today: death is usually caused by cardiovascular collapse, concurrent infection, irreversible hypoglycaemia or malignant hyperthermia. Good case management of withdrawal, whether mild or severe, requires constant vigilance to detect complications. Second, detoxification is an opportunity to help people change. Good therapy can steer the learning experience in the desired direction. A colleague relates the clinical anecdote of two cases which did not have the benefit of addiction therapy during detoxification. One, a film director in his 40s, the other a retired builder, were referred to her clinic during the same month following inpatient admissions for reasons quite unrelated to alcohol dependence. During both inpatient stays, alcoholic delirium was the consequence of the abrupt and unreported cessation of alcohol consumption. At their first consultation, both patients related their frightening experiences, the one concluding "I must never start drinking again", the other concluding "I must never stop drinking again".

KEY WORKS AND SUGGESTIONS FOR FURTHER READING

Edwards, G., Gross, M.M., Keller, M., Moser, J. & Room, R. (Eds) (1977). *Alcohol-related Disabilities*. Geneva: World Health Organization.

This publications gives a good account of the thinking that separated alcohol dependence from alcohol-related problems. There are useful definitions and reference to some of the classic studies of alcohol withdrawal problems.

Stahl, S.M. (1996). *Essential Pharmacology: Neuroscientific Basis and Practical Applications*. Cambridge: Cambridge University Press.

This is a richly illustrated book which offers a very understandable account of neurochemical mechanisms. The book is not specific to alcohol but rather gives an excellent overview of the principal neurochemical pathways and the mechanisms of pharmacotherapies for mental illness problems.

Heather, N. & Robertson, I. (1997). *Problem Drinking*, 3rd edn. Oxford: Oxford University Press.

This easy to read book summarizes the evidence which supports the view that problem drinking is primarily a learned behaviour. An understanding of these arguments is necessary in order to set the management of withdrawal symptoms in the broader treatment context.

Institute of Medicine (1990). *Broadening the Base of Treatment for Alcohol Problems*. Washington, DC: National Academy Press.

This book contains some interesting analysis of key issues that have challenged the expanding alcohol treatment field. Detoxification services are mentioned in several sections but it is the introduction to needs analysis and cost benefits that may be of particular interest.

REFERENCES

Alldredge, B.K. & Lowenstein, D.H. (1993). Status epilepticus related to alcohol abuse. *Epilepsia*, **34**, 1033–1037.

Araujo, L., Goldberg, P., Eyma, J., Madhusoodanan, S., Buff, D.D., Shamim, K. & Brenner, R. (1996). The effect of anxiety and depression on completion/withdrawal status in patients admitted to substance abuse detoxification program. *Journal of Substance Abuse Treatment*, **13**, 61–66.

Brewer, C. (1995). Second-line and "alternative" treatments for alcohol withdrawal: α-agonists, β-blockers, anticonvulsants, acupuncture and neuro-electric therapy. *Alcohol and Alcoholism*, **30**, 799–803.

Brower, K.J., Mudd, S., Blow, F.C., Young, J.P. & Hill, E.M. (1994). Severity and treatment of alcohol withdrawal in elderly versus younger patients. *Alcoholism: Clinical and Experimental Research*, **18**, 196–201.

Brown, S.A. & Irwin, M. (1991). Changes in anxiety among abstinent male alcoholics. *Journal of Studies on Alcohol*, **52**, 55–61.

Bullock, M.L., Culliton, P.D. & Olander, R.T. (1989). Controlled trial of acupuncture for severe recidivist alcoholism. *Lancet*, **••**, 1435–1438.

Carroll, K.M. (1997). Integrating psychotherapy and pharmacotherapy to improve drug abuse outcomes. *Addictive Behaviours*, **22**, 233–245.

Cook, C.H. & Thomson, A.D. (1997). B-complex vitamins in the prophylaxis and treatment of Wernicke–Korsakoff syndrome. *British Journal of Hospital Medicine*, **57**, 461–465.

Davidson, R. (1992). The Prochaska and DiClemente model: reply to the debate. *British Journal of Addiction*, **87**, 833–835.

Driessen, M., Arolt, V., John, U., Veltrup, C. & Dilling, H. (1996). Psychiatric comorbidity in hospitalized alcoholics after detoxification treatment. *European Addiction Research*, **2**, 17–23.

Duncan, D. & Taylor, D. (1996). Chlormethiazole or chlordiazepoxide in alcohol detoxification. *Psychiatric Bulletin*, **20**, 599–601.

Edwards, G. (1990). Withdrawal symptoms and alcohol dependence: fruitful mysteries. *British Journal of Addiction*, **85**, 447–461.

Edwards, G. & Gross, M.M. (1976). Alcohol dependence: provisional description of a clinical syndrome. *British Medical Journal*, **1**, 1058–1061.

Essardas, D.H., Santolaria, F.J., Reimers, G.E., Jorge, J.A., Lopez, B.N., Hernandez, M.F. et al. (1994). Alcohol withdrawal syndrome and seizures. *Alcohol and Alcoholism*, **29**, 323–328.

Glue, P. & Nutt, D. (1990). Overexcitement and disinhibition: dynamic neurotransmitter interactions in alcohol withdrawal. *British Journal of Psychiatry*, **157**, 491–499.

Green, L. & Gossop, M. (1988). Effects of information on the opiate withdrawal syndrome. *British Journal of Addiction*, **83**, 305–309.

Gross, M.M., Rosenblatt, S.M., Chartoff, S., Hermann, A., Schachter, M., Sheinkin, D. & Broman, M. (1971). Evaluation of acute alcoholic psychoses and related states. *Quarterly Journal of Studies on Alcohol*, **32**, 611–619.

Gross, M.M., Lewis, E. & Nagarajan, M. (1973). An improved quantitative system for assessing the acute alcoholic psychoses and related states (TSA and SSA). In M.M. Gross (Ed.), *Advances in Experimental Medicine and Biology, Vol 35. Alcohol Intoxication and Withdrawal: Experimental Studies*. New York: Plenum.

Gross, M.M. (1977). Psychobiological contributions to the alcohol dependence syndrome: a selective review of recent research. In G. Edwards, M.M. Gross, M. Keller, J. Moser & R. Room (Eds), *Alcohol-related Disabilities*. WHO Offset Publication No. 32. Geneva: World Health Organization.

Hershon, H.I. (1977). Alcohol withdrawal symptoms and drinking behavior. *Journal of Studies on Alcohol*, **38**, 953–971.

Hosein, I.N., de Freitas, R. & Beaubrun, M.H. (1978). Intramuscular/oral lorazepam in acute alcohol withdrawal and incipient delirium tremens. *Current Medical Research and Opinion*, **5**, 632–636.

Isbell, H., Fraser, H.F., Wikler, A., Belleville, M.A. & Eisenman, A.J. (1955). An experimental study of the etiology of "rum fits" and delirium tremens. *Quarterly Journal on Studies of Alcohol*, **16**, 1–33.

Johnston, A.L., Thevos, A.K., Randall, C.L. & Anton, R.F. (1991). Increased severity of alcohol withdrawal in inpatient alcoholics with a coexisting anxiety diagnosis. *British Journal of Addiction*, **86**, 719–725.

Kramp, P. & Hemmingsen, R. (1979). Delirium tremens: some clinical features, Part I. *Acta Psychiatrica Scandinavica*, **60**, 393–404.

Kramp, P., Hemmingsen, R. & Rafaelsen, O.J. (1979). Delirium tremens: some clinical features, Part II. *Acta Psychiatrica Scandinavica*, **60**, 405–422.

Marlatt, A. (1985).   Relapse prevention: theoretical rationale and overview of the model. In A. Marlatt & J. Gordon (Eds), *Relapse Prevention*. London: Guilford.

Mayo-Smith, M.F. & Bernard, D. (1995).   Late-onset seizures in alcohol withdrawal. *Alcoholism: Clinical and Experimental Research*, **19**, 656–659.

Metcalfe, P., Sobers, M. & Dewey, M. (1995).   The Windsor Clinical Alcohol Withdrawal Assessment Scale (WCAWAS): investigation of factors associated with complicated withdrawals. *Alcohol and Alcoholism*, **30**, 367–372.

Milby, J.B., Gurwitch, R.H., Wiebe, D.J., Ling, W., McLellan, T. & Woody, G.E. (1986).   Prevalence and diagnostic reliability of methadone maintenance detoxification fear. *American Journal of Psychiatry*, **143**, 739–743.

Morgan, M.Y. (1995).   The management of alcohol withdrawal using chlormethiazole. *Alcohol and Alcoholism*, **30**, 771–774.

Mortimer, R. & Edwards, J.G. (1994).   Detoxification in a community-based alcohol recovery unit and psychiatric department of a general hospital. A comparative study. *Psychiatric Bulletin*, **18**, 218–220.

Phillips, G.T., Gossop, M. & Bradley, B. (1986).   The influence of psychological factors on the opiate withdrawal syndrome. *British Journal of Psychiatry*, **149**, 235–238.

Prochaska, J.O. & DiClemente, C.C. (1984).   *The Transtheoretical Approach: Crossing the Traditional Boundaries of Therapy*. Homewood: Dow Jones/Irwin.

Raimo, E.B. & Schuckit, M.A. (1998).   Alcohol dependence and mood disorders. *Addictive Behaviours*, **23**, 933–946.

Raistrick, D., Bradshaw, J., Tober, G., Weiner, J., Allison, J. & Healey, C. (1994).   Development of the Leeds Dependence Questionnaire. *Addiction*, **89**, 563–572.

Rankin, H., Stockwell, T. & Hodgson, R. (1982).   Cues for drinking and degrees of alcohol dependence. *British Journal of Addiction*, **77**, 287–296.

Ritson, B. & Chick, J. (1986).   Comparison of two benzodiazepines in the treatment of alcohol withdrawal: effects on symptoms and cognitive recovery. *Drug and Alcohol Dependence*, **18**, 329–334.

Salloum, I.M., Cornelius, J.R., Daley, D.C. & Thase, M.E. (1995).   The utility of diazepam loading in the treatment of alcohol withdrawal among psychiatric inpatients. *Psychopharmacology Bulletin*, **31**, 305–310.

Schuckit, M.A., Tipp, J.E., Reich, T., Hesselbrock, V.M. & Bucholz, K.K. (1995).   The histories of withdrawal convulsions and delirium tremens in 1648 alcohol dependent subjects. *Addiction*, **90**, 1335–1347.

Shaw, J.M., Sellers, G.S., Kaplan, H.L. & Sandor, P. (1981).   Development of optimal treatment tactics for alcohol withdrawal. I. Assessment and effectiveness of supportive care. *Journal of Clinical Psychopharmacology*, **1**, 382–388.

Shaw, G.K. (1995).   Detoxification: the use of benzodiazepines. *Alcohol and Alcoholism*, **30**, 765–770.

Stockwell, T., Hodgson, R., Edwards, G., Taylor, C. & Rankin, H. (1979).   The development of a questionnaire to measure severity of alcohol dependence. *British Journal of Addiction*, **74**, 79–87.

Stockwell, T., Bolt, L., Milner, I., Pugh, P. & Young, I. (1990).   Home detoxification for problem drinkers: acceptability to clients, relatives, general practitioners and outcome after 60 days. *British Journal of Addiction*, **85**, 61–70.

Stockwell, T. (1994).   Alcohol withdrawal: an adaptation to heavy drinking of no practical significance? *Addiction*, **89**, 1447–1453.

Sullivan, J.T., Sykora, K., Schneiderman, J., Naranjo, C.A. & Sellers, E.M. (1989).   Assessment of alcohol withdrawal: the revised clinical institute withdrawal assessment for alcohol scale (CIWA-Ar). *British Journal of Addiction*, **84**, 1353–1357.

Tabakoff, B. (1990).   One man's craving is another man's dependence. *British Journal of Addiction*, **85**, 1253–1254.

Tober, G. (1992).   What is dependence and why is it important? *Clinical Psychology Forum*, **41**, 14–16.

Tsaung, J.W., Irwin, M.R., Smith, T.L. & Schuckit, M.A. (1994).   Characteristics of men with alcoholic hallucinosis. *Addiction*, **89**, 73–78.

Vinson, D.C. & Menezes, M. (1991).   Admission alcohol level: a predictor of the course of alcohol withdrawal. *Journal of Family Practice*, **33**, 161–167.

Wetterling, T., Kanitz, R., Besters, B., Fischer, D., Zerfass, B., John, U. et al. (1997).   A new rating scale for the assessment of the alcohol-withdrawal syndrome (AWS scale). *Alcohol and Alcoholism*, **32**, 753–760.

Whitfield, C.L., Thompson, G., Lamb, A., Spencer, V., Pfeifer, M. & Browning-Ferrando, M. (1978). Detoxification of 1024 alcoholic patients without psychoactive drugs. *Journal of the American Medical Association*, **239**, 1409–1410.

Wilkens, L., Ruschulte, H., Ruckoldt, H., Hecker, H., Scroder, D., Piepenbrock, S. & Leuwer, M. (1998). Standard calculation of ethanol elimination rate is to sufficient to provide ethanol substitution therapy in the postoperative course of alcohol-dependent patients. *Intensive Care Medicine*, **24**, 459–463.

Williams, D. & McBride, A.J. (1998). The drug treatment of alcohol withdrawal symptoms: a systematic review. *Alcohol and Alcoholism*, **33**, 103–115.

World Health Organization (1992). *The ICD-10 Classification of Mental and Behavioural Disorders: Clinical Descriptions and Diagnostic Guidelines*. Geneva: WHO.

Chapter 27

Pharmacological Treatments

Jonathan Chick
Alcohol Problems Clinic, Royal Edinburgh Hospital, Edinburgh, UK

Synopsis

For years, the only medications that could help prevent relapse in alcohol dependence were the deterrent drugs such as disulfiram, and even those appeared only to be effective when taken under supervision. Based on research into the neurochemical pathways involved in animal models of alcohol preference and dependence, three types of drugs have been developed which are safe in humans and have been found to reduce relapse rates in alcohol dependence, at least under certain conditions: acamprosate, opioid antagonists and some serotonin-enhancing drugs. The use in practice of these medications, as well as that of disulfiram, is described in this chapter, together with a summary of their proposed mode of action, their effectiveness, their unwanted effects, the characteristics of patients most likely to respond (although information here is often lacking) and their interaction with other therapies. Other chapters deal with the use of medication in treating alcohol withdrawal, and in preventing and treating alcohol-induced brain and liver disorders.

Treating an addiction with another drug sometimes alarms sufferers, their families and therapists. Is it not substituting one addiction with another? The drug therapies tested to reduce relapse during outpatient treatment, to be described in the main section of this chapter, have not been shown to be abused for their psychotropic effects, and do not prolong a dependent state because of cross-tolerance with alcohol, as occurs with benzodiazepines. Neither do they worsen the psychomotor retardation caused by ethanol if the person drinks. Evidence about their mode of action, safety and efficacy will be presented.

DETERRENT MEDICATION

Mode of Action

Disulfiram, if taken regularly in a sufficient dose, causes an unpleasant reaction 15–20 minutes after alcohol enters the body. The reaction is due to accumulation of the intermediate metabolite of ethanol, acetaldehyde. The patient flushes, experiences headache,

International Handbook of Alcohol Dependence and Problems. Edited by N. Heather, T.J. Peters and T. Stockwell.
© 2001 John Wiley & Sons Ltd.

pounding in the chest or head, tightness in breathing, nausea and perhaps vomits. Hypotension can be dangerous, but deaths have been exceedingly rare, with documented cases usually being individuals who had received large doses and/or had pre-existing heart disease. The efficacy of disulfiram depends on deterring the patient from drinking because of fear or distaste for the reaction.

In the typical dose of 200 or 250 mg/day, some individuals will have only a mild reaction if they drink alcohol. Probably some patients, at varying frequency and without declaring it to the therapist or without it being obvious, consume small amounts of alcohol. This was the likely explanation for the finding that the urinary marker of recent ethanol consumption, 5-hydroxytryptophol, can sometimes signal positive for ethanol in patients taking disulfiram, but normalizes if the dose of disulfiram is increased (Helander, 1998).

In the past, surgical implantation of disulfiram tablets under the skin was sometimes used as a longer-term deterrent. This is seldom used now, partly because the active drug was often not detectable in blood after about 2 weeks. However, when patients were told that there was a risk of a reaction for several months after the implant was inserted, many patients had long periods of abstinence, especially if they had tested it out and had a reaction in the early weeks. Local skin reactions occurred in some patients.

The antimicrobial drug metronidazole causes a disulfiram-like interaction with ethanol and has been used in treating alcohol dependence, as a deterrent. However, it has several, albeit infrequent, toxic effects and is not a drug to prescribe lightly. Calcium carbimide is a drug with similar properties to disulfiram, but it is out of production.

Evidence of Efficacy

Hughes & Cook (1997) and Wright & Moore (1990) reviewed published efficacy studies. It is only when compliance with the medication has been improved by supervision that randomized controlled studies show with consistency that disulfiram is associated with a better outcome on drinking measures than placebo. In some patients, it is the belief that if they drink while taking the tablet they will be ill that enhances abstinence. Thus, in the randomized controlled study analysed by Fuller & Williford (1980), there was no difference at the end of 1 year between groups who had received 1 mg disulfiram (insufficient to cause an ethanol reaction) and 250 mg.

Many patients do not test out the reaction. However, a difficulty in placebo-controlled studies is that telling subjects they may be prescribed a dummy may lead to a greater number of subjects testing it out. Of those who test it out, a proportion will not get much reaction, even on a dose of 200 mg or 250 mg. For those, the drug loses its effect. Thus, for the research subject and the investigator to remain blind to the treatment could be seen as preventing a test of one of the features of the disulfiram treatment package, namely, the instillation of fear to drink. This could be part of the explanation for the failure to show an effect of disulfiram in the all-patient analysis in the largest reported trial ($n = 605$) of unsupervised disulfiram (Fuller et al., 1986). Nevertheless, Fuller et al. found that amongst patients who attended all appointments (thus, a compliant group), such that there were sufficient detailed data on patterns of drinking, disulfiram 250 mg daily was associated with significantly fewer drinking days than disulfiram 1 mg or placebo.

There seems to be a tendency in some patients for disulfiram treatment to become less effective over time. For example, Chick et al. (1992) compared supervised disulfiram to vitamin C. The "blind" assessor rated more abstinent days and less total consumption in the 6 months of the trial in the disulfiram group. However, in the last month of the study the groups' mean consumption did not differ. This may be due to diminishing compliance, or a waning of the fear of the reaction.

Characteristics of Responders

The literature is contradictory in specifying who benefits from being offered disulfiram (Hughes & Cook, 1997). Having a partner or supervisor to aid compliance, and some incentive, would seem to be important. In a randomized trial comparing disulfiram vs. no medication in patients dependent on both cocaine and alcohol, patients allocated to disulfiram had longer periods of abstinence from alcohol and longer periods of abstinence from cocaine (Carroll et al., 1998). The authors speculated that the patients had the incentive to receive help to get off cocaine. When a methadone prescription is the incentive in methadone maintenance clinics, patients with coexisting opiate and alcohol dependence do better if they take disulfiram as a condition of their prescription (Liebson et al., 1978).

Interaction with Other Therapies

Trials have not applied randomized methods to compare whether disulfiram is more effective when combined with some psychosocial treatments rather than others. The largest treatment effect size in the disulfiram literature (although in a small sample of 42 patients) was seen by Azrin (1976) in a study in which supervised disulfiram was added to community reinforcement therapy (see Chapter 15) and marital behavioural therapy. Azrin found almost 100% abstinence over 2 years in the 20 disulfiram patients. In the studies of Azrin and colleagues (Azrin, 1976; Azrin et al., 1982), when disulfiram was shown to produce an added advantage, it had been part of a contract and ingestion was supervised.

Duckert & Johnsen (1987) studied the use of disulfiram combined with a behaviour therapy approach which permitted patients to choose their own goals, including "controlled drinking". Some patients used the disulfiram intermittently, and interspersed this with drinking; some patients used it to deal with high-risk situations they had identified in the psychological therapy. Compared to non-users of disulfiram, users consumed significantly less alcohol by the end of the study.

Disulfiram has been used with apparent success with acamprosate (see below), in a study where random allocation was made to either acamprosate or placebo, and some patients also chose to take disulfiram. The longest time to relapse was seen in patients taking both drugs (Besson et al., 1998).

Unwanted Effects

One or more unwanted effects, including drowsiness, headache or, less commonly, bad breath or skin rash, occurs in about every tenth patient.

Very rare but potentially fatal liver hypersensitivity has been reported. This type of liver reaction is reported in a number of other medications in common use over many years, e.g. chlorpromazine (Largactil). For disulfiram, death due to liver hypersensitivity is estimated to occur in 1 in 25,000 patients treated per year (Chick, 1999). Most cases have developed in the first 3 months of treatment. Overall, disulfiram is associated with improvement in liver function tests compared to control groups rather than worsening—presumably due to reduction of drinking (Chick et al., 1992).

Controlled studies have not found that there are more complaints of sexual dysfunction in patients taking disulfiram than in control groups. Peripheral neuropathy (almost always reversible) has been reported in rare cases following some months of treatment at doses of over 250 mg. There are a few reports of psychosis induced by disulfiram and a history of psychotic illness has been a contraindication in the licensing in some countries. The risk is so low and the need to help schizophrenic patients with alcohol problems is sometimes so pressing that in other countries that contraindication is changed to a "caution". There are many documented cases where improvement due to abstaining from alcohol has occurred in psychotic patients while taking disulfiram, and in a dose of up to 250mg/day there are no problems from unwanted effects or interactions with medication for the psychiatric illness (Larson, 1992).

Disulfiram slows the breakdown of a number of commonly prescribed medications, including some antidepressants such as amitryptiline and imipramine, and this can be therapeutic rather than harmful. However, with other affected compounds, such as anticonvulsants (e.g. phenytoin) and warfarin, there are risks of toxic effects and the combination should be avoided or extra plasma monitoring put in place. Unwanted effects of disulfiram have been reviewed in detail by Chick (1999).

Use in Practice

Disulfiram should not be given to patients with active or recent heart disease. Great caution must be used if prescribing to patients taking medication to lower blood pressure, when the hypotension resulting if the patient drank alcohol having been taking disulfiram would be exaggerated and extremely dangerous. Like many drugs metabolized in the liver, it should not be given in advanced liver disease. There is no consensus as to whether or not it should be given to people with mild or moderately abnormal liver enzyme tests. If it aids sobriety, then the liver damaged by alcohol can improve.

Disulfiram enables the individual to get used to life without alcohol and allows time for confidence to resume in the family and at work. It only works if taken consistently. It is suggested to patients that they recruit someone to help them remember to take it and see them take it, such as their partner, or a nurse or welfare officer at work, a high street pharmacist, or a nurse at the clinic or a Health Centre. This can be either daily or three times a week in a larger dose, so that at least 1400mg/week is taken. The tablet can be taken dispersed in water so that it can be seen to be swallowed.

It is common to prescribe disulfiram for 6 months, but many patients and their families ask to continue the method much longer. There are sometimes slips, even after long periods of abstinence when the disulfiram is ceased, and many patients keep a supply to use when they are at risk of drinking, for example, on a business trip away or at a social event.

Some clinics regard disulfiram as "a last ditch". Indeed, after numerous admissions and relapses, clinics may make further treatment conditional on supervised disulfiram. This was documented as successful in a controlled study by Sereny et al. (1986).

Sometimes an employer is prepared to reinstate an employee suspended because of an alcohol-related infringement if the employer knows that supervised disulfiram is being taken. When employees on their final warning were offered supervised disulfiram, they reduced their annual absenteeism rate from 10% to 2%. However, after the year's disciplinary period ended and some stopped the disulfiram, annual absenteeism of these employees rose again, towards but not reaching the previous level (Robichaud et al., 1979). While ethically repugnant to some physicians, supervised disulfiram can be effective as part of probation or when there is a deferral of sentence while the Court wait to see if good behaviour is maintained (Chick, 1998).

There is no consensus on whether or not blood tests to monitor liver function should be repeated at intervals. The very rare disulfiram-induced hepatitis mentioned above seems to commence very suddenly. It has been argued that even monthly blood tests cannot guarantee early detection of the reaction and that the rarity of the condition therefore does not justify frequent testing (Chick, 1999)

It is recognized practice to increase the dose of disulfiram, for example to 400 mg/day, if the patient finds the deterrent method useful in principle, but has tested out the alcohol reaction and the reaction has not been severe enough to act as a deterrent.

What to Tell Patients

Patients should be informed about the risks of the reaction, the need to avoid ethanol in foods or some medicines, and of the unwanted effects.

Patients may object that it is weakness to take a deterrent pill, instead of using "will-power". But they may agree that will-power is not always there when most needed. With the pills, a decision to drink or not still has to be made, but only once a day. An analogy can be made with recovery after a fracture—a splint permits stability to allow the fracture to heal.

THE OPIOID ANTAGONISTS

Mode of Action

The brain's own opiate transmitters, endorphins, are involved in the release of dopamine in the nucleus accumbens, which is believed to be part of the brain substrate of reward and addiction (see Chapter 6). There are drugs which antagonize endorphin transmission. Of these drugs, naltrexone and nalmefene reach the brain after having been taken by mouth and act for some 24 hours, making them potentially relevant for the clinical situation. Stimulating endorphin transmission is one of many acute actions of ethanol on the limbic system.

Naltrexone reduces ethanol-seeking in dependent animals. Several strains of alcohol-consuming animals show "catch-up drinking" after periods of imposed abstinence, much like the human reinstatement phenomenon. Naltrexone reduces catch-up drinking. Reid et al. (1996) have studied the durability of naltrexone's effects in alcohol-consuming rats. They found that the naltrexone-induced inhibition of ethanol drinking did not diminish when naltrexone was continued over some days. But when naltrexone was replaced by placebo, drinking immediately resumed at the level of the control rats. There was no carry-over of its effect. Part of naltrexone's action may be to reduce the positive, rewarding effects of ethanol, and studies of its effect on non-dependent drinking in humans, and its subjective correlates, have tended to support this (for a recent study and review, see Davidson et al., 1999). It could be that some alcohol-dependent individuals have particularly pronounced endorphin response to alcohol (Gianoulakis et al., 1996) and by blocking this, naltrexone can help prevent relapse in susceptible individuals after the first drink is taken.

Sinclair (1998) proposes that when drinking is repeated while positive effects of ethanol are blocked by the opioid antagonist, drinking behaviour will gradually be extinguished, as in a classical conditioning paradigm (see Chapter 14). Thus, naltrexone's action in reducing drinking will only appear if the subject consumes some ethanol on a number of occasions while premedicated with naltrexone. This has now been tested in a randomized controlled study, but the results have not appeared at the time of writing in a peer-reviewed journal.

A related hypothesis is that, as well as reducing positive experiences of drinking, naltrexone may also reduce the strength of conditioned positive associations of drinking, including positive thoughts about drinking and the intensity of positive cue-triggered urges to drink (O'Brien et al., 1998). But a test of this in the laboratory by Modesto-Lowe et al.

(1997) found that 1 week of pre-treatment with naltrexone did not reduce the desire to take alcohol expressed by patients with coexisting alcohol and cocaine dependence after watching a film about drinking.

In the follow-up studies of naltrexone on the treatment of alcohol dependence, subjects who lapse have been asked about their experiences after a drink is taken. In the study of O'Malley et al. (1992), amongst those who took at least one drink during the 3 month out-patient treatment period, subjects who were prescribed daily naltrexone reported lower levels of craving for alcohol compared to subjects who received placebo, and were more likely to give reasons for terminating drinking that were consistent with decreased incentive to drink (O'Malley et al., 1996a). Some patients who resume drinking while taking naltrexone reported that they felt less of the ethanol "high". Perhaps they then experience less impulse to carry on drinking (Volpicelli et al., 1995).

Evidence of Efficacy

Three double-blind randomized controlled studies of naltrexone in detoxified patients taking part in an outpatient treatment programme have been published at the time of writing and others are in press. They mostly show a reduced risk of relapse [defined as more than five US standard drinks (65 g ethanol) in a day], over a 3 month study duration. The same result was found for nalmefene (Mason et al., 1999).

In the two earliest studies that had the most unequivocal results, the effect size of naltrexone treatment in reducing the percentage of days drinking was 0.42 (Volpicelli et al., 1992) and 0.60 (O'Malley et al., 1992; for review, see Volpicelli et al., 1995). An effect size of 1.0 means success in all patients and 0.0 in none. For comparison, the mean effect size in reducing depressive symptoms in meta-analyses of studies of fluoxetine in the treatment of depression is around 0.4. In the first Veterans Administration hospital study of Volpicelli et al. (1992), naltrexone treatment was associated with greater reduction in craving than placebo, but not with a significantly greater rate of total abstinence. The effect in reducing relapse (defined as more than 5 drinks per day) was greatest when the subsample of those who had taken at least one drink during the study was examined. However, in the O'Malley study there was an advantage to naltrexone in the numbers of patients who reported achieving total abstinence as well as a reduction of drinking overall.

The marker of drinking, serum aspartate aminotransferase (AST) level, was significantly lower at 3 months in the naltrexone group compared to the placebo group for O'Malley et al. (1992), with a similar but non-significant trend for the less specific marker alanine amino-transferase. There was a non-significant trend in the study of Volpicelli et al. (1992) for lower serum AST and serum γ-glutamyl transferase (GGT) levels in the naltrexone group compared to the placebo group.

Subsequent analyses and further studies have found that compliance is critical. O'Brien et al. (1996) showed that the naltrexone treatment effect in the study of Volpicelli et al. (1992) was higher among those who complied with medication than among less compliant patients. In a later 3 month outpatient study at the same centre, the overall advantage of naltrexone treatment was only modest, with 35% of the naltrexone group relapsing over 3 months compared to 53% in the placebo group. However, among those who completed treatment, relapse occurred in only 25% of naltrexone-treated subjects compared to 53% of placebo subjects (Volpicelli et al., 1997).

Some clinicians have wondered whether, unlike the animal results of Reid et al. (1996; see above), the efficacy of naltrexone might wane with longer use. This has not yet been answered. Relating to appropriate length of treatment are the findings of O'Malley (1996b), who followed patients from the study quoted above (O'Malley, 1992) for 6 months after withdrawal of medication. Although there was no sudden peak of relapse, there was a tendency for the previous naltrexone-treated patients to relapse, so that after 6 months there was no statistically significant difference between the groups. While there are no controlled studies of longer than 3 months duration, it might nevertheless be appropriate in some patients to continue prescribing it for longer.

Characteristics of Responders

Peterson et al. (1996) compared response to drinking alcohol in young non-alcoholic men at high genetic risk of alcohol dependence with that in controls. They had a greater increase in heart rate after drinking, and peak production of plasma β-endorphin correlated with increased heart rate. They proposed that a subset of those at high risk for alcoholism might be characterized by heightened heart-rate response to ethanol mediated by endorphin production, and that these persons might differentially benefit from naltrexone treatment. Volpicelli et al. (1995) found that beneficial response to naltrexone in their original study was greater in those who initially had reported high levels of craving for alcohol and higher levels of somatic symptoms.

Jaffe et al. (1996), in a post-hoc analysis of the results of the naltrexone/placebo trial of O'Malley et al. (1992), found that naltrexone had additionally benefited patients who at intake to the study had high craving, poor learning ability and more severe dependence.

Interaction with Other Therapies

In their study of random allocation to naltrexone or placebo, O'Malley et al. (1992) found that there was a greater advantage of naltrexone to placebo in patients who, in the psychotherapy arm of the trial, had been randomly allocated to cognitive-behavioural therapy rather than to supportive therapy. Balldin et al. (1998) designed a similar study, and found a response to naltrexone *only* in those allocated to cognitive-behavioural therapy, and no effect in those in the "treatment-as-usual" group.

Unwanted Effects

Early speculation that opiate antagonists might cause dysphoria seemed to be supported by statements from heroin addicts given naltrexone, even when they were apparently some weeks free of heroin. Placebo-controlled studies in alcohol-dependent patients have consistently only revealed one unwanted effect that is commoner in naltrexone-treated patients—nausea. Headache, dizziness and weight loss have also been found to be commoner in naltrexone-treated than placebo groups. Neither depression nor inability to feel pleasure have are associated with the use of naltrexone by alcohol-dependent patients. There are only anecdotal reports of alterations (increase and decrease) in sexual performance or desire. Data have been systematically collected on patients who have taken naltrexone for up to a year, and no cumulative harm has been detected (Croop et al., 1997).

Use in Practice

Naltrexone is prescribed as one 50 mg tablet each morning. To reduce the risk of early side-effects, a half tablet is usually given for the first 3 or 4 days. Naltrexone is to aid those who are striving to remain completely abstinent. Despite the data from the studies quoted above showing that its effect was greatest in those who had had a lapse, at the time of writing there is no published controlled study showing naltrexone as an aid to moderating drinking. If patients drink while taking naltrexone, they are advised to continue the drug but also put into play all methods they can to terminate the lapse and regain abstinence. Because regular compliance is necessary if an overall effect of naltrexone is to be seen, a sustained-release injection is being developed (Kranzler et al., 1998). Naltrexone is metabolized in the liver and should not be used when there is hepatic decompensation.

ACAMPROSATE (CALCIUM ACETYL HOMOTAURINATE)

Mode of Action

The inhibitory neurotransmitter γ-aminobutyric acid (GABA) and the excitatory transmitter glutamate are known to be important in alcohol dependence (see Chapter 6). Acamprosate acts in a dose-dependent way to reduce glutamate transmission by acting at the NMDA receptor complex. It may also reduce activity of the voltage-operated calcium channels, which are over-active after alcohol withdrawal (Littleton, 1995). It does this without any benzodiazepine-like tranquillizing action.

Indicators of excessive brain glutamate activity can be detected in the cerebrospinal fluid of alcohol-dependent patients at least a month following withdrawal from alcohol (Tsai et al., 1998), and this may contribute to what Begleiter & Porjesz (1979) proposed might be a "sub-acute withdrawal syndrome". They referred to the psychological and physiological parameters (e.g. irritability, anxiety, depression, sleep EEG, temperature control, cortisol response to stressors and electrophysiological signs of nervous system hyperexcitability) which are abnormal during withdrawal and still abnormal up to 4 months later.

Acamprosate reduces drinking in alcohol-dependent animals, and reduces the reinstatement of drinking behaviour and withdrawal symptoms in animals re-exposed to alcohol after a period of abstinence. It does not substitute for ethanol or benzodiazepines in animals in the sense that they will seek out acamprosate, that is, it is not in itself rewarding (reviewed by Littleton, 1995). Although acamprosate has been called an anti-craving medication, that conscious experience of craving is not felt by many drinkers who relapse. It may be more accurate to say that acamprosate may reduce drinking by altering the sub-acute withdrawal state, and perhaps drinking triggered by priming doses of alcohol and cues to drinking that have been conditioned via the GABA–glutamate system.

Evidence of Efficacy

The first randomized controlled study of acamprosate in recently detoxified patients found that 33% of acamprosate-treated patients relapsed during the 3 month outpatient period, compared to 66% of placebo patients (Lhuintre et al., 1985). The effect was subsequently seen to be dose-related in a larger 12 month study (Paille et al., 1995). The dose-related effect was also shown by Pelc et al. (1997). Other large randomized controlled studies, each in at least 200 alcohol-dependent newly abstinent patients, have shown acamprosate's efficacy, typically enhancing complete abstinence by some 20% above the rate achieved in the placebo group (i.e. approximately doubling the proportion of complete abstainers) for up to 1 year (e.g. Whitworth et al., 1996; Sass et al., 1996; Poldrugo, 1997). These studies also found that the cumulative total of days of abstinence was significantly greater in the acamprosate-treated patients. Some of these studies (e.g. Whitworth et al., 1996) followed patients into the year after medication was withdrawn, without evidence of sudden relapse.

Whereas the Swiss study by Besson et al. (1998) of 110 patients found that the advantage of acamprosate over placebo persisted until the end of the 12 month study, the smaller, earlier Swiss study (Ladewig et al., 1993) had found that a significant trend to advantage was detected only in the first 3 months.

With regard to objective markers of alcohol consumption, Paille et al. (1995) found the self-report data showing acamprosate-treated patients drank less overall was corroborated by significantly lower GGT levels during the 1 year follow-up compared to placebo-treated patients. Corroboration by significantly greater improvement in GGT was found in the Italian study (Poldrugo, 1997) and the Swiss study of Besson et al. (1998).

The large UK multicentre study (Chick et al., 2000) is the only study known to the author in which acamprosate was not associated with statistically significantly better outcome than placebo. Another large study (Lhuintre et al., 1990) was less clear in terms of self-reported abstinence than the other studies quoted above, but nevertheless found an advantage to acamprosate in terms of serum GGT.

Characteristics of Responders

Data in the efficacy studies just quoted have been analysed to tease out which type of patient is most likely to benefit from acamprosate. None has been revealed. Lesch & Walter (1996) have proposed the more "pure" alcohol-dependent patients without psychiatric disorders or evidence of early childhood behaviour disorder related to brain injury.

Interaction with Other Therapies

No interaction with type of outpatient therapy has been found. Acamprosate has been used safely while patients are prescribed antidepressants. In the study of Besson et al. (1998), patients who requested it were permitted to also take disulfiram. Those patients who were randomly allocated to acamprosate and also took disulfiram did better than those who were not also taking disulfiram. Although it could be that those who chose to take disulfiram as well as the study medication were specially well motivated, it may be that the drug effects are important: taking acamprosate may reduce the need to drink, and disulfiram reinforces the conscious determination to avoid alcohol.

Unwanted Effects

Diarrhoea and abdominal discomfort are the only common (approximately 10%) unwanted effects reported, and this is usually mild. Acamprosate is excreted via the kidney without being metabolized in the liver. Thus, in mild to moderate liver disease (before kidney function is affected) it is safe. It has no abuse potential and does not interact harmfully with alcohol.

Use in Practice

In the studies showing efficacy of acamprosate, patients met criteria for alcohol dependence, expressed a goal of abstinence and commenced the drug within a week or two after the last drink. Its advantage over placebo emerges in the first 2 months after withdrawal. It has not been tested as a stand-alone treatment, although in some of the above studies the psychosocial treatment offered was not intensive. Until more precise information is available, these points should guide its use.

SEROTONERGIC AND NORADRENERGIC MEDICATIONS (ANTIDEPRESSANTS)

Mode of Action

Numerous animal studies have implicated serotonin (5-HT) transmission in alcohol preference and dependence (Le et al., 1996; see Chapter 6). Specific 5-HT-reuptake inhibitors (SSRIs) reduce volitional drinking in animals, but their effect in reducing drinking in non-depressed alcohol-dependent patients is equivocal, is more predictable in non-dependent drinkers, and tends to be short-lived (reviewed by Lejoyeux, 1996; Pettinati, 1996). In particular, no effect of fluoxetine was seen in the large, well-designed and analysed controlled study of Kranzler et al. (1995).

For citalopram, the results are more positive, and Angelone et al. (1998) found that citalopram and fluvoxamine were associated with 52% and 56%, respectively, of complete abstinence compared to placebo of 30% over 16 weeks (reanalysed here to the intention to treat sample).

When depressive symptoms are present in the newly detoxified patients, SSRIs and other antidepressants have been found to help more consistently. Imipramine helped depressive symptoms in alcoholics with a primary depressive illness, and if depression lifted, drinking was seen to improve (McGrath et al., 1996). Cornelius et al. (1997) found severely depressed patients recovered more from their depression, drank less and had more abstinent days if they took fluoxetine in a 3 month study, although rates of attaining complete abstinence were not significantly different statistically; however, there was a trend: fluoxetine 28%, placebo 15%. Desipramine, a tricyclic antidepressant that enhances transmission via noradrenaline more than via serotonin, reduced relapse in alcohol-dependent patients who also had major depression, but not if they did not meet major depression criteria (Mason et al., 1994). Powell et al. (1995), in a group of male alcoholics followed for 6 months, found that nortryptiline, another noradrenergic antidepressant, was associated with reduction of drinking greater than placebo, not in depressives but in those with antisocial personality disorder, who tended, if they were in the placebo group, to have the worst outcome (antisocial personality disorder is closer to Type II than Type I; see Chapter 4). Buspirone, the 5-HT$_{1A}$ partial agonist, is a treatment for anxiety disorders, and it also reduces ethanol drinking in rats who have been regularly taking ethanol for many weeks independent of the anxiolytic effect of the drug. Kranzler et al. (1994) found that buspirone, started in a low dose with gradual increase to a full dose to avoid initial unwanted effects, reduced drinking as well as anxiety in anxious alcohol-dependent patients. Subsequent studies led to the conclusion that buspirone is only indicated if patients have significant anxiety.

Lithium is not a treatment for alcohol dependence itself, but is effective if there is primary manic-depressive disorder.

Characteristics of Responders

As discussed above, psychiatric disorders such as depression or anxiety disorder predict response to serotonin drugs. There is evidence that post-traumatic stress disorder responds to these drugs, and there are patients whose alcohol dependence is linked to this disorder.

An argument has been put forward that impulsive, socially disorganized, early onset patients ("Type B" or "Type I", see Chapter 4) would be those who would respond to serotonin-enhancing drugs, but there has been little clinical support so far. If anything, the opposite is emerging. Kranzler et al. (1996) found type B alcoholics drank more when taking fluoxetine than placebo, and Pettinati et al. (2000) found that the SSRI sertraline slightly improved the outcome for Type A alcoholics (later onset, more socially stable, less severe) but did not do so in Type B.

Interactions with Other Therapies

Kranzler et al. (1996), in a controlled study of fluoxetine, found an association between poorer response to cognitive therapy and taking fluoxetine in Type B patients. Such associations may occur by chance and require replication in specifically designed studies.

Unwanted Effects

Tihonen et al. (1996) reported an advantage to citalopram in self-report, relatives' report and GGT after 3 months treatment, with a higher drop-out rate in the placebo group than the citalopram group. They only presented data on patients who had taken a full week of drug therapy, which may have excluded some of those who had unwanted effects from the drug (numbers excluded were not published). Initial side-effects of SSRIs (nausea, agitation, insomnia) cause people to stop treatment. One reason why fluoxetine may have emerged as more effective than placebo in the small placebo-controlled study of fluoxetine of Janiri et al. (1996) is because small doses of benzodiazepine were allowed.

OTHER COMPOUNDS INVESTIGATED

Benzodiazepine tranquillizers substitute partly for alcohol. When alcohol dependence is related to severe chronic anxiety persisting some weeks into abstinence, a long-acting benzodiazepine, such as chlordiazepoxide or diazepam, may permit a better quality of life and reduce the risk of relapse to drinking. However, dependence on the benzodiazepine is likely and the anxiety condition may remain chronic. Benzodiazepines should be avoided in impulsive individuals or those with a history of drug misuse, since abuse may develop, and should be avoided in persons with a history of aggression. The medication is best used as an occasional aid, rather than a regular prescription, e.g. to enable a severely phobic patient to travel by bus or train. The occasions when specialists in alcohol dependence recommend long-term benzodiazepines are rare (see review by Lejoyeux et al., 1998).

Tiapride is a selective D2 dopamine antagonist which was shown in outpatient samples of anxious/depressed alcoholic patients to be associated with better outcome after 6 months (see Shaw et al., 1994). It is licensed for this in some countries. However, two larger, more methodologically sound studies showed no evidence of efficacy. These have been reported at meetings but are not yet published.

Carbamazepine, chiefly known as an anticonvulsant but with mood-stabilizing properties too, was found to lengthen the time to first drink in small placebo-controlled study (Mueller et al., 1997).

GHB (γ-ydroxybutyric acid) is a sedative that can be habit-forming. It has been shown to reduce relapse rates in studies lasting 6 months (Gallimberti et al., 1992). Its abuse potential may limit its acceptance as a treatment for alcohol dependence (Addolorato et al., 1996).

Animal models have found that preparations from the plant St John's Wort (*Hypericum*), which is prescribed in some countries for mild depression, reduces ethanol-seeking behaviour and consumption in laboratory animals, but there are no published controlled studies of its use in alcohol-dependent patients.

SUMMARY

New medications are beginning to find their place in preventing relapse in alcohol dependence, but have only been tested where psychological therapy is also offered. In time, whether or not they might have a place in primary care, with minimal psychological therapy, will be tested. At best, these treatments are only an aid to establishing a change in lifestyle. A medication to enable an individual to regain control of drinking, so that thereafter alcohol can be enjoyed in moderation, has not yet been identified. However, if the erratic nature of the journey to an acceptance of abstinence and adjustment to that way of life can be smoothed by taking specific medications, then their place is assured.

KEY WORKS AND SUGGESTIONS FOR FURTHER READING

O'Brien, C.P. & McLellan, A.T. (1996).   Myths about the treatment of addiction. *Lancet*, **347**, 237–240.

A challenging argument for viewing addictions as diseases meriting investigation of their biological causes and biological treatments.

Kranzler, H. (2000).   Pharmacotherapy of alcoholism: gaps in knowledge and opportunities for research. *Alcohol and Alcoholism*, **35**, 537–547.

Raimo, E.B. & Schuckit, M. (1998).   Alcohol dependence and mood disorders. *Addictive Behaviours*, **23**, 933–946.

An exploration of the complex relationship between alcohol dependence and mood disorders, with implications for treatment.

REFERENCES

Addolorato, G., Castelli, E., Stefanini, G.F., Casella, G., Caputo, F., Marsigli, L., Bernardi, M., Gasbarrini, G. & the GHB Study Group (1996).   An open multicentric study evaluating 4-hydroxybutyric acid sodium salt in the medium-term treatment of 179 alcohol-dependent subjects. *Alcohol and Alcoholism*, **31**, 341–345.

Angelone, S.M., Bellini, L., Di Bella, D. & Catalano, M. (1998).   Effects of fluvoxamine and citalopram in maintaining abstinence in a sample of Italian detoxified alcoholics. *Alcohol and Alcoholism*, **33**, 151–156.

Azrin, N.H. (1976).   Improvements in the community reinforcement approach. *Behaviour Research and Therapy*, **14**, 339–348.

Azrin, N.H., Sisson, R.W., Meyers, R. & Godley, M. (1982).   Alcoholism treatment by disulfiram and community reinforcement therapy. *Journal of Behaviour Therapy and Experimental Psychiatry*, **13**, 105–112.

Balldin, J., Berglund, M. & Borg, S. (1998).   The Swedish naltrexone study, present results. *European Psychiatry*, **14**(Suppl. 14), 154s (Abstract).

Begleiter, H., Porjesz, B. (1979). Persistence of a subacute withdrawal syndrome following chronic alcohol intake. *Drug and Alcohol Dependence*, **4**, 353–357.

Besson, J., Aeby, F., Kasas, A., Lehert, P. & Potgieter, A. (1998). Combined efficacy of acamprosate and disulfiram in the treatment of alcoholism: a controlled study. *Alcoholism: Clinical and Experimental Research*, **22**, 573–579.

Carroll, K.M., Nich, C., Ball, S.A., McCance, E. & Rounsaville, B.J. (1998). Treatment of cocaine and alcohol dependence with psychotherapy and disulfiram. *Addiction*, **93**, 713–728.

Chick, J., Gough, K., Falkowski, W. et al. (1992). Disulfiram treatment of alcoholism. *British Journal of Psychiatry*, **161**, 84–89.

Chick, J. (1999). Safety issues concerning the use of disulfiram in treating alcohol dependence. *Drug Safety*, **20**, 427–435.

Chick, J. (1998). Treatment of alcoholic violent offenders—ethics and efficacy. *Alcohol and Alcoholism*, **33**, 20–25.

Chick, J., Howlett, H., Morgan, M.Y. & Ritson, B. (2000). United Kingdom Multicentre Acamprosate Study (UKMAS): a 6 month prospective study of acamprosate versus placebo in preventing relapse after withdrawal from alcohol. *Alcohol and Alcoholism*, **35**, 176–187.

Cornelius, J.R., Salloun, I.M., Ehler, J.G. et al. (1997). Fluoxetine reduced depressive symptoms and alcohol consumption in patients with comorbid major depression and alcohol dependence. *Archives of General Psychiatry*, **54**, 700–705.

Croop, R., Faulkner, E.B. & Labriola, D.F. (1997). The safety profile of naltrexone in the treatment of alcoholism—results from a multicentre usage study. *Archives of General Psychiatry*, **54**, 1130–1135.

Davidson, D., Palfai, Y., Bird, C. & Swift, R. (1999). Effects of naltrexone on alcohol self-administration in heavy drinkers. *Alcoholism: Clinical and Experimental Research*, **23**, 195–203.

Duckert, F. & Johnsen, J. (1987). Behavioural use of disulfiram in the treatment of problem drinking. *International Journal of the Addictions*, **22**, 445–454.

Fuller, R.K. & Williford, W.O. (1980). Life-table analysis of abstinence in a study evaluating the efficacy of disulfiram. *Alcoholism: Clinical and Experimental Research*, **4**, 298–301.

Fuller, R.K., Branchey, L., Brightwell, D.R. et al. (1986). Disulfiram in the treatment of alcoholism: a Veterans Administration cooperative study. *Journal of the American Medical Association*, **256**, 1449–1455.

Gallimberti, L., Ferri, M., Ferrara, S.D., Fadda, F. & Gessa, G.L. (1992). γ-Hydroxybutyric acid in the treatment of alcohol dependence: a double blind study. *Alcoholism: Clinical and Experimental Research*, **16**, 673–676.

Gianoulakis, C., Krishnan, B. & Thavundayil, J. (1996). Enhanced sensitivity to pituitary β-endorphin to ethanol in subjects at high risk of alcoholism. *Archives of General Psychiatry*, **53**, 250–257.

Helander, A. (1998). Monitoring relapse drinking during disulfiram therapy by assay of urinary 5-hydroxytryptophol. *Alcoholism: Clinical and Experimental Research*, **22**, 111–114.

Hughes, J.C. & Cook, C. (1997). The efficacy of disulfiram—a review of outcome studies. *Addiction*, **92**, 381–396.

Jaffe, A.J., Rounsaville, B., Chang, G., Schottenfield, R.S., Meyer, R.F. & O'Malley, S.S. (1996). Naltrexone, relapse prevention and supportive therapy with alcoholics: an analysis of patient treatment matching. *Journal of Consulting and Clinical Psychology*, **64**, 1044–1063.

Janiri, L., Gobbi, G., Manelli, P., Pozzi, G., Serretti, A. & Tempesta, E. (1996). Effects of fluoxetine at antidepressant doses on short-term outcome of detoxified alcoholics. *International Journal of Clinical Psychopharmacology*, **11**, 109–117.

Kranzler, H.R., Burleson, J.A., Boca, F.K., Babor, T.F., Korner, P., Brown, P. & Bohn, M.J. (1994). Buspirone treatment of anxious alcoholics. *Archives of General Psychiatry*, **51**, 720–731.

Kranzler, H.R., Burleson, J.A., Korner, P., del Boca, F.K., Bohn, M.J., Brow, J. & Liebowitz, N. (1995). Placebo-controlled trial of fluoxetine as an adjunct to relapse prevention in alcoholics. *American Journal of Psychiatry*, **152**, 391–397.

Kranzler, H.R., Burleson, J.A., Brown, J. & Babor, T.F. (1996). Fluoxetine treatment seems to reduce the beneficial effect of cognitive-behavioural therapy in Type B alcoholics. *Alcoholism: Clinical and Experimental Research*, **20**, 1534–1541.

Kranzler, H.R., Modesto-Lowe, V. & Nuwayser, E.S. (1998). Sustained-release naltrexone for alcoholism treatment: a preliminary study *Alcoholism: Clinical and Experimental Research*, **22**, 1074–1079.

Ladewig, D., Knecht, T., Lehert, P. & Fend, A. (1993). Acamprosat—ein Stabilisierungsfaktor in der Langzeitentwohnung von Alkoholabhangigen. *Therapeutische Umschau*, **50**, 182–187.

Larson, E.W., Lincy, A., Rommans, T.A. & Morse, R.M. (1992). Disulfiram treatment of patients with both alcohol dependence and other psychiatric disorders: a review. *Alcoholism: Clinical and Experimental Research*, **16**, 125–136.

Lê, A.D., Tomkins, D.M. & Sellers, E.M. (1996). Use of serotonin (5-HT) and opiate-based drugs in the pharmacotherapy of alcohol dependence: an overview of the preclinical data *Alcohol and Alcoholism*, **31**(Suppl. 1), 27–32.

Lejoyeux, M. (1996). Use of serotonin (5-hydroxytryptamine) reuptake inhibitors in the treatment of alcoholism. *Alcohol and Alcoholism*, **31**(Suppl. 1), 69–76.

Lejoyeux, M., Solomon, J. & Ades, J. (1998). Benzodiazepine treatment for alcohol-dependent patients. *Alcohol and Alcoholism*, **33**, 563–575.

Lesch, O.M. & Walter, H. (1996). Subtypes of alcoholism and their role in therapy. *Alcohol and Alcoholism*, **31**(Suppl. 1), 59–62.

Liebson, I., Tommasello, A. & Bigelow, L.G. (1978). A behavioural treatment of alcoholic methadone patients. *Annals of Internal Medicine*, **89**, 342–344.

Littleton, J. (1995). Acamprosate in alcohol dependence: how does it work? *Addiction*, **90**, 1179–1188.

Lhuintre, J.P., Moore, N.D., Saligaut, C. et al. (1985). Ability of calcium bis-acetyl homotaurinate, a GABA agonist, to prevent relapse in weaned alcoholics. *Lancet*, **1**, 1015–1016.

Lhuintre, J.P., Moore, N., Tran, G. et al. (1990). Acamprosate appears to decrease alcohol intake in weaned alcoholics. *Alcohol and Alcoholism*, **25**, 613–622.

Mason, B.J., Ritvo, E.C., Morgan, R.O., Salvato, F.R., Goldberg, G., Welch, B. & Mantero-Atienza, E. (1994). A double-blind, placebo-controlled pilot study to evaluate the efficacy and safety of oral nalmefene HCL for alcohol dependence. *Journal of the American Medical Association*, **18**, 1162–1167.

Mason, B.J., Kocsis, J.H., Ritvo, E.C. & Cutler, R.B. (1996). A double-blind, placebo-controlled trial of desimipramine for primary alcohol dependence stratified for the presence or absence of major depression. *Journal of the American Medical Association*, **275**, 761–767.

McGrath, P.J., Nunes, E.V., Stewart, J.W. et al. (1996). Imipramine treatment of alcoholics with primary depression: a placebo-controlled clinical trial. *Archives of General Psychiatry*, **53**, 232–240.

Mason, B.J., Salvato, F.R., Williams, L.D., Ritro, E.C. & Cutler, R.V. (1999). A double-blind, placebo-controlled study of oral nalmefene for alcohol dependence. *Archives of General Psychiatry*, **56**, 719–724.

Modesto-Lowe, V., Burleson, J.A., Hersh, D., Bauer, L.O. & Kranzler, H.R. (1997). Effects of naltrexone on cue-elcitied craving for alcohol and cocaine. *Drug and Alcohol Dependence*, **49**, 9–16.

Muellet, T.I., Stout, R.L., Rudden, S., Brown, R.A., Gordon, A., Solomon, D.A. & Recupero, P.R. (1997). A double-blind placebo-controlled pilot study of carbamazepine for the treatment of alcohol dependence. *Alcoholism: Clinical and Experimental Research*, **21**, 86–92.

O'Brien, C.P., Volpicelli, L.A. & Volpicelli, J.R. (1996). Naltrexone in the treatment of alcoholism: a clinical review. *Alcohol*, **13**: 35–39.

O'Malley, S.S., Jaffe, A.J., Chang, G., Schottenfeld, R.S., Meyer, R.E. & Rounsaville, B. (1992). Naltrexone and coping skills therapy for alcohol dependence, a controlled study. *Archives of General Psychiatry*, **49**, 881–887.

O'Malley, S.S., Jaffe, A.J., Rode, S. & Rounsaville, B.J. (1996a). Experience of a "slip" among alcoholics treated with naltrexone. *American Journal of Psychiatry*, **153**, 281–283.

O'Malley, S.S. (1996b). Six month follow-up of naltrexone and psychotherapy for alcohol dependence. *Archives of General Psychiatry*, **53**, 217–224.

Paille, F.M., Guelfi, J.D., Perkins, A.C., Royer, R.J., Steru, L. & Perot, P. (1995). Randomised multi-centre trial of acamprosate in a maintenance programme of abstinence after alcohol detoxification. *Alcohol and Alcoholism*, **30**, 239–247.

Pelc, I., Verbanck, P., Le, Bon., M., Gavrilovic, M., Lion, K. & Lehert P. (1997). Efficacy and safety of acamprosate in the treatment of detoxified alcohol-dependent patients: a 90-day dose finding study. *British Journal of Psychiatry*, **171**, 73–77.

Peterson, J.B., Pihl, R.O., Gianoulakis, C., Conrod, P., Finn, P.R., Stewart, S.H., LeMarquand, D.G. & Bruce, K.R. (1996). Ethanol-induced change in cardiac and endogenous opiate function and risk for alcoholism. *Alcoholism: Clinical and Experimental Research*, **20**, 1542–1552.

Pettinati, H.M. (1996). Use of serotonin selective pharmacotherapy in the treatment of alcohol dependence. *Alcoholism: Clinical and Experimental Research*, **20**, 23–29.

Pettinati, H.M., Volpicelli, J.R., Kranzler, H.R., Luck, G., Rubstalis, M.R. & Cnaan, A. (2000). Sertraline treatment for alcohol dependence: interactive of medication and alcoholic subtype. *Alcoholism: Clinical and Experimental Research*, **24**, 1041–1049.

Poldrugo, F. (1997). Acamprosate treatment in a long-term community based alcohol rehabilitation programme. *Addiction*, **92**, 1537–1547.

Powell, B.J., Campbell, J.L., Landon, J.F. et al. (1995). A double-blind placebo-controlled study of nortryptiline and bromocriptine in male alcoholics subtyped by comorbid psychiatric disorders. *Alcohol: Clinical and Experimental Research*, **19**, 462–468.

Reid, L.D., Gardell, L.R., Chattopadhyay, S. & Hubbell, C.L. (1996). Periodic naltrexone and propensity to take alcoholic beverage. *Alcohol: Clinical and Experimental*, **20**, 1329–1334.

Robichaud, C., Strickland, D., Bigelow, G. et al. (1979). Disulfiram maintenance employee alcoholism treatment: a three phase evaluation. *Behaviour Research and Therapy*, **17**, 618–621.

Sass, H., Soyka, M., Mann, K. & Ziegelgansberger, W. (1996). Relapse prevention by acamprosate: results from a placebo controlled study in alcohol dependence. *Archives of General Psychiatry*, **53**, 673–680.

Sereny, G., Sharma, V., Holt, S. & Gordis, E. (1986). Mandatory supervised Antabuse therapy in an out-patient alcoholism program: a pilot study. *Alcoholism: Clinical and Experimental Research*, **10**, 290–292.

Sinclair, J.D. (1998). New treatment options for substance abuse from a public health standpoint. *Annals of Medicine*, **30**, 406–411.

Shaw, G.K., Waller, S., Majumdar, S.K., Alberts, J.L., Latham, C.J. & Dunn, G. (1994). Tiapride in the prevention of relapse in recently detoxified alcoholics. *British Journal of Psychiatry*, **165**, 515–523.

Tihonen, J., Ryynänen, O.-P., Kauhanen, J., Hakola, H.P.A. & Salaspuro, M. (1996). Citalopram in the treatment of alcoholism: a double-blind placebo controlled study. *Pharmacopsychiatry*, **29**, 27–29.

Tsai, G.E., Ragan, P., Chang, R., Chen, S., Linnoila, M.I. & Coyle, J.T. (1998). Increased glutamatergic neurotransmission and oxidative stress after alcohol withdrawal. *American Journal of Psychiatry*, **155**, 726–732.

Volpicelli, J.R., Alterman, A.I., Hayashida, M. & O'Brien, C.P. (1992). Naltrexone in the treatment of alcohol dependence. *Archives of General Psychiatry*, **49**, 876–880.

Volpicelli, J.R., Volpicelli, L.A. & O'Brien, C.P. (1995). Medical management of alcohol dependence: clinical use and limitations of naltrexone treatment. *Alcohol and Alcoholism*, **30**, 789–798.

Volpicelli, J.R., Rhines, K.C., Rines, J.S., Volpicelli, L.A., Alterman, A.I. & O'Brien, C.P. (1997). Naltrexone and alcohol dependence: role of subject compliance. *Archives of General Psychiatry*, **54**, 737–742.

Whitworth, A.B., Fischer, F., Lesch, O., Nimmerrichter, A., Oberauer, H., Platz, A., Walter, H. & Fleischhacker, W.W. (1996). Comparison of acamprosate and placebo in long-term treatment of alcohol dependence. *Lancet*, **347**, 1438–1442.

Wright, C. & Moore, R.D. (1990). Disulfiram treatment of alcoholism. *American Journal of Medicine*, **88**, 647–655.

Chapter 28

Cognitive-behavioral Alcohol Treatment

George A. Parks
G. Alan Marlatt
and
Britt K. Anderson
Addictive Behaviors Research Center, University of Washington,
Seattle, WA, USA

Synopsis

What follows is the first of two chapters devoted to a cognitive-behavioral approach to the treatment of alcohol abuse and dependence. The goal of this chapter is to provide a state-of-the-art overview of this therapeutic approach to alcohol treatment, about which more detailed discussions are available elsewhere (Mackay et al., 1991; Kadden, 1994). The next chapter in this two-part series will present a cognitive-behavioral model of Relapse Prevention Therapy (RPT). The present chapter begins by placing cognitive-behavioral approaches to alcohol treatment within the context of various conceptual models of addictive behaviors. The four primary models include the moral *model, the* disease *or* medical *model, the* spiritual *or* enlightenment *model, and the* compensatory *model, which differ in their determination of responsibility for the development and resolution of addictive behaviors. Stages in the acquisition and change of alcohol-related problems are then presented. Alcohol problems and related consequences lie on a continuum and can range from mild difficulties to more severe dependency. It is important that treatment be appropriate for both the level of dependency and degree of motivation that exists for each individual. The basic principles of cognitive-behavioral alcohol treatment are also discussed. Based on social learning theory, alcohol dependence is conceptualized as a learned behavior that represents a maladaptive coping mechanism for life's stressors. Practice guidelines for a cognitive-behavioral approach with clients and the scope, duration, and aims of cognitive-behavioral alcohol treatment are explained. This approach necessitates an objective and non-judgmental therapeutic style that allows for collaboration and flexibility between therapist and client. Additionally, assessment and goal setting are ongoing activities during the course of therapy and guide the overall process. The next section summarizes behavioral therapy*

International Handbook of Alcohol Dependence and Problems. Edited by N. Heather, T.J. Peters and T. Stockwell.
© 2001 John Wiley & Sons Ltd.

and cognitive therapy *assessment and intervention strategies, both of which constitute the ingredients of this approach. Behavioral assessment involves a functional analysis of the drinking behavior, which evaluates the situational antecedents, the intensity and frequency of the drinking behavior itself and the consequences that may be reinforcing the problematic behavior. Behavioral treatment techniques include aversive approaches designed to reduce the reinforcing aspects of alcohol through electric shock, nausea-inducing drugs or imagery, cue exposure therapy, relaxation training, contingency management, which involves restructuring one's environment, and coping skills training. In contrast, cognitive assessment focuses on the manner in which behavior is mediated by thoughts and internal events. Clients are asked to self-monitor and record their thoughts and expectancies related to drinking, so that faulty beliefs can be challenged. Cognitive treatment techniques include teaching appraisal of situations that represent a risk for heavy drinking, problem-solving training to cope with life's demands, and cognitive restructuring to confront negative thoughts. Both behavioral and cognitive techniques rely heavily on the use of role-plays, modeling, homework and feedback to facilitate the learning process. A contemporary cognitive-behavioral alcohol therapy protocol developed by Monti and colleagues (Kadden et al., 1995; Monti et al., 1989) is briefly described. Finally, the chapter concludes with a discussion of the potential benefits of cognitive-behavioral alcohol treatment and a brief review of empirical support for the efficacy of alcohol treatments based on this theoretical approach.*

CONCEPTUAL MODELS OF ADDICTIVE BEHAVIORS

In order to highlight the unique contribution to alcohol treatment that a cognitive-behavioral approach can provide, a brief discussion of various conceptualizations of the etiology and treatment of alcohol dependence follows. Each of these models of addictive behavior makes different predictions about the nature, course and outcome of alcohol treatment. These predictions influence not only therapist behaviors, but also the clients' beliefs about treatment entry, staying in treatment, treatment success and relapse (Marlatt et al., 1997; Miller et al., 1996: see the Section 6 Overview for a more complete discussion of conceptual models).

A model of helping and coping created by Brickman et al. (1982) helps to clarify four divergent conceptual approaches to the development and modification of addictive behaviors in general and alcohol dependence in particular. In their presentation, Brickman and his associates asked the following two questions: (a) to what extent is an individual considered personally responsible for the initial development of the addictive behavior problem?; and (b) to what extent is the person responsible for and capable of changing the behavior problem on his/her own, without treatment? Based on answers to these two questions, four general models of helping and coping were formulated which can readily be applied to addictive behaviors, including alcohol dependence (Marlatt, 1992).

These four models consist of: the *moral* model, in which a person is held responsible for both acquiring and changing his/her alcohol problem; the *disease* or *medical* model, where a person is held responsible for neither the acquisition nor the change of his/her alcohol problem; the *spiritual* or *enlightenment* model, where a person is held responsible for the development of his/her alcohol problem but is not responsible for changing it; and finally, the *compensatory* model, where a person is not held responsible for the development of his/her alcohol problem but is seen as responsible for changing their problem and considered capable of doing so.

The *disease* model of alcohol dependence, or "alcoholism", remains the dominant conceptual model or paradigm of both alcohol and drug treatment, especially in the USA.

However, this situation is changing in response to empirical evidence, managed care cost containment policies and greater pressures to demonstrate treatment efficacy and effectiveness (Miller & Hester, 1986). Therapies based on a cognitive-behavioral approach have recently been developed and tested as alternatives treatments or as adjuncts to more traditional alcohol and drug treatment program based on the disease model (Cook, 1988a, b).

A COGNITIVE-BEHAVIORAL APPROACH TO ALCOHOL TREATMENT

The moral, disease and spiritual models of addictive behaviors represent three alternative approaches to alcohol treatment. It is within the fourth and final model in Brickman's typology, the *compensatory* model, that we place cognitive-behavioral approaches to alcohol treatment. This perspective is called the compensatory model because, while an individual is not considered responsible for the development of alcohol abuse or dependence, he/she is believed to be capable of compensating for it. Both self-change and change through the assistance of others are seen as valid alternatives. Cognitive-behavioral approaches to alcohol dependence are based largely on the principles of social learning theory, as elaborated by Bandura (1969, 1986, 1997). The major assumption of the cognitive-behavioral model is that addictive behaviors, including alcohol dependence, are learned, maladaptive habit patterns acquired through the interactive processes of classical conditioning, instrumental learning and cognitive mediation (see Chapter 17). From this point of view, addictive behaviors are maladaptive coping responses when they become the central means individuals use to cope with the stress of life's demands.

Strong reinforcers that reward alcohol use with immediate consequences, such as euphoric feelings of pleasure (positive reinforcement) or the reduction or elimination of negative states, such as anxiety and pain (negative reinforcement), maintain these excessive behaviors or addictive habits. The alcohol dependence syndrome is characterized by both the presence of immediate gratification and the experience of delayed negative consequences. The reinforcement dynamics of this biphasic effect of drinking contributes to an individual's overgeneralized use of alcohol and interferes with his/her efforts to abstain from drinking or to engage in controlled or moderate consumption.

Defining alcohol dependence as a maladaptive *habit* rather than as alcoholism, a disease-based addiction, does not diminish the disorder's intensity or resistance to change. Indeed, over-learned habits, such as the excessive drinking characteristic of alcohol dependence, can become nearly or completely involuntary. The drinker may perform them with little conscious awareness or attention. Because alcohol use is effective in increasing pleasure and decreasing pain, attempts to abstain in the absence of viable alternative coping behaviors will lead to increased stress and distress. An individual's ongoing stress and unmet needs may then motivate the resumption of excessive drinking and the reinstatement of alcohol dependence, despite the predictably severe negative consequences of this behavior.

In this model of addictive behaviors, the development of alcohol abuse or dependence is seen as a result of the interaction of biological, psychological and sociocultural forces. In this *biopsychosocial* model, biological factors, such as genetic vulnerability and substance-induced physiological changes; psychological factors, such as expectancies, attributions and coping skills; and sociocultural factors, such as family history, peer influences, cultural and ethnic background, advertising and the media, all influence the development of addictive behaviors (Donovan, 1988). This biopsychosocial model of addictive behaviors describes alcohol dependence as a complex disorder with multiple determinants in systematic interaction during its development, maintenance and treatment. Therefore, cognitive-behavioral alcohol treatments must be designed to effectively address the interaction of these multiple factors as they influence alcohol dependence at different stages of its development and amelioration.

In addition to having biological and sociocultural causes and consequences, addictive behaviors, such the excessive drinking characteristic of alcohol abuse or dependence, are temporarily effective, yet ultimately maladaptive, coping mechanisms. Cognitive-behavioral alcohol treatment views therapy as a habit change process during which clients gradually replace addictive behaviors with new and more adaptive coping skills. The overall goal of cognitive-behavioral approaches to treatment is to help clients meet life's demands without resorting to the excessive use of alcohol and its associated problems. In this model, relapse is defined as a mistake or error in a process of new learning. It may also be thought of as a temporary setback in the journey from being controlled by alcohol dependence to the recovery of life-style balance, self-control and personal freedom that characterize health and well-being (a more thorough discussion of cognitive-behavioral Relapse Prevention Therapy follows in Chapter 29).

MOTIVATION AND STAGES OF CHANGE

Effective cognitive-behavioral alcohol treatment requires that both therapist and client understand the stages that occur when one acquires an abusive or dependent pattern of drinking and the stages that occur when drinking behavior changes to a moderate level of consumption or is eliminated entirely. Cognitive-behavioral therapy is based on an empirical, developmental model of alcohol use disorders, which attempts to delineate the natural history of excessive drinking and alcohol-related problems. As therapist and client refine this understanding, they collaborate to generate an effective treatment plan for either individual or group therapy formats. This developmental approach to alcohol treatment takes advantage of recent research examining drinking behavior, the development of alcohol problems, and variability in current patterns of drinking from a longitudinal perspective (Marlatt et al., 1988; Vaillant, 1995).

The potential development of alcohol dependence or other alcohol-related problems begins with exposure and experimentation with alcohol, often during childhood or adolescence. Whether an alcohol-related problem of any type develops depends on a variety of biopsychosocial factors including genetic vulnerability, family dynamics, peer relations, conduct problems, media depictions of drinking, and access to alcohol. Most individuals who drink do so with little or no problem; some individuals experience occasional mild to moderate alcohol-related problems; and a few unfortunate others progress to the development of alcohol abuse or dependence disorders (IOM, 1990; Marlatt, 1992). Therefore, rather than the overly simplistic notion of either having or not having the disease of alcoholism, the cognitive-behavioral developmental perspective views alcohol use and alcohol-related problems as existing on a continuum of use and severity of consequences. This analysis is consistent with the notion of a spectrum of alcohol-related problems, each of which is best addressed by a different level of treatment, ranging from prevention and brief intervention to more intensive treatment (IOM, 1990).

Just as the development of alcohol-use disorders occurs in stages, it also seems that individuals go through as series of predictable *stages of change* when trying to alter their drinking behavior. In our previous work on relapse prevention (Marlatt & Gordon, 1985; Marlatt & Parks, 1982), we proposed that habit change is a *journey* that occurs in three stages. These stages consist of *preparation* for the journey, involving motivation and commitment; *departure*, involving cessation or quitting the addictive behavior; and finally, the *maintenance* stage, involving coping with the challenges one will encounter to resume excessive drinking. It is during the maintenance stage that clients must work the hardest to maintain their motivation and commitment over the long term and avoid the problem of relapse (see Chapter 29).

A related stages of change model, first applied to smokers and later to other addictive behaviors, has been developed and refined by Prochaska & DiClemente (1992). An important point illustrated by both stages of change models is that therapeutic interventions, to be maximally effective, should be relevant to the stage of change a client is experiencing. Cognitive-behavioral alcohol treatment includes ongoing assessment of a client's motivation at various stages of change, and strategically integrates motivational enhancement interventions throughout the course of therapy (Baer et al., 1999; Miller & Rollnick, 1991; also see Chapter 30). Cognitive and behavioral assessment and intervention strategies designed specifically for the action, maintenance, and relapse stages are gradually introduced as client motivation increases during the preparation or determination stage of change (Prochaska & DiClemente, 1992; also see Chapter 29).

PRINCIPLES OF COGNITIVE-BEHAVIORAL ALCOHOL TREATMENT

As stated earlier, the theoretical heritage of cognitive-behavioral alcohol treatment derives from the social learning approach to understanding human behavior, more recently referred to as social cognitive theory (Bandura, 1969, 1986, 1997). Based on a tradition of empirical studies and theoretical hypothesis testing, the social cognitive approach has evolved within psychology from earlier behavioral theories but departs from a strictly behavioral approach to human problems by incorporating the principles of reciprocal determinism, observational learning, social cognition and self-regulation. Cognitive-behavioral alcohol treatment combines behavioral and cognitive interventions in an overall approach that emphasizes self-management and rejects labeling clients with traits like "alcoholic" or "drug addict", which are often promoted by moral and disease models of addiction. The psychoeducational philosophy of this approach focuses on enhancing client motivation, providing new knowledge about drinking and its consequences, and fostering coping skills to empower a person to maintain long-term freedom from excessive and problematic alcohol use.

The first principle of cognitive-behavioral alcohol treatment is that the excessive drinking characteristic of alcohol abuse and dependence disorders is conceptualized as a set of socially learned behaviors with multiple determinants. These determinants include genetic factors, past learning, situational antecedents, cognitive processes and immediate positive and delayed negative consequences. This treatment approach focuses on: (a) situational antecedents of excessive drinking, such as time of day, place, people, activities; (b) internal states, such as anxiety, depression or other unpleasant emotions or painful sensations that may increase the likelihood of excessive drinking; (c) cognitive processes, such as expectancies about the rewarding effects of alcohol and attributions infusing alcohol with the power of a magic elixir to transform moods; and (d) the reinforcing consequences that serve to maintain drinking behavior at an excessive level. Cognitive-behavioral alcohol treatment integrates classical conditioning mechanisms (see Chapter 14), instrumental learning (see Chapter 15), and social-cognitive processes (see Chapter 16) in the understanding of the etiology of excessive drinking and its therapeutic techniques of treatment. Consistent with a social learning analysis of excessive drinking, alcohol dependence can be treated most effectively by a combination of both behavioral and cognitive techniques.

A second basic principle of this treatment approach is that alcohol abuse or dependence and other addictive behaviors are viewed as maladaptive mechanisms for coping with stress. This *adaptive orientation* views stress as resulting from an imbalance between environmental demands (stressors) and an individual's coping resources. The client's level of stress, vulnerability to stress and repertoire of coping responses that reduce or eliminate the need for excessive drinking as a coping mechanism are essential factors in cognitive-behavioral alcohol treatment. As an individual faces the demands of stressful living, an increasing imbalance may occur that taxes or exceeds his/her ability to adapt, master or at least tolerate these circumstances without resorting to excessive drinking. To the extent that effective cognitive or behavioral coping skills are not possessed or implemented, excessive alcohol use may be seen as an effective short-term coping strategy, even at the expense of long-term negative consequences.

The third basic principle of a cognitive-behavioral alcohol treatment is that drinking behavior can be understood as existing on a continuum of use and severity of consequences which may not always be perfectly correlated. This continuum ranges from abstinence with no alcohol-related problems, at one extreme, to alcohol dependence with many alcohol-related problems at the other extreme, with many intermediate locations on the continuum between these two endpoints. This principle contrasts with the traditional model of alcoholism as a progressive disease, which assumes the potential for addiction to be present or absent and, if present, to intensify in severity as time goes on. From a cognitive-behavioral point of view, alcohol consumption is viewed as a learned behavior, determined by the same processes regardless of where an individual's drinking falls on the continuum of use and severity of consequences. The learning processes involved in alcohol consumption, including important biopsychosocial factors, determine drinking at all levels of the continuum and are no different from the learning processes that govern the acquisition and change of other non-addictive behaviors. This continuity of learning processes in human behavior allows the cognitive-behavioral therapist to help clients replace the habit of excessive drinking with the cognitive and behavioral skills to cope with the stress of life's demands.

CLINICAL PRACTICE GUIDELINES

The essence of cognitive-behavioral alcohol treatment is the movement from a *disease model* of deficits, powerlessness and loss of control to a *competence model* based on enhanced motivation, increased awareness, skill acquisition and social support (Marlatt & Parks, 1999). Traditional approaches to the treatment of alcoholism initiate therapy by using confrontational techniques designed to "break through the denial system" and force clients into accepting a diagnostic label such as "alcoholic". In contrast, a cognitive-behavioral approach attempts to foster a sense of objectivity or detachment in the way individuals approach their alcohol-related problems (see Chapter 30). By relating to the client as a colleague or co-therapist, cognitive-behavioral therapists hope to encourage a sense of cooperation and openness during the therapy process. Using this approach helps clients learn to perceive their excessive drinking as something they *do*, rather than as an indication of someone they *are*. By adopting this objective and detached approach, clients may be able to free themselves from any guilt and defensiveness that would otherwise bias their view of their alcohol-related problem and their ability to change their excessive drinking behavior.

Cognitive-behavioral therapists encourage clients to take an active role in treatment planning and decision-making processes throughout the course of treatment and to assume progressively more personal responsibility for their treatment at every stage of the therapy program. Within-session exercises and between-session homework assignments, such as bibiliotherapy and self-monitoring, are carefully explained and demonstrated by the therapist so that the client understands their rationale and importance. Over time, the client becomes his/her own therapist as he/she gains new knowledge and masters new skills.

Self-control or self-management is the ultimate goal of treatment and, after termination of the therapy proper, the client is in charge of aftercare planning and the implementation of an individually tailored relapse prevention program (see Chapter 29). The overall goals of cognitive-behavioral alcohol treatment are: (a) to increase and maintain motivation for change; (b) to enhance awareness and choice concerning drinking behavior; and (c) to develop coping skills and self-control capacities.

SCOPE, DURATION AND AIMS OF COGNITIVE-BEHAVIORAL ALCOHOL TREATMENT

Cognitive-behavioral alcohol treatment begins with a thorough biopsychosocial assessment of the client. Utilizing a multivariate, biopsychosocial model in treatment requires a comprehensive and integrated assessment of the client, focusing on social and medical history, level of alcohol dependence, alcohol-related problems, drinking behaviors, coping skills deficits, psychiatric comorbidity and social support (see Chapter 3). A comprehensive pre-treatment assessment involves the multiple systems of physiological, cognitive, psychological, behavioral, and social factors. While begun prior to treatment, assessment is an ongoing interactive process between therapist and client that contributes to the development of a treatment plan matching the person to an appropriate type and intensity of cognitive-behavioral treatment. Assessment includes continuous monitoring of the client's progress throughout therapy and frequent feedback about currently achieved and anticipated treatment outcomes.

Cognitive-behavioral alcohol treatment employs a public health approach that matches clients to levels of care, depending on the severity of alcohol abuse or dependence and on factors such as psychiatric comorbidity, other drug use, cognitive or neurological impairment and criminal conduct. A stepped-care approach offers interventions ranging in intensity and duration, from psycho-educational programs and brief interventions (see Chapter 31) to intensive outpatient treatment or on to medically supervised inpatient alcohol treatment. Initial matching of clients to treatments is determined by comprehensive assessment results. Ongoing assessment of clients determines whether a specific course of treatment should be continued and whether a client should be moved backward or forward in terms of the intensity and duration of treatment needed (see Chapters 24, 25).

Cognitive-behavioral alcohol treatment also allows for some flexibility with regard to the ultimate goal of therapy. Considerable controversy has existed concerning the appropriateness of "controlled drinking" as a goal for alcoholics or alcohol-dependent individuals (Marlatt et al., 1993; Heather & Robertson, 1983). However, in clinical practice the goals of abstinence or moderation are often determined more by program policy or consumer choice than by objective assessment or research findings (Marlatt et al., 1997). Obviously, alcohol treatment will not work unless the person begins and continues therapy. Insisting on a goal of abstinence may create a high threshold for treatment entry and continuation. Harm reduction approaches to alcohol treatment (Marlatt, 1998) and motivational interviewing (Miller & Rollnick, 1991; see also Chapter 30) attempt to provide consumers with low-threshold access to treatment services. While the harm reduction approach includes abstinence as the ideal goal for alcohol-dependent individuals, consistent with the stages of change model, any progress toward abstinence is viewed as therapeutic progress. From a cognitive-behavioral point of view, abstinence, moderation or even attenuated drinking can be appropriate goals of alcohol treatment for clients, depending on their unique characteristics and life circumstances (Jarvis et al., 1995).

Although clients may not initially choose or accept abstinence as their treatment goal, over time they may decide that it is in their best interest not to drink. They will often then begin to ask their therapist for interventions aimed at drinking cessation, rather that moderation or attenuation. The ultimate therapeutic objective is to help clients create those outcomes that are desirable to the client, that reduce harm and that are safe and attainable. Jarvis, Tegbutt & Mattick (1995) suggest the following factors as guidelines for choosing appropriate goals for alcohol treatment: medical complications, alcohol-induced organic brain damage, cognitive impairment, psychiatric comorbidity, physical withdrawal, severity of alcohol dependence, drinking history, social support and partner preference (see also Heather & Robertson, 1989).

BEHAVIORAL ASSESSMENT

Cognitive-behavioral alcohol treatment utilizes assessment techniques and clinical interventions that integrate traditional behavioral therapy strategies with cognitive therapy interventions. Early behavioral therapy approaches to alcohol treatment focused primarily on the clinical application of the principles of classical conditioning and instrumental learning. While this approach has since been viewed as overly simplistic, it has served a useful heuristic purpose and several key aspects of behavioral therapy continue to be central to the contemporary and more mediational cognitive-behavioral approach to alcohol treatment.

The cornerstone of assessment in behavioral therapy is the functional analysis of behavior. This assessment method continues to be fundamental in the practice of effective cognitive-behavioral alcohol treatment. Functional analysis is a behavioral assessment procedure which involves observing and measuring the *antecedents* of drinking behavior, the rate and pattern of alcohol consumption *behavior* itself, and the *consequences* of alcohol use that reinforce drinking. The first step in the functional analysis of alcohol consumption is to determine and help the client understand the most frequent and potent antecedents for his/her drinking behavior. This is done while teaching the client that selective attention, subjective interpretations and expectancies are cognitive factors that determine the choice and meaning of drinking situations. A second step in the functional analysis of alcohol consumption is to instruct clients in observing and measuring the frequency, quantity, duration and intensity of drinking behavior and its associated temporal and situational patterns. Finally, consequences that serve to maintain drinking behavior are assessed and discussed, including positive physiological consequences such as increased pleasure and decreased pain, emotional consequences such as tension reduction and greater emotional expressiveness, and social consequences such as peer approval and acceptance.

Useful behavioral assessment techniques include self-monitoring of drinking behavior, as well as questionnaires and structured interviews like the Comprehensive Drinking Profile, the Brief Drinking Profile, and the Timeline Follow-back Method (Donovan & Marlatt, 1988; Sobell & Sobell, 1993). A cognitive-behavioral approach to alcohol treatment also requires the assessment of level of alcohol dependence and the nature and severity of any alcohol-related problems (Allen & Columbus, 1995; Donovan & Marlatt, 1988).

BEHAVIORAL THERAPY INTERVENTIONS

Aversive Therapies

Aversive therapies are designed to reduce the reinforcing properties of drinking by changing the valence of drinking-related cues from positive to negative through counter-conditioning procedures. In this technique, an aversive unconditioned stimulus is paired with a reinforcing conditioned stimulus, such as alcohol use. The goal of this classical conditioning procedure is for the client to experience an aversive conditioned response to alcohol and to avoid drinking after the conditioning has occurred. Two forms of aversive stimuli that have been shown to reduce a person's desire to drink are electric shock and nausea-inducing drugs, such as disulfiram (Antabuse) and calcium carbimide. Nausea-inducing drugs are more effective than electric shock, although both of these aversive techniques pose both ethical and procedural problems (Chapter 27).

A more cognitive-behavioral version of aversive therapy involves imaginal pairing of unpleasant events with alcohol, rather than actual *in vivo* pairing. This procedure, called covert sensitization, includes three phases (Rimmele et al., 1989). In the first phase, the client is guided through positive imagery of drinking and then an aversive response such as vomiting. In the second phase, the aversive imagery is paired with suggestions of non-drinking alternatives, allowing the client to escape the negative consequences if he/she chooses not to continue drinking. Finally, in phase three, non-drinking alternatives are given prior to the experience of any aversive consequences, allowing the client to avoid them if he/she chooses not to drink in the first place. Despite their promise and empirical support, aversion therapies may be useful only for initial abstinence and have not been utilized very heavily by alcohol treatment providers.

Cue Exposure

Classical conditioning approaches to behavioral therapy suggest that alcohol-dependent drinkers may develop conditioned craving responses to drinking-related antecedent stimuli because of their drinking history. This suggests that cue reactivity must be addressed during treatment in order for dependent drinkers to learn to anticipate and cope with cravings for alcohol and urges to drink without a return to excessive consumption. Traditional treatment programs usually do everything they can to minimize or eliminate all tempting stimuli from the protected environment of the therapeutic setting. Clients are discouraged from ever mentioning the possibility of encountering temptations to drink excessively. Without preparation or warning, exposure to cues associated with past heavy drinking can be an overwhelming and discouraging experience that is often interpreted by clients as an indication that the treatment has failed or that treatment effects have worn off. The presence of alcohol cues may disrupt the coping responses of dependent drinkers, with those who are more dependent showing greater impairment in their coping behaviors.

Cue exposure may be most effective when paired with response prevention and coping skills training designed to prepare clients for the temptations they will encounter in the course of their everyday lives (Monti et al., 1989; Marlatt, 1990). Extensive research is currently under way assessing the efficacy of incorporating cue exposure therapy into cognitive-behavioral skills training, in order to improve the effectiveness of treatment outcome (Rohsenow et al., 1994, Drummond et al., 1995).

Relaxation Training

To the degree that stress causes unpleasant physical sensations and associated dysphoric moods, it is a high-risk situation for excessive alcohol use. An important coping skill for clients to learn is how to use the physical and emotional signs of stress as cues to "stop, look and listen" and to try something to cope besides heavy drinking. Relaxation training is a fundamental coping skill in the repertoire of a person trying to avoid excessive drinking. It can help clients to reduce their anxiety and tension when facing stressful situations and minimize their typical levels of motor and psychological tension. Relaxation training can also assist a person to remain calm and to think clearly in circumstances that require effective problem solving and fast action. Many individuals believe in the tension-reducing properties of alcohol, whether or not they are true, and, without an alternative means to relax, excessive drinking may be a person's only means of coping with painful sensations and unpleasant emotions. Relaxation training fosters general stress-reduction and can be taught to clients using various techniques that either reduce muscle tension, develop deep breathing skills or focus on the use of pleasant imagery (Monti et al., 1989). In addition to relaxation training, both meditation and exercise have been shown to have similar stress-reducing properties.

Contingency Management

Contingency management procedures assist clients to re-structure their environment to decrease the rewards associated with alcohol use and increase the costs of excessive drinking. The principles of contingency management are based on operant or instrumental learning approaches to human behavior (see Chapter 15). Contingency management techniques include providing incentives for compliance with alcohol treatment and positive reinforcement from spouses or friends for sobriety. This approach is combined with punishment, in the form of withdrawal of attention and approval contingent on the resumption of excessive drinking, and provisions for social support, recreational activities and vocational counseling.

The Community Reinforcement Approach to alcohol treatment is a contingency management intervention strategy that has demonstrated its effectiveness in both inpatient and outpatient settings (Hunt & Azrin, 1973; Smith & Meyers, 1995). It is compatible with either moderation or abstinence treatment goals. The program involves a functional analysis of drinking behavior, basic skills training, problem-solving training, drinking refusal training, and social, recreational and vocational counseling, including marital therapy where indicated.

Skills Training

Behavioral and cognitive skills training techniques, sometimes called coping skills training, form the cornerstone of cognitive-behavioral alcohol treatment. Monti et al. (1989) have categorized these coping skills as either *intra*personal or *inter*personal and have developed a session-by-session manual for skills training in their treatment protocol. Individuals with a history of heavy drinking may be deficient in coping skills, such as rational thinking, problem solving, assertiveness or effective conflict resolution. A functional analysis of drinking identifies deficits in those skills the client needs to learn and practice in order to regain abstinence or maintain moderate use in situations previously associated with excessive drinking.

A series of behavioral skills, such as blood alcohol discrimination, pacing of drinking, drinking refusal and setting moderation goals, have been used in behavioral self-control training to help clients whose goal is moderation rather than abstinence. In addition, clients whose goals are moderation or abstinence can benefit from social skills acquisition, such as communications training, assertiveness training, creating and maintaining social support networks and vocational training. Interpersonal skills training is often necessary because many individuals lacking in social skills use alcohol excessively as a way of coping with stressful situations involving others, especially interpersonal conflict (Marlatt & Parks, 1982).

Monti et al. (1989) provide modules on a number of specific interpersonal skills, as well as guidelines for how to conduct skills training sessions. In this regard, verbal instructions introducing skills are followed by modeling, role-playing and active practice by clients until mastery in analog therapy situations is achieved. Homework assignments provide clients with practice of new social skills in real-life situations where excessive drinking is a definite risk. Success and failure in coping with these situations is debriefed in individual or group therapy sessions, allowing for both a review of previously taught skills and feedback to the client on his/her efforts. Interpersonal skills are also important to the acquisition and maintenance of social support during the process of acquiring greater mastery of social skills.

COGNITIVE ASSESSMENT

A major strength of cognitive-behavioral alcohol treatment lies in the integrated combination of behavioral and cognitive intervention strategies. An initial step in the conduct of cognitive assessment and intervention is to persuade clients of the important role that thoughts and other internal events play in excessive drinking. While behavioral assessment involves the functional analysis of antecedents, behavior and consequences, cognitive assessment involves a focusing of attention on the mediation of behavior by internal events, such as self-talk and mental images.

One way to get the idea of cognitive mediation across to clients is to use the notion popularized by rational-emotive behavioral therapy, that "people are disturbed not by things, but by the views which they take of them" (Ellis et al., 1988). Most clients readily understand that their drinking-related attitudes, beliefs and expectations are important contributors to their excessive drinking when a few examples are analyzed using the ABCs of rational-emotive behavioral therapy. This involves identifying the activating event (A), exploring the client's interpretation of the event by discussing his/her beliefs, expectations, automatic thoughts and self-talk (B), and demonstrating how these beliefs and expectations take the form of internal dialogue or self-talk and contribute to the consequence of excessive drinking (C).

Once the rationale for cognitive assessment and intervention has been firmly established, clients are asked to begin self-monitoring their thoughts and other internal events in those situations that have in the past been related to excessive drinking. Clients are also taught about the importance of assessing and changing their cognitive appraisal of events. They are encouraged to examine and challenge their beliefs and expectancies about the transforming effects of alcohol and to develop greater self-efficacy expectations for mastery of life events without heavy drinking. Cognitive assessment falls within the intrapersonal skills domain of Monti et al. (1989), which includes a number of specific training modules to be briefly reviewed below. The Daily Thought Record and the Daily Record of Cravings are cognitive therapy techniques designed to help clients self-monitor their drinking-related thoughts (Beck et al., 1993). In addition, a number of questionnaires and interview methods have been devised to help therapist and client assess cognitive factors related to alcohol dependence, including alcohol outcome and self-efficacy expectancies (Allen & Columbus, 1995).

COGNITIVE THERAPY INTERVENTIONS

Appraisal

An initial cognitive intervention strategy is to assess the client's characteristic manner of evaluating whether various situations pose a risk for excessive drinking and, if they do, why they do. This strategy is consistent with the notion that people respond not to the *actual* situation, but to the situation as they *perceive* it to be. The importance of the appraisal process in understanding and treating alcohol problems is based on the work of Lazarus et al. (1974) and, more specifically, on the work of Sanchez-Craig et al. (1987). In this model, two types of appraisal are important to assess. *Primary* appraisal is the process by which a situation is judged beneficial, harmful, or irrelevant to the task of avoiding excessive drinking. *Secondary* appraisal refers to one's ability to identify and implement behavioral alternatives to coping with stress without drinking.

Based on this analysis of the relevance of appraisal for effective coping, Sanchez-Craig et al. (1987) suggest performing a functional analysis of the client's beliefs, expectations and attributions regarding drinking and their relationship to the emotions and behavioral intentions the client experiences. Given this information on the appraisal process, clients are taught new, more adaptive ways to appraise situations and are encouraged to reconsider attributions made about their appraisal of past negative events. The reappraisal process follows the basic formula of all cognitive-behavioral interventions. That is, clients first become aware of their thoughts and related behaviors by learning to identify situations in which they are likely to drink excessively. Additionally, they are taught how their primary and secondary appraisals influence this process. Then clients are taught to generate new, more effective cognitive strategies and to rehearse these strategies in both treatment and real life until mastery is achieved. This approach to reappraisal is consistent with both rational-emotive behavioral therapy (Ellis et al., 1988) and with the use of overt verbal instructions to modify the self-statements of clients used in Meichenbaum's (1977) stress inoculation training approach to control impulsivity and schizophrenic behavior.

Problem-solving Training

Cognitive and behavioral coping skills training focuses on specific thoughts or situations related to the likelihood of excessive drinking. In addition to this situation-specific strategy, cognitive-behavioral alcohol treatment combines training in general problem solving, with specific skills training that focuses on the client's unique challenges and resources regarding his/her drinking. Adopting a problem-solving orientation to these situations (D'Zurilla & Goldfried, 1971) gives clients greater flexibility and adaptability in new stressful situations, rather than having to rely solely on the rote learning of a number of discrete coping skills that may or may not generalize across various settings and situations. In this sense, maintaining abstinence from alcohol or moderating drinking may be largely dependent on the ability of clients to use problem solving to cope effectively with the demands of those life situations previously associated with excessive drinking.

D'Zurilla & Goldfried (1971) describe five general stages that focus on key cognitive processes that have been seen as a prescription for effective problem solving in situations involving the risk of excessive drinking. In real life, problem solving may not take place in such a sequential manner. There might be substantial overlap between the stages; a client may jump back and forth from stage to stage or even work on different stages simultaneously. Nevertheless, the stages listed below can be seen as a method for effective problem solving and are usually helpful in the education of clients who have problem-solving deficits.

D'Zurilla & Goldfried (1971) recommend five steps for effective problem solving: (a) identifying a client's style of approaching problems and helping him/her to improve a maladaptive general orientation to problems is vital for effective problem solving; (b) assisting a client in the skill of problem definition allows him/her to formulate a problem in a clear, simple and unambiguous form, thereby facilitating a solution; (c) teaching a client the skill of generating alternative solutions to the problem is a vital step and is often facilitated by teaching the technique of brainstorming; (d) helping a client to weigh the consequences of various alternative solutions with the assistance of a decision matrix or decision balance sheet; and (e) verification, where the client and therapist evaluate the outcome of the client's problem-solving effort, allowing for feedback and correction if needed. Eventually, it is assumed that the client will select a viable solution and the verification of its effectiveness should result in increased self-efficacy for mastering life events without excessive drinking.

Cognitive Restructuring

Problem-solving training helps clients to better identify and resolve the everyday challenges they face in their efforts to achieve their therapeutic and life goals. Cognitive or "thought" restructuring gives clients a cognitive skill that focuses their awareness on identifying those beliefs, patterns of thinking, attributions and expectations that are related to excessive drinking and alcohol-related problems. During this procedure, clients engage in ongoing self-monitoring and written recording of internal states, such as inner dialogue or self-talk related to excessive drinking. Through this process of client self-assessment, client and therapist try to create a functional analysis of the antecedent events, beliefs and consequences that form a client's typical pattern of excessive drinking. Client handouts and recording forms are often used to assist clients in making a systematic analysis of the relationship between their thinking and their problematic drinking.

Awareness of internal states and the relationships between certain ways of thinking and excessive alcohol use lays the foundation for cognitive restructuring. The next step is teaching clients how to "restructure" or alter their thinking by first interrupting a sequence of "negative" thoughts and then by challenging those thoughts, eventually leading to new, more adaptive ways of thinking. Clients are taught to "stop, look and listen" for thoughts leading to excessive drinking, especially as they face situations and circumstances where heavy alcohol consumption used to occur. Strategies to identify negative thinking are combined with in-session and/or in-group practice in discussing these beliefs, expectations and attributions and challenging them. Negative thinking is challenged, based either on the rationality of its content, on the evidence supporting it or on the presence of distortion or errors in thinking (Ellis et al., 1988; Beck et al., 1993).

A CONTEMPORARY COGNITIVE-BEHAVIORAL ALCOHOL TREATMENT PROTOCOL

Monti et al. have developed a cognitive-behavioral coping skills therapy protocol that systematically combines the cognitive and behavioral assessment and intervention elements previously described into treatment manuals for practitioners (Kadden et al., 1995; Monti et al., 1989). These manuals guide therapists engaged in the treatment of individuals with alcohol abuse and dependence disorders to an understanding of a social learning approach to alcohol consumption, an appreciation of the rationale for coping skills training, and the creation of a session-by-session treatment program, including both assessment and intervention procedures. They divide their coping skills training program into interpersonal and intrapersonal components, which roughly correspond to behavioral and cognitive therapy interventions. This cognitive-behavioral alcohol treatment protocol has been applied in both inpatient and outpatient settings, using both individual and group therapy formats. A version of this protocol was chosen as the cognitive-behavioral intervention in the Project MATCH study (Kadden et al., 1995).

POTENTIAL BENEFITS OF COGNITIVE-BEHAVIORAL ALCOHOL TREATMENT

Cognitive-behavioral alcohol treatment avoids the stigma and shame of labeling clients as "alcoholic" because clients are instead viewed as individuals with drinking behavior problems, or bad habits, that are not their fault but that can be changed with knowledge, effort and support. This approach to treatment creates a low threshold for treatment entry, fosters openness and cooperation in clients, and increases the likelihood of continued treatment compliance. Another benefit of this science-based approach to alcohol treatment is that specific, yet flexible, treatment goals can be derived and modified, depending on the nature and severity of a client's alcohol dependence and his/her stage in the habit change process. This is true in part because assessment of the nature and severity of the alcohol-related problem and feedback to the client occur at the onset of treatment and are an ongoing process during therapy. Since therapeutic goals are made explicit and agreed upon by therapist and client in advance, it is readily apparent to both the therapist and the client whether a treatment intervention is effective in achieving its desired results as therapy progresses. Finally, because cognitive-behavioral alcohol treatment is an empirically-derived approach and endeavors to evolve and improve as new evidence accumulates from efficacy and effectiveness studies, the intervention components and protocols of cognitive-behavioral alcohol treatment are designed to be evaluated and modified by the results of ongoing clinical research trials and the outcome effectiveness of active treatment programs.

EMPIRICAL SUPPORT FOR COGNITIVE-BEHAVIORAL ALCOHOL TREATMENT

Cognitive-behavioral therapies are often recommended as "what works" best for the treatment of a number of mental and medical disorders, including substance use disorders such as alcohol abuse and dependence, because these science-based protocols have been supported by outcome research testing their efficacy through randomized controlled experimental designs (Nathan & Gorman, 1998; Chambless & Hollon, 1998). Specifically, empirical support for the efficacy of cognitive-behavioral therapies as preferred treatments for drug abuse (Carroll, 1996) and for alcohol use disorders (Miller & Hester, 1986; Hester & Miller, 1995; Nathan & Gorman, 1998) is very strong. For example, Hester & Miller (1995), in their comprehensive review of alcohol treatment outcome studies, listed the following six cognitive-behavioral therapy techniques among their top 10 interventions with the strongest empirical evidence: social skills training, community reinforcement approach, behavioral contracting, aversion therapy (nausea), relapse prevention, and cognitive therapy. There is substantial evidence that constituent ingredients or components of a more integrated cognitive-behavioral alcohol treatment program are effective when applied to drug and alcohol problems. This evidence will be reviewed in Chapter 29 on Relapse Prevention Therapy (Marlatt & Parks, 1999; Carroll, 1996; Irvin et al., 1999). For the purposes of this chapter, let us end with the following statement of endorsement for this therapeutic approach by Monti and colleagues as they discuss the efficacy of cognitive-behavioral treatment for both substance and alcohol use disorders:

> Since the essential core elements in CSST (Coping and Social Skills Training) have a strong theoretical base as well as solid empirical support from research treatment outcome studies, they should be an integral part of any state-of-the-art intervention for clients with addictive behaviors in general, and of alcohol prevention and treatment in particular (Monti et al., 1995).

KEY WORKS AND SUGGESTIONS FOR FURTHER READING

Broadening the Base of Treatment for Alcohol Problems. Institute of Medicine (1990). Washington, DC: National Academy Press.

This report highlights the continuum of alcohol-related problems and disorders that can range from mild difficulties to severe dependency. The importance of matching treatment intensity to problem intensity is emphasized.

Kadden, R. et al. (1995). *Cognitive-behavioral Coping Skills Therapy Manual: A Clinical Research Guide for Therapists Treating Individuals with Alcohol Abuse and Dependence.* National Institute on Alcohol Abuse and Alcoholism Project MATCH Monograph Series. Bethesda, MD: US Department of Health and Human Services.

This manual was developed for Project MATCH and is a modified version of the treatment approach developed by Monti and his colleagues. The manual provides guidelines for 22 cognitive-behavioral therapy sessions that can be combined in an individualized manner.

Sobell, M.B. & Sobell, L.C. (1993). *Problem Drinkers: Guided Self-change Treatment.* New York: Guilford.

The Sobells describe the nature and scope of problem drinking and provide a detailed description of a guided self-change treatment approach.

Monti, P.M. et al. (1989). *Treating Alcohol Dependence.* New York: Guilford.

This book presents 27 cognitive-behavioral treatment sessions for alcohol-dependent clients. It formed the basis of the Project MATCH CBT manual. This treatment approach is geared towards a group setting and incorporates the development of both interpersonal and intrapersonal coping skills.

Jarvis, T.J., Tebbutt, J. & Mattick, R.P. (1995). *Treatment Approaches for Alcohol and Drug Dependence: An Introductory Guide.* Chichester: Wiley.

This book describes basic treatment approaches without going into the detail of specific session-by-session instructions. It addresses general topics such as assessment, motivational enhancement and goal setting, as well as more specific techniques.

REFERENCES

Allen, J.P. & Columbus, M. (1995). *Assessing Alcohol Problems: A Guide for Clinicians and Researchers.* National Institute on Alcohol Abuse and Alcoholism Treatment Handbook, Series 4, Bethesda, MD: US Department of Health and Human Services.

Baer, J.S., Kivlahan, D.R. & Donovan, D.M. (1999). Integrating skills training and motivational therapies: implications for the treatment of substance dependence. *Journal of Substance Abuse Treatment,* **17**(1–2), 15–24.

Bandura, A. (1969). *Principles of Behavior Modification.* New York: Holt, Rinehart & Winston.

Bandura, A. (1997). *Self-efficacy: The Exercise of Control.* San Francisco, CA: W.H. Freeman.

Bandura, A. (1986). *Social Foundations of Thought and Action: A Social Cognitive Theory.* Englewood Cliffs, NJ: Prentice Hall.

Beck, A.T., Wright, F.D., Newman, C.F. & Liese, B.S. (1993). *Cognitive Therapy of Substance Abuse.* New York: Guilford.

Brickman, P., Rabinowitz, V.C., Karuza, J., Coates, D., Cohn, E. & Kidder, L. (1982). Models of helping and coping. *American Psychologist,* **37**(4), 368–384.

Carroll, K.M. (1996). Relapse prevention as a psychosocial treatment: a review of controlled clinical trials. *Experimental and Clinical Psychopharmacology*, **4**(1), 46–54.

Chambless, D.L. & Hollon, S.D. (1998). Defining empirically supported therapies. *Journal of Consulting and Clinical Psychology*, **66**, 7–19.

Cook, C.C.H. (1988a). The Minnesota model in the management of drug and alcohol dependency: miracle method or myth? Part I: The philosophy and the programme. *British Journal of Addiction*, **83**, 625–634.

Cook, C.C.H. (1988b). The Minnesota model in the management of drug and alcohol dependency: miracle method or myth?: Part II: evidence and conclusions. *British Journal of Addiction*, **83**, 735–748.

Donovan, D.M. (1988). Assessment of addictive behaviors: implications of an emerging biopsychosocial model. In D.M. Donovan & G.A. Marlatt (Eds), *Assessment of Addictive Behaviors* (pp. 3–50). New York: Guilford.

Donovan, D.M. & Marlatt, G.A. (1988). *Assessment of Addictive Behaviors*. New York: Guilford.

Drummond, D.C., Tiffany, S.T., Glautier, S. & Remington, B. (Eds). (1995). *Addictive Behavior: Cue Exposure Theory and Practice*. Chichester: Wiley.

D'Zurilla, T.J. & Goldfried, M.R. (1971). Problem solving and behavior modification. *Journal of Abnormal Psychology*, **78**, 107–126.

Ellis, A., McInerney, J.F., DiGiuseppe, R. & Yeager, R.R. (1988). *Rational-emotive Therapy with Alcoholics and Substance Abusers*. Boston, MA: Allyn and Bacon.

Heather, N. & Robertson, I. (1989). *Problem Drinking*, 2nd edn. Oxford: Oxford University Press.

Heather, N. & Robertson, I. (1983). *Controlled Drinking*, revised edn. New York: Methuen.

Hester, R.K. & Miller, W.R. (Eds) (1995). *Handbook of Alcoholism Treatment Approaches: Effective Alternatives*; 2rd edn. Boston MA: Allyn & Bacon.

Hunt, G.M. & Azrin, N.H. (1973). A community-reinforcement approach to alcoholism. *Behaviour Research and Therapy*, **11**, 91–104.

Institute of Medicine (IOM) (1990). *Broadening the Base of Treatment for Alcohol Problems*. Washington, DC: National Academy Press.

Irvin, J.E., Bowers, C.A., Dunn, M.E. & Wang, M.C. (1999). Efficacy of relapse prevention: a meta-analytic review. *Journal of Consulting and Clinical Psychology*, **67**(4), 563–570.

Jarvis, T.J., Tebbutt, J. & Mattick, R.P. (1995). *Treatment Approaches for Alcohol Aand Drug Dependence: An Introductory Guide*. Chichester: Wiley.

Kadden, R.M. (1994). Cognitive-behavioral approaches to alcoholism treatment. *Alcohol Health and Research World*, **18**(4), 279–286.

Kadden, R., Carroll, K., Donovan, D., Conney, N., Monti, P., Abrams, D., Litt, M. & Hester, R. (1995). *Cognitive-behavioral Coping Skills Therapy Manual: A Clinical Research Guide for Therapists Treating Individuals with Alcohol Abuse and Dependence*. National Institute on Alcohol Abuse and Alcoholism, Project MATCH Monograph Series. Bethesda, MD: US Department of Health and Human Services.

Lazarus, R.S., Averill, J.R. & Opton, E.M. (1974). The psychology of coping: issues of research and assessment. In G.V. Coelbo, D.A. Hamburg & J.E. Adams (Eds), *Coping and Adaption* (pp. 249–315). New York: Basic Books.

Mackay, P.W., Donovan, D.M. & Marlatt, G.A. (1991). Cognitive and behavioral approaches to alcohol abuse. In R.J. Frances & S.I. Miller (Eds), *Clinical Textbook of Addictive Disorders* (pp. 452–481). New York: Guilford.

Marlatt, G.A. (Ed.) (1998). *Harm Reduction: Pragmatic Strategies for Managing High-risk Behaviors*. New York: Guilford.

Marlatt, G.A. (1992). Substance abuse: implications of a biopsychosocial model for prevention, treatment, and relapse prevention. In J. Grabowski & G.R. VandenBos (Eds), *Psychopharmacology: Basic Mechanisms and Applied Interventions* (pp. 131–162). Washington, DC: America Psychological Association.

Marlatt, G.A. (1990). Cue exposure and relapse prevention in the treatment of addictive behaviors. *Addictive Behaviors*, **15**, 395–399.

Marlatt, G.A., Larimer, M.E., Baer, J.S. & Quigley, L.A. (1993). Harm reduction for alcohol problems: moving beyond the controlled drinking controversy. *Behavior Therapy*, **24**, 461–504.

Marlatt, G.A., Baer, J.S., Donovan, D.M. & Kivlahan, D.R. (1988). Addictive behaviors: etiology and treatment. In M.K. Roszenweig & L.W. Porter (Eds), *Annual Review of Psychology*, Vol. 39 (pp. 223–252). Palo Alto, CA: Annual Reviews Inc.

Marlatt, G.A. & Gordon, J.R. (Ed.) (1985). *Relapse Prevention: Maintenance Strategies in the Treatment of Addictive Behaviors*. New York: Guilford.

Marlatt, G.A. & Parks, G.A. (1982). Self-management of addictive behaviors. In F.H. Kanfer & P. Karoly (Eds), *Self-management of Behavior Change: From Theory to Practice* (pp. 443–488). New York: Pergamon.

Marlatt, G.A. & Parks, G.A. (1999). Keeping "what works" working: cognitive-behavioral relapse prevention therapy with substance abusing offenders. In E.J. Latessa (Ed.), *Strategic Solutions: The International Community Corrections Association Examines Substance Abuse* (pp. 161–233). Lanham, MD: American Correctional Association.

Marlatt, G.A., Tucker, J.A., Donovan, D.M. & Vuchinich, R.E. (1997). Help-seeking by substance abusers: the role of harm reduction and behavioral-economic approaches to facilitate treatment entry and retention. In L.S. Onken, J.D. Blaine & J.J. Boren (Eds), *Beyond the Therapeutic Alliance: Keeping the Drug-dependent Individual in Treatment*. National Institute on Drug Abuse Research Monograph 165, 44–84. Rockville, MD: US Department of Health and Human Services.

Meichenbaum, D.H. (1977). *Cognitive-behavioral Modification*. New York: Plenum.

Miller, W.R. & Hester, R.K. (1986). The effectiveness of alcoholism treatment. What research reveals. In W.R. Miller & N. Heather (Eds), *Treating Addictive Behaviors: Processes of Change* (pp. 175–203). New York: Plenum.

Miller, W.R. & Rollnick, S. (1991). *Motivational Interviewing: Preparing People to Change Addictive Behaviors*. New York: Guilford.

Miller, W.R., Westerberg, V.S., Harris, R.J. & Tonigan, J.S. (1996). What predicts relapse? Prospective testing of antecedent models. *Addiction*, **91**(Suppl.).

Monti, P.M., Abrams, D.B., Kadden, R.M. & Conney, N.L. (1989). *Treating Alcohol Dependence*. New York: Guilford.

Monti, P.M., Rohsenow, D.J., Colby, S.M. & Abrams, D.B. (1995). Coping and social skills training. In R.K. Hester & W.R. Miller (Eds), *Handbook of Alcoholism Treatment Approaches: Effective Alternatives*, 2nd edn (pp. 221–241). Boston, MA: Allyn and Bacon.

Nathan, P.E. & Gorman, J.M. (1998). *A Guide to Treatments that Work*. New York: Oxford University Press.

Prochaska, J.O. & DiClemente, C.C. (1992). In search of how people change: applications to addictive behaviors. *American Psychologist*, **47**, 1102–1114.

Rimmele, C.T., Miller, W.R. & Dougher, M.J. (1989). Aversion therapies. In R.K. Hester & W.R. Miller (Eds), *Handbook of Alcoholism Treatment Approaches* (pp. 128–140). New York: Pergamon.

Rohsenow, D.J., Monti, P.M., Rubonis, A.V., Sirota, A.D., Niaura, R.S., Colby, S.M., Wunschel, S.M. & Abrams, D.B. (1994). Cue reactivity as a predictor of drinking among male alcoholics. *Journal of Consulting and Clinical Psychology*, **62**, 620–626.

Sanchez-Craig, M., Wilkinson, D.A. & Walker, K. (1987). Theory and methods for secondary prevention of alcohol problems: a cognitively based approach. In W.M. Cox (Eds), *Treatment and Prevention of Alcohol Problems* (pp. 287–331). Orlando, FL: Academic Press.

Sobell, M.B. & Sobell, L.C. (1993). *Problem Drinkers: Guided Self-change Treatment*. New York: Guilford.

Smith, J.E. & Meyers, R.J. (1995). The Community Reinforcement Approach. In R.K. Hester & W.R. Miller (Eds), *Handbook of Alcoholism Treatment Approaches: Effective Alternatives*; 3rd edn. Boston, MA: Allyn & Bacon.

Vaillant, G.E. (1995). *The Natural History of Alcoholism* (revised edn). Cambridge: Harvard University Press.

Chapter 29

Relapse Prevention Therapy

George A. Parks
Britt K. Anderson
and
G. Alan Marlatt
Addictive Behaviors Research Center, University of Washington,
Seattle, WA, USA

Synopsis

What follows is the second of two chapters devoted to a cognitive-behavioral approach to the treatment of alcohol abuse and dependence. In Chapter 28, we provided an overview of this therapeutic approach by placing it within a typology of conceptual models, summarizing the main principles of cognitive-behavioral alcohol treatment and reviewing both cognitive and behavioral assessment and intervention techniques that are the constituent ingredients of this empirically-supported form of therapy. The goal of this chapter is to present an overview of a cognitive-behavioral approach to the problem of relapse, Relapse Prevention Therapy (RPT).

The chapter begins by introducing a conceptual model of relapse prevention and discussing the cyclical nature of long-term behavioral change. From this perspective, relapse is a natural part of the process of change and does not represent failure. Rather, lapses or relapses represent opportunities for clients to gain a greater understanding of their unique challenges in changing drinking behavior and to learn new skills to better cope in the future. High-risk situations represent difficult circumstances in which goals of abstinence or moderation may be tested. Common across a range of addictive behaviors, they can be broadly described as interpersonal or intrapersonal situations in which one's sense of control is threatened. The process of relapse, from the experience of high-risk situations to an initial lapse, is then presented. Positive outcome expectancies regarding the effects of alcohol, degree of self-efficacy and the acquisition of effective coping skills all play a role in this process. Additionally, when a lapse occurs there is often an abstinence violation effect, composed of guilty feelings and a sense of inherent powerlessness, which can interact with these other factors and trigger a relapse. A client may unknowingly contribute to a relapse through several covert antecedents that lead him/her to a high-risk situation. For example, the desire for the pleasurable effects of alcohol, a lack of life-style balance, the experience of urges and craving, and cognitive factors such as rationalization, denial and apparently irrelevant decisions, all

International Handbook of Alcohol Dependence and Problems. Edited by N. Heather, T.J. Peters and T. Stockwell.
© 2001 John Wiley & Sons Ltd.

may represent links in the chain leading up to a relapse. A thorough analysis of a relapse experience will reveal these steps and contribute to a greater understanding of the relapse process.

RPT intervention strategies are then discussed. Specific RPT strategies are designed to address the immediate precursors of relapse and include assessment of high-risk situations and coping skills, training of new coping skills, challenging positive outcome expectancies associated with alcohol use, and coping with lapses and the abstinence violation effect. Global RPT strategies are focused on broader issues of life-style balance and awareness of covert determinants of relapse. These include an assessment and emphasis on life-style balance, coping with the desire for indulgence through substitute indulgences, coping with cravings for alcohol and urges to drink, and coping with cognitive distortions to minimize the likelihood of relapse. Finally, two empirical reviews of RPT are discussed. Both support the use of RPT as an effective treatment for alcohol problems.

THE NATURE OF RELAPSE

What is the best way to conceptualize the *maintenance stage* of habit change? One approach is to consider the maintenance stage as a period following treatment and successful abstinence or moderation, during which therapeutic effects wear off over time. In this theory of treatment decay, one would expect the risk of relapse to increase over time as treatment effects wear off. Therefore, booster sessions of alcohol treatment are typically recommended to bolster the lagging effects of the initial therapy. Relapse Prevention Therapy (RPT) provides an alternative view of the maintenance stage of habit change as an opportunity for new learning to occur. Since drinking is a learned behavior from a cognitive-behavioral point of view, the maintenance stage can be conceptualized as a time to practice "unlearning" old drinking behaviors and replacing these previously dominant responses by experimenting with new learning. Using this theoretical model, one would expect the risk of relapse to decrease over time as clients learn to avoid errors and to acquire and more firmly establish new responses related to alcohol.

In RPT, quitting drinking or exerting control over alcohol consumption is like embarking on an extended journey, with the act of departure (quitting or moderating) only the first of many steps (see discussion of stages of change in Chapter 28). If clients and therapists believe that habit change is successful once drinking has ceased or is moderated, little attention and effort will be placed on the demands of the perilous journey of maintaining change ahead. From a stages of change perspective, after a client has made a successful change in drinking behavior, usually through a series of advances and setbacks, the focus shifts to the stability of the changes achieved. In the maintenance stage, therapeutic gains from the action stage will be consolidated and clients will attempt to identify and implement strategies to avoid relapse. During the first 90 days, when rise of relapse is highest, a client must work hard to maintain his/her motivation and commitment to the ultimate goal of abstinence or sustained moderation. Research has demonstrated that most of the variance in long-term treatment outcome can be attributed to events that occur *after* the action stage, or *after* treatment has been completed (Cronkite & Moos, 1980). This research underscores the need for RPT during both the action and maintenance stages of change and the need for aftercare and social support following the termination of alcohol treatment.

Failure to maintain the changes achieved during the *action stage* of change may lead the client to the *relapse stage*. Although traditionally viewed an indication of treatment failure or the gradual extinction of treatment effects, a cognitive-behavioral view of relapse conceptualizes it as a fluid and dynamic process that is best understood as a natural transition in the habit change process. Relapse prevention and relapse management strategies are necessary at the action, maintenance and relapse stages in order for habit change to be successful in the long run. Cognitive-behavioral *relapse prevention strategies* are designed to cope with the high-risk situations that precede a slip or lapse and *relapse management strategies* are designed to prevent a slip or lapse from becoming a full-blown relapse.

Since change is a cyclical process, most clients will not be completely successful on their first attempt to alter their drinking behavior. Therefore, RPT is also designed to teach clients not to be demoralized or to view relapse as a failure, but to re-ignite their motivation and commitment to change and to risk beginning the journey again. The lessons learned from each lapse or even relapse may bring clients closer to stable maintenance if they are viewed as opportunities to learn, rather than failures, dead ends, or an indication that the disease of alcoholism is incurable.

HIGH-RISK SITUATIONS FOR RELAPSE

After a client completes treatment, he/she experiences a sense of perceived control while maintaining abstinence from drinking or a moderated level of alcohol consumption. The longer the period of successful abstinence or moderation, the greater the individual's perception of control and self-efficacy is likely to be. Abstinence or moderation will usually continue until the person encounters a *high-risk situation* or *relapse trigger*. A high-risk situation is defined as any internal or external event or factor that poses a threat to the individual's sense of perceived control or ability to cope with the immediate situation or its subjective consequences (e.g. elicitation of negative emotions).

In an analysis of 311 initial relapse episodes obtained from clients with a variety of addictive behavior problems (alcohol, smoking, heroin addiction, compulsive gambling and overeating), three high-risk situations were identified that were associated with almost three-quarters of all the relapses reported: negative emotional states, interpersonal conflict, and social pressure (Cummings et al., 1980). Overall, these high-risk factors can be more specifically divided into *intrapersonal* and *interpersonal* determinants. *Intra*personal determinants refer to those precipitating factors that do not require the presence of another person and include negative emotional states, negative physical states, positive emotional states, testing personal control and urges and temptations. *Inter*personal determinants refer to those precipitating factors that require the current or recent presence of another person and include interpersonal conflict, direct and indirect social pressure, and positive emotional states experienced in social settings.

THE RELAPSE PROCESS: THE PATH FROM HIGH-RISK SITUATIONS TO RELAPSE

If a client has learned and can implement an effective coping response to deal with a high-risk situation (e.g. assertiveness in response to direct social pressure, or relaxation to reduce anxiety and tension), the probability of relapse may decrease significantly (see Figure 29.1). The RPT model proposes that when a person copes effectively with a high-risk situation, he/she is likely to experience an increased sense of mastery and a perception of self-control or self-efficacy. The concept of *self-efficacy* (Bandura, 1977, 1997) refers to an individual's expectation concerning his/her capacity to cope effectively with a specific situation or a particular task. As the duration of abstinence or moderation increases, clients have the experience of coping effectively with one high-risk situation after

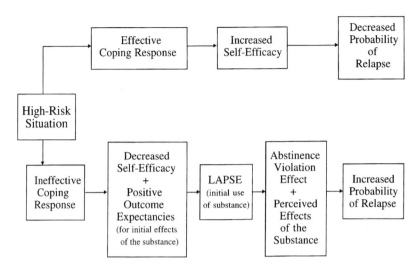

Figure 29.1   A cognitive-behavioral model of the relapse process

another. However, what happens if a client has not learned or cannot execute an effective coping response when exposed to a high-risk situation? The RPT model predicts that failure to effectively cope with a high-risk situation is likely to create decreased self-efficacy and possibly engender a sense of helplessness and powerlessness to cope with other life demands.

As self-efficacy decreases, clients are likely to focus more narrowly on the anticipated immediate positive effects of drinking, especially if they recall that alcohol helped them cope in the past. Attraction to the immediate gratification of excessive drinking becomes dominant in a person's mind and the reality of the delayed negative effects of drinking fade. Research has demonstrated that positive outcome expectancies for the effects of alcohol are potent determinants of excessive use (Marlatt & Rohsenow, 1980). The combination of being unable or unwilling to cope effectively with a high-risk situation, combined with positive outcome expectancies for the effects of drinking, greatly increases the probability of an initial lapse or slip.

After a lapse has been experienced, many clients may experience a further decrease in self-efficacy coupled with the tendency to give up trying to cope and give in to further temptations to continue to drink. To account for this reaction to the transgression of an absolute rule, we have proposed a mechanism called the *abstinence violation effect* (AVE) which is termed the *rule violation effect* (RVE) when applied more broadly to moderation as a goal (Marlatt & Gordon, 1985). The AVE is characterized by two key factors: *cognitive dissonance* (a discrepancy between one's identity as an abstainer and one's current drinking behavior) and an *attribution* of the cause of the lapse to *internal uncontrollable factors* (blaming oneself for lack of willpower). The final factor to be considered concerning the immediate determinants of relapse is the initial intoxicating effects of drinking alcohol experienced by the person following the lapse or slip. It is likely that the immediate outcome of drinking will be a "high" or euphoric state (positive reinforcement) or perhaps a reduction in any negative emotional or physical states (negative reinforcement). These initial effects of the lapse interact with the AVE to further increase the probability of relapse by priming the person to continue engaging in excessive drinking.

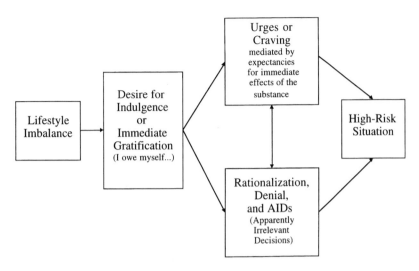

Figure 29.2   Relapse set-ups: covert antecedents of relapse situations

RELAPSE SET-UPS: COVERT ANTECEDENTS OF RELAPSE

In many, perhaps most, relapse episodes, clients report they were not expecting a high-risk situation to occur or were not well prepared to cope effectively with it when it did occur. Usually, after extensive debriefing and analysis of relapse episodes, the lapse or subsequent relapse appears to be the last link in a chain of events that preceded exposure to the high-risk situation itself. It seems as if, perhaps unknowingly, even paradoxically, the client has set him/herself up for relapse (see Figure 29.2).

Why would a person set him/herself up for relapse? The immediate gratification of drinking is a welcome relief from the relative deprivation of abstinence or the restraints of moderation and the individual may believe that it is difficult to cope with life's demands without excessive drinking. For many clients, the instant gratification of excessive drinking may outweigh the cost of any anticipated future negative consequences. Cognitive distortions, such as denial and rationalization, make it easier to set up one's own relapse episode with the added benefit of not having to take responsibility for it.

Research studies and clinical experience suggest that the degree of balance in a person's daily life has a significant impact on the desire for indulgence and immediate gratification. *Life-style imbalance* is the first covert antecedent in a chain of events that can lead to a relapse set-up. A key aspect of life-style balance is the number of daily activities perceived as required by external demands, or *shoulds*, and those activities perceived as engaged in for enjoyment and pleasure, or *wants*. If shoulds are much greater that wants, a client may experience a sense of relative self-deprivation and a corresponding *desire for indulgence* or immediate gratification. More broadly conceived, life-style balance refers to the amount of stress in a person's daily life compared with stress-reducing activities, such as social support, exercise or meditation.

Relapse set-ups are also caused by affective and cognitive processes that mask a client's actual intentions and move the client closer to a high-risk situation. Affectively, the desire for indulgence may be experienced as an urge or craving for alcohol. An urge is defined as the relatively sudden impulse to engage in a pleasurable act. Craving is defined as the sub-jective desire to experience the expected effects of a given behaviour. While the disease model of alcoholism views craving as a result of acute withdrawal or an internal physio-logical need for alcohol, the RPT model recognizes that both craving and urges may also be elicited by conditioned environmental cues associated with withdrawal or past alcohol use and that urges and cravings are mediated by the expectation of immediate pleasure or reduced pain associated with drinking (Rohsenow et al., 1994).

In addition to affective processes, covert antecedents of a relapse episode are influ-enced by three cognitive factors: rationalization, denial, and apparently irrelevant decisions (AIDs), which are associated with the chain of events preceding exposure to a high-risk situation. A *rationalization* is an explanation or an seemingly legitimate excuse to engage in drinking behaviour. *Denial* is a similar defense mechanism in which an individual will deny the existence of any motive to engage in a drinking and may also deny awareness of the delayed negative consequences of resuming excessive drinking. Both rationalization and denial are cognitive distortions that occur with little awareness and may promote a client's covert planning of exposure to a high-risk situation. AIDs stand for a number of mini-decisions made over time, each of which seems innocent or irrelevant to relapsing in and of itself (e.g. a man decides to visit his old friends at the neighborhood bar) but in com-bination bring the client closer to exposure to a relapse triggering high-risk situation. One of the primary goals of RPT is to train clients to recognize *early warning signs* that precede exposure to a high-risk situation, and to execute intervention strategies before it is too late to do anything and the temptations in the high-risk situation become too compelling to resist.

RPT INTERVENTION STRATEGIES

RPT intervention strategies represent a menu of treatment alternatives aimed at both the immediate and covert aspects of relapse that can be individually tailored to various clini-cal populations, to particular addictive behaviors including alcohol dependence, and to dif-ferent treatment settings. These strategies can be grouped into three categories: coping skills training, cognitive therapy and life-style modification. *Coping skills training strategies* include behavioral and cognitive techniques to effectively cope with high-risk situations and to enhance self-efficacy. *Cognitive therapy* procedures are designed to provide clients with ways of reframing the habit change process (i.e. to view it as a learning process and as a journey), to correcting cognitive distortions and to introduce coping imagery to deal with urges and craving. Finally, *life-style modification* strategies (e.g. meditation, exercise, spiritual practices) are designed to strengthen the client's global coping capacity and to reduce the frequency and intensity of the desire for indulgence and the experience of urges and craving.

Initially, RPT assessment and intervention strategies are designed to teach clients to anticipate and cope with the possibility of relapse. Clients are taught to recognize and cope with high-risk situations that may precipitate a lapse and to modify cognitions and other reactions to prevent a single lapse from developing into a full-blown relapse. Because these procedures are focused on the immediate precipitants of the relapse process, they are referred to collectively as *specific intervention strategies* (Figure 29.3). As clients master these techniques, clinical practice extends beyond a microanalysis of the relapse process and the initial lapse and involves strategies designed to modify the client's life-style and to identify and cope with covert determinants of relapse (early warning signals, cognitive dis-tortions and relapse set-ups). As a group, these procedures are called *global intervention strategies*.

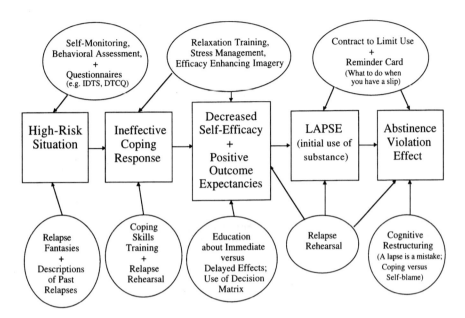

Figure 29.3 Specific relapse prevention therapy intervention strategies

SPECIFIC RPT INTERVENTION STRATEGIES

Assessment of High-risk Situations

Autobiographies

One of the first homework assignments in RPT is for clients to write a brief autobiography describing the history and development of their alcohol problem. Clients are asked to focus on their subjective image of themselves as they progressed through the stages of habit acquisition leading to alcohol abuse or dependence. The following points are emphasized: a description of parental and extended family alcohol and drug use habits, a description of the first episode of drinking to drunkenness, the role of alcohol and drugs in the client's adult life up to the present, factors associated with any increases in the severity of the client's drinking problem, the self-image of the client as a drinker, and any previous attempts to quit or moderate on one's own or with the assistance of treatment. The purpose of this technique is to identify high-risk situations and to get a baseline assessment of the client's self-image while engaging in excessive drinking. Clients are also asked to write a brief essay describing their future as an ex-drinker or a moderate drinker.

Past Relapses

Most clients in treatment will have tried either on their own or in previous treatment to abstain from alcohol or moderate their use. Asking clients to describe past relapses may provide important clues to future high-risk situations and deficits in coping skills. The therapist and the client can classify the descriptions of past relapses into the categories previously presented in order to determine the situational or personal factors that had the greatest impact. It is also useful to determine the client's attitude toward these past "failures" to remain abstinent or to drink moderately, because many clients develop negative attitudes toward future change attempts, based on attributions that they have a deficit in willpower or self-control. *Cognitive reframing* of past relapses will be necessary to reduce the client's fear of the prospect of yet another failure. The therapist can encourage the client to attribute past relapses as due to a lack of skill or effort, not to immutable internal factors.

Relapse Fantasies

This guided imagery technique involves asking the client to imagine as vividly as possible what it would take to resume drinking. Clients are asked to repeat this technique either in a therapy session or on his/her own as homework for as many possible relapse scenarios as he/she can envision. If a client denies that relapse is a possibility or has difficulty using his/her imagination, the therapist and client can brainstorm together, perhaps using any past relapses as a guide. Questionnaire techniques to be described below can also be used to gain a better understanding of a client's unique profile of high-risk situations.

Self-Monitoring

When clients who are still drinking alcohol or using drugs enter therapy, prior to quitting they are asked to self-monitor their use on a daily basis by keeping track of drinking, the situational context in which it occurs, and the immediate consequences of the behaviour. In most cases, RPT programs are initiated after abstinence or moderation has been achieved by some means. In this situation, self-monitoring of tempting high-risk situations for excessive drinking is a useful technique. Clients are asked to keep track of exposure to situations or personal factors that cause them to have urges or craving to resume drinking excessively.

Questionnaires for Assessing High-risk Situations

The *Inventory of Drug-Taking Situations (IDTS)* developed by Annis, Turner & Sklar (1997b) is a 50-item self-report questionnaire which provides a profile of a client's high-risk situations by measuring those circumstances in which a client has used alcohol heavily in the past year. Clients are asked to indicate their frequency of heavy drinking in each of 50 specific situations. The eight high-risk categories previously described are divided into three areas: *negative situations* (unpleasant emotions, physical discomfort, conflict with others), *positive situations* (pleasant times with others, pleasant emotions), and *temptation situations* (urges and temptations, social pressure to use, testing personal control). Research has documented the utility of the IDTS as a reliable and valid instrument for helping therapists and clients recognize situations in which the client has had alcohol problems in the past and to begin working on acquiring coping skills specific to those situations.

Another excellent tool for assessing a client's specific high-risk situations and coping deficits is the *Substance Abuse Relapse Assessment* (SARA) (Schonfeld, Peters & Dolente, 1993). This structured interview technique based on the RPT model yields the frequency and pattern of substance use for the 30 days preceding the last use of the substance; has the client describe the antecedents of substance abuse including places, activities and companions; assesses coping skills; identifies the most problematic substance in the client's lifetime; identifies the consequences of substance use; and, in a final section, describes the client's responses to previous slips or lapses. SARA also provides the client and therapist with instructions on how to develop an individualized substance abuse behavior chain.

Assessing Coping Skills

The Situational Competency Test (SCT)

The SCT is a role-play technique developed by Chaney, O'Leary & Marlatt (1978), requiring clients to give a verbal response to a series of high-risk situations presented by a narrator on audio tape. The client is presented with a series of high-risk scenarios drawn from the categories of high-risk situations previously described. In the initial use of the SCT, four scoring measures were used: *latency, duration, compliance* and *specification of new behavior. Latency* is defined as the elapsed time from the termination of the recorded situation to the beginning of the subject's verbal response. *Response duration* is taken as the frequency of words in the response. *Compliance* is a dichotomous score indicating whether or not the subject gave in to the situation without attempting to engage in an alternative coping response.

Specification of new behavior is also a dichotomous score indicating whether the description of the problem-solving behavior or coping response was given in enough detail for someone else to be able to use the description as a guide to perform the behavior. This technique is a good way to assess coping skills deficits and to begin the process of coping skills training.

Coping Skills Training

Stimulus Control

This behavioral technique is particularly important in the early phase of the maintenance stage of habit change, before self-efficacy has increased and before new, more effective coping skills for handling high-risk situations have been learned. The situational cues previously associated with drinking are likely to create craving, urges and temptations to resume the old pattern of excessive alcohol consumption. Several stimulus control strategies can be easily learned and applied while more extensive coping skills training is under way. The first option is *avoidance* of those high-risk situations that have been identified in the assessment as having the highest problem potential. While this my not be practical in all cases, there are many situations that can be avoided with some forethought and vigilance. Where avoidance is not possible, or when a high-risk situation appears to occur unexpectedly, *escape* is the next best option. Some preparation may be necessary to prepare a client with escape plans for the most probable high-risk situations. Finally, if neither avoidance or escape is possible, *delay* of action may be a final stop-gap measure to buy time until escape is possible.

Coping Skills

Once the high-risk situations have been identified, the client can then be taught to respond to these situational cues as discriminative stimuli ("highway signs") for behavior change. The cornerstone of the RPT approach to maintaining behavior change is *coping skills training* (e.g. Chaney, O'Leary & Marlatt, 1978). For clients whose coping responses are blocked by fear or anxiety, the therapist should attempt to disinhibit the behavior through an appropriate anxiety-reduction procedure, such as systematic desensitization or general relaxation training. For clients who show deficiencies in their coping skills repertoire, however, the therapist attempts to teach them new coping skills, using a systematic and structured approach. The RPT approach combines training in general problem-solving ability with specific skill training focused on the client's unique challenges and resources. Adopting a problem-solving orientation to stressful situations (D'Zurilla & Goldfried, 1971) gives clients greater flexibility and adaptability in new problem situations, rather than having to rely solely on the rote learning of a number of discrete skills that may or may not generalize across various settings and situations. Coping skills training methods incorporate components of direct instruction, modeling, behavioral rehearsal, therapist coaching and feedback from the therapist.

Relapse Rehearsal

Sometimes a therapist and a client can do coping skills training *in vivo*, in which the therapist accompanies the client while he/she is exposed to high-risk situations in real-life settings. However, the therapist can also make use of imagery or role-plays to represent the high-risk situation. This procedure, called *relapse rehearsal*, is similar to the relapse fantasy technique mentioned earlier. In the relapse rehearsal procedure, the therapist goes beyond the imagined scenario of relapse to include scenes in which the client can imagine or practice engaging in appropriate coping responses. This behavioral procedure, known as covert modeling, can also be used to help clients cope with their reactions to a lapse. Relapse rehearsal can be extended into a role-playing procedure, either in individual therapy or in the context of RPT group work.

Stress Management

In addition to teaching the clients to respond effectively when confronted with specific high-risk situations, there are a number of additional relaxation training and stress management procedures the therapist can draw upon to increase the client's overall capacity to cope. Relaxation training may provide the client with an increased perception of control overall, thereby reducing the stress "load" that any given situation may pose for the individual. Such procedures as progressive muscle relaxation training, meditation, exercise and various stress management techniques are extremely useful in aiding the client to cope more effectively with the hassles and demands of daily life.

Assessing Self-efficacy

The *Drug-Taking Confidence Questionnaire* (DTCQ) (Annis, Sklar & Turner, 1997a) is available to measure a client's confidence in avoiding heavy drinking or drug use across the same eight high-risk categories and 50 specific risk situations included in the IDTS. Clients using the DTCQ are asked to imagine themselves in each of the 50 risky situations and to indicate on an accompanying scale how confident they are that they would be able to resist the urge to drink heavily or use a specific drug. Studies of clients' confidence in coping with risky situations have found that clients are less likely to relapse in situations where they have a high level of confidence in their ability to cope. The DTCQ allows therapists to gauge a client's self-efficacy in coping with high-risk situations at different stages in the treatment process, providing a measure of the client's progress.

Enhancing Self-efficacy

In terms of the relapse prevention model, *self-efficacy* refers to the judgments or expectations about one's capacity to cope with specific high-risk situations. Until a high-risk situation is encountered, there is little threat to this perception of control, since urges and temptations are minimal or absent. If a coping response is successfully performed, the individual's judgment of efficacy will be strengthened for coping with similar situations as they arise on subsequent occasions. Guided imagery can be used to enhance efficacy in a manner similar to relapse rehearsal. In this procedure, the therapist gently guides the client who is experiencing anxiety or having trouble generating successful coping strategies with subtle prompts that can later be internalized by the client. Efficacy-enhancing imagery is used to augment coping skills training and to assess the client's current level of self-efficacy and coping skills mastery.

Challenging Positive Outcome Expectancies

Positive outcome expectancies for the immediate effects of alcohol play an influential role in the relapse process. As a reminder of its potent effects, this phenomenon is called the *problem of immediate gratification* or *PIG*. The image of a hungry and insatiable PIG provides clients with a vivid reminder of the costs of impulsive consumption. Education about both the immediate and delayed effects of alcohol use may help offset the tendency to exaggerate the positive effects of drinking and to minimize its negative effects. A decision matrix can be an important resource to reduce the PIG phenomenon and the myopia of having outcome expectancies that focus only on the immediate positive effects of drinking. The decision matrix cells concerning both immediate and long-term effects of drinking or not drinking can serve as a potent reminder that alcohol use has its costs.

Coping with Lapses and the AVE

The occurrence of a lapse, while not a catastrophe, cannot be viewed as a totally harmless event. It is a moment of crisis that combines both danger and opportunity, with the most dangerous period immediately following the slip. There are several recommended strategies, or *relapse emergency procedures*, to employ whenever a lapse occurs. These can be presented to clients in summary form by the use of a *reminder card* that should be kept handy in the event that a lapse occurs. Since specific coping strategies will vary from client to client, therapists may wish to help a particular client prepare an individualized reminder card that fits that person's unique set of vulnerabilities and resources.

The following strategies for coping with lapse and the AVE are adapted from *Relapse Prevention* (Marlatt & Gordon, 1985):

1. *Stop, look and listen.* The first thing to do when a lapse occurs is to *stop* the ongoing flow of events and to *look* and *listen* to what is happening. The lapse is a warning signal indicating that you are in danger.
2. *Keep calm.* The first reaction to a lapse may be one of feeling guilty and blaming oneself for what has happened. This is a normal reaction and is to be expected. Give yourself enough time to allow this reaction to arise and to pass away, just like an ocean wave that builds in strength, peaks at a crest, and then ebbs away.
3. *Renew your commitment.* After a lapse, the most difficult problem to deal with is motivation. You may feel like giving up. Think back over the reasons why you decided to change your behavior in the first place. Renew your commitment.
4. *Review the situation leading up to the lapse.* Don't yield to the tendency to blame yourself for what happened. Instead, look at the slip as a specific unique event. Ask yourself the following questions. What events led up to the slip? Were there any early

warning signals that preceded the lapse? What was the nature of the high-risk situation that triggered the slip?

5. *Implement your plan for recovery.* After a slip, you must turn your renewed commitment into a plan of action to be carried out immediately. First, get rid of all alcohol or other stimuli associated with drinking. Second, remove yourself from the high-risk situation if at all possible. If necessary, find an alternative means of gratifying your need for satisfactions.

6. *Ask for help.* Make it easier on yourself if you find that you need help: ask for it! Ask your friends who are present to help in any way they can. If you are alone, call your therapist or AA sponsor and seek out their assistance and support. If you know about a crisis center, give them a call for assistance.

After the lapse has occurred, the client should be reassured that the therapist or RPT group will not censure or blame him/her for the mistake, as often occurs in traditional programs. Instead, clients should receive compassion and understanding, along with encouragement to learn everything possible about how to cope with similar situations in the future through a thorough debriefing of the lapse and its consequences. Clients are taught to review the details of the of the events and thoughts that led to the high-risk situation, to develop and practice new coping responses that are likely to be more effective in future situations, and to reframe their reactions to the slip as an error that is correctable with effort on their part and not as a sign of failure or moral weakness.

GLOBAL RPT INTERVENTION STRATEGIES

Providing clients with behavioral coping skills training and cognitive strategies to effectively cope with high-risk situations and lapses is vital to the success of any relapse prevention program. However, simply teaching clients to cope with one high-risk situation after another is not enough for long-term success in habit change. Even if every situation could be identified, teaching the client to cope effectively with each situation is likely to be time consuming and inefficient. In addition, the coping skills training and cognitive therapy procedures previously described are, by necessity, specific to the situations encountered and their unique cognitive and emotional consequences. In order to develop a more comprehensive and effective program of habit change, it is necessary to: (a) help the clients develop a more balanced life-style in order to increase their overall capacity to cope with stress, as well as incrementally to increase self-efficacy; and (b) teach clients how to identify and anticipate the early warning signals that preceded exposure to high-risk situations and to implement coping strategies designed to reduce the probability of a lapse or a relapse (Figure 29.4).

Assessment of Lifestyle Balance

As stated earlier, the degree of balance or imbalance in a person's daily life has a significant impact on the desire for indulgence and immediate gratification. The first step in applying global RPT intervention strategies is to assess the client's quality of life with a focus on areas of life-style imbalance. A good place to start assessing life-style balance is by paying attention to the areas of life previously mentioned by the client. Areas to explore include, but are not limited to: physical health, including chronic illness; exercise and nutrition; psychological health, including co-occurring psychological conditions, such as DSM-IV Axis I disorders and DSM-IV Axis II disorders; interpersonal factors, including family

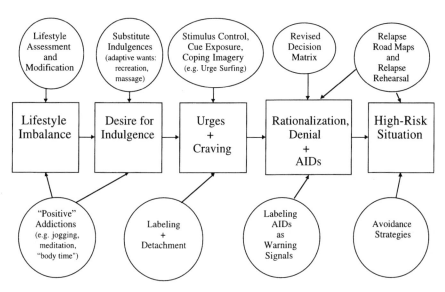

Figure 29.4 Global relapse prevention therapy intervention strategies

dynamics and the extent and quality of other social support; employment, including job satisfaction and security; the client's current financial situation, including savings and debt; and the client's spiritual beliefs and practices. In addition to clinical interviews, two life-style questionnaires designed for use in substance abuse treatment are available: *The Health and Daily Living Form* and the *Lifestyle Assessment Questionnaire* (Murphy & Impara, 1996). Both instruments can be used as therapist-administered structured interviews or as self-report questionnaires.

Increasing Life-style Balance

Once life-style imbalance has been assessed and its implications have been thoroughly discussed with the client, a comprehensive self-management program to improve the client's overall life-style and to increase his/her capacity to cope with the experience of more pervasive stress factors is begun. Life-style modification procedures are designed to identify and circumvent the covert antecedents of relapse that set-up exposure to high-risk situations and to promote life-long habit change to create greater mental, emotional, physical and spiritual well being.

The specific life-style modifications recommended in the RPT approach depend on the client's unique needs and abilities. A program of exercise, meditation, enhanced social activities, or weekly massages to reduce muscle tension are among the many possibilities. Some clients are simply encouraged to create some time and space in their daily routine for discretionary activities to reduce stress and enhance pleasure.

Coping with the Desire for Indulgence: Substitute Indulgences

As life-style imbalance is likely to create a desire for indulgence, one effective strategy is to search for activities that might be *substitute indulgences* that are not harmful or addictive. In this regard, Glasser (1974) has described behaviors such as excessive drinking and drug abuse as negative addictions that initially feel good, but produce long-term harm. Conversely, Glasser describes "positive addictions" (e.g. running, meditation, hiking, hobbies) as producing short-term discomfort or even pain while creating long-term benefits to physical health and to psychological well-being. Positive addictions often become wants as clients begin to gain mastery and look forward to engaging in these activities as a source of pleasure. An added benefit of positive addictions is that they often involve developing new skills and social relationships, which may increase a person's self-efficacy and create social networks with peers who model and support a healthy life-style.

Coping with Craving for Alcohol and Urges to Drink

Stimulus Control

Despite one's best attempts to modify life-style and to learn and practice positive addictions and substitute indulgences, occasional urges and cravings do arise. Quite often, urges and craving are conditioned responses triggered by external cues, such as the sight of others engaged in drinking. The frequency of these externally triggered urges and craving can be reduced by using *stimulus control techniques* designed to minimize exposure to these cues. In some circumstances, simply avoiding the situation is the best strategy. Using a highway metaphor for habit change, avoidance strategies can serve as an *emergency detour* allowing the client to escape exposure by a last-minute defensive maneuver. Later, when coping skills are better learned and more effective, it may be less dangerous to venture down that high-risk road. In any case, viable avoidance strategies may serve a person well for a time and enhance his/her sense of self-efficacy and personal choice while more sophisticated coping strategies are being learned.

Cue Exposure

Stimulus control techniques such as avoidance are at best short-term solutions to the challenges posed by urges and craving. Eventually, the client will have to learn and master effective techniques to cope with these tempting situations. One emerging approach in this regard is *cue exposure* (Drummond et al., 1995). Traditional treatment programs do everything they can to minimize or eliminate all tempting stimuli from the protected environment of the therapeutic setting. Without preparation or warning, exposure to cues associated with addictive behaviors can be an overwhelming and discouraging experience and is often interpreted by the client as an indication that the treatment has failed or that treatment effects have worn off. Cue exposure treatments administered in either analog situations or *in vivo* can assist clients to avoid lapse when they cannot avoid drinking cues.

Coping Imagery

In addition to contemporary approaches, such as cue exposure, it is often helpful when teaching clients to cope with urges and craving to emphasize that the discomfort and agitation associated with these conditioned internal sensations is expected and natural. Most people have the mistaken idea that once an urge or craving begins, it will increase in intensity until drinking occurs. In helping clients to cope with the seemingly overwhelming power of growing urges and craving, it is helpful to teach them that these conditioned responses will rise in intensity, reach a peak, and then subside. In this respect, urges and craving can be compared to waves on the ocean; they rise, they crest, and then they fall, in a repeated cycle. *Urge surfing* uses the wave metaphor to help clients gain control over these seemingly unmanageable events. The client is taught to label these urges or craving as an ocean wave that reaches a peak, crests, and then subsides. Clients visualize learning to "ride the wave" through the peak experience of craving to its eventual decline. Clients are initially taught the urge surfing technique through guided imagery and then encouraged to try it on their own whenever they are exposed to alcohol cues.

Self-monitoring

Another way to foster detachment and disidentification with urges and craving is to have clients use *self-monitoring procedures* to keep track of these experiences. The *craving diary* is a technique used in a number of RPT programs to gain information and to help cope with craving. The client is asked to keep track of the internal and external cues that stimulated a craving, his/her mood, the strength of the craving, how long it lasted, coping skills used, and how successful or unsuccessful these coping strategies were.

Craving Cards

Just as a reminder card is used to automate the client's emergency response to a lapse, *craving cards* are designed to help clients cope with intense urges and cravings at a time when they may have trouble generating adaptive thoughts and behavioral coping skills. These cards include both general and specific suggestions for how the client can survive an urge and craving emergency without a lapse. A sample card might include tips on recognizing and labeling cravings, brief instructions for relaxation techniques, positive self-statements that encourage continued abstinence, tips on how to use distraction and incompatible responses, an abbreviated decision balance sheet, and emergency escape directions, including phone numbers of individuals willing to offer social support.

Coping with Cognitive Distortions

Urges and cravings usually do not operate at a conscious level, but are likely to be masked by the cognitive distortions and defense mechanisms described in the discussion of covert antecedents of high-risk situations. As such, these dimly perceived sensations and strong emotions fueled with forbidden desires set-up the possibility of relapse by allowing for *apparently irrelevant decisions* (AIDs) to bring the person closer to exposure to a high-risk situation. Teaching clients to become vigilant for these early warning signals and to engage in explicit self-talk that questions their motivations and intentions can help them to recognize and acknowledge the direct relevance of these AIDs to the increased risk of relapse. By acknowledging to oneself that these mini-decisions actually represent urges and craving to return to excessive drinking, one is better able to recognize them as early warning signals on the road to relapse. Deliberately labeling the true nature of urges and craving before they motivate apparently irrelevant decisions is a good way to foster detachment and a stronger sense of self-efficacy.

EMPIRICAL SUPPORT FOR
RELAPSE PREVENTION THERAPY

In this section, we will described two recent reviews which provide evidence for the therapeutic efficacy of treatments derived from the RPT model in their ability to effectively help clients overcome alcohol dependence and other addictive behavioral problems.

Carroll (1996) reviewed more than 24 randomized controlled trials evaluating the effectiveness of RPT as a psychosocial treatment for substance abuse. Her selection criteria included "only those randomized controlled trials that evaluated a treatment approach defined as *relapse prevention* or evaluated a coping skills approach that explicitly invoked the work of Marlatt" (Carroll, 1996, p. 46). After reviewing these studies, Carroll concluded:

> Across different substances of abuse, there is evidence for the effectiveness on substance use outcomes for relapse prevention over no-treatment control conditions, mixed findings when compared with attention and discussion control conditions, and findings that relapse prevention appears comparable, but not better than, other active treatments. (Carroll, 1996, p. 51).

In her review, Carroll (1996) discusses three areas that emerged as having particular promise for the effective application of RPT. First, Carroll notes that while RPT may not always prevent relapse better than other active treatments, several investigations suggest that RPT is more effective than available alternatives in relapse management (i.e. reducing the intensity of lapse episodes if they do occur). Second, numerous studies, especially those comparing RPT to other psychotherapies, have found RPT to be particularly effective at maintaining treatment effects over long-term follow-up measurement. In addition, Carroll's review suggests the presence of what she calls "delayed emergence of effects for relapse prevention", in which clients actually improve in coping ability over time (Carroll, 1996, p. 52). Finally, Carroll (1996) suggests that relapse prevention may be most effective "for more impaired substance abusers, including those with more severe levels of substance abuse, greater levels of negative affect, and greater perceived deficits in coping skills" (Carroll, 1996, p. 52).

Narrative reviews of substance abuse treatment studies, such as the one by Carroll (1996), serve a useful purpose for both researchers and clinicians, but conclusions from descriptive analysis are not readily quantified and may be subject to various interpretations. On the other hand, *meta-analytic reviews* of treatment outcome studies use statistical techniques to measure and quantify treatment effects, allowing more precise comparisons and conclusions regarding the relative effectiveness of different treatment alternatives (Lipsey & Wilson, 1993). A meta-analytic review of the efficacy of Relapse Prevention Therapy has been recently completed and will be summarized below.

Irvin, Bowers, Dunn & Wang (1999) selected 17 controlled studies with 72 hypotheses in order to evaluate the overall effectiveness of RPT as a substance abuse treatment and to identify moderator variables that may reliably impact the outcome of treatment. Six moderator variables were studied: treatment modality; theoretical orientation of prior therapy delivered before relapse prevention; treatment setting; type of outcome measure used to determine effectiveness; medication as an adjunct to relapse prevention; and finally, type of substance use disorder treated by the RPT interventions.

In their discussion of the results of the meta-analytic review of RPT outcome studies, Irvin et al. (1999) conclude that "relapse prevention is highly effective for both alcohol-use and substance-use disorders". They go on to say that the effect size for this finding was significant and the available evidence indicates the overall effectiveness of RPT as a substance abuse treatment for both habit cessation and maintenance. Additionally, relapse prevention appears to be most effective when applied to alcohol or poly-substance use disorders, combined with adjunctive use of medications, and when evaluated immediately following treatment using uncontrolled pre–post tests (Irvin et al., 1999). These two treatment outcome reviews provide encouraging evidence on the effectiveness of RPT as a treatment for alcohol problems. Overall, RPT appears to be a promising intervention for use in alcohol and substance abuse treatment.

KEY WORKS AND SUGGESTIONS FOR FURTHER READING

Marlatt, G.A. & Gordon, J.R. (1985). *Relapse Prevention: Maintenance Strategies in the Treatment of Addictive Behaviors.* New York: Guilford.

Part I of this book presents a detailed exposition of the relapse prevention model that forms the basis of RPT. Part II presents application of RPT with specific addictive behaviors such as alcohol, smoking, and weight control. This is still the most complete presentation of RPT in print.

Wanigaratne, S., Wallace, W., Pullin, J., Keaney, F. & Farmer R. (1990). *Relapse Prevention for Addictive Behaviors: A Manual for Therapists.*

This manual is a practical introductory guide to conducting RPT with any type of addictive behavior. Written in a clear and engaging style, it presents an overview of the relapse prevention model as well as descriptions of how to implement both specific and global RPT interventions for individuals or groups.

Annis, H.M., Herie, M.A. & Watkin-Merek, L. (1996). *Structured Relapse Prevention: An Outpatient Counselling Approach.* Toronto: Addiction Research Foundation of Ontario.

A treatment manual and videotape developed by Helen Annis and her colleagues at the Addiction Research Foundation that presents a systematic protocol for use in outpatient settings. The five major components of SRP include assessment, motivational interviewing, treatment planning, initiation of change and maintenance of change.

Annis, H.M., Turner, N.E. & Sklar, S.M. (1997). *IDTS: Inventory of Drug-Taking Situations.* Toronto: Addiction Research Foundation of Ontario.

This manual provides guidelines for using the IDTS, which assesses a client's most problematic triggers for relapse based on the taxonomy of high-risk situations developed by Marlatt. The IDTS is available as a paper and pencil questionnaire or as computerized software.

Swanson, J. & Cooper, A. (1994). *The Complete Relapse Prevention Skills Program.*

This program based on the RPT model offers clinicians and clients a package of user-friendly yet sophisticated tools to prevent and manage relapse. The program includes an integrated set of clinician's guides as well as client pamphlets, workbooks and videotapes.

Roberts, L.J., Shaner, A. & Eckman, T. (1999). *Overcoming Addictions: Skills Training for People with Schizophrenia.*

A therapist manual with accompanying video offering a step-by-step approach to RPT with clients presenting with co-occurring substance use and mental disorders. The best resource currently available for RPT coping skills training.

REFERENCES

Annis, H.M., Sklar, S.M. & Turner, N.E. (1997a). *DTCQ—Drug-Taking Confidence Questionnaire.* Toronto: Addiction Research Foundation of Ontario.
Annis, H.M., Turner, N.E. & Sklar, S.M. (1997b). *IDTS—Inventory of Drug-Taking Situations.* Toronto: Addiction Research Foundation of Ontario.

Bandura, A. (1977). Self-efficacy: toward a unifying theory of behavioral change. *Psychological Review*, **84**, 191–215.

Bandura, A. (1997). *Self-Efficacy: The Exercise of Control*. San Francisco, CA: W.H. Freeman.

Carroll, K.M. (1996). Relapse prevention as a psychosocial treatment: a review of controlled clinical trials. *Experimental and Clinical Psychopharmacology*, **4**(1), 46–54.

Chaney, E.F., O'Leary, M.R. & Marlatt, G.A. (1978). Skill training with alcoholics. *Journal of Consulting and Clinical Psychology*, **46**, 1092–1104.

Cronkite, R. & Moos, R. (1980). The determinants of post-treatment functioning of alcoholic patients: a conceptual framework. *Journal of Consulting and Clinical Psychology*, **48**, 305–316.

Cummings, C., Gordon, J.R. & Marlatt, G.A. (1980). Relapse: strategies of prevention and prediction. In W.R. Miller (Ed.), *The Addictive Behaviors*, Oxford: Pergamon.

Drummond, D.C., Tiffany, S.T., Glautier, S. & Remington, B. (1995). *Addictive Behaviour: Cue Exposure Theory and Practice*. Chichecter: Wiley.

D'Zurilla, T.J. & Goldfried, •• (1971). Problem solving and behavior modification. *Journal of Abnormal Psychology*, **78**, 107–126.

Glasser, W. (1974). *Positive Addictions*. New York: Harper and Row.

Irvine, J.E., Bowers, C.A., Dunn, M.E. & Wang, M.C. (1999). Efficacy of relapse prevention: a meta-analytic reviews. *Journal of Consulting and Clinical Psychology*, **67**(4), 563–570.

Lipsey, M. & Wilson, D.B. (1993). The efficacy of psychological, educational, and behavioral treatment: confirmation from meta-analysis. *American Psychologist*, **48**(12), 1181–1209.

Marlatt, G.A. (1978). Craving for alcohol, loss of control, and relapse: a cognitive-behavioral analysis. In P.E. Nathan, G.A. Marlatt & T. Loberg (Ed.), *Alcoholism: New Directions in Behavioral Research and Treatment*. New York: Plenum.

Marlatt, G.A. & Gordon, J.R. (Ed.) (1985). *Relapse Prevention: Maintenance Strategies in the Treatment of Addictive Behaviors*. New York: Guilford.

Marlatt, G.A. & Parks, G.A. (1982). Self-Management of addictive behaviors. In F.H. Kanfer & P. Karoly (Ed.), *Self-Management of Behavior Change: From Theory to Practice* (pp. 443–488). New York: Pergamon.

Marlatt, G.A. & Rohsenow, D.J. (1980). Cognitive processes in alcohol use: expectancy and the balanced placebo design. In N.K. Mello (Ed.), *Advances in Substance Abuse*, Vol. 1. Greenwich, CT: JAI Press.

Murphy, L.L. & Impara, J.C. (1996). *Buros Desk Reference to Assessment of Substance Abuse*. Lincoln, NE: University of Nebraska Press.

Rohsenow, D.J., Monti, P.M., Rubonis, A.V., Sirota, A.D., Niaura, R.S., Colby, S.M., Wunschel, S.M. & Abrams, D.B. (1994). Cue reactivity as a predictor of drinking among male alcoholics. *Journal of Consulting and Clinical Psychology*, **62**, 620–626.

Schonfeld, L., Peters, R.H. & Dolente, A.S. (1993). *SARA—Substance Abuse Relapse Assessment*. Odessa, FL: Psychological Assessment Resources Inc.

Chapter 30

Motivational Interviewing

Stephen Rollnick
*Department of General Practice, University of Wales College
of Medicine, Cardiff, UK
and*
Jeff Allison
Jeff Allison Training Consultancy, Edinburgh, UK

Synopsis

This chapter begins with the context in which motivational interviewing was developed: the often conflict-ridden encounters in alcohol counselling in which poor motivation, denial and resistance were viewed as ingrained qualities of clients themselves. A psychologist trained in client-centred counselling, William R. Miller, developed the hypothesis that the way clients were spoken to could either enhance or minimize motivation to change. The method that emerged provided counsellors with the skills to reduce resistance and explore the uncertainty about change (ambivalence) so common among problem drinkers. It is guided by the notion that motivation to change should not be imposed from without, in the form of counsellor arguments for change, but elicited from within the client. This chapter outlines the practice of motivational interviewing, starting with three central concepts—readiness, ambivalence and resistance. It then turns to the principles and three core skill areas—empathic listening, eliciting self-motivating statements and responding to resistance. The chapter concludes with a brief review of research evidence and a discussion of the opportunities and limitations of motivational interviewing.

Every therapist knows that motivation is a vital element of change. Nowhere is this clearer than in the treatment of addictive behaviours, which are, if one thinks about it, fundamentally motivational problems. Addictive behaviours are by definition highly motivated, in that they persist against an accumulating tide of aversive consequences. When one continues to act despite great personal risk and cost, something is overriding common sense. In the context of war, we call it bravery or heroism. In the context of pleasure, we call it addiction (Miller, 1998).

It is a common experience for alcohol counsellors to sigh at the inability of clients to change their lives. Conversations about them abound with frustration—about the hardships they

---

International Handbook of Alcohol Dependence and Problems. Edited by N. Heather, T.J. Peters and T. Stockwell.

face in the outside world and about difficult encounters in the consulting room. Traditionally, lack of progress in alcohol treatment has been attributed to client failings, with lack of motivation often seen as the main culprit. The counsellor, often with a clear sense of where the client is going wrong, tries to steer the person in the right direction. The response is often passivity, disagreement or outright denial.

Motivational interviewing presents the counsellor with a quite different perspective: low motivation is not just a client problem but a shifting state that is very sensitive to the behaviour of the counsellor. Progress in counselling is more likely to occur if the client is given room to breathe, if motivation to change is not imposed from without, but elicited from within in an atmosphere free of conflict. How these tasks are achieved is the subject of this chapter, the principal aims of which are to describe the origins and content of motivational interviewing and to briefly consider some new directions for practice and research.

THE ORIGINS OF MOTIVATIONAL INTERVIEWING

When a client says, ". . . you don't seem to understand, it's not just the alcohol, it's my marriage as well . . .", how should a counsellor respond? How might the counsellor influence the course of the conversation to the satisfaction of both parties?

It was questions like these that were asked by a group of clinicians in the early 1980s in seminars with William R. Miller in Bergen, Norway. The answers pointed to something which was quite different to everyday practice in addiction treatment at the time, particularly in North America: instead of attributing client resistance and poor motivation to the client, Miller, a client-centred psychotherapist, suggested that a confrontational interviewing style could enhance and reinforce these problems. Stated positively, *the counsellor could use empathic listening to minimize resistance and increase motivation for change.* What emerged was an outline of motivational interviewing (Miller, 1983) which must have struck a chord in the field. Ten to 15 years later, this variant of client-centred counselling had become one of the most popular approaches to the treatment of alcohol problems. The method was subsequently revised and enlarged (Miller & Rollnick, 1991), a research base emerged, and attempts were made to adapt the method to other client groups and settings. There are numerous unanswered questions about the effective ingredients of motivational interviewing and its relation to other treatment approaches. Nevertheless, its central principle, that motivation to change should be elicited from people, not somehow imposed on them, has clearly proved useful in a treatment culture with a history of sometimes coercive solutions to the problem of the unmotivated problem drinker.

THE DEFINITION AND SPIRIT OF MOTIVATIONAL INTERVIEWING

Motivational interviewing has been described as a counselling *style* (Rollnick & Miller, 1995). Matters of technique have thus been rendered secondary to an *atmosphere of constructive conversation about behaviour change*, in which the counsellor uses empathic listening initially to understand the client's perspective and minimize resistance. Upon this foundation of non-confrontational interviewing, strategies and techniques are used to explore the person's value system and its relation to the addictive problem, and to elicit motivation from the client. Since so many clients feel intense *ambivalence* about change, working with this conflict in a constructive way often becomes the central focus.

This activity is not viewed as equivalent to non-directive counselling; it also involves being directive. Counsellors need to provide clear structure to the session. They frequently also have a clear view about what direction they would like the client to take. Typically this involves gently coaching the client to explore the conflicts and contradictions so prevalent in addiction problems. By summarizing these for the client, and giving the person room to reflect, it is assumed that motivation to change is more likely to be enhanced. The definition of motivational interviewing provided by Rollnick & Miller (1995) is: *a directive, client-centred counselling style for helping clients explore and resolve ambivalence about behaviour change.* Before turning to the more technical "how to" aspects of motivational interviewing, the use of this counselling style will be illustrated with reference to three concepts that have guided the development of the method. Awareness of them ensures that the method is viewed, not as a set of techniques, but as a skilful listening task in the first instance.

Three Useful Concepts

Readiness

One useful way to view motivation is as a state of readiness to change, which fluctuates and can be influenced by others (Miller & Rollnick, 1991). The stages of change model (DiClemente & Prochaska, 1998), which emerged almost simultaneously with motivational interviewing, provided a construct, readiness to change, which proved useful for the understanding and conduct of a motivational interviewing session. There are a number of ways of conceptualizing readiness. One is to think in terms of stages of change, as Prochaska & DiClemente (1998) have done. Despite debates about its measurement and scientific status (see Davidson, 1998), this stage-based framework has been a source of inspiration to counsellors because it indicates that people have different needs, depending on their stage of change, and that simply moving stages during counselling might be beneficial. Another way of conceptualizing readiness is to view it as a continuum (Rollnick, 1998). Although obviously oversimplified, with no reference being made to a circular process, the notion of a continuum of readiness highlights the need to maintain *congruence* with the client's readiness on an ongoing basis in counselling (Rollnick et al., 1999). Moreover, jump ahead of the client and resistance will be the outcome.

Counsellor awareness of shifting readiness is invaluable for the skilful use of motivational interviewing. The therapist's role is to keep in step with the client. In this difficult terrain, either party, with equal ease and suddenness, might lose his/her footing. Debates on the purpose of the counselling, the route to be taken, doubts about the importance of the goal and one's capacity to reach it, all serve to make the task ever more fraught. Not only is the client usually cautious but the counsellor, often with limited time for the journey, may run ahead of the client's readiness, shouting encouragement and entreaties backwards across an ever-broadening gulf. If the gulf becomes too great, the conversation, in all but name, is ended, and it is not uncommon for both parties to blame the other for failure and wasting time. It is sensitivity to readiness that enables the so-called resistance behaviours of the client to be kept to a minimum and for rapport to be sustained through difficult passages. In motivational interviewing, the counsellor always walks beside the client, in step with his/her readiness to change.

Ambivalence

This concept was placed at the centre of the description of motivational interviewing (Miller & Rollnick, 1991) because it provided counsellors with a conceptual anchor for dealing with the uncertainty about behaviour change that pervades so many counselling sessions. If change is a process, and if all change is preceded by some degree of ambivalence, then ambivalence is a normal and defining state endured by all in degrees. It is doubtless the case that change is not made without inconvenience, even from worse to better. Such inconvenience may be hard to comprehend from the perspective of the outsider, especially when the behaviour is perceived by others as problematic and therefore surely troublesome to the individual. But for the person with the "problematic" behaviour, change may be effortful and enervating, not least because it may demand a reconfiguration of beliefs concerning the particular role that the behaviour fulfils and its attendant value. As Miller has noted in conversation with an "ambivalent client", ". . . it's almost like giving up a part of yourself, in a way, to think about changing . . . it's offensive to think about that because it's like sacrificing part of who you've become . . . (it's) . . . a letting go of something that (is) dear to you . . ." (Miller, Rollnick & Moyers, 1998). It is the *inter-relationship of ambivalence about change and the client's goals and core values* that is the substance of motivational interviewing.

Where problematic alcohol use is the focus of discussion, many conversations about change demand a period of discomforting ambivalence wherein the client may feel a range of emotions perhaps hitherto unrecognized and inexperienced. To feel, at once, that, "I don't want to and I want to!" is both the source of immobilization and mobilization. It is the problem and the solution; it is the explanation of inaction and the seed of action. To increase the probability of change—the client's readiness—the counsellor's task is to encourage the client to change the balance of "weights" from one clause, "I don't want to . . ." to the other, "I want to . . ."; to shift commitment from one posture to the other. In motivational interviewing the shift is attempted by harnessing the client's own motivation, by gentle coaching, not by using a clever argument or therapeutic technique. It is the client who is encouraged to express a recognition of problems and express concern about these problems, who talks with determination to make changes and with hope and optimism in his/her own ability to achieve his/her goals; these are the cognitive, affective and behavioural domains of motivation for change. Clients hear themselves articulating a desire for change—not the counsellor's words, but theirs. In traditional alcohol counselling, many a counsellor has fallen into the trap of overtly taking sides, of trying to persuade an ambivalent client about the advantages of change or about the dangers of continued drinking. The outcome is often a more entrenched client who defends the "no change" position with even greater authority! Motivational interviewing provides a counselling style that avoids this problem of postural confrontation and helps, first, the counsellor to avoid eliciting defensiveness whilst maintaining direction and, second, the client to explore his/her ambivalence about change without experiencing the process as hostile and insensitive.

For many clients, the experience of hearing themselves exploring personal discrepancies out loud provokes strong emotions; for some, such turmoil is so disturbing and painful that a strong desire to quickly re-establish a sense of internal continuity results in attempts to "fight back", using the counsellor as a foil. During this period of heightened ambivalence, the counsellor's overarching need is, in one sense, to remove him/herself from the debate, to distance him/herself from the client's competing voices. The role and tasks of a "chair" are most apt here. Particularly through the skilful employment of reflection, the counsellor moderates the articulated "voices" of the client, acknowledging the many divergent viewpoints.

Resistance

The connection between expressions of ambivalence and resistance can be illustrated thus; the client says, "I'd like to do it, but I can't"; to which the counsellor responds, "But if you succeeded for a month last time, maybe you can do better this time?"; to which the clients replies, "Yes, but I can't because . . .". The conversation then continues, *ad nauseam*, in a spiral of wills, the two combatants locked as wrestlers until one party is exhausted and submits. Such activity has little connection with effective addiction counselling and certainly no similarity in style with motivational interviewing.

What is resistance? In the description of motivational interviewing, resistance is viewed as observable behaviour that arises when the counsellor loses demonstrable congruence with the client (Miller & Rollnick, 1991). In short, in its most active form, it is often a consequence of counsellor behaviour and therefore amenable to change—provided that the counsellor understands the dynamic process in which he/she is engaged. Resistance may be conceived of as a general reluctance to make progress, or as opposition to the counsellor or what the counsellor thinks is best, or as the client's expectations as to the posture of the agency the counsellor represents, or even, more traditionally, as "denial". Conceived of another way—from the position and perspective of the client—resistance might be viewed as we might view resistance movements in war: as an heroic defence and counteraction to a perceived or quite palpable threat. What might the client be defending or maintaining? His/her self-esteem, personal values or the articulating of a particularly important opinion—one, perhaps, that expresses a core belief held dear by the client. Most commonly, the threat is an injunction, not always expressly stated but felt nonetheless, "Think differently, act differently!" Such injunctions rarely elicit the response, "Of course, whatever you say. You're absolutely right". Responding constructively to rapport damaged by miscommunication and confusion is particularly important in the early stages of counselling. This skill is at the heart of motivational interviewing.

THE PRACTICE OF MOTIVATIONAL INTERVIEWING

Principles

Express Empathy

Empathic listening is the fundamental principle that ensures that the counsellor remains in step with the needs and aspirations of the client. Its practice, enhanced considerably by the use of reflective listening, involves both simple summary statements, designed to ensure parity with the client, and more complex statements that enable the skilled counsellor to gently but directively highlight elements of the client's dilemma that might encourage resolution of ambivalence.

Avoid Argument and Roll with Resistance

These two principles highlight the need to avoid non-constructive conversations, which resemble a battle of wills. Guidance is provided in the outline of motivational interviewing about how to achieve greater harmony in the counselling session.

Support Self-efficacy

There is strong research support for the importance of self-efficacy as a predictor of success in changing behaviour (Miller & Rollnick, 1991). Put simply, developing a sense that, "I can cope in this situation" and "I will do this in that difficult situation" will be of benefit to clients. In a motivational interviewing session, emphasis is placed on eliciting this inner conviction, rather than imposing it from without. This does not mean that the counsellor cannot make suggestions. Rather, suggestions are made and specific problems discussed in the context of a brainstorming session in which the client is encouraged to take charge of decision making.

Deploy Discrepancy

In the exploration of the client's personal values and aspirations for the future, a particular state of discomfort, termed discrepancy, can arise from the contrast between what the person wants from life and the self-destructive nature of the addiction problem. "I like the drink but it's getting me nowhere and tearing my life apart. I have no future", is a common expression from the exasperated client in addiction counselling. In motivational interviewing this kind of discomforting realization is not viewed as a problem to be avoided, but as something that can be a catalyst for change. The development of the discrepancy principle is not a pointer to the use of clever technique for creating discomfort, but to the value of allowing clients to see how the problem might be at odds with what is dear to them and their hopes for the future. Its practice requires a sensitivity and ability to empathize that is critical for avoiding the ethical challenge that therapy should not be making clients feel uncomfortable. A useful protective guideline can be phrased thus: the more discrepancy is deployed, the deeper should be the quality of empathic listening.

The Method

Empathic Listening Skills

These skills form the basis of motivational interviewing. Definitions of open questions, affirmation, summarizing and reflective listening can be found in Miller & Rollnick (1981). Reflective listening is the principal vehicle for conveying empathy with the client and the most amenable to skilful use. Discussion about ambivalence, decision-making and behaviour change can be fraught with tension, both between and within the two parties involved. The use of simple reflective listening can ensure that the client feels understood in the often confusing discussion that takes place. One guideline suggested by therapists is that one should aim for using three reflective listening statements for every open question asked of the client. More complex reflective listening statements serve other purposes, e.g. to guide the client to explore particular topics and to respond to resistance.

In the example below, a client is engaged in talking about ambivalence. The counsellor's task is not to jump ahead to any other topic but merely to allow the client to explore this conflict. Simple reflective listening statements are used to do this.

COUNSELLOR: So what have you noticed about the effect of alcohol on your mood?
CLIENT: It's like my saviour, because you see it is sometimes the only time I really feel at peace with myself, like really relaxed.
COUNSELLOR: It comes over you and you feel so different.
CLIENT: Yes, and this goes on for a long time. There can be all hell breaking loose around me and I won't let it touch me.
COUNSELLOR: It protects you from all sorts of troubles.
CLIENT: For a while and then it's like my punishment is not far away, like the time will come when I feel upset, little things, and I get upset and even angry.
COUNSELLOR: You get this lovely lift and you also get these darker moments.
CLIENT: Exactly, but they don't just last for a moment. You should see what I am like the next day, I feel really down, like my life is a roller coaster of highs and lows, and the drink is my master. I don't like that.

Eliciting Self-motivating Statements

This complex sounding task is really quite simple: instead of presenting arguments for change to the client, the counsellor elicits these from the client. This is not a technical matter of eliciting these statements and ignoring arguments for not changing, but of giving the client time to express ambivalence free of distraction in an atmosphere in which the counsellor's main task is to listen and understand. In the dialogue noted above, reflective listening was used to do just this, and the last statement from the client is a self-motivating statement and an expression of concern about drinking.

More complex reflective listening statements (see Miller & Rollnick, 1991) have been identified that assist the counsellor to extend, highlight or even redirect the focus of discussion. Thus, new meanings can be added to reflective statements, which amount to subtle interpretations. Particularly useful is the double-sided reflection, where the counsellor looks for contrasting feelings and captures them in a single brief statement; e.g. "So you feel like it's killing you sometimes, and it also gives you so much pleasure".

It is in using these more complex reflections that an element of directiveness is added to the encounter. One can, for example, highlight certain issues and not others, thus obliging the client to respond accordingly. How and when reflections are used in this way depends on the specific circumstances and quality of the rapport between the parties. Some counsellors argue that it is best to use simple reflections in the early part of a counselling session and turn to more complex interpretations only when the rapport is strong enough. In any event, a useful guideline is not to try to be clever in using artful reflections but to track very carefully what the client is saying. Self-motivational statements usually emerge quite naturally from this process.

Responding to Resistance

Responding constructively to resistance, which can be viewed as damaged rapport, is particularly important in the early stages of an encounter, when the possibilities for miscommunication are so common. Being frank about the counsellor's role and motives, and then focusing on the client's agenda using reflective listening statements, can do a great deal to diffuse tension and misunderstanding. One of the most common mistakes made by counsellors is to assume greater readiness to change then felt by the client. Resistance will be the outcome. Similar, and very common in the alcohol field, is the tendency to focus on alcohol at all costs, when the client is equally or more concerned about something else. The outcome will be damaged rapport and disengagement.

Responding to resistance is not merely a technical matter. The counsellor's attitude should reflect acknowledgement of the client's need to maintain dignity, self-respect and to be heard and acknowledged. Upon this basis of respect, the counsellor responds to resistance by coming alongside the client, thereby undermining the oppositional nature of the interaction. Reflective listening is the most useful way of doing this. In the example below, the counsellor focuses on "an alcohol problem" to begin with, receives defensiveness from an angry client in response and then repairs the damage using reflective listening.

COUNSELLOR: I understand that you have come to see me about your drinking, is that correct?

CLIENT: No it's not. I thought that would happen here, like you go on just like my wife— drinking, drinking, drinking, as if it's all due to drinking. I tell you, if all you want to do is talk about drinking, I may as well go home. It's just a waste of my time. (*A single misdirected closed question has earned the counsellor the reward of a battle. In the dialogue that follows, the counsellor resists the temptation to argue back, and uses reflective listening to come alongside the client and diffuse the tension.*)

COUNSELLOR: For you, there's a much bigger picture. It's not just the alcohol that's bothering you.

CLIENT: That's right, because time and time again I get told that my drinking is a problem, like it's the only thing that matters.

COUNSELLOR: Other things also matter and you don't want them to be sidelined in our meeting today.

CLIENT: No that's exactly right, I want to talk about other things as well.

COUNSELLOR: Tell me, taking your time, about these other things.

Summary

There is more technical depth to the practice of motivational interviewing than described above. However, at its heart is an attempt to have a quiet and constructive discussion about change in which the client drives the process as much as possible. The counsellor will actively look for opportunities to explore ambivalence about drinking and will try to understand what broader values and issues are important to the client. How the client's aspirations coexist or conflict with the drinking problem will often provide the fuel for decision-making and change.

THE RESEARCH BASE

Research on motivational interviewing initially focused on the use of this counselling style when feeding back the results of a "Drinker's Check-Up" assessment (Bien et al., 1993; Brown & Miller, 1993; Miller et al., 1998). The generally positive results that emerged have since been supplemented by other studies in other settings, e.g. among heroin users (Saunders et al., 1995), heavy drinkers in a hospital setting (Heather et al., 1996) and smokers in primary care (Butler et al., 1999). In Project MATCH, a brief four-session version of motivational interviewing turned out to be as effective as more intensive treatments for problem drinkers (Project MATCH Research Group, 1997), although this study was largely unable to establish how to match individual clients to different treatments. Studies outside of the addictions field, e.g. among patients with diabetes (Smith et al., 1997) have also emerged.

The question, "Is motivational interviewing effective?" can be answered in different ways. The Project MATCH findings clearly suggest that it is comparable in effectiveness to two other standard approaches to treatment (cognitive-behavioural therapy and a 12-Steps approach; see also Chapter 24, this volume). Fewer studies have compared it to no treatment. In general health care settings, two studies have noted a tendency for motivational interviewing to be effective among those designated as less ready to change (Heather et al., 1996; Butler et al., 1999). However, little is known about what elements of the method are particularly effective. One study suggests that an effective element is the absence of confrontational statements from the counsellor which elicit resistance and lead to poorer client outcome (Miller, Benefield & Tonigan, 1993). Much of the uncertainty about effective mechanisms and counsellor behaviour can be resolved by studying session content as well as outcome. To this end, attempts are now being made to provide researchers with a coding system for analysing audio-taped sessions, called the Motivational Interviewing Skills Coding (MISC) system (W.R. Miller, personal communication). Treatment outcome researchers should benefit from being able to better control the quality of the method under study.

OPPORTUNITIES AND LIMITATIONS

Despite the positive outcome of controlled trials and the apparent popularity of motivational interviewing, the commitment of counsellors to developing and extending their empathic listening skills will be critical to its survival. Without this commitment, motivational interviewing could be mistakenly viewed or practised as a set of simple techniques applied on or to clients. This approach is unlikely to be of enduring benefit to the field, since it involves discarding the use of the one element of motivational interviewing, empathic listening, which has stood the test of numerous research efforts. Until the acquisition of these listening skills is placed at the centre of pre-qualification training for counsellors and emphasized throughout their professional development, motivational interviewing will have a limited role in the field of alcohol counselling.

Counsellors are usually taught different methods as relatively distinct entities, then left to integrate them in everyday practice. Whether this is the most productive training strategy is an open question. It might be tempting to take the results of Project MATCH and argue that, since there was little difference in effectiveness across treatments, there is a case for integrating different methods into a single broad model of addiction counselling. The findings of the UK Alcohol Treatment Trial (see Chapter 28, this volume) will certainly contribute to this debate. If there were to be a move towards integrating treatment approaches, which is compatible with developments like the *transtheoretical* stages of change model (Miller & Heather, 1998), motivational interviewing might serve as a useful base for such a method.

Consultations and conversations about whether or not to change behaviour are obviously not unique to the addictions field. Interest has been shown in using motivational interviewing to grapple with motivation challenges among, for example, patients with diabetes, eating disorders, heart disease and clients in correctional and psychiatric settings. Often however, consultation time is shorter in these settings, and practitioners have less experience of using empathic listening skills and less time to learn them. Attempts have therefore been made to simplify motivational interviewing while retaining its essential client-centred foundation (see e.g. Rollnick et al., 1999).

CONCLUSION

If motivational interviewing has made a contribution to the alcohol field, it has been the realization that empathic listening can become a highly sophisticated skill, capable of helping client and counsellor manoeuvre through the sometimes entangled jungle of mixed emotions, motivations and conflicts that lie at the heart of so many drinking problems. Helping clients to find out what they really want and value, and how alcohol fits in, requires a deftness of touch in the consulting room that motivational interviewing has attempted to harness.

KEY WORKS AND SUGGESTIONS FOR FURTHER READING

In addition to consulting the original text on motivational interviewing (see Miller & Rollnick, 1991, listed in References) the reader may wish to examine the following:

Davies, P. (1979).   Motivation, responsibility and sickness in the psychiatric treatment of alcoholism. *British Journal of Psychiatry*, **134**, 449–458.

Davies, P. (1981).   Expectations and therapeutic practices in outpatient clinics for alcohol problems. *British Journal of Addiction*, **76**, 159–173.

These two papers by Davies provide a vivid account of what went on in traditional alcoholism treatment. They provided some of the impetus for developing motivational interviewing.

Miller, W.R. & Heather, N. (Eds) (1998). *Treating Addictive Behaviours*, 2nd edn. New York: Plenum.

This edited volume contains many useful reviews and critiques, including a detailed examination of the stages of change model, a chapter on motivation by William R. Miller and one on common processes across treatments by Stephen Rollnick.

Orford, J. (1985). *Excessive Appetites: A Psychological View of Addictions.* New York: Wiley.

An interesting account of different behaviours to which people can become excessively attached, with the concept of ambivalence close to the heart of the book.

www.motivationalinterview.com

A website produced by the International Association of Motivational Interviewing Trainers, which contains updates on research, bibliography, news of training events and a trainer's newsletter.

REFERENCES

Bien, T., Miller, W. & Boroughs, J. (1993). Motivational interviewing with alcohol outpatients. *Behavioural & Cognitive Psychotherapy*, **21**, 347–356.

Brown, J. & Miller, W. (1993). Impact of motivational interviewing on participation in residential alcoholism treatment. *Psychology of Addictive Behaviours*, **7**, 211–218.

Butler, C., Rollnick, S., Cohen, D., Russell, I., Bachmann, M. & Stott, N. (1999). Motivational consulting versus brief advice for smokers in general practice: a randomized trial. *British Journal of General Practice*, **49**, 611–616.

DiClemente, C.C. & Prochaska, J. (1998). Toward a comprehensive, transtheoretical model of change: stages of change and addictive behaviours. In W.R. Miller & N. Heather (Eds), *Treating Addictive Behaviours*, 2nd edn. New York: Plenum.

Davidson, R. (1998). The transtheoretical model: a critical overview. In W.R. Miller & N. Heather (Eds), *Treating Addictive Behaviours*, 2nd edn. New York: Plenum.

Egan, G. (1994). *The Skilled Helper: A Problem Management Approach to Helping.* Pacific Grove, CA: Brooks/Cole.

Heather, N., Rollnick, S., Bell, A. & Richmond, R. (1996). Effects of brief counselling among male heavy drinkers identified on general hospital wards. *Drug & Alcohol Review*, **15**, 29–38.

Miller, W.R. (1983). Motivational interviewing with problem drinkers. *Behavioural Psychotherapy*, **1**, 147–172.

Miller, W.R. & Heather, N. (Eds) (1998). *Treating Addictive Behaviours*, 2nd edn. New York: Plenum.

Miller, W.R. & Rollnick, S. (1991). *Motivational Interviewing: Preparing People to Change Addictive Behaviour.* New York: Guilford.

Miller, W.R., Benefield, R.G. & Tonigan, J.S. (1993). Enhancing motivation for change in problem drinking: a controlled comparison of two therapist styles. *Journal of Consulting and Clinical Psychology*, **61**, 455–461.

Miller, W., Sovereign, G. & Krege, B. (1988). Motivational interviewing with problem drinkers: II. The drinker's check-up as a preventative intervention. *Behavioural Psychotherapy*, **16**, 251–268.

Miller, W.R., Rollnick S. & Moyers, T. (1998). *Motivational Inteviewing.* Professional Training Videotape Series. Albuquerque, NM: University of New Mexico.

Miller, W.R. (1998). Enhancing motivation for change. In W.R. Miller & N. Heather (Eds), *Treating Addictive Behaviours*, 2nd edn. New York: Plenum.

Prochaska, J. & DiClemente, C. (1998). Comments, criteria and creating better models: in response to Davidson. In W.R. Miller & N. Heather (Eds), *Treating Addictive Behaviours*, 2nd edn. New York: Plenum.

Project MATCH Research Group (1997). Matching alcohol treatment to client heterogeneity: Project MATCH posttreatment drinking outcomes. *Journal of Studies on Alcohol*, **58**, 7–29.

Rollnick, S. (1998). Readiness, importance and confidence: critical conditions of change in treatment. In W.R. Miller & N. Heather (Eds), *Treating Addictive Behaviour*, 2nd edn. New York: Plenum.

Rollnick, S. & Miller W.R. (1995). What is motivational interviewing? *Behavioural & Cognitive Psychotherapy*, **23**, 325–334.

Rollnick, S., Mason, P. & Butler, C. (1999). *Health Behavior Change: A Guide for Practitioners*. Edinburgh: Churchill Livingstone.

Saunders, W., Wilkinson, C. & Phillips, M. (1995). The impact of a brief motivational intervention with opiate users attending a methadone programme. *Addiction*, **90**, 415–422.

Smith, D.E., Heckemeyer, C.M., Kratt, P.P. & Mason, D.E. (1997). Motivational interviewing to improve adherence to a behavioral weight-control program for older obese women with NIDDM: a pilot study. *Diabetes Care*, **20**, 53–54.

Truax, C.B. & Carkhuff, R.R. (1967). *Toward Effective Counseling & Psychotherapy*. Chicago, IL: Aldine.

Chapter 31

Brief Interventions

Nick Heather
*Centre for Alcohol and Drug Studies, University of Northumbria at,
Newcastle Newcastle upon Tyne, UK*

Synopsis

Brief interventions are not merely a passing fancy in the alcohol problems field but a crucial and permanent addition to the range of strategies used to combat alcohol-related harm. It is important to distinguish between two classes of brief intervention—brief treatment and opportunistic brief intervention. Brief treatment is offered to people who are seeking help for an alcohol problem and is delivered in specialist treatment centres; opportunistic brief intervention is delivered among their other duties by generalist workers and is aimed at people who must be identified as excessive drinkers in settings where they have attended for reasons other than to seek help for an alcohol problem. Brief treatment is usually longer than opportunistic brief intervention, is aimed at problem drinkers with relatively more severe problems and derives from an evidence base quite different from that applying to opportunistic brief intervention. The latter is best seen as part of a public health approach to alcohol-related harm.

Interest in brief treatment originated from trials of treatment for alcohol problems beginning in the 1970s, showing no differences in outcome between briefer and more intensive modalities. Evidence in favour of brief treatment was greatly strengthened by the findings of Project MATCH, which reported no clinically significant differences in overall outcome between a four-session treatment (Motivational Enhancement Therapy: MET) and two more intensive, 12-session treatments. Project MATCH did report some client–treatment matches that favoured the use of either MET or more intensive approaches. Questions relating to the relative effectiveness and cost-effectiveness of brief and more intensive treatment are currently being investigated in the UK Alcohol Treatment Trial. Perhaps the main potential of brief treatment is its ability to deliver more cost-effective treatment programmes in times of limited resources for health care funding and competition for these limited resources from different branches of health care.

The impetus for interest in opportunistic brief interventions against excessive drinking comes partly from a trial reported in 1979 of brief advice on smoking cessation by general medical practitioners (GPs). This showed that, if brief advice were routinely implemented by GPs throughout the UK, the gains to public health would be enormous. A similar logic under-

International Handbook of Alcohol Dependence and Problems. Edited by N. Heather, T.J. Peters and T. Stockwell.

pinned a series of trials of alcohol opportunistic brief intervention in primary health care and has also been applied to other generalist settings, such as general hospital wards, accident and emergency departments, social services, educational institutions, criminal justice settings and the workplace. A number of reviews and meta-analyses of opportunistic brief intervention have reached positive conclusions but several important research and practical issues remain to be addressed. In particular, efforts to achieve widespread implementation of opportunistic brief interventions by the medical and nursing professions have so far been largely unsuccessful, but research on this implementation process is proceeding. It is argued in this chapter that, especially given the reluctance by governments to introduce preventive control measures against excessive drinking, the widespread, routine and enduring implementation of opportunistic brief intervention by the medical and other professions represents the best chance of achieving a significant reduction in alcohol-related harm among the population at large.

The term "brief interventions" is much in vogue in alcohol treatment circles these days. Research on brief interventions and applications in practice attract attention in many countries of the world and among international organizations in the alcohol field. Some may conclude that brief interventions are merely a current fad in alcohol treatment, a passing fashion like others before it that will be superseded in time by some other popular idea. This chapter will argue that this is not the case—that brief interventions have an indispensable and crucial role to play in the response to alcohol problems and should be regarded as a permanent addition to the range of methods used to counter alcohol-related harm.

The chapter will review the origins of interest in brief interventions and the various justifications for their use. Obstacles that have been encountered in disseminating and implementing brief interventions—in other words, in translating research findings into practice—will be discussed. However, the chapter will be mostly focused on reviewing research evidence on the effectiveness and cost-effectiveness of brief interventions. Readers interested in clinical descriptions of brief interventions and how-to-do-it guides should look elsewhere (Bien, Miller & Tonigan, 1993; Heather, 1995a; NIAAA, 1995; Rollnick, Mason & Butler, 1999).

TWO DOMAINS OF BRIEF INTERVENTION

Before proceeding, it is necessary to clarify one outstanding issue. Despite their popularity, there is still much confusion about the precise nature of brief interventions and their aims. The main source of confusion is a failure to make a clear distinction between two different forms of activity that have been called brief interventions: the distinction between their use with people who are actively seeking help for an alcohol problem and with those who are not. As argued in more detail elsewhere (Heather, 1995b), although the two types of intervention may in some senses be seen as lying along a single continuum, there are dangers in confusing the evidence relating to these domains, not least the danger that evidence in favour of brief interventions in non-specialist settings like general medical practice will be interpreted as evidence that more intensive interventions in specialist alcohol treatment settings are unnecessary.

To avoid adding to this confusion, this chapter will employ different terms to describe these two sorts of brief intervention activity—opportunistic brief interventions and brief treatment. Opportunistic brief interventions (OBIs) are those that take place in community settings and are delivered by non-specialist personnel, such as general medical practitioners and other primary health care staff, hospital physicians and nurses, social workers, probation officers and other generalist professions. They need consist of only a few minutes advice and encouragement but may also take somewhat longer than this. They are directed almost exclusively at excessive drinkers who are not complaining about or seeking help for an alcohol problem, and who therefore have to be identified by opportunistic screening or some other identification process. These drinkers will normally show only mild alcohol dependence and relatively low levels of alcohol problems. As we shall see, reasons for interest in OBIs, the forms they take, the evidence underlying their application in practice and their role in the treatment and prevention of alcohol problems are quite different from those applying to the other domain of brief interventions.

As the name suggests, brief treatment (BT) consists of relatively briefer forms of treatment delivered by therapists or counsellors working in alcohol or addiction specialist agencies to those who are seeking, or have been mandated or persuaded to seek, help for their alcohol problems. Although described as brief, these treatments are normally longer and more intensive than OBIs. Since clients are self-selected by their attendance at specialist alcohol treatment agencies, screening and identification are unnecessary. Clients offered BT will usually show higher levels of dependence and alcohol-related impairment than those typically offered OBI in generalist settings, although not as high as other clients of specialist treatment centres. Another difference is that evidence supporting the use of BT comes mainly from studies that find no differences in effectiveness between briefer and more intensive, conventional forms of treatment, whereas evidence in favour of OBIs comes from studies that compare their effects with those of no intervention or, at least, even more minimal intervention. Thus, the task of judging the strength of the evidence is crucially different in each case.

BRIEF TREATMENT

Origins of Interest in Brief Treatment

The key event in stimulating interest in BT among alcohol treatment specialists was the publication in 1976–1977 of the results of a treatment trial carried out at the Maudsley Hospital in London (Edwards et al., 1977). Following a comprehensive 3 hour assessment, 100 married, male, problem drinkers were randomly allocated to receive either conventional inpatient or outpatient treatment, complete with the full panoply of services available at a leading psychiatric institution and lasting several months, or to a single counselling session with a psychiatrist involving the client and his wife and delivered "in constructive and sympathetic terms". At follow-up 1 and 2 years later, no statistically significant differences were found between these two groups in drinking behaviour, alcohol-related problems, social adjustment or any other outcome measure. This lack of difference in outcome between BT and intensive treatment was repeated in a follow-up of this cohort 12 years after entry to treatment (Edwards et al., 1983).

The results of this study shocked many people involved in providing alcohol problems treatment, leading to pessimism about the benefits of conventional treatment and whether it could be said to work at all (see e.g. Heather, Robertson & Davies, 1985). While such a nihilistic reaction to the findings of the Maudsley study has generally been abandoned, several subsequent studies, as we shall see, have supported its main implication that brief, inexpensive treatment can often be as beneficial as a full, conventional treatment programme and have led to a major re-evaluation of the necessary requirements for effective treatment of alcohol problems.

Studies of Intensive vs. Briefer Treatment

Following Edwards et al.'s (1977) report, their study was criticized on several grounds. Tuchfeld (1977) suggested that the overall finding of no differences between groups might disguise an interaction in the outcome data, such that those with more severe dependence might do relatively better with more intensive treatment. This appeared to be borne out in the second year follow-up data from the Maudsley study (Orford & Edwards, 1977) in which gamma alcoholics (see Chapter 4) benefited more from intensive treatment and non-gamma alcoholics seemed to do better with brief advice. While this hypothesis was not confirmed in a retrospective analysis of level of dependence and outcome in the original sample by Edwards & Taylor (1994), the idea that briefer treatment is more suited to clients with lower degrees of dependence, while more intensive treatment is still necessary for those with more severe dependence, has been a durable principle among treatment practitioners. Unfortunately, although it may be consistent with common sense, there is little research evidence to support this principle.

A related criticism of the Maudsley study was that, as shown by their intact marriages, the clients were relatively socially stable and, moreover, showed little evidence of psychiatric disturbance. Both these factors are known to be associated with a good prognosis from treatment (Gibbs & Flanagan, 1977; McLellan et al., 1983). Thus, it may be that these clients would have responded well to any kind of intervention, including brief advice. If the trial had been conducted among clients of lower social stability and/or with significant psychiatric problems, who often comprise a substantial proportion of clients in routine treatment programmes, differences between the effects of intensive and briefer treatment may have been greater (Kissin, 1977). Another obvious point is that, since the study was confined to men, the findings could not be applied to female problem drinkers.

These alleged deficiencies of the Maudsley study were addressed in a further comparison of intensive and brief treatment by Chick et al. (1988), which included women and unmarried clients. Following assessment, 152 attenders at an alcohol problems clinic in Edinburgh were randomly allocated to extended inpatient or outpatient treatment or to one of two forms of brief intervention—"simple advice", consisting of no more than 5 minutes standardized advice to stop drinking, or "amplified advice", in which a psychiatrist was given 30–60 minutes to increase the client's motivation to make a radical change in drinking behaviour. At follow-up 2 years later, those who had received extended treatment did not show a higher rate of abstinence, which was nearly always the explicit goal of treatment, than those given the briefer interventions, or any greater improvement in employment or relationship status. However, the extended treatment group was functioning better in that clients had accumulated less harm from their drinking during the follow-up period. Remarkably, no differences were apparent between the simple and amplified advice groups.

Also at the Maudsley Hospital, Drummond et al. (1990) gave 40 clients of an alcohol problems clinic a thorough assessment followed by brief advice. Clients were then randomized to receive outpatient counselling at the clinic or referral back to their general medical practitioners for medical monitoring. At a 6-month follow-up, both groups showed substantial improvements on a range of relevant measures and no significant differences in outcome were detected.

In another study of intensive vs. BT among clients of specialist alcohol treatment services in New Zealand, Chapman & Huygens (1988) reported no differences in effectiveness between a single session of advice and either 6 weeks of inpatient treatment or 6 weeks of twice-weekly outpatient treatment. However, this study and those of Edwards et al. (1977) and Chick et al. (1988) have been criticized by Mattick & Jarvis (1994) on the grounds that the treatments under investigation were not delivered as they were intended. Thus, a substantial proportion of clients in the BT groups in fact received additional treatment, either because they were deemed to need it or sought it themselves, while some of those in the intensive groups received only brief help because they dropped out of regular treatment. Mattick & Jarvis argued that these factors would tend to obscure potential differences between intensive and brief treatment.

Studies of Moderation-orientated Treatment

In addition to comparisons of brief and intensive treatment among those referred to specialist alcohol problems clinics, there is another set of studies that compare the effects of different intensities of treatment aimed at a moderation goal among problem drinkers with less severe impairment. These studies are included here under the heading of BT because clients are seeking help but are channelled into treatment by unconventional means, often by self-referral through media advertisements.

A series of studies by William R. Miller and his colleagues from the University of New Mexico (Miller & Taylor, 1980; Miller, Taylor & West, 1980; Miller, Gribskov & Mortell, 1981) compared the effects of a self-help manual based on cognitive-behavioural principles and accompanied by minimal therapist contact with various types of cognitive-behavioural therapy, delivered on an outpatient basis in either individual or group formats. None of these studies showed any advantage for conventional behavioural treatment. Rates of improvement for both minimal and intensive approaches were high (60–70%) and stable at a 2 year follow-up (Miller & Baca, 1983). Other studies (e.g. Carpenter, Lyons & Miller, 1985; Skutle & Berg, 1987; Sannibale, 1988) have reported comparable findings among various populations of problem drinkers in different countries. Following these earlier studies, Miller and his colleagues developed a brief motivational intervention aimed at media-recruited heavy drinkers (the *Drinker's Check-up)* and reported some evidence for its effectiveness (Miller, Sovereign & Krege, 1988). In a study of conjoint therapy among moderately severe problem drinkers, using both moderation and abstinence goals, Zweben, Pearlman & Lee (1988) found no differences in outcome at an 18-month follow-up between a single conjoint session of advice and the provision of eight conjoint sessions. Neither this study nor those of Drummond et al. (1990) and Miller & Baca (1983) found any relationship between severity of dependence and the relative effectiveness of brief vs. intensive treatment.

It must be pointed out that sample sizes in the studies reviewed so far in this section were typically small, so that the conclusion of equivalence between treatments becomes hazardous because of low statistical power to detect real differences in effectiveness. If widespread implementation of a form of treatment in a health care system is envisaged, even a small superiority of one treatment over another becomes important, especially if considerations of cost-effectiveness are introduced into the argument. It may need very large samples to detect these small effect sizes.

Project MATCH

The hypothesis that BT is generally as effective as more intensive treatment has gained considerable support from the results of Project MATCH, the largest study of the effects of treatment for alcohol problems ever carried out (Project MATCH Research Group, 1997a,b, 1998). The project involved 10 treatment sites in the USA and a total of 1726 clients, divided into two parallel but independent clinical trials—an outpatient arm ($n = 952$) and an aftercare arm ($n = 774$). It was designed to assess the benefits of matching clients showing alcohol dependence or abuse to three different treatments with respect to a variety of client attributes. Clients within each arm of the study were randomly assigned to three 12-week, manual-guided interventions: Twelve-step Facilitation Therapy (TSF), an approach following the principles of Alcoholics Anonymous and founded on the idea that alcoholism is a spiritual and medical disease; Cognitive-behavioural Coping Skills Therapy (CBT), an approach based on social learning theory; and Motivational Enhancement Therapy (MET), a less intensive form of therapy based on the principles of motivational psychology. Each of these modalities was delivered by trained therapists on a one-to-one basis. CBT and TSF consisted of 12 weekly sessions, while MET consisted of four sessions spread over 12 weeks.

Project MATCH was primarily concerned with client–treatment matches (i.e. interactions between the effects of treatments and characteristics of clients) and the main effects of treatment were not the focus of the study. However, these main effects are of great interest for present purposes. The overall conclusion was that there were no clinically meaningful differences in success rates among the three treatments studied. This basic finding, which was undoubtedly surprising to many in the field, has the important implication that a briefer treatment, MET, was no less effective than two more intensive treatments, CBT and TSF. This applied across the entire range of clients in the sample and not only to those of lower dependence or problem severity. This is an important point because, as we have seen, the consensus on the effectiveness of BTs before Project MATCH was that they should be confined to clients with lower levels of dependence and problems.

Equally important, since MET consisted of only one-third the number of sessions available in the two more intensive treatments, it would seem at first sight that it was the more cost-effective treatment. In times of limited funding for health care services in all countries of the world and of fierce competition for these limited resources among different areas of health care, the cost-effectiveness of treatment becomes a matter of paramount concern for service delivery. If two or more treatments do not differ in effectiveness, it is obviously a rational strategy to prefer the cheaper treatment. In fact, Cisler et al. (1998) showed that MET was somewhat more than one-third as expensive to deliver as the other treatments, but nevertheless concluded that it was clearly the most cost-effective option.

We have noted that there were no interactions between the relative effectiveness of MATCH treatments and level of alcohol dependence. But were there any other indications of what types of client might be especially suited to either briefer or more intensive forms of treatment? A few matching effects discovered by the project are relevant to this issue:

1. *Network support for drinking.* In the outpatient arm only, those individuals with a social network supportive of drinking (i.e. those with lots of heavy-drinking friends) did better with TSF than MET. Interestingly, this effect did not emerge until the 3 year follow-up (Project MATCH Research Group, 1988), implying that it took time for the behavioural changes in question to come about, but when it did emerge it was the largest matching effect identified in the trial. An analysis of the data by Longabaugh et al. (1998) showed that this effect was mediated by involvement with *Alcoholics Anonymous*. The clear implication here is that outpatients with social networks supportive of drinking will benefit especially from a Twelve-step programme, because that is the most effective means of eliminating heavy-drinking friends and acquaintances from the social network.

2. *Client anger.* Also specific to the outpatient arm, the finding here was that clients initially high in anger reported more days of abstinence and fewer drinks per drinking day if they had received MET than if they had received CBT (Project MATCH Research Group, 1997b). This effect persisted from the 1 year to the 3 year follow-up point (Project MATCH Research Group, 1998). This can be understood as a conse-

quence of the deliberately non-confrontational nature of MET, and high client anger at initial assessment is clearly a positive indicator for the offer of MET.

3. *Readiness to change.* Perhaps the chief matching hypothesis relevant to the effects of MET was that clients with lower "readiness to change" in terms of Prochaska & DiClemente's (1992) stages of change model would do better with MET than with CBT, whereas the reverse would apply to those who had reached the action stage of change. This was because the motivational content of MET was thought to be more helpful to clients who were still ambivalent about changing their drinking behaviour but less relevant to those who had already decided to make this change. There was some evidence to support this hypothesis from the outpatient arm of the trial but the matching effect in question was "time-dependent", i.e. it did not meet the MATCH investigators' stringent criterion that a matching effect should be robust over time throughout the follow-up period (Project MATCH Research Group, 1997a). Nevertheless, it is worth observing that, at the follow-up one year after the end of treatment, the hypothesis was supported by the data; if the investigators had carried out only one follow-up, as is often the case in treatment trials, and restricted analysis to clients' drinking status at that time, the readiness to change matching hypothesis would have been regarded as confirmed.

Returning to treatment main effects, note that the two major criticisms made of previous work on brief vs. intensive treatment (see above) cannot be applied to Project MATCH. First, the great majority of clients received a substantial "dose" of treatment, there was no switching between modalities and the number of sessions received by CBT and TSF clients was substantially greater than that received by MET clients. Second, because of the very large sample sizes in the two arms of the study, needed to test specific matching hypotheses, there is very little possibility of insufficient statistical power to detect genuine main effects of treatment, even very minor effects.

Nevertheless, there are some difficulties in interpreting the MATCH findings as unequivocally supportive of the effectiveness of BT for the normal run of clients attending specialist alcohol services. First, a commonly-voiced criticism of the trial is that various factors—including the intensive 8 hour pre-treatment assessment, the five follow-up visits during the first year after the end of treatment, the exclusion of clients with polydrug dependence or low social stability, the additional treatment obtained by many clients outside the trial, the high levels of therapist qualifications and training, and the rigorous quality control over treatment delivery—could have blunted any potential differences between the outcomes of the treatments studied (see Heather, 1999). Differences between treatments that were obscured by the conditions of a rigorous research trial, so the argument runs, might well exist in the "real world" of day-to-day treatment delivery and, especially, to differences between briefer and intensive treatment. While there are reasons for believing that some of the grounds for this criticism are misplaced or exaggerated (Heather, 1999), they must be carefully considered in evaluating the evidence in favour of BT.

Second, deductions from research findings from one country to another must always be accompanied by considerable caution. This is because of different treatment systems as well as wider cultural influences affecting drinking behaviour and attitudes to alcohol. Ideally, implications for practice of the MATCH findings should explored in research within the treatment systems of other countries before they are considered relevant to practical applications. As one illustration of this point, MATCH findings have little bearing on the outcome of clients in moderation-orientated programmes since, although abstinence may have been urged with different degrees of emphasis in the three treatments, moderation was never an explicit goal of any of them. This particular limitation must be borne in mind when thinking about the implications of the findings in countries like the UK, Australia and some others, where the moderation goal is offered to a sizeable minority of clients in treatment for alcohol problems.

Finally, it should be emphasized that MATCH was a pragmatic trial aimed primarily at decision-making rather than theoretical advance. It was also aimed explicitly at discovering treatment–client matches, not at evaluating the comparative effectiveness of different treatment modalities. For these reasons, the factors of treatment type and treatment intensity were deliberately confounded in the design. Thus, accepting for the moment that the results show MET to be as effective as the two more intensive treatments, we cannot be sure whether this was because of the specifically motivational nature of MET or whether it would apply to BT, of roughly the same intensity as MET, in general. To decide this issue, another trial would be necessary which added to the MATCH design either an intensive form of MET or briefer forms of CBT and TSF. All we can conclude from the MATCH results is that, given the qualifications and reservations expressed above, a briefer treatment in the form of MET is as effective as more intensive treatments represented by CBT and TSF.

The UK Alcohol Treatment Trial

Implications of MATCH findings for treatment of alcohol problems in the UK are currently being explored in a trial funded by the Medical Research Council—the United Kingdom Alcohol Treatment Trial (UKATT). The starting point for UKATT is the finding from Project MATCH that has been the focus of the preceding section of this chapter— that a briefer treatment in the form of MET was as effective in reducing harmful drinking as two more intensive treatments. Thus, the general hypothesis it was aimed to test was that, in the UK treatment system, MET would be as effective as more intensive treatment. Another hypothesis flows from this: in the UK treatment system, MET will be more cost-effective than more intensive treatment.

According to Popper (1959), good science proceeds by the attempt to *falsify* hypotheses. In other words, researchers should subject their hypotheses to the most stringent test possible by inventing experiments where the hypothesis is thought least likely to be confirmed. How does this apply to the hypothesis that MET is as effective as, and therefore more cost-effective than, more intensive treatment? An obvious response to this question is the view that MET should be tested against the most effective form of intensive treatment available or, in other words, the form that is best supported by the research literature.

The conclusion reached by UKATT investigators from recent reviews of the literature (Holder et al., 1991; Thom et al., 1994; Miller et al., 1995; Finney & Monahan, 1996) was that, among relatively intensive treatment modalities, those with the most favourable results tend to contain a strong social or, at least, interpersonal element (see UKATT Research Team, in press). In the light of this evidence and based on feasibility work, a treatment modality called *social behaviour and network therapy* (SBNT) was developed by integrating a number of strategies used previously in other approaches reported in the literature. These strategies, which are all focused on the central aim of helping the client to build positive social support for a change in drinking, were drawn from network therapy (Galanter, 1993), behavioural marital therapy (e.g. McCrady et al., 1991), unilateral family therapy (e.g. Thomas & Ager, 1993), social aspects of the community reinforcement approach (e.g. Sisson & Azrin, 1989), relapse prevention (e.g. Chaney, O'Leary & Marlatt, 1978) and social skills training (e.g. Oei & Jackson, 1980). However, SBNT represents the first treatment modality in which these various methods and treatment principles have been brought together within a unified social treatment with theoretical coherence.

In the UKATT, SBNT is carried out over eight sessions, combining core and elective topics, and lasting 50 minutes each. This is compared with a version of MET scheduled for three 50-minute sessions in weeks 1, 2 and 8 of the treatment period. The UKATT version of MET is a modified form of that used in Project MATCH (Miller et al., 1992), with changes designed to make MET more relevant to the UK treatment context and to the requirements of UKATT (see UKATT Research Team, in press).

There are a few other characteristics of UKATT that are relevant to the issue of brief vs. intensive treatment and to an exploration of the implications of Project MATCH findings. First, without sacrificing internal validity, the investigators have made very effort to increase the external validity of the trial (i.e. its relevance to routine treatment provision in the UK). This has been done by reducing the pre-treatment assessment as far as possible, by scheduling only two follow-up assessments during the first year post-treatment, by limiting exclusion criteria to include as many clients as possible who would normally receive treatment at UK specialist centres, and by selecting therapists from treatment personnel employed by the treatment services in which the research is taking place. Screening and identification of potential clients for the trial is carried out by non-UKATT clinical staff in conjunction with routine assessment procedures in place in the participating treatment centres.

Second, despite the emphasis on the main effects of treatment in UKATT, it is possible that interactions in the data will be found indicating which types of client are more likely to benefit from SBNT than from MET and which do as well or better with the briefer as with the more intensive treatment. The discovery of some relevant matching effects in Project MATCH suggests this possibility. Thus, specific matching hypotheses will be tested in UKATT and follow-up data will also be inspected for possible matching effects that were not predicted and could be further examined in another study. The interactions investigated will also include therapist–treatment matches, i.e. the possibility that some therapist characteristics are associated with better outcomes with MET and some others with SBNT.

Finally, since the issue of the relative cost-effectiveness of a briefer and a more intensive treatment is of prime importance in UKATT, an economic evaluation has been built into the design of the trial and relevant data from clinical sites and clients is being gathered concurrently with all other data. It is very unlikely that the results of the UKATT will be the "last word" on the issue of brief vs. intensive specialist treatment for alcohol problems, but the investigators hope that these results, when they begin to appear in 2003, can be used to improve the effectiveness and efficiency of treatment services.

Conclusions Regarding Brief Treatment

In considering the conclusions that may be drawn from this short review of evidence on the relative effectiveness of brief and intensive treatment for alcohol problems, it cannot be emphasized too strongly that the cost-effectiveness of treatment should already be a matter of paramount concern to treatment providers and will remain so in future. It is often pointed out that the total availability of health care resources is diminishing because of developments in expensive medical technology and of demographic changes due to the greater longevity of the population. Even in wealthy industrialized societies and in times of economic prosperity, there will never be enough resources to meet all society's demands for health care. Increasingly, those responsible for funding treatment services will expect to see evidence, not only that services are effective in helping people recover from alcohol-related disabilities, but that resources devoted to the treatment of alcohol problems would not be more beneficially diverted to other areas of health care. If we can bring about equivalent gains in health and adjustment for lower costs, there can surely be no rational objection in principle to implementing briefer forms of treatment.

From a clinical viewpoint, the very least that can be concluded from the evidence is that many clients do not need protracted and relatively expensive treatment programmes to show marked improvements in drinking behaviour. If we can clearly identify these clients, precious resources can be released for the treatment of those who do need more intensive help. The weight of accumulated evidence supports the offer of briefer forms of moderation-orientated treatment with clients who have comparatively less severe alcohol problems and levels of dependence (cf. Mattick & Jarvis, 1993, 1994). Brief treatment of this kind may be especially suited to problem drinkers who refer themselves for help, rather than those who have been coerced or persuaded by others to attend a treatment service.

If, despite the evidence, such a policy is regarded as risky because there may be some less severely-affected individuals who nevertheless need a more intensive and/or abstinence-based approach to improve or avoid further deterioration, BT could be implemented as the first step in a *stepped care* model of treatment (Sobell & Sobell, 1993; Breslin et al., 1997). This is an approach in which clients are systematically followed-up after treatment and those who have not benefited are offered successively more intensive treatments. Clients with characteristics for which there is clear evidence that more intensive approaches will be needed can be immediately assigned to higher steps in the sequence, and experience gained from outcomes of the stepped care programme can be used gradually to improve the efficiency of the treatment model. It will be seen that the stepped care model contains within it a built-in mechanism for the cost-effective use of resources. Outcome research on this model is urgently needed.

With regard to the treatment of those with more severe levels of dependence and/or more serious alcohol problems, conclusions from the evidence are less certain. Project MATCH (see above) produced evidence that clients with high levels of anger and resentment at intake to treatment benefit more from a briefer, motivational approach (MET) than from cognitive-behavioural therapy or a 12-step approach. On the other hand, clients with heavy-drinking social networks seem to fare better with a more intensive approach, like TSF, that seeks, among other things, to modify the social network. The intuitively-appealing idea that clients who are less ready to change drinking behaviour will benefit more from MET than from more intensive treatment needs further support before it can be regarded as secure. Beyond this, and despite the findings of Project MATCH on the overall equivalence of brief and intensive treatment outcome, the evidence does not yet justify the offer of MET as the standard treatment for alcohol problems. It is hoped that the results of UKATT will help to clarify this issue, at least as far as treatment in the UK is concerned.

OPPORTUNISTIC BRIEF INTERVENTIONS

Origins of Interest in Brief Opportunistic Interventions

Although several influences have conspired to create an interest in opportunistic brief interventions (OBIs) against excessive drinking, a key event was the publication of a paper in the smoking cessation field. Russell et al. (1979) allocated 2138 smokers attending their general practitioners (GPs) in London to one of four groups: (1) a non-intervention control; (2) a questionnaire-only group; (3) a group given simple advice by the GP to stop smoking; and (4) a group advised to stop smoking, given a leaflet to assist them and warned that they would be followed-up. The proportion of smokers in group 4 who stopped smoking during the first month and were still not smoking 1 year later was 5.1%, and this was significantly greater than the corresponding proportions in the other groups. From a clinical point of view, this success rate seems unacceptably low. However, as Russell and colleagues pointed out, over 90% of people in Britain visit their GP at least once in 5 years and the average number of attendances, by smokers and non-smokers alike, is over three per year. Figures from other countries are likely to be similar. Thus, if the simple routine given in group 4 of this study were consistently applied by all GPs in the UK, the yield would exceed half a million ex-smokers per year, a figure that could not be matched by increasing the number of specialist withdrawal clinics in the country from about 50 to 10,000.

This scenario provides the main justification for OBI in the smoking field and is applicable in principle to any area of heath care in which a change in behaviour is targeted, including excessive drinking. Stimulated by the Russell et al. (1979) findings, during the 1980s researchers in the alcohol field began to apply the same logic to OBI by GPs designed to reduce the alcohol consumption of heavy-drinking patients to "safe" or low-risk levels (i.e. under levels recommended by medical authorities.) The first study of this kind, carried out in Scotland by Heather and colleagues (1987), failed to find a clear effect of GP advice to cut down drinking, but this study probably had insufficient statistical power to detect such an effect. However, in a much larger study, Wallace, Cutler & Haines (1988) used 47 group practices throughout the UK. Excessive drinkers in the intervention group received an assessment interview about alcohol consumption, problems and dependence, and were then given advice and information about how to cut down drinking plus a drinking diary. Up to five repeat consultations were scheduled. Patients in the control group received assessment and usual care. At 1 year follow-up, the proportion of men with excessive alcohol consumption had fallen by 44% in the treatment group compared with 26% in the controls, with corresponding proportions among women of 48% and 29%. The public health potential of OBIs was highlighted by Wallace et al. (1988) when they calculated that consistent implementation of their intervention programme by GPs throughout the UK would result in a reduction from excessive to low-risk levels of the drinking of 250,000 men and 67,500 women each year.

Aims and Characteristics

The crucial aims and characteristics of OBIs, and the ways in which these differ from those of brief treatment, should now be apparent. First, the main aim is a reduction in hazardous and harmful drinking in the population at large; the justification for OBIs in practice rests, not on an impressively high success rate among the individuals who receive them, but on a relatively low success rate with a high *impact* through widespread implementation in a primary health care system. For this reason, OBI is best described as part of the public health approach to alcohol-related harm (Heather, 1996). It can easily be demonstrated that, because their numbers are so large, reducing drinking among people with comparatively mild problems and dependence results in a much greater reduction in the total sum of alcohol-related harm in a society than reducing problems among severely dependent and seriously affected individuals. Once more to use the UK as an example, the latest *General Household Survey* in 1996 (Office of National Statistics, 1998) showed that 28% of adult (16+) males and 13% of adult females reported drinking over the limits recommended by the Royal College of Physicians (1987). Among young (16–24) men and women, the figures rose to 35% and 21%, respectively. There are reasons for believing that even these figures may be underestimates but they nevertheless reveal the enormous extent of excessive drinking in the UK general population and the gains to public health and welfare if the drinking of a substantial proportion of these excessive drinkers could be reduced. This does not mean, of course, that the problems of the more severely dependent should be ignored, but merely that interventions to curtail alcohol-related harm should be widened to embrace the much larger group of low-dependence drinkers (Institute of Medicine, 1990).

Second, although the main impact of OBIs is on public health, it is obviously expected that individual excessive drinkers will derive benefit from them. The main way in which this can be achieved is through the related goals of secondary prevention—the prevention of existing alcohol problems from getting worse—and early intervention—the attempt to modify hazardous or harmful drinking before the stage is reached where more intensive treatment for alcohol problems is needed. It is here that the two domains of brief intervention are linked, since, to the extent that OBIs are successful, the load on specialist treatment services will be lightened. In this particular respect, OBI and BT can be thought of as points along a continuum of intervention characterized by increasing intensity. There is no reason also why OBI should not be the starting point in a stepped care model of alcohol intervention (see above), bridging generalist and specialist services.

With regard to defining characteristics, we have already noted that the principal targets of OBIs are drinkers who are not explicitly complaining of, or overtly seeking help for, problems with alcohol. These interventions applied in routine practice are called "opportunistic" (Heather, 1998) because the opportunity created by attendance in settings where people are presenting for some other purpose is used to identify hazardous or harmful drinkers and offer them advice and counselling, e.g. primary health care, general medical wards, social work agencies, criminal justice settings, etc. For this reason, the over-riding task in delivering OBIs is in most cases motivational, since drinkers who may have recognized little or no harm from their drinking must be convinced that their drinking is actually or potentially harmful and persuaded to modify it. In the language of the stages of change model (Prochaska & DiClemente, 1992), the intervention aims to move them from the precontemplation or contemplation stages to the preparation and action stages.

It also follows from the opportunistic nature of OBIs that excessive drinkers must be identified as such before advice or counselling can be offered. This can be done by using questionnaires (see Chapter 25, this volume), laboratory markers (see Chapter 12, this volume), drinking history or simple enquiry, but these methods will not be described here. We may merely note that an instrument has been specially developed for this purpose [the Alcohol Use Disorders Identification Test (AUDIT): Saunders et al., 1993] and is being increasingly used in many parts of the world.

It has already been explained that OBIs are normally directed at a goal of reduced, moderate drinking rather than total abstinence. This is because an insistence on abstinence would be a major disincentive for behaviour change among the great majority of individuals who are the targets of OBIs. The evidence shows that the use of the moderation goal is highly effective in this population (Bien, Miller & Tonigan, 1993) and, indeed, that the abstinence goal is counterproductive (Sanchez-Craig & Lei, 1986). There is, however, no reason in principle why the abstinence goal cannot be employed in OBIs if the drinker prefers it or if it is advisable for some other reason.

Lastly, although the origins of OBIs in the primary health care setting were stressed above, they can be, and have been, applied in other settings, medical and non-medical, in various parts of the world. Medical settings include general hospital wards (Chick et al., 1985; Elvy, Wells & Baird, 1988; Heather et al., 1996), accident and emergency departments (Antti-Poika et al., 1988; Dunn, Donovan & Gentilello, 1997), somatic outpatient clinics (Persson & Magnusson, 1989), hypertension clinics (Maheswaran et al., 1992), obstetric clinics and practices (Chang et al., 1999) and health screening programmes (Kristenson et al., 1983; Romelsjö et al., 1989; Nilssen, 1991). Non-medical settings include social services (Gorman et al., 1990; Shawcross et al., 1996), the workplace (Babor & Grant, 1992; Higgins-Biddle & Babor, 1996; Richmond et al., 1999), educational institutions (Machona, 1992;

Higgins-Biddle & Babor, 1996), the criminal justice system (Baldwin, 1990) and even taverns and bars (Reilly et al., 1998).

Effectiveness of Opportunistic Brief Interventions

The research literature on the effectiveness of brief interventions has been reviewed a number of times (Bien, Miller & Tonigan, 1993; Fremantle et al., 1993; Heather, 1995a; Kahan, Wilson & Becker, 1995; Wilk, Jensen & Havighurst, 1997; Poikolainen, 1999). These reviews have included studies based on different definitions of brief intervention, have been concerned with somewhat different research questions and have used different review methods and meta-analytic techniques. Nevertheless, the overall conclusion from these reviews strongly favours the effectiveness of OBI. In terms of effect size, Fremantle et al. (1992) estimated that OBIs consisting of assessment of alcohol consumption and the provision of information and advice are effective in reducing consumption by 20% compared with no intervention. Wilk et al. (1997) calculated that heavy drinkers who received an OBI were twice as likely to moderate their drinking 6–12 months after intervention as heavy drinkers who had received no intervention.

The most recent of the above-mentioned reviews will be considered here in somewhat more detail. Poikolainen (1999) confined his meta-analysis to studies of OBI in primary health care and identified 14 data sets meeting his criteria. The main purpose of the review was to distinguish and separately analyse studies of very brief intervention (5–20 minutes) and more extended (several visits) brief intervention. The somewhat surprising conclusion was that extended brief interventions were effective among women but that other brief interventions (very brief interventions among women and extended or very brief interventions among men) appeared effective is some studies but not in all. However, the average effect of OBIs could not be reliably estimated in these other studies because of statistical heterogeneity, due probably to methodological weaknesses, the use of different outcome measures and the varying components of the brief interventions themselves. The main conclusions from Poikolainen's review are that there is a need for increased methodological rigour and uniformity in future studies of OBI, and that, for the time being, we must rely on the results of individual studies to reach generalized conclusions regarding the effectiveness of OBI.

When individual studies are inspected, it appears that the largest and most rigorous trials (e.g. Wallace et al., 1988; Israel et al., 1996; Fleming et al., 1997) show beneficial effects of OBI for men as well as women. Perhaps the strongest body of evidence in favour of OBI comes from the WHO clinical trial of brief intervention (Babor & Grant, 1992), an international collaboration involving 10 countries and 1655 heavy drinkers recruited from a combination of various, mostly medical settings. Either by a combined analysis of all the data or by confining attention to the larger and better designed studies (see Heather, 1994), it was clearly established that, among male excessive drinkers at least, an OBI delivered at the primary care level and consisting of 5 minutes' simple advice, based on 15 minutes of structured assessment, was effective in reducing alcohol consumption compared to non-intervention controls, with concomitant improvements in health. In the WHO study no additional benefit of more extended counselling was observed.

This positive verdict on OBI should not be taken to mean that its overall effectiveness can be accepted without qualification or that there are no outstanding matters that need clarification in research. As Poikolainen (1999) points out, it may well be that certain kinds of OBI are effective in certain contexts, while other kinds are not and, if so, we need to know what the characteristics of successful interventions are, especially with respect to the issue of the optimal length and intensity of intervention for different categories of excessive drinker. We also need more information on the longer-term effects of OBI beyond the conventional follow-up point of 1 year, the economic costs and benefits of OBI (see below), and whether or not the widespread implementation of OBI can be shown to reduce alcohol-related harm in the community at large.

Another crucial issue is the extent to which the findings of research apply to the implementation of OBI in regular, routine practice. The most prominent and positive trials of OBI in the literature (e.g. Wallace et al., 1988; Anderson & Scott, 1992; Fleming et al., 1997) are *efficacy* rather than *effectiveness* trials, i.e. they provided a test of brief interventions under optimum research conditions, rather than under real-world conditions of routine primary health care (Flay, 1986). For example, excessive drinkers entering the study were identified and recruited by the research team, rather than by the busy physician in the normal course of his/her practice, and this may have resulted in more motivated patients being selected for study (cf. Kahan et al., 1995). Edwards & Rollnick (1997) demonstrated that subjects lost to controlled trials of OBI, due to unavailability for study or drop-out from follow-up, differed systematically from those included in ways that would probably be associated with a poorer response to intervention. In a project in which OBI was investigated in naturalistic general practice settings (Richmond et al., 1995), far fewer patients returned for consultation following assessment, and the beneficial effects of brief intervention, although still arguably present, were weaker than those reported in efficacy studies. More effectiveness trials of OBI are clearly needed.

From a clinical perspective, Rollnick, Butler & Hodgson (1997) introduced several "concerns from the consulting room" into the discussion of OBI and were especially critical of a simple "advice-giving" framework for intervention. They argued that medical practitioners and nurses might not be satisfied with the evidence on which this framework is based, due to small effect sizes of intervention and to the disjunction in aims between a public health approach to alcohol problems and the practitioners' over-riding interest in the welfare of the individual patient. If true, this would create obvious barriers to the implementation of OBI in practice. So too, practitioners might experience difficulty in interpreting evidence about harmful consumption when counselling their patients, especially those who may be drinking above medically recommended levels but who have not experienced any significant alcohol-related harm. Lastly, Rollnick et al. maintain that advice giving, in the sense of direct persuasion and information, is likely to be ineffective or even counterproductive and is, in any case, bedevilled by practical problems and uncertainties about putative public health gains. The authors offer a number of solutions to the problems they describe, including incorporating into intervention programmes the guidance on what to do with more severely dependent drinkers that many practitioners demand and widening brief alcohol interventions to embrace other health behaviours and personal concerns in a "patient-centred approach". At the very least, the case for offering to practitioners a relatively more intensive, motivational approach to brief interventions is well made by Rollnick and his colleagues.

Cost–benefits

A theme of this chapter has been the need to include economic considerations in evaluations of the potential of brief interventions. For example, one of the best arguments in favour of implementing OBIs in practice must surely be that they can save money for the health care system, either by early intervention among drinkers who might eventually need expensive treatment for end-organ damage or simply by limiting the extent of current alcohol-related harm in the community. While Fremantle et al. (1993) calculated that the direct cost of a brief intervention delivered to an excessive drinker was less than £20, no study has yet been designed explicitly to investigate the possible economic benefits of OBI. However, several studies have produced findings that are relevant to this issue.

In the Malmö study in Sweden, Kristenson et al. (1983) found that, compared to a non-intervention control group, excessive drinkers who had received an OBI showed a 80% reduction in sick absenteeism from work in the 4 years following the intervention, a 60% reduction in hospital days over 5 years and a 50% reduction in mortality from all causes over 6 years following intervention. In their American study, Fleming et al. (1997) found that men in the brief intervention group reported less than half the total number of hospital days in the 12 months following intervention than men in the control group. In Canada, Israel et al. (1996) reported that intervention group patients showed significantly reduced physician visits in the year following counselling compared to controls.

In a review of evidence relevant to the introduction of the managed care system in the USA, Holder, Miller & Carina (1995) estimated that, for every US$10,000 dollars spent on brief alcohol or drug abuse intervention, US$13,500–US$25,000 would be saved in medical spending for the managed care provider. What is needed now is a study designed specifically to test the hypothesis that OBI produces "cost-offsets" for the health care system, i.e. reductions in the use of health services following intervention that meet the costs of the intervention itself and produce additional financial gains for the health service. Studies from a wider economic perspective that includes possible gains to social services, the criminal justice system and industrial productivity are also needed.

Implementing Opportunistic Brief Interventions

The effort to implement OBI in settings other than health care has hardly begun, and this discussion will therefore focus on medical and nursing practice. Partly inspired by the promising research findings that have been reviewed in this chapter, there has been a great deal of attention over the years to the implementation of OBI in routine medical practice in several countries of the world. Unfortunately, as in other fields of health care, many studies have documented a wide gap between actual and recommended good practice based on research evidence. As but one illustration of this, Kaner et al. (1999a) reported findings from a questionnaire survey of general medical practitioners (GPs) in the English Midlands. The results showed that GPs did not to make routine enquiries about alcohol, with 67% enquiring only "some of the time". The fact that 65% of GPs had managed only 1–6 patients for excessive drinking in the last year is striking in view of evidence that approximately 20% of patients presenting to primary health care are likely to be at least hazardous drinkers (Anderson, 1993). Given figures on GPs' average list size in the UK, this suggests that the majority of GPs may be missing as many as 98% of the excessive drinkers presenting to their practices. The situation regarding the detection of excessive drinkers among patients on general hospital wards is comparable. For example, in a study designed to establish whether housemen took an adequate drinking history from their patients, Barrison et al. (1980) noted a failure to record alcohol consumption in 39% of cases; furthermore, in only 37% of the medical notes studied was an accurate history of consumption obtained, while in the remainder only an inaccurate descriptive estimate was recorded. There is little reason to believe that the situation is better in countries other than the UK.

Thus, there is little evidence that medical practitioners have increased their levels of enquiry, identification and intervention regarding excessive drinking over the past 20 years. If the medical profession is too busy or otherwise unwilling to take on this work, the nursing profession represents an engine of great potential in this implementation process (Deehan et al., 1998). It may also be true that medical practitioners are now more likely than they were to see alcohol interventions as a legitimate part of their work, and that changes are taking place within the medical profession with respect to preventive work in general, although these changes will inevitably take time to be fully realized. Meanwhile, ways must be sought to ensure a more adequate response to alcohol problems in medical and nursing practice.

A great deal has been written on the barriers to greater involvement of medical practitioners in OBI and to possible incentives that might be helpful in this regard, but space does not permit a full examination of these ideas (but see Chapter 9 in Raistrick, Hodgson & Ritson, 1999). What can be said is that the best way to implement OBI among the medical and nursing professions is itself an empirical issue. Phase III of the *WHO International Collaborative Project on the Identification and Management of Alcohol-related Problems in Primary Health Care* included a randomized controlled trial of ways to encourage the uptake and utilization of a brief intervention package by GPs (Gomel et al., 1998). In the UK arm of this WHO project (Lock et al., 1999), a total of 729 GPs were randomly allocated to one of three strategies for marketing OBI: direct mail, telemarketing or a personal marketing interview. Personal marketing transpired to be the most effective dissemination strategy but telemarketing was the most cost-effective. In a second component of this study (Kaner et al., 1999b), 128 GPs who had agreed to take part in the trial were randomized to one of three groups: (a) training and support; (b) training and no support; (c) a control group that received the intervention programme with written guidelines only. Results showed that trained and supported GPs were significantly more likely to implement the OBI programme at no greater cost than incurred in the other groups. Results from other countries participating in this WHO collaborative project have been published (Hansen et al., 1999) or are awaited.

Following on from these findings and a large amount of other relevant research, Phase IV of the WHO Collaborative Project is concerned with the development of strategies for the widespread, routine and enduring implementation of screening and brief intervention in the primary health care systems of countries taking part. The WHO Phase IV study is an example of action research in which the overall objective is to make a significant difference to the "real-world" conditions under which OBI is disseminated and implemented. At the time of writing, a total of 12 countries, mostly from Europe, are represented in the study.

Conclusions Regarding Opportunistic Brief Intervention

With regard to smoking cessation, Chapman (1993) has argued that the effects of brief interventions in medical practice are likely to be modest compared with whole population preventive strategies, like higher taxation on cigarettes, increased environmental restrictions on smoking and advertising restrictions; by analogy, the same argument could be applied to excessive drinking. However, this argument misses the point that there is no necessary competition between OBI strategies and preventive control measures; indeed, there are good reasons to believe they these strategies could reinforce each other and work to mutual benefit in the attempt to reduce harmful drinking. It is easy to see, for example, how the widespread implementation of alcohol OBI by the medical, nursing and other professions could facilitate the introduction of effective control measures, by helping to create a climate of opinion in which such measures become more politically acceptable. On the other hand, an environment that does not support and encourage excessive drinking would assist efforts to instigate lasting behaviour changes in OBIs.

In any case, if environmental and other control measures for alcohol continue to be resisted by governments, which is likely to be the case for some time yet, widespread implementation of OBI is probably the only alternative for impacting on alcohol-related public health. Given the formidable barriers to this implementation that have been described in the literature, it is clear that this will be no easy task but it is nevertheless a task that should be started sooner rather than later. In the same way that it took over 30 years for brief advice against cigarette smoking to be fully accepted as an essential contribution to public health, it may take a similar period for OBI against excessive drinking to be widely accepted and implemented in practice.

KEY WORKS AND SUGGESTIONS FOR FURTHER READING

Bien, T.H., Miller, W.R. & Tonigan, J.S. (1993). Brief interventions for alcohol problems: a review. *Addiction*, **88**, 315–336.

Despite being now somewhat out of date and tending to conflate brief treatment and opportunistic brief interventions, this is a very useful review of theory and practice regarding brief interventions.

Heather, N. (1995a). Brief intervention strategies. In R.K. Hester & W.R. Miller (Eds), *Handbook of Alcoholism Treatment Approaches: Effective Alternatives*, 2nd edn. Needham Heights, MA: Allyn & Bacon.

A guide to brief interventions for practitioners plus a narrative review of the research literature.

National Institute on Alcohol Abuse and Alcoholism (1995). *The Physician's Guide to Helping Patients with Alcohol Problems*. Washington, DC: National Institutes of Health.

A how-to-do-it guide for medical practitioners in the USA.

Rollnick, S., Mason, P. & Butler, C. (1999). *Health Behaviour Change: A Guide for Practitioners*. Edinburgh: Churchill Livingstone.

A recent and highly recommended guide to the negotiation of behaviour change, including drinking, in health care settings.

Rollnick, S., Butler, C. & Hodgson, R. (1997). Brief alcohol interventions in medical settings: concerns from the consulting room. *Addiction Research*, **5**, 331–342.

An articulate and in many ways persuasive critique of the "advice-giving" model of opportunistic brief interventions.

REFERENCES

Anderson, P. (1993). Effectiveness of general practice interventions for patients with harmful alcohol consumption. *British Journal of General Practice*, **43**, 386–389.

Anderson, P. & Scott, E. (1992). The effect of general practitioners' advice to heavy drinking men. *British Journal of Addiction*, **87**, 891–900.

Anitt-Poika, I., Karaharju, E., Roine, R. & Salaspuro, M. (1988). Intervention of heavy drinking: a prospective and controlled study of 438 consecutive injured male patients. *Alcohol & Alcoholism*, **23**, 115–121.

Babor, T.F. & Grant, M. (Eds) (1992). *Project on Identification and Management of Alcohol-related Problems. Report on Phase II: A Randomized Clinical Trial of Brief Interventions in Primary Health Care*. Geneva: World Health Organization.

Baldwin, S. (Ed.) (1990). *Alcohol Education and Offenders*. London: Batsford.

Barrison, I.G., Viola, L. & Murray-Lyon, I.M. (1980). Do housemen take an adequate drinking history? *British Medical Journal*, **281**, 1040.

Bien, T.H., Miller, W.R. & Tonigan, J.S. (1993). Brief interventions for alcohol problems: a review. *Addiction*, **88**, 315–336.

Breslin, F.C., Sobell, M.B., Sobell, L.C., Buchan, G. & Cunningham, J.A. (1997). Toward a stepped care approach to treating problem drinkers: the predictive utility of within-treatment variables and therapist prognostic ratings. *Addiction*, **92**, 1479–1489.

Carpenter, R.A., Lyons, C.A. & Miller, W.R. (1985). Peer-managed self-control program for prevention of alcohol abuse in American Indian high school students: a pilot evaluation study. *International Journal of the Addictions*, **20**, 299–310.

Chaney, E.F., O'Leary, M.R. & Marlatt, G.A. (1978). Skill training with alcoholics. *Journal of Consulting & Clinical Psychology*, **48**, 419–426.

Chang, G., Wilkins-Haug, L., Berman, S. & Goetz, M.A. (1999). Brief intervention for alcohol use in pregnancy: a randomized trial. *Addiction*, **94**, 1499–1508.

Chapman, P.L.H. & Huygens, I. (1988). An evaluation of three treatment programmes for alcoholism: an experimental study with 6- and 18-month follow-ups. *British Journal of Addiction*, **83**, 67–81.

Chapman, S. (1993). The role of doctors in promoting smoking cessation. *British Medical Journal*, **307**, 518–519.

Chick, J., Lloyd, G. & Crombie, E. (1985). Counselling problem drinkers in medical wards: a controlled study. *British Medical Journal*, **290**, 965–967.

Chick, J., Ritson, B., Connaughton, J., Stewart, A. & Chick, J. (1988). Advice vs. extended treatment for alcoholism: a controlled study. *British Journal of Addiction*, **83**, 159–170.

Cisler, R., Holder, H.D., Longabaugh, R., Stout, R.L. & Zweben, A. (1998). Actual and estimated replication costs for alcohol treatment modalities: case study from Project MATCH. *Journal of Studies on Alcohol*, **50**, 503–512.

Deehan, A., Templeton, L., Taylor, C., Drummond, C. & Strang, J. (1998). Are practice nurses an unexplored resource in the identification and management of alcohol misuse? Results from a study of practice nurses in England and Wales in 1995. *Journal of Advanced Nursing*, **28**, 592–597.

Drummond, D.C., Thom, B., Brown, C., Edwards, E. & Mullan, M. (1990). Specialist vs. general practitioner treatment of problem drinkers. *Lancet*, **336**, 915–918.

Dunn, C.W., Donovan, D.M. & Gentilello, L.M. (1997). Practical guidelines for performing alcohol interventions in trauma centers. *Journal of Trauma: Injury, Infection & Critical Care*, **42**, 299–304.

Edwards, A.G.K. & Rollnick, S. (1997). Outcome studies of brief alcohol intervention in general practice: the problem of lost subjects. *Addiction*, **92**, 1699–1704.

Edwards, G. & Taylor, C. (1994). A test of the matching hypothesis: alcohol dependence, intensity of treatment and 12 month outcome. *Addiction*, **89**, 553–561.

Edwards, G., Duckitt, E., Oppenheimer, E., Sheehan, M. & Taylor, C. (1983). What happens to alcoholics? *Lancet*, **30**, 269–271.

Edwards, G., Orford, J., Egert, S., Guthrie, S., Hawker, A., Hensman, C., Mitcheson, M., Oppenheimer, E. & Taylor, C. (1977). Alcoholism: a controlled study of "treatment" and "advice". *Journal of Studies on Alcohol*, **38**, 1004–1031.

Elvy, G.A., Wells, J.E. & Baird, K.A. (1988). Counselling problem drinkers in medical wards: a controlled study. *British Journal of Addiction*, **83**, 83–89.

Finney, J.W. & Monahan, S.C. (1996). The cost-effectiveness of treatment for alcoholism: a second approximation. *Journal of Studies on Alcohol*, **57**, 229–243.

Flay, B.R. (1986). Efficacy and effectiveness trials (and other phases of research) in the development of health promotion programs. *Preventive Medicine*, **15**, 451–474.

Fleming, M.F., Barry, K.L., Manwell, L.B., Johnson, K. & London, R. (1997). Brief physician advice for problem alcohol drinkers: a randomized controlled trial in community-based primary care practices. *Journal of the American Medical Association*, **277**, 1039–1045.

Fremantle, N., Gill, P., Godfrey, C., Long, A., Richards, C., Sheldon, T. et al. (1993). *Brief interventions and Alcohol Use*. Effective Health Care Bulletin No. 7. Leeds, UK: Nuffield Institute for Health.

Galanter, M. (1993). *Network Therapy for Alcohol and Drug Abuse: A New Approach in Practice*. New York: Basic Books.

Gibbs, L. & Flanagan, J. (1977). Prognostic indicators of alcoholism treatment outcome. *International Journal of the Addictions*, **12**, 1097–1141

Gomel, M.K., Wutzke, S.E., Hardcastle, D.M. et al. (1998). Cost-effectiveness of strategies to market and train primary health care physicians in brief intervention techniques for hazardous alcohol use. *Social Science & Medicine*, **47**, 203–211.

Gorman, D.M., Werner, J.M., Jacobs, L.M. & Duffy, S.W. (1990). Evaluation of an alcohol education package for non-specialist health care and social workers. *British Journal of Addiction*, **85**, 223–233.

Hansen, L.J., de Fine Olivarius, N., Beich, A. & Barfod, S. (1999). Encouraging GPs to undertake screening and brief intervention in order to reduce problem drinking: a randomized controlled trial. *Family Practice*, **16**, 551–557.

Heather, N. (1994). Brief interventions on the world map. Comments on WHO Project on Identification and Management of Alcohol-related Problems; Report on Phase II: a randomized clinical trial of brief interventions in primary health care. *Addiction*, **89**, 665–667.

Heather, N. (1995a). Brief intervention strategies. In R.K. Hester & W.R. Miller (Eds), *Handbook of Alcoholism Treatment Approaches: Effective Alternatives*, 2nd edn. Needham Heights, MA: Allyn & Bacon.

Heather, N. (1995b). Interpreting the evidence on brief interventions for excessive drinkers: the need for caution. *Alcohol & Alcoholism*, **30**, 287–296.

Heather, N. (1996). The public health and brief interventions for excessive alcohol consumption: the British experience. *Addictive Behaviors*, **21**, 857–868.

Heather, N. (1998). Using brief opportunities for change in medical settings. In W.R. Miller & N. Heather (Eds), *Treating Addictive Behaviors*, 2nd edn. New York: Plenum.

Heather, N. (1999). Some common methodological criticisms of Project MATCH: are they justified? *Addiction*, **94**, 36–39.

Heather, N., Campion, P., Neville, R. & MacCabe, D. (1987). Evaluation of a controlled drinking minimal intervention for problem drinkers in general practice (the DRAMS Scheme). *Journal of the Royal College of General Practitioners*, **37**, 358–363.

Heather, N., Robertson, I. & Davies, P. (1985). *The Misuse of Alcohol: Crucial Issues in Dependence, Treatment and Prevention.* London: Croom Helm.

Heather, N., Rollnick, S., Bell, A. & Richmond, R. (1996). Effects of brief counselling among male heavy drinkers identified on general hospital wards. *Drug & Alcohol Review*, **15**, 29–38.

Higgins-Biddle, J.C. & Babor, T.F. (1996). *Reducing Risky Drinking: A Report on the Early Identification and Management of Alcohol Problems through Screening and Brief Intervention.* Prepared for the Robert Wood Johnson Foundation. Farmington, CT: University of Connecticut Health Center.

Holder, H.D., Longabaugh, R., Miller, W.R. & Rubonis, A.V. (1991). The cost effectiveness of treatment for alcohol problems: a first approximation. *Journal of Studies on Alcohol*, **52**, 517–540.

Holder, H.D., Miller, T.R. & Carina, R.T. (1995). *Cost Savings of Substance Abuse Prevention in Managed Care.* Berkeley, CA: Center for Substance Abuse Prevention.

Institute of Medicine (1990). *Broadening the Base of Treatment for Alcohol Problems.* Washington, DC: National Academy Press.

Israel, Y., Hollander, O., Sanchez-Craig, M., Booker, S., Miller, V., Gingrich, R., & Rankin, J.G. (1996). Screening for problem drinking and counseling by the primary care physician-nurse team. *Alcoholism: Clinical & Experimental Research*, **20**, 1443–1450.

Kahan, M., Wilson, L., & Becker, L. (1995). Effectiveness of physician-based interventions with problem drinkers: a review. *Canadian Medical Association Journal*, **152**, 851–859.

Kaner, E., Heather, N., McAvoy, B., Haighton, C. & Gilvarry, E. (1999a). Intervention for excessive alcohol consumption in primary health care: attitudes and practices of English general practitioners. *Alcohol & Alcoholism*, **34**, 559–566.

Kaner, E.F.S., Haighton, C.A., McAvoy, B.R., Heather, N. & Gilvarry, E. (1999b). A RCT of three training and support strategies to encourage implementation of screening and brief alcohol intervention by general practitioners. *British Journal of General Practice*, **49**, 699–703.

Kissin, B. (1977). Comments on "Alcoholism: a controlled trial of 'treatment' and 'advice'." *Journal of Studies on Alcohol*, **38**, 1804–1808.

Kristenson, H., Ohlin, H., Hulten-Nosslin, M., Trell, E. & Hood, B. (1983). Identification and intervention of heavy drinking in middle-aged men: results and follow-up of 24:60 months of long-term study with randomized controls. *Alcoholism: Clinical & Experimental Research*, **20**, 203–209.

Lock, C.A., Kaner, E.F.S., Heather, N., McAvoy, B.R. & Gilvarry, E. (1999). A randomized trial of three marketing strategies to disseminate a screening and brief alcohol intervention programme to general practitioners. *British Journal of General Practice*, **49**, 695–698.

Longabaugh, R., Wirtz, P.W., Zweben, A. & Stout, R.L. (1998). Network support for drinking, Alcoholics Anonymous and long-term matching effects. *Addiction*, **93**, 1313–1333.

Machona, A.M. (1992). Harare, Zimbabwe. In T.F. Babor & M. Grant (Eds), *Project on Identification and Management of Alcohol-related Problems. Report on Phase II: A Randomized Clinical Trial of Brief Interventions in Primary Health Care* (pp. 211–220). Geneva: World Health Organization.

Maheswaran, R., Beevers, M. & Beever, D.G. (1992). Effectiveness of advice to reduce alcohol consumption in hypertensive patients. *Hypertension*, **19**, 79–84.

Mattick, R.P. & Jarvis, T. (Eds) (1993). *An Outline for the Management of Alcohol Problems: Quality Assurance Project*. National Drug Strategy Monograph Series No. 20. Canberra: Australian Government Publishing Service.

Mattick, R.P. & Jarvis, T. (1994). Brief or minimal intervention for "alcoholics"? The evidence suggests otherwise. *Drug & Alcohol Review*, **13**, 137–144.

McCrady, B.S., Stout, R.L., Noel, N.E., Abrams, D.B & Nelson, H.F. (1991). Comparative effectiveness of three types of spouse-involved behavioural alcoholism treatment: outcomes 18 months after treatment. *British Journal of Addiction*, **86**, 1415–1424.

McLellan, A.T., Luborsky, L., Woody, G.E., Druley, K.A. & O'Brien, C.A. (1983). Predicting response to alcohol and drug abuse treatments: role of psychiatric severity. *Archives of General Psychiatry*, **40**, 620–625.

Miller, W.R. & Baca, L.M. (1983). Two-year follow-up of bibliotherapy and therapist-directed controlled drinking training for problem drinkers. *Behavior Therapy*, **14**, 441–448.

Miller, W.R. & Taylor, C.A. (1980). Relative effectiveness of bibliotherapy, individual and group self-control training in the treatment of problem drinkers. *Addictive Behaviors*, **5**, 13–24.

Miller, W.R., Brown, J.M., Simpson, T.L. et al. (1995). What works? A methodological analysis of the alcohol treatment outcome literature. In R.K. Hester & W.R. Miller, (Eds), *Handbook of Alcoholism Treatment Approaches: Effective Alternatives*. Needham Heights, MA: Allyn & Bacon.

Miller, W.R., Gribskov, C.J. & Mortell, R.L. (1981). Effectiveness of a self-control manual for problem drinkers with and without therapist contact. *International Journal of the Addictions*, **16**, 1247–1254.

Miller, W.R., Sovereign, R.G. & Krege, B. (1988). Motivational interviewing with problem drinkers: II. The Drinker's Check-up as a preventive intervention. *Behavioural Psychotherapy*, **16**, 251–268.

Miller, W.R., Taylor, C.A. & West, J.C. (1980). Focused vs. broad-spectrum behavior therapy for problem drinkers. *Journal of Consulting & Clinical Psychology*, **48**, 590–601.

Miller, W.R., Zweben, A., DiClemente, C. & Rychtarik, R. (1992). *Motivational Enhancement Therapy: A Clinical Research Guide for Therapists Treating Individuals with Alcohol Abuse and Dependence*. Project MATCH Monograph Series, Vol. 2, DHHS Publication No. (ADM) 92–1894. Washington, DC, Department of Health & Human Services.

National Institute on Alcohol Abuse and Alcoholism (1995). *The Physician's Guide to Helping Patients with Alcohol Problems*. Washington, DC: National Institutes of Health.

Nilssen, O. (1991). The Tromsø Study: identification of and a controlled intervention on a population of early-stage risk drinkers. *Preventive Medicine*, **20**, 518–528.

Oei, T.P.S. & Jackson, P. (1980). Long-term effects of group and individual social skills training with alcoholics. *Addictive Behaviors*, **5**, 129–136.

Office of National Statistics (1998). *Living in Britain: Results from the 1996 General Household Survey*. London: The Stationery Office.

Orford, J. & Edwards, G. (1977). *Alcoholism: A Comparison of Treatment and Advice with a Study of the Influence of Marriage*. Maudsley Monographs No. 26. Oxford: Oxford University Press.

Persson, J. & Magnusson, P.-H. (1989). Early intervention in patients with excessive consumption of alcohol: a controlled study. *Alcohol*, **6**, 403–408.

Poikolainen, K. (1999). Effectiveness of brief interventions to reduce alcohol intake in primary health care populations: a meta-analysis. *Preventive Medicine*, **28**, 503–509.

Popper, K.R. (1959). *The Logic of Scientific Discovery*. London: Hutchinson.

Prochaska, J.O. & DiClemente, C.C. (1992). Stages of change in the modification of problem behaviors. In M. Hersen, R.M. Eisler & P.M. Miller (Eds), *Progress in Behavior Modification*. Newbury Park, CA: Sage.

Project MATCH Research Group (1997a). Matching alcoholism treatments to client heterogeneity: Project MATCH posttreatment drinking outcomes. *Journal of Studies on Alcohol*, **58**, 7–29.

Project MATCH Research Group (1997b). Project MATCH secondary *a priori* hypotheses. *Addiction*, **92**, 1655–1682.

Project MATCH Research Group (1998). Matching alcoholism treatments to client heterogeneity: Project MATCH three-year drinking outcomes. *Alcoholism: Experimental & Clinical Research*, **22**, 1300–1311.

Raistrick, D., Hodgson, R. & Ritson, B. (Eds) (1999). *Tackling Alcohol Together: the Evidence Base for UK Alcohol Policy*. London: Free Association Books.

Reilly, D., Van Beurden, E., Mitchell, E., Dight, R., Scott, C. & Beard, J. (1998). Alcohol education in licensed premises using brief intervention strategies. *Addiction*, **93**, 385–398.

Richmond, R., Heather, N., Wodak, A., Kehoe, L. & Webster, I. (1995). Controlled evaluation of a general practice-based brief intervention for excessive drinking. *Addiction*, **90**, 119–132.

Richmond, R.L., Kehoe, L., Hailstone, S., Wodak, A. & Uebel-Yan, M. (1999). Quantitative and qualitative evaluations of brief interventions to change excessive drinking, smoking and stress in the police force. *Addiction*, **94**, 1509–1521.

Romelsjö, A., Andersson, L., Barrner, H., Borg, S., Granstrand, C., Hultman, O. et al. (1989). A randomized study of secondary prevention of early stage problem drinkers in primary health care. *British Journal of Addiction*, **84**, 1319–1327.

Rollnick, S., Butler, C. & Hodgson, R. (1997). Brief alcohol interventions in medical settings: concerns from the consulting room. *Addiction Research*, **5**, 331–342.

Rollnick, S., Mason, P. & Butler, C. (1999). *Health Behaviour Change: A Guide for Practitioners*. Edinburgh: Churchill Livingstone.

Royal College of Physicians (1987). *A Great and Growing Evil: The Medical Consequences of Alcohol Abuse*. London: Tavistock.

Russell, M.A.H., Wilson, C., Taylor, C., & Baker, C.D. (1979). Effect of general practitioners' advice against smoking. *British Medical Journal*, **283**, 231–235.

Sannibale, C. (1988). The differential effect of a set of brief interventions on the functioning of a group of "early-stage" problem drinkers. *Australian Drug & Alcohol Review*, **7**, 147–155.

Sanchez-Craig, M. & Lei, H. (1986). Disadvantages of imposing the goal of abstinence on problem drinkers: an empirical study. *British Journal of Addiction*, **81**, 505–512.

Saunders, J.B., Aasland, O.G., Babor, T.F. et al. (1993). Development of the Alcohol Use Disorders Identification Test (AUDIT): WHO Collaborative Project on early detection of person with harmful alcohol consumption, II. *Addiction*, **88**, 791–804.

Shawcross, M., Robertson, S., Jones, A., Maciver, J. & de Souza, R. (1996). *Family and Alcohol Project: Report on a Pilot Project*. Edinburgh: Lothian Regional Council Social Work Department.

Sisson, R.W. & Azrin, N. (1989). Family members' involvement to initiate and promote the treatment of problem drinkers. *Journal of Behaviour Therapy & Experimental Psychiatry*, **17**, 15–21.

Skutle, A. & Berg, G. (1987). Training in controlled drinking for early-stage problem drinkers. *British Journal of Addiction*, **82**, 493–501.

Sobell, M.B. & Sobell, L.C. (1993). Treatment for problem drinkers: a public health priority. In J.S. Baer, G.A. Marlatt & R.J. McMahon (Eds), *Addictive Behaviors Across the Lifespan: Prevention, Treatment and Policy Issues*. Newbury Park, CA: Sage.

Thom, B., Franey, C., Foster, R., Keaney, R. & Salazar, C. (1994). *Alcohol Treatment Since 1983: A Review of Research Literature*. Report to the Alcohol Education & Research Council. London: Centre for Research on Drugs and Health Behaviour.

Thomas, E.J. & Ager, R.D. (1993). Unilateral family therapy. In T.J. O'Farrell (Ed.), *Treating Alcohol Problems: Marital and Family Interventions*. New York: Guilford.

Tuchfeld, B.S. (1977). Comments on "Alcoholism: a controlled trial of 'treatment' and 'advice'", *Journal of Studies on Alcohol*, **38**, 1808–1813.

UKATT Research Team (in press). United Kingdom Alcohol Treatment Trial: hypotheses, design and methods. *Alcohol and Alcoholism.*

Wallace, P., Cutler, S. & Haines, A. (1988).   Randomised controlled trial of general practitioner intervention in patients with excessive alcohol consumption. *British Medical Journal*, **297**, 663–668.

Wilk, A.I., Jensen, N.M. & Havighurst, T.C. (1997).   Meta-analysis of randomized control trials addressing brief interventions in heavy alcohol drinkers. *Archives of Internal Medicine*, **12**, 274–283.

Zweben, A., Pearlman, S. & Li, S. (1988).   A comparison of brief advice and conjoint therapy in the treatment of alcohol abuse: the results of the Marital Systems study. *British Journal of Addiction*, **83**, 899–916.

Chapter 32

Treating Comorbidity of Alcohol Problems and Psychiatric Disorder

Kim T. Mueser
Dartmouth Medical School, Hanover, NH, USA
and
David Kavanagh
Department of Psychiatry, Royal Brisbane Hospital, Herston,
Queensland, Australia

Synopsis

Alcohol use disorders have an increased prevalence in persons with psychiatric disorders. The comorbidity between substance misuse and psychiatric disorders is highest for antisocial personality disorder, schizophrenia and bipolar disorder, followed by anxiety and affective disorders. Because anxiety and affective disorders are the most prevalent psychiatric illnesses, the large majority of people with comorbid psychiatric and alcohol use disorders have an anxiety or affective disorder.

Treatment of alcohol and psychiatric comorbidity must be tailored to patients' insight and motivation to address their substance abuse, eschewing confrontational strategies that can threaten the therapeutic alliance and provoke symptom relapses. The concept of stages of treatment provides an overarching heuristic in treating comorbid disorders. According to this model, patients progress through a series of stages in the process of recovery from alcohol misuse problems, and are responsive to interventions appropriate to that stage. The different stages include engagement, persuasion, active treatment, *and* relapse prevention. *Awareness of patients' stage of treatment can improve outcomes by optimizing treatments appropriate to patients' motivational states.*

In recent years there has been a movement towards treating alcohol misuse and psychiatric disorders in an integrated fashion, in which both disorders are treated

International Handbook of Alcohol Dependence and Problems. Edited by N. Heather, T.J. Peters and T. Stockwell.

simultaneously by the same clinicians. The necessity of integrated treatment stems from problems in non-integrated treatment approaches, in which patients either failed to receive one or both types of treatment, or treatment by different providers was not coordinated and was often contradictory. Integrated treatment is especially critical for patients with severe mental illness such as schizophrenia, who often receive little or no treatment for their substance use problems. Several other features of effective treatment for alcohol misuse in people with severe mental illness include assertive outreach, comprehensiveness, attention to safe and protective living environments and a long-term commitment.

The treatment of anxiety and affective disorders has also moved towards integrated models, although somewhat more slowly than in people with severe mental illness. Where the anxiety or affective disorder is unremitting or recurrent, we expect that treatment will be more effective if it teaches patients not only to manage each disorder but to maintain control of alcohol use during an exacerbation of their symptoms. However, the integrated treatment will rarely need to be as intensive or long-term as in severe mental disorders, and will usually rely heavily on patients' self-management skills.

Treatment of comorbidity of alcohol-related problems and antisocial personality disorder sometimes raises particular concern among therapists and often involves more severe alcohol abuse than in other comorbid disorders. However, current data suggest that once the severity of the alcohol-related problems is controlled, treatment for alcohol abuse or dependence in this population may be as effective as in the general community.

Optimal treatment of comorbidity with alcohol abuse or dependence requires clinicians with skills in the management of both disorders and full access to treatment resources required for each one. Problems with the management of comorbidity will not be addressed fully until clinician training and service structures allow a complete integration of patient management.

Psychiatric comorbidity in people with alcohol abuse or dependence presents multi-faceted challenges for practitioners. One set of challenges involves accurate detection. Practitioners need to ensure that their primary focus of referral or treatment does not blind them to comorbidity. Psychiatric disorders can go undetected in a person with severe alcohol problems, due to the prominence of alcohol-related symptoms. Conversely, in psychiatric settings, alcohol problems can be overlooked in the context of severe psychiatric symptoms or functional impairment. There can also be uncertainty when diagnosing a psychiatric disorder in a person with alcohol misuse, due to the overlap in symptoms and the similar consequences of both disorders. A further set of challenges is posed by the selection and delivery of appropriate treatments for people with comorbid problems. Different or additional interventions for the psychiatric symptoms may be required, and the treatment of alcohol abuse or dependence may need to be tailored to the specific psychiatric disorder. This complexity underscores the importance of both recognizing and treating psychiatric comorbidity in people with an alcohol use disorder.

We begin with a review of the epidemiology of alcohol and psychiatric disorder comorbidity, in which we include both large community-based surveys of alcohol and psychiatric comorbidity and studies in treatment settings. Next, we describe the principles of treating patients with alcohol misuse and comorbid psychiatric disorders. As these principles differ according to the type of disorder, we discuss treatment strategies separately for three broad classes of disorders: severe mental disorders (such as schizophrenia), anxiety and affective disorders, and antisocial personality disorder.

EPIDEMIOLOGY OF ALCOHOL AND PSYCHIATRIC DISORDER COMORBIDITY

Studies examining substance misuse and psychiatric comorbidity generally fall into one of two types: community-based surveys and studies of patients in treatment settings (e.g. in a psychiatric hospital, or at an outpatient clinic for alcohol disorders). Each type of study has its own advantages and disadvantages. The primary advantage of community-based surveys is that they provide the most accurate estimate of comorbidity for the *population* of people with a particular disorder. If the population comorbidity is estimated from samples of patients in treatment rather than from a community survey, the true level of comorbidity will be overestimated because the psychiatric and the alcohol use disorders can independently propel the person into treatment (a phenomenon known as "Berkson's Fallacy"; Berkson, 1949). The major limitation of community surveys is that very large numbers of people must be sampled in order to assess enough people with disorders that occur at low base rates in the general population, such as bipolar disorder or schizophrenia.

The primary advantage of comorbidity studies that are conducted in treatment settings is that they provide the best estimates of comorbidity for patients who are receiving treatment for at least one of their disorders. Such information has practical value to clinicians who need to know about the extent and nature of comorbidity in their patients. A drawback to surveys of patients in treatment is that the observed comorbidity rates depend heavily on the specific treatment setting (e.g. inpatient, outpatient, emergency room) and the demographic characteristics of the patients receiving treatment (Galanter, Castaneda & Ferman, 1988; Mueser et al., 1990). Estimates of comorbidity from surveys in both community and treatment settings are also subject to geographical variations in substance use and changes in substance preferences and normative levels of use over time: both of these effects can be substantial (Becker, 1967; Johnson & Muffler, 1992; Jenner et al., submitted for publication; Mueser, Yarnold & Bellack, 1992).

Community-based Surveys

Two large community-based surveys of alcohol and psychiatric disorder comorbidity have been conducted over the past 15 years in the USA, the Epidemiologic Catchment Area (ECA) Study (Regier et al., 1990) and the National Comorbidity Survey (NCS; Kessler et al., 1996). Another large survey was recently completed in Australia (National Survey of Mental Health and Well-being; MHW; Teeson et al., 2000).

The ECA Study was a large survey that included over 20,000 people throughout the USA. This study oversampled people in different institutional settings, including state psychiatric hospitals, Veterans Administration Medical Centers, general hospitals, jails and nursing homes. This oversampling provided enough people with severe mental disorders to evaluate comorbidity with alcohol use disorders. For all participants, interviews were conducted to evaluate recent and lifetime substance misuse and psychiatric disorders. The NCS and MHW studies involved structured interviews with over 8000 and over 10,000 community residents, respectively. Oversampling of patients in institutional settings was not done, so few people with schizophrenia-spectrum and bipolar disorder were evaluated. However, the MHW survey was supplemented by a separate study of 980 people with psychotic disorders (Jeblensky et al., 1999).

In all of the community surveys, alcohol use disorders were often comorbid with drug use disorders. For example, in the ECA study the odds ratio (OR) for drug use disorder in people with an alcohol use disorder was 7.1; 21.5% of people with a lifetime alcohol use disorder also had a lifetime drug use disorder.

The three community samples also showed high rates of comorbidity between alcohol misuse and psychiatric disorders. The most common types of psychiatric disorders in the general population are anxiety disorders and affective disorders. Alcohol problems are associated with increased rates of both psychiatric disorders. For example, in the ECA study the lifetime rate of anxiety disorders for the general population was 14.6%, and 8.3% had an affective disorder. Among people with an alcohol disorder, the rate of anxiety disorders increased to 19.4% (OR = 1.5) and affective disorders rose to 13.4% (OR = 1.9). The combination of high population rates and increased risks with alcohol disorders means that anxiety and affective disorders are the most common comorbid problems in people with alcohol abuse or dependence.

Relatively low rates of some psychiatric disorders in the general population result in lower absolute rates of dual diagnosis in the general community, even though the proportional increase in risk is sometimes considerably higher. In the ECA study, the highest proportional increase was in antisocial personality disorder (ASPD; OR = 21.0), followed by bipolar disorder (OR = 5.1) and schizophrenia (OR = 3.3). As a result, the life-time incidence of alcohol misuse in people with schizophrenia was 33.7%, in bipolar disorder it was 43.6%, and in ASPD 73.6% had an alcohol disorder at some time in their lives.

Treatment-based Surveys

Most studies examining alcohol misuse and psychiatric comorbidity have been conducted in treatment settings. In general, these studies also show high rates of comorbidity, in some cases even higher rates than in the community-based studies, as expected from Berkson's Fallacy. Across numerous studies of people receiving treatment for severe mental disorders (including schizophrenia, schizoaffective disorder, bipolar disorder and major depression), the lifetime rate of alcohol misuse is often over 40% (Duke, Pantelis & Barnes, 1994; Fowler et al., 1998; Mueser et al., 1990, 1992, 2000; Rosenthal, Hellerstein & Miner, 1992b; Shaner et al., 1993; Stone et al., 1993). Although fewer treatment-based studies have been conducted of the prevalence of alcohol use disorders among people in treatment for anxiety disorders, the available evidence suggests similarly high rates (Kushner, Sher & Beitman, 1990; Stewart, 1996).

Just as research has documented high rates of alcohol misuse in treatment-seeking psychiatric patients, people in treatment for alcohol-related problems also have high rates of psychiatric comorbidity. For example, Ross et al. (1988) evaluated lifetime psychiatric disorders in 501 people who sought treatment for alcohol or drug misuse. Of these people, 84.2% also had a psychiatric disorder. The most common disorders were anxiety disorders (61.9%), ASPD (46.9%) and affective disorders (33.7%). Similar findings have been reported by Powell et al. (1982) and Hesselbrock et al. (1985).

Summary of Epidemiology of Alcohol Misuse–Psychiatric Comorbidity

Numerous studies show that alcohol use disorders have a high comorbidity with psychiatric disorders. Treated samples tend to have higher rates of comorbidity than community samples. Rates of alcohol misuse comorbidity tend to be highest for ASPD, followed by severe mental disorders such as schizophrenia and bipolar disorder, followed by other affective disorders and anxiety disorders. Because severe mental disorders and ASPD have a relatively low prevalence in the general population compared to anxiety and depression, the majority of patients with an alcohol misuse–psychiatric comorbidity have anxiety or affective disorders.

TREATMENT

In recent years there has been a growing recognition of the importance of providing treatment for alcoholism that is tailored to patients' level of insight and motivation to work on their substance misuse. Rather than emphasizing direct confrontation of patients who deny problems related to their substance misuse, social pressure to acknowledge the evils of alcohol abuse and immediate endorsement of abstinence as a treatment priority, motivational approaches initially focus on relationship formation and harm reduction. While motivational strategies have gained some ascendance in the treatment of primary substance misuse, their importance has been even more rapidly accepted in work with individuals with comorbid disorders, whose psychiatric disorders are often inextricably tied to their use of alcohol and drugs.

Stages of Treatment

A useful overarching heuristic in work with all comorbid disorders is provided by the concept of stagewise treatment. The *stages of treatment* are based on the observation that people with an alcohol misuse problem who change their behavior over the course of treatment typically progress through a series of stages, and that each stage is characterized by different attitudes, behaviors and goals. By understanding a patient's current stage of treatment, the clinician can optimize treatment so that it matches his/her current level of motivation, and avoid driving the person away from treatment by attempting interventions that are mismatched to his/her motivation. Four stages of treatment have been identified: engagement, persuasion, active treatment and relapse prevention (Mueser, Drake & Noordsy, 1998; Osher & Kofoed, 1989). We provide a brief description of each stage of treatment, including the goal of each stage, and examples of interventions appropriate to that stage.

Engagement Stage

Efforts to change another person's behavior are doomed to failure if a therapeutic alliance has not first been established. Therefore, at the engagement stage the primary goal of treatment is to establish a working alliance (or therapeutic relationship) between the patient and clinician. A working alliance can be operationally defined as regular contact (e.g. weekly) between the patient and clinician (McHugo et al., 1995). Until this relationship is established, no efforts are directed at changing the substance misuse. A wide range of strategies exist for engaging the patient in treatment, including assertive outreach, resolving a crisis, attending to basic needs (e.g. medical, housing), and legal constraints (e.g. outpatient commitment).

Persuasion Stage

At the persuasion stage, the clinician has a working alliance with the patient, but the focus of the relationship is not on addressing the patient's substance misuse. Therefore, at this stage the patient is still actively misusing substances, or has only recently begun to cut down on substance use. The goal of this stage is to convince the patient that his/her substance misuse is an important problem, and to marshal motivation to begin working on that problem.

Motivational interviewing (Miller & Rollnick, 1991) is one useful strategy for helping patients understand the negative impact of their substance use on their own personal goals. Persuasion groups (Mueser & Noordsy, 1996), in which patients are provided with an opportunity to share their experiences with substance use with a minimum of direct confrontation or social censure, can help patients develop motivation to address their substance misuse. Commitment to work on substance misuse can be operationally defined as an actual reduction in substance misuse (McHugo et al., 1995), or another change in behavior that is associated with a reduction in risk (e.g. ceasing intravenous administration of a drug). In many cases, the duration of these attempts may at first be inhibited by the self-control skills the patient can marshal: in these instances, re-engagement occurs in close conjunction with training in skills to deal with situations in which previous lapses occurred.

Miller & Rollnick (1991) emphasize that commitment to change is a function of both motivation and self-efficacy or confidence in being able to change. As Bandura (1986) noted, past achievements are much more powerful influences on self-efficacy than verbal persuasion that is unrelated to past performance. The attention of patients is drawn to successful aspects of past control attempts, rather than to their ultimate failure to deal with the substance-related problems up to now. While a sense of self-efficacy tends to have limited generalization across performance domains (Bandura, 1986), commitment to change may sometimes be aided by success in another domain, such as work-related skills that open up options for a viable substance-free life-style.

The current cognitive abilities of some patients are so limited that their behavior is governed primarily by currently salient stimuli, rather than by behavioral plans. Commitment to change then becomes a fleeting phenomenon that is restricted by an inability to sustain attention or recall information. The effects of skills training or even of persuasion groups may then be relatively small. A temporary reduction in substance intake or risk of harm may sometimes be achieved in these patients by cueing them to engage in activities that are inconsistent with substance use (e.g. helping the person buy groceries on the day they receive disability payments, or scheduling an outing at a time where they are at particular risk of misuse). In cases where the substance misuse is restricted to a narrow range of situations, or where an ongoing structured environment can be created, behavioral scheduling and reinforcement can have a significant impact. However, unless the cognitive deficit is reduced by the changes in substance intake, the impact of this supportive environmental intervention will necessarily be as ephemeral as the patient's attention and memory.

Active Treatment Stage

Once the patient has begun to reduce his/her substance use, the motivation to work on substance misuse is harnessed, and the goal of treatment shifts to further reduction of substance use or the maintenance of abstinence. Many of the strategies developed for people with a primary substance use disorder can be used with dually diagnosed patients once they reach the active treatment stage. Examples of interventions at this stage of treatment include cognitive-behavioral counseling to address "high-risk" situations, self-help groups, and social skills training to address substance use situations. Structured activities, such as work preparation or leisure pursuits that decrease opportunities for using substances and divert attention from substance use, can assist in development of substance control.

Relapse Prevention Stage

In relapse prevention, the patient has achieved substance control for a substantial period (e.g. at least 6 months). The goals are to both guard against a relapse of substance misuse and to extend the gains made to other areas of functioning, such as social relationships, work and housing. Awareness of vulnerability to relapse can be achieved through continued participation in self-help groups, or individual or group work with substance misuse as a focus. The focus in the relapse prevention stage on other areas of functioning, such as relationships, leisure activities and work, reflects the belief that the better a patient's life is, the less vulnerable he/she will be to a relapse of substance misuse.

Integrated Dual Diagnosis Treatment

Until recently, patients with substance misuse and mental disorders had their two disorders treated separately, when treated at all. These traditional treatment models followed a policy of either sequential or parallel treatment. In sequential treatment, patients first receive treatment for one disorder, followed by treatment for the other disorder. In the most extreme version of sequential treatment, a disorder that is considered "primary" is treated initially, and the second is only treated if it does not remit after treatment of the first. In parallel treatment, patients receive treatment for both disorders simultaneously from different groups of professionals, including specialists in the management of substance misuse and others who treat mental health problems. Both approaches assume that each disorder can be treated in isolation of the other. Sequential treatment assumes an absence of substantial reciprocal interaction between the disorders; parallel treatment assumes an absence of problematic interactions between treatments.

By the late 1980s, problems with traditional approaches to treating comorbid substance abuse and mental disorders were widely recognized and their ineffectiveness was broadly accepted—at least in the case of comorbidity with severe mental disorders (Polcin, 1992; Ridgely, Goldman & Willenbring, 1990). The separation of mental health and substance abuse treatment resulted in many patients never receiving services for one of their comorbid disorders, due to restrictive eligibility criteria or inadequate detection or management by the treatment provider. Sequential treatment approaches tend to be ineffective because significant comorbid disorders tend to have a web of reciprocal influence that makes the treatment of one disorder in isolation difficult. Parallel treatment approaches are problematic because different treatment providers usually fail to integrate their interventions, which can result in contradictory or incompatible treatments (e.g. the use of strong interpersonal confrontation is favored by some substance misuse professionals, but eschewed by most professionals who treat severe mental disorders). In addition, deficiencies in communication between the therapists who are involved in parallel treatment present substantial problems for patient management, especially when these therapists work in different agencies (Kavanagh et al., 2000).

The recognition of problems with traditional approaches to dual diagnosis treatment has led to the development of integrated treatment models for severe mental disorders and substance misuse (Drake et al., 1991; Kavanagh, 1995; Minkoff, 1989; Rosenthal, Hellerstein & Miner, 1992a). At the core of integrated treatment models is the assumption that the same clinician or team of clinicians treats both the mental disorders and the substance misuse simultaneously. When deciding whether an intervention is appropriate at a particular stage, clinicians working within this approach take into account the total picture of symptoms, cognitive abilities and context, rather than focusing on progress within a single problem dimension.

Severe Mental Disorders

The evidence for integrated treatment is currently strongest in the context of severe mental disorders. A recent review was completed of 36 studies of integrated treatment for dual disorders involving severe mental illness (Drake et al., 1998d). Many of the studies were limited by small sample sizes, lack of experimental design, short treatment and follow-up periods, and the use of assessments not validated for people with severe mental illness. However, several trends in findings were apparent. First, the simple addition of substance abuse groups to standard mental health treatment had little effect on outcomes. Second, as reported in primary substance abuse treatment, successful engagement in treatment was associated with improved outcomes. Third, programs that provided integrated dual diagnosis treatment, in which both substance misuse and mental illness were treated simultaneously, tended to have superior outcomes to traditional parallel or sequential treatment approaches (Carmichael et al., 1998; Drake et al., 1997; Godley, Hoewing-Roberson & Godley, 1994).

Research on the critical ingredients of effective dual diagnosis treatment programs is sparse. However, in addition to the use of motivational enhancement strategies described above, most integrated programs share a number of common features, including assertive outreach, comprehensiveness, attention to stable housing and a long-term perspective (Mueser et al., 1998b). We briefly describe these core components below.

Assertive Outreach

Patients with severe mental disorders and alcohol misuse frequently are in and out of treatment, and they often become non-compliant during exacerbations of their substance misuse. In order to involve them in treatment, assertive outreach in the community to engage patients in their natural living environments is often necessary. In the absence of assertive outreach, it is difficult or impossible to engage many patients in dual diagnosis treatment.

Outreach to patients with psychotic disorders requires special delicacy, as substance misuse often worsens these symptoms, clouding judgment and increasing social withdrawal. It is critical that outreach in the early stages of treatment is focused on establishing a relationship with the patient while avoiding confrontation, and persuasion work aimed at developing insight into the effects of substance use. Patients often stop taking prescribed medications for their psychiatric illness when they misuse substances, in part for fear of those medications interacting with the substance they use, and education about these interactions may be necessary to achieve psychiatric stabilization.

In addition to the importance of assertive outreach for engaging patients in treatment, outreach can also be helpful later in the course of treatment. Meeting with patients in the community can provide the clinician with valuable information about the possible effects of the patient's environment on his/her continued substance misuse or threats to relapse. In addition, assertive outreach can provide valuable information about patients' ongoing substance misuse and the availability of social supports.

The benefits of outreach are supported by the results of a study recently completed by Drake et al. (1998b). Dually diagnosed patients at seven different mental health centers were randomly assigned to either standard case management teams or assertive community treatment (ACT; Stein & Santos, 1998) teams, and provided with integrated treatment over 3 years. The primary difference between the ACT and standard case management teams was in the intensity of services and extent of outreach provided. While patients in both treatment groups improved, those who received ACT improved more in their alcohol misuse outcomes.

Comprehensiveness

People with severe mental disorders and substance misuse have multiple needs in addition to their substance misuse problems. Effective, integrated dual diagnosis treatment programs attend to these needs and provide services to address functioning in a wide range of areas other than substance misuse. Typically, impairments in other areas of functioning interact with substance abuse, requiring rehabilitation in order to successfully address the substance misuse.

One important area requiring attention is problems in social relationships. Impairments in social functioning are a core characteristic of schizophrenia, and are common in other disorders such as bipolar disorder (American Psychiatric Association, 1994). Substance abuse may facilitate social functioning in these individuals by providing opportunities for social interactions and shared leisure activities with others (Salyers & Mueser, in press). However, with increased substance misuse and negative consequences, relationships with others often become strained, and social exclusion occurs (Drake, Brunette & Mueser, 1998a). Therefore, social skills training has been advocated to help dually diagnosed patients develop skills for dealing with substance use situations more effectively, and to establish relationships with people who do not misuse substances (Bellack & DiClemente, 1999; Bellack et al., 1997). Data from one quasi-controlled study has supported the effects of social skills training for dually diagnosed patients (Jerrell & Ridgely, 1995).

Another area in need of attention in a comprehensive program is family relationships. Substance abuse in patients with severe mental illness is associated with increased problems in family relationships (Dixon, McNary & Lehman, 1995; Salyers & Mueser, in press), violence directed towards relatives (Steadman et al., 1998), and housing instability and homelessness (Susser, 1989). Family treatment aims at educating families about dual disorders, stress reduction, improved adherence to treatment, and harm reduction (and preferably abstinence) from substance use (Mueser & Fox, 1998). Without family intervention, many dually diagnosed patients eventually lose the support of their relatives and the benefits of the buffering role families play in shielding patients from stress, and consequently suffer a worse course of their disorders (Caton et al., 1994; 1995). Although controlled research on family intervention has been shown to be effective for both substance use disorders (Stanton & Shadish, 1997) and severe mental illness (Baucom et al., 1998; Mueser & Glynn, 1999), similar research has not evaluated family treatment for dually diagnosed patients.

Comprehensive treatment also needs to attend to patients' involvement in meaningful, structured tasks, such as school or work. Ample evidence shows that supported employment models of vocational rehabilitation improve work outcomes of patients with severe mental illness (Bond et al., 1997; Drake et al., 1999). Competitive work can decrease the opportunity patients have for using substances and improve self-esteem through involvement in a socially approved activity. In addition, the ability of patients with severe mental illness to benefit from a supported employment program is unrelated to having comorbid substance misuse problems (Sengupta, Drake & McHugo, 1998).

Two other areas that require attention include teaching patients illness management skills and supported housing. Patients often report using substances to manage their symptoms (Addington & Duchak, 1997; Carey & Carey, 1995), and one study reported that trait negative affect in schizophrenia is associated with substance misuse (Blanchard et al., 1999). Many patients need help in developing more effective strategies for coping with their psychiatric symptoms, negative mood states and personal life stress in order to avoid resorting to substance use. Furthermore, they need assistance in learning how to recognize and respond to the early warning signs of psychotic relapse, which, if not attended to, may worsen substance misuse and increase vulnerability to full-blown relapses of either or both disorders. Programs have been designed and empirically validated for facilitating patient coping and preventing relapses (e.g. Perry et al., 1999). Although psychological strategies to manage symptoms often form an important part of integrated treatment for dual diagnosis (Kavanagh et al., 1998), their specific effects on dually diagnosed patients have not yet been evaluated in a controlled trial.

Safe and Protective Living Environments

Substance misuse does not occur in a vacuum, and dual diagnosis treatment must attend to the effects of the environment on patients' continued substance use. Indeed, evidence from one study shows that dually diagnosed patients with numerous substance users in their social networks have a poorer prognosis than similar patients with fewer users (Trumbetta et al., 1999). Although there is broad recognition of the importance of the environment to the treatment of dual disorders (Osher & Dixon, 1996), the solutions to the problem are varied, and depend heavily on the resources available to the treatment providers.

Short-term residential facilities appear to be ineffective because patients relapse immediately upon discharge (Bartels & Drake, 1996). In some settings, treatment agencies arrange for safe housing through contacts in the community (e.g. Drake et al., 1997). Family treatment or social network intervention, focused on engaging other people in the patients' social milieu and decreasing opportunities for substance use, may be helpful. Last, when a social environment appears refractory to change, endeavoring to either move the patient to another setting, or arrange for him/her to spend less time there (such as by going to work or training programs) may decrease some of the deleterious effects of the environment on substance misuse.

Long-term Commitment

Just as a psychotic disorder is a persistent problem for many patients, so is substance misuse. Research on integrated treatment programs for dually diagnosed patients suggests that the best outcomes are usually achieved by programs that provide longer-term treatment, rather than short-term intervention (Drake et al., 1998c). Therefore, patients with chronic dual diagnoses are most likely to benefit in programs that have a long-term commitment to their treatment.

It is possible that individuals who have recently developed a psychosis, and whose substance misuse is of a briefer duration, may benefit from shorter-term interventions focused on substance misuse (White et al., 1999). Pilot testing suggests that such interventions, which employ both motivational and educational strategies, have great promise (Kavanagh et al., in press) and are in need of further evaluation in large-scale controlled trials.

Anxiety and Depression or Dysthymia

Despite the prevalence of anxiety or depression in alcohol misuse, there is remarkably little in the research literature to guide us on management of the comorbidity. Almost all of the existing treatment trials focus on pharmacotherapy for the anxiety or mood disorder

(Cornelius et al., 1997; McGrath et al., 1996; Tollefson, Montague & Tollefson, 1992), rather than the efficacy or effectiveness of psychological interventions. At present there is no controlled trial to demonstrate a superiority for integrated treatment, and some commentators continue to advocate parallel (Oei & Loveday, 1997) or sequential treatment (Scott, Gilvarry & Farrell, 1998) in the absence of such a study.

It is perhaps less immediately obvious that the treatment of anxiety or depression should be integrated with alcohol intervention than is the case with a pervasive and severe disorder such as schizophrenia. However, we do know that both the psychological treatment of alcohol misuse (Lennox, Scott-Lennox & Bohlig, 1993; Project MATCH Research Group, 1997) and the pharmacological treatment of depression (Worthington et al., 1996) tend to be less effective when conducted in the presence of the other disorder than when the comorbidity is not present.

Treatment design in anxiety and depression has been strongly influenced by the notion of primacy or independence of the disorders. This has largely been because of the high rate of spontaneous recovery of anxiety or depressive symptoms during treatment for alcohol dependence. For example, Brown & Schuckit (1988) found that 42% of people entering inpatient alcohol dependence treatment had a depressive syndrome, but only 6% had clinical levels of depression after 4 weeks of abstinence. This has led a number of commentators to recommend either that treatment for the anxiety or depression should be delayed to provide an opportunity for remission (Oei & Loveday, 1997), or that a decision on the order of treatment should be made in response to assessment of which disorder is primary (Scott et al., 1998).

Schuckit et al. (1997) have argued that it is possible to distinguish depressive episodes that have clearly been independent of alcohol use by applying a retrospective time-line technique. "Independent" depression either precedes the development of alcohol dependence or occurs during at least one period of sustained abstinence. Depression that is not clearly independent is assumed to be secondary to the alcohol misuse. The notion is that assessment of independence may assist in determining whether treatment of the depression is necessary.

However, recent data suggests that even in "non-independent" depression, treatment with desipramine (Mason et al., 1996) or with cognitive-behavioral therapy (Brown et al., 1997) can improve the depression and the outcome of treatment for alcohol dependence. Indeed, the assumption that non-independent depression is truly secondary may often be unsound. Depression that occurs during alcohol misuse can be of independent origin. The terminology "independent" is also potentially misleading, since it suggests a lack of inter-relationship with the alcohol problem. Most often, the true situation is likely to be one of mutual influence, or of co-occurring problems whose primary or secondary status shifts over time (Hodgkins et al., 1999). A search for the single primary problem may in these cases be inappropriate.

Some of the issues are illustrated by a recent self-report study on post-traumatic stress disorder (PTSD) and concurrent substance misuse (Brown, Strout & Gannon-Rowley, 1998). Participants reported that their two disorders tended to be functionally related, so that as each worsened or improved, the other changed in parallel. When this relationship is present, whether one disorder is secondary or both are primary problems may be less important than their linkages and co-variation. If treatment of one disorder is successful, the other may well show an improvement or even a remission. But the delay of the second treatment is likely to impede the effectiveness of the first, especially if the person is attempting to reduce or stop his/her consumption in the community with limited support for the attempt. Furthermore, the opportunity to train the person in skills to deal with the comorbidity, should it recur, is lost if the second problem resolves before the comorbidity issue has been addressed in treatment.

A wide search of existing literature found only two controlled trials on the treatment of coexisting depressive symptoms and alcohol misuse (Brown et al., 1997; Turner & Wehl, 1984). Each of the studies attested to the effectiveness of cognitive-behavioral therapy (CBT) for depression in parallel with treatment of the alcohol problems. In Turner & Wehl's (1984) study, CBT gave superior alcohol and mood outcomes to the standard alcohol treatment alone, but only in an individual rather than group format. In Brown et al.'s (1997) study of people receiving treatment for alcohol dependence, CBT for depression achieved better reductions in depressive symptoms during treatment and better alcohol outcomes from 3–6 months post-treatment than did relaxation training. Neither of the studies was restricted to people with major depression, and the cut-off on depressive symptoms was relatively low (e.g. Brown et al., 1997; a Beck Depression Inventory score ≥ 10). We still await a controlled trial consisting entirely of patients who are experiencing a major depressive episode or dysthymic disorder.

Research in clinical depression is available for pharmacotherapies. These studies suggest that, while the effectiveness of some antidepressants is reduced by the presence of alcohol problems (Worthington et al., 1996), drugs such as imipramine (McGrath et al., 1996) and fluoxetine (Cornelius et al., 1997) are more effective than placebos for the treatment of comorbid depression. Alcohol-related outcomes have tended to be better for dual-diagnosis patients whose depression responded to the pharmacological treatment.

Research into the treatment of comorbid anxiety is even less well advanced. Buspirone has shown better alcohol and anxiety outcomes than placebos in three out of four double-blind trials on people with comorbid anxiety and alcohol misuse (Kranzler et al., 1994; Malcolm et al., 1992; Tollefson, Lancaster & Montague-Clouse, 1991; Tollefson et al., 1992), and an open-label case series with sertraline produced promising symptomatic and alcohol-related outcomes in PTSD (Brady, Sonne & Roberts, 1995). There are no controlled trials of psychological interventions for alcohol and anxiety problems in the published literature. Multiple case series on the integrated treatment of PTSD and substance abuse problems (Kuhne, Nohner & Baraga, 1986; Najavits et al., 1998) suggest that a combined approach will prove to be effective, and a series of three case studies by Lehman, Brown & Barlow (1998) suggest that standard cognitive-behavioral treatment of panic disorder may sometimes result in improvements, not only of the panic symptoms but also of secondary alcohol misuse.

On theoretical grounds, we expect that an integrated treatment will be more effective in anxiety and depression, just as it is in severe mental disorder. Integration of treatment is likely to be most critical in cases where the anxiety or depression is either unresponsive to treatment or is prone to recurrence. In these cases, it may be especially important to train participants to maintain their self-management of alcohol use in the face of anxiety or dysphoria, and to prevent a lapse in alcohol control from precipitating a full relapse of both disorders.

However, there are likely to be important differences between the design of integrated interventions for alcohol disorders and anxiety and depression and the structure of treatments in psychosis. People with comorbid anxiety or depression tend to be more cognitively intact and have more functional abilities than people with psychotic disorders, including skills in self-monitoring and self-management of behavior. They are also more likely to have financial and other resources, such as social supports, and their comorbid disorder has a better chance of complete remission. As a result of these factors, the treatment may not always need to be as extensive as that described in the previous section. In some cases of low alcohol dependence, such as the single cases of panic disorder and alcohol abuse treated by Lehman et al. (1998), simply drawing attention to the alcohol misuse by initial assessment and ongoing alcohol monitoring may be sufficient to trigger self-management of the problem. In most cases, some skills training or support will be required to help them succeed at an attempt to control their alcohol intake.

In anxiety disorders, the disorder itself does not impede the development of motivation in the same way as in a disorder such as schizophrenia, and in some anxiety disorders such as phobias there is a relatively low chance of recurrence after treatment. In contrast, depression shares both of these problems with the severe mental disorders. Engagement needs to overcome the pessimism, lack of self-efficacy and lack of expected reward value that are associated with both dysphoria and negative symptoms. This may sometimes result in an extended engagement stage. Major depression, bipolar disorder and schizophrenia also share a high risk of relapse after resolution of an acute episode. However, we expect that treatment of alcohol–depression comorbidity will rarely need to be as extended as in the more severe disorders, and that it will typically focus less on assertive follow-up and more on self-monitoring and self-management.

An effective psychological intervention for the anxiety and depressive aspects of the comorbid problems should at this stage be guided by what we know about effective treatment of these disorders when alcohol misuse is not also present. That is, the treatment of anxiety is likely to be dominated by exposure-based procedures, with cognitive therapy for negative cognitions that are impeding treatment progress (Brown & Barlow, 1992). Treatment of depression is likely to focus on cognitive therapy (Beck et al., 1979) or interpersonal therapy (Klerman et al., 1984). In each case, the therapy will be modified to deal with the comorbidity (e.g. Beck et al., 1993; Scott et al., 1998), in terms of both the specific targets of the treatment and the timing of particular treatment components.

Full integration with a cognitive-behavioral alcohol intervention would not end with a minor modification of existing treatments that were essentially presented in parallel by the same therapist. Such an approach would not assist participants to make the conceptual links that were required, and could lead to excessive demands on them at some points of the intervention. Rather, the combined intervention would meld the treatments for the two disorders more fully. For example, engagement would focus on the combined disorder, self-monitoring would encompass both problems, and early success would be attempted in both problem areas. Skills training would routinely encompass both problems: e.g. in depression, increasing pleasurable activities that were inconsistent with alcohol use would help to boost mood and allow a test of pessimistic cognitions, but would also decrease periods of time when the person was at risk of alcohol misuse. Minimization of relapse risk would include training in early detection and prevention of recurrence of either problem, but would particularly focus on reduction in risk of recurrence of the comorbidity. Some examples of these integrated treatments already exist (Kuhne et al., 1986; Najavits et al., 1998); we expect to see a proliferation of these interventions and the further development of an empirical basis for their use over the coming years.

Antisocial Personality Disorder (ASPD)

Epidemiologic studies indicate that the highest psychiatric–substance misuse comorbidity is with ASPD. There is a large literature showing that ASPD is related to a more severe course of alcohol and drug use disorders, including an earlier age of misuse, more binge drinking and more physical and legal consequences (Cadoret, Troughton & Widmer, 1984; Epstein et al., 1994; Penick et al., 1984). Indeed, the importance of ASPD is illustrated by the fact that it has been at the backbone of all major typologies of alcoholism, ranging from the delta/gamma subtypes (Jellinek, 1960) to Cloninger's (1987) Type I/II distinction, to Babor's et al.'s (1992) Type A/B distinction (see Chapter 4, this volume).

Early studies of differential treatment response for substance misuse suggested that patients with comorbid ASPD had a worse prognosis (e.g. Kadden et al., 1989; Rounsaville et al., 1987; Woody et al., 1985). However, the conclusions reached by these studies may be incorrect because of the confounding effects of substance use severity on treatment outcomes. Patients with substance misuse and ASPD tend to have more severe substance disorders. Their poor prognosis may be a reflection of their more severe substance misuse, rather than their ASPD. In line with this interpretation, research does not indicate that patients with ASPD have a worse response to substance misuse treatment once the severity of their disorder has been statistically controlled (Alterman & Tarter, 1986; Cacciola et al., 1994; McKay et al., in press). In fact, one study suggested that patients with ASPD and substance misuse responded quite well to a highly structured cognitive-behavioral treatment program for substance use disorder (Brooner et al., 1998).

CONCLUSIONS

Surveys of both community and treatment samples show there is a high rate of substance misuse and psychiatric comorbidity. Co-occurring alcohol and drug use tend to be highest in people with antisocial personality disorder (ASPD), followed by patients with severe mental illnesses such as schizophrenia or bipolar disorder, followed by patients with affective or anxiety disorders, whose substance misuse nevertheless exceeds that of people in the general population. Recognition of the importance of comorbidity has developed recently, and consequently the research base upon which recommendations can be made is rather slim. Nevertheless, several points must be stressed that are supported by a broad consensus. Perhaps the most important step involves the recognition of both disorders. With rates of comorbidity so high, a careful evaluation should be conducted to ensure proper diagnosis. In alcohol and drug treatment settings, this involves an assessment of psychiatric disorders, of which the most common in those settings are affective and anxiety disorders. In psychiatric treatment settings, assessments should routinly screen for substance use disorders.

A second principle of treatment is that motivational strategies should be used in order to match the intervention to patients' motivational states. Dually diagnosed patients tend to be highly sensitive to interpersonal stress, and confrontational approaches risk increasing their psychiatric symptoms and driving them away from treatment. Awareness of the patient's level of motivation to work on substance misuse maximizes the chances of successfully engaging patients in treatment and ensuring that selected interventions are optimally timed.

Third, it is best if both substance misuse and psychiatric disorders are treated simultaneously, by the same treatment providers. Dually diagnosed patients often "fall between the cracks" of the substance misuse and psychiatric treatment systems, and fail to receive one or both needed treatments (Kavanagh et al., 1998). Furthermore, since both disorders tend to worsen the other, effective treatment of one disorder requires knowledge and coordination with treatment of the other. Concurrent treatment of both disorders avoids the common trap of attempting to distinguish which disorder is "primary" and which is "secondary" when such distinctions are often difficult or impossible to make.

Finally, effective treatment of substance misuse and psychiatric comorbidity requires that treatment for the psychiatric disorder be specialized for that disorder. Over the past several decades significant advances have been made in the treatment of different psychiatric disorders. Knowledge of empirically validated interventions, both pharmacological and psychological, is critical in order to effectively treat the psychiatric illness (and hence the substance misuse as well). In this regard, the nature of dual diagnosis treatment must be informed by the specific psychiatric disorder, as well the individual characteristics of the patients.

Recognition of the high comorbidity of substance misuse and psychiatric disorders has grown tremendously over the past decade and clinicians are now aware of the importance of assessing both disorders in their patients. Research on effective treatment of comorbidity is still in its infancy, but it has provided important guidelines for integrating the treatment of both disorders. As our knowledge of the treatment of dual disorders grows, traditional distinctions between the psychiatric and substance misuse fields, including training, requirements for the credentialing of professionals, administration and funding should hopefully break down. Ultimately this may lead to the integration of the service systems themselves. Whole systems are needed to treat whole people. The movement afoot towards providing integrated mental health and substance misuse treatment bodes well for the outcomes of patients with comorbid disorders.

KEY WORKS AND SUGGESTIONS FOR FURTHER READING

Daley, D.C., Moss, H.B. & Campbell, F. (1993). *Dual Disorders: Counseling Clients with Chemical Dependency and Mental Illness*, 2nd edn. Center City, MN: Hazeldon.

Provides a useful survey of the problem of dual diagnosis and describes a modified 12-step treatment to these disorders.

Drake, R.E., Mercer-McFadden, C., McHugo, G.J., Mueser, K.T., Rosenberg, S.D., Clark, R.E. & Brunette, M.F. (Eds) (1998). *Readings in Dual Diagnosis*. Columbia, MD: International Association of Psychosocial Rehabilitation Services.

A selection of previously published articles and book chapters on dual disorders, with sections including overview, etiology, assessment, clinical issues, treatment and special issues.

Drake, R.E. & Mueser, K.T. (Eds) (1996). *Dual Diagnosis of Major Mental Illness and Substance Abuse Disorder II: Recent Research and Clinical Implications*. New Directions in Mental Health Services, Vol. 70. San Francisco, CA: Jossey-Bass.

A series of articles on the assessment and treatment of persons with dual disorders, with primary focus on severe mental illness. Chapters include: prevalence, assessment, treatment, group treatment, housing, family support and cost-effectiveness of treatment.

Graham, H.L. (1998). The role of dysfunctional beliefs in individuals who experience psychosis and use substances: implications for cognitive therapy and medication adherence. *Behavioural and Cognitive Psychotherapy*, **26**, 193–208.

Describes the application of cognitive therapy to clients with psychosis and substance use disorders.

Kavanagh, D.J., Young, R., Boyce, L., Clair, A., Sitharthan, T., Clark, D. & Thompson, K. (1998). Substance Treatment Options in Psychosis (STOP): a new intervention for dual diagnosis. *Journal of Mental Health*, **7**, 135–143.

Lehman, A. & Dixon, L. (Eds), *Double Jeopardy: Chronic Mental Illness and Substance Abuse*. Chur, Switzerland: Harwood Academic.

A compilation of invited chapters on dual disorders organized into three sections: background and diagnostic issues, treatment and social system issues.

Mercer-McFadden, C., Drake, R.E., Clark, R.E., Verven, N., Noorsdy, D.L. & Fox, T.S. (1999). *Substance Abuse Treatment for People with Severe Mental Disorders: A*

Program Manager's Guide. Concord, NH: New Hampshire–Dartmouth Psychiatric
Research Center.

Information for program planners on establishing and financing dual disorder services.

Mueser, K.T., Drake, R.E. & Wallach, M.A. (1998).   Dual diagnosis: a review of etiological theories. *Addictive Behaviors*, **23**, 717–734.

Reviews different theories accounting for the high prevalence of substance use disorders in persons with schizophrenia and bipolar disorder.

Onken, L.S., Blaine, J.D., Genser, S. & Horton, A.M. Jr (1997).   *Treatment of Drug-
dependent Individuals with Comorbid Mental Disorders.* National Institute on Drug
Abuse Research Monograph No. 172, NIH Publication No. 97–4172, Rockville, MD:
National Institutes of Health.

Surveys the problem of alcohol and drug use disorders in persons with mental illness.
Chapters cover a broad range of topics, including the effects of depression on substance
misuse treatment, assessment problems, anxiety disorders and substance misuse comorbidity, cigarette smoking comorbidity, treatment of severe mental illness and substance
misuse, and substance use and HIV risk in persons with severe mental illness.

Roberts, L.J., Shaner, A. & Eckman, T.A. (1999).   *Overcoming Addictions: Skills Training
for People with Schizophrenia.* New York: Norton.

Describes a social skills training program for persons with schizophrenia and substance
use disorders.

REFERENCES

Addington, J. & Duchak, V. (1997).   Reasons for substance use in schizophrenia. *Acta Psychiatrica
Scandinavica*, **96**, 329–333.
Alterman, A.I. & Tarter, R.E. (1986).   An examination of selected typologies: hyperactivity, familial,
and antisocial alcoholism. In M. Galanter (Ed.), *Recent Developments in Alcoholism*, Vol. IV (pp.
169–189). New York: Plenum.
American Psychiatric Association (1994).   *Diagnostic and Statistical Manual of Mental Disorders
(DSM-IV)*, 4th edn, revised. Washington, DC: American Psychiatric Association.
Andrews, G., Hall, W., Teeson, M. & Henderson, S. (1999).   *The Mental Health of Australians: National
Survey of Mental Health and Well-being, Report 2.* Canberra: Mental Health Branch, Common-
wealth Department of Health and Aged Care.
Babor, T.F., Hofmann, M., DelBoca, K., Hesselbrock, V., Meter, R.E., Dolinsky, Z.S. & Rounsaville, B.
(1992).   Types of alcoholics, I. Evidence for an empirically derived typology based on indicators
of vulnerability and severity. *Archives of General Psychiatry*, **49**, 599–608.
Bandura, A. (1986).   *Social Foundations of Thought and Action: A Social Cognitive Theory.* Englewood Cliffs, NJ: Prentice-Hall.
Bartels, S.J. & Drake, R.E. (1996).   A pilot study of residential treatment for dual diagnoses. *Journal
of Nervous and Mental Disease*, **184**, 379–381.
Baucom, D.H., Shoham, V., Mueser, K.T., Daiuto, A.D. & Stickle, T.R. (1998).   Empirically supported
couple and family interventions for adult mental health problems. *Journal of Consulting and
Clinical Psychology*, **66**, 53–88.
Beck, A.T., Rush, A.J., Shaw, B.F. & Emery, G. (1979).   *Cognitive Therapy of Depression.* New York:
Guilford.
Beck, A.T., Wright, F.D., Newman, C.F. & Liese, B.S. (1993).   *Cognitive Therapy of Substance Abuse.*
New York: Guilford.
Becker, H.S. (1967).   History, culture, and subjective experience: an exploration of the social bases
of drug-induced experiences. *Journal of Health and Social Behavior*, **8**, 163–176.

Bellack, A.S. & DiClemente, C.C. (1999). Treating substance abuse among patients with schizophrenia. *Psychiatric Services*, **50**, 75–79.

Bellack, A.S., Mueser, K.T., Gingerich, S. & Agresta, J. (1997). *Social Skills Training for Schizophrenia: A Step-by-step Guide*. New York: Guilford.

Berkson, J. (1949). Limitations of the application of four-fold tables to hospital data. *Biological Bulletin*, **2**, 47–53.

Blanchard, J.J., Squires, D., Henry, T., Horan, W.P., Bogenschutz, M., Lauriello, J. & Bustillo, J. (1999). Examining an affect regulation model of substance abuse in schizophrenia: the role of traits and coping. *Journal of Nervous and Mental Disease*, **187**, 72–79.

Bond, G.R., Drake, R.E., Mueser, K.T. & Becker, D.R. (1997). An update on supported employment for people with severe mental illness. *Psychiatric Services*, **48**(3), 335–346.

Brady, K.T., Sonne, S.C. & Roberts, J.M. (1995). Sertraline treatment of comorbid posttraumatic stress disorder and alcohol dependence. *Journal of Clinical Psychiatry*, **56**, 502–505.

Brooner, R.K., Kidorf, M., King, V.L. & Stoller, K. (1998). Preliminary evidence of good treatment response in antisocial drug abusers. *Drug and Alcohol Dependence*, **49**(3), 249–260.

Brown, P.J., Strout, R.L. & Gannon-Rowley, J. (1998). Substance use disorder PTSD comorbidity: patient's perceptions of symptom interplay and treatment issues. *Journal of Substance Abuse Treatment*, **15**, 445–448.

Brown, R.A., Evans, D.M., Miller, I.W., Burgess, E.S. & Mueller, T.I. (1997). Cognitive-behavioral treatment for depression in alcoholism. *Journal of Consulting and Clinical Psychology*, **65**, 715–726.

Brown, S.A. & Schuckit, M.A. (1988). Changes in depression among abstinent alcoholics. *Journal of Studies on Alcohol*, **49**, 412–417.

Brown, T.A. & Barlow, D.H. (1992). Comorbidity among anxiety disorders: implications for treatment and DSM-IV. *Journal of Consulting and Clinical Psychology*, **60**, 835–844.

Cacciola, J.S., Rutherford, M.J., Alterman, A.I. & Snider, E.C. (1994). An examination of the diagnostic criteria for antisocial personality disorder in substance abusers. *Journal of Nervous and Mental Disease*, **182**, 517–523.

Cadoret, R., Troughton, E. & Widmer, R. (1984). Clinical differences between antisocial and primary alcoholics. *Comprehensive Psychiatry*, **25**, 1–8.

Carey, K.B. & Carey, M.P. (1995). Reasons for drinking among psychiatric outpatients: relationship to drinking patterns. *Psychology of Addictive Behaviors*, **9**, 251–257.

Carmichael, D., Tackett-Gibson, M., O'Dell, L., Jayasuria, B., Jordan, J. & Menon, R. (1998). *Texas Dual Diagnosis Project Evaluation Report 1997–1998*. College Station, TX: Public Policy Research Institute, Texas A&M University.

Caton, C.L., Shrout, P.E., Eagle, P.F., Opler, L.A., Felix, A.F. & Dominguez, B. (1994). Risk factors for homelessness among schizophrenic men: a case-control study. *American Journal of Public Health*, **84**(2), 265–270.

Caton, C.L.M., Shrout, P.E., Dominguez, B., Eagle, P.F., Opler, L.A. & Cournos, F. (1995). Risk factors for homelessness among women with schizophrenia. *American Journal of Public Health*, **85**, 1153–1156.

Cloninger, C.R. (1987). Neurogenetic adaptive mechanisms in alcoholism. *Science*, **236**, 410–416.

Cornelius, J.R., Salloum, I.M., Ehler, J.G., Jarret, P.J., Cornelius, M.D., Perel, J.M., Thase, M.E. & Black, A. (1997). Fluoxetine in depressed alcoholics. *Archives of General Psychiatry*, **54**, 700–705.

Dixon, L., McNary, S. & Lehman, A. (1995). Substance abuse and family relationships of persons with severe mental illness. *American Journal of Psychiatry*, **152**, 456–458.

Drake, R.E., Antosca, L.M., Noordsy, D.L., Bartels, S.J. & Osher, F.C. (1991). New Hampshire's specialized services for the dually diagnosed. In K. Minkoff & R.E. Drake (Eds), *New Directions for Mental Health Services*, Vol. 50 (pp. 57–67). San Francisco, CA: Jossey-Bass.

Drake, R.E., Brunette, M.F. & Mueser, K.T. (1998a). Substance use disorder and social functioning in schizophrenia. In K.T. Mueser & N. Tarrier (Eds), *Handbook of Social Functioning in Schizophrenia* (pp. 280–289). Boston, MA: Allyn & Bacon.

Drake, R.E., McHugo, G.J., Bebout, R.R., Becker, D.R., Harris, M., Bond, G.R. & Quimby, E. (1999). A randomized clinical trial of supported employment for inner-city patients with severe mental illness. *Archives of General Psychiatry*, **56**, 627–633.

Drake, R.E., McHugo, G.J., Clark, R.E., Teague, G.B., Xie, H., Miles, K. & Ackerson, T.H. (1998b).

Assertive community treatment for patients with co-occurring severe mental illness and substance use disorder: a clinical trial. *American Journal of Orthopsychiatry*, **68**(2), 201–215.

Drake, R.E., Mercer-McFadden, C., McHugo, G.J., Mueser, K.T., Rosenberg, S.D., Clark, R.E. & Brunette, M.F. (Eds) (1998c). *Readings in Dual Diagnosis*. Columbia, MD: International Association of Psychosocial Rehabilitation Services.

Drake, R.E., Mercer-McFadden, C., Mueser, K.T., McHugo, G.J. & Bond, G.R. (1998d). Review of integrated mental health and substance abuse treatment for patients with dual disorders. *Schizophrenia Bulletin*, **24**(4), 589–608.

Drake, R.E., Yovetich, N.A., Bebout, R.R., Harris, M. & McHugo, G.J. (1997). Integrated treatment for dually diagnosed homeless adults. *Journal of Nervous and Mental Disease*, **185**(5), 298–305.

Duke, P.J., Pantelis, C. & Barnes, T.R.E. (1994). South Westminster schizophrenia survey: alcohol use and its relationship to symptoms, tardive dyskinesia and illness onset. *British Journal of Psychiatry*, **164**, 630–636.

Epstein, E.E., Ginsburg, B.E., Hesselbrock, V.M. & Schwarz, J.C. (1994). Alcohol and drug abusers subtyped by antisocial personality and primary or secondary depressive disorder. In T.F. Babor, V. Hesselbrock, R.E. Meyer & W. Shoemaker (Eds), *Types of Alcoholics: Evidence from Clinical, Experimental and Genetic Research*, Vol. 708 (pp. 187–201). New York: New York Academy of Sciences.

Fowler, I.L., Carr, V.J., Carter, N.T. & Lewin, T.J. (1998). Patterns of current and lifetime substance use in schizophrenia. *Schizophrenia Bulletin*, **24**, 443–455.

Galanter, M., Castaneda, R. & Ferman, J. (1988). Substance abuse among general psychiatric patients: place of presentation, diagnosis and treatment. *American Journal of Drug and Alcohol Abuse*, **14**, 211–235.

Godley, S.H., Hoewing-Roberson, R. & Godley, M.D. (1994). *Final MISA Report*. Bloomington, IL: Lighthouse Institute.

Hesselbrock, M.N., Meyer, R.E. & Keener, J.J. (1985). Psychopathology in hospitalized alcoholics. *Archives of General Psychiatry*, **42**(11), 1050–1055.

Hodgkins, D.C., el-Guebaly, N., Armstrong, S. & Dufour, M. (1999). Implications of depression on outcome from alcohol dependence: a three-year prospective follow-up. *Alcoholism: Clinical and Experimental Research*, **23**, 151–157.

Jeblensky, A., McGrath, J., Herrman, H., Castle, D., Gureje, O., Morgan, V. & Korten, A. (1999). People living with psychotic illness: an Australian study 1997–98. Banberra, Australia: Department of Health and Aged Care.

Jellinek, E.M. (1960). Alcoholism: a genus and some of it species. *Canadian Medical Association Journal*, **83**, 1341–1345.

Jerrell, J. & Ridgely, M. (1995). Evaluating changes in symptoms and functioning of dually diagnosed clients in specialized treatment. *Psychiatric Services*, **46**(3), 233–238.

Johnson, B.D. & Muffler, J. (1992). Sociocultural aspects of drug use and abuse in the 1990s. In J.H. Lowinson, P. Ruiz, R.B. Millman & J.G. Langrod (Eds), *Substance Abuse: A Comprehensive Textbook*, 2nd edn (pp. 118–137). Baltimore, MD: Williams and Wilkins.

Kadden, R., Cooney, N., Getter, H. & Litt, M. (1989). Matching alcoholics to coping skills or interactional therapies: posttreatment results. *Journal of Consulting and Clinical Psychology*, **57**(6), 698–704.

Kavanagh, D.J. (1995). An intervention for substance abuse in schizophrenia. *Behaviour Change*, **12**, 20–30.

Kavanagh, D.J., Greenaway, L., Jenner, L., Saunders, J., White, A., Sorban, J., Hamilton, G. and members of the Dual Diagnosis Consortium (2000). Contrasting views and experiences of health professionals on the management of comorbid substance abuse and mental disorders. *Australian and New Zealand Journal of Psychiatry*, **34**, 279–289.

Kavanagh, D.J., Young, R., White, A., Saunders, J.R., Wallis, J. & Ceait, A. (in press). SOS—a brief intervention for substance abuse in early psychosis. In H. Graham, K. Mueser, M. Birchwood & A. Copello (Eds), *Substance Misuse in Psychosis: A Handbook of Approaches to Treatment and Service Delivery*. Chichester: John Wiley.

Kavanagh, D.J., Young, R., Boyce, L., Clair, A., Sitharthan, T., Clark, D. & Thompson, K. (1998). Substance Treatment Options in Psychosis (STOP): a new intervention for dual diagnosis. *Journal of Mental Health*, **7**, 135–143.

Kessler, R.C., Nelson, C.B., McGonagle, K.A., Edlund, M.J., Frank, R.G. & Leaf, P.J. (1996). The epidemiology of co-occurring addictive and mental disorders: implications for prevention and service utilization. *American Journal of Orthopsychiatry*, **66**(1), 17–31.

Klerman, G.L., Weissman, M.M., Rounsaville, B.J. & Chevron, E.S. (1984). *Interpersonal Psychotherapy of Depression*. New York: Basic Books.

Kranzler, H., Burleson, J., DelBoca, F., Babor, T., Korner, P., Brown, J. & Bohn, M. (1994). Buspirone treatment of anxious alcoholics. *Archives of General Psychiatry*, **51**, 720–731.

Kuhne, A., Nohner, W. & Baraga, E. (1986). Efficacy of chemical dependency treatment as a function of combat in Vietnam. *Journal of Substance Abuse Treatment*, **3**, 191–194.

Kushner, M., Sher, K. & Beitman, B. (1990). The relation between alcohol problems and the anxiety disorders. *American Journal of Psychiatry*, **147**(6), 685–695.

Lehman, C.L., Brown, T.A. & Barlow, D.H. (1998). Effects of cognitive-behavioral treatment for panic disorder with agoraphobia on concurrent alcohol abuse. *Behavior Therapy*, **29**, 423–433.

Lennox, R.D., Scott-Lennox, J.A. & Bohlig, E.M. (1993). The cost of depression-complicated alcoholism: health-care utilization and treatment effectiveness. *Journal of Mental Health Administration*, **20**, 138–152.

Malcolm, R., Anton, R.F., Randall, C.L., Johnston, A., Brady, K. & Thevos, A. (1992). A placebo-controlled trial of buspirone in anxious inpatient alcoholics. *Alcoholism: Clinical and Experimental Research*, **16**, 1007–1013.

Mason, B.J., Kocsis, J.H., Ritvo, E.C. & Cutler, R.B. (1996). A double-blind, placebo-controlled trial of desipramine for primary alcohol dependence stratified on the presence or absence of major depression. *Journal of the American Medical Association*, **275**, 761–767.

McGrath, P.J., Nunes, E.V., Stewart, J.W., Goldman, D., Agosti, V., Ocepek-Welikson, K. & Quitkin, F.M. (1996). Imipramine treatment of alcoholics with primary depression. *Archives of General Psychiatry*, **53**, 232–240.

McHugo, G.J., Drake, R.E., Burton, H.L. & Ackerson, T.H. (1995). A scale for assessing the stage of substance abuse treatment in persons with severe mental illness. *Journal of Nervous and Mental Disease*, **183**(12), 762–767.

McKay, J., Alterman, A.I., Cacciola, J.S. & Mulvaney, F. (in press). Prognostic significance of antisocial personality disorder in cocaine dependent patients entering continuing care. *Journal of Nervous and Mental Disease*.

Miller, W. & Rollnick, S. (1991). *Motivational Interviewing: Preparing People to Change Addictive Behavior*. New York: Guilford.

Minkoff, K. (1989). An integrated treatment model for dual diagnosis of psychosis and addiction. *Hospital and Community Psychiatry*, **40**(10), 1031–1036.

Mueser, K.G., Yarnold, P.R., Levinson, D.F., Singh, H., Bellack, A.S., Kee, K., Morrison, R.L. & Yadalam, K.G. (1990). Prevalence of substance abuse in schizophrenia: demographic and clinical correlates. *Schizophrenia Bulletin*, **16**, 31–56.

Mueser, K.T., Drake, R.E. & Noordsy, D.L. (1998). Integrated mental health and substance abuse treatment for severe psychiatric disorders. *Journal of Practical Psychiatry and Behavioral Health*, **4**(3), 129–139.

Mueser, K.T. & Fox, M.A. (1998). Dual diagnosis: how families can help. *Journal of the California Alliance for the Mentally Ill*, **9**, 53–55.

Mueser, K.T. & Glynn, S.M. (1999). *Behavioral Family Therapy for Psychiatric Disorders*, 2nd edn. Oakland, CA: New Harbinger.

Mueser, K.T. & Noordsy, D.L. (1996). Group treatment for dually diagnosed clients. In R.E. Drake & K.T. Mueser (Eds), *Dual Diagnosis of Major Mental Illness and Substance Abuse Disorder II: Recent Research and Clinical Implications* (pp. 31–51). New Directions for Mental Health Services, Vol. 70. San Francisco, CA: Jossey-Bass.

Mueser, K.T., Yarnold, P.R. & Bellack, A.S. (1992). Diagnostic and demographic correlates of substance abuse in schizophrenia and major affective disorder. *Acta Psychiatrica Scandinavica*, **85**, 48–55.

Mueser, K.T., Yarnold, P.R., Rosenberg, S.D., Swett, C., Miles, K.M. & Hill, D. (2000). Substance use disorder in hospitalized severely mentally ill psychiatric patients: prevalence, correlates, and subgroups. *Schizophrenia Bulletin*, **26**, 179–192.

Najavits, L.M., Weiss, R.D., Shaw, S.R. & Muenz, L.R. (1998). "Seeking safety": outcome of a new cognitive behavioral psychotherapy for women with posttraumatic stress disorder and substance dependence. *Journal of Traumatic Stress*, **11**, 437–456.

Oei, T.P.S. & Loveday, W.A.L. (1997). Lifetime diagnosis of major depression as a multivariate predictor of treatment outcome for inpatients with substance abuse. *Drug and Alcohol Review*, **16**, 261–274.

Osher, F.C. & Dixon, L.B. (1996). Housing for persons with co-occurring mental and addictive disorders. In R.E. Drake & K.T. Mueser (Eds), *Dual Diagnosis of Major Mental Illness and Substance Abuse Disorder II: Recent Research and Clinical Implications* (pp. 53–64). New Directions for Mental Health Services, Vol. 70. San Francisco, CA: Jossey-Bass.

Osher, F.C. & Kofoed, L.L. (1989). Treatment of patients with psychiatric and psychoactive substance use disorders. *Hospital and Community Psychiatry*, **40**, 1025–1030.

Penick, E.C., Powell, B.J., Othmer, E., Bingham, S.F., Rice, A.S. & Liese, B.S. (1984). Subtyping alcoholics by coexisting psychiatric syndromes: course, family history, outcome. In D.W. Goodwin, K. Teilman-Van Dusen & S.A. Mednick (Eds), *Longitudinal Research in Alcoholism* (pp. 167–196). Boston, MA: Kluwer-Nijhoff.

Perry, A., Tarrier, N., Morriss, R., McCarthy, E. & Limb, K. (1999). Randomised controlled trial of efficacy of teaching patients with bipolar disorder to identify early symptoms of relapse and obtain treatment. *British Medical Journal*, **318**, 149–153.

Polcin, D.L. (1992). Issues in the treatment of dual diagnosis clients who have chronic mental illness. *Professional Psychology: Research and Practice*, **23**(1), 30–37.

Powell, B.J., Penick, E.C., Othmer, E. et al. (1982). Prevalence of additional psychiatric syndromes among male alcoholics. *Journal of Clinical Psychiatry*, **43**, 404–407.

Project Match Research Group (1997). Matching alcoholism treatments to client heterogeneity: Project MATCH posttreatment drinking outcomes. *Journal of Studies on Alcohol*, **58**, 7–29.

Regier, D.A., Farmer, M.E., Rae, D.S., Locke, B.Z., Keith, S.J., Judd, L.L. & Goodwin, F.K. (1990). Comorbidity of mental disorders with alcohol and other drug abuse: results from the Epidemiologic Catchment Area (ECA) study. *Journal of the American Medical Association*, **264**, 2511–2518.

Ridgely, M.S., Goldman, H.H. & Willenbring, M. (1990). Barriers to the care of persons with dual diagnoses: organizational and financing issues. *Schizophrenia Bulletin*, **16**(1), 123–132.

Rosenthal, R., Hellerstein, D. & Miner, C. (1992a). A model of integrated services for outpatient treatment of patients with comorbid schizophrenia and addictive disorders. *American Journal on Addictions*, **1**(4), 339–348.

Rosenthal, R.N., Hellerstein, D.J. & Miner, C.R. (1992b). Integrated services for treatment of schizophrenic substance abusers: demographics, symptoms, and substance abuse patterns. *Psychiatric Quarterly*, **63**, 3–26.

Ross, H.E., Glaser, F.B. & Germanson, T. (1988). The prevalence of psychiatric disorders in patients with alcohol and other drug problems. *Archives of General Psychiatry*, **45**, 1023–1031.

Rounsaville, B.J., Dolinsky, Z.S., Babor, T.F. & Meyer, R.E. (1987). Psychopathology as a predictor of treatment outcome in alcoholics. *Archives of General Psychiatry*, **44**, 505–513.

Salyers, M.P. & Mueser, K.T. (in press). Social functioning, psychopathology, and medication side effects in relation to substance use and abuse in schizophrenia. *Schizophrenia Research*.

Schuckit, M.A., Tipp, J.E., Bergman, M., Reich, W., Hesselbrock, V.M. & Smith, T.L. (1997). Comparison of induced and independent major depressive disorders in 2945 alcoholics. *American Journal of Psychiatry*, **154**, 948–957.

Scott, J., Gilvarry, E. & Farrell, M. (1998). Managing anxiety and depression in alcohol and drug dependence. *Addictive Behaviors*, **23**, 919–931.

Sengupta, A., Drake, R.E. & McHugo, G.J. (1998). The relationship between substance use disorder and vocational functioning among persons with severe mental illness. *Psychiatric Rehabilitation Journal*, **22**(1), 41–45.

Shaner, A., Khalsa, M.A., Roberts, L., Wilkins, J., Anglin, D. & Hsieh, S.C. (1993). Unrecognized cocaine use among schizophrenic patients. *American Journal of Psychiatry*, **150**, 758–762.

Stanton, M.D. & Shadish, W.R. (1997). Outcome, attrition, and family-couples treatment for drug abuse: a meta-analysis and review of the controlled, comparative studies. *Psychological Bulletin*, **122**(2), 170–191.

Steadman, H.J., Mulvey, E.P., Monahan, J., Robbins, P.C., Appelbaum, P.S., Grisso, T., Roth, L.H. &

Silver, E. (1998).   Violence by people discharged from acute psychiatric inpatient facilities and by others in the same neighborhoods. *Archives of General Psychiatry*, **55**, 393–401.

Stein, L.I. & Santos, A.B. (1998).   *Assertive Community Treatment of Persons with Severe Mental Illness*. New York: Norton.

Stewart, S.H. (1996).   Alcohol abuse in individuals exposed to trauma: a critical review. *Psychological Bulletin*, **120**, 83–112.

Stone, A.M., Greenstein, R.A., Gamble, G. & McLellan, A.T. (1993).   Cocaine use by schizophrenic outpatients who receive depot neuroleptic medication. *Hospital and Community Psychiatry*, **44**(2), 176–177.

Susser, E., Strvening, E.L. & Conover, S. (1989).   Psychiatric problems in homeless men: lifetime psychosis, substance use, and current distress in new arrivals at New York City Shelters. *Archives of General Psychiatry*, **46**, 845–850.

Teeson, M., Hall, W., Lynskey, M. & Degenhardt, L. (2000).   Alcohol and drug use disorders in Australia: implications of the National Survey of Mental Health and Well-being. *Australian and New Zealand Journal of Psychiatry*, **34**, 206–213.

Tollefson, G.D., Lancaster, S.P. & Montague-Clouse, J. (1991).   The association of buspirone and its metabolite 1 pyrimidinylpiperazine in the remission of comorbid anxiety with depressive features and alcohol dependency. *Psychopharmacology Bulletin*, **27**, 163–170.

Tollefson, G.G., Montague, C.J. & Tollefson, S.L. (1992).   Treatment of comorbid generalised anxiety in a recently detoxified alcoholic population with a selective serotonergic drug (buspirone). *Journal of Clinical Psychopharmacology*, **12**, 19–26.

Trumbetta, S.L., Mueser, K., Quimby, E., Bebout, R. & Teague, G.B. (in press).   Social networks and clinical outcomes of dually diagnosed homeless persons. *Behavior Therapy*.

Turner, R.W. & Wehl, C.K. (1984).   Treatment of unipolar depression in problem drinkers. *Advances in Behaviour Research and Therapy*, **6**, 115–125.

White, A., Kavanagh, D.J., Wallis, G., Young, R. & Saunders, J. (1999).   *Start Over and Survive (SOS) Treatment Manual: Brief Intervention for Substance Abuse in Early Psychosis*. Brisbane: University of Queensland.

Woody, G.E., McLellan, A.T., Luborsky, L. & O'Brien, C.P. (1985).   Sociopathy and psychotherapy outcome. *Archives of General Psychiatry*, **42**, 1081–1986.

Worthington, J., Fava, M., Agustin, C., Alpert, J., Nierenberg, A.A., Pava, J.A. & Rosenbaum, J.F. (1996).   Consumption of alcohol, nicotine, and caffeine among depressed outpatients. *Psychosomatics*, **37**, 518–522.

Chapter 33

Natural Recovery from Alcohol Problems

Harald K.-H. Klingemann
*University of Applied Sciences, School of
Social Work, Berne, Switzerland*

Synopsis

*Disputes regarding the dogma of abstinence or the claim that it is possible to revert to con-
trolled drinking illustrate a deep-seated lack of belief in the individual's chances of changing
without treatment. However, when people do change from substance misuse, most of them
change on their own. Features common to the successful quitting of alcohol, gambling,
overeating and drug taking are mostly ignored. In general, the hypothesis of "spontaneous
recovery" challenges the concept of addiction as a disease that is in principle irreversible and
progressive. At the same time, the spectrum of definitions of the different terms describing
this phenomenon is varied. In clinical usage, "spontaneous remission" simply means
"an improvement in the patient's condition without effective treatment"; psychological
working definitions emphasize the individual's own cognitive achievement; from a sociological viewpoint, the primary consideration is the exit from a deviant career without
formal intervention. Theoretically, the increasing adoption in the clinical domain of
Prochaska & DiClemente's (1983) stages of change model has been described as an important paradigm shift.*

*The variety of theoretical aspects of self-change is also associated with numerous
practical problems of research methodology, which are outlined in this chapter after a
discussion of definitional issues. Studies in this area have been mostly conducted either
from a survey/cohort perspective or from a qualitative in-depth approach attempting to
"zoom in" on the change process. Canadian population surveys have suggested that about
78% of interviewees with alcohol problems had overcome them without professional
treatment. A considerable proportion had reverted to moderate, controlled consumption.
Intensive case studies in smaller samples highlight, among other things, the role of
social support and control and the influence of life events or stress factors in the motivation
to overcome problem use, and point to an impressively creative potential of individual coping
strategies.*

International Handbook of Alcohol Dependence and Problems. Edited by N. Heather, T.J. Peters and
T. Stockwell.
© 2001 John Wiley & Sons Ltd.

This chapter not only provides a review of self-change research but also outlines treatment and policy implications. Policy planners in the addiction field find themselves faced with growing criticism of the increasing and costly impact of professional therapy and the abstinence dogma in various spheres of life. Under-utilization of the resources of numerous treatment services also raises questions about the reasons for "treatment rejection" and supports the view that, from the study of clinical populations only it is not possible to understand the needs of the much more important hidden population of problem drinkers. In this context, the concept of "assisted natural remission" is introduced and illustrated by various forms of bibliotherapy. Finally, psychological models and perspectives on change need to be complemented by a sociological approach. This views the societal climate of opinion (discrimination, judgements of different types of deviance in the general population and in the media) and objective features of the treatment system (barriers to treatment and perceptions of available programs) as key parameters which can promote or impede individual chances for change.

"SELF-HEALING": TABOO IN RESEARCH AND THERAPY?

Michael Caine, his days of philandering and heavy drinking well and truly behind him, says that he is too old to mess around with women. The 65 year-old actor's film career has taken on a new life with his portrayal of a sleazy impresario in *Little Voice*, winning a Golden Globe award and sparking speculation that an Oscar might be next. "I used to do a bottle of vodka a day in the 1960s—no problem. You are just topping yourself up", Caine told *The Times* of London in an interview. Meeting the model Shakira Baksh changed all that. "I stopped when I met my wife", he said. "Romance took over and, of course, women do not like drunks" (*International Herald Tribune*, p. 20; "People", February 2, 1999).

The idea that alcoholics can overcome their dependence without extensive professional help has been, and to some extent still is, met with disbelief among many professionals in the treatment and social care field, as well as among the general public. The tenet, "once an alcoholic, always an alcoholic" is shared not just by adherents of Alcoholics Anonymous, and disputes regarding the dogma of abstinence or the claim that it is possible to revert to controlled drinking or drug-taking illustrate the deep-seated lack of belief in the individual's chances of change without treatment. As a rule, features common to the progression of individual drug and alcohol careers, on the one hand, and to "privately organized remission processes" in people with eating disorders and smokers, on the other (Tinker & Tucker, 1997), are mostly ignored. Although this *Handbook* is about alcohol problems, we will also address other problem areas, because there are many informative studies of natural remission covering a range of substances, and results point to similarities between various types of recovery, consequently supporting an underlying concept of addiction.

In general, the notion of "spontaneous recovery" contradicts the concept of addiction as a disease that is, in principle, irreversible and progressive. Similar attitudes are found in the sociological labelling approach, which for a long time focused one-sidedly on the progressive consolidation of deviant careers and viewed the individual as a victim of stigmatization by the agencies of social control (Sack, 1978).

DEFINITIONS

Concepts such as "spontaneous remission" and "natural recovery" are not in any way new, neither are they confined to specific types of addiction, such as alcoholism or drug consumption. The relative significance of attempts at self-change, as compared with success rates in treatment in the clinical domain, was the subject of early studies of the neuroses (Eysenck & Rachman, 1973). Coping strategies, creative avoidance and self-protection mechanisms in schizophrenics have also been treated in various ways in psychiatric research and related very broadly to psychological and behavioural approaches to coping behaviour (Böker et al., 1984). In addition to cognitive models of personality (see Miller, 1981), the sociology of life histories (Kohli, 1978), the principles of humanistic psychology (Hay, 1984) and psychoanalytical interpretations of self-destructive behaviour (Battegay, 1988) have been offered as primary theoretical concepts, irrespective of the specific problem area concerned.

The spectrum of definitions of the different terms related to the phenomenon is therefore equally varied. In clinical usage, "spontaneous remission" means simply "an improvement in the patient's condition without effective treatment" (Roizen, Cahalan & Shanks, 1978). Psychological working definitions emphasize the individual's own cognitive achievement ("self-initiated recovery or change in behaviour"; Marlatt & Gordon, 1985). From a sociological viewpoint, the primary consideration is the exit from a deviant career without formal intervention (Stall, 1983). "Natural" and "spontaneous" are increasingly being replaced as keywords by neutral terms, such as "untreated recovery". Nevertheless, common to all these conceptualizations is the assumption that an *unwanted* condition is overcome without professional help.

These approaches can be seen in perspective if self-destructive behaviour is viewed in functional terms as an, albeit unsuccessful, attempt at self-change. Thus, Lange (1981) concludes, again from observations of schizophrenics, that the development of a psychosis in many patients might be interpreted in wholly positive terms as a defensive reaction against a society which suppresses self-realization and thus is viewed as an attempt at self-change.

A variety of theoretical aspects are also associated with numerous practical problems of research methodology. Hidden or unregistered study populations cannot be recruited by means of conventional sampling techniques, while alternative "active case finding" strategies have also their limitations. Snowball procedures reflect local communication networks, while recruitment through the media generates other selective effects—responding to a media call is already a sign of a basic willingness to change and of a more severe problem at hand. Along these lines, a systematic comparison of media recruitment and survey sampling among natural remitters from problem alcohol use from a large-scale German study showed that media recruitment leads to biased samples, with more severely dependent subjects and fewer controlled drinking remitters; media-recruited individuals also believed more strongly than general population survey subjects that treatment would take too much time and effort (Rumpf et al., 2000). Both active case-finding and media calls only reach people who are or were *aware* of their addiction.

An ethical problem in this research area is the risk that successful "spontaneous remitters" will once again be destabilized or discriminated against *through the research contacts*. Finally, the recording and measurement of the processes of change in life histories or variations in addictive behaviour place heavy demands on study instruments or analytical methods, with little opportunity for using standardized procedures.

THE STATE OF RESEARCH

Major starting points for the discussion of self-change phenomena in addiction research are the literature reviews by Smart (1975) in the field of alcoholism, by Waldorf & Biernacki (1979) on overcoming heroin addiction, and the attempt at a comparative review of self-change in eating disorders, nicotine, alcohol and heroin addiction by Stall & Biernacki

(1986). Overall, it can be seen that self-change is not a rare phenomenon and that success rates approximate to those of professional treatment (cf. Blomqvist, 1996). Figures for specific self-change rates naturally vary with the definitional criteria used. We end up with very different remission rates if we choose, for instance, life-long abstinence or return to moderate drinking as reference points, and if we compare subjects with a long drinking history with mildly dependent cases. Taking into account the fact that treatment provision reaches only a minority of those with problems, and bearing in mind the considerable variation in addictive behaviour according to numerous longitudinal studies (Fillmore et al., 1988), this finding is hardly surprising. Canadian population surveys have suggested that about 78% of interviewees with alcohol problems had overcome them without professional treatment. A considerable proportion (38–63%, depending on the survey) had reverted to moderately controlled consumption (Sobell, Cunningham & Sobell, 1996a). Even when eating disorders, medication misuse and gambling addiction were included, only 12% of those interviewed in a population sample by McCartney (1996) had resorted to professional treatment (mainly general practitioners and self-help groups).

Intensive case studies in smaller samples highlight, among other things, the role of social support and control and the influence of life events or stress factors on the motivation to overcome problem use, and point to the creative potential of individual control strategies (Blackwell, 1983). The analytical phase model of self-change, proposed by Stall & Biernacki (1986), has proved to be a useful framework for integrating numerous individual events. In this model, the first phase of remission involves the emergence of a motivation for change; the second phase, the public negotiation of a new, non-stigmatized identity; and the third phase, the stabilization of what has been achieved. According to Stall & Biernacki, in the decision phase, persistent financial and health problems may be considered a specific trigger for the motivation for change, but so can the stress from social sanctions. In the second phase, when sometimes far-reaching changes in lifestyle are instigated but are complicated by withdrawal reactions, the mobilization of social resources is important. In this context, Granfield & Cloud (in press) have introduced the concept of "recovery capital", which is used to refer to the total sum of one's resources (social, physical and human) that can be brought to bear in an effort to overcome alcohol and drug dependency—maintaining bridges with non-using family members and friends, relying on a supportive "safety net" and the commitments of other people, and relying on legal rights with respect to labour market employment, to mention just a few elements. This recovery capital tends to be distributed unevenly between social classes, an aspect that has been little studied (Granfield & Cloud, in press). These more sociologically-orientated approaches to individual life-history change processes correspond to the six-stage model of Prochaska & DiClemente in the clinical domain (see Prochaska, Norcross & DiClemente, 1994), which has to some extent been described as a paradigm shift (Burman, 1997) and has gained broad acceptance in research. It involves a more detailed analytical distinction between "precontemplation" (no change is considered), "contemplation" (medium-term intention to change), "preparation" (immediate intention to change and initial preparatory action), "action" (attempts at changing behaviour) and "maintenance" (continued efforts to change behaviour and continuous support of the new behaviour).

After a lengthy period of neglect of the whole area of spontaneous recovery, a change began during the 1990s which, once again, made discussion of the importance of self-change respectable. Policy planners in the addiction field found themselves faced with growing criticism of the increasing (and also costly) impact of professional therapy, and of the abstinence dogma, in various spheres of life (Peele, 1989). Economic considerations in the financing of treatment sparked interest in so-called minimal intervention, such as long-term, low-intensity case monitoring (Stout et al., 1999) and "assisted spontaneous remissions". The low acceptance or under-utilization of the resources of numerous treatment services also raised questions about the reasons for treatment rejection and supported the view that it was not possible to understand, from the study of clinical populations only, the needs and possibilities for change among the much more important "hidden problem group". A successful outreach for this group implied, also, the increasingly pragmatic recognition of the concept of harm reduction or low-threshold intervention which, on its part, was also based on a more realistic assessment of the possibilities and acceptance of professional forms of therapy. The idea of harm minimization is not in any way new in the alcohol area, but has gained increasing significance, particularly in view of interesting parallels with other drugs (Plant, Single & Stockwell, 1997).

These general developments have also stimulated research efforts, offered a wider framework for understanding addiction-related change processes or divorced them from a fixation on therapy (Miller, 1998), and encouraged discussion and re-assessment of research available so far. An example from the most recent past is the re-assessment of Vaillant's (1983, 1995) unique long-term study on the natural history of alcoholism.

Taken as a whole, these more recent studies largely confirm the stage model mentioned earlier, which stresses cognitive cost–benefit processes (Prochaska & DiClemente, 1983). This finding also appears to apply in cross-addiction and cross-cultural comparisons. Tinker & Tucker (1997), in their study of overcoming problems of obesity with and without treatment support, observed a combination of short- and long-term, predominantly negative, influences on motivation similar to self-remission processes from studies of addiction problems. In an interview study in Sweden, similar behaviour-orientated control strategies were found in alcohol, tobacco and drug spontaneous remitters (e.g. altered life conception, change in social contacts) (Mariezcurrena, 1996). In an English study which, for the first time, compared smoking, eating disorders, alcoholism and gambling addiction, the overriding importance of subjective will-power and motivation for change (awareness of reasons for change, particularly social pressure and change in life circumstances, such as new job, etc.) was apparent (McCartney, 1996). Social-class-specific opportunities and forms of treatment-free remission were found in a small mixed sample of drug and alcohol addicts (Granfield & Cloud, 1996) and also in a large-scale analysis of problem drinkers (Humphreys, Moos & Finney, 1995). According to this, middle-class addicts with good social networks and, in particular, an intact feeling of self-worth developed into moderate/controlled alcohol consumers, whereas members of the lower social class, subscribing to a "hitting bottom" syndrome, became abstinent significantly more often (Humphreys et al., 1995). With regard to the "abstinence strategy" and "controlled drinking" types of self-change, interesting distinctions can be drawn in life-event profiles. According to King & Tucker (1998), a 4 year group comparison showed that abstaining spontaneous remitters exhibited a steady decrease in the number of reported negative life events, whereas controlled drinking spontaneous remitters (but also stabilized for many years) reported an increase in the fourth year. The authors postulate that:

> . . . as their drinking remained normalized and less central as a life problem, the moderation drinkers were increasingly able to tolerate some instability and change without resuming problem drinking . . . by comparison, the environments of abstainers were increasingly uneventful . . . (p. 541).

According to the only Swiss study available, it was possible to identify motivation, implementation and stabilization phases from an in-depth analysis of the life histories of heroin and alcohol spontaneous remitters, as well as the significance of cognitive decision and learning processes. As this is one of the few comparative prospective studies, main results from the first (1989) and second (1992/1993 and 1996) phases of the research will be highlighted in somewhat greater detail. The 30 heroin and 30 alcohol spontaneous remitters generally went through a conscious phase of preliminary deliberation, with an objectively high "loss stress" (i.e. the number of negatively experienced life events during the year preceding spontaneous recovery), which progressed to a serious motivation for change through additional, in most cases positive and social, triggers. Contrary to previous findings, support played *no* role in the decision implementation (although it probably did in medium-term stabilization). The spontaneous remitters tend to withdraw in this vulnerable phase and are unaware of informal and professional help provision or reject it as inappropriate. They apply an impressive repertoire of implementation techniques and everyday methods. Specifically, spontaneous remitters resort to distancing techniques (e.g. throwing away the contents of the bar; changing the journey home to avoid passing the pub, etc.), drug-related substitution ideas (e.g. instead of alcohol, new cosmo-organic nutrition, coffee consumption, etc.), the imagination of effects (e.g. anticipated effects of further consumption; a belief that one is specifically vulnerable to alcohol), and individual behaviour management (e.g. hobbies, reading) (Klingemann, 1992).

These concrete resources used in implementing change have generally received little attention in research; one exception is the extensive narrative material in the study by Burman (1997) of 38 male and female alcoholic spontaneous remitters. Burman's typology of self-change strategies, similar in many respects to the Swiss study, included: "bargaining with time—a trial commitment", "programmed self-talks and public announcements", "preserving painful memories" and "journalling".

Overall, the self-remission process in alcohol and heroin spontaneous remitters appeared to follow a *similar* basic pattern. However, differences were apparent which pointed to a more difficult course of self-remission, but also a more stable natural recovery, in heroin spontaneous remitters. According to the findings from the first study, heroin spontaneous remitters had a harder task in the first place to achieve control because, for example, of initial stress levels and persistent craving problems. However, the prognosis for this group was more favourable in terms of medium-term stabilization than that for alcohol spontaneous remitters; the self-assessment of their future progress, as well as that of others, was more positive than in the alcohol reference group. This was all the more surprising because the stress situation of heroin spontaneous remitters at the time of the interview always appeared relatively more precarious than in the reference group. This could be tentatively explained by the relatively more pronounced cognitive support and social orientation of the self-remission decision in the preliminary phase, as well as the establishment of primarily *non*-substance drug substitutes (e.g. religion, relationships) in the stabilization phase among heroin remitters. It is precisely the combination of the pressure from continuing public stigmatization, on the one hand, and perceived primary group support, on the other, which might be interpreted as an ideal basis for challenging the inner-directed remitter to pursue new goals in life.

A comparison of alcohol and heroin cases ($n = 30$ in each group, 100% retrieval) in a follow-up study 4 years later confirmed the tendency for a more positive outcome for self-change in the latter group. Only three out of 30 non-treated heroin remitters reported a fully-blown relapse (with an additional three cases indicating a lapse) compared to nine out of 30 non-treated alcohol remitters (with two additional lapses). Natural recovery from alcohol problems seems to be much more difficult than quitting illicit drug use. Alcohol remitters continue to be confronted with risk situations and easy availability, whereas the drug world is far less culturally integrated.

Future Research Priorities

Having outlined some of the more important research findings in this area of work, we will now indicate where we think future research is especially needed.

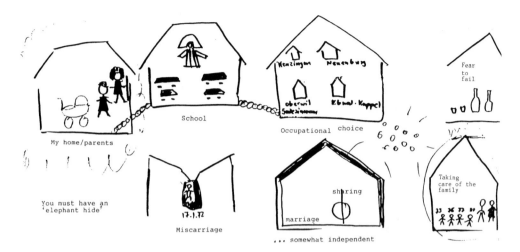

Figure 33.1 'Biographical drawing' of a spontaneous remitter from problem alcohol use (female 35 years old, works in a kindergarten). From Klingemann (1990), with permission

1. *Prospective longitudinal studies*, which help answer questions of causal relationship, and a better integration of qualitative and quantitative approaches. A clear-cut survey approach falls short of the very complicated life histories of spontaneous remitters. The combined use of open-ended questions, narrative approaches, projective methods and standardized questionnaires seems to be promising. If one looks at the complicated ups and downs of the life-charts of spontaneous remitters, one realizes that one can never hope to capture these transitions, passages and career shifts with a series of simple questionnaire items. Figure 33.1, taken from the Swiss study mentioned above, illustrates this very clearly (see also the first use of this method by Alasuuntari, 1986, with a sample of blue-collar alcoholics in Finland).

2. *Improvements in methodological design*, such as the incorporation of control groups and validity tests by interviews with collaterals. Comparing different "true" stories of recovery helps to get a better understanding of how individuals managed to quit. Collaterals tend to be more distanced; quitters may exaggerate their problems of the past to see themselves as "heroes".

3. *Comparative studies*, which include various problem areas—particularly licit and illicit drugs, but also eating disorders, medication misuse and substance-unrelated addictions (e.g. gambling addiction)—in an integrated research design. Above all, increased attention should be paid to the question of multiple problem solutions. Is it easier for people who quit drinking also to stop smoking? Does one success experience carry over to other types of addiction and encourage people to work on other problems as well?

4. *Increased attention to societal conditions*, which might promote or impede individual change. By way of example, mention may be made of the varying degrees of stigmatization of addiction and other social problems by the public and the different ways the media portray alcoholics, drug addicts and gamblers, which in turn will influence perceived chances of change and willingness to help such people.

5. *Investigation of change processes in different cultural contexts*. The few findings available so far do not point to distinct cultural differences but, on the contrary, underline the overriding dominant role of cognitive appraisal processes in very different

countries such as the USA, Switzerland, Canada (Sobell et al., 1999) and Australia (Brady, 1995). It seems that health problems, life objectives, support and pressure from collaterals are *leitmotivs*, which show up almost universally. However, the different focus and development of alcohol (Klingemann, Takala & Hunt, 1992) and drug (Klingemann & Hunt, 1998) treatment systems already indicate significant influences on remission rates and individual control strategies. If little alcohol treatment is available in a specific country and access is difficult in terms of cost and admission criteria, natural recovery rates may be higher than in countries with elaborate treatment systems and guaranteed individual rights to proper treatment. Natural recovery from smoking is the rule, with no specific treatment offered in most cases (Steward, 1999).

CONCLUSIONS FOR TREATMENT AND FOR ALCOHOL POLICY

The provisional demonstration of effective self-change processes does not in any way make professional intervention superfluous. What is required, however, is harmonization of various treatment programmes and specific interventions tailored to the needs of groups targeted for spontaneous remissions at critical points. Finfgeld (1998) discusses how health care providers might promote the process of change and help people to "reinvest in themselves" by, for instance, teaching life management skills and providing accurate problem information.

Bibliotherapy can be regarded as the most prominent case of "assisted spontaneous remission". The basic idea is that written material can assist the individual in the recovery process. This material can be categorized according to the way it is administered, the underlying didactic impetus/content, the target group it is intended should use the manual, and the producer/source. More precisely, we can distinguish between self-help manuals, which are entirely self-administered, those that require minimal contact with a therapist, and manuals used in the context of regular therapeutic meetings. As to the last-named, drinking diaries have been developed to provide doctors with an interactive and cost-effective method of responding to low-dependence problem drinkers they encounter in their practice. In Scotland, the DRAMS scheme (Drinking Responsibly and Moderately with Self-Control) was tested (Heather, 1986) and subsequently adopted also in different cultural contexts (e.g. in Switzerland; Noschis, 1988).

Furthermore, self-help material may be based explicitly on the principles of self-management and stages of change theory to facilitate the transition to the action and maintenance stages. The material may simply help to monitor and structure personal observations of drinking occasions and quantities consumed, or the written material can be simply of a general informative nature, with no stepwise or didactic programme whatever. Self-help manuals are available for both problem drinkers and their partners (Barber & Gilbertson, 1998). While all this material is produced by professionals for people ready to change, there are also cases of "natural bibliotherapy", when spontaneous remitters keep a diary themselves or use related books or materials not produced by professionals as a self-help manual in the strict sense.

> At the time we always drank a lot at Christmas, heavily, and so it wasn't that nice for the kids. I was always in a bad mood and it seemed that the whole world was against me—and then it struck me—I thought, "Now I've really got to do something about this". Anyway, on the 24th we were in a library with our daughter to take a book back—I still don't know exactly how it happened—there was this shelf—I still had a headache from the night before and I was a little

unsteady on my feet but something drew—no idea how it happened—either way, something drew me to this shelf and at head height there were various books: "ways away from alcohol"—this book, that book, lots of books on drugs and such like—and then I simply picked up two books, took them home and started reading on Saturday night right through into Sunday—I was reading and crying and from then on I knew, as I had already known, "You've got to do something". And the book—incredibly well-written because—well there it was at the beginning—you should only read it when you haven't touched a drop. And so I waited another day (laughs) to get everything out of my system, and then I began to read. And there were so many things in the book that you know full well yourself—but that it takes the book to show you—that's how it is. And then you do the test and insert the points and at the end you add them up and see how many you have. And then you are shocked—5 points is critical and I had 22—it gave me courage (laughs) and then you want to flick back through the pages but when you read further—the very next paragraph—it says stop, don't do it: "why are you flicking back through the pages?". And you laugh because the book caught you out, and then you get to thinking, "How would it be if I stopped drinking altogether?" (Case No. 112, Klingemann, 1992).

Studies by Heather (1986), Heather, Kissoon-Singh and Fenton (1990) and others (e.g. Miller & Taylor 1980) clearly demonstrate the benefits of self-help manuals compared with other forms of brief low-threshold interventions, such as the use of telephone help-lines. However, as the short case description above illustrates, "it is necessary to establish whether it is the self-management ingredients of a self-help manual that make for effective bibliotherapy or the act of reading any reasonably relevant and well-intentioned material" (Heather, 1986, p. 338). Finally, cognitive impairment by alcohol diminishes the capability for self-regulation and monitoring of one's own behaviour and limits the use of these manuals mainly to low-dependence cases.

In this context, addicts' perceptions of treatment programmes are highly instructive and highlight corrections that are necessary to available help. Happel, Fischer & Wittfeld (1993) observed that self-activated forms of strategy and control to achieve remission frequently contradict concepts shared by official drug professionals. Thus, for example, a positive view of the period of addiction in one's own life history is instead depicted as "persistent thinking about addiction", and everyday methods of coping with the problem are often not recognized or picked up by the professional treatment provider. As a result, demands for unconventional support of the individual's own efforts and greater utilization of the skills of those affected can be made. More recent research also points to the fact that cognitive appraisal processes may generally be considered as a basis of motivation for change, irrespective of the specific remission strategy later chosen involving treatment or self-change. Often astonishing similarities between the everyday methods of spontaneous remitters and the methods of paid therapists (Tinker & Tucker, 1997) can be noted.

What can therapists learn from spontaneous remitters? Is it possible to replicate or integrate powerful motivators and facilitators of change in real life in treatment activities? Blomqvist (1996) shows the practical and political limits of such a transfer in practice by pointing out that: ". . . many such activities are most likely to lose their authenticity when explicitly used for therapeutic purposes, thereby creating a 'problem of imitation'", and warns, ". . . the same idea may be taken as an argument for restricting treatment offers to the most destitute cases, whose prospect of encountering in their 'natural environment' experiences that may promote change are extremely poor" (p. 1830).

Case material from a Swiss study illustrates this point nicely. Could Yvonne's bottle trick be used by others or copied by therapists?

"OK", I said, about 3 or 4 years ago, "I can't go on like this". I made up my mind I wanted to be a writer, a journalist, and you just can't do that on alcohol, I couldn't write like that. And then I got out a bottle of whisky and I said to myself, "There must be a way", and I looked at the bottle for a long time and I got the idea that you could dilute it. And then I started, on the first day I had a little drink, a small glass, just like I always had these little drinks, I poured it from the full bottle and then water, I poured a little glass of water in. And so on, every day I had a glass, two, three glasses till nothing was left in the bottle except water, but the taste of whisky, that was still in the bottle and every day I poured myself a drink or two, until there was only water left . . . I drank that, thinking that it was "whisky"—and so it was for me . . . And then I started drinking coffee—by the litre! (laughs) (subject aged 54, cutter, excerpts from the tape-recorded summary of the auto-remission; Klingemann, 1992).

People's perceptions of available treatment programmes and their own everyday methods are not the only factors that determine whether self-change or expert advice is sought. We also need to consider the physical and geographical problems of access, stigmatization/reputation of treatment, and costs and time demands for a potential patient. Copeland (1997) describes the gender-specific aspects of these limitations. The increasing acceptance of concepts such as "harm reduction" and "low-threshold interven-tion" is a reflection of the effort to improve general accessibility to treatment and overcome specific barriers, such as time schedules, costs, the possibility of bringing children along, and rigid admission criteria. Happel et al. (1993) urge greater individualization in the treatment system, and complaints about poor gender-specific provision are consistent with the conclusions from an analysis of remission processes (Lind-Krämer & Timper-Nittel, 1991).

Reflecting definitions of spontaneous remission discussed at the outset, basic questions are raised as to what should be considered to be "treatment" and what community reac-tions to alcohol and drug problems are legitimate and effective. Do material support and aids to survival or the use of complete treatment programmes smooth the path to success-ful self-change in the medium term, or do they undermine the potential for self-help and self-change (Blomqvist, 1996)? The provision of minimal intervention in conjunction with proactive alcohol prevention in the community context is a highly promising avenue (Sobell et al., 1996b). However, the decisive factor is the acceptance by populations that already have an initial impetus for change (spontaneous remitters in the contemplation/appraisal phase), and that would not benefit from costly outpatient or inpatient care to begin with.

In addition to these therapeutic perspectives, we need to consider the important role of the conditions for a *self-change-friendly societal climate* in the broader sense. More specifi-cally, the perception of possibilities for change by the addict as well as by others and willingness to talk about it interact closely with images of addictive behaviour held by the general public. The major discrepancy between the objective prevalence of self-change processes and their public visibility and evaluation is illustrated by a comparison between groups with different experiences of treatment and consumption behaviour in a Canadian study. Whereas 53% of interviewees who had overcome their dependence without treat-ment knew of similar cases, only 14% in one (admittedly non-representative) population group were aware of self-change cases. The other study groups (third parties in respect of spontaneous remitters, unsuccessful spontaneous remitters and treatment cases) fell between these two extremes (Cunningham, Sobell & Sobell, 1998).

What is the reason for a distortion of awareness to such an extent that even people whose sensitivity to self-change processes is heightened by their own experience still under-estimate the phenomenon? An important factor is the problem-specific stigma. While only 5% of spontaneous remitters in the Canadian study had inhibitions about telling others they had stopped smoking, 24% of interviewees considered it inadvisable to declare pub-licly that they had abandoned an alcohol career (Cunningham et al., 1998). In his study, Klingemann (1992) showed how people react when they learn that someone has overcome a problem with alcohol or heroin. First, among both heroin and alcohol spontaneous remit-ters, it was primarily employers and colleagues, as well as neighbours—in other words, groups which can hand out "rewards" or "punishments" to the individual—who were not informed about the self-change. Second, successful heroin spontaneous remitters who "confessed" to self-change reported negative reactions far more frequently than alcohol spontaneous remitters, which again points to differing degrees of stigmatization.

A reduced potential for stigmatization and increased social support, together with an increased belief in self-efficacy on an individual level, can improve the chances of remission for addicts. They, too, are consumers of mass media messages (Elwood & Ataabadi, 1997), a circumstance which is used in research as a recruitment strategy, but which in public work and prevention is given too little consideration. Last, if these findings are seen at a macrosocial level, then undoubtedly the way in which social problems are presented in the public (media) arena (Widmer, Boller & Coray, 1997) can exert a considerable influence on collective stereotypes and the willingness to provide informal support and help.

National alcohol policy and prevention campaigns can have a definite effect at this level and promote a favourable climate for self-change. An interesting example is the prevention campaign "Handle with Care" run in 1999. This publicity campaign by the Swiss Federal Office of Public Health used slogans and TV advertisements focusing on binge drinking situations (bowling evening, birthday party, disco, etc.). An attempt was made here to induce a transition from the precontemplation to the contemplation phase. In addition, the situational reference does not require continuous monitoring of one's behaviour but it increases the individual awareness of the problem and reinforces relevant avoidance and control strategies. Close attention should, however, be paid to ensuring that the threshold of inhibition for seeking treatment in more serious cases is not *raised* as a result of the propagation of self-help potential among the public (Cunningham et al., 1998).

Finally, from a macrosocietal perspective, one might also assume that more general cultural values and societal belief systems will influence chances for self-change. One might plausibly assume that individually-centred, achievement-orientated Western societies in particular offer good preconditions for self-change philosophies, with active individuals believing in their abilities to resolve the problem situated at the centre. In contrast to this, the disease concept tends as a rule to imply a more passive patient role and expensive expert involvement or, as in the case of the AA movement, even demands an acknowledgement of powerlessness over alcohol and a life-long, ongoing recovery process. Welfare agencies, collective approaches, the belief in state intervention and expert knowledge place far less emphasis on the individual potential for remission and would probably tend more to impede self-change processes. Burman (1997) illustrates this point in her qualitative study in respect of the assessment of self-help groups by spontaneous remitters:

> Many respondents resisted the mandatory labelling, as well as the philosophy of powerlessness over alcohol and recovering as an endless process. As one man stated: "I can't keep seeing myself as an alcoholic if I'm ever going to close that door, *take control* and move on with my life" (p. 47, emphasis added).

ACKNOWLEDGEMENT

Work on this chapter was carried out while the author was affiliated to the Swiss Institute for the Prevention of Alcohol and Other Drug Problems (SIPA).

KEY WORKS AND SUGGESTION FOR FURTHER READING

Blomqvist, J. (1996).   Paths to recovery from substance misuse: change of lifestyle and the role of treatment. *Substance Use and Misuse*, **31**, 1807–1852.

This review article provides an excellent overview of natural recovery research. Blomqvist argues for the integration of outcome research and research on spontaneous recovery and raises the issue of the definition of "treatment".

Moos, R.H. (1994). Treated or untreated, an addiction is not an island unto itself. *Addiction*, **89**, 507–509.

The title says it all. Best to be read after a comprehensive review article.

Vaillant, G.E. (1996). A long-term follow-up of male alcohol abuse. *Archives of General Psychiatry*, **53**, 243–249.

For those who do not have time to read Vaillant's (1995) book, this article presents the complex study in a nutshell and raises core questions about the natural history of alcoholism from a clinical perspective.

Brady, M. (1995). *Giving Away the Grog. Aboriginal Accounts of Drinking and Not Drinking*. Canberra: Commonwealth Department of Human Services and Health.

This is a fine collection of narratives of Australian aborigines, which illustrates change processes in an unfamiliar cultural context.

Peele, S. (1989). *Diseasing of America—Addiction Treatment Out of Control*. Lexington, MA: Lexington Books).

A provocative book, especially for a North American readership used to the 12-step philosophy and the "war on drugs" rhetoric. More a policy book than a scientific reader, the book suggests why natural recovery research has sparked so much controversy.

Miller, W.R. (1998). Why do people change addictive behavior? The 1996 H. David Archibald Lecture. *Addiction*, **93**, 163–172.

This article puts the influential transtheoretical model of change by Prochaska and his colleagues into perspective and focuses on the concept of "assisted natural recovery", touching upon principles of motivational interviewing, self-efficacy and brief intervention.

Klingemann, H., Sobell, L., Barker, J. et al. (2001). *Promoting Self-change from Problem Substance Use: Practical Implications for Policy, Prevention and Treatment*. Dordrecht: Kluwer Academic.

This book offers an up-to-date review of self-change from problem use of licit and illicit drugs, and from gambling, and provides a "tool-box" for the practice-oriented reader.

REFERENCES

Alasuuntari, P. (1986). Alcoholism in its cultural context: the case of blue-collar men. *Contemporary Drug Problems*, **13**, 641–686.
Barber, J.G. & Gilbertson, R. (1998). Evaluation of a self-help manual for the female partners of heavy drinkers. *Research on Social Work Practice*, **8**(2), 141–151.
Battegay, R. (1988). *Autodestruktion*. Bern: Verlag Hans Huber.
Blackwell, J.St. (1983). Drifting, controlling and overcoming: opiate users who avoid becoming chronically dependent. *Journal of Drug Issues*, **13**, 219–236.
Blomqvist, J. (1996). Paths to recovery from substance misuse: change of lifestyle and the role of treatment. *Substance Use and Misuse*, **31**, 1807–1852.
Böker, W., Brenner, H., Gerstner, G., Keller, F., Müller, J. & Spichtig, L. (1984). Self-healing strategies among schizophrenics: attempts at compensation for basic disorders. *Acta Psychiatrica Scandinavia*, **69**, 373–378.

Brady, M. (1995). *Giving Away the Grog. Aboriginal Accounts of Drinking and Not Drinking.* Canberra: Commonwealth Department of Human Services and Health.

Burman, S. (1997). The challenge of sobriety: natural recovery without treatment and self-help groups. *Journal of Substance Abuse*, **9**, 41–61.

Copeland, J. (1997). A qualitative study of barriers to formal treatment among women who self-managed change in addictive behaviours. *Journal of Substance Abuse Treatment*, **14**, 183–190.

Cunningham, J.A., Sobell, L.C. & Sobell, M.B. (1998). Awareness of self-change as a pathway to recovery for alcohol abusers: results from five different groups. *Addictive Behaviors*, **23**, 399–404.

Elwood, W.N. & Ataabadi, A.N. (1997). Influence of interpersonal and mass-mediated interventions on injection drug and crack users: diffusion of innovations and HIV risk behaviors. *Substance Use and Misuse*, **32**, 635–651.

Eysenck, H.J. & Rachman, S.J. (1973). *Neurosen und Heilmethoden. Einführung in die moderne Verhaltensthetapie* [The Causes and Cures of Neurosis]. Berlin-Ost: Verlag der Wissenschaft.

Fillmore, K.M., Hartka, E., Johnstone, B.M., Speiglman, R. & Temple, M.T. (1988). Spontaneous remission from alcohol problems: a critical review. Unpublished manuscript, University of California at Berkeley, CA.

Finfgeld, D.L. (1998). Self-resolution of drinking problems as a process of reinvesting in self. *Perspectives in Psychiatric Care*, **34**, 5–15.

Granfield, R. & Cloud, W. (1996). The elephant that no one sees: natural recovery among middle-class addicts. *Journal of Drug Issues*, **26**, 45–61.

Granfield, R. & Cloud, W. (in press). *Social Structure and Natural Recovery: the Role of Social Capital in Facilitating Self-change.* New York: New York University Press.

Happel, H.-V., Fischer, R. & Wittfeld, I. (1993). *Selbstorganisierter Ausstieg. Überwindung der Drogenabhängigkeit ohne professionelle Hilfe (Endbericht).* Frankfurt: Integrative Drogenhilfe an der Fachhochschule Ffm L.V.

Hay, L.L. (1984). *You Can Heal Your Life.* London: Eden Grove Editions.

Heather, N. (1986). Change without therapists. The use of self-help manuals by problem drinkers. In W.R. Miller & N. Heather (Eds), *Treating Addictive Behaviors* (pp. 331–359). New York/London: Plenum.

Heather, N., Kissoon-Singh, J. & Fenton, G.W. (1990). Assisted natural recovery from alcohol problems: effects of a self-help manual with and without supplementary telephone contact. *British Journal of Addiction*, **85**, 1177–1185.

Humphreys, K., Moos, R.H. & Finney, J.W. (1995). Two pathways out of drinking problems without professional treatment. *Addictive Behaviors*, **20**, 427–441.

King, M.P. & Tucker, J.A. (1998). Natural resolution of alcohol problems without treatment: environmental contexts surrounding the initiation and maintenance of stable abstinence or moderation drinking. *Addictive Behaviors*, **23**, 537–541.

Klingemann, H. (1990). "Der Freitag, wo alles kaputt war" oder "Die Macht des Positiven"? Eine dimensionale Analyse "natürlicher Heilungen" bei kritischem Alkohol- und Heroinkonsum. *Zeitschrift für Soziologie*, **19**(6), 444–457.

Klingemann, H. (1992). Coping and maintenance strategies of spontaneous remitters from problem use of alcohol and heroin in Switzerland. *International Journal of the Addictions*, **27**, 1359–1388.

Klingemann, H., Takala, J.-P. & Hunt, G. (Eds) (1992). *Cure, Care, or Control—Alcoholism Treatment in Sixteen Countries.* New York: State University of New York Press.

Klingemann, H. & Hunt, G. (Eds) (1998). *Drug Treatment Systems in an International Perspective: Drugs, Demons and Delinquents.* Thousand Oaks, CA: Sage.

Kohli, M. (1978). *Soziologie des Lebenslaufs.* Soziologische Texte, Vol. 109: N.F. Darmstadt-Neuwied: Luchterhand.

Lange, H.U. (1981). Anpassungsstrategien, Bewältigungsreaktionen und Selbstheilversuche bei Schizophrene. *Fortschritte der Neuroligie Psychiatrie*, **49**, 275–285.

Lind-Krämer, R. & Timper-Nittel, A. (1991). *Geschlechtsspezifische Analyse von Drogenabhängigkeit.* Projektgruppe Rauschmittelfragen, Forschungsprojekt "Amsel", Abschlussbericht, Vol. 2. Frankfurt: Jugendberatung und Jugendhilfe e.V.

Mariezcurrena, R. (1996). Recovery from addictions without treatment: an interview study. *Scandinavian Journal of Behaviour Therapy*, **25**, 57–84.

Marlatt, G.A. & Gordon, J.R. (Eds) (1985). *Relapse Prevention: Maintenance Strategies in the Treatment of Addictive Behaviors*. New York: Guilford.

McCartney, J. (1996). A community study of natural change across the addictions. *Addiction Research*, **4**, 65–83.

Miller, L. (1981). Predicting relapse and recovery in alcoholism and addiction: neuropsychology, personality, and cognitive style. *Journal of Substance Abuse Treatment*, **8**, 277–291.

Miller, W.R. (1998). Why do people change addictive behavior? The 1996 H. David Archibald Lecture. *Addiction*, **93**, 163–172.

Miller, W.R. & Taylor, C.A. (1980). Focused vs. broad spectrum behavior therapy for problem drinkers. *Journal of Consulting and Clinical Psychology*, **48**, 590–601.

Noschis, K. (1988). Testing a self-help instrument with early-risk alcohol consumers in general practice: a progress report. *Contemporary Drug Problems*, **15**(3), 365–382.

Peele, S. (1989). *Diseasing of America—Addiction Treatment Out of Control*. Lexington, MA: Lexington Books.

Plant, M., Single, E. & Stockwell, T. (1997). *Alcohol: Minimising the Harm*. London: Free Association Books.

Prochaska, J.O. & DiClemente, C.C. (1983). Stages and processes of self-change of smoking: toward an integrative model of change. *Journal of Consulting and Clinical Psychology*, **51**, 390–395.

Prochaska, J.O., Norcross, J.C. & DiClemente, C.C. (1994). Transtheoretical therapy: toward a more integrative model of change. *Psychotherapy: Theory, Research and Practice*, **19**, 276–288.

Roizen, R., Cahalan, D. & Shanks, P. (1978). Spontaneous remission among untreated problem drinkers. In D.B. Kandel (Eds), *Longitudinal research on drug use* (pp. 197–221). New York: Wiley.

Rumpf, H.-J., Bischof, G., Hapke, U., Meyer, C. & John, U. (2000). Studies on natural recovery from alcohol dependence: sample selection bias by media solicitation. *Addiction*, **2000**, 765–775.

Sack, F. (1978). Probleme der Kriminalsoziologie. In R. König (Ed.), *Handbuch der empirischen Sozialforschung, Vol. 12. Wahlverhalten, Vorurteile, Kriminalität*. Stuttgart: Ferdinand Enke Verlag.

Smart, R.G. (1975). Spontaneous recovery in alcoholics: a review and analysis of the available research. *Drug and Alcohol Dependence*, **1**, 277–285.

Sobell, L.C., Cunningham, J.A. & Sobell, M.B. (1996a). Recovery from alcohol problems with and without treatment: prevalence in two population surveys. *American Journal of Public Health*, **86**(7), 966–972.

Sobell, L.C., Cunningham, J.C., Sobell, M.B., Agrawal, S., Gavin, D.R., Leo, G.I. & Singh, K.N. (1996b). Fostering self-change among problem drinkers: a proactive community intervention. *Addictive Behaviors*, **21**, 817–833.

Sobell, L.C., Klingemann, H., Toneatto, T., Sobell, M.B., Agrawal, S. & Leo, G.I. (1999). *Cross-cultural qualitative analysis of factors associated with natural recoveries from alcohol and drug problems*. Paper presented at the KBS thematic meeting, Les Diablerets, Switzerland, 7–12 March.

Stall, R. (1983). An examination of spontaneous remission from problem drinking in the bluegrass region of Kentucky. *Journal of Drug Issues*, **13**, 191–206.

Stall, R. & Biernacki, P. (1986). Spontaneous remission from the problematic use of substances: an inductive model derived from a comparative analysis of the alcohol, opiate, tobacco and food/obesity literatures. *International Journal of the Addictions*, **21**, 1–23.

Steward, C. (1999). Investigation of cigarette smokers who quit without treatment. *Journal of Drug Issues*, **29**, 167–186.

Stout, R.L., Rubin, A., Zwick, W., Zywiak, W. & Bellino, L. (1999). Optimizing the cost-effectiveness of alcohol treatment: a rationale for extended case monitoring. *Addictive Behaviors*, **24**, 17–35.

Tinker, J.E. & Tucker, J.A. (1997). Motivations for weight loss and behavior change strategies associated with natural recovery from obesity. *Psychology of Addictive Behaviors*, **11**, 98–106.

Vaillant, G.E. (1983). *The Natural History of Alcoholism: Cases, Patterns, and Paths to Recovery*. Cambridge, MA: Harvard University Press.

Vaillant, G.E. (1995). *The Natural History of Alcoholism Revisited*. Cambridge, MA: Harvard University Press.

Waldorf, D. & Biernacki, P. (1979). Natural recovery from heroin addiction: a review of the incidence literature. *Journal of Drug Issues*, **9**, 281–289.

Widmer, J., Boller, B. & Coray, R. (Eds) (1997). *Drogen im Spannungsfeld der Öffentlichkeit*. Basel: Helbing & Lichtenhan.

Chapter 34

Alcoholics Anonymous and Other Mutual Aid Groups

Chad Emrick
University of Colorado Health Sciences Center, Denver, CO, USA

Synopsis

Alcoholics Anonymous was founded in the USA in 1935. Currently, there are an estimated nearly 2,000,000 active members worldwide in nearly 99,000 groups in over 140 countries. Since the mid-1940s, a number of other mutual aid groups for alcoholics developed outside of North America, including the Abstainer Clubs in Poland, Links in Sweden, Vie Libre and Croix d'Or in France, Clubs for Alcoholics in Treatment in Italy, Club of Treated Alcoholics in Croatia, Freundeskreise in Germany, 24-Hours Movements in Mexico, and Danshu-Tomo-no-Kai and the All Nippon Sobriety Association in Japan. More recently, alternatives to AA have emerged in North America: Women for Sobriety, Secular Organizations for Sobriety, Rational Recovery, and Moderation Management, for example.

The philosophy, structure, and therapeutic processes of AA are centered around the organization's Twelve Steps and Twelve Traditions. Alternative mutual-aid groups possess varied structures and processes, many of which differ from those of AA. This variability broadens the opportunity each individual has for finding a compatible mutual aid group.

Substantial cross-cultural variation is found in the demographic characteristics of AA members. Also, there is international variability in the degree to which alcohol-troubled individuals use mutual aid groups other than AA.

Treatment outcome studies have found that, compared to alcohol-troubled patients who do not go to AA within the context of professional treatment, those who go to AA during or after professional treatment are more likely to improve in drinking behavior and have improved psychological health. AA's effectiveness can be traced to members' learning to use therapeutic and adaptive processes to deal with life. Besides leading to improvements in the lives of its members, AA and other mutual-aid groups have the advantage of being considerably less costly than professional treatment.

International Handbook of Alcohol Dependence and Problems. Edited by N. Heather, T.J. Peters and T. Stockwell.
© 2001 John Wiley & Sons Ltd.

Attendance at AA meetings may occur without a member becoming actively involved in the therapeutic processes of the organization. To facilitate effective involvement in AA and other mutual-aid groups, health care providers need to familiarize themselves with the philosophy, structure and therapeutic processes of each group. Knowledge needs to be acquired regarding: how to integrate mutual aid groups with professional treatment; how to direct individual clients to specific groups, given the heterogeneity of individual groups within a mutual aid organization; how to facilitate mutual aid group involvement with individuals who belong to special populations; and how to match individuals to mutual aid groups. With regard to the last item, AA-orientated treatment appears to be most useful for outpatients whose social interactional systems support drinking and for those who have relatively low levels of anger at the start of treatment. For inpatients who are relatively high in their dependence on alcohol, an AA-orientated aftercare treatment may be most suitable. For outpatients who have been involved in AA prior to professional treatment, encouraging them once again to go to AA offers an approach that is more compatible to the drinker than are methods that are not 12-step-group focused.

Alcoholics Anonymous and other mutual aid groups are not always helpful to alcohol-troubled individuals. Sometimes, people with alcohol problems need to be assisted in finding alternative treatments, either of a professional or mutual-aid sort.

Recent research has yielded a virtual explosion of new understanding concerning the therapeutic processes, effectiveness and suitable utilization of AA and, by extension, other mutual aid groups. Health care providers are now able to provide wiser counsel than ever about mutual aid groups when dealing with their patients who have alcohol problems.

The primary purpose of this chapter is to inform health care workers and other interested readers about Alcoholics Anonymous. Pertinent findings from recent quantitative research on AA are exploited in this effort and observations from relevant contemporary clinical writings are used to amplify these findings. This information is given application to care-givers for making maximum use of AA. Alternatives to AA are explored in order to broaden the perspective with regard to mutual aid groups for alcohol-troubled individuals.

HISTORICAL DEVELOPMENT OF AA AND OTHER MUTUAL AID GROUPS

AA was founded in the USA in 1935 by two chronic alcoholics, Bill W. and Dr Bob S. Several ideas stemming from the founders' contacts with Moral Rearmament (a Christian evangelical movement) helped shape the philosophy and structure of the organization. In 1938 and 1939, this philosophy was codified in the Twelve Steps. In 1950, AA's organizational structure was codified in the Twelve Traditions. Growth of the organization was very slow until around 1940, when several US articles were published about AA. Since then, this organization has enjoyed rapid development. It has grown into a worldwide organization with an estimated nearly 2,000,000 active members in nearly 99,000 groups in over 140 countries (personal communication, General Service Office of Alcoholics Anonymous, November 4, 1999).

Since the mid-1940s, a number of other mutual aid groups for alcoholic-troubled individuals have been established outside of North America. While all of them differ in organization and functioning from AA, each was "influenced, positively or negatively, by the example of AA" (Room, 1998, p. 133). Abstainer Clubs were formed in Poland; Links emerged in Sweden; Vie Libre and Croix d'Or were established in France; Clubs for Alcoholics in Treatment (CATs) took root in Italy; Club of Treated Alcoholics emerged in Croatia; traditional temperance-based organizations, as well as Freundeskreise, found life in the state of Hesse in Germany; 24-Hours Movements were established in Mexico; and Danshu-Tomo-no-Kai and the All Nippon Sobriety Association came into existence in Japan.

In North America, the development of alternatives to AA is a relatively recent phenomenon. The pioneers of these alternatives defected from AA for a variety of reasons, "including dislike of the sexism, the powerlessness concept, rigidity, religiosity, the cult-like atmosphere, and the all powerful God approach" (Kasl, 1992, p. 163). Jean Kirkpatrick founded Women for Sobriety (WFS) in 1976 (see Kaskutus, 1996). This organization addresses the special needs of female problem drinkers by taking a holistic approach to health and fostering autonomy from men. In 1985, two organizations that promote a secular approach to alcohol problems were founded: James Christopher started Secular Organizations for Sobriety (SOS), also called Save our Selves (see Connors and Dermen, 1996); and Jack Trimpey established Rational Recovery (RR) (see Galanter, Egelko & Edwards, 1993; Trimpey, 1996). As with AA, all these alternatives view abstinence as the goal of recovery from alcohol problems. As a counterpoint to these groups, an organization that promotes harm reduction as its members' goal was formed by Audrey Kishline in the early 1990s (Kishline, 1994). This organization, Moderation Management®, provides group support for the establishment of moderate drinking practices.

AA'S PHILOSOPHY, STRUCTURE AND THERAPEUTIC PROCESSES

AA's philosophy, although rooted in the Judeo-Christian tradition, contains thought elements that are consonant with a variety of religious and philosophical traditions. Thus, people with a wide spectrum of beliefs can find a home in this organization. The organization itself is structured around the Twelve Steps and the Twelve Traditions (Alcoholics Anonymous World Services, 1986) (see Appendix). Therapeutic processes are played out in "working" the steps, having (for some members) one-to-one guidance and support from a senior member (identified as a "sponsor"), and participating in group meetings that possess therapeutic processes akin to those found in professionally led psychotherapy groups (Emrick, Lassen & Edwards, 1977).

The process of going through the Twelve Steps is adumbrated here for the reader who is unfamiliar with these steps. In Step One, members adopt the perspective that they cannot control their drinking behavior through conscious, deliberate effort. In Step Two, members incorporate the belief that only a Power greater than oneself can help them become free of alcohol dependence. In Step Three, members surrender to this Higher Power—and in so doing let go of their struggle with drinking behavior as well as with the thoughts, feelings, physical sensations, and behavioral predispositions that are associated with such behavior. In Step Four, members undertake a self-analysis of fear, guilt and resentment that are often major contextual factors in drinking behavior. One's resentments are given especial attention and members are guided through procedures for developing a less blaming, more self-responsible perspective with regard to resentments and associated actions. In Step Five, members share the product of their self-analysis with their Higher Power and another individual. In Steps Six and Seven, more letting go of an active struggle with one's inner life is prompted. Whatever behaviors are identified in Steps Four and Five as dysfunctional are viewed as beyond the scope of the individual to change directly. Rather, the individual lets go of a deliberate struggle, "turning over" these behaviors to a Higher Power to effect change. In Steps Eight and Nine, members extend the development of responsibility to their interpersonal relationships. Responsibility is taken for harm caused others (by omission and commission), and restitution to those one has harmed is undertaken, unless restitution efforts would bring harm either to the member or someone else. Because self-awareness is inevitably limited, members are encouraged, once they have made amends for the harmful actions of which they are aware, to look the harmed individual square in the face and ask him/her to identify harmful acts that the member has forgotten. Responsibility is then extended to these behaviors. In Steps Ten and Eleven, activities are engaged that serve to maintain the therapeutic gains achieved in taking the earlier steps. Finally, in Step Twelve, the healing gained through involvement in the program (referred to as a "spiritual awakening") is maintained by helping newcomers to the organization and by serving to sustain the organization itself. Increasing one's awareness of, acceptance of and enactment of the paradoxes of life is at the core of spiritual awakening within the context of active AA involvement. A member's philosophical perspective on life becomes infused with such paradoxical truths as "in order to win, one has to lose" and "in order to give, one has to receive". It is from this place of awareness that experienced members help new members and contribute through service activities to the maintenance of the organization.

The Twelve Traditions of AA are intended to preserve AA as an organization that is completely dedicated to helping individuals live life free of alcohol. Central to AA is an essentially anarchistic organizational structure. There are no permanent leaders, and leaders are instructed to "serve but never govern". Each group maintains autonomy, owns no property, and receives income only from voluntary contributions. Members are to avoid identifying themselves to the public media as members of AA. AA does not "give endorsements, make alliances, or enter public controversies" (Alcoholics Anonymous World Services, 1976, p. xix). AA is not to solicit new members through any promotional activity. By virtue of its organizational structure, AA has been able to avoid usurpation of power by any individual or faction of members. Such avoidance has been strongly contributive to AA's remarkable success as a social movement.

Although AA's essential organizational structure and therapeutic processes are notably consistent throughout its multinational operations, interesting variations are found across countries and within different regions of a country. The International Collaborative Study of Alcoholics Anonymous (Mäkelä et al., 1996) investigated AA in eight societies, offering fascinating facts concerning AA's international variation. For example, 30–50% of AA members in Iceland, Mexico, Poland and German-speaking Switzerland view the Higher Power referred to in the Twelve Steps as a Christian God, while only 13% perceive the Higher Power construct in this fashion in Sweden. The Higher Power construct is viewed as the "AA fellowship or the power of the group", not a metaphysical entity, by 59% of Swedish members and 47% of Icelandic members, whereas only 34% of Mexican members impute this quality to the construct. Recitation of the Lord's Prayer at the end of meetings is a common practice in many parts of the USA and in some Icelandic groups, but is rare or non-existent in Austria, Finland, France, Poland, Sweden and Switzerland. Even the practice of having a sponsor guide a member through the Twelve Steps has international variation. In the USA and Mexico, for example, more than 70% of the members have a sponsor, whereas in Poland, only 30% do.

STRUCTURE AND PROCESSES OF ALTERNATIVE MUTUAL AID GROUPS

Alternatives to AA differ in some remarkable ways from AA with respect to their organizational structure and therapeutic processes. These differences are so numerous that just a few of them can be identified in this chapter. The reader is guided to Room (1998) and

Emrick et al. (1977) for a fuller treatment of these differences. Women for Sobriety groups, for example, discourage talk about one's drinking history. In stark contrast, story-telling in AA is to be limited to one's drinking and the effects drinking has had on the member's life. AA members are to avoid commenting directly on each other's statements (i.e. there is the rule of "no crosstalk"), while the Mexican 24-Hours Movements meetings encourage members to be directly aggressive with fellow members, believing that such confrontation is conducive to change. Only individuals with alcohol use problems can become a member of AA (with spouses and friends belonging to an auxiliary group: Al-Anon). In contrast, family members are invited to join Vie Libre in France and the Clubs movements in Croatia and Italy. In Japan, cultural beliefs lend to wives being *expected* to become members of Danshu-Tomo-no-Kai or the All Nippon Sobriety Association. Finally, in contrast to the emphasis AA places on developing a relationship with a Higher Power, the Swedish Links movement downplays any reference to a Higher Power; and SOS and RR are distinctly void of any reference to a Higher Power.

Differences in structure and function across mutual aid groups, such as those identified here, benefit individuals with alcohol problems by increasing the opportunity each has for finding a compatible mutual aid group.

WHAT ARE THE DEMOGRAPHIC CHARACTERISTICS OF THE CURRENT AA MEMBERSHIP?

The demography of AA membership varies considerably across nations, with "historical contingencies and internal differences in the national movements" shaping the membership (Mäkelä et al., 1996, p. 102). The International Collaborative Study of Alcoholics Anonymous (see Mäkelä et al., 1996) found, for example, that women comprise only 10% of the membership in Mexico, whereas 44% of the membership in Austria are female, with this disparity not being related directly to the prevalence of female problem drinkers in these countries. Demographic diversity is reflected in the fact that in Mexico and Iceland, around 30% of AA members are under the age of 30, compared to less than 10% of the membership in Austria, Finland, Sweden and German-speaking Switzerland. With respect to socioeconomic levels, AA members in Mexico include a number of urban workers and rural poor, and Japan draws in those who are "less well-off" (Room, 1998, p. 136). Similarly, in Finland, Iceland and Switzerland the membership is drawn significantly from the working class. In contrast, members in Austria and, to some degree, Sweden are typically from the higher socioeconomic levels (Mäkelä et al., 1996). Clearly, cultural factors help shape the demographics of AA's membership.

Besides at-large cultural variables, contextual variables more proximal to the individual impact the mutual aid group affiliation process. These more proximal contextual factors have such complex and inconsistent relationships with AA affiliation (see Emrick, 1999) that health care providers have little in the way of clear-cut guidelines for determining, in advance, who will be a good match for AA or other mutual aid groups. Nevertheless, there are a couple of trends within the AA data set that health care providers might wish to reflect upon when working with a patient toward the possibility of involvement in AA. These trends indicate that the more severe an individual's drinking or other identified problem, and the less that person has available in the way of interpersonal supports for abstinence in the "natural" environment (particularly for an outpatient), the more likely the individual is to join AA. These trends notwithstanding, health care practitioners would do well to hold to the position that any given patient *may* or *may not* be a suitable candidate for AA or other mutual aid group.

HOW OFTEN ARE AA AND OTHER MUTUAL AID GROUPS USED BY ALCOHOL ABUSERS?

Although AA appears to be increasingly utilized, the extension of AA into the population of individuals with alcohol use disorders may still be quite modest, with a penetration rate of perhaps less than 10% in the USA, for example (Hasin & Grant, 1995; Hasin, 1994). At the same time, of alcohol-troubled individuals who *do* seek the support of mutual help groups in the USA, the vast majority go to AA inasmuch as this organization has an over-whelming hegemony among mutual help groups in North America. In fact, it is estimated that 95% of the groups that exist for problem drinkers in North America are AA (Room, 1998). The nearly total reliance on AA for mutual help among alcohol-dependent individuals extends to some other countries as well, such as Iceland, Australia and New Zealand. There are some countries, however, in which alternative mutual help groups are utilized as much or more so than AA. For example, in Austria, only about 50% of the mutual help groups are AA; and in Poland, 47% of individuals who go to mutual help groups attend AA. Still lower proportions of AA groups among all available mutual help groups are found in Sweden (24%), Germany (17%) and Italy (14%). In Japan, just 14% of individuals who go to mutual help groups go to AA, with the proportion of problem drinkers who seek the support of mutual help groups being even lower in France (11%).

HOW EFFECTIVE IS AA?

Even though AA is widely used by problem drinkers in some cultures to assist them in dealing with their alcohol problems, and although many health care providers, at least in North America, strongly endorse the effectiveness of AA, is such use and such endorse-ment warranted? Certainly humans are capable of engaging in widely shared behaviors that are not particularly the most constructive. Is this the case with AA?

By now, ample research data have accumulated that document the effectiveness of AA as a resource for helping individuals maintain an alcohol-free lifestyle. In effect, research evidence substantiates the experiential knowledge that AA members and health care providers possess concerning the effectiveness of 12-step groups.

Outcome Studies

A strong element in the expanding structure of positive AA findings consists of data that emerged from a meta-analysis of 107 studies on AA (Emrick et al., 1993). The results of this analysis suggest "that professionally treated patients who attend AA during or after treatment are more likely to improve in drinking behavior than are patients who do not attend AA, although the chances of drinking improvement are not overall a great deal higher" (Emrick et al., 1993, p. 57). Also, a positive relationship between AA affiliation and psychological health was observed.

Most salient among the recent original research findings on AA's effectiveness are the findings of investigators at the Center for Health Care Evaluation in Menlo Park, CA, USA. In one of these studies (Humphreys, Moos & Cohen, 1997), 515 subjects from an original sample of 631 individuals with previously untreated drinking problems were followed up at 1 year. Of those in the sample who attended AA meetings but did not receive inpatient or outpatient professional treatment, significant improvement was found on all measures of drinking problems, as well as on several other measures of functioning. A total of 395 subjects in this sample were followed up at 8 years, at which time it was found that the number of AA meetings attended during the first 3 years of follow-up was positively related to remission from alcohol problems 8 years after the beginning of the project. AA attendance in the first 3 years of the study also predicted, at 8-year follow-up, lower levels of depression as well as higher-quality relationships with friends and partners or spouses. Humphreys et al. (1997) concluded that, compared with professionally delivered inpatient or outpatient treatment, "AA probably helped more people more substantially in this sample" (p. 237).

This same research group evaluated the effects of different types of aftercare treatment 1 year after inpatient treatment in a large sample of veterans (Finney, Moos & Humphreys, 1999; Moos et al., 1999; Ouimette, Moos & Finney, 1998; Ouimette et al., 1999). Followed up were 3018 veterans who had been treated for substance abuse in an inpatient setting. The majority of patients, all of whom were male, were non-Caucasian; 83% of the sample were dependent on alcohol, with about 52% of those with alcohol problems being dependent on other substances. They were evaluated with regard to their outcome status approximately 1 year after being discharged from the inpatient program. Participation in AA or NA in the 3 months prior to the 1-year follow-up was associated with a greater likelihood of being abstinent, free of substance use problems, free of significant distress and psychiatric symptoms, and employed. These findings held even when controlling for the influence of aftercare treatment, and they applied to dually diagnosed patients as much as to those with only substance use disorders (for the latter, see Ouimette et al., 1999). Statistical analyses suggested that 12-step involvement after inpatient treatment helped maintain the gains made during inpatient treatment (Finney et al., 1999). These results led the researchers to conclude that, "Overall, 12-step attendance and involvement were more strongly related to positive outcomes than was outpatient treatment attendance" (Ouimette et al., 1998, p. 519).

Treatment Cost

Humphreys & Moos (1996) took another angle toward assessing the effectiveness of AA. They compared the per-person treatment costs for problem drinkers who sought help from a professional outpatient alcoholism treatment provider with the costs of treatment for drinkers who initially chose to go to AA. Costs were assessed for a three-year period. Over the course of the study, some individuals within both groups required detoxification and inpatient/residential treatment. Furthermore, some drinkers who initially went to AA also had outpatient treatment and vice versa. When all cost factors were calculated, those individuals who initially attended AA incurred per-person treatment costs that were 45% lower than the costs for those who initially sought outpatient treatment. If nothing else, AA appears to be as effective as professional outpatient treatment, while being considerably less costly, in helping at least some individuals with alcohol problems.

Mechanisms of Effectiveness of AA

The mounting research evidence in support of the effectiveness of AA begs the question: what are the mechanisms which mediate the effectiveness of AA? Several recent research efforts provide fascinating and enlightening data pertaining to the operational ingredients in AA's effectiveness (see Emrick, 1999). These data indicate that the more present and active an individual's connection is with AA, the more the member uses a variety of therapeutic/adaptive processes including behavioral change processes, such as avoidance of high-risk situations and the use of active cognitive and behavioral coping strategies. AA's benefits can thereby be traced to the increased utilization of therapeutic/adaptive processes that occurs within the context of increased involvement in AA.

AA GROUP AFFILIATION VS. GROUP INVOLVEMENT

Given that AA's therapeutic benefits are awarded most to those individuals who become actively involved in the organization, reflecting the axiom that "you get out of it only what you put into it," researchers and health care providers need to take into account an individual's degree of participation in AA when assessing that person's responses to the organization. Practitioners and researchers may find it helpful to avail themselves of one or more instruments that have been developed for arriving at a quantitative determination of the degree to which their patients/subjects are actively involved in AA. A number of these instruments exist, most notably those developed by Tonigan, Connors & Miller (1996), and Humphreys, Kaskutas & Weisner (1998). Researchers are encouraged to develop similar instruments for determining the degree of involvement in other mutual aid groups.

FACILITATION OF INVOLVEMENT IN AA AND OTHER MUTUAL AID GROUPS

Since AA and other mutual aid groups can be a vital resource in the recovery of individuals from alcohol abuse and dependence, health care practitioners need to prepare their clients for participation in these organizations. Empirical support for this suggestion comes from two recent major research efforts, both of which show that 12-step-orientated treatment results in a higher percentage of patients involving themselves in 12-step groups and that this involvement, in turn, produces higher abstinence rates (Project MATCH Research Group, 1998; Humphreys et al., 1999).

To be successful in their efforts, professionals need to have an accurate understanding of the philosophy of each mutual aid group. If AA is the target of attention, for example, practitioners need to understand that AA is *not*, according to Miller & Kurtz (1994), an organization that asserts that:

> (1) There is only one form of alcoholism or alcohol problem; (2) moderate drinking is impossible for everyone with alcohol problems; (3) alcoholics should be labeled, confronted aggressively or coerced into treatment; (4) alcoholics are riddled with denial and other defense mechanisms; (5) alcoholism is purely a physical disorder; (6) alcoholism is hereditary; (7) there is only one way to recover; or (8) alcoholics are not responsible for their condition or actions (p. 165).

Practitioners can also assist their patients in becoming beneficially involved in AA and other mutual aid groups by offering basic instruction concerning the structure and therapeutic processes of the mutual aid group at issue. If AA is the focus of attention, health care professionals may facilitate involvement by having contact with their patients' sponsors, encouraging individuals to pick a home group, and encouraging clients to attend AA meetings frequently (particularly at the beginning of participation).

Learning How to Integrate AA, Other Mutual Aid Groups and Professional Treatment

Health care professionals can further enhance the effective use of AA and other mutual aid groups by acquiring knowledge about how best to integrate mutual aid groups and professional treatment (see e.g. Zweben, 1995). Integration is advised because alcohol-dependent individuals who combine these two systems of care appear to have better outcomes (at least with respect to alcohol abuse) than do those who utilize only one type of help. Professionals need to learn the language and culture of AA and other mutual aid groups in order to understand where the two systems differ and where the commonalities in concepts and processes exist. For example, both systems facilitate the development of cognitive and behavioral change processes; only the language used to foster this development differs. By possessing a working knowledge of the language and culture of both systems, health care providers can become more skilled in aiding their patients' use of both forms of help, simultaneously, alternately or sequentially. As recent research data suggest, the most effective way to promote use of both types of care is to fashion a professional treatment approach that is consonant with that found in the mutual aid group environment (Humphreys et al., 1999).

Even when focusing on mutual aid groups alone, health care professionals should keep in mind that patients may benefit from the language and culture of one mutual aid group more than another. Still other patients may find a combinatorial approach most helpful. That is, they may derive greatest benefit from attending AA along with another mutual aid group. Consistent with this consideration, Kaskutus (1996) found that about one-third of the members of Women for Sobriety attended AA concurrently with WFS involvement. Likewise, Connor & Dermen (1996) found that 35% of the members of SOS attended AA along with SOS.

Tailoring Facilitation Efforts to Specific Groups

Professionals may enhance their referral effectiveness by becoming familiar with the unique characteristics of specific groups within a mutual aid organization. This recommendation is based on the fact that heterogeneity has been found across different groups within AA (see, e.g. Montgomery, Miller & Tonigan, 1993). Because of such heterogeneity, a patient may find one particular group within a mutual aid organization to be compatible with individual needs, while other groups may be inappropriate. Helping patients understand the heterogeneity of groups and, therefore, the need to attend several groups before deciding which one(s) best fit(s), is a service health care providers are encouraged to offer.

Becoming Knowledgeable about Special Population Considerations

Recent reports identify points of consideration (as well as, in some case, guidelines) for facilitating AA involvement among individuals with special characteristics, viz. veterans with PTSD, lesbians, adolescents, persons with dual disorders, women, non-affiliative substance abusers, and individuals within a particular ethnic group (see Emrick, 1999). Health care providers need to become knowledgeable about, and sensitive to, these special population issues in order to be effective maximally in facilitating AA group involvement among their patients. Obviously, similar attention to special population considerations must be given with regard to other mutual aid groups as well.

Matching Patients to AA and Other Mutual Aid Groups

An intuitively appealing, although practically difficult, approach to facilitating the utilization and effectiveness of AA and other mutual aid groups is that of finding appropriate matches for these groups. Results from Project MATCH, a major, multi-site study conducted in the USA, suggest three matching strategies health care providers might keep in mind when considering a referral to AA:

1. For drinkers who have a social support system that is supportive of drinking, facilitating participation in AA (through Twelve-Step Facilitation Therapy) appears to result in better drinking outcome than does trying to motivate the individual to give up drinking (through Motivational Enhancement Therapy) or providing treatment based on cognitive-behavioral theory (i.e. Cognitive Behavioral Coping Skills Therapy) (Project MATCH Research Group, 1998; Longabaugh et al., 1998).
2. Alcohol-dependent individuals who are angry at the start of treatment may benefit more from a non-confrontational approach to acquire motivation to change their drinking behavior (i.e. Motivational Enhancement Therapy) than from treatment that encourages them to attend AA (i.e. Twelve-Step Facilitation Therapy). Actively encouraging angry patients to attend AA may provoke an angry response, thereby lowering the chance of a good treatment outcome (Project MATCH Research Group, 1998).
3. Those inpatients who have relatively high dependence on alcohol may benefit more from a 12-step-group orientated aftercare treatment than from treatment based on cognitive-behavioral theory (Project MATCH Research Group, 1997).

An intriguing addendum to these matching strategies is found in a recent publication by Winzelberg & Humphreys (1999). In their study of 3018 male substance abusing inpatients, clients who were low in religious behaviors were less likely to be referred to a 12-step mutual aid group. However, such individuals had a favorable response to 12-step-group referrals and subsequently experienced better substance abuse outcome. It appears, therefore, that health care providers should not be wary of encouraging their less religious clients to get involved in 12-step groups. As Winzelberg & Humphreys state, ". . . a non-religious patient may benefit from referral to AA or NA more than either the clinician or the patient expects" (p. 794).

Although not of the stature of a proposed matching strategy, another Project MATCH finding merits notation. Problem drinkers treated in residential settings who were strong in seeking meaning in life had better drinking outcome, at least for a period of time, when they were given aftercare treatment that was orientated toward AA participation rather than comparison aftercare treatments (Tonigan, Miller & Connors, 1997b). Because this finding is quite tentative, further research needs to be undertaken before the "meaning in life" variable can serve as a guide in making clinical decisions. Nonetheless, clinicians are encouraged to be sensitive to the interplay between a patient's search for meaning in life and the treatment that patient receives.

MATCHING AA MEMBERS TO PROFESSIONAL TREATMENT

How are health care providers to approach their patients who have been involved previously in AA but who are now seeking the services of a professional? Does prior AA involvement affect what type of treatment will be most helpful? Again, Project MATCH data offer us a suggestion (Tonigan, Miller & Connors, 1997a). It appears that for outpatients who have been involved in AA prior to professional treatment, encouraging them through Twelve-Step Facilitation Therapy to resume or maintain involvement in AA offers a more compatible approach than does offering Motivational Enhancement Therapy or therapy based on cognitive-behavioral theory.

Matching strategies along these lines may be identified for other mutual aid groups should researchers and clinicians undertake collaborative efforts to mine these groups for relevant data.

AA AND OTHER MUTUAL AID GROUPS ARE NOT ALWAYS HELPFUL

The health care practitioner must ever keep in mind that any intervention possesses the potential to harm people if it also holds the power to help some people. Should a health care provider assume that AA or another mutual aid organization "can't hurt", he/she may fail to intervene appropriately if a client/patient claims to be worsening through his/her involvement in a mutual aid community.

If health care practitioners assess that a mutual aid group is having iatrogenic effects for a patient, they need to work with that patient to reverse such effects. One obvious corrective course is to assist the patient in finding alternative treatments. To insist on a patient's continued attendance at a particular mutual aid group when the patient is being harmed by such attendance is equivalent to instructing a patient to stay on medication that is not only failing to improve that patient's condition but is also causing harmful side-effects. Good medical and other professional practice proscribes such behavior.

CONCLUSION

This chapter has covered a wide spectrum of issues concerning AA and other mutual aid groups. Information has been presented regarding the historical development of AA and other mutual aid groups: the philosophy, structure and therapeutic processes of AA and other mutual help groups; the demographics of mutual aid group membership; the degree to which AA and other mutual aid groups are being used; the effectiveness of AA; the distinction between mere attendance at mutual aid group meetings and active involvement in a mutual aid community; ways to enhance the utilization of mutual aid groups; referral of AA-involved patients to appropriate professional treatment; and the limits of AA and other mutual aid groups.

In this author's opinion, a virtual explosion of new understandings concerning AA and other mutual aid groups has arisen from the research reviewed in this chapter. Health care providers, armed with considerably greater knowledge than ever before about AA and other mutual aid groups, can now offer their patients even wiser counsel regarding such groups.

ACKNOWLEDGEMENTS

The author is very indebted to Nancy Moore, who not only brought her expert computer and editing skills to the preparation of the manuscript, but also provided invaluable support and encouragement throughout the project. Through Scott Tonigan PhD, I was guided to the most significant current research activity pertaining to AA. His scholarly, compassionate support is deeply valued.

KEY WORKS AND SUGGESTIONS FOR FURTHER READING

Alcoholics Anonymous World Services Inc. (1976). *Alcoholics Anonymous: The Story of How Many Thousands of Men and Women Have Recovered from Alcoholism*, 3rd edn. New York: Alcoholics Anonymous World Services, Inc.

This book is known in AA as "*The Big Book*". Functioning as "The Bible" of AA, it presents a conceptual model of alcoholism, details the method of recovery that AA members are to follow, offers advice to spouses and employers of alcoholics, gives guidance on how to re-establish family relationships after the cessation of drinking, and presents the stories of a number of individuals who have experienced recovery through the fellowship of AA.

Alcoholics Anonymous World Services (1986). *12 + 12: Twelve Steps and Twelve Traditions*. New York: Alcoholics Anonymous World Services.

This book, written by Bill Wilson, a co-founder of AA, presents a codification of the organizational principles and practices of AA. Anyone wishing to understand how AA operates and the principles underlying its activities must read this book.

Kurtz, E. (1979). *Not-God: A History of Alcoholics Anonymous*. Center City, MN: Hazelden Educational Materials.

Written by an historian of American civilization, this is an authoritative account of the philosophical and social development of AA within the contexts of American history and the history of religious ideas. This is a must read for anyone who wishes to acquire a profound understanding of the history and philosophy of AA.

Mäkelä, K. et al. (1996). *Alcoholics Anonymous as a Mutual-help Movement: A Study in Eight Societies*. Madison, WI: University of Wisconsin Press, 1996.

This book is a report of the International Collaborative Study of Alcoholics Anonymous that investigated AA in eight countries. The purpose of the investigation was to analyze AA as an international mutual aid movement that is adaptive to cultural context. A history of the organization, including its expansion internationally, precedes an analysis of AA from the conceptual frameworks of AA as a social movement and social network, AA as a belief system, and AA as a system of interaction. Also addressed are AA's relationship to professional treatment and other alcohol-focused mutual help movements, as well as the application of the Twelve Steps of AA to problems other than alcohol.

McCrady, B.S. & Miller, W.R. (1993). *Research on Alcoholics Anonymous: Opportunities and Alternatives*. New Brunswick, NJ: Rutgers Center of Alcohol Studies.

This volume contains the papers presented at a 1992 conference of scholars and scientists who focused on the current state of knowledge about AA and explored issues concerning future research on AA. Included in this book are papers on how change occurs in AA, the contexts of this change, how change among AA members can be measured, and how studies of AA can be designed. This books contains an extensive appendix that details the responses of conference participants to 10 questions concerning future research on AA.

Project MATCH Research Group (1998). Matching alcoholism treatments to client heterogeneity: Project MATCH three-year drinking outcomes. *Alcoholism: Clinical and Experimental Research*, **22**, 1300–1311.

This article reports data from Project MATCH, a monumental clinical trial conducted in the USA that sought to identify possible optimal matches between client intake characteristics and types of treatments. This particular paper presents the analysis of data collected at 3 year follow-up and can serve as a door to numerous other publications that have emerged from this clinical trial. Given that one of the treatments investigated in Project MATCH targets the facilitation of AA involvement as its main goal, this project is highly relevant to the issue of how professional treatment relates to AA attendance and affiliation.

Room, R. (1998). Mutual help movements for alcohol problems in an international perspective. *Addiction Research*, **6**, 131–145.

This article adumbrates the historical development of AA and other mutual aid groups for alcohol-troubled individuals throughout the world. Informative differentiations among the groups are made with respect to organizational structure, principles and practices; the philosophical underpinnings of the groups; and the basis of group membership.

Symposium (1999). A comparative evaluation of substance abuse treatment. *Alcoholism: Clinical and Experimental Research*, **23**, 528–572.

This series of papers reports the findings of a major prospective naturalistic study of US male veterans following inpatient treatment for substance abuse. The results of this investigation strongly demonstrate the effectiveness of AA participation during aftercare, at least for the sample studied. Also receiving empirical support is the contribution to good outcome made by the delivery of professional treatment that is conceptually consistent with AA.

REFERENCES

Alcoholics Anonymous World Services (1976). *Alcoholics Anonymous: The Story of How Many Thousands of Men and Women have Recovered from Alcoholism*, 3rd edn. New York: Alcoholics Anonymous World Services.

Alcoholics Anonymous World Services (1986). *12 + 12: Twelve Steps and Twelve Traditions*. New York: Alcoholics Anonymous World Services.

Connors, G.J. & Dermen, K.H. (1996). Characteristics of participants in Secular Organizations for Sobriety (SOS). *American Journal of Drug and Alcohol Abuse*, **22**, 281–295.

Emrick, C.D. (1999). Alcoholics Anonymous and other 12-step groups. In M. Galanter & H.D. Kleber (Eds), *Textbook of Substance Abuse Treatment*, 2nd edn (pp. 403–411). Washington, DC: American Psychiatric Press.

Emrick, C.D., Lassen, C.L. & Edwards, M.T. (1977). Non-professional peers as therapeutic agents. In A.S. Gurman & A.M. Razin (Eds), *Effective Psychotherapy: A Handbook of Research* (pp. 120–161). Oxford: Pergamon.

Emrick, C.D., Tonigan, J.S., Montgomery, H. & Little, L. (1993). Alcoholics Anonymous: what is currently known? In B.S. McCrady & W.R. Miller (Eds), *Research on Alcoholics Anonymous: Opportunities and Alternatives* (pp. 41–76). New Brunswick, NJ: Rutgers Center of Alcohol Studies.

Finney, J.W., Moos, R.H. & Humphreys, K. (1999). A comparative evaluation of substance abuse treatment. II. Linking proximal outcomes of 12-step and cognitive-behavioral treatment to substance use outcomes. *Alcoholism: Clinical and Experimental Research*, **23**, 537–544.

Galanter, M., Egelko, S. & Edwards, H. (1993). Rational recovery: alternative to AA for addiction? *American Journal of Drug and Alcohol Abuse*, **19**, 499–510.

Hasin, D.S. (1994). Treatment/self-help for alcohol-related problems: relationship to social pressure and alcohol dependence. *Journal of Studies on Alcohol*, **55**, 660–666.

Hasin, D.S. & Grant, B.F. (1995). AA and other help-seeking for alcohol problems: former drinkers in the US general population. *Journal of Substance Abuse*, **7**, 281–292.

Humphreys, K., Kaskutas, L.A. & Weisner, C. (1998). The Alcoholics Anonymous Affiliation Scale: development, reliability, and norms for diverse treated and untreated populations. *Alcoholism: Clinical and Experimental Research*, **22**, 974–978.

Humphreys, K. & Moos, R.H. (1996). Reduced substance-abuse-related health care costs among voluntary participants in Alcoholics Anonymous. *Psychiatric Services*, **47**, 709–713.

Humphreys, K., Moos, R.H. & Cohen, C. (1997). Social and community resources and long-term recovery from treated and untreated alcoholism. *Journal of Studies on Alcohol*, **58**, 231–238.

Humphreys, K., Huebsch, P.D., Finney, J.W. & Moos, R.H. (1999). A comparative evaluation of substance abuse treatment: V. Substance abuse treatment can enhance the effectiveness of self-help groups. *Alcoholism: Clinical and Experimental Research*, **23**, 558–563.

Kasl, C.D. (1992). *Many Roads, One Journey: Moving Beyond the Twelve Steps*. New York: HarperCollins.

Kaskutus, L.A. (1996). Pathways to self-help among Women for Sobriety. *American Journal of Drug Alcohol Abuse*, **22**, 259–280.

Kishline, A. (1994). *Moderate Drinking: The Moderation Management Guide for People Who Want to Reduce Their Drinking*. New York: Three Rivers Press.

Kurtz, E. (1979). *Not-God: A History of Alcoholics Anonymous*. Center City, MN: Hazelden Educational Materials.

Longabaugh, R., Wirtz, P.W., Zweben, A. & Stout, R.L. (1998). Network support for drinking, Alcoholics Anonymous and long-term matching effects. *Addiction*, **93**, 1313–1333.

Mäkelä, K., Arminen, I., Bloomfield, K. et al. (1996). *Alcoholics Anonymous as a Mutual Help Movement: A Study in Eight Societies*. Madison, WI: University of Wisconsin Press.

McCrady, B.S. & Miller, W.R. (Eds) (1993). *Research on Alcoholics Anonymous: Opportunities and Alternatives*. New Brunswick, NJ: Rutgers Center of Alcohol Studies.

Miller, W.R. & Kurtz, E. (1994). Models of alcoholism used in treatment: contrasting AA and other perspectives with which it is often confused. *Journal of Studies on Alcohol*, **55**, 159–166.

Montgomery, H.A., Miller, W.R. & Tonigan, J.S. (1993). Differences among AA groups: implications for research. *Journal of Studies on Alcohol*, **54**, 502–504.

Moos, R.H., Finney, J.W., Ouimette, P.C. & Suchinsky, R.T. (1999). A comparative evaluation of substance abuse treatment: I. Treatment orientation, amount of care, and 1-year outcomes. *Alcoholism: Clinical and Experimental Research*, **23**, 529–536.

Ouimette, P.C., Moos, R.H. & Finney, J.W. (1998). Influence of outpatient treatment and 12-step group involvement on one-year substance abuse treatment outcomes. *Journal of Studies on Alcohol*, **59**, 513–522.

Ouimette, P.C., Gima, K., Moos, R.H. & Finney, J.W. (1999). A comparative evaluation of substance abuse treatment. IV. The effect of comorbid psychiatric diagnoses on amount of treatment, continuing care, and 1-year outcomes. *Alcoholism: Clinical and Experimental Research*, **23**, 552–557.

Project MATCH Research Group (1997). Project MATCH secondary *a priori* hypotheses. *Addiction*, **92**, 1671–1698.

Project MATCH Research Group (1998). Matching alcoholism treatments to client heterogeneity: Project MATCH three-year drinking outcomes. *Alcoholism: Clinical and Experimental Research*, **22**, 1300–1311.

Room, R. (1998). Mutual help movements for alcohol problems in an international perspective. *Addiction Research*, **6**, 131–145.

Tonigan, J.S., Connors, G.J. & Miller, W.R. (1996). Alcoholics Anonymous Involvement (AAI) scale: reliability and norms. *Psychology of Addictive Behavior*, **10**, 75–80.

Tonigan, J.S., Miller. W.R. & Connors, G.J. (1997a). *Prior Alcoholics Anonymous Involvement and Treatment Outcome: Matching Findings and Causal Chain Analyses*, Vol. 8. Project MATCH Monograph. Bethesda, MD: NIAAA.

Tonigan, J.S., Miller, W.R. & Connors, G.J. (1997b). *The Search for Meaning in Life as a Predictor of Treatment Outcome*, Vol. 8. Project MATCH Monograph. Bethesda, MD: NIAAA.

Trimpey, J. (1996). *Rational Recovery: The New Cure for Substance Addiction*. New York: Pocket Books.

Winzelberg, A. & Humphreys, K. (1999). Should patients' religiosity influence clinicians' referral to 12-step self-help groups? Evidence from a study of 3018 male substance abuse patients. *Journal of Consulting and Clinical Psychology*, **67**, 790–794.

Zweben, J.E. (1995). Integrating psychotherapy and 12-step approaches. In A.M. Washton (Ed.), *Psychotherapy and Substance Abuse: A Practitioner's Handbook* (pp. 124–140). New York: Guilford.

APPENDIX

The Twelve Steps of Alcoholics Anonymous

1. We admitted we were powerless over alcohol—that our lives had become unmanageable.
2. Came to believe that a Power greater than ourselves could restore us to sanity.
3. Made a decision to turn our will and our lives over to the care of God *as we understood Him*.
4. Made a searching and fearless moral inventory of ourselves.
5. Admitted to God, to ourselves and to another human being the exact nature of our wrongs.
6. Were entirely ready to have God remove all these defects of character.
7. Humbly asked Him to remove our shortcomings.
8. Made a list of all persons we had harmed, and became willing to make amends to them all.
9. Made direct amends to such people wherever possible, except when to do so would injure them or others.
10. Continued to take personal inventory and when we were wrong promptly admitted it.
11. Sought through prayer and meditation to improve our conscious contact with God, *as we understood Him*, praying only for knowledge of His will for us and the power to carry that out.
12. Having had a spiritual awakening as the result of these steps, we tried to carry this message to alcoholics, and to practice these principles in all our affairs.

The Twelve Traditions of Alcoholics Anonymous

1. Our common welfare should come first; personal recovery depends upon AA unity.
2. For our group purpose, there is but one ultimate authority—a loving God as He may express Himself in our group conscience. Our leaders are but trusted servants; they do not govern.
3. The only requirement for AA membership is a desire to stop drinking.
4. Each group should be autonomous except in matters affecting other groups or AA as a whole.
5. Each group has but one primary purpose—to carry its message to the alcoholic who still suffers.
6. An AA group ought never endorse, finance or lend the AA name to any related facility or outside enterprise, lest problems of money, property and prestige divert us from our primary purpose.
7. Every AA group ought to be fully self-supporting, declining outside contributions.
8. Alcoholics Anonymous should remain forever non-professional, but our service centers may employ special workers.
9. AA, as such, ought never be organized; but we may create service boards or committees directly responsible to those they serve.
10. Alcoholics Anonymous has no opinion on outside issues; hence the AA name ought never be drawn into public controversy.
11. Our public relations policy is based on attraction rather than promotion; we need always maintain personal anonymity at the level of press, radio and films.
12. Anonymity is the spiritual foundation of all our traditions, ever reminding us to place principles before personalities.

Part VI

Prevention of Alcohol Problems

Edited by Tim Stockwell

EDITOR'S INTRODUCTION

A major development in the field of alcohol prevention towards the end of the twentieth century was the gradual emergence of "harm minimization" as a guiding principle. This term has its origins in relation to the prevention of blood-borne viruses and overdoses associated with the illegal use of injectable drugs, mostly opiates (Midford & Lenton, 1996). It refers to the impact of a range of strategies that can reduce the risk of death and illness to injecting drug users. Harm minimization for illicit drugs is politically unacceptable in some countries, being associated, rightly or wrongly, with "going soft" on drug users and with attempts to legalize drugs. There is growing acceptance of the term in relation to the prevention of alcohol problems where, in most countries, there is no question other than that alcohol will continue to be widely available and used by the majority of the population (Plant, Single & Stockwell, 1997). Even as applied to alcohol, however, the term is still controversial and some of the contributors to the following chapters would probably distance themselves from it on the grounds that it may be mistaken for "going soft" on alcohol availability.

Harm minimization for alcohol problems is best characterized as the development of specific evidence-based strategies that reduce the occurrence of serious harms *without necessarily* requiring abstinence or reducing overall alcohol consumption. Examples of harm minimization strategies will be presented here which do not require a reduction in consumption to be effective, e.g. the introduction of non-breakable glassware at potentially violent drinking places. Most harm minimization strategies, however, do require a degree of reduction in alcohol consumption, at least in some high-risk situations, e.g. before driving a motor vehicle or operating machinery. The reader is also referred to Section IV and, in particular, Chapters 20 and 21 for "total consumption" vs. "high-risk" approaches to reducing alcohol problems.

Harm minimization can usefully be seen as an alternative to the total consumption approach, which has dominated alcohol policy for some 25 years (Bruun et al., 1975; Edwards et al., 1994). This refers to the policy goal of reducing the total consumption of a population as a means for reducing related problems. This position is discussed in detail in the first two chapters of this section and a number of practical and scientific difficulties are identified. For example, at what point does one stop reducing both availability and consumption? The total consumption approach alone gives no guidance regarding what are optimal levels, providing instead the somewhat open-ended principle that "less is best". Furthermore, in some countries at least, public opinion is not sympathetic to prevention strategies that impact on the drinking of all people by making alcohol more expensive or less convenient to purchase (Stockwell et al., 1997). It will be argued that the harm minimization approach to alcohol prevention offers the way out of an impasse that has afflicted the field for over two decades: effective policies (e.g. price controls) are politically dangerous and unpopular, while popular strategies (e.g. public and school-based education) are relatively ineffective. It is important to note, however, that in some countries with a tradition of tight controls on alcohol availability (e.g. Sweden), the idea of reducing consumption by price controls may be quite acceptable to the general public. Harm minimization principles can also be applied alongside efforts to control population consumption, but the fundamental goal must remain as to whether harm is minimized and whether the means to achieve this are broadly acceptable and non-discriminatory.

Increasing the price of alcohol by raising taxes is the classic case of an effective but unpopular and even politically dangerous strategy. The opening chapter of this section (Österberg, Chapter 35) describes how studies from numerous countries using data from several decades have in almost every instance shown that alcohol behaves like most other commodities in that its consumption is negatively responsive to price. It is known that beer consumption is less responsive to price changes than is consumption of wine and spirits but, nonetheless, an increase in the price of beer is almost invariably associated with a decrease in its consumption. Naturally, the extent of this responsiveness (referred to by economists as "elasticity") varies across place and time, reflecting as it does the varying nature of both supply and demand for alcohol in different parts of the world. There is evidence for example that, when the physical availability of alcohol is tightly regulated, consumption is less responsive to price changes. It is known that price elasticities also vary for different types of drinker (e.g. people who drink less tend to be less affected by price changes) and for different types of beverage. As well as the net or average price of alcoholic drinks, it becomes critical also for public health and safety to consider the distribution of alcohol taxes across different beverages. Among the thousands of alcoholic beverages available in developed markets (e.g. Ponicki et al., 1995), there are usually a few that occupy the basement in terms of quality but not alcohol content. These can be preferentially selected by high-risk drinkers and greatly limit the benefits from across-the-board price increases (e.g. Stockwell et al., 1998). It is arguable, therefore, that redistributing alcohol taxes, rather than simply increasing them, can have public health benefits. It is also clear, however, that studies reviewed in this section show a direct link between changes in alcohol taxes and in serious alcohol-related harms without needing to invoke the idea of controlling total consumption.

The second chapter (Stockwell & Gruenewald, Chapter 36) in this section extends the concept of alcohol's availability beyond its economic accessibility. The "effective" price of alcohol includes such aspects of physical availability as convenience, e.g. in terms of distance travelled or time taken to purchase alcohol in a given locality. It is clear that while dramatic changes in both physical and economic availability can result in dramatic changes in national levels of harm, local factors can modify these consequences in important ways. If a drinker lives close by an area in which large numbers of premises compete for custom by offering heavily discounted drink at certain times ("happy hours"), then even a 20% increase in alcohol taxes may make little difference to their drinking patterns. The elucidation of the effects of changes in physical availability at the local level (principally the density of liquor outlets, the hours and days of trading) is a demanding analytic task. The places where people live, purchase alcohol, drink it and then (on occasion) experience serious alcohol-related harm are usually overlapping and often quite separate. Population-level studies to examine the impacts of changes in physical availability need to be mindful of the effects of such local factors as traffic flows and the socioeconomic profiles of adjoining neighbourhoods. Despite these complexities, a strong case can be made for utilizing local and regional controls on the physical availability of alcohol to limit alcohol-related harm. Other local factors though need to be taken into account if this knowledge is to be operationalized into effective local policy—and more research is required to facilitate that process.

It is easy to be lured into imagining a world in which wise, evidence-based and benevolent regulation of alcohol markets occurs so that price, outlet density, trading hours and serving practices are all arranged so that alcohol-related harm is minimized. This, of course, happens only in dreamland. Regulators have to be mindful of consumers' demands for reasonable access to alcohol, which plays an important part in the leisure time of a great part of the voting public in many societies. They must also be mindful of the livelihoods of the many people working in the different sectors of the manufacture and sale of alcohol. Dramatic changes in alcohol policies can even lose elections, may result in substantial job losses and usually result in an upsurge of illegal supplies. The issue then comes down to how best to develop an effective system of alcohol regulation at the national and local level that facilitates pleasurable low-risk use, minimizes harm to health and sustains a major industry. Chapter 37 (Homel, McIlwain & Carvolth) provides a penetrating analysis of the ways in which regulatory systems, local communities and alcohol suppliers can (but often fail to) create safer drinking environments. Numerous evidence-based strategies are outlined for creating lower-risk environments, ranging from safer glassware and more peaceable security staff to more proactive local police. The importance of local politics, as both the medium through which effective community action can occur and as an obstacle to its sustained implementation, is made starkly evident. The glare of public scrutiny on these matters is only intense when local people and businesses are being badly inconvenienced. Effective regulation of licensed premises to minimize violence is rarely a high priority for local regulators.

Drink–driving countermeasures are reviewed in Chapter 38 (McKnight & Voas). In alcohol prevention these stand out as rare examples where scientific evidence and popular opinion are as one. Measures such as rigorously implemented random breath testing and low blood-alcohol levels for drivers are demonstrably effective in saving lives and are highly publicly acceptable in those countries where they have been implemented. As a specific, evidence-based set of measures that reduce alcohol-related harm without reducing the availability or total consumption of alcohol, drink–driving prevention is an example *par excellence* of harm minimization in practice. The necessity of drink–driving countermeasures is usually well understood by communities; the potential harms are serious and can impact on all road users, while the intervention itself is applied without fear or favour in a way that only minimally inconveniences drivers with a legal blood alcohol limit. Other local prevention initiatives are not so readily accepted. Treno & Holder (Chapter 39) analyse six successful examples of community action to reduce alcohol-related problems in order to identify the ingredients of success. It is useful to consider this chapter in combination with the others from this section, where evidence for specific types of strategies (controls on price, availability, situational risk factors and so on) is summarized. Treno & Holder largely focus on the processes that seem to be successful in mobilizing a community to engage in evidence-based community action on alcohol. It is not enough to know what can work but also how to get it to happen (this simple truth also applies at the national policy level).

The last three chapters deal in different ways with the more subjective issues around the communication of alcohol's effects, both positive and negative. Midford & McBride (Chapter 40) provide a distinctly harm minimization-based analysis of school-based alcohol education. They overview the somewhat patchy results from alcohol education efforts in general and arrive at a set of well-documented principles to underpin more effective approaches in the future. In particular, they caution against an unrealistic goal of total abstinence in favour of providing advice to children on low-risk drinking—in terms of both how much to drink and coping strategies to reduce the risk of negative consequences, e.g. unwanted pregnancies, being driven by a drunk driver. Promising early results are outlined from a harm minimization approach to alcohol prevention in schools. Chapters 41 (Boots & Midford) and 42 (Hill & Casswell) deal with the issues of public communications about alcohol: the first from public health proponents intending to reduce consumption and/or harm, the second from the alcohol industry to increase sales through advertising and sponsorship. Boots & Midford identify media advocacy as a key strategy for public health activists to influence public and political debates about alcohol and its control. In a complementary way, Hill & Casswell review the evidence for a relationship between total and high-risk alcohol use and alcohol promotions. It is clear that associations can be shown such that young people who are more aware of alcohol promotions are more likely to go on to drink in a high-risk fashion. However, associations can always be explained away if one is determined to be sceptical. A safe and rational position at this point of time is to suppose that all public messages and information influence the overall context with alcohol is consumed, the effects of alcohol are understood and alcohol prevention policies are implemented—or neglected.

While good science must continue in the field of alcohol prevention, it is also clear that little progress in the implementation of effective strategies will be achieved unless public awareness of the issues is high and, in turn, impacts on the making of local, regional and public policy. Public health advocacy on alcohol-related harm is vital if prevention strategies are to happen. As recommended in Chapter 36, there is an important role to be played in the dissemination of accurate local, regional and national data on high-risk alcohol consumption and serious alcohol-related harms (see e.g. Chikritzhs et al., 1999). A range of mutually supportive strategies is outlined in this section, which can be understood within the framework of harm minimization. It is suggested here and elsewhere (e.g. Plant et al., 1997) that harm minimization is an optimal stance for public health advocacy on the need for specific and effective strategies to reduce serious alcohol-related harms.

REFERENCES

Bruun, K., Edwards, G., Lumio, M., Mäkelä, K., Pan, L., Popham, R.E., Room, R., Schmidt, W., Skog, O.-J., Sulkunen, P. & Österberg, E. (1975). *Alcohol Control Policies in Public Health Perspective.* Helsinki: Finnish Foundation for Alcohol Studies.

Chikritzhs, T., Jonas, H., Heale, P., Dietze, P., Hanlin, K. & Stockwell, T. (1999). *Alcohol-caused Deaths and Hospitalisations in Australia, 1990–1997.* National Alcohol Indicators, Bulletin No. 1. Perth, Western Australia: National Drug Research Institute, Curtin University of Technology.

Edwards, G., Anderson, P., Babor, T.F., Casswell, S., Ferrence, R., Giesbrecht, N., Godfrey, C., Holder, H.D., Lemmens, P., Mäkelä, K., Midanik, L.T., Norström, T., Österberg, E., Romelsjö, A., Room, R., Simpura, J. & Skog, O.-J. (1994). *Alcohol Policy and the Public Good.* New York: Oxford University Press.

Midford, R. & Lenton, S. (1996). Clarifying "harm reduction"? *Drug & Alcohol Review*, **15**, 411–414.

Plant, M., Single, E. & Stockwell, T. (1997). *Alcohol: Minimising the Harm. What Works?* London: Free Association Books.

Ponicki, W., Holder, H., Gruenewald, P. & Romelsjo, A. (1995). Altering alcohol price by ethanol content: results from a Swedish tax policy in 1992. *Addiction*, **92**, 859–870.

Stockwell, T., Single, E., Hawks, D. & Rehm, J. (1997). Sharpening the focus of alcohol policy from aggregate consumption to harm and risk reduction. *Addiction Research*, **5**, 1–9.

Stockwell, T., Masters, L., Phillips, M., Daly, A., Gahegan, M., Midford, R. & Philp, A. (1998). Consumption of different alcoholic beverages as predictors of local rates of night-time assault and acute alcohol-related morbidity. *Australian & New Zealand Journal of Public Health*, **22**, 237–242.

Chapter 35

Effects of Price and Taxation

Esa Österberg
*National Research and Development Centre for Welfare and
Health, Helsinki, Finland*

Synopsis

This chapter starts with a general discussion of the role of alcohol taxation, on the one hand as a means of curbing total alcohol consumption and alcohol-related problems, and on the other hand as a means to collect revenues to the coffers of the state and/or local authorities.

Next, the effects of changes in alcohol prices on alcohol consumption and related problems are scrutinized. This means that econometric studies of effects in changes of alcohol prices on alcohol consumption are reviewed. In this connection, results of studies on both changes in alcohol prices on total alcohol consumption and the consumption of different categories of alcoholic beverages are summarized. Econometric studies looking at the relation between changes in alcohol prices and alcohol-related problems are also reviewed. In addition, studies dealing with the relationship between alcohol prices, on the one hand, and alcohol consumption and alcohol-related problems, on the other, are discussed.

Price elasticities are not inherent attributes of alcoholic beverages. Therefore, one should not expect studies relating to different regions, periods and categories of alcohol beverages to produce similar elasticity values. In the interpretation of elasticity values, the points of departure should be the social, cultural and economic circumstances affecting drinking alcohol in each country and period. This means that the factors producing certain kinds of elasticities and the factors behind the changes in elasticity values are discussed.

Alcohol taxation is one way to curb alcohol consumption and alcohol-related problems and/or to collect tax revenues. The state or local authorities can not, however, decide at will the tax burden of alcoholic beverages. Therefore this chapter also discusses the feasibility of alcohol taxation.

The sale of alcoholic beverages at prices higher than their production and distribution costs is a generally accepted custom. Quite often the purpose and rationale for special taxes on alcoholic beverages are not, however, explicitly stated. In practice, taxing alcoholic beverages has been a well-established means of raising government revenue. In some countries, alcoholic beverages have been susceptible to such taxation because of their status as luxury commodities, offering a credible justification to tax them. In some other countries, alcoholic

International Handbook of Alcohol Dependence and Problems. Edited by N. Heather, T.J. Peters and T. Stockwell.
© 2001 John Wiley & Sons Ltd.

beverages have been suitable objects for excise taxes because of their nature as an every-day commodity offering a wide tax basis, and in some countries they have been taxed because of their detrimental social and public health consequences, and the external costs they impose on the state and the society. The rationale for levying a special tax on alcoholic beverages is seldom questioned, and what discussion there is on the subject usually revolves around how expensive alcoholic beverages should be relative to other commodities, and whether taxes should vary according to the alcohol content of the beverages and to the different alcoholic beverage categories, i.e. distilled spirits, wines and beer (Bruun et al., 1972; see also Crooks, 1989; Baker & McKay, 1990; Cook & Moore, 1993a).

Taxation of alcoholic beverages has traditionally been an important source of state revenue in many countries. Between 1911 and 1917, for example, in the USA the federal revenues from alcoholic beverages each year amounted to over one-third of the total receipts from taxes levied by the government (Landis, 1952). Similar figures can also be found on the other side of the Atlantic Ocean, for instance from The Netherlands, the UK and the Nordic Countries, Denmark, Finland, Iceland, Norway and Sweden. The relative importance of alcohol taxation as a source of state income has declined in most countries during the twentieth century, particularly after the advent of modern income taxation. In many countries the share of alcohol taxes in state budgets has declined also because of decreases in alcohol tax rates both in nominal but especially in real terms. For instance, in recent decades Ireland, which amongst the Western countries has shown the highest shares of alcohol taxes of total state revenues, has experienced a clear decrease in its alcohol tax incomes in relation to total state incomes. In 1970 this share was still 16.5% but dropped to 10.4% in 1978 (Davies & Walsh, 1983). In 1996 the share was estimated to be 5.0% (Hurst et al., 1997). Despite these trends, alcohol tax revenues are still of considerable fiscal significance in many countries (Hurst et al., 1997, p. 562).

From the consumers' point of view, excise duties on alcoholic beverages are factors which are increasing prices of alcoholic beverages and sometimes putting an extra pressure on household budgets. If an increase in alcohol taxes and alcohol prices leads to a large decrease in alcohol consumption, then the share of alcohol expenditure in family budgets may also decrease. However, the dilemma for policy makers who view alcohol taxation as a means on preventing alcohol problems is worsened when higher prices on alcoholic beverages result in only a small drop in alcohol consumption and a substantial increase in household alcohol expenditure. In this case lowering the amount of alcohol that a heavy drinker consumes by increasing alcohol taxes will usually mean that his/her family will suffer greater financial hardships. This is not, however, necessarily the case. If higher alcohol taxes and prices mean people spend more money on alcoholic drinks, then the state will collect more alcohol tax revenue. And, in principle at least, this could mean that other forms of taxation will fall or, consequently, that more public services becomes available. The taxation question, then, is largely a matter of who pays excise taxes on alcohol and how these tax revenues are employed—if employed wisely, the outcome can be a greater measure of prosperity for all.

Raising prices of alcoholic beverages with special taxes or limiting alcohol availability in some other way will not only affect the drinker or the state; the alcohol industry and its employees will also be hit. Understandably, those engaged in the production and distribution of alcoholic beverages therefore feel that they must have as big a say in alcohol control policy as possible. This is particularly true in countries where the alcohol industry is fettered by stringent control measures. But even in such countries there exists a difference between the short term and the long term. Limiting the availability of alcoholic beverages may result in a number of brewery and distillery workers or wine growers losing their jobs in the short term. However, those displaced may find employment elsewhere and the long-term outcome may well be increased general prosperity (Österberg, 1982). On the other hand, there are also instances where alcoholic beverage taxes are used in support of agricultural, cultural or economic objectives in a country. For instance, in Australia the wine industry is exempt from excise taxes because it is considered to be a primary producing industry on which the livelihood of many small grape growers is dependent. In addition, in that country no excise tax is levied on spirits used for fortifying wine (Hurst et al., 1997). In the European Union there is a minimum excise tax rate on wine but this rate has been set to zero, because the wine industry makes a significant contribution to the domestic economy in many wine-growing EU member states.

On the other side of the coin, it can be concluded that alcohol has significant adverse effects on the physical, psychological and social health of individuals, families and communities throughout the world. Alcohol is a dependence-producing drug and this dependence is associated with an increased risk of morbidity and mortality. Moreover, alcohol is also an intoxicant and drunkenness is associated with an increased risk of injury and mortality, both to the drinker and to others. The adverse effects of drinking alcohol are diffuse and costly and are not confined to a minority of easily identified heavier drinkers. This is sometimes called the "preventive paradox", describing the fact that alcohol problems cannot be eliminated simply by getting rid of heavy alcohol consumers, because lighter drinkers also suffer from alcohol problems. And as the number of light drinkers is much larger than the number of heavy drinkers, their share or the total burden of alcohol problems is important. The impact of alcohol on all-cause mortality is affected, amongst other things, by the prevalence of different diseases and injuries, the age structure of the population and the level of alcohol consumption at the societal level. The impact of alcohol is therefore culturally and temporally specific. At younger ages, for instance, deaths from traffic accidents and violence predominate (World Health Organization, 1995).

In research conducted at both the societal and individual level, alcohol has been found to increase the risk of death from a number of specific causes, including: injury from traffic accidents and other trauma; violence; suicide; poisonings; liver cirrhosis; cancers of the upper aerodigestive tract; cancer of the liver; breast cancer; haemorrhagic stroke; alcoholic psychosis; alcohol dependence; pancreatitis; malnutrition; neurological disorders; alcoholism; and fetal alcohol syndrome. On the other hand, alcohol consumption has been found to reduce the risk of coronary heart disease and ischaemic stroke. The reduced risk for coronary heart disease has been found at the level of one drink every second day, and there is little additional reduction of risk beyond consumption levels of about one to two drinks a day (World Health Organization, 1995).

Epidemiological data on the contribution of alcohol use to the prevalence of disease are mainly found in developed countries, with limited data available for developing countries. The best available estimates are found in *The Global Burden of Disease* (Murray & Lopez, 1996), which estimates that alcohol contributed to 3.5% of the global burden of disease and disability and 1.5% of total deaths in 1990. Alcohol is ranked fourth among the top 10 risk factors for disease and disability for men, following malnutrition, poor water supply and sanitation, and unsafe sex. The contribution of alcohol use to overall disease and disability varies greatly by region: it is highest in the established market economies (10.3%), Latin America (9.7%) and the former Soviet Union (8.3%). It is lowest in the Middle East (0.4%) and India (1.6%). Globally, alcohol is estimated to have caused about three-quarters of a million more deaths than it averted, with more than 80% of this excess mortality occurring in developing countries. The burden of social problems from drinking is mostly unmeasured, but qualitative evidence suggests it is large in the developing as well as the developed world.

Alcohol control policies, i.e. legal, economic and physical factors which bear on the availability of alcohol, seek to reduce the harmful effects of alcohol use whilst recognizing its real and perceived benefits. Across space and historical time and within the context of culturally determined value systems, administrative formulae and beliefs as to the fundamental nature of the target issues, these problems have provoked an extraordinary diversity of policy responses. A number of policies have also been demonstrated to be effective in the reduction of alcohol-related harm, amongst them excise taxes on alcoholic beverages.

ECONOMETRIC STUDIES

The effect of changes in prices of alcoholic beverages on alcohol consumption has been more extensively investigated than any other potential alcohol control measure. The most widely employed research approaches have relied on econometric methods. According to different reviews, econometric studies dealing with all alcoholic beverages or a certain category of alcoholic beverages are currently available in at least the following countries: Australia, Belgium, Canada, Denmark, Germany, Finland, France, Ireland, Italy, Kenya, The Netherlands, New Zealand, Norway, Poland, Portugal, Spain, Sweden, the UK and the USA (see Huitfeldt & Jorner, 1972; Lau, 1975; Ornstein, 1980; Ornstein & Levy, 1983; Godfrey, 1986; Olsson, 1991; Clements & Selvanathan, 1991; Yen, 1994, Edwards et al., 1994; Österberg, 1995). This list of countries also shows that our knowledge of the effects of changing alcohol prices on alcohol consumption chiefly derives from Western industrialized nations.

In econometric studies, the responsiveness or sensitivity of quantity demanded of the determinants of demand is measured by elasticity. The sensitivity of the quantity demanded to changes in prices, when other determinants remain unchanged, is called the price elasticity of demand, or own-price elasticity.

The values of price elasticities for alcoholic beverages estimated in different studies have consistently shown that when other factors remain unchanged, a rise in the price of alcoholic beverages has generally led to a drop in alcohol consumption, and that a decrease in price of alcoholic beverages has usually led to a rise in alcohol consumption. In other words, alcoholic beverages appear to behave on the market like most other commodities and in the way presupposed by the theory of consumer demand. On the other hand, in studies dealing with different geographical regions and periods, different values of income and price elasticities have been found with respect to both total alcohol consumption and the consumption of different categories of alcoholic beverages. These variations are partly due to the methods applied, the accuracy of the basic data, and the statistical factors of uncertainty relating to the elasticities. However, disparities in elasticity values also stem from differing social, cultural and economic circumstances prevailing in different regions and in different periods. Therefore, when looking at the results of different studies, it is not possible to find any general, typical or mean elasticity value for all alcoholic beverages, or even for beer, wines or spirits separately, because elasticities describing the reactions of the consumers to price increases are not inherent attributes of alcoholic beverages, but rather reflections of the prevailing drinking habits and culture.

On a very general level, it may be said that consumer preferences are linked to the benefits consumers derive from using different commodities, in this case, drinking alcoholic beverages, and consumer preferences are therefore reflected in elasticity values. When taking into account the many different uses of alcoholic beverages—as intoxicants, thirst quenchers, drinks with meals, medicines or means of recreation and enjoyment—it is not surprising that the demand for all alcoholic beverages or a certain category of alcoholic beverages may respond very differently to a certain change in price in different countries and in different periods. Therefore, the interpretation of elasticity values calls for a close examination of drinking habits and the uses to which alcoholic beverages are put in a certain society at a certain point in time.

If the demand for a given category of alcoholic beverages is price-elastic, that is, relatively sensitive to price changes, a rise in price will have a strong diminishing effect on its consumption, and decrease the share of personal disposable income allocated to that beverage category. Consequently, a decline in price will have a strong increasing effect on its consumption, and raise the share of personal disposable income allocated to that beverage category. Alcoholic beverages can also be price-inelastic, that is, relatively insensitive to price changes. In this case, a price increase would have only a small impact on the consumption of this beverage category, and increase the share of personal disposable income allocated to those beverages. A decline in price will have a relatively small positive effect on the consumption of this beverage category and decrease the share of personal disposable income allocated to those beverages. If the demand for alcoholic beverages is unit price-elastic, a rise in price will have a diminishing effect on alcohol consumption of equal proportion and keep the share of personal disposable income allocated to alcoholic beverages fairly constant. Consequently, a percentage reduction in prices increases the consumption of alcoholic beverages by the same percentage and keeps the share of personal disposable income allocated to alcoholic beverage constant.

So far, discussions of small or large effects of price on alcohol consumption in this chapter have concerend unit changes in the consumpiton of alcoholic beverages. Even in circumstances where the demand for alcoholic beverages is price-inelastic, a large absolute change in the price of alcoholic beverages will still have a larger effect on alcohol consumption than only a slight change in alcohol prices in situations where alcohol demand is price-elastic. Degree of price change as well as the value of the price elasticity must be jointly taken into account when predicting the impact of changing prices of alcoholic beverages on alcohol consumption.

The value of price elasticity denotes the way consumers have reacted to changes in prices during the study period. If alcohol prices have, for instance, fallen steadily during that period, the estimated price elasticity may not necessarily apply to a situation of increasing alcohol prices, because the assumption that elasticities are symmetrical may not be valid as far as alcoholic drinks are concerned. A symmetrical elasticity would mean that a given rise or fall in alcohol prices produces an equivalent effect in the opposite direction on consumption. However, since some people may become addicted to alcohol, it is quite possible that a rise in alcohol consumption introduced by a cut in prices would not be checked by an equivalent increase in alcohol prices (Bruun et al., 1975).

EFFECTS OF CHANGING PRICES ON CONSUMPTION

There are great differences between countries in the way alcohol consumers have reacted to changes in prices of alcoholic beverages (see Edwards et al., 1994, pp. 112–114). This is something that is to be expected because of the differences in drinking habits between countries. But, to make it more difficult, even the results of economic studies dealing with one and the same country do not present a very clear picture. For instance, in the USA estimated price elasticities for beer range from almost zero to -1.39, available estimates of price elasticities for wine range from -0.44 to -1.78, and the estimated price elasticities for distilled spirits range from 0.08 to -2.03 (Österberg, 1995, p. 149).

In a review of price elasticities for alcoholic beverages, Ornstein (1980) wanted to see whether the weight of the evidence indicated that beer, wine, and distilled spirits were price-elastic, price-inelastic or unit price-elastic, and whether they were substitutes, complements or unrelated in consumption. He also discussed the possibility of identifying a range of "true" elasticities for the USA (and Canada) by a comparison of diverse studies (Ornstein, 1980). In a later review, Ornstein & Levy (1983), using the same data as Ornstein (1980), reconsidered the range of price-elasticity estimates in the USA. After a detailed description, comparison, evaluation and discussion of 20 studies, they reported that their "summary estimates of own-price elasticities for beer, wine, and distilled spirits were –0.3, –1.0 and – 1.5, respectively. These are crude at best, particularly for wines, but seem the best available" (Ornstein & Levy, 1983, p. 343; see also Leung & Phelps, 1993). In her reviews of demand models from 1989 and 1990, Godfrey (1989, 1990) discussed three alcohol demand studies in the UK as well as her own estimates and the elasticities used by the treasury in their alcohol tax revenue calculations. These figures show that in the UK the demand for beer has generally been price-inelastic (i.e. a given percentage change in the price of beer produces a smaller percentage change in demand for beer, not that demand is unresponsive to price changes) and the demand for wines and spirits has been more responsive to prices than beer (Godfrey, 1989). Later studies accord with this interpretation (see Österberg, 1995, p. 150).

It has been argued that alcohol control measures other than taxes and prices affect the values of price elasticities. This argument seems to be reasonable, since lifting of other alcohol control measures gives alcohol prices more regulative power. In Sweden, Huitfeldt & Jorner (1972) have shown that lifting the "motbok" connected with the Bratt rationing system—where the possibility of buying distilled spirits in Sweden was individually regulated until 1955—in fact led to a rise in the value of the price elasticity for distilled spirits. It can, therefore, be argued that the more restricted the availability of alcoholic beverages, the smaller is the influence of a unit change in prices of alcoholic beverages on alcohol consumption (Huitfeldt & Jorner, 1972).

In Finland, Ahtola, Ekholm & Somervuori (1986) studied the changes in the values of price elasticities for alcoholic beverages for the period 1955–1980. They found that the value of price elasticities was decreasing over time and interpreted this to show that alcoholic beverages have come to be seen more and more as an everyday commodity. In the mid-1950s, the total alcohol consumption per capita in Finland was under 2 litres in terms of 100% alcohol, while at the beginning of the 1980s it was over 6 litres. These figures could also be interpreted to show that the value of price elasticity has a tendency to decrease as incomes and the standard of living rise.

Econometric studies use as their material factual changes in alcohol prices, which are normally relatively small. It can therefore be asked if they have any predictive value in cases where changes in alcohol prices are dramatic. An unusual example of the effects of radical price changes on consumption comes from Denmark. Due to food shortages during World War I, the price of Danish *akvavit* was raised more than 10 times and the price of beer was almost doubled. These drastic price increases reduced per capita consumption of alcohol by 75% within 2 years. The decrease was mostly due to the diminished consumption of distilled spirits, especially *akvavit*, and only later did the consumption of beer increase to change Denmark from a spirit-drinking country to a beer-drinking country. Not only was the total alcohol consumption affected, but also the rate of registered cases of delirium tremens declined to one-thirteenth, and deaths due to chronic alcoholism to one-sixth of their previous rates (Bruun et al., 1975).

Other examples of great price changes are not as dramatic as the Danish one. They have, however, taken place more recently. For instance, a 10% increase in the real price of alcoholic beverages in Finland in 1975 put an end to the increase in alcohol consumption that had continued in the country since the early 1960s (Salo, 1987, 1990). In Sweden, the marked increase in consumption which followed the abolition of the Bratt system in 1955 was halted and eventually reversed by radical increases in prices. In 1957 and 1958, for instance, the real price of distilled spirits went up by more than 30%. This contributed to a decline in spirits consumption from 0.8 litres per capita per month in 1956 to 0.6 litres in 1958, i.e. a decrease of one-quarter (Huitfeldt & Jorner, 1972).

EFFECTS ON DIFFERENT POPULATION GROUPS

In econometric studies based on time series data, the values of price elasticities reflect in many ways the average reactions of consumers to changes in prices. It is particularly the treatment of alcohol consumers as a group that has raised doubts about the validity of the estimated elasticity values. Although it can be inferred from econometric studies that a rise in the price of alcoholic beverages reduces alcohol consumption, it cannot be determined who the people are that have reduced their alcohol consumption and by how much. However, the use of individual data can shed light on debates that cannot be solved by using aggregate data. One good example is the disagreement about whether or not heavy drinkers are responsive to changes in prices of alcoholic beverages. This is an important issue, because in both public discussions and in the alcohol literature it is often asserted that increases in prices of alcoholic beverages will only affect light or moderate drinkers and will have no effect on heavy drinkers or problem drinkers, because they are either addicted to or physically dependent on alcohol. Consequently, unwillingness to raise prices is likely to be provoked if the effect on pricing policy is felt mainly by moderate drinkers and leaves the heavy drinkers to carry out as before.

In the early 1970s many bars, taverns and restaurants in Western countries initiated a variety of sales programmes to attract more customers. These programmes, called "happy hours", included some kind of price reduction; it might be two beverages for the price of one, a 25% reduction for all beverages, free beverages for a particular type of patron, or "all-you-can-drink" specials. Consequently, happy hours offer one possibility to study the effect of decreasing prices on alcohol consumption. In the USA, Babor et al. (1978) conducted an observational study of the drinking habits of 16 regular bar patrons, in happy hour and non-happy-hour times. Happy-hour patrons drank 9.6 drinks per day, while non-happy-hour patrons drank only 3.7 drinks, despite the fairly small reduction in drink prices during the happy hour. Furthermore, happy hour patrons engaged in more drinking sessions, which also lasted longer (Babor et al., 1978). In another experimental study, 34 men who were admitted to McLean Hospital in Boston for 30 days were studied (Babor et al., 1980). Those 34 men consisted of 14 heavy drinkers and 20 fairly light drinkers. Their patterns of drinking were tested under happy-hour or non-happy-hour conditions. As expected, both light and heavy drinkers drank more when drinks were less expensive. In the happy hour condition, light drinkers drank about twice as much and heavy drinkers about 2.4 times as much as in the non-happy-hour condition. Both light and heavy drinkers had longer episodes of drinking under happy hour conditions, but heavy drinkers also increased their short drinking episodes.

Surveys have also been used to study the effects of changing alcohol prices on alcohol consumption. In 1981 the effect of price on consumption was studied in Scotland by means of two surveys, one before and one after a rise in the price of alcoholic beverages (Kendell et al., 1983). According to this study, the impact of the price increase was strongest among the heaviest drinkers, for both men and women. Heavy drinkers also experienced the largest reduction in the number of adverse effects related to alcohol consumption. In the USA, Grossman et al. (1987) and Coate & Grossman (1988) have studied the price sensitivity of young people's demand for alcohol, using data from the National Health and Nutrition Examination Surveys, cycles I and II. Both studies conclude that youth beer consumption is inversely related to the price of beer, and that the effects of higher prices are not limited to infrequent or light drinkers. Instead, the results provide weak evidence that heavy drinkers are more sensitive to price changes than moderate drinkers (Grossman, Coate & Arluck, 1987; Coate & Grossman, 1988). A similar kind of study by Laixuthai and Chaloupka (1993) found that higher beer excise taxes significantly reduce both the frequency of youth drinking and the probability of heavy drinking. This study, like the other studies mentioned above, also implies that a tax increase will result in larger reductions amongst frequent and fairly frequent young drinkers than amongst infrequent young drinkers. Furthermore, it is interesting to note that, like some studies based on time series data, this study shows that there is an interplay between price controls and other measures affecting alcohol availability. It was shown that the price sensitivity of youth drinking fell after the legal minimum drinking age of 21 years came into force in all states (Laixuthai & Chaloupka, 1993). More recently in the USA Chaloupka and Wechsler (1996) have studied the effects of beer prices on drinking and binge drinking among students in colleges and universities, using a nationally representative sample from the year 1993. They found that price had a statistically significant effect on underage drinking and binge drinking among female students but not among male students.

PRICE CHANGES AND ALCOHOL-RELATED PROBLEMS

Seeley (1960) wrote about the relationship between the price of alcoholic beverages and death by liver cirrhosis in Ontario. He used alcohol consumption as an intermediate variable and was able to conclude that deaths from liver cirrhosis rose and fell with average alcohol consumption, and that average alcohol consumption rose and fell inversely with the price of alcoholic beverages. One development in the field in later years has been to link changes in the price of alcoholic beverages directly to alcohol-related problems. In this way one is able to get indirect evidence of the effects of price policy on heavy consumers. The other benefit of this kind of study design is that it takes care of problems caused by the possible substitution of recorded and unrecorded alcohol consumption. Furthermore, in recent studies full price instead or monetary price is often used. In this context, the full price of alcoholic beverages includes not only the monetary price of alcoholic beverages but also a wide variety of other costs of drinking and heavy drinking, such as the time costs of obtaining alcoholic beverages.

In the USA Cook (1981) adopted Simon's (1966) approach, using as a quasi-experiment the changes in state liquor excise-tax rates legislated between 1960 and 1975 in licence states. A follow-up study by Cook & Tauchen (1982) sought to improve this method while still taking advantage of the underlying quasi-experiment. They considered not only the relationship between spirit consumption and tax changes but also cirrhosis and car accidents in relation to tax changes. The Cook (1981) study discovered that states which raised their liquor tax had a greater reduction or smaller increase in cirrhosis mortality than other states in the corresponding year. In the Cook & Tauchen (1982) study the median price elasticity for liquor was −1.8 and it was concluded that liquor consumption, including that of heavy drinkers as indicated by cirrhosis mortality, is quite responsive to price and that a liquor tax increase tends to reduce the fatality rate of car accidents (see also Chaloupka et al., 1992; Sloan, Reilly & Schenzler, 1994). In addition, Sloan and his colleagues (1994) also considered the effects of changing prices of alcoholic beverages on a variety of other death rates related to alcohol use, including deaths from diseases primarily related to alcohol, motor vehicle traffic accidents, homicides, suicides, diseases where alcohol is a contributing factor, and other accidental deaths. They found that higher alcoholic beverage prices do not lead to significant reductions in deaths primarily related to alcohol. Schweitzer, Intriligator & Salehi (1983) developed an econometric model of alcoholism that could incorporate its causes, effects and possible control. According to them, such a model should give more complete and more direct insights into the problems of alcoholism than previous demand studies. They used cross-sectional data on 35 US states in 1975 to estimate a simultaneous model of beer and spirits consumption, alcoholism, and alcohol-related mortality. According to their results, a rise in the price of spirits lowers alcoholism, but a rise in the price of beer appears to increase it.

Saffer & Grossman (1987a, b) examined the impact of beer excise taxes on youth motor vehicle fatality rates. Both studies concluded that increases in beer taxes significantly reduce youth motor vehicle fatalities. Chaloupka, Saffer & Grossman (1993) continued this research tradition. They concluded that higher beer excise taxes are among the most effective means to reduce drinking and driving in all segments of the population. More recent studies using individual data also conclude that increases in beer taxes are effective in reducing drinking and driving and involvement in non-fatal traffic accidents. For example, Kenkel (1993), using the 1985 National Health Interview Survey, estimated that a 10% increase in the price of alcoholic beverages would reduce the probability of drinking and driving by about 7% for males and 8% for females, with even larger reductions among those 21 years and under.

Several recent studies have examined the impact of the price of alcoholic beverages on homicides and other crimes and family violence. Using annual state-level data on violent crime rates, Cook & Moore (1993b) were able to conclude that higher beer taxes would lead to significant reductions in rapes and robberies but would have little impact on homicides and assaults. In an analysis of the Uniform Crime Reports data, Chaloupka & Shaffer (1992) considered the impact of beer taxes on a variety of crime rates, including total crime, violent crime, property crime, homicide, rape, assault, robbery, burglary, larceny and motor vehicle theft rates. They concluded that increases in beer taxes led to statistically significant reductions in nearly every crime rate, with the exception of the assault rate. An analysis of vital statistics data on homicide rates resulted in that higher alcoholic beverage prices would lower homicide rates (Sloan, Reilly & Schenzler, 1994). More recently, the impact of beer taxes and other alcohol control policies on domestic violence directed at children has been studied. It was estimated that there is a significant inverse relationship between child abuse and other violence towards children and the price of beer (Markowitz & Grossman, 1998).

CROSS-ELASTICITIES

In econometric analyses of demand, the estimation of cross-elasticities—i.e. of the change in demand for one type of alcoholic beverage caused by a change in the price of some other type of alcoholic beverage—has proved to be an extremely difficult task. Although the price changes in the cases studied in the Nordic countries have mostly been within a modest range, they nevertheless seem to result in some substitution of one type of beverage for another (Nyberg 1967; Huitfeldt & Jorner 1972). When discussing cross-price elasticities in North America, Ornstein (1980) finds that reported elasticities are inconsistent both within and across different studies. His overall conclusion was that consumption of each beverage category is significantly related to its own price and little affected by changes in the price of substitute alcoholic beverages (Ornstein, 1980). According to Godfrey (1989), the UK estimates of demand models based upon time series data have in general been unsuccessful in identifying the cross-substitution effects with accuracy, even in the case of close substitutes, and all cross-price elasticities found have been very small.

The cross-elasticities estimated in econometric studies may also be of little use in actual alcohol policy-making. The estimated elasticities are derived from aggregate data using average price rates. However, it has been observed in many studies that heavy consumers usually prefer the cheaper beverages in each type of alcoholic beverage. Under such circumstances, the substitution between different types of alcoholic beverage is perhaps not so much determined by changes in the average price of each type as by changes in prices of the cheapest brands in each type (Bruun et al., 1975).

Because all alcoholic beverages include ethyl alcohol, they are potential substitutes for each other. A substitution between different classes of alcoholic beverages means that alcohol is substituted by alcohol, that is, with the same substance from the public health point of view. Alcoholic beverages also serve as substitutes for other commodities and thus they can be replaced by other commodities. This means that the level of alcohol consumption is related to the prices of alcoholic beverages relative to other commodities. When discussing other commodities as substitutes for alcoholic beverages, it should be noted that the substitution process may equally well lead to either unhealthier or healthier drinking habits. A rise in wine prices may result in a substitution of commercially produced wine by soft drinks, by self-produced wine, by "moonshine" or even by drugs. Although a rise in alcohol prices can lead to a shift in consumption to illegal alcohol or drugs, it should be remembered that these types of substitution processes are affected by restrictions and limitations of those beverages or drugs to which consumers are apt to move. In all probability, the more decisive factors in these substitutions are the control measures that bear upon the availability of those substitutes, and it is scarcely conceivable that illicit traffic of alcohol could be altogether eliminated by cutting the prices of legally produced alcohol. Furthermore, if prices of legally produced alcohol are kept constant or lowered because of the possible undesirable substitution for illegal alcoholic beverages, the harmful effects of the legitimate alcohol may exceed the socially acceptable level of alcohol problems.

OVERVIEW AND DISCUSSION

This chapter has reviewed the role of alcohol taxation as a means of curbing total alcohol consumption and alcohol-related problems. In this connection, the results of studies on both changes in alcohol prices on total alcohol consumption and on the consumption of different categories of alcoholic beverages have been summarized. Also econometric and other studies looking at the relation between changes in alcohol prices and alcohol-related problems have been examined. The evidence presented in this chapter suggests that alcohol price levels do have an independent effect on the level of alcohol consumption and alcohol-related problems. Consumers of alcoholic beverages seem to be responsible for the prices of these beverages, and heavy drinkers are no exceptions of this rule. On the contrary, in many studies the impact of the price increase was strongest among the heaviest drinkers. Price elasticities are not, however, inherent attributes of alcoholic beverages. Therefore, studies relating to different regions, periods and categories of alcoholic beverages do not produce similar elasticity values. In the interpretation of elasticity values, the points of departure should be the social, cultural and economic circumstances affecting drinking alcohol in each country and period.

The rationale for levying a special tax on alcoholic beverages is seldom questioned, and what discussion there is on the subject usually revolves around how expensive alcoholic beverages should be relative to other commodities. The level of taxation varies greatly in different countries (see e.g. Hurst et al., 1997). In most countries, however, the tax counted per litre of alcohol is higher in the form of distilled spirits than in the form of beer or wine. In this context, Japan seems to be one of the rare exceptions. Wine and beer taxes are nearer each other but, at least in the industrialized countries, beer seems to be taxed, on average, a little bit harder than wine. Because beer and wine are more expensive beverages to produce than distilled spirits in terms of the alcohol content, equal tax rates per litre of alcohol would mean that ethyl alcohol would be cheaper in the form of distilled spirits than in the form of wine or beer. From an economic perspective, the principle of taxing alcoholic beverages on the basis on alcohol strength, both within each beverage category and across different beverage categories, is often held as the most effective solution, because other solutions lead to a distortion of the allocation of resources within the alcohol sector (see e.g. Baker & McKay, 1990).

Even if increases in alcohol taxes mean lower alcohol consumption and lower problem rates, it is not always easy to use alcohol taxes as an instrument of public health. For instance, Edwards et al. (1994) mention four objections to this kind of policy. First, and particularly in a developing country, a price increase imposed on commercial beverages may stimulate illicit or home production. That danger should be heeded and monitored but, as noted in this chapter, allowing commercial production to go unfettered because of this fear also carries its own risks. Second, the budgetary authorities may view the tax obtained from beverage alcohol as a valuable and easily collectable revenue, and be reluctant to impose tax increases for fear of a consequent net loss in state incomes. Only a knowledge of the elasticities that pertain in particular circumstances can answer that question, but in most situations a price increase will swell rather than depress the tax take. The third objection to taxation as a control measure is that such an approach is not socially equitable, with tax increases imposing a proportionally greater burden on the poorer segment of the population. The evidence available does not, however, totally support this contention, since alcohol taxes will in many circumstances impose a lower relative burden on low-income groups than most other commodity taxes. The fourth point to be considered is that the efficacy of fiscal control may, in some circumstances, be eroded where borders are long or open. That speaks to the need for a strong voice to be given to health advocacy at the international level when trade and customs deals are being struck.

KEY WORKS AND SUGGESTIONS FOR FURTHER READING

Bruun, K., Edwards, G., Lumio, M., Mäkelä, K., Pan, L., Popham, R.E., Room, R., Schmidt, W., Skog, O.-J., Sulkunen, P. & Österberg, E. (1975). *Alcohol Control Policies in Public Health Perspective*, Vol. 25. Helsinki: Finnish Foundation for Alcohol Studies.

This monograph gives the basic evidence for alcohol taxes and prices as measures of controlling alcohol availability. It also places price control in the context of other measures affecting alcohol availability and sheds light on the whole idea of why alcohol consumption should be controlled.

Edwards, G.A.P., Babor, T.F., Casswell, S., Ferrence, R., Giesbrecht, N., Godfrey, C., Holder, H.D., Lemmens, P., Mäkelä, K., Midanik, L.T., Norström, T., Österberg, E., Romelsjö, A., Room, R., Simpura, J. & Skog, O.-J. (1994). *Alcohol Policy and the Public Good*. New York: Oxford University Press.

The chapter on alcohol prices in this monograph could be described as an updated version of the price chapter in Bruun et al. (1995). It summarizes the research evidence up to the early 1990s.

Hurst, W., Gregory, E. & Gussman, T. (1997). *Alcoholic Beverage Taxation and Control Policies. International Survey*. Ninth edition. Ottawa: Brewers' Association of Canada.

Brewers Association of Canada has surveyed alcohol taxation each third year since the beginning of the 1970s. A good source for those who wish to know how alcoholic beverages are taxed and what trends one can find in alcohol tax levels in industrialized countries.

Ornstein, S.I. & Levy, D. (1983).   Price and income elasticities and the demant for alcohol beverages. In M. Galanter (Ed.). *Recent Developments in Alcoholism*, Vol. 1 (pp. 303–345). New York: Plenum.

A review of econometric studies in North America. It gives good descriptions of the studies conducted and is a quick way to become familiar with different kinds of practical solutions and problems in studies on the effects on alcohol consumption of changing alcohol prices.

Godfrey, C. (1989).   Factors influencing the consumption of alcohol and tobacco: the use and abuse of economic models. *British Journal of Addiction*, **84**, 1123–1138.

Another review of demand models. A good discussion of economic theory, estimation techniques and statistical testing. Alcohol and tobacco receive special attention as commodities with dependence-inducing characteristics.

REFERENCES

Ahtola, J., Ekholm, A. & Somervuori, A. (1986).   Bayes estimates for the price and income elasticities of alcoholic beverages in Finland from 1955 to 1980. *Journal of Business and Economic Statistics*, **4**, 199–208.

Babor, T.F., Mendelson, H., Greenberg, I. & Kuehnle, J. (1978).   Experimental analysis of the "happy hour": effects of purchase price on alcohol consumption. *Psychopharmacology*, **58**, 34–41.

Babor, T.F., Mendelson, J.H., Uhly, B. & Souza, E. (1980).   Drinking patterns in experimental and barroom settings. *Journal of Studies on Alcohol*, **41**, 635–651.

Baker, P. & MacKay, S. (1990).   *The Structure of Alcohol Taxes: A Hangover from the Past?* London: Institute for Fiscal Studies.

Bruun, K., Edwards, G., Lumio, M., Mäkelä, K., Pan, L., Popham, R.E., Room, R., Schmidt, W., Skog, O.-J., Sulkunen, P. & Österberg, E. (1975).   *Alcohol Control Policies in Public Health Perspective*, Vol. 25. Helsinki: Finnish Foundation for Alcohol Studies.

Chaloupka, F.J. & Saffer, H. (1992).   Alcohol, illegal drugs, public policy and crime. Presented at Annual Meeting of Western Economic Association. San Francisco, CA, July.

Chaloupka, F.J., Saffer, H. & Grossman, M. (1993).   Alcohol control policies and motor vehicle fatalities. *Journal of Legal Studies*, **22**, 161–186.

Chaloupka, F.J. & Wechsler, H. (1996).   Binge drinking in college: the impact of price, availability, and alcohol control policies. *Contemporary Economic Policy*, **14**, 112–124.

Chaloupka, F.J., Grossman, M., Becker, G.S. & Murphy, K.M. (1992).   Alcohol addiction: An econometric analysis. Presented at the Annual Meeting of the Allied Social Science Associations, Anaheim, CA, December.

Clements, K.W. & Selvanathan, S. (1991).   The economic determinants of alcohol consumption. *Australian Journal of Agricultural Economics*, **35**, 209–231.

Coate, D. & Grossman, M. (1988).   Effects of alcoholic beverage prices and legal drinking ages on youth alcohol use. *Journal of Law and Economics*, **31**, 145–171.

Cook, P.J. (1981).   The effect of liquor taxes on drinking, cirrhosis, and auto fatalities. In M. Moore & D. Gerstein (Eds), *Alcohol and Public Policy: Beyond the Shadow of Prohibition* (pp. 255–285). Washington, DC: National Academy of Sciences.

Cook, P.J. & Moore, M.J. (1993a).   Drinking and schooling. *Journal of Health Economics*, **12**, 411–430.

Cook, P.J. & Moore, M.J. (1993b).   Economic perspectives on reducing alcohol-related violence. In S.E. Martin (Ed.), *Alcohol and Interpersonal Violence: Fostering Multidisciplinary Perspectives* (pp. 193–212). Washington, DC: US Government Printing Office.

Cook, P.J. & Tauchen, G. (1982).   The effect of liquor taxes on heavy drinking. *Bell Journal of Economics*, **12**, 379–390.

Crooks, E. (1989).   *Alcohol Consumption and Taxation*. London: Institute for Fiscal Studies.

Davies, P. & Walsh, D. (1983).   *Alcohol Problems and Alcohol Control in Europe*. New York: Gardner.

Edwards, G.A.P., Babor, T.F., Casswell, S., Ferrence, R., Giesbrecht, N., Godfrey, C., Holder, H.D., Lemmens, P., Mäkelä, K., Midanik, L.T., Norström, T., Österberg, E., Romelsjö, A., Room, R., Simpura, J. & Skog, O.-J. (1994). *Alcohol Policy and the Public Good*. New York: Oxford University Press.

Godfrey, C. (1986). *Factors Influencing the Consumption of Alcohol and Tobacco—A Review of Demand Models*. York, UK: Addiction Research Centre for Health Economics.

Godfrey, C. (1989). Factors influencing the consumption of alcohol and tobacco: the use and abuse of economic models. *British Journal of Addiction*, **84**, 1123–1138.

Godfrey, C. (1990). Modelling demand. In A. Maynard & P. Tether (Eds), *Preventing Alcohol and Tobacco Problems*, Vol. 1 (pp. 35–53). Aldershot: Avebury.

Grossman, M., Coate, D. & Arluck, G.M. (1987). Price sensitivity of alcoholic beverages in the United States: Youth alcohol consumption. In H.D. Holder (Ed.), *Advances in Substance Abuse: Behavioral and Biological Research: Control Issues in Alcohol Abuse Prevention: Strategies for States and Communities* (pp. 169–198). Greenwich, CT: JAI.

Huitfeldt, B. & Jorner, U. (1972). *Efterfrågan på rusdrycker i Sverige* (The Demand for Alcoholic Beverages in Sweden). Rapport från Alkoholpolitiska utredningen (Report from the Alcohol Policy Commission). Stockholm: Government Official Reports.

Hurst, W., Gregory, E. & Gussman, T. (1997). *Alcoholic Beverage Taxation and Control Policies. International Survey*. Ninth edition. Ottawa: Brewers Association of Canada.

Kendell, R.E., de Roumanie, M. & Ritson, E.B. (1983). Effect of economic changes on Scottish drinking habits, 1978–82. *British Journal of Addiction*, **78**, 365–379.

Kenkel, D.S. (1993). Driving, driving and deterrence: the effectiveness and social costs of alternative policies. *Journal of Law and Economics*, **36**, 877–913.

Laixuthai, A. & Chaloupka, F.J. (1993). Youth alcohol use and public policy. *Contemporary Policy Issues*, **11**, 70–81.

Landis, B.Y. (1952). Some economic aspects of inebriety. In *Alcohol, Science and Society*. New Haven, CT: Quarterly Journal of Studies on Alcohol.

Lau, H.-H. (1975). Cost of alcoholic beverages as a determinant of alcohol consumption. In R.J. Gibbins, Y. Israel & H. Kalant (Eds), *Research Advances in Alcohol and Drug Problems*, Vol. 22 (pp. 211–245). New York: Wiley.

Leung, S.F. & Phelps, C.E. (1993). "My kingdom for a drink . . . ?" A review of estimates of the price sensitivity of demand for alcoholic beverages. In M.E. Hilton & G. Bloss (Eds), *Economics and the Prevention of Alcohol-related Problems*. Research Monograph No. 25, NIH Pub. No. 93–513 (pp. 1–32). Rockville, MD: National Institute on Alcohol Abuse and Alcoholism.

Markowitz, S. & Grossman, M. (1998). *Alcohol Regulation and Violence towards Children*. Working Paper No. 6359. Cambridge, MA: National Bureau of Economic Research.

Murray, C.J.L. & Lopez, A.D. (Eds) (1996). *The Global Burden of Disease. A Comprehensive Assessment of Mortality and Disability from Diseases, Injuries, and Risk Factors in 1990 and Projected to 2020*. Global Burden of Disease and Injury Series, Vol. 1. Cambridge, MA: Harvard School of Public Health.

Nyberg, A. (1967). *Alkoholijuomien kulutus ja hinnat* (Consumption and Prices of Alcoholic Beverages), Vol. 15. Helsinki: Finnish Foundation for Alcohol Studies.

Olsson, O. (1991). *Prisets och inkomstens betydelse för alkoholbruk, missbruk och skador* (The Effect of Prices and Income on Alcohol Consumption and Related Problems). Stockholm: Swedish Council for Information on Alcohol and other Drugs (CAN).

Ornstein, S.I. (1980). Control of alcohol consumption through price increases. *Journal of Studies on Alcohol*, **41**, 807–818.

Ornstein, S.I. & Levy, D. (1983). Price and income elasticities and the demant for alcohol beverages. In M. Galanter (Ed.), *Recent Developments in Alcoholism*, Vol. 1 (pp. 303–345). New York: Plenum.

Österberg, E. (1982). Alcohol and Economics. In E.M. Pattison & E. Kaupfman (Eds), *Encyclopedic Handbook of Alcoholism* (pp. 415–425). New York: Gardner.

Österberg, E. (1995). Do alcohol prices affect consumption and related problems? In H. Holder & G. Edwards (Eds), *Alcohol and Public Policy: Evidence and Issues* (pp. 145–163). Oxford: Oxford University Press.

Saffer, H. & Grossman, M. (1987a). Beer taxes, the legal drinking age, and youth motor vehicle fatalities. *Journal of Legal Studies*, **16**, 351–374.

Saffer, H. & Grossman, M. (1987b).   Drinking age laws and highway mortality rates: cause and effect. *Economic Inquire*, **25**, 403–417.

Salo, M. (1987).   *Alkoholijuomien anniskelukulutuksen määrän kehitys vuosina 1969–1986 ja eräitä anniskelua koskevia kysyntämalleja* (Developments on On-premises Retail Sales of Alcoholic Beverages, 1968–1986, and Some Demand Models for On-premises Retail Sales). Research Report No. 9, Alko, Helsinki: Economic Research and Planning.

Salo, M. (1990).   *Alkoholijuomien vähittäiskulutuksen analyysi vuosilta 1969–1988* (An Analysis of Off-premises Retail Sales of Alcoholic Beverages, 1969–1988). Research Report No. 15. Alko, Helsinki: Economic Research and Planning.

Schweitzer, S.O., Intriligator, M.D. & Salehi, J. (1983).   Alcoholism: an econometric model of its causes, its effects and its control. In M. Grant, M. Plant & A. Williams (Eds), *Economics and Alcohol* (pp. 107–127). London: Croom Helm.

Seeley, J.R. (1960).   Death by liver cirrhosis and the price of beverage alcohol. *Canadian Medical Association Journal*, **83**, 1361–1366.

Simon, J.L. (1966).   The price elasticity of liquor in the US and a simple method of determination. *Econometrica*, **34**, 193–205.

Sloan, F.A., Reilly, B.A. & Schenzler, C. (1994).   Effects of prices, civil and criminal sanctions, and law enforcement on alcohol-retaled mortality. *Journal of Studies on Alcohol*, **55**, 454–465.

World Health Organization (1995).   *Alcohol and Health—Implications for Public Health Policy*. Report of a WHO Working Group, Oslo, 9–13 October. Oslo: World Health Organization.

Yen, S.T. (1994).   Cross-section estimation of US demand for alcoholic beverage. *Applied Economics*, **26**, 381–392.

Chapter 36

Controls on the Physical Availability of Alcohol

Tim Stockwell
National Drug Research Institute, Curtin University of Technology, Perth, Western Australia
and
Paul Gruenewald
Prevention Research Center, Berkeley, CA, USA

Synopsis

This chapter reviews the evidence regarding the circumstances under which changes in the physical availability of alcohol achieved through changes in the legal drinking age, outlet densities and trading hours can affect high-risk drinking and alcohol-related harm. With the growing reluctance of governments to use controls on alcohol's physical availability to reduce problems, this form of availability has tended to increase in both developed and developing countries over the past two decades. In developed countries this has not always been associated with an obvious increase in alcohol-related problems. Such markets are often "saturated". Alcohol is available to broad segments of society, from a great number of places and at all hours of the day and night. In these contexts, availability is but one of a complex array of influences on drinking behaviour and is expressed in different problems in different contexts. In developing countries this level of market "saturation" has not yet been achieved. Given the limited research currently available, the likely consequences of greatly increased physical availability of alcohol in these markets can only be inferred from studies of markets in developed countries.

In general terms, the research evidence suggests that each of the main forms of physical availability have powerful impacts on local levels of serious harm. However, in each case there are important contingencies that condition the development of such problems. This leads to substantial possibilities for local variation in problems related to the use of alcohol in different contexts. This is least of a problem with regard to legal drinking ages. Increases in the legal drinking age have been consistently found to reduce levels of serious harm associated with the affected age groups (teenagers and young adults). These laws, however, are controversial and

International Handbook of Alcohol Dependence and Problems. Edited by N. Heather, T.J. Peters and T. Stockwell.

often difficult to change. It appears that significant and readily achievable benefits may be obtained from a more vigorous enforcement of existing laws.

The effects of greater densities of alcohol outlets on levels of local problems, on the other hand, appear to be strongly context dependent. This dependence poses difficult methodological problems for alcohol researchers. Current evidence suggests that different relationships of outlet densities to problems may be observed across different sized areas of analysis, for different types of problems and for different types of licensed outlets. With this in mind, it appears that the regulation of licensed premises will move towards the use of local data to determine the risks associated with decisions that affect license density.

The effects of hours and days of sale on alcohol related problems are also found to be important from a harm reduction perspective. Large changes in the times at which alcohol is available (e.g. days of sale) are consistently related to expected changes in problem levels. Smaller changes (e.g. hours of sale) have only recently been found to have significant local impacts. It is suggested that local planners take special notice of the potential for late night trading to affect the local alcohol environment from a public health and safety point of view.

Future research should develop and refine models that can be applied at the local, state and national levels at which critical decisions about alcohol availability are made. Regulatory mechanisms are required which enable levels of problem consumption and harm to be monitored and incorporated into planning and policy formation. These steps will move the field towards effective approaches for the reduction of serious alcohol-related harm.

One of the most significant powers at the disposal of government to limit alcohol-related problems is the ability to control both the physical and economic availability of alcohol. There are many ways in which alcohol can be made less available through government intervention, whether at the local, state or national levels. These powers, however, are often controversial and may cut across the perceived interests of a number of important stakeholders. The manufacturing and retail arms of the alcohol industry attempt to maximize profits from sales of alcohol, state and national governments become dependent on alcohol tax revenues as part of their tax base, and many members of the voting public in Western-style democracies prefer to have ready access to affordable alcohol. Of course, stakeholders who advocate the minimization of the adverse consequences of alcohol consumption on public health, safety and order are also members of this community. These stakeholders may advocate for greater government controls on the physical and economic availability of alcohol; however, active expression of this public interest in a form that is politically potent, readily understood and supported by ordinary citizens is relatively rare.

Alcohol's availability varies markedly across the globe and it is still possible to find countries where alcohol is either completely prohibited or in which there are discrete localities or regions where the sale of alcohol is prohibited. However, while the evidence has mounted regarding the public health significance of alcohol, the 1990s in particular have witnessed a global expansion of alcohol's availability. This expansion has been marked by a growth in both the nature of availability within traditional alcohol consuming countries and the sheer number of countries in which alcohol is now readily available. Jernigan (1997) has documented strategies used by some alcohol companies to create new markets in the developing world. The rapid globalization of world trade, supported by major international treaties such as the General Agreement on Tariffs and Trade, has effectively restricted the extent to which individual governments can heavily tax alcohol or otherwise restrict access (see Österberg, Chapter 35, this volume). In most Western countries there has been an increase in the number and type of outlets at which alcohol can be sold, in the number and range of alcohol products and in the days and hours of sale. In many countries without a long tradition of public access to alcohol, availability has been introduced and expanded with little in the way of regulatory controls on the manner of its sale and promotion. Unrestricted sales of alcohol in street-corner kiosks in Estonia and the ubiquitous street vending machines in Japan are but two examples of this trend (Jernigan, 1997).

Opponents of controls on availability of alcohol are quick to point out that the pattern of deregulation established in the latter half of the twentieth century has, at least in some instances, been accompanied by declining levels of per capita consumption in some developed countries (see Chapter 19). For example, Duffy & Plant (1986) report that the substantial relaxation of Scotland's liquor licensing laws in 1976 were not associated with increased alcohol consumption in comparison with neighbouring England (these laws permitted trading on Sundays and later trading hours during the week). Deregulation of liquor licensing in Victoria, Australia, in the late 1980s resulted in a dramatic increase in the number of liquor licenses issued but was associated with a decline in overall alcohol consumption (Storey et al., 1998). So are reductions in alcohol availability a potent weapon for achieving reductions in alcohol-related harm? We believe they are. However, we also believe that research endeavours to elucidate the relationships between availability and use are highly complex, demand a great deal of the alcohol researcher and are unlikely to provide simple answers to the question, "Do reductions in availability reduce alcohol-related problems?" While the answer to this question is usually "yes" it is also sometimes "no", depending on the local context. Consideration of local context is often missing from much of the research literature. Thus, reported failures to obtain "significant" effects of changes in availability on use or problems often border on scientific anecdote; attempts to support a null finding in the absence of adequate theory or experimental control. The studies cited above are cases in point. There is no *a priori* reason to believe that Sunday sales should affect use unless one argues that such sales uniquely contribute to alcohol access (e.g. by permitting sales that would not otherwise take place on other days). Similarly, deregulation of licenses may or may not affect access to alcohol, depending upon the geographic distribution of outlets, their locations with respect to consumers and the current "saturation" of the markets themselves (i.e. the degree to which demand is already met by current availability). Sunday sales, and greater numbers of alcohol outlets, may sometimes be irrelevant to access (individuals being so able to purchase alcohol at other times and places).

The evidence in relation to specific types of controls will be discussed here and it will be noted that there are multiple influences on levels of alcohol consumption and harm at the population level, so that simplistic conclusions from single examples can frequently be misleading. We will indicate how both theory and research must be enriched to deal with the contingent relationships of alcohol availability, use and problems.

AVAILABILITY THEORY

Historically, efforts to control alcohol's availability so as to reduce alcohol-related harms have been based on the view that "less is best", i.e. the less that alcohol is available the better for public health and safety. The idea that level of alcohol-related harm in a society is closely associated with degree of alcohol availability is sometimes referred to as the "Availability Theory". The theory was first articulated on the basis of a growing body of epidemiological research in 1975 (Bruun et al., 1975). The major conclusion of this World Health Organization report was that population levels of alcohol-related harm are directly related to the levels of per capita alcohol consumption and, hence, the control of alcohol consumption through restrictions on alcohol availability becomes legitimate and a pressing public health concern. To paraphrase Single (1988), there are three separate but linked propositions contained within Availability Theory:

1. The greater the availability of alcohol in a society, the higher the average consumption of its population.
2. The higher the average consumption of a population, then the greater number there will be of excessive drinkers.
3. The greater the number of excessive drinkers in a population, the greater the extent of adverse health and social problems stemming from alcohol use.

From a modern perspective, these propositions present a deterministic view that runs counter to many of our experiences as alcohol researchers. In general, the research does not seem to support the notions that greater availability *invariably* leads to greater levels of drinking, and that changes in average drinking levels *invariably* lead to greater "excessive" drinking and problems, even if in practice they usually do. There remain significant empirical questions regarding these assertions. The relationships between availability and drinking problems are complex and multifaceted. Greater availability may and may not be related to greater use, and may be related to problems independent of use. Increases in average drinking levels may and may not be related to greater "excessive" drinking. "Excessive" drinking itself may and may not be related to greater problems. What we suggest is that, when viewed from the perspective of contemporary research, each proposition of the theory needs qualification and should be understood as a conditional, not absolute, description of the relationship between drinking and harm.

Contemporary research into the relationships of alcohol availability to use and problems has placed the three basic propositions of Availability Theory in a new context. The basic questions asked with regard to these propositions are:

*   What are the mechanisms that relate decreases in availability to decreases in use?
*   Are the effects of changes in availability restricted to "excessive" consumers?
*   Are the greatest health consequences always incurred by "excessive" drinkers?

Contemporary answers to these questions are:

*   The "full price" of alcohol consists of both its real price and the convenience costs of obtaining this good, and these "full prices" affect levels of use (Grossman, 1988).
*   Changes in availability affect both drinking patterns and routine drinking activities of all consumers (Gruenewald, Millar & Treno, 1993).
*   Traditional definitions of "excessive drinkers" as persons who on average, over all days, drink significant amounts of alcohol (e.g. more than 60 g) in fact exclude the many people who experience alcohol-related harm as a consequence of occasional "binges"— the so-called "prevention paradox" (Kreitman, 1986; Stockwell et al., 1996).

While some of the important implications of these observations will be discussed below, it is essential to recognize that this work has altered the entire context in which these scientific issues are discussed. The deterministic sense displayed by the original propositions of Availability Theory has been altered by contingent views of availability's effects. Changes in availability affect drinking only to the degree that they affect the "full price" of alcohol; this need not always be the case for all consumers (Abbey et al., 1993). Changes in availability may not affect use, but may still affect routine drinking activities related to problems; reducing availability at bars and restaurants reduces crashes independent of drinking levels (Gruenewald et al., 1996a, 1999). Changes in availability may not effect the overall volume of alcohol defined on external criteria as "excessive" but may influence the frequency of high risk or "excessive" drinking occasions. This leads us to the following expansion of the basic propositions of Availability Theory:

1. Greater availability of alcohol in a society will increase the average consumption of its population when such changes reduce the "full price" of alcohol, i.e. the real price of beverages at retail markets plus the convenience costs of obtaining them.
2. Greater availability of alcohol in a society will directly affect alcohol-related harm when such changes affect the distribution of "routine drinking activities"; behaviours drinkers engage in when consuming alcohol (e.g. drinking at bars vs. at home; drinking socially vs. alone).
3. Greater average consumption in a population will be related to increases in drinking among some segments of the population along one or more of the several basic dimensions of drinking; rates of abstention, frequencies of use, quantities consumed and variances in drinking levels.
4. Greater adverse health and social problems stemming from alcohol use will appear across the drinking population, focused in those subpopulations most exposed to risk. These risks will be distributed differently across population subgroups, depending upon differences in routine drinking activities (2, above) and drinking patterns (3, above).

In this chapter evidence will be outlined for the view that some restrictions on alcohol's availability do indeed usually reduce alcohol consumption and related harm. However, the limitations of the original propositions of Availability Theory will also be discussed including the idea that extreme forms of restriction sometimes produce adverse outcomes. Future directions will then be provided for developing an optimal regulatory system for alcohol's local availability, in which consumer demand for alcohol is balanced against public health and safety concerns.

FORMS OF ALCOHOL AVAILABILITY

The means for controlling alcohol's availability can be usefully divided into those that reduce economic availability and those that reduce physical availability.

Economic availability is essentially the price of alcoholic drinks as a proportion of disposable income among potential consumers. The retail price of alcohol is directly influenced by levels of taxation, formal and informal controls on drink prices, the costs of production, levels of consumer demand and the cost of any related services supplied along with alcoholic beverages (e.g. live entertainment on licensed premises). As discussed in Chapter 35 (Österberg), the price of alcohol appears to have an influence on level and pattern of consumption and, beyond noting that this relationship is mediated by a complex array of other factors, it will not be discussed further here.

Physical availability is essentially the availability of alcohol in one's physical environment mediated by the likelihood that one will come into contact with these sources of drink. Thus, the physical availability of alcohol is principally determined by local liquor licensing laws and the nature of their enforcement, but may be strongly modified by other aspects of human behavior. Licensing laws may govern permitted hours of sale, persons who may be licensed, numbers and types of outlets, persons to whom alcohol may be sold, types and strengths of alcohol beverages sold, permitted locations of alcohol outlets, the physical characteristics of premises, and the range of other services or products that may be provided. In many instances, how these laws are enforced in practice falls short of both the intention and the letter of the law. In particular, laws regarding service to underage and intoxicated customers are frequently ignored (Lang et al., 1996; Rydon et al., 1996; Grube, 1997) and local outlet densities grow disproportionately large as outlets concentrate along geographic boundaries between wealthy and poor areas (Gruenewald et al., 1999) and are "grandfathered" into urban planning areas (LaScala, Gerber & Gruenewald, 2000). It is vital, therefore, to understand regulatory systems and strategies as well as the legal context when considering the extent of alcohol's availability.

It is also vital to understand that the effects of physical availability are, unlike beverage prices, local rather than global. Alcohol beverage prices are relatively homogenous with respect to the physical geography of nations, states, provinces, counties, communities and neighbourhoods (e.g. varying by a factor of 83 within markets and less than 1.1 between neighbourhoods in a recent community-based study in the USA; Gruenewald et al., 1999). Beverage availability, on the other hand, is typically quite homogenous on large scales (e.g. at the state level in the USA) but heterogeneous at the smaller scales of communities and neighbourhoods (in the same study, varying by a factor of 300). Hence, while it is a simple matter of beverage choice that enables consumers to off-set price increases (by selecting less expensive beverages; Gruenewald & Treno, 2000), it is a more complicated matter to off-set the effects of reduced availability (by selecting alternative establishments, taking on additional travel time, altering travel schedules, and so on). Of course, it becomes a very difficult matter to overcome sparse levels of availability when they are encountered (e.g. in the more arid regions of Western Australia). For these reasons, the impacts of availability policy on the use of alcohol may be as heterogeneous as patterns of availability themselves. The reduction of one outlet in an urban area has significantly different meaning and implications than the reduction of one outlet in a rural outpost. Similarly, the reduction of one outlet on one side of town has different meaning and implications than the reduction of one outlet on another. The outlet in the rural outpost may be the only one for 300 miles. The bar closed at the end of the street may be frequented by most of the neighbourhood, the bar across town rarely used.

For these reasons, although the formulation of economic policies (e.g. beverage taxes, mark-ups, etc.) tend to take place on a more global level (at the levels of states and nations), the formulation of policies to influence physical availability of alcohol can and often does occur at all levels of governance. Thus, it is rarely the case that the price of alcoholic drinks may be influenced at the local level (in Australia this does occasionally occur, often through informal agreements). On the other hand, outlet licensing laws and regulations typically allow input from local communities who wish to restrict the hours and days of sale of alcohol. In the USA, planning and zoning regulations may be used to restrict the distribution of alcohol outlets in community areas and, at the urban level, are the primary determinants of local distributions of availability. At the other extreme, international agreements may restrict labelling and taxation of alcoholic products or ban sales of alcohol altogether. For all these reasons, it is important to be clear about the geographic parameters of a particular alcohol control measure.

AVAILABILITY, DRINKING AND HARM: A SUMMARY AND DISCUSSION OF THE RESEARCH EVIDENCE

Three key areas of research into the physical availability of alcohol will be discussed in turn; the legal drinking age, outlet densities and hours and days of sale. Research in these areas is most well developed and deserving of thorough review. Other major methods for influencing economic availability (e.g. price controls; Österberg, Chapter 35, this volume) and otherwise intervening in the drinking process itself (e.g. responsible beverage service practices; Homel et al., Chapter 37, this volume) have been discussed in other chapters and will not be taken up again here.

Before discussing these three key areas of research, however, it is important at the outset to consider the general arguments that have been used historically to link population levels of drinking (i.e. per capita measures of consumption) to high-risk drinking and alcohol-related harm. Along with Availability Theory, these general arguments serve as a backdrop to all contemporary discussions of alcohol availability, use and harm.

General Considerations: Availability Theory vs. the Single Distribution Theory

After some decades of work, there is now a large and impressive literature which establishes that, with very few exceptions, per capita alcohol consumption and alcohol-related harm are associated at the national, regional and, sometimes, local levels. The major review *Alcohol Policy and the Public Good* (Edwards et al., 1994) was a collaborative exercise in which the scientific literature available at that time was carefully examined. A major conclusion was that average level of consumption is associated with levels of harmful social and health consequences. At the population level it was observed that per capita alcohol consumption was related to levels of cirrhosis mortality, suicide and alcohol-related traffic crashes. Since that review, other studies have found these relationships to vary according to the specific types of beverage and alcohol-related harm considered. For example, it appears that beer sales are more closely related to drinking and driving, while spirits sales are more closely related to suicide and cirrhosis mortality rates (Kerr, 2000; Gruenewald & Ponicki, 1995a, b; Gruenewald, Ponicki & Mitchell, 1995). These findings, however, do not detract from the central point that alcohol sales, in total or beverage specific, remain correlated with specific problems. As such, relationships between beverage specific sales and problems are also contingent upon and qualified by drinking behaviours of consumers that link consumption of some beverages in some contexts to specific problems. Thus, Gruenewald et al. (1999) show that even greater levels of specificity apply within local community areas where, as in Perth, Western Australia, sales of high-alcohol beers are uniquely associated with drinking and driving (among all beer sold).

These scientific findings, relatively uncontroversial in and of themselves, and based on the rather reasonable tenets of Availability Theory, are nevertheless politically contentious because of their serious implications for the alcohol beverage industry. If these findings were used to inform government policy (e.g. through higher taxes, fewer retail outlets, restricted hours and days of sale), profits of the beverage industry would no doubt suffer. Thus, critics of these observations, and Availability Theory in general, frequently cite scientific criticisms that have been successfully levelled at a related theory, sometimes referred to as the Single Distribution Theory or, alternatively, the Ledermann Model (1956) after the French epidemiologist who originated it. The latter asserts there is a simple mathematical relationship between the level of per capita consumption and the number of excessive drinkers in any given population, increases in the former directly leading to increases in the latter (and, not surprisingly, increases in related problems). Although subsequent analyses have demonstrated that there is no such consistent and precise relationship (e.g. Skög, 1985), and these demonstrations are sometimes cited as a failure of Availability Theory, it should be noted that the two theoretical positions and the relevant facts bearing upon them are somewhat unrelated. Availability Theory, at least as represented by its contemporary adherents, advocates that an overall relationship does exist between alcohol sales and problem levels, but does not advocate that this relationship is a simple one. Rather, as noted above, it is advocated that a set of contingent mechanisms exist relating overall measures of consumption to patterns of use and problems, conditional upon a variety of social, economic, political and psychological conditions that bear upon the use of alcohol in different settings by different individuals.

In conjunction with this point, more recent research points to the quite reasonable possibility that changes in availability do not have to affect alcohol sales *per se* in order to affect a change in both patterns and rates of alcohol problems. The archetypal example here is a law that effectively closes all on-premise alcohol outlets, but otherwise preserves the availability of alcohol. Would rates of alcohol-related traffic crashes then change? All evidence appears to point to the affirmative; reducing on-premise outlet densities will lead to reductions in alcohol-related crashes (Scribner et al., 1994; Gruenewald et al., 1996). On the other hand, would such a change alter beverage use? The evidence on this point is ambiguous. At the largest scales (e.g. states in the USA), reductions in availability affect use (Gruenewald, Ponicki & Holder, 1993). At smaller scales (e.g. neighbourhoods within communities in the USA), there is little evidence that availability affects use (Gruenewald et al., 2000), but considerable changes in the distribution of availability effect substantial changes in the distribution of drunken driving crashes (Gruenewald et al., 1996). Thus, moving well beyond the Lederman model and its detractors, contemporary approaches to Availability Theory suggest a much more diversified and precise picture of the contingent relationships among these aspects of access to and use of alcohol.

Clearly, a more sophisticated view of alcohol availability, patterns of use and harm is required. These patterns of use should include not only traditional measures of drinking, but also more contemporary measures of routine drinking behaviours. One need not change drinking levels *per se* to alter the characteristics and rates of drinking problems. The contingent nature of drinking and problems assures that this is the case. One need only successfully argue that changes in availability affect aspects of drinking behavior that bear upon harm. Availability Theory, developed along these lines, will enable researchers to explore these aspects of human drinking behaviors and develop rational policy based on a deeper understanding of the contingent causes of drinking problems.

The Legal Drinking Age

Policies to restrict the minimum drinking age at which licensed sales to underage youth are permitted are intended to restrict youth access to alcohol and prevent the early onset and rapid development of drinking problems among youth and young adults. To date the research focus has been upon the determination of the extent to which raising the minimum drinking age results in reduction in use and problems among young adults. It is of some interest in this regard to also determine the effects of lower minimum drinking ages on later alcohol problems and the development of alcohol dependence. This is a rather limited area of current study and one that deserves considerable further investigation. A related issue of some importance concerns the effectiveness of laws concerning the age at which it is legal to allow a child to drink alcohol in private settings (e.g. it is an offence in the UK to give alcohol to a child less than 5 years of age). There is some cross-sectional evidence indicating that early onset of alcohol use is related to alcohol dependence (Grant, 1996). Some longitudinal evidence (Reifman et al., 1998) also indicates that the age at which a child first consumes alcohol predicts whether he/she will drink above recommended levels later in life. However, the extent to which laws governing such private behaviour can ever be enforced other than in the most extreme cases is probably small and this issue has not been a major focus of research or policy.

By contrast, there is now a strong and consistent body of knowledge in relation to the impact of drinking age laws for public drinking and making legal purchases of alcohol. This was influential in assisting community advocacy groups such as Mothers Against Drink Driving (MADD) to push successfully for the drinking age to be raised to 20 or 21 in many US States in the 1980s, following experiences with earlier periods of relaxation

(Wagenaar, 1993). These drinking age laws stand as the highest in the world, being shared with Malaysia, South Korea and Ukraine (International Center on Alcohol Policy, 1998). Most countries for which information is available have 18 as the legal drinking age and a handful of European countries have adopted 16 (Austria, Belgium, France, Italy and Spain).

There is persuasive evidence that changes to the minimum legal drinking age directly result in corresponding changes in levels of a variety of problems relating to alcohol intoxication, including road traffic fatalities, juvenile crime, serious assault and drunkenness convictions for the affected age groups (Wagenaar, 1993). The US General Accounting Office (1987) conducted a systematic review of this topic and, on the basis of 14 studies judged to be methodologically sound, estimated reductions in fatal road crashes among young drivers to be 5–28%. In one study of changes in drinking age laws across four Australian states, reductions were significantly associated with increases in assaults. Following the drop in drinking age from 21 to 18 in Western Australia in 1970, rates of serious assault increased by 231% for juveniles in comparison with Queensland (Smith, 1988).

Changes to drinking age laws are often controversial, with strongly divided opinions in the community. In 1999 the government of New Zealand introduced a Bill to lower the legal drinking age from 19 to 18, despite public opinion polls indicating a majority of opinion was against this change. Analyses of public opinion from various countries indicate divided views on this issue (Lang et al., 1995). An alternative strategy that enjoys strong public support is to enforce existing underage drinking laws more effectively. A number of studies have employed young people who either are underage or appear underage to attempt to purchase alcohol on licensed premises. In both the USA (Grube, 1997) and Australia (Lang et al.,1996), these studies indicate that the first attempt to purchase alcohol is successful on about 50% of occasions, suggesting that after four tries the chance of at least one success rises above 90%. The Community Trials Project in California included a successful component to reduce underage drinking. The evaluation of this component found that law enforcement, rather than server training, was the most effective ingredient. Police-operated underage stings were most effective in reducing underage access to alcohol (Grube, 1997).

An additional strategy to reduce alcohol-related harm for young drivers is to have a 2 or 3 year probationary license period for new drivers, during which not only are there stricter speeding restrictions but a zero permitted blood alcohol level. As reviewed in Chapter 38 (McKnight & Voas), there is some evidence in support of the effectiveness of the enforcement of drinking and driving laws when this is based upon principles of deterrence specific to drinking and driving in a particular locality.

In summary, worldwide drinking age laws vary between 16 and 21 years. Public opinion regarding these laws is usually divided, so they are difficult and controversial to change. Raising and lowering the age limits are clearly associated with, respectively, increases and decreases in levels of serious alcohol-related harm for young people. Similar effects can be achieved through enforcement and regulation strategies, although it should be noted that this requires concerted local effort and commitment, which may not always be forthcoming.

Outlet Density

Although associations between densities of licensed premises, alcohol consumption and harm are widely reported, it is a complex statistical task to establish causal relationships between changes in the density of licensed premises and these outcomes. The multifaceted determinants of drinking and problems in local settings are such that observed statistical associations (or failures to obtain such associations) may be due to a host of unmeasured characteristics relating human activities to drinking places and problems. Notwithstanding this, controls on numbers of licensed premises are a common feature of many licensing systems.

Evidence for an association between outlet density, drinking and harm comes from two major sources: cross-sectional studies that compare cities, counties or other geographic areas at one point in time or longitudinal studies which examine the relationships between trends in outlet density, consumption and harm. A few studies have managed, in effect, to combine the power of both approaches and conduct cross-sectional time series analyses of trends across both time and place.

Cross-sectional Studies

Many cross-sectional studies have found associations between density of licensed outlets, levels of alcohol consumption and harm. Several North American studies have examined data from defined geographical areas and shown that outlet density is related to levels of some alcohol problems. For example, Watts & Rabow (1983) examined alcohol availability, alcohol sales and problems across the 213 cities of California. They found that cities with high problem rates were those with the greatest availability of alcohol, as measured by outlet density per head of population. In particular, there was a strong association between the density of taverns or "beer parlours" with rates of public drunkenness arrests, on the one hand, and between liquor stores and liver cirrhosis rates, on the other.

A few state-level studies of increasing rigour were conducted in the 1990s, including Nelson's (1990) detailed study of cross-sectional relationships between beverage prices, outlet densities and alcohol use and Gruenewald, Madden & Janes's (1992) study of beverage specific availability, beverage prices and use. The findings were relatively consistent; greater beverage prices and lower outlet densities were related to lower sales of alcohol. It is noteworthy that Gruenewald et al. (1992) were able to show that both beer prices and densities of beer outlets significantly affected beer sales. However, these studies need to be interpreted with caution, since they failed to account for spatial autocorrelation among geographic units, a factor that can strongly bias statistical estimates from cross-sectional models. The tendency of data from one unit to resemble (or contrast) data from adjacent areas violates the assumption of unit independence underlying classical statistical models used to analyse these data. Failure to adjust for significant autocorrelation can result in false conclusions. The degree of spatial autocorrelation appears to increase on smaller spatial scales (e.g. community-level vs. state-level analyses; Chou, 1991). For example, Stevenson et al. (1999) did not find significant autocorrelations in a study of alcohol consumption and assaults at the postcode level for New South Wales, Australia, while Gruenewald et al. (1996) have found significant autocorrelation at the neighbourhood level of analysis within communities in California.

Scribner, MacKinnon & Dwyer (1994) and Jewell & Brown (1995) demonstrated significant cross-sectional relationships between outlet densities and alcohol-related motor vehicle accidents. Parker & Rebhun (1995), Scribner, MacKinnon & Dwyer (1995), and Speer et al. (1998) demonstrate significant cross-sectional relationships between outlet densities, homicide and assaults. All these studies are noteworthy for their control of variation in sociodemographic characteristics across geographic areas. Thus, in a pairing of studies unique to this area, Gorman et al. (1998) reported that the geographic distribution of assaults is unrelated to the distribution of outlets (at the city level within states). By contrast, Speer et al. (1998) found that the geographic distribution of assaults was related to the distribution of outlets, although at the neighborhood level within cities. The geographic scale of analysis would appear to be central to the different results in these two studies. It is to be noted, however, that these studies did not control for the effects of spatial auto-correlation and should also be treated with caution.

An important direction in recent years has been towards small area analysis of patterns of consumption and harm in local neighbourhoods. This kind of work is of great potential value to local policy makers in relation to critical local licensing decisions, e.g. the issuing of new licenses, extensions of trading hours and zoning. Several recent studies have employed sophisticated spatial techniques, not only to control for spatial auto-correlation but also to examine whether problems that occur in neighbourhoods are a function of adjoining areas with high densities of liquor outlets (so-called "spatial lag effects"). Gruenewald et al. (1996) studied the geographic patterning of alcohol-related crashes across four communities in California. It was found that alcohol-related crashes most often took place in neighbourhoods containing the largest densities of restaurants (not bars). In addition, the analysis of spatial lag effects revealed that rates of alcohol-related crashes in target neighborhoods were directly related to outlet densities in adjacent neighbourhoods.

Three other studies have used similar geostatistical techniques to examine the relationships between outlet densities and violence. It appears that rates of youth violence in minority neighbourhoods are related to greater off-premise outlet densities (Alaniz, Cartmill & Parker, 1998), rates of alcohol-related pedestrian injuries are greater in neighbourhoods near on-premise outlets (LaScala, Gerber & Gruenewald, 2000), and rates of violent assaults are greater in high-density outlet areas selling greater proportions of specific beverage types (i.e. high-alcohol beer and spirits; Stevenson, Lind & Weatherburn, 1999). A more recent fourth study (Gorman et al., in press b) has replicated the observation that outlet densities are related to violence in neighbourhood areas, but added to this is the observation that rates of violence are also related to the sociodemographic characteristics of adjacent neighborhoods. Thus, not only is the level of impoverishment of target neighbourhoods relevant to rates of violence, but the impoverishment of other adjacent nearby neighbourhoods is also important. Finally, using a related technique (generalized potentials), a fifth study by Wieczorek & Coyle (1998) has begun to identify the types of community neighbourhoods in the USA that are more likely to produce drunken drivers (i.e. areas with larger populations of youthful, lower educated, White males with unskilled jobs).

Going beyond the dichotomous characterization of outlets as on- or off-premises, specific types of on-premises drinking environments are another important contextual factor. Stockwell et al. (1992a) examined a unique set of data regarding alcohol-related harm (assaults, road crashes and drink–driving offences) and consumption (alcohol sales recorded for taxation purposes) at the level of individual licensed premises. Comparing on the basis of units of alcohol sold per premises, it was found that among on-premises establishments, nightclubs, taverns and "hotels" (large venues devoted almost entirely to drinking in Australia) were at high risk for having customers involved in drinking and driving offences, crashes and assaults. That is, drink-for-drink, these outlets sold to more consumers who were likely to be involved in these high-risk problem outcomes. A further study demonstrated that the highest risk premises were those whose patrons were more likely to have high blood alcohol levels on exiting (Stockwell et al., 1992b). Gruenewald et al. (1999) also conducted analyses on these data and detected significant relationships between the types of beverages sold at individual premises and patterns of drink–driving offences—increases over time in sales of lower strength beers from these premises were associated with reductions in drinking and driving offences.

The above studies begin to form the basis for providing empirical evidence upon which to base licensing decisions, both in terms of general principles and also of specific situations on a particular locality. For example, in Australia, a more relaxed approach might be taken by licensing authorities to the issuing of licenses for "low-risk" premises and tighter controls on hotels and nightclubs. Communities might act to site new premises in "low-risk" rather than "high-risk" locations. It is interesting to note that in the example of deregulation of licensing in Victoria, Australia, discussed above, the great increase in licensed venues was in a low-risk category—small restaurants and wine bars (Storey et al., 1998).

The future of policy applications from this approach, of course, awaits much further research. Much needs to be learned regarding the types of specific local factors that may either protect against or facilitate the occurrence of harm. For example, in a recent study by Gruenewald & Treno (2000), it is demonstrated that the effects of outlet densities on alcohol-related crash rates are strongly contingent upon local traffic flow and the available pool of drinking drivers. Effects of outlets are strongest in areas of communities where there is considerable traffic flow and which are near to larger populations of drinking drivers (spatial lags). Thus, the contextual dependence of these effects on local conditions again supports the view presented here of the contingent nature of availability. It also provides the first indications of an effective direction for local outlet policy. One could imagine a future in which local communities assess specific neighbourhood characteristics before licensing alcohol outlets, placing new outlets in low-risk areas.

Longitudinal Studies

One problem with cross-sectional studies is that the demonstrated associations cannot tell us whether increases in outlet density stimulate demand for alcohol or whether they are merely responsive to a higher level of demand from consumers. Other problems include a failure to take into account the density of outlets in geographical as well as population terms, biases due to alcohol consumption by non-resident visitors to community neighbourhoods, difficulties in obtaining sufficient observations for statistically powerful analyses of geographic data, and the problem of ignoring correlated changes in the real price of alcohol. Some longitudinal studies have been conducted that overcome some of these methodological difficulties.

Within the USA Gruenewald, Ponicki & Holder (1993) collectively analysed a 10 year panel of data available from 38 states, employing cross-sectional time series analyses. The results of the study demonstrated a significant effect of outlet densities upon alcohol sales. Elasticities related to outlet densities (on a per-person basis) were 0.411 for spirits and 0.378 for wine. Importantly, the study also showed that the geographic spread between outlets and people was similarly and independently significant, with greater distances being related to reductions in alcohol use. The time series approach was consistent with the notion that increases in outlet density frequently preceded increases in per capita alcohol consumption. The converse of consumption stimulating increases in densities was not confirmed. In other words the number of licensed premises per unit population appears to drive consumption more than the converse. A major limitation still of this study was the lack of sales data for beer—only sales of spirits and wine were available for analysis. It should be noted, however, that a number of earlier, less sophisticated, studies that examined outlet density and beer sales also found positive relationships (see Gruenewald, Madden & Janes, 1992).

Gruenewald et al. (2000) replicated this study at the neighbourhood level in analyses of six communities over 5 years and found quite different results. At this geographic level, neither outlet densities nor beverage prices were related to rates of self-reported abstention, or frequencies and quantities consumed. As these authors suggest, the scale of the spatial processes underlying access to alcohol (e.g. how far one typically drives when shopping) interacts with the effects of changing outlet densities (i.e. for a change in local outlet density to "matter", it must either increase or decrease the convenience of obtaining alcohol for a significant number of people). It appears that very local planning and zoning activities can have substantive effects on problems proximally related to outlets (e.g. crashes and violence). More global interventions are required to attack problems (e.g. heavy drinking) less closely related to the local distribution of outlets.

Outlet Density: Summary

These studies strongly suggest that limits on outlet density may be an effective means of controlling alcohol problems and needs to be taken more seriously as an effective policy tool for the reduction of alcohol-related harm. Clearly, further research into the effectiveness of these policies needs to be conducted. In future, research on this topic will need to be better informed by theoretical models of the manner in which availability, consumption and harm interact across different harm domains. It would seem that each problem studied at the community and neighbourhood level will require its own theoretical analysis. For example, models of alcohol-related crashes, in which the relationships between sources of drinkers, sources of drink and driving patterns are the focus of attention (Gruenewald et al., 1996), cannot be directly extended to studies of alcohol-related violence. There the dynamics of aggressive interactions within alcohol environments matter a great deal (Parker & Auerhahn, 1998) and the relationships between locations of violent acts, residences of victims and offenders, and alcohol outlets are key. Further development, empirical testing and refinement of these different models hold the promise of providing a rational basis for decisions about outlet densities at the local area level.

HOURS AND DAYS OF SALE

It is important to make a distinction between the related issues of the hours of trading and the number of days of trading. It will be argued here that the evidence for an effect of the number of drinking days is stronger than an effect of trading hours, although recent evidence suggests even the latter represents an important issue to be considered in the local regulation of licensed premises.

A number of Scandinavian studies have focused on natural experiments involving the introduction of the closure of liquor stores for a whole day, usually Saturday or Sunday. In Sweden, Olsson & Wikström (1982) found reductions in levels of drunkenness, domestic and public violence following the Saturday closure of stores, although not, interestingly, any reduction in the total consumption of alcohol. Similar experiments in Norway (Nordlund, 1985) and Finland (Österberg and Säilä, 1991) also yielded evidence of significant reductions in problems associated with alcohol intoxication, with either small or non-existent effects on overall consumption. More recently, the effects of closures of liquor stores and bars on social security pay-days in Aboriginal communities and other restrictions have been studied in Australia (Gray, 2000). In most instances there have been parallel reductions observed in alcohol consumption and alcohol-related harm, although in one case, as in the Scandinavian examples, only harm indicators were affected and not consumption *per se*. It should also be noted that other restrictions were also introduced in these communities, such as the rationing of cask wine sales. Collectively, these studies point to the need for a better understanding of the unique local contexts in which such experiments in alcohol availability occur. It is interesting that overall consumption throughout the whole week is not always reduced by closures on a single day, while problem incidents are. As noted in the intro-duction, this represents an important variation on traditional Availability Theory and prompts the additional investigation of the key contextual variables that contribute to the reductions in problems.

In relation to variations in trading hours, a significant contribution has been made to this literature by the Australian researcher Ian Smith in the late 1980s. He published a series of studies which documented changes in alcohol-related harm in different states before and after a relaxation in pub trading or liquor store trading hours. His analyses clearly show that small alterations in trading hours shift the pattern of road traffic accidents, so that a peak occurs shortly after the new closing time. In some instances they show a significant increase in accidents in comparison with a control state on the day when extended trading hours occur (Smith, 1988). What they do not show, however, is an overall increase in total numbers of accidents across all times. This means that it is impossible to rule out the expla-nation that peoples' drinking and driving habits have simply shifted or been redistributed across the whole week. Much research in this area, as with that concerned with outlet den-sities, has failed to take into account a number of variables. The absence of a dramatic increase in alcohol problems in Scotland following a substantial deregulation of trading hours in 1976 was highly influential in persuading the Clayson Committee (1984) to rec-ommend similar deregulation in England and Wales. During the period after the deregu-lation, Scotland experienced a particularly severe recession that was greater in severity than that of its neighbours. An independent study conducted in Edinburgh in 1978 (Kendell et al., 1983), found that there was a substantial drop in alcohol consumption in accord with a rise in the real price of alcohol. As noted in the Introduction, these are additional cases of scientific anecdote driving policy decisions. None of the original studies were sufficiently well performed to justify the confirmation of "null effects" used to defend the policy change. None of the original studies considered alternative impacts of the change under consid-eration (e.g. drinking levels), or examined mechanisms suspected to mediate the outcomes of the studies, or took into account the geographic bases and likely geostatistical problems (e.g. process scale and map resolution) that could affect observed outcomes.

A detailed study of the impact of extended trading hours in the city of Fremantle, Western Australia, during the 1987 Americas Cup failed to demonstrate any significant changes in rates of alcohol problems or consumption levels for local residents, although it did suffer from some inherent weaknesses in design (McLaughlin & Harrison-Stewart, 1992). Due to the enormous influx of visitors to the area it was not, of course, possible to examine overall rates of drink–driving and assault offences in any meaningful way. In fact, it appeared that the local residents made very little use of the extended hours. The only exception here was that those residents who reported the heaviest typical levels of con-sumption were more likely to take advantage of the opportunity to drink in hotels after midnight. This finding parallels that of another of Ian Smith's studies, in which it was deter-mined that persons who frequented hotels and taverns in Perth with early morning opening tended to have higher rates of problem drinking (Smith, 1986).

More recent Australian studies have examined in finer detail the impacts of experimental extensions of trading hours of nightclubs in Darwin (D'Abbs, 1993) and of "hotels" (i.e. bars or pubs) in Perth, Western Australia (Chikritzhs et al., 1997). The former study found significant evidence of an increase in late night and early morning violence and public drunkenness, which resulted in the permitted hours being reduced once more. In the Perth study, specific data were obtained on drink–driving offences, assaults and alcohol sales asso-ciated with specific premises before and during the granting of permits for individual premises to trade until 1 p.m. instead of midnight. In comparison with premises that did not apply for these permits, those granted extended trading evidence substantial increases in alcohol sales, assaults on or near their premises and alcohol-related road crashes involving customers who had last drunk there. While the partially controlled design of this study limits the extent to which economic confounding will have affected the results, the findings still leave open the possibility that the later trading hours for some premises simply shifted across time and place and the overall impact was not great. However, it should also be considered that, at the local community and planning levels, it is highly significant information that trading hours have these impacts. It is likely that local communities will wish to shift serious alcohol-related problems elsewhere. Furthermore, in many locations emergency services and public transport are thinner on the ground and more expensive in the early hours of the morning; another consideration for local planners.

In summary, the international experience with trading hours and days appears to demonstrate that modifications in these have some impacts on the patterning of problems of alcohol intoxication, across both time and place. In both instances, this fact should be considered in the local regulation of alcohol availability and the planning of public transport and emergency services. In the case of large changes in temporal availability of alcohol (i.e. whole days), there is evidence of parallel changes in problem occurrences, although not always in overall weekly alcohol consumption. In relation to small variations in late night trading hours, there is suggestive but not conclusive evidence that later trading hours may increase problem rates and consumption. Local contextual factors are likely to be critical in this respect and warrant further attention from researchers.

REGULATORY APPROACHES TO THE MINIMIZATION OF ALCOHOL-RELATED HARM

A common compromise response to the Temperance Movement in many parts of the world in the early twentieth century was for governments to assume ownership of alcohol supply and retail outlets. In both North America and Scandinavia, many state and national governments established government alcohol monopolies, with the intention of curbing the worst excesses of commercial alcohol sales and related harms. Over the past 50 or so years, a number of these monopolies have been converted to enable private licensed sales of alcohol. In response, a substantial evaluation literature has sprung up regarding the impact of privatization on per capita consumption and harm. A recent review of this literature (Her et al., 1999) noted that there was substantial blurring between the nature of the operation of private and government-owned alcohol retail systems. Some private systems were heavily regulated and some government monopolies were highly commercially orientated in their operation (see also Janes & Gruenewald, 1991). In addition, in nearly all instances privatization promoted a long-term increase in per capita consumption. It was recommended that further studies also examine more systematically the impacts of such major changes in regulatory style on indices of alcohol-related harm.

In the discussions of the importance of the major means of influencing the physical availability of alcohol, among the themes that have emerged is the importance of local contextual factors in determining the net outcome of a particular change in alcohol's availability. It follows that if general principles from the international literature cannot always be applied to every specific context, systems should be established at the local level for monitoring the occurrence of alcohol-related harm across key domains, such as violent crime, drink–driving, injury, death and illness. The application of Geographic Information System technology to this area (Midford et al., 1998; Wieczorek and Hansen, 1997) and the utilization of local level indicators (Stockwell et al., 1998) could facilitate a rational and empirically-based approach to minimizing harm at the local level. An encouraging trend in this area has been for liquor licensing laws in some English-speaking countries, such as

Canada, New Zealand and Australia, to adopt the minimization of alcohol-related harm as the principle objective. The existence of strategies that can be targeted successfully at high-risk drinking environments to make them safer places (see Homel et al., Chapter 37) suggests the need for strong local information bases on serious harm which can target these strategies and assist in their evaluation. Health, police and liquor-licensing authorities could be assisted to apply this information in the regulation of the conduct of liquor licensees (see Rydon & Stockwell, 1997). In fact, when this strategy is pursued at the local level, it has been shown to be successful in forming policy in community areas (Reynolds, Holder & Gruenewald, 1997; Gruenewald, Roeper & Millar, 1996b). Examples of local harm indicators that appear to be most relevant here are rates of assaults, road crashes and hospital injury presentations between the hours of 9 p.m. and 4 a.m. (Brinkman et al., 2000).

There has been increasing interest in the 1990s in the development and application of community-based indicators for monitoring alcohol-related harm and the effectiveness of responses at the local level (see Gruenewald et al., 1997; Holder, 1998). An important reason for the need to develop local monitoring systems is that with the increasing emphasis in some countries on harm minimization as a primary objective of liquor licensing laws, local licensing issues are increasingly contested and defended against this principle. As an example, in one Australian jurisdiction (Gull Petroleum vs. Health Department of Western Australia, 1999) it has been ruled that applications of general principles from the research literature in relation to alcohol's commercial availability do not constitute expert testimony, and that local factors and research are the sole determining legitimate sources of evidence.

CONCLUSIONS

Some important lessons can be learned from a review of the literature on the macro relationships between alcohol availability, alcohol consumption and alcohol-related harm. While the relationships under study are not fully determinate, in most instances it has been found that changes in the physical availability of alcohol can be influential in affecting local, regional and state levels of alcohol-related use and problems. There are many challenges to be addressed by researchers and policy makers in the future, principally to examine the specific impacts of different types of change to alcohol's availability on different patterns and levels of drinking with attendant problems. It will be important to examine the moderating effects of different drinking settings, the routine activities of the actors in these settings and to develop the technology for monitoring local, state and national harm indicators.

The major scientific challenges will be: (a) to determine what are the primary processes in communities that influence the production of alcohol-related harm; and (b) to develop models that can be used to estimate the amount of alcohol-related harm associated with different types and distributions of alcohol outlets. Although simple direct relationships between alcohol availability and harm are unlikely to be uncovered in community settings, in-depth scientific investigations into the community systems underlying alcohol-related problems will reveal the contingent relationships that result in alcohol-related harm.

An important challenge for the development of evidence-based alcohol policy will be to determine a means to establish optimum geographic distributions of different types of alcohol outlets for a range of different community contexts. In this regard it should be noted that the local effects of distributions of alcohol outlets on one problem (e.g. traffic crashes) may be quite different from the local effects on another (e.g. violence). Thus, over-concentrations of outlets in downtown retail areas may contribute relatively little to alcohol-related crashes (Gruenewald & Treno, 2000) but very much to increased rates of violence

(Gorman et al., in press b). The dispersion of these same outlets into areas of greater traffic flow may aggravate alcohol-related crash rates while mitigating violent events. Although it is much too early for the scientific research evidence to speak comprehensively to these issues, that they can be broached in current scientific discourse represents a major step forward in the field. Next steps will require much more detailed understanding of the genesis and distribution of alcohol-related problems across community areas.

A fundamental challenge for policy in the area of regulating alcohol availability will be to determine effective mechanisms whereby local distributions of outlets can be regulated to minimize alcohol-related harm while within the context of "fair" competitive practices (balancing retail access against secondary costs of distribution and use). Even with the best scientific evidence in hand, policy makers must balance the needs for sensible community growth (e.g. in retail and residential sectors) against the secondary costs related to availability in the context of local community values. These values may tend toward the reduction of alcohol-related problems along one or another dimensions important to community residents. Thus, one community could balance the costs of drunken driving events against the benefits of the substantial tax base created through greater retail growth; another could balance local rates of pedestrian injury relative to efficient traffic flow through dense retail areas; still another may consider violence related to outlet over-concentration to be so problematic as to require the implementation of severe distance requirements (spreading out outlets relative to one another). Regardless of the concern of community residents, students of this area should be prepared to build the scientific foundations upon which such decisions can be made.

KEY WORKS AND SUGGESTIONS FOR FURTHER READING

Edwards, G., Anderson, P., Babor, T.F. et al. (1994). *Alcohol Policy and the Public Good*. Oxford: Oxford University Press.

> To date, the major review of studies relating to alcohol availability and harm. An international group of scientists under the auspices of WHO each contribute chapters on a wide range of alcohol policy issues, summarizing the available evidence.

Gruenewald, P.J., Treno, A.J., Taff, G. & Klitzner, M. (1997). *Measuring Community Indicators: A Systems Approach to Drug and Alcohol Problems*. Thousand Oaks, CA: Sage.

> An introduction and guide for researchers interested in measuring local levels of alcohol use and harm for the purpose of evaluating prevention strategies and policies.

Stockwell, T. (Ed.) (1995). *Alcohol Misuse and Violence, 5. An Examination of the Appropriateness and Efficacy of Liquor Licensing Laws across Australia*. Canberra: Australian Government Publishing Service.

> While the focus of this multi-authored book is on recommendations for Australian policy, it contains several reviews of key literatures on alcohol availablity and harm, not only in relation to violence. It also summarizes surveys of public opinion regarding policy options on alcohol availability.

Holder, H.D. (1998). *Alcohol and the Community: Systems Approach to Prevention*. London: Cambridge University Press.

> An overview of the design, implementation and outcomes from the most comprehensively evaluated community alcohol intervention trial ever conducted. Efforts to reduce alcohol's availability were one of four major strategies adopted. Offers a systems view

of how control policies might be integrated with other regulatory and education strategies.

REFERENCES

Abbey, A., Scott, R.O. & Smith, M.J. (1993).   Physical, subjective, and social availability: their relationship to alcohol consumption in rural and urban areas. *Addiction*, **88**, 489–499.

Alaniz, M.L., Cartmill, R.S. & Parker, R.N. (1998).   Immigrants and violence: the importance of neighborhood context. *Hispanic Journal of Behavioral Sciences*, **20**, 155–174.

Brinkman, S., Stockwell, T., Chikritzhs, T. & Mathewson, P. (2000).   An indicator approach to the measurement of alcohol related violence. In P. Williams (Ed.), *Alcohol, Young People and Violence.* Canberra: Australian Institute of Criminology, Research and Public Policy.

Bruun, K., Edwards, G., Lumio, M., Makela, K., Pan, L., Popham, R. et al. (1975).   *Alcohol Control Policies in Public Health Perspective.* The Finnish Foundation for Alcohol Studies, Vol. 25. Helsinki: Forssa.

Chikritzhs, T., Stockwell, T. & Masters, L. (1997).   *Evaluation of the Public Health and Safety Impact of Extended Trading Permits for Perth Hotels.* Technical Report, National Centre for Research into the Prevention of Drug Abuse, Division of Health Sciences. Perth: Curtin University of Technology.

Chou, Y.H. (1991).   Map resolution and spatial autocorrelation. *Geographical Analysis*, **23**, 228–246.

Clayson, C. (1984).   Licensing law and health: the Scottish experience. Action on Alcohol Abuse Policy Forum: Licensing Law and Health, 4 December, London.

D'Abbs, P., Forner, J. & Thomsen, P. (1993).   *Darwin Nightclubs: A Review of Trading Hours and Related Issues.* Darwin: Menzies School of Public Health.

Duffy, J.C. & Plant, M.A. (1986).   Scotland's liquor licensing changes; an assessment. *British Medical Journal*, **292**, 36–39.

Edwards, G., Anderson, P., Babor, T.F. et al. (1994).   *Alcohol Policy and the Public Good.* Oxford: Oxford University Press.

Gorman, D.M., Speer, P.W., Labouvie, E.W. & Subaiya, A.P. (1998).   Risk of assaultive violence and alcohol availability in New Jersey. *American Journal of Public Health*, **88**, 97–100.

Gorman, D.M., Speer, P.W., Gruenewald, P.J. & Labouvie, E.W. (in press).   Neighborhood structure, alcohol availability and violent crime: a test of social disorganization and routine activities theory. *Journal of Studies on Alcohol.*

Grant, B.F. (1996).   Prevalence and correlates of drug use and DSM-IV drug dependence in the United States: results of the National Longitudinal Alcohol Epidemiologic Survey. *Journal of Substance Abuse*, **8**, 195–210.

Gray, D. (2000).   Indigenous Australians and liquor licensing restrictions. *Addiction*, **95**, 1469–1472.

Grossman, M. (1998).   Health economics of prevention of alcohol-related problems. Paper presented at the Workshop on Health Economics of Prevention and Treatment of Alcohol-Related Problems, National Institute on Alcohol Abuse and Alcoholism, Washington, DC.

Grube, J.W. (1997).   Preventing sales of alcohol to minors: results from a community trial. *Addiction*, **92**, S251–S260.

Gruenewald, P.J. (in press).   The epiphenomena of beverage specific effects. *Addiction.*

Gruenewald, P.J., Madden, P. & Janes, K. (1992).   Alcohol availability and the formal power and resources of state alcohol beverage control agencies. *Alcoholism: Clinical and Experimental Research*, **16**, 591–597.

Gruenewald, P.J., Millar, A.B. & Treno, A.J. (1993).   Alcohol availability and the ecology of drinking behavior. *Alcohol Health & Research World*, **17**, 39–45.

Gruenewald, P.J., Ponicki, W.R. & Holder, H.D. (1993).   The relationship of outlet densities to alcohol consumption: a time series cross-sectional analysis. *Alcoholism: Clinical and Experimental Research*, **17**, 38–47.

Gruenewald, P.J. & Ponicki, W.R. (1995a).   The relationship of the retail availability of alcohol and alcohol sales to alcohol-related traffic crashes. *Accident Analysis and Prevention*, **27**, 249–259.

Gruenewald, P.J. & Ponicki, W.R. (1995b). The relationship of alcohol sales to cirrhosis mortality. *Journal of Studies on Alcohol*, **56**, 635–641.

Gruenewald, P.J., Ponicki, W.R. & Mitchell, P.R. (1995). Suicide rates and alcohol consumption in the United States: 1970–1989. *Addiction*, **90**, 1063–1075.

Gruenewald, P.J., Millar, A.B., Treno, A.J., Yang, Z., Ponicki, W.R. & Roeper, P. (1996a). The geography of availability and driving after drinking. *Addiction*, **91**, 967–983.

Gruenewald, P.J., Roeper, P. & Millar, A. (1996b). Access to alcohol: geography and prevention for local communities. *Alcohol Health & Research World*, **20**, 244–251.

Gruenewald, P.J. & Treno, A.J. (2000). Local and global alcohol supply: economic and geographic models of community systems. *Addiction*, **95**, 5537–5550.

Gruenewald, P.J., Treno, A.J., Taff, G. & Klitzner, M. (1997). *Measuring Community Indicators: A Systems Approach to Drug and Alcohol Problems*. Thousand Oaks, CA: Sage.

Gruenewald, P.J., Millar, A.B., Ponicki, W.R. & Brinkley, G. (2000). Physical and economic access to alcohol: the application of geostatistical methods to small area analysis in community settings. In R. Wilson & M. DuFour (Eds), *Small Area Analysis and the Epidemiology of Alcohol Problems*. NIAAA Monograph, Rockville, MD: NIAAA.

Gruenewald, P.J., Stockwell, T., Beel, A. & Dyskin, E.V. (1999). Beverage sales and drinking and driving: The role of on-premise drinking places. *Journal of Studies on Alcohol*, **60**, 47–53.

Gull Petroleum v. Health Department of WA, Liquor Licensing Court of Western Australia, April, 1999.

Her, M., Giesbrecht, N., Room, R. & Rehm, J. (1999). Privatizing alcohol sales and alcohol consumption: evidence and implications. *Addiction*, **94**(8), 1125–1139.

Holder, H.D. (1998). *Alcohol and the Community: A Systems Approach to Prevention*. London: Cambridge University Press.

International Center for Alcohol Policies (1998). *Drinking Age Limits*. ICAP Reports 4, March. Washington, DC: International Center for Alcohol Policies.

Janes, K. & Gruenewald, P.J. (1991). The role of formal law in alcohol control systems: a comparison among states. *The American Journal of Drug and Alcohol Abuse*, **17**, 2.

Jernigan, D. (1997). *Thirsting for Markets—The Global Impact of Corporate Alcohol*. San Rafael, CA: The Marin Institute for the Prevention of Alcohol and Other Drug Problems.

Jewell, R.T. & Brown, R.W. (1995). Alcohol availability and alcohol-related motor vehicle accidents. *Applied Economics*, **27**, 759–765.

Kendell, R.E., De Roumanie, M. & Ritson, E.B. (1983). Effect of economic changes on Scottish drinking habits, 1978–82. *British Journal of Addiction*, **78**(4), 365–379.

Kerr, W.C. (in press). Beverage-specific alcohol consumption and cirrhosis mortality in a group of English-speaking beer drinking countries. *Addiction*.

Kreitman, N. (1986). Alcohol consumption and the Preventive Paradox. *British Journal of Addiction*, **81**(3), 353–364.

Lang, E., Stockwell, T. & Whitehead, M. (1995). In T. Stockwell (Ed.), *Alcohol Misuse and Violence Report No 5: A Review of the Appropriateness and Efficacy of Liquor Licensing Laws across Australia*. Canberra: Australian Government Publishing Service.

Lang, E., Stockwell, T., Rydon, P. & Beel, A. (1996). The use of pseudo patrons to assess compliance with licensing regarding underage drinking. *Australian Journal of Public Health*, **20**(3), 296–300.

LaScala, E.A., Gerber, D. & Gruenewald, P.J. (2000). Demographic and environmental correlates of pedestrian injury collisions: a spatial analysis. *Accident Analysis and Prevention*, **32**, 651–658.

Ledermann, S. (1956). *Alcohol, Alcoholism, Alcoholisation*, Vol 1. Connees scientifiques de caractere physiologique, economique et social. Institute National d'Etudes Demographique, Travaus et Documents, Cah. No. 29. Paris: Presses Universitaires de France.

Mclaughlin, K.L. & Harrison-Stewart, A.J. (1992). The effect of a temporary period of relaxed licensing laws on the alcohol consumption of young male drinkers. *International Journal of the Addictions*, **27**(4), 409–423.

Midford, R., Masters, L., Phillips, M., Daly, A., Stockwell, T., Gahegan, M. & Philp, A. (1998). Alcohol consumption and injury in Western Australia: a spatial correlation analysis using geographic information systems. *Australian and New Zealand Journal of Public Health*, **22**(1), 80–85.

Nelson, J.P. (1990). State monopolies and alcoholic beverage consumption. *Journal of Regulatory Economics*, **2**, 83–98.

Nordlund, S. (1985).   Effects of Saturday closing of wine and spirits shops in Norway. Presented at the 31st International Institute on the Prevention and Treatment of Alcoholism, Rome, June 2–7.

Olsson, O. & Wikström, P.H. (1982).   Effects of the experimental Saturday closing of liquor retail stores in Sweden. *Contemporary Drug Problems*, **11**(3), 325–353.

Österberg, E. & Säilä, S. (Eds) (1991).   *Natural experiments with decreased availability of alcoholic beverages: Finnish alcohol strikes in 1972 and 1985.* Helsinki: Finnish Foundation for Alcohol Studies.

Parker, R.N. & Rebhun, L.A. (1995).   *Alcohol and Homicide: A Deadly Combination of Two American Traditions.* Albany, NY: State University of New York Press.

Parker, R.N. & Auerhahn, K. (1998).   Alcohol, drugs, and violence. *Annual Reviews of Sociology*, **24**, 291–311.

Rabow, J., Watts, R.K. & Hernandez, A.C.R. (1993).   Alcoholic beverage licensing practices in California: a study of a regulatory agency. *Alcoholism: Clinical and Experimental Research*, **17**, 241–245.

Reifman, A., Barnes, G.M., Dintcheff, B.A., Farrell, M.P. & Uhteg, L. (1998).   Parental and peer influences on the onset of heavier drinking among adolescents. *Journal of Studies on Alcohol*, **59**(3), 311–317.

Reynolds, R.I., Holder, D. & Gruenewald, P.J. (1997).   Community prevention and alcohol retail access. *Addiction*, **92**(2), S155–S171.

Rydon, P., Stockwell, T., Lang, E. & Beel, A. (1996).   "Pseudo-drunk" patron evaluation of bar-staff compliance with Western Australian liquor law. *Australian Journal of Public Health*, **20**(3), 290–295.

Rydon, P. & Stockwell, T. (1997).   Local regulation and enforcement strategies for licensed premises. In M. Plant, E. Single & T. Stockwell (Eds), *Alcohol: Minimizing the Harm—What Works?*, New York: Free Association Books.

Scribner, R.A., MacKinnon, D.P. & Dwyer, J.H. (1994).   Alcohol outlet density and motor vehicle crashes in Los Angeles County cities. *Journal of Studies on Alcohol*, **55**, 447–453.

Scribner, R.A., MacKinnon, D.P. & Dwyer, J.H. (1995).   The risk of assaultive violence and alcohol availability in Los Angeles County. *American Journal of Public Health*, **85**, 335–340.

Single, E.W. (1988).   The availability theory of alcohol related problems. In C.D. Chaudron & D.A. Wilkinson (Eds), *Theories on Alcoholism* (pp. 325–351). Toronto: Addiction Research Foundation.

Skög, O.-J. (1985).   *The distribution of Alcohol Consumption. Part III: Evidence of a Collective Drinking Culture.* Oslo: National Institute for Alcohol Research.

Smart, R. & Mann, R. (1992).   Alcohol and the epidemiology of liver cirrhosis. *Alcohol Health and Research World*, **16**, 217–222.

Smith, D.I. (1988).   Effect on traffic accidents of introducing Sunday alcohol sales in Brisbane, Australia. *International Journal of the Addictions*, **23**(10), 1091–1099.

Smith, D.I. (1986).   Comparison of patrons of hotels with early opening and standard hours. *International Journal of the Addictions*, **21**, 155–163.

Speer, P.W., Gorman, D.M., Labouvie, E.W. & Ontkush, M.J. (1998).   Violent crime and alcohol availability: relationship in an urban community. *Journal of Public Health Policy*, **19**, 175–190.

Stevenson, R.J., Lind, B. & Weatherburn, D. (1999).   The relationship between alcohol sales and assault in New South Wales, Australia. *Addiction*, **94**(3), 397–410.

Stockwell, T., Somerford, P. & Lang, E. (1992a).   The relationship between license type and alcohol related problems attributed to licensed premises in Perth, Western Australia. *Journal of Studies on Alcohol*, **53**(5), 495–498.

Stockwell, T., Rydon, P., Gianatti, S., Jenkins, E., Ovenden, C. & Syed, D. (1992b).   Levels of drunkenness of customers leaving licensed premises in Perth, Western Australia: a comparison of high and low "risk" premises. *British Journal of Addiction*, **87**, 873–881.

Stockwell, T., Hawks, D., Lang, E. & Rydon, P. (1996).   Unravelling the preventive paradox. *Drug and Alcohol Review*, **15**(1), 7–15.

Stockwell, T., Masters, L., Phillips, M., Daly, A., Midford, R., Gahegan, M. & Philp, A. (1998).   Consumption of different alcoholic beverages as predictors of local rates of assault, road crash and hospital admission. *Australian and New Zealand Journal of Public Health*, **22**(2), 237–242.

Storey, H., Broderick, G. & Hamilton, M. (1998).   *Control Act 1987: Review.* Melbourne: State Government of Victoria.

US General Accounting Office (1987).   *Drinking Age Laws: An Evaluation Synthesis of Their Impact on Highway Safety.* Washington, DC: US Superintendant of Documents.

Wagenaar, A. (1993).   Research effects public policy: the case of the legal drinking age in the United States. *Addiction*, **88**(Suppl.), 75s–81s.

Watts, R.K. & Rabow, J. (1983).   Alcohol availability and alcohol-related problems in 213 California cities. *Alcoholism: Clinical and Experimental Research*, **7**, 47–58.

Wieczorek, W.F. & Coyle, J.J. (1998).   Targeting DWI prevention. *Journal of Prevention & Intervention in the Community*, **17**, 15–30.

Wieczorek, W.F. & Hansen, C.E. (1997).   New modeling methods: geographic information systems and spatial analysis. *Alcohol Health & Research World*, **21**, 331–339.

Chapter 37

Creating Safer Drinking Environments

Ross Homel
Gillian McIlwain
School of Criminology and Criminal Justice, Griffith University,
Brisbane, Queensland, Australia
and
Russell Carvolth
Alcohol, Tobacco and Other Drug Services, Queensland Health,
Brisbane, Queensland, Australia

Synopsis

The focus of the chapter is violence and crime in the licensed drinking environment. The central argument is that creating safer licensed environments is primarily a regulatory problem, not just an "alcohol problem", and that formal enforcement is a necessary but not sufficient tool for creating a culture of compliance. A system of regulation that is responsive to industry conditions will rely on the interaction of formal regulation, which is the political domain; informal regulation; mobilizing civil society; and self-regulation, taming the market.

To be effective, regulatory systems must reduce situationally specific risk factors in the licensed environment that are related primarily to management practices and to "hidden deals" between licensees and regulators. Effective regulation will ensure that the physical environment is attractive and sends a message to patrons about appropriate behaviour; that it does not irritate or frustrate people by being crowded, excessively noisy, hot or smoky; that provocation related to forms of entertainment is minimized; and that non-salty food is freely available. The social environment will not be permissive, having clear limits concerning sexual and other behaviours; drinking to intoxication, especially by large numbers simultaneously, will be discouraged; trained, peace-loving security and bar staff will be employed; and people identified as regularly aggressive will be kept out.

There is limited evidence that formal enforcement through visible, random checks on licensees can be effective, as can undercover policing combined with warnings to managers.

International Handbook of Alcohol Dependence and Problems. Edited by N. Heather, T.J. Peters and T. Stockwell.
© 2001 John Wiley & Sons Ltd.

There is consistent evidence that mobilizing local community groups and agencies through organized community action can bring about major reductions in aggression and violence in and around venues, although the effects have not been demonstrated to be permanent in any locality. Critical ingredients of community action include: strong directive leadership during the establishment period; the mobilization of community groups concerned about violence and disorder; the implementation of a multi-agency approach involving licensees, local government, police, health and other groups; the use of safety audits to engage the local community and identify risks; a focus on the way licensed venues are managed (particularly those that cater to large numbers of young people); the "re-education" of patrons concerning their role as consumers of "quality hospitality", and attention to situational factors, including serving practices, that promote intoxication and violent confrontations.

Approaches available to regulators include licensing provisions; policy development; cooperation with the industry to develop standards; developing formal and informal codes of practice; education, publicity and information campaigns (especially at the local level); incentives for responsible operators; and working with the community. These approaches can usefully be arranged in an enforcement pyramid, the broad base representing frequently used approaches based on suasion, cooperation and negotiation, the sharp end representing the ultimate but infrequently used sanctions, such as the closure of an establishment. In addition, to ensure transparency and accountability in this most difficult of regulatory arenas, a system of responsive regulation will accord a central place to community empowerment and to the role of public interest groups.

Fights are known to occur in or around pubs and taverns, and sometimes people get hurt. Usually young men are involved, and usually they're drunk—or so people assume. Fights like this are a problem, of course, especially if one's son or daughter is involved, but unless the injuries are really serious, it seems no one worries too much—least of all the police, who dislike the messy business of trying to get statements from people who can't stand up straight and are frequently uncooperative, incoherent or violently ill (Homel & Tomsen, 1991).

However, the enforcement problem can take on a new dimension if lots of fights and incidents of disorderly conduct occur in a local "hot spot" on a regular basis. Downtown entertainment areas in many towns and cities often take on this character, becoming notorious for law-and-order and public safety problems that make extra attention from regulatory authorities and local government politically unavoidable. But then the response is often purely political: sweeping the streets clean of the human riff-raff in a series of well publicized blitzes for public relations purposes, rather than attending to the underlying problems of how venues and the surrounding public space are managed and regulated.

Despite the often blasé attitudes of the regulators, there is an emerging awareness in the research literature that a serious public health issue is at stake (e.g. Stockwell et al., 1995). One feature of assault victimization found in all crime victim surveys, including those analysed by Homel & Mirrlees-Black (1997) in Queensland, is the extremely high rates of victimization of teenagers and young adults. The survey data also highlight the importance of environmental or situational factors as risk factors for young people. In general, those who go out for entertainment at night, particularly to hotels and nightclubs, have a higher than average risk of assault. The same pattern applies to teenagers: about half of male and female teenage victims are assaulted in places they go to regularly (away from a home environment) which provide leisure or entertainment. Many of these places, especially for those aged 18 years or over, are licensed venues. It follows that one important strategy for reducing violence is to increase the safety of leisure and entertainment venues, including hotels and nightclubs, especially for young patrons.

I argue in this chapter that creating safer licensed environments is primarily a regulatory problem, not just an "alcohol problem". A fundamental assumption is that whatever the effects of alcohol, its role is mediated by cultural, personal and contextual factors that are still the subject of active research. To quote Homel, Tomsen & Thommeny (1992: 681), who conducted observational studies of aggression and violence in licensed venues in Sydney:

> A key assumption was that there is a complex (but nevertheless real) relation between violence and public drinking (not the mere ingestion of ethanol) which is imbedded in Australian history and culture and reproduced in institutional arrangements and regulatory and police practices regarding drinking. In our research we aimed to transcend the narrow debate about the effects of ethanol *the substance* by focusing on the *total environment* of drinking and its regulation (or lack of regulation) by management, police and other public officials. Thus, we considered features of the external regulation of licensed premises as well as more directly observable characteristics such as physical layout, patron mix and social atmosphere.

If safety in licensed environments is a regulatory problem, it is a problem not much different in its essential nature from, say, persuading small businesses to comply with environmental laws or nursing home proprietors to maintain minimum prescribed standards of care. There are of course specific features of drinking environments that might make them problematic for the safety of their patrons (or staff), and it is very important that these be understood if wise regulations are to be devised. Nursing home regulations will not suffice for nightclubs.

One difficulty historically is that licensing and other laws relevant to the licensed environment have often not been very wise, in the sense that the known risk factors, such as simultaneous binge drinking by a large number of patrons, have not influenced the legal provisions (Stockwell, 1997). An even greater difficulty is that in many countries the laws, inadequate as they might be, have not been enforced very well. These difficulties have led in other fields both to extensive law reform and to the creation of complex mechanisms for persuading the target population if they cannot be coerced. In the licensed environments arena, the trend has been partly to new laws but even more to alternative regulatory models that rely in some way on new forms of "non-legal" persuasion or on legal measures that fall short of prosecution (Stockwell, 1995). In recent years an important element in the search for new kinds of regulatory "levers" to effect change has been the use of community action techniques.

This chapter is mainly about this search for new forms of regulation through community action. The focus is the licensed environment, especially hotels, taverns and nightclubs that provide entertainment for young people, since these are more likely to be sites of alcohol-related harm (Casswell, Zhang & Wyllie, 1993; Stockwell, Somerford & Lang, 1992). The perspective is Australian, although I draw on all the published international research of which I am aware. I begin with a brief review of what is known about risk and protective factors in the licensed environment, and then examine the literature from North America and Australia on community initiatives. I conclude that although promising new regulatory forms are emerging, no-one has yet succeeded in demonstrating a permanent reduction in disorder, crime and violence through community action. This may reflect failures of implementation or, in other cases, the failure of the formal apparatus of state control—police and liquor licensing authorities—to "follow through" with consistent enforcement in the aftermath of a community initiative.

The search for a satisfactory system of regulation requires "praxis in concrete institutional arenas" (Ayres & Braithwaite, 1992). Slogans like "zero tolerance" will not suffice, neither will any rigid adherence to a single doctrine, regardless of context. It is clear that community action *can* reduce aggressive incidents and injuries. The challenge is to institu-tionalize the critical ingredients, especially the power of community groups to act as cred-ible watchdogs, in forms that are sensitive to the political environment and to local conditions.

RISK AND PROTECTIVE FACTORS

While methods of preventing alcohol-related crime at large "one-off" or irregular public events have some relevance to the present discussion, the primary focus of this chapter is on the slightly different issue of the prevention of violence that may occur routinely in and around licensed venues.[1] Consequently, the discussion in this section is based on the review chapter on "safer bars" by Graham & Homel (1997) (with some reference also to Chapter 22 by Graham & West, this volume), and the earlier studies by Graham et al. (1980) and by Homel and his colleagues (Homel, Tomsen & Thommeny, 1992; Homel & Clark, 1994; Tomsen, Homel & Thommeny, 1991).

The Physical Environment

Using the Environment to Create Expectations about Behaviour

Attractive, nicely furnished, well-maintained premises give a message to the patron that the managers do not anticipate physical violence and associated damage to furnishings. Graham et al. (1980) found in their study of bars in Vancouver that aggression was signif-icantly correlated with poorly maintained, unclean, unattractive bar environments. In Sydney (Homel & Clark, 1994), a relationship was found between bar cleanliness and aggression.

Avoiding Physical Environment Features that Irritate or Frustrate People

Aggression in bars has been found to be associated with poor ventilation and smoky air, inconvenient bar access and inadequate seating, high noise level and crowding (Graham et al., 1980; Graham, 1985; Homel & Clark, 1994). A plausible link between these aspects of the environment and aggressive behaviour is the role of these factors in irritating, frustrating or otherwise provoking bar patrons, particularly highly intoxicated bar patrons.

In a study of crowding, Macintyre & Homel (1997) concluded that, for any given level of patron density (people per square metre), some venues exhibited higher levels of crowd-ing (unintended low-level physical contacts) than others. The more crowded venues tended to be the more violent, and in these high-risk establishments crowding increased more rapidly with patron density than in low-risk venues. Crowding appeared to arise partly from inappropriate pedestrian flow patterns caused by poor location of entry and exit doors, dance floors, bars and toilets.

---

[1] For research and guidelines on the maintenance of order at large public events and in public places, see: Alcoholic Liquor Advisory Council (1996); Bjor, Knutsson & Kuhlhorn (1992); Department of Tourism, Sport & Racing (1999); Dunstan & McDonald (1996); Ramsay (1989, 1990, 1991); Magnificent Events Company (1996).

Minimizing Provocation Related to Games and Entertainment

Graham et al. (1980) found that aggression was more likely in bars where there was dancing and pool playing (no relationship with aggression was found for other games such as darts and shuffleboard). Gibbs (1986) in his review article used the example of pool playing to demonstrate how formal and informal rules can be used to structure bar environments in order to reduce both frequency and severity of aggression. His suggestions included limits on betting, establishing protocols regarding appropriate behaviour around pool games, and keeping observers of the game out of any disputes that arise.

Safer Glassware and Other Harm Reduction Strategies

Shepherd (1994) observed that some of the more severe injuries resulting from bar fights were caused by using broken glasses or bottles as weapons, and suggested the substitution of tempered glass. Many venues do use plastic glasses on a routine basis.

Encouraging Eating with Drinking

The availability of food (especially full meals) has been associated with reduced risk of aggression in bars (Graham, 1985; Homel & Clark, 1994). This may be because the types of bars that serve food are less likely to have aggressive patrons; they are more likely to have a positive social atmosphere; and because eating while drinking slows absorption of alcohol, reducing the blood alcohol level the drinker reaches (Wedel et al., 1991).

The Social Environment and Social Control

Creating a Social Atmosphere with Clear Limits

The "permissiveness" of the environment has been shown to be associated with aggressive behaviour (Graham et al., 1980; Homel & Clark, 1994; Hauritz et al., 1998). This includes overall decorum expectations, abusive swearing, sexual activity among patrons, sexual competition, prostitution, drug use and dealing, male rowdiness, and male roughness and bumping. Management and staff behaviour is also important: there is greater aggression where bar staff are very permissive and do not engage in responsible serving practices (e.g. serving underage patrons) (Homel & Clark, 1994), or where staff exercise little control over patrons' behaviour (Graham et al., 1980). Aggression has also been found to be more likely in bars where drunkenness is frequent (Graham et al., 1980; Homel & Clark, 1994) and where there are discount drinks and other drink promotions (Homel et al., 1992).

Discouraging Drinking to Intoxication

A high proportion of intoxicated patrons is associated (in complex ways) with aggression. High levels of intoxication signal a generally permissive environment, but there is also a consistent relationship between drunkenness and aggression in a number of studies (Graham & West, Chapter 22, this volume) that suggests a variety of causal paths. In addition, the *severity* of aggression is related to levels of drunkenness (Graves et al., 1981).

Fostering a Positive Social Atmosphere

Positive atmospheres that are friendly rather than tense and hostile, that include quiet laughter and small talk rather than hostile talk, and where patron boredom is low, are associated with a lower risk of aggression (Graham et al., 1980; Homel & Clark, 1994).

Employing Trained Peace-loving Staff

Aggression has been found to occur in response to venue staff exercising social control such as refusing service and otherwise intervening with intoxicated patrons (Felson, Baccaglini & Gmelch, 1986; Graves et al., 1981; Homel & Clark, 1994). Bouncers, in particular, have been identified as sometimes *increasing* the harm associated with bar-room aggression (Homel et al., 1992; Marsh & Kibby, 1992).

Keeping out Aggressive People

Certain bars are violent because they are frequented by aggressive people (Graham & West, Chapter 22, this volume; Tomsen et al., 1991). Therefore, a necessary feature of safer bars is the capability to recognize and ban, if necessary, persistent trouble-makers.

PREVENTION PROGRAMS

To be effective, prevention programs must reduce multiple risk factors in the licensed environment. It may not much matter which particular risk factors are manipulated, provided that several of the features discussed in the previous section are covered. However, whatever else is done, controls on the incidence of intoxication, particularly mass intoxication, must probably be implemented for violence to decline substantially (Hauritz et al., 1998; Homel & Clark, 1994).

Responsible Server Programs

These programs employ a variety of techniques to prevent intoxication, including observing patrons and being able to recognize intoxication; promoting non-alcoholic and low-alcohol drinks; serving well-priced, attractive and well-marketed food low in salt content; and training staff in techniques for monitoring patrons and adjusting service as necessary. Training is also provided in refusal of service to patrons who are intoxicated or who show signs of becoming intoxicated. Bar staff are trained in offering positive alternatives, such as soft drinks or food at discounted prices, and both management and staff are trained in negotiation techniques with patrons who are becoming difficult or aggressive. The importance of a well-publicized "house policy" to provide a positive context for responsible serving practices and for negotiation with patrons is emphasized (Simpson et al., 1987).

The small number of rigorous evaluations of responsible serving programs that have been published have reported mixed results. On the positive side, Saltz (1987), in an evaluation of an experimental 18 hour training programme in a USA Navy base, reported that the likelihood of a customer being intoxicated was cut in half, although for the establishment as a whole absolute consumption and the rate of consumption were not affected. On the other hand, Lang et al. (1998b) studied a responsible serving training program of 1–2 hours duration in seven sites. They found that there was no significant reduction in patrons with blood alcohol levels greater than 0.15% (i.e. those who were "very drunk"), or in the number of drinking and driving offences from the intervention sites. Researchers who pretended to be drunk were rarely refused service, and identification was rarely checked.

Lang et al. (1998b) attribute the disappointing results to poor implementation of the training and a lack of support among managers. They argue that server training should be mandatory, and that licensing laws must be routinely enforced if the goals of responsible service are to be met. It is noteworthy that in most of the programmes in the USA, responsible serving programmes are supported by legal sanctions or are embedded in broader community interventions. The crucial role of enforcement is highlighted by Jeffs & Saunders (1983), who reported the positive impact in an English seaside resort of the impact of uniformed police dropping in at random intervals two or three times a week and very conspicuously checking (in an amiable way) for under-age drinkers or intoxicated patrons. McKnight & Streff (1994) in the USA show that intensive undercover police operations, preceded by education of licensees about the enforcement activities, after-visit reports to licensees not cited, and media publicity, resulted (in comparison with a control county) in greatly increased refusals of service to "pseudopatrons" simulating intoxication and a marked decline in drunk drivers who had been served at the target establishments.

The great problem that is faced in most countries is that enforcement of licensing laws is not a high priority and therefore is not well resourced. Moreover, in some countries, such as Australia, the licensing area has been a seedbed for the corruption of police and other officials (Homel, 1996). For these and other reasons, "enforcement" approaches that do not depend solely on agencies of the state have become attractive in recent years.

Community Action Projects

Community approaches emphasize regulation of alcohol-related disorder and violence through procedures that empower residents, business people and citizen groups to resolve problems with licensed establishments and to take effective action at the local level. Resources and reports that are available to understand and implement this approach include: Alcohol Advisory Council of Western Australia (1989); Braun & Graham (1997); Eastern Sydney Area Health Service (1995); Gilling (1993); Lakeland & Durham (1991); Lang, Keenan & Brooke (1998a); Marsden & James (1992); Parkdale Focus Community (1995); Robinson & Tether (1990); Robinson, Tether & Teller (1989); Shane & Cherry (1987); Standing Conference on Crime Prevention, (1986); Tether & Robinson (1986); the St Kilda Project (1997); Victorian Community Council Against Violence (1990); Welsh (1996).

There is a theoretical literature on community action, mainly from the USA and Canada, that emphasizes its complexity and difficulty (e.g. Giesbrecht et al., 1990; Giesbrecht and Ferris, 1993; Giesbrecht, Krempulec and West, 1993; Holder, 1992). Giesbrecht, Krempulec & West (1993) argue that the complexity arises from the "unstable mix" of processes such as research, community action, evaluation, and the type and level of intervention. The authors argue that by tackling the four main sources of problems faced by community projects, this unstable mix may be overcome. The four problems are: the ideologies and agendas of main parties; the difficulties faced by evaluators when the dynamics of implementation are beyond their control; the failure to train community members in "how-to-do" community-based interventions; and meeting goals because of funding problems, ill-defined timelines, political interference, poor methodology, and conflict among project participants (Lang, Keenan & Brooke, 1998a).

Giesbrecht et al. (1993) argue that problems might be overcome by locating the research agenda within a health promotion framework, which is seen as relevant to a wide range of agencies, programs and services at a community level. The bottom line, according to the authors, is the ability of such projects to facilitate manageable partnerships; to ensure scientific rigor in a dynamic context; and to impart skills and resources to community members so that they can realize worthy and realistic goals.

Despite the difficulties, community action can be demonstrated to work. Putnam, Rockett & Campbell (1993) report the results of a very comprehensive community intervention on Rhode Island which resulted in a 21% reduction in Emergency Room assault injury rates in the intervention site compared with a 4% increase for the comparison communities. Motor vehicle crash injuries were also reduced. The community intervention involved server training as well as publicity campaigns, local task force activities, and community forums, and was supported by training of police and increased levels of enforcement with respect to alcohol-related accidents and crimes.

Undoubtedly the most wide-ranging and well-resourced attempt to date to reduce alcohol-related accidental injuries and deaths through community-based methods has been the work of Harold Holder and his colleagues in the USA (Holder et al., 1997a,b). This 5-year project carried out in three experimental communities consisted of five mutually reinforcing components: community mobilization; promotion of responsible beverage service for bar staff and managers/licensees of on-premises alcohol outlets; deterrence of drinking and driving through local enforcement; reduction in retail availability of alcohol to minors; and reductions in the number and density of alcohol outlets to limit general access to alcohol. The project did not target particular groups, but was based on the assumption that changes in the social and structural contexts of alcohol use can alter individual behaviour.

The community mobilization process involved working as much as possible with existing community coalitions, tailoring programme materials for each site, generating as far as possible resources from within the communities, and channelling existing community resources, skills and interests, rather than only introducing them from the outside. As Treno & Holder (1997, p. S176) observe, ". . . the Community Trials Project was composed of three independent replications of a generic prevention design . . . in which implementation approaches were designed within each community . . .".

The project brought about a 10% reduction in alcohol-involved traffic crashes, a significant reduction in underage sales of alcohol, and increased adoption of local ordinances and regulations to reduce concentrations of alcohol outlets. The specific aspect of the project of most relevance to the present chapter was the responsible beverage service (RBS) component:

> The general operating principle of this component was to create a combination of incentives and disincentives that would strongly encourage on-premise licensees to provide server training in responsible beverage serving practices and to strengthen their policies related to preventing intoxication and keeping intoxicated patrons from driving (Holder et al., 1997b, p. S162).

Saltz & Stanghetta (1997) conclude that this component achieved modest success as measured by the number of businesses trained, by the introduction of limited law enforcement around service to intoxicated patrons where none had existed previously, and by increases in levels of community debate about RBS policies. However, these program elements did not produce significant changes in serving practices. Saltz & Stanghetta argue that to achieve any impact, it is essential to involve the hospitality industry; to avoid voluntary RBS training; and (once again) to reinforce mandatory training with enforcement of the law around service to intoxicated patrons.

The Australian Experience

Perhaps as a response to the vacuum created by an inadequate regime of legal regulation, community action projects targeting licensed premises have proliferated in recent years in Australia. Examples include the Westend Forum in Melbourne (Melbourne City Council, 1991); Eastside Sydney Project (Lander, 1995); the St Kilda Project (1997); the Tennant Creek Project (a community collaboration against striptease shows; Boffa et al; 1994); the

Kings Cross Licensing Accord (New South Wales Health Department, 1997); the Armidale Community Alcohol Strategy Committee (Cope, 1995); the Halls Creek initiative (Douglas, 1995), and several projects in South Australia (Fisher, 1993; Walsh, 1993). Limited evaluation data are available for these projects, although most show at least qualitative signs of impact, and some (like the Halls Creek project) suggest falls in alcohol consumption and reductions in crime and alcohol-related presentations at hospital.

Stockwell (1997), Boots et al. (1995) and Felson et al. (1997) report three recent Australian initiatives that have been evaluated: the "Freo Respects You" project in Fremantle, Western Australia, the COMPARI (Community Mobilization for the Prevention of Alcohol-Related Injury) project in Geraldton, Western Australia, and the "Geelong Accord" in Victoria. Recent work that colleagues and I have conducted in Queensland is summarized in the next section.

"Freo Respects You" was a collaborative project involving the hospitality industry, police, and liquor licensing and health authorities. The project was designed to increase levels of responsible service of alcohol in participating premises by providing incentives for drinkers to avoid excessive intake (e.g. offering competitively priced, reduced alcohol-drinks and good food); avoiding incentives for intoxication (e.g. very cheap, high-strength drinks); instituting policies to minimize the harm of being intoxicated (e.g. transport schemes) and establishing policies to minimize intoxication by refusing service to intoxicated customers. The other major component of the intervention was a series of training programs for licensees, managers and bar staff covering liquor licensing laws, strategies for dealing with drunk customers and the development of responsible house policies.

An evaluation of the project revealed that there was a significant increase in the awareness of bar staff's obligations under the Liquor Act and an increase in the rate at which bar staff at participating premises requested age ID. There were small improvements in the responsible house policies of some of the participating premises, including the provision of free non-alcoholic drinks for drivers and lower-priced reduced-alcohol beers. However, discounting of full-strength drinks continued and bar staff reported that they were serving obviously drunk customers. Stockwell (1997) suggests that the Fremantle Project was hindered by the fact that there was insufficient "ownership" of the project by licensed operators and that only medium- to high-risk premises participated.

The COMPARI project in Geraldton commenced in 1991. A local community taskforce was established in 1992, involving police, local government, health and education officers and the local public. The taskforce was encouraged to develop a sense of ownership through actively seeking alternative funding from local government and the regional health authority (Midford et al., 1994). Unfortunately, the evaluation found that, with regard to measures of alcohol-related harm, there was no evidence of a positive impact from the COMPARI project. Key informant interviews indicated that community awareness of alcohol issues had increased, along with improved knowledge about associated harm. There was, however, only minimal impact among young people. In line with experience with similar projects undertaken elsewhere, community participation was found to be highest during the early part of the project, following which numbers gradually reduced. Community leadership and organization, however, were judged to have improved as the project developed. The survey of community attitudes found a statistically significant increase in support for local council having a role in alcohol issues. There was an increased level of awareness of the project and the various activities, especially the "skipper" campaign, alcohol-free concerts and the campaign around the establishment of a new tavern.

The "Geelong Local Industry Accord," was a cooperative effort beginning in 1991, involving police, the Liquor Licensing Commission, hotel and nightclub licensees, and local government, although in practice police appear to have taken on the main leadership role (Felson et al., 1997; Kelly, 1993; Rumbold et al., 1998). Essentially the Accord is a code of practice that facilitates self-regulation by licensees throughout the region. "Best practice" provisions included specified types of photo-identification, minimum $5 cover charges after 11.00 p.m., no passouts from venues with an entry charge, no underage patrons and responsible service of alcohol (including elimination of gimmicks that promote rapid and excessive consumption of alcohol). A key strategy of the Accord was to stop "pub-hopping" by means of entry and exit controls.

No before–after measures of alcohol and drug related harm were available but police records suggest that reported assault and property damage rates reduced after the Accord was implemented (Rumbold et al., 1998). Moreover, in comparison with two other regional centres, practices in Geelong venues were significantly better in terms of responsible drinking promotions, amenities and responsible serving practices, although no differences were found with respect to crowding or overall levels of intoxication. In comparison with other community-based initiatives, the Geelong Accord seems to have maintained a positive impact over a period of several years. Rumbold et al. (1998) attribute this "longevity" to several factors, particularly the fact that the Accord was developed and resourced entirely within the local community, and the levels of stability in the local liquor industry and amongst police, local government and liquor licensing personnel.

It seems that the Fremantle, Geraldton and Geelong initiatives were mostly "top-down" rather than community-initiated interventions, despite the levels of cooperation achieved at the local level. In fact, most "community" projects seem to require at least some external resources or initiative to get them going, even if the level of community involvement and empowerment eventually achieved is quite high. As Midford et al. (1994) conclude, the "top-down" and "bottom-up" approaches both have strengths and weaknesses, and in practice should be seen as complementary rather than mutually exclusive.

The Queensland Safety Action Projects

The Surfers' Paradise Safety Action Project was a community-based initiative in 1993, designed to reduce violence in and around licensed venues in the central business district of the main tourist area on Queensland's Gold Coast. (Homel et al., 1997). Key features of the implementation included channelling funding through local government; creating a representative steering committee and community forum; forming task groups to address safety of public spaces, management of venues and security and policing; encouraging nightclub managers to introduce a Code of Practice, regulating serving and security staff, advertising, alcohol use and entertainment; and regulating managers through "risk assessments" and through a community-based monitoring committee. More subtle but equally important aspects of the implementation included: rehabilitating the image of nightclub managers and integrating them into the local business community; using managers committed to the reform process from another city to encourage and bring pressure to bear on local licensees; employing a Project Officer who was female and who had considerable interpersonal skills; and balancing the conflicting political agendas of participating agencies.

The evaluation showed a marked initial impact of the project, with reductions in practices that promote the irresponsible use of alcohol (such as binge-drinking incentives) and improvements in security practices, entertainment, handling of patrons and transport policies. Physical and verbal aggression inside and outside venues, based on structured observations pre- and post-implementation and on police and security data, showed substantial declines. Male and female drinking rates and drunkenness declined markedly, but there was no change in prices for drinks or admission. There were dramatic improvements in publicity to patrons about house policies and associated improvements in server practices, the physical environment (e.g. clean toilets and accessible bars) and security practices (e.g. ID checks at door).

However, there are indications that displacement of problem patrons may have been at least partly responsible for the impact of the project. In addition, observational data collected 2 years after completion of the project indicated that violence and drunkenness levels had returned to pre-project levels, and that compliance with the Code of Practice had almost ceased (Homel et al. 1997). Licensees attributed the deterioration to a failure on the part of regulators to deal with "cowboy operators" who flouted the Code of Practice and engaged in dangerous but (at least in the short term) profitable practices.

In 1995 the Surfers' Paradise Safety Action Project was replicated in Cairns, Townsville and Mackay in North Queensland (Hauritz et al., 1998). Many of the features of the Surfers' Paradise project were incorporated in the replications, but not all features were present at all sites, while others that seemed important in Surfers' (such as a community monitoring committee) were introduced quite late in some of the projects.

Using structured observational methods in 1994 and 1996, big reductions were observed in each city on overall physical and non-physical aggression. Paralleling this, there were marked improvements on most indicators of host responsibility practices, especially practices to control consumption. Publicity to patrons improved, with an increase in the use of underage drinking warnings, Patron Care signs and other forms of publicity. Presumably as a result of these initiatives, some drinking measures showed marked changes. Male and female drinking rates were not judged to have changed significantly, and neither did the estimated levels of female drunkenness, but male drunkenness appeared to decline sharply. These results imply that staff intervened in a firm way when serving men in order to prevent intoxication.

The fact that the situation in Surfers' Paradise was badly deteriorating in the 1994–1996 period suggests that the improvements observed in the replication projects were not part of a more general trend.

GUIDELINES FOR SOCIAL POLICY AND BEST PRACTICE

From the Queensland safety action research, features that characterize successful community interventions include: strong directive leadership during the establishment period; the mobilization of community groups concerned about violence and disorder; the implementation of a multi-agency approach involving licensees, local government, police, health and other groups; the use of safety audits to engage the local community and identify risks; a focus on the way licensed venues are managed (particularly those that cater to large numbers of young people); the "re-education" of patrons concerning their role as consumers of "quality hospitality"; and attention to situational factors, including serving practices, that promote intoxication and violent confrontations.

In a review of the experience of many communities with action on alcohol and drug issues, Lang et al. (1998a) emphasize the importance of ownership and control of programmes by the communities themselves, in contrast to control by outside "experts". They propose guidelines for community action based on a philosophy of: harm reduction; using community diversity as an asset (providing a wealth of social resources to address issues of concern); encouraging broad community and organizational collaboration allowing the sharing of resources to achieve common goals; and accommodating the dynamic nature of community action, emphasizing ongoing reassessment.

The themes of "grass roots" action and interagency collaboration also emerged from the UK Home Office working group on violence associated with licensed premises (Standing Conference on Crime Prevention, 1986), together with a number of other practical management strategies. The working group recommended the development of local interagency liaison groups, such as "Pub Watch" (see below); an investigation of the relationship between licensing hours and violence; that premises should be encouraged to become more family-orientated to help reduce age segregation; that "difficult" pubs should be run as community ventures with a local community management structure; and that attempts be made to involve the liquor industry in identifying and disseminating good practices among members.

The authors identified a number of good practices that came to their attention during the course of the research. One example was communication and cooperation between police, industry, local government, tenant associations and local resident action groups, evolving into local Licensing Forums or Committees. This process has resulted in some pubs becoming seen as part of the community and to a great extent self-policing. The report notes that problem premises are well known to industry, police, local authorities and local residents, so a cooperative approach at the grass roots level to monitor and deal with such premises is required.

A comprehensive summary of possible prevention strategies that builds on recent literature is provided by Braun & Graham (1997). These authors also provide examples of specific measures and a summary of the evidence for their impacts. Their overall emphasis is on ways of mobilizing and empowering the community. Consequently, they focus on creating coalitions linking community groups with representatives from key commercial and government agencies, including the police, liquor licensing authority, taxi/bus services and retail associations. The role of these coalitions includes auditing licensed venues and the surrounding neighbourhood to identify problems and develop measures to reduce risks to personal safety. The authors emphasize that community mobilization needs to be supported by legal, regulatory and enforcement methods.

Many of Braun & Graham's principles encourage licensees to lift their horizons and accept responsibility for behaviour within community settings beyond their own establishments. With support from external organizations such as the police, they need to assume responsibility for monitoring their customers and ensuring that bar staff serve in a responsible manner. Thus, bar staff should be trained in responsible practices and door staff should also be registered and trained. The authors observe that strict enforcement of the liquor laws is necessary to increase perceptions that there will be adverse consequences from serving underage or intoxicated customers.

Braun & Graham document several valuable techniques for effective harm reduction. One key proposal concerns the formation of a town planning committee aiming to limit harm through effective environmental design. The committee's role would be to consider appropriate locations for services, such as fast food outlets and transportation, in relation to licensed venues. Other proposals involve mobilizing licensees to monitor and report violent offences by their customers. One such measure is Pub Watch, which is a communication system for licensees to warn each other about any disorderly incidents in their area via a "ring-around" arrangement. Pub Watch is closely linked to Pub Ban schemes, which involve banning known offenders. Pub Ban can be supported by the creation of an incidence register of bar fights, which would fully document the occurrence of fights in or near licensed establishments.

CONCLUSION: TOWARD BETTER REGULATORY MODELS FOR CREATING AND MAINTAINING SAFE DRINKING ENVIRONMENTS

There are many signs from the emerging literature on community action and formal enforcement that disorder and violence in the licensed environment can indeed be reduced. There is less compelling evidence that anyone has yet succeeded in effecting a permanent reduction in these problems. So the challenge is to build on the successes and learn from the failures, in order to devise systems of regulation that continue to work over time. There is certainly no shortage of good ideas with which to experiment.

The most important lessons from the literature concern *systems* of regulation. The importance of consistent and vigorous enforcement from police and liquor licensing authorities is clear, from the examples of both success and failure in achieving and maintaining reductions in violence. However, there are lessons as well for other forms of regulation: those deriving from the persuasive powers of agency and citizen partnerships at the local community level, and those relating to the practices that are best implemented by licensees and managers themselves. Getting the balance right between these three levels—formal regulation, which is the *political* domain; informal regulation, mobilizing *civil society*; and self-regulation, taming the *market*—is one of the primary challenges for those interested in the prevention of violence and associated problems in and around licensed venues.

On the basis of their experience with safety action projects, Hauritz et al. (1998) developed a model of the change process that posited parallel but interacting processes at the three levels of regulation. This model, perhaps in modified form, is proposed as a tool for any person or group concerned with reducing violence and crime in the licensed environment.

Hauritz and her colleagues assumed that certain *antecedent conditions*, such as a political environment emphasizing deregulation of liquor licensing or a lack of faith by licensees in the formal system of regulation, lead to a range of *problem behaviours*. These behaviours could include cut-throat competition between venues and irresponsible drinks promotions, a police crack-down on symptoms (arresting drunks in the streets), rather than dealing with problem venues, and a fragmented local response. These conditions and problems create a climate conducive to the development of a range of *intervention strategies* at each of the three levels of regulation. Strategies could include interagency cooperation, community mobilization and the formation of a licensed venues association to promote compliance with a code of practice and to "legitimize" the role of licensees as part of the local business community. These interventions produce certain positive *outcomes*, such as reduced violence or legislative reform, which can be *reinforced* if key players and organizations are rewarded through career enhancement or positive publicity. The reinforcers of positive change are more likely to have a continuing effect if key reforms are institutionalized through legislation or community-based monitoring systems. They referred to this process of institutionalization as *mechanisms to safeguard change*.

A crucial philosophy that guided Hauritz and her colleagues and which, in the light of the failed projects in the literature, may be an important guideline for future interventions, was the need to be *situationally specific* in the analysis of problems and the formulation of solutions. The theoretical basis is "situational crime prevention" (Clarke, 1997, p. 4), which involves a shift from thinking in terms of offenders and their motivations to offences and their settings. In the case of licensed premises this implies a focus on all the management practices that give rise to unsafe environments. As previously emphasized, alcohol-serving practices are only one aspect of unsafe environments. Other aspects include such things as physical design, selection and training of security staff, the permissiveness of the social climate in venues, and the hidden "deals" between managers and regulators. The relevance of situational theory to these kinds of issues can be illustrated not only by the traditional typology that was focused on the physical environment, but by Clarke & Homel's (1997) recent extension of situational methods to include techniques for removing excuses, or inducing guilt or shame. These include: *rule setting* (e.g. through codes of practice); *stimulating conscience* (e.g. by encouraging managers to regard themselves as responsible businessmen); *controlling disinhibitors* (e.g. by controlling alcohol through server intervention);

and *facilitating compliance* (e.g. by creating a regulatory environment in which it is financially worthwhile for licensees to adhere to the code of practice).

A focus on venue management leads not only "inward" to specific contexts, but "outward" to the local community and to the larger arena in which laws and regulations are created and enforced (or not). The concept of "responsive regulation" (Ayres & Braithwaite, 1992) is particularly useful in this context. Ayres & Braithwaite propose regulatory approaches that are responsive to industry context and structure, regulatory culture, and history, and which incorporate, as key ideas, "tit-for-tat" strategies that combine punishment and persuasion in an optimum mix; "tripartism" (empowering citizen associations) as a way of solving the dilemma of regulatory capture and corruption; and "enforced self-regulation", in which private sets of rules written by business (such as codes of practice), are publicly ratified and, when there is a failure of private regulation, are publicly enforced.

Central to their model is an "enforcement pyramid" of penalties, from the frequently used techniques of persuasion and warning letters through to the infrequently used techniques of license suspension and revocation ("capital punishment" of alcohol outlets). The ideological basis of their ideas is ". . . a replacement of the liberal conception of the atomized free individual with a republican conception of community empowerment" (p. 17). Tripartism fosters the participation of community associations by giving them full access to all the information available to the regulator; by giving them a seat at the negotiating table; and by giving them the same standing to sue or prosecute as the regulator. Thus, they propose a model in which no one element, whether it be self-regulation, formal enforcement or citizen involvement, can operate effectively without the others.

There are many questions that must be addressed in each community as new forms of regulation are developed. An excellent general reference, whether or not readers are Australian, is the extensive report prepared by Stockwell et al. (1995), focusing on the appropriateness and efficacy of liquor licensing laws across Australia. This report particularly contrasts the complex and fragmentary nature of the Australian regulations with the Canadian situation. However, no jurisdiction has a monopoly on best practice, so to conclude this chapter some questions are raised and ideas proposed that may assist in the "praxis" of responsive regulation (Ayres & Braithwaite, 1992, p. 99).

A fundamental question is whether any form of regulation beyond effective police or licensing authority enforcement is really required. Why not just devise clearer and more comprehensive laws, and ensure that the authorities have the resources and motivation to enforce them (Solomon & Prout, 1994)? Is it really necessary to complicate the regulatory problem by emphasizing the community and self-regulation layers?

The critical role of formal enforcement has already been noted, although the evidentiary base is still thin. The paper by Jeffs & Saunders (1983) suggests that some form of visible, random enforcement in licensed venues can be quite effective, while the research of McKnight & Streff (1994) suggests that an undercover police presence, combined with warnings to managers, can be a potent deterrent. More evidence on the effects of enforcement in a variety of settings is urgently required, addressed particularly to the appropriate balance between visible and covert methods. But, as Solomon & Prout observe (p. 79), when it comes to law enforcement, "resources and priorities" are the problem. This reflects the fact that in many jurisdictions it is just not politically feasible to expect that police or licensing officers will be particularly zealous in law enforcement. The industry is too important economically to jeopardize good relations, so probably the most that can be expected of formal enforcement is that it will be used to support and reinforce other regulatory measures.

The overall aim of regulation should not be to "catch crooks," but to develop *a culture of compliance*. Of course a few heads on stakes might be essential occasionally to get the attention of unruly and anarchistic operators, but generally less savage techniques will be appropriate. The options, apart from prosecution, include persuasion and non-prosecution enforcement measures. Approaches available to regulators include: *licensing provisions* (e.g. imposing conditions in specific cases); *policy development* (e.g. advocating for change in licensing authority priorities); *cooperation with the industry to develop standards* (e.g. what exactly are the maximum acceptable degrees of "permissiveness" in a nightclub?); *developing formal and informal codes of practice* (working with a representative industry body if possible); *education, publicity and information campaigns* (especially at the local level, and designed and implemented with full industry cooperation); *incentives for responsible operators* (lower license fees for exemplary performance?); and, of course, *working with the community*.[2]

These approaches can usefully be arranged in an enforcement pyramid, the broad base representing frequently used approaches based on suasion, cooperation and negotiation, the sharp end representing the ultimate but infrequently-used sanctions, such as the closure of an establishment (the business equivalent of capital punishment). Many specific techniques that are used, at least occasionally, in some jurisdictions have already been noted. Others that are used in allied fields, such as environmental regulation, include: *abatement notices* (to control "nuisance practices"); *show-cause notices* (an operator is given time to make written representations why further action should not be taken); *enforcement notices* (setting out the grounds on which it is issued and the action required to comply); and *on-the-spot fines*. An increasingly common practice in environmental regulation is the *environmental management plan*, which can be issued by the regulator or voluntarily by the operator. The issuer devises objectives and strategies for compliance, stipulates a timetable and proposes performance indicators and monitoring and reporting mechanisms. Some of these techniques are already used by liquor licensing authorities but all could be used more frequently, with a greater emphasis on experimentation and evaluation.

But "head office" busyness will never be enough. All regulatory arenas are littered with the putrescent remains of cost cutting, shady deals and blatant corruption. The liquor licensing field, for obvious historical and cultural reasons, is particularly prone to regulatory capture and to official misconduct. For this reason, more than any other, a system of responsive regulation will give a central place to community empowerment and to the role of public interest groups. It does seem however, as Ayres & Braithwaite (1992) sadly observe, that the ideal of a full partnership role at the negotiating table with industry and government for such interest groups is as yet too remote to be promoted as a realistic goal. But the literature on community action *has* taught us that in the present political environment in at least some countries, local groups can be credible watchdogs, if not full partners, and can also bark loud enough to be effective "terriers for reform".

KEY WORKS AND SUGGESTIONS FOR FURTHER READING

Ayres, I. & Braithwaite, J. (1992).   *Responsive Regulation: Transcending the Deregulation Debate.* New York: Oxford University Press.

This is essential reading for anyone interested in grappling with the theoretical and practical issues involved in effective regulation of any industry.

---

[2] I am indebted to my wife, Beverley, for valuable insights into the world of environmental regulation.

Braun, K. & Graham, K. (1997). *Community Action for Safer Bars: Summary of Relevant Literature and Examples of Strategies Aimed at Reducing Violence in Licensed Establishments.* Toronto: Addiction Research Foundation.

A valuable document that sets out in detail what we can learn from the research literature about strategies to reduce violence.

Homel, R. (1997). *Policing for Prevention: Reducing Crime, Public Intoxication and Injury.* Crime Prevention Studies No. 7. Monsey, NY: Criminal Justice Press.

This edited volume has several chapters on policing licensed venues (especially the chapters by Stockwell, Felson, Homel and Macintyre).

Graham, K. & Homel, R. (1997). Creating safer bars. In M. Plant, E. Single & T. Stockwell (Eds), *Alcohol: Minimizing the Harm* (pp. 171–192). London: Free Association Press.

This chapter summarizes the evidence on risk and protective factors for violence in licensed venues.

Hauritz, M., Homel, R., McIlwain, G., Burrows, T. & Townsley, M. (1998). Reducing violence in licensed venues through community safety action projects: the Queensland experience. *Contemporary Drug Problems*, **25**, 511–551.

A recent paper that presents evidence that reductions in violence through community action are achievable. It includes a model of the community change process.

Lang, E., Keenan, M. & Brooke, T. (1998). *Guidelines for Community Action on Alcohol and Drug Issues, and Annotated Bibliography.* Melbourne: Turning Point Drug and Alcohol Centre.

This document combines community action guidelines with a comprehensive annotated bibliography.

Stockwell, T. (Ed.) (1995). *Alcohol Misuse and Violence: An Examination of the Appropriateness and Efficacy of Liquor Licensing Laws across Australia.* Report No. 5, Commonwealth Department of Health, Housing, Local Government and Community Services. Canberra: Australian Government Publishing Service.

The most comprehensive document available on the many facets of liquor licensing regulation as it relates to violence. Although Australian, it is relevant to problems faced in many countries.

REFERENCES

Alcohol Advisory Council of Western Australia (1989). *Licensed Premises: Your Right to Object.* Perth, WA: Alcohol Advisory Council of Western Australia.

Alcoholic Liquor Advisory Council (1996). *Good Times: Managing a Successful Public Event.* Auckland: Alcoholic Liquor Advisory Council.

Ayres, I. & Braithwaite, J. (1992). *Responsive Regulation: Transcending the Deregulation Debate.* New York: Oxford University Press.

Bjor, J., Knutsson, J. & Kuhlhorn, E. (1992). The celebration of Midsummer Eve in Sweden—a study in the art of preventing collective disorder. *Security Journal*, **3**(3), 169–174.

Boffa, J., George, C. & Tsey, K. (1994). Sex, alcohol and violence: a community collaborative action against striptease shows. *Australian Journal of Public Health*, **18**(4), 359–366.

Boots, K., Cutmore, T., Midford, R., Harrison, D. & Laughlin, D. (1995). *Community Mobilisation for the Prevention of Alcohol-related Injury. Project Evaluation Report. Reducing Alcohol-related*

Harm: What Can Be Achieved by a Three Year Community Mobilisation Project. Bentley WA: National Centre for Research into the Prevention of Drug Abuse, Curtin University of Technology.

Braun, K. & Graham, K. (1997). *Community Action for Safer Bars: Summary of Relevant Literature and Examples of Strategies Aimed at Reducing Violence in Licensed Establishments*. Toronto: Addiction Research Foundation.

Casswell, S., Zhang, J.F. & Wyllie, A. (1993). The importance of amount and location of drinking for the experience of alcohol-related problems. *Addiction*, **88**, 1527–1534.

Clarke, R. (1997). *Situational Crime Prevention: Successful Case Studies*, 2nd edn. Guilderland, NY: Harrow and Heston.

Clarke, R. & Homel, R. (1997). A revised classification of situational crime prevention techniques. In S.P. Lab (Ed.), *Crime Prevention at a Crossroads* (pp. 17–30). Cincinnati, OH: Anderson Publishing Co. and Academy of Criminal Justice Sciences.

Cope, K. (1995). Developing an alcohol strategy from the grassroots up—the Armidale Community Alcohol Strategy Committee. In R. Midford (Ed.), *National Workshop on Community-based Alcohol Harm Prevention*. Bentley WA: National Centre for Research into the Prevention of Drug Abuse, Curtin University of Technology.

Department of Tourism, Sport and Racing: Liquor Licensing Division and Queensland Police (1999). *A Planning Guide for Event Managers: Alcohol Safety and Event Management*. Brisbane, Queensland: Queensland Government.

Douglas, M. (1995). Alcohol abuse in Halls Creek: the process of change. In R. Midford (Ed.), *National Workshop on Community-based Alcohol Harm Prevention*. Bentley WA: National Centre for Research into the Prevention of Drug Abuse, Curtin University of Technology.

Dunstan, G. & McDonald, R. (1996). Situational crime prevention and the art of celebration. Paper presented at the Last Night First Light Conference, Byron Bay, Australia.

Eastern Sydney Area Health Service (1995). *Preventing Alcohol-related Violence: A Community Action Manual*. Sydney: St Vincent's Hospital.

Felson, R.B., Baccaglini, W. & Gmelch, G. (1986). Bar-room brawls: aggression and violence in Irish and American bars. In A. Campbell & J.J. Gibbs (Eds), *Violent Transactions: The Limits of Personality*. Oxford: Basil Blackwell.

Felson, M., Berends, R., Richardson, B. & Veno, A. (1997). Reducing pub hopping and related crime. In R. Homel (Ed.), *Policing for Prevention: Reducing Crime, Public Intoxication and Injury* (pp. 115–132). Crime Prevention Studies, No. 7. Monsey, NY: Criminal Justice Press.

Fisher, J. (1993). Partnership for personal safety: preventing violent crime in and around licensed premises. Presented at the National Conference on Crime Prevention, Griffith University, Brisbane.

Gibbs, J. (1986). Overview. In A. Campbell & J. Gibbs (Eds), *Violent Transactions: The Limits of Personality*. Oxford: Basil Blackwell.

Giesbrecht, N., Conley, P., Denniston, R., Glicksman, L., Holder, H., Pederson, A., Room, R. & Shain, M. (Eds) (1990). *Research, Action, and the Community: Experiences in the Prevention of Alcohol and Other Drug Problems*. OSAP Prevention Monograph No. 4. Rockville, MD: US Department of Health and Human Services.

Giesbrecht, N. & Ferris, J. (1993). Community-based research initiatives in prevention. *Addiction*, **88**(Suppl.), 83–93.

Giesbrecht, N., Krempulec, L. & West, P. (1993). Community-based prevention research to reduce alcohol-related problems. *Alcohol Health & Research World*, **17**(1), 84–88.

Gilling, D. (1993). The multi-agency approach to crime prevention: the British experience. Presented at the National Conference on Crime Prevention, Griffith University, Brisbane.

Graham, K. (1985). Determinants of heavy drinking and drinking problems: the contribution of the bar environment. In E. Single & T. Storm (Eds), *Public Drinking and Public Policy*. Toronto: Addiction Research Foundation.

Graham, K. & Homel, R. (1997). Creating safer bars. In M. Plant, E. Single & T. Stockwell (Eds), *Alcohol: Minimizing the Harm* (pp. 171–192). London: Free Association Press.

Graham, K., LaRoque, L., Yetman, R., Ross, T.J. & Guistra, E. (1980). Aggression and barroom environments. *Journal of Studies on Alcohol*, **41**, 277–292.

Graves, T.D., Graves, N.B., Semu, V.N. & Sam, I.A. (1981). The social context of drinking and violence in New Zealand's multi-ethnic pub settings. In T.C. Harford & L.S. Gaines (Eds), *Social Drinking Contexts*. Research Monograph No. 7. Rockville, MD: NIAAA.

Hauritz, M., Homel, R., McIlwain, G., Burrows, T. & Townsley, M. (1998). Reducing violence in licensed venues through community safety action projects: the Queensland experience. *Contemporary Drug Problems*, **25**, 511–551.

Holder, H.D. (1992). Undertaking a community prevention trial to reduce alcohol problems: translating theoretical models into action. In H.D. Holder & J.M. Howard (Eds), *Community Prevention Trials for Alcohol Problems* (pp. 227–243). Westport, CT: Praeger.

Holder, H.D., Saltz, R.F., Grube, J.W., Treno, A.J., Reynolds, R.I., Voas, R.B. & Gruenewald, P.J. (1997a). Summing up: lessons from a comprehensive community prevention trial. *Addiction*, **92**(2), S293–S301.

Holder, H.D., Saltz, R.F., Grube, J.W., Voas, R.B., Gruenewald, P.J. and Treno, A.J. (1997b). A community prevention trial to reduce alcohol-involved accidental injury and death: overview. *Addiction*, **92**(2), S155–S171.

Homel, R. (1996). Review of T. Stockwell (Ed.), *An Examination of the Appropriateness and Efficacy of Liquor-Licensing Laws across Australia*. Canberra: AGPS. *Addiction*, **91**(8), 1231–1233.

Homel, R. & Clark, J. (1994). The prediction and prevention of violence in pubs and clubs. *Crime Prevention Studies*, **3**, 1–46.

Homel, R., Hauritz, M., Wortley, R., McIlwain, G. & Carvolth, R. (1997). Preventing alcohol-related crime through community action: the Surfers Paradise Safety Action Project. In R. Homel (Ed.), *Policing for Prevention: Reducing Crime, Public Intoxication, and Injury* (pp. 35–90). Crime Prevention Studies No. 7. Monsey, NY: Criminal Justice Press.

Homel, R. & Mirrlees-Black, C. (1997). *Assault in Queensland*. Brisbane: Queensland Criminal Justice Commission.

Homel, R. & Tomsen, S. (1991). Pubs and violence: violence, public drinking, and public policy. *Current Affairs Bulletin*, **68**(7), 20–27.

Homel, R., Tomsen, S. & Thommeny, J. (1992). Public drinking and violence: not just an alcohol problem. *Journal of Drug Issues*, **22**, 679–697.

Jeffs, B.W. & Saunders, W.M. (1983). Minimizing alcohol related offences by enforcement of the existing licensing legislation. *British Journal of Addiction*, **78**, 67–77.

Kelly, W. (1993). *Geelong "Local Industry Accord": A Partnership in Crime Prevention*. Geelong Local Industry Accord, Best Practices Committee. Geelong: Australia.

Lakeland, G. & Durham, G. (1991). AHB and community organisation: building a coalition in preventing alcohol problems. A paper prepared for the Perspectives for Change Conference, Wellington, New Zealand.

Lander, A. (1995). *Preventing Alcohol-related Violence: A Community Action Manual*. Sydney: Eastern Sydney Area Health Service and St Vincent's Alcohol & Drug Service.

Lang, E., Keenan, M. & Brooke, T. (1998a). *Guidelines for Community Action on Alcohol and Drug Issues, and Annotated Bibliography*. Melbourne: Turning Point Drug and Alcohol Centre.

Lang, E., Stockwell, T., Rydon, P. & Beel, A. (1998b). Can training bar staff in responsible serving practices reduce alcohol-related harm? *Drug and Alcohol Review*, **17**, 39–50.

Macintyre, S. & Homel, R. (1997). Danger on the dance floor: a study of interior design, crowding and aggression in nightclubs. In R. Homel (Ed.), *Policing for Prevention: Reducing Crime, Public Intoxication, and Injury* (pp. 91–113). Crime Prevention Studies No. 7. Monsey, NY: Criminal Justice Press.

Magnificent Events Company (1996). *Concept Plans for Managing Dysfunctional Events at Bondi Beach on Christmas Day and New Year's Day*. Bond University, Queensland: Australian Institute of Dramatic Arts.

Marsdon, G. & James, R. (1992). *From Pain to Power: Resident Action for the Prevention of Alcohol-related Problems*. Perth: National Centre for Research into the Prevention of Drug Abuse, Curtin University of Technology.

Marsh, P. & Kibby, K. (1992). *Drinking and Public Disorder*. A report of research conducted for the Portman Group by MCM research. London: Portman Group.

McKnight, A.J. & Streff, F. M (1994). The effect of enforcement upon service of alcohol to intoxicated patrons of bars and restaurants. *Accident Analysis and Prevention*, **26**(1), 79–88.

Melbourne City Council (1991). *Westend Forum Project—1990/91. Final Report.* Melbourne, Victoria: Melbourne City Council.

Midford, R., Laughlin, D., Boots, K. & Cutmore, T. (1994). *Top down or bottom up: is one approach better for developing a community response to alcohol harm?* Paper presented at the APSAD Conference, *Alcohol, Drugs and the Family.* Melbourne, VIC: October 11–13.

New South Wales Health Department (1997). *Kings Cross Licensing Accord.* Sydney: New South Wales Health Department.

Parkdale Focus Community (1995). *Liquor Licensing and the Community: Resolving Problems with Licensed Establishments.* Toronto: Parkdale Focus Community.

Putnam, S.L., Rockett, I.R. & Campbell, M.K. (1993). Methodological issues in community-based alcohol-related injury prevention projects: attribution of program effects. In T.K. Greenfield & R. Zimmerman (Eds), *Experience with Community Action Projects: New Research in the Prevention of Alcohol and Other Drug Problems.* Center for Substance Abuse Prevention Monograph 14. Rockville, MD: US Department of Health and Human Services.

Ramsay, M. (1989). *Downtown Drinkers: The Perceptions and Fears off the Public in a City Centre.* Crime Prevention Unit Paper 19. London: Home Office.

Ramsay, M. (1990). *Lagerland Lost: An Experiment in Keeping Drinkers off the Streets in Central Coventry and Elsewhere.* Crime Prevention Unit Paper 22. London: Home Office.

Ramsay, M. (1991). A British experiment in curbing incivilities and fear of crime. *Security Journal,* **2**(2), 120–125.

Robinson, D. & Tether, P. (1990). *Preventing Alcohol Problems: Local Prevention Activity and the Compilation of "Guides to Local Action".* Geneva: World Health Organization.

Robinson, D., Tether, P. & Teller, J. (Eds) (1989). *Local Action on Alcohol Problems.* London: Tavistock/Routledge.

Rumbold, G., Malpass, A., Lang, E., Cvetkovski, S. & Kelly, W. (1998). *An Evaluation of the Geelong Local Industry Accord: Final Report.* Melbourne: Turning Point Alcohol and Drug Centre.

St Kilda Project (1997). *Tool Kit. A Resource Guide for Community Groups Wishing to Develop a Harm Reduction Response to Alcohol and Other Drug Use.* St Kilda, Victoria: St Kilda Project & City of Port Phillip.

Saltz, R. (1987). The roles of bars and restaurants in preventing alcohol-impaired driving: an evaluation of server education. *Evaluation in Health Professions,* **10**(1), 5–27.

Saltz, R.F. & Stanghetta, P. (1997). A community-wide Responsible Beverage Service program in three communities: early findings. *Addiction,* **92**(2), S237–S249.

Shane, P. & Cherry, L. (1987). *Alcohol Problem Prevention through Community Empowerment: A Review and Summary of the Castro Valley Prevention Planning Project.* Alameda, CA: Alameda County Health Care Services Agency.

Shepherd, J. (1994). Violent crime: the role of alcohol and new approaches to the prevention of injury. *Alcohol and Alcoholism,* **29**(1), 5–10.

Simpson, R., Brunet, S., Solomon, R., Stanghetta, P., Single, E. & Armstrong, R. (1987). *A Guide to the Responsible Service of Alcohol: Manual for Owners and Managers.* Toronto: Addiction Research Foundation.

Solomon, R. & Prout, L. (1994). A summary of provisions contained in Australian liquor laws of possible relevance to violence. In T. Stockwell (Ed.), *Alcohol Misuse and Violence: An Examination of the Appropriateness and Efficacy of Liquor Licensing Laws across Australia* (pp. 57–84). (Report No. 5: Presented at the National Symposium on Alcohol Misuse and Violence.) Prepared for the Commonwealth Department of Health, Housing, Local Government and Community Services. Canberra, Australia: Australian Government Publishing Service.

Standing Conference on Crime Prevention (1986). *Report of the Working Group on the Prevention of Violence Associated with Licensed Premises.* London: Home Office.

Stockwell, T. (Ed.) (1995). *Alcohol Misuse and Violence: An Examination of the Appropriateness and Efficacy of Liquor Licensing Laws across Australia.* Report No. 5, Commonwealth Department of Health, Housing, Local Government and Community Services. Canberra: Australian Government Publishing Service.

Stockwell, T. (1997). Regulation of the licensed drinking environment: a major opportunity for crime prevention. In R. Homel (Ed.), *Policing for Prevention: Reducing Crime, Public Intoxication and Injury* (pp. 7–34). Crime Prevention Studies No. 7. Monsey, NY: Criminal Justice Press.

Stockwell, T., Norberry, J. & Solomon, R. (1995). Proposed directions for future reforms of
    licensing laws. In T. Stockwell (Ed.), *Alcohol Misuse and Violence: An Examination of the Appro-
    priateness and Efficacy of Liquor Licensing Laws across Australia* (pp. 287–308). (Report No. 5:
    presented at the National Symposium on Alcohol Misuse and Violence.) Prepared for the Com-
    monwealth Department of Health, Housing, Local Government and Community Services. Can-
    berra: Australian Government Publishing Service.

Stockwell, T., Somerford, P. & Lang, E. (1992). The relationship between license type and alcohol-
    related problems attributed to licensed premises in Perth, Western Australia. *Journal of Studies on
    Alcohol*, **53**, 495–498.

Tether, P. & Robinson, D. (1986). *Preventing Alcohol Problems. A Guide to Local Action*. London:
    Tavistock.

Tomsen, S., Homel, R. & Thommeny, J. (1991). The causes of public violence: situational vs. other
    factors in drinking related assaults. In D. Chappell, P. Grabosky & H. Strang (Eds), *Australian
    Violence: Contemporary Perspectives*. Canberra: Australian Institute of Criminology.

Treno, A.J. & Holder, H.D. (1997). Community mobilization: evaluation of an environmental
    approach to local action. *Addiction*, **92**(2), S173–S187.

Victorian Community Council Against Violence (1990). *Inquiry into Violence in and Around
    Licensed Premises*. Melbourne: Victorian Community Council Against Violence.

Walsh, B. (1993). Communities working together side by side to create safe seaside suburbs. Pre-
    sented at Australian Institute of Criminology Conference, Melbourne.

Wedel, M., Pieters, J.E., Pikaar, N.A. & Ockhuizen, T. (1991). Application of a three-compartment
    model to a study of the effects of sex, alcohol dose and concentration, exercise and food con-
    sumption on the pharmacokinetics of ethanol in healthy volunteers. *Alcohol and Alcoholism*, **26**(3),
    329–336.

Welsh, M. (1996). *The St. Kilda Project. A Community Response to Alcohol and Other Drug Issues*.
    Final Report, December 1996. St. Kilda: City of Port Phillip.

Chapter 38

Prevention of Alcohol-related Road Crashes

A. James McKnight
Transportation Research Associates, Annapolis, MD, USA
and
Robert B. Voas
Pacific Institute for Research and Evaluation, Calverton, MD, USA

Synopsis

Countermeasures to alcohol-related road crashes are considered within four categories: reducing alcohol consumption by reducing alcohol availability; separating drinking from driving; apprehending and removing the drinking driver from the road; and preventing the recurrence of drinking and driving among drink–driving offenders. This chapter is organized around those four elements of the impaired driving problem.

Traditional efforts to reduce drinking and driving have centered on the enforcement of impaired driving laws. Over the last two decades, however, the science of alcohol safety has expanded to include efforts to limit drinking as well as driving after drinking. This has occurred as research has demonstrated the effectiveness of making alcohol less available, particularly to youth, in reducing alcohol-related crashes. Efforts to reduce consumption have taken three forms: (a) limiting total consumption by regulating sales through prohibition of sales to minors in certain locations or jurisdictions and through the manipulation of price through excise taxes; (b) controlling the conditions of service (e.g. limiting "happy hours"); and (c) designing information campaigns to discourage heavy drinking.

It is possible for individuals to drink heavily and not be exposed to causing alcohol-related crashes if they do not have access to a vehicle. Programs to achieve this outcome include: public education efforts to persuade the drinkers themselves to take steps to avoid driving after drinking; programs to encourage servers, peers and hosts to prevent intoxicated individuals from driving; and organized efforts by alcohol outlets and community organizations to make provisions for alternative transportation. Public education efforts are most effective where they publicize other strategies that depend upon public awareness for their effectiveness.

International Handbook of Alcohol Dependence and Problems. Edited by N. Heather, T.J. Peters and T. Stockwell.
© 2001 John Wiley & Sons Ltd.

Action to reduce alcohol-related crashes has been the enforcement by the police of impaired driving laws which, as traffic volumes have grown and laws more complex, has become a specialized task in many jurisdictions. A new enforcement science has developed that focuses on (a) identifying vehicles driven by impaired drivers, (b) detecting signs of drinking, (c) measuring impairment, and (d) measuring BAC levels. There is now compelling evidence for the effectiveness of reduced BAC levels and their enforcement through highly visible means.

Many strategies have been developed to prevent a drink–driver from re-offending. Three general areas of action can be distinguished: (a) applying traditional penalties, such as jail and fines directed at causing sufficient discomfort to deter the individual from repeating the offense; (b) suspending the driver's license to prevent future drinking and driving; and (c) requiring attendance at treatment or educational programs directed at assisting the offender to avoid future impaired driving and promoting recovery from dependence on alcohol. Unfortunately, most current remedial programs have shown limited success, as one-third to one-half of the drivers convicted of impaired driving repeat the offense.

Preventive efforts directed toward previous offenders can use sanctions to limit driving, including license suspension and revocation, vehicle impoundment and jail. Although the immediate effect of these sanctions is to reduce driving, they are also expected to create an unpleasant condition that deters future alcohol-impaired driving. Ignition interlocks are a promising technical development that has been found to be more effective than license suspension. Once the interlock is removed, however, there is little reduction in recidivism. There is limited take-up of this option by drivers in the USA unless the only alternative given is jail.

This chapter identifies a range of effective and less effective strategies for the reduction of serious injury and death on the roads caused by alcohol-impaired driving.

The contribution of alcohol impairment to death and injury on the highway has been well established through comparisons of blood alcohol levels among drivers in fatal crashes and non-crash-involved drivers using the roads at the same times and places. The first risk curve based on such comparisons, showing the increase in crash probability associated with increased BAC, produced by Borkenstein et al. (1974), has generally been confirmed by several investigators since that time (Hurst, 1973). The relationship of blood alcohol and risk of death in road crashes is exponential, with risk increasing sharply at blood alcohol levels between 0.08% and 10%. The most recent estimates for the USA (Zador, 1991) indicated that the relative risk of involvement in a single-vehicle fatal crash increased nine times in the BAC range from 0.05 to 0.09. In this BAC range, the corresponding risk curve for drivers 16–20 years old rises even more sharply. The relationships found in fatal crash accident data are reinforced by the results of laboratory research showing performance in a wide range of tasks, evidencing a marked decline at the same blood alcohol levels (Moskowitz & Robinson, 1988). In the USA, this increased risk results in a comprehensive cost to society of $115 billion or approximately 95 cents per 1-ounce drink. Forty cents of that cost is borne by non-drinking drivers (Miller, Lestina & Spicer, 1998).

Countermeasures to alcohol-related road crashes have fallen into four categories (Table 38.1) representing separate phases: reducing alcohol consumption by reducing alcohol availability; separating drinking from driving; apprehending and removing the drinking driver from the road; and preventing the recurrence of drinking and driving among drink–driving offenders. This chapter is organized around those four elements of the impaired driving problem.

Table 38.1 Countermeasures to alcohol-related road crashes

Reducing consumption	Separating drinking from driving	Removing the impaired driver from the road	Preventing recurrence of drinking and driving
Reduce availability MLDA	Information and education Public information School-based programs	Enforcement methods Identifying vehicles Sobriety checkpoints Detecting impairment	Specific deterrence Jail sentences Fines
Conditions of sale Civil liability Alcohol control laws	Individual interventions Individual intervention Host intervention Peer intervention Server intervention	Chemical Testing Evidential sensors Preliminary sensors Passive sensors BAC limits	Offender remediation Assessment Education and counseling Treatment
	Alternative transportation programs Designated driver programs Safe ride programs	Media advocacy	Incapacitation License actions Vehicle actions

REDUCING CONSUMPTION

Traditional efforts to reduce drinking and driving have centered on the enforcement of impaired driving laws. Over the last two decades, however, the science of alcohol safety has expanded to include efforts to limit drinking as well as driving after drinking. This has occurred as research has demonstrated the effectiveness of making alcohol less available, particularly to youth, in reducing alcohol-related crashes. This has brought traffic safety into the broader public health arena. Efforts to reduce consumption have taken three forms: (a) limiting total consumption by regulating sales through prohibition of sales to minors in certain locations or jurisdictions and through the manipulation of price through excise taxes; (b) controlling the conditions of service (e.g. limiting "happy hours"); and (c) designing information campaigns to discourage heavy drinking.

Reducing Availability

The general availability of alcohol and its price (discussed elsewhere in this volume) is a factor in all alcohol abuse problems including impaired driving. However, perhaps the best evidence for the relationship of availability to alcohol-related crash involvement is provided by the minimum legal drinking age (MLDA) law in the United States. Though almost all developed nations set a minimum age below which it is illegal to purchase, possess, or consume alcoholic beverages, the USA's age limit of 21 is the highest in the world. The relationship of age to the effects of alcohol-impaired crash risk evident in crash–risk curves shows a relatively steeper rise in the likelihood of fatality for teenage drivers than for adults (Beirness, Simpson & Mayhew, 1993; Zador, 1991). The relationship reflects a combination of lowered tolerance to alcohol, as observed in laboratory studies relating blood alcohol to performance for various age groups (Moscowitz & Burns, 1976), and the relation of inexperience and immaturity to crash risk in general (Mercer, 1986).

Enactment of the MLDA law by the 50 states was stimulated by federal legislation withholding highway funds from states failing to lower the limits for drivers under age 21. Although the purchase of alcohol by underage individuals occurs in on- and off-premises settings, the enforcement of alcohol control laws has taken place primarily in the latter. Over-the-counter sale of alcohol to underage customers in the USA appears to be widespread (Preusser & Williams, 1991). Enforcement is lax, with many more actions against underage drinkers than against outlets (Wagenaar & Wolfson, 1995). It principally takes the form of infrequent "stings", in which purchases are attempted by underage customers working with the police—often underage police. When such enforcement results in well-publicized action against stores, the result has been a decline in illegal sales (McKnight, 1991). Although not strongly enforced, prohibitions against sales to those under age 21 and sanctions for possession by the underage individuals have appeared to combine to reduce significantly underage alcohol-related highway deaths. The National Highway Traffic Safety Administration (NHTSA) reports that the MLDA laws saved 17,000 lives between 1982 and 1997.

Conditions of Sale

Several programs have been introduced to prevent impairment by limiting the locations and times or the methods by which alcohol may be sold or served to prospective drivers. McKnight & Streff (1994) found intoxication of patrons to be associated with risky practices, such as selling doubles, triples, and beer by the pitcher. These risky practices include the hours when alcohol may be sold, the amount of alcohol served (e.g. beer pitchers), the alcohol content (e.g. doubles and triples), the reduced price promotions (e.g. "happy hours"), and the price discounts (e.g. two for one). Some measures are introduced at the discretion of the establishment; others are legislated, generally at the community level. In the USA, sports facilities have been examined as sources of alcohol-impaired driving. Voas et al. (1998d) found that 10% of the drivers came from some sporting events, although they made up only 2% of all over-the-limit drivers. Efforts undertaken at a national level have succeeded in limiting the sale of alcoholic beverages during sports events, particularly toward the end, just before patrons drive home. Although formal evaluation has been lacking, some reduction in beer sales when accompanied by an increase in food and non-alcoholic beverage sales has been reported (NHTSA, 1986). Other measures that have been taken to restrict the availability of alcohol more generally, such as limiting the density of outlets, have been concerned more with the overall consumption of alcohol than with individual episodes of drinking. Although there is general agreement that availability effects consumption and, by extension, alcohol problems, it has been difficult to assess the effect of laws and practices that lower availability (for a review of available studies, see Gruenewald, 1993.)

Research discloses that a leading source of intoxicated drivers are licensed on-premises drinking establishments, such as bars and restaurants, with the proportion of arrested drivers ranging from one-third to half (Wolfe, 1975; Damkot, 1979; Ontario Ministry of Transport and Communications, 1980; Palmer, 1986; Foss et al., 1990). Rydon, Lang & Stockwell (1993) studied risk factors associated with drinking leading to a wide range of harmful incidents (violence, injury, illness) and concluded that "the most significant risk factors were the amount of alcohol consumed and whether obviously intoxicated customers continued to be served". What makes a licensed establishment a highly attractive target for alcohol-impaired driving countermeasures is that the dispensing of alcohol is under the control of servers who are sober and, therefore, in a position to identify seriously impaired drivers.

The early 1980s saw the widespread introduction of programs intended to enable and encourage those who sell alcohol to withhold it from patrons who are, or might become, impaired by alcohol. Efforts to gain intervention by sellers have taken two general forms: legal sanctions against sellers who dispense alcohol irresponsibly, and training programs that teach sellers how to behave responsibly.

Sanctions against the irresponsible sale of alcoholic beverages has itself taken two forms: (a) civil liability laws that allow victims of irresponsible service of alcohol to collect financial damages from sellers; and (b) alcohol control laws imposing administrative and criminal penalties for the illegal sale of alcohol to the underaged and intoxicated. Alcohol prevention measures involving licensed establishments have been summarized by Mosher (1991).

Civil Liability

Laws allowing victims of irresponsible service to collect damages date back to the 1800s and were enacted primarily to protect wives and children from abuse and neglect resulting from the sale or service of alcohol to an establishment's patrons. As the arrival of the automobile shifted the primary locus of harm from the home to the highway, these "dram shop" laws were increasingly applied to the victims of road accidents. Some jurisdictions have passed laws specifically addressing the service of alcohol; other jurisdictions allow suits to be brought under common liability laws. Yet, still other jurisdictions specifically exempt alcohol sellers from liability for damages resulting from the sale of alcohol.

Beyond providing financial compensation to the victims of irresponsible alcohol service, dram shop laws are expected to deter such service and the harm it causes. However, the potential deterrent effect of dram shop laws has been compromised by the extremely low likelihood of a successful suit being brought and by the protection offered to offending establishments by liability insurance. Holder et al. (1990) pointed out that, "the pooling of risk can dilute incentives to adopt preventive serving practices". They noted no relationship between dram shop law and server training, age checking, or refusal of service. Attempts to evaluate the effect of dram shop law upon accidents are thwarted by the antiquity if the law, which prevents pre- and post-comparisons, and fundamental differences among jurisdictions in other alcohol-related measures, which complicate cross-sectional comparisons.

Alcohol Control Laws

In many jurisdictions, it is illegal to sell an alcoholic beverage to purchasers, including the *underage* and the *intoxicated*, considered to be at risk of injury. Violations can result in criminal actions and fines against sellers and administrative action, such as fines and license suspensions, against the establishments.

Service of alcohol to already-intoxicated customers occurs almost entirely in on-premises bars and restaurants. Enforcement of laws prohibiting service to an intoxicated customer is even more rare than enforcement of laws prohibiting sales to an underage customer. Unpublished data collected by Mothers Against Drunk Driving show only one case of the former for every 15 of the latter. Most actions against servers appear to occur when the illegal service resulted in some form of harm, rather than from routine enforcement activity. Effective enforcement requires observing actual service to intoxicated patrons, an activity that demands more time than mounting a sting. Yet, the impact upon service to the intoxicated and the incidence of drink–driving can be highly cost-beneficial. An enforcement activity in which plain clothes officers cited licensed establishments that were serving visibly intoxicated patrons showed a three-fold increase in refusals of service to pseudopatrons simulating signs of intoxication and a one-fourth drop in the percentage of arrested drivers coming from bars and restaurants (McKnight & Streff, 1994). The savings in accident costs were estimated at $90 for each enforcement dollar.

The efficiency of alcohol-control efforts can be enhanced by focusing enforcement on establishments that are the most persistent violators. Arrested drivers queried for the sources of their last drinks can identify the greatest sources of trouble. As early as 1977, the California Department of Beverage Control undertook a program targeting establishments identified by motorists convicted of alcohol-impaired driving as sources of their last drink (Mosher & Wallack, 1979). Presently, several communities, as part of their alcohol-control efforts, target establishments that are the last-drink source in information collected by police or other agencies processing alcohol-impaired drivers.

SEPARATING DRIVING FROM DRINKING

It is possible for individuals to drink heavily and not be exposed to causing alcohol-related crashes if they do not have access to a vehicle. This reduces the proportion of fatal crashes that are alcohol-involved in Third World countries where per capita ownership of motor vehicles is low. In industrialized nations such as the USA, where most drinkers own vehicles, programs directed at separating drinking and drinking and driving offer significant potential for reducing the harm associated with heavy drinking. Such programs generally fall into three categories: public education efforts to persuade the drinkers themselves to take steps to avoid driving after drinking; programs to encourage servers, peers and hosts to prevent intoxicated individuals from driving; and organized efforts by alcohol outlets and community organizations to make provisions for alternative transportation.

Information and Education

The most direct way of getting drivers to avoid alcohol-impaired driving may be through the dissemination of information. From the earliest recognition of an alcohol-impaired driving problem, messages exhorting drivers not to drink before driving or not to drive after drinking have been delivered through many programs in different forms. The method of delivery ranges from public information announcements warning, "if you drink, don't drive", to lengthy educational programs addressing all aspects of the issue.

Public Information

Public information about drinking and driving has been distributed to the driving public through a variety of media including posters; mail-outs; and messages transmitted through the radio, television and print media as paid advertisements and public service announcements (PSAs), which can be widely distributed at low cost. Although messages crafted through formative research (Atkin, 1989) influence knowledge and attitudes, the challenge is getting the media to disseminate them in places and at times where they will reach the public. Gaining sponsorship for paid advertisements and the cooperation of news media seem to offer greater chances of reaching the intended audience. Public information programs disseminating information about drinking and driving have not evidenced a beneficial effect upon alcohol-related crashes (Wilde et al., 1971; Haskins, 1985; Atkin, 1989).

Detecting the small effect that can be anticipated from the relatively small amount of information would require a tightly controlled experiment involving many thousands of drivers—requirements that are largely incompatible.

Where public information has proved most valuable is publicizing alcohol safety efforts that depend upon public awareness for their implementation. These include: (a) enactment and heightened enforcement of laws and regulations for which the general deterrence value obviously depends on public awareness; (b) the availability of alternatives to driving while alcohol-impaired, including designated driver and safe-ride programs; and (c) the means by which drivers can check on their level of sobriety–impairment as they drink. In this context, the role of public information is that of a delivery mechanism for other countermeasures that are themselves effective in reducing alcohol-related crashes and violations.

School-based Programs

Most of the educational efforts to prevent alcohol-impaired driving have been within secondary education programs. Few adults enroll in alcohol- or driving-related courses except when required, doing so because of a traffic offense (see Preventing Recurrence of Drinking and Driving). Driver education courses have devoted up to several classroom hours to the prevention of drinking–driving among licensed teenagers. Improvements in measures of knowledge, attitude and self-reported behavior (KAB) have been covered in several studies summarized by Mann et al. (1986). The use of alcohol-involved crashes or citations as evaluative criteria is precluded by the small samples involved. One area in which education has been particularly effective among teenagers is intervention in the drinking or driving of other teenagers at events where alcohol is available. As previously noted, teenagers, as a group, tend to be more willing to intervene in the drinking of their peers than are adults, who are typically more reluctant to intrude in the behavior of other adults. Programs giving instruction and role-playing practice in intervention skills have also shown KAB improvement.

Much of the development, implementation, and evaluation of educational programs has taken place in the USA, as an element of secondary school driver education. Two developments over the past decade have diminished the treatment of alcohol-impaired driving in secondary schools. One is the elimination of driver education from many school systems, which is the result of a tightened economy. Although alcohol-impaired driving is often taught in health education courses, it is less extensively treated than in driver education courses. The second development reducing treatment of alcohol-impaired driving has been an increase of the legal drinking age from 18 to 21. The fact that secondary school students cannot drink legally and will not be allowed to for some time has led many to believe that education in the use of alcohol is unnecessary.

Individual Intervention

Attempts to encourage direct intervention in further drinking or in driving by the alcohol-impaired have been directed toward social hosts, peers and servers of alcohol.

Host Intervention

The 1996 National Roadside Survey (Voas et al., 1998d) revealed that US drivers coming from the homes of friends accounted for 45% of those with BACs greater than 0.01, although making up only 27% of the drivers surveyed. Drinking in private parties is characteristic of drivers who are under age 25, male, unemployed and drinking with others (Chang & Lapham, 1996). Private gatherings rank second behind licensed establishments as sources of drivers arrested for drinking, which accounts for about a quarter of all those arrested for driving while intoxicated (DWI). However, DWIs from unlicensed drinking locations are relatively more likely to be involved in accidents than those from licensed establishments (Lang & Stockwell, 1991).

Efforts to ensure responsible service of alcohol by social hosts have lagged behind those directed at servers in licensed establishments. First, their wide dispersion leaves efforts to encourage intervention largely to mass media communications. Second, social hosts are not subject to the same legal sanctions as licensed establishments; service to intoxicated guests is not a criminal offense. In the USA, 27 states have statutory or case laws making social hosts liable for injury to third parties, although in more than half the law applies only to service of minors. However, social host liability suits are rare, and, the public does not appear to support social host liability.

The literature reveals little effort to develop, conduct or evaluate prevention programs for social hosts. One program was administered to 271 adults in 18 locations around the USA and evaluated through pre- and post-measures KAB (McKnight, 1987). The pattern of behavior change observed was similar to that found among servers; that is, significant gains were being reported in alcohol service practices but not in preparation for or subsequent dealing with intoxicated guests. The analysis of attitudes disclosed a general disinclination of hosts to interfere with the drinking of adult guests. Two influences were of concern: appearing to be inhospitable and the belief that interference would lead to resentment and loss of friendship.

Peer Intervention

Efforts to enlist the associates of the alcohol-impaired driver in preventing harm from overdrinking are epitomized by the phase, "friends don't let friends drive drunk". The idea of peer intervention includes both keeping drivers from getting drunk and keeping drunks from getting behind the wheel. In most drinking contexts, peers are able to observe drinkers more closely, and thus can recognize the signs of impaired behavior more quickly than servers or hosts.

Although the concept of peer intervention applies to all drinkers, it has been most frequently advanced and studied within the underage population, whose drinking tends to occur surreptitiously in automobiles, remote outdoor locations or homes lacking adult supervision. Lee et al. (1997) found that, of teenagers who drank, 83% did so in someone else's home, 46% outdoors, 41% in a moving vehicle, 38% in their own home and only 22% in a bar or restaurant. Jones-Webb et al. (1997) found that adolescents drinking in homes consumed fewer drinks than those drinking in public places, even after controlling for demographic differences. Wagenaar et al. (1996) found that young people obtained alcohol primarily through purchases by persons of legal age; purchases by those under the legal age and home supplies accounted for most of the rest.

The disinclination of adult hosts to intervene in the drinking of other adults does not appear to be as true of the youths. An evaluation of a secondary school alcohol program found that those completing the program reported no less drinking-and-driving behavior than those taking a standard driver education program and a no-treatment control. However, they appeared to be more likely to intervene in the drinking and driving of their peers (McKnight et al., 1979). Collins & Frey (1992) surveyed college students and found that 87% had intervened with someone. The most frequent form of intervention was driving others home, followed by preventing them from driving, telling them not to drive, having someone else drive, offering to follow them, and threatening to prevent them from driving. Attempts to intervene were successful 80–89% of the time; success did not vary as a function of gender (same or opposite) or the relationship to an intervener. Similar results were reported by Monto et al. (1992), who found that two-thirds of the college students had intervened with others; the incidence of intervention was unrelated to gender, age or race.

Peer intervention instruction has been evaluated through a random experiment. The treatment group was given an alcohol segment containing the peer intervention program, and the control group was given an alcohol program of equal length but without intervention instruction (McKnight et al., 1984). Although pre-post knowledge gains were found for both groups, attitude and enduring intervention behavior change were found only among students receiving intervention training.

Server Intervention

The 1980s saw the rise of server training as a way to reduce the harm resulting from irresponsible service of alcohol. Typically, training programs for wait-persons and bartenders take only a few hours and address: (a) the safety, health, and economic problems of irresponsible service; (b) the laws and regulations governing service; (c) the prevention of alcohol problems through better serving practices, age identification and alternative beverages; and (d) the prevention of impaired driving by identifying impairment, refusing service and providing transportation. Programs for managers also included instruction in promotion, service and transportation policies. By 1990, server training had become something of a cottage industry. The early history and development of programs has been extensively reviewed by Christy (1989).

The effectiveness of server training has been evaluated by Russ & Geller (1986); Gliksman & Single (1988); Mosher et al. (1989); McKnight (1991); Howard-Pitney et al. (1991); Stockwell, Land & Rydon (1993); Rydon et al. (1996); and Saltz & Stanghetta (1997). Most programs have led to significant improvement in server knowledge and attitude, as well as intervention in the form of discouraging overconsumption and encouraging alternative beverages. Improved management practices have included not permitting multiple drink orders, requiring individual drink requests rather than "rounds", and limiting the number of drinks available at last call. However, success in reducing the risk of drink–driving has not been forthcoming. Service to intoxicated patrons and "pseudopatrons" simulating signs of intoxication has not been significantly reduced. These outcomes contrast markedly with those achieved through enforcement of alcohol control laws.

Obstacles to intervention by servers are formidable, including difficulty in observing signs of intoxication while busily engaged in talking and delivering (McKnight, 1991), conflict with a service orientation and possible loss of patron gratuities, patron persistence in seeking service and the "customer is always right" tradition, and frequent lack of management support. Countering these disincentives to intervention requires strict enforcement of alcohol control laws. One of the few programs to evidence a beneficial effect was carried out by a Navy NCO club where tight management control could be exercised (Saltz, 1986).

Despite the lack of demonstrated effectiveness, a number of jurisdictions have mandated the training of servers as a condition of licensing. The results have been no more encouraging than those of optional training. Molof & Kimball (1994) found no apparent change in the rate of drinking or the mean BAC or percentage of patrons with BACs greater than 0.10 associated with the Oregon mandatory training law. However, legislation mandating

server training has generally been tied to a reduction in licensee liability for damages resulting from illegal service by trained servers. To the extent that it relieves management of
liability for harm resulting from illegal and harmful service, it cannot be viewed as a step
toward the responsible sale of alcohol.

Alternative Transportation Programs

Drivers who are too impaired to operate a motor vehicle safely must find another way to
get home or to another destination. Two forms of alternative transportation are designated
driver programs and ride programs.

Designated Driver Programs

Any vehicle driven to a drinking event is a potential source of alcohol-impaired driving.
McKnight et al. (1995) conducted in-depth interviews of 600 individuals convicted of
drink–driving and retraced the decisions involving the event leading to their arrest. They
found that once the individuals left home, impaired driving became almost inevitable. This
finding indicates the importance of having a designated driver available when the possibility of heavy drinking exists. National surveys reveal that most Americans are aware of
the designated driver concept and that 93% reported that using a designated driver is good
or excellent idea (Winsten, 1994). Roadside surveys conducted in 1986 and 1996 found that
the proportion of drivers acting as designated drivers had increased from 5% to 25% (Fell,
Voas & Lange, 1997). In a telephone survey, Lange, Voas & O'Rourke (1998) found that
only 15.3% of their respondents were unfamiliar with the "designated driver" term.
However, the definition offered by 25.9% of those familiar with the term did not require
a designated driver to be identified before the planned drinking event or to avoid consuming alcohol during the event. Apsler, Harding & Goldfein (1987) conducted a national
study of commercial establishments that claimed to have designated driver programs that
offered free soft drinks to the designated drivers and found participation by drivers to be
low. The study of decisions leading to alcohol-impaired driving by McKnight et al. (1995)
showed that many who agree to serve as designated drivers renege after drinking, even
though it means riding with a drunk driver.

Some have expressed concern that the presence of a designated driver might encourage
the owner-drivers to drink more than they would otherwise, making them a greater danger
if either they or the designated drivers change their minds. Apsler et al. (1987) could not
determine if the presence of a designated driver resulted in increased drinking by peers or
if the reported designated drivers actually did the driving. In a later study, Harding &
Caudill (1997) found drinkers reporting small, but significant, increases in consumption
when drinking outside the home when with a designated driver. Therefore, it would appear
that a designated driver program is not as effective as a countermeasure for preventing
alcohol-impaired driving as originally envisioned. It seems to work best when designated
drivers are non-drinkers and drive their own cars to drinking events, thus helping to ensure
that they will indeed do the driving.

Safe Ride Programs

Several communities have organizations that provide free rides largely to individuals who
drive while being alcohol impaired. Harding, Apsler & Goldfein (1988) surveyed 335 ride

services in response to calls from their passengers or the drinking establishments serving them. They found the biggest obstacle to be the inability of more than 15% of these programs to transport the driver's vehicle. Drivers were reluctant to leave their vehicles behind or return to the drinking location to collect their vehicles. The literature failed to assess their value in reducing alcohol-impaired driving, including whether or not their availability increased consumption among potential clients. Ross (1992b) has suggested that one approach to individuals could be to provide them with free taxi rides to drinking establishments. This would ensure their inability to drive away and, consequently, a heavy drinker would be forced to find alternative transportation to return home, as the vehicle would not be at the drinking location.

REMOVING THE IMPAIRED DRIVER FROM THE ROAD

The historic area for action to reduce alcohol-related crashes has been the enforcement by the police of impaired driving laws. British laws against driving horse-drawn carriages existed in the nineteenth century. US laws against drink–driving were enacted at the end of the first decade of the twentieth century. Initially, enforcement duty fell on all police officers. As the number of vehicles on the roadways increased and the traffic laws multiplied, however, the larger urban departments began to establish traffic divisions with specific responsibilities to supervise driver compliance with traffic regulations. In the 1950s and 1960s, as the role of alcohol in the most serious crashes came to be recognized, some departments formed special drink–driving enforcement units. This specialization became more necessary as the impaired driving laws became more complex and the technology of detection and blood alcohol concentration testing became more intricate.

Enforcement Methods

The immediate goal of enforcing alcohol-impaired driving laws is to remove dangerous drivers from the road. However, the ultimate objective is to deter potentially impaired drivers from driving after heavy drinking. Deterrence depends upon both an effective enforcement system and sufficient media coverage to make the public aware of the enforcement effort, which is discussed below. A new enforcement science has developed that focuses on: (a) identifying vehicles driven by impaired drivers; (b) detecting signs of drinking; (c) measuring impairment; and (d) measuring BAC levels.

Identifying Vehicles Driven by Impaired Operators

Current roadside breath-test surveys indicate that approximately 17% of drivers on weekend evenings in the USA have been drinking and 8% have BACs greater than 0.05, making them potentially liable to arrest for impaired driving (Voas et al., 1998d). The first problem for enforcement is to identify the vehicles driven by the over-the-limit drivers. Traditionally, traffic patrol officers come across drinking drivers in the course of enforcing speeding and other traffic regulations. However, without specialized training, they generally miss half or more of the high-BAC drivers with whom they come in contact (Taubenslag & Taubenslag, 1975). Consequently, apprehension rates are low. Borkenstein (1975) estimated that drivers with BAC greater than 0.10 were apprehended only once in 2000 trips by officers trained to detect the special impaired driving cues developed by the NHTSA.

Where high-intensity DUI enforcement operations involving special patrols of specially trained officers are implemented, the apprehension rate rises to about 1 in 300 trips (Voas & Hause, 1987; Beitel, Sharp & Glauz, 1975).

Sobriety Checkpoints

Another approach to contacting impaired drivers is random stopping and assessment of every driver using the road at times and locations where drinking and driving is common. In this procedure, drivers are stopped at random and the officer conducts a brief interview at the driver's window to determine whether there is evidence of drinking. If such evidence is detected, the driver is invited out of the vehicle for further observation. In Australia and Sweden, this random-stopping procedure is coupled with an immediate screening breath test that all motorists are required to provide. In the state of Victoria, large bus-like mobile units are stationed at checkpoints. These units provide facilities in which breath tests can be administered to two or more suspects at a time, and initial paperwork can be done on those drivers who are over the limit. This Australian random-testing procedure has been shown to be effective in reducing alcohol-related crashes (Homel, 1988; Homel, McKay & Henstridge, 1995; Span & Stanislaw, 1995).

In the USA, the Fourth Amendment to the US Constitution precludes random stopping except in structured checkpoint operations. However, even in such operations, the Fourth Amendment is currently interpreted as precluding mandatory breath testing of all individuals stopped. Therefore, a behavioral element is a part of the decision-making process at American checkpoint operations. By surveying drivers passing through checkpoints, Lund & Jones (1987), Ferguson, Wells & Lund (1993) and Wells et al. (1997) have found that officers miss as many of 50% of the drivers who have BACs higher than the 0.10 limit, partially because of the relatively brief 30–60 second interview permitted at the checkpoint. Despite this limitation, research has clearly demonstrated that, in the USA, checkpoints are effective in reducing alcohol-impaired driving crashes (Ross, 1992a; Levy, Shea & Asch, 1989; Foss et al., 1997; Lacey, Jones & Fell, 1997; Voas, Rhodenizer & Lynn, 1985; Stuster & Blowers, 1995).

The impact of this checkpoint technique on drinking-and-driving accidents throughout the USA has been generally limited because sobriety checkpoints are viewed by enforcement agencies as expensive and complex to mount (Ross, 1992a). However, Stuster & Blowers (1995) have demonstrated that checkpoints employing relatively few officers (four to six) can be as effective as the much larger checkpoints that are normally mounted. Most communities should be able to use small checkpoints at least once or twice a month. Currently, however, checkpoints are primarily mounted three or four times a year during national holidays. In states such as California, Tennessee and North Carolina, where the state police assist communities in operating several checkpoints each month throughout the year, there is considerable evidence of their effectiveness (Lacey et al., 1997; Foss et al., 1997; Stuster & Blowers, 1995).

Detecting Impairment

In Australia and Sweden, any driver stopped can be tested for alcohol (Homel, 1988). In Britain, drivers can be tested under three conditions: when in a crash, when committing a traffic offense, or when an officer suspects drinking. Ross (1973), in a detailed study of the British Road Safety Act, indicated that this procedure was highly effective in reducing nighttime crashes. In the USA, whatever the reason for stopping the vehicle, the officer must have probable cause to believe the driver is impaired before requiring a BAC test. This is a three-step process: (a) assessment for visible signs of drinking; (b) a sobriety test; and (c) a chemical test.

Visible Signs

The first step in the measurement process involves a brief interview of the driver in his/her vehicle, during which an officer makes an initial determination as to whether the driver is likely to be impaired. The research literature does not encourage confidence in the ability of people to correctly estimate alcohol impairment in relation to legal BAC limits. Physicians examining suspected drinking drivers in Scandinavia identified as impaired only about 50% of those with BACs greater than 0.10. Studies by Langenbucher & Nathan (1983) and Pisoni & Martin (1989) showed only police officers to be reasonably accurate in classifying drinkers in terms of impairment. Work by Pagano & Taylor (1980), Taubenslag & Taubenslag (1975), Vingilis, Adlaf & Chung (1982), Jones & Lund (1985) & Compton (1985), by contrast, found that even the police were highly inaccurate.

Teplin & Lutz (1985) developed a scale for using observable signs to enable hospital staff to judge the presence of alcohol in accident victims arriving at emergency rooms. They found a correlation of 0.83 between the *number* of signs observed and BAC level. Use of prescribed cut-off points yielded probabilities of correctly identifying impaired victims ranging between 0.72 and 0.87. Much of the correlation reported came from accuracy identifying victims with very high blood alcohol levels. McKnight et al. (1997) undertook a study in which 1250 drinkers with 0.08–0.12% BAC were judged by casual observers in social situations. Observers correctly identified alcohol-impaired drinkers (>0.04), true positives, over half the time, and misidentified the unimpaired as impaired, false positives, about a quarter of the time. Those trained in using cues and observing only a few drinkers at a time were the most accurate. In judging intoxication (BAC > 0.08%), observers were as accurate, but more conservative, with true positives at slightly more than 50% and false positives less than 10%. Cues of intoxication were slurring of speech, fumbling objects, sloppy appearance and clothing, rudeness, hostility and stumbling, in order of increasing impairment.

Sobriety Tests

Once an initial determination has been made that the driver may be impaired through an interview at the driver's window, the officer invites the driver out of the vehicle to conduct a set of "sobriety tests". For decades, police have used a variety of performance tests to assess the degree of impairment for drivers suspected of alcohol-impaired driving. The admissibility of these tests as evidence relied entirely upon court acceptance of their validity as indices of inability to drive safely. A set of Standardized Field Sobriety Tests (SFSTs) was developed in the NHTSA by Tharp, Burns & Moskowitz (1981), based upon measured relationships between performance on various tasks and measured blood alcohol level. The three tests showing the most reliable relationships are: (a) the *horizontal gaze nystagmus (HGN)* test, a method for observing the irregularities in pupillary motion of the eye tracking a stimulus moving horizontally across a field of view; (b) the *walk-and-turn (WAT)* test, which determines the ability of an individual to remember directions, walk a straight line and execute a turn in place; (c) the *one-leg-stand (OLS)* test, which determines the ability of an individual to count in a prescribed manner while maintaining balance on one foot.

The US government funded the training of officers throughout the country in using these standardized tests. Several studies have indicated that they are useful to the police in apprehending impaired drivers (Burns & Dioquino, 1997; Anderson, Schweitz & Snyder, 1983). These tests play two roles in drink-driving enforcement. First, they provide probable cause to require a breath test, which is considered more intrusive than a sobriety test. Second, they provide evidence of impairment when suspects refuse to take a breath test, results of the breath test are challenged, or the defense claims that the results of the breath test do not provide a true indication of impairment.

Of the three SFST measures, HGN is by far the most reliable indicator of blood alcohol level and the only one that can identify drivers just above the statutory limits of 0.08% and 0.10% (Perrine et al., 1992). Moreover, it is the primary measure with any validity in identifying drivers at the low BACs, including the 0.04% level imposed on drivers of commercial vehicles and the even lower levels called for under "zero tolerance" laws (McKnight et al., 1997).

Chemical Testing

For the first half of the twentieth century, the primary basis for convicting operators of driving while impaired was through the testimony of the arresting officers regarding their appearance and behavior. However, since World War II, a movement has grown based on the work earlier in the century of Widmark (1932) to define the offense in terms of blood alcohol concentration. The first country to do so was Norway in 1936, which defined the impaired driver offense as operating a vehicle with a 0.05 BAC (Voas, 1982). This *per se* definition of the impaired driving offense has gradually been adopted by European nations, the USA and Austria over the last 30 years. The ability to use a particular BAC limit as a definition of impaired driving depended upon the development of accurate and inexpensive methods to measure blood alcohol levels. Initially, BACs were measured either in blood or in urine. However, the development of an inexpensive breath test device, the "Breathalyzer", by Borkenstein & Smith (1961) in the 1950s (which could be operated by police officers with minimal training) increased the availability and ease of BAC measurement and extended the utility of the *per se* definition of impaired driving. Initially, the breath test was primarily used in the USA, with Europe continuing to use blood samples.

A significant advance occurred in the mid-1960s, with the development of disposable breath-test devices that could be used by the police in the field. This permitted Sweden to initiate its innovative program of sobriety checkpoints, where drivers were stopped at random and tested using these disposal devices. Field units using either a semiconductor or a fuel cell sensor were developed in the early 1970s. These permitted an even more convenient and accurate method of breath testing, using small hand-held units about the size of a cigarette package, which police could use in the field (Moulden & Voas, 1975). The availability of these devices made programs such as the Random Testing in Australia possible.

A final technological development in the breath-testing field was the production of passive breath test units, which could be integrated with police flash lights to allow officers to rapidly screen motorists at the roadside (Voas, 1983; Lund & Jones, 1987). Thus, in current enforcement, three types of breath-test devices can be distinguished: (a) evidential test used to collect data for presentation in court; (b) preliminary breath tests used by officers in the field to confirm that drivers are over the limit before taking them to the police station for an evidential test; and (c) passive sensors used by officers early in their investigation to determine whether there is evidence of heavy drinking.

Evidentiary Breath Testers (EVTs)

If there is probable cause to suspect that a driver is over the limit, the individual may be taken to the police station for an evidential breath test. These semi-automatic test devices are generally set to perform a calibration, take two breath samples and print the result. In the USA, the NHTSA has established model specifications for these devices (NHTSA, 1992). The operator must ensure that the suspect takes nothing into his/her mouth for 20 minutes before the test. The operator must also inform the suspect before the test that refusal will result in license suspension.

Preliminary Breath Testers (PBTs)

PBTs are small hand-held units that can be carried in the field by police officers and used to measure BACs. These devices assist the police in determining whether there is probable cause to arrest a potential offender to then be arrested and taken to the police station for an evidential test. These devices have proved to be accurate evidential breath-test machines used for collecting court data (Frank & Flores, 1989). Distribution of preliminary breath testers to police officers has been shown to increase the number of arrests of alcohol-impaired driving offenders. An econometrics study by Saffer & Chaloupka (1989) showed that states with PBT had lower alcohol-related fatality rates than did states without these laws.

Passive Alcohol Sensors (PASs)

Since evidential and preliminary breath testers insert a small tube into the mouth to collect the sample, their use is generally viewed as a "search" under the US Constitution and, therefore, must be "reasonable". This means that the officer must suspect drinking and have probable cause to arrest the offender before requiring either an EVT or a PBT. The PAS, on the other hand, collects expired air from 2–6 inches in front of the driver's face. This expired air is mixed with ambient air, so the measurement lacks precision; however, it is reasonably sensitive to the presence of alcohol (Voas, 1983). The ability of police officers to detect drinking through their sense of smell is limited by the fact that ethanol, the active impairing drug, is essentially odorless. What the nose detects is the additional substances in different types of drinks (e.g. Bourbon, Scotch, vodka), their special tastes. Further, olfactory sensitivity varies considerably among officers. As a result, passive sensing can be useful for detecting drinking when officers have limited contact with the driver, such as at checkpoints, or when enforcing zero tolerance laws where low BACs must be detected. Farmer et al. (1999), in the 1996 National Roadside Survey, demonstrated that using a passive sensor on randomly stopped nighttime drivers detected 37% of the drivers with BACs between 0.05 and 0.08, 63% of the drivers with BACs between 0.08 and 0.10, and 73% of the drivers with BACs of at least 0.10. Since, as noted above, officers typically miss 50% of the drivers with BACs greater than 0.10 at checkpoints, passive sensors offer the possibility of increasing significantly the detection rates in such operations.

BAC Limits

In most countries, the police have the right to require the driver to take a breath test if they have stopped the vehicle legally. In the USA, however, the Fourth Amendment requires that "searches be reasonable". Therefore, an officer can require a driver to provide a breath sample for a BAC test only if he/she has probable cause to make an arrest. If there is probable cause, the US Supreme Court in the Smerber vs. California case determined that a chemical test involved the collection of physical evidence and, therefore, could be forced on the driver. However, most police departments did not want to get involved in restricting offenders and forcibly taking blood samples. Therefore, "implied consent" legislation was passed by the states under which drivers implicitly agreed to submit to a measure of their blood alcohol when they accept a license to drive. This allows the Department of Motor Vehicles to suspend that driver's permit if he/she refuses to take the test. The significance of the EVT was further enhanced when 40 states adopted the administrative license revocation (ALR) laws. The ALR laws provide that, if a breath test is taken and found to be higher than the state BAC limit, the offender will also have his/her license administratively suspended.

The specific levels that define the maximum BAC at which one may legally drive vary considerably from one country to another, as well as between jurisdictions within some countries. For example, in North America and some European countries, the legal limit is relatively high, 0.08–0.10%. In Australia, New Zealand and some Scandinavian countries, 0.05% is the legal limit. A review by Moskowitz, Burns & Williams (1985) revealed that alcohol impairment begins at as little as a 0.02 BAC. Analyses of roadside survey and crash data by Zador (1991) and Hurst (1973) have shown that at a BAC of 0.05 or greater, there is a significant increase in the risk of involvement in an alcohol-related fatal crash. However, only about 10% of fatal crashes in the USA involve BACs of less than 0.10 (NHTSA, 1998). Blood alcohol concentrations above this level account for most of those at a highly elevated relative risk and also the largest numbers of alcohol-related fatalities.

A recent trend in the USA has been to establish lower BAC limits for youthful drivers. These so-called "zero tolerance" laws make it illegal for those under age 21 to operate a vehicle with any alcohol in their systems. Reductions in nighttime single-vehicle accidents following passage of zero tolerance laws have been reported (Blomberg, 1992; Hingson, Heeren & Winter, 1994; Hingson, Heeren & Morelock, 1986; Hingson et al., 1991; Voas, Tippetts & Fell, under review). However, the extent to which the laws are actually enforced is open to question. Very low BACs rarely evidence themselves in observable driving behavior; therefore, few arrests appear to occur at low levels. Voas, Lange & Tippetts (1998a) found that police principally used the zero tolerance law in the state of California to cite young drivers over the adult limit. Thus, the total number of drinking and driving arrests showed only a small increase. Further, there was little evidence that young drivers targeted by the law perceived a significant increase in risk of apprehension. Still, the California zero tolerance law was associated with a decline in the number of underage drinking drivers in fatal crashes—possibly because the law changed peer attitudes regarding drinking and driving.

Media Advocacy

It is generally accepted that new laws and enforcement programs must be publicized to be effective. If the public is unaware of a change in the law or an increase in its enforcement, it is unlikely that it will effect their drinking and driving.

Studies such as that by Blomberg (1992) and Voas & Hause (1987) in Stockton, California, demonstrated that publicity doubled the impact of new laws and new enforcement efforts. Two types of approaches have been used to publicize special programs or laws.

The traditional approach to publicizing new laws has been to create public service announcements (PSAs) through a series of steps: (a) identifying the target group at which the law or program is aimed; (b) identifying the media that reaches that target group; (c) developing an appeal that will gain the attention of the target group (such as well-known athletic figures); and (d) creating a message that is to be conveyed. The strength of this approach is it provides relatively professional, high-quality messages. Its weakness is that the station manager must be persuaded to run the PSAs at times when the target audience is likely to be watching. This may require considerable effort by community public relations personnel.

A more recent alternative is to apply "media advocacy" procedures, which begin with the collection of data relevant to a community, such as the number of drivers killed in the last year. Community spokespersons announce the information at news conferences. This interesting new information is released to the media through community leaders. The appearance of these leaders on local television or in local newspapers serves to persuade the public that the issue is important in their community and that action is supported by the local leadership. Appearing on television and in local papers serves to commit the participating leaders to the prevention program and facilitates recruiting them into the community coalition dealing with the problem. This process is also designed to motivate action organizations, such as the police, by featuring officers and police chiefs in news events and having community spokespersons praise the department, indicating the importance of the department's enforcement actions. Thus, although the media advocacy effort ultimately delivers a message to the drinking driver target group, in the process it also helps to organize and empower community leaders to take action to support the program. A community-wide media program described by Holder & Treno (1997) provided a demonstration of this process.

PREVENTING RECURRENCE OF DRINKING AND DRIVING

Once impaired drivers have been identified and removed from the road, it is possible to move from the general deterrence aimed at all operators on the highway to specific deterrence, using remedies frequently tailored to the characteristics of an individual driver and his/her offense. Three general areas of action can be distinguished: (a) applying traditional penalties such as jail and fines, directed at causing sufficient discomfort to deter the individual from repeating the offense; (b) suspending the driver's license to prevent future drinking and driving; and (c) requiring attendance at treatment or educational programs directed at assisting the offender to avoid future impaired driving and promoting recovery from dependence on alcohol. Because a drinking–driving conviction allows the state to identify high-risk drivers, and because it brings these drivers under the control of the courts, communities are presented with a special opportunity to attack the impaired-driving problem. Unfortunately, in the USA, most current remedial programs have shown limited success, as one-third to one-half of the drivers convicted of impaired driving repeat the offense.

Specific Deterrence

Traditional penalties, such as jails and fines, have generally been justified on two bases: (a) a *general deterrent* effect on those not yet convicted of impaired driving; and (b) a *specific deterrent* effect on offenders currently suffering the penalties by promoting avoidance of future offenses. Because of these two bases for justifying traditional penalties, arguments over sanctions are often confused by the conflicting opinions of those focusing on general, as compared to specific, deterrence. A further confusion is presented by the interests of the government and the courts in using fines to promote "self-sufficiency" in the criminal justice effort by paying for such activities such as breath tests, police patrols and court expenses.

Jail Sentences

There is limited evidence for the general deterrent effectiveness of jail sentences for reducing impaired driving by the public as a whole (Nichols & Ross, 1989; Zador et al., 1988; Jones et al., 1988). However, there is little evidence that this sanction has a specific deterrent effect on the offenders who are actually incarcerated (Voas, 1986; Simpson, Mayhew & Beirness, 1996). Moreover, its use for DWI offenders is limited by the cost of incarceration and overcrowded jails (Voas, 1985). Nevertheless, the availability of jail sanctions is an important motivational tool for the courts. It provides a penalty for failure to conform to the probation requirements established by the court (Voas et al., 1999). Lower cost, alternative confinement procedures, such as electronic house arrest, have been shown as ineffective in reducing recidivism (Jones et al., 1996). Finally, the authority to impose a jail sanction may provide the legal basis for referring offenders to residential treatment programs. Programs such as the DWI Center in Prince Georges County, Maryland, have significantly reduced DWI recidivism in first and multiple offenders (Voas & Tippetts, 1990).

Fines

Other than an early report by Homel (1988) in Australia, there is no reliable evidence that fines have any general or specific deterrent effect on impaired driving. However, they can play an important role in helping to finance some essential enforcement activities such as breath testing. Yet, many fines are either uncollected or paid over a long time as courts tend to accept defendant pleads that they are either indigent or do not have the funds to pay the fines. Further, fines are frequently waived to allow the offender to pay for the required treatment program.

Offender Remediation

A variety of programs have been developed and administered to cope with alcohol-impaired driving. For the lack of a better term, "remedial" will be applied to the educational, counseling and treatment programs designed to deal the population of drivers found guilty of alcohol-impaired driving.

Assessment

Convicted drinking drivers in the USA represent a heterogeneous group (Perrine, Peck & Fell, 1989). Some offenders can be classified as high-risk drivers who drink; others might be classified as problem drinkers who drive. It has been hypothesized that some first offenders are apprehended for drink–driving because they lack an understanding of the effect of alcohol on performance and they lack knowledge of the law. Other offenders are apprehended principally because they are addicted to alcohol and have little or no control over their drinking. Because of wide variations in the characteristics of first offenders, courts have established the capability to conduct presentencing investigations, using interviews and brief questionnaires to separate first offenders into two broad classes: *social drinkers* and *problem drinkers*. Those identified through this assessment process as *social drinkers* are assigned by the courts to a relatively brief educational program involving 10–12 hours of instructions over 3–4 weeks. Offenders assessed to be *problem drinkers* are assumed to have limited conscious control of their drinking; therefore, they require intensive treatment to overcome their alcohol abuse or dependence problem (Wells-Parker & Popkin, 1994). Several reviews of the assessment instruments used in this process have demonstrated that they are reasonably accurate in discriminating between *social* and *problem* drinkers (Popkin et al., 1988; Lapham, Skipper & Simpson, 1997).

Education and Counseling

Drivers not previously found guilty of an alcohol offense are generally given the opportunity to participate in programs involving some combination of education or counseling to avoid or shorten the period of license suspension. Perhaps the first well-documented remedial effort designed to deal specifically with alcohol-impaired driving was that reported by Steward & Malfetti (1970). Although the substance of education and counseling programs varies from one program to another, the most common focal points are: (a) the effects of alcohol—from its general effect upon health and everyday functioning to its specific effects upon safe operation of motor vehicles; (b) the relationship between amount and rate of consumption to the blood alcohol level and impairment; (c) the laws governing drinking and driving and the sanctions for which violators are at risk; and (d) the influences that lead to heavy drinking and ways of neutralizing them.

The effectiveness of various court-mandated remedial programs in reducing drink–driving recidivism among DUI offenders has been extensively studied. The results of these studies have been reviewed and synthesized (Voas, 1972; Struckman-Johnson & Mushill, 1976; Swenson & Clay, 1977; Mann et al., 1983). These reviewers found that, although most of the studies faced serious methodological problems that undermined their conclusiveness, certain programs evidenced some small impact upon recidivism when compared with the absence of any program.

The alternative to education and counseling programs is generally suspension of licenses. McKnight & Voas (1991) found that without some form of education, counseling or treatment program, the effects of suspension upon alcohol-impaired driving lasted only as long as the driver was incapacitated by the license suspension. Further, this could be attributed to a reduction in driving exposure rather than any selective effect upon drink–driving itself. An extensive meta-analysis of 215 independent evaluations of remedial programs by Wells-Parker et al. (1995) found remedial programs yielding an average reduction of 8–9%, both in recidivism for alcohol-impaired driving offenses and in alcohol-related accidents. Alternatively, licensing sanctions alone "tended to be associated with reduction in occurrence of non-alcohol . . . crashes". The effects of the individual interventions could not be readily differentiated because the evaluations addressed varying combinations of remediation. Moreover, the populations addressed varied considerably from one intervention to another. However, educational programs for first offenders predominated.

Treatment

Historically, first offenders were considered candidates for education and counseling, with treatment being considered only after two or more convictions. More recently, however, many jurisdictions are providing assessment programs in which drivers are screened at the outset to determine the nature and extent of their drinking problem. The requirements of effective treatment for alcohol dependency goes beyond drink–driving and is addressed separately in another chapter of this volume.

For many, alcohol-impaired driving is a symptom of a more fundamental alcohol dependency. Recognition that many convicted drink–drivers exhibit drinking problems and are alcohol-dependent dates back to the late 1960s (Waller et al., 1967; Selzer et al., 1967). Successful treatment of alcohol-dependent drivers requires a more intensive and extensive form of remediation than education or counseling. Where education and counseling generally focuses upon separating drinking from driving, treatment addresses the use of alcohol itself. Indeed, a large segment of the patient population being treated for alcohol dependency has entered treatment because of an alcohol-impaired driving conviction.

Incapacitation

Although most drivers in fatal crashes do not have records of alcohol-impaired driving, being convicted of a prior offense raises the risk of being involved in an alcohol-related fatal crash (Simpson et al., 1996; Hedlund & Fell, 1995). Preventive efforts directed toward previous offenders can use sanctions to limit driving, including license suspension and revocation, vehicle impoundment and jail. Although the immediate effect of these sanctions is to reduce driving, they are also expected to create an unpleasant condition that deters future alcohol-impaired driving. In addition, participation in the remedial programs discussed earlier is often motivated almost entirely by the requirement to complete such programs as a condition for relief from sanctions.

License Actions

Research supports for the effectiveness of license suspension as a way to reduce DWI recidivism and alcohol-related crashes among individuals convicted of impaired driving (Peck, Sadler & Perrine, 1985; Nichols & Ross, 1989; McKnight & Voas, 1991; Ross, 1992a). This action is, however, only partially effective because the effects of suspension are generally confined to the period of the suspension itself, and for first offenders these periods are usually relatively short. A second offense is considered indicative of a fundamental alcohol problem and is typically accompanied by a much longer suspension. Further, multiple offenses can result in revocation of the driver's license, thus requiring drivers to seek licenses as new drivers. Yet even the longer suspension and revocation periods may not be sufficient to provide an opportunity for treatment interventions to have an impact on impaired driving.

Driving on a suspended license is common because it cannot be detected by the police unless drivers are apprehended for another infraction. It estimated that up to 75% of US drivers suspended for DWI continue to drive to some extent (Nichols & Ross, 1989; Ross & Gonzales, 1988). Where special insurance coverage is required for license reinstatement, it is common for drivers to continue operating on a suspended license rather than seek reinstatement (Voas & Tippetts, 1996b). However, a combination of reduced and/or more careful driving leads to lower accident and recidivism rates for drivers on suspension (Blomberg, Preusser & Ulmer, 1987; Voas, Tippetts & Taylor, 1998c; Voas & Tippetts, 1996a).

Many states offer drivers the opportunity to regain licenses before the end of a suspension period where the suspension would cause a hardship. Popkin et al. (1983) found that, as might be expected, drivers receiving hardship licenses had a higher incidence of accidents and violations than those not legally permitted to drive. Voas & McKnight (1991) found that the availability of a hardship license had little effect in reducing the general deterrent value of the license suspension penalty. A study by Wells-Parker & Cosby (1987) revealed that the hardship imposed by suspension rarely involved loss of employment. However, the net effect of hardship licensing depends upon the balance between the costs of higher accident rates and the benefits of increased mobility, a trade-off not yet calculated.

Administrative License Suspension

It is well established that the deterrent effect of any penalty is benefited by certainty and immediacy (Ross, 1984). License suspension through the court system often involves extensive delay of, and frequently escape from, adverse consequences. To overcome this problem, many jurisdictions have passed laws allowing the drivers' licensing agency to suspend licenses administratively for drivers showing blood alcohol levels greater than the legal limit. Forty of the 50 states in the USA have enacted what has come to be known as Administrative License Revocation (ALR) laws, although licenses are typically suspended rather than revoked. Some jurisdictions allow police to confiscate licenses on the spot and others require an action by the Department of Motor Vehicles. In some jurisdictions, the suspension is immediate; in others, the drivers are permitted to continue driving for a short period. Based on a decision of the US Supreme Court, all ALR laws require that offenders have the opportunity to request a hearing.

Zador et al. (1988) and Klein (1989) have demonstrated that the ALR law has a general deterrent effect, as evidenced by a reduction in alcohol-impaired driving offenses among the general driving public following passage of laws. Voas et al. (1998c) and Beirness et al. (1997) have shown that ALR laws have also reduced recidivism among convicted alcohol-impaired driving offenders. Zobeck & Williams (1994) reviewed 46 studies on administrative license suspension as part of a meta-analysis of literature on the effects of alcohol-impaired driving control efforts, and found an average reduction of 5% in alcohol-related crashes and a reduction in fatal crashes of 26%.

Vehicle Actions

There is considerable evidence that, in the USA, efforts to prevent high-risk, impaired driving offenders from driving on public roads by suspending their driving privileges are failing. Evidence of this is shown by the large number of suspended drivers who are apprehended while operating a vehicle illegally and who do not reinstate their licenses when eligible to do so. The Department of Motor Vehicles in California estimates that there are close to 1 million suspended drivers in that state and that only 16% of the suspended drivers attempt to reinstate their licenses when eligible (Tashima & Helander, 1999). Voas & Tippetts (1994) found that half of the first offenders suspended for 90 days in the state of Washington were still suspended 4 years later. To deal with this illicit driving problem, states are beginning to pass legislation aimed at depriving the DUI offenders who are caught driving a vehicle while suspended (Voas, 1992).

Ignition Interlocks

The most permissive vehicle action for preventing DUI offenders from driving while impaired is placing interlocks in the ignition to prevent an impaired driver from operating the vehicle. Before the engine can be started, the driver must provide an alcohol-free breath sample. After the initial test to start the vehicle, the system is designed to require tests every few minutes, thus preventing a confederate from starting the engine for an alcohol-impaired driver (Voas & Marques, 1992). Unlike license suspension or other forms of immobilization, interlocks permit cars to be driven if the operator is not at a BAC < 0.03.

Eight studies of interlock programs conducted under the authority of a local court or a motor vehicle department has found them to be more effective than full license suspension in preventing recidivism among alcohol-impaired drivers (Voas et al., 1999). However, seven of the studies found that, once the interlock is removed, offenders have the same recidivism rate as suspended offenders. A major problem for the implementation of alcohol interlocks in the USA is that only a small proportion (generally less than 10%) of DUI offenders are willing to install them in order to drive legally. Only when the court is willing to make the alternative incarceration are the majority of drink–driving offenders motivated to accept an interlock (Voas et al., in press).

Vehicle Impoundment

A more severe form of vehicle action is impounding the vehicle of an offender so that it cannot be operated by either the offender or anyone else. Vehicle impoundment laws are generally applied to multiple alcohol-impaired driving offenders or to those convicted of driving while suspended. Studies of these laws in California (DeYoung, 1997), Ohio (Voas, Tippetts & Taylor, 1997, 1998b), and the province of Manitoba, Canada (Beirness et al., 1997), have demonstrated that impounding a vehicle for 1–6 months at the time of arrest reduces recidivism of multiple DUI offenders.

One problem of using vehicle impoundment or forfeiture is that it involves taking private property. In many cases, it is the property of someone other than the offender, because approximately half of those apprehended for unlicensed driving are operating vehicles owned by others. The vehicle license plate, on the other hand, is state property. A law enacted in Minnesota permits the police officer to seize the vehicle license plate when an individual is apprehended for their third alcohol-impaired driving offense, immobilizing the car without actually taking possession of it. The plate is destroyed and offenders cannot register another vehicle or obtain a plate until they can demonstrate that their drivers' licenses have been reinstated. A study by Rodgers (1994) indicated that this law reduced recidivism among third-time offenders.

KEY WORKS AND SUGGESTIONS FOR FURTHER READING

U.S. Government Accounting Office (1989). *Surgeon General's Workshop on Drunk Driving: Background Papers, December 14–16, 1988.* Washington, DC: Office of the Surgeon General, US Department of Health and Human Services, Public Health Service.

This collection of papers provides authoritative summaries of the key issues: causes of drink driving, prevalence, effectiveness of different prevention strategies and discussions of legal issues.

National Institutes of Health (Public Health Service) (1996). *Alcohol Health & Research World. Vol. 20(4).* Springfield, VA: National Technical Information Service, US Department of Commerce.

Another set of authoritative reviews.

Ross, H.L. (1981). *Deterring the Drinking Driver: Legal Policy and Social Control,* 2nd edn. Lexington, MA: Lexington Books.

A classic text that provides theories that have guided policing practices in this area for the past three decades.

Ross, H.L. (1992). *Confronting Drunk Driving: Social Policy for Saving Lives.* New Haven, CT: Yale University Press.

This book in many ways updates the previous one in light of accumulated evidence regarding what works in the prevention of drink–driving.

REFERENCES

Anderson, T.E., Schweitz, R.M. & Snyder, M.B. (1983). *Field Evaluation of a Behavioral Test Battery for DWI.* Technical Report DOT-HS-806-475. Washington, DC: National Highway Traffic Safety Administration.

Apsler, R., Harding, W. & Goldfein, J. (1987). *The review and assessment of designated driver programs as an alcohol countermeasure approach.* Final Report HS 807 108, February). Washington, DC: US Department of Transportation, National Highway Traffic Administration.

Atkin, C.K. (1989). Advertising and marketing: mass communication effects on drinking and driving. In *Surgeon General's Workshop on Drunk Driving: Background Papers. Washington, DC, December 14–16, 1988* (pp. 15–34). Rockville, MD: US Department of Health and Human Services, Public Health Service, Office of the Surgeon General.

Beirness, D.J., Simpson, H.M. & Mayhew, D.R. (1993). Predicting crash involvement among young drivers. In H.-D. Utzelmann, G. Berghaus & G. Kroj (Eds), *Alcohol, Drugs and Traffic Safety— T92. Proceedings of the 12th International Conference* (pp. 885–890). Cologne: Verlag TUV Rhineland.

Beirness, D.J., Simpson, H.M., Mayhew, D.R. & Jonah, B.J. (1997). The impact of administrative license suspension and vehicle impoundment for DWI in Manitoba. In C. Mercier-Guyon (Ed.), *Proceedings of the 14th International Conference on Alcohol, Drugs and Traffic Safety* (pp. 919–925). Annecy, France: Centre d'Etudes et de Recherches en Medecine du Trafic.

Beitel, G.A., Sharp, M.C. & Glauz, W.D. (1975). Probability of arrest while driving under the influence of alcohol. *Journal of Studies on Alcohol,* **36**, 109–115.

Blomberg, R. (1992). *Lower BAC Limits for Youth: Evaluation of the Maryland 0.02 Law.* DOT HS 806 807. Washington, DC: US Department of Transportation.

Blomberg, R., Preusser, D. & Ulmer, R. (1987). *Deterrent Effects of Mandatory License Suspension for DWI Convictions.* DOT-HS-807-138. Washington, DC: National Highway Traffic Safety Administration.

Borkenstein, R.F. (1975). Problems of enforcement, adjudication and sanctioning. In S. Israelstam & S. Lambert (Eds), *Alcohol, Drugs and Traffic Safety* (pp. 655–662). Toronto: Addiction Research Foundation of Ontario.

Borkenstein, R.F., Crowther, R.F., Shumate, R.P., Ziel, W.B. & Zylman, R. (1974). The role of the drinking driver in traffic accidents (The Grand Rapids study). *Blutalkohol,* **II**(1), 1–132.

Borkenstein, R.F. & Smith, H.W. (1961). The breathalyzer and its application. *Medicine, Science and the Law,* **1**, 13.

Burns, M. & Dioquino, T. (1997). *Florida Validation Study of the Standardized Field Sobriety Test (SFST) Battery.* Project No. AL-97-05-14-01. ••: State Safety Office, Department of Transportation, State of Florida.

Chang, I. & Lapham, S.C. (1996). Validity of self-reported criminal offenses and traffic violations in screening of driving-while-intoxicated offenders. *Alcohol and Alcoholism,* **31**, 583–590.

Christy, C.C. (1989). Server Intervention/Responsible Beverage Service (SI/RBS): A Source Document Addressing Related Literature. Unpublished doctoral thesis, George Peabody College for Teachers, Vanderbilt University, Nashville, TN.

Collins, M.D. & Frey, J.H. (1991). Drunken driving and informal social control: the case of peer intervention. *Deviant Behavior,* **13**, 73–87.

Compton, R.P. (1985). *Pilot Test of Selected DWI Procedures for Use at Sobriety Checkpoints.* Technical Report DOT-HS-806-724. Washington, DC: National Highway Traffic Safety Administration.

Damkot, D.K. (1979). Alcohol and the rural driver. In *Incurrence in Alcoholism*. Vol. VI (pp. 319–325). New York: Grune and Stratton.

DeYoung, D.J. (1997). *An Evaluation of the Specific Deterrent Effect on Vehicle Impoundment on Suspended, Revoked and Unlicensed Drivers in California*. Final Report No. DOT HS 808 727. Washington, DC: Department of Transportation, National Highway Traffic Safety Administration (NHTSA).

Farmer, C.M., Wells, J.K., Ferguson, S.A. & Voas, R.B. (1999). Field evaluation of the PAS III passive alcohol sensor. *Journal of Crash Prevention and Injury Control*, **1**(1), 55–61.

Fell, J., Voas, R.B. & Lange, J.E. (1997). Designated driver concept: extent of use in the USA. *Journal of Traffic Medicine*, **25**(3–4), 109–114.

Ferguson, S.A., Wells, J.K. & Lund, A.K. (1993). The role of passive alcohol sensors in detecting alcohol-impaired drivers at sobriety checkpoints. Paper presented at the Insurance Institute for Highway Safety, Arlington, VA.

Foss, R.D., Beirness, D.J., Tolbert, W.G., Wells, J.K. & Williams, A.F. (1997). Effect of an intensive sobriety checkpoint program on driving–driving in North Carolina. In C. Mercier-Guyon (Ed.), *Proceedings of the 14th International Conference on Alcohol, Drugs and Traffic Safety* (pp. 943–948). Annecy, France: Centre d'Études et de Recherches en Medecine du Trafic.

Foss, R.D., Voas, R.B., Beirness, D.J. & Wolfe, A.C. (1990). *Minnesota 1990 State-wide Drinking and Driving Roadside Survey*. Contract No. 525493. St. Paul, MN: Minnesota Department of Public Safety, Office of Traffic Safety.

Frank, J.F. & Flores, A.L. (1989). *The Accuracy of Evidential Breath Testers at Low BACs*. Report No. DOT HS 807 415. Washington, DC: National Highway Traffic Safety Administration.

Gliksman, L. & Single, E. (1988). A field evaluation of server intervention programs: accommodating reality. Paper presented at the Canadian Evaluation Society Meetings, Montreal.

Gruenewald, P.J. (1993). Alcohol problems and the control of availability: theoretical and empirical issues. In M.E. Hilton & G. Bloss (Eds), *Economics and the Prevention of Alcohol-related Problems*. Research Monograph No. 25, NIH Pub. No. 93-3513 (pp. 59–90). Bethesda, MD: National Institute on Alcohol Abuse and Alcoholism.

Harding, W.M., Apsler, R. & Goldfein, J. (1998). *A Directory of Ride Service Programs*. Final Technical Report, DOT HS 807 290. Washington, DC: US Department of Transportation, National Highway Traffic Safety Administration.

Harding, W.M. & Caudill, B.D. (1997). Does the use of designated drivers promote excessive alcohol consumption? In C. Mercier-Guyon (Ed.), *Proceedings of the 14th Annual Conference on Alcohol, Drugs and Traffic Safety, Volume 3. Annecy, France, 21–26 September 1997* (pp. 1359–1364). Annecy, France: Centre d'Études et de Recherches en Médecine du Traffic.

Haskins, J.B. (1985). The role of mass media in alcohol and highway safety campaigns. *Journal of Studies on Alcohol*, **10**, 184–191.

Hedlund, J. & Fell, J. (1995). Persistent drinking drivers in the US. In *39th Annual Proceedings of the Association for the Advancement of Automotive Medicine*. (pp. 1–12). Chicago, IL: Association for the Advancement of Automotive Medicine.

Hingson, R., Heeren, T. & Morelock, S. (Eds) (1986). *Preliminary Effects of Maine's 1982 0.02 Laws to Reduce Teenage Driving after Drinking*. London: Royal Society of Medicine Services.

Hingson, R., Heeren, T. & Winter, M. (1994). Lower legal blood alcohol limits for young drivers. *Public Health Reports*, **109**(6), 739–744.

Hingson, R., Howland, J., Heeren, T. & Winter, M. (1991). Reduced BAC limits for young people (impact on night fatal) crashes. *Alcohol, Drugs and Driving*, **7**(2), 117–127.

Holder, H.D., Janes, K., Mosher, A.M., Musty, R.E. & Voas, R.B. (1990). *Alcoholic Beverage Server Liability and the Reduction of Alcohol-involved Problems*. Berkeley, CA: Prevention Research Center.

Holder, H.D. & Treno, A.J. (1997). Media advocacy in community prevention: news as a means to advance policy change. *Addiction*, **92**(2), S189–S199.

Homel, R. (1988). *Policing and Punishing the Drinking Driver. A Study of General and Specific Deterrence*. New York: Springer-Verlag.

Homel, R., McKay, P. & Henstridge, J. (1995). The impact on accidents of random breath testing in New South Wales, 1982–1992. In C.N. Kloeden & A.J. Mclean (Eds), *Proceedings of the 13th International Conference on Alcohol, Drugs and Traffic Safety, Adelaide, 13 August–19 August 1995*,

Vol. 2 (pp. 849–855). Adelaide: NHMRC Road Accident Research Unit, University of Adelaide 5005.

Howard-Pitney, B., Johnson, M.D., Altman, D.G., Hopkins, R. & Hammond, N. (1991). Responsible alcohol service: a study of server, manager, and environmental impact. *American Journal of Public Health*, **81**(2), pp 197–198.

Hurst, P.M. (1973). Epidemiological aspects of alcohol in driver crashes and citations. *Journal of Safety Research*, **5**(3), 130–148.

Jones, I.S. & Lund, A.K. (1985). Detection of alcohol-impaired drivers using passive alcohol sensor. *Journal of Police Science and Administration*, **145**(2), 153–160.

Jones, R.K., Joksch, H.C., Lacey, J.H. & Schmidt, H.J. (1988). *Field Evaluation of Jail Sanctions for DWI*. Final Report No. DOT HS 807 325. Washington, DC: Department of Transportation, National Highway Traffic Safety Administration (NHTSA).

Jones, R.K., Lacey, J.H., Berning, A. & Fell, J.C. (1996). Alternative sanctions for repeat DWI offenders. In *40th Annual Proceedings of the Association for the Advancement of Automotive Medicine* (pp. 307–315). Des Plaines, IL: Association for the Advancement of Automotive Medicine.

Jones-Webb, R., Toomey, T., Miner, K., Wagenaar, A.C., Wolfson, M. & Poon, R. (1997a). Why and in what context adolescents obtain alcohol from adults: a pilot study. *Substance Use & Misuse*, **32**(2), 219–228.

Jones-Webb, R., Short, B.J., Wagenaar, A.C., Toomey, T.L., Murray, D.M., Wolfson, M. & Forster, J.L. (1997b). Environmental predictors of drinking and drinking-related problems in young adults. *Journal of Drug Education*, **27**(1), 67–82.

Klein, T. (1989). *Changes in Alcohol-involved Fatal Crashes Associated with Tougher State Alcohol Legislation*. Final Report under Contract No. DTNH-122-88-C-07045. Washington, DC: National Highway Traffic Safety Administration.

Lacey, J.H., Jones, R.K. & Fell, J.C. (1997). The effectiveness of the "Checkpoint Tennessee" program. In C. Mercier–Guyon (Ed.), *Alcohol, Drugs and Traffic Safety*, Vol. 2 (pp. 969–975). Annecy, France: Centre d'Etudes et et Recherches en Médecine du Trafic.

Lang, E. & Stockwell, T. (1991). Drinking locations of drink-drivers: a comparative analysis of accident and non-accident cases. *Accident Analysis & Prevention*, **23**(6), 573–584.

Lange, J.E., Voas, R.B. & O'Rourke, P. (1998). What is a designated driver anyway? Results of a California survey on definitions and use of designated drivers. *Journal of Traffic Medicine*, **26**(3–4), 101–108.

Langenbucher, J.W. & Nathan, P.E. (1983). Psychology, public policy, and the evidence for alcohol intoxication. *American Psychologist*, ••, 1070–1077.

Lapham, S.C., Skipper, B.J. & Simpson, G.L. (1997). A prospective study of the utility of standardized instruments in predicting recidivism among first DWI offenders. *Journal of Studies on Alcohol*, **58**, 524–530.

Lee, J.A., Jones-Webb, R., Short, B. & Wagenaar, A.C. (1997). Drinking location and risk of alcohol-impaired driving among high school seniors. *Addictive Behaviors*, **22**(3), 387–393.

Levy, D., Shea, D. & Asch, P. (1989). Traffic safety effects of sobriety checkpoints and other local DWI programs in New Jersey. *American Journal of Public Health*, **79**(3), 291–293.

Lund, A.F. & Jones, I.S. (1987). Detection of impaired drivers with a passive alcohol sensor. In P.C. Noordzij & R. Roszbach (Eds), *Alcohol, Drugs and Traffic Safety '86* (pp. 379–382). New York: Excerpta Medica.

Mann, R.E., Vingilis, E.R., Leigh, G., Anglin, L. & Blefgen, H. (1986). School-based programmes for the prevention of drinking and driving: issues and results. *Accident Analysis and Prevention*, **18**(4).

Mann, R.E., Vingilis, E.R., Leigh, G. & deGenova, K. (1983). A critical review on the effectiveness of drinking-driving rehabilitation programs. *Accident Analysis and Prevention*, **15**, 441–461.

McKnight, A.J. (1987). *An Evaluation of a Host Responsibility Program*. Washington, DC: National Highway Traffic Safety Administration.

McKnight, A.J. (1991). Factors influencing the effectiveness of server-intervention education. *Journal of Studies on Alcohol*, **52**(5), 389–397.

McKnight, A.J., Langston, E.A., McKnight, A.S., Resnick, J.A. & Lange, J.E. (1995). *Why People Drink and Drive: The Bases of Drinking-and-driving Decisions*. Publication No. DOT HS 808 251. Washington, DC: US Department of Transportation, National Highway Traffic Safety Administration.

McKnight, A.J., Marques, P.R., Langston, E.A. & Tippetts, A.S. (1997).   Estimating blood alcohol level from observable signs. *Accident Analysis and Prevention*, **29**(2), 247–255.

McKnight, A.J., Mason, R.W., McPherson, L. & Oates, J.F. Jr. (1984).   *Evaluation of Peer Intervention Training for High School Alcohol Safety Education*. Washington DC: National Highway Traffic Safety. Administration.

McKnight, A.J., Preusser, D.F., Psotka, J., Katz, D.B. & Edwards, J.M. (1979).   *Youth Alcohol Safety Education Criteria Development*. NTIS Publication No. PB80-17894-0. Washington, DC: US Department of Transportation.

McKnight, A.J. & Streff, F.M. (1994).   The effect of enforcement upon service of alcohol to intoxicated patrons of bars and restaurants. *Accident Analysis and Prevention*, **26**(1), 79–88.

McKnight, A.J. & Voas, R.B. (1991).   The effect of license suspension upon DWI recidivism. *Alcohol, Drugs and Driving*, **7**(1), 43–54.

Mercer, G.W. (1986).   *Age vs. Driving Experience as Predictors of Young Drivers' Traffic Accident Involvement*. Vancouver: Ministry of the Attorney General.

Miller, T.R., Lestina, D.C. & Spicer, R.S. (1998).   Highway crash costs in the United States by driver age, blood, alcohol level, victim age, and restraint use. *Accident Analysis and Prevention*, **30**(2), 137–150.

Molof, M.J. & Kimball, C. (1994).   *A Study of the Implementation and Effects of Oregon's Mandatory Alcohol Server Training Program*. Eugene, OR: Oregon Research Services Inc.

Monto, M.A., Newcomb, M.D., Rabow, J.E. & Hernandez, A.C.R. (1992).   Social status and drunk driving intervention. *Journal of Studies on Alcohol*, **53**(1), 63–68.

Mosher, J.F. (1991).   *Responsible Beverage Service: An Implementation Handbook for Communities*. Palo Alto, CA: Health Promotion Resource Center.

Mosher, J.F., Delewski, C., Saltz, R.F. & Hennessey, M. (1989).   *Monterey/Santa Cruz Responsible Beverage Project: Final Report*. San Rafael, CA: Marin Institute for the Prevention of Alcohol and other Drug Problems.

Mosher, J.F. & Wallack, L.M. (1979).   *The DUI Project: A Description of an Experimental Program to Address Drinking–Driving Problems*. Sacramento, CA: California Department of Alcoholic Beverage Control.

Moskowitz, H. & Burns, M.M. (1976).   ••.

Moskowitz, H., Burns, M.M. & Williams, A.F. (1985).   Skills performance at low blood alcohol levels. *Journal of Studies on Alcohol*, **46**(2), 482–485.

Moskowitz, H. & Robinson, C. (1988).   *Effects of Low Doses of Alcohol on Driving-related Skills: A Review of the Evidence*. Report No. DOT HS 807 280. Washington, DC: National Highway Traffic Safety Administration.

Moulden, J.V. & Voas, R.B. (1975).   *Breath Measurement Instrumentation in the US*. Technical Report DOT-HS-801-621. Washington, DC: National Highway Traffic Safety Administration.

National Highway Traffic Safety Administration (1986).   *Techniques of Effective Alcohol Management: Findings from the First Year*. Washington, DC: National Highway Traffic Safety Administration.

National Highway Traffic Safety Administration (1992).   Model specifications for breath alcohol ignition interlock devices (BAIIDs). *57 Federal Register*, **67**, 11772–11787.

National Highway Traffic Safety Administration (NHTSA) (1998).   *Fatality Analysis Reporting System data files, 1982–1997*. Washington, DC: National Highway Traffic Safety Administration, National Center for Statistics and Analysis.

Nichols, J.L. & Ross, H.L. (1989).   The effectiveness of legal sanctions in dealing with drinking drivers. In *Surgeon General's Workshop on Drunk Driving: Background Papers* (pp. 93–112). Washington, DC: US Department of Health and Human Services, Public Health Service, Office of the Surgeon General.

Ontario Ministry of Transport and Communications (1980).   *The 1979 Ontario roadside BAC survey: Summary report, Interministerial Committee on Drinking and Driving*. Toronto: Ontario Ministry of Transport and Communications.

Pagano, M.R. & Taylor, S.P. (1980).   Police perceptions of alcohol intoxication. *Journal of Applied Social Psychology*, **10**(2), 166–177.

Palmer, J.W. (1986).   *Minnesota Roadside Survey: Alcohol-positive Drivers*. Saint Cloud, MN: Saint Cloud University.

Peck, R.C., Sadler, D.D. & Perrine, M.W. (1985). The comparative effectiveness of alcohol rehabilitation and licensing control actions for drunk driving offenders: a review of the literature. *Alcohol, Drugs and Driving: Abstracts and Reviews*, **1**(4), 15–40.

Perrine, M.W., Foss, R.D., Vélez, C., Voas, R.B. & Meyers, A.R. (1992). Validity and inter-rater reliability of the field sobriety test. *Alcoholism: Clinical & Experimental Research*, **16**(2), 417 (Abstr. 377).

Perrine, M.W., Peck, R.C. & Fell, J.C. (1989). Epidemiologic perspectives on drunk driving. In USPHS, Office of the Surgeon General (Ed.) *Surgeon General's Workshop on Drunk Driving: Background Papers* (pp. 35–76). Washington, DC: US Department of Health and Human Services.

Pisoni, D.B. & Martin, C.S. (1989). Effects of alcohol on the acoustic-phonetic properties of speech: perceptual and acoustic analyses. *Alcoholism: Clinical and Experimental Research*, **13**(4), 577–587.

Popkin, C., Li, L., Lacey, J., Stewart, R. & Waller, P. (1983). *An Initial Evaluation of the North Carolina Alcohol and Drug Education Traffic Schools*, Vol. 1. Chapel Hill, NC: Highway Safety Research Center, University of North Carolina.

Popkin, C.L., Kannenberg, C.H., Lacey, J.H. & Waller, P.F. (1988). *Assessment of Classification Instruments Designed to Detect Alcohol Abuse*. Washington, DC: National Highway Traffic Safety Administration.

Preusser, D.F. & Williams, A.F. (1991). *Sales of Alcohol to Underage Purchasers in Three New York Counties and Washington, DC*. Washington, DC: Insurance Institute for Highway Safety.

Rodgers, A. (1994). Effect of Minnesota's license plate impoundment law on recidivism of multiple DWI violators. *Alcohol, Drugs and Driving*, **10**(2).

Ross, H. & Gonzales, P. (1988). The effect of license revocation on drunk-driving offenders. *Accident Analysis and Prevention*, **20**(5), 379–391.

Ross, H.L. (1973). Law, science and accidents: the British Road Safety Act of 1967. *Journal of Legal Studies*, **2**, 1–78.

Ross, H.L. (1984). *Deterring the Drinking Driver: Legal Policy and Social Control*, 2nd edn. Lexington, MA: Lexington Books.

Ross, H.L. (1992a). Are DWI sanctions effective? *Alcohol, Drugs and Driving*, **8**(1), 61–69.

Ross, H.L. (1992b). *Confronting Drunk Driving: Social Policy for Saving Lives*. New Haven, CT: Yale University Press.

Russ, N.W. & Geller, E.S. (1986). *Evaluation of a Server Intervention Program for Preventing Drunk Driving*. Blacksburg, VA: Virginia Polytechnic Institute and State University, Department of Psychology.

Rydon, P., Lang, E. & Stockwell, T. (1993). High risk drinking settings: the association of serving and promotional practices with harmful drinking. *Addiction*, **88**, 1519–1526.

Rydon, P., Stockwell, T., Lang, E. & Beel, A. (1996). Pseudo-drunk-patron evaluation of bar-staff compliance with Western Australian liquor law. *Australian and New Zealand Journal of Public Health*, **20**, 31–34.

Saffer, H. & Chaloupka, F. (1989). Breath testing and highway fatality rates. *Applied Economics*, **21**, 901–912.

Saltz, R.F. (1986). Server intervention: will it work? *Alcohol Health & Research World*, **10**(4), 12–19.

Saltz, R.F. & Stanghetta, P. (1997). A community-wide responsible beverage service program in three communities: early findings. *Addiction*, **92**(2), S237–S249.

Selzer, M.L., Payne, C.E., Westervelt, F.H. & Quinn, J. (1967). Automobile accidents as an expression of psychopathology in an alcoholic population. *Quarterly Journal of Studies in Alcoholism*, **28**, 517–528.

Simpson, H.M., Mayhew, D.R. & Beirness, D.J. (1996). *Dealing with Hard Core Drinking Driver* (107 pp.). Ottawa: Traffic Injury Research Foundation.

Span, D. & Stanislaw, H. (1995). Evaluation of the long-term impact of a deterrence-based random breath testing program in New South Wales. In C.N. Kloeden & A.J. Mclean (Eds), (1995). *Proceedings of the 13th International Conference on Alcohol, Drugs and Traffic Safety, Adelaide, 13 August–19 August 1995*, Vol. 2 (pp. 840–844). Adelaide: NHMRC Road Accident Research Unit, University of Adelaide 5005.

Steward, E.I. & Malfetti, J.L. (1970). *Rehabilitation of the Drunken Driver*. New York: Teachers College Press.

Struckman-Johnson, D.L. & Mushill, E.F. (1976). *Program Level Evaluation of A.S.A.P. Diagnosis, Referral and Rehabilitation efforts. Vol. II: Analysis of A.S.A.P. Diagnosis and Referral Activity.* Washington, DC: US Department of Transportation.

Stuster, J.W. & Blowers, M.A. (1995). *Experimental Evaluation of Sobriety Checkpoint Programs.* DTNH22-91-C-07204. Washington, DC: National Highway Safety Administration.

Swenson, P.R. & Clay, T.R. (1977). *An Analysis of Drinker Diagnosis, Referral and Rehabilitation Activity, ASAP Phoenix, Arizona.* Washington, DC: National Highway Traffic Safety Administration.

Tashima, H.N. & Helander, C.J. (1999). *1999 Annual Report of the California DUI Management Information System.* CAL-DMV-RSS-99-179. Sacramento, CA: California Department of Motor Vehicles, Research and Development Section.

Taubenslag, W.N. & Taubenslag, M.J. (1975). *Selective Traffic Enforcement Program (STEP).* Washington, DC: National Highway Traffic Safety Administration.

Teplin, L.A. & Lutz, G.W. (1985). Measuring alcohol intoxication: the development, reliability and validity of an observational instrument. *Journal of Studies on Alcohol,* **46**(6).

Tharp, V.K., Burns, M. & Moskowitz, H. (1981). *Development and Field Test of Psychophysical Tests for DWI Arrests.* Final Report No. DOT-HS-805-864. Washington, DC: Department of Transportation, National Highway Traffic Safety Administration.

Vingilis, E.R., Adlaf, E.M. & Chung, L. (1982). Comparison of age and sex characteristics of police-suspected impaired drivers and roadside-surveyed impaired drivers. *Accident Analysis and Prevention,* **14**, 425–430.

Voas, R.B. (1972). *ASAP Program Evaluation Methodology and Overall Program Impact.* Technical Report DOT-HS-880-874. Washington, DC: National Highway Traffic Safety Administration.

Voas, R.B. (1982). *Drinking and Driving: Scandinavian Tough Penalties and United States Alternatives.* Final Report on NHTSA Contract DTNH22-82-P-05079. Washington, DC: National Highway Traffic Safety Administration.

Voas, R.B. (1983). Laboratory and field tests of a passive alcohol sensing system. *Abstracts & Reviews in Alcohol & Driving,* **4**(3), 3–21.

Voas, R.B. (1985). *The Drunk Driver and Jail.* Technical Report DOT-HS-806-761. Washington, DC: National Highway Traffic Safety Administration.

Voas, R.B. (1986). Evaluation of jail as a penalty for drunken driving. *Alcohol, Drugs and Driving: Abstracts and Reviews,* **2**(2), 47–70.

Voas, R.B. (1992). *Final Report on Assessment of Impoundment and Forfeiture Laws for Drivers Convicted of DWI.* NHTSA Contract No. DTNH22-89-4-07026. Washington, DC: National Highway Traffic Safety Administration.

Voas, R.B. & Hause, J.M. (1987). Deterring the drinking driver: the Stockton experience. *Accident Analysis and Prevention,* **19**(2), 81–90.

Voas, R.B., Lange, J.E. & Tippetts, A.S. (1998a). Enforcement of the zero tolerance law in California: a missed opportunity? In *Association for the Advancement of Automotive Medicine, 42nd Annual Proceedings, Charlottesville, VA, October 5–7, 1998* (pp. 369–383). Des Plaines, IL: Association for the Advancement of Automotive Medicine.

Voas, R.B. & Marques, P.R. (1992). Model specifications for breath alcohol ignition interlock devices (BAIIDs). *Federal Register,* **57**(67), 11772–11787.

Voas, R.B., Marques, P.R., Tippetts, A.S. & Beirness, D.J. (1999). The Alberta Interlock Program: the evaluation of a province-wide program. *Addiction,* **94**, 1857–1867.

Voas, R.B. & McKnight, A.J. (1991). *An Evaluation on Hardship Licensing for DWIs. Volume II: Effect on General and Specific Deterrence.* Final Report under NHTSA Contract No. DTNH22-84-C-07292. Landover, MD: National Public Services Research Institute.

Voas, R.B., Rhodenizer, A.E. & Lynn, C. (1985). *Evaluation of Charlottesville Checkpoint Operations.* Final Report under DOT Contract DTNH-22-83-C-05088. Washington, DC: National Traffic Safety Administration.

Voas, R.B. & Tippetts, A.S. (1990). Evaluation of treatment and monitoring programs for drunken drivers. *Journal of Traffic Medicine,* **18**, 15–26.

Voas, R.B. & Tippetts, A.S. (1994). Unlicensed driving by DUIs—a major safety problem? TRB ID No. CR077. Paper presented at the 73rd Annual Meeting, Transportation Research Board, Landover, MD.

Voas, R.B. & Tippetts, A.S. (1996a). Are licensing sanctions effective at reducing impaired driving? In *Transportation Research Circular: Progress and Promise in Alcohol, Other Drugs and Transportation* (pp. 16–18). Washington, DC: Transportation Research Board.

Voas, R.B. & Tippetts, A.S. (1996b). Unlicensed driving by DUIs—A major safety problem. In *Transportation Research Circular; Progress and Promise in Alcohol, Other Drugs and Transportation* (pp. 38–39). Washington, DC: Transportation Research Board, National Transportation Safety Board.

Voas, R.B., Tippetts, A.S. & Fell, J. (submitted for publication). Minimum drinking age and zero tolerance laws: do they reduce alcohol-related crashes? *American Journal of Public Health*.

Voas, R.B., Tippetts, A.S. & Taylor, E. (1997). Temporary vehicle immobilization: evaluation of a program in Ohio. *Accident Analysis and Prevention*, **29**(5), 635–642.

Voas, R.B., Tippetts, A.S. & Taylor, E. (1998b). Temporary vehicle impoundment in Ohio: a replication and confirmation. *Accident Analysis and Prevention*, **30**(5), 651–655.

Voas, R.B., Tippetts, A.S. & Taylor, E.P. (1998c). Impact of Ohio administrative license suspension. In *Association for the Advancement of Automotive Medicine, 42nd Annual Proceedings, Charlottesville, VA, October 5–7, 1998* (pp. 401–415). Des Plaines, IL: Association for the Advancement of Automotive Medicine.

Voas, R.B., Wells, J., Lestina, D., Williams, A. & Greene, M. (1998d). Drinking and driving in the United States: the 1996 National Roadside Survey. *Accident Analysis and Prevention*, **30**(2), 267–275.

Wagenaar, A.C. & Wolfson, M. (1995). Deterring sales and provision of alcohol to minors: a study of enforcement in 295 countries in four states. *Public Health Reports*, **110**(4), 419–427.

Wagenaar, A.C., Toomey, T.L., Murray, D.L., Short, B.J., Wolfson, M. & Jones-Webb, R. (1996). Sources of alcohol for underage drinkers. *Journal of Studies on Alcohol*, **57**(3), 325–333.

Waller, J.A., King, E.M., Nielson, G. & Turkel, H.W. (1967). Alcohol and other factors in California highway fatalities. Paper presented at the Eleventh Annual Meeting of the American Association of Automotive Medicine, Springfield, IL.

Wells, J.K., Greene, M.A., Foss, R.D., Ferguson, S.A. & Williams, A.F. (1997). Drinking drivers missed at sobriety checkpoints. *Journal of Studies on Alcohol*, **58**(5), 513–517.

Wells-Parker, E., Bangert-Drowns, R., McMillen, R. & Williams, M. (1995). Final results from a meta-analysis of remedial interventions with DUI offenders. *Addiction*, **90**(7), 907–926.

Wells-Parker, E. & Cosby, P.J. (1987). *Impact of Driver's License Suspension on Employment Stability of Drunken Drivers*. Social Research Report Series 87-3. Mississippi State University, Social Science Research Center.

Wells-Parker, E. & Popkin, C. (1994). Deterrence and rehabilitation: Rehabilitation and screening—research needs for the next decade. *Journal of Traffic Medicine*, **23**, 71–78.

Widmark, E.M.P. (1932). *Die theoretischen Grundlagen und die praktsch Verwendbarkeit der gerichlich-medizinischen Alkoholbetimmung*. Berlin: Urban und Schwarzenberg.

Wilde, C.J.S., Hoste, J.L., Sheppard, D. & Wind, G. (1971). Road safety campaigns: design and evaluation. In *Organization for Economic Cooperation and Development* (p. 75). Paris: ••.

Winsten, J.A. (1994). Promoting designated drivers: the Harvard Alcohol Project. *American Journal of Preventive Medicine*, **10**(Suppl. 1), 11–14.

Wolfe, A.C. (1975). Characteristics of late-night, weekend drivers: results of the US national roadside breath-testing survey and several local surveys. In S. Israelstam & S. Lambert (Eds), *Proceedings of the 6th International Conference on Alcohol, Drugs, and Traffic Safety* (pp. 411–449). Toronto: Addiction Research Foundation of Ontario.

Zador, P.K., Lund, A.K., Field, M. & Weinberg, K. (1988). *Alcohol-impaired Driving Laws and Fatal Crash Involvement*. Washington, DC: Insurance Institute for Highway Safety.

Zador, P.L. (1991). Alcohol-related relative risk of fatal driver injuries in relation to driver age and sex. *Journal of Studies on Alcohol*, **52**(4), 302–310.

Zobeck, T.S. & Williams, G.D. (1994). *Evaluation Synthesis of the Impacts of DWI Laws and Enforcement Methods: Final Report*. Contract No. ADM-281-89-0002. Rockville, MD: Office of Policy Analysis, National Institute on Alcohol Abuse and Alcoholism (NIAAA).

Chapter 39

Prevention at the Local Level

Andrew J. Treno
and
Harold D. Holder
Prevention Research Center, Berkeley, CA, USA

Synopsis

The prevention of alcohol problems at the local level has a relatively short but rich history compared to the community efforts to reduce other health problems. For example, health professionals concerned with the prevention of chronic diseases have accumulated over 20 years of experience in local programs designed to reduce cardiovascular disease (CVD). Typically, these have been directed toward either high-risk subsets of the population, carried out in clinical settings or in worksites, or directed at the entire populations in communities. Based upon the successes of studies, similar programs have been developed over the past 10 years or so to address problem drinking and alcohol-related problems. However, few of these have been characterized by: (a) the development of a careful baseline planning and pre-intervention period; (b) well-defined community-level alcohol-involved problems as targets; (c) a long-term implementation and monitoring period; (d) a follow-up or final scientific evaluation of changes in target problems; and (e) an empirically documented successful result in the target that can be attributed to the intervention. Thus it is difficult to say with certainty whether these programs have been effective.

This chapter presents the project designs and findings of programs designed to address problem drinking and alcohol-related problems and include all five of the above characteristics. Specifically, for each study we consider the presence of a baseline measurement period, the specific problem targeted and its operationalization, the implementation and monitoring period, the structure of scientific evaluation of expected program effects, and the extent to which such effects were found to be attributable to program efforts.

The chapter is organized in the following manner. It begins by presenting a brief discussion of the pre-history of local alcohol programs. Here we note the success of local efforts addressing other chronic health problems, such as heart disease, smoking and adolescent pregnancy, and note that the success of such programs provided optimism concerning the potential for local efforts to combat problem drinking and alcohol-related problems. The chapter then notes that alcohol programs designed to alter individual use of alcohol, either through school-based education or the media campaigns following the chronic

International Handbook of Alcohol Dependence and Problems. Edited by N. Heather, T.J. Peters and T. Stockwell.
© 2001 John Wiley & Sons Ltd.

health problem model, have found only limited success. As an alternative approach, the chapter then discusses a number of alcohol programs designed around environmental approaches. The chapter concludes with a summary of what is currently known about the efficacy of local alcohol programs and a discussion of potential areas for future research.

The reduction of alcohol problems in the community through local efforts has had a rich but brief history and shares a common heritage with community prevention concerning other health problems. Thus, these efforts have attracted increased interest among researchers, community organizers and funding agencies. However, this flurry of interest should not detract from important differences in philosophies and strategies motivating these diverse programs or important characteristics of target problems. Most of these studies have been directed toward either high-risk subsets of the population, carried out in clinical settings or in worksites, or directed at the entire populations in communities, and involve some combination of community organization and health education. Moreover, most have addressed chronic health problems, such as cardiovascular disease.

Based upon the successes of studies evaluating chronic health problems, similar programs were developed to address problem drinking and alcohol-related problems. However, there is reason to believe that such strategies are unlikely to be effective in the prevention of alcohol-related problems. First, these interventions involve high-risk medical conditions. Second, they assume that individuals have the power to rationally control their behavior. Clearly, a number of factors make the case of alcohol different from that of CVD. For example, there are both greater needs and greater opportunities for regulating behaviors associated with alcohol-related problems than behavior associated with CVD. Moreover, the acute effects of alcohol in producing alcohol problems are more closely linked in time and space to the consumption of alcohol than are the dietary patterns associated with CVD, the chronic disease expression. Finally, norms associated with drinking differ dramatically from those associated with problematic dietary patterns.

Here we review community prevention efforts that address the entire community and which use strategies and approaches that go beyond educational programs to attempt changes in the local social, economic or physical environment related to risky drinking. Thus, we do not review school-based programs that are located within the community, which address drinking and related problems in the schools using only informational approaches. As noted elsewhere in this *Handbook*, education-only strategies have produced modest results. Of course, a number of reasons likely underlie these less-than-impressive results, including high rates of absenteeism, drop-outs among high-risk youth, limited time to devote to such problems, and social rootedness of drinking in US culture in general and among youth in particular (Grube, 1997).

As an alternative to such traditional approaches, local communities have developed community-wide programs to address alcohol problems. Adopting broader environmental approaches, such programs have differed from more traditional approaches in that they attempt to seek policy change, seek to bring about system-level community level change, use the media to target policy makers, and seek to mobilize the broader community to pursue desired changed. While such alternative approaches appear promising, only recently have there been systematic attempts to evaluate such efforts (Holder et al., 1997). For this reason local policy makers find themselves attempting to implement policy changes in the absence of a scientific basis supporting such changes. This chapter presents a summary of what is currently known about the effectiveness of such local prevention programs. In discussing the findings of such program evaluations, we consider the presence of a baseline measurement period, the specific problem targeted and its operationalization, the implementation and monitoring period, the structure of scientific evaluation of expected program effects, and the extent to which such effects were found to be attributable to program efforts (see Table 39.1 for summary). The studies considered here generally meet a number of criteria to qualify for inclusion. First, they are community-wide in their focus, as opposed to being targeted at high-risk groups. Second, they seek to bring about community-level system change. Third, to the extent that they use media strategically, such use is targeted at key community leaders in the pursuit of policy change. Fourth, they seek to mobilize the entire community in the pursuit of such change. In keeping with the international orientation of this collection, we discuss selected projects conducted in the USA, Scandinavia, Australia and New Zealand. Specifically, we discuss the Lahti Project, the Compari Project, the Saving Lives Project, the CMCA Project, the New Zealand CAP Project and the Community Trials Project. These projects, representative of a variety of cultural differences, illustrate various environmental approaches to the reduction of alcohol-related problems. For evaluation of programs that are more focused on bringing about individual-level change through the use of persuasion targeted at high-risk groups, the reader is directed toward other chapters included in this volume.

The logic behind targeting communities, as opposed to individuals, is compelling. First, substance use occurs largely within community contexts. That is, particularly in the case of alcohol, communities provide structures (e.g. zoning of alcohol establishments) through which alcohol is typically obtained. Second, many of the costs associated with alcohol are born collectively at the community level in the form of car crashes and alcohol-related violence.

A fundamental distinction may be made between the manner in which traditional and environmental approaches conceptualize communities. Specifically, traditional approaches view communities as catchment areas, while environmental approaches view communities as systems. From the catchment area perspective, the community is viewed largely as a collection of target groups with adverse behaviors and associated risks. Prevention operates largely through educational efforts to reduce the demand for alcohol. The strategy is thus to find, and treat or serve, those most at risk. No particular structural change is proposed and those outside the targeted groups are left unaffected. As an alternative, Holder (1997) has proposed a systems approach to the reduction of alcohol problems that operates by changing the community structures that provide the context in which alcohol consumption occurs. Such supply-orientated approaches may provide advantages over demand approaches, in that they do not require the identification of at-risk individuals or even their active cooperation. Moreover, since most alcohol-related problems do not involve alcoholics, this approach may be particularly effective in the case of alcohol. Here the view is that the problem is created by the system, rather than by problem individuals. Thus, rather than attempt to reduce alcohol-related problems through the education and treatment of problem drinkers, efforts may be directed toward affecting policy makers in positions to implement zoning restrictions governing outlet densities. More broadly, collective risk is thus reduced through interventions affecting community processes that influence alcohol use. In our review of community alcohol projects, the distinction between demand-orientated catchment area approaches and supply-orientated systems approaches will be a major point of reference.

THE COMMUNITY ACTION PROJECT

The Community Action Project (CAP), conducted between October 1982 and March 1985 in six New Zealand (four experimental, two control) communities, was targeted at increasing support among the general public for public policies, as well as attitudes and behavior, supportive of moderate alcohol use through the use of print media (Casswell & Gilmore, 1989).

Table 39.1   Effectiveness of local prevention programs

Project	Baseline	Target Problem	Implementation	Evaluation	Result
CAP	Data collected pre- and post-intervention	Public support for alcohol policy Attitudes supportive of moderate alcohol use	Two sites media only, two sites media and community organization, two sites control	Quasi-experimental design Analyzed project history community survey, key informant interviews	Declining public support for alcohol policy relative to advertising, availability, and price in comparison communities Increased support for restrictions on sales and age limits in media and community organization sites
Lahti	Data collected pre- and post-intervention	Prevention of alcohol-related harm	Experimental site, two comparison sites Experimental site exposed to modular activities corresponding to problem construction, key person interviews, education and information, heavy drinking, social support, alcohol supply, and evaluation	Local newspapers and community survey	Changes in community perceptions relative to alcohol Increased program awareness
COMPARI	Time series data collected pre- and post-intervention	Alcohol problem reduction through changes in context of use	Project activities in one site corresponded to networking and support, community development, alternative options health education, health marketing and policy institutionalization	ARIMA modeling of alcohol sales, assaults, traffic crashes and alcohol-related morbidity	No significant differences found

Table 39.1 (*continued*)

Project	Baseline	Target Problem	Implementation	Evaluation	Result
Saving Lives	Data collected pre- and post-intervention	Reductions in alcohol-impaired driving and related problems	Project designed locally in six experimental communities matched to five comparison sites. Included a host of program activities	Quasi-experimental design modeling fatal and injury crashes, seatbelt use and traffic sitations	25% Reduction in fatal crashes relative to rest of state
CMCA	Data collected at baseline and at 2.5 years after intervention implementation	Reduction in youth access	Randomized 15-community trial (7 experimental and 8 control) collected at baseline and at follow-up after a 2.5 year intervention. Included decoy operations, keg registration, restrictions on hours of sale, responsible beverage service programs, education programs, etc.	Quasi-experimental design examined youth telephone surveys, merchant surveys, apparent minor surveys, and media and process data	Increased ID checking Decreased provision of alcohol to minors Decreased consumption
Community Trials	Data collected pre-intervention and throughout the project	Reductions in alcohol-related injuries and death	Interventions inplemented in three sites matched to three comparison sites, targeted at community mobilization, reduction of drink–driving, youth access, availability and responsible beverage service	Quasi-experimental design examined community survey, youth survey, roadside survey, local media, intoxicated patron, apparent minor, and project history data	10% reduction in alcohol involved car crashes 43% Reduction in violence, lower alcohol sales to youth

The project design was quasi-experimental. Cities were matched in terms of size and overall ethnic breakdown and economic composition. Of six cities selected, four were exposed to the mass media campaign. Two of these were also exposed to the community organization campaign. Two served as controls. In the four experimental communities, the mass media campaign was utilized to influence drinking behavior at the individual level among young males. In the two experimental sites, which included the community organization program, a full-time project organizer was employed. These project organizers worked with local community organizations in support of project goals. Additionally, social service personnel were used to establish task-orientated work groups. This project attempted to operate at the individual level by supporting healthy behaviors, at the community level by increasing support for policy change, and at the policy level by affecting both advertising and alcohol availability. Efforts were made to affect access by influencing licensing. Beverage service practices were influenced by contact with both the police and the alcohol service industry. Community organizers attempted to influence policy through the city government process.

The project evaluation was conducted using process data, documenting the project's history, survey data, key informant interviews, analysis of local print media and surveys with independent random samples from each of the six participating surveys. Data were collected pre- and post-intervention for all six communities.

Results of the survey analysis of attitudes toward three policy areas (alcohol advertising, availability and price) were somewhat equivocal. While no change could be found in the two experimental conditions, declining support for these policies were found in the comparison sites. A significant difference was, however, found for support for restrictions dealing with alcohol sales in supermarkets and age limits in the intensive intervention site. These findings have generally been interpreted as suggesting that the project efforts prevented further liberalization of attitudes toward alcohol, as found in the comparison communities. A number of non-policy related items were also considered. In general, these results suggested a shift toward predicted change in the intensive intervention sites.

THE LAHTI PROJECT

The Lahti Project was conducted in Lahti, Finland and was aimed at the prevention of alcohol-related harm. The project started in the autumn of 1992 and continued until 1995 (Homila, 1995, 1997). The project involved members of most sectors of the community and was coordinated through the city's health bureau. The work was organized into modules corresponding to the following activities: constructing alcohol problems in the community; group interviews of key persons; education and information; health care intervention for heavy drinkers; social support; influencing the supply of alcohol; and evaluation. The core of the project consisted of seven researchers, information experts and the local coordinator, who met approximately every 2 months. Project coordinators maintained a minimum of weekly contact.

Baseline project measures consisted primarily of pre-intervention surveys of drinking surveys conducted in Lahti and two comparison communities, which were repeated during the post-intervention period. Additionally, the content of alcohol-related newspaper articles was examined.

The project's program evaluation showed some community-level effects. These were primarily in community perceptions and attitudes relative to alcohol, as well as overall awareness of the program. The results were less conclusive in terms of behavioral outcomes, as no statistically significant change in drinking levels could be found (Homila, 1997). Thus, while the project demonstrated efficacy in mobilizing community level efforts, less could be said about program outcomes.

THE COMPARI PROJECT

The Community Mobilization for the Prevention of Alcohol Related Injury (COMPARI) project was conducted in the Western Australian regional city of Geraldton between

January 1992 and February 1995. Based on the view that most alcohol problems are not the results of actions of alcoholics, the project was designed to reduce alcohol injury by focusing not on heavy drinkers or alcoholics, but rather on the general context of use in the community. After completion of the university-managed demonstration project, the project was transferred to local control. It currently operates under a contract awarded by the government and is the only non-metropolitan alcohol and drug program undertaking community-wide activities in Western Australia (Midford et al., 1998).

COMPARI project activities may be broadly classed into five areas: (a) networking and support (e.g. coordinating local committee on domestic violence); (b) community development (e.g. giving project presentations to community service groups); (c) alternative options health education (e.g. underage youth disco); (d) health marketing (e.g. media campaign presenting safe partying tips); and (e) policy institutionalization (e.g. implementation of guidelines to license applications to serve liquor on council property and the development and delivery of a training package in the responsible serving of alcohol).

The project was evaluated using ARIMA modeling techniques. Several time series were analyzed. These included wholesale alcohol sales, assaults, traffic crashes and hospital morbidity, weighted to reflect likely association with alcohol. These analyses failed, however, to demonstrate an impact. Specifically, alcohol consumption remained relatively flat, as did most harm indicators. One harm indicator approached but did not attain significance, possibly due to the short length of the series. Whether more post-intervention data will demonstrate an effect is not known.

THE SAVING LIVES PROJECT

The Saving Lives Project was conducted in six communities in Massachusetts and was designed to reduced alcohol-impaired driving and related problems such as speeding. In each community a full-time coordinator from within city government organized a task force representing various city departments. Each project was funded at $1 per inhabitant annually, with half of the funds paying the coordinator, police enforcement, program activities and educational materials. Programs were designed locally and involved a host of activities, media campaigns, business information programs, speeding and drink–driving awareness days, speed watch telephone hotlines, police training, high-school peer-led education, Students Against Drunk Driving chapters, college prevention programs, etc. The program evaluation involved a quasi-experimental design and utilized five comparison communities as controls, which, while slightly more affluent that experimental sites, had similar demographic characteristics, rates of traffic citations and fatal crashes. Project monitoring considered, as measures, fatal and injury crashes, seat belt use, telephone surveys and traffic citations. While some baseline differences were found, comparison communities roughly reflected the characteristics of the experimental sites. Evaluation indicated that during the 5 program years, Saving Lives cities experienced a 25% greater decline in fatal crashes than the rest of Massachusetts.

THE CMCA PROJECT

The Communities Mobilizing for Change on Alcohol (CMCA) was designed to reduce the flow of alcohol to youth under age 21. In simplified form, the project identified five core components: (a) influences on community policies and practices; (b) community policies; (c) youth alcohol access; (d) "youth alcohol consumption", and subsequently; (e) "youth alcohol problems". Although the project was clearly community-wide in terms of the community institutions involved, the project was thus focused on one particular target group, youth.

The CMCA project recruited 15 communities (defined by school districts with at least 200 students in the ninth grade and who drew students from no more than three municipalities) in Minnesota and western Wisconsin before using randomization to determine which would be the intervention communities and which would form the comparison group. Pairs of communities (along with one group of three, due to there being an odd number of communities) were created by matching on their size, state, proximity to a college or university, and baseline data from an alcohol purchase survey. One member community of each pair was then selected to be the intervention site when the time came to begin the community organizing. In the end, there were seven intervention sites and eight comparisons, ranging in size from approximately 8000 to 65,000 people with an average of about 20,000.

The project involved activating the communities that could, in turn, select interventions designed to influence underage access to alcohol. Such interventions could include decoy operations with alcohol outlets, citizen monitoring of outlets selling to youth, keg registration, developing alcohol-free events for youth, shortening hours of sale for alcohol, responsible beverage service training, and developing educational programs for youth and adults. The CMCA project hired a part-time local organizer from within each community who was trained and supervised by project staff.

Evaluation data were collected at baseline, and again about 2.5 years after beginning the intervention. These data included surveys of 9th and 12th grade students at baseline, 12th graders at follow-up, telephone surveys of 18–20 year-olds, surveys of alcoholic beverage merchants, and a survey of outlets using 21 year-old women who appeared to be younger, to see if they would be sold or served alcohol without having identification. Other data sources included monitoring of mass media and process-orientated data, both qualitative and quantitative, to capture how the intervention moved ahead and the obstacles staff and communities faced in reaching their objectives.

Merchant survey data revealed that they increased checking for age identification, reduced their likelihood of sales to minors, and reported more care in controlling sales to youth (Wagenaar et al., 1996). The telephone survey of 18–20 year-olds showed a lower frequency of providing alcohol to other minors, and lower likelihood of buying and consuming alcoholic beverages themselves (Wagenaar et al., 2000).

PREVENTION RESEARCH CENTER'S COMMUNITY TRIALS PROJECT

The Community Trials Project (Holder et al., 1997) was a five-component community-level intervention conducted in three experimental communities matched to three comparisons. The five interacting components included: (1) a "community knowledge, values, and mobilization" component, to develop community organization and support for the goals and strategies of the project; (2) a "responsible beverage service practices" component, to reduce the risk of intoxicated and/or underage customers in bars and restaurants; (3) a "reduction of underage drinking" component, to reduce underage access; (4) a "risk of drinking and driving" component, to increase local driving while intoxicated (DWI) enforcement efficiency and reduce drink–driving; and (5) an "access to alcohol" component, to reduce the availability of alcohol. Each component of the project was successfully implemented in each of three experimental communities.

In all three experimental communities, indigenous local program staff were hired during the first project year. A project coordinator (a trained and experienced community organizer) provided regular on-site technical assistance with community mobilization. An orientation early in the first year of the project presented overall project goals in detail, along with the five prevention components and their rationale. During the second project year, training in media advocacy was given to local staff. Additional assistance was provided by a professional advisor on political/legislative action, alcohol problem prevention and community organization and activism. In each community, active coalitions were in place at the onset of the project. During the second year, accompanying local staff training, a series of coalition trainings on project research rationales and component designs was given by PRC scientific staff.

While broad-based community coalitions provided general support for environmental approaches, component-specific strategies were developed and intervention plans formulated by designated task forces for each component. For example, in the Northern California site, policy implementation took the form of increased DUI enforcement, mandatory training for Conditional Use Permit (CUP) holders,[1] implementation of responsible beverage service (RBS) standards at community events, incorporation of coalition recommendations regarding zoning amendments (e.g. distance requirements), and enforcement efforts in support of the California Zero-Tolerance law.[2] In another site, implementation included increased arrests for DUI, introduction and use of passive DUI breathalyzers, DUI sweeps, establishment of clerk training, and both on-site and off-site police stings. In the third site, implementation included strengthened DUI enforcement, clerk trainings, adoption of density regulations (i.e. distance requirements), and the establishment of underage stings that involve police use of underage buyers to determine whether retail outlets were in compliance with underage drinking laws.

Project effects were measured in terms of both component-specific intermediary effects and project outcomes. Due to the project's design, project outcomes could not be linked to specific project interventions. Intermediary effects, however, could. The goal of the RBS component was to reduce the likelihood of customer intoxication at licensed on-premises establishments. Thus, the component's potential contribution to lowering intoxication and injuries was evaluated using trained associates, who entered a sample of on-premises establishments and ordered a number of drinks sufficient to require intervention on the part of the server. In preliminary analyses, however, no significant differences in server intervention were observed between experimental and comparison sites (Saltz & Stanghetta, 1997). Similarly, the evaluation of the youth access component was accomplished through the use of underage purchase surveys, involving the use of adults judged by a panel to look underage, in purchase attempts. The evaluation of the effects of these activities showed that randomly selected outlets in the experimental sites were about equally likely as those in comparison sites to sell alcohol to an apparent minor on pre-test. On post-test, experimental community outlets were about half as likely to sell alcohol to an apparent minor as those in comparison sites.

The activities of the risk of drink–driving component were evaluated by considering changes in alcohol-involved traffic crashes. Evaluation results indicated that this component's activities were associated with a statistically significant impact corresponding to an overall reduction in alcohol-involved crashes, i.e. 78 crashes over a 28-month intervention period, representing an annual reduction of 10%. The activities of the alcohol access com-

---

[1] Sales of alcohol are licensed as a Conditional Use by municipal governments in California. Conditional User Permits (CUPs) are given conditional upon outlets remaining in conformity with planning and zoning regulations and other license conditions.

[2] "Zero Tolerance" is maintained by law in California toward any underage driver having any detectable blood alcohol level. In this cricumstance the law requires license revocation until age 21.

ponent were evaluated in terms of the response of communities to density issues. The range of local responses to these efforts included the reconsideration of alcohol policies by city councils, the adoption of new ordinances regulating outlets (i.e. distance requirements), changes in state administrative policies regarding license review (allowing greater local input), and citizen participation in licensing hearings. The impacts of these responses included alterations of regulations regarding special event permits (e.g. banning alcohol at some public activities), successful protests of licenses (eliminating sales of alcohol from some premises), and reductions in outlet densities. Overall, the project demonstrated decreases in self-reported DUI and a 43% decrease in emergency room assault injuries in intervention communities relative to comparison communities (Holder et al., 2000).

In sum, relative to the three comparison communities, it was shown that component 1 (community mobilization) affected media coverage of alcohol-related stories and provided support for other program developments; component 2 led to the training of a substantial number of managers and servers; component 3 led to pressure on retailers to reduce sales to underage youth and the implementation of police stings; component 4 led to significant increases in police enforcement activity against drink–driving; and component 5 led to community action directed at regulating alcohol outlets (Holder et al., 1997). Additionally, in a summary article, Holder and his colleagues (1997) characterize the preliminary overall findings of their project as follows: (a) community mobilization was able to accomplish the implementation of the planned interventions; (b) there was significant community support for those interventions, especially when there were research results to support them; (c) there were increases in media coverage of alcohol-related trauma and control policies as a result of training of community members; and (d) there were reductions in sales of alcoholic beverages to underage decoys. The primary outcome of interest, alcohol-involved traffic crashes, was estimated (via time-series analysis with matched comparison communities) to have dropped by about 10% annually over the 28 months intervention period for which data were available.

As a summary of these experiences, the researchers highlighted six points as being essential to mobilizing communities to support preventive interventions:

1. Explaining the research base for interventions is important to community actors.
2. Existing community coalitions may take their own lead and require project staff to guide them to reconsider specific interventions.
3. Pre-existing community support for project interventions is key to rapidly developing intervention programs.
4. Existing support for project interventions among community leaders may be used to focus mobilization efforts.
5. Community conditions may provide unforeseen opportunities for intervention and to galvanize public support (e.g. local festivals).
6. Media events may generate project enthusiasm.

These experiences were seen to parallel those of other international (Midford et al., 1995; Gorman & Speer, 1996) and US (Hingson et al., 1996; Wagenaar & Perry, 1994) community interventions.

CONCLUSIONS

This review of community approaches to the prevention of alcohol problems at the local level can draw important conclusions. First, the case studies reviewed here demonstrate the potential of a well-defined, theory-driven community action approach to reduce local alcohol problems. Each of these examples, and other local efforts not discussed here, show that local initiatives can be efficacious.

Second, community action projects are just that, projects that seek to address the total community system and are not naturally limited to a specific target group or service group. These are not projects in which a local program to provide services to a specific target group happens to be located in a community. These are efforts to involve community leadership in designing, implementing and supporting approaches to reduce problems across the community in total.

Third, community projects can effectively involve leaders and citizens, i.e. they encourage local participation. Thus, in each of the community projects, mobilization as an effort to engage the community in an action project to actually reduce alcohol problems is an essential element. These programs are designed to increase a sense of and actual local ownership.

Fourth, each of these community projects described involved a partnership between the community and researchers. As Holder & Reynolds (1998) have observed, such partnerships work best when each of the participants receives the respect and appreciation of the other, i.e. there is a recognition of what each partner brings to the relationship. Each of these projects represented instances in which researchers participated in the design, supported the implementation of program activities, and conducted the process and quantitative evaluation for the local program. Such evaluations not only contribute to increasing the scientific basis of community action projects designed to reduce alcohol problems, but also increase the level of solid information that can be shared with the community about the results of their own effort.

Fifth, local programs are designed or implemented uniformly. These projects reflect unique and important cultural differences. However, as shown in this review, they all share in common the five elements described in the introduction.

Sixth, community projects confirm the research evidence that changes in attitudes and beliefs are easier to attain than changes in either individual behavior (e.g. rates of problem drinking) or outcome measures (e.g. alcohol-related car crashes). A number of factors may account for this. Traditional attempts to treat and serve isolated high-risk groups have ignored the fact that most alcohol problems are not produced by members of such groups. Members of high-risk groups may be hard to find or resistant to change and the cost associated with the treatment/service approach may be prohibitive.

Recommendations based upon local prevention efforts suggest that alcohol problems are best considered in terms of the community systems that produce them. Local prevention strategies have the greatest potential to be effective when prior scientific evidence is utilized. Many of the local projects described here implemented a series of interventions that prior research had indicated were likely to reduce alcohol-related problems. Thus, complementary system strategies that seek to restructure to total alcohol environment are more likely to be effective than single intervention strategies. Finally, prevention strategies with the natural capacity for long-term institutionalization are to be favored over interventions that are only in place for the life of the project.

ACKNOWLEDGEMENTS

Research and preparation for this article were supported by the center for Substance Abuse Prevention (CSAP) and the National Institute on Alcohol Abuse and Alcoholism (NIAAA) under Grant No. AA09146.

KEY WORKS AND SUGGESTIONS FOR FURTHER READING

Allamani, A., Casswell, S., Graham, K., Holder, H., Holmila, M., Larsson, S. & Nygaard, P. (Eds) (2000). Community Action and the Prevention of Alcohol-Related Problems at the Local Level. *Substance Use and Misuse*, **35** (Special Issue, 1, 2) 1–202.

A good summary of community action programs from around the world, as well as a description of the history of local efforts to reduce alcohol problems at the total community level.

Casswell, S. & Gilmore, L. (1989). An evaluated community action project. *Journal of Studies on Alcohol*, **50**, 339–346.

Paper that demonstrates the essential steps in developing local prevention initiatives, based upon experiences in New Zealand.

Hawks, D., Stockwell, T. & Casswell, S. (1993). Helping research and policy meet, *Addiction*, **88** (Suppl.), 5S–7S.

An description of how public policy becomes implemented in practice and the partnership of policy advocates with researchers.

Hingson, R., McGovern, T., Howland, J., Heeren, T., Winter., M. & Zakocs, R. (1996). Reducing alcohol-impaired driving in Massachusetts: the Saving Lives program. *Ameican Journal of Public Heath*, **86**, 791–797.

Paper describing the interventions and results of a series of local efforts to reduce traffic problems in communities in the USA.

Holder, H.D. (1997). *A Community Systems Approach to Alcohol Problem Prevention*. Cambridge: Cambridge University Press.

Book which describes a systems approach to community prevention of alcohol problems. The book can be used by researchers and local prevention professionals in planning effective prevention strategies in the community.

Homila, M. (Ed.) (1997). *Community Prevention of Alcohol Problems*. London: Macmillan.

Describes the design and results of a community prevention project in Finland. Excellent illustration of the use of qualitative and quantitative information in evaluation.

REFERENCES

Casswell, S. & Gilmore, L. (1989). An evaluated community action project. *Journal of Studies on Alcohol*, **50**, 339–346.

Gorman, D.W. & Speer, P.W. (1996). Preventing alcohol abuse and alcohol-related problems through community interventions: a review of evaluation studies. *Psychology and Health*, **11**, 95–131.

Grube, J.W. (1997). Preventing alcohol sales to minors: results from a community trial. *Addiction*, **92**, S251–S260.

Hingson, R., McGovern, T., Howland, J., Heeren, T., Winter., M. & Zakocs, R. (1996). Reducing alcohol-impaired driving in Massachusetts: the Saving Lives program. *American Journal of Public Heath*, **86**, 791–797.

Holder, H.D. (1997). *A Community Systems Approach to Alcohol Problem Prevention*. Cambridge: Cambridge University Press.

Holder, H.D. & Reynolds, R. (1998). Science and alcohol policy at the local level: a respectful partnership. *Addiction*, **93**(10), 1467–1473.

Holder, H.D., Gruenewald, P.J., Ponicki, W.R. et al. (2000). Effect of community-based interventions on high-risk drinking and alcohol-related injuries. *Journal of the American Medical Association*, **284**, 2341–2347.

Holder, H.D., Saltz, R.F., Grube, J.W., Voas, R.B., Gruenewald, P.J. & Treno, A.J. (1997). A community prevention trial to reduce alcohol-involved accidental death and injury: overview. *Addiction*, **92** (Suppl. 2), S155–S171.

Homila, M. (1995). Community action on alcohol: experiences of the Lahti Project in Finland. *Health Promotion International*, **10**(4), 283–291.

Homila, M. (Ed.) (1997). *Community Prevention of Alcohol Problems*. Geneva: World Health Organization.

Midford, R., Boots., K., Masters, L. & Chikritzhs, T. (1998). Time series analysis of outcome measures from a community alcohol harm reduction project in Australia. Presented at the 1998 Kettil Brun Society's Fourth Symposium on Community Action, Research and the Prevention of Alcohol and Other Drug Problems, Russell, New Zealand, February 8–13.

Saltz, R.F. & Stanghetta, P. (1997). A community-wide responsible beverage service program in three communities: early findings. *Addiction*, **92**, S237–S249.

Wagenaar, A.C. & Perry, C.L. (1994). Community strategies of the reduction of youth drinking: theory and application. *Journal of Research on Adolescence*, **4**(2), 319–345.

Wagenaar, A.C., Murray, D.M., Gehan, J.P. et al. (2000). Communities mobilizing for change on alcohol: outcomes from a randomized community trial. *Journal of Studies on Alcohol*, **61**, 85–94.

Wagenaar, A., Toomey, T.L., Murray, D.M., Short, B.J., Wolfson, M. & Jones-Webb, R. (1996). Sources of alcohol for underage drinkers. *Journal of Studies on Alcohol*, **57**, 325–333.

Chapter 40

Alcohol Education in Schools

Richard Midford
and
Nyanda McBride
National Drug Research Institute, Curtin University of Technology,
Perth, Western Australia

Synopsis

Young people typically initiate alcohol use while at school and their drinking is the cause of major social and public health problems. As a consequence, there is obvious appeal to school-based alcohol education. However, to date, success has been limited.

School alcohol education dates from the late nineteenth century, but drug education as a whole expanded considerably during the 1950s and 1960s. Programmes of that era emphasized abstinence and drew on behaviour theory as the basis for their change strategies. So-called "scare tactics" paired fear arousal with use, in an attempt to establish negative attitudes to alcohol and other drugs. Another approach involved providing "factual" information on the negative consequences of use. Evaluations of these programmes indicated that they were largely ineffective in changing behaviour. This spurred two developments during the 1970s, affective programmes and abuse prevention. The former sought to reduce alcohol and other drug use by enhancing personal development, but again research evidence indicated little impact. The latter sought to prevent the problematic consequences associated with use and could be considered harm reduction. In America, official support for abuse prevention was short-lived and abstinence-focused programmes resurfaced during the 1980s. However, this time interventions drew on social influence approaches, which sought to boost resistance to use through social skills training. Harm-reduction education tended to be adopted more in Europe and Australasia. Here there is greater acceptance of the logic of using such an approach with alcohol, because the drug is legally available and use by young people is prevalent.

The evolution of alcohol education has in the main been driven by failure to achieve the desired behaviour change. In part, this failure was due to an unrealistic emphasis on abstinence, further compounded by poor science. There are, however, indications that recent alcohol education programmes are more rigorous, have goals other than abstinence and have achieved behaviour change. Reviews and meta-analyses of recent alcohol and other drug education programmes indicate that successful programmes tend to include interactive social

International Handbook of Alcohol Dependence and Problems. Edited by N. Heather, T.J. Peters and
T. Stockwell.

skills training and normative belief components, whereas programmes that do not have a sustained effect tend to rely on didactic resistance training.

Most alcohol education for young people is classroom-based. However, school health promotion research has indicated that health behaviour is best shaped by an integrated, "whole-of-school" approach. A number of studies have involved the community in drug education programmes, on the basis that the cues from the social environment are critical in establishing adolescent patterns of alcohol use and strategies to reduce adolescent access to alcohol can only be enacted at a community level. The benefits of such a community-wide approach are promising, but need to be seen in the context of the resources involved.

Alcohol education has developed considerably in the last decade, but particular programmes are often adopted because they are aggressively marketed, rather than because they are demonstrably effective. Alcohol education in the future needs to be more realistic about its goals and accountable for its achievements. An approach that is broadly useful has to acknowledge that the majority of young people will drink and that education should equip them to handle drinking situations in a way that reduces harm.

THE ATTRACTION OF SCHOOL-BASED ALCOHOL EDUCATION

In Western industrialized societies, young people typically start drinking alcohol in their early teenage years, well before they reach legal drinking age (Johnston et al., 1989). The 1996 American National Household Survey on Drug Abuse (Substance Abuse and Mental Health Services Administration, 1997) estimated that 38.3% of males and 39.4% of females in the 12–17 year-old age group had tried alcohol. The prevalence of use is much higher in other countries. A survey conducted in 1997 estimated that 73% of Norwegian 15–16 year-olds had drunk alcohol (Grytten, 1997). The National Drug Household Survey in Australia indicated that not only have most teenagers tried alcohol, but the age at which they first started drinking has progressively decreased over the past 30 years (Jones, 1993). In the UK, a survey of 15 and 16 year-old students found that 77.9% reported that they had been intoxicated from drinking and that 48.3% had been intoxicated within the last 30 days (Miller & Plant, 1996). On their last occasion of drinking, the average number of standard drinks consumed by the male English students in this study was 8.5 (Miller & Plant, 1996). Such worldwide research consistently indicates that the majority of young people not only drink, but also that they are starting to drink at a younger age, that they drink in a risky manner and that they disproportionately experience acute health and social problems because of drinking (McBride, Midford & Farringdon, 1998). As a consequence, there is obvious appeal to school-based alcohol education. Schools are places of learning. The great majority of youth are attending school when they start drinking and, as Hansen (1993) comments, are a captive audience. Accordingly, if schools educate young people about alcohol, they will make better decisions, which in turn will prevent problems. Such logic has led to the development of numerous school-based prevention programmes, but to date the success of these programmes has been limited.

WHAT MAKES ALCOHOL EDUCATION DIFFERENT?

Alcohol education is inextricably a part of drug education, because alcohol is a drug and many of the education issues are common across the spectrum of drug use. However, alcohol is a drug with unique status, which influences what will be effective education for young people. Alcohol is widely available, is socially acceptable and consumption by adults is both legal and prevalent, whereas it is axiomatic that illicit drug use is illegal and societal norms prohibiting use are much stronger. This means that young people face a more salient range of choices about drinking. Should I drink? When should I start drinking? How much should I drink? In what circumstances should I drink? Given this different set of decisional demands, alcohol education is arguably a more complex task than general drug education. This can be taxing for educators, because young people are likely to want education that is immediately useful in making these decisions and be more discerning of the information they receive, because of their own experiences with alcohol. Alcohol's status as a legal drug makes it easier to talk openly about use and prevention. However, it can also make it more difficult to bring about behaviour change. Educators have to contend with an environment in which adult drinking is prevalent and there are strong and pervasive media images that portray drinking as an attractive, even necessary, adult behaviour (Perry & Kelder, 1992; Petosa, 1992). Given such desirable associations, it is not surprising that so many young people are attracted to drinking.

The social influence approach, based on resisting the social pressures to use drugs, seems to have been quite effective in preventing cannabis use among young people (Perry & Kelder, 1992), yet this approach has been less successful in reducing alcohol use. Perry & Kelder attribute this lack of success to the perception by young people that alcohol use is normative. Support for this hypothesis is provided by a study by Hansen & Graham (1991). These researchers found that students who received social influence education that corrected misperceptions as to the amount of alcohol consumed by young people, consumed significantly less alcohol than those who received no such education. These results indicate that students were basing their own drinking behaviour on an inflated judgement of what was usual consumption by others in their age group. Given the difficulties for alcohol education in a permissive context, Perry & Kelder (1992) suggest that one way to curtail use in young people may be to establish conservative norms. This would seem beyond the scope of alcohol education programmes in pluralistic societies, as the influences that establish normative drinking behaviour go well beyond what is taught in the classroom. Education may be a useful way to impart skills to young people, but those skills will be used in a social context and policy makers and educators really have to grapple with what can be achieved by alcohol education within this broader context. Is abstinence a realistic or even a desirable goal for most young people, given that in Western industrialized societies most will drink as adults? Alternatively, should alcohol education aim to better prepare young people to make responsible decisions about drinking, as advocated by Beck (1998) and Milgram (1996), so that harmful consequences are reduced or eliminated?

THE HISTORICAL DEVELOPMENT OF ALCOHOL EDUCATION

Beck (1998) reported that, in America, provision of formal school-based alcohol education dates from the 1880s, when the temperance movement sought to take preventative action against alcohol, tobacco and other drugs, by teaching youth about their dangers. Leaders of this movement were very successful in gaining support for compulsory temperance education in schools and by 1901 every American state and territory had mandated compulsory temperance education (Mezvinsky, 1961). These programmes focused strongly on abstinence and taught that alcohol was both dangerous and seductive. Any amount of use amounted to abuse, because it led to physical harm and moral degeneration.

During this same period, approaches to alcohol education on the other side of the Atlantic varied considerably and reflected the values and norms of the society in which they occurred. The development of alcohol education in Norway, for example, echoed what occurred in America to a remarkable degree. Education started in primary schools in the late nineteenth century and was strongly linked to the temperance movement (Waahlberg, 1988). However, dissatisfaction with the narrow focus of such education led to progressively greater involvement of teachers and a broadening of the information provided. The French provided compulsory alcohol education in schools, but students were encouraged only to abstain from drinking spirits. The message in relation to fermented beverages such as wine and beer was "drink in moderation". Beck (1998) considered that this early French approach to alcohol education constituted the first harm reduction approach by a government in this area.

The temperance movement, and the school alcohol education programmes it supported, probably reached their peak of influence in America during the Prohibition years of the 1920s and early 1930s. The repeal of Prohibition in 1933 signalled the failure of a solely abstinence-orientated approach to alcohol, and prohibitionist approaches to alcohol education were rapidly abandoned. Where some form of education continued, there was increased emphasis on responsible decision making and informed choice. However, two factors led to an overall decline in alcohol education over the next three decades. Lender & Martin (1987) indicated that the societal backlash against prohibition approaches meant that many schools provided little or no education on alcohol. Coupled with this, the post-prohibition drug bureaucrats, led by Harry Anslinger, considered that illicit drugs, particularly cannabis, constituted the greater problem (Beck, 1998). Anslinger asserted, in a series of public appearances and radio broadcasts, that cannabis use led to killings, sex crimes and insanity and this use of sensationalism and scare tactics, coupled with disregard for contrary scientific evidence, characterized drug education campaigns for several decades (Schlosser, 1994; Wallack, 1980). Drug education based on information was discouraged in this climate, as knowledge was considered to encourage experimentation (Anslinger & Tomkins, 1953).

In the early 1960s, the previously dominant view, that no education was good prevention, was increasingly challenged. As a consequence, drug education as a whole expanded considerably during the decade. Programmes during this period drew on behaviour theory in developing their change strategies. Typically, so-called factual information was provided on the harmful effects of drug use in order to establish negative attitudes and a fear of use. Some of these programmes emphasized the provision of objective information. However, others continued to use scare tactics in the belief that such an approach would maximize fear arousal. Fear arousal approaches have generally lacked credibility with their target group when the images and messages they presented were extreme and inconsistent with that groups' personal experiences of drug use (Coggans & Watson, 1995). However, even without the hyperbole, information-only approaches have made little impact and, in a review of drug education from this period, Kinder et al. (1980) indicated that there was:

> ... little to support the notion that presenting factual information is an appropriate and effective method of changing attitudes and behaviours (p. 1044).

This acknowledged failure spurred two developments during the 1970s, affective programmes and abuse prevention (Gorman, 1996; Beck, 1998). Affective programmes sought to reduce alcohol and other drug use by enhancing personal development. Many programmes were not drug-specific but rather focused on personal development, with the objective of ensuring that young people were properly equipped to make positive, healthy choices (Sharp, undated). Programmes typically included training in self-esteem, decision-making, values clarification, stress management and goal setting. Again, the evidence indicated that these programmes did not demonstrably succeed in changing behaviour (Hansen, 1993). This was not surprising, according to Dielman (1994), because, like the information programmes that preceded them, these affective programmes had use or abuse reduction as their stated goal, but were evaluated against a completely different dependent variable, such as increase in self-esteem. In addition, this model makes assumptions that alcohol and drug use by young people is driven by individual deficiency and that the problem can be addressed by enhancing self-esteem or improving decision-making skills. In the case of alcohol, this is a difficult position to defend. Use by adults must be considered normative and this sets up the expectation in young people that drinking alcohol is part of becoming an adult. In such a social context, alcohol consumption is actually conformist. The other major drug education development at this time, abuse prevention programmes, were based on the premise that drinking by young people would occur and that pragmatic programmes should seek to prevent or minimize the problematic consequences of such use. Such an approach today would be considered harm reduction, although it was not called that at the time.

Harm-reduction approaches have tended to be adopted more in Europe, Canada and Australasia, where they gained credibility initially because of their success in combating the spread of HIV among intravenous drug users. In America, there was a short period during the late 1970s when official support was given to harm reduction as a guiding principle in drug education, primarily because of the well-documented failure of previous abstinence-only approaches (Beck, 1998). However, abstinence re-emerged strongly within a few years, as a result of the influence of the "parent power movement" (Beck, 1998). This grass-roots movement convinced governments to only support non-use or "zero tolerance" education programmes, and US federal guidelines mandate that prevention programmes emphasize such an approach (Office for Substance Use Prevention, Alcohol, Drug Abuse, and Mental Health Administration, 1989).

The education programmes that were developed in the 1980s generally reflected this abstinence goal, but were more sophisticated in their methodology. The social influence model, developed from Bandura's (1977) social modelling theory and McGuire's (1964) work on resistance training, has dominated this most recent phase of alcohol and drug education. The approach is based on the belief that young people begin to smoke, drink and use other drugs because of social pressure to do so from a variety of sources, such as the mass media, their peers and even the image they have of themselves. In order to successfully resist the adoption of undesirable behaviour, young people need to be inoculated by prior exposure to counter-arguments and the opportunity to practise the desired coping behaviour.

The social influence model was initially used to prevent young people taking up smoking, and its success in this area led to the approach being used to reduce the uptake of other drugs, including alcohol (Perry & Kelder, 1992). Duryea et al. (1984) used an inoculation approach with ninth grade students in an American mid-west school and achieved significant gains in knowledge and responsible attitudes, but no assessment of actual drinking behaviour was included in the study. Other studies in which drinking behaviour was measured indicate that social influence or inoculation interventions have a limited impact on drinking behaviour. Gorman (1996) conducted a comprehensive review of alcohol education programmes based on this approach and found that only three of the 12 reviewed programmes reported consistently lower alcohol use, following intervention. However, there were methodological difficulties with each of these studies. He concluded that while social influence has become the pre-eminent model for drug education programmes, the evidence supporting the effectiveness of such an approach is sparse. In fact, he suggested there is little reason to indicate that such an approach would be effective, because many of the components of social influence programmes are the same as those that comprised the failed affective programmes of the 1970s. He also made the point that prevention education has, to date, been driven by the idea that alcohol use by young people is primarily caused by interpersonal factors. This is too simplistic, given the considerable literature on the role of environment in alcohol use and harm (Holder, 1992; Lang, 1994; Wittman, 1990). Other education approaches need to be trialled that take into consideration those environmental factors that are particularly salient to young people's choices about drinking.

THE CURRENT STATE OF KNOWLEDGE

Early reviews of drug education programmes were consistently damning of their methodology and achievements (Goodstadt, 1980; Kinder et al., 1980; Schaps et al., 1981). However, Dielman (1994) indicated that these programmes and the accompanying research were useful as both a foundation and an impetus for the development of better interventions. In more recent reviews and meta-analyses of contemporary drug education programmes, a picture is beginning to emerge as to what interventions are likely to make a difference. Tobler (1986) conducted a meta-analysis of 143 drug prevention programmes designed for young people and concluded that programmes that combined peer influence with specific skills training were the most effective, although programmes offering alternatives to drug use, such as sporting or social activities, were particularly useful for "at-risk" students. Bangert-Drowns (1988) conducted a meta-analysis of 33 school-based prevention programmes, which in the main focused on alcohol and emphasized education strategies. The evaluation examined changes in drug-related knowledge, attitudes towards drugs and drug use behaviour. He found that education increased drug-related knowledge and changed attitudes, but drug use behaviour only changed in students who had volunteered to participate in the education. He also found that mode of delivery was important. Programmes that used lectures as their only intervention had less influence on attitudes than those that used discussion. Use of peer leaders was associated with greater attitude change and Coggans & Watson (1995) considered that peer-led approaches could take advantage of factors such as peer modelling and normative attitudes and values. However, they recommended that peer leaders be selected very carefully. Students considered good role models by adults are not necessarily well regarded by the target group. Botvin (1990) considers that, ideally, peer leaders should be credible with high-risk adolescents, have good communication skills, show responsible attitudes, but at the same time be somewhat unconventional. Botvin (1990) considered that even ideal peer leaders are likely to lack the organizational and management skills possessed by effective professional teachers, and accordingly he has recommended that the best of both worlds could be achieved by using teachers and peer leaders in combination. The timing of drug education is likely to be critical, according to a number of researchers (Dielman, 1994; Duncan et al., 1994). Kelder et al. (1994) commented that primary prevention is most effective if instituted before behavioural patterns are established and more resistant to change. Dielman (1994) considered that alcohol education programmes should be undertaken when they are particularly salient to young people's life experiences, such as when they are starting to drink. The general consensus in the literature (Johnston, O'Malley & Bachman, 1989; Dielman, 1994; Duncan et al., 1994) is that the optimal time for initiating youth alcohol interventions is during the late primary/early high school years, as this is when experimentation starts. However, onset of use can vary in different populations and Dielman (1994) has suggested that the timing of programmes can be optimized for a particular population, by reference to the appropriate prevalence data.

Dusenbury & Falco (1995) considered that the research literature indicates that certain types of school-based education, "can achieve at least modest reductions in adolescent drug use" (p. 420). In order to identify the key elements of effective drug education, they reviewed school-based programmes conducted between 1989 and 1994 and interviewed 15 leading researchers in the area. From this process they identified 11 critical components for an effective programme. Ballard et al. (1994) undertook a very similar process of consultation and review in developing their 15 principles for drug education in schools. These principles are substantially evidence-based and Ballard et al. (1994) considered that they offer a framework for policy makers, school administrators, teachers, parents and other stakeholders to use when making decisions about the selection, design and implementation of drug education programmes. They are remarkably similar to Dusenbury & Falco's key elements and these two sets of critical components have provided the basis for the summary of effective drug education elements, contained in Table 40.1. In addition, three features of successful drug education programmes not mentioned in these two reviews, but consistently identified in other research, have been included in this table. These features are: appropriate timing of the intervention, to ensure that prevention programmes are initiated when prevalence of use by young people is still very low (Kelder et al., 1994); use of peer leaders to focus on the social factors that influence drug use (Coggans & Watson, 1995); fidelity of implementation to ensure that programmes are delivered as intended (Dielman, 1994). This set of critical components was derived from the broader drug education literature, but it clearly should be considered when undertaking alcohol education.

Table 40.1 Summary of critical elements in effective school-based drug education and prevention

Theme	Component	Source	Comment
Context	Drug education is best taught in the context of broader health skills	Ballard et al. (1994) Dusenbury & Falco (1995)	Ongoing, comprehensive, developmentally appropriate health programmes promote general competence and provide a context for understanding drug-related behaviour
Consistency	Drug education messages across the school environment should be consistent and coherent	Ballard et al. (1994)	School policies and practices should reinforce the objectives of drug education programmes
Basis in evidence	Drug education needs to be based on research as to effective curriculum practice and the needs of students	Ballard et al. (1994) Dusenbury & Falco (1995)	Effective programmes are based on an understanding of contemporary theory and research evidence as to what causes drug use and what factors provide protection
	Drug education programmes should be evaluated	Ballard et al. (1994) Dusenbury & Falco (1995)	Evaluation will provide formal evidence of the worth of the programme in contributing to short- and long-term goals, as well as improving the design of future programmes. The quality of evaluation studies should also be assessed
Timing of education	Prevention education is best delivered before behavioural patterns are established	Kelder et al. (1994)	Drug education programmes should start when prevalence of use by young people is still very low

continued overleaf

Table 40.1 (*continued*)

Theme	Component	Source	Comment
	Drug education programmes should be immediately relevant, developmentally appropriate and have sequence, progression and continuity	Ballard et al. (1994) Dusenbury & Falco (1995)	Programmes must be credible and useful to students, which means they need to be provided regularly at different stages of schooling
Education goals	Drug education strategies should relate to programme objectives	Ballard et al. (1994)	Strategies should be selected because they are expected to achieve the objectives of the programme
	Objectives for drug education should be linked to the overall goal of harm minimization	Ballard et al. (1994)	The concept of harm minimization encompasses a range of strategies, including non-use, which aim to reduce harmful consequences of drug use
Education strategies	Social resistance skills training	Dusenbury & Falco (1995)	Such an approach helps young people to identify pressures to use drugs and gives them the skills to make alternative responses
	Normative education	Dusenbury & Falco (1995)	This gives young people an accurate indication as to the extent of drug use in their peer group, which is typically lower than expected
	Interactive teaching techniques	Dusenbury & Falco (1995)	Techniques such as role play, group discussion and joint activities promote active involvement in the learning process
	Approaches to drug education should address the values, attitudes and behaviours of the community and the individual	Ballard et al. (1994)	Responsible decisions by students about drugs are more likely where peer and community groups demonstrate responsible attitudes and practices
	Drug education programmes should reflect an understanding of the interrelationship between individual, social context and drug in determining drug use	Ballard et al. (1994)	The drug experience is influenced by these three components and effective education programmes need to deal with these influences in an integrated manner
	Drug education programmes should focus on drug use that is most likely and most harmful	Ballard et al. (1994)	Generally, school-based drug education should concentrate on lawfully available drugs, because their use by young people is more likely. While illicit drug use disproportionately attracts media attention and public concern, it should be addressed in particular contexts or subgroups, where it is particularly prevalent and harmful

Table 40.1 (*continued*)

Theme	Component	Source	Comment
	Peer-led education	Coggans & Watson (1995)	Peers leaders are credible and effective in presenting the social factors that influence drug use
Collaborative approaches	Mechanisms should be developed to involve students, parents and the wider community in school-based drug education	Ballard et al. (1994) Dusenbury & Falco (1995)	Broadening school-based education by including family, community and media components will reinforce desired behaviours by providing a supportive environment
Sensitivity to different needs	Drug education should be responsive to developmental, gender, cultural, language, socioeconomic, and life-style differences	Ballard et al. (1994) Dusenbury & Falco (1995)	Drug education programmes that are sensitive to the different backgrounds of the young people they target will be more relevant and effective
Teachers	Teachers should be trained and supported to conduct drug education	Ballard et al. (1994) Dusenbury & Falco (1995)	The classroom teacher, with specific knowledge of students and the learning context, is best placed to provide contextual drug education. Programmes are most successful when teachers receive training and support, particularly in undertaking interactive teaching activities
	Drug education programmes and resources should be selected to complement the role of the classroom teacher	Ballard et al. (1994)	The classroom teacher is central to the delivery of effective drug education and should not be compromised by external programmes
Programme implementation	Drug education programmes should demonstrate adequate coverage, sufficient follow-up and ability to achieve long-term change	Ballard et al. (1994) Dusenbury & Falco (1995)	An adequate intervention, complemented by follow-up, is needed to counter effect decay and the ongoing influences to use drugs. Stand-alone and one-off interventions are not likely to be effective
	Fidelity of implementation	Dielman (1994)	Monitoring should be undertaken to ensure that programmes are delivered in the intended manner, as failure may occur because of inadequate implementation, rather than as a result of any deficiency in the design of the programme

THE IMPORTANCE OF PARENTS

The major influence that parents have on the drinking behaviour of their children is con-sistently identified in the literature. Drinking usually begins within the family, and Foxcroft & Lowe (1997) considered that good family function and positive family associations with alcohol fostered responsible drinking by young people. They found that higher consump-tion was associated with low family support, low family control, regular parental drinking and indifference to drinking by their children. McCallum (1990), in a review of the litera-ture, indicated that parents have a major influence on their children's drug use behaviour through modelling, attitudes and family relationships, although she noted that many parents were unaware of their degree of influence and how this could be used to bring about better choices (McCallum, 1996). Mallick, Evans & Stein (1998) suggested that the first step in getting parents involved in drug education is to make them more aware of their influence, and McCallum (1990) considered that parents would have more impact if they were con-fident about their contribution. Many parents feel ill-equipped to discuss drug matters with their children, or make representations about drug education policy, because of a lack of knowledge. Accordingly, programmes that inform, engage and support parents are a useful start in tapping their potential to contribute to the drug education process.

Mallick, Evans & Stein (1998) reported that parents see drugs as their greatest issue of concern in relation to their children. However, the basis for this predominantly stems from sensationalist media reporting, with all its attendant myths, exaggerations and simplistic prescriptions. As a consequence, parents' dealings with their children tend to be directive and based on the premise that "Just say no" is the only safe message, even though there is some acknowledgment that this may not be heeded. These researchers concluded that parents needed drug education themselves, so that they could assist effectively in the drug education of their children. Many in their study were receptive to this idea but the views and motivation of hard-to-reach parents were not gauged, even though the involvement of this group may be particularly beneficial. McCallum (1990) reported that the most promis-ing prevention programmes involved parents learning communication skills, setting limits and providing consistent support. Including families in school programmes reduced risk factors, improved family interaction habits and allowed early detection of problem behav-iour. However, involving families in on site programmes has proven difficult. Quinn (1996) has suggested that the media may be an effective way of reaching parents who would oth-erwise have little contact with the school, but such a mass communication approach has difficulty conveying the complexity of drug use issues. Parents in Mallick, Evans & Stein's (1998) study have reinforced this view, with suggestions that if the media reduced its sensational reporting of drug use and provided more balanced and accurate informa-tion, parents would be better informed, less fearful and more capable of addressing their children's drug issues in a balanced and effective manner.

WHOLE-OF-SCHOOL AND COMMUNITY-WIDE APPROACHES

An important recent trend in alcohol and other drug education is the increased emphasis given to whole-of-school and community approaches (Midford & McBride, 1999; Perry et al., 1996; Ballard, Gillespie & Irwin, 1994). This acknowledges that drug education occurs within a broader social setting and that greater benefit is likely to occur if there is contex-tual support for the formal curriculum programmes. McBride, Midford & Farringdon, (1998) suggested that whole-of-school approaches should ensure that the school policy and practices complement the education message; that services are provided for at-risk students and that the local school community, particularly parents, are involved in the education process. However, these authors also acknowledged that getting schools to adopt a comprehensive approach to drug education is difficult. There are an increasing number of educational issues vying for a place on the school agenda, and attracting broad support for an issue that is generally not seen as core business for a school is difficult, particularly if additional resources and training are not provided. Any effect achieved by intense whole-of-school programmes will also be more vulnerable to withdrawal of resources. A curriculum approach, however, is more achievable in terms of existing resources, more easily integrated into and maintained within existing teaching structures and offers greater coverage per unit cost. Evaluation of a national drug education programme in Australia (Midford & McBride, 1999) indicated that comprehensive and intense drug education in selected schools achieved a greater level of drug education activity than system-wide teacher training. However, this change only occurred in a few schools, whereas the global approach achieved less change, but in a greater number of schools. Midford & McBride (1999) suggested that the emphasis of a programme should be determined by its objectives, whether that be reach or intensity. Schools that have had little drug education will probably be best served by broad-based teacher training, which will create the skill base and motivation for further development. In contrast, those schools that have reached a certain level of accomplishment in drug education are more likely to have the capacity to undertake a more intense, whole-of-school approach.

Perry and her colleagues (Perry et al., 1996, Perry and Kelder, 1992, Perry and Murray, 1985) recognized the importance of the social environment in determining drug use by young people and suggested that, if schools are to be effective in achieving sustained change, their programmes have to be reinforced at the broader community level. They offered several reasons for undertaking community-wide prevention efforts in support of school drug education. Those students with a high risk of alcohol and drug use are likely to be alienated from the education process and thus may not be receptive to school-based programmes. They are also more likely to drop out of school early and thus not receive school-based education. Major social influences that affect alcohol and drug use by young people include parents, peers, significant adults in the community and the media. Most of these groups are not associated with the school and prevention messages may best come directly from these sources. The community also formally and informally regulates alcohol consumption by young people. There are laws that regulate access to alcohol and there are social norms as to acceptable drinking practices. These contribute in a major way to the patterns of consumption by young people and changes here may complement education programmes.

A good example of a broad community approach to alcohol education for young people is provided by Project Northland. This is a large, long-term, community-wide programme, conducted in six north-eastern counties of Minnesota. The project sought to prevent or reduce alcohol use among younger adolescents and has achieved a measure of success (Perry et al., 1996). At the end of 3 years, students in the school districts who received the intervention, reported lower onset of use and lower levels of use than students in the control districts. However, this must be seen in context. The achievements of a well-funded project implemented by highly motivated and capable researchers are not likely to be replicated in schools that do not receive this extra support. Follow-up of these students in high school also indicated that the initial positive results attenuated. Perry et al. (1998) reported that by the end of the 10th grade, there was no significant difference in alcohol consumption between students in the intervention and control districts. It would seem that although a number of normative and interpersonal factors were influenced by the initial 3 year intervention, these changes were not sufficient to maintain lower levels of use when the students reached high school. These results indicate that alcohol use may be particularly resistant to long-term change, which Perry et al. (1993) attribute to society not providing consistent, clear and compelling messages about adolescent alcohol use. However, the relevance, for older adolescents, of an abstinence-focused alcohol education approach also seems a factor, whether or not such a goal is reinforced at the local community level. Education programmes, no matter how comprehensive or well-resourced, cannot control all messages on alcohol. The perception gained by many young people via media images and personal experience is that alcohol is an integral part of adult life and learning how to drink is a part of becoming an adult (Petosa, 1992). It seems logical, therefore, to assume that as young people approach adulthood, an increasing number will drink alcohol.

Broadening and reinforcing curriculum-based health education with complementary community initiatives has been demonstrably successful (McBride & Midford, 1996), and there is a reasonable expectation that such an approach to alcohol education would also provide advantages. However, whole-of-school or community approaches have to resist making the same mistake of the early curriculum-based approaches. If the goal is unrealistic, adding extra components to the intervention will not make it any more likely that the goal will be achieved. Abstinence is clearly unrealistic as the only goal, and alcohol prevalence data clearly indicates it is not supported by broader community norms in Western industrialized societies (Grytten, 1997; Jones, 1993; Miller & Plant, 1996; Substance Abuse & Mental Health Services Administration, 1997). As a consequence, not only is the legitimacy of such a goal questionable, but programmes based on such a goal may actually be counterproductive. They provide the appearance that prevention education is being undertaken, while offering little to the large proportion of young people who are already drinking or who may be experiencing consequences from drinking by others.

PERSISTENCE WITH INEFFECTIVE APPROACHES

An example of a drug education programme with a long history of acceptance in schools, but a poor evaluation record in terms of achieving behaviour change, is DARE (Drug Abuse Resistance Education). The programme was developed in 1983 by the Los Angeles Police Department and the Los Angeles Unified School District, with the intention of teaching students the skills to resist drug use. It essentially uses a didactic approach to deliver a strong abstention message, although its distinguishing feature is that community police officers, rather than teachers, provide the education. Ennett et al. (1994) reported that DARE has been adopted by over 50% of school districts in America and the programme also has a significant international presence, with representation in almost 20 countries (Rogers, 1993). DARE has a high profile in the community and is relatively expensive to implement, because of the use of police officers to conduct the extracurricular education. This has meant that a number of evaluations of the programme have been conducted. Some have indicated that the programme is well regarded, such as the study by Donnermeyer & Wurschmidt (1997), which found that 97% of educators in a sample of mid-western schools conducting the DARE programme endorsed the programme. Other evaluations of the programme's impact in particular locations, such as that conducted by Dukes, Ullman & Stein (1995) with students in Colorado Springs, have indicated that the programme does influence students. In the Colorado Springs study, DARE improved self-esteem and institutional bonding and decreased endorsement of risky behaviours, although drug-using behaviour was not measured. A meta-analysis of eight methodologically rigorous DARE outcome evaluations, however, concluded that the programme's short-term effect on drug-using behaviour was small (Ennett et al., 1994). The authors noted the disparity between the programme's popularity and prevalence and its effectiveness, and indicated that this could mean that it was taking the place of other more beneficial drug education interventions. Lindstrom & Svensson (1998) reported similar findings in their evaluation of the Swedish equivalent of DARE, the VAGA programme. They found that students who had undertaken the programme were no different in their attitudes to drugs or actual drug-using behaviour than students who had not participated. On the basis of their findings, they questioned the emphasis of the programme and the use of limited police resources for this task. Australia is another country that has funded drug education programmes that have a high public profile but no proven efficacy. The Life Education programme receives several million dollars a year from government, business and service groups and has a high profile in the community, yet an evaluation of students exposed to the programme found no evidence that it reduced use of alcohol, analgesics or tobacco. Rather, the Life Education students were slightly more likely to use these substances (Hawthorne, Garrard & Dunt, 1995). In a later evaluation of the social impact of the programme in the Australian state of Victoria, Hawthorne (1996) reported that because the programme was institutionalized and reached a wide student audience, estimates could be made of its impact at the population level. In relation to alcohol use, Hawthorne (1996) reported that 22% of all Victorian boys' recent drinking could be attributed to participation in Life Education.

Well-publicized programmes such as DARE and Life Education seem to build up a momentum that is difficult to stop, even though the empirical evidence attests to their ineffectiveness. DARE continues to be the drug education programme of choice in America, despite over a decade of predominantly negative evaluations and a recent review commissioned by the American Department of Education, which concluded that it was among the least effective programmes in use (Silvia & Thorne, 1997). Past experience indicates that ineffective drug education programmes are eventually superseded, but this takes considerable time and is inherently wasteful of resources. Hawthorne's (1996) suggestion for preventing the institutionalization of ineffective programmes is to conduct a thorough evaluation prior to widespread implementation.

THE PROMISE OF HARM REDUCTION APPROACHES

Dielman (1994) considered that the early drug prevention programmes were not able to demonstrate an impact on behaviour, because they tended to adopt unrealistic goals, such as the prevention of any drug use. However, it is arguable that this aspect of drug education has changed much in recent times. Drug education research still tends to be framed in terms of abstinence outcomes, because the great majority of studies have taken place in the USA (Foxcroft et al., 1997), where federal guidelines mandate that prevention programmes emphasize "zero tolerance" and abstinence (Office for Substance Use Prevention, Alcohol, Drug Abuse and Mental Health Administration, 1989). While the research on harm reduction as a goal for drug education has had little support in the past, there is a particularly compelling logic for the use of such an approach with alcohol. The drug is legal, socially acceptable, readily available and problems tend to be associated with binge-drinking occasions (Single, 1996). Given these parameters, abstinence is unlikely and greater benefit should accrue from education to reduce binge-drinking and equip people with the skills to deal better with the risks associated with settings where such drinking occurs. Such an approach is even more applicable to young people, because of their lack of knowledge about alcohol, their inexperience with drinking and their greater propensity to binge-drink in high-risk settings.

McBride et al. (1998) and the Australian Drug Foundation (undated) found that alcohol education was more meaningful for students if it acknowledged their experiences with alcohol. In this regard, a harm reduction approach was received positively by students, because it was not judgemental about their experiences and offered something useful to all students, whether they had started drinking or not. Midford & McBride (1999) found that in Australia, teachers generally understood and were very supportive of the concept, because it permitted them to be more open in their discussions of drug use. Parents in Australia were also supportive of the approach in relation to alcohol, because they typically introduced their own children to alcohol at home and did not expect schools to impose a moralistic view of alcohol use (Australian Drug Foundation, undated). In a study of alcohol and other drug use in Nova Scotia, Canada, Poulin & Elliot (1997) indicated that for the 27% of students who reported at least one alcohol-related problem, a harm-reduction approach would be more relevant than trying to prevent use. Yet these researchers acknowledged that there was little evidence as to the effectiveness of school-based harm reduction programmes.

An alcohol education study by Shope et al. (1994) is one of the first to explore the harm-reduction benefits they may derive from education. These researchers found that while there was no difference in the level of alcohol use between intervention and control groups, the harms deriving from alcohol use did not increase as rapidly in an intervention subgroup with a prior history of unsupervised drinking, as they did in comparable controls. While curriculum materials used in the study contained a strong abstinence message and there was criticism of the small numbers in the subgroup that demonstrated change (Gorman, 1996), it does seem to indicate that harm reduction can be achieved by school drug education and that this is not necessarily linked to reduced consumption. A recent alcohol education research study in Australia, designed to teach harm-reduction skills (McBride et al., 2000) found that the intervention students were significantly more knowledgeable about alcohol after the first phase of the intervention than the control group. They also held attitudes that were significantly more supportive of safe alcohol use and harm reduction and consumed significantly less alcohol than the control group. Change in the level of alcohol harm experienced was not as dramatic, which was to be expected, given a retrospective reporting period longer than the interval between surveys and the gradual nature of behaviour change. However, one subgroup of intervention students, those who reported drinking with adult supervision, did experience significantly less harm than their non-intervention counterparts, subsequent to the intervention. These early findings are promising, and such evidence is very necessary if objective support is to be provided for what Duncan et al. (1994) considered to be a major paradigm shift in drug education, away from use-prevention to abuse prevention or harm reduction. They saw this as a rational response to the failure of efforts aimed at preventing drug use and a coherent organization of prevention resources, so as potentially to yield the greatest benefit to society. Demonstrable behaviour change lends further weight of argument to the benefit of this shift.

The essence of harm reduction is that it acknowledges that people will use drugs and gives priority to preventing harms rather than preventing use. Lenton & Midford (1996) define a harm reduction programme or policy as:

> . . . one in which (1) the primary goal is to reduce net health, social and/or economic harm without necessarily seeking to reduce use, and (2) it can be directly demonstrated against broadly agreed criteria, that net harm across these dimensions has been reduced, rather than claiming or inferring that harm has been reduced from changes in other indices (p. 412).

Some jurisdictions have accepted the logic of harm reduction, such as Canada and Australia, where harm reduction forms the basis of each country's respective national drug policy (Single, 1996; National Drug Strategy Committee, 1993). The approach was initially associated with reducing the harms associated with illicit drug use, which was resistant to traditional prevention and treatment methods. It has only more recently been seen as an appropriate goal for drug education (Duncan et al., 1994; Resnicow & Botvin, 1993). However, while the approach was successful in reducing the spread of HIV among the injecting drug population, there has been insufficient research carried out to determine whether it delivers more effective drug education than traditional abstinence or delayed onset approaches. Duncan et al. (1994) considered that preventing drug abuse or harmful drug use is a different task from preventing all drug use and, according to Resnicow & Botvin (1993) may make drug education more credible and more realistic. This also means that harm reduction may make drug education more effective in terms of achieving stated outcomes, as outcomes can be measured in terms of the amount of harm reduced, rather than in absolutist terms of whether or not abstention was achieved.

CONCLUSION

Drug education as a whole has developed considerably in the last decade and, as a part of this, there is greater understanding of the various influences involved. This is not to say that drug or alcohol education has become demonstrably more effective in changing behaviour. Rather, it seems that there is greater understanding at a component level of the forces that foster drinking and the programme elements that need to be included if a programme is to deal comprehensively and effectively with these forces.

In a recent meta-analysis of 55 school- or college-based drug education programme evaluations that met minimum methodological criteria, White & Pitts (1998) considered that 18 were methodologically sound studies and that 10 of these "sound" studies evidenced some impact on drug-using behaviour. Meta-analysis of 11 "sound" studies, with 1 year follow-up, indicated that the mean effect size was 0.037. This means that over a period of a year the best-researched drug education interventions were able to delay the onset of drug use or stop use in 3.7% of young people who would otherwise have used. Such a study has not been done separately with alcohol education programmes, but the effect size is likely to be even smaller, because both abstinence and use onset have proved more difficult to achieve in relation to alcohol. While this recent meta-analysis demonstrates that drug education programmes still have difficulty in changing behaviour, the authors identified promising individual approaches that produced slightly larger effects. The effective interventions were a mix of focused and generic training, although some elements that worked as part of one programme were also present in unsuccessful programmes. The great majority of programmes that had a longer-term impact were intense in their own right and supported by reinforcing messages. They also usually included booster sessions at a later stage of the programme. White & Pitts (1998), however, found that programmes rarely identified the separate contribution of each component element, which makes it difficult to tease apart why programmes work and optimize the composition of new initiatives.

The more recent drug education studies and reviews of the area indicate that sound school-based interventions do change behaviour and, while the change is small, it occurs at a population level, so the aggregate benefit of good programmes can be large if widely implemented. (McBride et al., 2000; Shope et al., 1994; White & Pitts, 1998). These findings reinforce the importance of assessing alcohol education in terms of utility. In this way there is some objective criterion to differentiate between those programmes that are simply well known or palatable and those that bring about meaningful change. This may seem self-evident, but the political and moral dimensions to drug education mean that certain approaches are more acceptable to the community. The American experience is that a great deal of money is spent on aggressively marketing programmes that either have not been evaluated or have been shown to be ineffective, rather than implementing proven programmes (Dusenbury, Falco & Lake, 1997; Hansen, Rose & Dyfoos, 1993).

Alcohol education will probably always be considered something that schools should provide, but in the past an emphasis on abstinence may have blinded educators to the inadequacies of the programmes chosen and, in the process, discredited the merit of education as a prevention measure. In the future, programmes need to be more realistic about their goals and accountable for their achievements. The benefit would be that schools spend time and money on education that has greater potential for bringing about useful change, and students are more likely to be provided with knowledge, values and skills that equip them to make better decisions about alcohol. In order to achieve these ends, there needs to be a broader range of research on alcohol education and this research must come to terms with the objectives of harm reduction. Beck (1998) pointed out that, because of historical movements aimed at prohibiting alcohol use, most research has evaluated how successful programmes have been at maintaining abstinence or delaying onset. As a consequence, evaluations may have assessed programmes as being ineffective because they did not achieve this. Such programmes may have actually achieved other benefits but typically these would not have been considered relevant. An even more concerning implication of this emphasis on abstinence is that other worthwhile goals, such as practising responsible decision making in relation to alcohol, or even just possessing the practical knowledge to be capable of making better decisions, have not been part of the research agenda. Within such a framework, they are not considered the legitimate business of alcohol education for young people. This continuing repetition of past mistakes suggests that it is timely for researchers to investigate less absolutist alternatives, on the basis that achieving some beneficial change is better than failing comprehensively to persuade young people that they should not drink at all. Alcohol consumption is an established aspect of Western industrialized societies. Accordingly, these societies have an obligation to educate and support their young people, so that they have the conceptual framework to be able to make responsible decisions about drinking as they grow older and the practical skills to implement those decisions.

KEY WORKS AND SUGGESTIONS FOR FURTHER READING

Beck, J. (1998).   100 years of "Just say no" vs. "Just say know". *Evaluation Review*, **22**(1), 15–45.

This article comprehensively reviews the history of American school-based drug education. Its particular contribution is that it provides an insight into how current approaches have been shaped by a long sequence of previous interventions and how future decisions need to be informed by past mistakes.

Dielman, T.E. (1994).   School-based research on the prevention of adolescent alcohol use and misuse: methodological issues and advances. *Journal of Research on Adolescence*, **4**(2), 271–293.

Dielman looks at why early school-based alcohol education approaches failed to achieve abstinence. He suggests that alcohol education programs need to be more realistic about what they can achieve and presents findings from his research, indicating that education can reduce alcohol harm.

Dusenbury, L. & Falco, M. (1995).   Eleven components of effective drug abuse prevention curricula. *Journal of School Health*, **63**(10), 420–425.

These two researchers comprehensively review recent school-based drug education programs and interview leading experts in prevention research to identify the key elements of effective drug education curricula. On the basis of their findings, they identify 11 critical components that contribute to effective programs.

Perry, C.C. & Kelder, S.H. (1992). Prevention. *Annual Review of Addictions Research and Treatment*, 463–472.

This is a review of primary prevention strategies used with youth. The paper is broad-ranging and explores how the effectiveness of school based programs can be enhanced by parallel media, community and public policy interventions.

White, D. & Pitts, M. (1998). Educating young people about drugs: a systematic review. *Addiction*, **93**(10), 1475–1487.

This is a very comprehensive meta-analysis of methodologically sound drug education studies. It provides a very useful summary as to the impact of drug education on drug using behaviour and identifies those components that consistently feature in the more successful programs.

REFERENCES

Anslinger, H.J. & Tompkins, W.F. (1953). *The Traffic in Narcotics*. New York: Funk and Wagnalls.

Australian Drug Foundation (undated). *Reducing the Risk 1. The Risk Reduction Approach to Alcohol Education*. Melbourne: Australian Drug Foundation.

Ballard, R., Gillespie, A. & Irwin, R. (1994). *Principles for Drug Education in Schools*. Belconnen, ACT: University of Canberra.

Bandura, A. (1977). *Social Learning Theory*. Englewood Cliffs, NJ: Prentice-Hall.

Bangert-Drowns, R.L. (1988). The effects of school-based substance abuse education—a meta-analysis. *Journal of Drug Education*, **18**(3), 243–264.

Beck, J. (1998). 100 years of "Just Say No" versus "Just Say Know". *Evaluation Review*, **22**(1), 15–45.

Botvin, G.J. (1990). Substance abuse prevention: theory, practice and effectiveness. In M. Tonry & J.Q. Wilson (Eds), *Drugs and Crime*, Vol. 13. Series: Crime and Justice: A Review of Research. Chicago, IL: University of Chicago Press.

Coggans, N. & Watson, J. (1995). Drug education: approaches, effectiveness and delivery. *Drugs: Education, Prevention and Policy*, **2**(3), 211–224.

Dielman, T.E. (1994). School-based research on the prevention of adolescent alcohol use and misuse: methodological issues and Advances. *Journal of Research on Adolescence*, **4**(2), 271–293.

Donnermeyer, J.F. & Wurschmidt, T.D. (1997). Educators perceptions of the DARE program. *Journal of Drug Education*, **27**(33), 259–276.

Dukes, R.L. Ullman, J.B. & Stein, J.A. (1995). An evaluation of DARE (Drug Abuse Resistance Education), using a Solomon four-groups design with latent variables. *Evaluation Review*, **19**(4), 409–435.

Duncan, D.F., Nicholson, T., Clifford, P., Hawkins, W. & Petosa, R. (1994). Harm reduction: an emerging new paradigm for drug education. *Journal of Drug Education*, **24**(4), 281–290.

Duryea, E., Mohr, P., Newman, I., Martin, G. & Egwaoje, E. (1984). Six-month follow-up results of a preventative alcohol intervention. *Journal of Drug Education*, **14**, 97–104.

Dusenbury, L. & Falco, M. (1995). Eleven components of effective drug abuse prevention curricula. *Journal of School Health*, **65**(10), 420–425.

Dusenbury, L., Falco, M. & Lake, A. (1997). A review of the evaluation of 47 drug abuse prevention curricula available nationally. *Journal of School Health*, **67**(4), 127–133.

Ennett, S.T., Tobler, N.S., Ringwalt, C.L. & Flewelling, R.L. (1994). How effective is Drug Abuse Resistance Education? A meta-analysis of Project DARE Outcome Evaluations. *American Journal of Public Health*, **84**(9), 1394–1401.

Foxcroft, D.R., Lister-Sharp, D. & Lowe, G. (1997).   Alcohol misuse prevention for young people: a systematic review reveals methodological concerns and lack of reliable evidence of effectiveness. *Addiction*, **92**(5), 531–537.

Foxcroft, D.R. & Lowe, G. (1997).   Adolescents' alcohol use and misuse: the socializing influence of perceived family life. *Drugs: Education, Prevention and Policy*, **4**(3), 215–229.

Goodstadt, M. (1980).   School-based drug education in North America: what is wrong? What can be done? *Journal of School Health*, **56**, 278–281.

Gorman, D.M. (1996).   Do school-based social skills training programs prevent alcohol use among young people? *Addiction Research*, **4**(2), 191–210.

Grytten, L. (1997).   *Rusmidler I Norge Alcohol and Drugs in Norway 1997*. Oslo: The Norwegian Directorate for the Prevention of Alcohol and Drug Problems and the National Institute for Alcohol and Drug Research.

Hansen, W.B. (1993).   School-based alcohol prevention programs. *Alcohol Health & Research World*, **17**(1), 54–60.

Hansen, W.B. & Graham, J.W. (1991).   Preventing alcohol, marijuana, and cigarette use among adolescents: peer pressure resistance training vs. establishing conservative norms. *Preventive Medicine*, **20**, 414–430.

Hansen, W.B., Rose, L.A. & Dyfoos, J.G. (1993).   *Causal Factors. Interventions and Policy Considerations in School Based Substance Abuse Prevention*, Washington, DC: US Congress, Office of Technology Assessment.

Hawthorne, G. (1996).   The social impact of Life Education: estimating drug use prevalence among Victorian primary school students and the statewide effect of the Life Education programme. *Addiction*, **91**(8), 1151–1159.

Hawthorne, G., Garrard, J. & Dunt, D. (1995).   Does Life Education's programme have a public health benefit? *Addiction*, **90**(2), 205–215.

Holder, H.D. (1992).   What is a community and what are implications for prevention trials for reducing alcohol problems? In H.D. Holder & J.M. Howard (Eds), *Community Prevention Trials for Alcohol Problems*. Westport, CT: Praeger.

Kelder, S.H., Perry, C.L., Klepp, K.I. & Lytle, L.L. (1994).   Longitudinal tracking of adolescent smoking, physical activity and food choice behaviour. *American Journal of Public Health*, **84**(7), 1121–1126.

Kinder, B., Pape, N. & Walfish, S. (1980).   Drug and alcohol education. A review of outcome studies. *International Journal of the Addictions*, **15**, 1035–1054.

Jones, R. (1993).   *Drug Use and Exposure in the Australian Community*. Canberra: Australian Government Publishing Service.

Johnston, L.D., O'Malley, P.M. & Bachman, J.G. (1989).   *Drug Use, Drinking and Smoking: National Survey Results from High School, College, and Young Adult Populations, 1975–1988*. National Institute on Drug Abuse, DHHS Publication No.(ADM) 89-1638. Washington, DC: Superintendant of Documents, US Government Printing Office.

Lang, E. (1994).   Community action regarding licensing issues. In T. Stockwell (Ed.), *Alcohol Misuse and Violence 5, An Examination of the Appropriateness and Efficacy of Liquor-Licensing Laws Across Australia*. Canberra: Australian Government Publishing Service.

Lender, M.E. & Martin, J.K. (1987).   *Drinking in America: A History*. New York: Free Press.

Lenton, S. & Midford, R. (1996).   Clarifying harm reduction? *Drug and Alcohol Review*, **15**, 411–413.

Lindstrom, P. & Svensson, R. (1998).   Attitudes towards drugs among youths: an evaluation of the Swedish DARE programme. *Nordisk Alkohol & Narkotikatidskrift*, **15**(English Suppl.).

McBride, N. & Midford, R. (1996).   Assessing organizational support for school health promotion. *Health Education Research Theory and Practice*, **11**(4), 509–518.

McBride, N., Midford, R. & Farringdon, F. (1998).   Alcohol harm reduction education in schools: An Australian efficacy study. In T. Stockwell (Ed.), *Drug Trials and Tribulations: Lessons for Australian Drug Policy*. Perth: National Centre for Research into the Prevention of Drug Abuse, Curtin University of Technology, Perth.

McBride, N., Midford, R., Farringdon, F. & Phillips, M. (2000).   Early results from a school alcohol harm minimisation intervention: the School Health and Alcohol Harm Reduction Project. *Addiction*, **95**(7), 1021–1042.

McBride, N., Midford, R., Woolmer, J. & Philp, A. (1998). *Youth Alcohol Forum: Evaluation Report.* Perth: National Centre for Research into the Prevention of Drug Abuse, Curtin University of Technology.

McCallum, T. (1990). Educating parents as drug educators. *Drug Education Journal of Australia,* **4**(3), 243–249.

McCallum, T. (1996). Who influences. *Youth Studies Australia,* **Spring**, 36–41.

McGuire, W.J. (1964). Inducing resistance to persuasion: some contemporary approaches. In L. Berkowitz (Ed.), *Advances in Experimental Social Psychology.* New York: Academic Press.

Mallick, J., Evans, R. & Stein, G. (1998). Parents and drug education: parents' concerns, attitudes and needs. *Drugs: Education, Prevention and Policy,* **5**(2), 169–176.

Mezvinsky, N. (1961). Scientific temperance instruction in the schools. *History of Education Quarterly,* **1**, 48–56.

Midford, R. & McBride, N. (1999). Evaluation of a national school drug education program in Australia. *International Journal of Drug Policy,* **10**(3), 177–193.

Milgram, G.G. (1996). Responsible decision making regarding alcohol: a re-emerging prevention/education strategy for the 1990s. *Journal of Drug Education,* **26**(4), 357–365.

Miller, P. M. & Plant, M. (1996). Drinking, smoking, and illicit drug use among 15 and 16 year-olds in the United Kingdom. *British Medical Journal,* **313**, 394–397.

National Drug Strategy Committee (1993). *National Drug Strategic Plan, 1993–97. Commonwealth Department of Health, Housing Local Government and Community Services.* Canberra: Australian Government Publishing Service.

Office for Substance Use Prevention, Alcohol, Drug Abuse and Mental Health Administration (1989). *Message and Material Review Process,* RPO726, Washington, DC: US Government Printing Office.

Perry, C.L. & Kelder, S.H. (1992). Prevention. *Annual Review of Addictions Research and Treatment,* 453–472.

Perry, C.L. & Murray, D.M. (1985). The prevention of adolescent drug abuse: implications from etiological, developmental, behavioural, and environmental models. *Journal of Primary Prevention,* **6**, 31–52.

Perry, C.L., Williams, C.L., Komro, K.A., Veblen-Mortenson, S., Forster, J.L., Bernstein-Lachter, R., Pratt, L.K., Munson, K.A. & Farbakhsh, K. (1998). Project Northland—Phase II: community action to reduce adolescent alcohol use. Paper presented at the Kettil Bruun Society's Fourth Symposium on Community Action Research, Russell, New Zealand, 8–13 February.

Perry, C.L., Williams, C.L., Veblen-Mortenson, S., Toomey, T.L., Komro, K.A., Anstine, P.S., McGovern, P.G., Finnegan, J.R., Forster, J.L., Wagenaar, A.C. & Wolfson, M. (1996). Project Northland: outcomes of a community-wide alcohol use prevention program during early adolescence. *American Journal of Public Health,* **86**(7), 956–965.

Perry, C.L., Williams, C.L., Forster, J.L., Wolfson, M., Wagenaar, A.C., Finnegan, J.R., McGovern, P.G., Veblen-Mortenson, S., Komro, K.A. & Anstine, P.S. (1993). Background, conceptualization, and design of a community-wide research program on adolescent alcohol use: Project Northland. *Health Education Research: Theory & Practice,* **8**(1), 125–136.

Petosa, R. (1992). Developing a comprehensive health promotion program to prevent adolescent drug abuse. In G. Lawson & A. Lawson (Eds), *The Prevention and Treatment of Adolescent Drug Abuse.* Gaithersburg, MD: Aspen.

Poulin, C. & Elliot, D. (1997). Alcohol, tobacco and cannabis use among Nova Scotia adolescents: implications for prevention and harm reduction. *Canadian Medical Association Journal,* **156**(10), 1387–1393.

Quinn, L. (1996). Mobilising parents. *Druglink,* **11**, 9–10.

Resnicow, K. & Botvin, G. (1993). School-based substance use prevention programs: why do effects decay? *Preventive Medicine,* **22**, 481–490.

Rogers, E.M. (1993). Diffusion and re-invention of project DARE. In T.E. Backer & E.M. Rogers (Eds), *Organizational Aspects of Health Communication Campaigns: What Works?* Newbury Park, CA: Sage.

Schaps, E., DiBartolo, R., Moskowitz, J., Palley, C.S. & Churgin, S. (1981). A review of 127 drug abuse prevention program evaluations. *Journal of Drug Issues,* **11**, 17–43.

Schlosser, E. (1994). Reefer madness. *Atlantic Monthly,* **274**(2), 45–63.

Sharp, C. (undated). *Alcohol Education for Young People: A Review of the Literature, 1983–1992. A report for the Alcohol Education and Research Council and the Portman Group.* London: National Foundation for Educational Research.

Shope, J.T., Kloska, D.D., Dielman, T.E. & Maharg, R. (1994). Longitudinal evaluation of an enhanced Alcohol Misuse Prevention Study (AMPS) curriculum for grades six–eight. *Journal of School Health*, **64**, 160–166.

Silvia, E.S. & Thorne, J. (1997). *School-based Drug Prevention Programs: A Longitudinal Study in Selected School Districts.* Research Triangle Park, NC: Research Triangle Park.

Single, E. (1996). Harm reduction as an alcohol-prevention strategy. *Alcohol Health and Research World*, **20**(4), 239–243.

Substance Abuse and Mental Health Services Administration (1997). *National Household Survey on Drug Abuse: Population Estimates 1996.* DHHS Pub. No.(SMA)97-3137. Rockville, MD: US Department of Health and Human Services.

Tobler, N.S. (1986). Meta-analysis of 143 adolescent drug prevention programs: quantitative outcome results of program participants compared to a control or comparison group. *Journal of Drug Issues*, **16**, 537–567.

Waahlberg, R.B. (1988). Alcohol and drug education. In O.J. Skog & R.B. Waahlberg (Eds), *Alcohol and Drugs: The Norwegian Experience*, Oslo: National Directorate for the prevention of Alcohol and Drug Problems.

Wallack, L. (1980). Mass media and drinking, smoking and drug taking. *Contemporary Drug Problems*, **Spring**, 49–83.

White, D. & Pitts, M. (1998). Educating young people about drugs: a systematic review. *Addiction*, **93**(10), 1475–1487.

Wittman, F.D. (1990). Environmental design to prevent problems of alcohol availability: concepts and prospects. In N. Giesbrecht, P. Conley, R.W. Denniston et al. (Eds), *Research, Action, and the Community: Experiences in the Prevention of Alcohol and Other Drug Problems.* OSAP Prevention Monograph No. 4, Rockville, MD: Office for Substance Abuse Prevention.

Chapter 41

Mass Media Marketing and Advocacy to Reduce Alcohol-related Harm

Kevin Boots
Health Department of Western Australia, Perth, Western Australia
and
Richard Midford
National Drug Research Institute, Curtin University of Technology,
Perth, Western Australia

Synopsis

The alcohol industry has for many years used large advertising and public relations budgets to implement sophisticated mass media marketing and advocacy campaigns to further the sale of alcohol. Public health agents are also increasingly advocating and marketing messages about alcohol: those that seek to encourage responsible drinking behaviour and reduce alcohol-related harm. Over time, mass media marketing and advocacy to reduce alcohol-related harm has begun to match the sophistication achieved by the purveyors of alcohol advertising. In the process, much has been learned by public health agents about both marketing and advocacy.

Marketing campaigns that use social marketing strategies, and that seek to reduce alcohol-related harm, compete for advertising space with other advertisers. Sometimes these campaigns also aim to increase the social pressure upon consumers to modify their behaviour by highlighting or seeking to create opposing social norms. More recent campaigns have benefited from the application of new social science theories (such as theories of individual behaviour change and of social marketing), from the use of formative evaluation and from the setting of realistic campaign objectives. The first part of this chapter provides an overview of mass media marketing and examines the current theories of individual behaviour change that underpin the social marketing approach. The two main methods of mass media marketing, advertising and "edutainment", are described, and their application to two recent mass media marketing campaigns are detailed.

International Handbook of Alcohol Dependence and Problems. Edited by N. Heather, T.J. Peters and T. Stockwell.
© 2001 John Wiley & Sons Ltd.

Unfortunately, an implicit tenet of the market-based, individual-focused health system is that those consumers who do not maintain health, or access health care services, are responsible for the consequences. Such an approach in its pure form does not acknowledge the structural determinants of health behaviour. In contrast to the marketing approach, mass media advocacy seeks to create change to the structural determinants of health. Mass media advocacy is a political activity that, along with coalition building and political lobbying, is used to influence decision-makers in order to achieve public health goals. It emphasizes the promotion of healthy behaviours and healthy public policy by influencing decision makers to accept the merit of health-promoting or -protecting policies or structures. The second part of this chapter illustrates the breadth of mass media advocacy activities undertaken by health advocates and provides a detailed example of successful advocacy to reduce alcohol-related harm.

Mass media marketing is most suited to issues that seek incremental change rather than those that directly challenge institutions such as the alcohol industry. Mass media advocacy, on the other hand, is a strategy well suited to challenging institutional practices and creating systemic change. However, in practice, both activities are often undertaken simultaneously. This is because the careful use of advertising can assist in advocating for structural change, and advocacy activity can reinforce or play a part in modifying individual behaviour. The apparent increase in success of these strategies can be attributed partly to improved implementation, partly to the new theories upon which they are now developed, and partly to improved evaluation methodology. Most importantly, however, has been the recognition that mass media marketing and mass media advocacy are more effective when they are only two of many elements within a broader change strategy.

In market-based societies the mass media has for many years been a fertile vehicle for the development and dissemination of alcohol advertising, and for political lobbying by the alcohol industry. Large advertising and public relations budgets, coupled with considerable expertise, have allowed the industry to refine its mass media marketing and advocacy activities with considerable precision. This means that the general public is receiving more sophisticated messages encouraging greater use of alcohol. However, public health agents have increasingly entered the fray by advocating and marketing different messages about alcohol; those that seek to encourage responsible drinking behaviour and reduce alcohol-related harm. Over time, mass media marketing and advocacy to reduce alcohol-related harm has begun to match the sophistication achieved by the purveyors of alcohol advertising. In the process, much has been learned about marketing and advocacy by public health agents in their attempts to have their messages heard in the mass media marketplace.

Mass media marketing and mass media advocacy are similar, in that they are both activities that use the mass media as a vehicle to achieve the same primary goal; that of creating change within the community. However, while change is central to both activities, the type of change targeted and the methods employed are quite different.

This difference in the target of change can be illustrated by reference to a model of change, such as that described by Thompson & Kinne (1990). In their "synthesis of change theories" model, Thompson & Kinne consider that the individual operates within a hierarchical community system. The community comprises component subsystems (such as health and police services) and functions within a broader contextual environment, influenced by such things as prevailing economic conditions. In Thompson & Kinne's model, the individual's behaviour is the end product of the successive influence of each of these components. They suggest that direct change to individual behaviour is brought about by a change in one or more of the subsystem levels within the community system. The reverse, however, also needs to be considered. The collective impact of individual behaviour can itself create change within community structures and the external environment. The target of mass media marketing is squarely on individual behaviour change, while the target of mass media advocacy is on the external environment and other structural determinants of the behaviour targeted.

The relative merit of these and other activities in reducing alcohol-related harm has been the subject of much empirical research over the years (Edwards et al., 1994). Andreasson and colleagues of the Stockholm North Centre for Addiction recently postulated that "if we were to construct a list of effective methods [to prevent alcohol problems], availability measures would be at the top and mass media campaigns at the bottom" (Andreasson et al., 1999). Although their ranking of 10 "prevention methods in the alcohol field according to effectiveness" did not consider the role of media advocacy, the targets of media advocacy (i.e. policies and economic conditions) were rated well above mass media campaigns in terms of influence on alcohol problems.

The worldwide dominance of market-based economies with associated values of "rugged individualism, self-determination, strong individual control and responsibility, and limited government involvement in social activity" (Wallack et al., 1993, p. 7) fosters a parallel approach to health care delivery. Within such a market framework, governments see their role as assisting individuals to make their own health-care choices. There is an expectation that the market-based health care system, when utilized in association with wise, thoughtful and prudent consumerism, rewards individuals by giving them personal control over their health and health-care needs. With equal services available to all, it is assumed that consumers will act in their own best interests; they will identify risks to their health and select health-care products that reduce risk to the extent that they would like.

This focus on the individual has been harnessed by public health practitioners through community interventions that use social marketing strategies. Marketing campaigns that seek to reduce alcohol-related harm compete for advertising space with other advertisers in the marketplace. One example from Australia of such competitive marketing occurred when a national football club promoting an anti-drink–drive message on their uniforms played a game of football against another sponsored by a brewery, within a competition named after a brand of beer. The purpose of social marketing is to compete in the marketplace against forces that have opposing aims, so as to modify consumer behaviour to promote health rather than illness. Sometimes these campaigns also aim to increase the social pressure upon consumers to modify their behaviour by highlighting or actually seeking to create opposing social norms.

The first part of this chapter provides a broad overview of mass media marketing and examines the current theories of individual behaviour change that underpin the social marketing approach. The two main methods of mass media marketing are then described and illustrated. These are advertising and the more recent strategy of "edutainment", which involves the placement of public health themes within popular entertainment.

Unfortunately, an implicit tenet of the market-based, individual-focused health system is that those consumers who do not maintain health, or access health care services, are responsible for the consequences. Such an approach in its pure form does not acknowledge the structural determinants of health behaviour and, as a consequence, there is a real danger of "blaming the victim" (Howat & Fisher, 1986). Social marketing campaigns that change social norms contribute to this by highlighting unhealthy behaviour as both preventable and deviant. A further danger associated with the social marketing of health is that such approaches may become the modern equivalent of the moralistic health crusades of yesteryear, which produced such legislation as the British "Act to Repress the Odious and Loathsome Sin of Drunkenness" in 1606 (Powell, 1988, p. 4).

The structural determinants of health behaviour not accounted for in social marketing campaigns include the impact of key events, secular trends, policies, economic conditions and technology on health outcomes (Thompson & Kinne, 1990). In contrast to the marketing approach, mass media advocacy seeks to create change to these systemic determinants. The importance of this aim is highlighted by Wallack et al. (1993), who noted that:

> For many communities, individual change is linked to social change and social change means addressing the power inequity that contributes to the problem. If power is defined as fundamental to improving health status, getting a message will not be a sufficient intervention. In this case, getting a voice will be the strategy. Unfortunately many of the populations that have the least power, the greatest health problems and the least resources for change are also the least visible to those who have the power to have an impact on disease-generating social conditions (p. 24).

The second part of this chapter examines the role and nature of mass media advocacy to reduce alcohol-related harm. Mass media advocacy is a political activity that, along with coalition building and political lobbying, is used to influence decision-makers in order to achieve public health goals. All three activities challenge the notion that health is a good or service that can be purchased or acquired by individuals according to personal choice. Rather, they emphasize the promotion of healthy behaviours and healthy public policy by influencing decision makers to accept the merit of health-promoting or -protecting policies or structures. This emphasis on the structural determinants of health makes mass media advocacy a potentially powerful tool. There are many reasons to use this tool, scores of different avenues to maximize the benefits of mass media advocacy and many examples of successful advocacy that has achieved the aim of reducing alcohol-related harm.

MASS MEDIA MARKETING

The mass media marketing of messages that aim to reduce alcohol-related harm is an activity that inherently supports and seeks to replicate product-marketing strategies that are associated with the free market economy and its focus on choice, on consumerism and on individuals. The methods used include those of advertising, "edutainment" and publicity.

Advertising is the major method used in the mass media marketing of messages that seek to reduce alcohol-related harm. Advertising may be paid or unpaid (such as public or community service announcements). It has frequently been used to: orientate the public to an issue, such as drink–driving; to teach new concepts or skills, such as how to pour a "standard drink" or to know what a "unit measure" is; to address specific problems, such as remaining under the legal blood alcohol limit; or to highlight the difference between hazardous consumption and safe consumption.

"Edutainment" refers to the deliberate placement of educational messages in media entertainment vehicles, such as television and radio soap operas, films, popular music, comics or novels, in order to achieve defined objectives (Egger, Donovan & Spark, 1993, p. 139). The main intention of edutainment is to have characters in mass media entertainment, particularly television soap opera characters with whom viewers identify, model certain behaviour that social marketers want replicated.

A third strategy used within mass media marketing is that of making publicity. Publicity is frequently used to supplement advertising or advocacy campaigns, but is seldom a strategy used in isolation. This strategy usually uses news networks and therefore, by definition, must present "new" (or at least "renewed") information. As a supplement to an advertising campaign, publicity will often result from an official "launch" of the campaign (frequently using a well-known identity or some form of gimmick) or from some controversy surrounding the campaign.

While edutainment is a new term, neither it nor advertising or publicity are recent phenomena. Groups such as temperance unions have been creating news and even sponsoring mass media advertising since the late nineteenth century, and popular entertainment, such as theatre, has been used as a vehicle to disseminate health-related wisdom since its inception. However, despite their long history, evidence of the effectiveness of early mass media marketing campaigns is difficult to find. According to Backer, Rogers & Sopory (1992, p. xiv), pre-1971 mass media health campaign evaluations mostly showed that the campaigns had failed. Montagne & Scott (1993) indicated that such old-style mass media campaigns in isolation mostly influenced knowledge and had little impact on behaviour. They also tended to target broad audiences, which reduced their ability to focus on specific issues. This meant that old-style campaigns were limited to reinforcing existing social attitudes and norms, such as not drinking and driving. In recent years, mass media marketing has been used as part of larger community-based drug prevention programmes (Pentz et al., 1989; Holder & Treno, 1997). These multi-component programmes have achieved a degree of success, although within such programmes it has been difficult to identify the specific contribution of mass media marketing. The strength of mass media marketing may be to reinforce community awareness of the problems created by alcohol use and prepare the ground for specific interventions (Holder & Treno, 1997). After investigating the efficacy of alcohol-related mass media marketing campaigns, Edwards et al. (1994) concluded that, "there is no present research evidence which can . . . justify expenditure of major resources on . . . mass media public education campaigns, unless these are placed in a broader context of community action" (p. 208). Consequently, it is within the context of broader community action that most examples of successful mass media marketing to reduce alcohol-related problems are found.

As components of such broader action, recent mass media marketing campaigns have, according to Backer et al. (1992, p. xiv), benefited from the application of new social science theories (such as theories of individual behaviour change and of social marketing), from the use of formative evaluation and from the setting of realistic campaign objectives. Each of these elements is described below, before examples of successful mass media advertising and edutainment campaigns are described.

Individual Behaviour Change

Two of the theories of individual behaviour change to have impacted on the development of mass media marketing campaigns are Bandura's (1986) social learning theory and Prochaska & DiClemente's (1992) "transtheoretical approach". Bandura (1986) was dissatisfied with the explanatory powers of the traditional deterministic theories of individual behaviour, which made no allowance for cognition and could not account for learning independently of behaviour. In his social learning theory, the individual is acknowledged as a thinking organism who makes conscious choices about how to interact with the environment. Some learning and change occurs through direct experience, but most occurs vicariously through observation and through modelling the actions of others. The individual can also be an agent for change and an object of change. This concept is known as reciprocal determinism (Nutbeam & Harris, 1998, p. 30) and is important in the understanding of the complex interplay between the individual and the environment and the development of social norms. Social norms are central to the ability of this theory to explain why some behaviours are acquired and others are not. An extension of this is that a change in norms will influence what behaviour people consider attractive and rewarding to learn. Bandura's

(1986) insights into the complex relationship between people and their environment have provided the theoretical foundations for advertising campaigns in recent years, while his recognition of the importance of "modelling" has been fundamental to the development of health-promoting edutainment.

A second model of change that is particularly relevant to mass media marketing, due to its usefulness in identifying and segmenting target groups, is the "transtheoretical approach" (Prochaska, Redding & Evers, 1997). This model suggests that people can be divided into population subgroups according to their stage of progression toward adopting a desired behaviour. The stages of change originally postulated by Prochaska and DiClemente (1992) are pre-contemplation, contemplation, preparation, action, maintenance and termination. The stages are sequential, moving from when an individual is not yet considering modifying his/her unhealthy behaviour, to when the problem behaviour is completely eliminated and the individual is not able to be tempted to return to the unhealthy behaviour. People in one stage will respond to different messages from those in another stage. For example, a marketing campaign teaching people the skills of controlled drinking will be useful to problem drinkers who have recognized that change in their drinking is needed and are thus in the preparation or action stages. It will not, however, be appropriate for problem drinkers in the pre-contemplation phase who are not aware that such skills could be useful to them.

Social Marketing

Another body of knowledge that has had a significant impact upon the mass media marketing of alcohol harm issues is that of "social marketing". Social marketing is derived from "commercial marketing", which has the three basic tenants of "consumer orientation, an integrated approach, and the pursuit of profitability or other predetermined objectives" (Hastings & Haywood, 1991). The interplay between product, price, place and promotion, the "marketing mix", is considered fundamental to the success or failure of the marketing strategy.

Social marketing theory has provided a model of the process involved in developing mass media campaigns. Three elements of this process are the accurate identification of the target group, the creation of the most effective message, and the selection of the most appropriate method and media (Egger, Donovan & Spark, 1993).

Social marketing recognizes that knowledge of the target audience is paramount to successful mass media marketing. While media campaigns are popularly thought to be able to achieve "mass reach", it is a myth that a message disseminated amongst an entire population will reach everyone in that population. As a consequence, if public health agents want to reach specific groups, such as binge drinkers, they need to know about this group. Information that they should collect includes the target group demographics, needs, attitudes, beliefs and knowledge of the media channels they access. To be effective, it is important to understand that there is rarely one universal market for a single message, but a variety of different target groups that require different programmes and messages. Segmentation is a useful strategy to help define a market and target a message to ensure best use of resources. Market segmentation involves breaking down the total market into various subgroups. Each group is defined in a way that implies some differences in their response to various marketing activities. For example the subgroups may have different needs requiring different product variations; different media channels may reach them; or they may respond to different advertising appeals. The basis for target audience segmentation may be demographic, geographic, psychographic, sociodemographic, epidemiological, behavioural, attitudinal, related to the benefits sought, or related directly to the stages of change identified by the "transtheoretical approach" of Prochaska & DiClemente (Egger, Donovan & Spark, 1993).

Social marketing theory also focuses on "getting the message right". Language, style and tone must be consistent, not only with the campaign objectives, but also to the background and life-style of the target audience. The message must be understood, accepted and suitably motivating to the target audience. An approach must be developed that differentiates the message from others and that presents the message in a fresh and timely manner.

Another area in which social marketing theory has supported the development of mass media campaigns has been through its identification and critique of the array of marketing methods and media. As well as choosing between advertising, edutainment and publicity mass media, marketers must choose between a variety of media, such as television, the Internet, print media such as newspapers and magazines, and outdoor media such as billboards and signs. The choices between the forms of media are generally made according to cost and ability of the medium to target the selected audience, while the choices between method are made in relationship to the change outcome sought.

Formative Evaluations

Recent mass media marketing campaigns also benefit from the widespread use of evaluation. Specific formative evaluation is now recognized as critical to campaign development (Simons-Morton, Donohew & Davis Crump, 1997), and the increasing use of process, output and outcome evaluation further contributes to the refinement of campaigns as they proceed. Formative evaluation is about undertaking research and product testing before campaign implementation in order to identify the best message, medium and method available within the existing resource constraints. After the creation of the marketing objectives, the translation of these objectives into the campaign is of critical importance. Formative evaluation should involve testing of the marketing mix (i.e. price, product, place and promotion) with the intended target audience, and will often be undertaken using focus groups, surveys or in-depth interviews. The social science theories described above provide insights into how campaigns should be developed, but without formative evaluation mass media marketing campaigns run the risk of missing their target. Likewise, process, output and outcome evaluation has allowed public health promoters to modify and improve their campaigns in line with their intended goals.

Achievable Objectives

Backer, Rogers & Sopory (1992, p. xiv) also suggest mass media campaigns have benefited by setting more modest achievable campaign objectives and recent projects, such as the New Zealand Community Alcohol Project, have benefited by setting "realistic objectives" (Casswell, Ransom & Gilmore, 1990). Early campaigns that sought to create individual behaviour change focused their outcome evaluations on identifying significant community-wide changes in behaviour. This simplistic approach did not acknowledge the complex nature of the process of change or the complexities involved in the communication of information. More often than not, there are a range of intermediary steps that can be identified between campaign implementation and large-scale community change. For example, a campaign targeting binge drinkers, who are unaware that their drinking behaviour is defined as "binge-drinking", will not engage the target group. Such a campaign, targeting a group of people in a "precontemplation" stage, should have problem awareness as the primary objective, not behaviour change. In this example, the outcome measures used to identify campaign "success" would vary according to the primary objective. Should the objective be behaviour change and the relevant outcome measures applied, the campaign will almost certainly be deemed a "failure" (even if the campaign resulted in 100% of the target group contemplating whether they are binge-drinkers).

The triad of modest achievable objectives, formative research and a basis in valid social science theory has been the foundation of numerous recent mass media marketing campaigns. One example that primarily used the method of advertising and one that primarily used edutainment are described below. They constitute examples of the "best practice" use of mass media marketing to reduce alcohol-related harm.

Mass Media Advertising and Edutainment to Reduce Alcohol-related Harm: Case Studies

An evaluation of the Danish National Campaigns on Alcohol presented in the mass media since 1990 provides an example of what can be achieved by a mass media campaign based on many of the principles outlined above. The campaign had three overall goals related to "sensible" alcohol consumption and an overall goal of reduction in total consumption. These goals were operationalized into four objectives that included increasing knowledge of, and the number of, people who followed the national recommended guidelines for consumption, and of increasing the number of local organizations active in support of the campaign.

Strunge (1998) reported the evaluation results for the years 1990–1996, during which annual mass media campaigns were developed and implemented. Awareness of the campaigns was high (around 70%) in each year except 1991, and was particularly high in 1990. This latter result was probably related to the provocative nature of the 1990 campaign, which resulted in additional publicity in the news media. Correspondingly, the lower 1991 result was seen to be the result of the lack of a provocative message, a smaller campaign budget (50% of the 1990 budget), lack of television advertising, and a longer time-lag (5 weeks) between the campaign closure and the evaluation.

The campaign was shown to have reached its knowledge objectives. Knowledge of the weekly unit guidelines was shown to increase steadily over the period from absolute zero in 1990 to 52% of the population in 1997. Knowledge of the unit contents of beer and wine (which is essential to know in order to calculate the weekly amounts consumed) was low for wine (35–42%), but high for beer (60–70%), with an annual but less marked increase during the period surveyed.

A small percentage of survey respondents indicated that the campaigns had directly influenced their behaviour (4–5%), and 12% of people surveyed in 1997 stated that they had reduced their alcohol consumption, with the majority reporting that health concerns were the motivation for this reduction.

In his description of the campaign, Strunge (1998) reveals that realistic goals were established, that the media campaign was supported by community action, that evaluation was an integral part of the campaign strategy, and that careful consideration was given to identifying the target group, the best advertising medium and an appropriate message. He concluded that "it is possible to generate positive awareness of alcohol information", and that "a continuous effort is necessary to maintain and increase the effects of the campaigns".

The Harvard Alcohol Project is an important alcohol harm-reduction project that has attempted to use edutainment to reduce alcohol-related problems. Beginning in 1988, the project sought to introduce the concept of a "designated driver" as a new social norm in the USA. A significant aspect of the project was the use of entertainment television to promote the designated driver concept. The slogan, "The Designated Driver is the Life of the Party" was used because:

1. It promotes a new social norm that the driver does not drink any alcohol.
2. It lends social legitimacy to the non-drinker's role.
3. It encourages people to plan ahead for transportation if they intend to drink.
4. It asks for only a modest shift in behaviour (Winsten, 1994).

By 1994, more than 160 prime-time television programmes had included the notion of the designated driver in a television episode, sometimes as a sub-plot, sometimes casually within the dialogue, and, on over 25 occasions, as the entire theme of the television show. In order to achieve this coverage, the project staff spoke with more than 250 producers and writers associated with all the leading prime time television entertainment shows and convinced them to support the project objectives.

Evaluation of the impact of the concept has been undertaken by using opinion polls that ask respondents about their use of designated drivers. DeJong (1997) reported that in 1993 64% of adults reported that "they and their friends assign a designated driver when they go out for social events where alcoholic beverages are consumed". Of those who assign a designated driver, two-thirds said that they always designate a driver.

DeJong & Winsten (1990) describe the Harvard Alcohol Project as "a mix of state-of-the-art advertising and public relations strategies". It is a product of social science research, such as social marketing theory, of thorough formative evaluation and of ongoing process, output and outcome evaluation, and of a comprehensive programme that included community organization and advocacy strategies.

Obstacles to "Successful" Mass Media Marketing

A range of obstacles to successful mass media marketing of alcohol-related messages can also be identified from the literature. These include, first, the complexity of changing individual behaviour through marketing, particularly in the substance use area; second, the suitability of the mass media as a means of prevention and the related fundamental differences between non-profit mass media marketing and commercial mass media marketing; and third, the power that the liquor industry has over the media through its considerable financial investment in advertising.

The complexity involved in changing individual behaviour through mass media marketing reduces the power of this strategy to reduce alcohol-related harm. The mass media, by its nature, has difficulty in targeting individuals whose behaviour social marketeers want to change. Even the very best population targeting strategy, with careful audience segmentation, still results in a scatter-gun approach, where many of the audience are not the target. Furthermore, the delay between uptake of the behaviour change sought and most of the health benefits to be received is often considerable. As Backer, Rogers & Sopory (1992) note:

> Preventive behaviour is a particularly difficult goal to achieve through mass media campaigns. An individual must change behaviour now to lower the probability of some unwanted future event that may not happen anyway (p. xiv).

The solution frequently used to address this delay, that of focusing marketing efforts on immediate benefits, will often result in campaigns to sell lesser, easy-to-gain benefits in favour of more significant longer-term benefits.

A second obstacle to the successful mass media marketing of alcohol harm-reduction messages is related to medium of the mass media itself. As a tool for educational purposes, the medium has significant constraints because most mass media outlets are privately owned and exist for the purposes of providing entertainment to its audience, with the sponsorship of its advertisers. Perry and Kelder (1992) suggest that:

> The mass media is primarily a private commercial entertainment medium which, as most research to date confirms, substantially limits its potential as a primary prevention method.

Related to this is the fundamental difference between non-profit mass media marketing and commercial mass media marketing. While commercial marketing principles have been useful in improving mass media marketing of alcohol health-related messages, the flexibility that commercial marketers have to change their product, price, promotion and/or place is simply not available to the public health field, which "cannot abandon its product and diversify its main interests just because its main product may not be very popular" (Tones, 1996). The need to reduce complex issues into the simple format demanded by the medium (such as the 30-second advertisement) is a third obstacle of the medium itself. However, one way to reduce the potential of this obstacle to nullify such mass media campaigns is to ensure that the campaign is part of a broader educational strategy, that utilizes a range of educational tools and methods to build on the attention created by mass media exposure.

Third, in most countries the liquor industry is one of the major advertisers within the mass media. Consequently, there is likely to be a level of self-censorship within the mass media against messages which could impact upon liquor sales. This censorship will affect paid advertising less than unpaid public or community service announcements, but will impact upon attempts to introduce "edutainment" to soap opera-style media. For example, Perry & Kelder (1992) suggest that:

> Even the Harvard project, while a model of cooperation, sponsored a message consistent with the alcohol industry of reducing liability rather than reducing the quantity consumed.

It is likely that anticonsumption messages will receive more hostile treatment from the mass media than those that do not directly challenge the consumption of alcohol.

Each of these obstacles indicate that mass media marketing is most suited to mainstream issues that seek incremental change, rather than those that directly challenge institutions such as the alcohol industry. Mass media advocacy, on the other hand, is a strategy well-suited to challenging institutional practices and creating systemic change.

MASS MEDIA ADVOCACY

The term "advocacy" has many connotations and has been defined in a number of ways, including:

> Advocacy is a catch-all word for the set of skills used to create a shift in public opinion and mobilize the necessary resources and forces to support an issue, policy or constituency (Wallack et al., 1993, p. 27).

> Public health advocacy—sometimes called public health lobbying—is an expression used most often to refer to the process of overcoming major structural (as opposed to individual or behavioural) barriers to public health goals (Chapman & Lupton, 1994, p. 6).

In this chapter, "advocacy" refers to the promotion of healthy behaviours and healthy public policy by influencing decision makers to accept the merit of processes, policies or structures that bestow a health advantage. A major tool used in this process is political lobbying, which is the presenting of arguments in favour of a particular policy course to those making the policy decision. Another is coalition building, which involves the development of groups and individuals in a community which have a common policy objective. A third is the use of mass media, typically the news media, to highlight and advance a particular public health issue. This approach has been promoted by Wallack (1990a) and is commonly referred to as "media advocacy".

A major challenge for health advocates is to move the debate from individually focused, simple definitions of problems to a level of complex sociopolitical conceptualization, where the targeted health problem is seen as a product of the interaction between the individual and the environment. According to Wallack et al. (1993):

> Advocacy is necessary to steer public attention away from disease as a personal problem to health as a social issue . . . (and) . . . advocacy is a strategy for blending science and politics with a social justice value orientation to make the system work better, particularly for those with the least resources (p. 5).

The most successful public health policy reformers have based their advocacy on sound research data and have utilized all three approaches to achieve their objectives. The approach has been successfully applied in the areas of smoking control (Erickson et al., 1990), workplace health promotion (Chapman & Lupton, 1994) and the alcohol, AIDS and nutrition areas (Wallack, 1990b).

The History and Politics of Advocacy

Advocacy is by no means a new process, as those involved in promoting prohibition on alcohol in the 1890s were engaged in just the same practices (Lewis, 1992). Advocacy was, however, generally confined to issues of patients' rights. In these issues, the role of advocates was to represent victims or sufferers of injustice by speaking on their behalf to the authority that controlled their circumstances. The definitions provided above reveal that the modern use of the term "advocacy" is much broader than that of patients' rights and less moralistic than temperance movement campaigns of the 1800s.

Advocacy is a political activity, because it encourages social change via a political route. Such change is likely to challenge the status quo and therefore the concept and practice of advocacy is often described in negative terms by those in government. Advocacy can target the laws of federal, state or local government, policies of governments or private institutions, or the actions of groups or industries that seek to oppose public health goals. However, the hostility provoked by any attempt to change the status quo is a significant barrier to advocacy goals.

Advocacy Strategies

While media advocacy is a subject of this chapter, there is increasing recognition that successful media advocacy is dependent upon the implementation of coalition building and political advocacy. As Wallack et al. (1993) note:

The reality is that mass media, whether public information campaigns, social marketing approaches, or media advocacy initiatives, are simply not sufficient to stimulate significant and lasting change on public health issues. The power for change comes from a broader advocacy that has widespread community support. Coalition building, leadership development, and extensive public participation form the foundation from which successful advocacy and media initiatives can make a difference (p. 27).

Media advocacy has been defined by a number of people. Some examples are:

Media advocacy refers to the strategic use of news media by those seeking to advance a social or public policy initiative (Holder & Treno, 1997, p. S190).

Media advocacy is the process of overcoming major structural (as opposed to individual or behavioural) barriers to public health goals (Chapman & Lupton, 1994, p. 6).

Media advocacy seeks to influence the selection of topics by the mass media and shape the debate about these topics. Media advocacy's purpose is to contribute to the development and implementation of social and policy initiatives that promote health and well-being and are based on the principles of social justice (Wallack et al., 1993, p. 73).

Media advocacy to reduce alcohol-related harm may be used for many different purposes. For example, it can be used to set a public agenda by heightening the profile of an alcohol-related problem through the presentation of research findings; it can be used to espouse the benefits or success of a programme or intervention in order to support its refunding; it can be used to publicly oppose or question the actions of members of the alcohol industry when those actions are likely to increase alcohol-related harm; it can support the call for increased resource allocation to address alcohol-related problems; or it can highlight the inadequacies of government action to address alcohol-related problems.

In practice, media advocacy can involve many different actions, from covert action such as releasing confidential information to the media, to overt actions such as issuing a media release related to concerns about an alcohol product like alcoholic ice-blocks. Chapman & Lupton (1994) provide a list of 66 advocacy issues, tips and discussion points, and illustrate these with numerous examples that provide public health workers with a comprehensive picture of media advocacy in practice. Examples include:

Advertising in advocacy. Careful use of advertising can support or even initiate news or current affairs coverage, as well as being an advocacy tool in its own right. For example, a large paid advertisement in the Australian newspapers called on state health ministers to introduce standard drinks labelling on alcohol containers (see example below). This advertisement was used to generate media releases in each state with local organizations available for interview, and consequently significant media coverage was gained.

Anniversaries. Health promoters can often create a "new" newsworthy story out of a story that occurred in the past by advertising an anniversary of an event or instituting a day of remembrance. Such events will probably be significant public events, such as gun massacres, notorious chemical spills or nuclear accidents, or the death of a famous person from a particular disease/condition. This is similar to "*piggy-backing*" which is the act of adding your issue to a similar current issue being run in the media. For example, in the event of a large chemical spill somewhere in the world, a local advocacy group may choose to parallel their concerns about a chemical warehouse in their area with this event. This act of "piggy-backing" will often be supported by the media and receive media coverage.

Creative epidemiology. This is a term used to describe the process of translating complex epidemiological data into media-friendly terms. For example, if 18,000 people per year die in Australia as a result of smoking (on average), 10 people die every day in Perth as a result of smoking. Large numbers can lose their impact and therefore it is often useful to localize and humanize statistics.

Letters to the editor. Like advertising, the writing of a letter to the editor of a newspaper is another form of undertaking media advocacy. It may also result in further public debate and media interest. Such letters, however, must fit within the guidelines issued by the newspaper and are more likely to be published if well written and topical.

Opinion polls. Opinion polls can be a very effective part of media advocacy, because they can form the basis of a media release. The use of polls to support your view is of course a standard ploy used by people for many years. Such polls are often treated sceptically by the public, but nevertheless they can be invaluable if used carefully. Even "quick and dirty" polls of small sample sizes, which ask questions that produce the "right" answers, when released before a decision making process is to begin, and when released by a respected organization, can prove effective. Polls by opponents of your view, or those of related issues, can also be valuable as an opportunity to present your case. A prompt response will be required to "piggy-back" on someone else's research.

Mass Media Advocacy to Reduce Alcohol-Related Harm: Case Study

An example of the role that media advocacy can play to reduce alcohol-related harm is described by Hawks (1996) and by Stockwell & Single (1997). They record the process, outputs and outcome of attempts to introduce compulsory "standard drinks" labelling on all Australian alcohol containers. Ultimately successful and the first such regulation in the world, this process was nevertheless complex and required considerable expertise, time and effort, as well as a mix of advocacy strategies, to effect the desired change.

In Australia the process of introducing the "standard drink" began in 1989 with a proposal for such labelling to the Ministerial Council on Drug Strategy. The initial proposal was followed by a lengthy period of consultation, during which research into the need for public education, and into identifying the amount of public support of the concept, was undertaken. Further submissions were developed and debated and considerable advocacy for change eventually resulted in the government decision to act, and the creation of a National Food Authority regulation that enshrined standard drink labelling on all alcohol containers. The latter and final event occurred in December 1995, 6 years after the first action was initiated. A single year during this period a single year (1994), included extensive media advocacy from public health advocates.

By 1994 public health advocates had established a formidable coalition that included a research organization, the National Centre for Research into the Prevention of Drug Abuse, and an advocacy agency, the Alcohol Advisory Council of Western Australia, and had the support of an industry group, the Winemakers Federation. The coalition undertook extensive "behind-the-scenes" political lobbying, using the research data collected to support the submissions that had been developed. Likewise, two large industry groups representing brewers and distillers also undertook considerable lobbying activity, producing a glossy brochure supporting their case and sending a delegation of representatives to meet with all relevant government ministers throughout Australia. To counter industry lobbying, and to support the other advocacy strategies, a concerted media advocacy strategy was implemented in 1994 in the lead-up to, and following, a meeting of the Ministerial Council on Drug Strategy (who were responsible for recommending such action to the government). A half-page advertisement supporting legislation of "standard drinks" was placed in Australia's major national newspaper by 19 individuals and organizations, and a series of press releases were issued during September and October 1994 that resulted in widespread media coverage. Public confirmation of government support for standard drink labelling occurred on 30 September 1994 and the regulation was created in December 1995.

Hawks (1996) and Stockwell & Single (1997) identify a number of factors that worked against, and a number of factors that worked for, the legislation of standard drink labelling. The key factors that worked against the development of the legislation were the lobbying and media advocacy activities of the liquor industry, which sought to discredit arguments for change, and that the Minister of Health at the time the campaign started was personally not in support of standard drink labelling. The key factors that encouraged the adoption of the legislation included, first, the existence of a national alcohol policy that, even in draft form in 1986, recommended the provision of information on alcohol content for consumers; second, the usefulness of the research in highlighting the need for standard drink labelling and of public support for it; third, the existence of two separate agencies that were able to finance relevant research and coordinate the advocacy strategy, respectively; and fourth, the impact of key individuals who linked the coalition through their roles and activities.

The experience of these authors provides important lessons about media advocacy. The first of these is that advocacy for major change usually requires considerable time and commitment. This is so even when health advocates hold "the high moral ground" (as in this example, where the opposition was identified by the public as tainted by the motive of financial profit). Furthermore, media advocacy and other advocacy strategies are essential to achieve change when change is likely to have powerful and financial opponents. Such opponents will almost certainly undertake advocacy of their own. Nevertheless, media advocacy requires extreme care during both its planning and its implementation. This was highlighted when the coalition used media advocacy to attack the liquor industry position, inadvertently criticizing the Winemakers' Federation, who subsequently threatened legal action against a coalition that it supported. Finally, key individuals can be critical to the success or failure of advocacy strategies, especially when they are at the centre of the flow of information and advocacy activity or have decision-making power.

Using Media Advocacy

The use of media advocacy should, therefore, be conditional on the fulfilment of two criteria. First, in using this strategy, consideration must be given to ensure that media advocacy is applied only in appropriate circumstances, i.e. those circumstances in which goals are likely to be achieved and in which the advocacy agency can withstand the inevitable opposition to their activities. The use of media advocacy can be, and has been, counterproductive to achieving the aims sought (see e.g. DeJong, 1996).

The second criterion, is to ensure that media advocacy is supported by other public health strategies wherever possible. The two other advocacy strategies noted earlier (coalition building and political lobbying) should not be seen to be less valuable than media advocacy, and all should be undertaken within the framework of a comprehensive public health strategy. The timely and skilled use of media advocacy within the framework of a comprehensive advocacy strategy is more likely to achieve the desired results than a stand-alone, opportunistic approach, even when it results in wide exposure.

COMBINING MASS MEDIA MARKETING AND ADVOCACY

While in this chapter we have sought to dissect the elements of mass media marketing independently of those of mass media advocacy, frequently both activities are undertaken simultaneously. It has already been noted that the careful use of advertising can assist in advocating for structural change. Similarly, advocacy activity can reinforce or play a part in modifying individual behaviour. This interplay is most transparent in the act of creating and disseminating publicity. Publicity is both a marketing method and an advocacy tool because the efforts to increase publicity about a topic are in themselves acts of advocacy, and the public display of activities aimed at creating structural change can reinforce an individual's thoughts or actions about a specific issue or behaviour.

The media advocacy activity undertaken in the Community Prevention Trial project by Holder and colleagues, and in the New Zealand Community Action Project of Casswell and colleagues, demonstrate the potential inter-relationship between mass media advocacy and mass media marketing.

Holder & Treno (1997) described how media publicity was used as part of a larger multi-community prevention project to highlight and support the specific prevention components that targeted drink–driving, underage drinking, responsible beverage service and alcohol availability. As part of the drink–driving component, local police departments were provided with additional breath-testing equipment and new passive sensor devices, which provided an additional aid in the detection of over-the-limit drivers with no observable symptoms of heavy drinking. Use of this equipment represented a new approach to the detection of drink–driving and was newsworthy within the affected communities because of its novelty, and because what was being done in each community had national practice ramifications. Holder & Treno (1997) considered that the news coverage encouraged increased enforcement efforts by police, because it indicated community support. In this respect the initiative should be considered media advocacy, because it sought a change in institutional practice. There is, however, also a marketing aspect to this example, because the media coverage was designed to increase the perceived risk of drink–driving detection at an individual level. Three conclusions were drawn from this media strategy:

1. Mass communication in itself is not enough to reduce alcohol-related trauma, but can be effectively used to reinforce specific environmental efforts to reduce high-risk alcohol-related activities, such as drink–driving.
2. Local communication is best presented through local news media and can focus public attention on alcohol-related problems without having to use professionally produced material.
3. Media advocacy can be taken up by community members if appropriate training is provided, which means that the capacity to use this prevention measure is capable of being institutionalized within the community.

The Community Action Project undertaken in New Zealand between 1982 and 1985 aimed to create change at both the individual and the community level (Casswell, Ranson & Gilmore, 1990). Utilizing an experimental design, it compared the impact of two levels of intervention, mass media campaigns only and mass media campaigns with parallel community action, against non-intervention control sites. The mass media intervention in the intervention sites consisted originally of advertisements focused at individuals, but subsequently, and with much controversy and publicity, was focused at the policy level. The project staff used the controversy associated with the original marketing campaign to stimulate debate, and as a result created even more publicity around the individual behaviour change sought. When the advertising agency was unwilling to support the development of policy-focused, advocacy-related advertising, further controversy developed. As a result of both the advertising and the associated controversy, the mass media campaign was identified as having a beneficial effect on the public support of a range of alcohol polices. In summary, Casswell et al. (1990) concluded that:

> The results suggest that the mass media campaign, despite having a focus on individual drinking behaviour, served the function of keeping alcohol problems on the public agenda and maintaining support for healthy public policies (p. 9).

CONCLUSION

The examples described in this chapter reveal the increasing sophistication with which mass media marketing and mass media advocacy are being applied to attempts to reduce alcohol-related harm. The activities described reveal that mass media marketing can be a significant element in changing individual behaviour, and that mass media advocacy can be a significant element in creating change to social structures that impact upon behaviour. Indeed, each strategy can be used to reinforce the impact of the other.

The increasing success of these strategies can be attributed partly to new theories upon which they are now developed, partly to implementation of improved techniques and practices, and partly to greater reflection upon past mistakes and successes. Most importantly, however, has been the recognition that mass media marketing and mass media advocacy are most effective when they are only two of many elements within a broader change strategy. Such a strategy also includes a range of other activities, such as community development and community mobilization, school and community education, health promotion, policy development and institutionalization, coalition building and political lobbying. In this context, mass media marketing and mass media advocacy have already proved themselves to be important elements of alcohol harm reduction research projects in the USA (Holder & Treno, 1997), Australia (Midford, Boots & Cutmore, 1999) and New Zealand (Stewart & Casswell, 1993). It is also the context within which "best practice" forms of mass media marketing and advocacy have been, and will continue to be, successfully employed to reduce alcohol-related harm.

KEY WORKS AND SUGGESTIONS FOR FURTHER READING

Atkin, C. & Wallack, L. (Eds) (1990). *Mass Communication and Public Health: Complexities and Conflicts*. Newbury Park, CA: Sage.

> The product of a conference convened in the USA to "explore how the mass media could become a more potent weapon to improve public health", this book is a collation of ideas and issues identified by a range of high-profile speakers. The subtitle, "Complexities and Conflicts", adequately describes the best aspect of this book: that is, it highlights the problems and difficulties (as well as positing solutions) experienced in the process of creating change through mass media marketing and advocacy.

Chapman, S. & Lupton, D. (1994). *The Fight for Public Health—Principles and Practice of Media Advocacy*. London: British Medical Journal Publishing Group.

If you want to know "how to do" media advocacy, read this book. An excellent book from experienced and successful practitioners, *The Fight for Public Health* is full of innovative ideas to advocate public health issues. In the words of another critic, "I only hope Chapman hasn't given away too many secrets for his own good".

Egger, G., Donovan, R. & Spark, R. (1993). *Health and the Media: Principles and Practices for Health Promotion*. Sydney: McGraw-Hill.

Originally conceived as material for a postgraduate distance-learning programme, this book is a comprehensive volume targeted at health professionals. It integrates the theories behind, and the knowledge gained from, many years of commercial marketing with a public health approach. It is an easy to read, practical and well-illustrated book that gives readers a step-by-step understanding of mass media marketing.

Wallack, L., Dorfman, L., Jernigan, D. & Themba, M. (1993). *Media Advocacy and Public Health—Power for Prevention*. Newbury Park, CA: Sage.

Wallack and colleagues understand the relationship between politics and health. Their book challenges the view that the role of public health practitioners is to facilitate change in individual behaviour. This thorough sociopolitical analysis provides readers with a framework within which to comprehend and implement advocacy activities that are also described and illustrated. This is a book that advocates advocacy with all the skill and determination that it encourages of its readers.

REFERENCES

Andréasson, S., Lindewald, B., Hjalmarsson, K., Larsson, J., Wallin, E. & Rehnman, L. (1999). Exploring new roads to prevention of alcohol and other drug problems in Sweden: the STAD project. In S. Casswell et al. (Eds), Kettil Bruun Society Thematic Meeting: Fourth Symposium on Community Action Research and the Prevention of Alcohol and other Drug Problems. Auckland, NZ: Alcohol and Public Health Research Unit.

Backer, T.E., Rogers, E.M. & Sopory, P. (1992). *Designing Health Communication Campaigns: What Works?* Newbury Park, CA: Sage.

Bandura, A. (1986). *Social Foundations of Thought and Action: A Cognitive Theory*. Englewood Cliffs, NJ: Prentice Hall.

Casswell, S., Ranson, R. & Gilmore, L. (1990). Evaluation of a mass-media campaign for the primary prevention of alcohol-related problem. *Health Promotion International*, **5**(1), 9–17.

Chapman, S. & Lupton, D. (1994). *The Fight for Public Health—Principles and Practice of Media Advocacy*. London: British Medical Journal Publishing Group.

DeJong, W. (1996). MADD Massachusetts vs. Senator Bourke: a media advocacy case study. *Health Education Quarterly*, **23**(3), 318–329.

DeJong, W. (1997). College students' use of designated drivers: the data are in. *Prevention Pipeline*, **Nov/Dec**, 25–27.

DeJong, W. & Atkin, C. (1995). A review of national television PSA campaigns for preventing alcohol-impaired driving, 1987–1992. *Journal of Public Health Policy*, **16**(1), 59–79.

DeJong, W. & Winsten, J.A. (1990). The use of mass media in substance abuse prevention. *Health Affairs*, **Summer**, 30–46.

Edwards, G. et al. (1994). *Alcohol Policy and the Public Good*. Oxford: World Health Organization.

Egger, G., Donovan, R. & Spark, R. (1993). *Health and the Media: Principles and Practices for Health Promotion*. Sydney: McGraw-Hill.

Erickson, A., Ricks, A., McKenna, J. & Romano, R. (1990). Past lessons and new uses of the media in reducing tobacco consumption. *Public Health Reports*, **105**, 244–257.

Hastings, G. & Haywood, A. (1991). Social marketing and communication in health promotion. *Health Promotion International*, **6**(2), 135–145.

Hawks, D. (1996). *Not Much to Ask for, Really! The Introduction to Standard Drink Labelling in Australia.* Unpublished report.

Holder, H.D. & Treno, A.J. (1997). Media advocacy in community prevention: news as a means to advance policy change. *Addiction,* **92**(2), S189–S199.

Howat, P. & Fisher, J. (1986). Should health education focus only on self-responsibility? *New Zealand Journal of Health, Physical Education and Recreation,* **19**(1), 10–15.

Lewis, M. (1992). *A Rum State: Alcohol and State Policy in Australia.* Canberra: Australian Government Publishing Service.

Midford, R., Boots, K. & Cutmore, T. (1999). COMPARI. In *Community Action to Prevent Alcohol Problems.* Copenhagen: World Health Organization.

Montagne, M. & Scott, D.M. (1993). Prevention of substance use problems: models, factors, and processes. *International Journal of the Addictions,* **28**(12), 1177–1208.

Nutbeam, D. & Harris, E. (1998). *Theory in a Nutshell: A Practitioner's Guide to Commonly Used Theories and Models in Health Promotion.* Sydney: University of Sydney.

Pentz, M.A., Dwyer, J.H., MacKinnon, D.P., Flay, B.R., Hansen, W.B., Wang, E.Y.I. & Johnson, C.A. (1989). A multicommunity trial for primary prevention of adolescent drug abuse: effects on drug prevention. *Journal of the American Medical Association,* **261**, 3259–3266.

Perry, C.L. & Kelder, S.H. (1992). Prevention. *Annual Review of Addictions Research and Treatment,* 453–472.

Powell, K.C. (1988). *Drinking and Alcohol in Colonial Australia, 1788–1901 for the Eastern Colonies.* National Campaign Against Drug Abuse Monograph Series, No 3. Canberra: Australian Government Publishing Service.

Prochaska, J.O. & DiClemente, C.C. (1992). Stages of change in the modification of problem behaviors. In M. Hersen, R.M. Eisler & P.M. Miller (Eds), *Progress in Behavior Modification.* Newbury Park, CA: Sage.

Prochaska, J.O., Redding, C.A. & Evers, K.E. (1997). The transtheoretical model and stages of change. In K. Glanz et al. (Eds), *Health Behaviour and Health Education: Theory, Research and Practice.* San Francisco, CA: Jossey-Bass.

Simons-Morton, B., Donohew, L. & Davis Crump, A. (1997). Health Communication in prevention of alcohol, tobacco, and drug use. *Health Education and Behaviour,* **October**, 544–554.

Stewart, L. & Casswell, S. (1993). Media advocacy for alcohol policy support: results from the New Zealand Community Action Project. *Health Promotion International,* **8**(3), 167–175.

Stockwell, T. & Single, E. (1997). Standard unit labelling of alcohol containers. In M. Plant, E. Single & T. Stockwell (Eds), *Alcohol: Minimising the Harm. What Works?* London: Free Association Books.

Strunge, H. (1998). Danish experiences of national campaigns on alcohol, 1990–1996. *Drugs: Education Prevention and Policy,* **5**(1), 73–79.

Thompson, B. & Kinne, S. (1990). Change theory: applications to community health. In N. Bracht (Ed.), *Health Promotion at the Community Level.* Newbury Park, CA: Sage.

Tones, K. (1996). Models of mass media: hypodermic, aerosol or agent provocateur? *Drugs: Education, Prevention and Policy,* **3**(1), 29–37.

Wallack, L. (1990a). Improving health promotion: media advocacy and social marketing approaches. In C. Atkin and L. Wallack (Eds), *Mass Communication and Public Health: Complexities and Conflicts.* Newbury Park, CA: Sage.

Wallack, L. (1990b). Two approaches to health promotion in the mass media. *World Health Forum,* **11**, 143–164.

Wallack, L., Dorfman, L., Jernigan, D. & Themba, M. (1993). *Media Advocacy and Public Health— Power for Prevention.* Newbury Park, CA: Sage.

Winsten, J.A. (1994). Promoting designated drivers: the Harvard Alcohol Project. *American Journal of Preventive Medicine,* **10**(Suppl. 1), 11–14.

Chapter 42

Alcohol Advertising and Sponsorship: Commercial Freedom or Control in the Public Interest?

Linda Hill
and
Sally Casswell
*Alcohol and Public Health Research Unit, University of Auckland,
Auckland, New Zealand*

Synopsis

Alcohol is marketed through an integrated mix of strategies: television, radio and print advertisements, point-of-sale promotions, the Internet, and the association of brands with a variety of sports and cultural events.

In all Western countries, the use of alcohol is promoted, despite policies to restrict alcohol sales through licensing and other laws. The question for policy makers is whether the active promotion of alcohol should be permitted, or to what extent it should be constrained in the public interest to reduce alcohol-related harm and health-care costs.

Policy decisions on laws banning broadcast alcohol advertising or industry self-regulation of advertising standards continue to be contested by vested industries and public health advocates, but this examination of national policy differences shows how outcomes are shaped by politico-legal contexts. Where permitted, the content of broadcast and other alcohol advertisements is often governed by industry codes of practice. However, it is argued that these are largely irrelevant to the way alcohol advertising and other promotional strategies work. The codes do not address the way modern marketing embeds alcohol brands and drinking in young people's lived experience through sports and other activities and in portrayals of the life-styles to which they aspire.

A review of a growing body of research concludes that alcohol advertising has a small but contributory effect to individual drinking behaviour and levels of alcohol-related harm, such as road fatalities. Of particular interest are studies of the responses of children and young

International Handbook of Alcohol Dependence and Problems. Edited by N. Heather, T.J. Peters and T. Stockwell.

*people, since industry profitability logically requires the continual recruitment of a new gen-
eration of young heavy drinkers. Research also shows the cumulative way that advertising
helps to shape perceptions about alcohol, contributing to the climate in which policy decisions are made.*

*This research evidence supports policy action against the promotion of alcohol and its
negative effects on health choices and on the social and physical environments in which those
choices are made. The authors call for an internationally coordinated response to some
alcohol marketing practices, while recognizing that politico-legal contexts will continue to
shape effective local strategies.*

In all countries in which alcohol is sold, its use is promoted through advertising and other
marketing practices. Arguments in support of alcohol advertising are often based on the
legality of drinking by adults and on their freedom to receive information about a legal
product (DISCUS, 1998; O'Neil, 1997; Starek, 1997; Pedlowe, 1998; Buchanan & Lev, 1989).
An alternative view is that advertising and marketing is inherent to the *sale* of alcohol,
which is regulated. This latter view underlies perspectives on alcohol advertising policy from
countries traditionally more focused on a collective responsibility to protect the public
interest, than on the pursuit of individual rights and freedoms.

In all Western countries, the sale of alcohol and the management of drinking venues and
outlets are routinely restricted and licensed by law. Alcohol may therefore best be described
as a regulated product, rather than a legal one. Advertising and other promotions are also
constrained by forms of state regulation or self-regulation by the advertising, media, hospitality and alcohol industries involved. This chapter reviews marketing practices in
different countries as outcomes of policy struggles over whether or what aspects of alcohol
promotion should be regulated by the state or left to voluntary industry codes.

This chapter locates alcohol marketing practices within the political economy through
the strategies and interests of the producing, retailing, advertising and media industries
involved. Available research on how children, young people and others respond to alcohol
advertisements on television, the most powerful of marketing media, is reviewed. Through
the mass media and through promotions that embed alcohol into lived experience, new
generations are recruited to drinking by linking alcohol brands to various adult life-styles
that young people aspire to. In considering restrictions on the promotion of alcohol in the
interest of public health, attention is given to politico-legal contexts underlying differing
policy approaches adopted in different countries.

REACHING NEW MARKETS AND NEW GENERATIONS

The globalization of alcohol ownership and production (Jernigan, 1997; Walsh, 1997) contributes to coherence between marketing strategies in particular countries, and to international organization to influence policy frameworks that constrain sales and marketing (Marin
Institute, 1998; Babor et al., 1996). A trend towards convergent patterns of drinking in European countries with traditionally different cultures around alcohol has been attributed to
beer and distilled spirits advertising that transcends national boundaries (Gual & Colum,
1997). The promotion of alcohol and the softening of policy constraints are no less important
in the "emerging markets" now being targeted in developing countries (Jernigan, 1997).

In English-speaking countries, about 10% of drinkers drink about half of the total
alcohol consumed; it is this sector that contributes most to the alcohol producers' markets
(Casswell, 1997). Young males are most likely to be recruited to be these heavy drinkers
and are disproportionately represented in statistics on alcohol-related harm, such as drink-

driving, injury and premature mortality (Shanahan & Hewitt, 1999; Wyllie, Millard & Zhang, 1996; Fillmore et al., 1998; Leino et al., 1998). This drinking distribution is maintained over time, despite drinking levels abating among most men as they reach their 30s. The logical implication is that the alcohol industry continually needs to recruit new generations of young heavy drinkers in order to maintain profitability.

The question for policy makers in all countries is whether the active promotion of alcohol should be permitted, or to what extent it should be constrained in the public interest to help reduce alcohol-related harm and health-care costs (van Iwaarden, 1985; Mosher & Jernigan, 1989).

SHAPING THE SOCIAL CLIMATES AROUND ALCOHOL

Running counter to greater public awareness of risks and health-care costs associated with drinking have been pressures to deregulate the sale of alcohol. This is partly an effect of a wider politics of deregulation, but also of efforts to promote a public discourse in which alcohol is "normalized" as part of everyday life and drinking is seen as a matter of individual choice and responsibility. This choice is informed and created by direct and indirect means: not only advertisements and promotions but the unproblematic portrayal of drinking in entertainment and editorializing on television, radio, film and print. In these ways the alcohol industry acts as a "drug educator" (Stewart & Casswell, 1990), reaffirming drinking cultures, inculcating new generations and creating an environment supportive of industry when policy decisions are taken on alcohol regulation and public health strategies (Casswell, 1997, 1995a,b).

The impact of marketing on beliefs about the benefits of alcohol (Synder & Blood, 1992; Slater & Domenech, 1995) impairs the efforts of health promotion by creating what Wallack (1983) has described as a "hostile environment". Such an effect occurs not only through the impact directly on the beliefs of the younger drinker but may be shown in the attitudes of parents, family, the creators of health promotion communications and all those who might be expected to bring social influence to bear on the drinking culture. Such an effect is also likely on the decisions of policy makers. Print and broadcast media act as an indirect link between policy makers and the public, and decisions by policy makers to allow marketing of alcohol send a meta-message about the social climate surrounding alcohol to the public. Reciprocal effects are also likely and there may be influence on policy makers' subsequent decisions about other public policies which have a direct impact on drinking and related harm (McCombs & Shaw, 1972; Partanen & Montonen, 1988; Postman et al., 1988; van Iwaarden, 1985).

Content analyses of advertising show little portrayal of harmful consequences of drinking (Breed & DeFoe, 1979; Atkin & Block, 1981; Thomson et al., 1994) and Mosher & Wallack (1979) concluded that alcohol advertising was misleading, given the absence of accurate health information. Health promotion campaigns in the absence of broadcast advertising have been found to influence the social climate around alcohol (Casswell et al., 1990) but there is often a marked imbalance between the extent of commercial marketing and of health promotion material (Wallack, 1983; Thomson et al., 1994).

COMMERCIALIZED BROADCAST MEDIA

The alcohol industry promotes brands known world-wide alongside others that symbolize local loyalties, using an integrated mix of marketing strategies and media.

Television now reaches into most homes in Western countries and is rapidly increasing its audiences in developing countries. In many countries the broadcast media were established by the state, allowing early technical development to be funded by taxpayers. In the deregulatory 1980s and 1990s there has been pressure to move broadcasting to private ownership, with increased licensing of private stations and channels and increased commercialization of much state broadcasting. The resulting competition increases commercial pressures to liberalize alcohol advertising constraints.

In the New Zealand example, the stages in the restructuring and commercialization of broadcasting were paralleled by policy changes to permit first broadcast advertising for alcohol outlets, then corporate or sponsorship advertisements by alcohol producers and, from 1992, advertisements for alcohol brands were permitted in exchange for free air time for alcohol health promotion advertisements (Thomson et al., 1994; Casswell et al., 1993; Casswell, 1995a). Television alcohol ads quadrupled between 1991 and 1993 (Wyllie et al., 1996). In 1997 alcohol industry exposure in all media was around 10 times alcohol health promotion exposure (Hunter, 1997). The two companies that dominate the New Zealand alcohol market are large accounts for the media and advertising industries, who therefore have a strong investment in supporting their clients' lobby for alcohol advertising to continue under a voluntary code.

Radio, with its lower costs, attracts advertising by local drinking venues and alcohol outlets, as well as by major brands. In a New Zealand study, the four most common categories of advertisement were discounts for bulk purchase at bottle stores, discounted drinks in drinking venues, free drinks with meals, and bar tabs as prizes (Maskill & Hodges, 1997)—all promotions that may be considered to encourage hazardous drinking. None are covered by the current code on alcohol advertising. Moreover, the line between programme content, commentary and advertising messages is less clear-cut on radio than for television or print—sometimes deliberately so.

POINT-OF-SALE PROMOTIONS

The point-of-sale promotions featured in radio advertising are also of concern to inspectors and health promoters encouraging responsible management of licensed premises (Hill & Stewart, 1996). Price has been shown to be an effective mechanism for curbing consumption levels and intoxication, particularly among young and lower-income drinkers (Edwards et al., 1994). Discounting and price wars, "happy hours", "free drinks for females", "shooters", "yard glasses", "all-you-can-drink" evenings and some pub entertainments will have the contrary effect. The most problematic of these practices are usually in hotels, pubs and clubs, where young men do much of their heavy drinking and experience most alcohol-related problems (Casswell, Zhang & Wyllie, 1993; Stockwell et al., 1992). Since such promotions are advertised to attract customers, it may be a question of strategy whether these should be banned as irresponsible advertising or as irresponsible management reflecting on suitability to hold a licence to sell alcohol.

PROMOTING ALCOHOL THROUGH SPORTS AND CULTURE

Where alcohol advertising is banned, or partially banned, on the broadcast media, other marketing practices take on greater importance—as has been noted with the international tobacco industry (Deeks, 1992), from which alcohol borrows many of its strategies. Much research focuses on broadcast advertising, but by the early 1990s more than half of all advertising expenditure was other forms of promotion (Stewart & Rice, 1995). Most effective among these is marketing through sporting activities that attract young males, the group most likely to be—or to learn to be—heavier drinkers.

In New Zealand and Australia, there is a long-standing association between beer and those "old signifiers of masculine potency" and national pride, rugby players (Star, 1993; Hill, 1999; Phillips, 1984). The problem of "lager louts" at home and away games shows similar British linkages between football, nationalism and alcohol. Sports clubs are the social centre of many small communities in which youngsters learn about sports but also about drinking (Rekve, 1997). In Australasia, problematic and underage drinking in clubs and at sports events has become a focus of public health and regulatory concern, and of new cross-sectoral initiatives for alcohol health promotion.

In the USA, deals between beer sellers and baseball parks date back to the 1870s, but modern sports marketing of alcohol took off in 1970, the year tobacco advertising on television was restricted and Philip Morris took over Miller Breweries, sponsors of The Braves. High-powered sales techniques from the cigarette brand wars were applied to marketing alcohol as well as cigarettes through sports. These included market segmentation and targeting, image-oriented life-style marketing and an integrated mix of promotion types for each brand. The phenomenal growth of Miller led Anheuser-Busch and Coors to follow suit (Buchanan & Lev, 1989) in strategies now adopted world-wide.

Alcohol sponsorship deals for sports events, teams and clubs now routinely involve naming rights ("Smirnoff League", "Coors Extra Gold Motor Spectacular") and mentions in sports commentaries; signage on clothing, sports grounds and products retailed to fans; and opportunities for direct marketing through product donations and exclusive "pourage rights". Packages worth millions of dollars are concluded between sports federations and alcohol corporates to be the official beer of the World Cup or the Olympics (Baird, 1998). Sponsorship money is the price of entry to an event and its marketing opportunities, but high "leverage" spending on related media and retail promotions ensures maximum exposure and maximum sales.

A study of motor racing highlights promotional opportunities that move beyond passive absorption of images to embed the product in the lived experience and everyday activities of consumers and potential consumers, tapping into social processes that establish and reinforce cultural identity (Buchanan & Lev, 1989). Television commercials increasingly meet inattention, saturation or resistance (Clark, 1989), but sports sponsorship accesses audiences when they are most receptive to "experiential learning" about a product—while having a good time at an exciting branded event. Sports events attract large numbers of the right kind of audience—the young men likely to be heavier drinkers. Sponsorship agreements detail promotional opportunities evaluated by the number of carefully crafted "impressions" bombarding potential customers, together with on-site opportunities to try the product (Buchanan and Lev, 1989). Many events are family affairs, and alcohol "impressions" are also made on young people well below the drinking age, helping form in adolescence the attitudes and preferences that are taken on into later life (Kelder et al., 1994).

> It is one thing that adult fans are being exposed to it, but it is something completely different that 5 year-olds are walking around with a Liverpool T-shirt with Carlsberg written on it. . . . Building up a loyalty to label commodities among children and young people can be an investment that will provide an income for several decades (Rekve, 1997).

Global communications technology takes live and recorded sport into the homes of millions of potential customers. This makes sports, particular those signifying manhood and national pride, into a revenue-generating vehicle that delivers mass audiences for product promotions, as corporate, sporting and commercial broadcasting interests meet. Collaborations between the industries involved have included filming for best inclusion of alcohol signage, sometimes by the advertiser's agencies for supply to minor broadcasters. Home audiences, like event participants, see sponsorship brand logos and signage on sports fields and clothing in a different light from regular advertisements (Buchanan & Lev, 1989).

Football and motor sports are traditional routes to mass beer markets among young working-class males, but premium beers and spirits-based products seek niche markets by targeting diverse consumer identities through other sports, such as athletics, ice hockey, basketball, skiing, snowboarding. Specialist sport marketers now research and select sports to sponsor that will deliver particular target markets (Taylor, 1999). For those to whom there is more to life than sport, alcohol producers are also targeting rock music. Ballantine's follow up snowboarding events with live concerts, noting that young people are inspired by music, sport and modern technology (Rekve, forthcoming). Wine industries target older drinkers, including women, through a range of cultural events, and by promoting a sophisticated "culture" around wine itself.

WORLD WIDE WEB MARKETING

Alcohol is being embedded in virtual lives, as well as sporting ones. A German website for Ballantine's offers free animation software, allowing web surfers to socialize in an interactive bar. Surfers are asked to respect local drinking age laws in entering the bar. US beer websites also make a virtual game out of age identification. Carlberg's website provides Top 10 listings for various pop genres, next to hyperlinks to on-line supermarkets for beer supplies. All these features are devices of mass customization designed to attract high and repeat usage by browsers in the targeted audience group (Watson et al., 1998). A 1997 study concluded that the visual and interactive nature of the Internet puts unprecedented power in the hands of alcohol marketers, especially in reaching and influencing the young (Montgomery, 1997).

The US ban on broadcast tobacco advertising is interpreted as applying to *all* electronic media, meaning the absence of major tobacco producers on the Internet, in contrast with the growing presence of major alcohol producers.

SELLING LIFE-STYLES AND FANTASIES

Modern advertising targets mass and niche markets by associating brands with consumer identities and desired life-styles, sometimes through devices as simple as placing a brand logo at the end of life-style images.

> A beer is a beer is a beer . . . So therefore it is all about brands . . . We are not selling beer, we are selling image (Asia Pacific Breweries CEO, in Jernigan, 1997, pp. 9–10).

Dominant images in beer advertising are masculinity and national pride, presented through different models of male identity (Hill, 1999; Law 1997; Thomson et al., 1994; Postman et al., 1988). Adulthood is marked by new patterns of socializing, and alcohol is a powerful symbol of this—and of masculinity itself. This is explicit in a recent New Zealand beer slogan: "Lion Red—what it means to be a man" (Hill, 1999).

Some beer ads use subtle and acceptable imagery that nevertheless evokes known stereotypes of masculinity. Others use humour to present extreme stereotypes in ways that allow the drinker to claim the brand while distancing himself psychologically from his own drinking (Abrahamson, 1998; Law, 1997). The effectiveness of linking masculinity with sports was demonstrated in a US study of male teenagers who consistently preferred televized beer advertisements with sports content, compared with those without (Slater et al., 1995). Themes of masculinity and regionalism are also evoked in some spirits ads, particularly for whisky. Others employ less gendered messages about partying, and increasingly adopt swirling, magical imagery conveying the "mind-altering" qualities of alcohol (Hill, 1999).

Image advertising is responded to positively, especially by younger recipients (Covell, 1992; Kelly & Edwards, 1998). Research has shown that advertising becomes increasingly salient to young people over the age-span 10–14 years (Aitken et al., 1988) and 10–13 year-old males were more likely than older teenagers to say that alcohol advertising was an important source of information about drinking, and did encourage teenagers to drink (Wyllie et al., 1998b). Effective advertising operates at the symbolic, intuitive level of consciousness (Lannon & Cooper, 1983) and by linking attractive people with aspirational life-styles (Breed & DeFoe, 1979; Atkin & Block, 1981; Madden & Grube, 1994). This includes social camaraderie or "mateship" (Lieberman & Orlandi, 1987; Wyllie et al., 1997), so important for young people, which provides vicarious reinforcement for alcohol use (Bandura, 1977).

RELATIONSHIP BETWEEN ADVERTISING, CONSUMPTION AND HARM

A considerable body of research has attempted, using a variety of methodologies, to investigate whether there is a discernible link between advertising and consumption at either the aggregate or the individual level. These research data have played an important part in the policy debate around alcohol advertising and several analyses have been funded by industry sources (e.g. Strickland, 1982; Calfee & Scherega, 1994). Mosher & Jernigan (1989) have, however, described proof of the direct impact of advertising on drinking practices and problems as tangential from the standpoint of a public health model that stresses the need for consistency throughout the environment.

In the 1970s and early 1980s, much of the research on effects centred on econometric analysis of expenditure on advertising in relation to aggregate consumption data. This body of research produced some conflicting results, although the analyses from Britain covering the period from the mid-1950s to the late 1970s showed positive relationships for some beverages (McGuiness, 1980, 1983; Duffy, 1981). Other studies showed no effects (Bourgeois & Barnes, 1979; Ornstein & Hanssens, 1985; Grabowski, 1976), including a recent analysis of four European countries in the 1970s and 1980s (Calfee & Scherega, 1994). This approach is limited by the degree to which advertising expenditure varies, and Saffer (1993) suggested that, in many countries in which analyses have been carried out, advertising was already at high levels. He has instead looked at countries in which advertising bans have been implemented, compared with those in which they have not, carrying out cross-country time series analysis (Saffer, 1991). This showed an impact on both consumption and motor vehicle fatalities. The comparison of 17 countries for the period 1970–1983 found, for example, that the countries with a ban on spirits advertising had 16% lower consumption and 10% lower motor vehicle fatalities than countries with no such ban. This study contrasted with earlier investigations that found no effect of more partial and short-term bans (Smart & Cutler, 1976; Makowsky & Whitehead, 1991; Schweitzer et al., 1983; Ogborne & Smart, 1980). A later regression analysis by Saffer (1997), comparing different regions of the USA using quarterly data from 1986–1989 and controlling numerous other relevant variables, found an impact of advertising on motor vehicle fatalities which was significant (although smaller than that of price).

Other research has looked for effects at the individual level. Experimental studies in which consumption behaviour was measured following exposure to alcohol advertising showed mixed results, but those showing more sophistication in design, with participants unaware of the purpose of the study and naturalistic settings (Atkin, 1995), have shown some positive effects. Some effect was shown on blood alcohol levels after viewing print advertisements for alcohol, but only if the advertisements were viewed while the people were already drinking (McCarty & Ewing, 1983). Other studies of print advertisements showed no effect on later consumption (Kohn et al., 1984). Television advertising, which might be expected to be more powerful in its effects, has been investigated in a number of studies with mixed results. For example, male college students shown advertising embedded in television programmes in relatively naturalistic settings were more likely to choose alcohol rather than soft drink (Kohn & Smart, 1984) and were likely to drink more (Wilks et al., 1992). However, the effects differed, depending on the timing and the number of ads shown, and a study using a less naturalistic situation showed no effect (Sobell et al., 1986).

An immediate impact of advertising on drinking, as measured in the previous studies, would not be expected if a more cumulative effect of advertising is assumed (Gerbner et al., 1986). In this perspective, which assumes a gradual effect over many thousands of exposures, it is more likely that an impact would be measured on the cognitions which arise when processing the advertising messages (Petty & Caccioppo, 1981). Two recent studies have measured such an effect on beliefs. Following repeated exposure to beer advertising, college students rated alcohol as more beneficial and less risky (Synder & Blood, 1992) and reported more positive assessments of the benefits of beer (Slater & Domenech, 1995). Such positive beliefs were predictive of plans about future alcohol use (Slater et al., 1995), although exposure of school children to advertisements did not effect expectancies of drinking (Lipsitz et al., 1993).

The effect of repeated exposure to advertising is also measured in the many surveys that compare participants who have been highly exposed and who report greater awareness or more positive responses to advertisements, with those who do not. This has been a very popular approach since the late 1970s, beginning with a large research programme funded by the US Bureau of Alcohol, Tobacco and Firearms (Atkin & Block, 1981, 1984). All of the many cross-sectional analyses of such survey data have found evidence of a positive relationship between self-reported exposure and/or response to advertising and positive beliefs and reports of consumption. In Atkin & Block's work, those who reported seeing the most advertisements tended to perceive the typical drinker as somewhat more fun-loving, happy and good-looking, and in turn this was associated with more favourable values regarding the amounts, situations and benefits of drinking (Atkin & Block, 1981, 1984). There were also differences in the levels of drinking reported by those who were more exposed and recalled advertising more. An analysis of 1227 people, mostly aged 12–22 years, found 33% of the half who were more exposed were drinking at least 5–6 drinks per week, compared with 16% of the less exposed (Atkin et al., 1983). Other studies have demonstrated an association between positive beliefs, expectancies of future drinking and/or current drinking behaviour (Strickland, 1982; Atkin et al., 1983; Grube & Wallack, 1994; Wyllie et al., 1998a,b). The likelihood that these associations reflect a causal effect of advertising on drinking has been strengthened by the use of structural equation modelling (Bentler, 1993) to analyse the more recent surveys. This found that the data are good fits to models assuming a causal pathway between advertising and expectations of future drinking (Grube & Wallack, 1994) and positive beliefs and consumption levels (Wyllie et al., 1998a,b).

Two published analyses of longitudinal data have similarly found an impact of response to advertising on consumption. In the first, the numbers of alcohol advertisements recalled at age 15 in response to a question about the portrayal of alcohol in the media significantly predicted heavier drinking among males aged 18 (Connolly et al., 1994). In the second analysis, liking for advertising measured at age 18 predicted heavier drinking and experience of more alcohol-related problems at age 21 (Casswell & Zhang, 1998).

A review of the evidence of the effects of advertising published in 1994 suggested that alcohol advertising had a small but contributory effect on drinking behaviour (Edwards et al., 1994). The evidence published since that review further strengthens that conclusion.

LAWS RESTRICTING ADVERTISING

In many but not all Western countries, alcohol is being promoted on a falling market. A decline in aggregate consumption since the 1970s in part reflects the impact of preventative interventions to reduce alcohol-related harm (WHO, 1998; Stockwell et al., 1997; Moskowitz, 1989). These include excise taxes affecting price, drink–driving laws, responsible server training, mass media alcohol awareness campaigns and health promotion in schools and communities (Holder, 1994; Holder & Edwards, 1995; Stewart, 1997). Contributing market factors may include competition from soft drinks and a wider choice of items attractive to the youth market.

The alcohol industry has adopted marketing strategies developed by the tobacco industry, particularly in regard to attracting the young (Vaidya et al., 1996; Pollay et al., 1996; Meier, 1991). Research evidence led to widespread bans on broadcast advertising of tobacco on the logic that "any other measures . . . would not work as well if they had to compete with stylish and powerful tobacco advertising" (Secretary of State for Health, 1998). Similar policy conclusions can be reached from the growing body of research showing the contribution of alcohol advertising to alcohol-related harm.

All Western countries, to a greater or lesser extent, place constraints on alcohol advertising, using a mixture of state legislation and industry self-regulation (see Appendix). Outcomes reflect policy struggles in specific political and cultural contexts, and systems remain in flux as decisions continue to be contested. Restrictions by law are most common for banning alcohol advertisements from the broadcast media. Despite commercial pressures and the wider deregulatory climate, the trend is towards seeking stricter rather than more lenient controls in both regulatory or self-regulatory systems (Montonen, 1996).

Norway permits no alcohol advertising at all; France does not permit television advertising. Belgium has no advertising on state television, bans spirits advertising on commercial channels and all alcohol advertising on radio. Other countries, such as Austria and Ireland, ban broadcast advertising of spirits, or of beverages above a particular alcohol content, which may exclude just spirits, as in Spain and Finland, or all beverages except lower-alcohol beers, as in Denmark and Sweden. New Zealand, Italy and Portugal restrict alcohol advertising to later hours of viewing, and this has also been proposed by the German Minister of Health. Behind some of these outcomes are unsuccessful efforts to secure more restrictive legislation.

Until recently, the major spirits producers in the UK, the US and Germany maintained voluntary bans against advertising on television. The UK 30 year voluntary ban on advertising "dark spirits" on radio or television was abandoned in 1995 because of falling sales, particularly for whisky. The US spirits ban in 1948 (following a radio ban from 1936) was a closed-door commitment by industry to avert Senate proposals to ban all alcohol advertising on television. The ban was breached in 1996 by the Canadian company Seagram, following a sharp decline in its Asian markets. It was then lifted by the Distilled Spirits

Council on the argument that other alcoholic beverages had an "unfair" advantage (DISCUS, 1996). Spirits advertisements were accepted by local and cable channels but by only one national network, Black Entertainment Television. This continuing situation represents an informal response by the networks to a high level of public controversy and political opposition (Center for Science in the Public Interest, 1998).

However, all efforts to formally restrict spirits advertising on US television have foundered. President Clinton, Rep. Joseph Kennedy and 16 state administrations applied for action by the Federal Communications Commission, the body that banned tobacco broadcast advertising. This was declined (Quello, 1997; Hundt, 1997). A 1997 bill asking Congress to "just say no" to advertising spirits on "any medium of electronic communication" failed to achieve sufficient support. A further bill was tacitly premised on a view of drinking as a "legal" adult activity; it argued for a ban on all alcohol advertising because of its harmful impact on children. Finally, in 1998 the Federal Trade Commission (FTC) was directed by Congress to investigate whether advertising practices by eight major alcohol producers targeted those under the legal drinking age.

The argument undermining these efforts to achieve a ban was that the First Amendment to the Constitution provides some, if lesser, protection for commercial speech. Restriction by government must pass three tests: the government interest must be substantial, the restriction must directly advance that interest, and it must not be more extensive than necessary to do so (Starek, 1997). The onus that this puts on government agencies to prove causal relationships undermines any "threat" of regulation by law. However, US courts may consider state restrictions constitutional if they relate to unlawful behaviour—such as sales to under-age drinkers (Starek, 1997). Hence the shift in tactical direction to a more limited inquiry into advertising standards.

This lack of success in countering alcohol advertising contrasts with strong state-level regulation of alcohol sales, reflecting contemporary societal concerns about drinking as well as a strong temperance tradition (Room, 1989). It is attributable in part to a particular US constitutional protection and related politico-legal discourse, which makes particular arguments available while limiting others. It has meant, for example, that warning labels on alcohol containers have been an achievable strategy, whereas television advertising bans have not. Warning labels, implemented first for tobacco products, then for alcohol in 1988, are consistent with discourses on freedom of commercial speech and on information requirements for efficient markets. However, this discourse also enabled the labelling of wine bottles with messages about health benefits of moderate alcohol consumption.

Research shows that alcohol container warning labels have had some success in increasing awareness, reaching target audiences and, to a more limited extent, influencing individual behaviour (Greenfield, 1997). Health warnings on television alcohol advertising could also influence beliefs regarding the risks and benefits of alcohol use in the long term (Slater & Domenech, 1995). This has several times been included in bills, without success, as has removing tax deductibility for company expenditure on alcohol advertising (Mosher, 1982). In 1992 the Advertising Tax Coalition and the State Advertising Coalition helped defeat an amendment in the US House of Representatives and 14 state initiatives to tax advertising (Saffer, 1997). Saffer estimated that such a move on advertising would reduce motor vehicle fatalities by about 1300 per year in the USA.

Across the border, Canada has a very different regulatory tradition. The sale of alcohol is strongly regulated by each province; drinking venues are licensed and sales by the bottle are a state monopoly. The Canadian Radio and Television Commission (CRTC) bans spirits advertising on television, although this is under pressure following Seagram's actions in the USA. Radio and television advertising are permitted for beer and wine and come under a

CRTC code (Canadian Radio and Television Commission, 1996). However, the content of all alcohol advertisements is also regulated by each provincial Act. A distinctive issue is the prohibition of prizes, gifts or premiums with the purchase of alcohol (ASC, 1999).

France also has a strong stand against the promotion of alcohol, although its regulation of alcohol sales is light. Despite challenges under European treaties, the Loi Evin has banned alcohol advertising on television, ads directed at the young or on sports fields, most alcohol sports sponsorship, and also restricts radio advertising. To obtain change in the "simplistic and seductive discourse" that underlay earlier alcohol advertising images of leisure, sun, sex and success (Craplet, 1997), alcohol advertisement content is restricted to product characteristics and facts about consumption, production and region of origin. In most countries, however, the content of alcohol advertisements comes under voluntary codes, not state regulation.

INDUSTRY SELF-REGULATION OF ADVERTISING STANDARDS

In Australia, New Zealand, Ireland and some other countries where alcohol advertising is permitted on broadcast media, self-regulation through voluntary codes variously involves the media, advertising and alcohol industries (ASA, 1998; ASB, 1998; ASAI, 1999), and stands alongside more general rules on advertising standards.

Self-regulation in the USA is weakly organized in comparison with other countries, which regulatory theory would attribute to lack of a credible threat of state regulation (Ayres & Braithwaite, 1992). Advertising and media industry codes do not mention alcohol; separate voluntary codes cover beer, wine and most recently spirits, with complaints going to the industry organization that wrote the code. The only independent body to have considered alcohol advertising is the Federal Trade Commission (FTC), responsible for market competition and consumer choice but also for complaints about "unfair or deceptive" practices and "conduct injurious to consumers". In investigating advertising practices by eight large beer and spirits companies, it found that half the companies were not in compliance with their code, and two companies targeted those under the legal drinking age in a quarter of their advertisements. Nevertheless, the FTC recommended continuance of self-regulation, but with third-party review of complaints (FTC, 1999; Wiecking, 1999).

In theory, a voluntary code can be monitored by the public, but the effectiveness of this will depend on widespread knowledge of the code and a sufficiently independent complaints body with powers of sanction. Only Ireland's current code fits this description, although its sanctions are seldom used. Most advertising campaigns are designed as short bursts to avoid saturation effects, so complaints decisions must be fast. "Pre-vetting" may increase effectiveness, but industry self-regulation against its vested interests not infrequently leads to under-regulation and under-enforcement (Baggott, 1989). In Australia, self-regulation of alcohol advertising collapsed following strong criticism (Saunders & Yap, 1991; Rearck Research, 1991), and it was 2 years before a new code was negotiated. These problems are inherent, since the essence of self-regulation is that compliance with codes is voluntary (Montonen, 1996). Legislation may provide a formal framework that requires self-regulation, but no existing code of alcohol advertising standards is supported by state monitoring or sanctions, as for some other areas of business activity (Boddewyn, 1995; Baggott, 1989; Grabosky, 1995).

Recommendations to strengthen self-regulatory systems still do not address the content of industry codes, or the demonstrated "creativity" by which advertisement design continually outwits any restrictions (Clark, 1989).

CONTESTED CONTENT AND SCOPE OF VOLUNTARY CODES

Most voluntary codes on alcohol advertising fail to address the full range of promotional activities, and pay little attention to sports. Codes typically prohibit the portrayal of excessive drinking, underage drinkers, promises of social or sexual success and similar matters. However, the scope and the content of industry codes remain hotly contested ground between industry and public health advocates. Additions and refinements result from complaints, reviews and controversial advertisements.

The use of frog cartoons and Halloween imagery by major beer brands has been controversial in the USA (Leiber, 1998; Center for Alcohol Advertising, 1998), leading to recent changes in the Beer Institute's code (1999). In Britain there has been a similar outcry over cartoon characters on "alcopop" containers. But alcopops themselves are considered by many to be a product designed to attract children (Board of Science and Education, 1999; *The Globe*, 1997). Soft drinks mixed with colourless, tasteless spirits or liqueurs have long acted as a "bridge" drink (Clark, 1989). Alcopops are made attractive to teenage tastes by similar packaging to soft drinks and by being instantly ready.

In the USA, as efforts at the national level met frustration, resistance to local advertising developed in communities. In Baltimore, Chicago and Los Angeles, neighbourhood campaigns resulted in city ordinances banning alcohol billboards in inappropriate locations, such as near school playgrounds. These were contested in court. Once again, a policy struggle over alcohol advertising and responsible practices turned on what grounds and what level of power was required to restrict constitutional freedoms. In April 1999, however, a federal bill was passed allowing cities to adopt more restrictive regulation of billboards than under previous state law.

Sport has become another "arena in which the alcohol industry tests the limits of alcohol regulations and the elasticity of ethical rubberbands" (Rekve, forthcoming). In Europe and Scandinavia, national television channels can be viewed from neighbouring countries and language presents little barrier to basic marketing messages. Alcohol advertising at major sporting events frequently circumvents alcohol advertising bans or codes of practice in different countries. In countries that permit broadcast alcohol advertisements and those that do not, the association between alcohol and sports is pursued through the mass media in ways that most codes do little to restrain.

These controversies highlight questions about exactly what marketing practices a code should cover. What is "alcohol advertising", as opposed to programme content (Casswell, 1995b), or drinking venue management, or packaging and delivery, or corporate sponsorship of community activities? Although television commands the widest attention, it is by no means the only medium used to market alcohol, neither are formal advertisements always considered by advertisers as the most effective means (Casswell, 1995b; Clark, 1989). The wider the range of activities and the greater the number of players, however, the less effective self-regulation is likely to be (Ayres & Braithwaite, 1992).

CODES IRRELEVANT TO HOW ADVERTISING AND PROMOTION WORKS

An effect of industry self-regulation through voluntary codes is that the struggle over policy is diverted from the essential question of whether it serves the public interest to allow promotion of products that have considerable adverse impact on public health. Instead, energy is focused on continually refining the letter of codes, the detail of what does or does not constitute responsible advertising and what forms of marketing should be covered, in constant reaction to unacceptable practices. However, most codes are irrelevant to the way successful advertising actually works to reinforce current behaviour and the wider culture around drinking, and to recruit new generations of drinkers.

For example, codes on advertising standards commonly state that actors in alcohol ads must be adults. This restriction has little meaning, since studies of advertising for other products show that children generally desire what they see being enjoyed by a child a couple of years older (Clark, 1989). The young consume more television and more advertising than adults, like it more and are more influenced by it (Craplet, 1997; Eigen, 1996). To attract alcohol brand allegiance in the key market of young adult males, many advertisements simply depict the young adult life-styles that adolescents aspire to and associate them with the brand. Alcohol advertising has no need to show underage drinkers, sexual or other success—or even the product—when what it is selling is desired life-styles and fantasies.

Similarly, while codes explicitly prohibit the portrayal of intoxication, research suggests that advertisements do communicate the concept of intoxication (Rantila, 1993) and young recipients perceive intoxication and heavy consumption (Wyllie et al., 1997).

Moreover, the alcohol industry finds ample opportunities to associate its products positively with desired life-styles, of young people and others, as they are actually being lived. It is no longer appropriate to consider the effects of mass media advertising in isolation from other marketing tools (Stewart & Rice, 1995).

CONCLUSIONS

In the alcohol research field it is recognized that public health is a collective activity. Health goals for populations require ensuring that all public policies take health effects and health economics into account in setting priorities and in shaping social and physical environments, so that the healthy choice is the easy choice (Milio, 1988; Lehto, 1997). Marketing of alcohol, the research suggests, has a negative effect on the environment which helps shape individuals' choices.

Control strategies adopted at the level of the state face the increasing globalization of the alcohol industry and its marketing strategies. Policy and forms of regulation dictate the forms of promotion and circumventory tactics adopted by alcohol advertisers, but discussion about which marketing strategy, or which policy intervention or health promotion strategy, is more effective misses a key point. Modern marketing delivers through integrated packages of promotions, in which one type complements and "leverages" another. Regulatory practices and health promotion need similarly to consider and cover all the bases.

The ground contested between public health advocates and the alcohol industry can shift from the detail of legislation or codes of practices to the ideological climate in which policy decisions are made, or to shaping public opinion in ways that can affect the political acceptability of certain strategies to protect the public health. Such efforts on the part of the liquor and hospitality industries are no less important to the promotion of alcohol and the profitability of the industries than the marketing strategies themselves.

The need to develop an internationally coordinated response is increasingly clear (Eurocare, 1998), particularly with regard to broadcasting and to Internet promotions. Research evidence in this chapter supports policy action against the promotion of alcohol on the powerful broadcast media. In many countries, cultural linkages between sport, alcohol, masculinity and nationalism need to be targeted by health promoters and policy-makers.

One possible strategy is Norway's current promotion of sport as an "alcohol-free zone", with a local club focus on young players, family involvement and safety.

Nevertheless, at the national level, one strategy does not fit all. Different responses adopted by comparable countries provide valuable opportunities to learn from the experiences of others. However, responses are necessarily embedded in local contexts, and these will shape choices of national strategy that are both politically possible and likely to be effective.

NOTE

The focus of this chapter does not include fair trading and product description laws (both general and specific to alcohol) that impact on advertising and labelling, which are often elaborate in regard to wine. Neither does it cover—but readers may interested to note—a US trade law limiting vertical integration of alcohol and hospitality industries through restrictions on producers contributing financially to advertising by alcohol retail outlets and venues.

ACKNOWLEDGEMENT

This work was supported by programme funding from the Health Research Council of New Zealand and the Alcohol Advisory Council.

KEY WORKS AND SUGGESTIONS FOR FURTHER READING

Casswell, S. (1995a). Does alcohol advertising have an impact on the public health? *Drug and Alcohol Review*, **14**, 395–404.

Draws on recent New Zealand and international research to examine a number of questions about the possible public health impact of policy which allows alcohol to be advertising on the broadcast media. The 1994 Leonard Ball Oration.

Casswell, S. & Zhang, J.F. (1998). Impact of liking for advertising and brand allegiance on drinking and alcohol-related aggression: a longitudinal study. *Addiction*, **93**, 1209–1217.

Analysis of alcohol data from a longitudinal study of childhood development showed a measurable impact of advertising during a time of decline in aggregate alcohol consumption in New Zealand.

Buchanan, D.R. & Lev, J. (1989). *Beer and Fast Cars: How Brewers Target Blue-collar Youth through Motor Sport Sponsorships.* Washington, DC: AAA Foundation for Traffic Safety.

Uncovers the many ways in which the association of alcohol with sport embeds drinking and brands to enjoyable lived experiences. Readers will readily recognize these strategies being used in relation to other sports and cultural events. For a general audience.

Clark, E. (1989). *The Want Makers. Lifting the Lid of the World Advertising Industry.* London: Hodder and Stoughton.

A classic analysis of advertising strategies, for a general audience, with case studies of US alcohol and tobacco advertising.

Internet web-sites.

Readers are recommended to explore Internet addresses for various industry websites and advertising standards codes. Examples of campaigns against alcohol advertising can be found at: http://www.cspinet.org/booze/index.html (Centre for Science in the Public Interest, Washington); and http://www.apolnet.web.net/index.html (Alcohol Policy Network, Toronto); or check out how alcohol advertising appeals to kids by searching "Budweiser frog".

REFERENCES

Abrahamson, M. (1998). Humour and mundane reason about alcohol drinking. Paper presented to the 24th Annual Alcohol Epidemiology Symposium of the Kettil Bruun Society, Florence, 1–5 June.

Advertising Standards Authority Inc. (ASA) (1998). *Advertising Codes of Practice.* Wellington, New Zealand: ASA.

Advertising Standards Authority of Ireland (ASAI) (1999). *Code of Advertising Standards for Ireland: Alcoholic Drinks.* http://www.asai.ie/ (as at May 1999).

Advertising Standards Authority. (1999). *The British Codes of Advertising and Sales Promotion.* http://www.asa.org.uk (as at May 1999).

Advertising Standards Board (ASB) (1998, July). *The Alcohol Beverages Advertising Code (ABAC) and Complaints Management System.* Sydney: ASB.

Advertising Standards Canada (ASC) (1999). *Les Normes Canadienne de la Publicité.* http://www.canad.com/ (as at May 1999).

Aitken, P.P., Eadie, D.R., Leathar, D.S., McNeill, R.E. & Scott, A.C. (1988). Television advertisements for alcoholic drinks do reinforce under-age drinking. *British Journal of Addiction,* 83, 1399–1419.

Atkin, C. (1995). Survey and experimental research on alcohol advertising. In S.E. Martin (Ed.), *Effects of the Mass Media on the Use and Abuse of Alcohol.* NIAAA Research Monograph 28. Bethesda, MD: US Department of Health and Human Services.

Atkin, C. & Block, N. (1981). *Content and Effects of Alcohol Advertising.* US National Technical Information Service.

Atkin, C. & Block, N. (1984). The effects of alcohol advertising. In T.C. Kinnear (Ed.), *Advances in Consumer Research* (pp. 688–693). Provo, UT: Association for Consumer Research.

Atkin, C., Neuendorf, K. & McDermott, S. (1983). The role of alcohol advertising in excessive and hazardous drinking. *Journal of Drug Education,* 13, 313–323.

Ayres, I. & Braithwaite, J. (1992). *Responsive Regulation: Transcending the Deregulation Debate.* New York: Oxford University Press.

Babor, T.E., Edwards, G. & Stockwell, T. (1996). Science and the drinks industry: cause for concern. *Addiction,* 91, 5–9.

Baggott, R. (1989). Regulatory reform in Britain: the changing face of self-regulation. *Public Administration,* 67, 435–454.

Baird, R. (1998). Big brands join £60m FA package. *Marketing Week,* 21(16), 9.

Bandura, A. (1977). *Social Learning Theory.* Englewood Cliffs, NJ: Prentice-Hall.

Beer Institute. (1999). *Advertising and Marketing Code, Washington, DC.* http://www.beerinst.org/education/advert.html (as at 25.10.99).

Bentler, P.M. (1993). *EQS: Structural Equations Program Manual.* Los Angeles, CA: BMDP Statistical Software.

Board of Science and Education (1999). *Alcohol and Young People.* London: British Medical Association.

Boddewyn, J.J. (1995). Advertising self-regulation: organization structures in Belgium, Canada, France and the United Kingdom. In W. Streeck & P.C. Schmitter (Eds), *Private Interest Government: Beyond State and Market.* London: Sage.

Bourgeois, J.C. & Barnes, J.G. (1979). Does advertising increase consumption? *Journal of Advertising Research*, **19**, 19–29.

Breed, W.A. & DeFoe, J.R. (1979). Themes in magazine alcohol advertisements. *Journal of Drug Issues*, **9**, 511–522.

Buchanan, D.R. & Lev, J. (1989). *Beer and Fast Cars: How Brewers Target Blue-collar Youth through Motor Sport Sponsorships*. Washington, DC: AAA Foundation for Traffic Safety.

Calfee, J.E. & Scheraga, C. (1994). The influence of advertising on alcohol consumption: a literature review and an econometric analysis of four European nations. *International Journal of Advertising*, **13**, 287–310.

Canadian Radio and Television Commission (CRTC) (1996). *Code for Broadcasting Advertising of Alcoholic Beverages*. http://www.crtc.gc.ca/ENG/general/codes/alcohole.htm (CRTC, 1998).

Casswell, S. (1995a). Does alcohol advertising have an impact on the public health? *Drug and Alcohol Review*, **14**, 395–404.

Casswell, S. (1995b). Public discourse on alcohol: implications for public policy. In H.D. Holder & G. Edwards (Eds), *Alcohol and Public Policy: Evidence and Issues*. Oxford: Oxford University Press.

Casswell, S. (1997). Public discourse on alcohol. *Health Promotion International*, **12**, 251–257.

Casswell, S. & Zhang, J.F. (1998). Impact of liking for advertising and brand allegiance on drinking and alcohol-related aggression: a longitudinal study. *Addiction*, **93**, 1209–1217.

Casswell, S., Ransom, R. & Gilmore, L. (1990). Evaluation of a mass-media campaign for the primary prevention of alcohol-related problems. *Health Promotion International*, **5**, 9–17.

Casswell, S., Stewart, L. & Duignan, P. (1993a). The negotiation of New Zealand alcohol policy in a decade of stabilised consumption and political change: The role of research. *Addiction*, **88**(Suppl.), 9S–17S.

Casswell, S., Zhang, J.F. & Wyllie, A. (1993b). The importance of amount and location of drinking for the experience of alcohol related problems. *Addiction*, **88**, 1527–1534.

Center for Alcohol Advertising (1998). *Hands off Halloween, 1998: History of Hands off Halloween and the Responsible Merchants Campaign*. Berkeley, CA: Center for Alcohol Advertising.

Center for Science in the Public Interest (1998). *A Rough Chronology of Broadcast Liquor Advertising Controversy, 1996–1998*. http://www.cspinet.org/booze/chronolo.htm

Clark, E. (1989). *The Want Makers. Lifting the Lid of the World Advertising Industry*. London: Hodder and Stoughton.

Connolly, G., Casswell, S., Zhang, J.F. & Silva, P.A. (1994). Alcohol in the mass media and drinking by adolescents: a longitudinal study. *Addiction*, **89**, 1255–1263.

Covell, K. (1992). The appeal of image advertisements: age, gender, and product differences. *Journal of Early Adolescence*, **12**, 46–60.

Craplet, M. (1997). Alcohol advertising: the need for European regulation. *Commercial Communications: The Journal of Advertising and Marketing Policy and Practice in the European Community*, **9**, 1–3.

Deeks, J. (1992). Who's choking smoking? Advertising, sponsorship and government regulation of the tobacco industry. In J. Deeks & N. Perry (Eds), *Controlling Interests: Business, the State and Society in New Zealand*. Auckland: Auckland University Press.

Distilled Spirits Council of the US (DISCUS) (1996). *Fact Sheet: Beverage Alcohol Advertising: A Constitutionally Protected Right*. http://www.discus.health.org (dated 25.10.96, sighted 13.5.99).

Distilled Spirits Council of the US (DISCUS) (1998). *A Code of Good Practice for Distilled Spirits Advertising and Marketing*. http://www.discus.health.org/newcode.htm (dated 4.3.1998, sighted 13.5.99).

Duffy, M. (1981). The influence of prices, consumer incomes and advertising upon the demand for alcoholic drink in the United Kingdom: an econometric study. *British Journal on Alcohol and Alcoholism*, **16**, 200–208.

Edwards, G., Anderson, P., Babor, T. et al. (1994). *Alcohol Policy and the Public Good*. Oxford: Oxford University Press.

Eigen, L.D. (1996). The young and restless: Generation X and alcohol policy. Paper presented to Alcohol Policy X Conference, Toronto, 5 May.

Eurocare (1998). *Counterbalancing the drinks industry: a summary of the Eurocare report on alcohol policy in the European Union*. http://www.eurocare.org/counterbalancing/ (November 1998).

Federal Trade Commission (FTC) (1999). *Self-regulation in the Alcohol Industry: A Review of Industry Efforts to Avoid Promoting Alcohol to Underage Consumers.* http://www.-ftc.gov/reports/alchol/alcholreport.htm (September).

Fillmore, K.M., Golding, J.M., Graves, K.L,, Kniep, S., Leino, E.V., Romelsjo, A., Shoemaker, C., Ager, C.R., Allebeck, P. & Ferrer, H.P. (1998). Alcohol consumption and mortality. III. Studies of female populations. *Addiction*, **93**, 219–230.

Gerbner, G., Gross, L. & Morgan, M. (1986). Living with television: the dynamics of the cultivation process. In J. Bryant & D. Zillman (Eds), *Perspectives on Media Effects* (pp. 17–40). Hillsdale, NJ: Erlbaum.

Grabosky, P.N. (1995). Using non-governmental resources to foster regulatory compliance. *Governance*, **8**, 527–550.

Grabowski, H. (1976). The effects of advertising on inter-industry distribution of demand. *Explorations in Economic Research*, **3**, 21–75.

Greenfield, T.K. (1997). Warning labels: evidence on harm-reduction from long-term American surveys. In M. Plant, E. Single & T. Stockwell (Eds), *Alcohol: Minimising the Harm*. London: Free Association Books.

Grube, J.W. & Wallack, L. (1994). The effects of television beer advertising on children. *American Journal of Public Health*, **84**, 254–259.

Gual, A. & Colom, J. (1997). Why has alcohol consumption declined in countries of southern Europe? *Addiction*, **92**(1), S21–S32.

Hill, L. (1999). What it means to be a Lion Red man: alcohol advertising and Kiwi masculinity. *Women's Studies Journal*, **1**, 65–85.

Hill, L. & Stewart, L. (1996). The Sale of Liquor Act, 1989: reviewing regulatory practices. *Social Policy Journal of New Zealand*, **7**, 174–190.

Holder, H.D. (1994). Public health approaches to the reduction of alcohol problems. *Substance Abuse*, **15**, 123–138.

Holder, H.D. & Edwards, G. (1995). *Alcohol and Public Policy*. Oxford: Oxford University Press.

Hundt, R. (1997). *Statement of FCC Chairman Reed Hundt on Broadcast Advertisements of Hard Liquor*. Washington: Federal Communications Commission, 9 July.

Hunter Monthly Media Expenditure Analysis (1997). *Estimated Industry Alcohol Advertising Expenditure and Alcohol Health Promotion Expenditure*. All media, December.

Jernigan, D. (1997). *Thirsting for Markets*. San Rafael, CA: Marin Institute.

Kelder, S.H., Perry, C.L. & Klepp, K.-I. (1994). Longitudinal tracing of adolescent smoking, physical activity and food choice behaviours. *American Journal of Public Health*, **84**, 1121–1126.

Kelly, K.J. & Edwards, R.W. (1998). Image advertisements for alcohol products: is their appeal associated with adolescents' intention to consume alcohol? *Adolescence*, **33**(129), 47–59.

Kohn, P.M. & Smart, R.G. (1984). The impact of television advertising on alcohol consumption: an experiment. *Journal of Studies on Alcohol*, **45**, 295–301.

Kohn, P.M., Smart, R.G. & Ogborne, A.C. (1984). Effects of two kinds of alcohol advertising on subsequent consumption. *Journal of Advertising*, **13**, 34–48.

Lannon, J. & Cooper, P. (1983). Humanistic advertising: a holistic cultural perspective. *International Journal of Advertising*, **2**, 195–213.

Law, R. (1997). Masculinity, place and beer advertising in New Zealand: the Southern Man campaign. *New Zealand Geographer*, **53**(2), 22–28.

Lehto, J. (1997). The economics of alcohol. *Addiction*, **92**(Suppl.), S55–S60.

Leiber, L. (1998). *Commercial and Character Slogan Recall by Children Aged 9–11 Years: Budweiser Frogs versus Bugs Bunny*. Berkeley, CA: Center on Alcohol Advertising.

Leino, E.V., Romelsjo, A., Shoemaker, C., Ager, C.R., Allebeck, P., Ferrer, H.P., Fillmore, K.M., Golding, J.M., Graves K.L. & Kneip, S. (1998). Alcohol consumption and mortality: studies of male populations. *Addiction*, **93**, 205–218.

Lieberman, L.R. & Orlandi, M.A. (1987). Alcohol advertising and adolescent drinking. *Alcohol Health and Research World*, **12**, 30–33, 43.

Lipsitz, A., Brake, G., Vincent, E.J. & Winters, M. (1993). Another round for the brewers: television ads and children's alcohol expectancies. *Journal of Applied Social Psychology*, **23**, 439–450.

Madden, P.A. & Grube, J.W. (1994). The frequency and nature of alcohol and tobacco advertising in televised sports, 1990–1992. *American Journal of Public Health*, **84**, 297–299.

Makowsky, C.R. & Whitehead, P.C. (1991).   Advertising and alcohol studies: a legal impact study. *Journal of Studies on Alcohol*, **52**, 555–567.

Marin Institute for the Prevention of Alcohol and Other Drug Problems (1998).   Big alcohol's smokescreen. *Newsletter*, **Winter**, 1–6.

Maskill, C. & Hodges, I. (1997).   *Alcohol Messages on New Zealand Radio, 1995/96*. Wellington: Alcohol Advisory Council.

McCarty, D. & Ewing, J.A. (1983).   Alcohol consumption while viewing alcoholic beverage advertising. *International Journal of the Addictions*, **18**, 1011–1018.

McCombs, M.E. & Shaw, D.L. (1972).   The agenda-setting function of the mass media. *Public Opinion Quarterly*, **36**, 176–187.

McGuiness, T. (1980).   An econometric analysis of total demand for alcoholic beverages in the UK, 1956–1975. *Journal of Industrial Economics*, **29**, 85–109.

McGuiness, T. (1983).   The demand for beer, wine and spirits in the UK, 1956–1979. In M. Grant, M. Plant & A. Williams (Eds), *Economics and Alcohol: Consumption and Controls*. London: Croom Helm.

Meier, K. (1991).   Tobacco truths: the impact of role models on children's attitudes towards smoking. *Health Education Quarterly*, **18**, 173–182.

Milio, N. (1988).   Masking healthy public policy: developing the science by learning the art; an ecological framework for policy studies. *Health Promotion*, **2**, 263–274.

Montgomery, K. (1997).   *Alcohol and Tobacco on the Web: New Threats to Young. Executive Summary*. Washington, DC: Center for Media Education (March).

Montonen, M. (1996).   *Alcohol and the Media*. WHO Regional Publications, European series No. 62. Genera: World Health Organization.

Mosher, J.F. (1982).   Federal tax law and public health policy: the case of alcohol-related tax expenditures. *Journal of Public Health Policy*, **34**(23), 260–283.

Mosher, J.F. & Jernigan, D.H. (1989).   New directions in alcohol policy. *Annual Review of Public Health*, **10**, 245–279.

Mosher, J.F. & Wallack, L.M. (1979).   Proposed reforms in the regulation of alcoholic beverage advertising. *Contemporary Drug Problems*, **Summer**, 87–106.

Moskowitz, J.M. (1989).   The primary prevention of alcohol problems: a critical review of the research literature. *Journal of Studies on Alcohol*, **50**, 54–88.

Ogborne, A.C. & Smart, R.G. (1980).   Will restrictions on alcohol advertising reduce alcohol consumption? *British Journal of Addiction*, **75**, 293–229.

O'Neil, R.M. (1997).   Mr Jefferson, distilled spirits and TV ads. *Commercial Speech Digest*, Washington DC: The Media Institute (Spring).

Ornstein, S. & Hanssens, D. (1985).   Alcohol control laws and the consumption of distilled spirits and beer. *Journal of Consumer Research*, **12**, 200–213.

Partanen, J. & Montonen, M. (1988).   *Alcohol and the Mass Media*. EURO Reports and Studies No. 108. Copenhagen: World Health Organization Regional Office for Europe.

Pedlowe, G. (1998).   Alcohol in emerging markets: identifying the most appropriate role for the alcohol industry. In M. Grant (Ed.), *Alcohol and Emerging Markets: Patterns, Problems and Responses*. Washington, DC: ICAP.

Petty, R. & Cacioppo, J. (1981).   *Attitudes and Persuasion: Classic and Contemporary Approaches*. Dubrique, IA: William C. Brown.

Phillips, J. (1984).   Rugby, war and the mythology of the NZ male. *New Zealand Journal of History*, **18**.

Pollay, R.W., Siddarth, S., Siegel, M., Haddix, A. et al. (1996).   The last straw? Cigarette advertising and realized market shares among youths and adults, 1979–1993. *Journal of Marketing*, **60**(2), 1–16.

Postman, N., Nystrom, C., Strate, L. & Weingartner, C. (1988).   *Myths, Men and Beer: An Analysis of Beer Commercials on Broadcast Television, 1987*. Falls Church: AAA Foundation for Traffic Safety.

Quello, R. (1997).   *Statement of Commissioner James H. Quello re: Proposed Notice of Inquiry on Broadcast Advertisement of Distilled Spirits*. Washington, DC: Federal Communications Commission (9 July).

Rantila, K. (1993).   Greimas och olreklamens magi [Greimas and the magic of beer commercials]. *Nordisk Alkoholtidskrift*, **10**, 70–80.

Rearck Research (1991). *A Study of Attitudes towards Alcohol Consumption, Labelling and Advertising.* A report prepared for the Dept of Community Services and Health, Canberra.

Rekve, D. (1997). *Status Report from a Joint Project between Alkokutt and the Norwegian Football Association.* Oslo: Alkokutt (March). http://www.alkokutt.no/english/

Rekve, D. (forthcoming). *Foul! Sports Sponsorship and the Drinks Industry: The Big Mis-Match.* Oslo: Alkokutt.

Room, R. (1989). Cultural changes in drinking and trends in alcohol problems indicators: Recent US experience. *Alcologia,* **1,** 83–89.

Saffer, H. (1991). Alcohol advertising bans and alcohol abuse: an international perspective. *Journal of Health Economics,* **10,** 65–79.

Saffer, H. (1993). Alcohol advertising bans and alcohol abuse: reply. *Journal of Health Economics,* **12,** 229–234.

Saffer, H. (1997). Alcohol advertising and motor vehicle fatalities. *Review of Economics and Statistics,* **79,** 431–442.

Saunders, B. & Yap, E. (1991). Do our guardians need guarding? An examination of the Australian system of self-regulation of alcohol advertising. *Drug and Alcohol Review,* **10,** 15–17.

Schweitzer, S.O., Intriligator, M.D. & Salehi, H. (1983). Alcoholism: an econometric model of its causes, its effects and its control. In M. Grant, M. Plant & A. Williams (Eds), *Economics and Alcohol: Consumption and Controls.* London: Croom Helm.

Secretary of State for Health. With Secretaries of State for Scotland, Wales and Northern Ireland *Smoking kills: A White Paper on Tobacco.* (1998). London: The Stationary Office (30 November).

Shanahan, P. & Hewitt, N. (1999). *Developmental Research for a National Alcohol Campaign.* Canberra: Summary report to the Commonwealth Department of Health and Aged Care.

Slater, M.D. & Domenech, M.M. (1995). Alcohol warnings in TV beer advertisements. *Journal of Studies on Alcohol,* **56,** 361–367.

Slater, M.D., Murphy, K., Beauvais, F., Rouner, D., van Leuven, J. & Domenech Rodriguez, M.M. (1995). *Modeling Predictors of Alcohol Use and Use Intentions among Adolescent Anglo Males: Social, Psychological, and Advertising Influences.* Annual Conference of the Research Society on Alcoholism, Steamboat Springs, CO, June.

Smart, R.G. & Cutler, R.E. (1976). The alcohol advertising ban in British Colombia: problems and effects on beverage consumption. *British Journal of Addiction,* **71,** 13–21.

Synder, L.B. & Blood, D.J. (1992). Caution: alcohol advertising and the Surgeon General's alcohol warnings may have adverse effects on young adults. *Journal of Applied Communication Research,* **20,** 37–53.

Sobell, L.C., Sobell, M.B., Riley, D.M., Klajner, F., Leo, G.I., Pavan, D. & Cancilla, A. (1986). Effect of television programming and advertising on alcohol consumption in normal drinkers. *Journal of Studies on Alcohol,* **47,** 333–339.

Star, L. (1993). Macho and his brothers: passion and resistance in sports discourse. *Sites,* **26,** 54–78.

Starek, R.B. (1997). *Advertising Alcohol and the First Amendment Address to the American Bar Association Section of Administrative Law and Regulatory Practice Committee on Beverage Alcohol Practice,* San Francisco, CA, 4 August.

Stewart, D.W. & Rice, R. (1995). Non-traditional media and promotions in the marketing of alcoholic beverages. In S.E. Martin (Ed.), *The Effects of the Mass Media on the Use and Abuse of Alcohol.* Bethesda, MD: US Dept of Health and Human Services.

Stewart, L. (1997). Approaches to preventing alcohol-related problems: the experience of New Zealand and Australia. *Drug and Alcohol Review,* **16,** 391–399.

Stewart, L. & Casswell, S. (1990). Creating a supportive environment for drinking: the alcohol industry as a drug educator. *Drug Education Journal of Australia,* **4**(3), 225–231.

Stockwell, T., Single, E. Hawkes, D. & Rehm, J. (1997). Sharpening the focus of alcohol policy from aggregate consumption to harm and risk reduction. *Addiction Research,* **5,** 1–9.

Stockwell, T., Somerford, P. & Lang, E. (1992). The relationship between licence type and alcohol related problems attributed to licensed premises in Perth, Western Australia. *Journal of Studies on Alcohol,* **53,** 495–498.

Strickland, D.E. (1982). Alcohol advertising: orientations and influence. *International Journal of Advertising,* **1,** 307–319.

Taylor, T. (1999).   Audience info the key to sports marketers. *Marketing News*, **33**(2), 10.

The Globe (1997).   *Alcopops under Fire in the European Union, 1* (pp. 10–11). London: Institute for Alcohol Studies.

Thomson, A., Casswell, S. & Stewart, L. (1994).   Communication experts' opinions on alcohol advertising in the electronic media. *Health Promotion International*, **9**, 145–152.

Vaidya, S.G., Naik, U.C. & Vaidya, J.S. (1996).   Effect of sports sponsorship by tobacco companies on children's experimentation with tobacco. *British Medical Journal*, **17 August**, 313.

van Iwaarden, M.J. (1985).   Public health aspects of the marketing of alcoholic drinks. In M. Grant (Ed.), *Alcohol Policies* (pp. 45–55). European Series No. 18. Copenhagen: WHO Regional Publications.

Wallack, L. (1983).   Mass media campaigns in a hostile environment: advertising as anti-health education. *Journal of Alcohol and Drug Education*, **28**, 51–63.

Walsh, B. (1997).   Trends in alcohol production, trade and consumption. *Addiction*, **92**(1), S61–S66.

Watson, R.T., Akselsen, S. & Pitt, L.F. (1998).   Attractors: building mountains in the flat landscape of the World Wide Web. *California Management Review*, **40**(2), 36–56.

Wiecking, F. (1999).   *FTC Report Downplays Failure of Alcoholic-beverage Advertisers to Comply with Their Own Advertising Standards.* Statement by Manager for Federal Affairs, Center for Science in the Public Interest, 10 September.

Wilks, J., Vardenega, A.T. & Callan, V.J. (1992).   Effect of television advertising on alcohol consumption and intentions to drive. *Drug and Alcohol Review*, **11**, 15–21.

Wine Institute (1999).   *Code of advertising standards, San Francisco.* http://www.-wineinstitute.org/adcodewi.htm (as at 25.10.99).

World Health Organization (1998).   *Health 21: An Introduction to the Health for All Policy Framework for the WHO European Region.* Copenhagen: WHO.

Wyllie, A., Millard, M. & Zhang, J.F. (1996a).   *Drinking in New Zealand: A National Survey, 1995.* Auckland: Alcohol & Public Health Research Unit.

Wyllie, A., Holibar, F., Casswell, S., Fuamatu, N., Aioluputea, K., Moewaka Barnes, H. & Panapa, A. (1997).   A qualitative investigation of responses to televised alcohol advertisements. *Contemporary Drug Problems*, **24**, 103–132.

Wyllie, A., Waa, A. & Zhang, J.F. (1996b).   *Alcohol and Moderation Advertising Expenditure and Exposure.* Auckland: Alcohol & Public Health Research Unit.

Wyllie, A., Zhang, J.F. & Casswell, S. (1998a).   Positive responses to televised beer advertisements associated with drinking and problems reported by 18–29 year-olds. *Addiction*, **93**, 749–760.

Wyllie, A., Zhang, J.F. & Casswell, S. (1998b).   Responses to televised alcohol advertisements associated with drinking behaviour of 10–17 year-olds. *Addiction*, **93**, 361–371.

APPENDIX: RESTRICTIONS ON ALCOHOL ADVERTISING: EXAMPLES SHOWING INTERNATIONAL DIVERSITY

Australia

The Australian Association of National Advertisers has set up an Advertising Standards Board and an Advertising Claims Board, and established a new code of ethics. It has no powers of enforcement; however, relying on "the willingness of advertisers to adhere voluntarily to ethical standards". A new code on liquor advertising was adopted in 1998 after a 2 year hiatus, during which only a general Commercial Television Industry Code of Practice applied. An earlier code collapsed in 1996 when the Competition and Consumers Commission revoked authorizations to the Media Council of Australia following public criticism.

Austria

Legal ban on spirits advertising on radio; otherwise a voluntary code.

Belgium

No commercial advertising on state television, and legal ban on spirits advertising on commercial television. No alcohol advertising on radio. In other media, voluntary guidelines prohibit the encouragement of "drinking to excess" and advertisements targeted at the under-21s.

Canada

A statutory body, the Canadian Radio and Television Commission, code governs alcohol ads. Also provincial codes on all alcohol advertising as part of regulations and guidelines under provincial Acts covering state monopoly over distribution and off-sales and state licensing of drinking venues. Detailed rules on giving out samples of alcohol. Restrictions on gifts, prizes and premiums.

Denmark

Television and radio advertisements are not permitted for alcohol over 2.25% alcohol by volume (i.e. low-alcohol beer may be advertised). Other media must not aim alcohol advertisements at minors. In 1999 negotiations for guidelines allowing corporate logos and light beer ads on sports clothes failed.

Finland

Formerly, legal ban on alcohol advertising. Now, advertising permitted of beer and wine up to 22% alcohol by volume.

France

A legal ban since 1987 on television ads. The Loi Evin bans ads for alcohol over 1% alcohol by volume on television and in publications for young people and in places where sports events are held. Ad content is also controlled by law, not a voluntary code. In other media, alcohol advertisements must focus on product characteristics only, advise that alcohol abuse is bad for your health, and be pre-approved.

Greece

There are no specific restrictions other than limitations on the number of ads per day for each brand on television and radio.

Germany

By voluntary agreement, most spirits are not advertised on television. On other media, a voluntary code is in operation, similar to that in the UK.

Italy

Alcohol advertisements on television may be shown only after 8 p.m. A voluntary code similar to that in the UK governs content.

Ireland

A legal ban on spirits advertising on television and radio, and alcohol advertisements may not be shown before sports programmes. The same ad may not appear more than twice per night on any one channel. On other media a voluntary code on alcohol is one of a set of codes of the Advertising Standards Authority of Ireland.

Luxembourg

Television and radio advertisements must not show alcohol being consumed "in excess or feature young people, or sportsmen or drivers consuming alcohol". Otherwise no restrictions.

New Zealand

Advertising standards shifted to self-regulation with commercialization of the broadcasting media, under an Advertising Standards Authority (ASA) set up by statute. Outlet ads, then sponsorship ads, then brand advertising in 1992, were permitted without reference to Parliament. A Broadcasting Standards Authority is responsible for "saturation" and alcohol in programme content. The ASA's Code on Liquor Advertising now covers all brand and sponsorship advertising. Ads are pre-vetted. The Complaints Board and review committees have some non-industry members.

Norway

Advertising of alcoholic beverages or alcoholic beverage products is prohibited, including in advertisements for other goods and services. This has limited alcohol marketing opportunities on sports grounds and on sports team clothing. Visiting international teams have been required to comply with this.

Portugal

No alcohol advertising on television before 10 p.m. and advertisements must not show alcohol being consumed.

Spain

A ban on television and radio advertising of spirits and alcohol over 23% alcohol by volume. Other alcohol advertisements may be shown only after 9.30 p.m. A ban on all television spirits advertising in the Basque country.

Sweden

Since July 1979, there has been a ban on beer, wine and spirits, except for beer under 2.25% alcohol, with restrictions on ad content on showing intoxication, etc. Some advertising of beer up to 3.5% showing only bottle and manufacturer. New proposals following a 1999 review are likely to tighten these regulations in 1999.

Switzerland

Law prohibits comparing or publishing alcohol prices and restricts advertising, especially at sports meetings or events for young people. Alcohol ads are restricted to information and descriptions directly related to the product. But this policy is undermined by ads, particularly on television, coming from neighbouring countries.

The Netherlands

In 1987 a bill to prohibit all alcohol advertising on broadcast media was defeated. Since 1990 the liquor industry, including retail, follows a voluntary code developed by the Stichting Zelfregulering Alcoholbranche. Its complaints committee can fine up to 50,000 guilders. Ads can be for individual brands but no corporate ads; sports sponsorship is limited. A moderation message must be included in 40% of audio-visual ads. Ads should not encourage minors to drink.

UK

The BBC does not carry advertising. Alcohol advertising on other television and radio stations is the responsibility of statutory bodies, the Independent Broadcasting Authority and the Cable Authority, whose codes of practice cover alcohol advertising. A 1965 voluntary agreement between manufacturers and TV companies not to advertise spirits was abandoned in 1995.

Alcohol advertising in other media comes under a voluntary code, the Advertising Standards Authority's British Code of Advertising and Sales Promotion, which now limits advertising where more than a quarter of the audience is like to be under 18. It also governs the way alcohol or people drinking is presented in ads for other products.

Under all codes, advertisements should not encourage excessive drinking, market to audiences under 18 or depict drinkers under 25, characters likely to appeal to those under 18, activities or location where alcohol would be unsafe, or suggest that alcohol enhances mental, physical or sexual capabilities, popularity, masculinity, femininity or sporting achievement.

In 1996, complaints about "alcopops", containing 5% alcohol and being marketed to young people alongside soft drinks, led the Portman Group to promote its own limited industry code. This averted a proposed ban on the words "lemonade" or "cola" on mixed drink containers.

USA

Beer and wine ads are permitted on radio and television, with alcohol industry codes for each. In California it is illegal to offer inducements to encourage drinking, such as give-aways recently offered in Budweiser ads.

Ads for spirits were kept off radio from 1936 and television from 1948 by a voluntary industry ban, broken in 1996 by Seagrams. Spirits ads now appear on local and cable channels, but are still refused by nearly all national networks. DISCUS wrote a code of conduct; its directors will consider any complaints.

A series of city ordinances restricting alcohol billboards met challenges in the Supreme Court but has now led to recent federal legislation allow greater city control over content and location.

South Africa

An Advertising Standards Authority of South Africa code of conduct governs advertising of alcohol. All forms of alcohol may be advertised freely on radio, television and in print. Sports sponsorship by the alcohol industry is very high, especially for cricket, rugby and soccer. In 1997 the Department of Health established a committee to look at counter-advertising and warning labels, and another to look at possible restrictions on broadcast advertising and sports sponsorships.

Sources: Institute for Alcohol Studies, London; Alcohol and Public Health Research Unit, New Zealand.

Author Index

Subject Index

Indexes compiled by Campbell Purton